S0-AEU-711

Approaching Ninety-Six

The Films I Love Viewing & Loved Doing

by

Carl Reiner

RANDOM CONTENT INK LLC
Beverly Hills, CA 90210

www.RandomContent.com

Published 2017
FIRST EDITION

Published by RANDOM CONTENT INK LLC
ISBN: *978-0-9995182-1-2*

Library of Congress Control Number: 2017959007

Book Design by: Carl Reiner and Aaron Davis

Any people depicted in images have given approval by their estate and trustees.

This book is printed on acid-free paper.

Because of the dynamic nature of the Internet, any web addresses or links contained in this book may have changed since publication and may no longer be valid.

Printed and bound in India by Replika Press Pvt. Ltd.

Approaching Ninety-Six

The Films I Love Viewing & Loved Doing

by

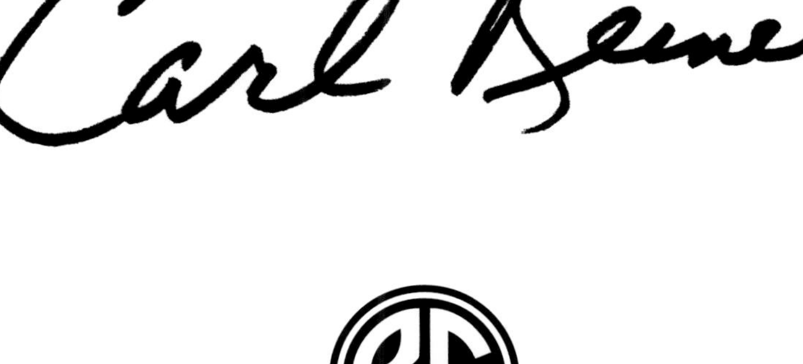

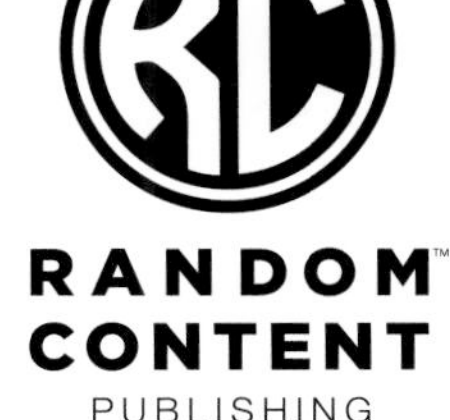

RANDOM™
CONTENT
PUBLISHING

Contents

the 50s

the 60s

Approaching Ninety-Six

the 70s

Contents Cont'd

the 80s

the 90s

Approaching Ninety-Six

Introduction

This second volume starts with the events that occurred in 1950, the year I joined Sid Caesar and Imogene Coca as a cast member on Max Liebman's "Your Show of Shows," and continues until it goes to the publisher, who expects it sometime this month.

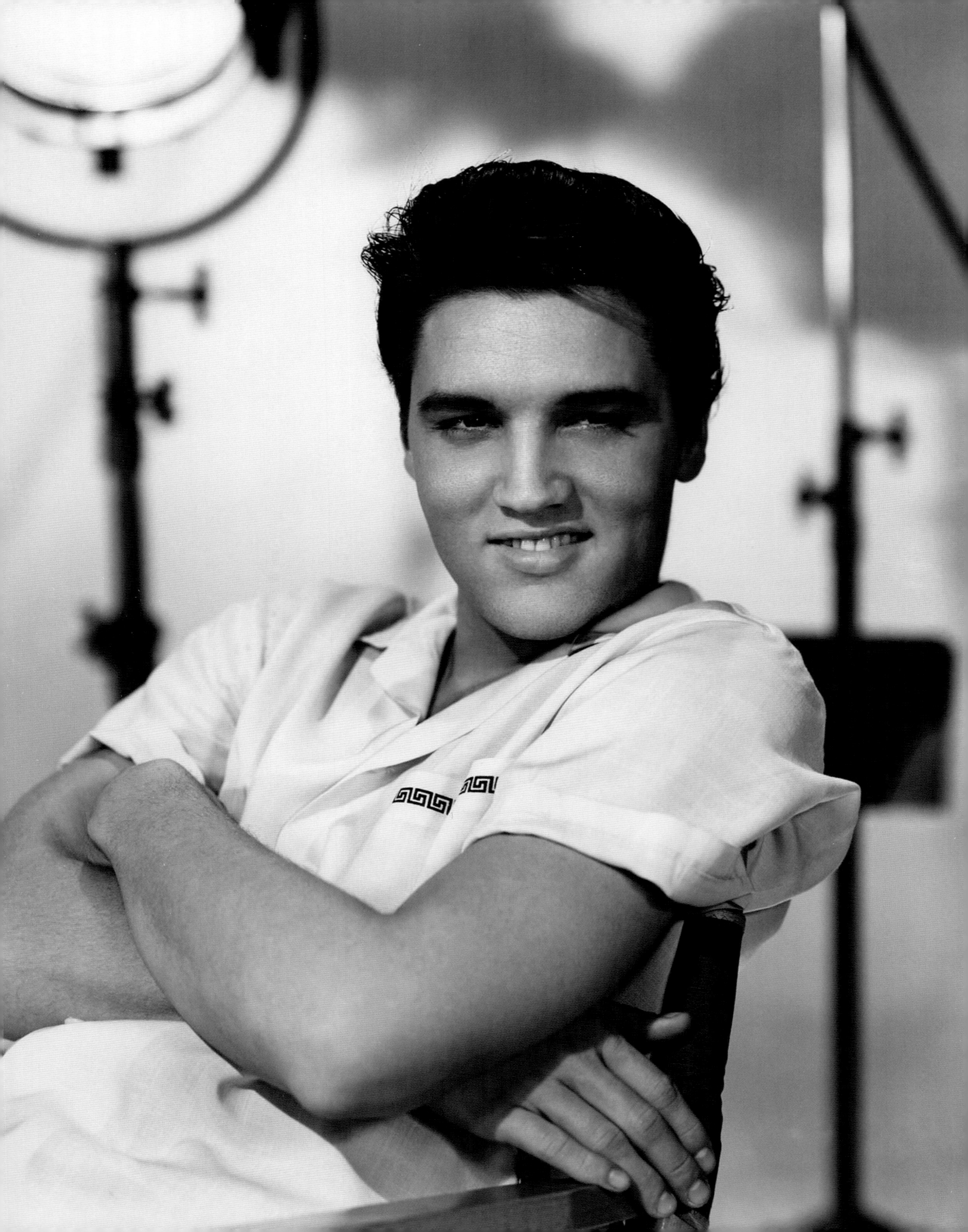

the 50s

A tycoon hires a tutor to teach his lover proper etiquette.

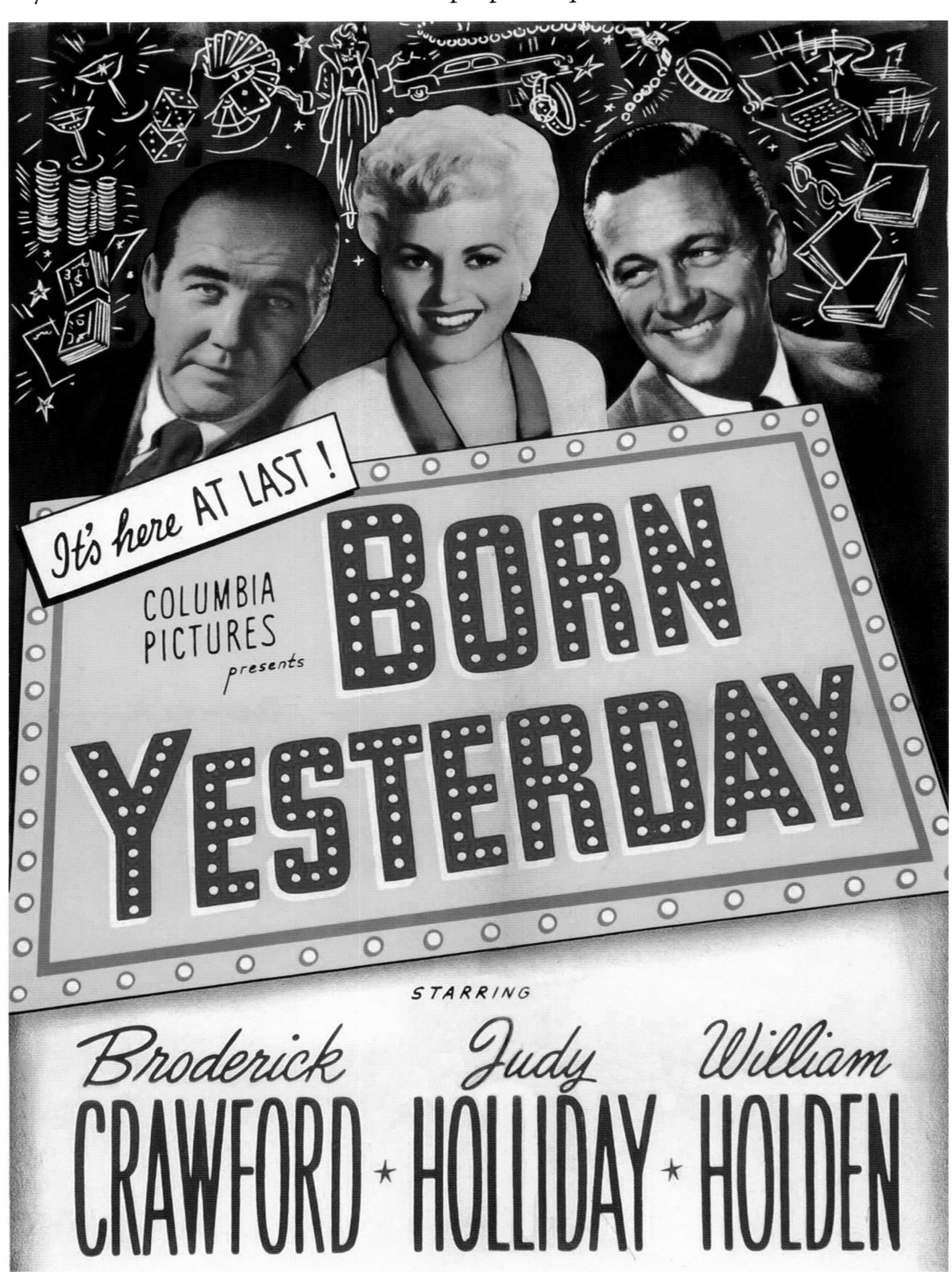

Jon Lyus of HeyUGuys wrote: "The moment Judy Holliday opens her mouth and screeches 'Whaaaaaaat????' in a thick New York accent it is hard to not fall in love with her."

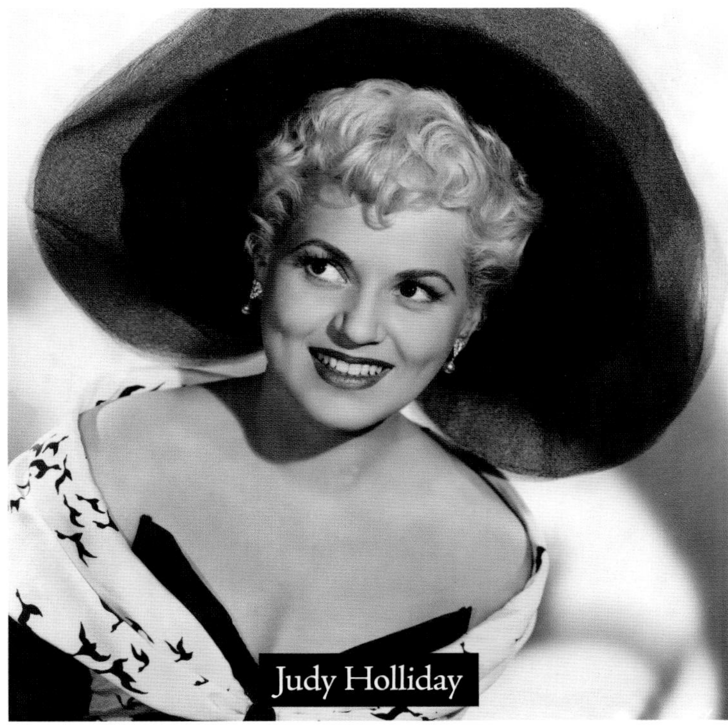
Judy Holliday

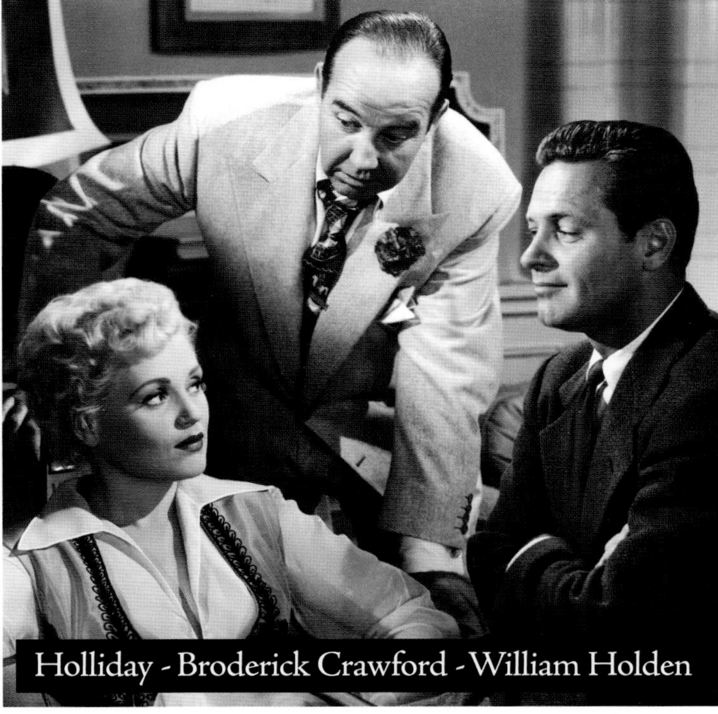
Holliday - Broderick Crawford - William Holden

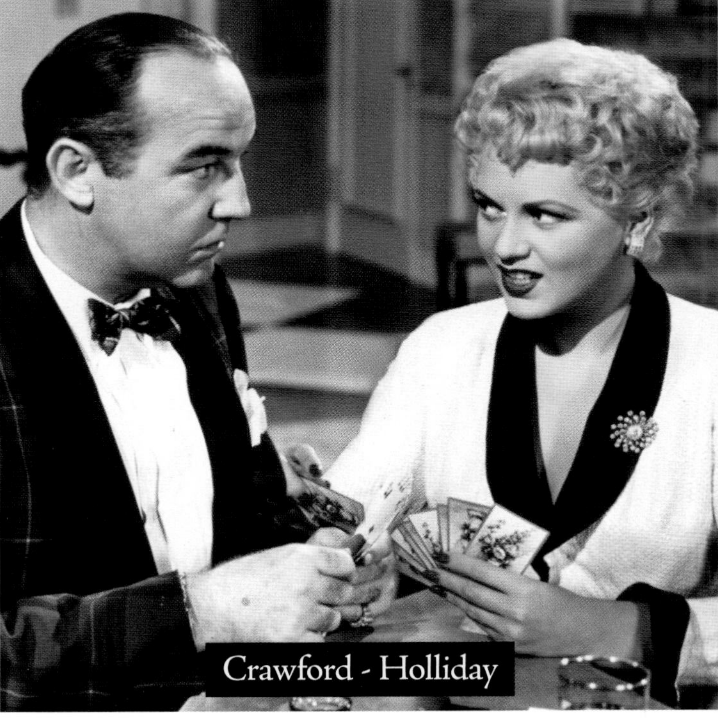
Crawford - Holliday

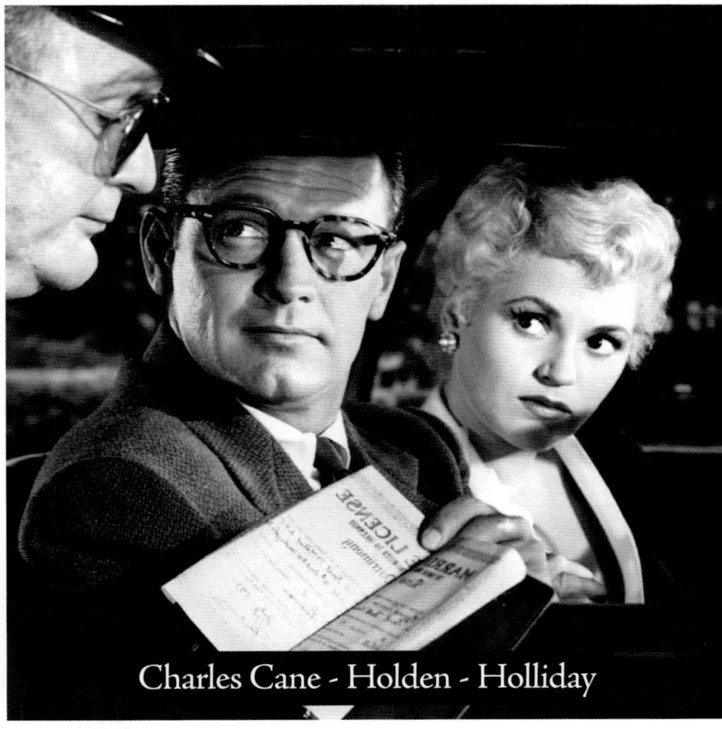

Charles Cane - Holden - Holliday

In 1965, I visited Judy Holliday in her apartment to offer her the leading roll in "The Art of Love," a film I was about to direct. She was lying on her living room floor explaining that she had a nagging pain in her back, but agreed to read the script and get back to me.

A few days after our meeting, forty-three year old Judy Holliday, one of the most talented and beloved actresses in our business, sadly passed away.

An ingénue insinuates herself into the company of an established but aging stage actress and her circle of theater friends.

BETTE DAVIS ANNE BAXTER GEORGE SANDERS CELESTE HOLM

ALL ABOUT EVE

Robert Hatch of The New Republic wrote: "What makes the picture seem so good and eminently worth seeing are the satirical touches in its detail and the performance of Bette Davis."

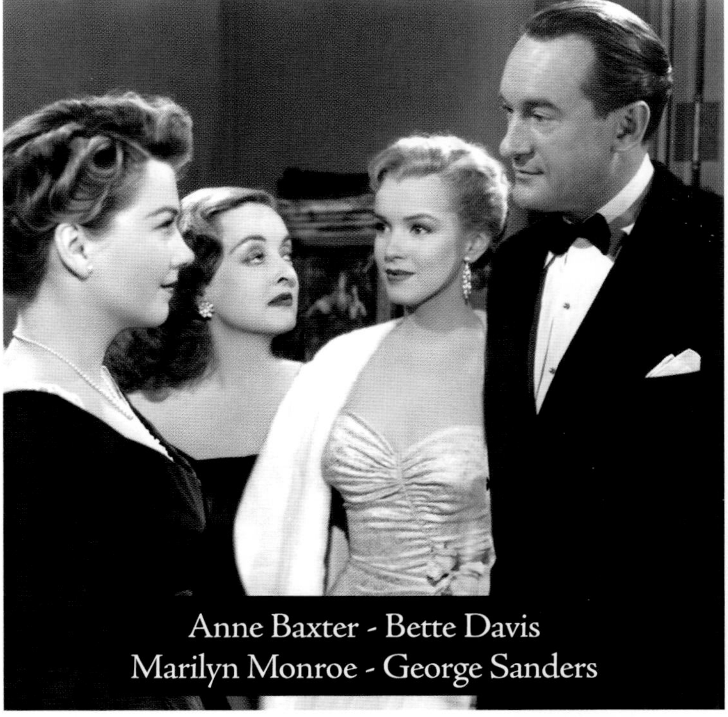
Anne Baxter - Bette Davis
Marilyn Monroe - George Sanders

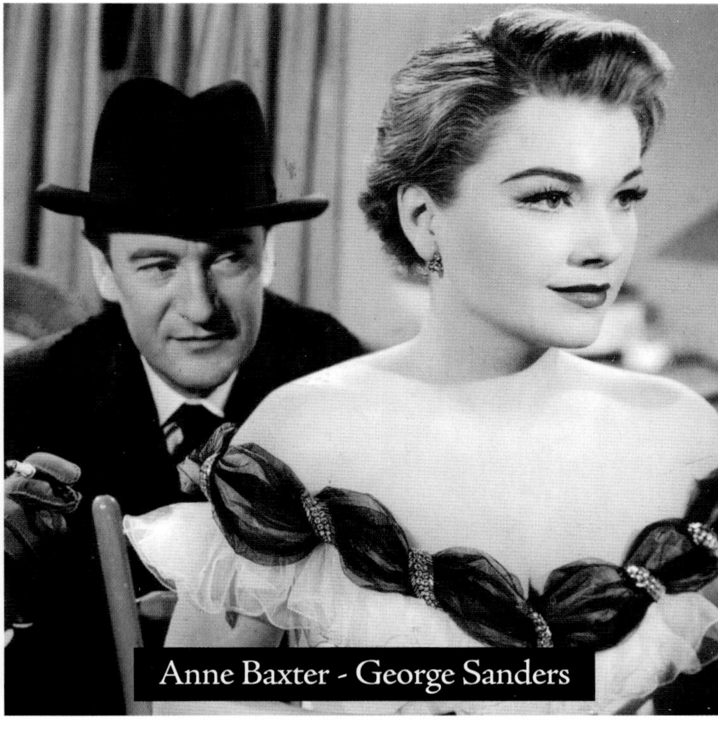
Anne Baxter - George Sanders

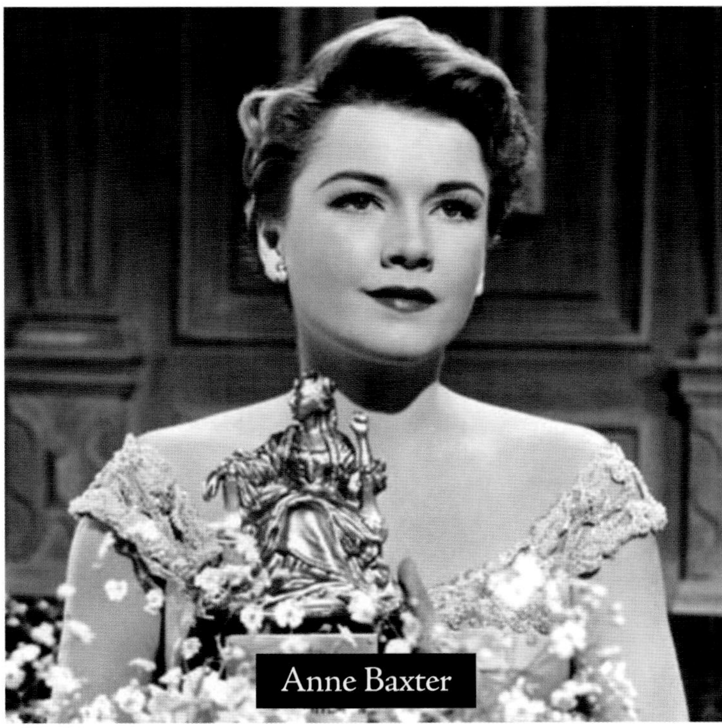
Anne Baxter

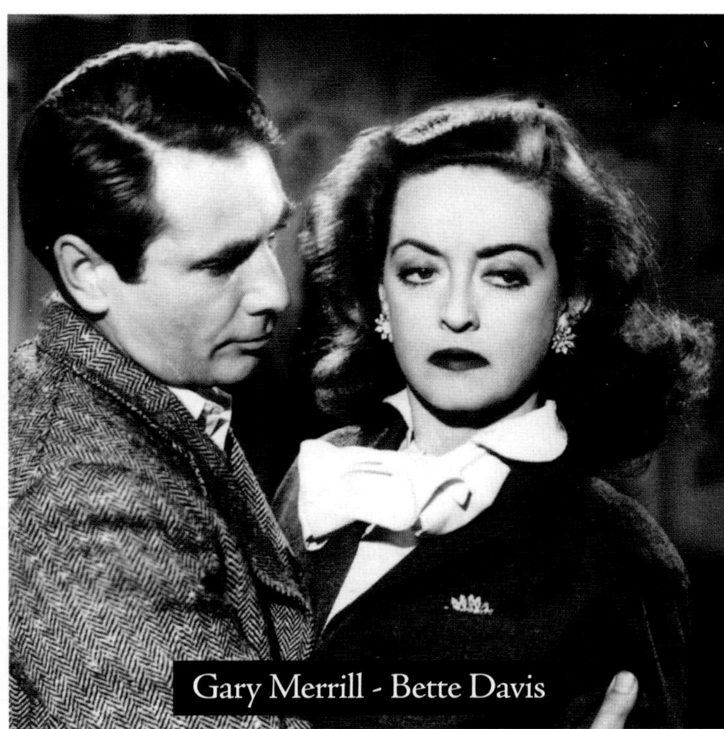
Gary Merrill - Bette Davis

Bette Davis appeared in 102 films and this film was her 61st and in my top five. How often has Bette Davis played a character who figuratively stabbed people in the back? Many times. And how often does she get to be the stabbee? Only once, and in "All About Eve," Anne Baxter is the one Bette deservedly attacks.

Yes, in the top left photo, playing a small part is Marilyn Monroe.

A screenwriter is hired to rework a faded silent film star's script, only to find himself developing a dangerous relationship.

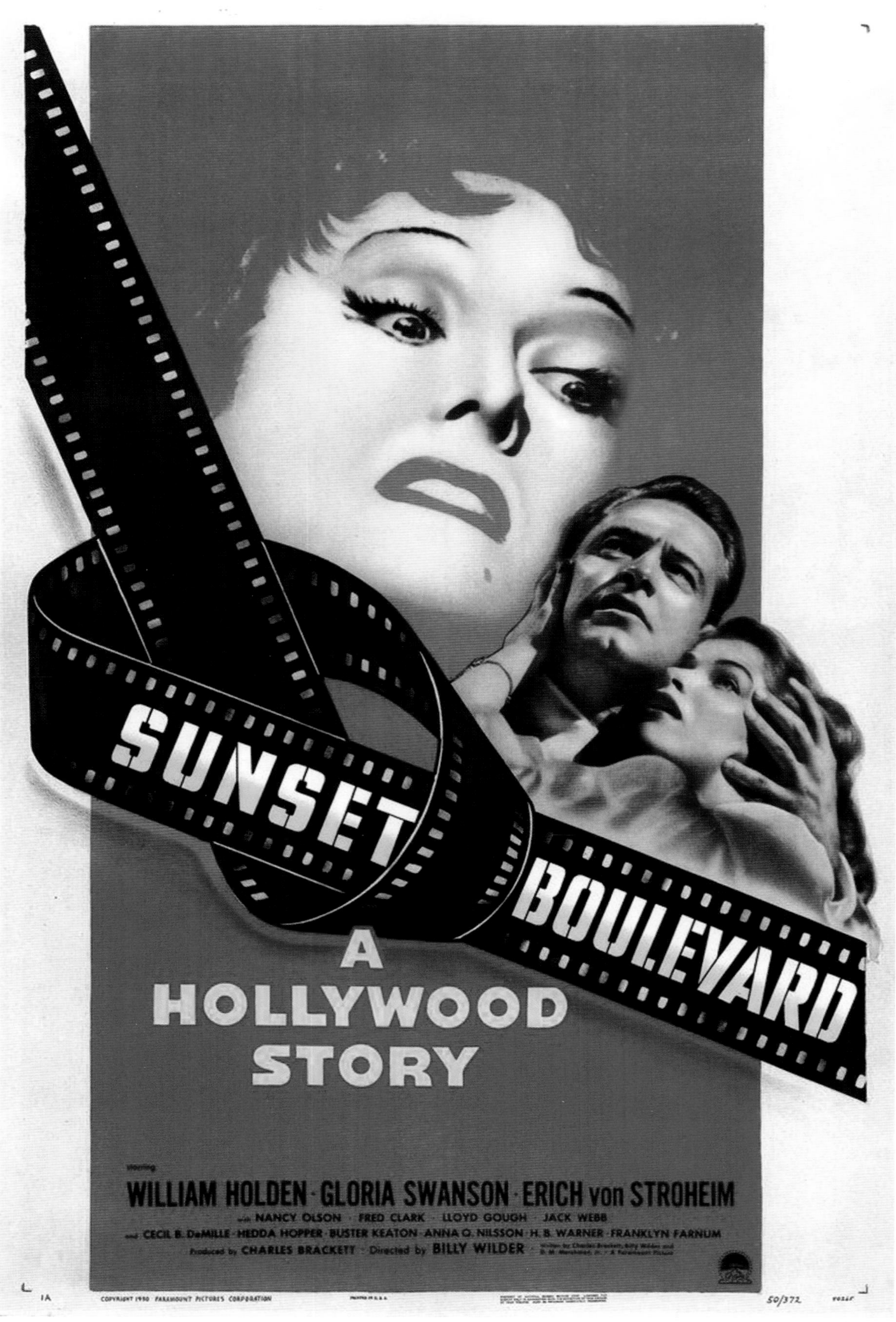

Don Druker of Chicago Reader wrote: "A tour de force for Swanson and Wilder."
Andrew Sarris of NY Observer wrote: "Best Hollywood movie ever made about Hollywood."

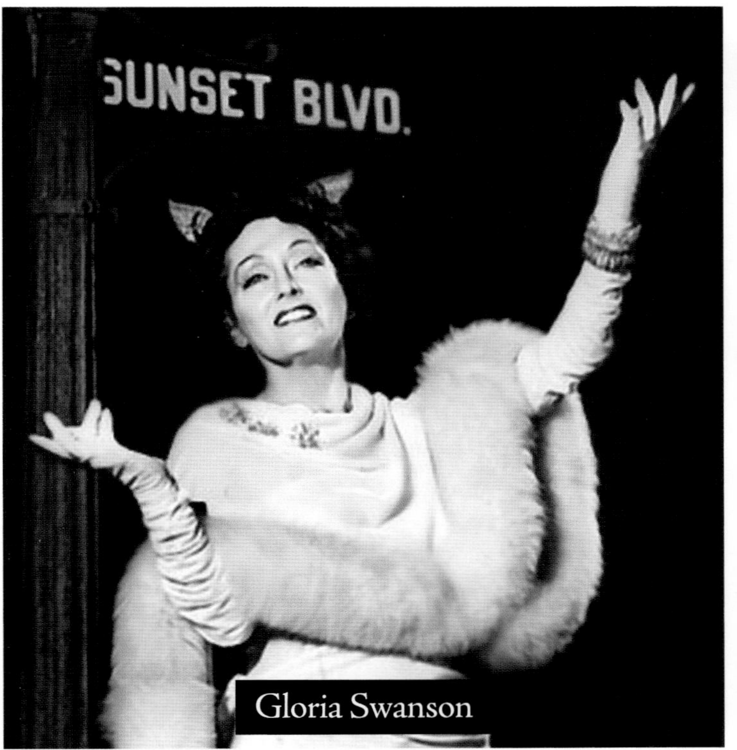

Gloria Swanson

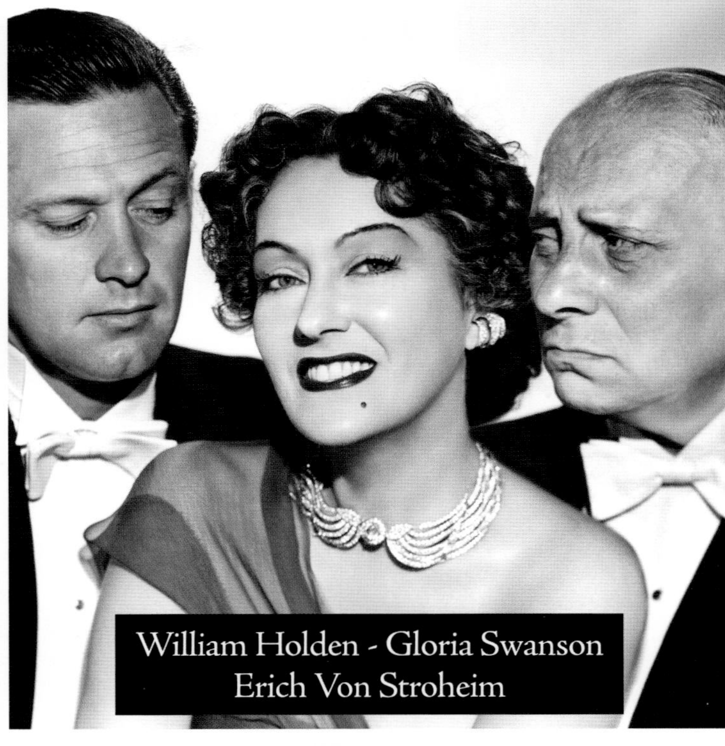
William Holden - Gloria Swanson
Erich Von Stroheim

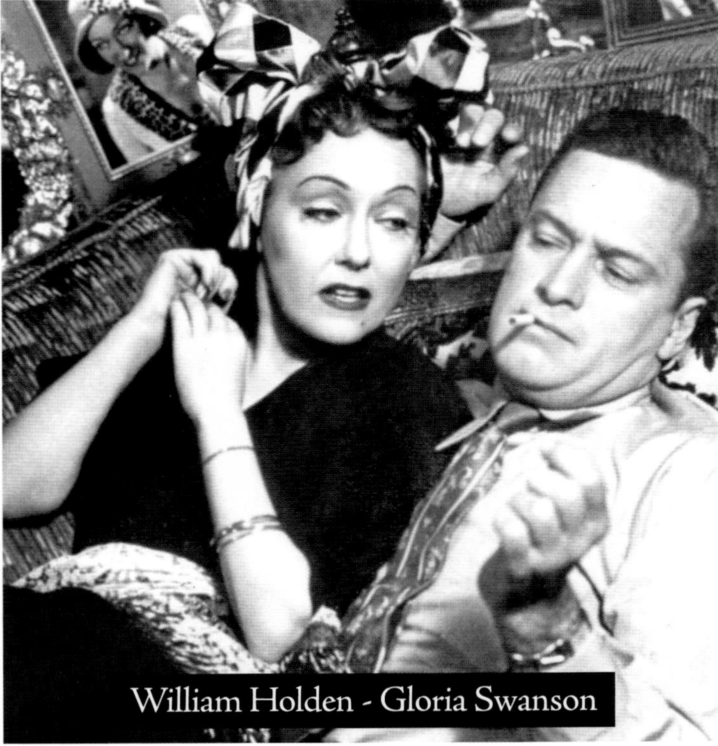
William Holden - Gloria Swanson

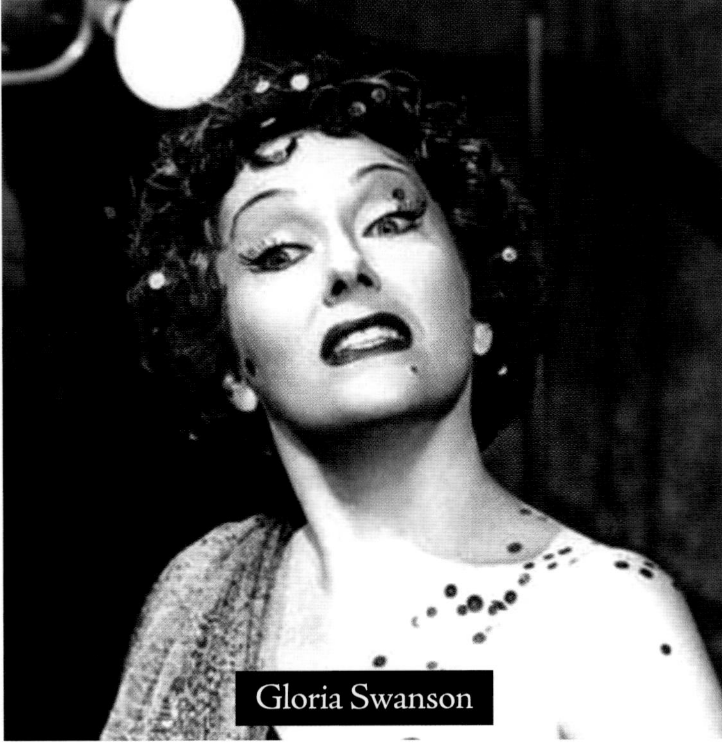
Gloria Swanson

In her distinguished sixty years on the silver screen, which encompassed fifty-four feature films, her performance in "Sunset Boulevard" was considered her very best. In it, on screen, Gloria Swanson played a vixen and off screen, she was a bit of a vixen, having an ongoing affair with the scion of one of America's wealthiest and most prestigious families.

An alien lands and tells the people of Earth that they must live peacefully or be destroyed as a danger to other planets.

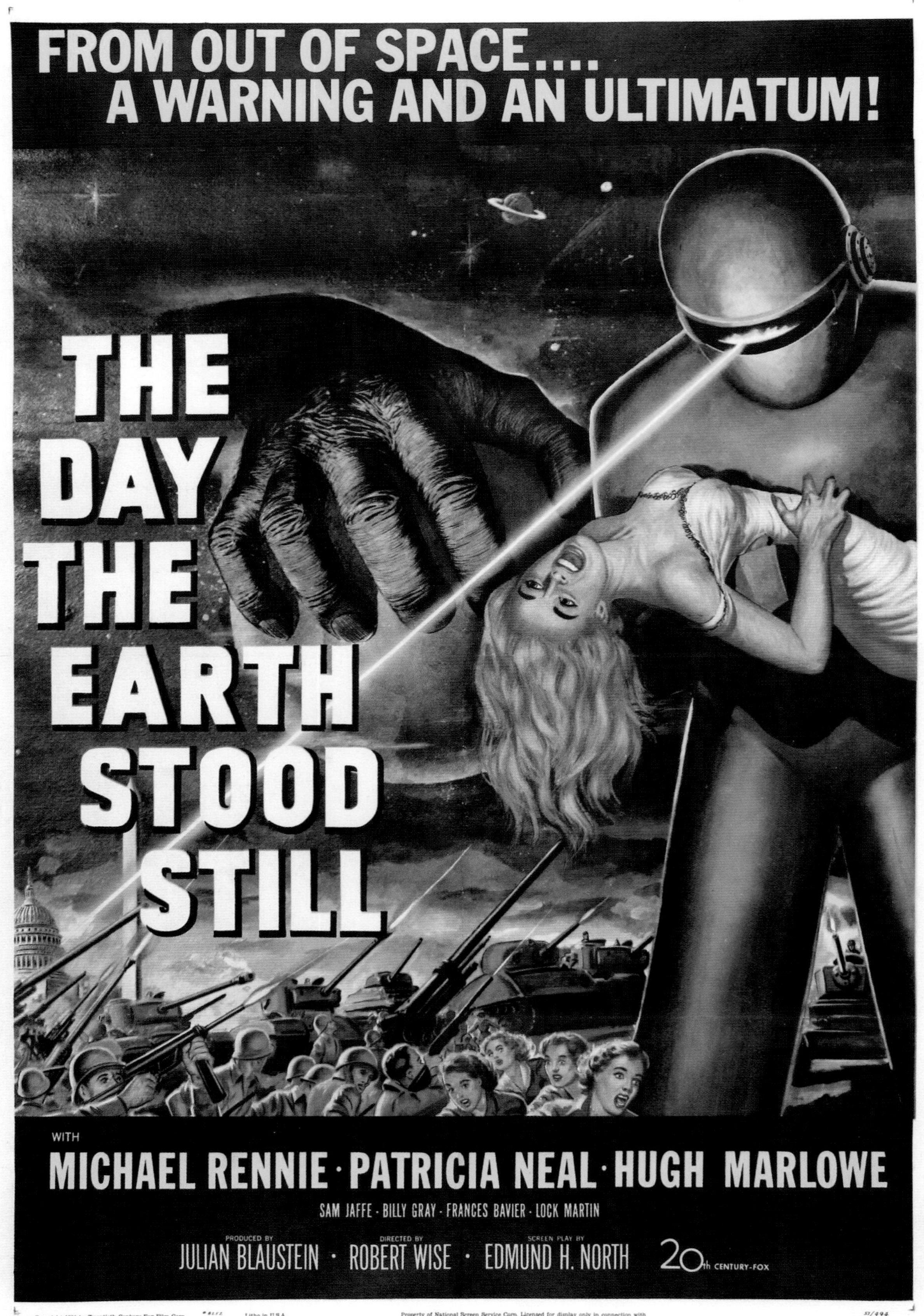

Time Out wrote: "Edmund H. North's intelligent script and Wise's smooth direction are serious without being solemn, while Bernard Herrmann's effectively alien-sounding score reinforces the atmosphere of strangeness and potential menace."

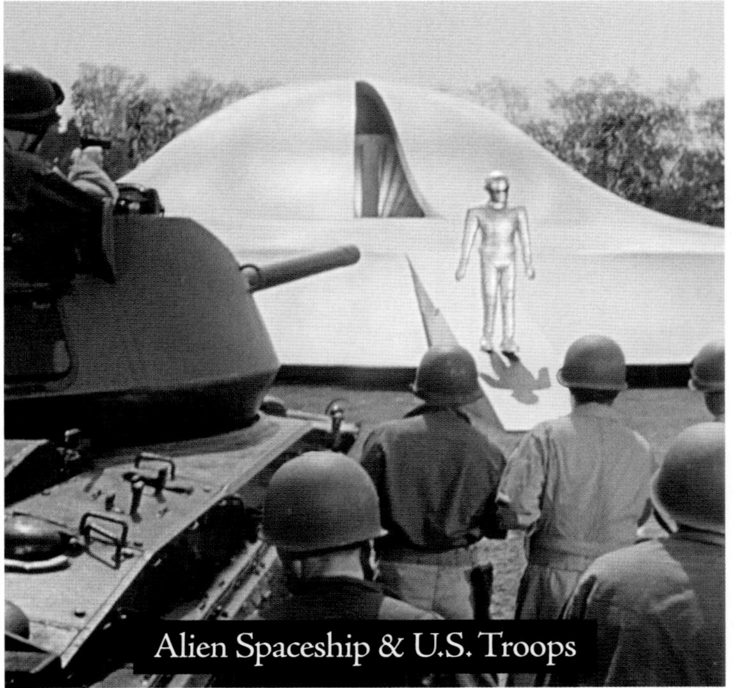
Alien Spaceship & U.S. Troops

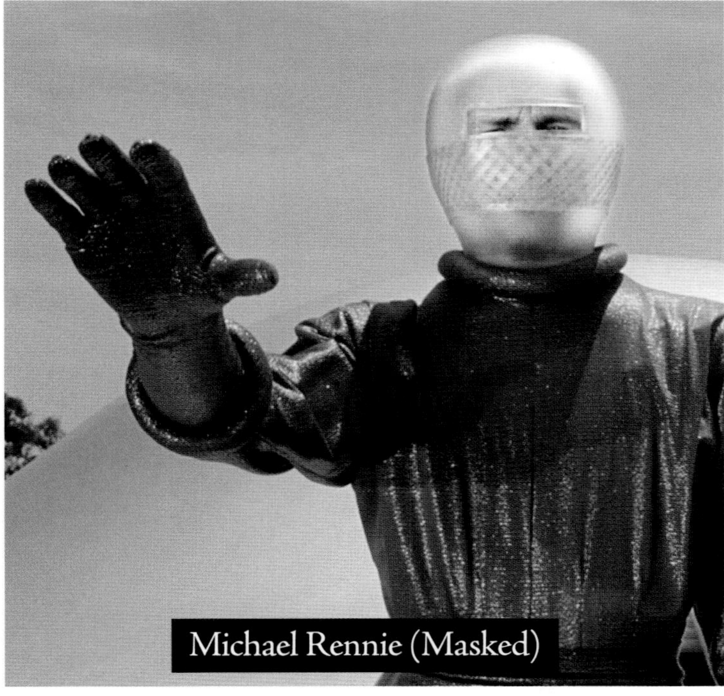
Michael Rennie (Masked)

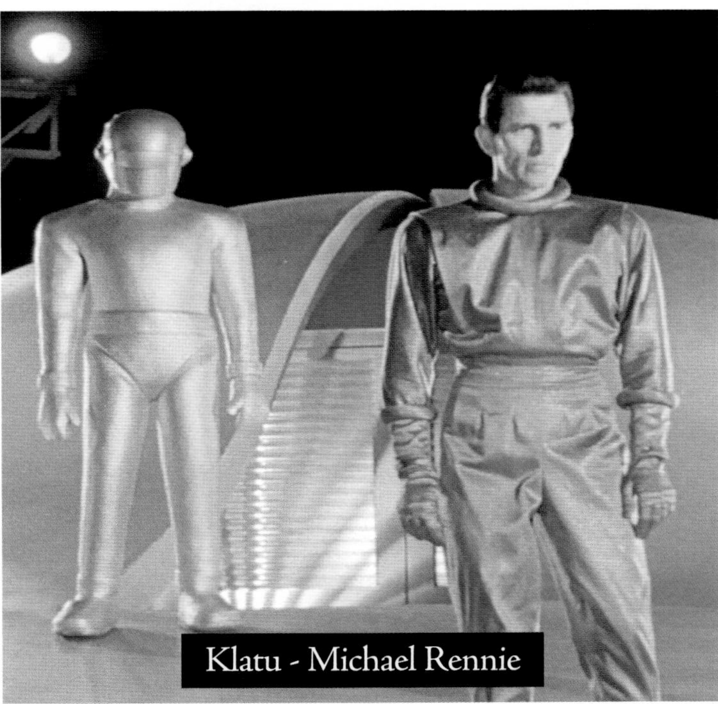
Klatu - Michael Rennie

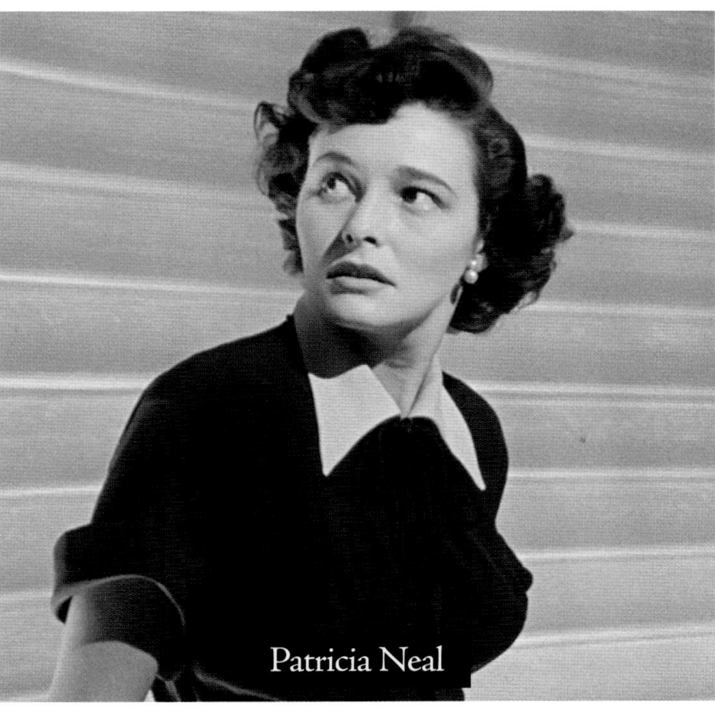
Patricia Neal

A spaceship with aliens from a distant planet comes to Earth to warn us that we face extinction unless we stop polluting the atmosphere. To this day I remember the words the aliens used, warning us Earthlings to mend our ways. Sid Caesar, Mel Brooks and everyone on "Your Show of Shows" kept repeating this phrase:

"Klacto nicto barada." "Klacto nicto barada." "Klacto nicto barada."

The daughter of a riverboat captain falls in love with a charming gambler, but their fairytale romance is threatened when his luck turns sour.

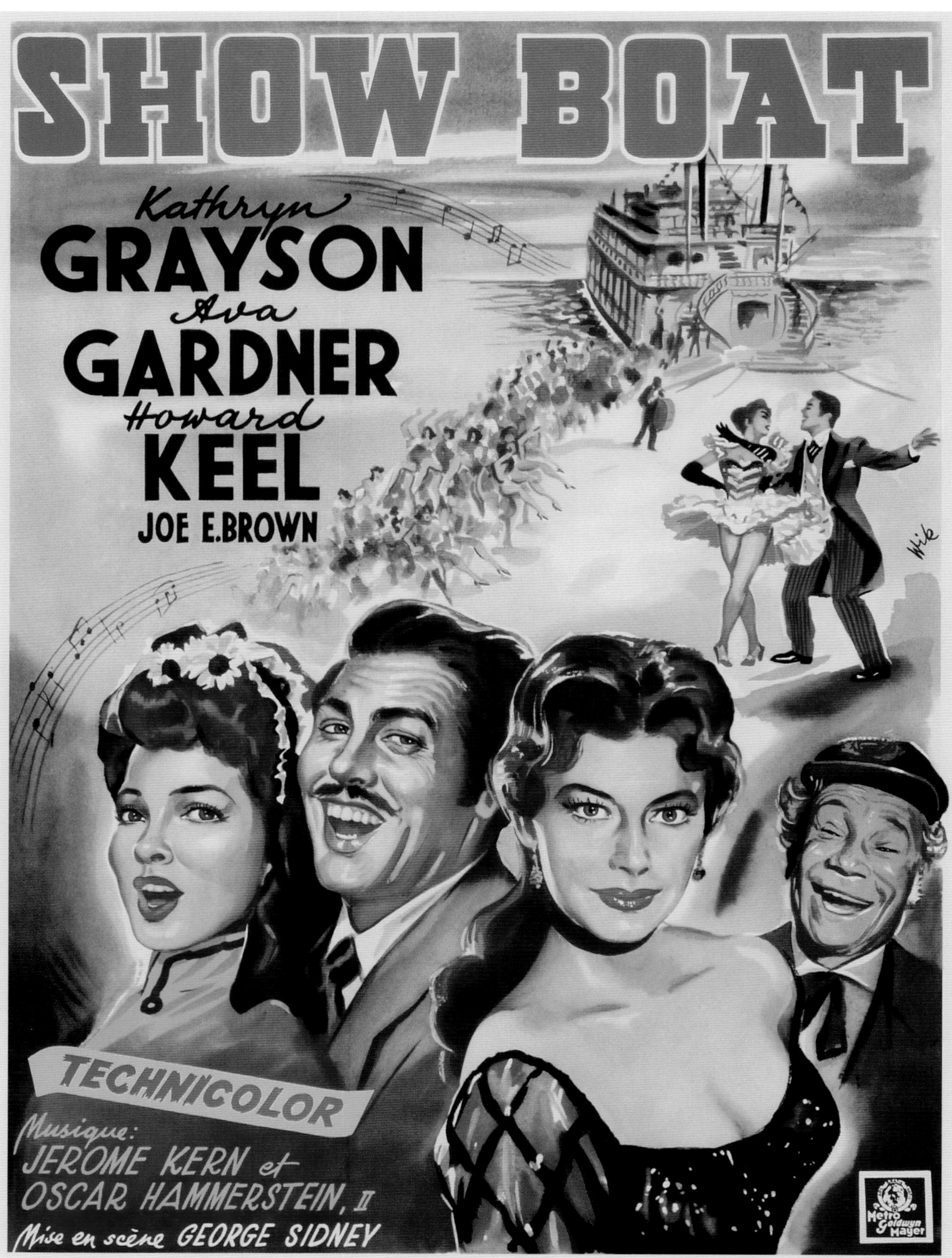

Michael Troudt wrote: "MGM's loving, lovely Technicolor adaptation of the groundbreaking stage musical retains most of Jerome Kern's music and strengthens the role of Julie, poignantly played by Ava Gardner; William Warfield also does well singing 'Ol' Man River.'"

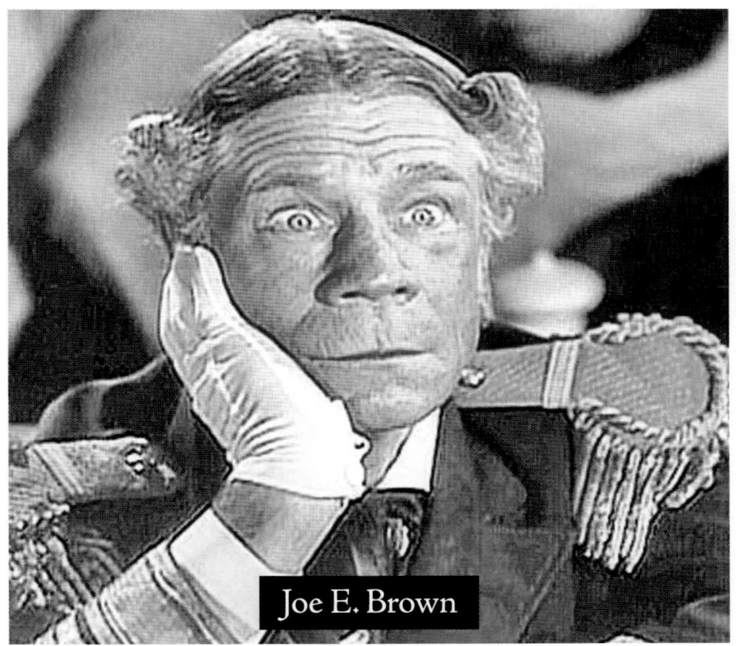
Joe E. Brown

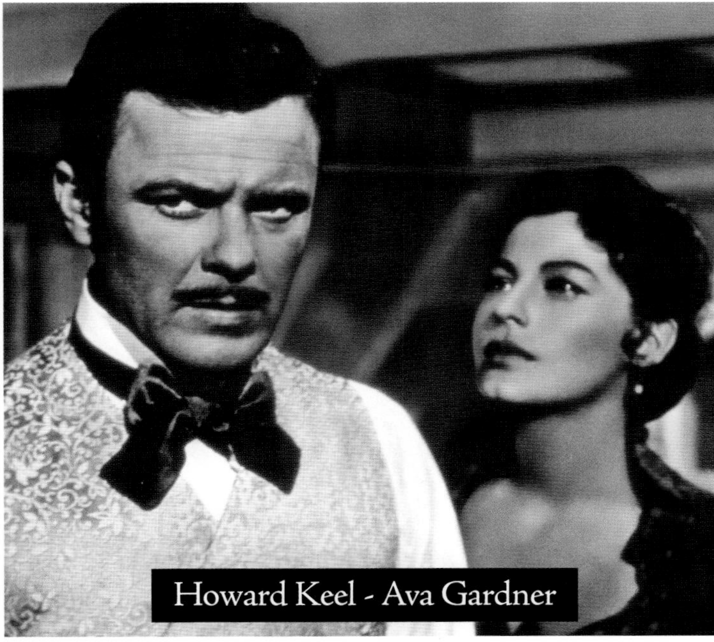
Howard Keel - Ava Gardner

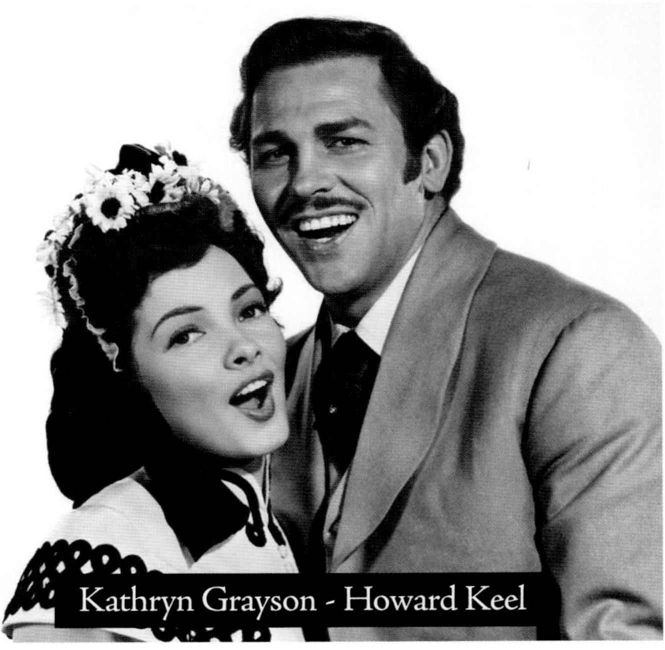
Kathryn Grayson - Howard Keel

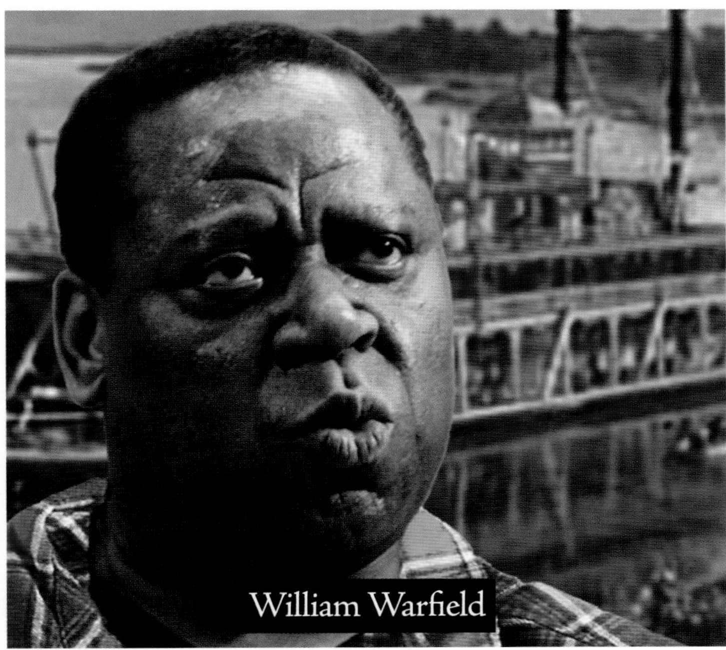
William Warfield

As the critic said, William Warfield, who sang "Ol' Man River," does it well, but not nearly as well as the brilliant Paul Robeson, who played the part in 1936.

In 1947, William Warfield and I toured the country as cast members of the Broadway musical, "Call Me Mister." We became good friends and I was happy when he was cast to play the lead in a touring version of George Gershwin's "Porgy & Bess," in which he co-starred with his wife, Leontyne Price. William Warfield became the first African-American to sing leading roles at The New York Metropolitan Opera.

A poor boy gets a job working for his rich uncle and ends up falling in love with two women.

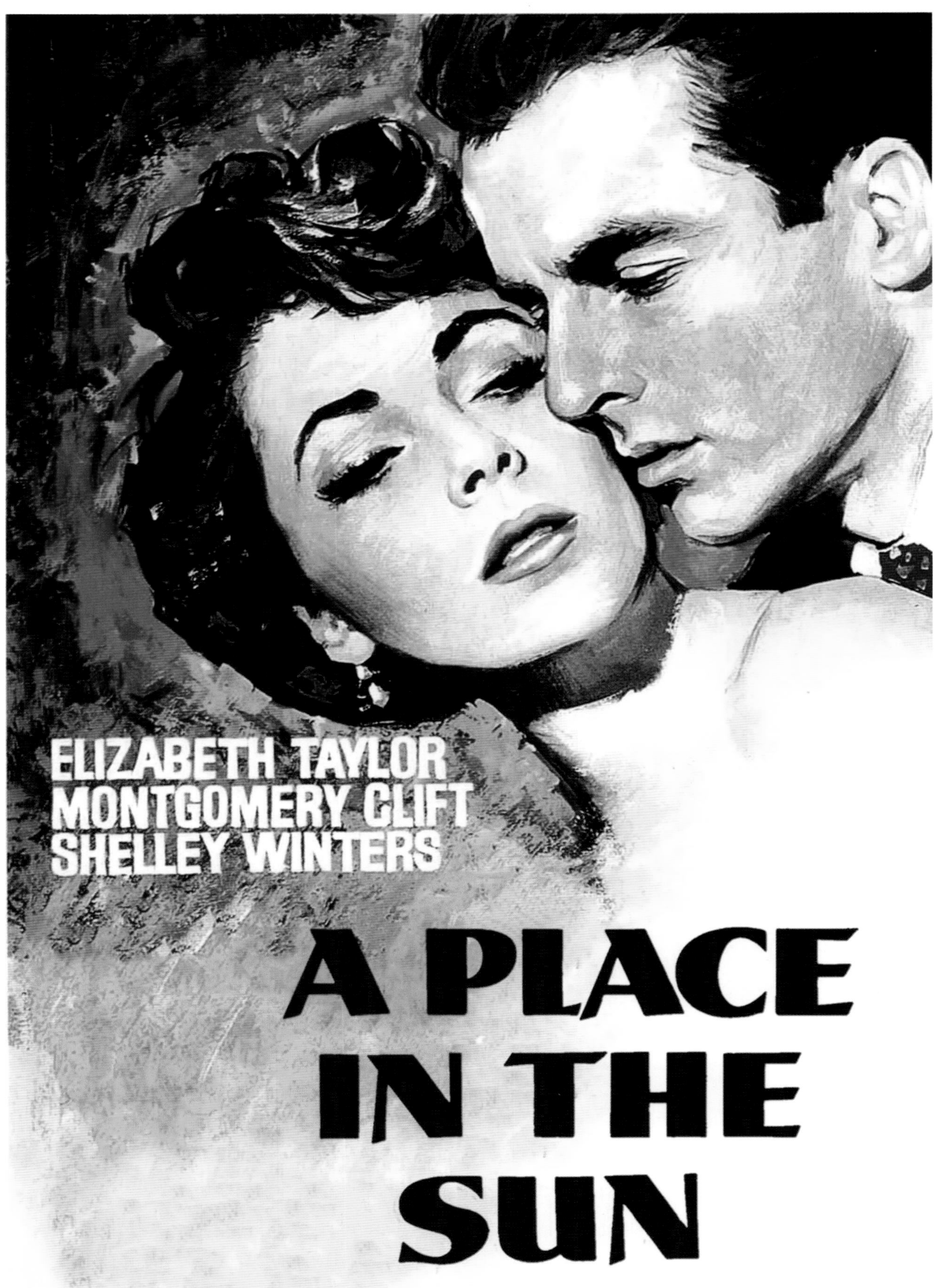

Evan Williams of The Australian wrote: "One of the great studio dramas and one of this column's favourite films, with haunting performances from Elizabeth Taylor and Montgomery Clift."

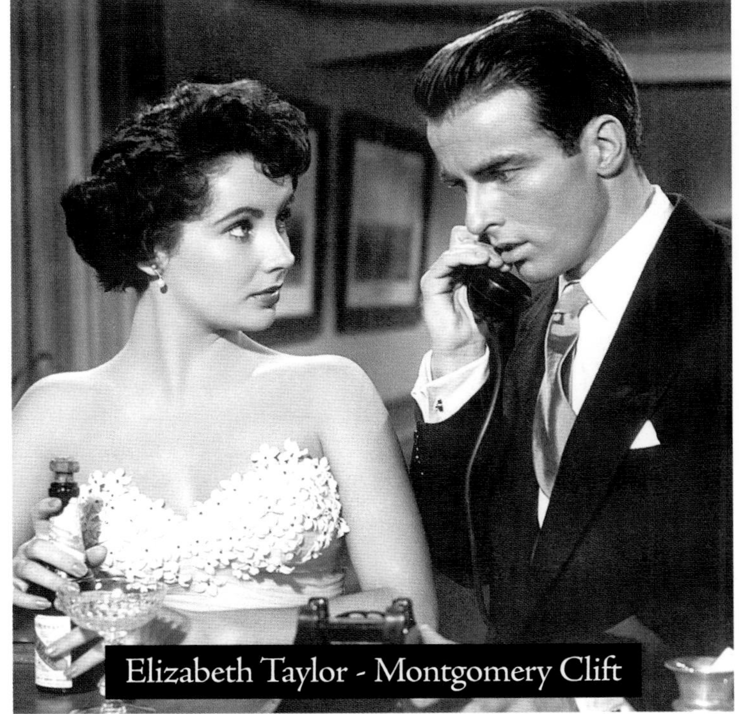
Elizabeth Taylor - Montgomery Clift

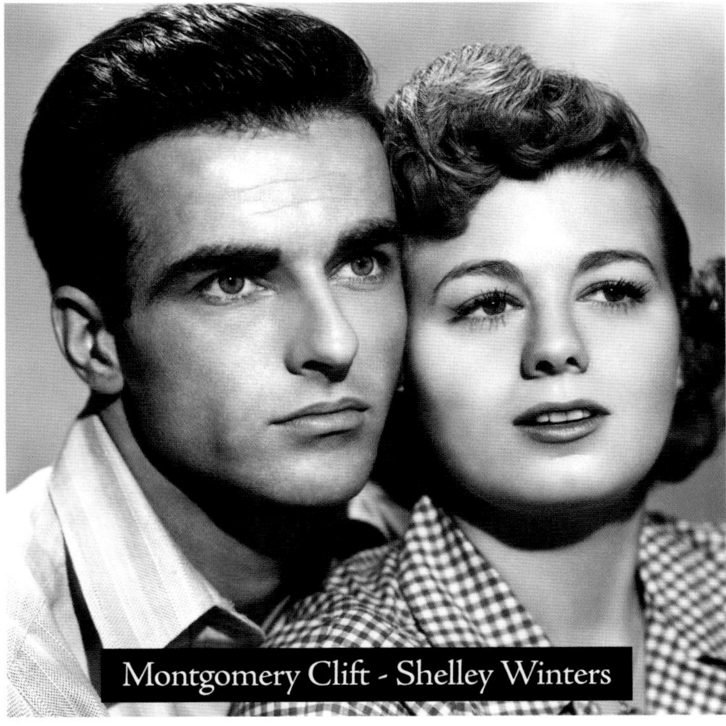
Montgomery Clift - Shelley Winters

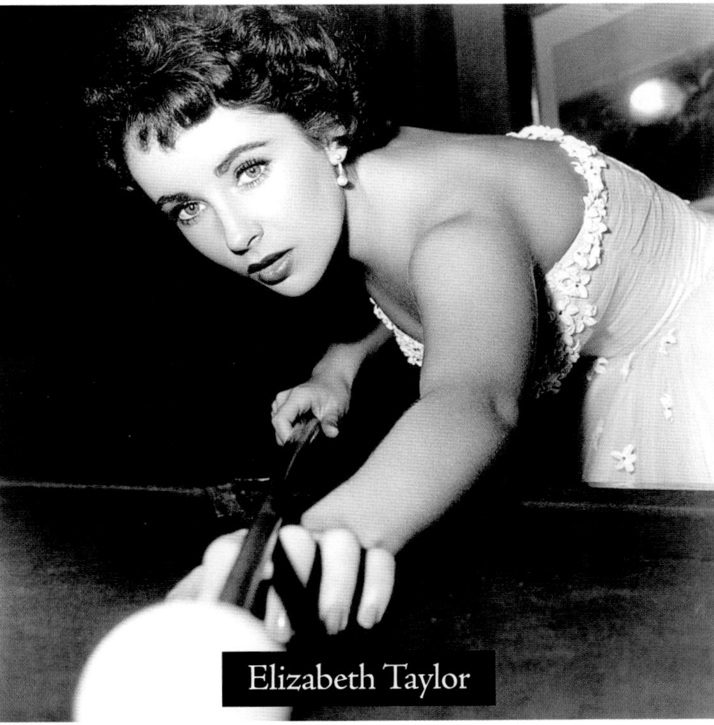
Elizabeth Taylor

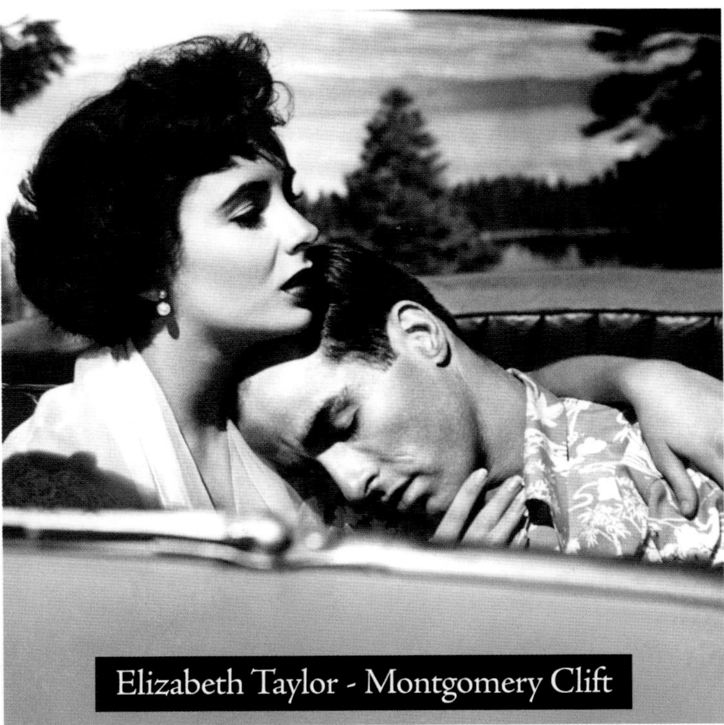
Elizabeth Taylor - Montgomery Clift

Monty Clift, an actor with tremendous charm and ability, nominated for 4 Oscars, among them "From Here to Eternity" and " Judgment at Nuremberg," passed away at the age of 45.

I had the great pleasure and slight displeasure of directing Shelley Winters in a movie adaptation of my stage adaptation of my novel, "Enter Laughing." Shelley was a great actress, but, as they say, "a handful."

A fierce Roman commander becomes infatuated with a beautiful Christian hostage and begins questioning the tyrannical leadership of the despot Emperor Nero.

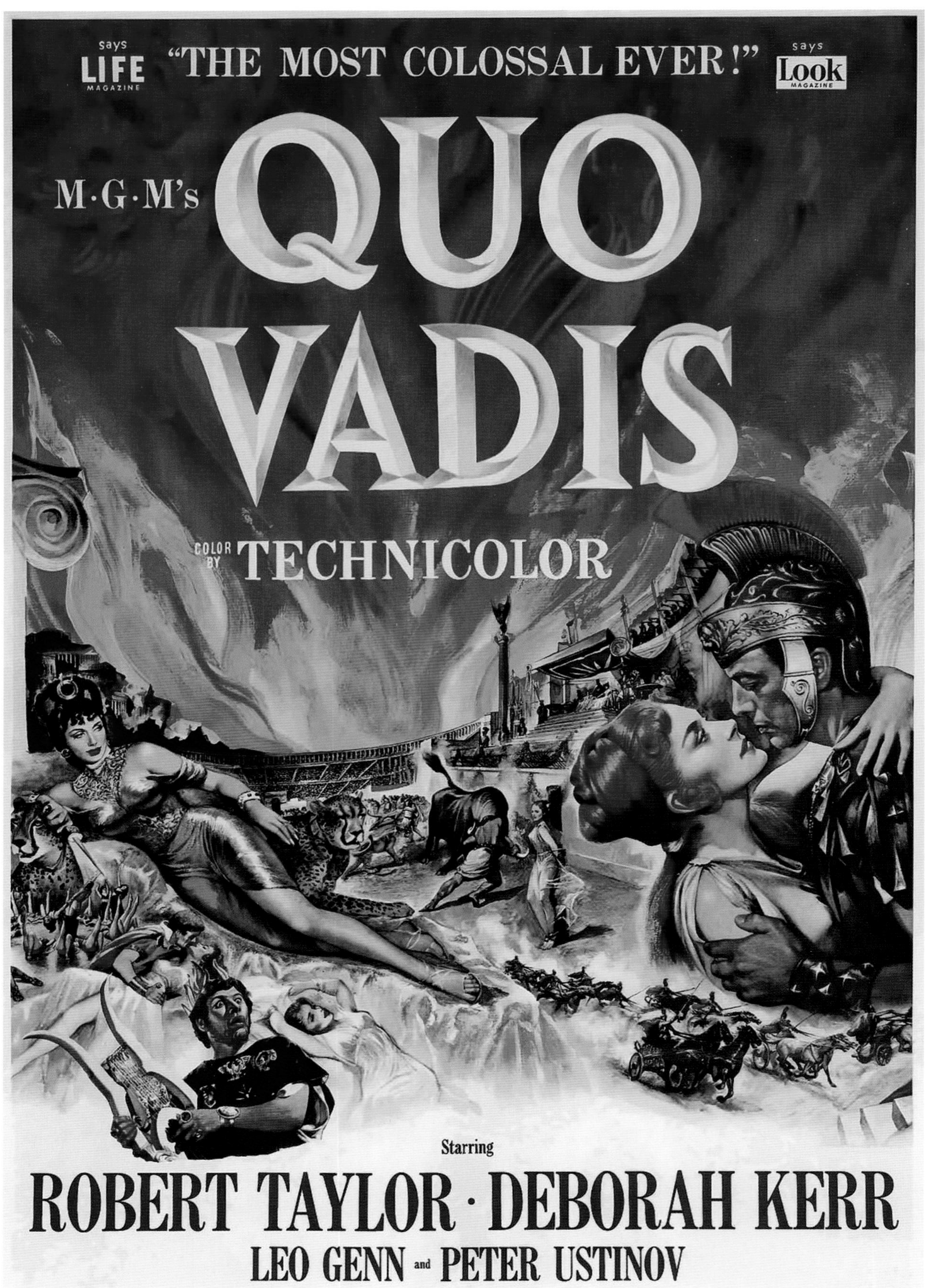

TIME Magazine wrote: "For sheer size, opulence and technical razzle-dazzle, 'Quo Vadis' is the year's most impressive cinematic sight-seeing spree."

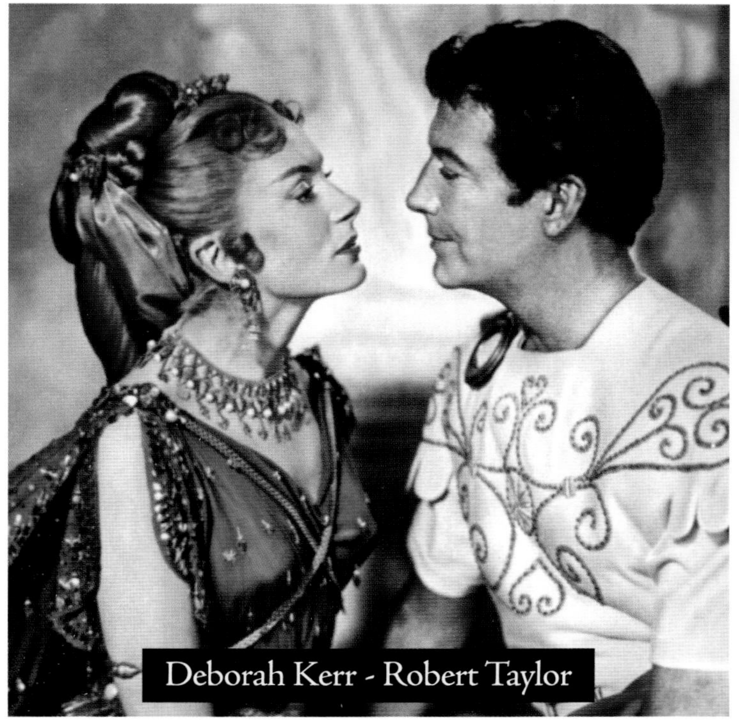
Deborah Kerr - Robert Taylor

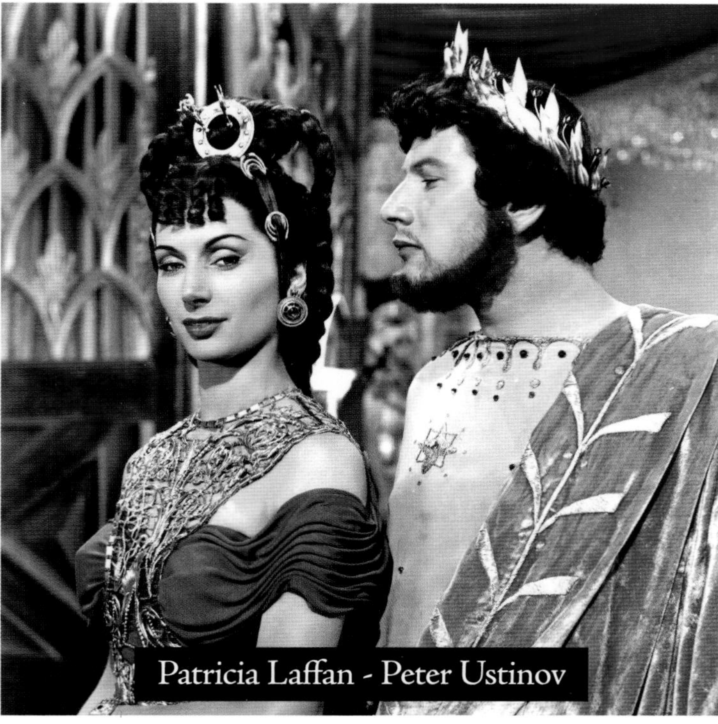
Patricia Laffan - Peter Ustinov

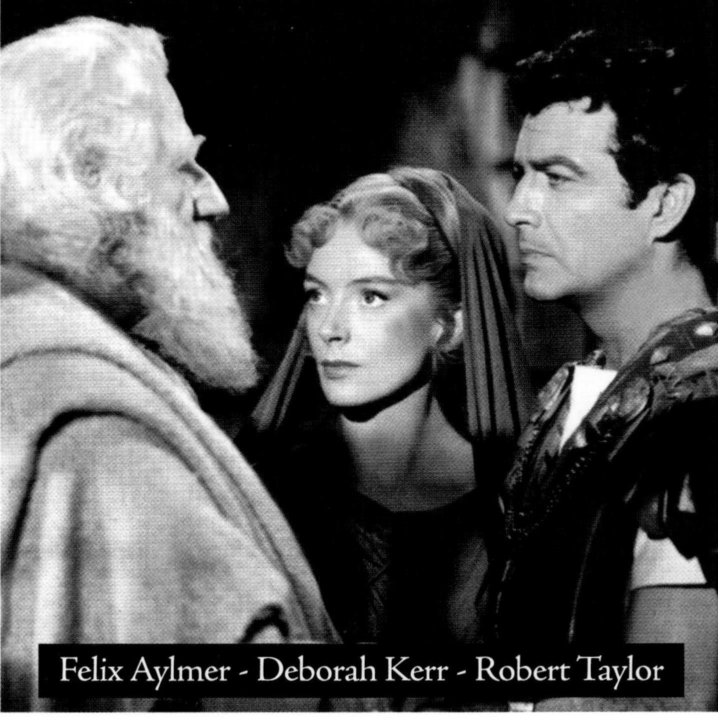
Felix Aylmer - Deborah Kerr - Robert Taylor

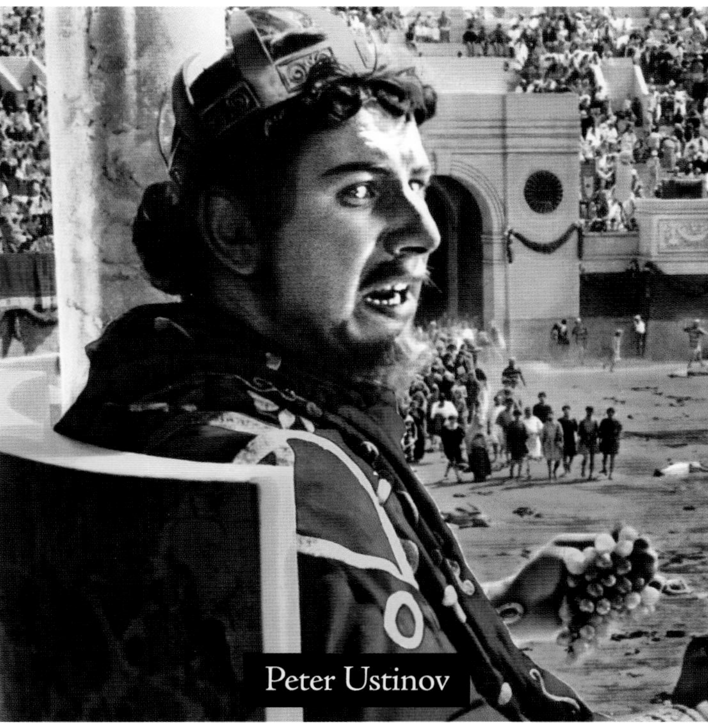
Peter Ustinov

"Quo Vadis" was produced in the era that spawned many historical events and was cast with wonderful actors, one being Peter Ustinov, who played the villainous Nero.

I had the opportunity to work with and know Peter Ustinov and unlike Nero, there wasn't a villainous bone in his body. He had a tremendous sense of humor and it was an extreme pleasure to be in his company.

Disturbed Blanche DuBois moves in with her sister in New Orleans and is tormented by her brutish brother-in-law while her reality crumbles around her.

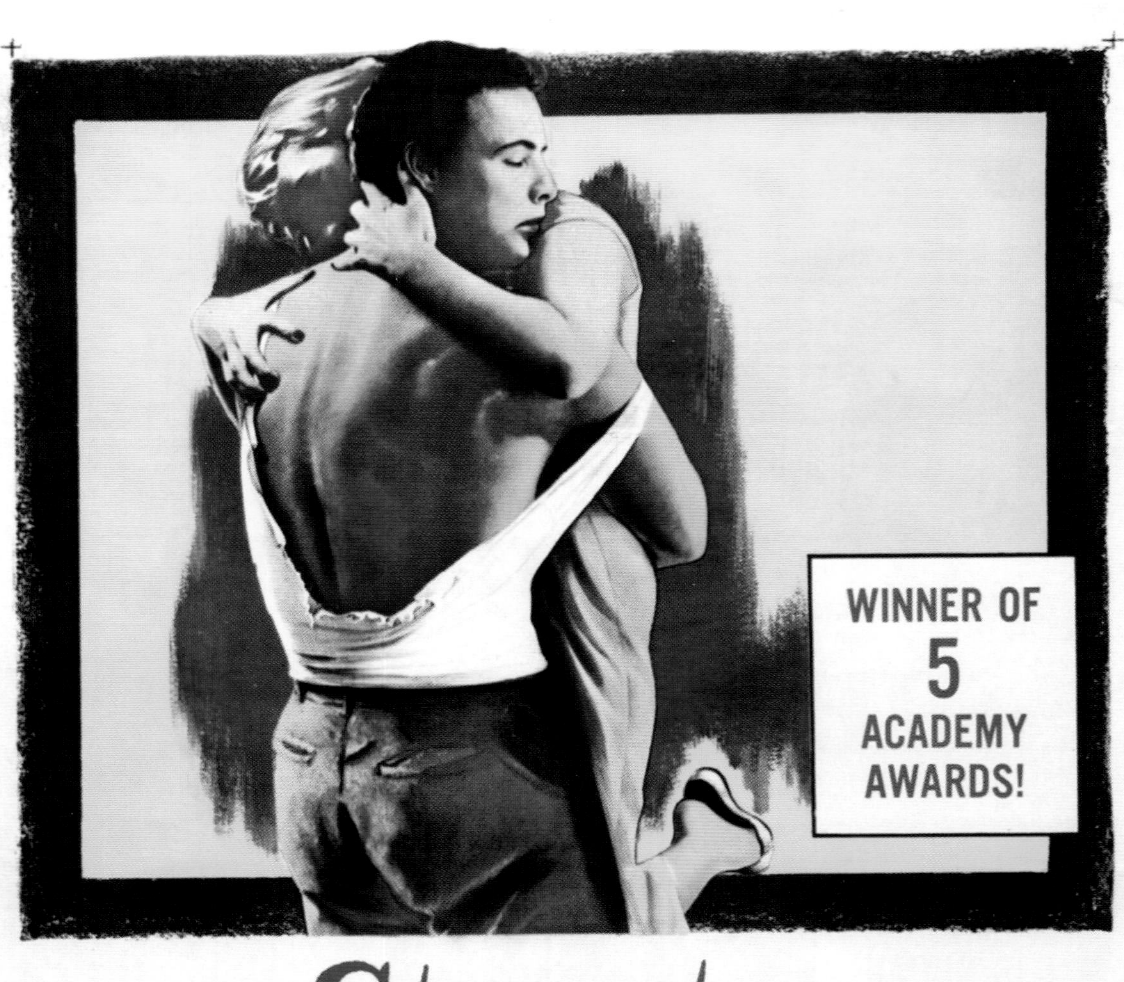

Bosley Crowther of The New York Times wrote: "Inner torments are seldom projected with such sensitivity and clarity on the screen."

Lloyd Rose of The Washington Post wrote: "Brando's performance as Stanley is one of those rare screen legends that are all they're cracked up to be."

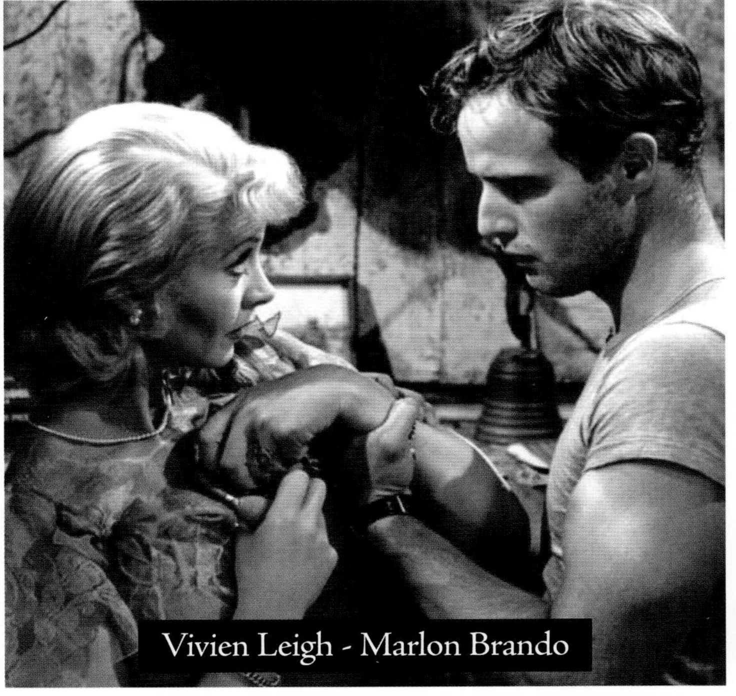

Vivien Leigh - Marlon Brando

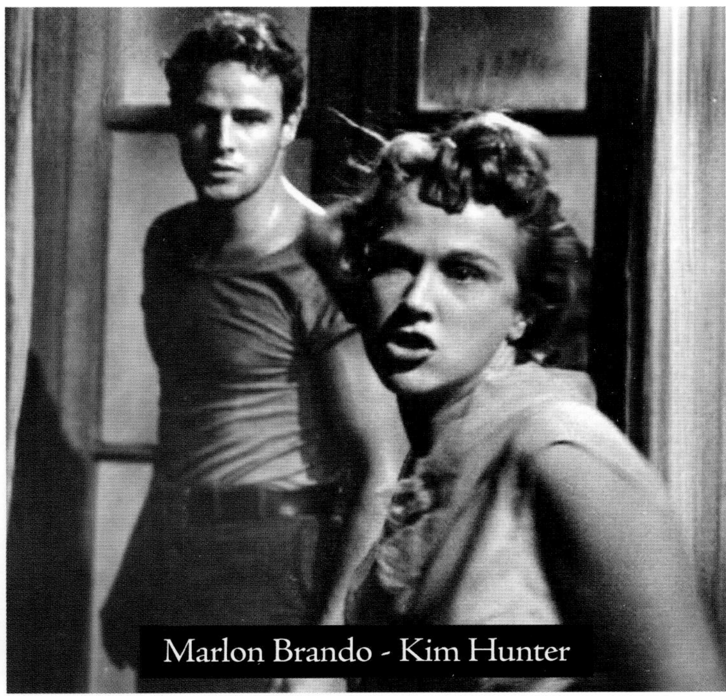

Marlon Brando - Kim Hunter

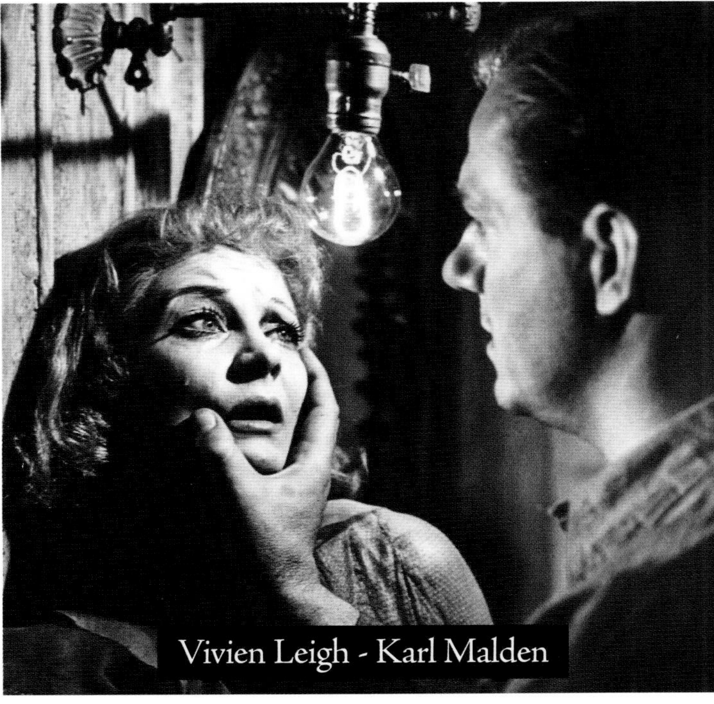

Vivien Leigh - Karl Malden

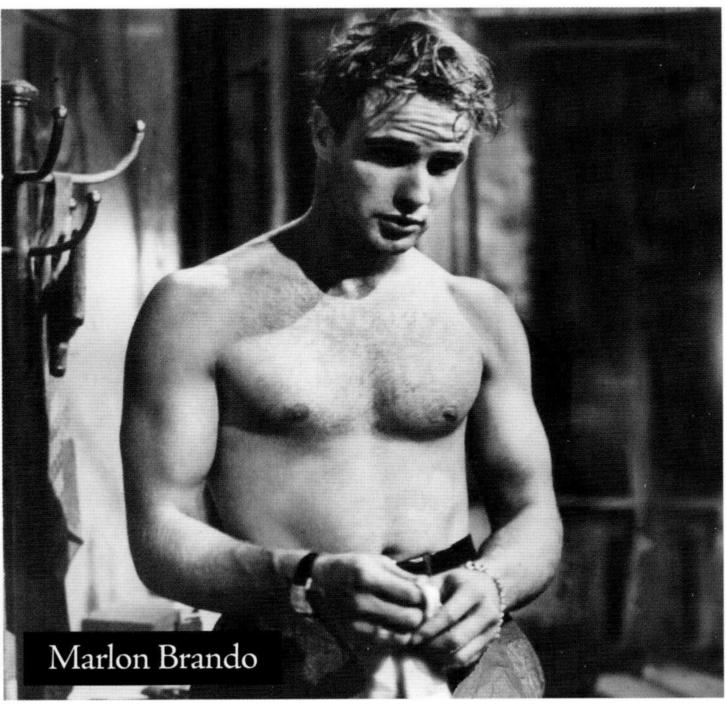

Marlon Brando

Atop every filmgoer's list of best actors you will no doubt find Marlon Brando's name. For his performance in "Streetcar Named Desire," he was nominated for an Academy Award.

Who can ever forget the scene where a disgruntled Brando says he is going to pack his bag and leave, then picks up a brown paper bag, tosses a t-shirt in it and leaves?

Three friends struggle to find work in Paris. Things become more complicated when two of them fall in love with the same woman.

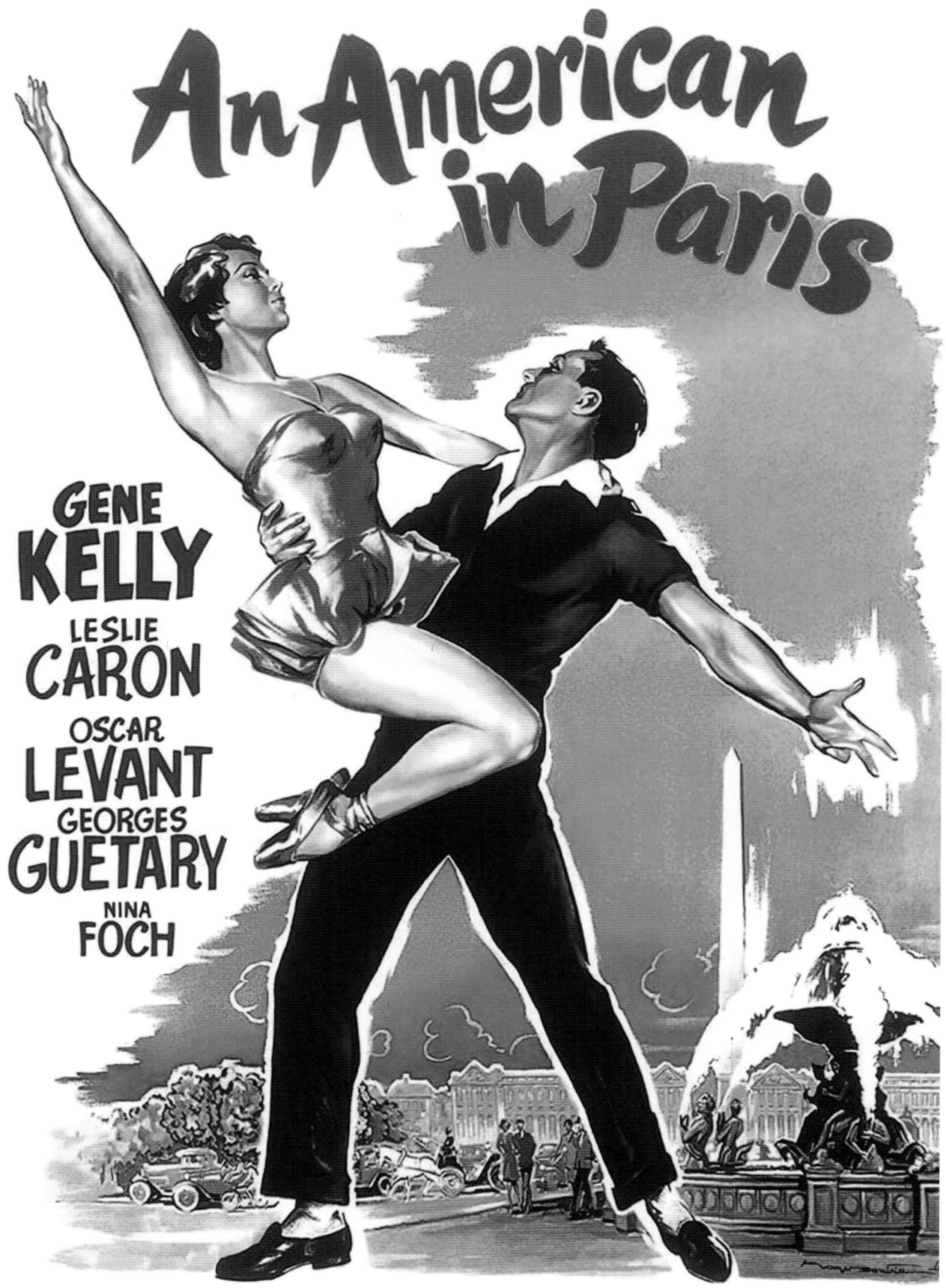

Kate Cameron of The New York Daily News wrote: "Inspired by the late George Gershwin's impressionistic musical suite of the same name, the picture is one of the finest musicals Hollywood has ever produced."

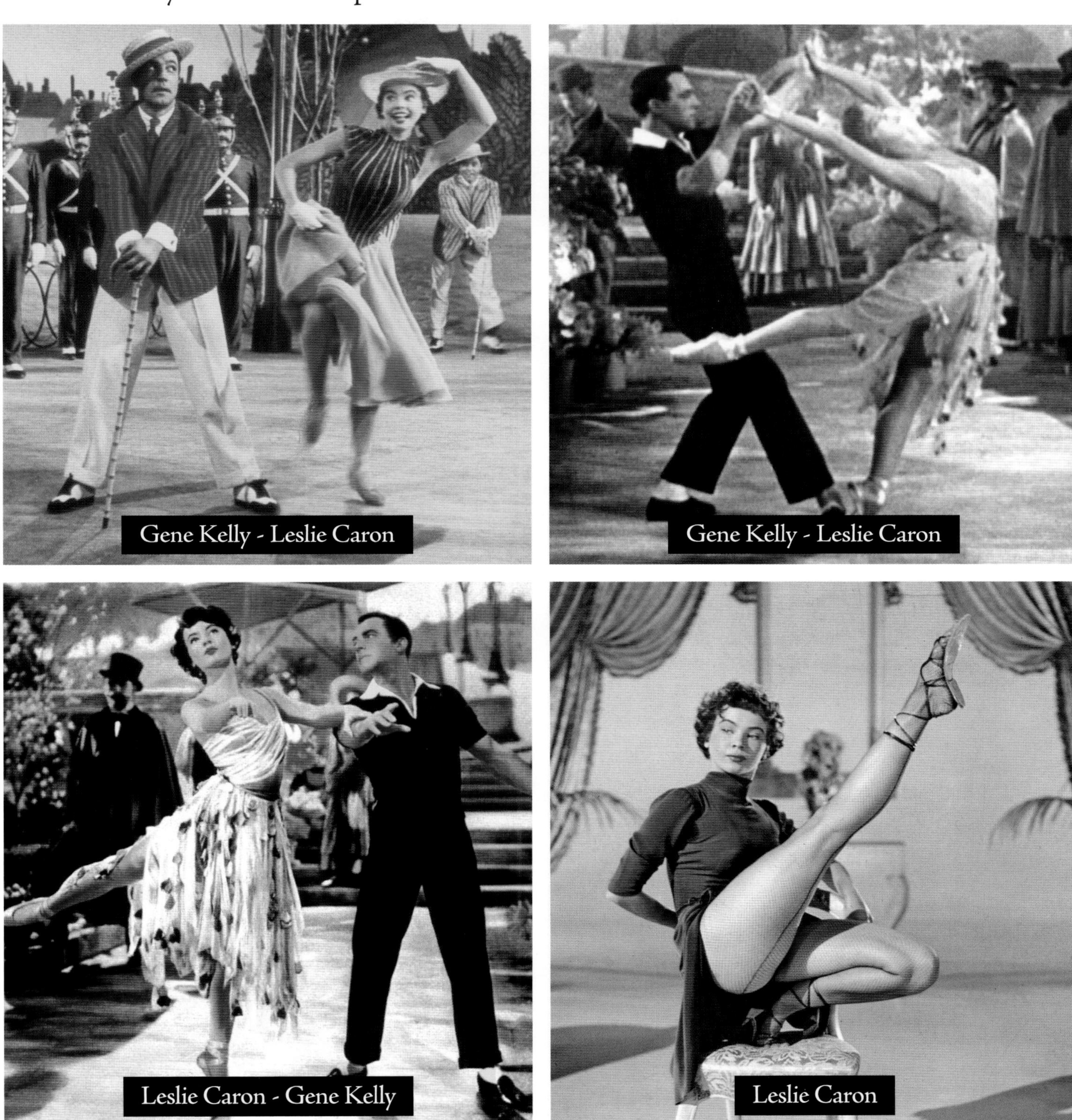

Gene Kelly - Leslie Caron

Gene Kelly - Leslie Caron

Leslie Caron - Gene Kelly

Leslie Caron

I expect that most choreographers would agree that Gene Kelly and Leslie Caron leading a troupe of dancers through the streets and parks of Paris has to be one of the greatest dance sequences ever filmed.

A silent film production company and cast make a difficult transition to sound.

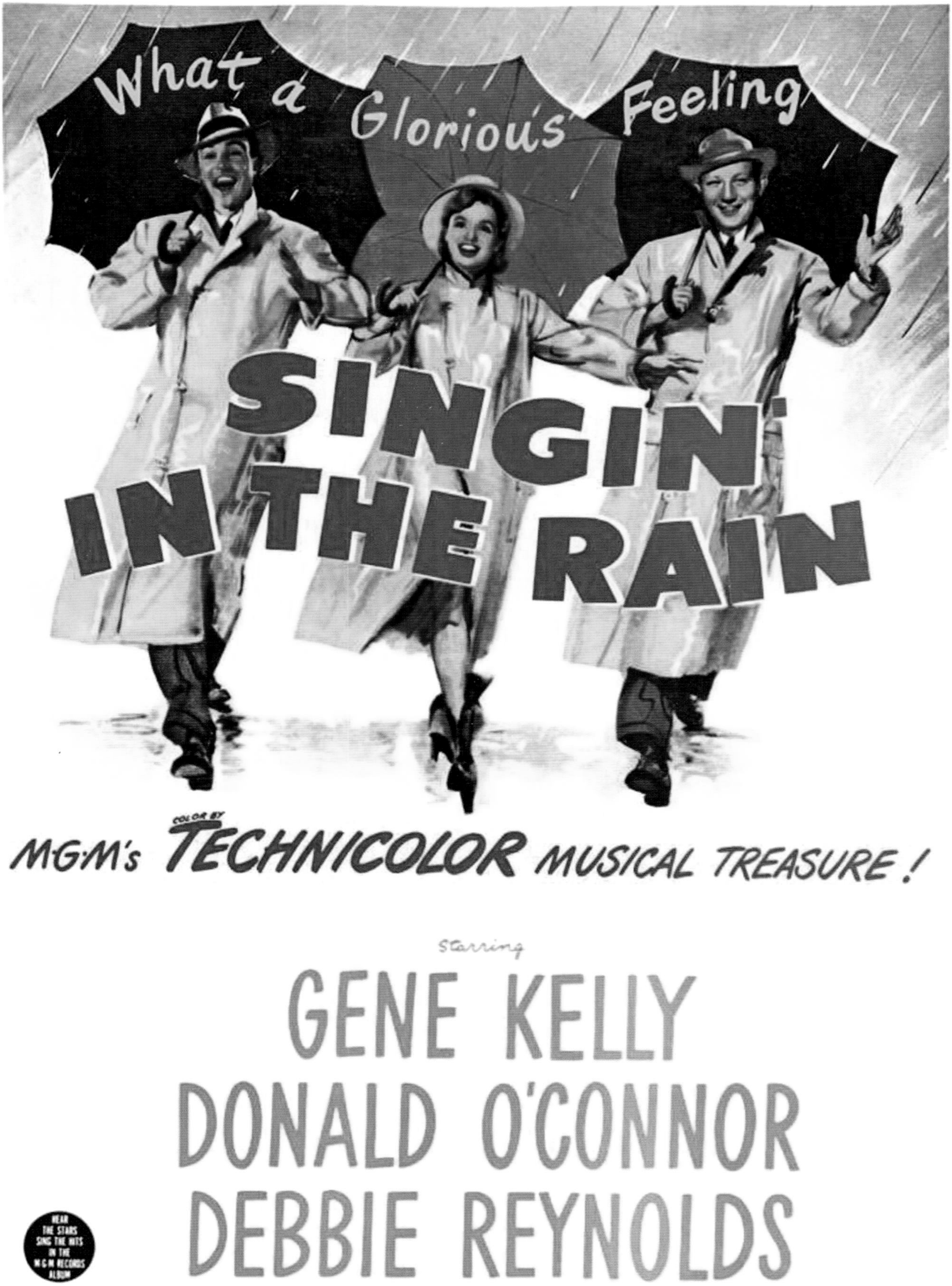

What a Glorious Feeling

SINGIN' IN THE RAIN

MGM's color by TECHNICOLOR MUSICAL TREASURE!

Starring

GENE KELLY
DONALD O'CONNOR
DEBBIE REYNOLDS

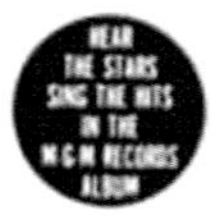

Dave Kehr of Chicago Reader wrote: "One of the shining glories of the American musical."

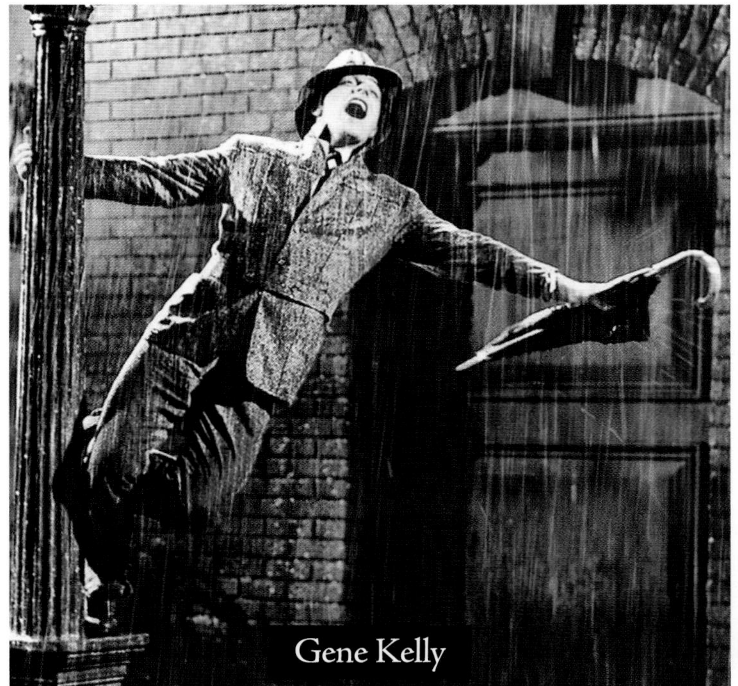
Gene Kelly

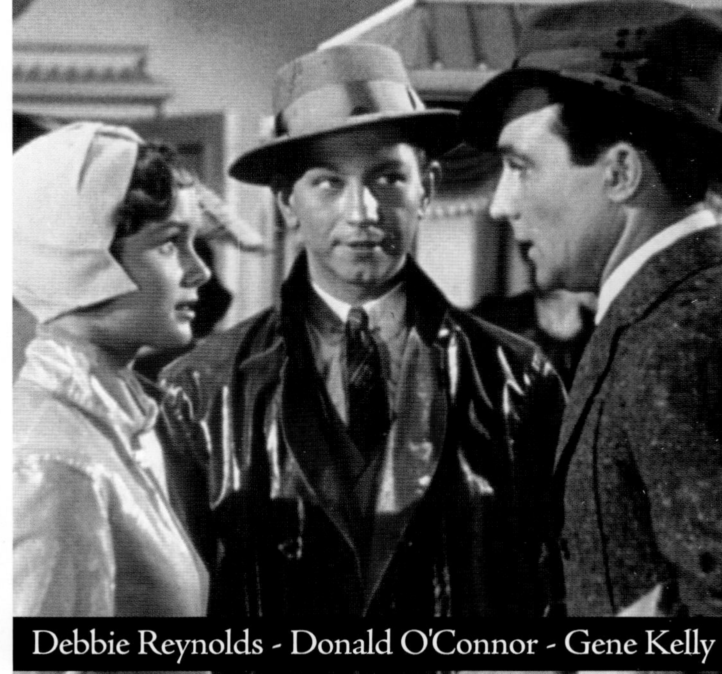
Debbie Reynolds - Donald O'Connor - Gene Kelly

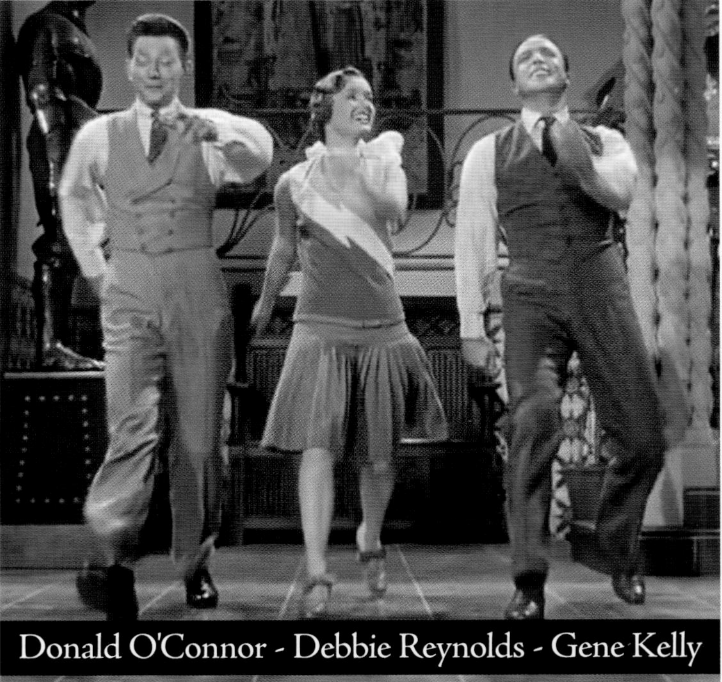
Donald O'Connor - Debbie Reynolds - Gene Kelly

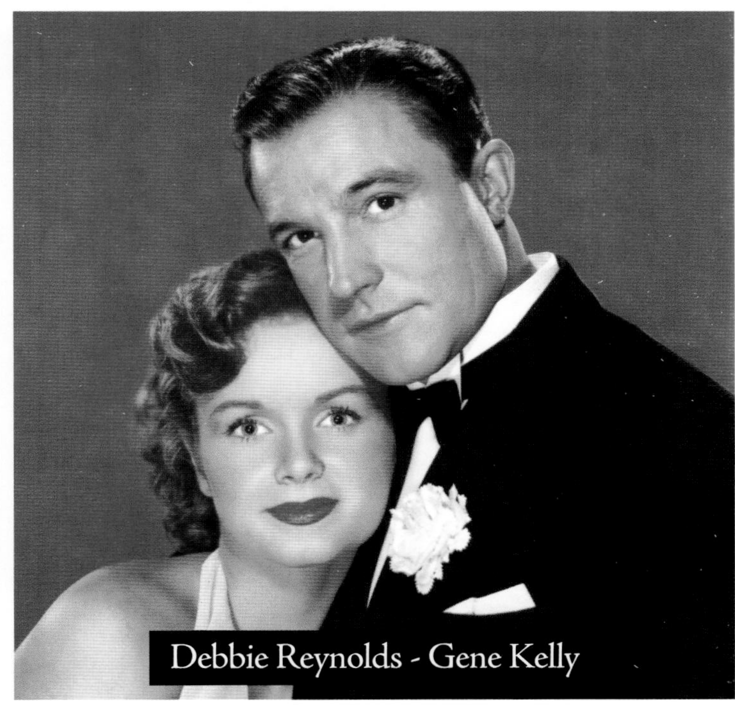
Debbie Reynolds - Gene Kelly

This film is an antidote to the blues. Though it was filmed over sixty-five years ago in 1952, it has never ceased to put a smile on my face. The miraculous thing about this delightful film is that twenty-year-old Debbie Reynolds, who danced so gracefully with Gene Kelly and Donald O'Connor, had never before danced.

I had the privilege of working with both Debbie Reynolds and her brilliant daughter, Carrie Fisher, and, like everyone, could not believe that they passed away but a day apart. I felt it to be a tragedy of Shakespearean proportions.

An emotionally remote recovering alcoholic and his dowdy, unambitious wife face a personal crisis when they take in an attractive lodger.

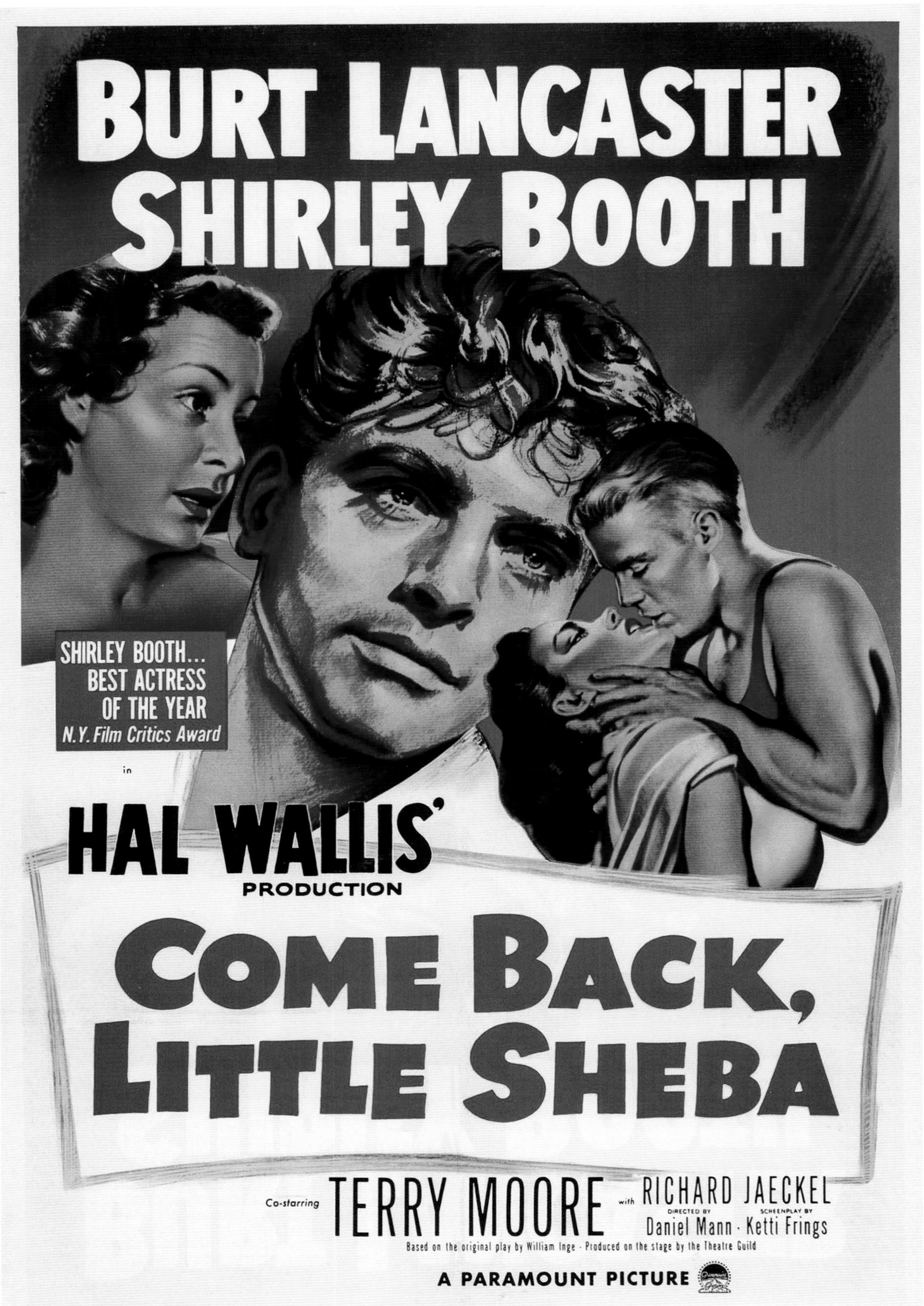

David Bezanson of Filmcritic.com wrote: "Among the best of several booze-obsessed Hollywood melodramas of the 1950s."

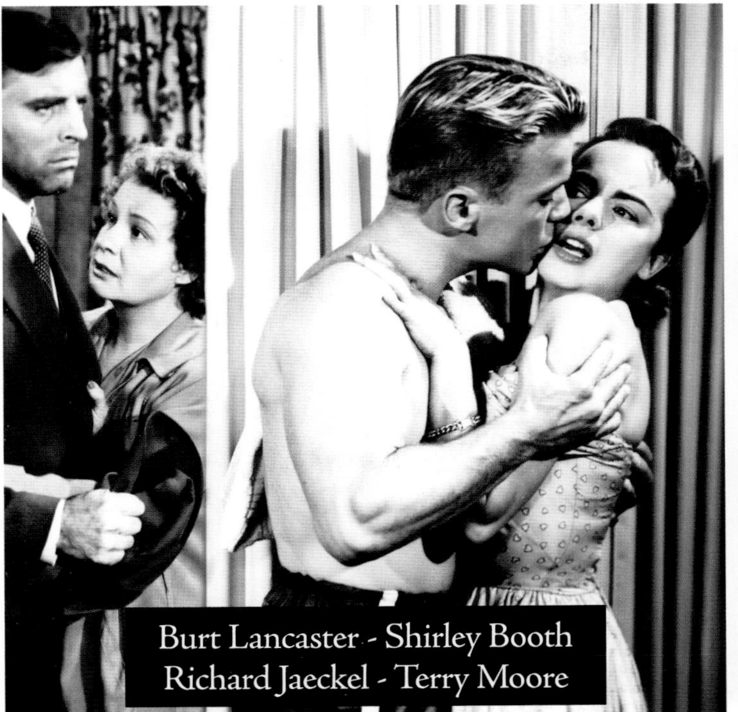

Burt Lancaster - Shirley Booth
Richard Jaeckel - Terry Moore

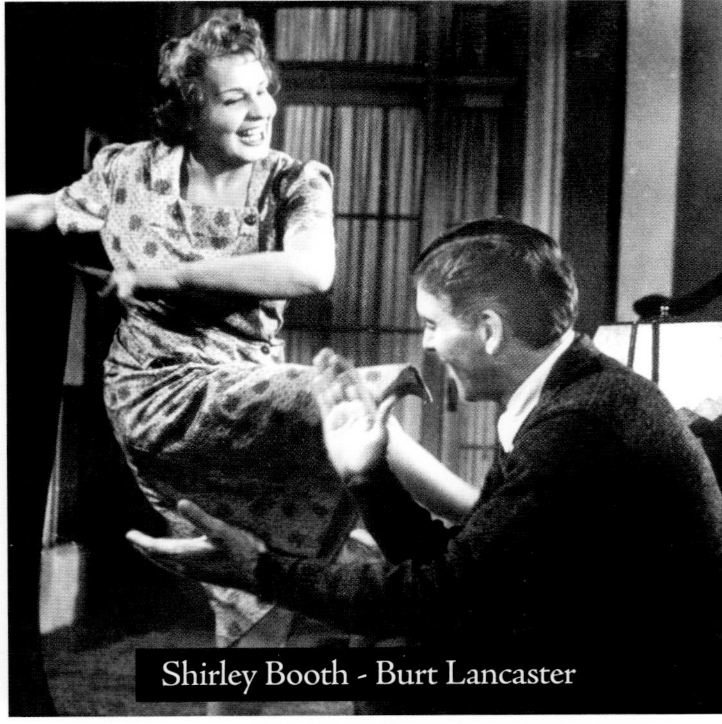

Shirley Booth - Burt Lancaster

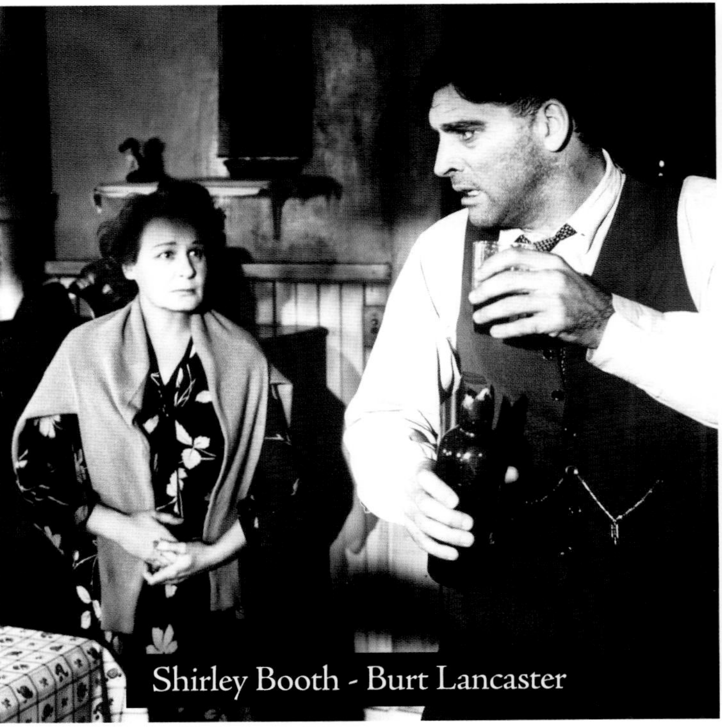

Shirley Booth - Burt Lancaster

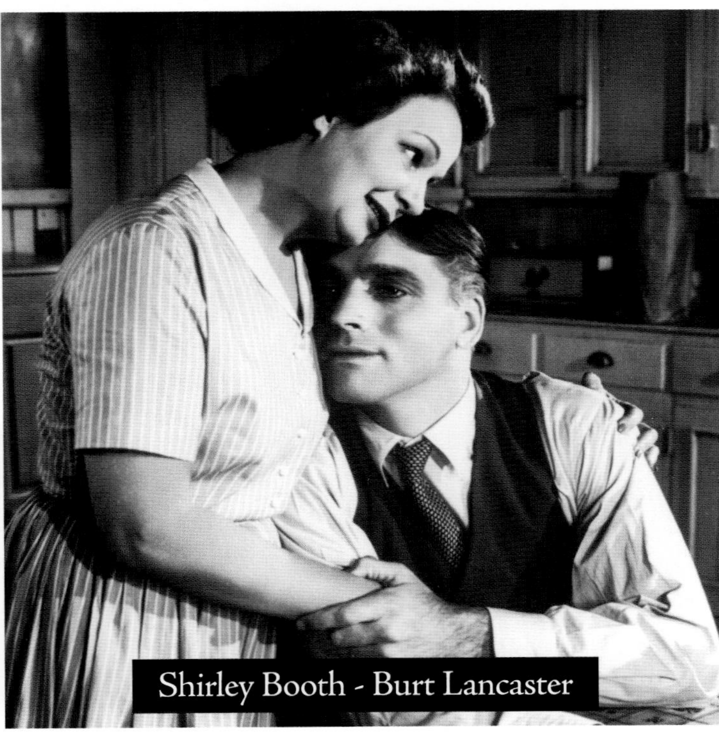

Shirley Booth - Burt Lancaster

For performing this role on Broadway, Shirley Booth received a Tony and for her film effort, she was awarded an Oscar. Shirley Booth had a long career which included 154 episodes of the TV show "Hazel," for which she won two Emmys.

'Sheeba' refers to her missing dog and all who have seen the film were touched by her calling out, "Come Back, Little Sheeba!"

A marshal, compelled to face a deadly enemy, finds that his own town refuses to help him.

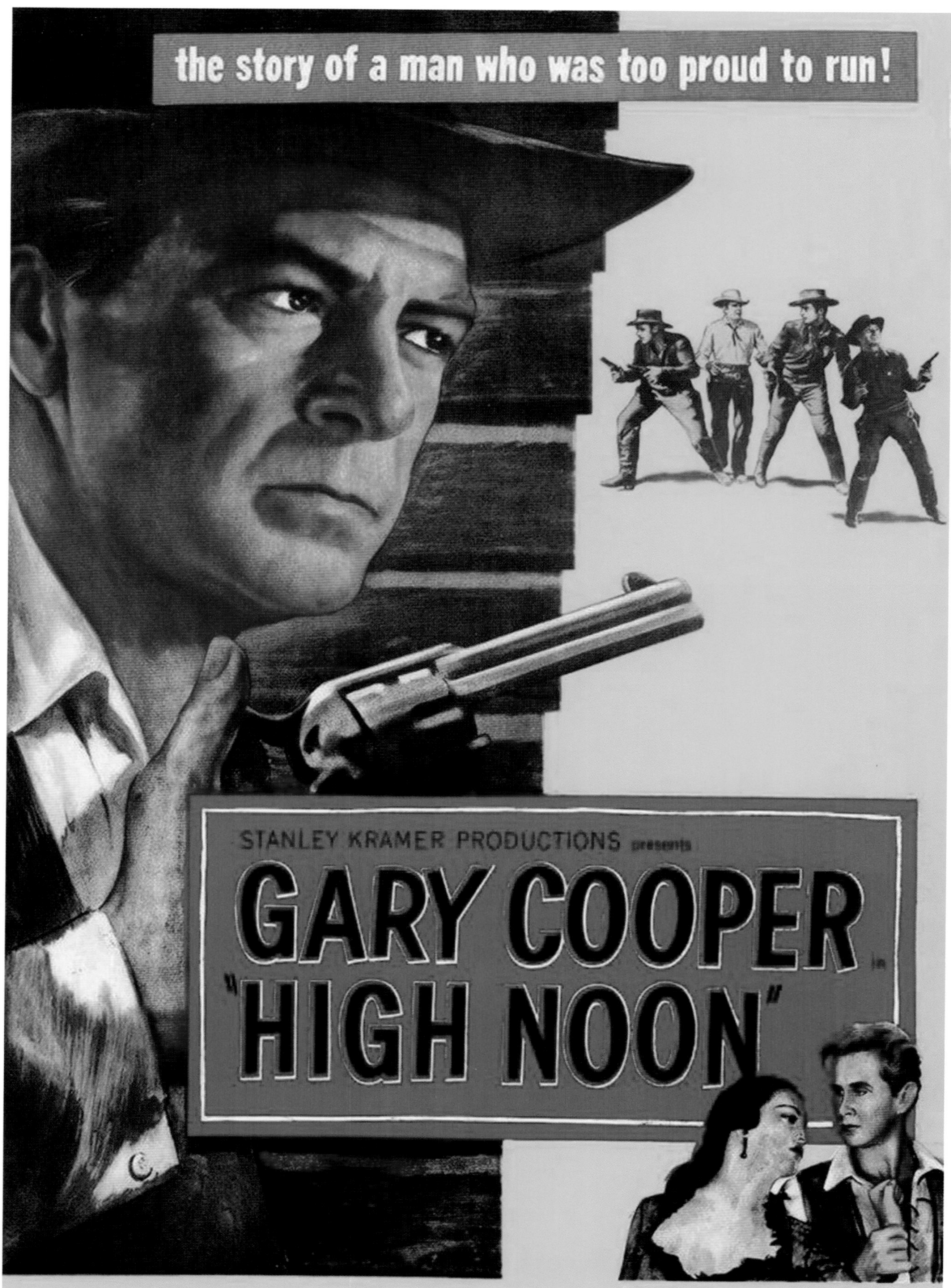

Michael Atkinson of Village Voice wrote: "Foreman was right after all: 'High Noon' is a scorching and sour portrait of American complacence and capacity for collaborationism."

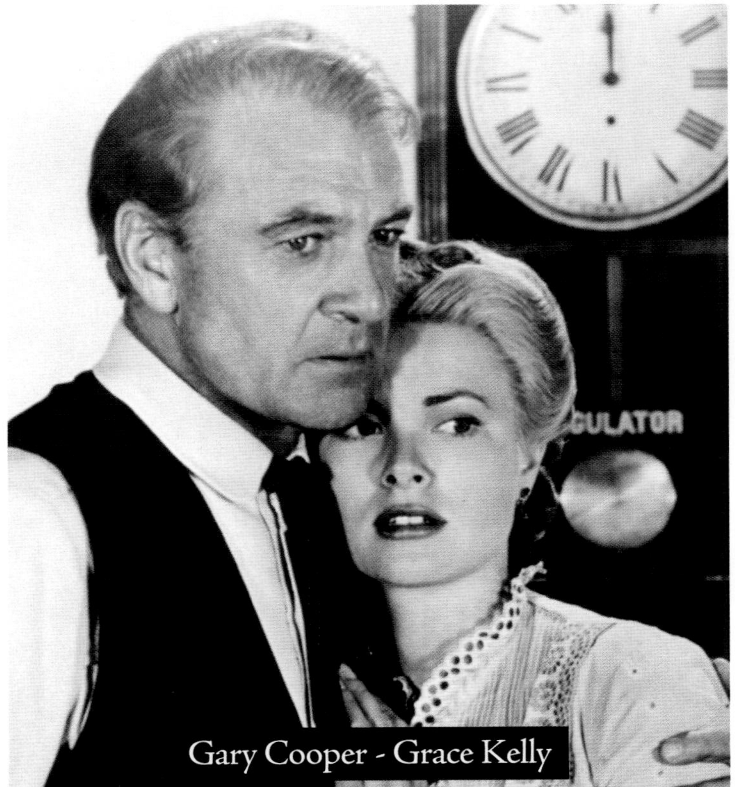
Gary Cooper - Grace Kelly

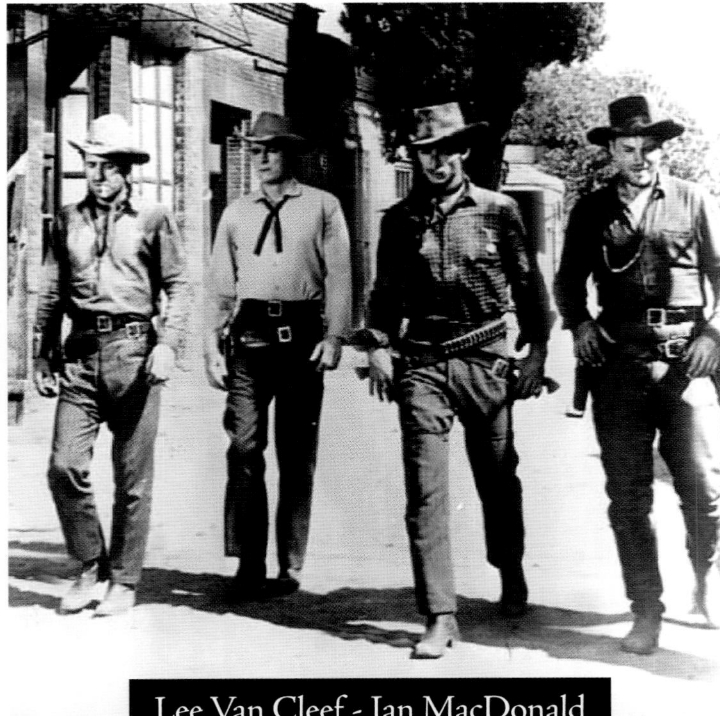
Lee Van Cleef - Ian MacDonald
Robert J. Wilke - Sheb Wooley

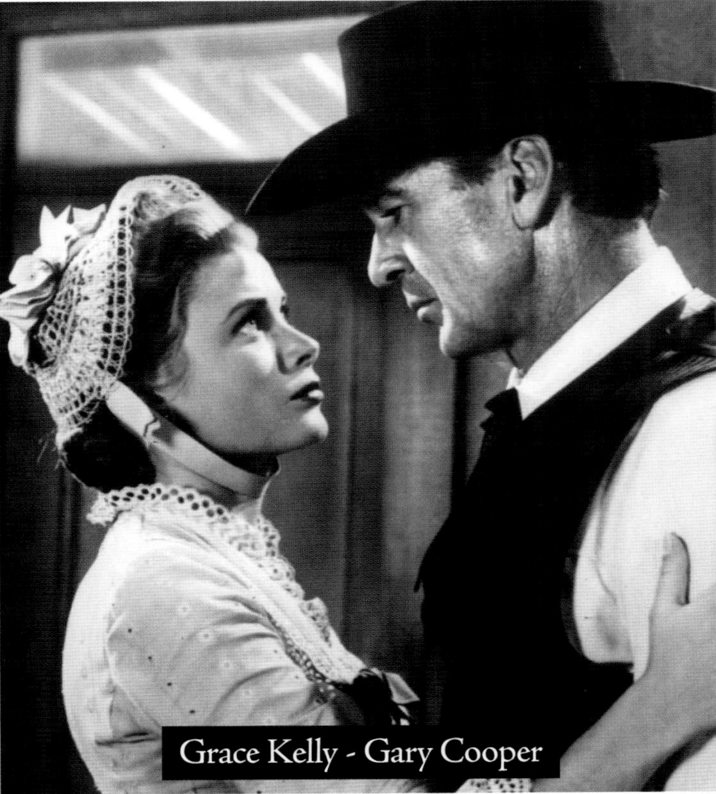
Grace Kelly - Gary Cooper

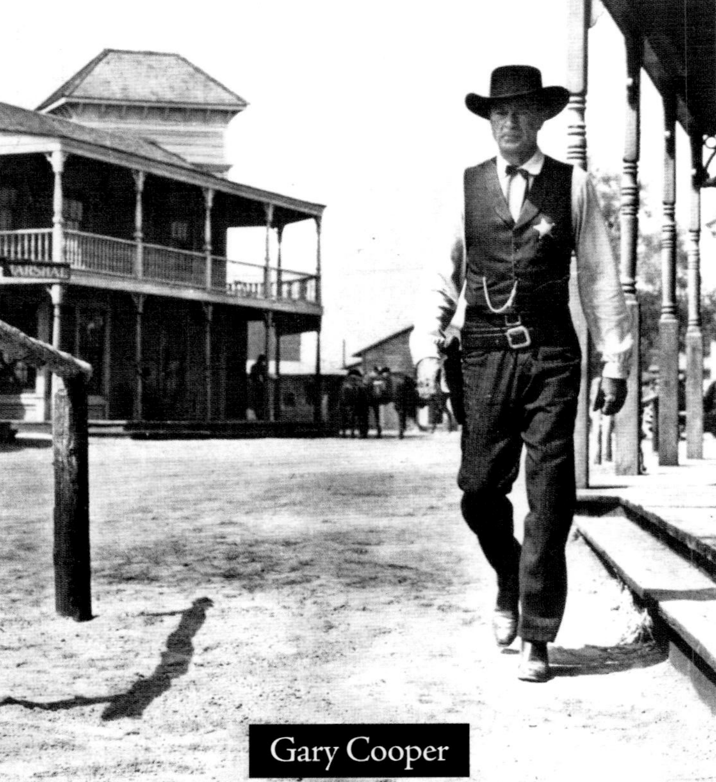
Gary Cooper

Gary Cooper made ninety-three feature films and won an Academy Award for "High Noon." Grace Kelly appeared in fourteen feature films and won one Oscar.

The story of Mexican revolutionary Emiliano Zapata, who led a rebellion against the corrupt, oppressive dictatorship of president Porfirio Diaz in the early 20th century.

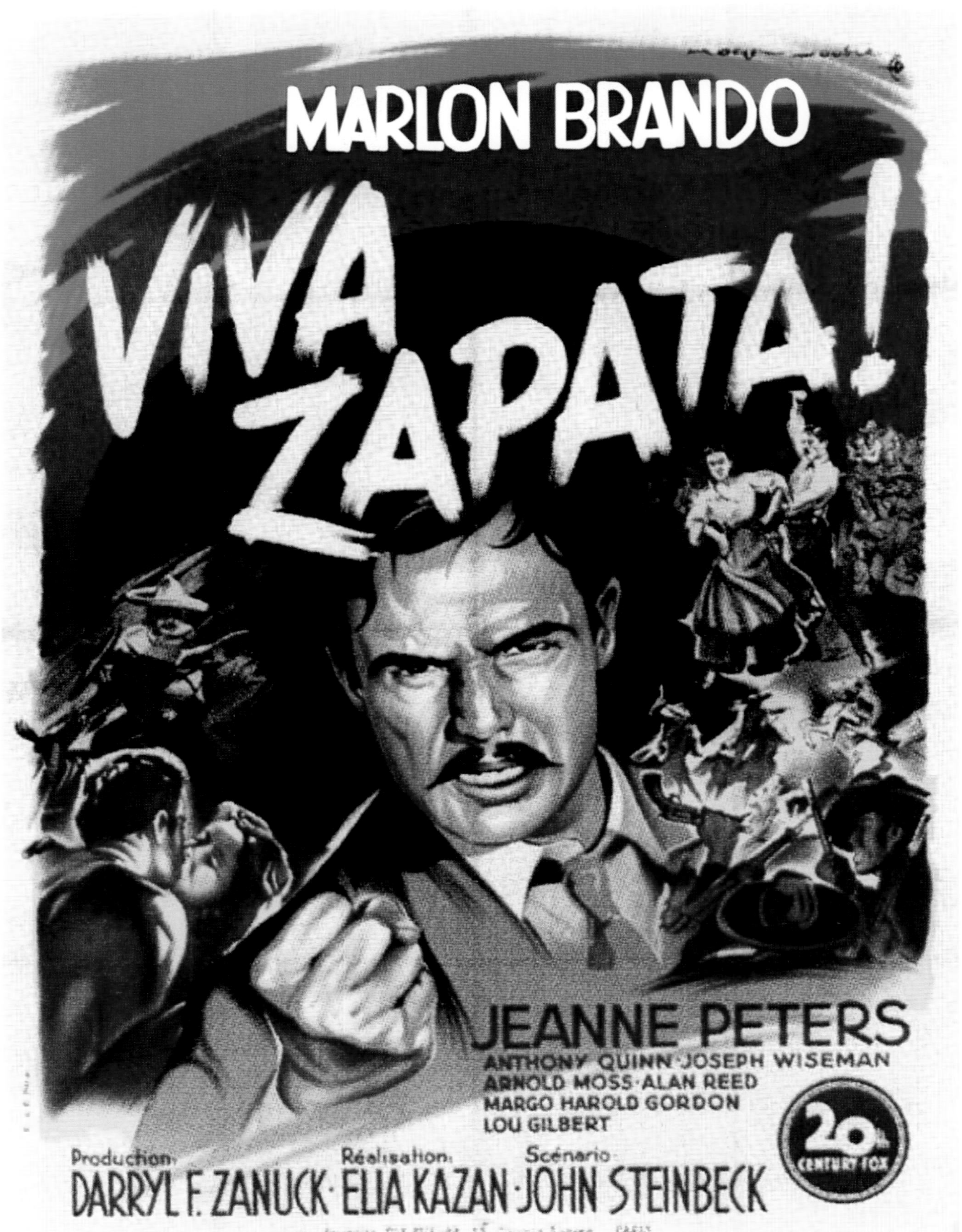

Bosley Crowther of The New York Times wrote: "Throbs with a rare vitality, and a masterful picture of a nation in revolutionary torment has been got by Director Elia Kazan."

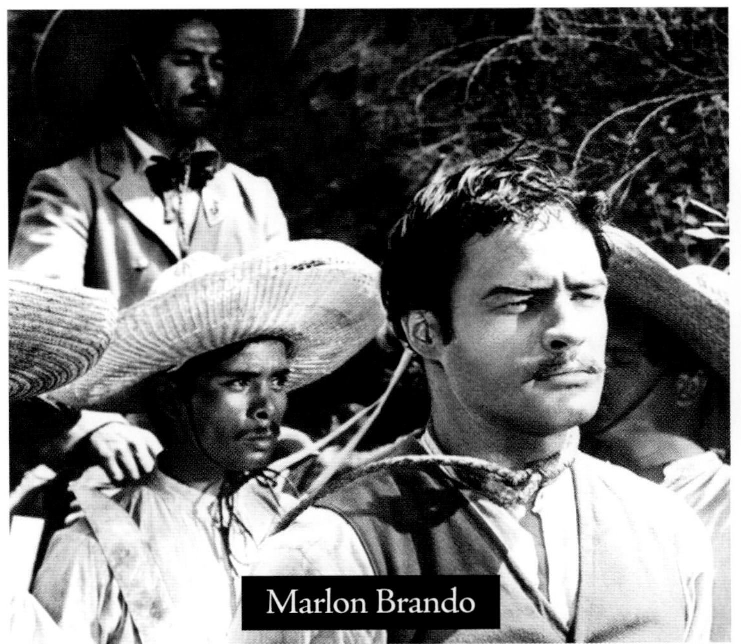
Marlon Brando

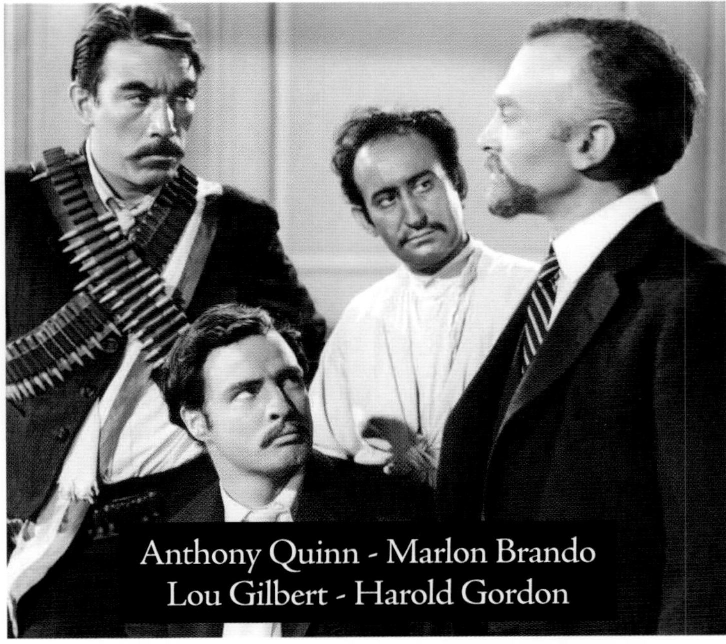
Anthony Quinn - Marlon Brando
Lou Gilbert - Harold Gordon

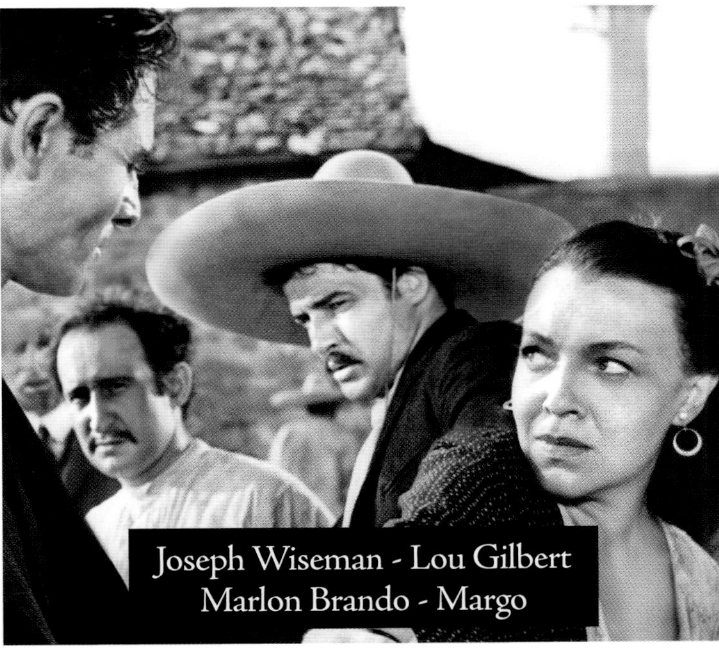
Joseph Wiseman - Lou Gilbert
Marlon Brando - Margo

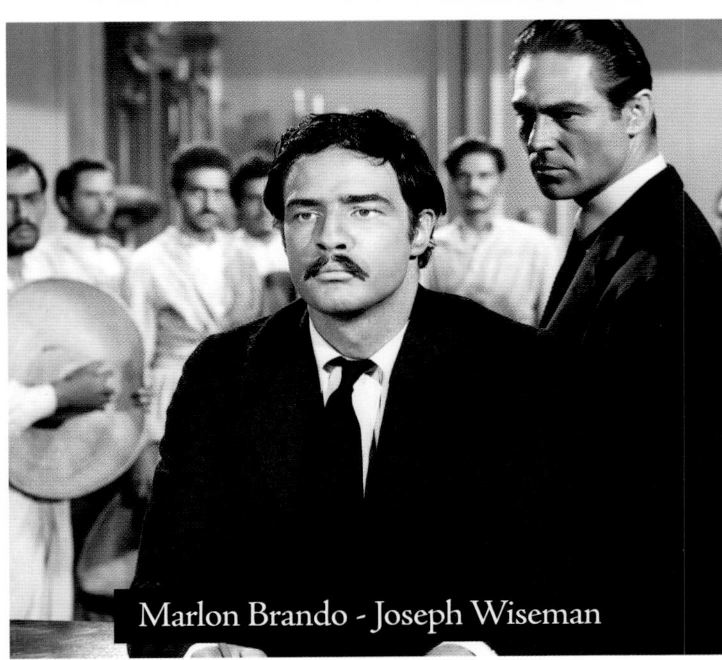
Marlon Brando - Joseph Wiseman

If ever you're curious about what is meant by someone saying "That actor was made to play the part," you have but to watch Marlon Brando as Zapata.

In 1947, when I was starring in the road company of "Call Me Mister," Marlon Brando was rehearsing with Talullah Bankhead for "The Eagle with Two Heads." He often sat in my dressing room waiting to meet his girlfriend, Nina Starkey, a dancer in our show. Three or four times he watched our show from the balcony and once asked me how I made my eyes sparkle when I was singing. "I don't make my eyes sparkle," I told him. "When I sing to the folks in the balcony, it's that large spotlight up there that puts the sparkle in my eyes."

Monsieur Hulot vacations at the beach, where he accidentally, but good-naturedly, causes havoc.

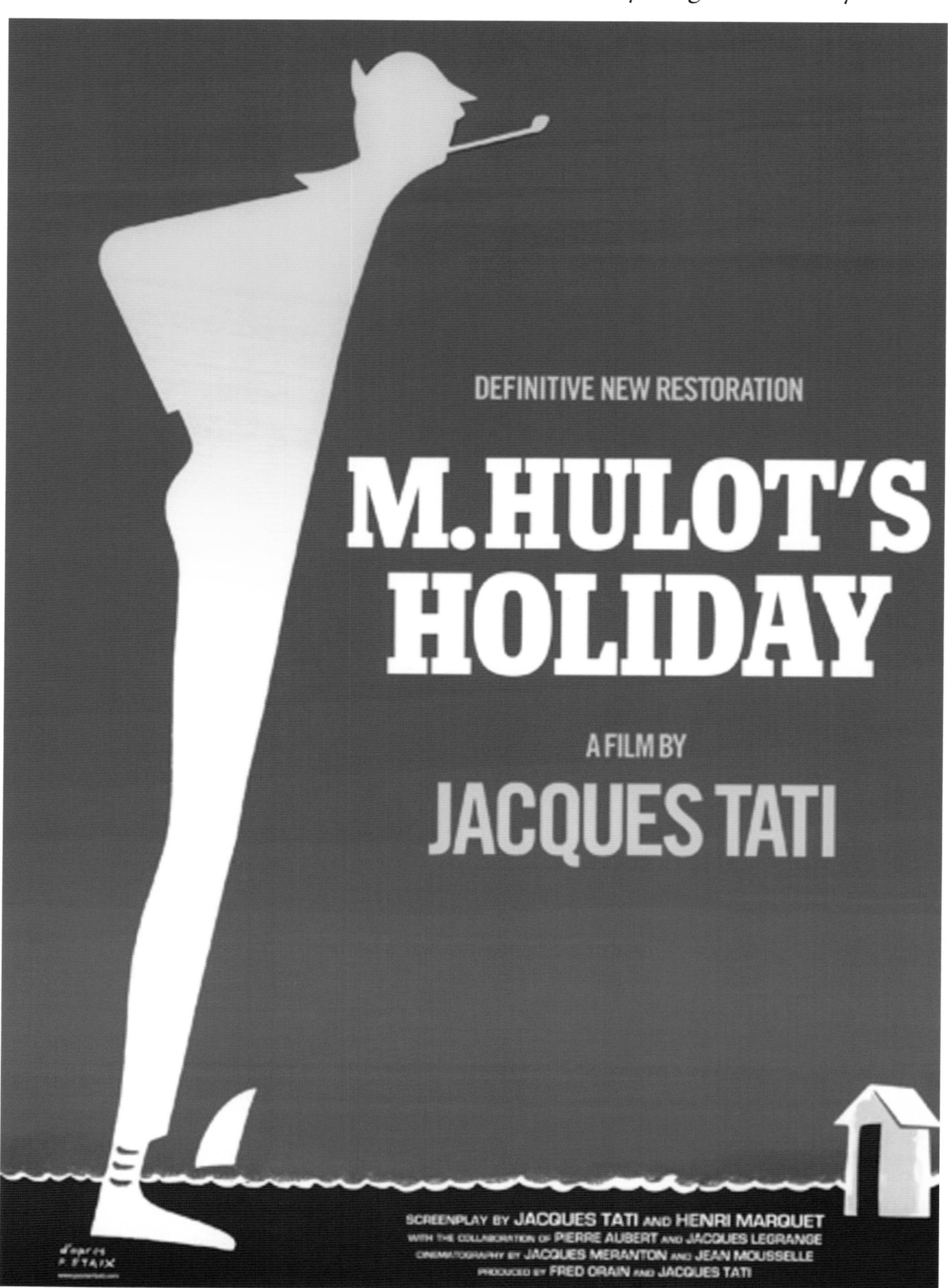

David Fear of Time Out wrote: "Jacques Tati's bumbling stick-bug of an alter ego is considered by many to be the funniest creation to come out of Gallic cinema."

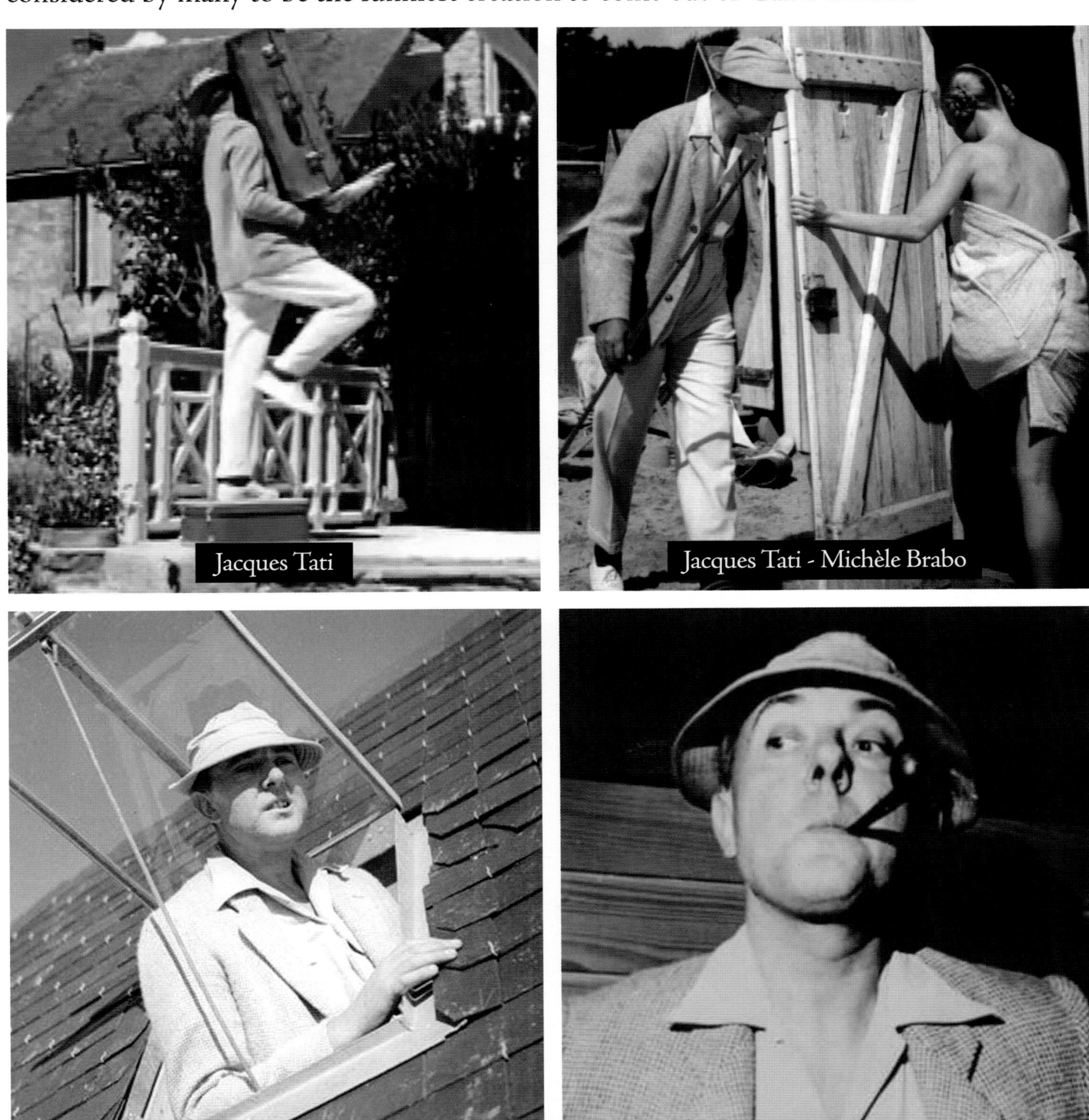

Jacques Tati

Jacques Tati - Michèle Brabo

Jacques Tati

Jacques Tati

If I were twenty-five years younger and you happened to knock on my door and ask me to do my impression of Jacques Tati leaning forward as he tip-toed up the street with long, angular, bounding strides, I would oblige. I daresay you would find it difficult not to smile.

In Hawaii in 1941, a private is cruelly punished for not boxing on his unit's team, while his captain's wife and second-in-command are falling in love.

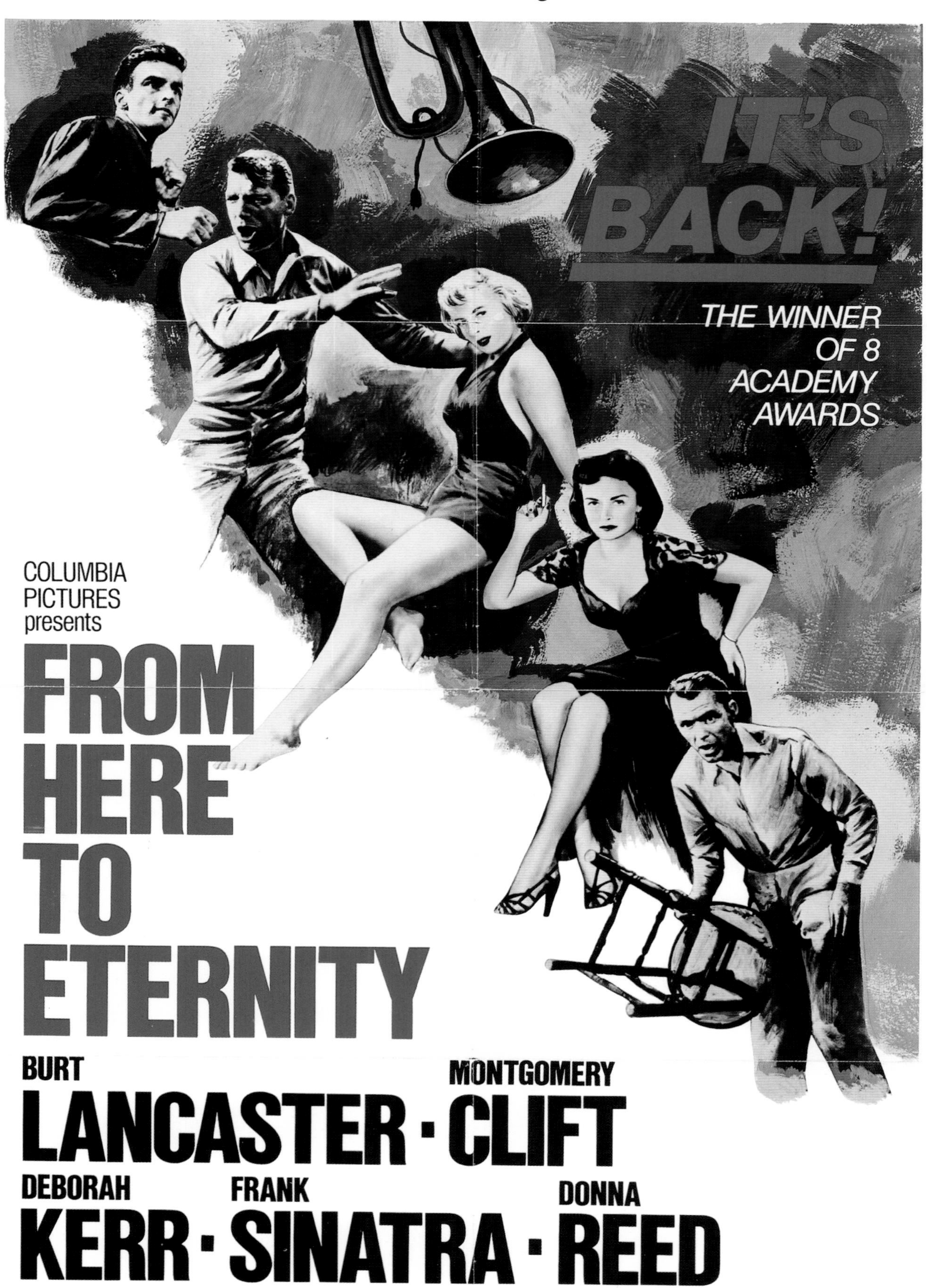

Kate Cameron of New York Daily News wrote: "There isn't a dull moment in the picture."

William Brogdon of Variety wrote: "It is an important film from any angle, presenting socko entertainment for big business."

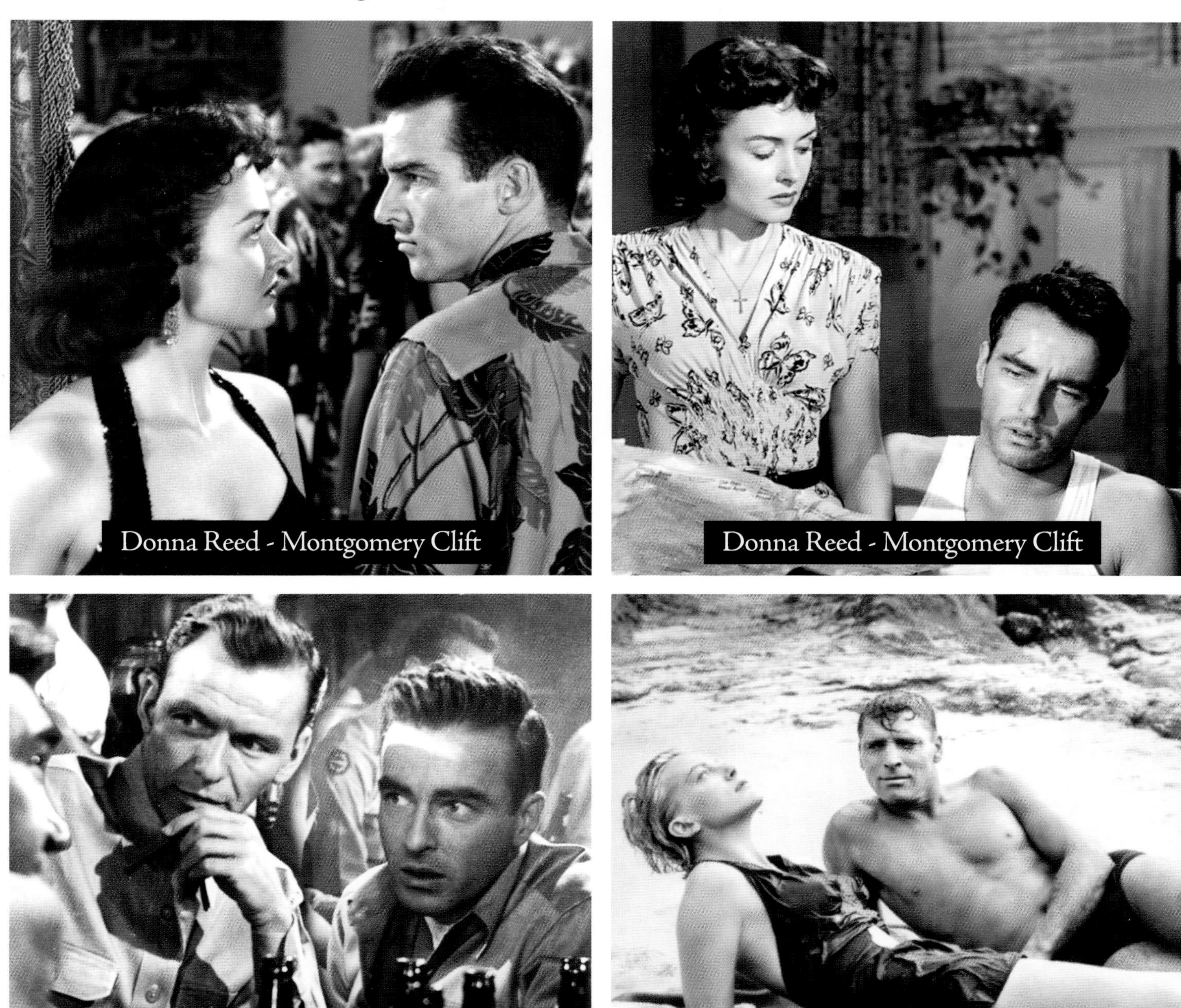

Donna Reed - Montgomery Clift

Donna Reed - Montgomery Clift

Frank Sinatra - Montgomery Clift

Deborah Kerr - Burt Lancaster

This film not only provided "socko entertainment," but it also provided a socko sketch for Sid Caesar and Imogene Coca to parody on "Your Show of Shows." I had difficulty not laughing out loud as I watched the stage hands slosh buckets of water on Sid and Imogene as they recreated the beach scene. I did laugh out loud when Sid romantically ad libbed, "Here we are amongst the ocean..."

The growing ambition of Julius Caesar is a source of major concern to his close friend Brutus. Cassius persuades him to participate in his plot to assassinate Caesar but they have both sorely underestimated Mark Antony.

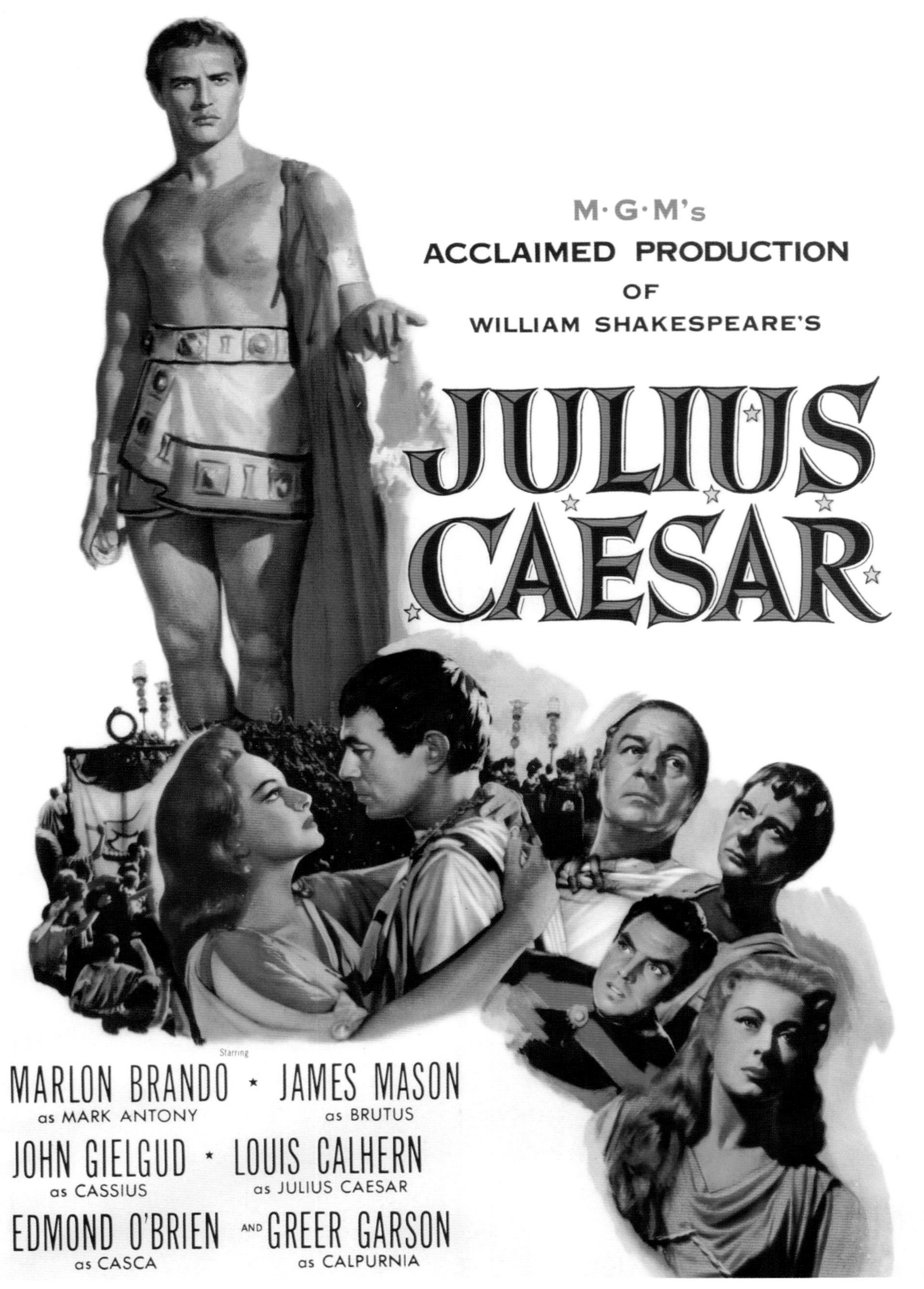

Time Magazine wrote: "The best Shakespeare that Hollywood has yet produced."

Variety wrote: "A tense, melodramatic story, clearly presented, and excellently acted by one of the finest casts assembled for a film."

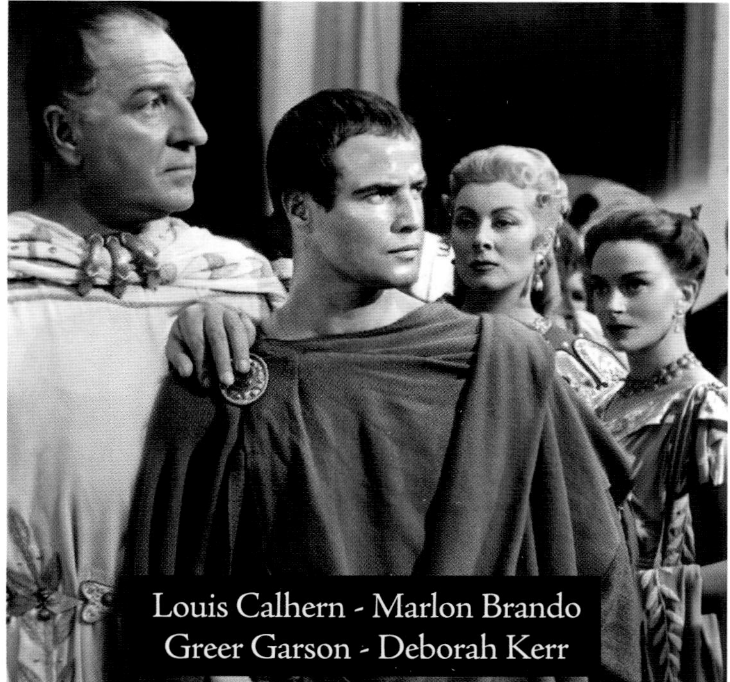
Louis Calhern - Marlon Brando
Greer Garson - Deborah Kerr

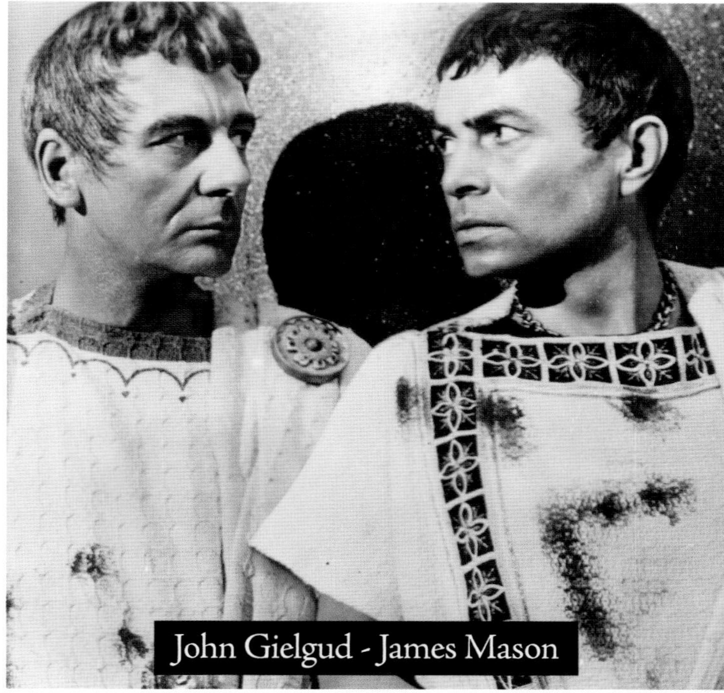
John Gielgud - James Mason

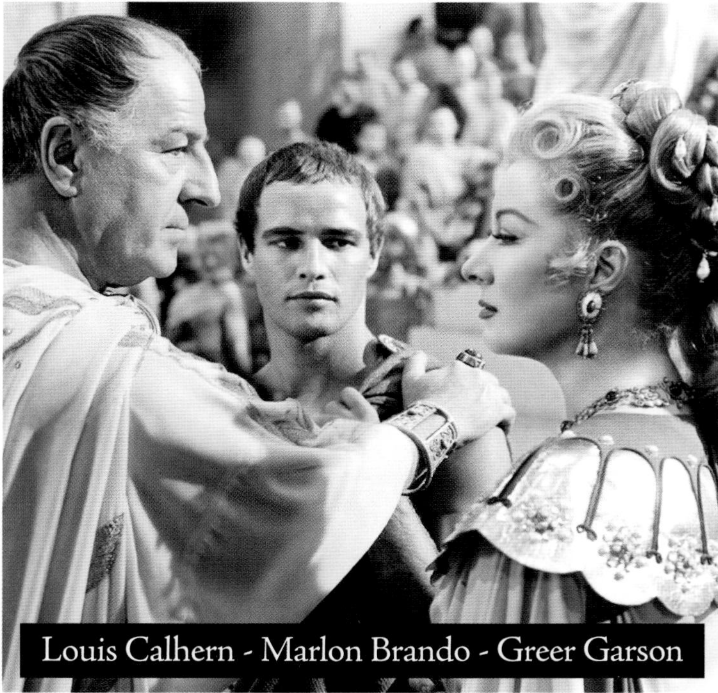
Louis Calhern - Marlon Brando - Greer Garson

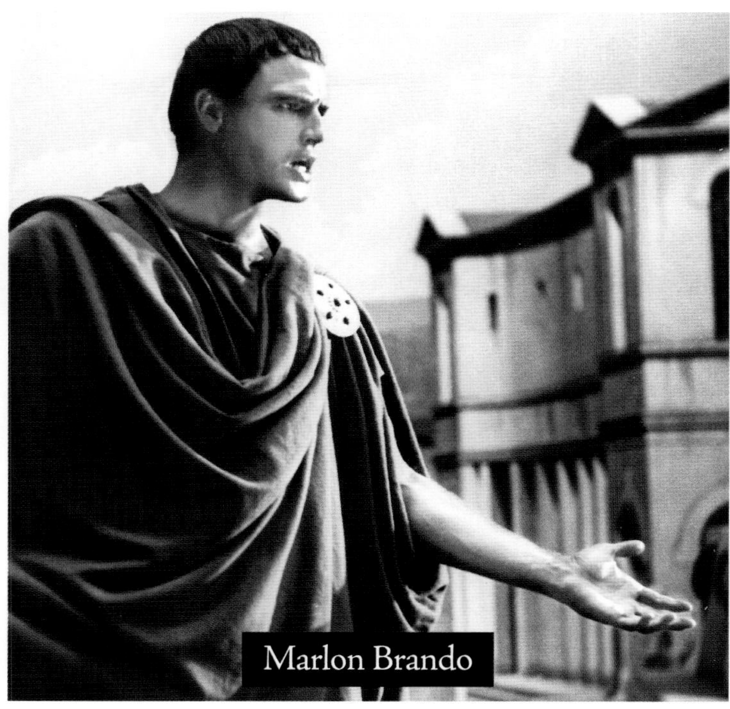
Marlon Brando

Everyone expected Louis Calhern, John Gielgud and James Mason to deliver Shakespeare's lines eloquently, but no one expected that Marlon Brando, who played Brutus and had mumbled his way through productions of "Cat On A Hot Tin Roof" and "Streetcar Named Desire," would enunciate his lines with such clarity, originality and heart-rending passion.

From the moment he said, "Friends, Romans, countrymen," we knew we were in for a treat.

An ex-husband and wife team star in a musical version of "The Taming of the Shrew;" off-stage, the production is troubled by quarreling ex-lovers and a gangster looking for his money.

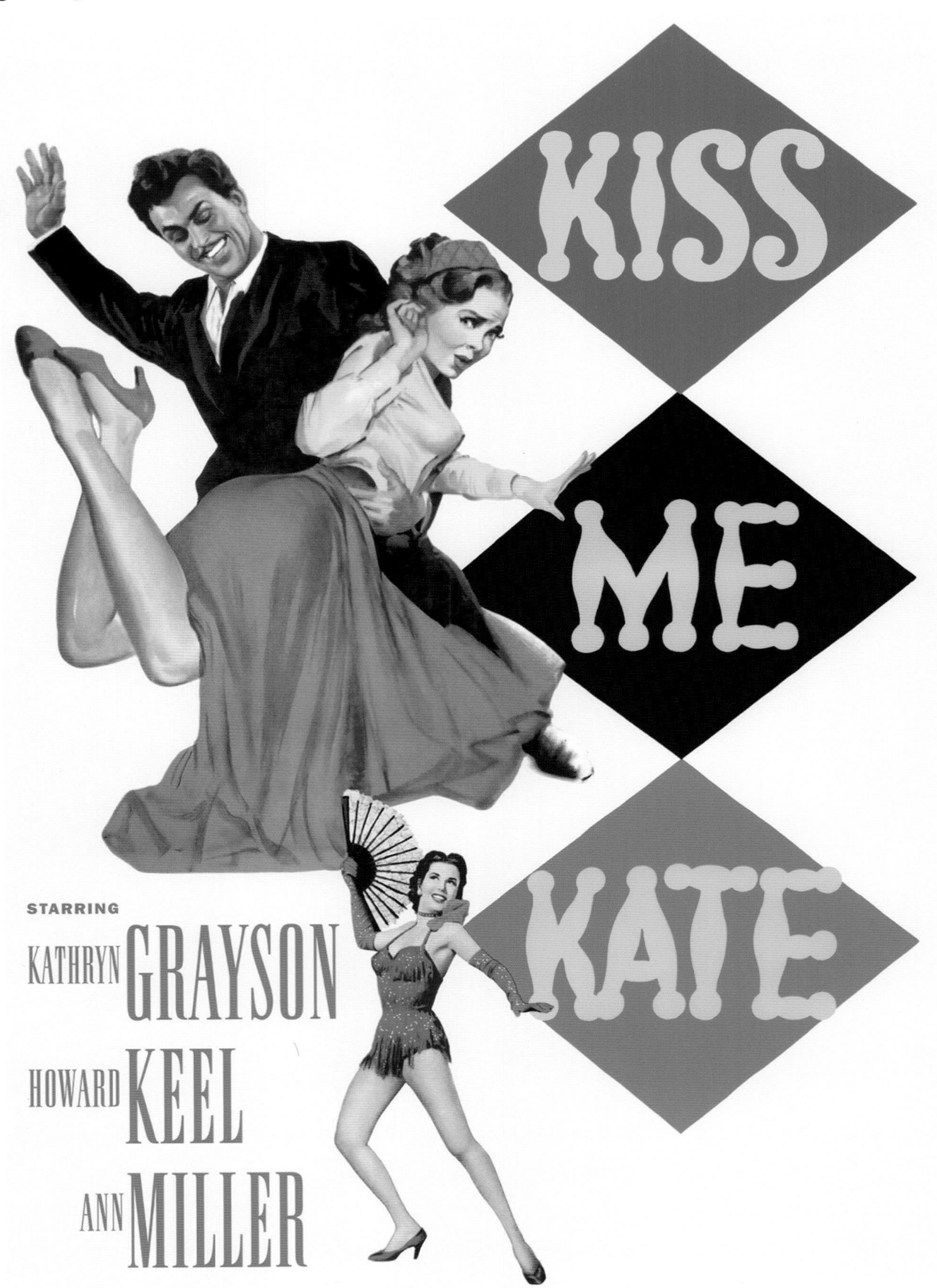

Nell Minow of Movie Mom wrote: "One of the all-time best movie musicals, with Fosse choreography and Cole Porter's vunderbar music."

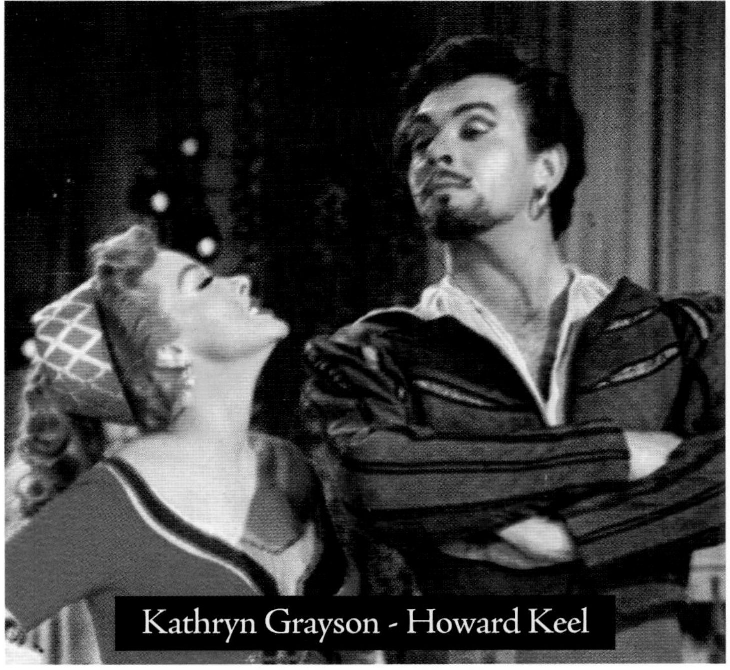
Kathryn Grayson - Howard Keel

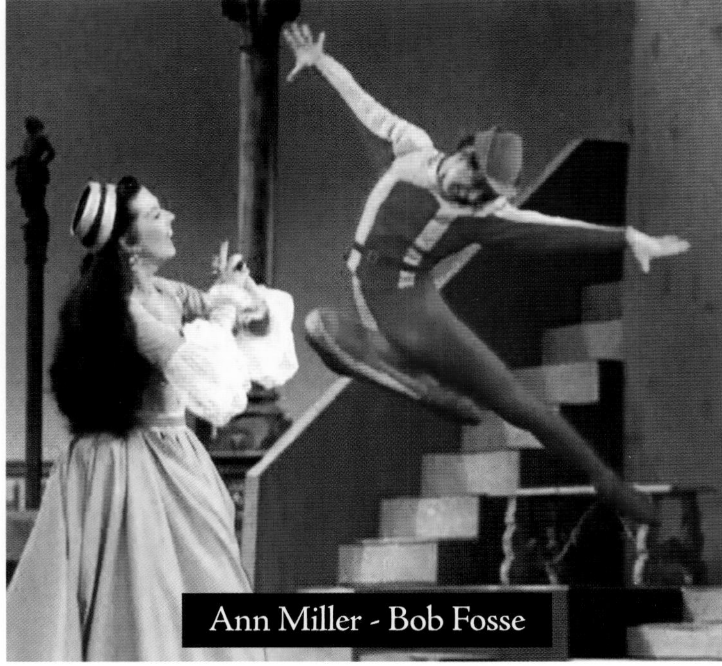
Ann Miller - Bob Fosse

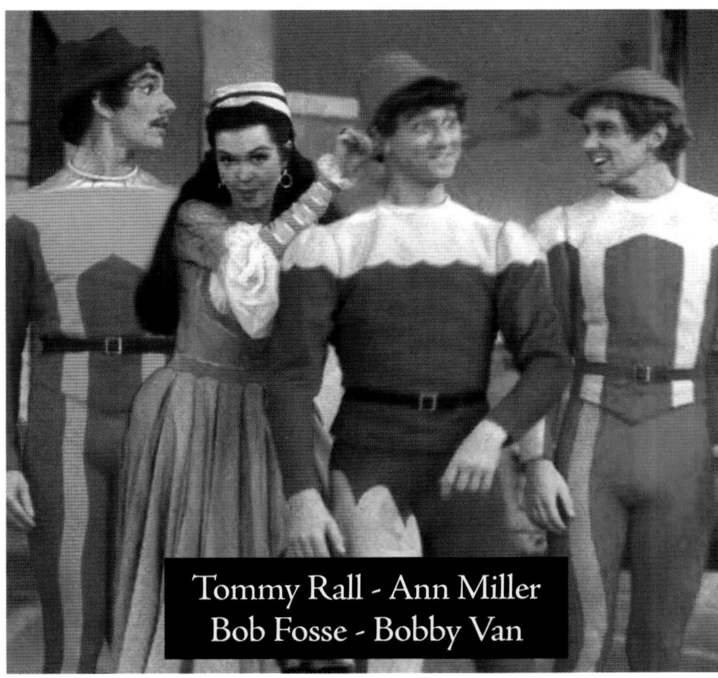
Tommy Rall - Ann Miller
Bob Fosse - Bobby Van

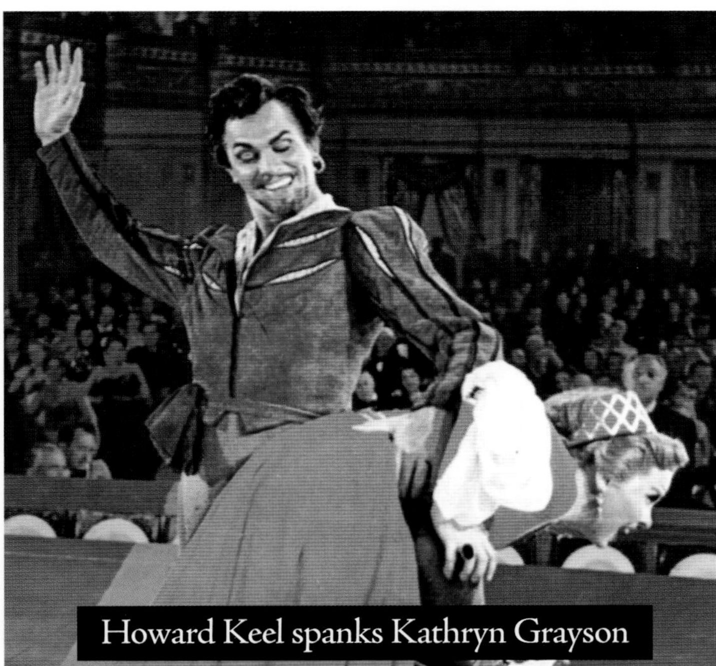
Howard Keel spanks Kathryn Grayson

Every aspect of this film is top drawer and in one of the drawers is the brilliant and athletic dancing of three major performers, Bob Fosse, who choreographed the show, and his two cohorts, Bobby Van and Tommy Rall.

Fosse and I were both in the cast of "Call Me Mister," Fosse as a dancer and I, a sketch actor. A year or so later Bob Fosse got his first offer to choreograph a Broadway show. I mentioned how proud his parents must be and he said that his father wasn't too thrilled. "What do you mean," his father asked him, "you're going to give away all your steps?"

A sheltered princess escapes her guards and falls in love with an American newsman in Rome.

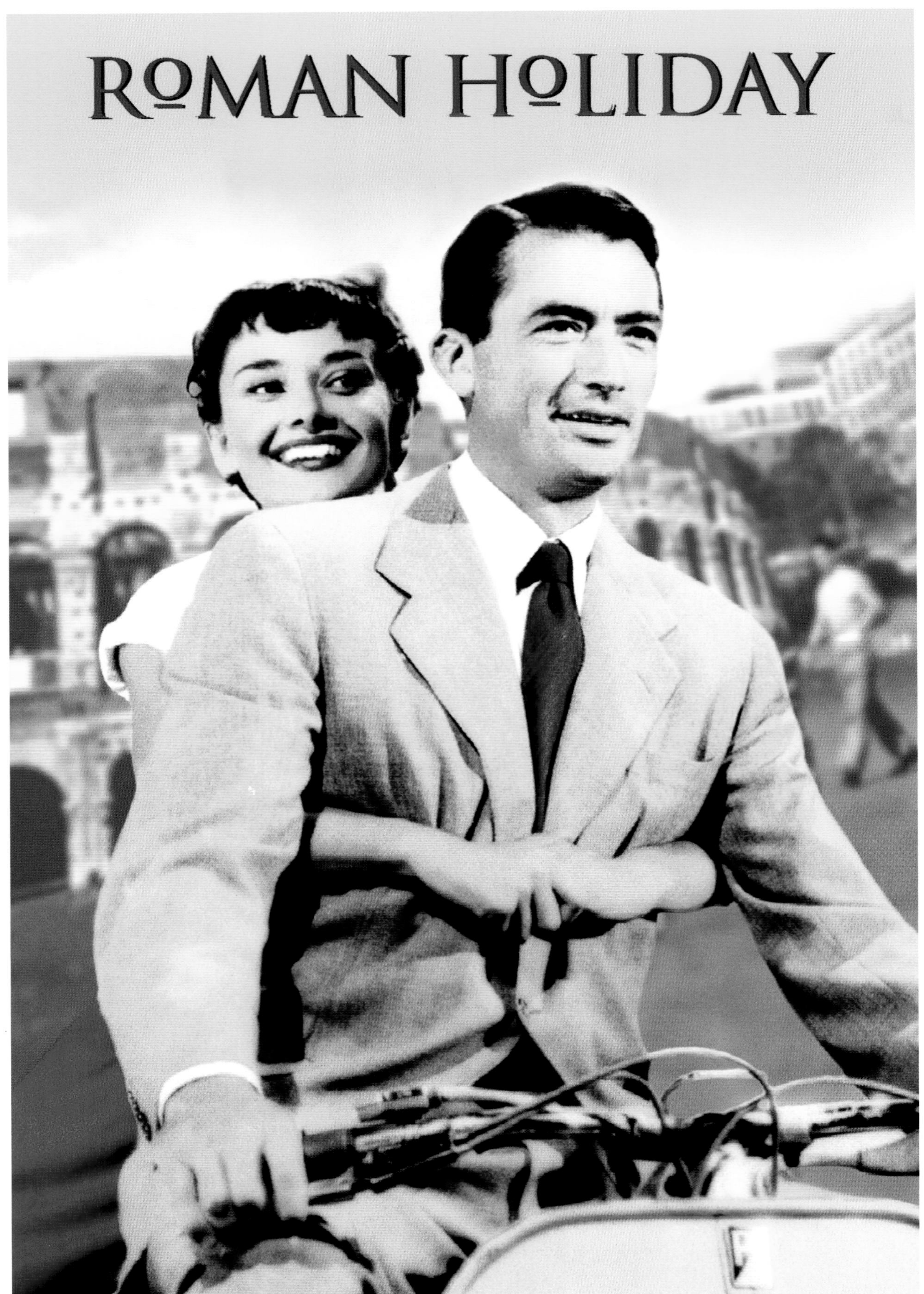

Time Magazine wrote: "The newcomer named Audrey Hepburn gives the popular old romantic nonsense a reality it has seldom had before."

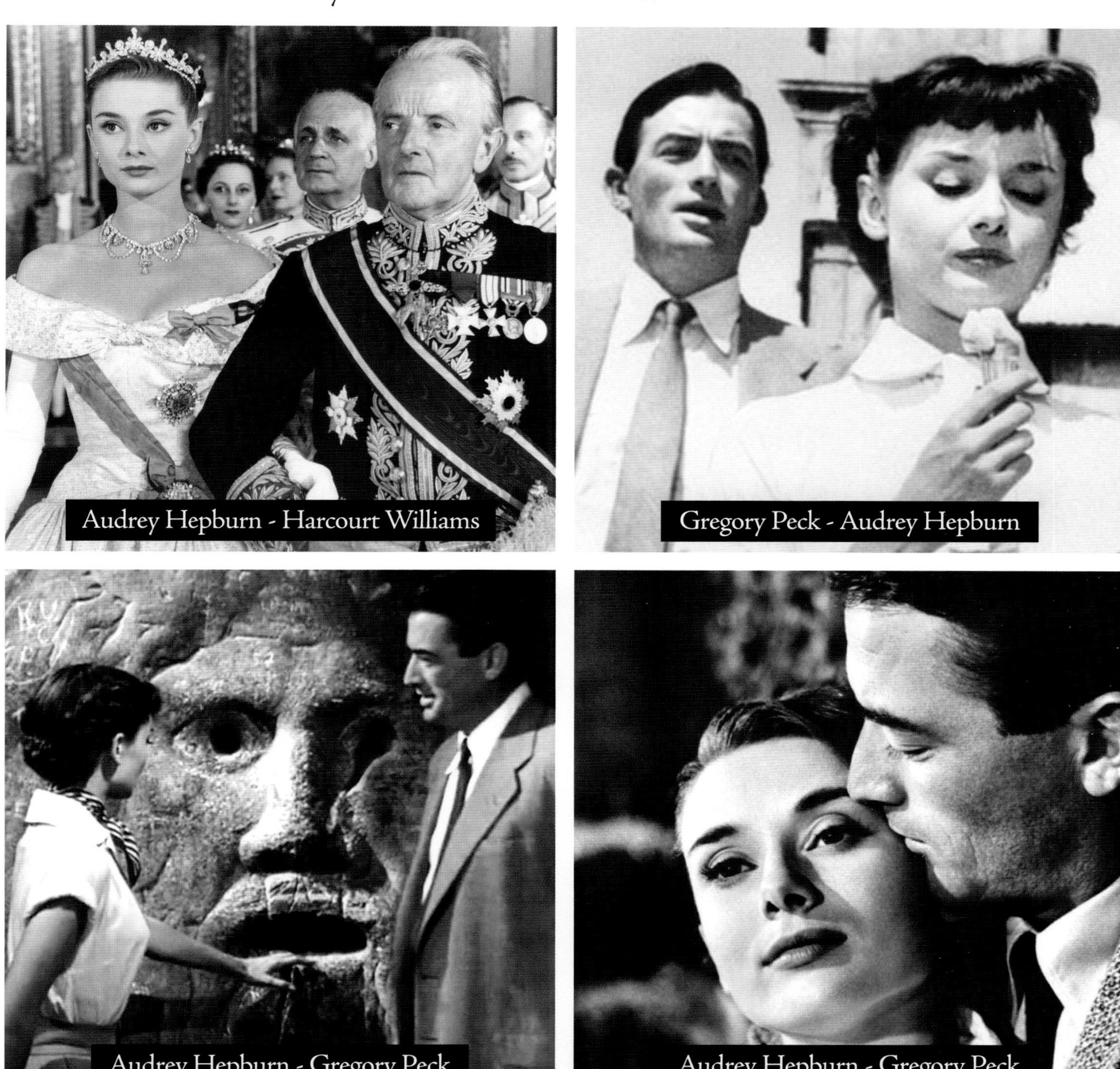

Audrey Hepburn - Harcourt Williams

Gregory Peck - Audrey Hepburn

Audrey Hepburn - Gregory Peck

Audrey Hepburn - Gregory Peck

In this scene, Gregory Peck relates to the naive princess that anyone who puts their hand in the mouth of a gargoyle and tells an untruth will have their hand bitten off. Knowing that she's lying about her royal birth, she chooses not to put her hand in. Gregory Peck thrusts his hand in and pretends it's being bitten off. Audrey screams and comes to his rescue, tugging at his arm, and helps him to extricate it. When she realizes she has been fooled, she beats at his chest but finally puts her head against it as she hugs him.

A weary gunfighter attempts to settle down with a homestead family, but a smoldering settler/rancher conflict forces him to act.

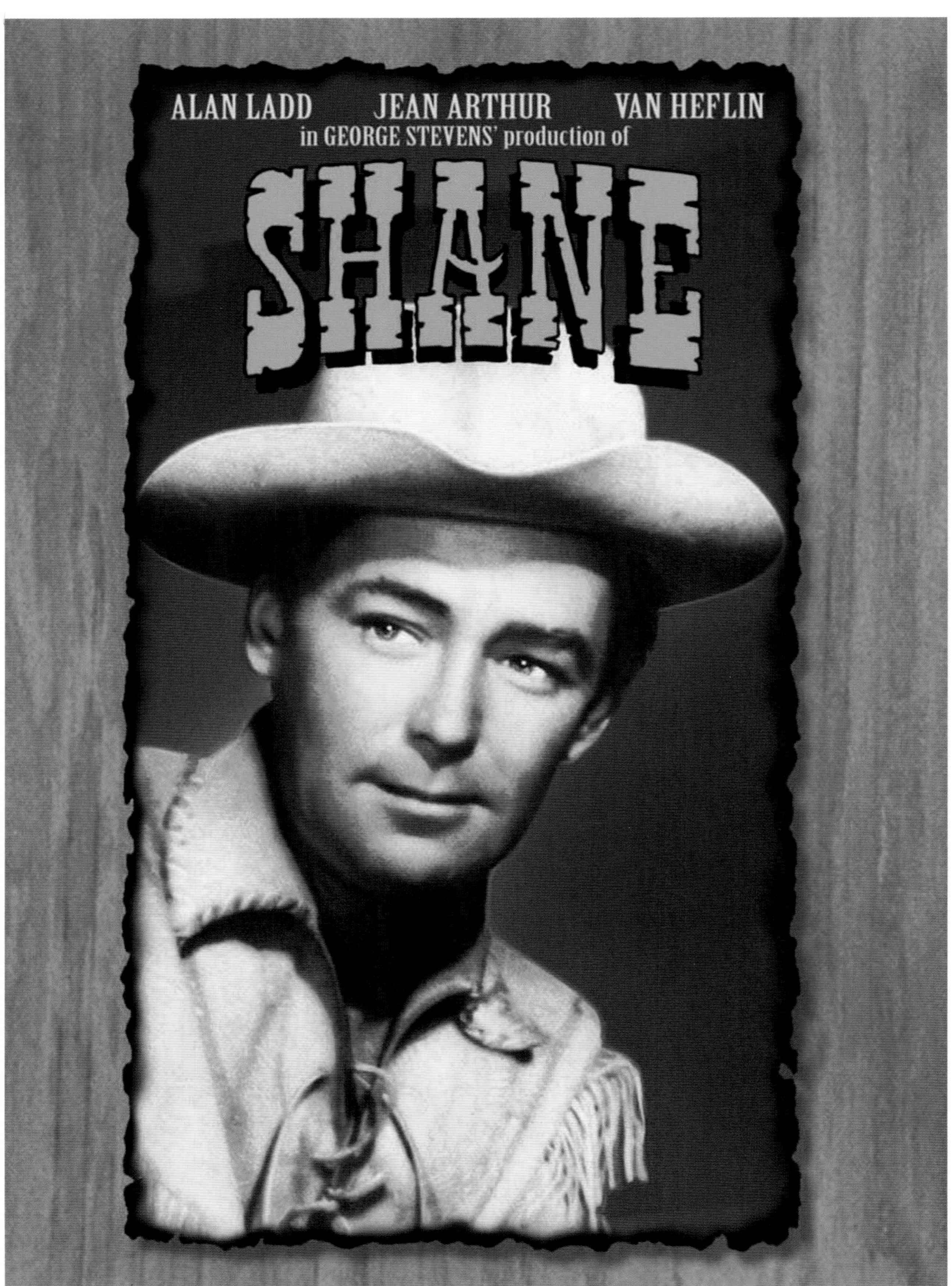

Woody Allen wrote in The New York Times: "'Shane' is in a class by itself. If I was making a list of the best American movies, 'Shane' would be on it."

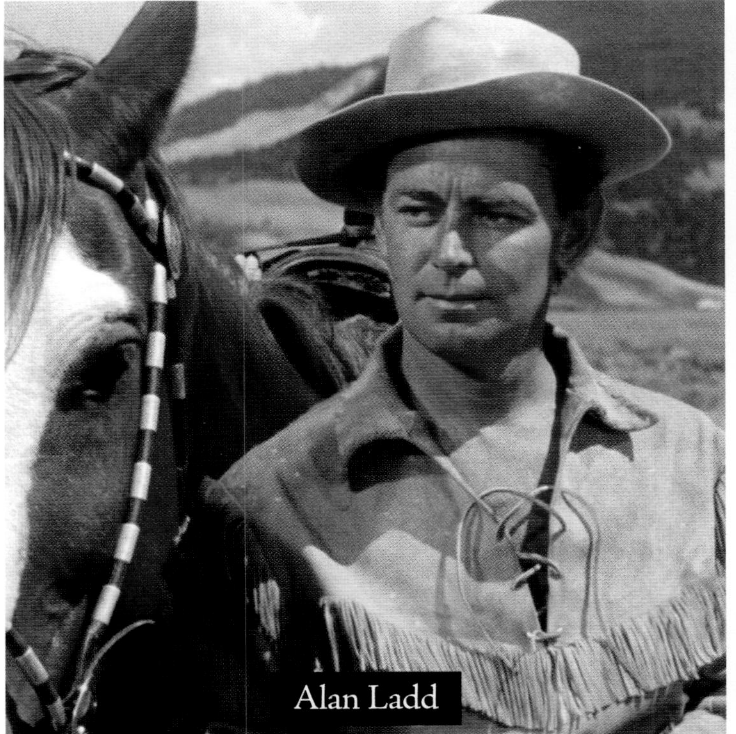

Alan Ladd

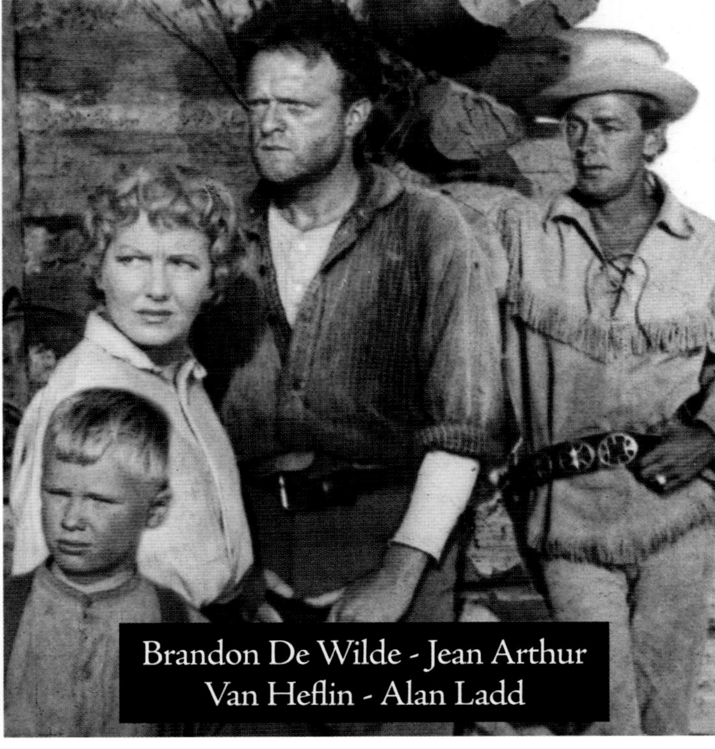

Brandon De Wilde - Jean Arthur
Van Heflin - Alan Ladd

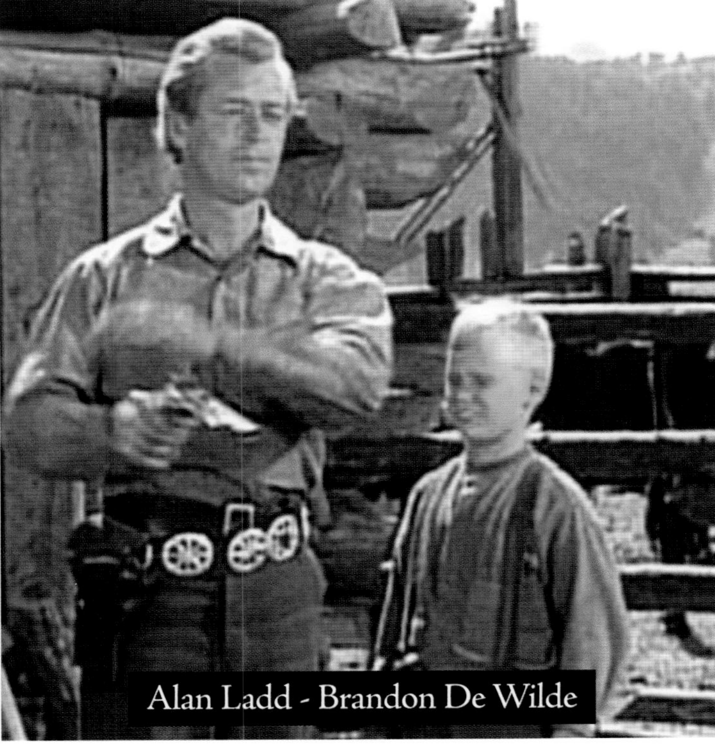

Alan Ladd - Brandon De Wilde

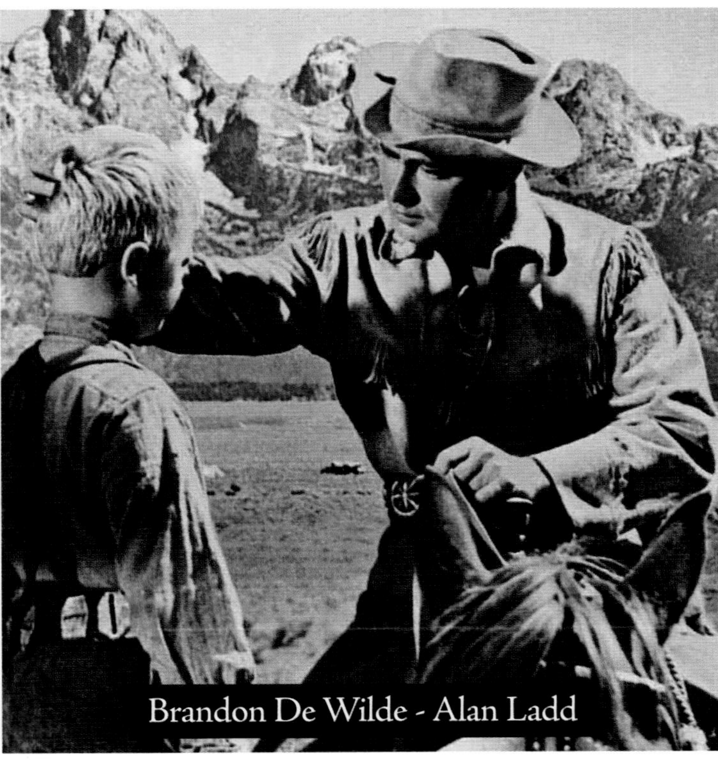

Brandon De Wilde - Alan Ladd

Alan Ladd was ably abetted by two very talented actors, Jean Arthur and Van Heflin.

Billy Crystal told me that his father, who owned a record company for which Billie Holiday recorded, had, when he was six years old, taken him to a theater to see "Shane" and, while sitting on her lap watching the film, they both unabashedly wept.

An ex-tennis pro improvises a brilliant plan B when the plot to murder his wife goes wrong.

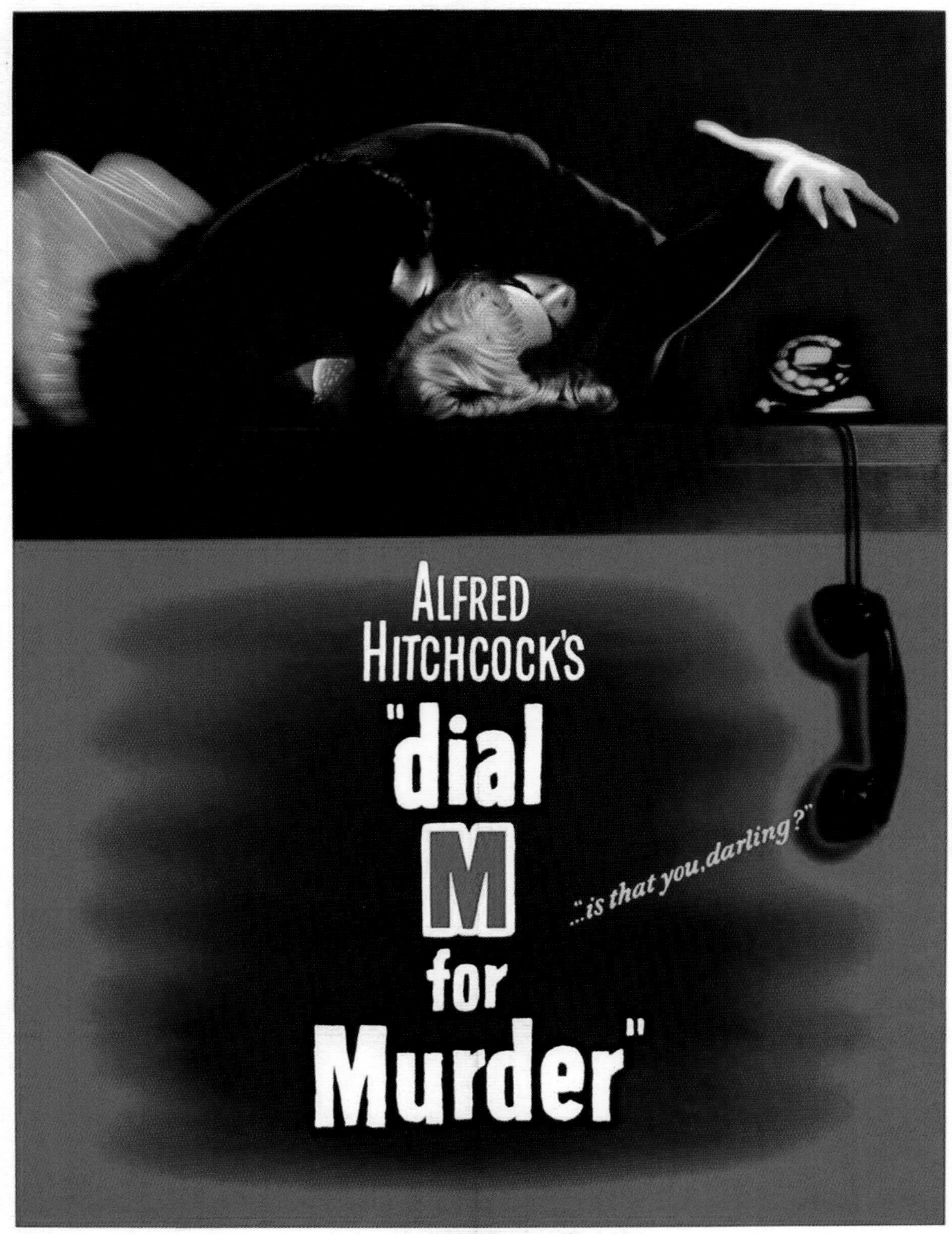

Tim Brayton of Antagony & Ecstasy wrote: "An exercise made by an enormously talented constructor of thrillers in the most fertile period of his career."

Philip French of Observer wrote: "Rather than let someone else mess with a play that has a formal perfection, Hitchcock did the adaptation himself, his only such credit while in Hollywood."

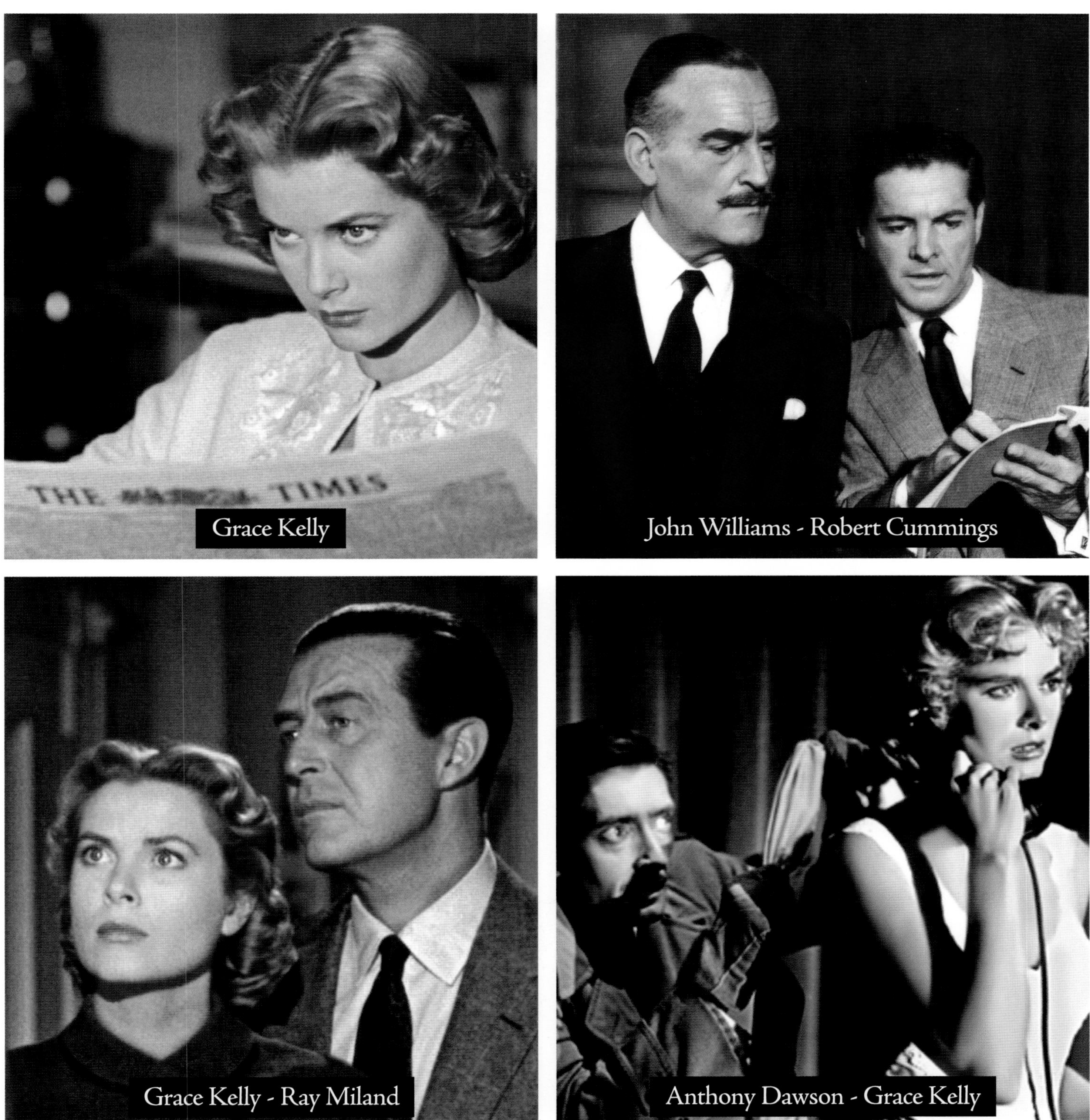

Grace Kelly

John Williams - Robert Cummings

Grace Kelly - Ray Miland

Anthony Dawson - Grace Kelly

If there was any doubt about the audience's love of "Dial M for Murder," you have only to know that it was remade ten times–two feature films and eight TV versions.

A wheelchair-bound photographer spies on his neighbours from his apartment window and becomes convinced one of them has committed murder.

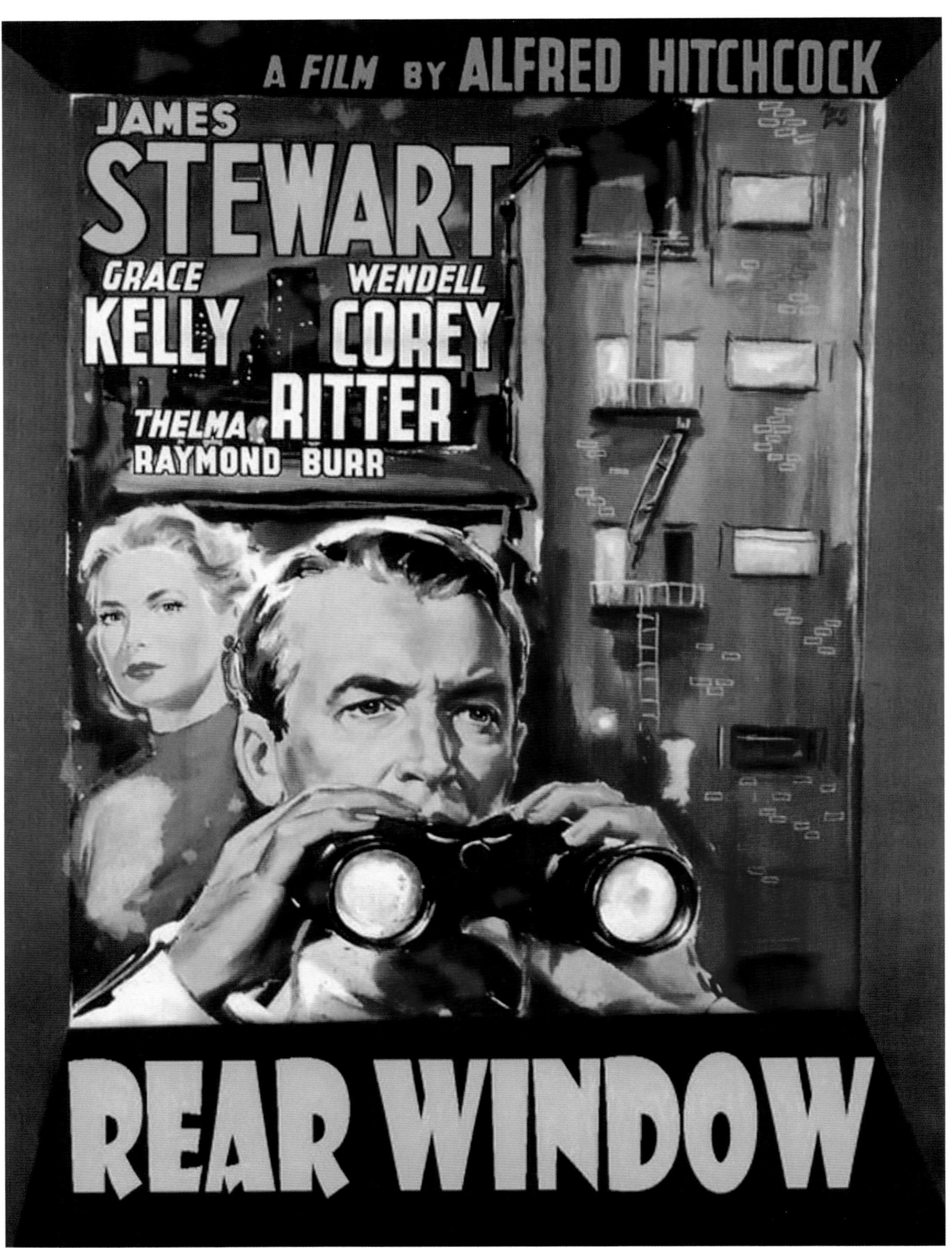

Michael Sragow of The New Yorker wrote: "It's one of Alfred Hitchcock's inspired audience-participation films: watching it, you feel titillated, horrified, and, ultimately, purged."

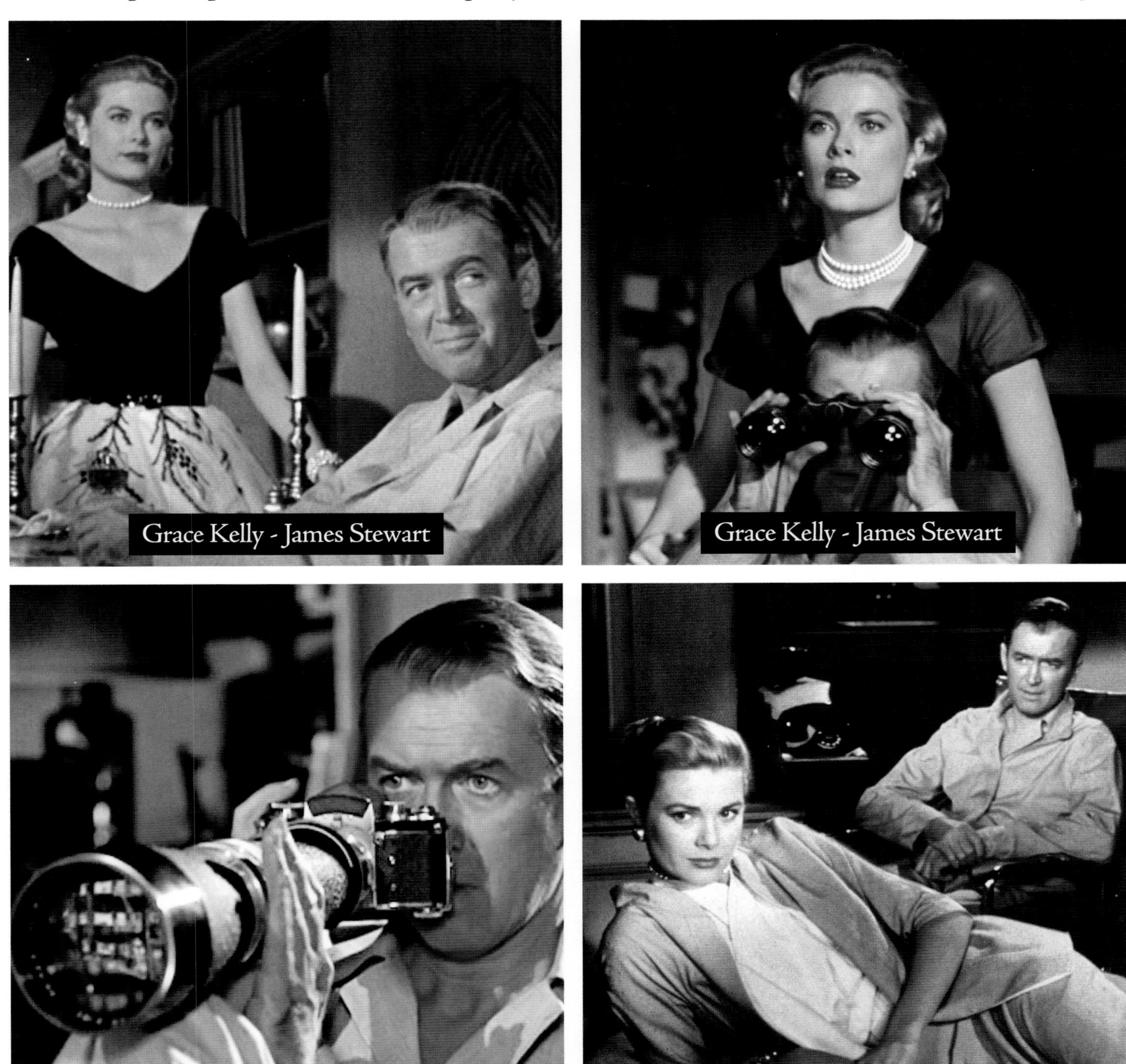

Grace Kelly - James Stewart

Grace Kelly - James Stewart

James Stewart

Grace Kelly - James Stewart

It was not hard to imagine why Prince Rainier of Monaco was smitten by Grace Kelly's beauty and would ask for her hand in marriage. I had the opportunity to meet Grace Kelly when her husband invited me and my wife to Monaco to play in his Pro-Am tennis tournament.

At the tournament I asked Princess Grace how she felt about being a princess and she said she didn't think of herself as a princess, but more like a producer.

Producer Ronny Graham finds himself in financial difficulties on the eve of opening night when a wealthy Texan offers to put up the money, if his daughter is cast in the show.

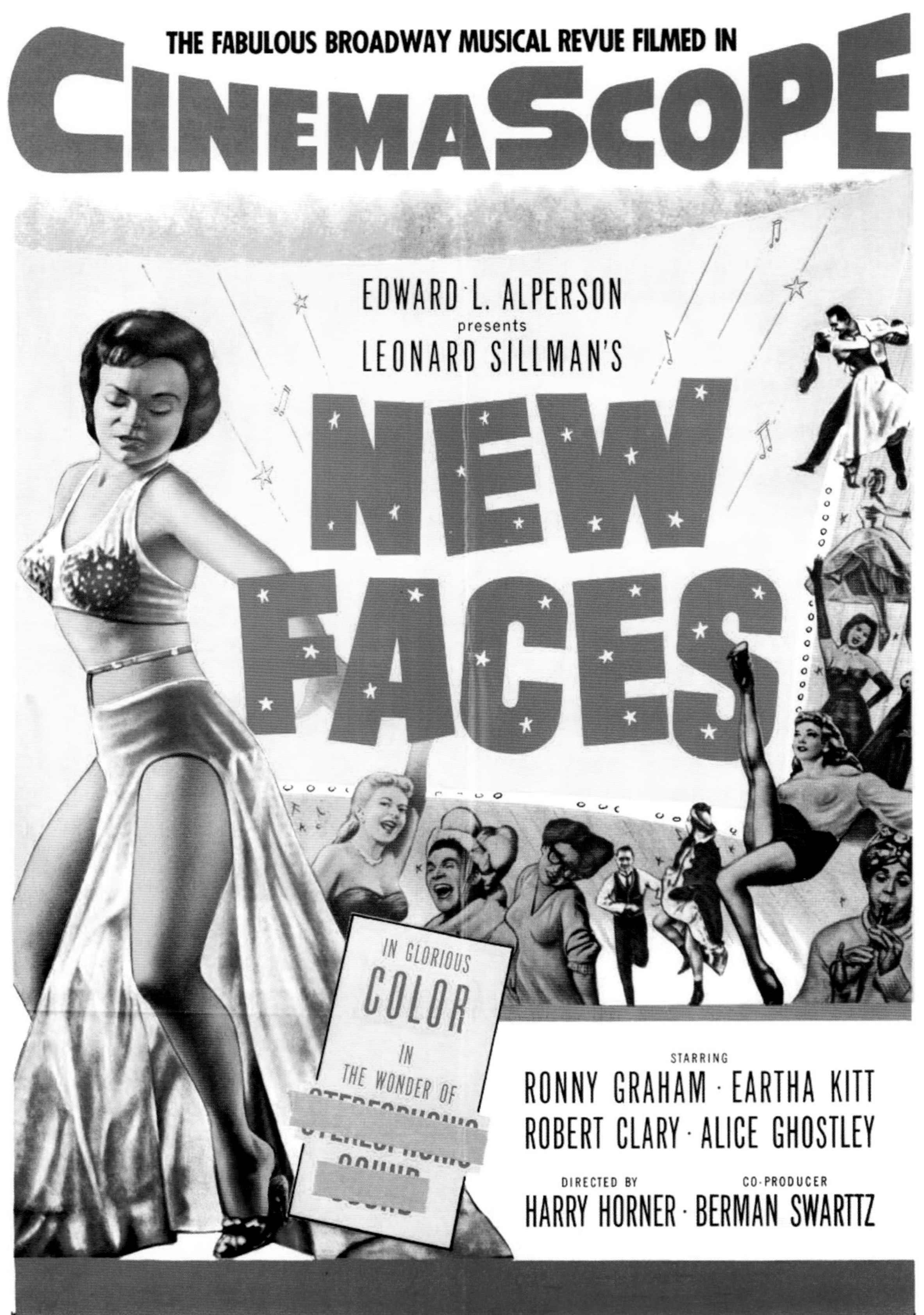

H.H.T. of The New York Times wrote: "Alice Ghostley delivers her stunning rendition of 'Boston Beguine.' Ronny Graham does a side-splitting burlesque of 'Death of a Salesman,' Eartha Kitt singing 'Monotonous' is anything but monotonous and the gravel-toned little Frenchman, Robert Clary, scampers through his numbers like a galvanized monkey."

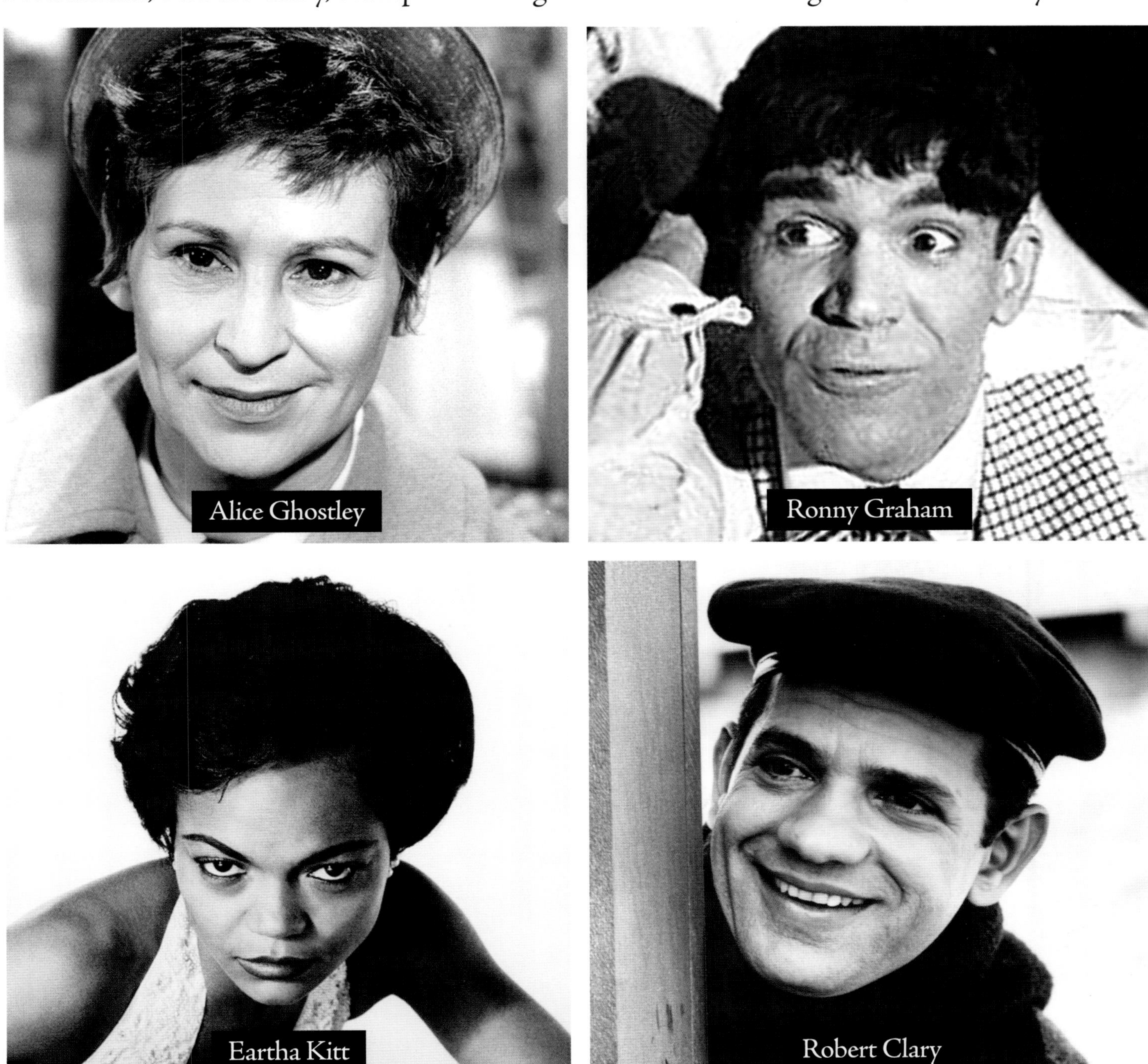

Alice Ghostley

Ronny Graham

Eartha Kitt

Robert Clary

Both Robert Clary and his audiences are eternally grateful for Robert's ability to live through the horror of the Nazi labor camp, Buchenwald. This extraordinarily talented singer-performer was kept alive by his Nazi captors so they might enjoy the command performances they ordered him to give.

With the writing of the show's hilarious sketches, the career of Mel Brooks was born.

In 1850 Oregon, when a backwoodsman brings a wife home to his farm, his six brothers decide that they want to get married too.

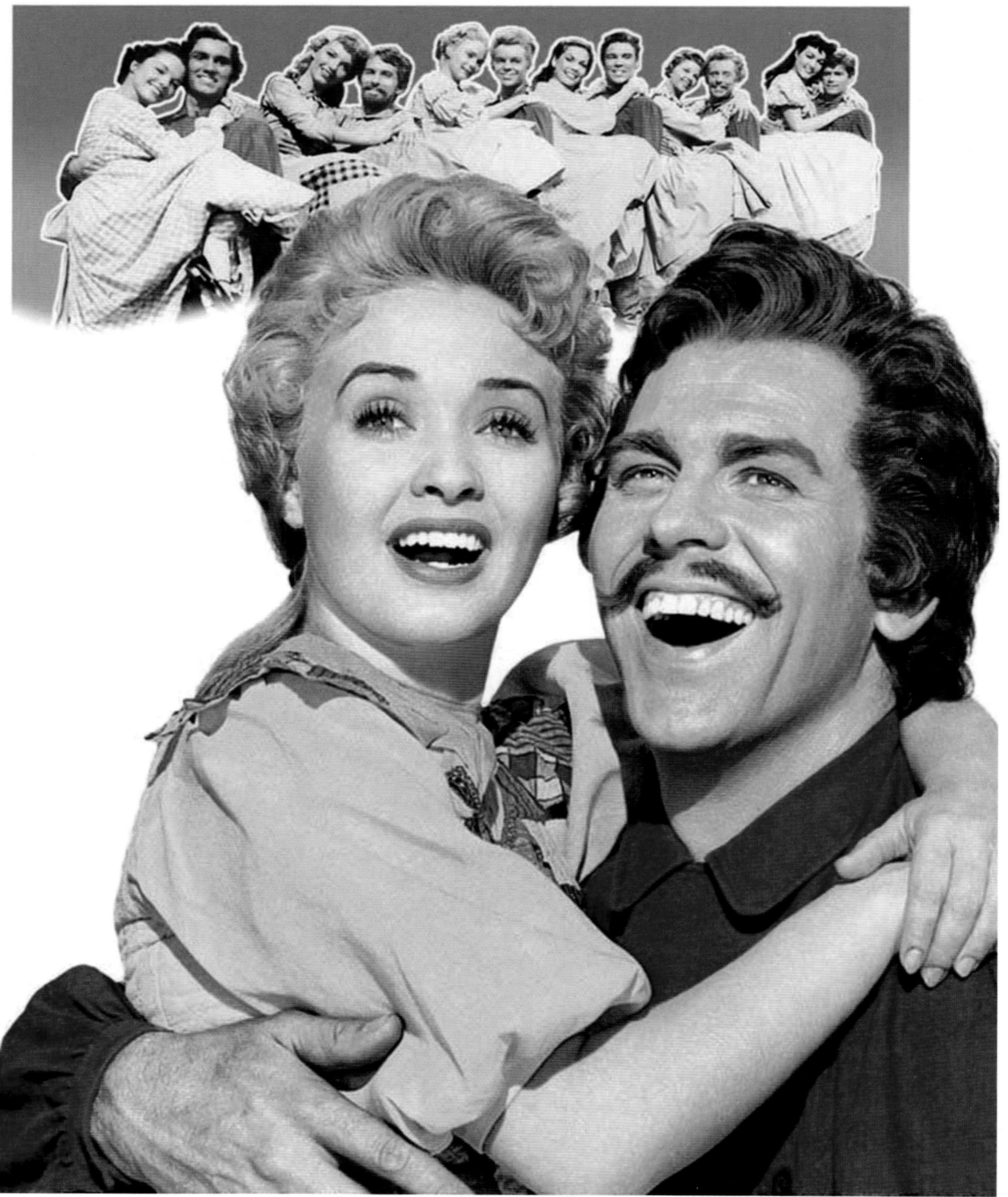

Variety wrote: "This is a happy, hand-clapping, foot-stomping country type of musical with all the slickness of a Broadway show."

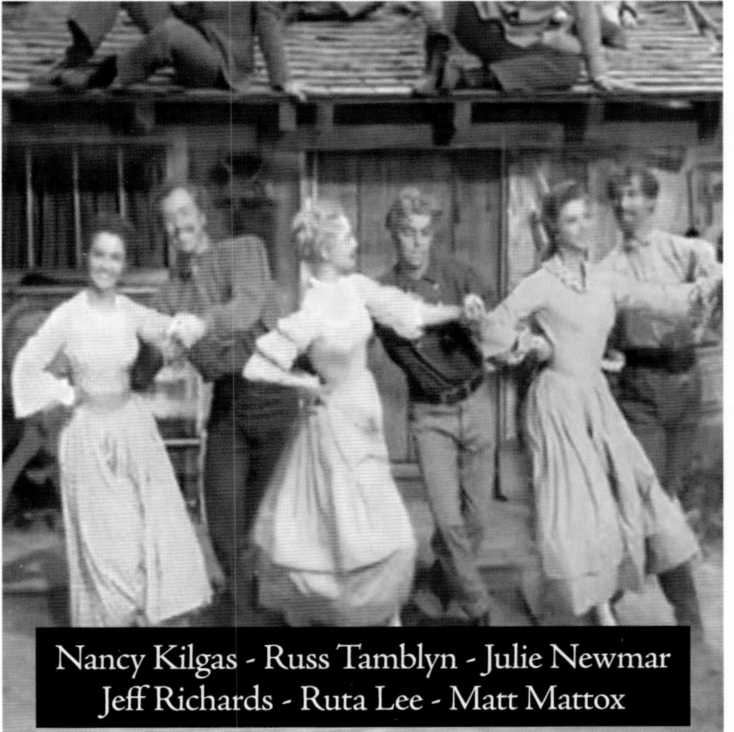

Nancy Kilgas - Russ Tamblyn - Julie Newmar
Jeff Richards - Ruta Lee - Matt Mattox

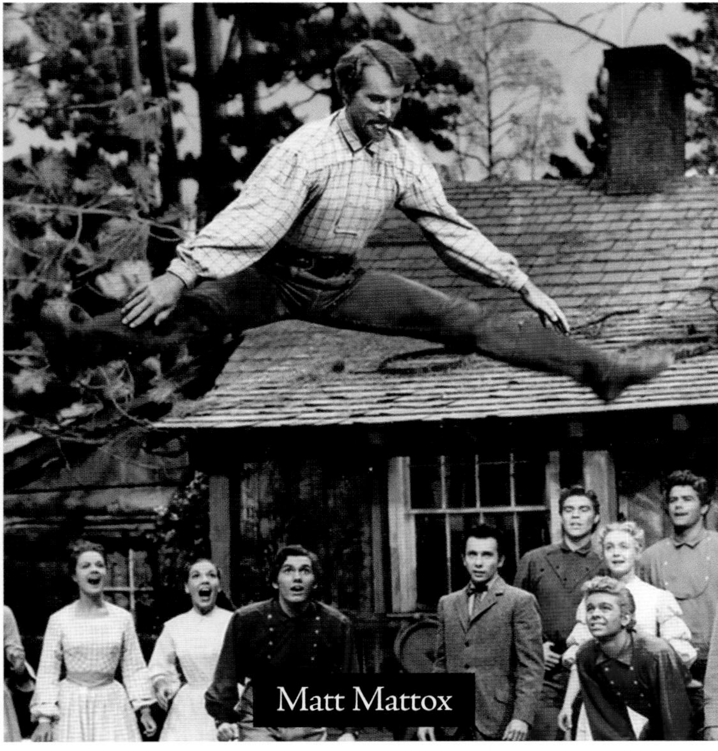

Matt Mattox

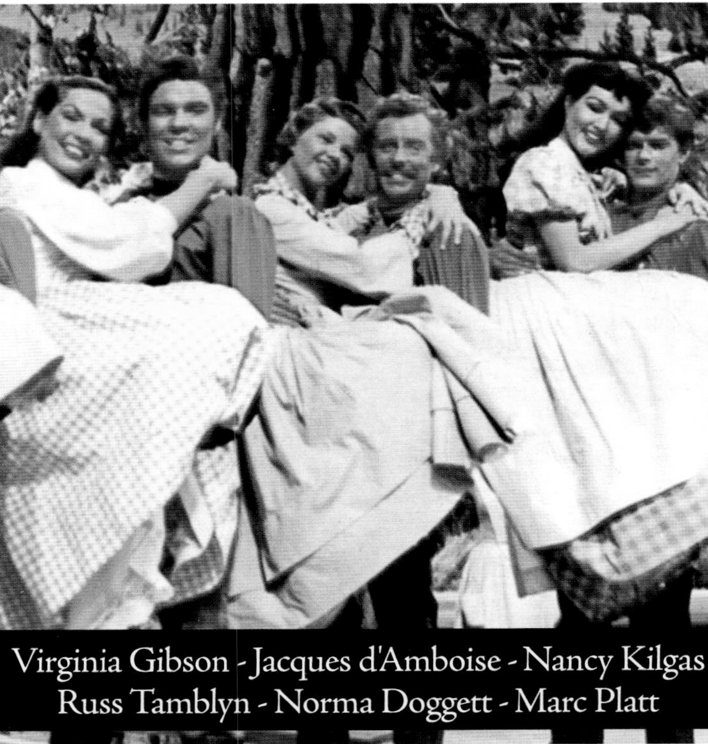

Virginia Gibson - Jacques d'Amboise - Nancy Kilgas
Russ Tamblyn - Norma Doggett - Marc Platt

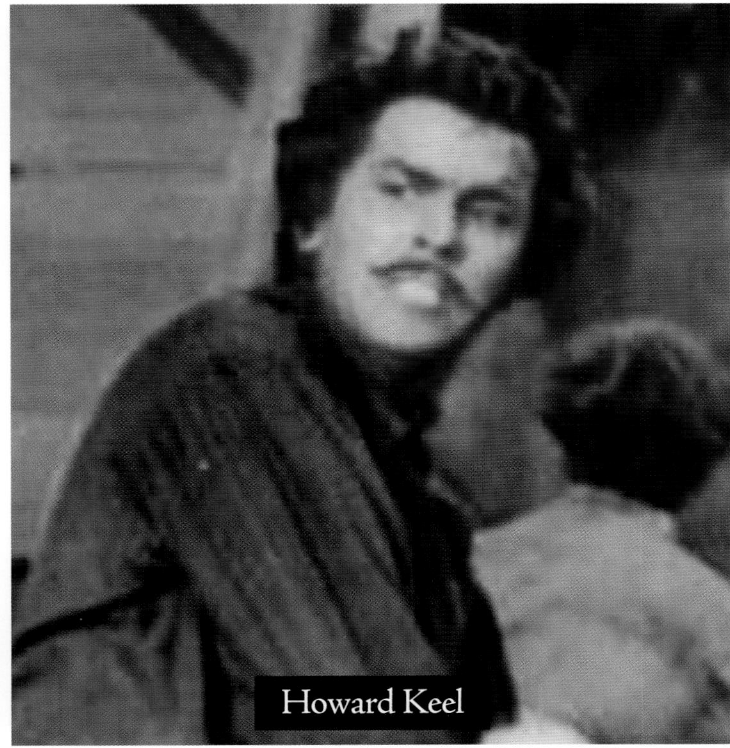

Howard Keel

The film's musical numbers were considered to have had the most difficult and dangerous choreography ever and the torturer in charge was the brilliant dance director, Michael Kidd. To prove that it was possible to do all the steps choreographed without breaking your leg, he went full out demonstrating each of his inventive leaps and landings.

An ex-prize fighter turned longshoreman struggles to stand up to his corrupt union bosses.

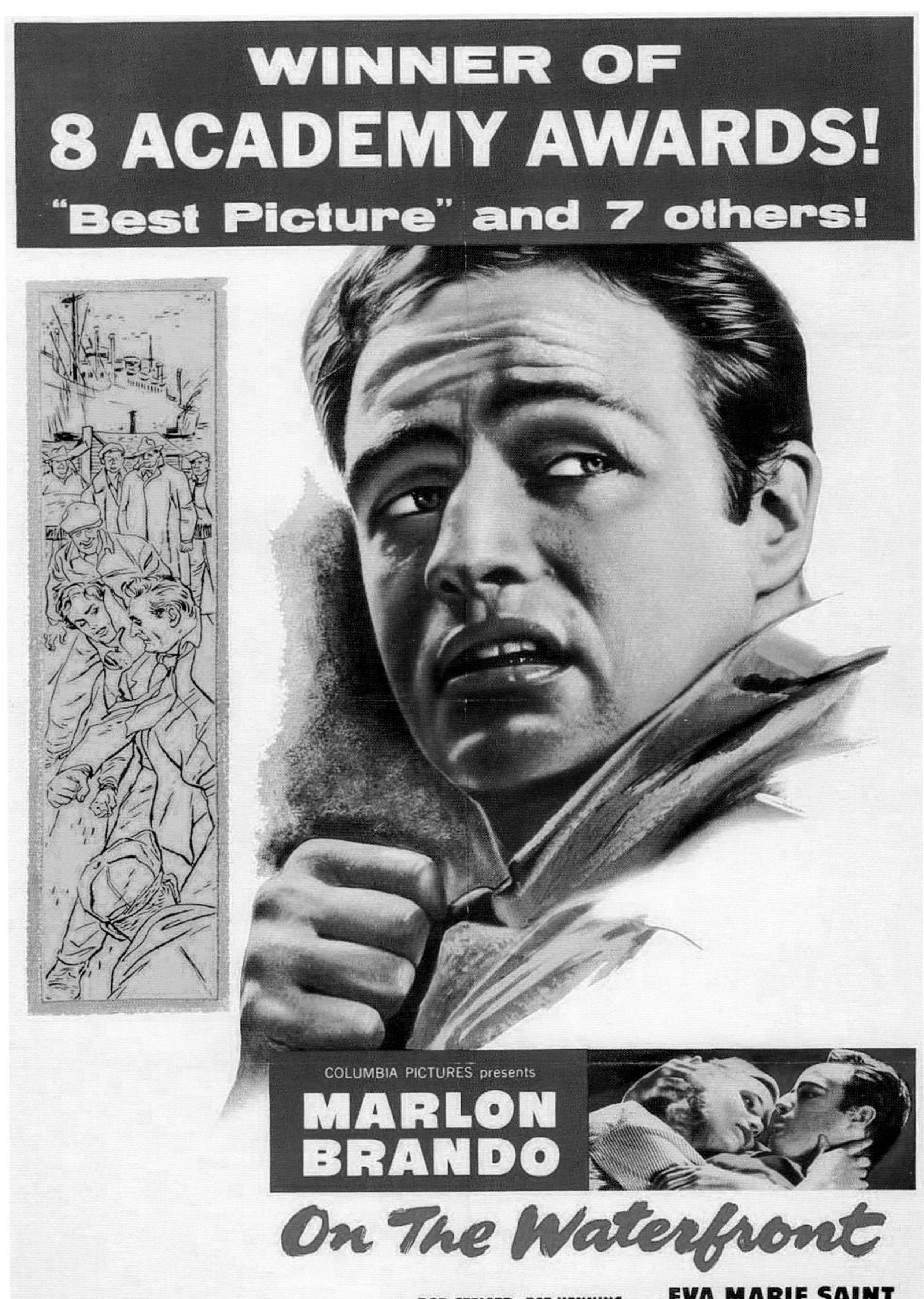

Matt Brunson of Creative Loafing wrote: "A powerful watch, thanks largely to an incredible cast, Leonard Bernstein's strong score, and a handful of iconic scenes, none better than the moving 'I coulda been a contender' sequence."

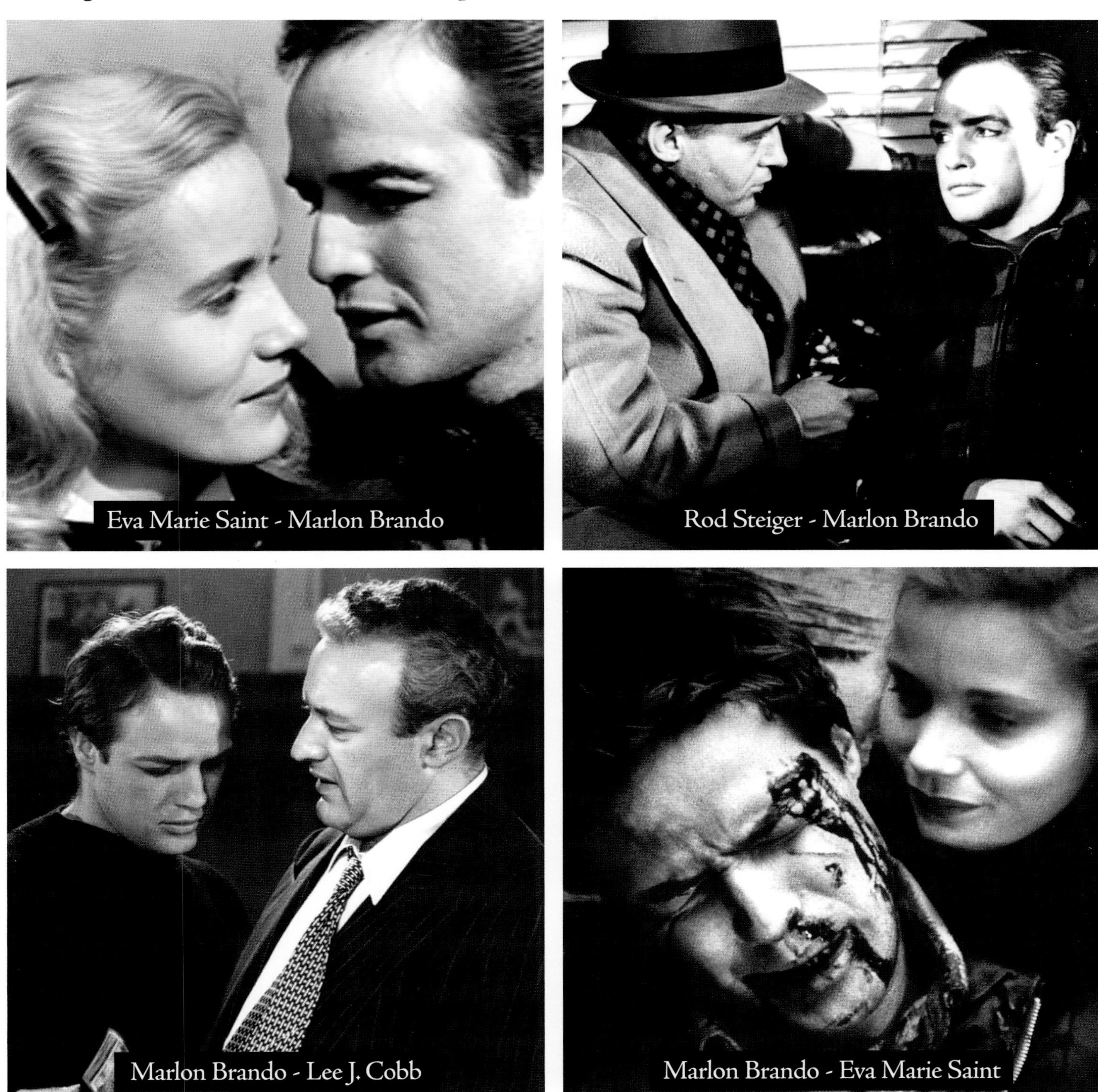
Eva Marie Saint - Marlon Brando

Rod Steiger - Marlon Brando

Marlon Brando - Lee J. Cobb

Marlon Brando - Eva Marie Saint

There is nothing I can tell you about this film that speaks louder than the poster, which informs us that a man standing up for his rights can win 8 Academy Awards, including Best Picture. Also speaking volumes are the words of a critic who acknowledges the most quotable line in the film, "I coulda been a contender. I coulda been somebody, instead of a bum."

When a U.S. Naval captain shows signs of mental instability that jeopardize the ship, the first officer relieves him of command and faces court martial for mutiny.

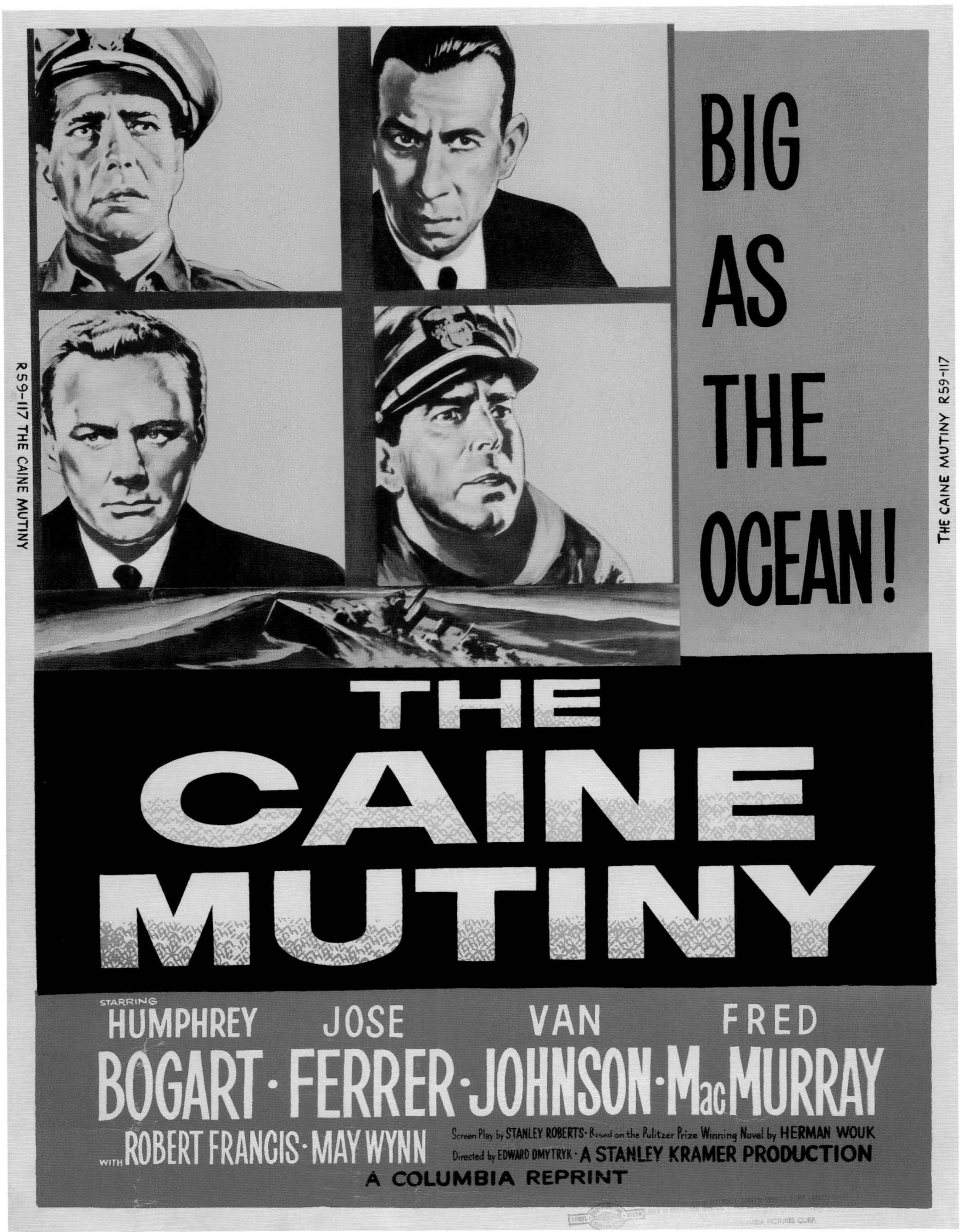

Daily Variety wrote: "The intelligent screenplay retains all the essence of Herman Wouk's novel."

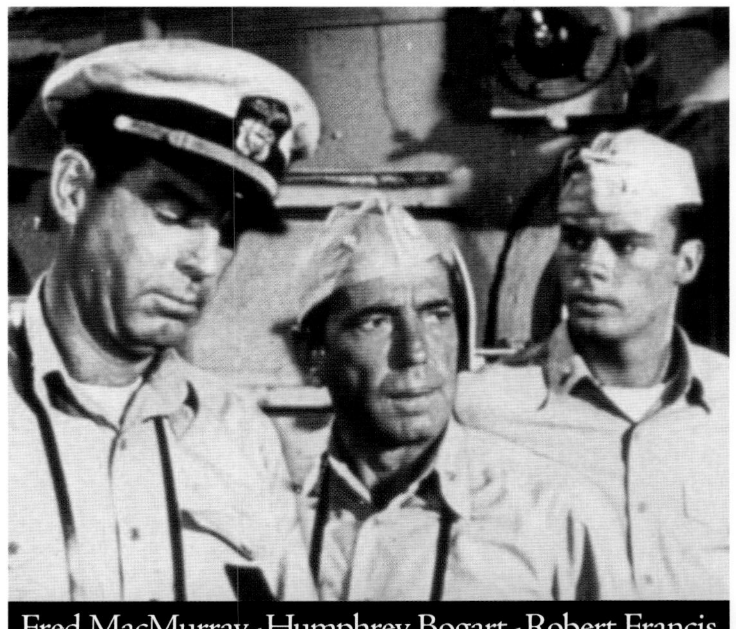
Fred MacMurray - Humphrey Bogart - Robert Francis

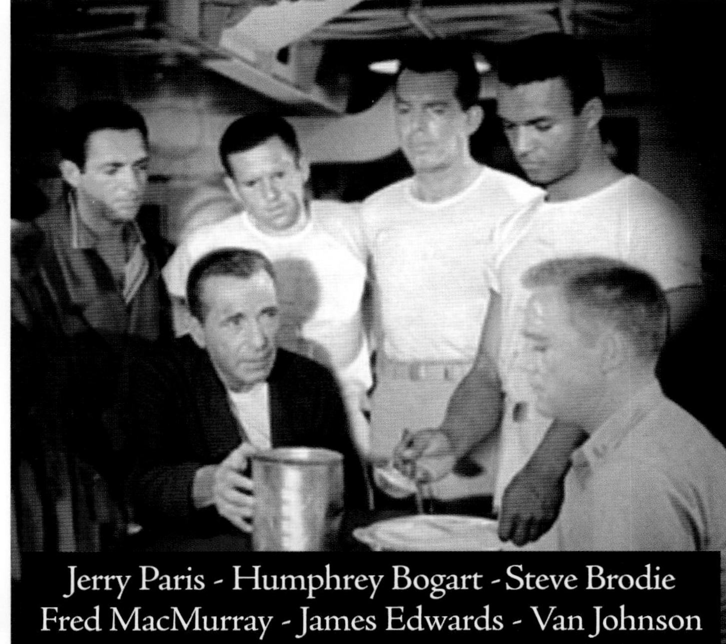
Jerry Paris - Humphrey Bogart - Steve Brodie
Fred MacMurray - James Edwards - Van Johnson

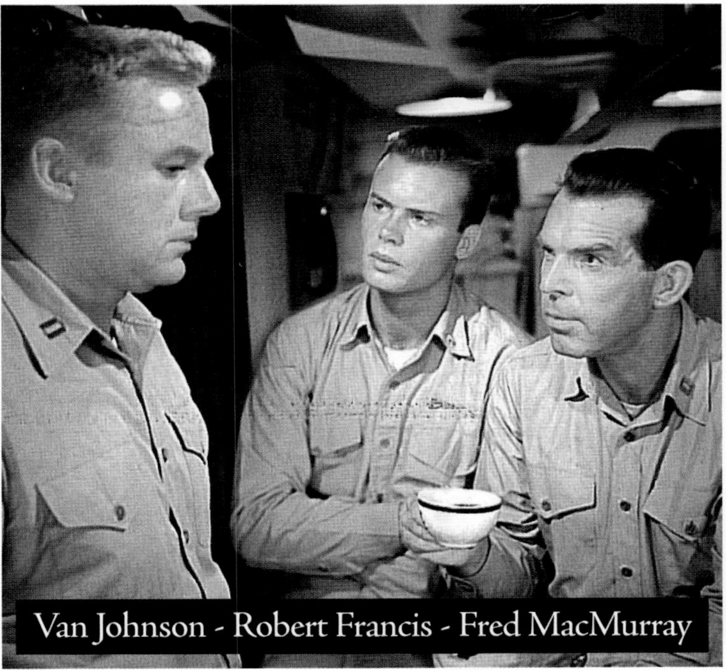
Van Johnson - Robert Francis - Fred MacMurray

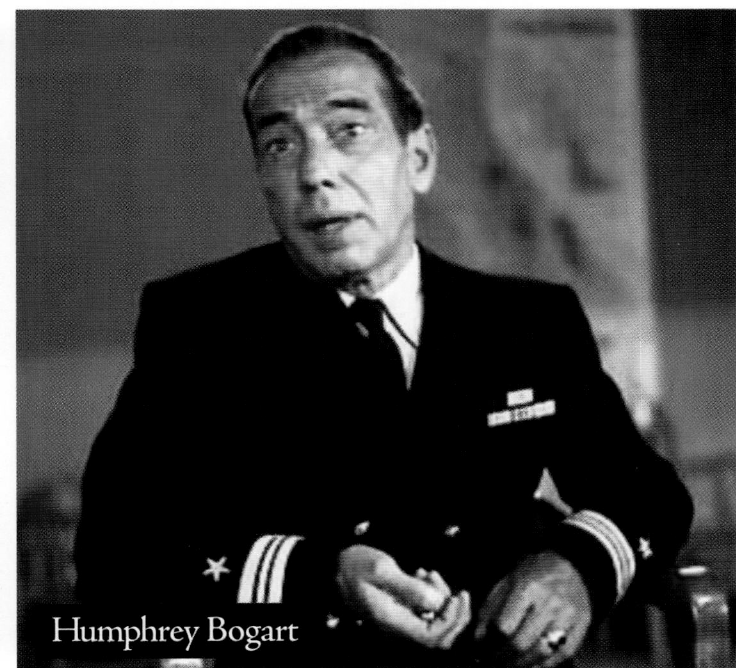
Humphrey Bogart

Etched in my memory is Capt. Queeg, commander of the USS Caine, rolling two steel balls in his palms as he was questioned about the mutiny aboard his ship.

Herman Wouk, the author of "The Caine Mutiny," and I were neighbors on Fire Island and one time I found myself chauffeuring him to New York, where I had a meeting with a publisher. Sitting in the front seat was the manuscript for my first novel, "Enter Laughing." On the drive Herman Wouk asked me if he might read it and, of course, I said he could. He read it and every time he giggled or laughed I looked over to see what I had written that evoked such a positive reaction from the country's #1 best-selling author.

A one-handed stranger comes to a tiny town possessing a terrible past that the townsfolk want to keep secret, by violent means if necessary.

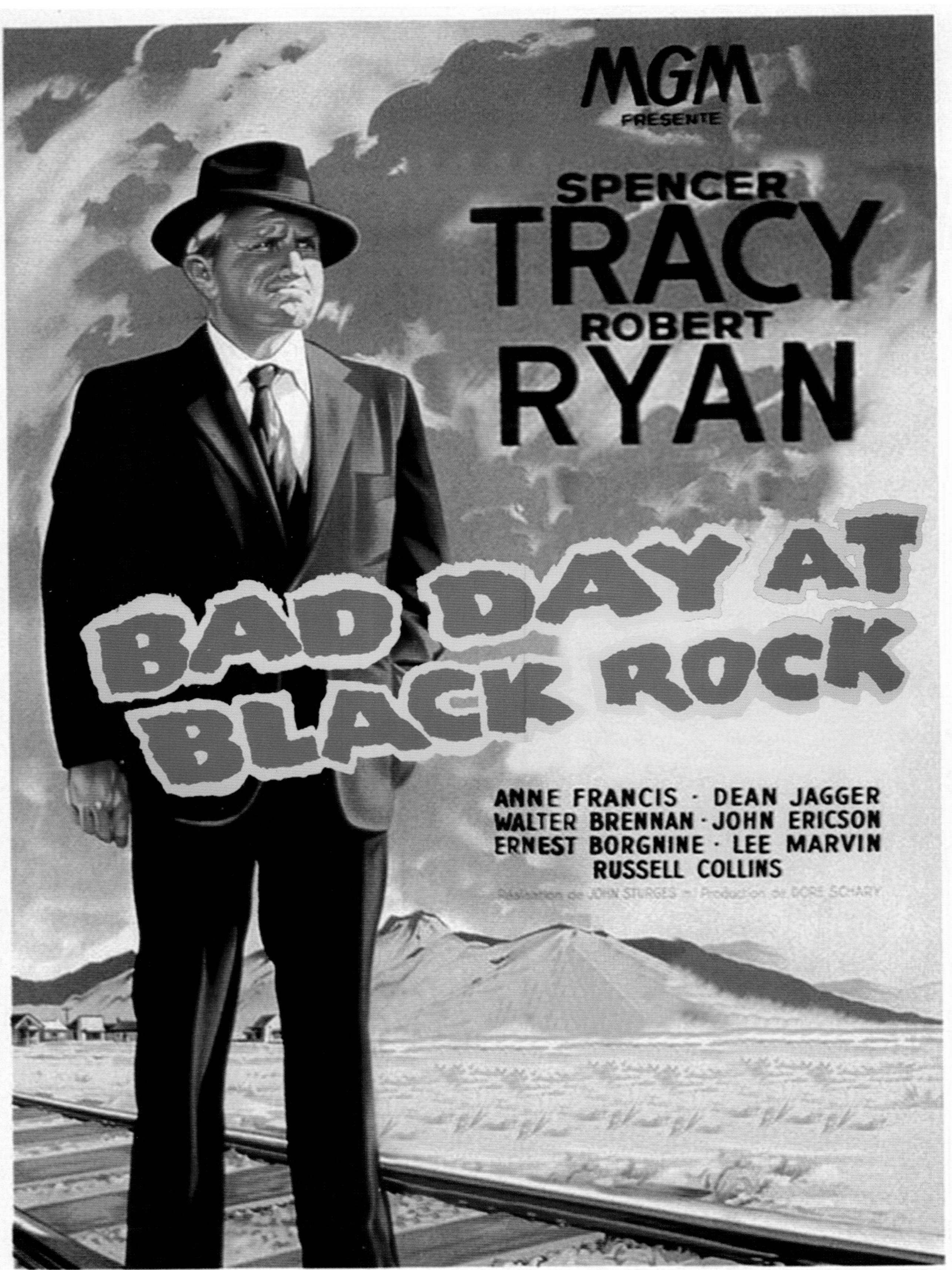

Variety wrote: "Considerable excitement is whipped up in this suspense drama, and fans who go for tight action will find it entirely satisfactory."

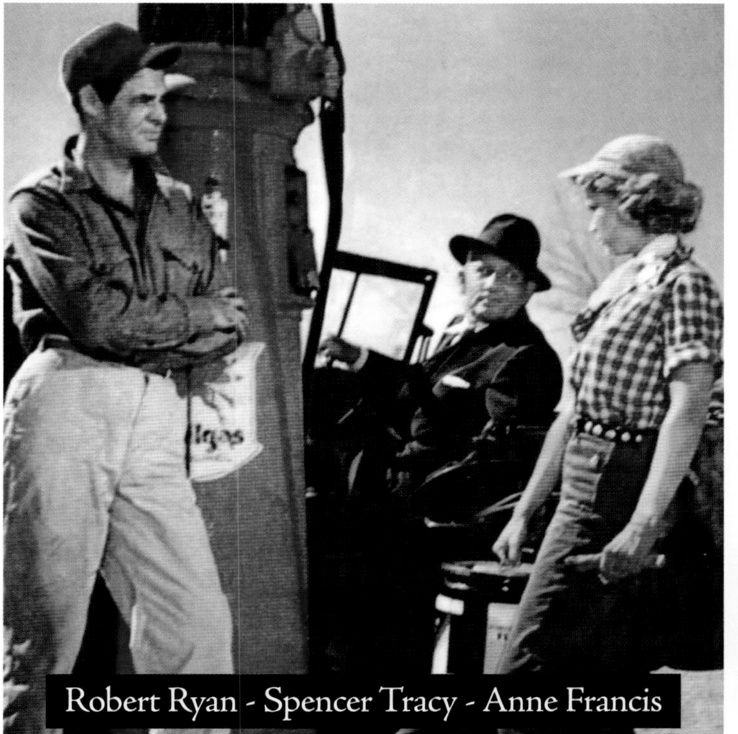
Robert Ryan - Spencer Tracy - Anne Francis

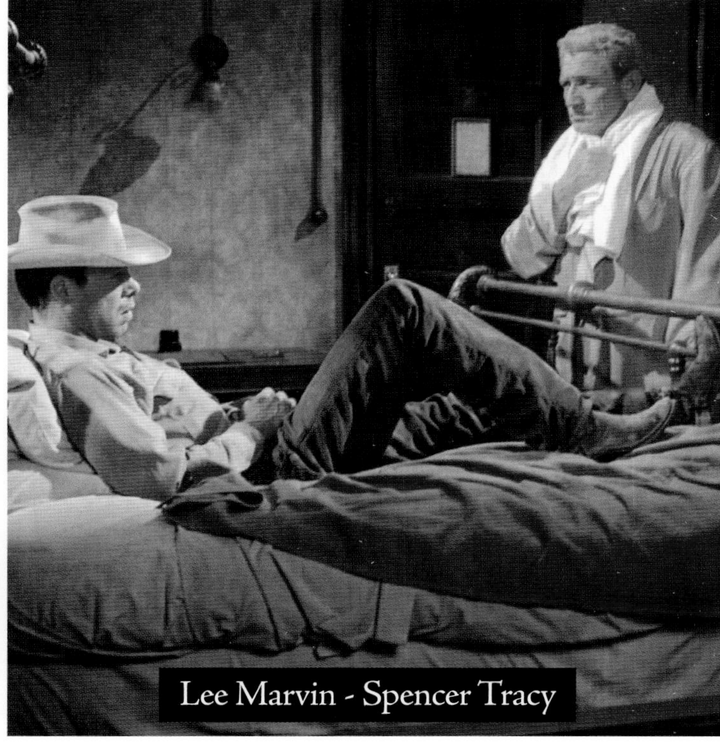
Lee Marvin - Spencer Tracy

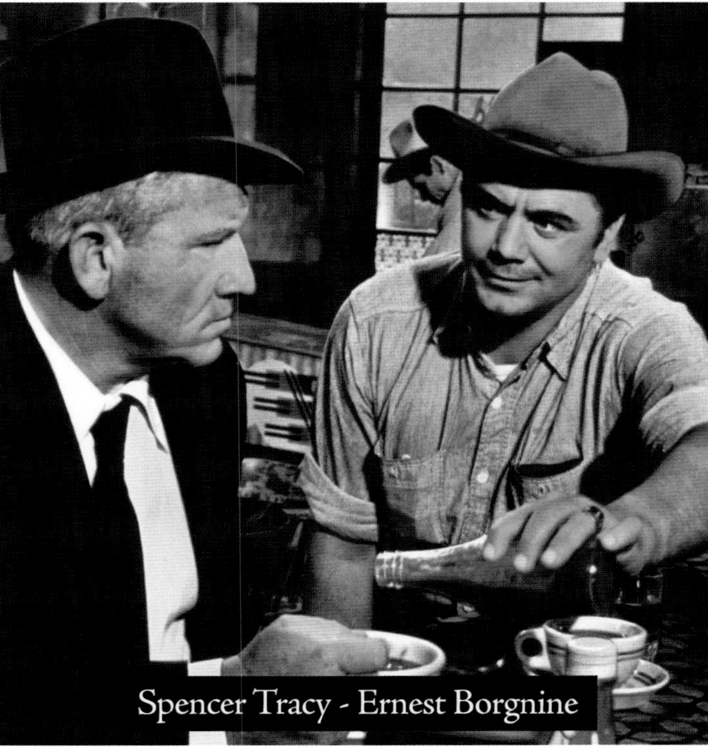
Spencer Tracy - Ernest Borgnine

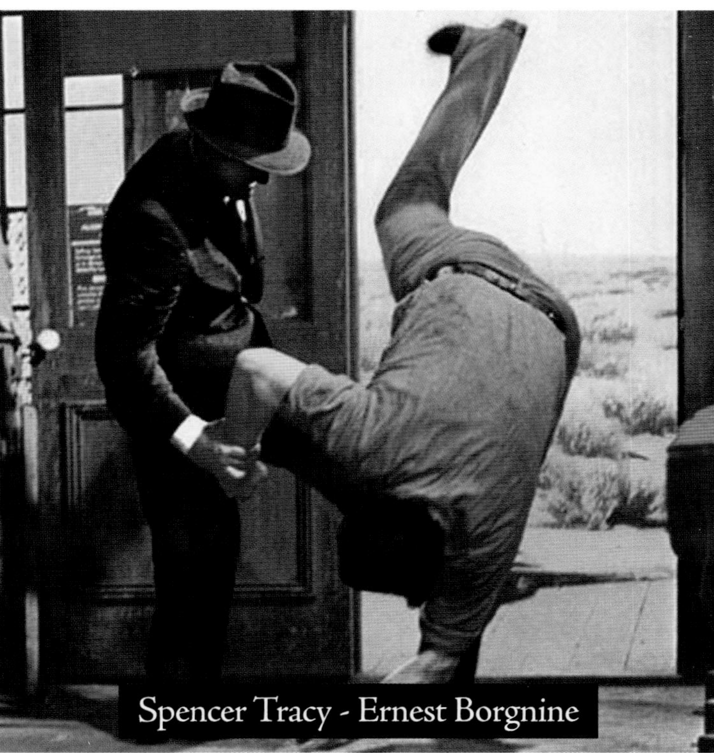
Spencer Tracy - Ernest Borgnine

This film was Hollywood's first production to directly tackle the unjust World War II internment of Japanese-American citizens.

In the last scene, we see Spencer Tracy, a veteran who lost his left arm fighting in Italy, use his right arm to knock the holy crap out of a bigoted racist.

A middle-aged butcher and a school teacher who have given up on the idea of love meet at a dance and fall for each other.

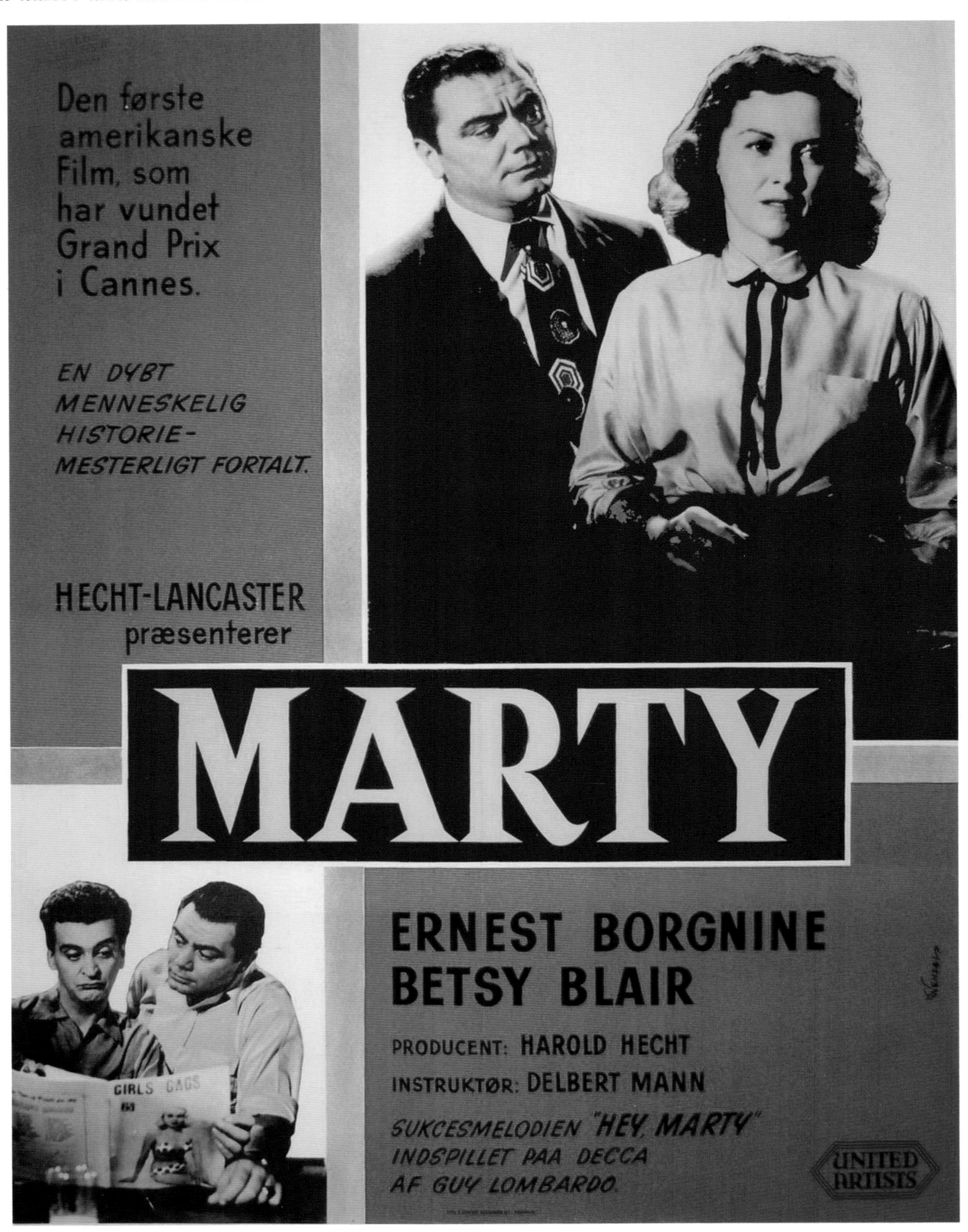

Kate Cameron of New York Daily News wrote: "It is a sentimental, heart-warming story of a couple of ugly ducklings who find compensation for their lack of good looks in each other's love."

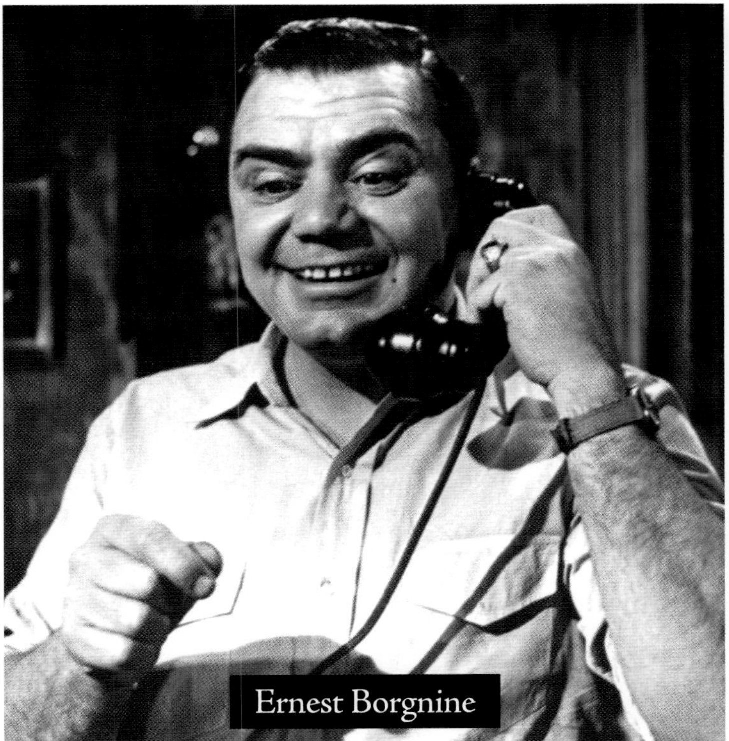
Ernest Borgnine

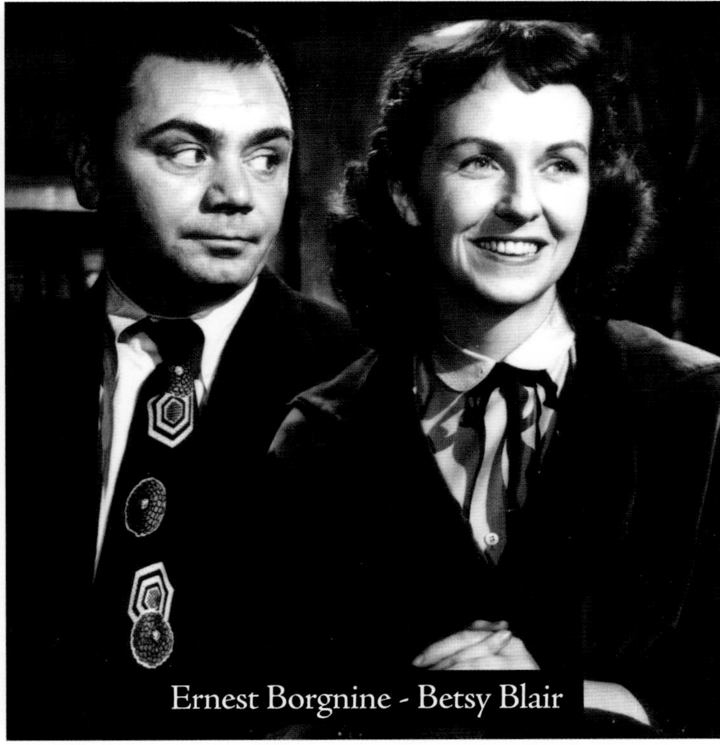
Ernest Borgnine - Betsy Blair

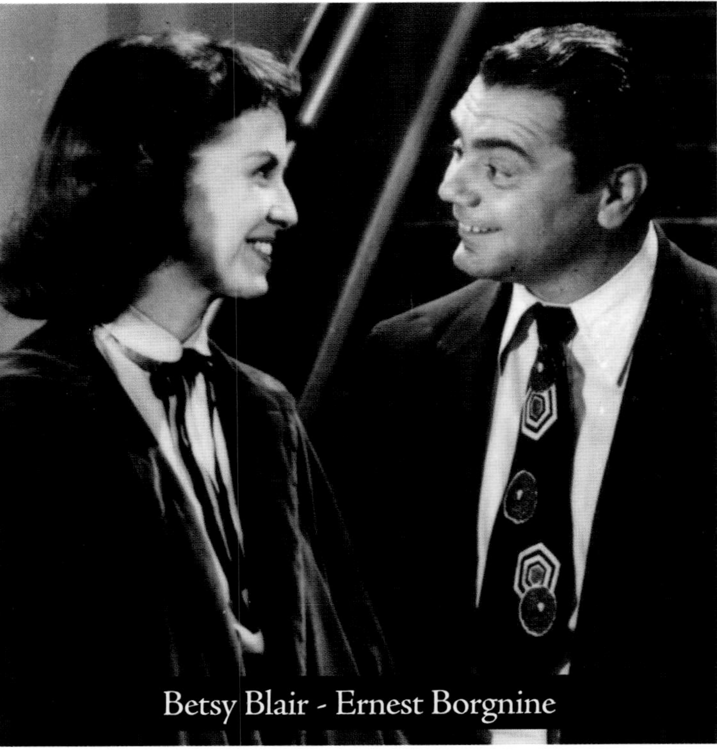
Betsy Blair - Ernest Borgnine

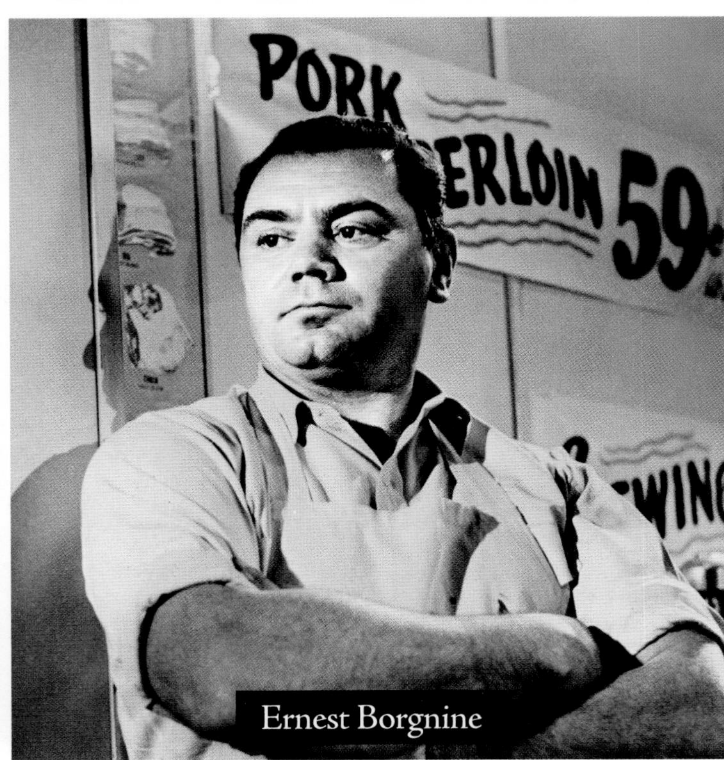

Ernest Borgnine

Paddy Chayefsky, the author of "Marty," is the only writer to have won three solo Academy Awards for Best Screenplay. He was one of the most renowned dramatists of the Golden Age of Television and a pioneer of the "slice of life" school of naturalism, among them "Network," "Hospital" and "The Americanization of Emily."

Four men plan a technically perfect crime, but the human element intervenes.

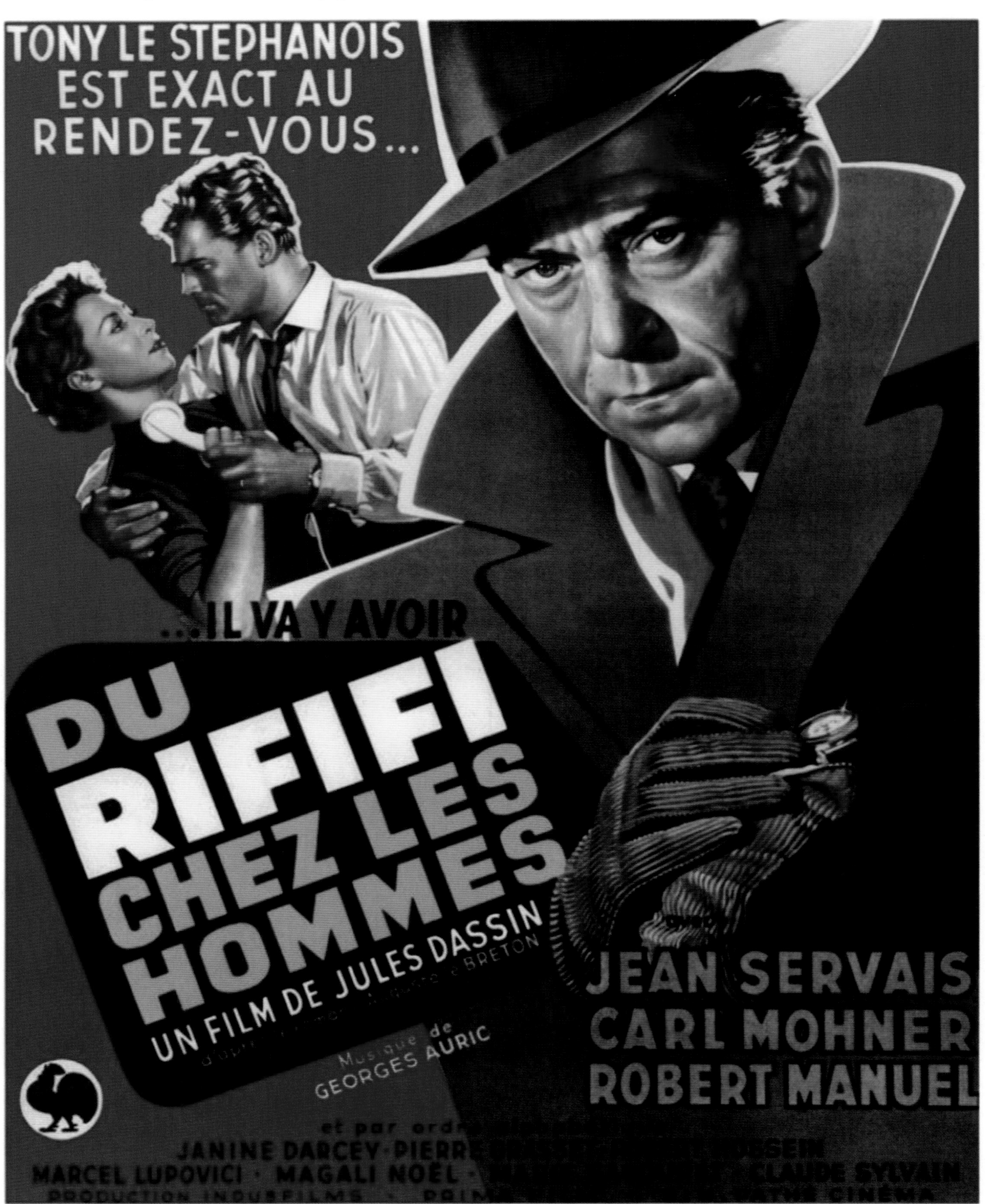

Variety wrote: "It took an experienced US director, Jules Dassin, who has lived in France some years, to give the French gangster pic the proper tension, mounting and treatment. This pic has something intrinsically Gallic without sacrificing the rugged storytelling."

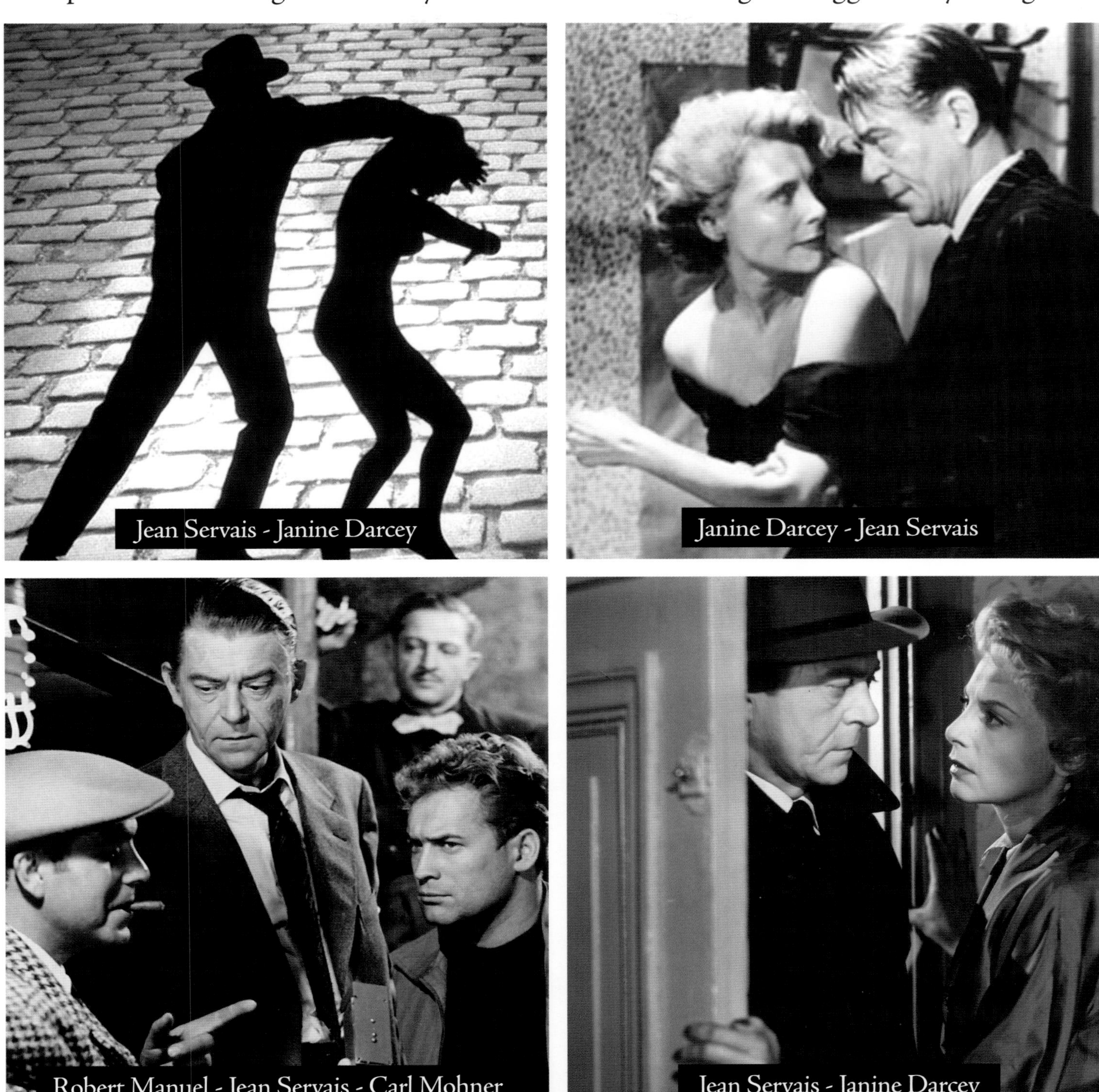

Jean Servais - Janine Darcey

Janine Darcey - Jean Servais

Robert Manuel - Jean Servais - Carl Mohner

Jean Servais - Janine Darcey

Jules Dassin, one of the leading American filmmakers of the postwar era, had to flee the country when the very 'Un-American' House Un-American Activities Committee branded him as a communist and made it difficult for him to find work. He settled in France, wrote and directed "Rififi," which set the table for all the film noirs to follow.

At the end of the Civil War, a Confederate team is ordered to rob a Union payroll train but the war ends leaving these men with their Union loot, until the Feds come looking for it.

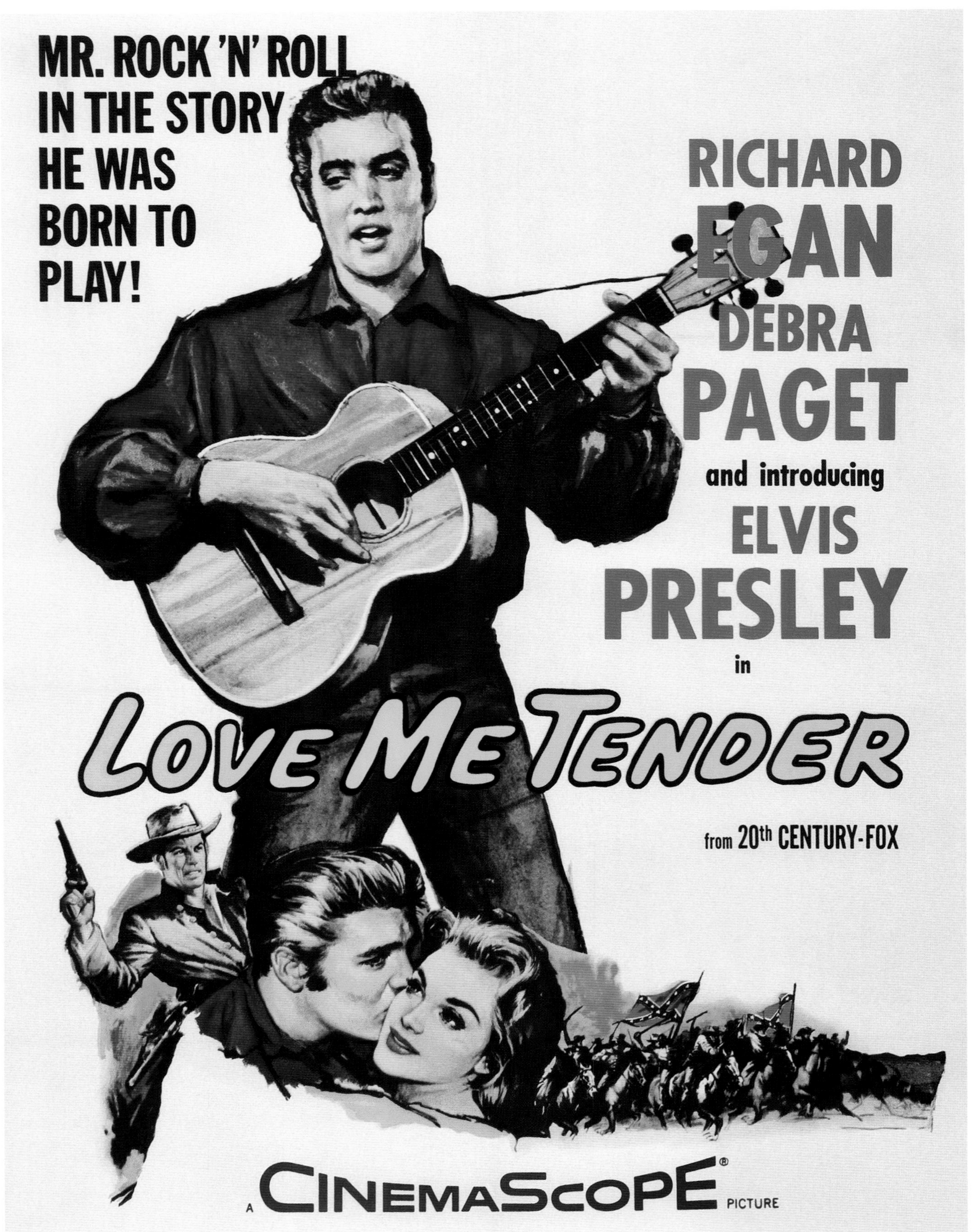

James Plath of Family Home Theater wrote: "Without The King, 'Love Me Tender' is a decent opera that has more stand-n-talk moments than shoot-'em-ups, but Elvis really does add interest."

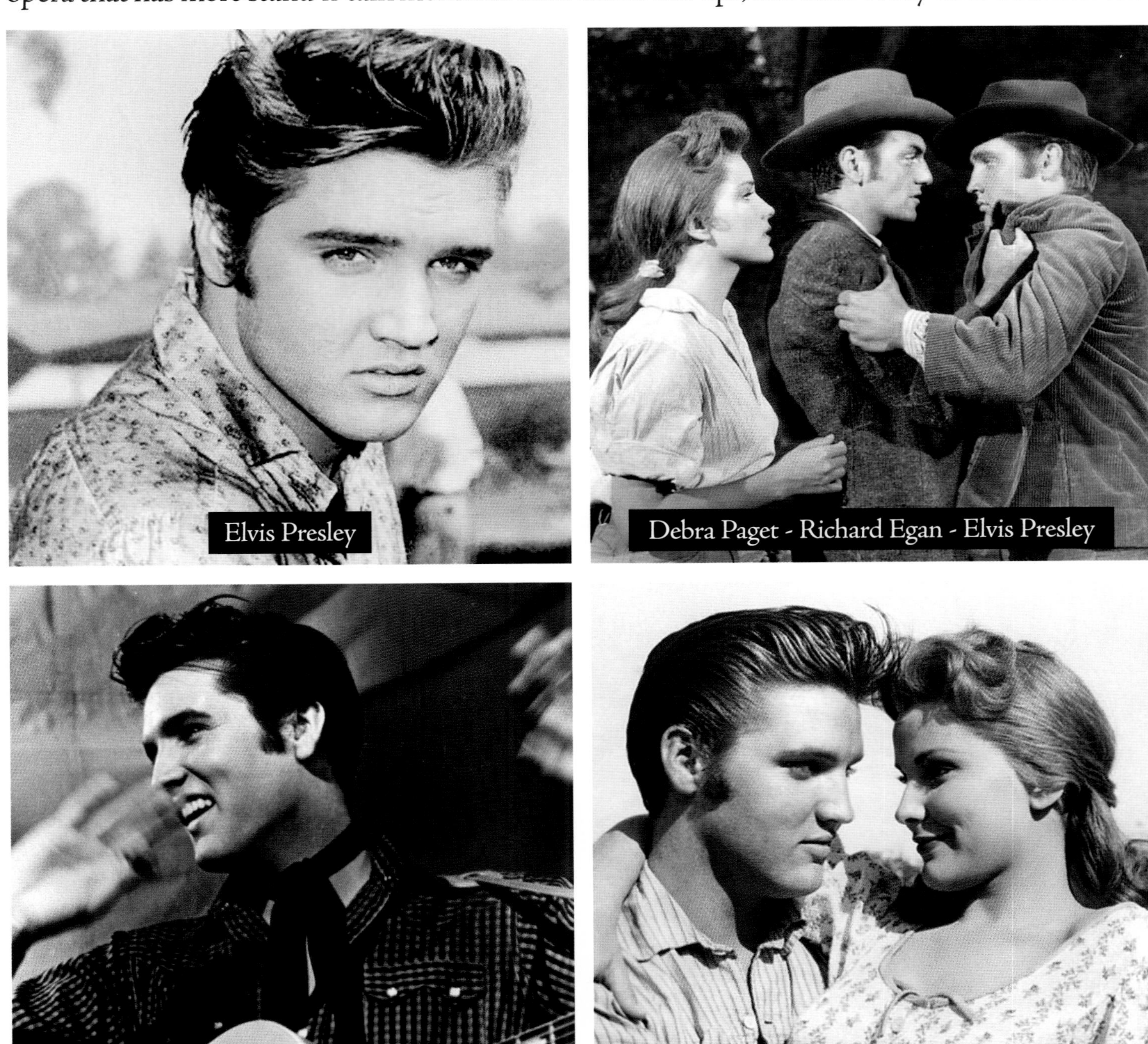

Elvis Presley

Debra Paget - Richard Egan - Elvis Presley

Elvis Presley

Elvis Presley - Debra Paget

When I saw this film, I was so taken with the natural acting ability of its star. Elvis had what Stanislavsky tried to teach his students. It was no surprise that Elvis would become who he became. My agent Harry Kalcheim traveled to Memphis to see Elvis perform and was so impressed that he took him on as a client. After appearances on "The Ed Sullivan Show," Elvis Presley became a force with which to reckon. At every lunch I had with Harry, he would talk about Elvis and once I asked him, "Harry, when you have lunch with Elvis, do you ever talk about me?"

Sprawling epic covering the life of a Texas cattle rancher and his family and associates.

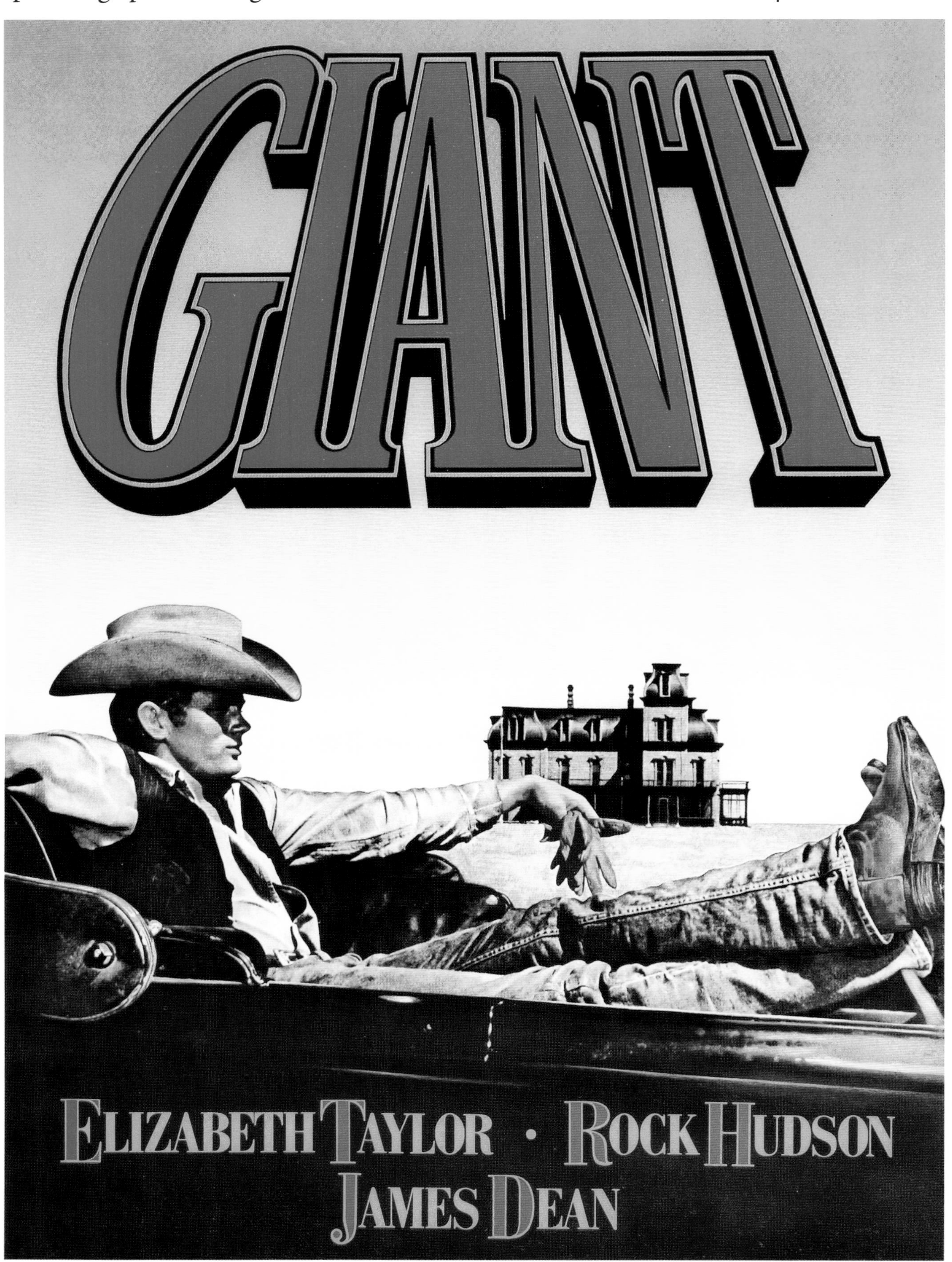

Serena Donadoni of Village Voice wrote: "Sweeping saga of American prosperity that reveals its racist underbelly; glorious star vehicle that upends rigid gender roles; modern western that questions the validity of frontier land ownership."

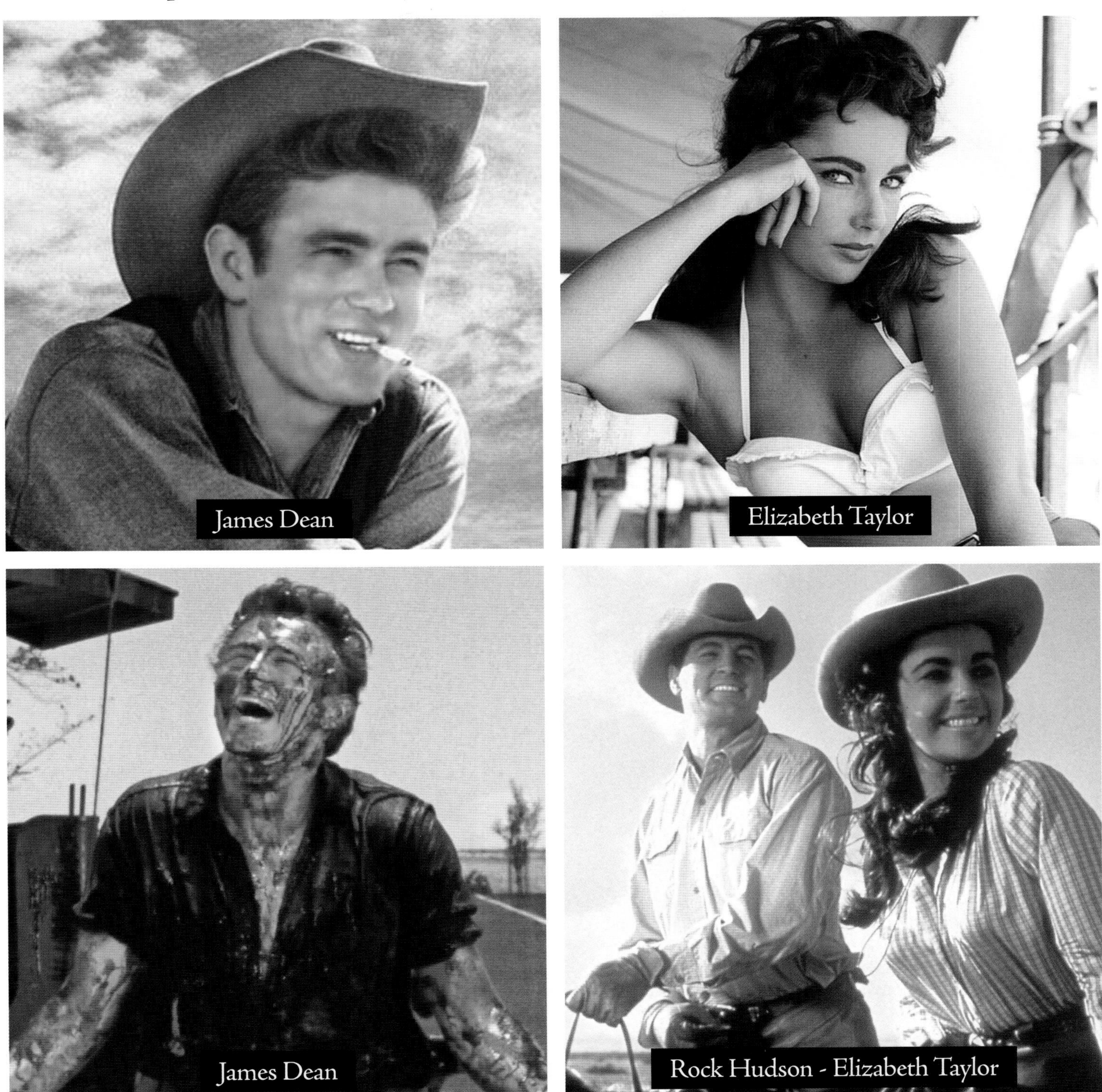

James Dean

Elizabeth Taylor

James Dean

Rock Hudson - Elizabeth Taylor

"Giant" is a 1956 American epic film which starred Elizabeth Taylor, Rock Hudson and James Dean. "Giant" was the last of James Dean's three films as a leading actor, and earned him his second Academy Award nomination. He might have earned a third, but before "Giant" was released, James Dean, then twenty-four, was killed in a car accident.

A spoiled heiress must choose between three suitors: her jazz musician ex-husband, a stuffy businessman, and an undercover tabloid reporter.

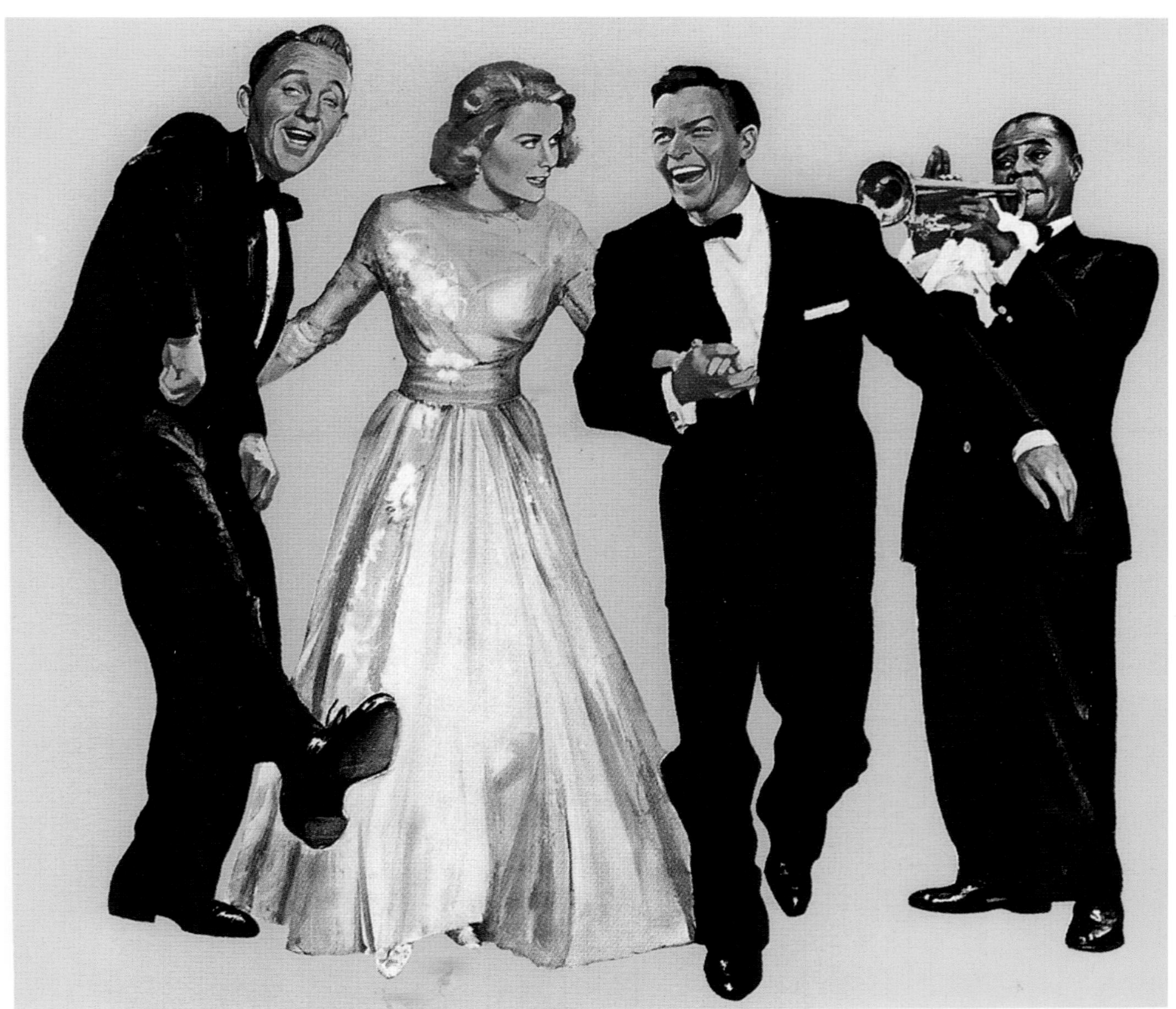

BING CROSBY ★ GRACE KELLY ★ FRANK SINATRA

in the hilarious low-down on high life

HIGH SOCIETY

co-starring

CELESTE HOLM · JOHN LUND

LOUIS CALHERN · SIDNEY BLACKMER

and LOUIS ARMSTRONG and His Band

Marjorie Baumgarten of Austin Chronicle wrote: "A musical remake of 'The Philadelphia Story,' 'High Society' features Cole Porter tunes, Frank Sinatra and Bing Crosby, and Grace Kelly in her final acting role."

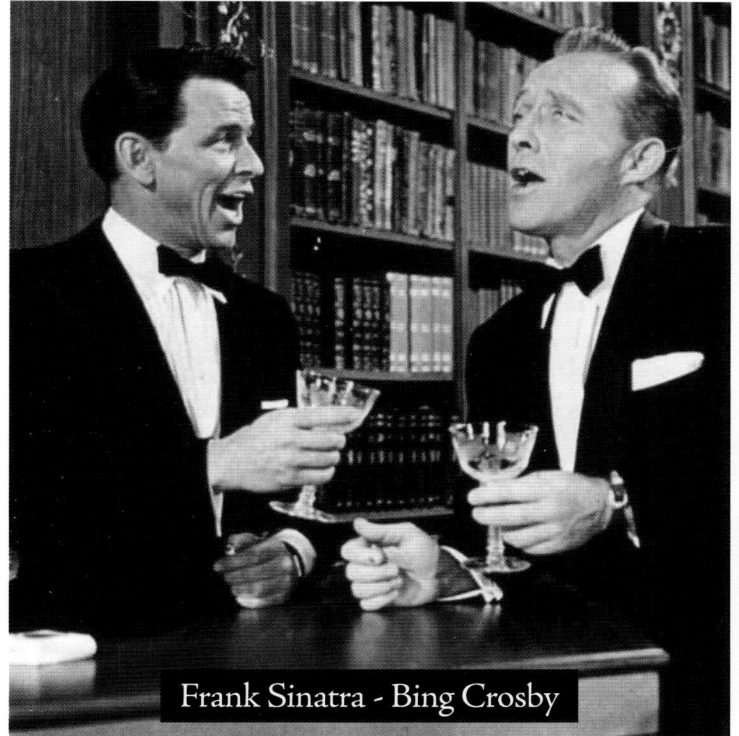
Frank Sinatra - Bing Crosby

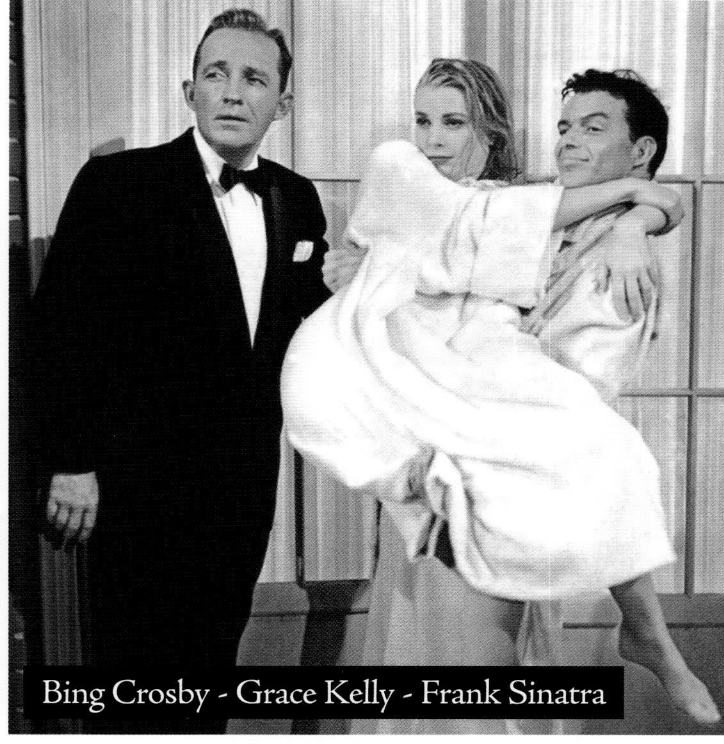
Bing Crosby - Grace Kelly - Frank Sinatra

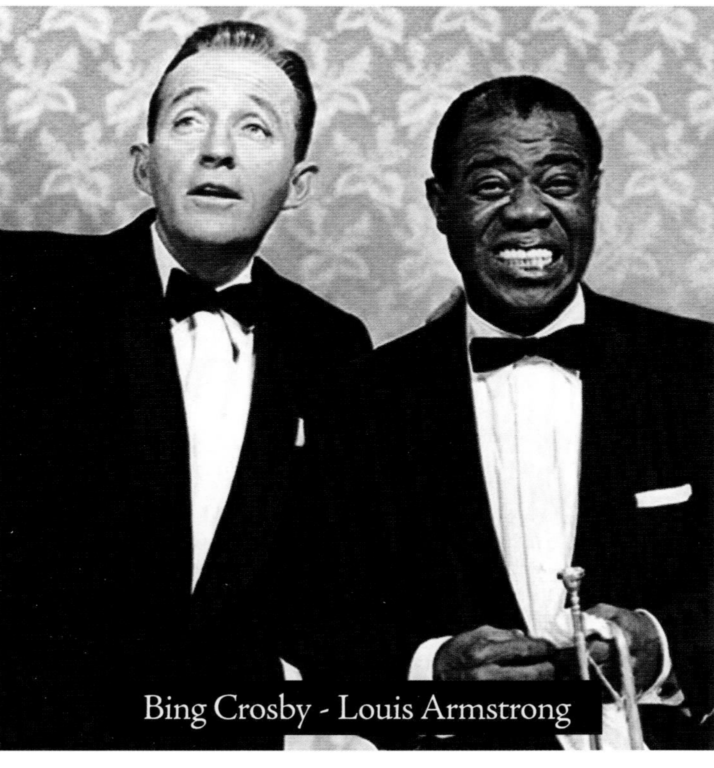
Bing Crosby - Louis Armstrong

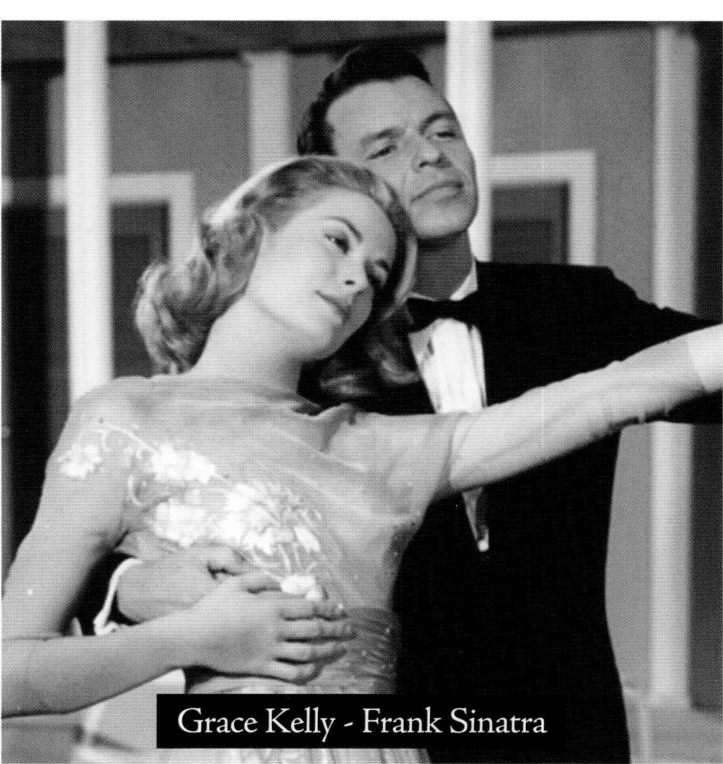
Grace Kelly - Frank Sinatra

My wife, Estelle, and I watched this movie at least a half dozen times just to hear Sinatra and Crosby sing "Did You Ever?" As a matter of fact, I'm going to play the song right now, so my publisher, Larry O'Flahavan, and my designer, Aaron Davis, know of what I speak.

A widow accepts a job as a live-in governess to the King of Siam's children.

RODGERS & HAMMERSTEIN'S

the KING and I

Music That's Everlasting: Hello Young Lovers • We Kiss In A Shadow • Whistle A Happy Tune • Getting To Know You Shall We Dance • March of The Siamese Children • I Have Dreamed • Something Wonderful • and many more!

Starring

DEBORAH KERR/YUL BRYNNER

with

Martin Benson RITA MORENO Rex Thompson

PRODUCED BY CHARLES BRACKETT/DIRECTED BY WALTER LANG/SCREENPLAY BY ERNEST LEHMAN

MUSIC BY RICHARD RODGERS/BOOK AND LYRICS BY OSCAR HAMMERSTEIN II

From Their Musical Play Based On "Anna And The King Of Siam" By Margaret Landon

CHOREOGRAPHY BY JEROME ROBBINS/FROM 20TH CENTURY-FOX/CINEMASCOPE/COLOR BY DE LUXE

Variety wrote: "All the ingredients that made Rodgers and Hammerstein's 'The King and I' a memorable stage experience have been faithfully transferred to the screen."

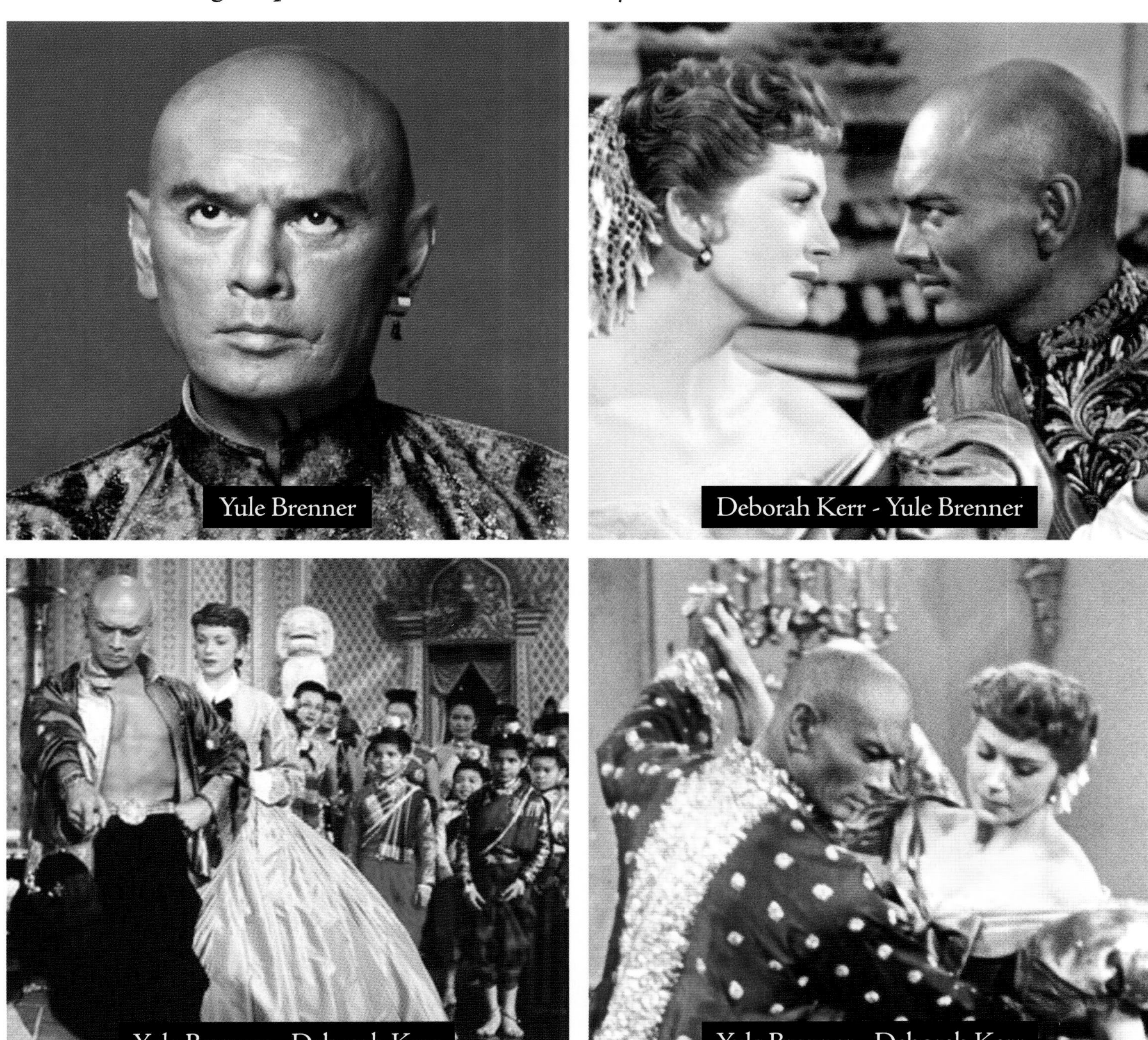

Yule Brenner

Deborah Kerr - Yule Brenner

Yule Brenner - Deborah Kerr

Yule Brenner - Deborah Kerr

I say the casting of Yule Brenner and Deborah Kerr for the leading roles was magic and so said The Academy, who awarded Yule an Oscar for Best Actor and Deborah a nomination for Best Actress.

Yule Brenner danced barefoot on a polished floor and on "Your Show of Shows," Sid Caesar, playing the King of Siam, danced barefoot. Halfway through the routine, Sid started hopping on one foot and screaming, "Damnit... who dropped a lit cigarette on my floor!?"

The line got even more belly laughs than the writers expected.

A juror holdout forces his opposers to reconsider the evidence to prevent a miscarriage of justice.

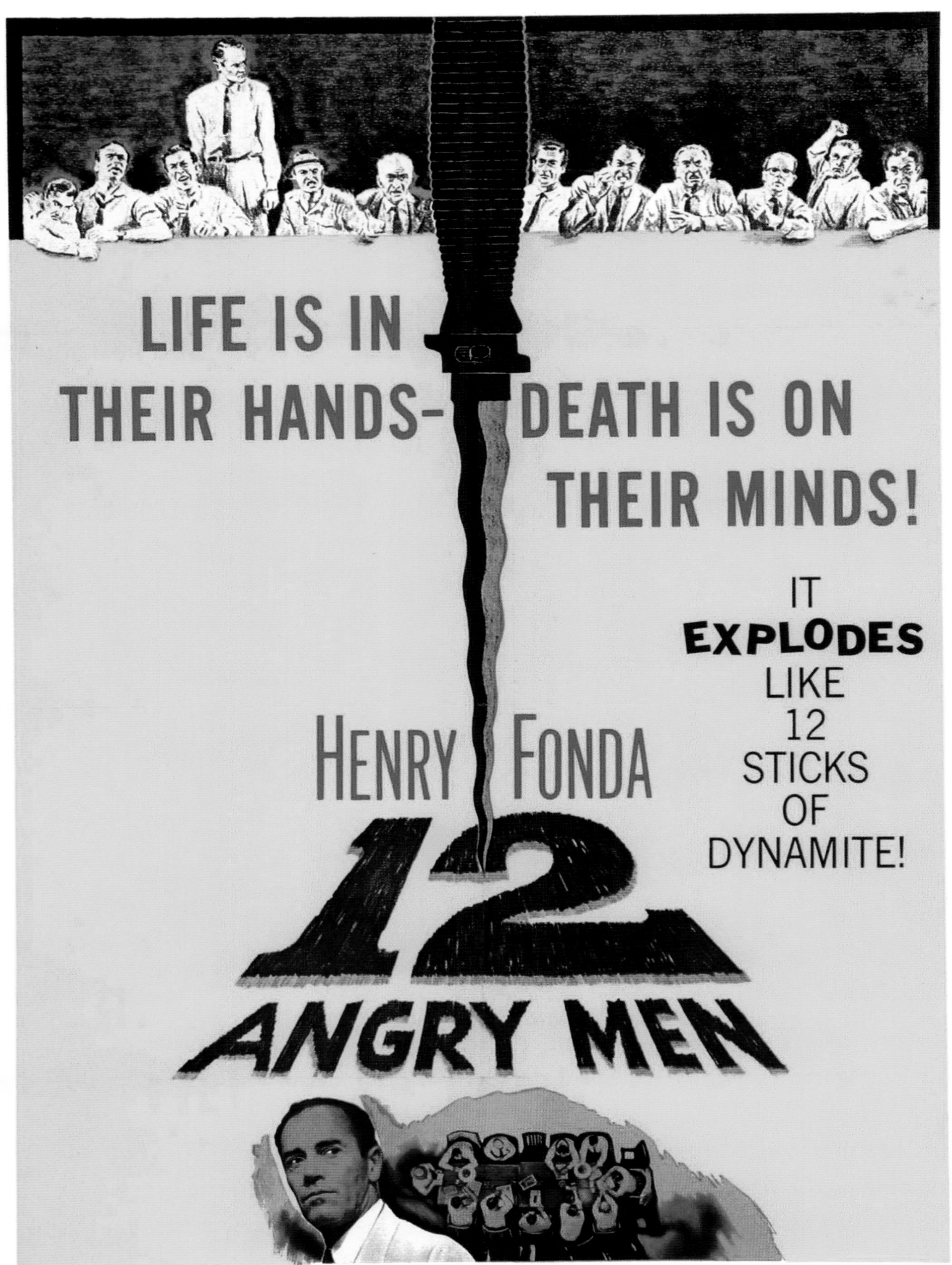

Christopher Machell of CineVue wrote: "Since its release, Reginald Rose's masterpiece has lost none of its impact. In this age of unreason, '12 Angry Men' remains sorely and urgently contemporary."

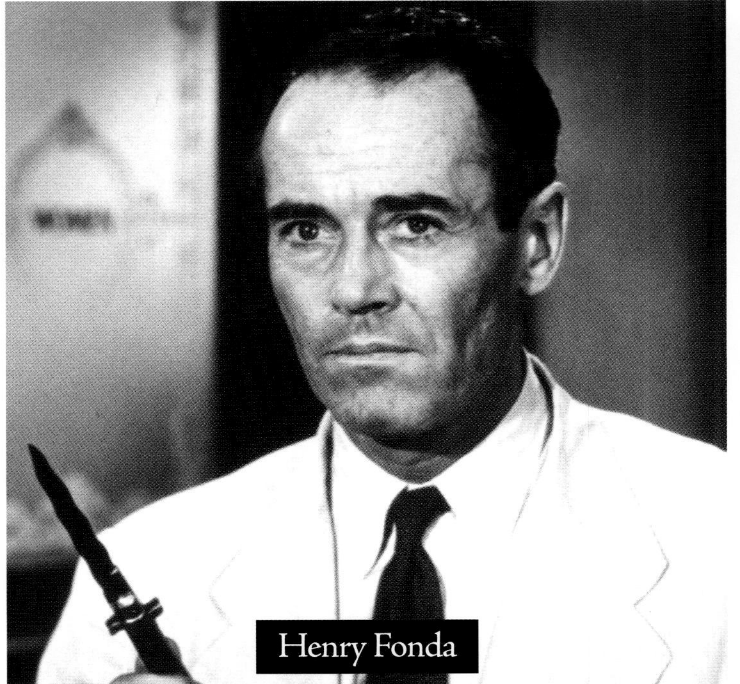
Henry Fonda

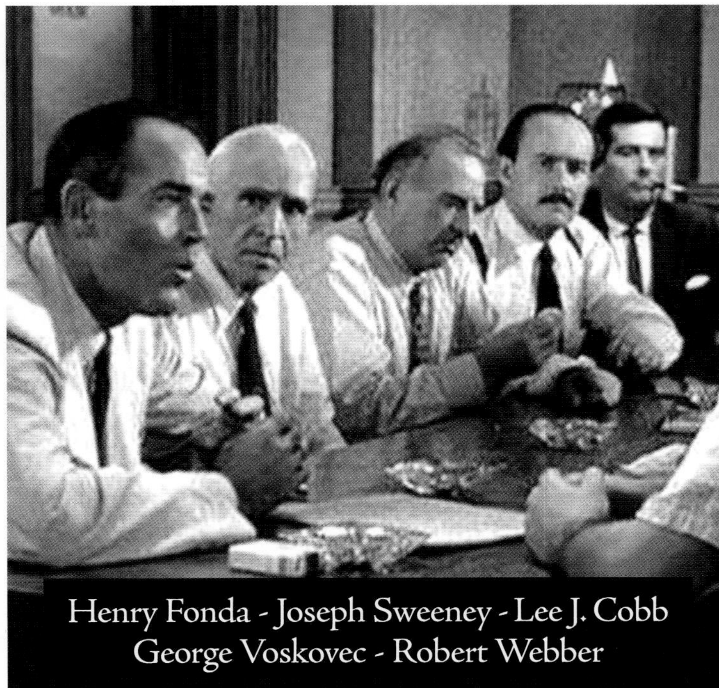
Henry Fonda - Joseph Sweeney - Lee J. Cobb
George Voskovec - Robert Webber

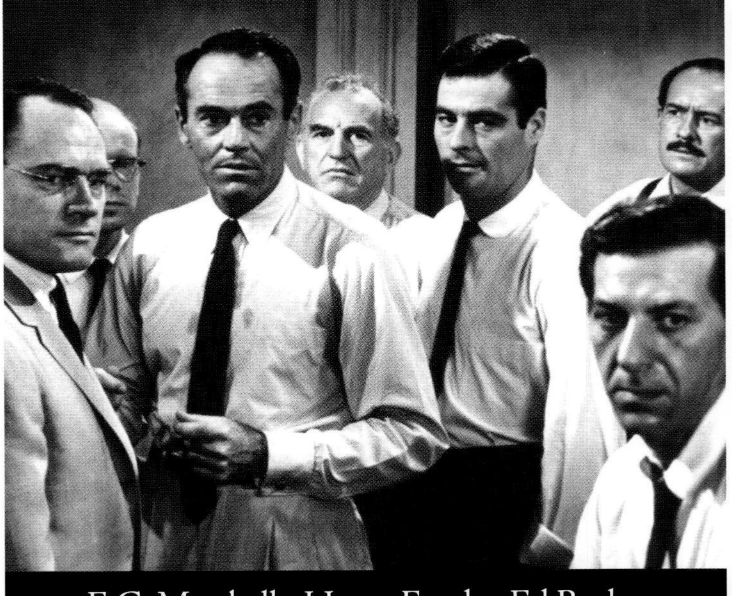
E.G. Marshall - Henry Fonda - Ed Begley
Robert Webber - Jack Klugman - George Voskovec

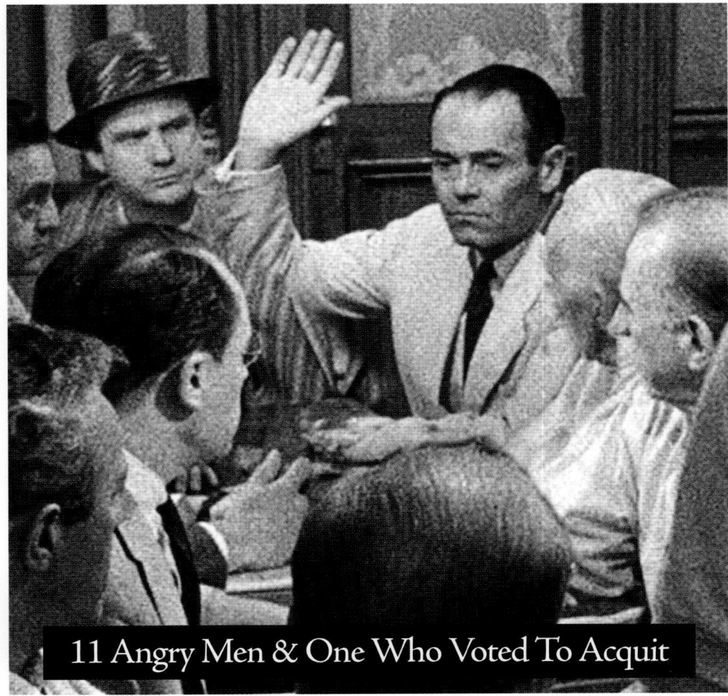
11 Angry Men & One Who Voted To Acquit

Every writer in the business saluted this extraordinary drama and its resourceful, brilliant author, Reginald Rose. I, as all of America, was riveted by his "12 Angry Men."

Reggie and I were friends and I was happy to send him an inscribed copy of my first novel, "Enter Laughing." I received a letter from him in which was enclosed thirty-five cents. The note read: "Carl, writers shouldn't give their books away for free. You should be paid for your work and that thirty-five cents is the royalty you would have received from your publisher."

A US air force major in Kobe confronts his own opposition to marriages between American servicemen and Japanese women when he falls for a beautiful performer.

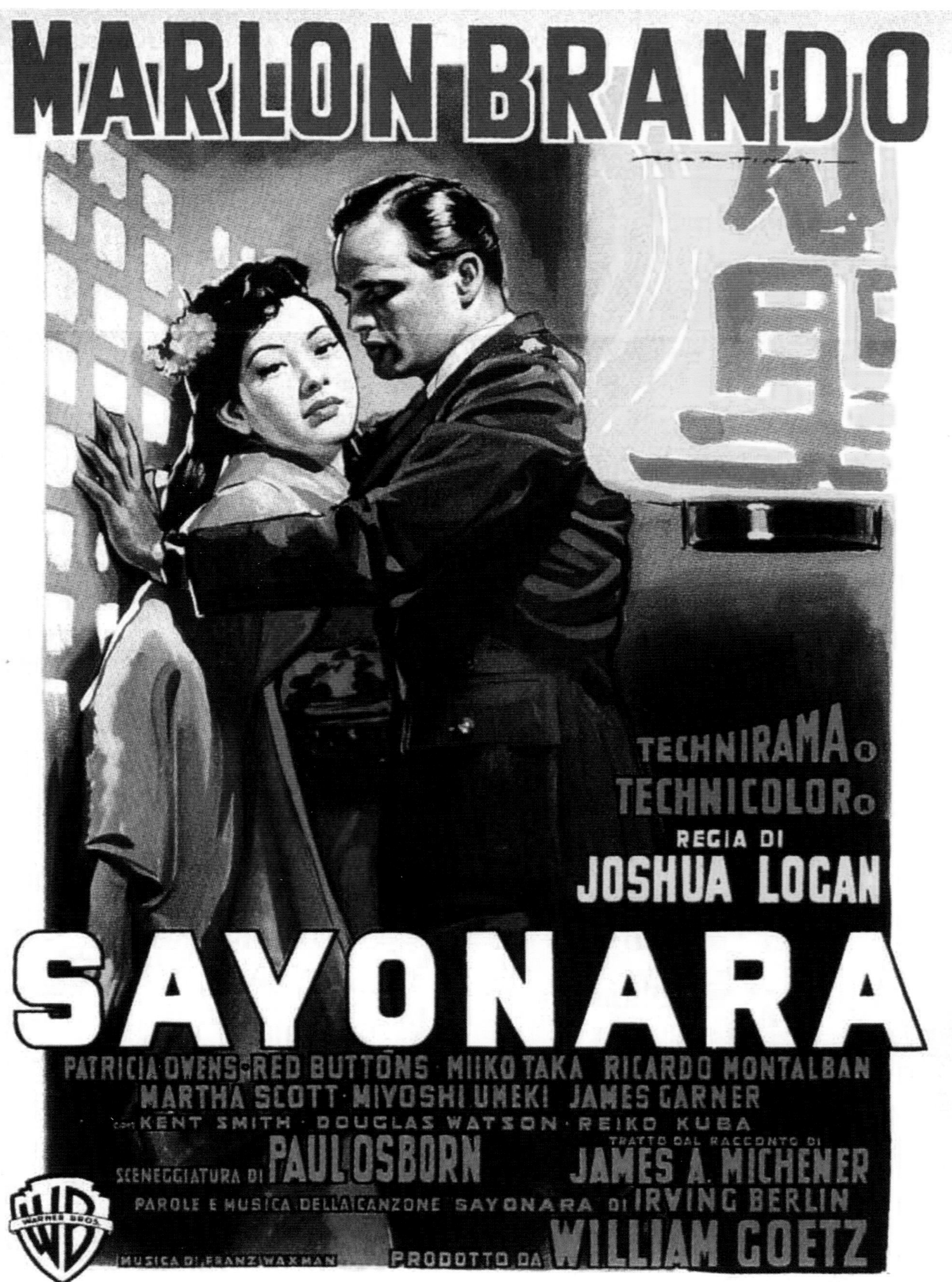

Emanuel Levy wrote: "Logan's message picture about interracial marriage is made more enjoyable by the then novelty of locations shooting in Japan as well as likable performances from Marlon Brando, Red Buttons, and rest of the cast."

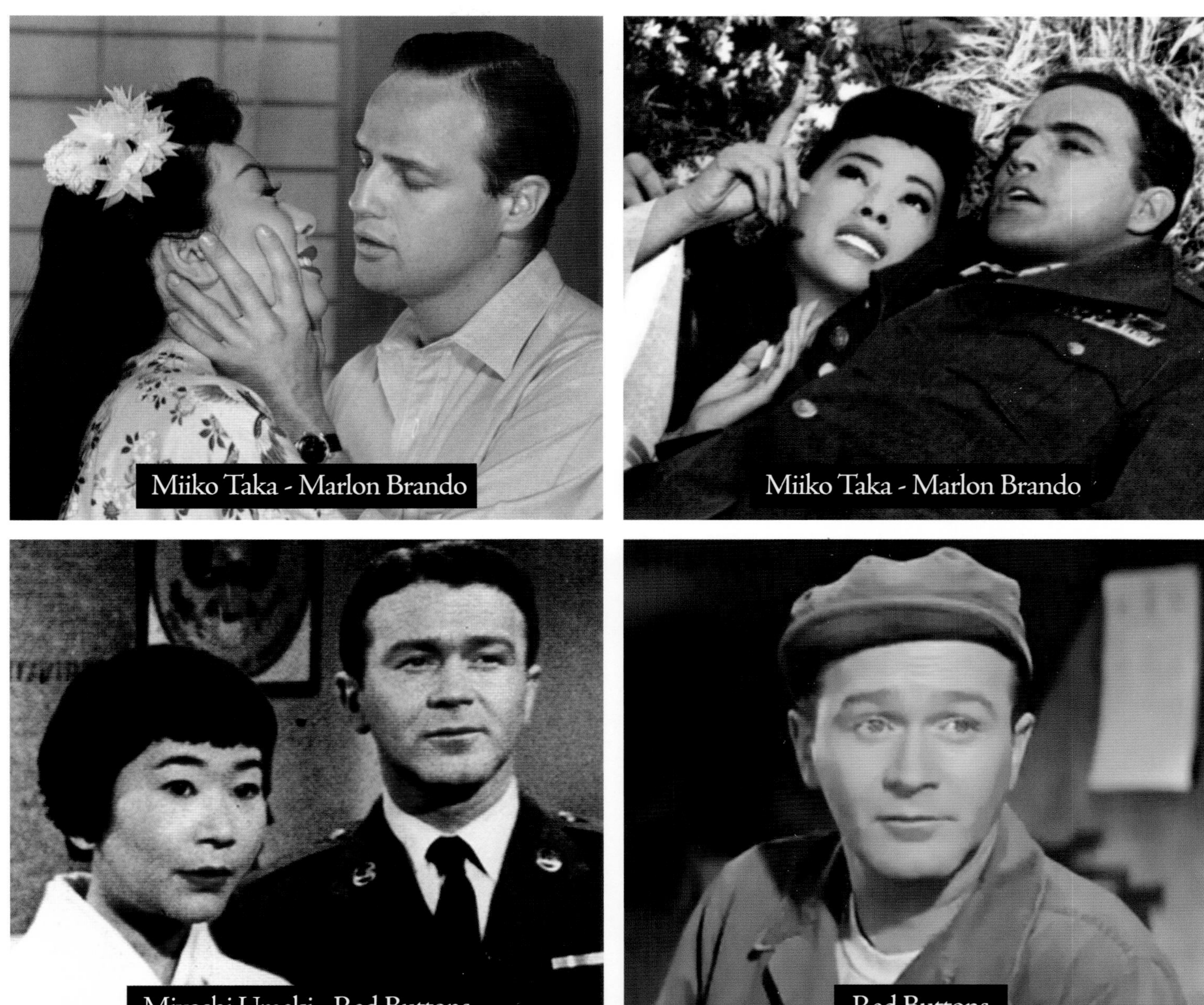

Miiko Taka - Marlon Brando

Miiko Taka - Marlon Brando

Miyoshi Umeki - Red Buttons

Red Buttons

"Sayonara" won four Academy Awards, including one for Red Buttons and one for Miyoshi Umeki. Red was then a successful comedian who did a routine about famous people who were never honored with a dinner. Among them were: "Moses, who said when he came out of Mount Sinai, 'The food in that hospital is terrible!' He never got a dinner!"

"Abraham Lincoln, who said, 'A house divided... is a condominium.' He never got a dinner!"

"Venus de Milo's mother, who once said to Venus, 'You never call me. Can't you pick up a phone?' She never got a dinner!"

"Joan Rivers, who said to Marcel Marceau, 'Can we talk?' She never got a dinner!"

After settling his differences with a Japanese P.O.W. camp commander, a British colonel co-operates to oversee his men's construction of a railway bridge for their captors - while oblivious to a plan by the Allies to destroy it.

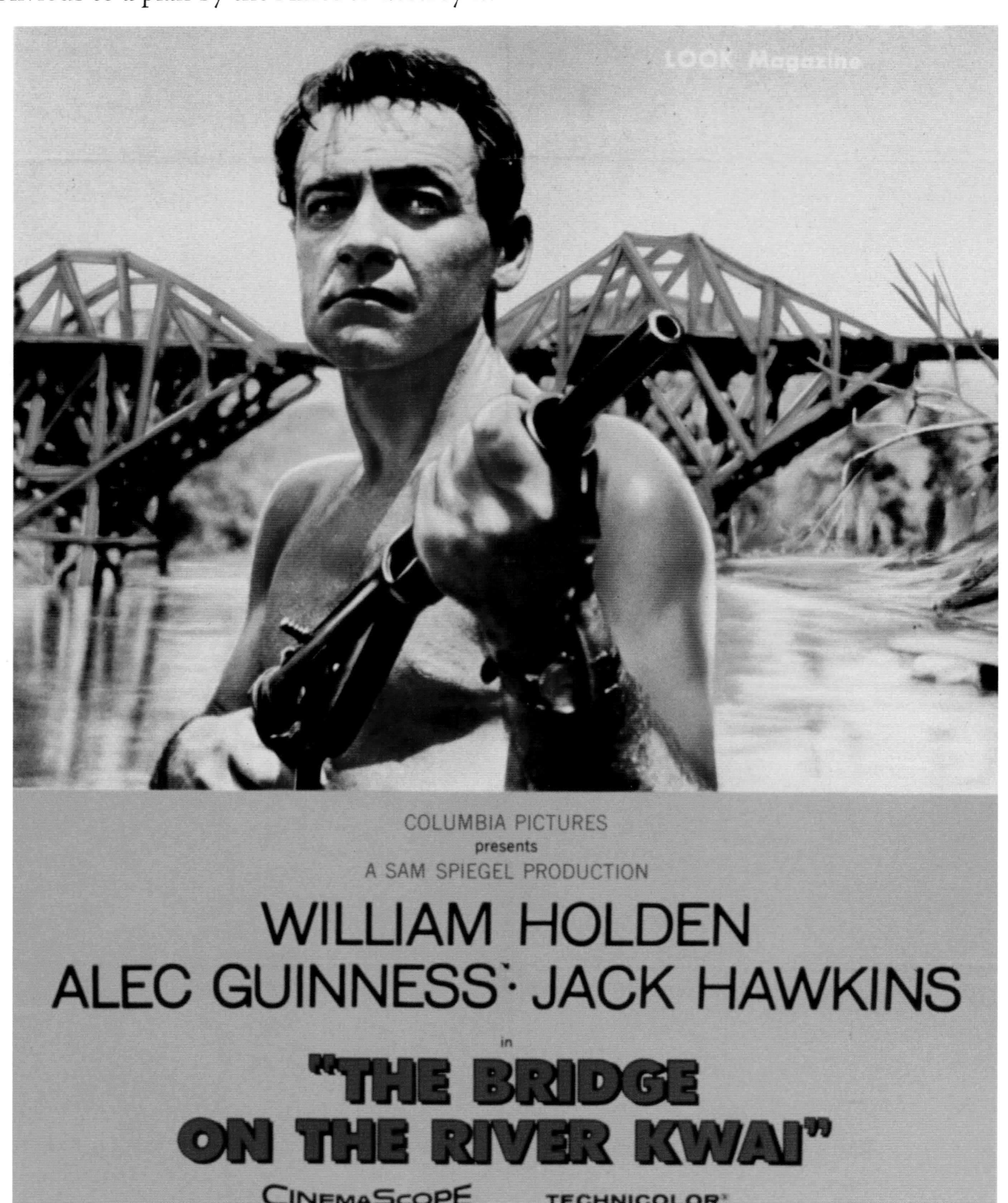

Philip Roth of The New Republic wrote: "Part of the success of 'The Bridge' is that its courageous hero is shown from all angles, in all kinds of mirrors. He is strong, stubborn, fallible, maniacal, silly, and wise; and in the end he is pathetic, noble, and foolish."

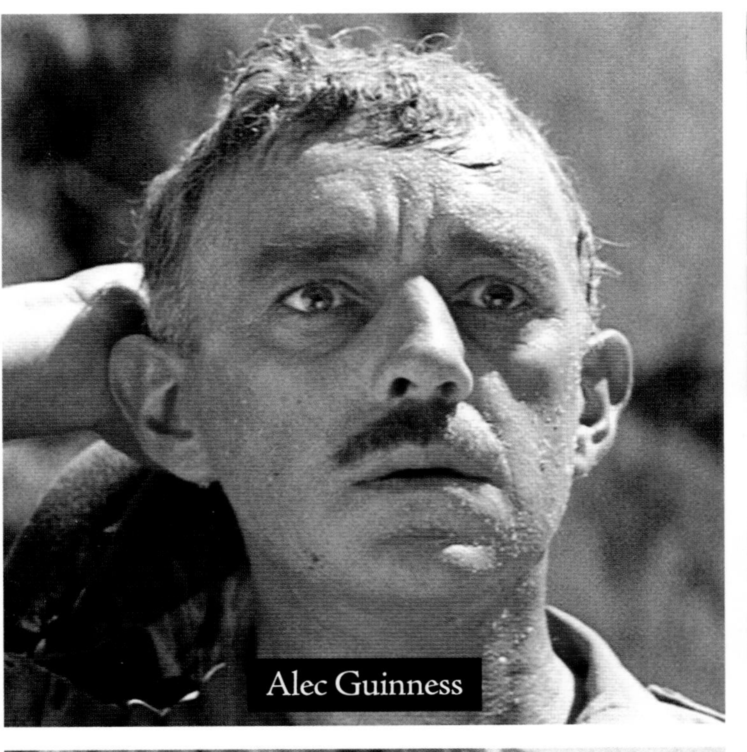
Alec Guinness

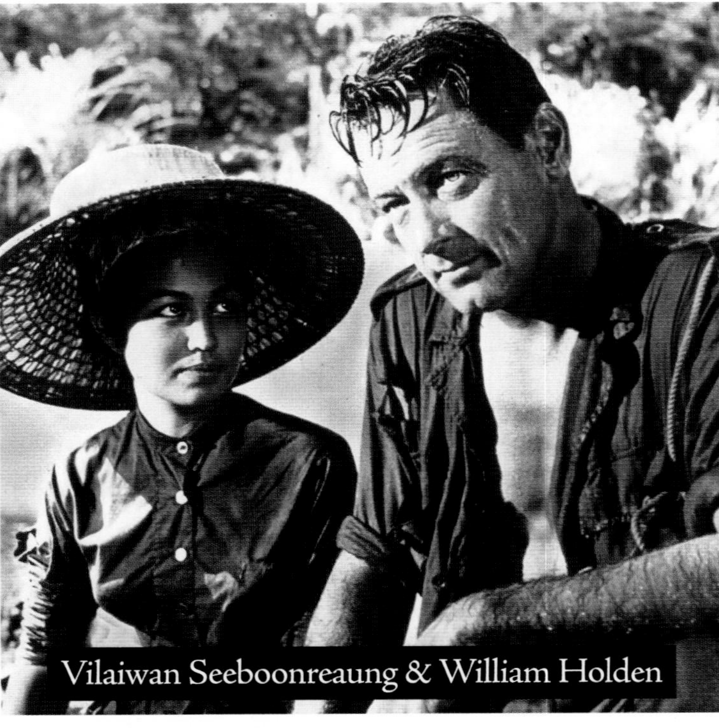
Vilaiwan Seeboonreaung & William Holden

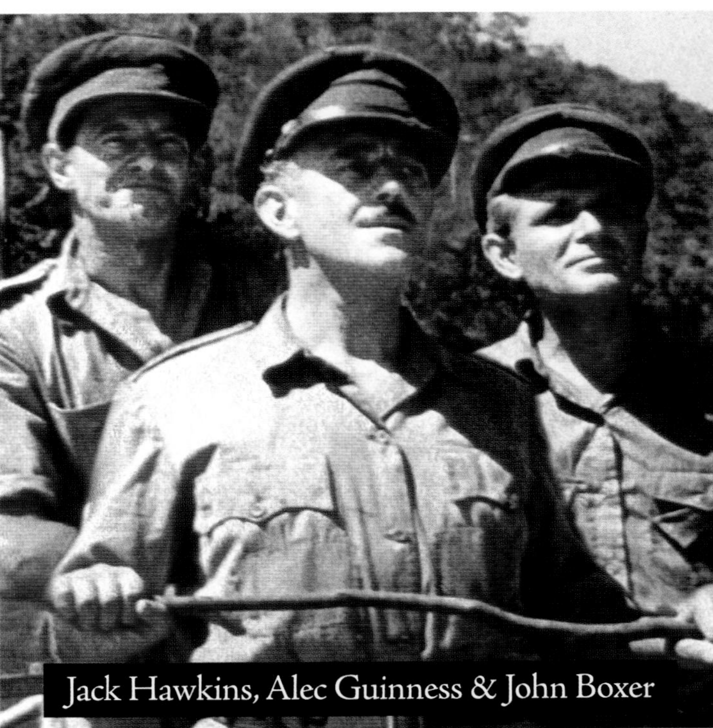
Jack Hawkins, Alec Guinness & John Boxer

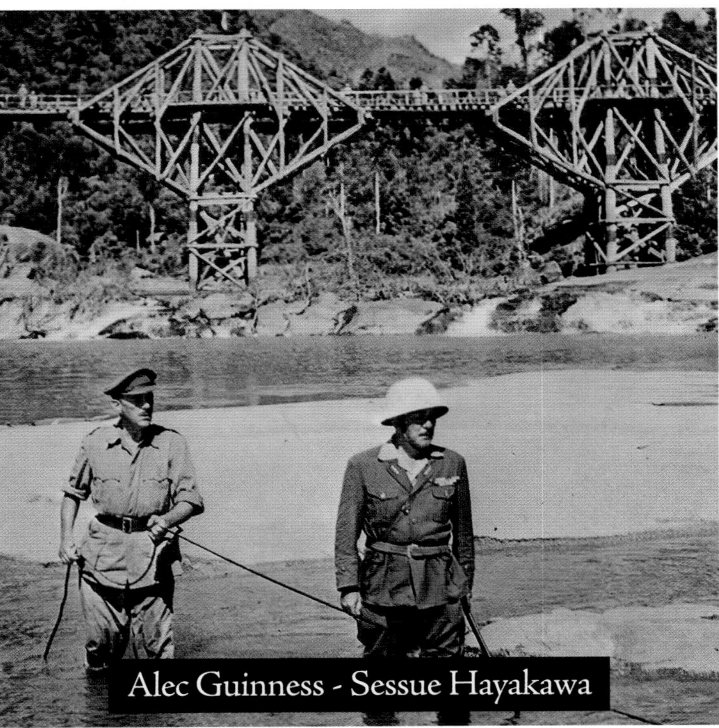
Alec Guinness - Sessue Hayakawa

This film won seven Academy Awards, including Best Picture. In 1997, the film was deemed "culturally, historically, or aesthetically significant" and selected for preservation by the Library of Congress. Sadly, in 1984, Carl Foreman and Michael Wilson, the blacklisted screenwriters, posthumously received Academy Awards. (Their blacklisters should hang their heads in shame.)

A British barrister must defend his client in a murder trial that has surprise after surprise.

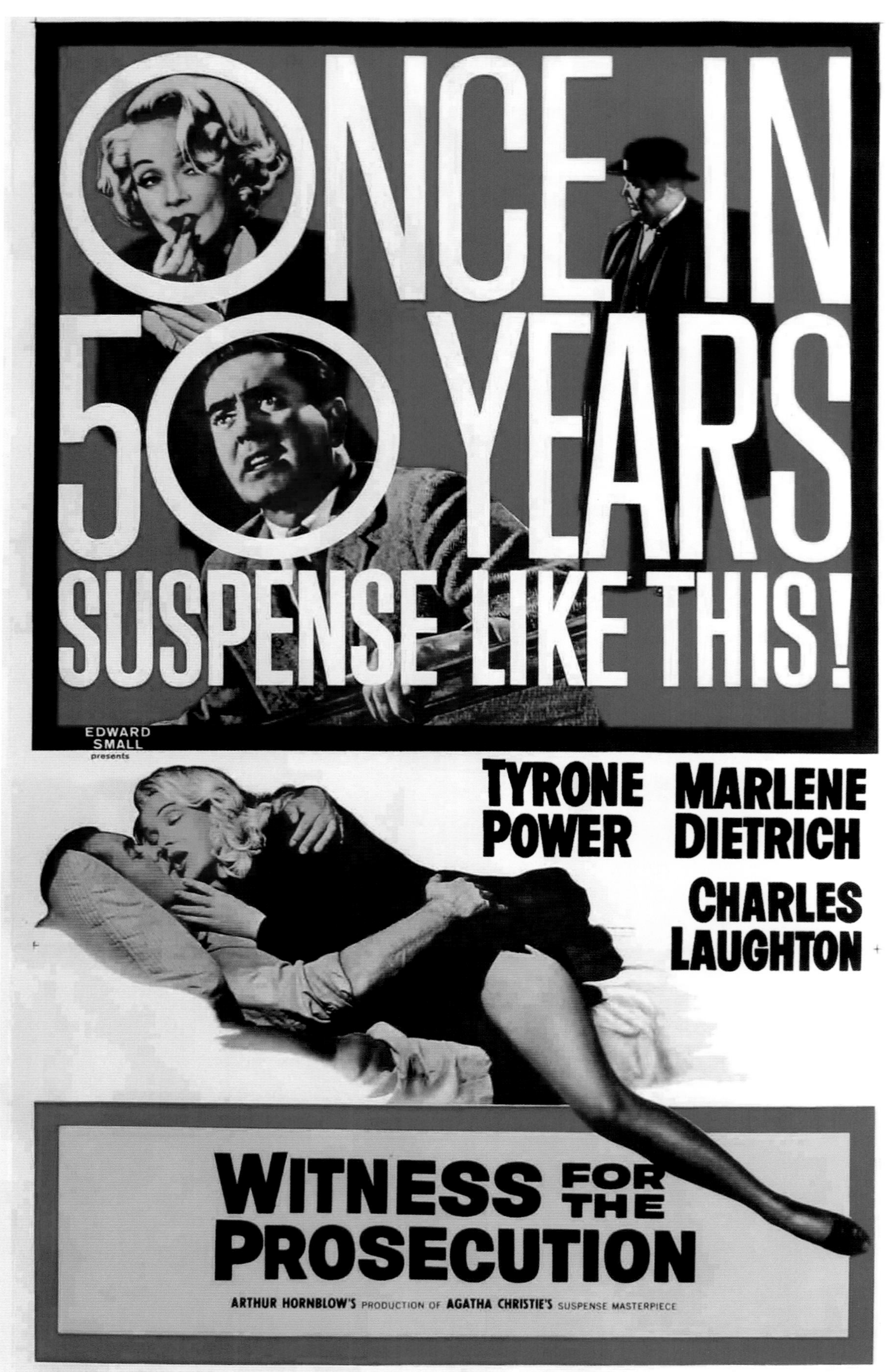

Bosley Crowther of The New York Times wrote: "The air in the courtroom fairly crackles with emotional electricity, until a staggering surprise in the last reel."

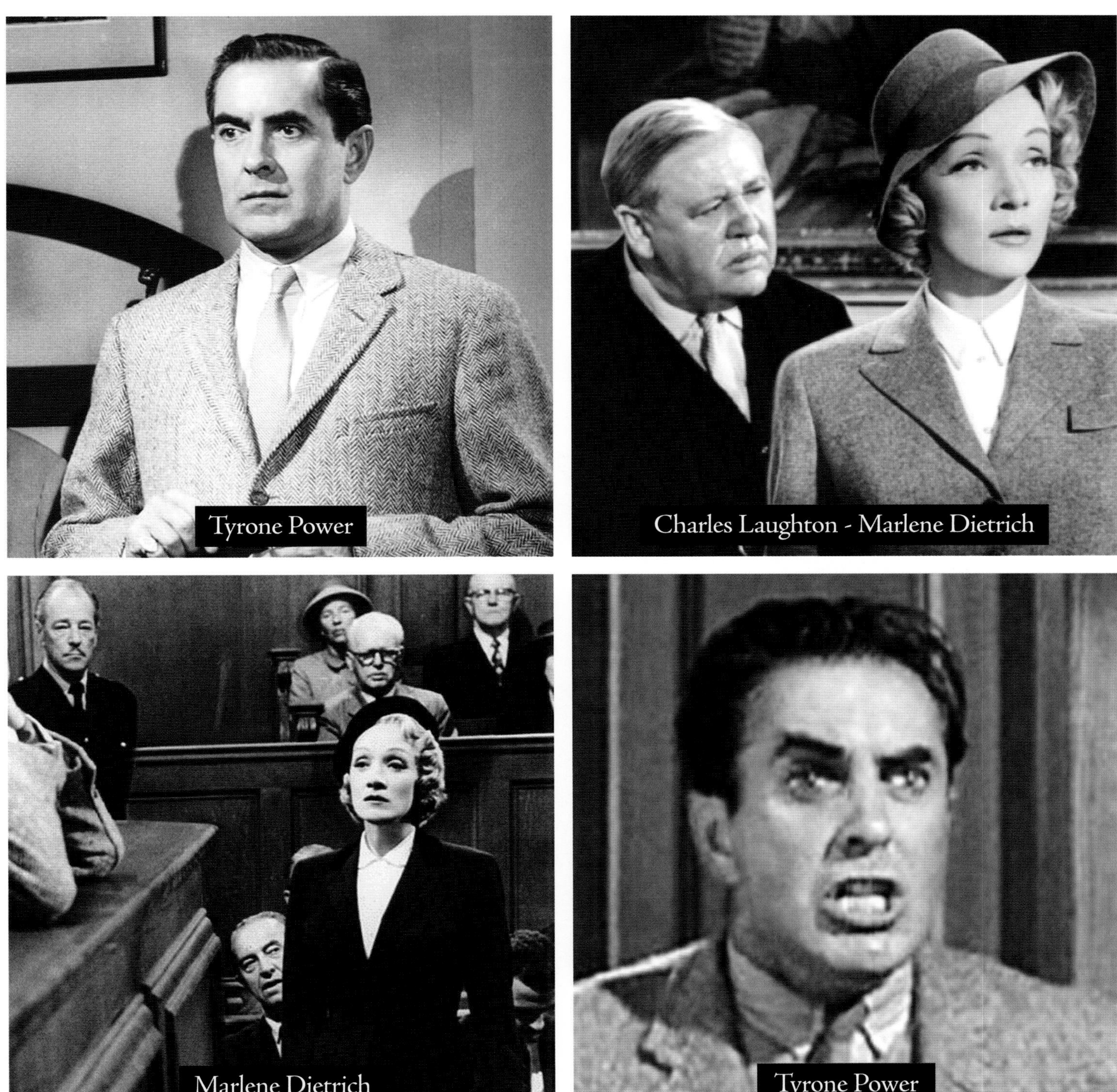

Tyrone Power

Charles Laughton - Marlene Dietrich

Marlene Dietrich

Tyrone Power

"Witness for the Prosecution," a witty, terse adaptation of Agatha Christie's hit play, was successfully brought to the screen by Billy Wilder. The film was included in AFI's list of Top Ten Courtroom Dramas.

Tragically, in 1958, while in Madrid filming "Solomon and Sheba," the forty-four year old Tyrone Power passed away.

A motley quintet of inept small-time thieves bungle a burglary in this Italian farce.

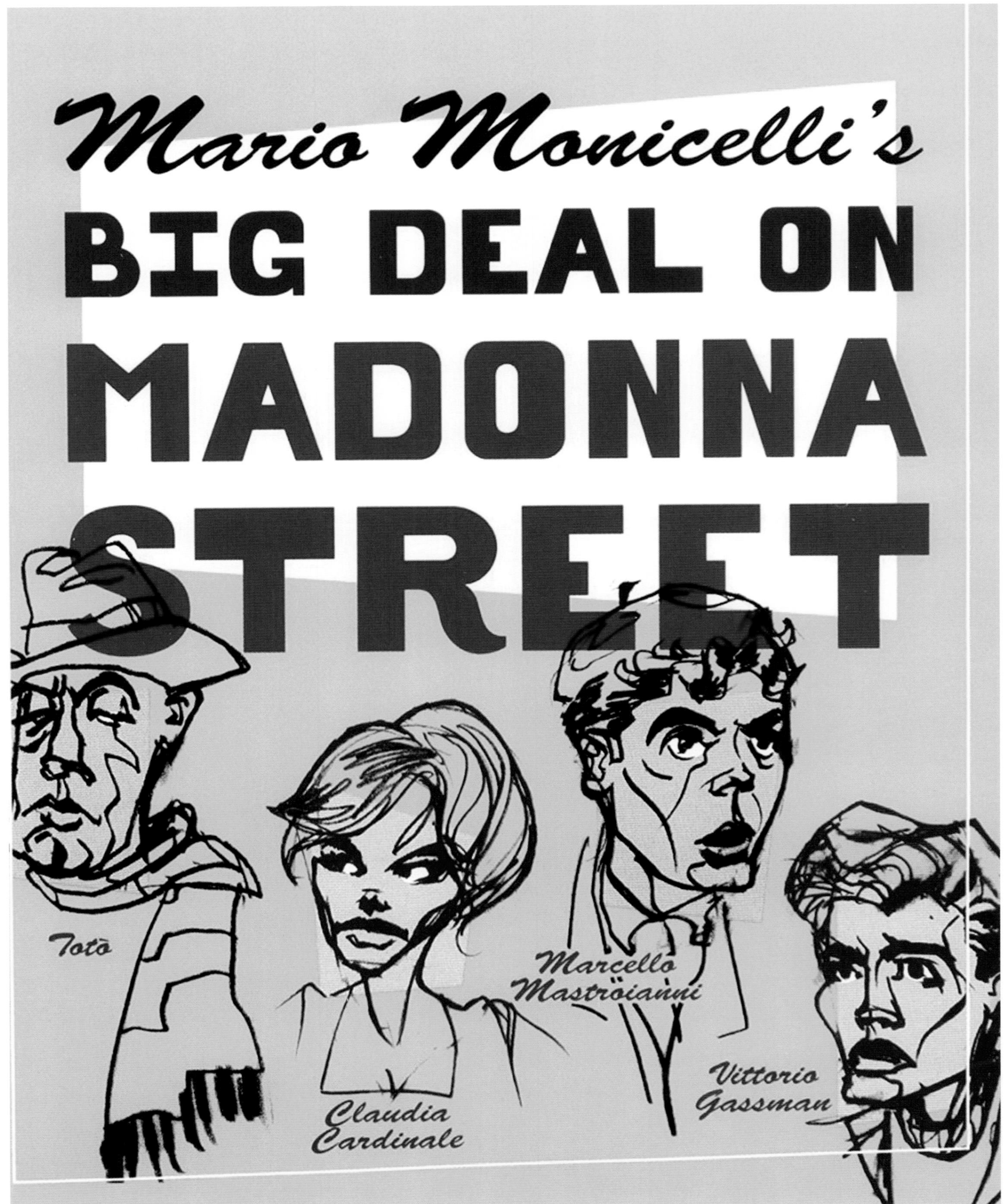

Emanuel Levy wrote: "Monicelli's seminal Italian comedy, a spoof of heist movies with great performances by Gassman, Mastroianni, Toto, and Cardinale, had major impact on many American satires, past and present."

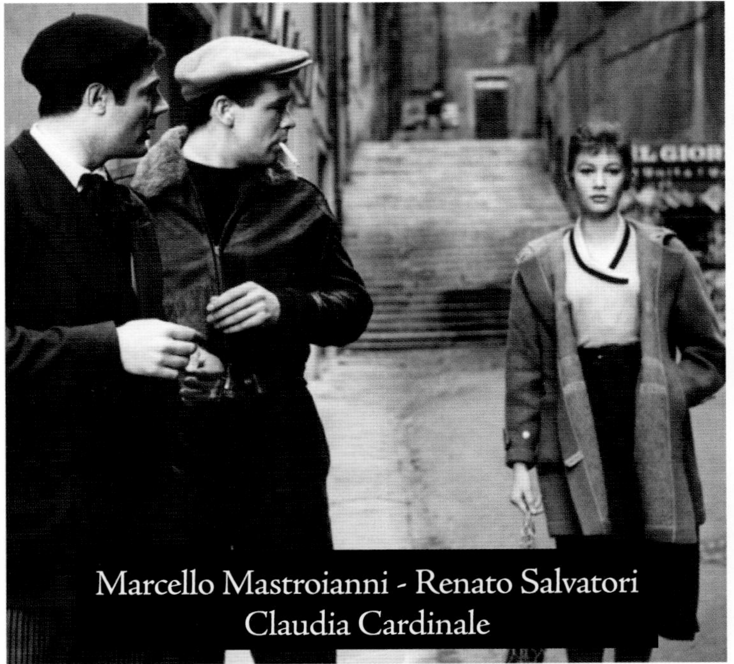
Marcello Mastroianni - Renato Salvatori
Claudia Cardinale

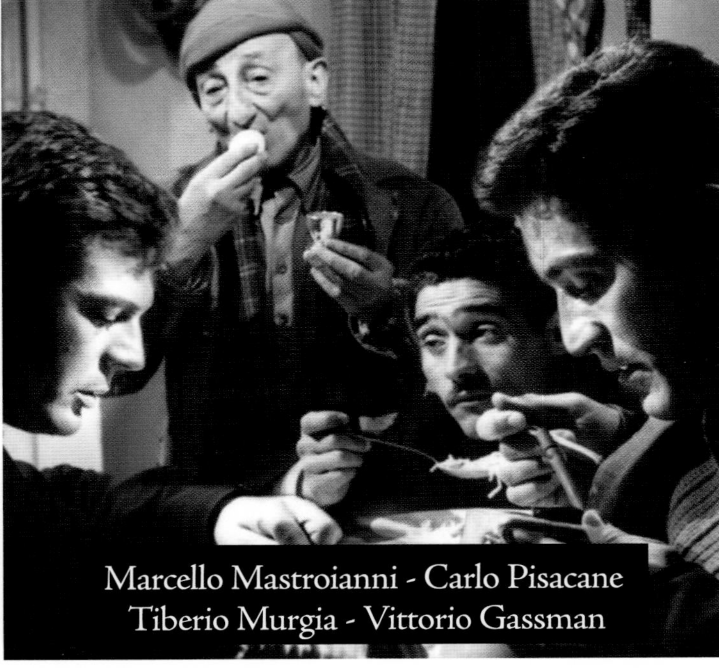
Marcello Mastroianni - Carlo Pisacane
Tiberio Murgia - Vittorio Gassman

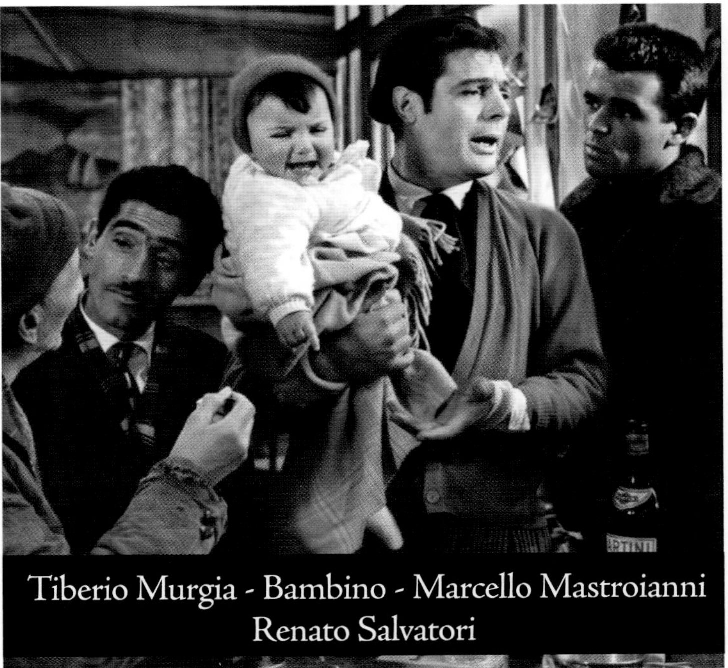
Tiberio Murgia - Bambino - Marcello Mastroianni
Renato Salvatori

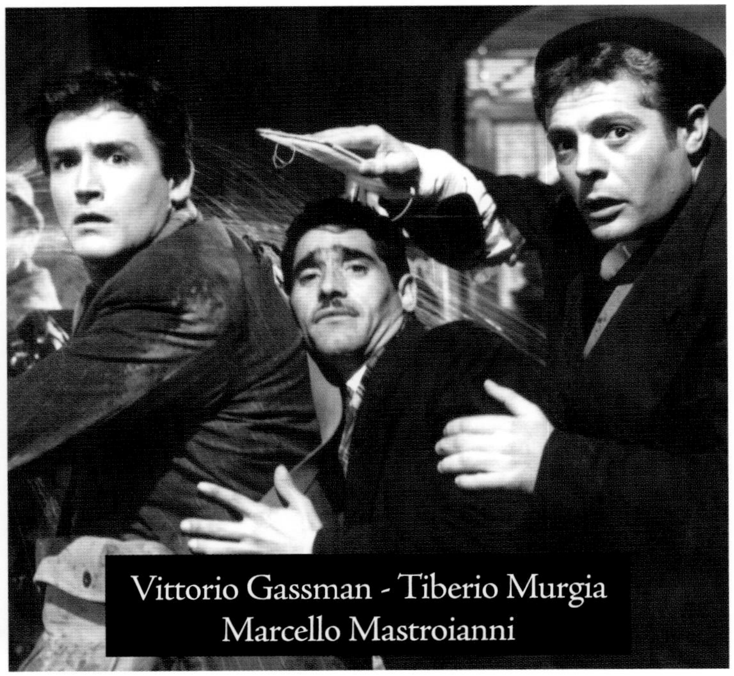
Vittorio Gassman - Tiberio Murgia
Marcello Mastroianni

This exquisite satire of the brilliant Jules Dassin's "Rififi" had the likes of Sid Caesar, Mel Brooks, Larry Gelbart, Neil Simon and me all agree that this was one of the funniest, if not the funniest, movie ever made. Vittorio Gassman, Renato Salvatori, Memmo Carotenuto and Marcello Mastroianni starred in it as the hapless would-be burglars. The love interest was handled by Claudia Cardinale. I've seen it a half-dozen times and Woody Allen, who wrote and directed "Small Time Crooks," must have seen "Big Deal" at least once.

Weary of the conventions of Parisian society, a rich playboy and a youthful courtesan-in-training enjoy a platonic friendship, but it may not stay platonic for long.

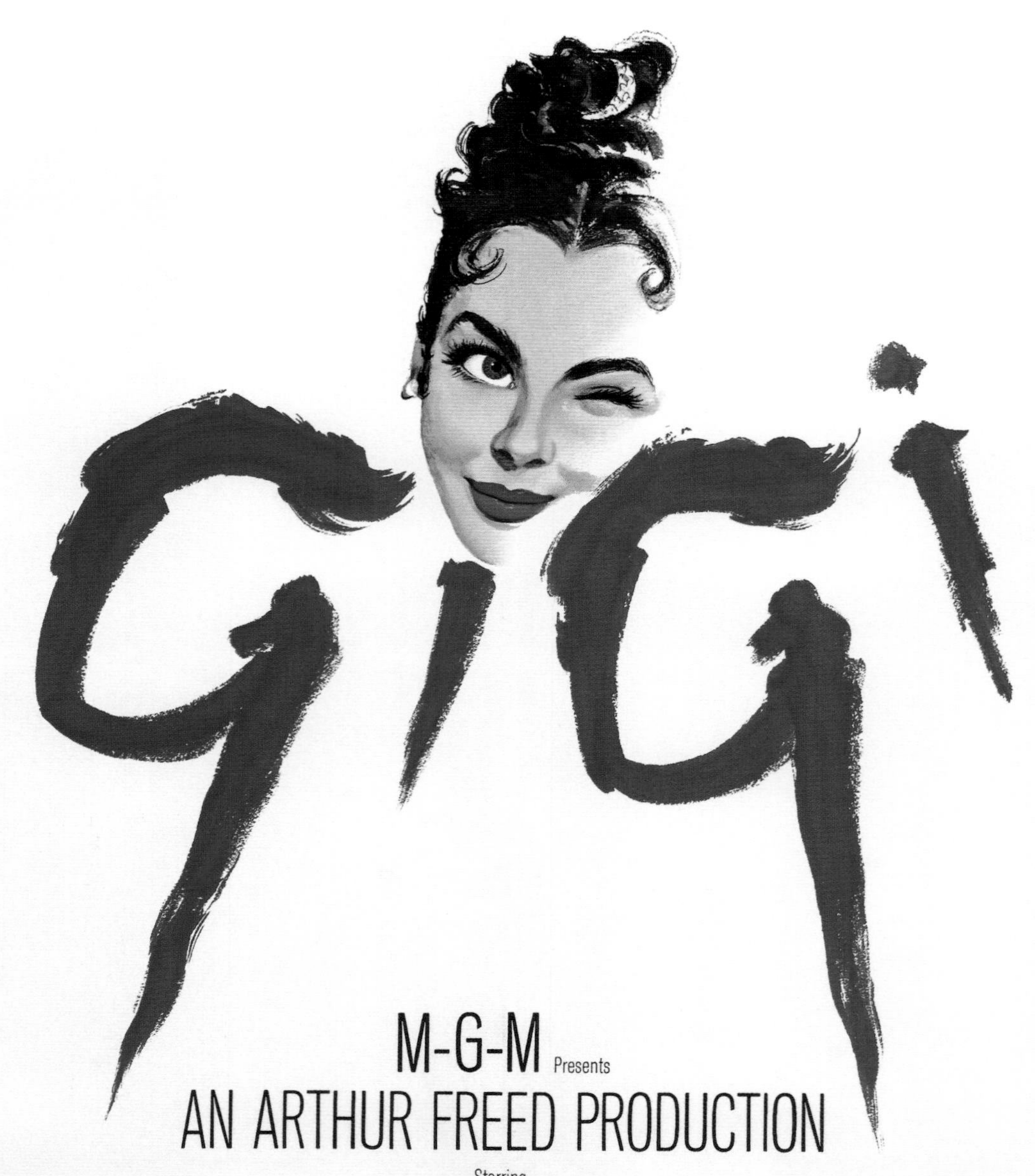

Bosley Crowther of The New York Times wrote: "'Gigi' is a charming entertainment that can stand on its own two legs, namely, those of Leslie Caron."

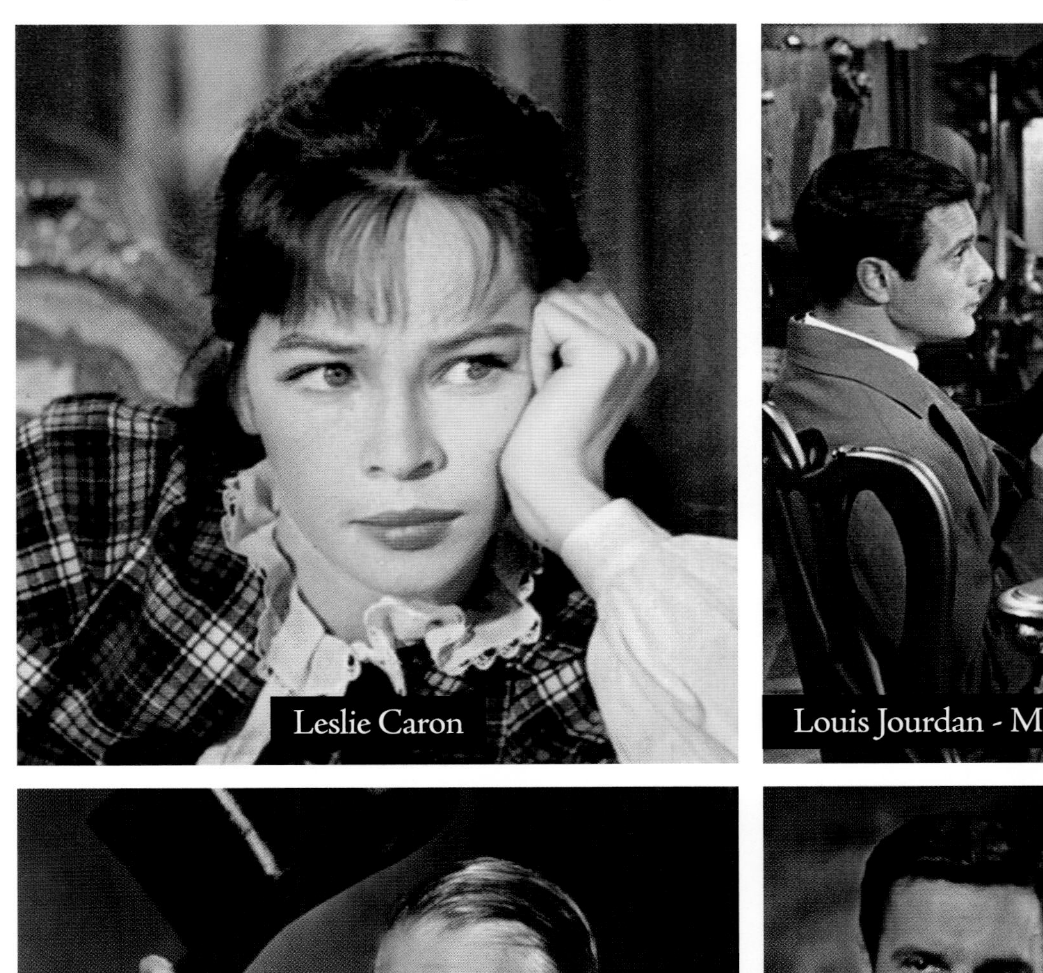

Leslie Caron

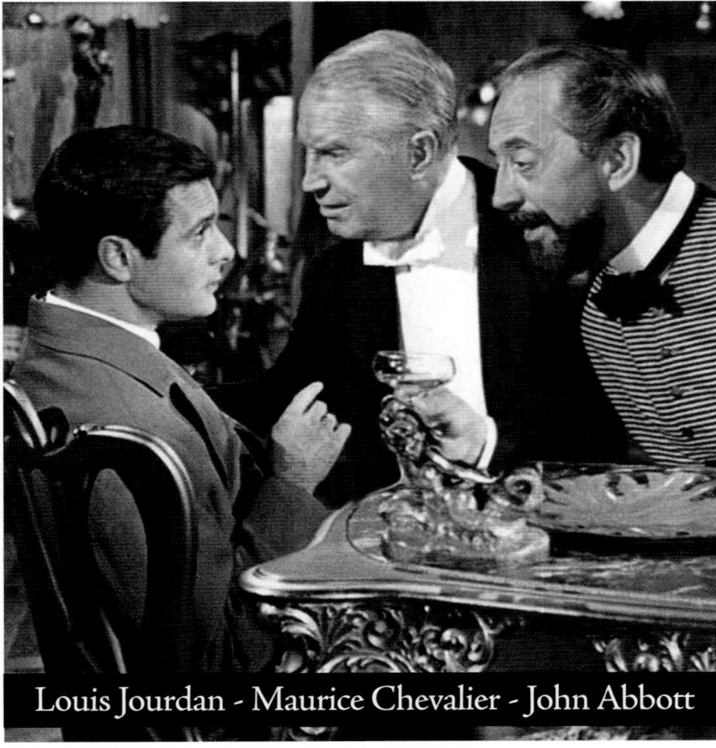

Louis Jourdan - Maurice Chevalier - John Abbott

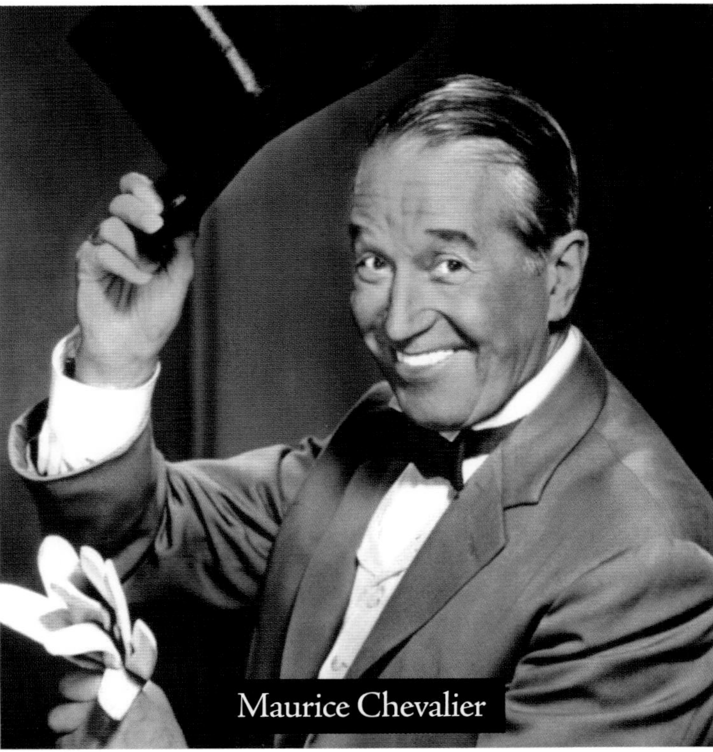

Maurice Chevalier

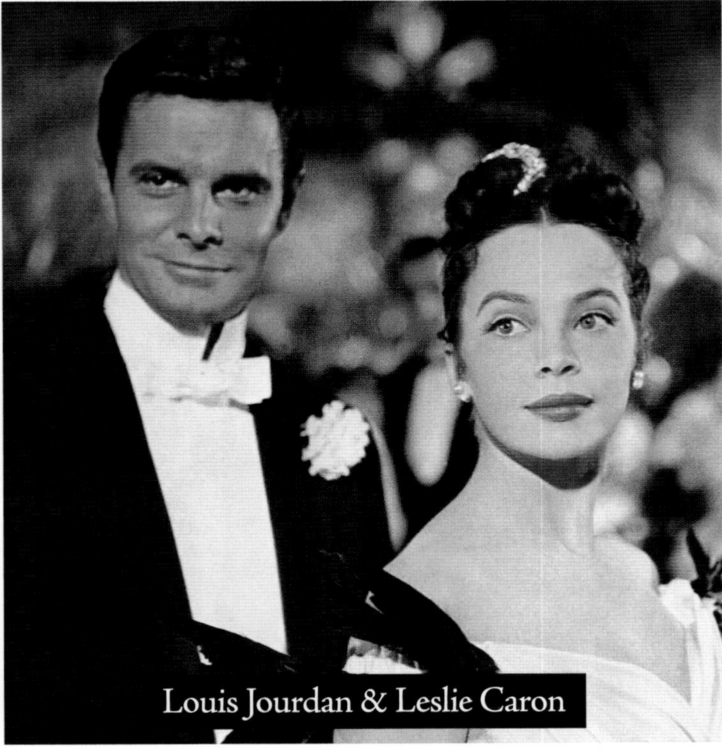

Louis Jourdan & Leslie Caron

My wife and I love this movie and, in particular, my wife loved Louis Jourdan, and fortunately she loved him a tad less than she loved me. If we record this book, you will hear me doing a spot on impression of Maurice Chevalier singing,

"Thank heaven for little girls... For little girls get bigger every day..."

Two escaped convicts chained together must learn to get along in order to elude capture.

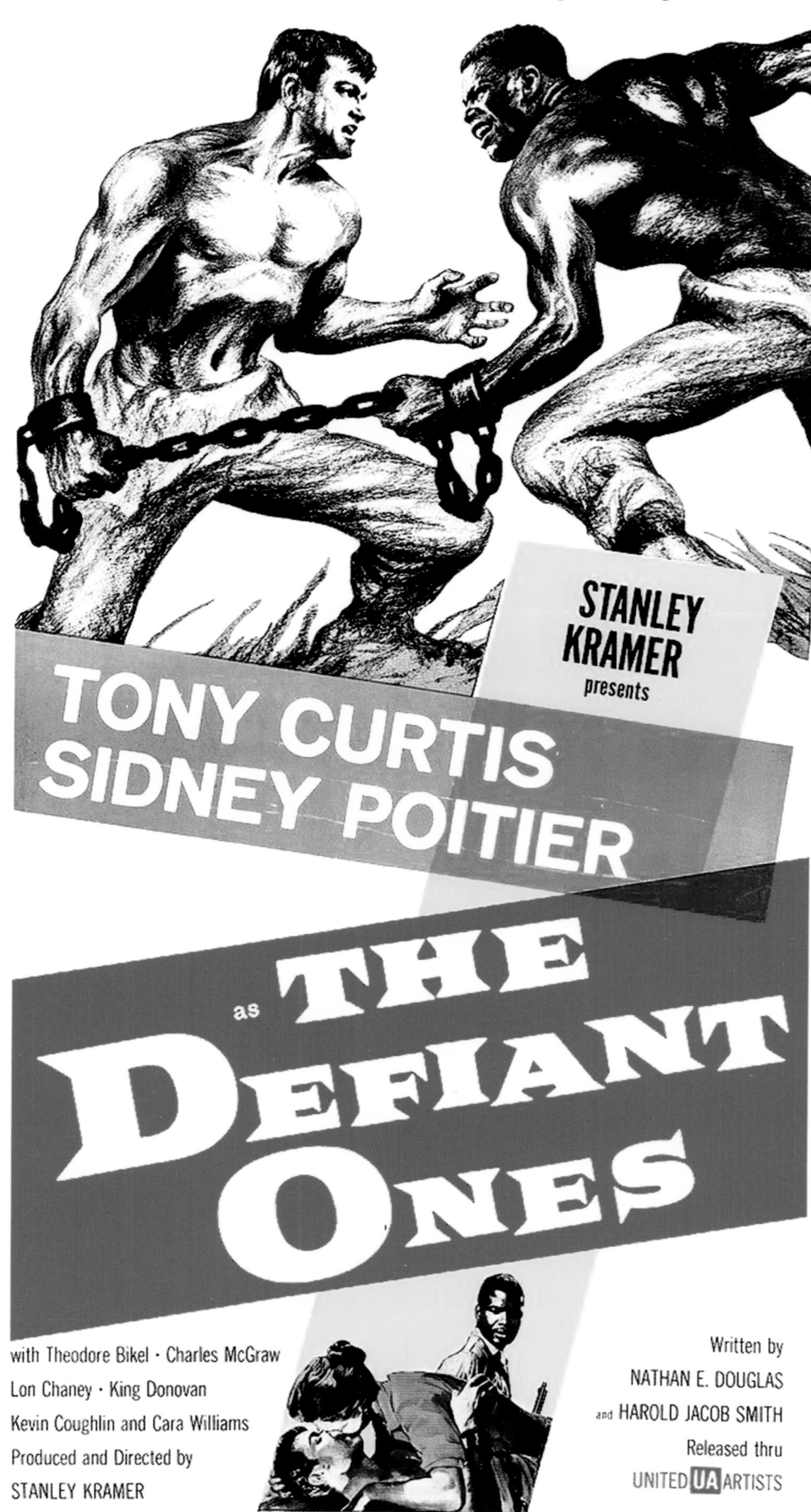

Bosley Crowther of The New York Times wrote: "This film is a remarkably apt and dramatic visualization of a social idea—the idea of men of different races brought together to face misfortune in a bond of brotherhood."

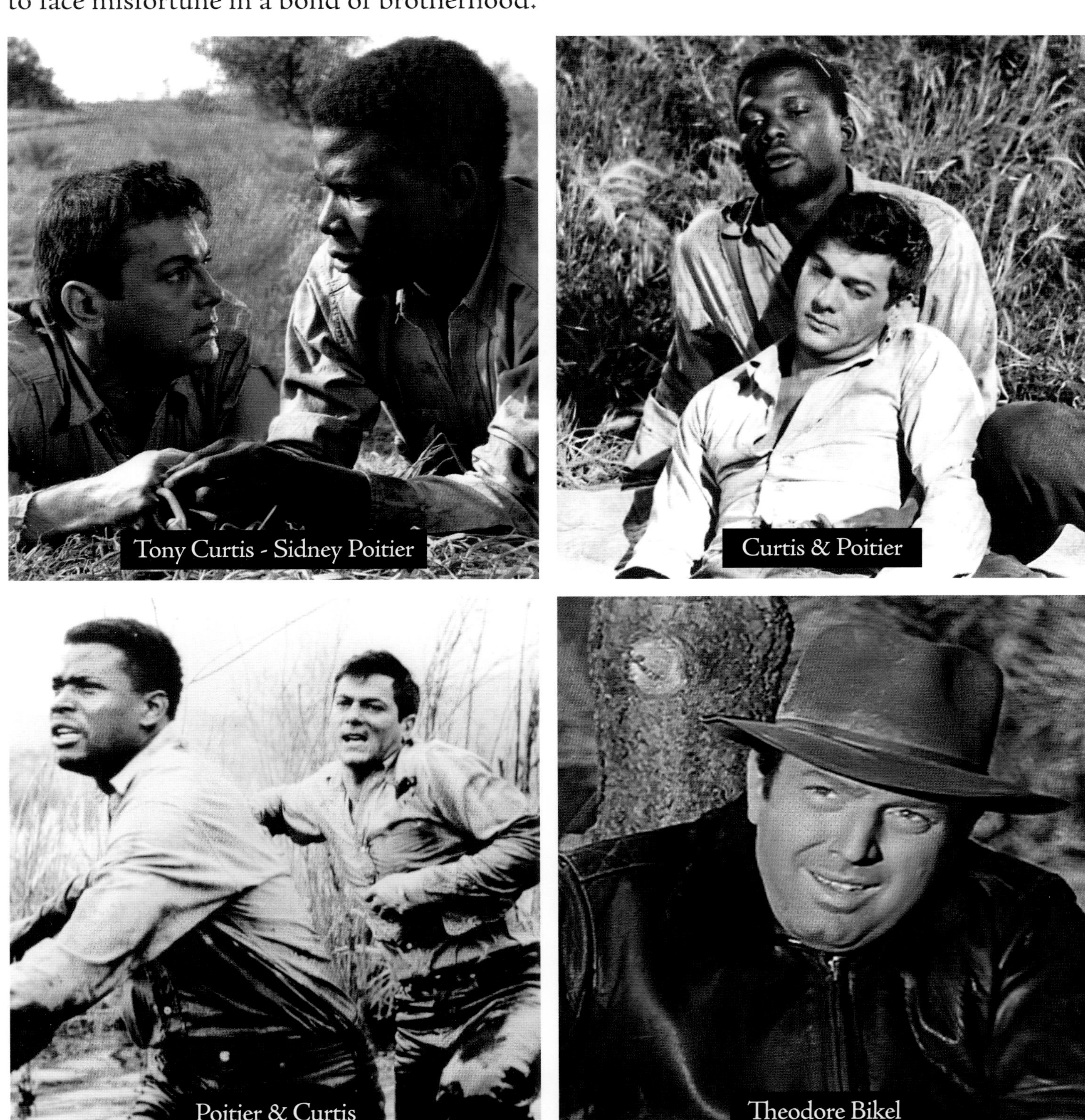

Tony Curtis - Sidney Poitier

Curtis & Poitier

Poitier & Curtis

Theodore Bikel

Besides being a fine actor, Theodore Bikel was an accomplished musician. He recorded over 20 albums of folk music, sang and spoke a half-dozen languages and it would be fair to call him a multi-multi-multi-multi-multi-multi-multi-multi-multi-multi-talented man.

When two male musicians witness a mob hit, they flee the state in an all-female band disguised as women, but further complications set in.

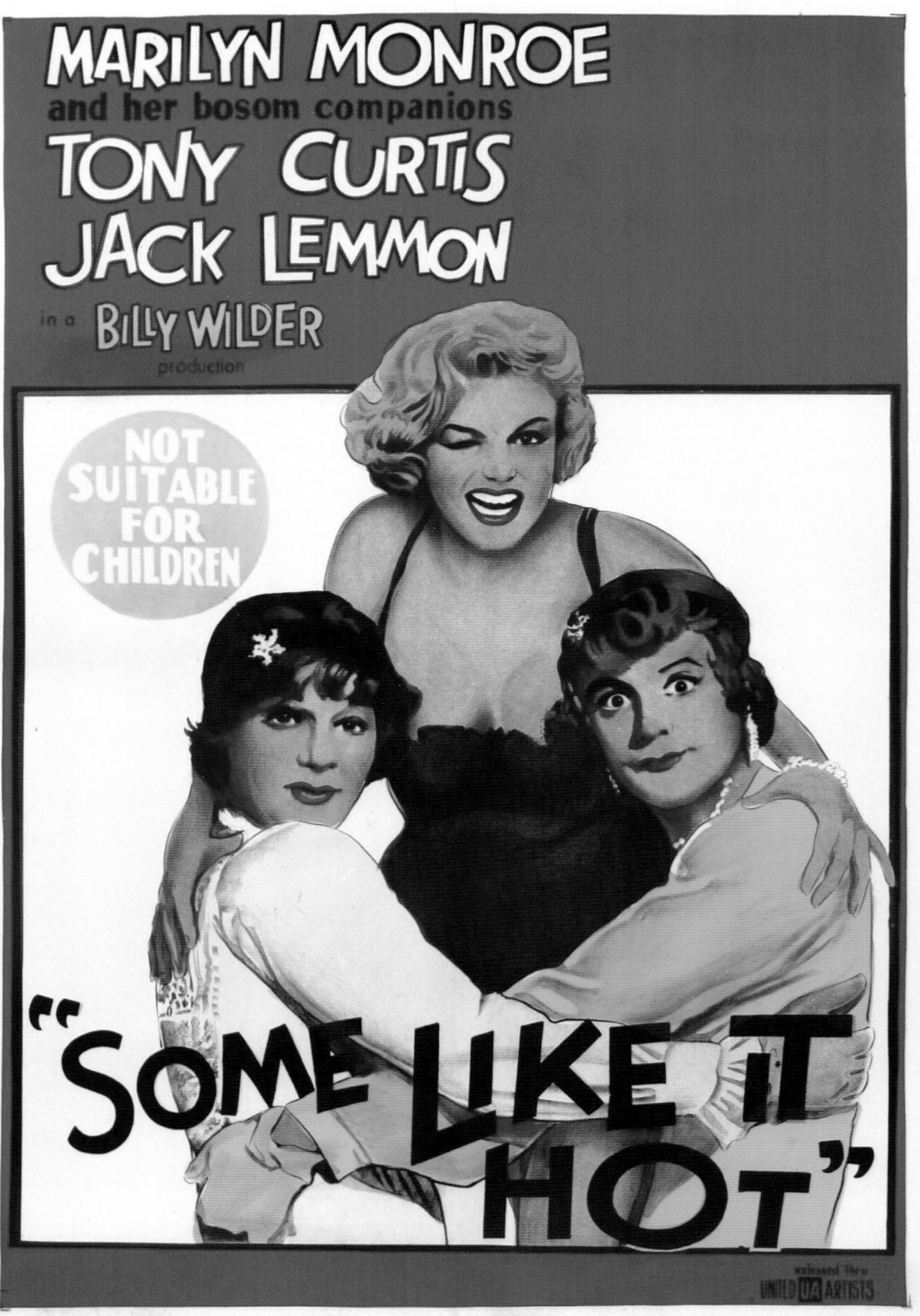

Variety wrote: "Pictures like this, with a sense of humor that is as broad as it can be sophisticated, come along only infrequently."

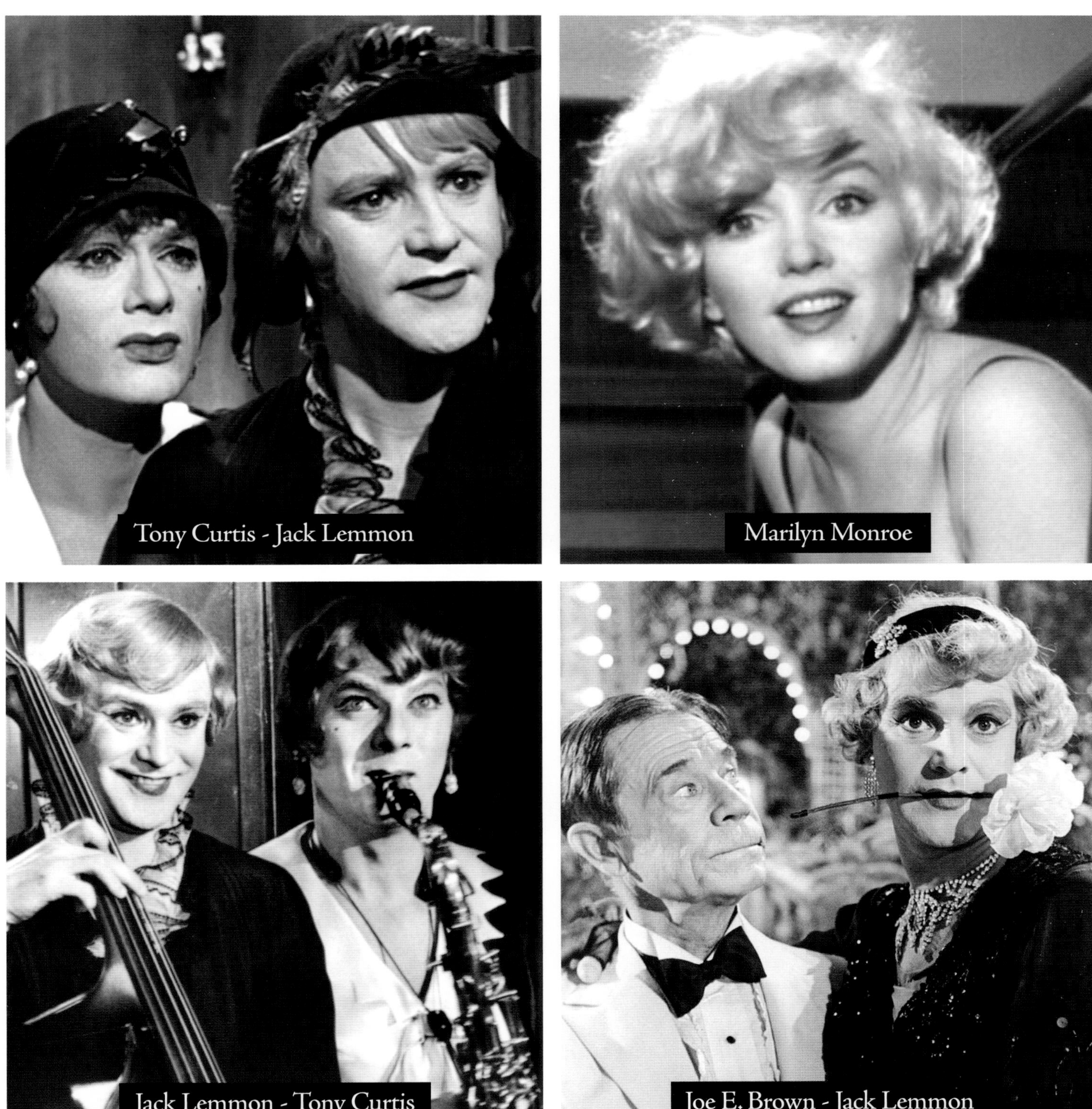

Tony Curtis - Jack Lemmon

Marilyn Monroe

Jack Lemmon - Tony Curtis

Joe E. Brown - Jack Lemmon

This film had three great performers and undoubtedly one of the funniest punch-lines ever. It was said by Joe E. Brown, who had fallen in love with Jack Lemmon, the blond bass player who was in hiding and dressed as a girl. At the end when Joe E. Brown professed his love for her, Lemmon admitted that he was a man, to which the still smitten Joe E. replied, "Well, nobody's perfect."

In a murder trial, the defendant says he suffered temporary insanity after the victim raped his wife. What is the truth, and will he win his case?

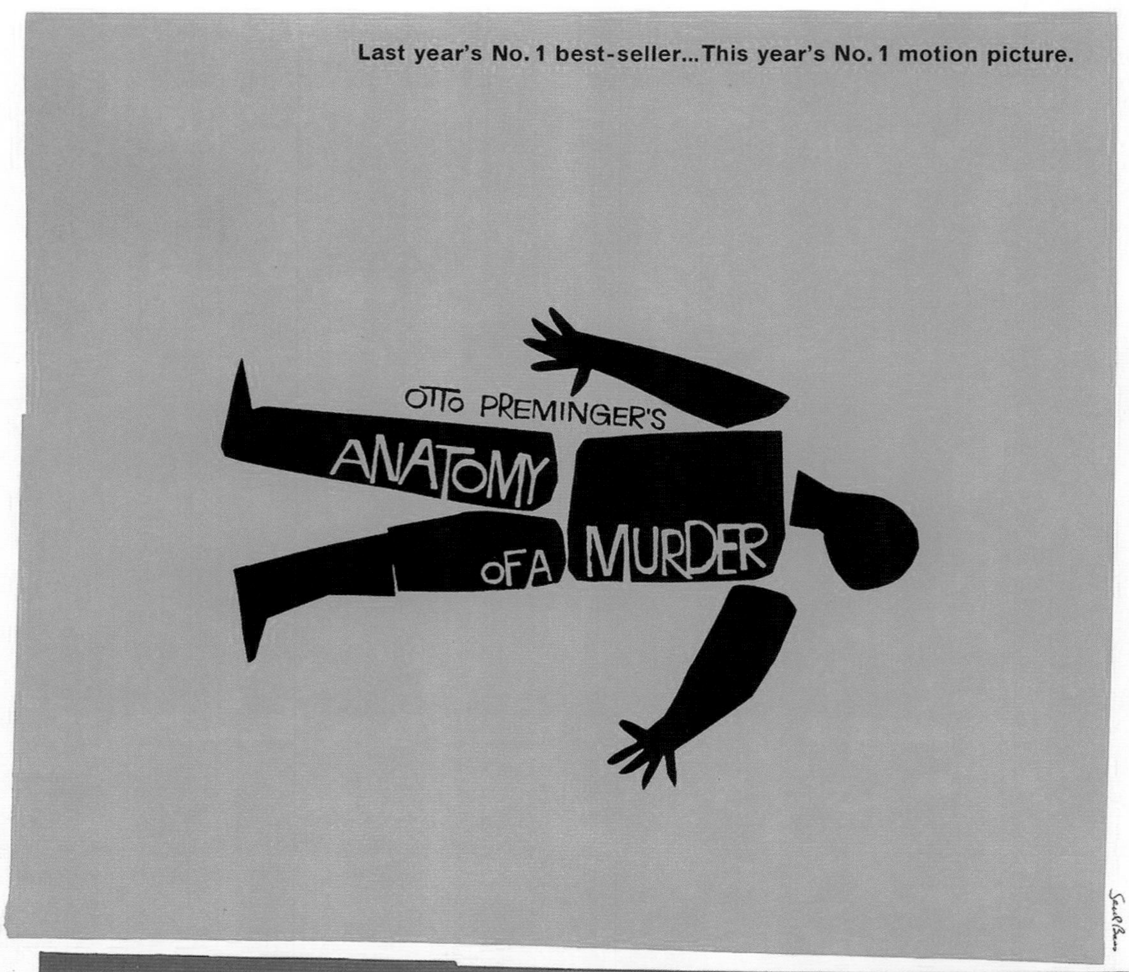

STARRING
JAMES STEWART
LEE REMICK
BEN GAZZARA
ARTHUR O'CONNELL
EVE ARDEN
KATHRYN GRANT

and JOSEPH N. WELCH as Judge Weaver

WITH
GEORGE C. SCOTT/ORSON BEAN/RUSS BROWN/MURRAY HAMILTON/BROOKS WEST screenplay by WENDELL MAYES from the best-seller by ROBERT TRAVER photography by SAM LEAVITT produced & directed by OTTO PREMINGER/a Columbia release

▸music by Duke Ellington◂

Jonathan Rosenbaum of Chicago Reader wrote: "As an entertaining look at legal process, this is spellbinding all the way, infused by an ambiguity about human personality and motivation."

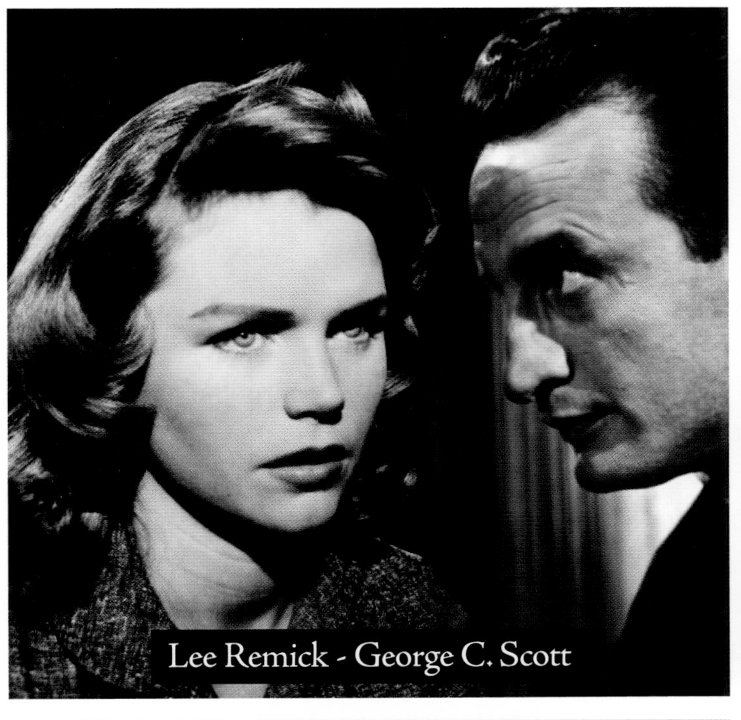
Lee Remick - George C. Scott

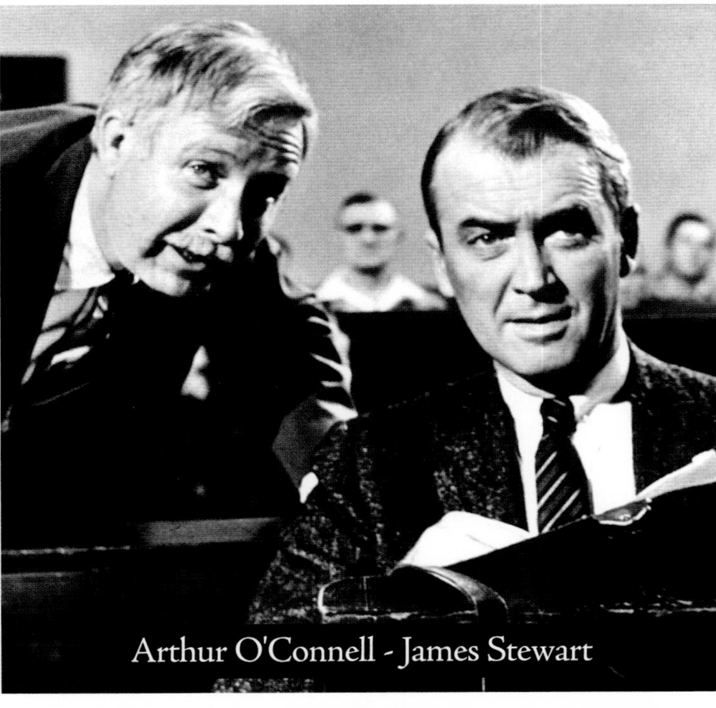
Arthur O'Connell - James Stewart

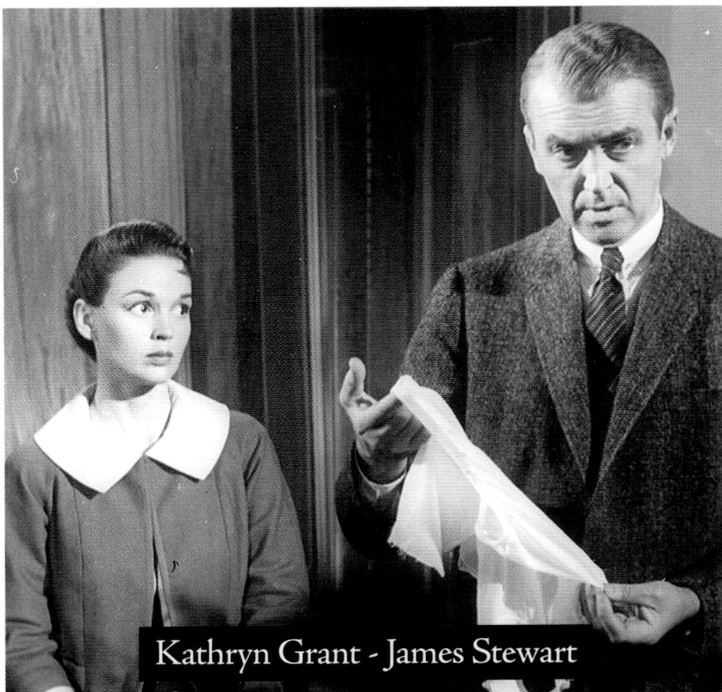
Kathryn Grant - James Stewart

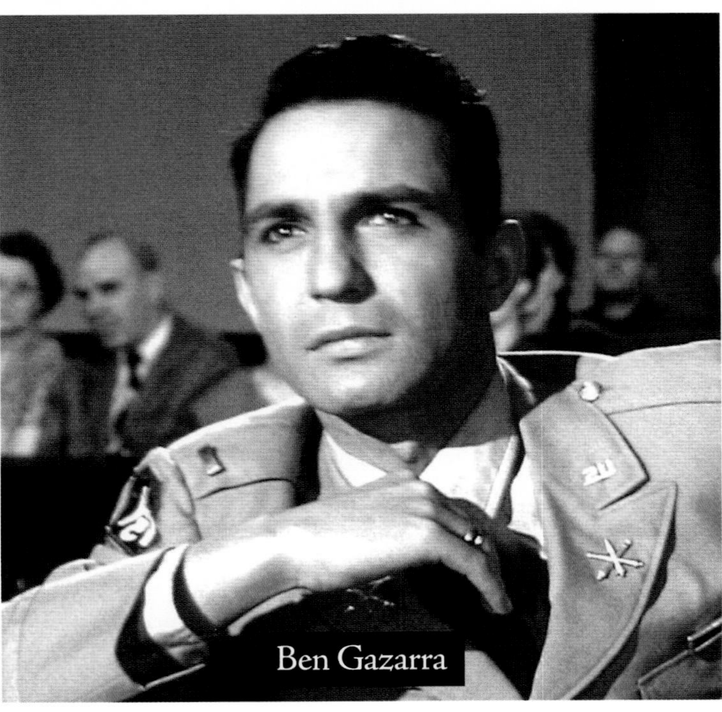
Ben Gazarra

"Anatomy of a Murder" was well received by members of the legal and educational professions. It demonstrated how a legal defense is developed in a difficult case. This is used as a teaching tool in law schools, as it encompasses, from the defense standpoint, all of the basic stages in the U.S. criminal justice system from client interview and arraignment through trial.

I knew from the beginning that the defense attorney would win the case, since that role was played by Jimmy Stewart and Jimmy Stewart never took a part where his character lost.

Harrowing story of a young Jewish girl who, with her family and their friends, is forced into hiding in an attic in Nazi-occupied Amsterdam.

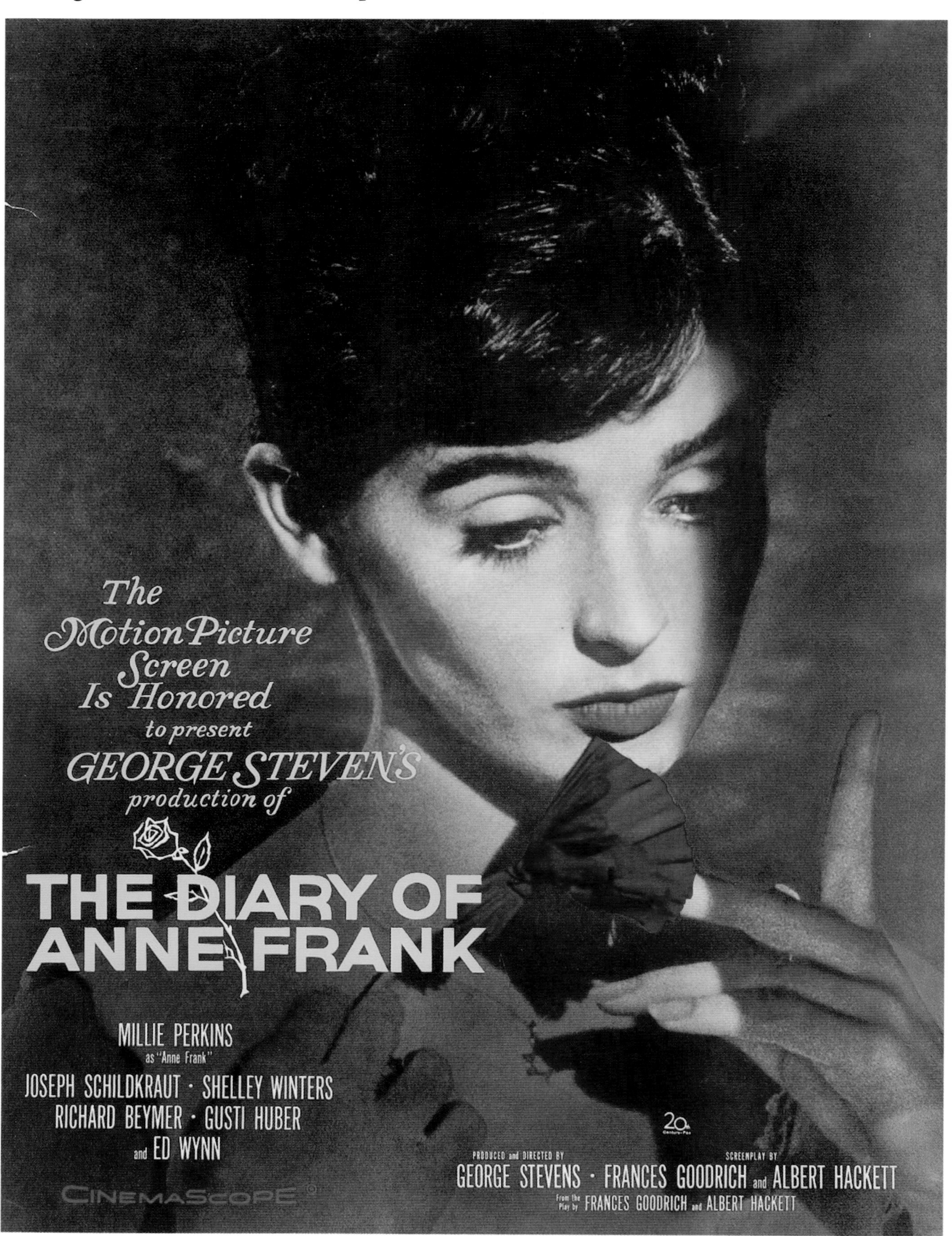

Peter Canavese of Groucho Reviews wrote: "Remains a potent statement about the horrors of war and a valid testament to the girl who could answer them by writing, 'I still believe, in spite of everything, that people are really good at heart.'"

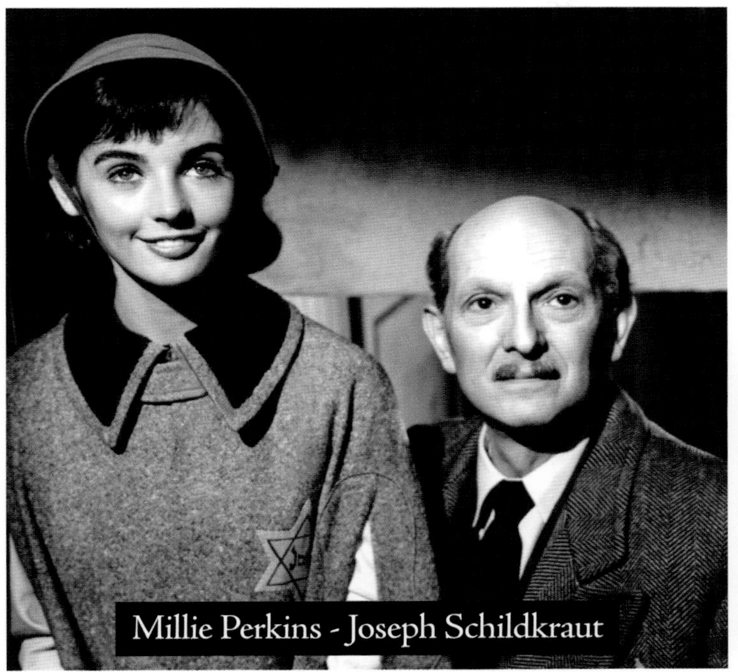
Millie Perkins - Joseph Schildkraut

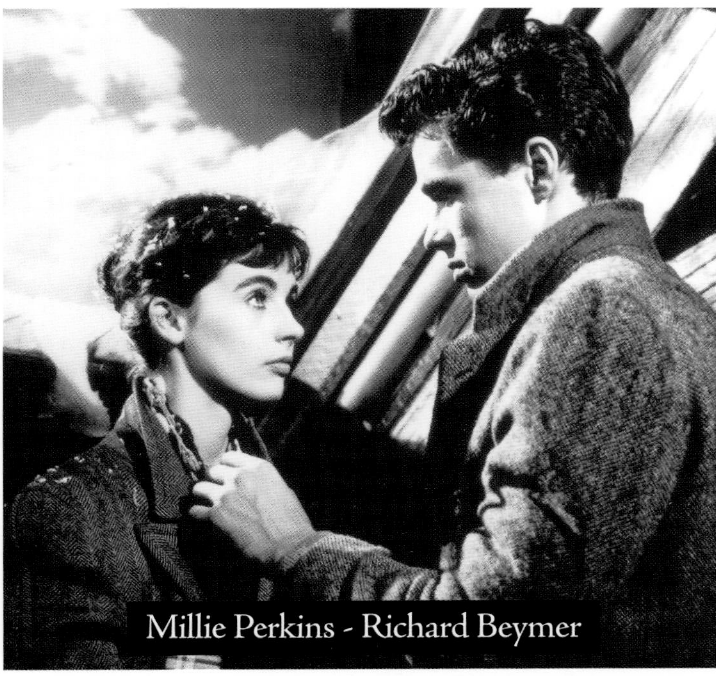
Millie Perkins - Richard Beymer

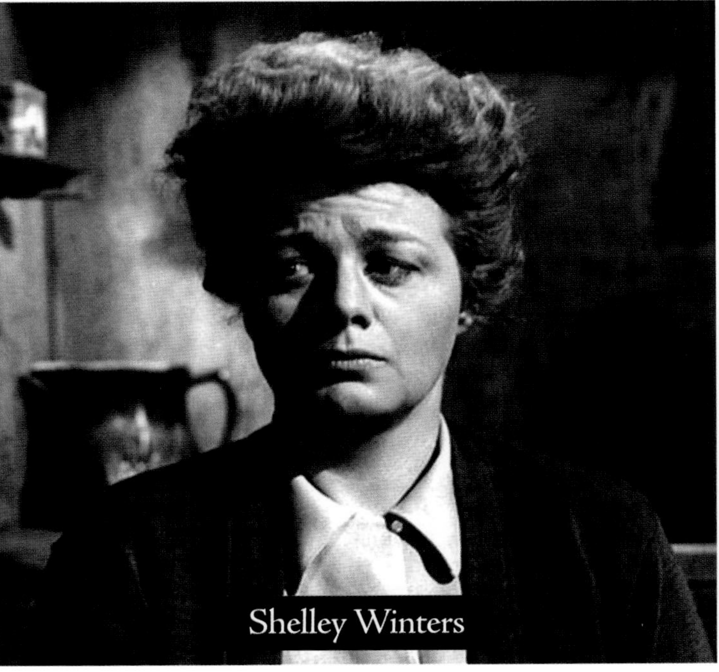
Shelley Winters

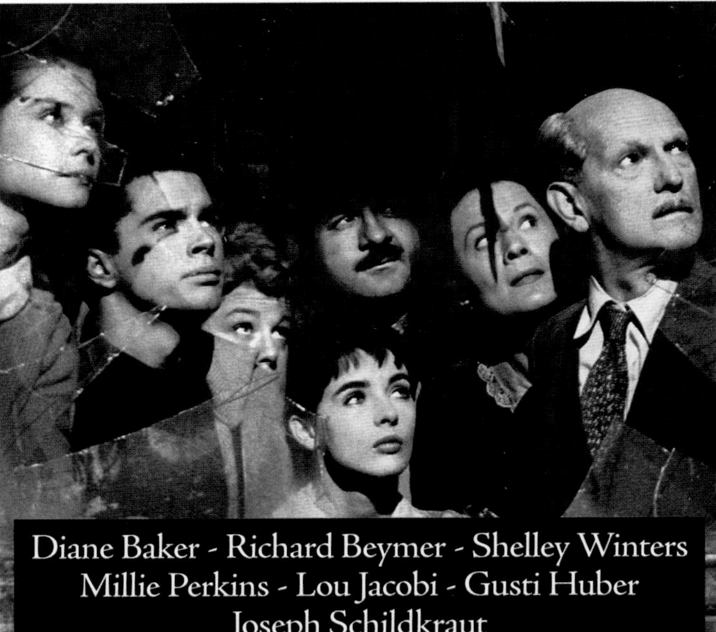
Diane Baker - Richard Beymer - Shelley Winters
Millie Perkins - Lou Jacobi - Gusti Huber
Joseph Schildkraut

After the Nazis had killed all of Otto Frank's family, he returned from his imprisonment at Auschwitz and published his daughter's diary.

The film's interiors were shot on a sound stage in Los Angeles, while the exteriors were shot on the street and in the house in which Anne Frank and her family lived.

In 1960, "The Diary of Anne Frank" won three Academy Awards, which included a Best Supporting Actress Award for Shelley Winters.

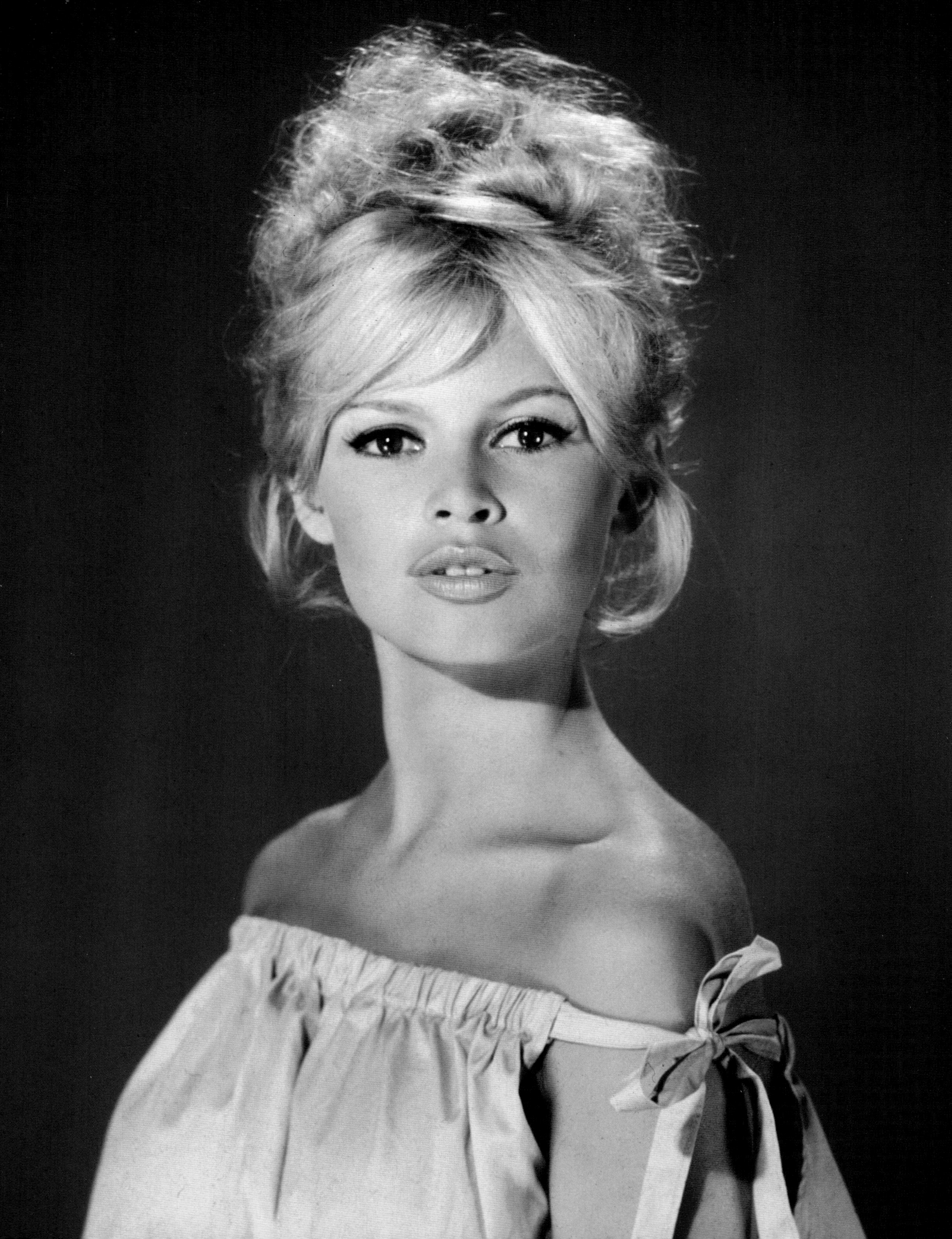

the 60s

Ella Peterson is a Brooklyn telephone answering service operator who tries to improve the lives of her clients by passing along bits of information she hears from other clients and falls in love with one of her clients.

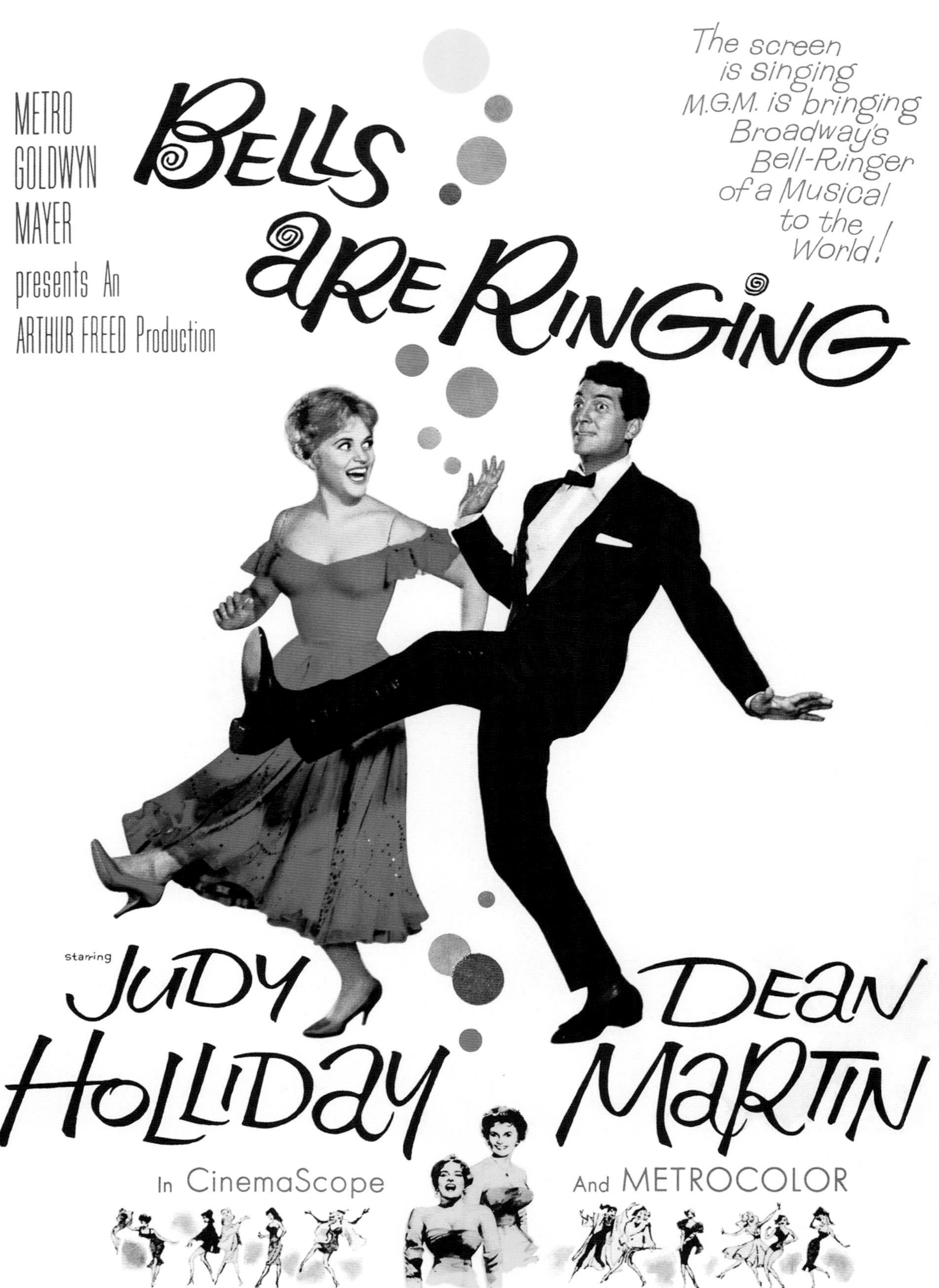

Carol Cling of Las Vegas Review-Journal wrote: "One of Hollywood's last old-fashioned Broadway adaptations, with Holliday as endearing as ever. Not exactly Minnelli's finest, but well worth catching for musicals fans."

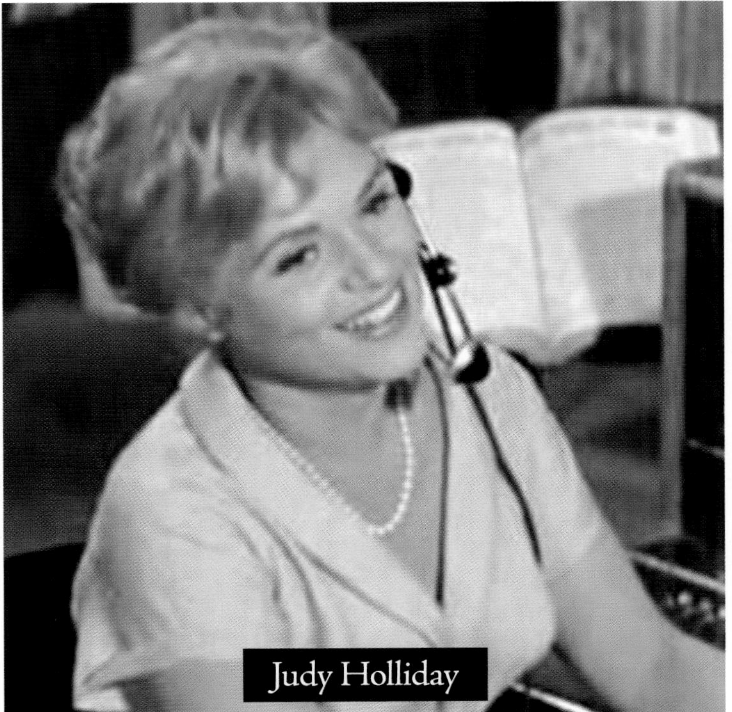
Judy Holliday

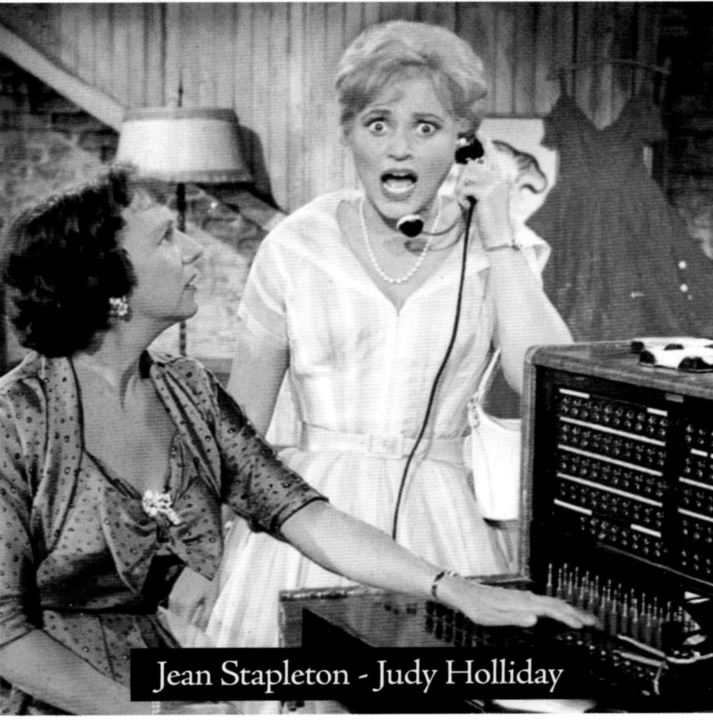
Jean Stapleton - Judy Holliday

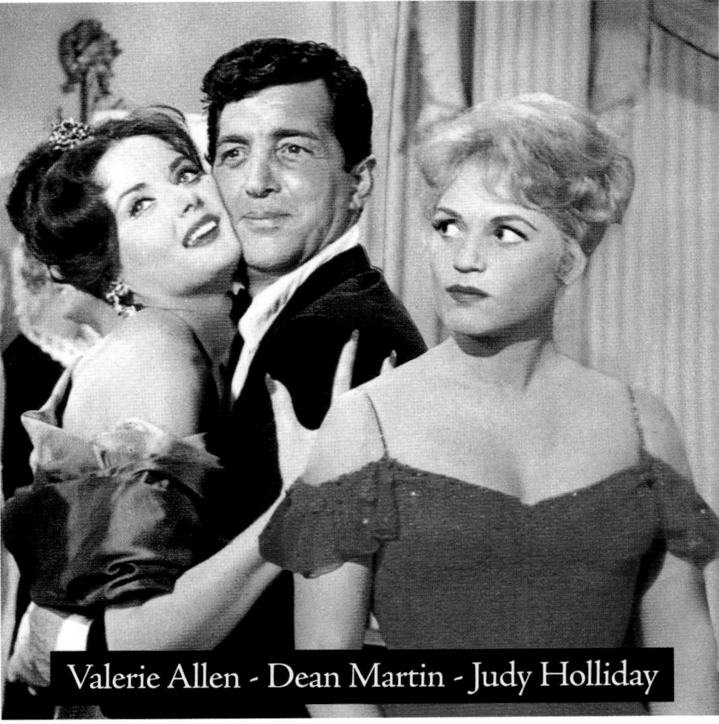
Valerie Allen - Dean Martin - Judy Holliday

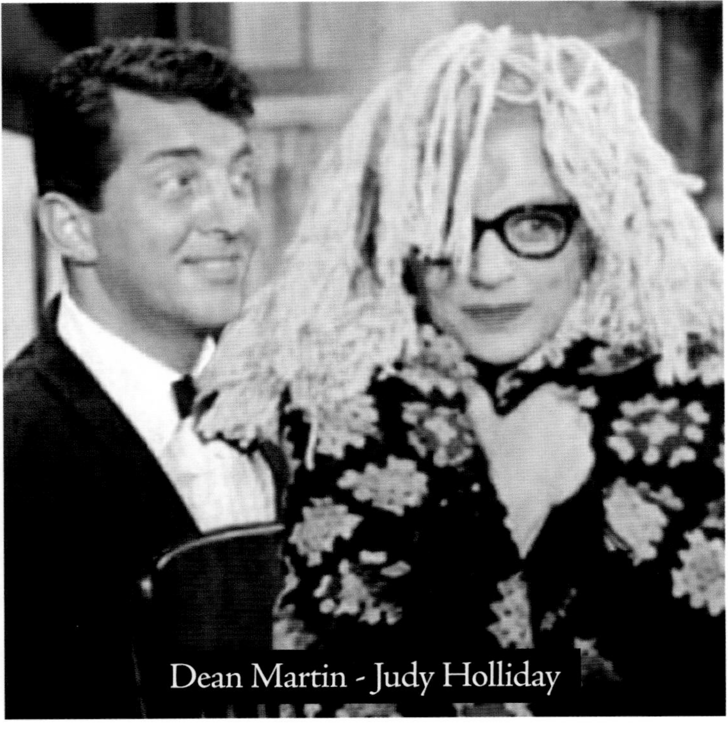
Dean Martin - Judy Holliday

I first became a fan of Judy Holliday when I saw her perform "Bells Are Ringing" on Broadway, which she did for two years. I am grateful that the Producers of the film chose to cast Judy Holliday in the role she originated, unlike the Producers of "My Fair Lady," who opted to use a non-singing star rather than the brilliant Julie Andrews, who originated the role.

As Elmer Gantry, Burt Lancaster plays a hard-drinking, fast-talking traveling salesman who, with a charismatic fervor, infuses biblical passages into his pitches to collect money, women and live a good-bad life at the expense of the suckers he euckered.

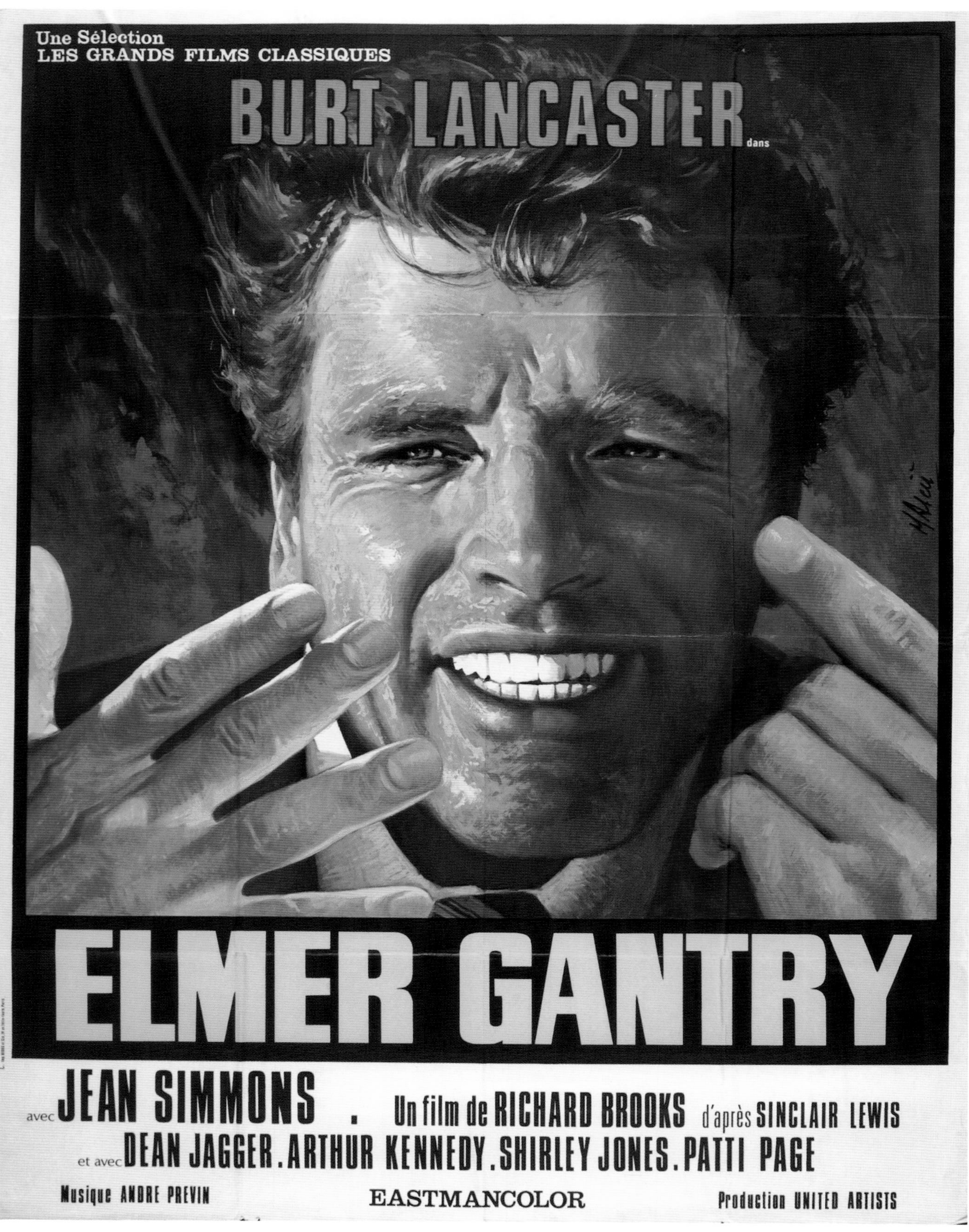

A.H. Weiler of The New York Times wrote: "The briskly paced drama of a religious opportunist, his colleagues and his times utilizes the tools of the motion picture in expert fashion."

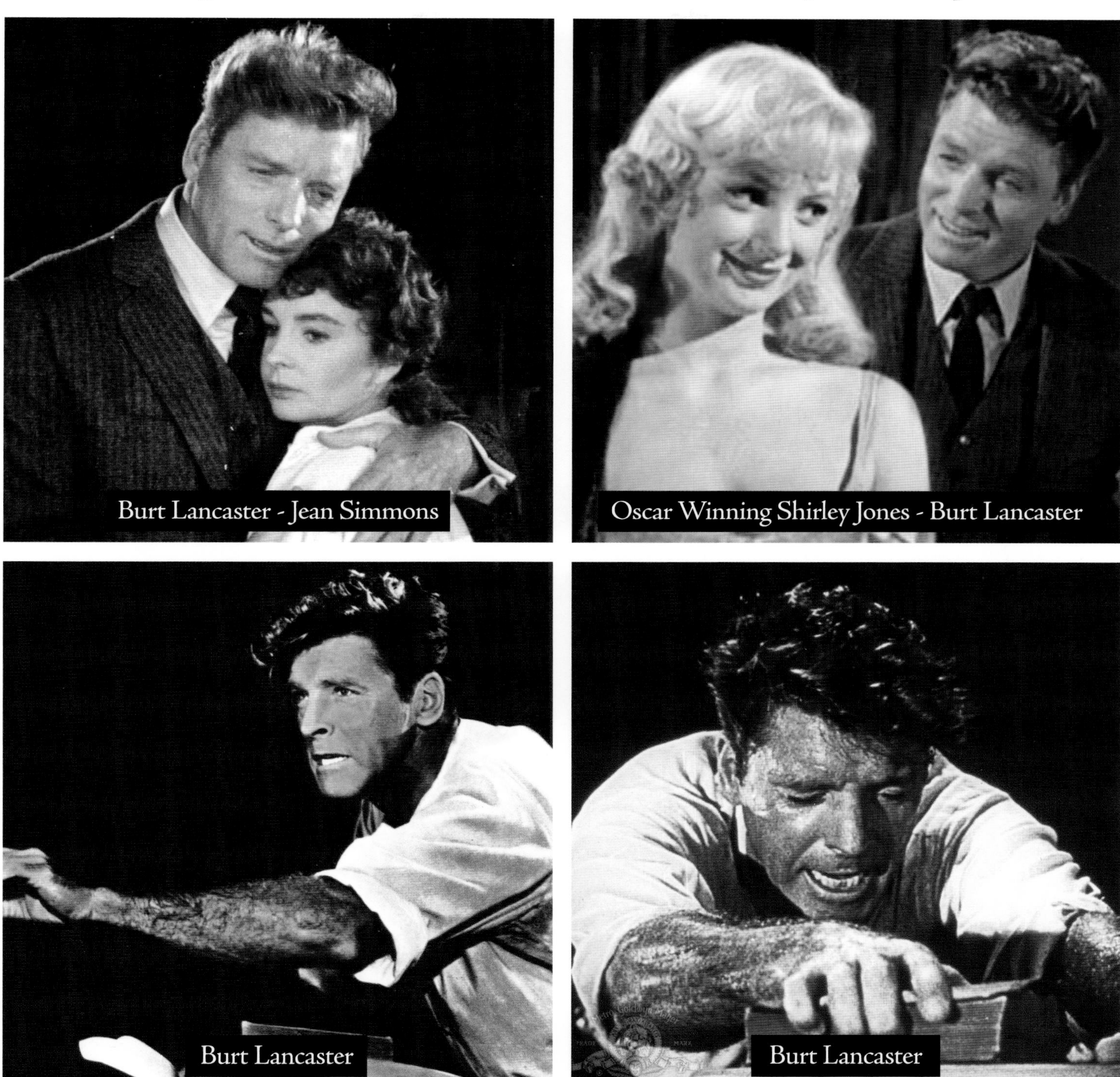

Burt Lancaster - Jean Simmons

Oscar Winning Shirley Jones - Burt Lancaster

Burt Lancaster

Burt Lancaster

In all of filmdom I can safely say that there is no one that comes near the physical abilities of Burt Lancaster. He was a circus performer in The Federal Theater Project specializing in aerobatic stunts on the horizontal bars. In his career, he made sixty-one films and in each one he never used a double to perform his derring-do. To promote the film "Trapeze," he set up parallel bars in theaters and entertained the audience with his acrobatics. I actually saw Burt Lancaster do his act at New York's Paramount Theater.

Jack Lemmon plays an office drudge at a New York insurance company. In order to climb the corporate ladder, he allows four managers to take turns borrowing his apartment for their various extramarital liaisons. These encounters are so noisy that his neighbors assume he's a playboy diddling different women every night.

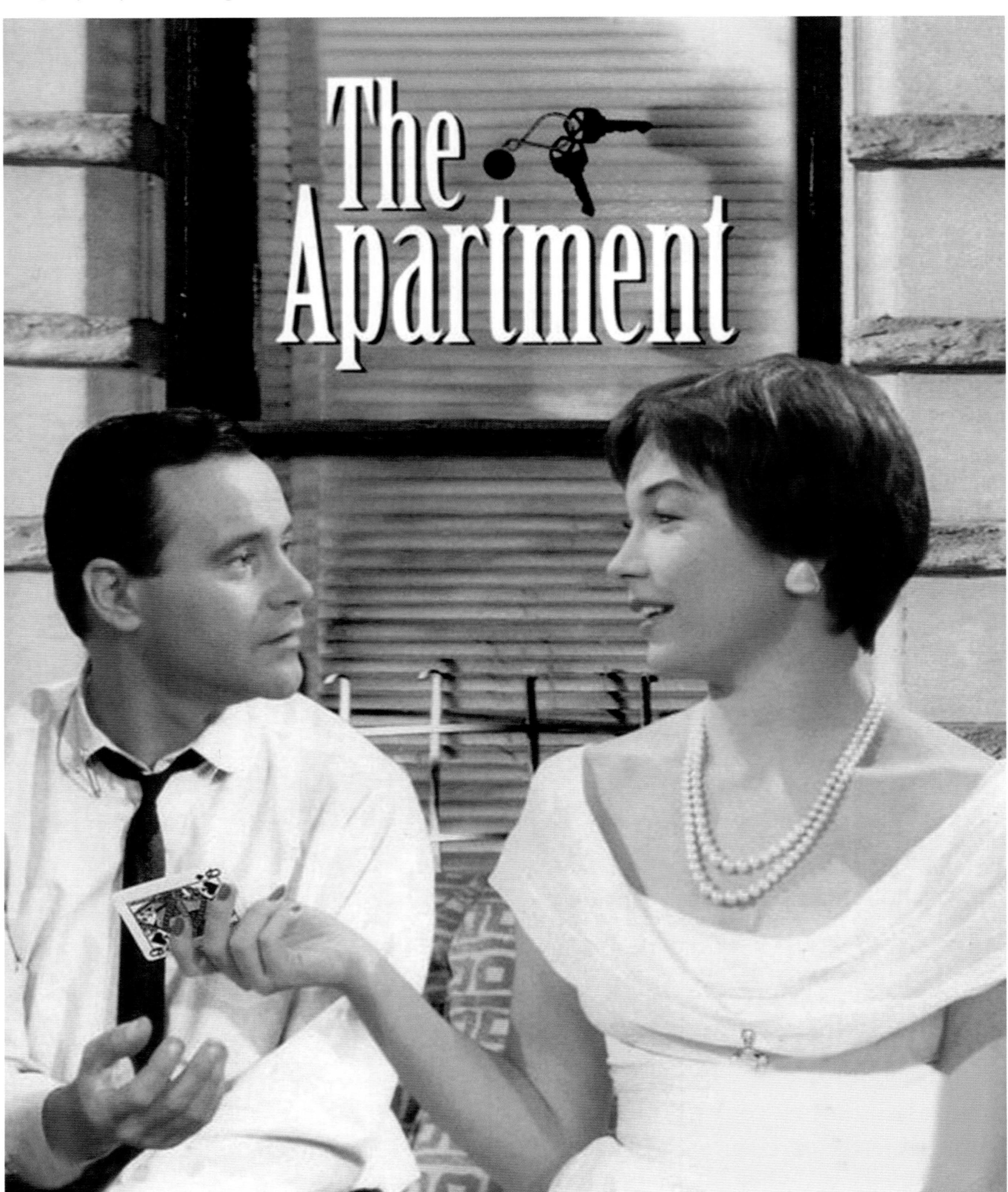

Time Magazine wrote: "A comedy of men's-room humours and water-cooler politics that now and then among the belly laughs says something serious and sad about the struggle for success, about what it often does to a man, and about the horribly small world of big business."

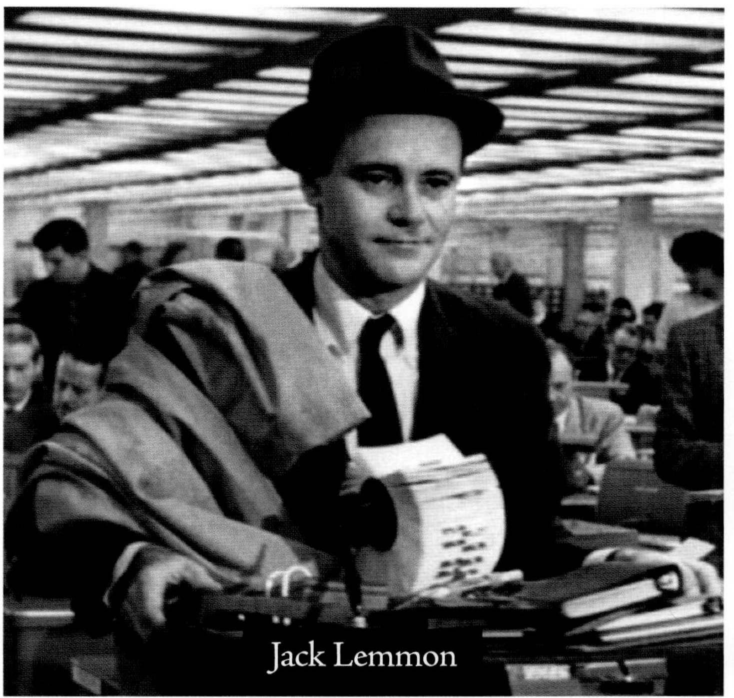
Jack Lemmon

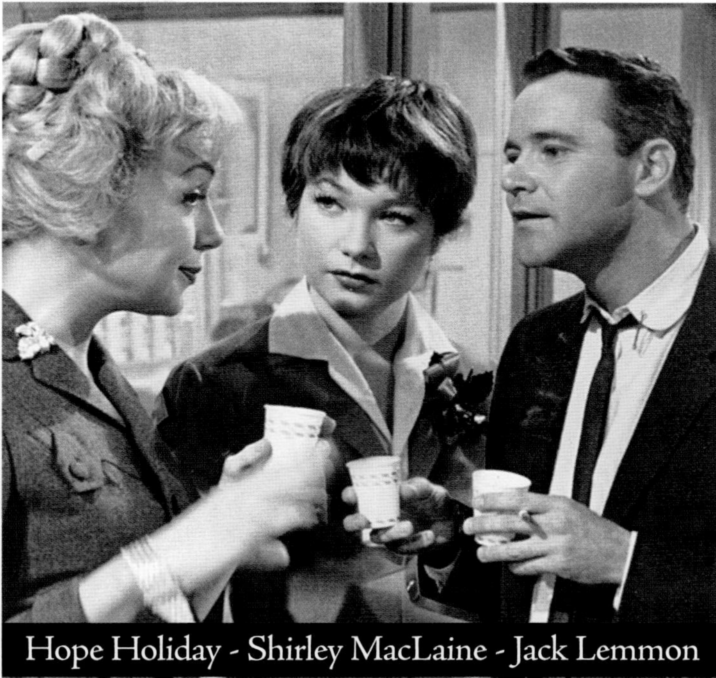
Hope Holiday - Shirley MacLaine - Jack Lemmon

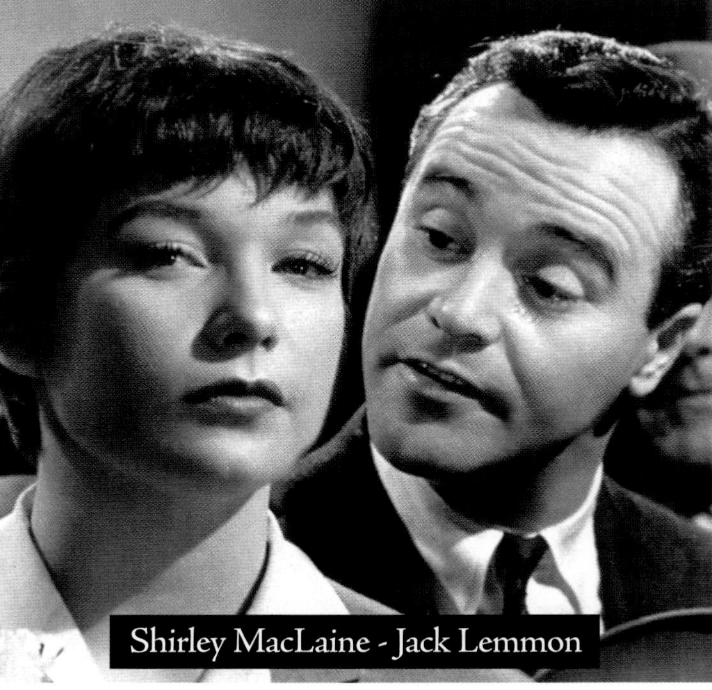
Shirley MacLaine - Jack Lemmon

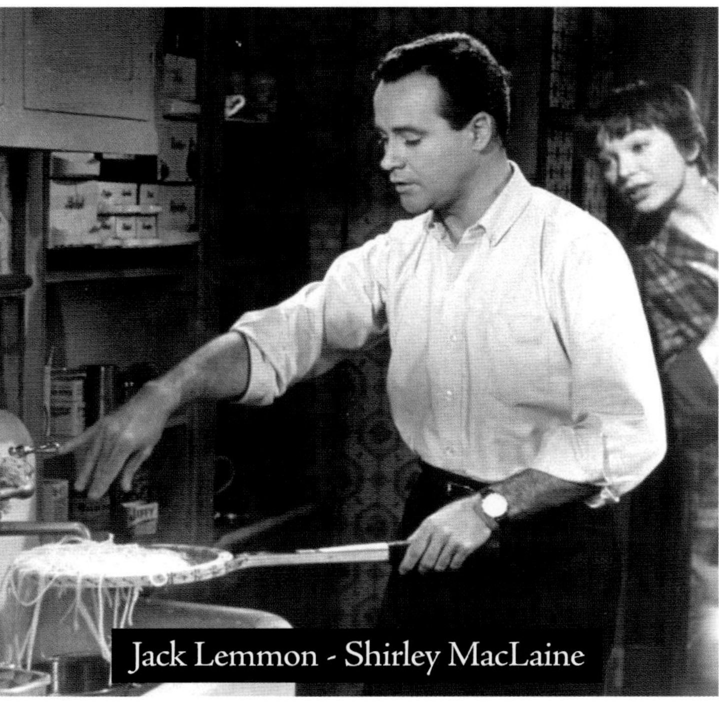
Jack Lemmon - Shirley MacLaine

Jack Lemmon was a Yale drama student when he came backstage to visit me at New Haven's Shubert Theater. He told me of his interest in theater and his thought of changing his name. I advised him to keep his name, keep studying and get good enough to make his mother and father and all the members of the Lemmon family proud of him.

In 1950, Jack Lemmon and I co-hosted the television series "Toni Twin Time."

The slave Spartacus leads a violent revolt against the decadent Roman Republic.

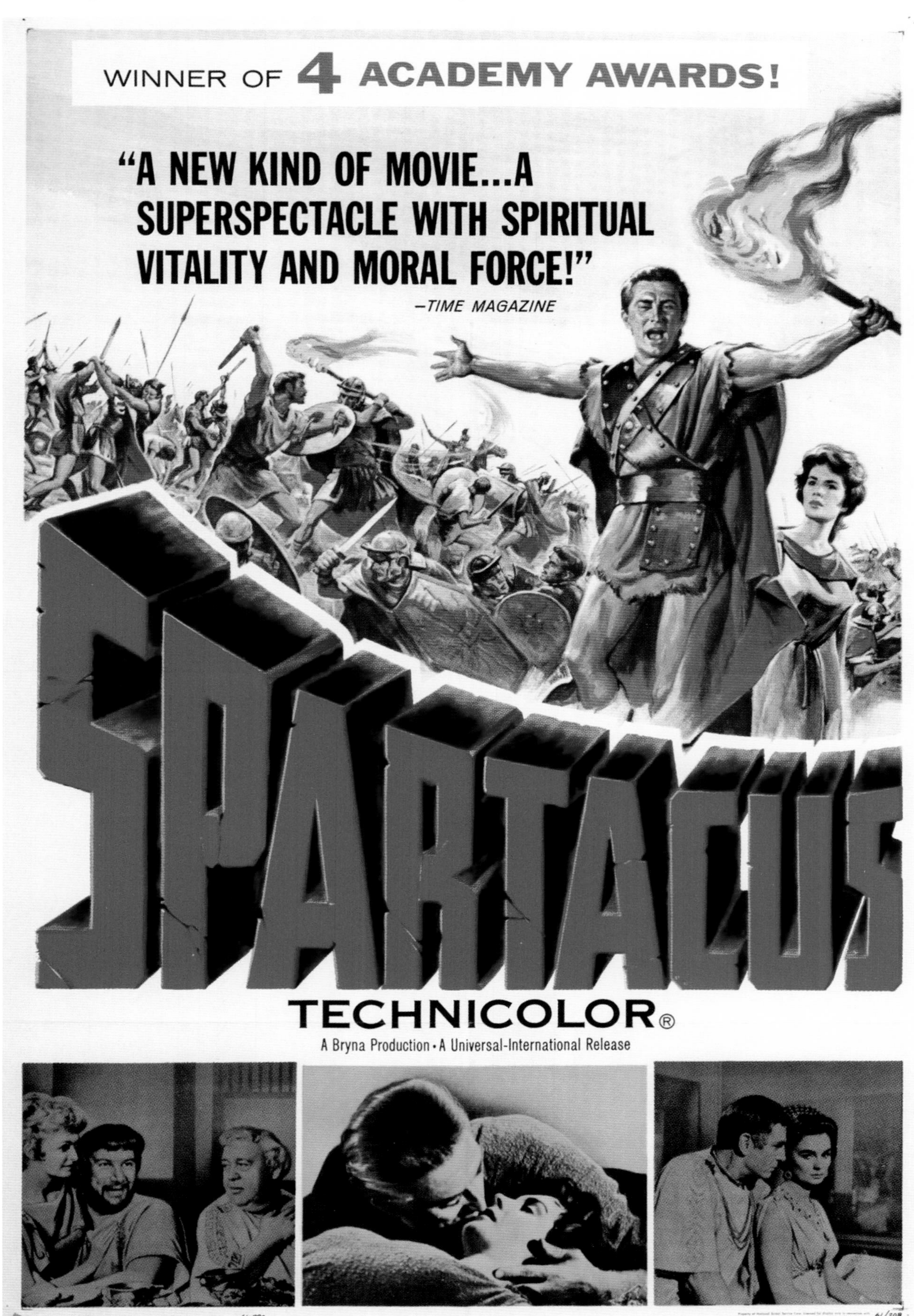

David Stratton of At the Movies wrote: "There have been other versions of the Spartacus story, including a silent epic and a more recent TV series, but Kubrick's film can't be beaten."

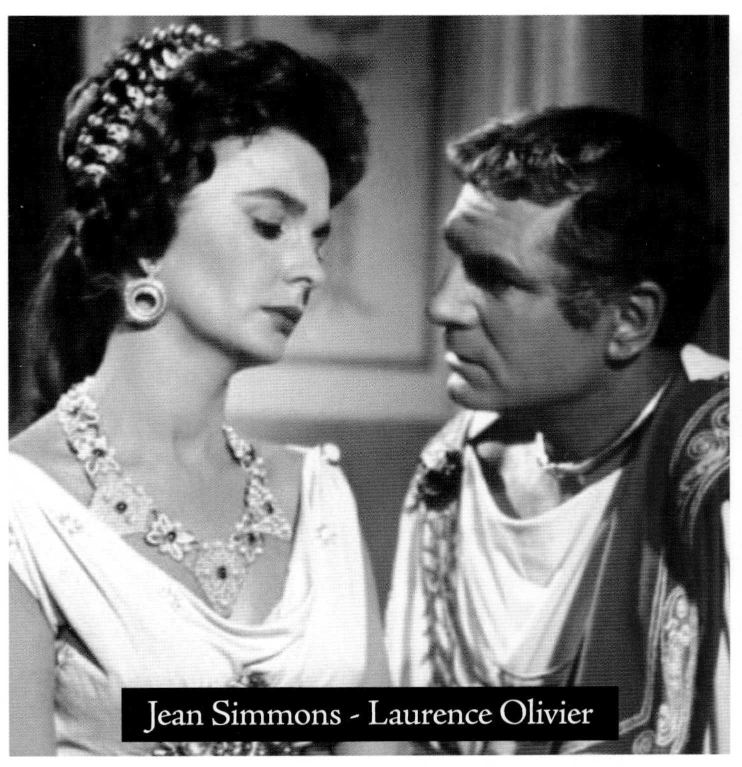
Jean Simmons - Laurence Olivier

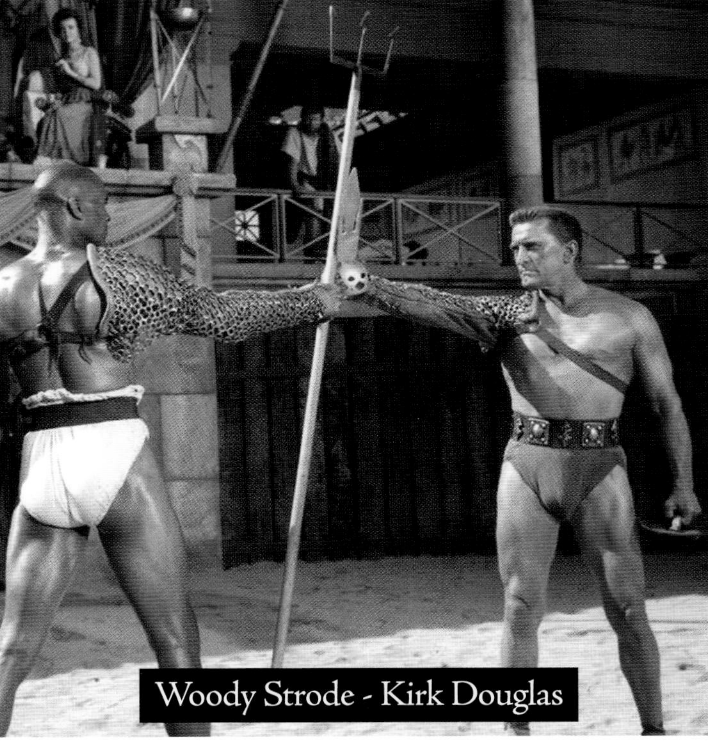
Woody Strode - Kirk Douglas

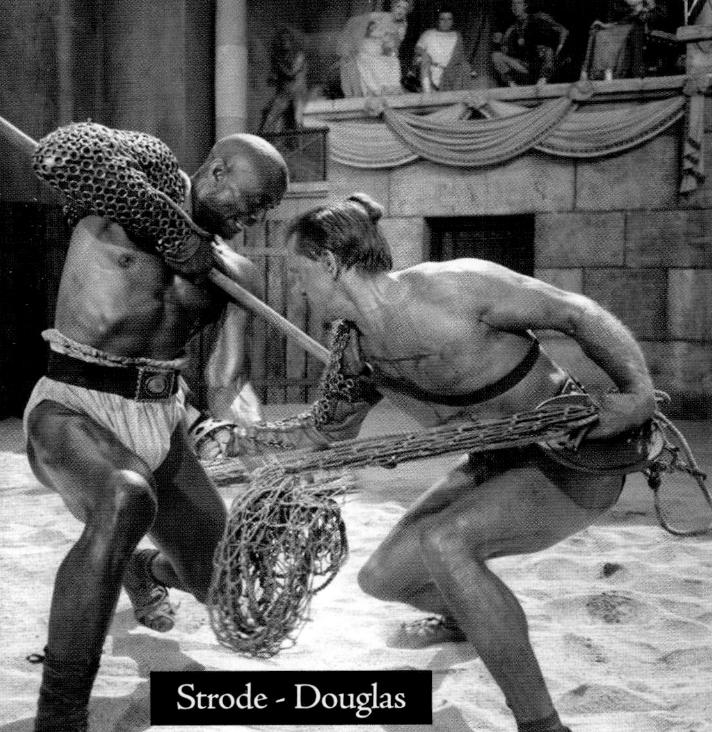
Strode - Douglas

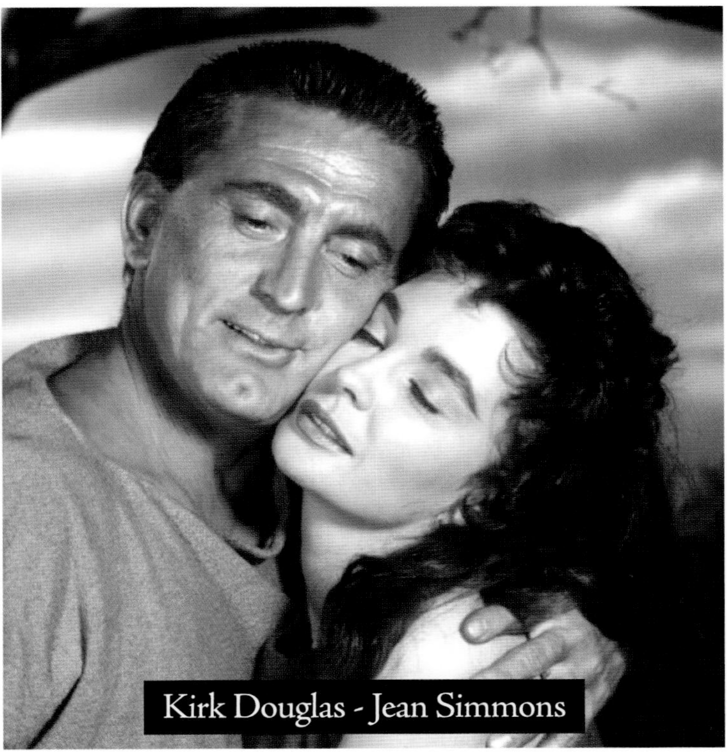
Kirk Douglas - Jean Simmons

One thing more that can't be beaten is Kirk Douglas' courage, in 1960, when he defied The House Un-American Activities Committee by crediting the screenplay to the blacklisted Dalton Trumbo. Another thing that can't be beaten is the spirit of Douglas, who at one hundred and one years of age still cherishes life with his wife, Anne, and his children, Michael, Joel and Peter.

In 1948, an American court in occupied Germany tries four Nazi judges for war crimes.

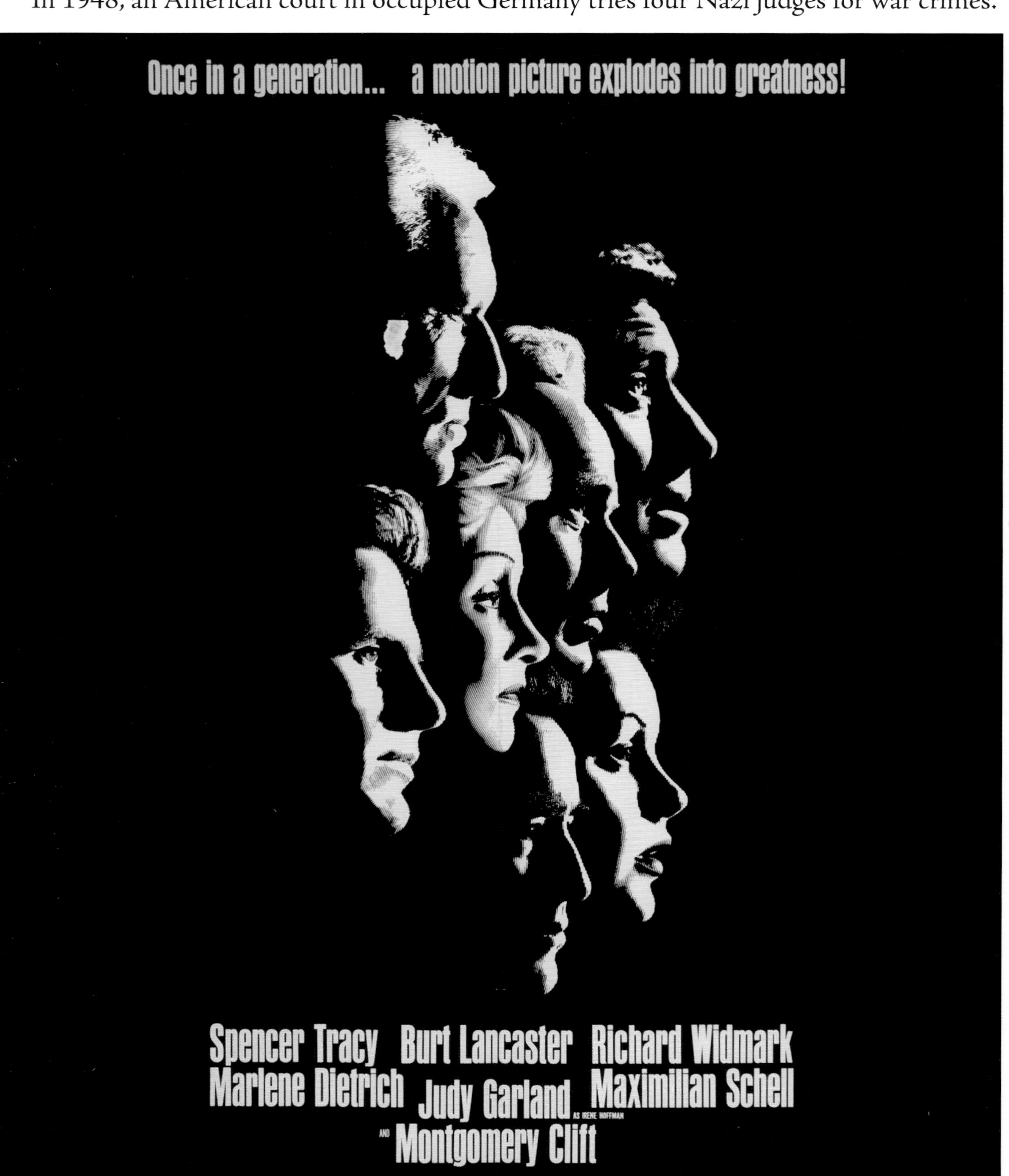

This film opens old wounds and singles out the German lawyers and judges, who did not rise to punish those responsible for the years of Nazi barbarism.

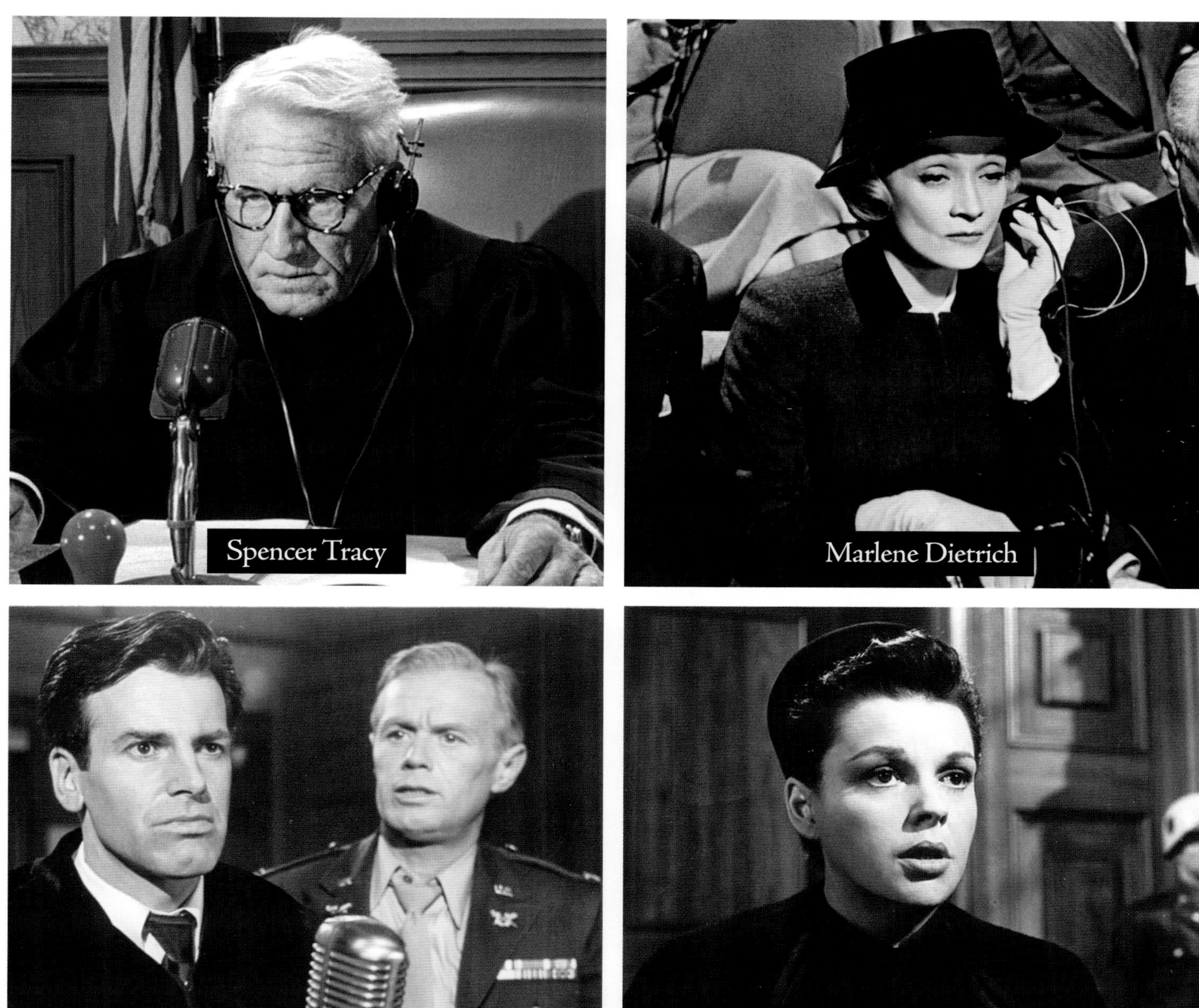

Spencer Tracy

Marlene Dietrich

Maximilian Schell - Richard Widmark

Judy Garland

Judy Garland, who all her life was a musical performer, doubted she could play this serious role. On her first day she is reported to have said to her director, Stanley Kramer, "Damn it, Stanley, I can't do it. I've dried up. I'm too happy to cry." "Judy," he argued, "there's nobody in the entertainment world today, actor or singer, who can run the complete range of emotions, from utter pathos to power, better than you! Now let's just do it!"

(*And boy did she ever do it.*)

Inspired by William Shakespeare's "Romeo and Juliet," two youngsters from rival New York City gangs fall in love, but tensions between their respective friends build toward tragedy.

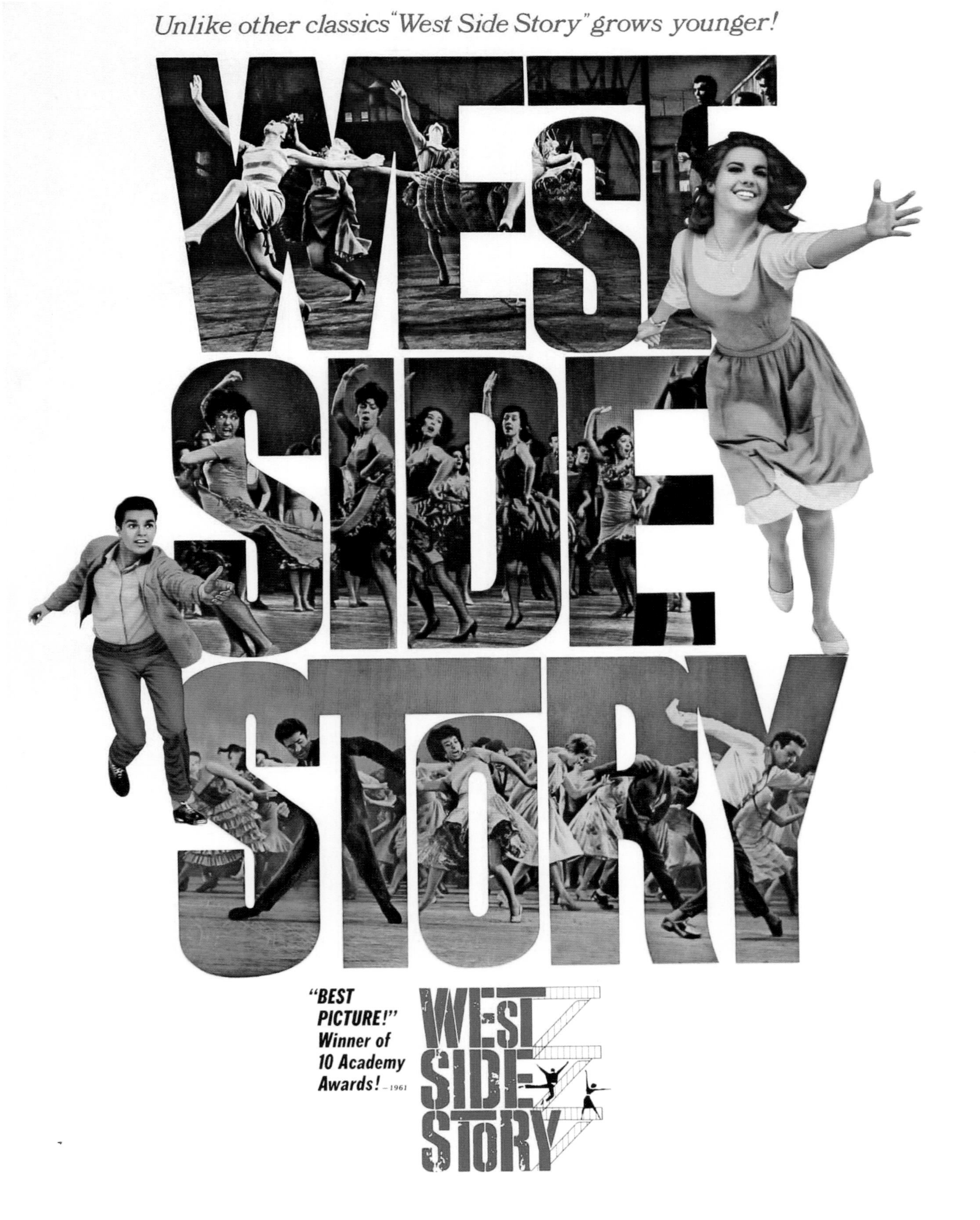

Unlike other classics "West Side Story" grows younger!

WEST SIDE STORY

"BEST PICTURE!" Winner of 10 Academy Awards! – 1961

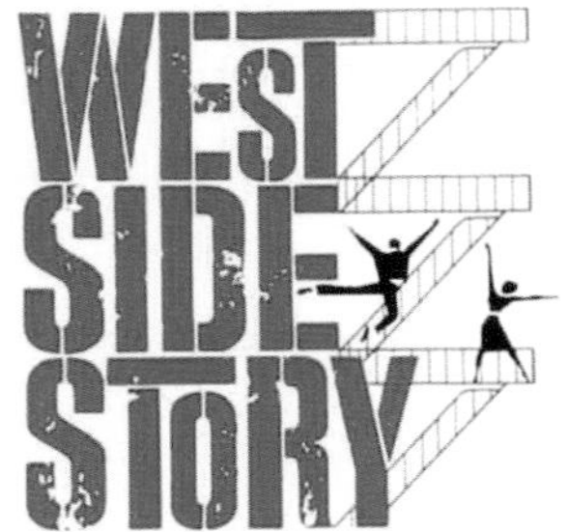

Whitney Williams of Variety wrote: "'West Side Story' is a beautifully-mounted, impressive, emotion-ridden and violent musical which, in its stark approach to a raging social problem and realism of unfoldment, may set a pattern for future musical presentations."

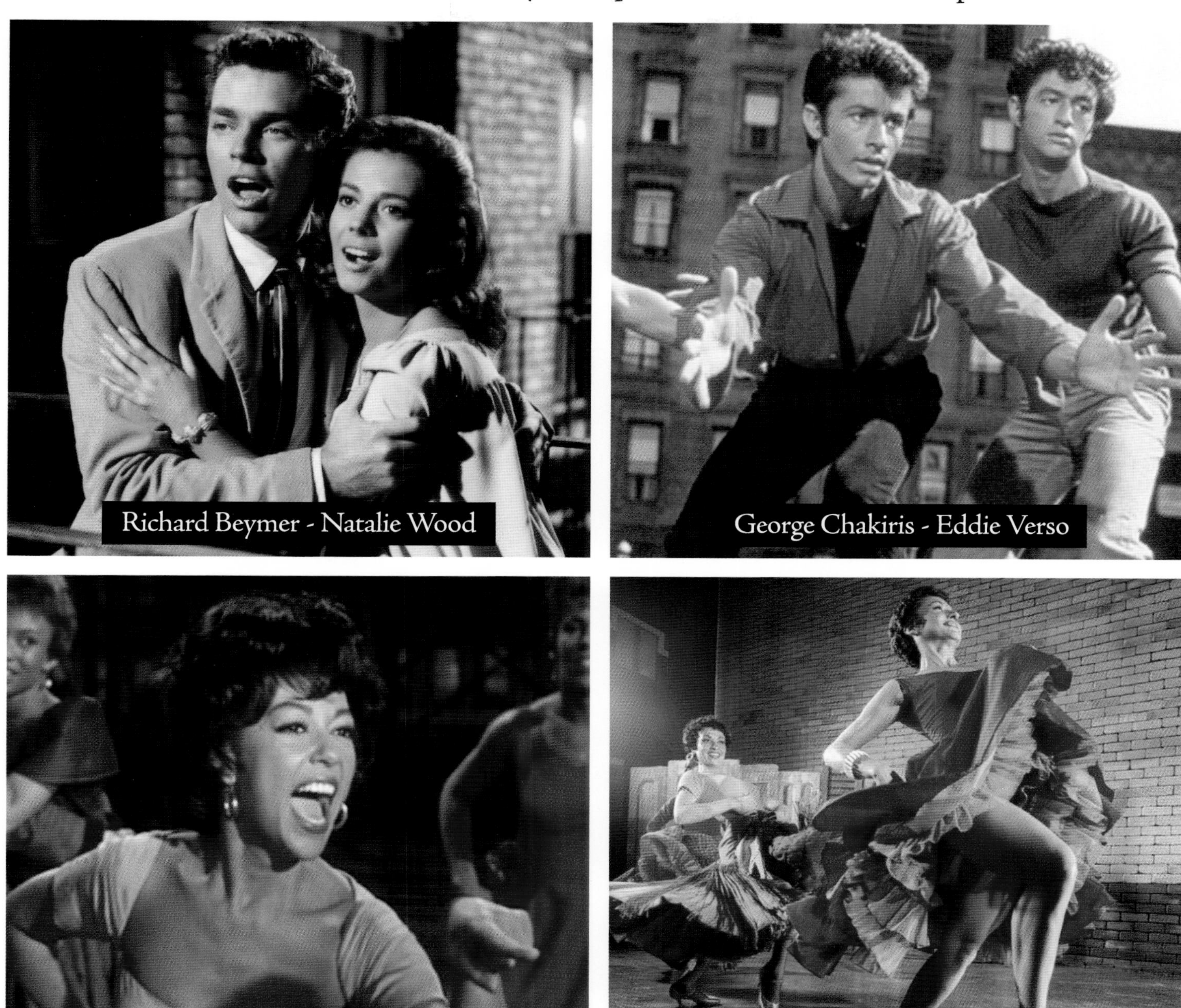

Richard Beymer - Natalie Wood

George Chakiris - Eddie Verso

Rita Moreno, In Film, 1962

Chita Rivera, B'way 1957

Natalie Wood and Richard Beymer were perfectly cast as the ill-fated lovers. George Chakiris, as Bernardo, leader of the "Sharks," won an Academy Award for Best Supporting Actor.

Jerome Robbins choreographed the dances that featured Rita Moreno. Documentaries were made on the lives of Rita Moreno and Chita Rivera, who played the role on Broadway.

If you haven't seen the documentaries on the careers of Rita Moreno and Chita Rivera, get copies of them, invite some friends over and you'll thank me.

A British team is sent to cross occupied Greek territory and destroy the massive German gun emplacement that commands a key sea channel.

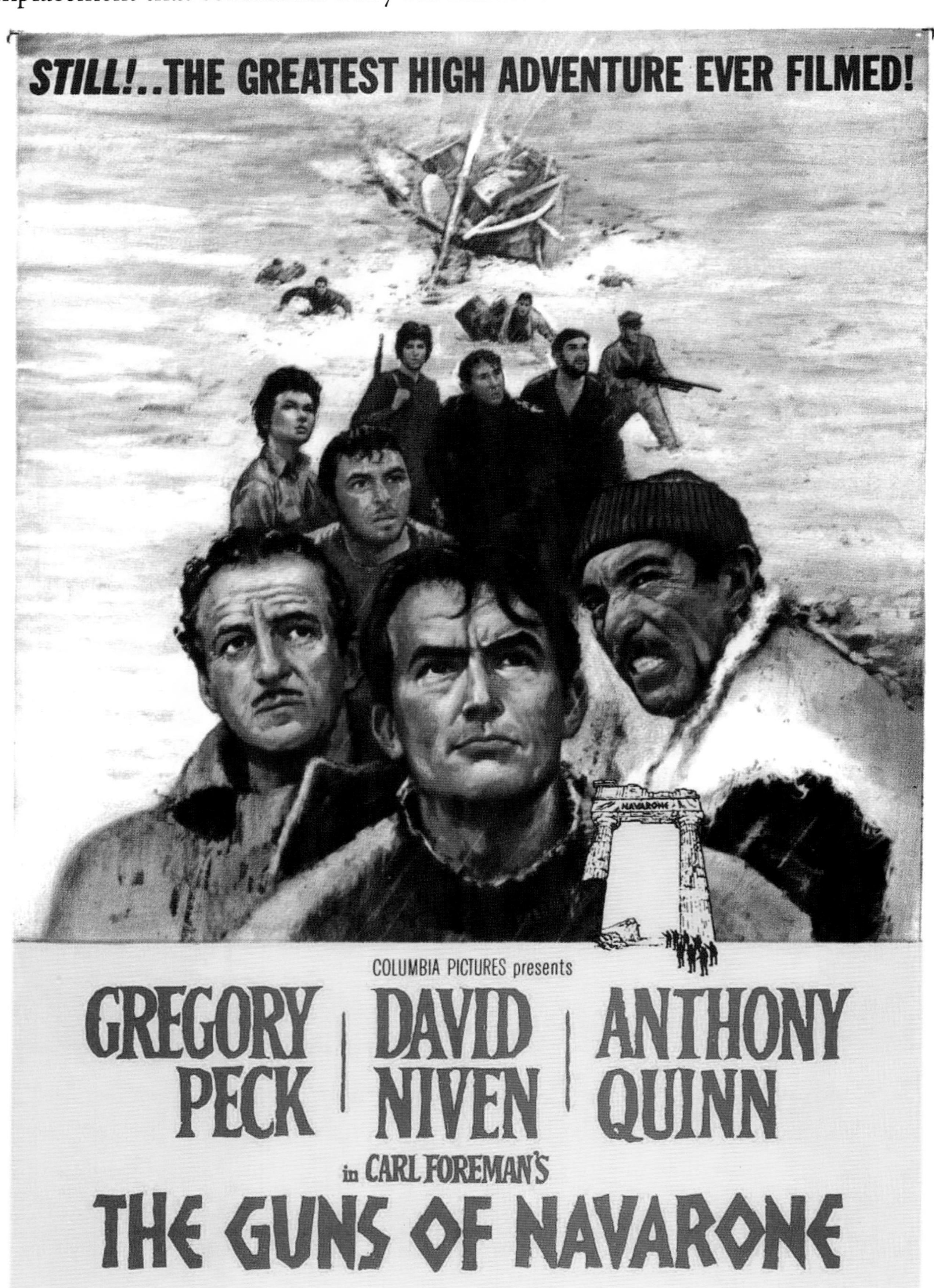

Emanuel Levy wrote: "One of the best WWII action-adventures, with an all-star cast headed by Gregory Peck, Anthony Quinn, and David Niven."

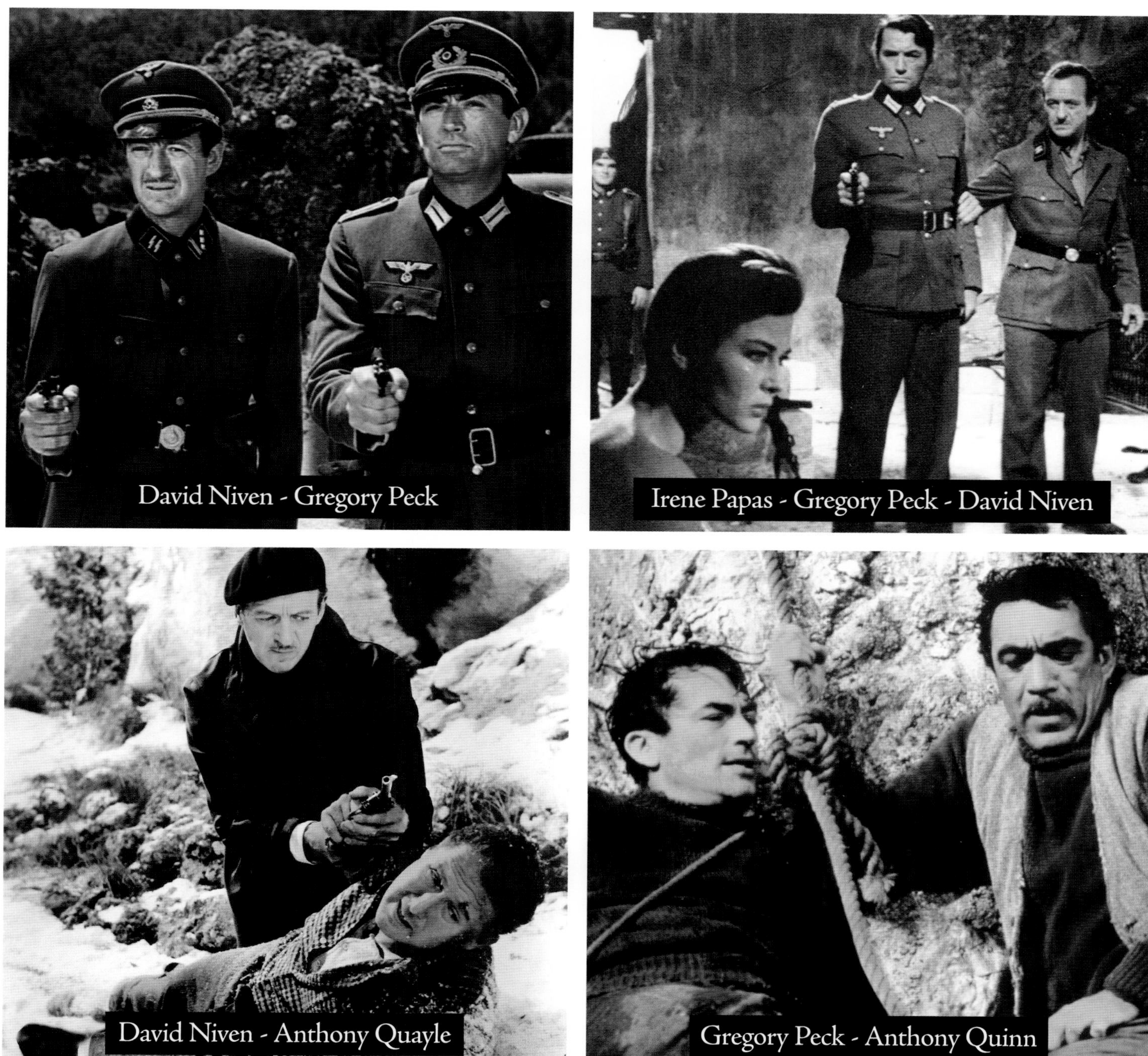

David Niven - Gregory Peck

Irene Papas - Gregory Peck - David Niven

David Niven - Anthony Quayle

Gregory Peck - Anthony Quinn

That "all-star cast" helped it become the top grossing film of 1961–twenty-nine million dollars.

I had the good fortune to meet David Niven when I did a supporting role in "Happy Anniversary," which starred him and Mitzi Gaynor. One day Niven happily commented, "This is the life... we get to eat lunch in a dining room. If we were in 'Lawrence of Arabia' we'd be in the desert eating sandwiches full of sand. Got to tell my agent this is the kind of quiet role I prefer."

His agent probably turned a deaf ear, for Niven's next job was a role in a very noisy film, "The Guns of Navarone."

The story of T.E. Lawrence, the English officer who successfully united and led the diverse, often warring, Arab tribes during World War I in order to fight the Turks.

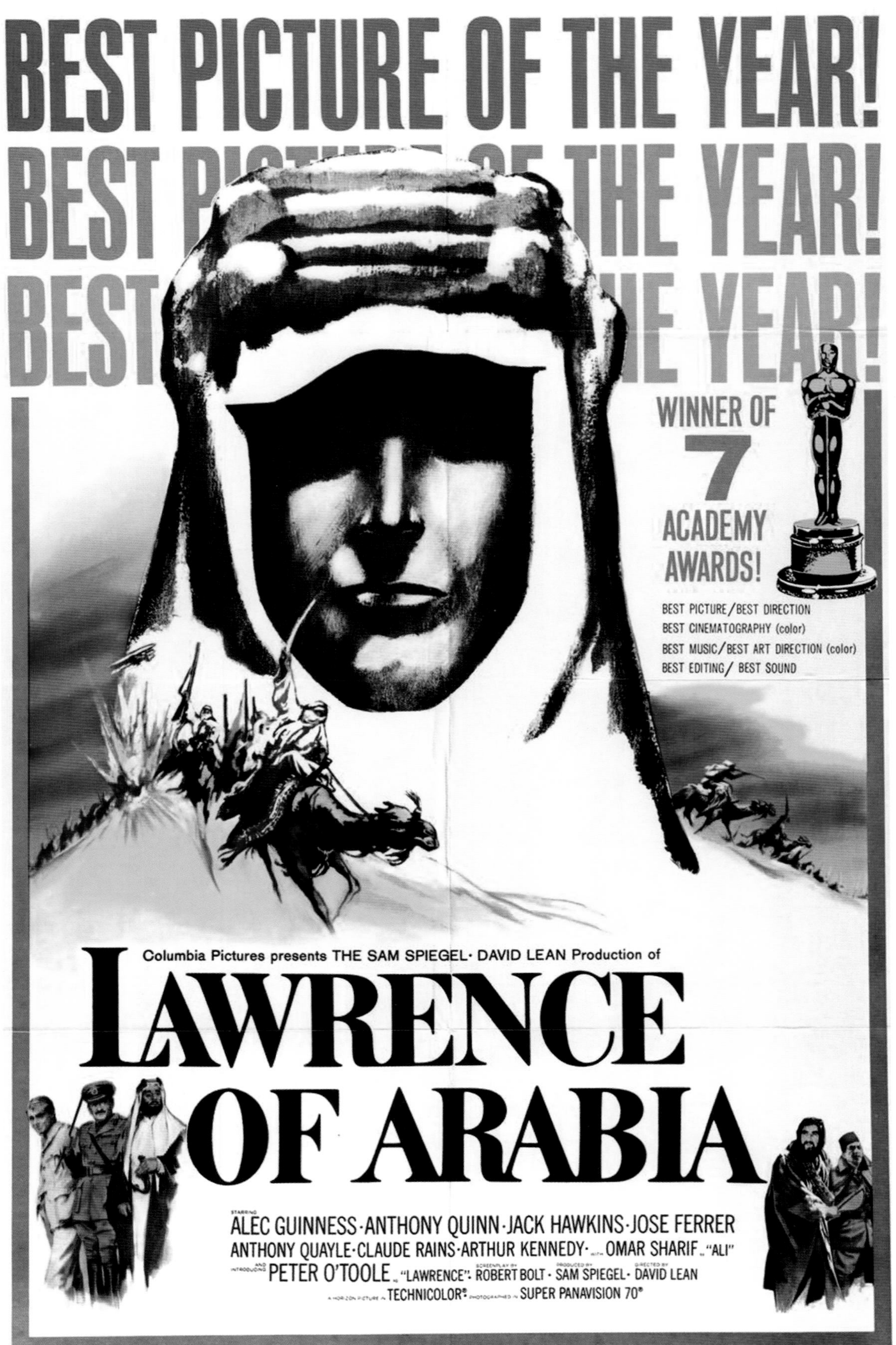

Time Magazine wrote: "It is O'Toole who continually dominates the screen, and he dominates it with professional skill, Irish charm and smashing good looks."

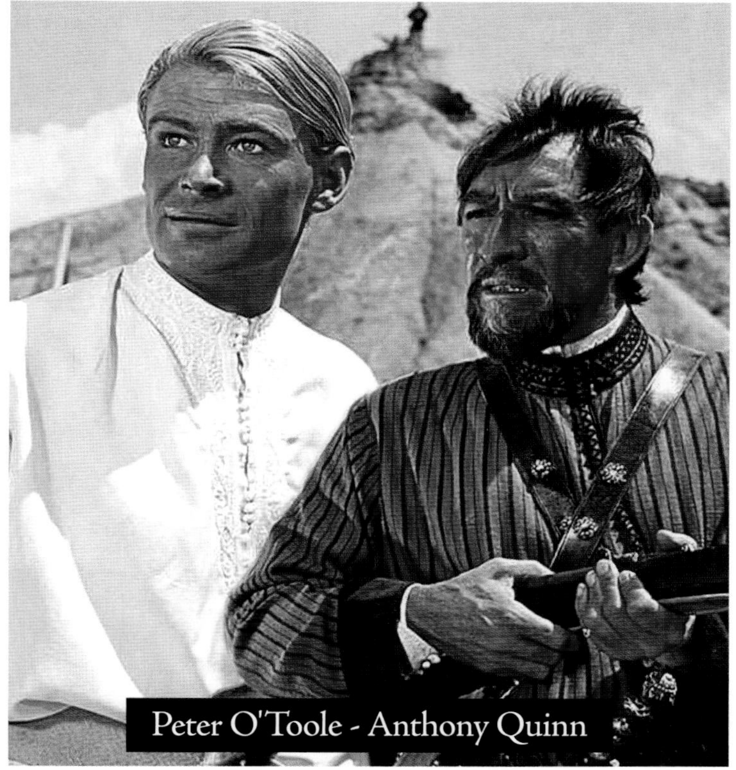

Peter O'Toole - Anthony Quinn

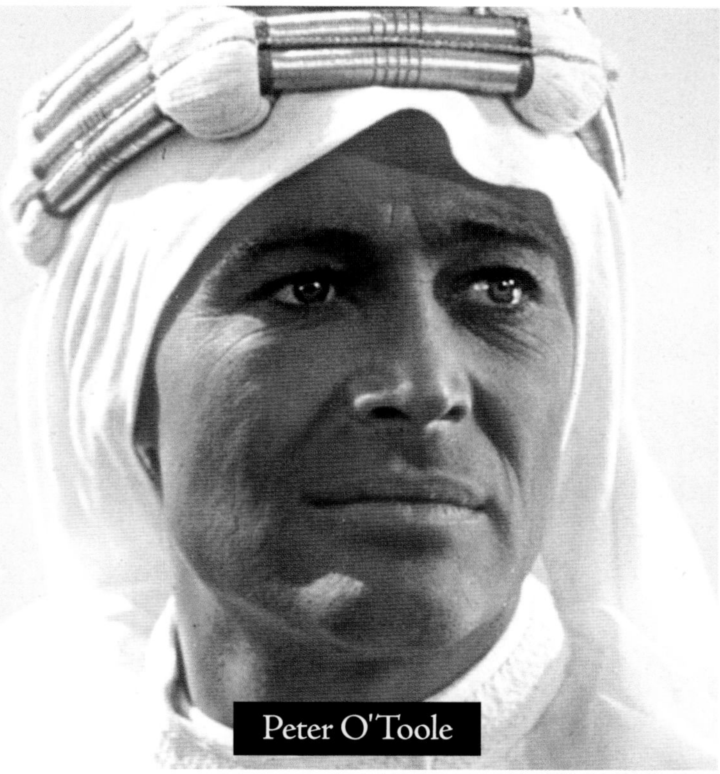

Peter O'Toole

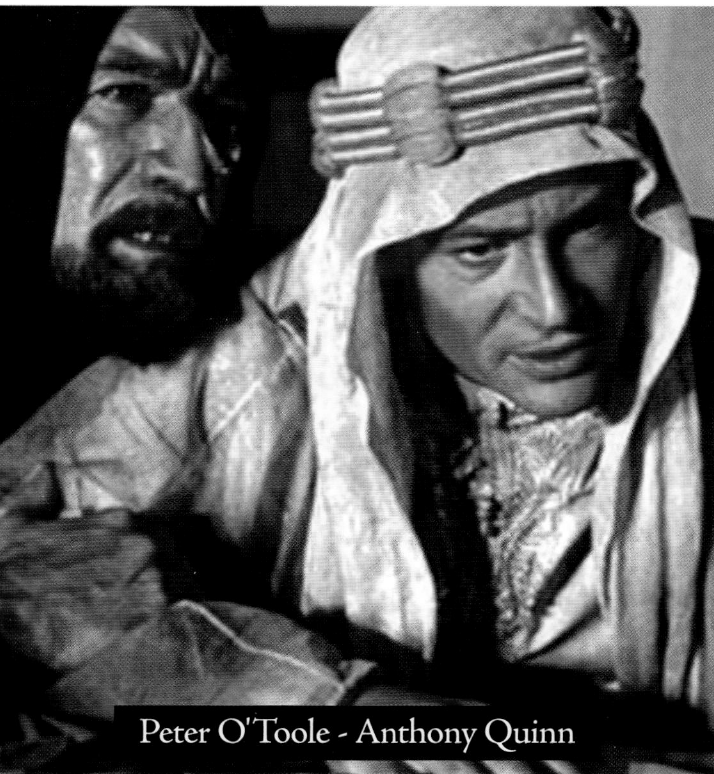

Peter O'Toole - Anthony Quinn

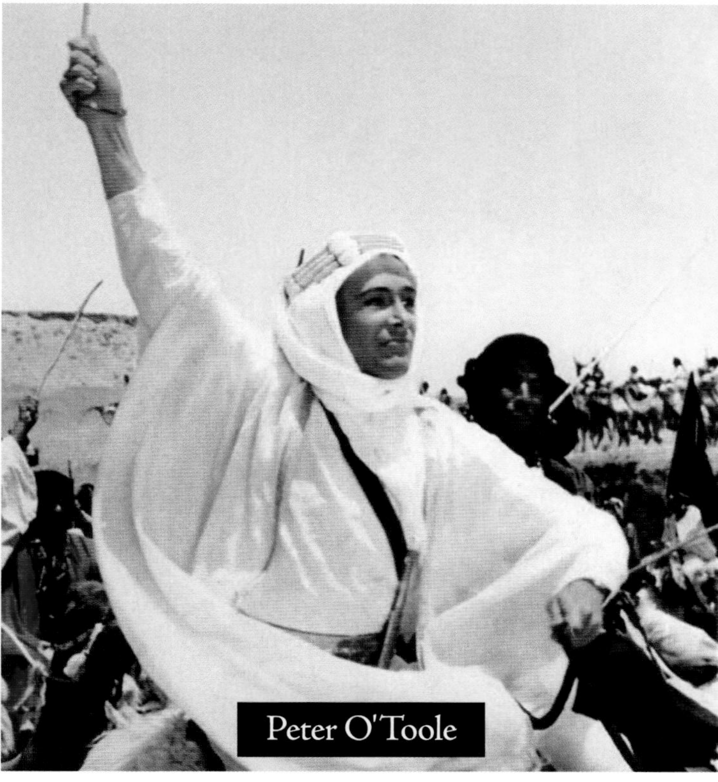

Peter O'Toole

The director, David Lean, unsure of himself, locked himself in his apartment because he was afraid he had made a bad film, and they had to break the door down in order to bring him the news that his film had grossed seventy million dollars and received great reviews.

Anne Sullivan's struggle to teach the blind and deaf Helen Keller how to communicate.

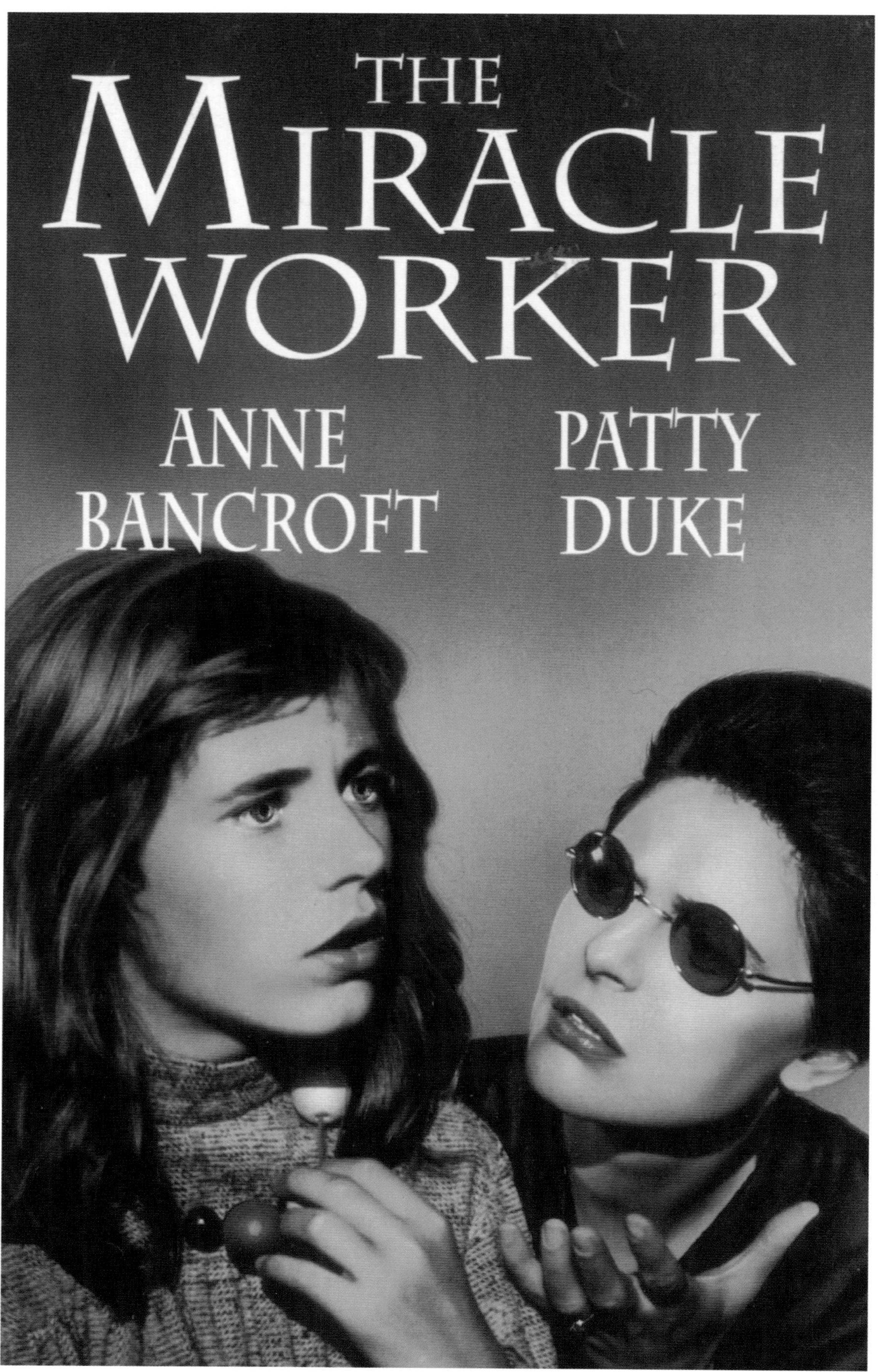

Don Druker of Chicago Reader wrote: "In William Gibson's 'The Miracle Worker,' Anne Bancroft is superb as Annie Sullivan, the teacher who finally reached into Helen Keller's darkness, and Patty Duke is chillingly real as the young Helen."

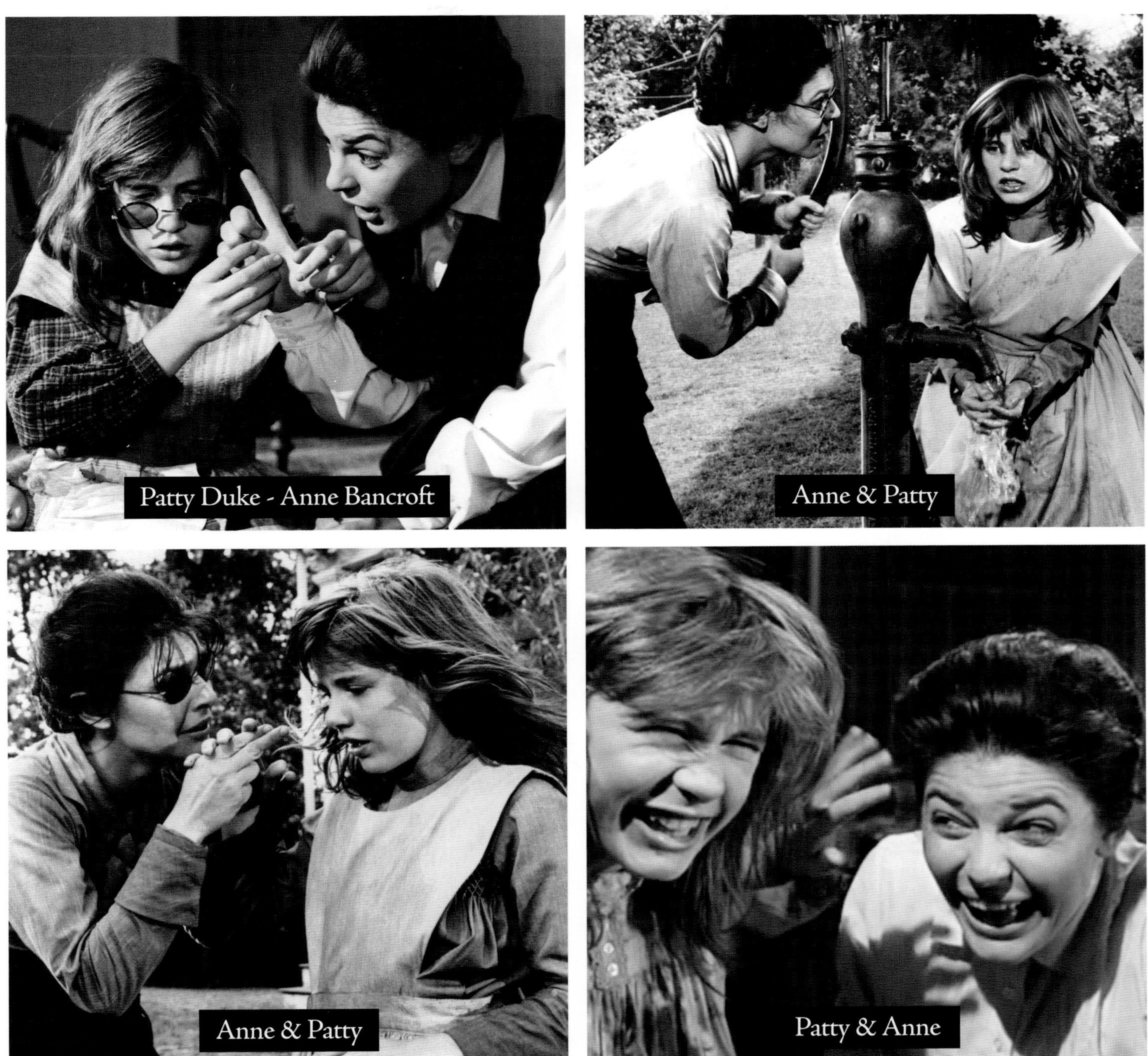

Patty Duke - Anne Bancroft

Anne & Patty

Anne & Patty

Patty & Anne

I was so moved when I saw Anne Bancroft and Patty Duke perform this on Broadway and even more moved when I saw the film, which allowed me to see, close-up, the torture and elation in their expressive faces.

I first saw Anne Bancroft perform, in 1958, on Broadway in "Two for the Seesaw," and I was, to coin a phrase, "blown away." In 1962, the crime of the century was committed when another actress was signed to play the role for which Anne Bancroft had won a Tony Award.

Harold Hill poses as a boys' band leader to con naive Iowa townsfolk.

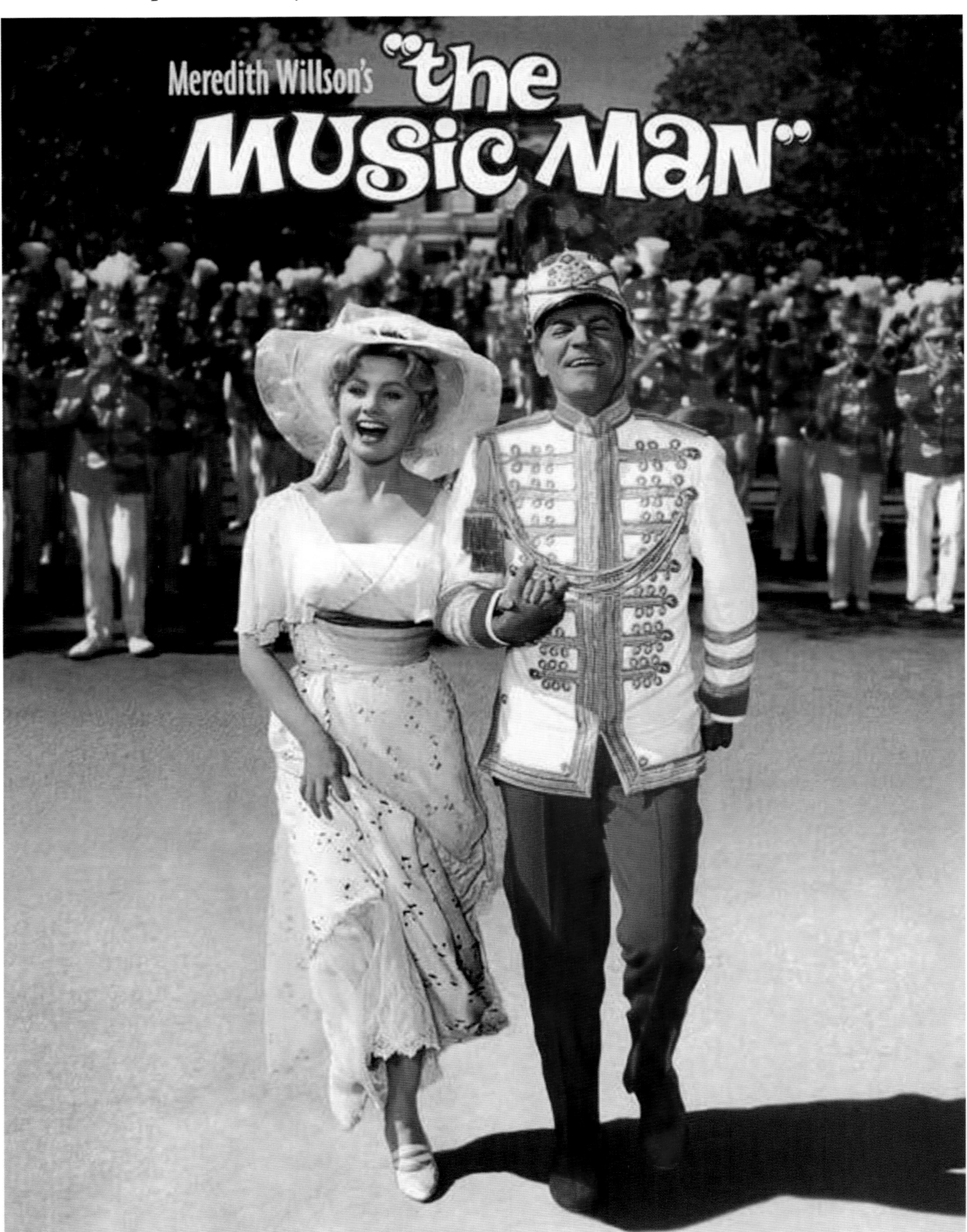

John J. Puccio of Movie Metropolis wrote: "A quintessential slice of Americana, featuring wonderful music, engaging characters, and an uplifting story."

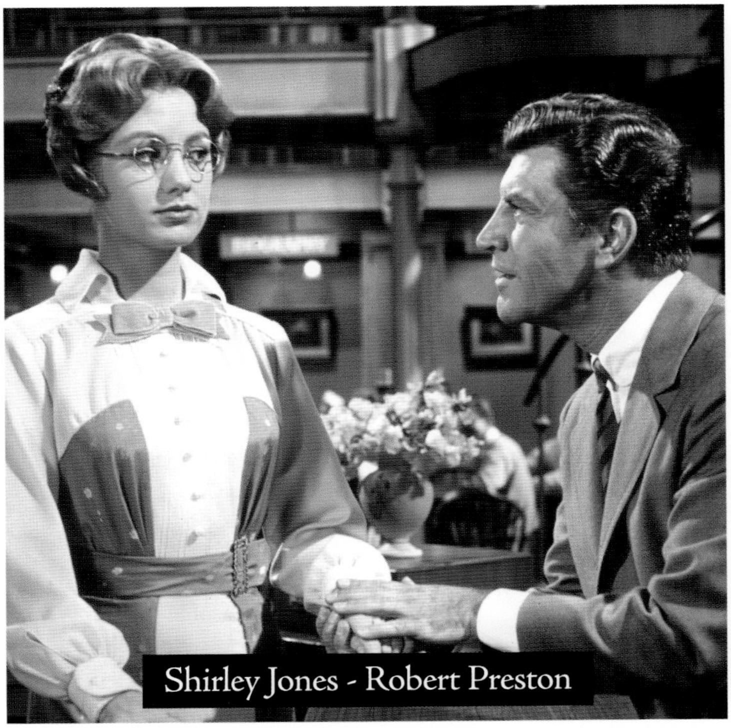

Shirley Jones - Robert Preston

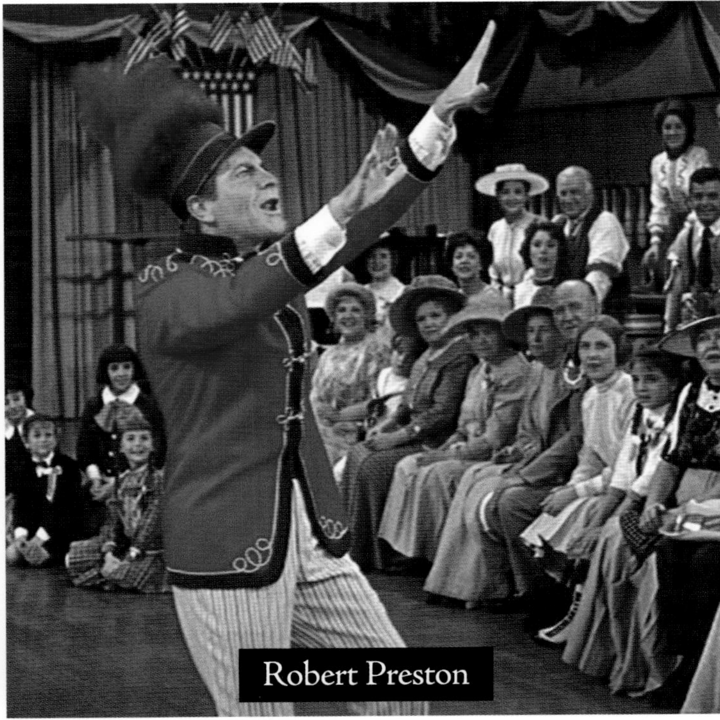
Robert Preston

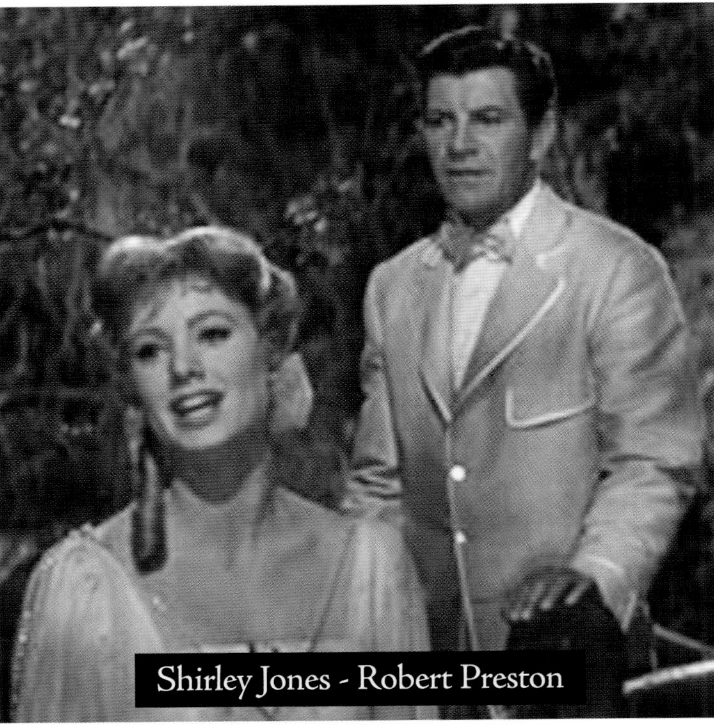
Shirley Jones - Robert Preston

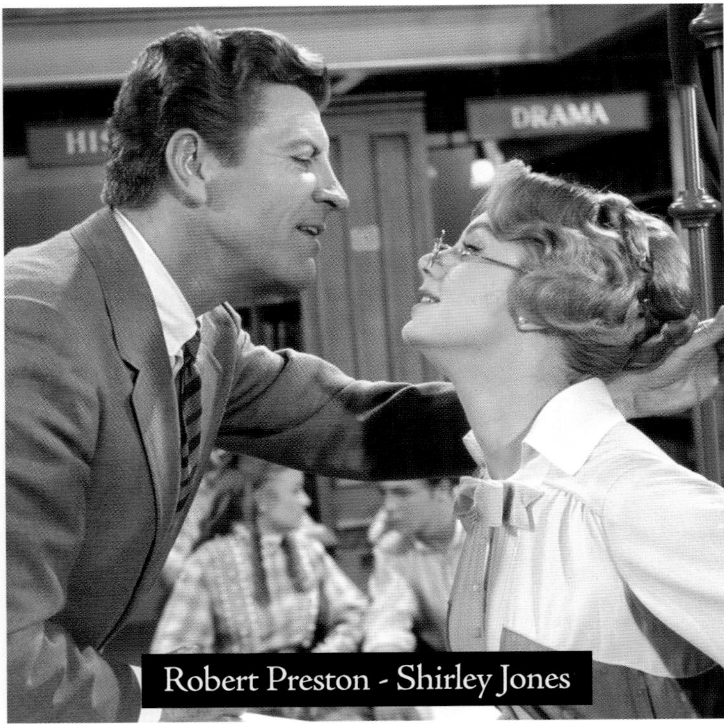

Robert Preston - Shirley Jones

"The Music Man," which co-starred Robert Preston and Barbara Cook, opened on Broadway in 1957 and remained there for three years. Preston remained with the musical for its entire run which ended in 1961 after 1,375-performances. He then went on to reprise his role as Harold Hill in the 1962 screen adaptation which co-starred Shirley Jones. Shirley's beautiful voice and presence and Preston's performances touched the hearts of all musical-loving Americans.

Atticus Finch, a lawyer in the Depression-era South, defends a black man against an undeserved rape charge, and his children against prejudice.

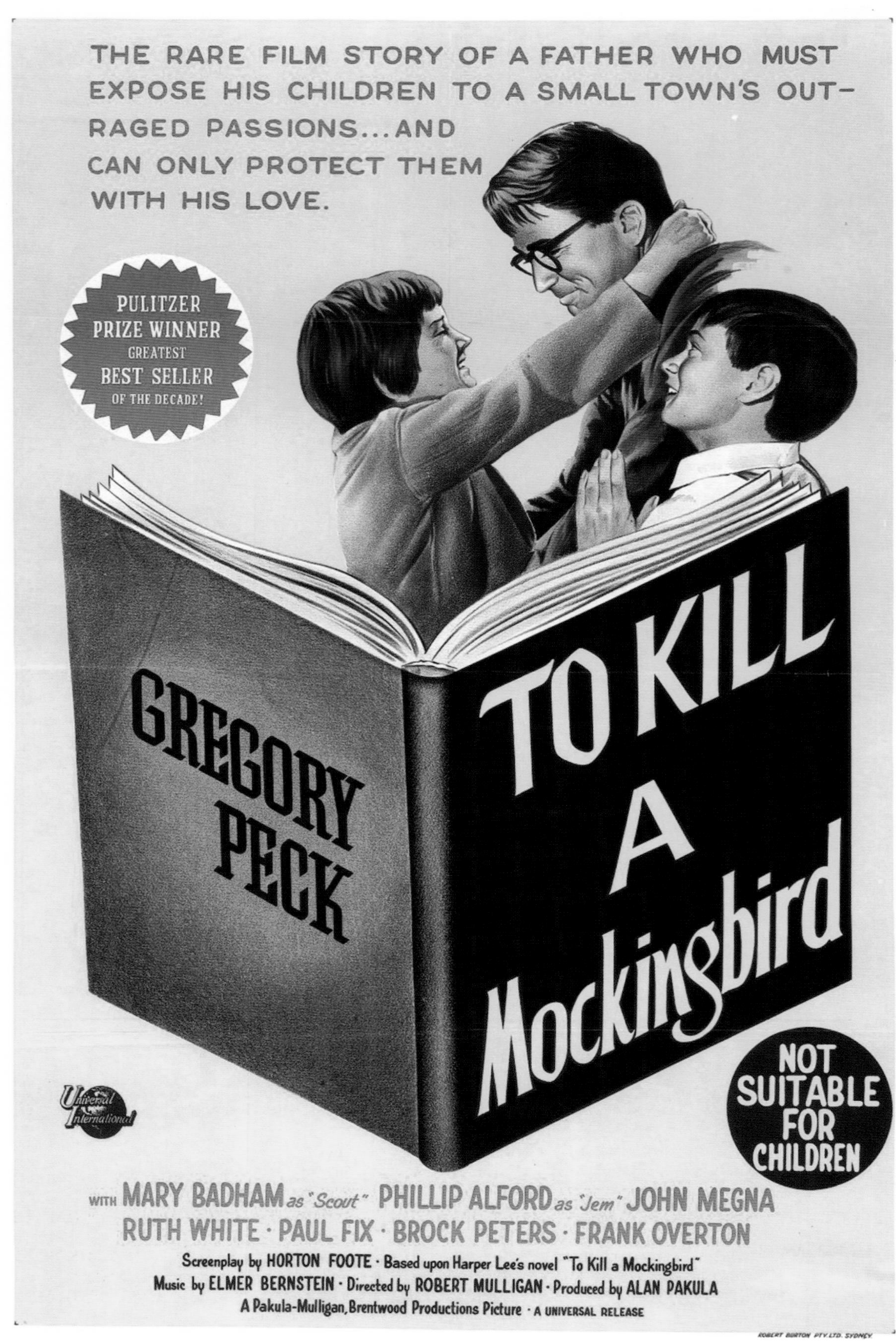

James Powers of Hollywood Reporter wrote: "'To Kill A Mockingbird' is a product of American realism, and it is a rare and worthy treasure."

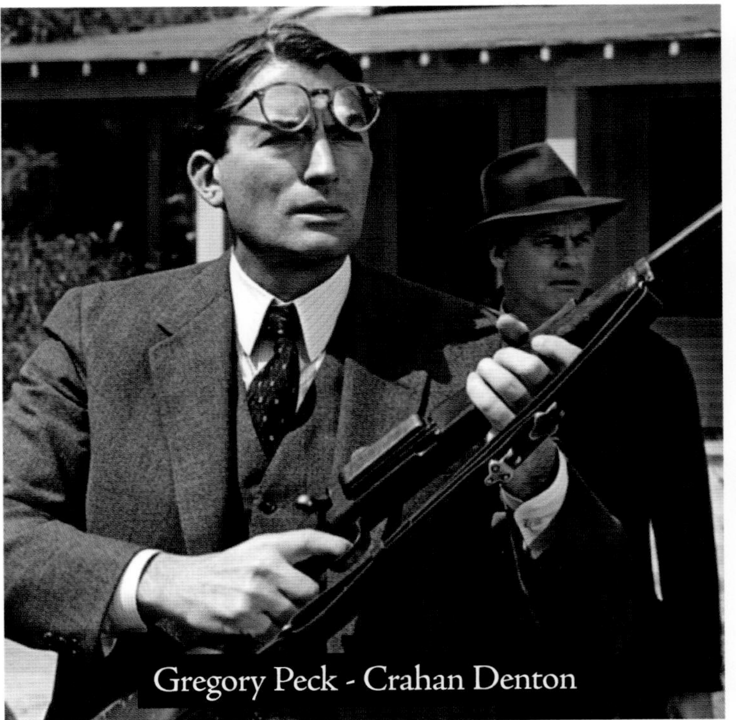
Gregory Peck - Crahan Denton

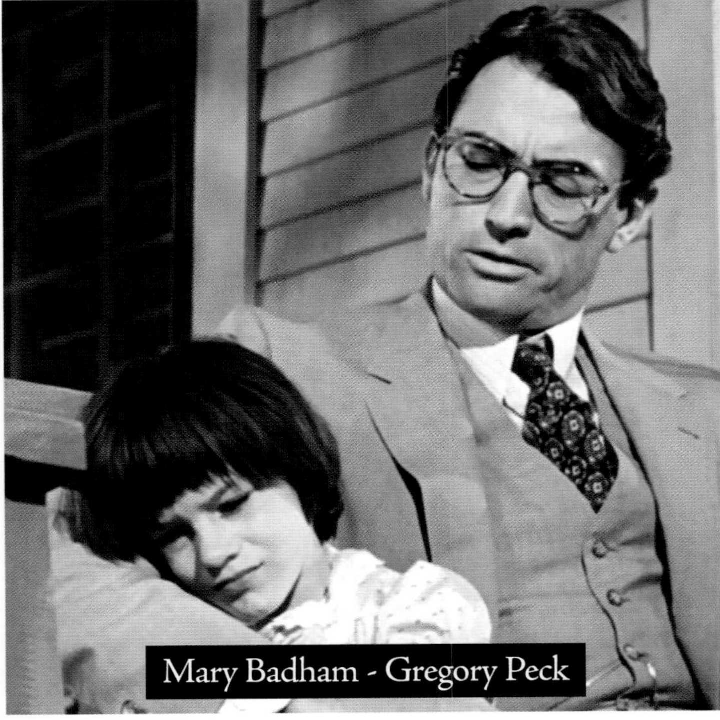
Mary Badham - Gregory Peck

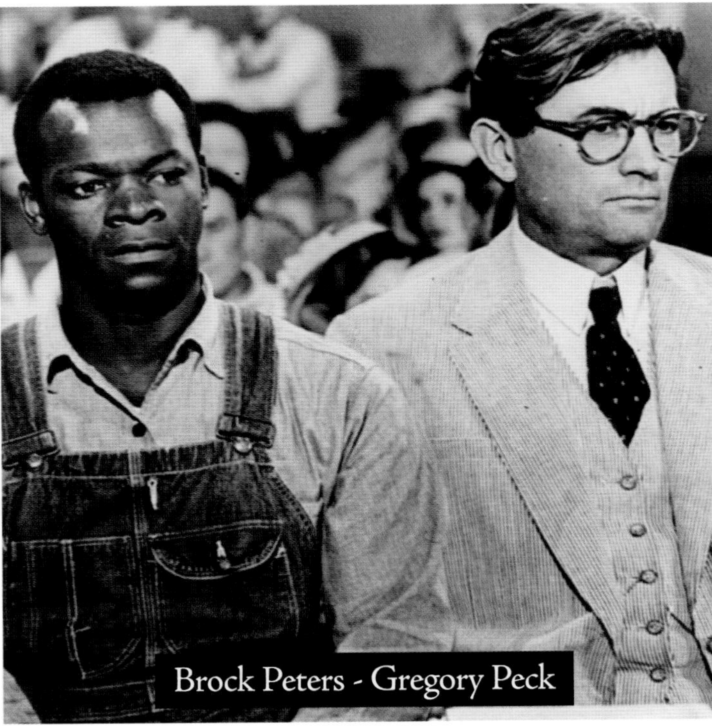
Brock Peters - Gregory Peck

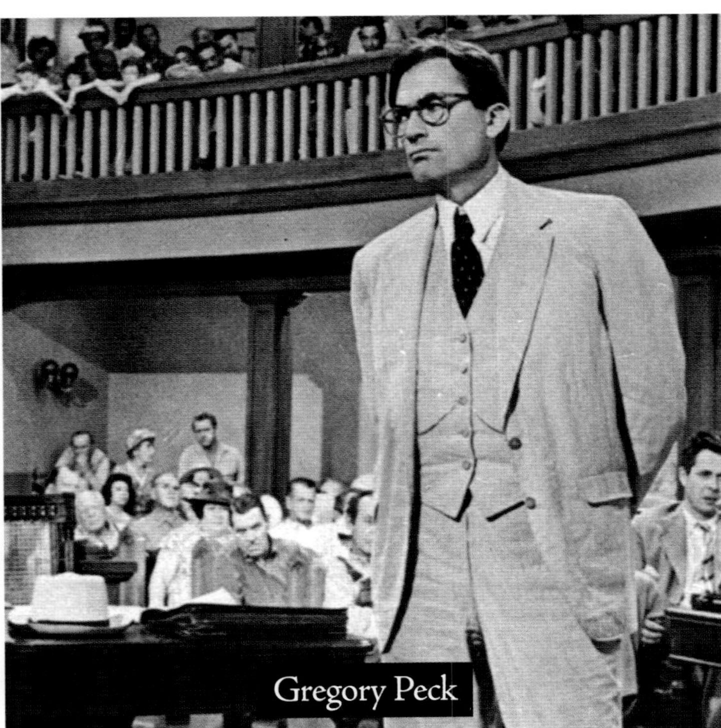
Gregory Peck

"To Kill a Mockingbird" deserved and received overwhelmingly positive reviews from critics. It was a box-office success, earning more than ten times its budget, winning three Academy Awards including Best Picture.

It dealt with the subject of racism that many left-wing, right-minded citizens felt needed to be addressed, and it was... well enough to change a few minds and laws.

A wealthy San Francisco socialite pursues a potential boyfriend to a small Northern California town that slowly takes a turn for the bizarre when birds suddenly begin to attack people.

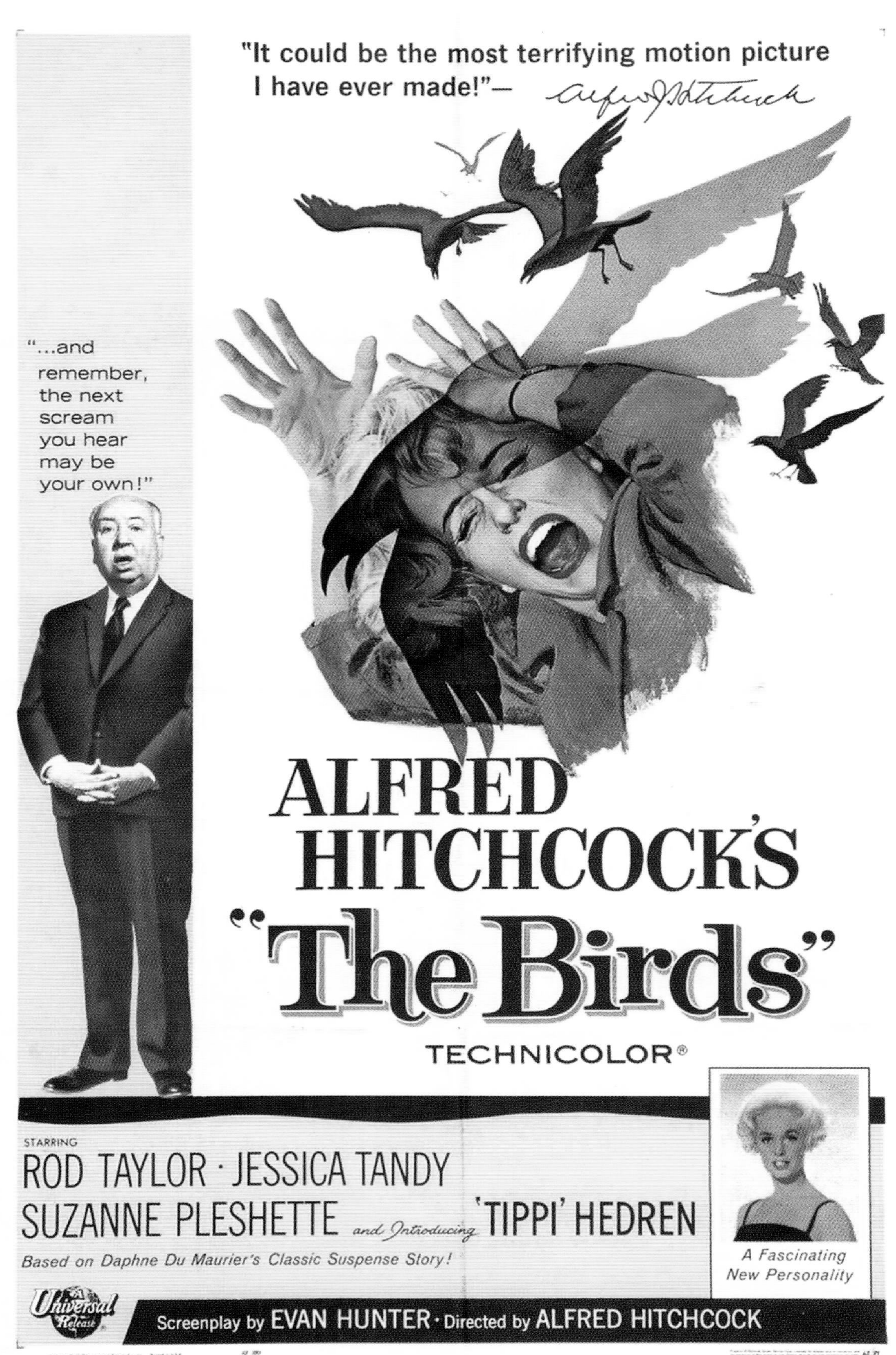

James Powers of The Hollywood Reporter wrote: "Hitchcock prolongs his prelude to horror for more than half the film, playing with audience suspense with comedy and romance while he sets his stage. The horror when it comes is a hair-raiser."

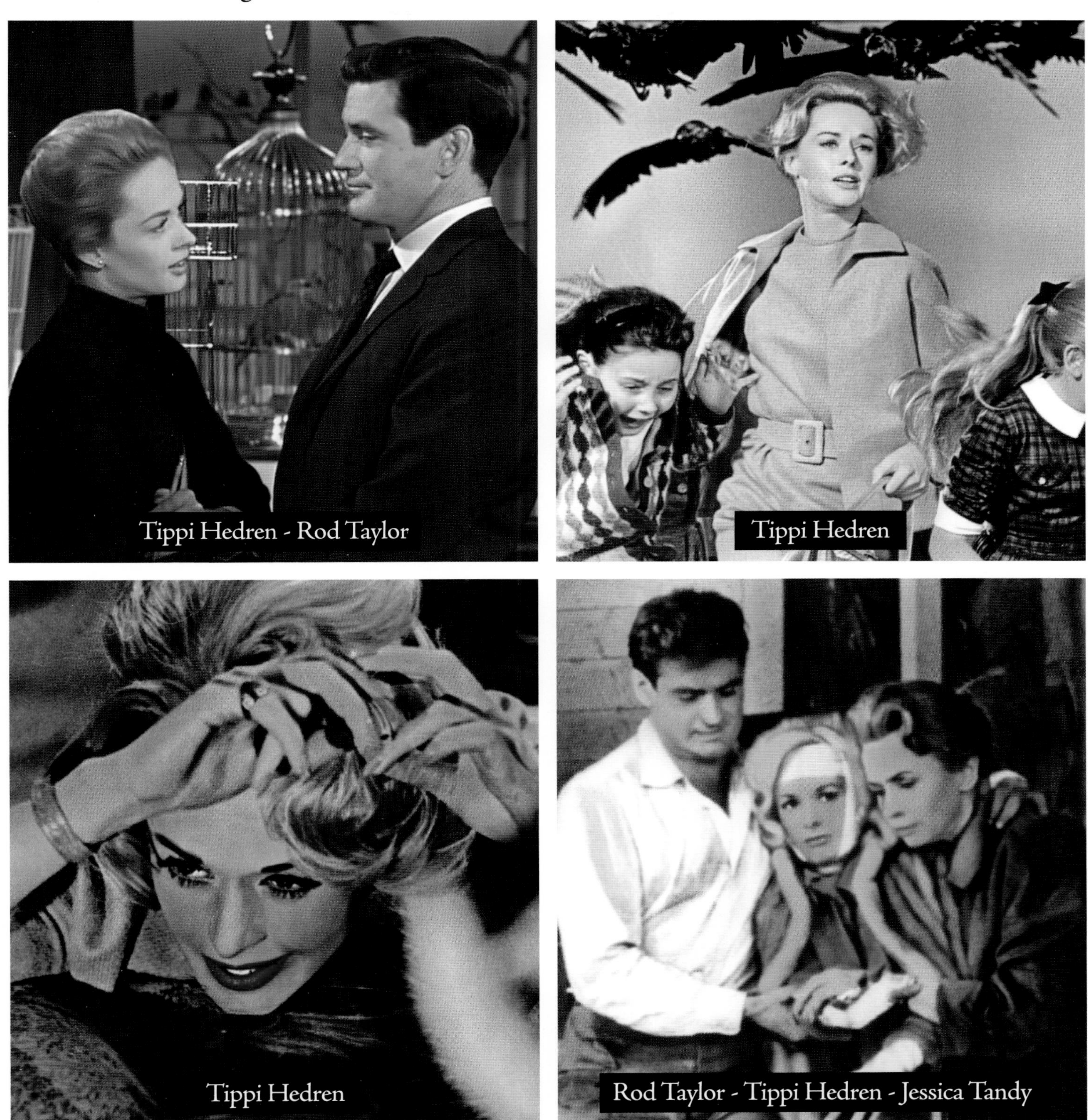

Tippi Hedren - Rod Taylor

Tippi Hedren

Tippi Hedren

Rod Taylor - Tippi Hedren - Jessica Tandy

Only Hitchcock could think of casting birds as murderous villains.

In 1968, I had the opportunity of campaigning with Tippi Hedren, Henry Fonda and other actors to support Lyndon Johnson's run for president... sadly, unsuccessfully.

Screenwriter Paul Javal's marriage to his wife Camille disintegrates during movie production as she spends time with the producer. Layered conflicts between art and business ensue.

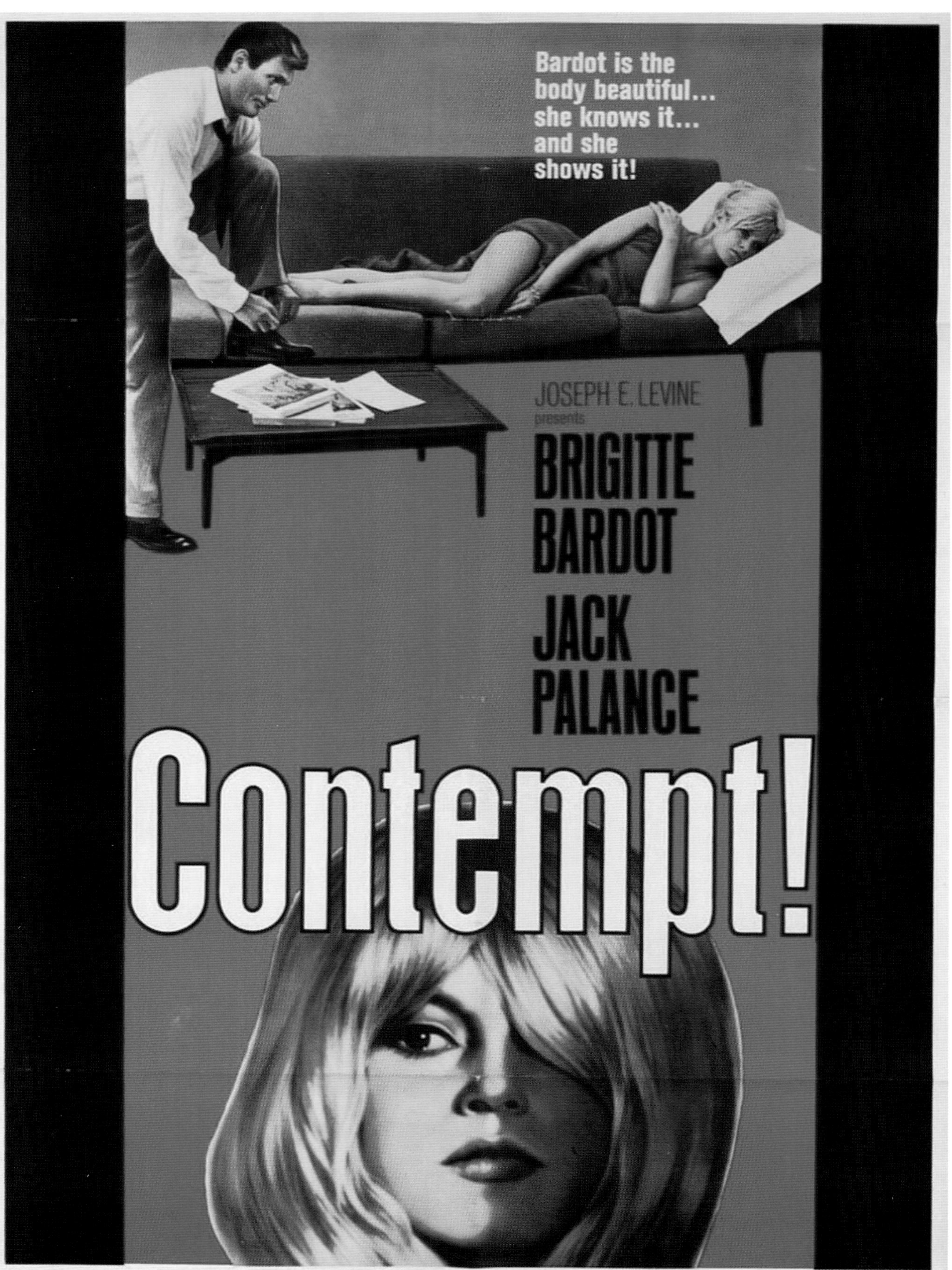

Stephanie Zacharek of The Village Voice wrote: "Possibly Godard's most melancholy film and probably his most beautiful."

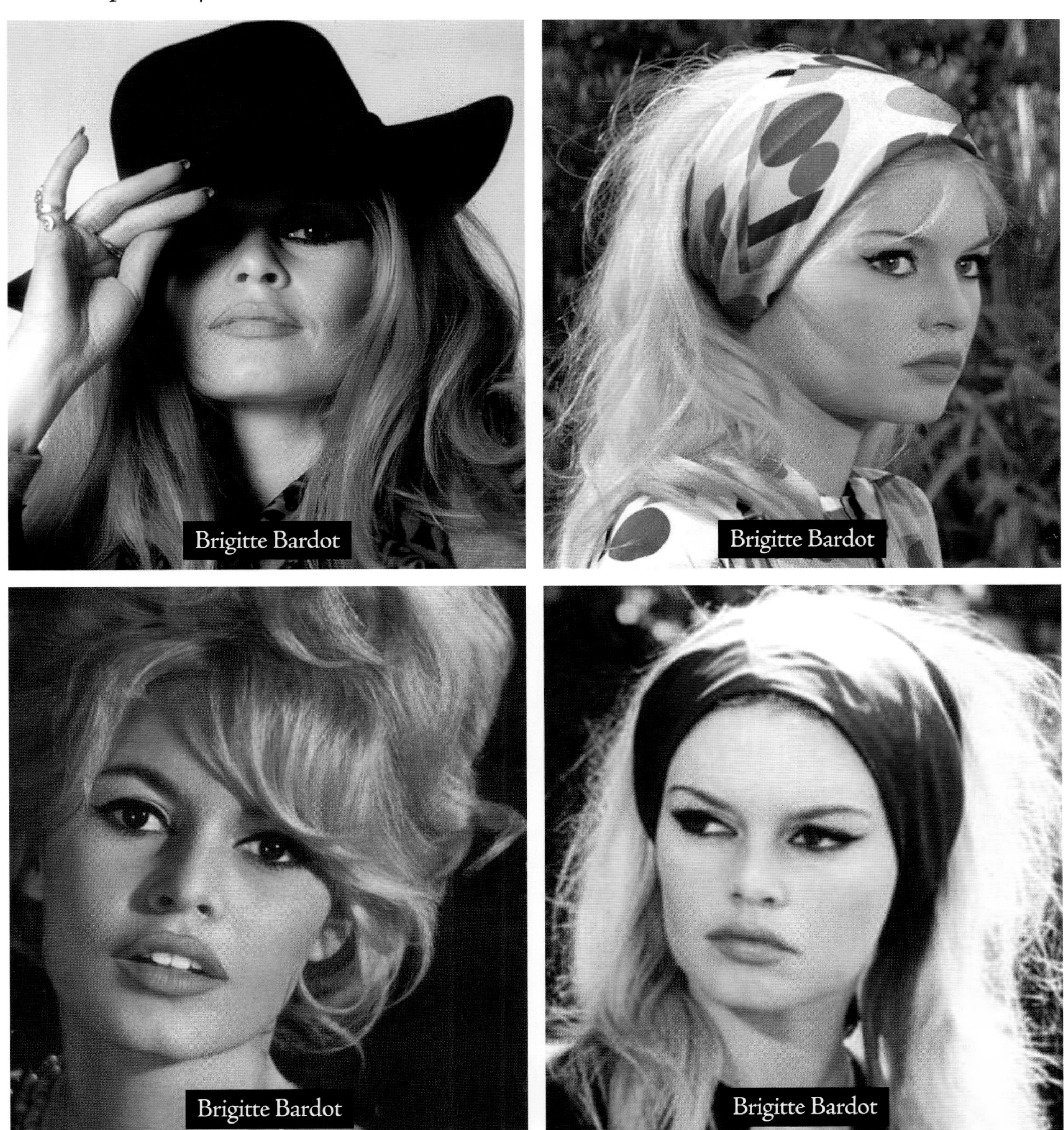

Brigitte Bardot

Brigitte Bardot

Brigitte Bardot

Brigitte Bardot

There is not one frame in the thirty-seven films that starred the beautiful, blonde-haired, brown-eyed Brigitte Bardot in which she was not lusted after by every red-blooded man and envied by every pink-blooded woman.

An insane general triggers a path to nuclear holocaust that a war room full of politicians and generals frantically try to stop.

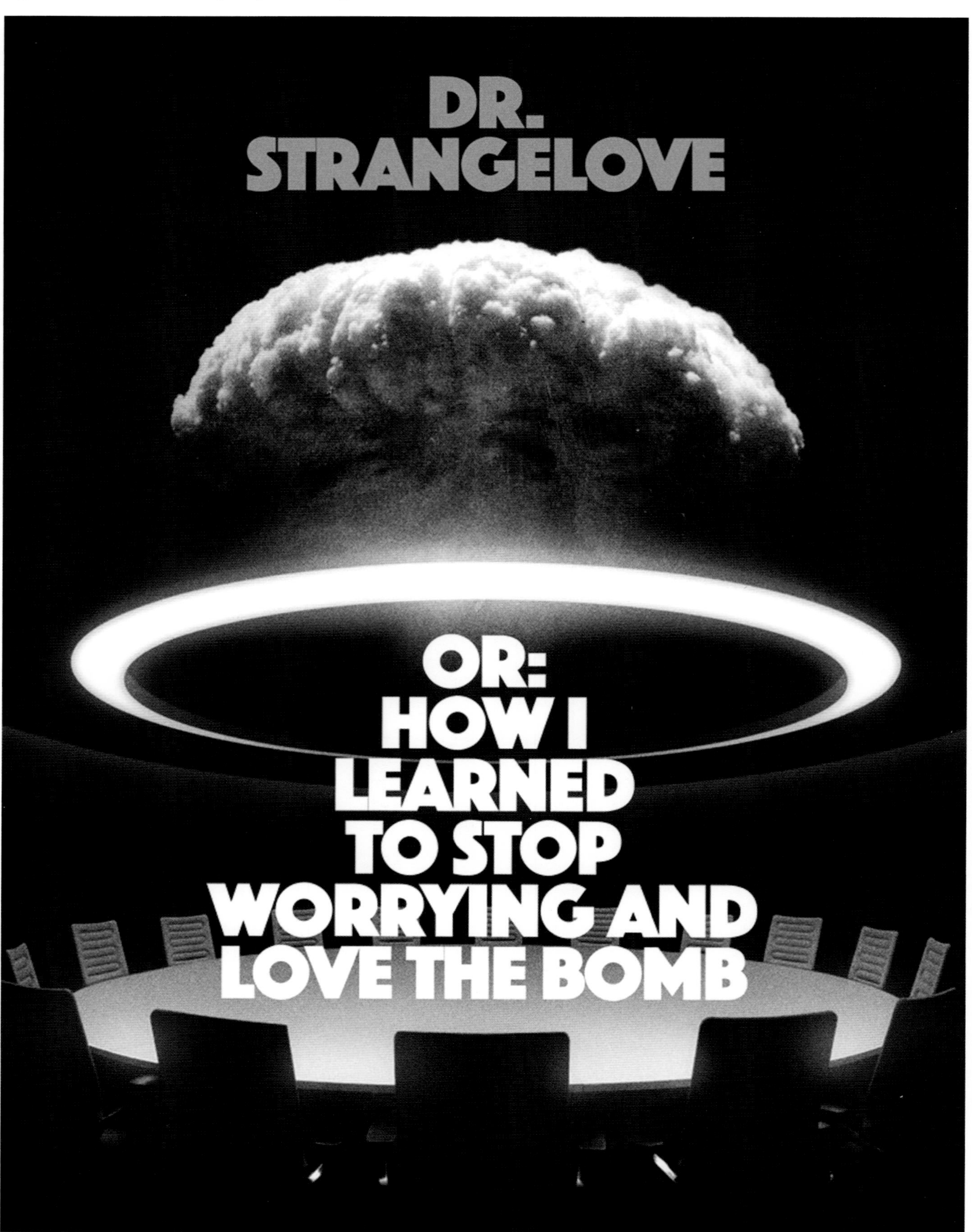

Geoff Andrew of Time Out wrote: "Perhaps Kubrick's most perfectly realized film, simply because his cynical vision of the progress of technology and human stupidity is wedded with comedy."

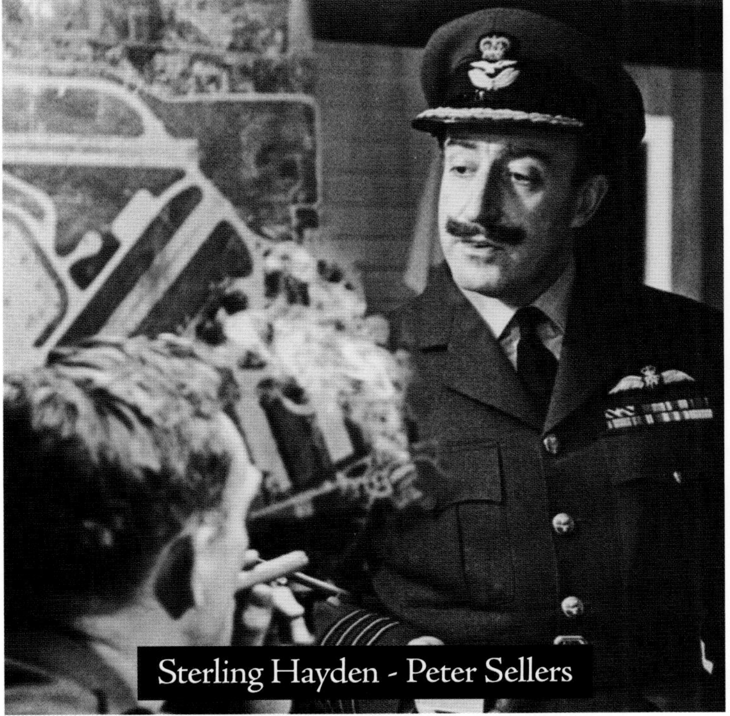
Sterling Hayden - Peter Sellers

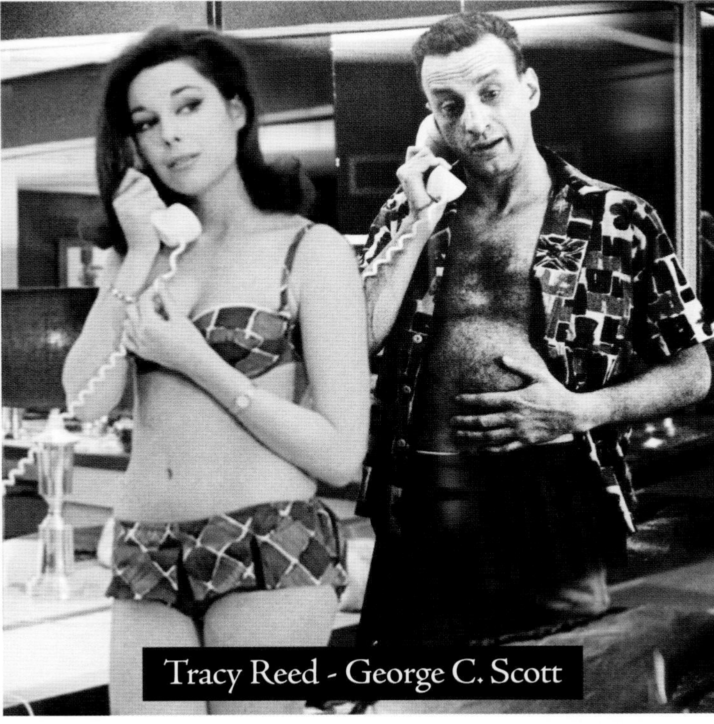
Tracy Reed - George C. Scott

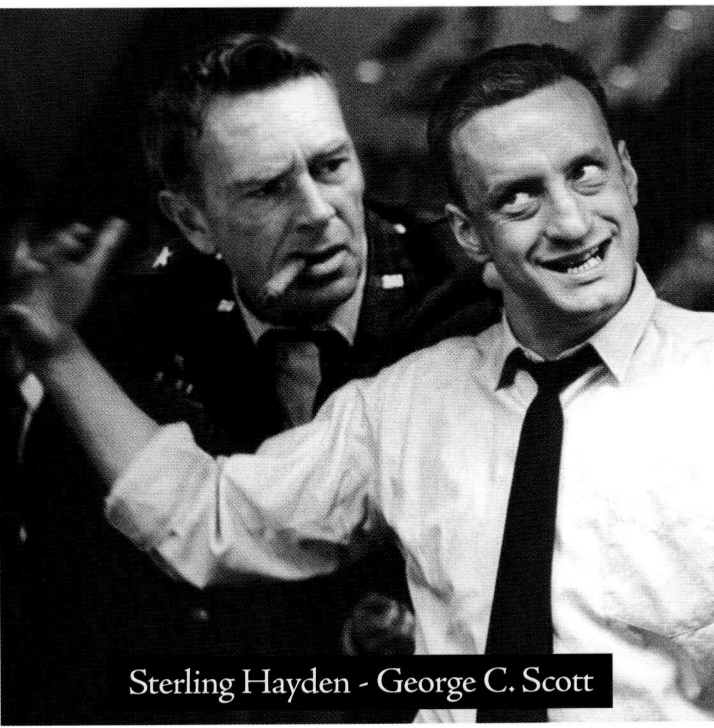
Sterling Hayden - George C. Scott

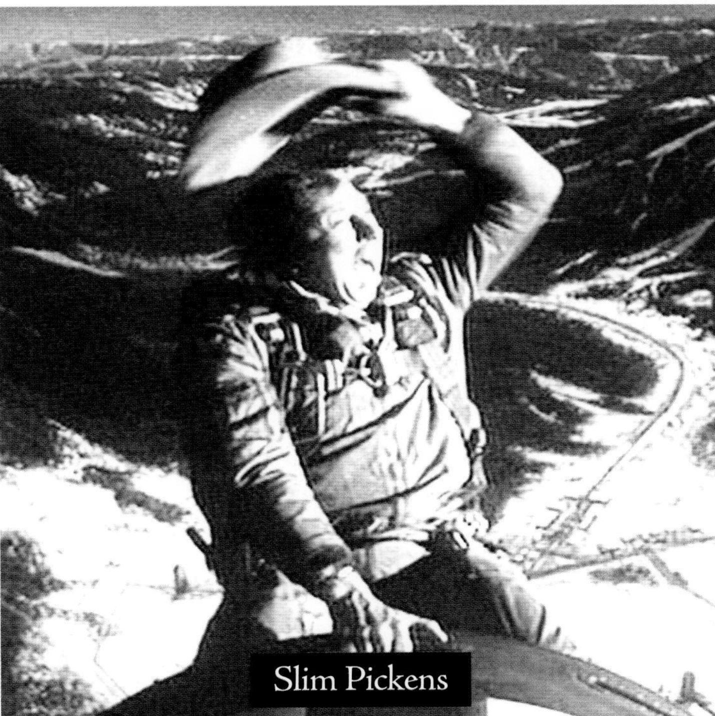
Slim Pickens

I'm happy to say that, so far, Slim Pickens falling to earth astride an atomic bomb has not become a reality... and, prayerfully, never will.

I doubt you'll find any devoté of film who will not agree that the single most versatile comic performer in the industry was Peter Sellers. To remind you of his brilliance, simply watch the seven films in which he portrayed master detective, Inspector Jacques Clouseau.

In turn of the century London, a magical nanny employs music and adventure to help two neglected children become closer to their father.

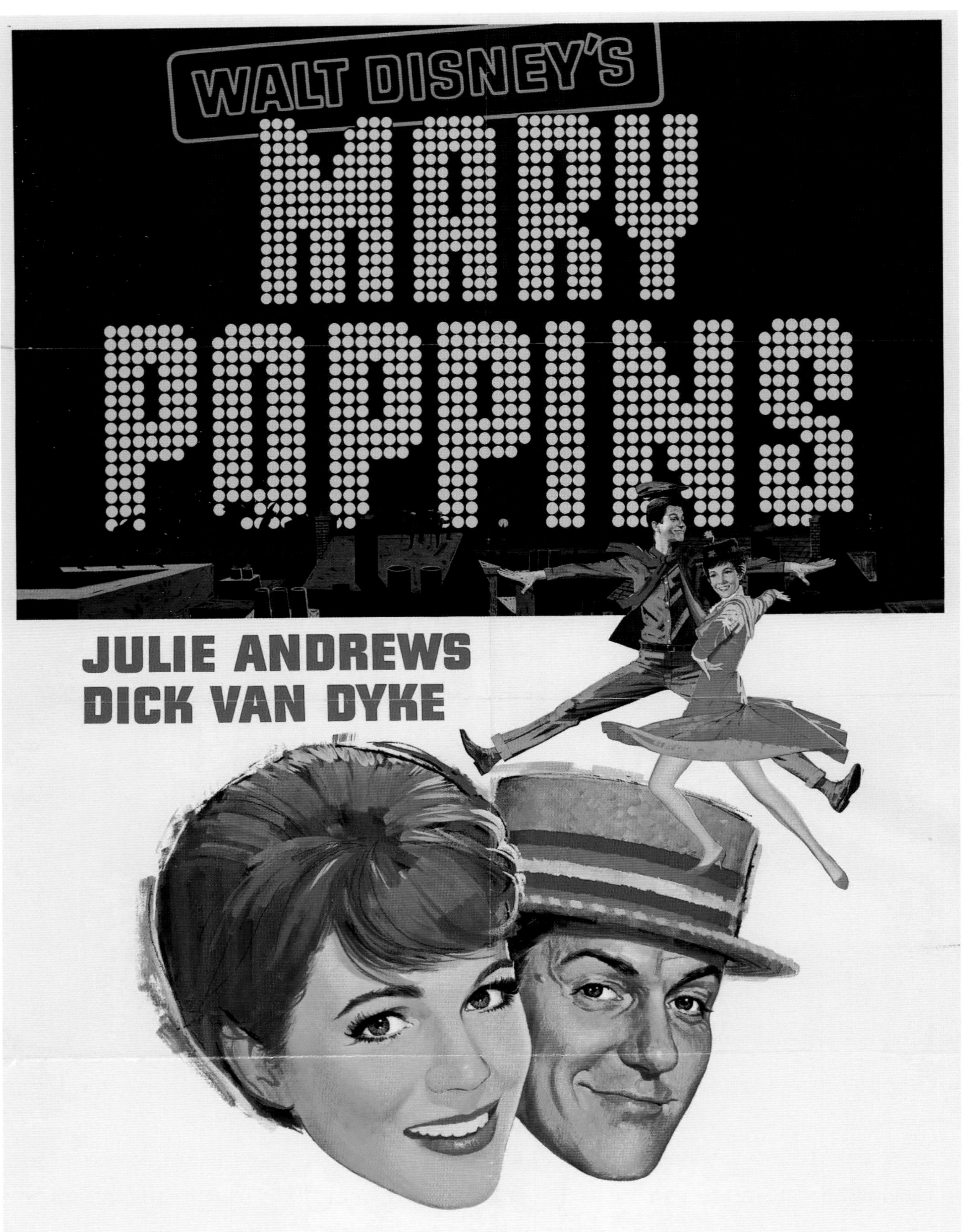

Variety wrote: "Julie Andrews' first appearance on the screen is a signal triumph and she performs as easily as she sings, displaying a fresh beauty nicely adaptable to the color cameras."

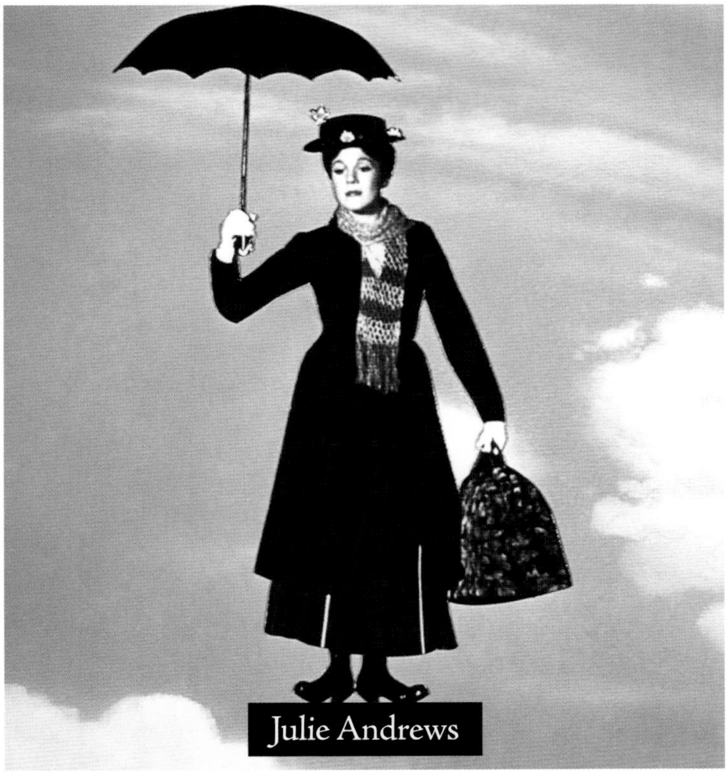

Julie Andrews

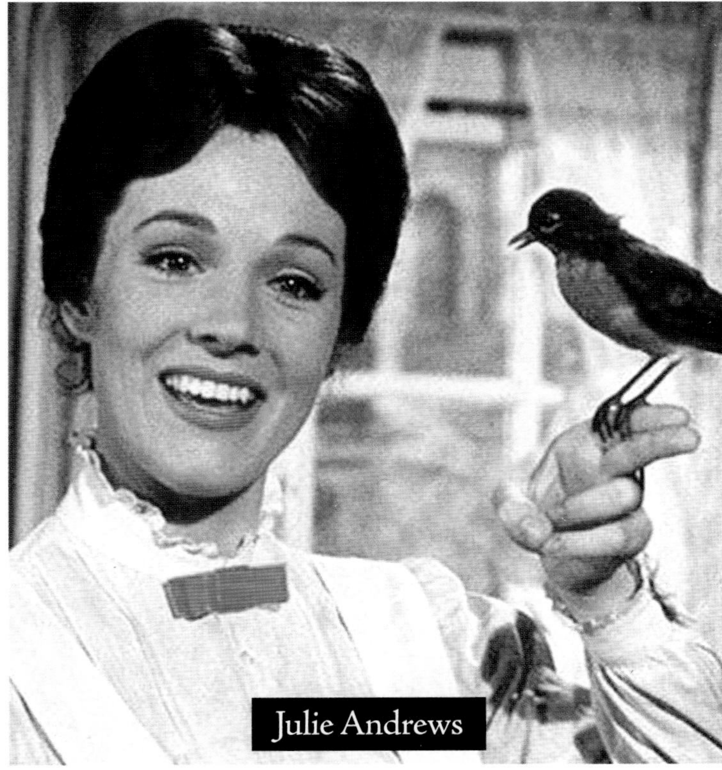

Julie Andrews

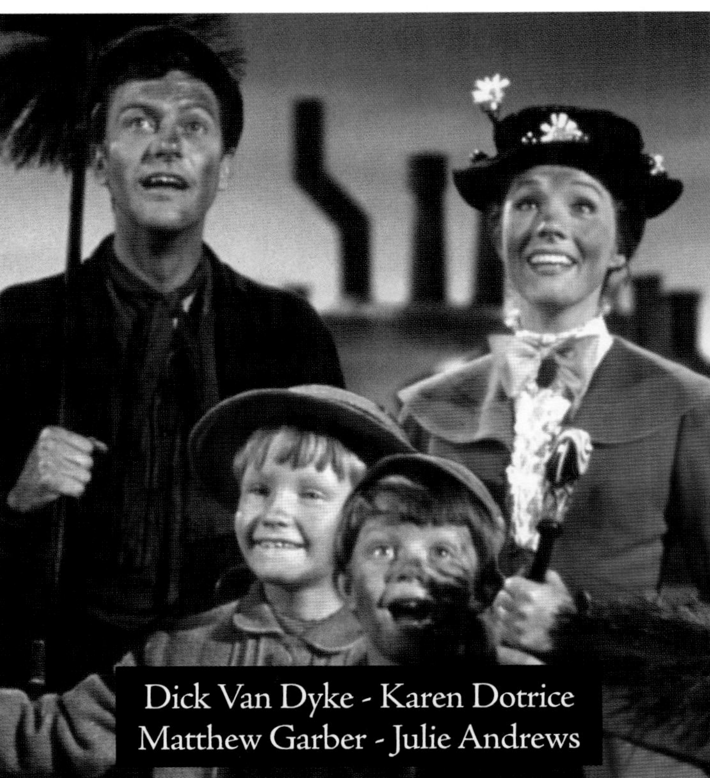

Dick Van Dyke - Karen Dotrice
Matthew Garber - Julie Andrews

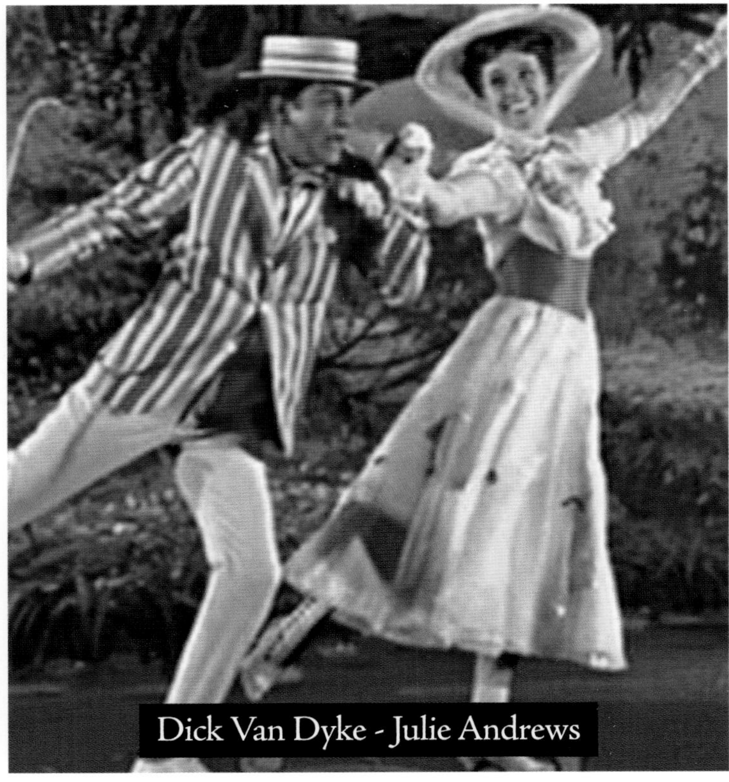

Dick Van Dyke - Julie Andrews

I have a fond memory of visiting the set of "Mary Poppins." It was a few weeks after Dick had performed in our last episode of "The Dick Van Dyke Show" and was on his way to conquering new fields, which he did with his usual elan.

A misogynistic and snobbish phonetics professor agrees to a wager that he can take a flower girl and make her presentable in high society.

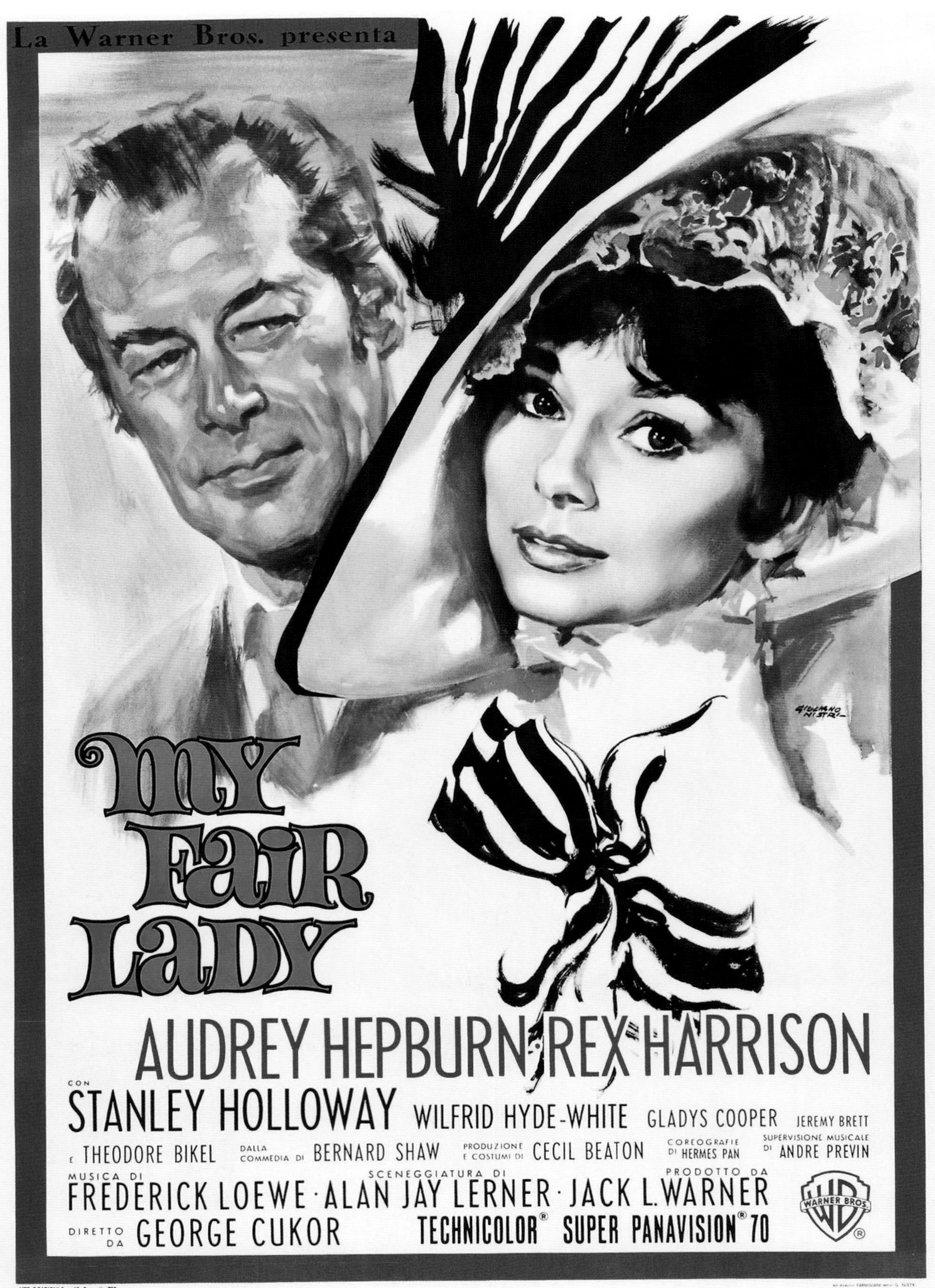

Time Magazine wrote: "In this literal, beautiful, bountiful version of the most gilt-edged attraction in theater history, Jack Warner has miraculously managed to turn gold into gold."

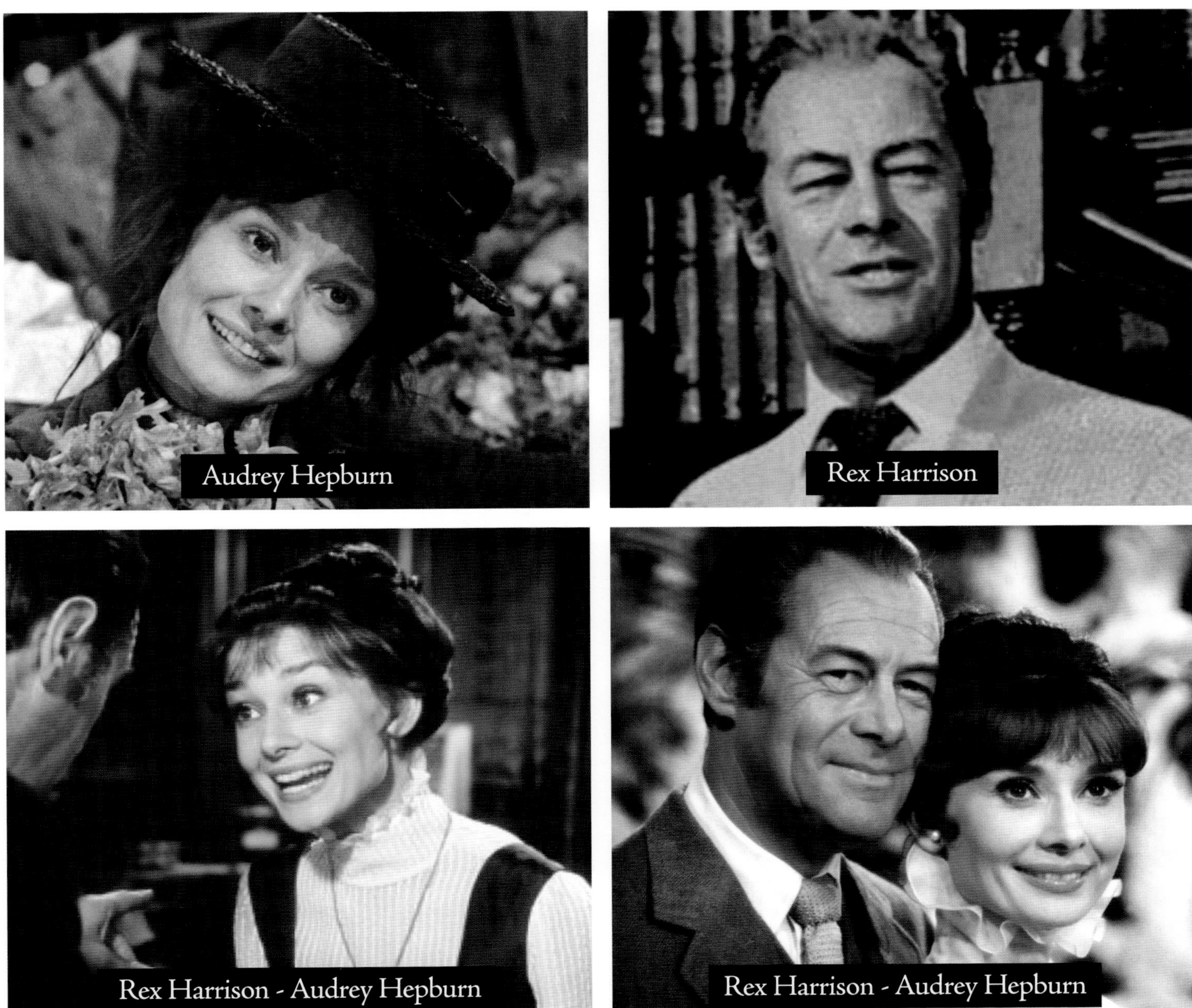

Audrey Hepburn

Rex Harrison

Rex Harrison - Audrey Hepburn

Rex Harrison - Audrey Hepburn

The studio heads who chose not to use Julie Andrews as Eliza Doolittle are not my favorite studio heads. They chose the beautiful Audrey Hepburn, because she was an established movie star. What she was not was a singer. She had to lip sync her songs to the voice of the opera star, Marni Nixon.

As a guest on "The Dinah Shore Show," I gave one of my better performances doing the shpreck-stimma (talk-singing) of Rex Harrison's second act soliloquy:

"I've grown accustomed to her face, She almost makes the day begin,
I've grown accustomed to the tune that, She whistles night and noon..."
Her smiles, her frowns, Her ups, her downs...

A woman leaves an Austrian convent to become a governess to the children of a widower.

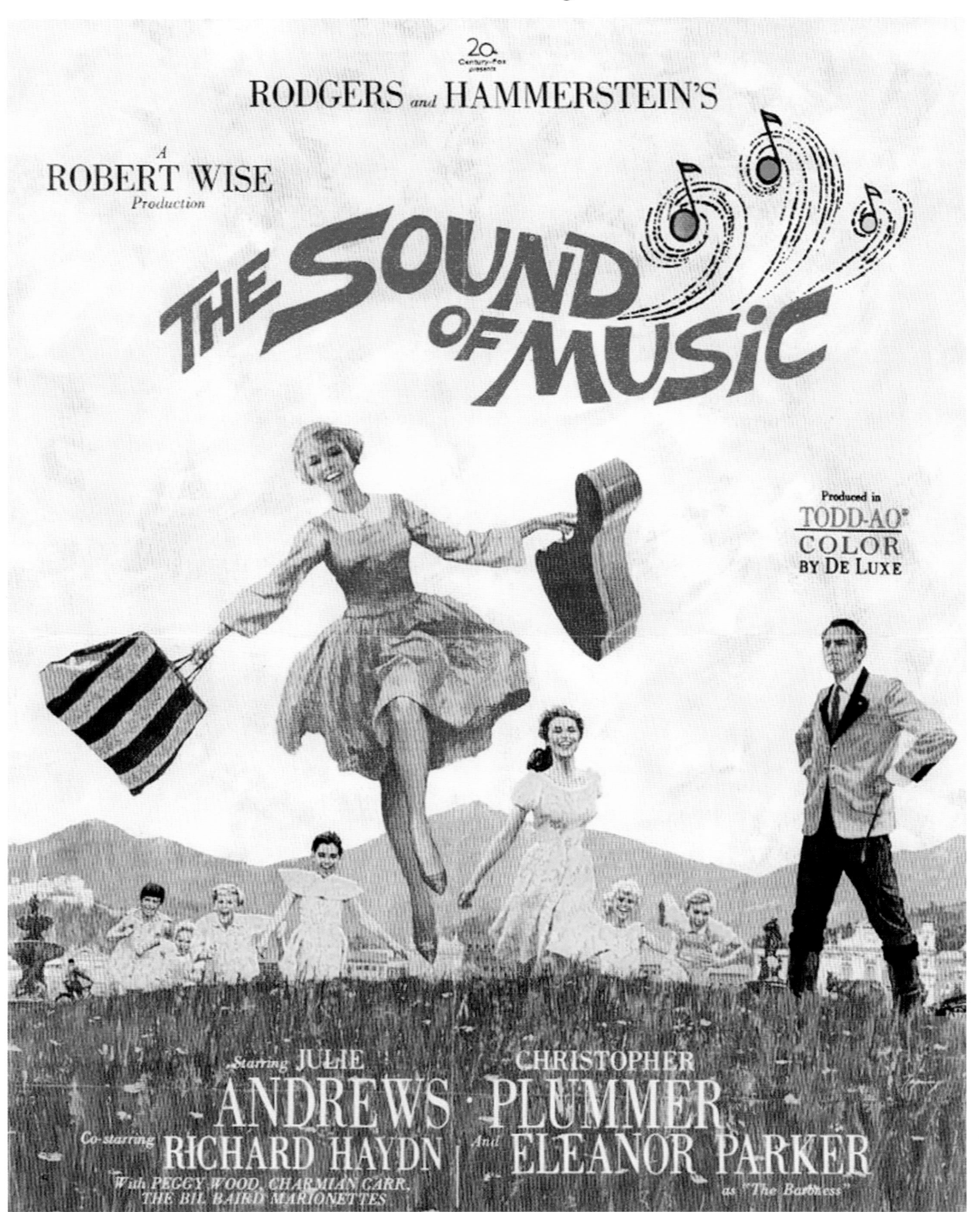

Tim Brayton of Antagony & Ecstasy wrote: "Arguably the best screen adaptation of a stage musical that has yet been made, and certainly the most improved over its source material."

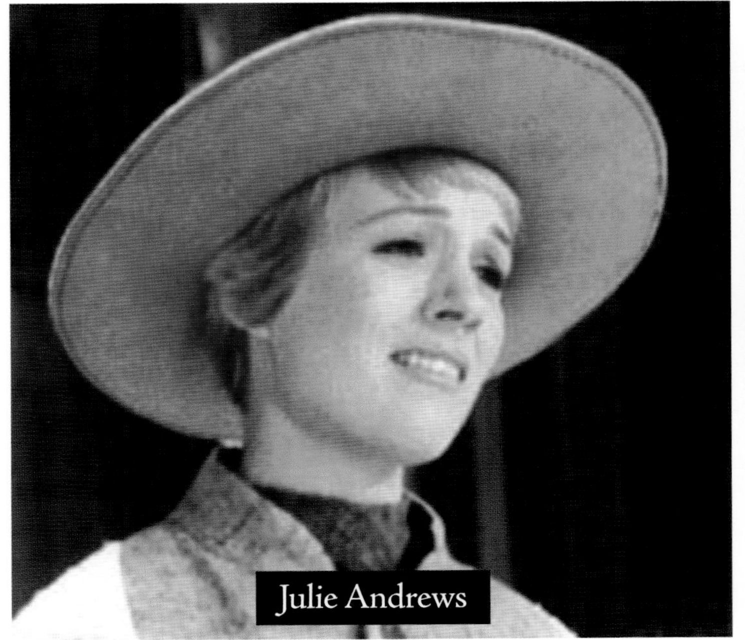

Julie Andrews

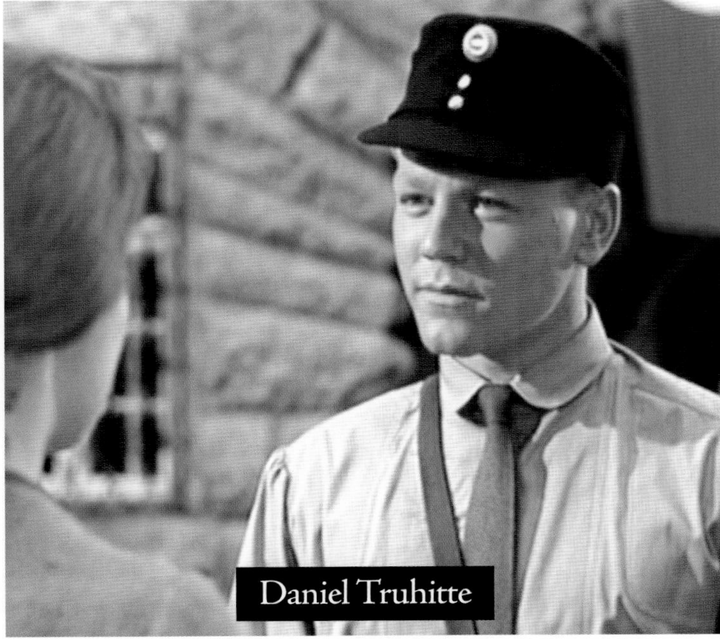

Daniel Truhitte

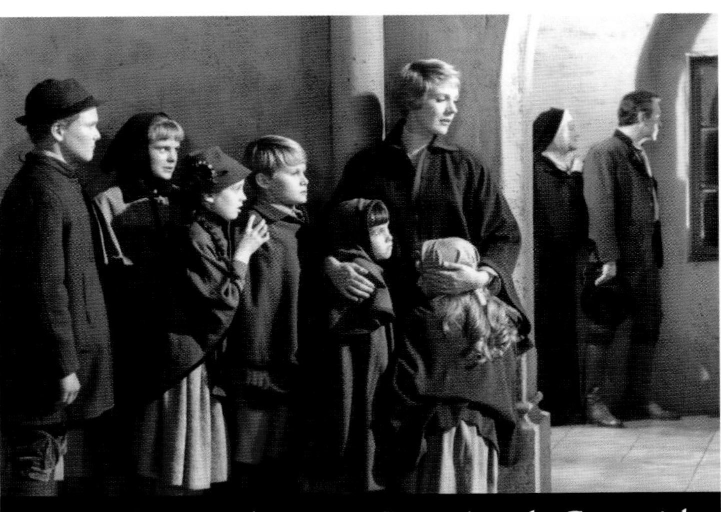

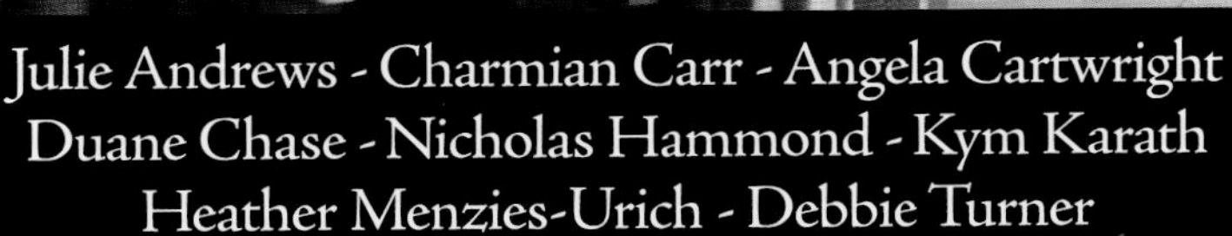

Julie Andrews - Charmian Carr - Angela Cartwright
Duane Chase - Nicholas Hammond - Kym Karath
Heather Menzies-Urich - Debbie Turner

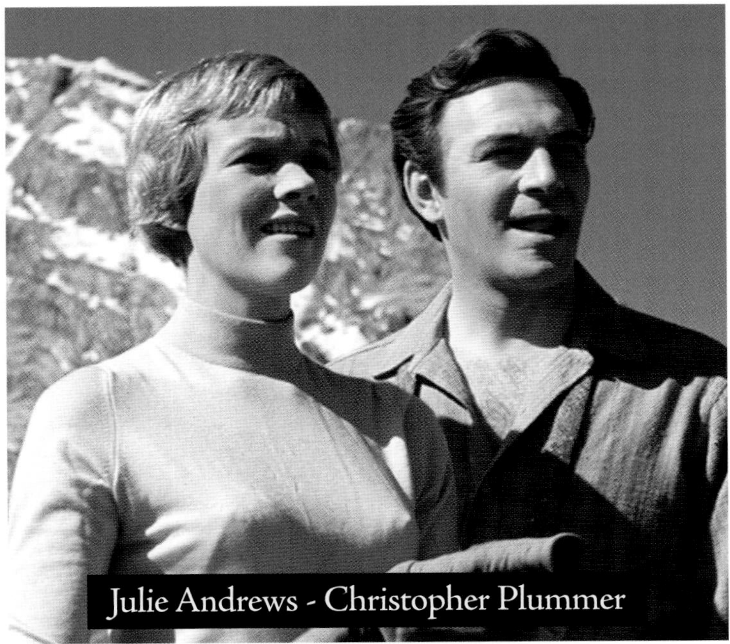

Julie Andrews - Christopher Plummer

I first met Julie Andrews at Longchamps restaurant in New York, where we had been invited to pose for a picture for a New York Magazine cover. She told me of an audition she had with Moss Hart, who was looking for someone to play the lead in his upcoming production of "My Fair Lady." She sighed and said how unlikely a choice she was for the part. I countered with, "From what I learned about you during this lunch, you're not an unlikely choice for the part, but a perfect choice to play Eliza Doolittle."

When my wife and I sat in a Broadway theater and heard her sing "*I Could Have Danced All Night*," I said, "I feel like I'm floating," and my wife replied, "Yes, floating, exactly how I feel."

Varied passengers aboard a ship bound for Germany represent a microcosm of 1930s society.

EVERYWHERE... EVERYONE'S CALLING IT THE MUST-SEE PICTURE OF THE YEAR!

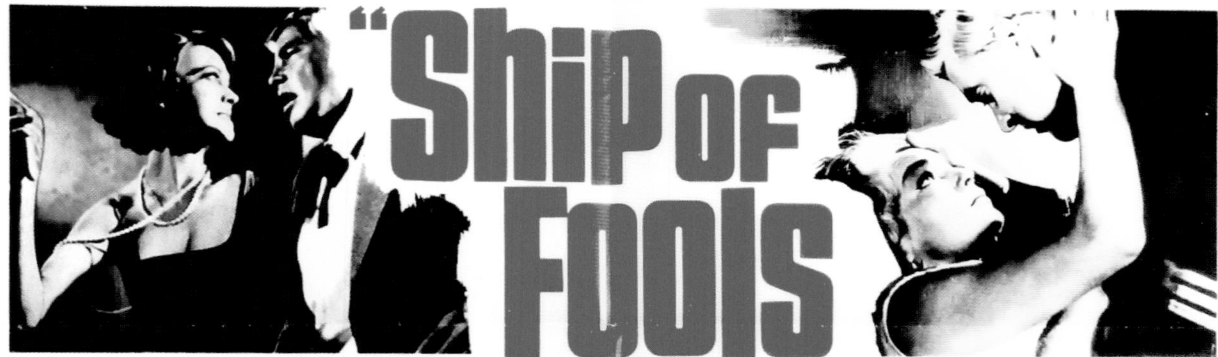

is AN EVENT! FASCINATING! MASTERFUL!" —TIME

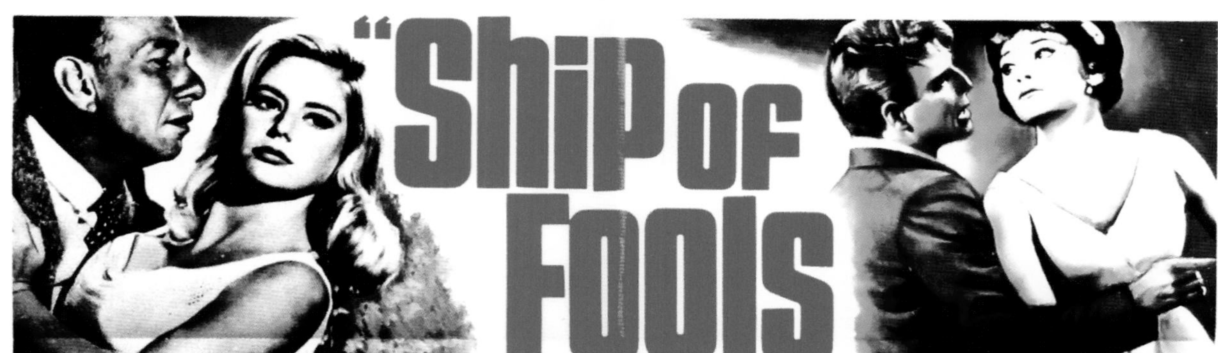

is A SUPERB PRODUCTION, MAGNIFICENTLY PLAYED!" —REDBOOK

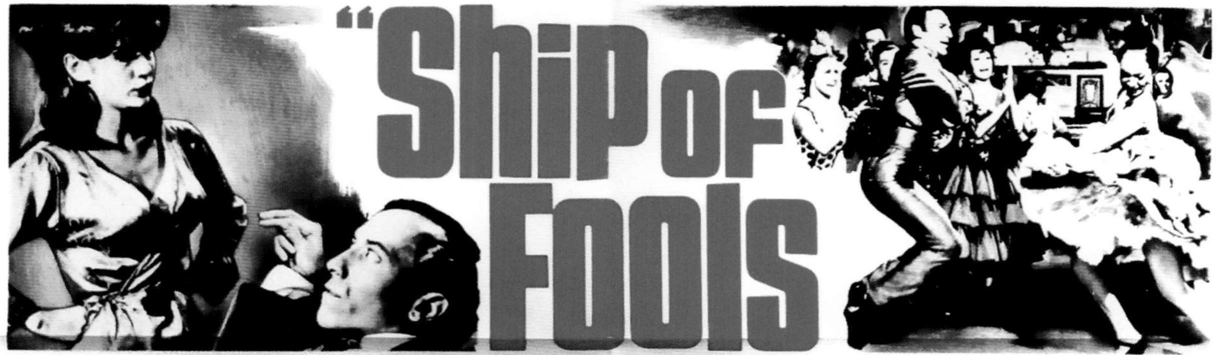

is FIRST-RATE! THOROUGHLY ENGROSSING!" —SATURDAY REVIEW

COLUMBIA PICTURES PRESENTS A STANLEY KRAMER PRODUCTION

VIVIEN LEIGH SIMONE SIGNORET JOSE FERRER LEE MARVIN OSKAR WERNER ELIZABETH ASHLEY

GEORGE SEGAL JOSE GRECO MICHAEL DUNN CHARLES KORVIN AND HEINZ RUEHMANN Co Starring LILIA SKALA

BASED ON KATHERINE ANNE PORTER'S "SHIP OF FOOLS"

Bosley Crowther of The New York Times wrote: "A powerful, ironic film."

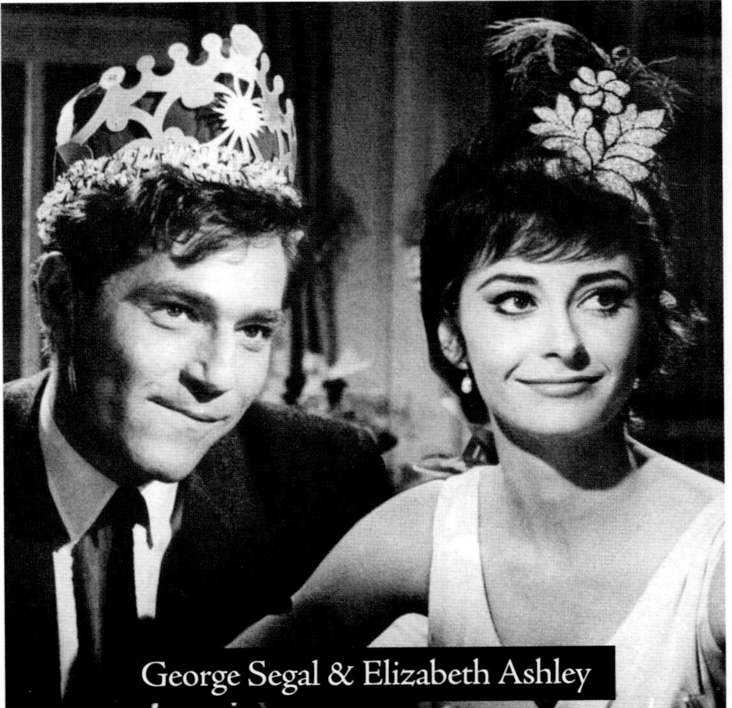
George Segal & Elizabeth Ashley

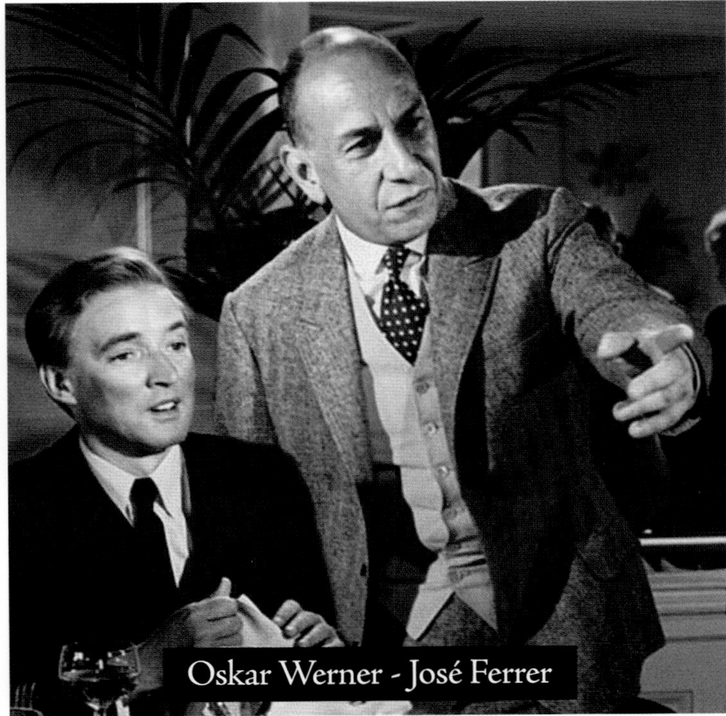
Oskar Werner - José Ferrer

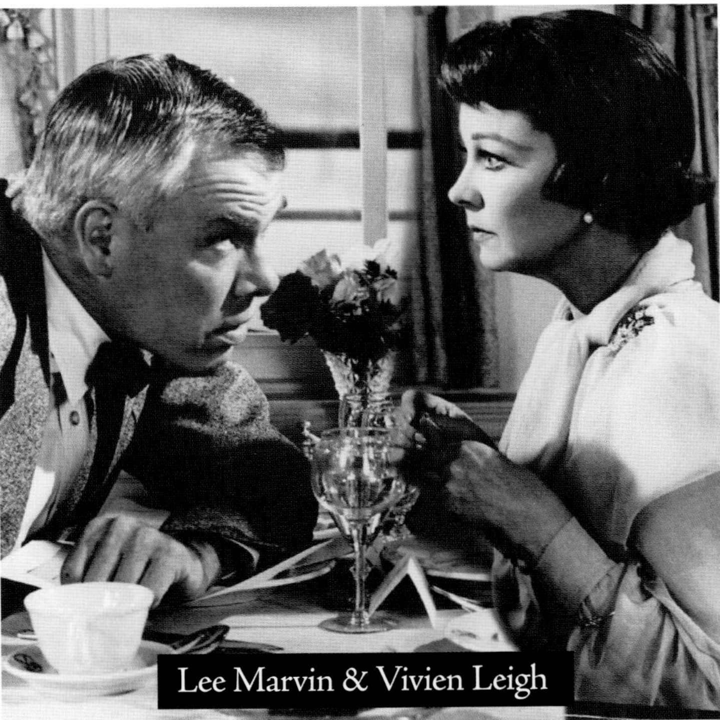
Lee Marvin & Vivien Leigh

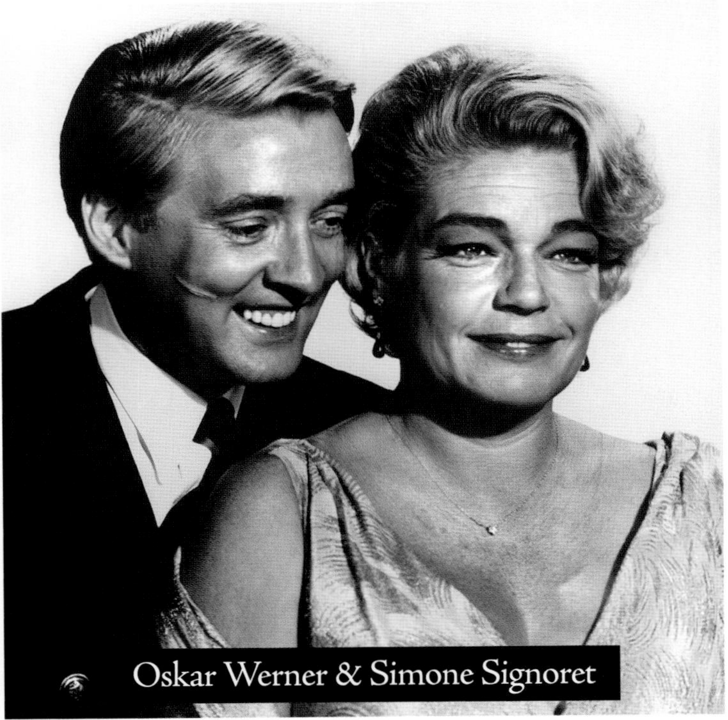
Oskar Werner & Simone Signoret

I enjoyed this film and was happy for the opportunity to see Simone Signoret, an actress who was a tremendous star in Europe. In later years, while performing on "The Dinah Shore Show," I did a comic singing impression of her husband, Yves Montand, a beloved internationally known star. The song I sang was a silly one, "Broken Cookies & Red Balloons." The following morning Simone Signoret phoned Dinah to tell her that while watching me impersonate her husband, she laughed so hard she fell out of bed.

Without hostile intent, a Soviet submarine runs aground off New England. The crew frightens the villagers while they search the town for a way to free their sub.

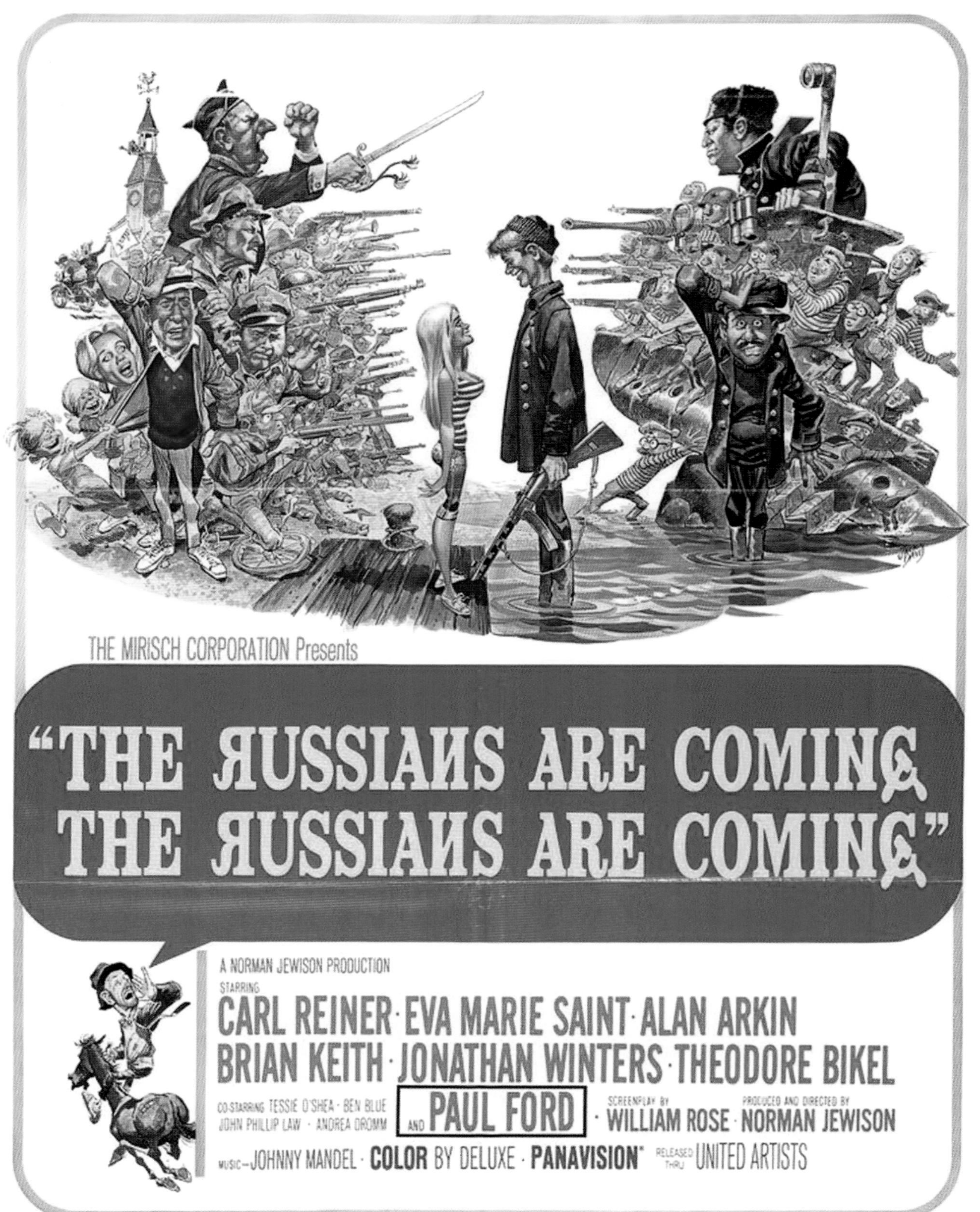

Marjorie Baumgarten of Austin Chronicle wrote: "The cast is great and the scene in which Carl Reiner and vaudeville vet Tessie O'Shea are lashed together is unforgettably funny."

When I was cast as the leading man to co-star with Eva Marie Saint, an actress who had co-starred with Marlon Brando, Paul Newman and Cary Grant, I felt like I had arrived!

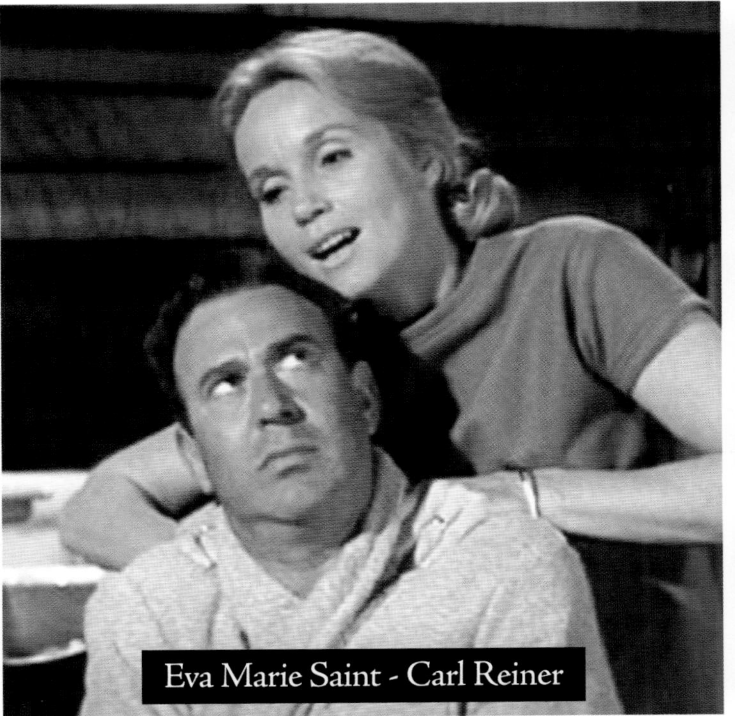
Eva Marie Saint - Carl Reiner

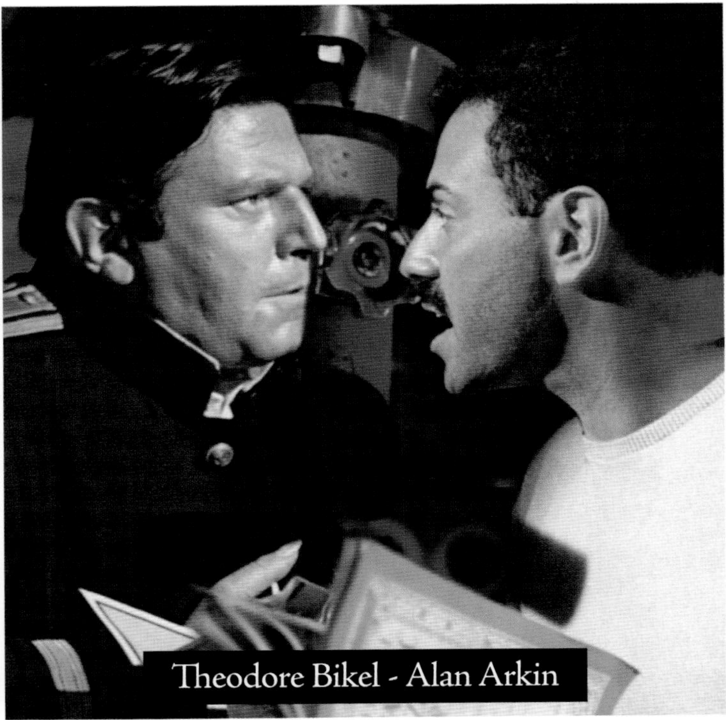
Theodore Bikel - Alan Arkin

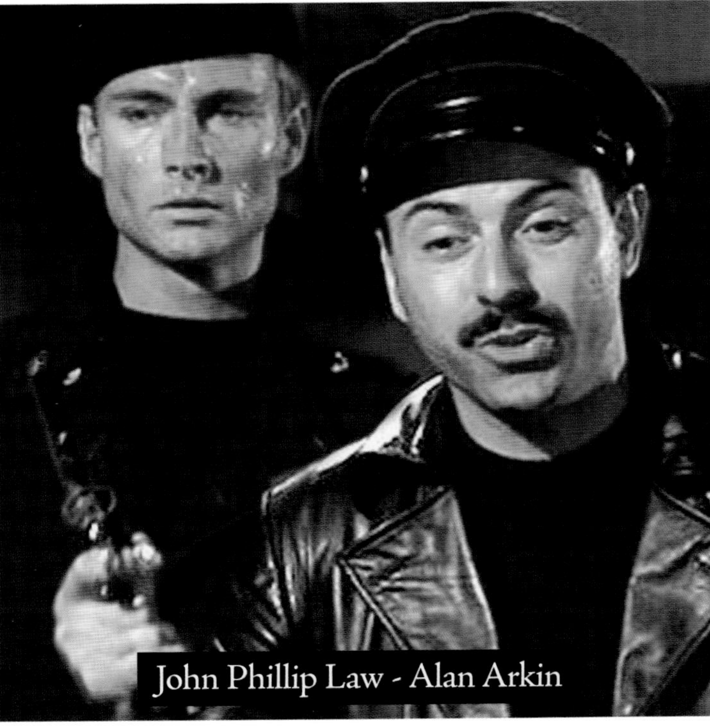
John Phillip Law - Alan Arkin

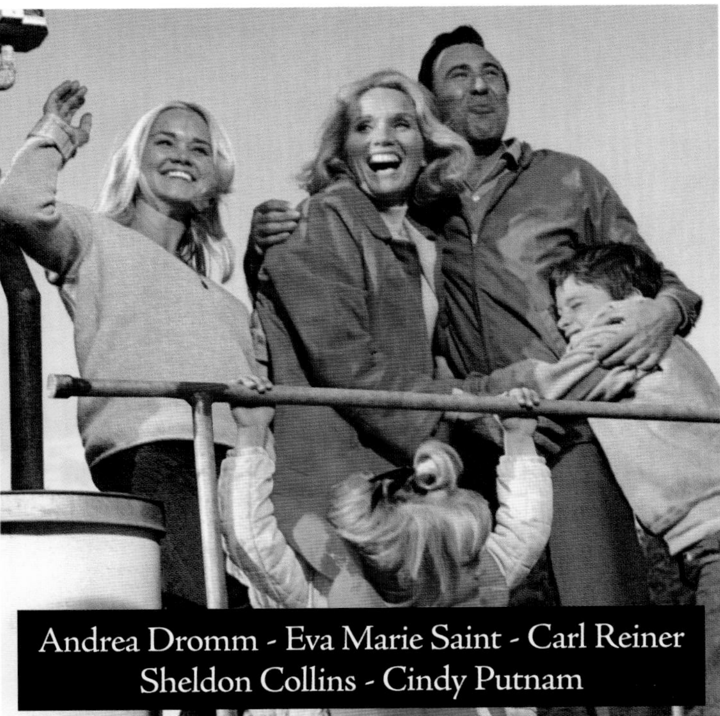
Andrea Dromm - Eva Marie Saint - Carl Reiner
Sheldon Collins - Cindy Putnam

Alan Arkin, who won an Oscar for his performance, had once written a beautiful, silly song that my wife, Estelle, sang in her nightclub act. It's entitled, "I Like You" and it starts with:

"I like you, Cuz you don't make me nervous, I met someone like you before, But only once or twice, Once or twice, And not very recently..." If you want to laugh, go to YouTube and watch Alan Arkin and Carol Burnett singing the rest of the lyrics of "I Like You."

A bitter, aging couple, with the help of alcohol, use a young couple to fuel anguish and emotional pain towards each other.

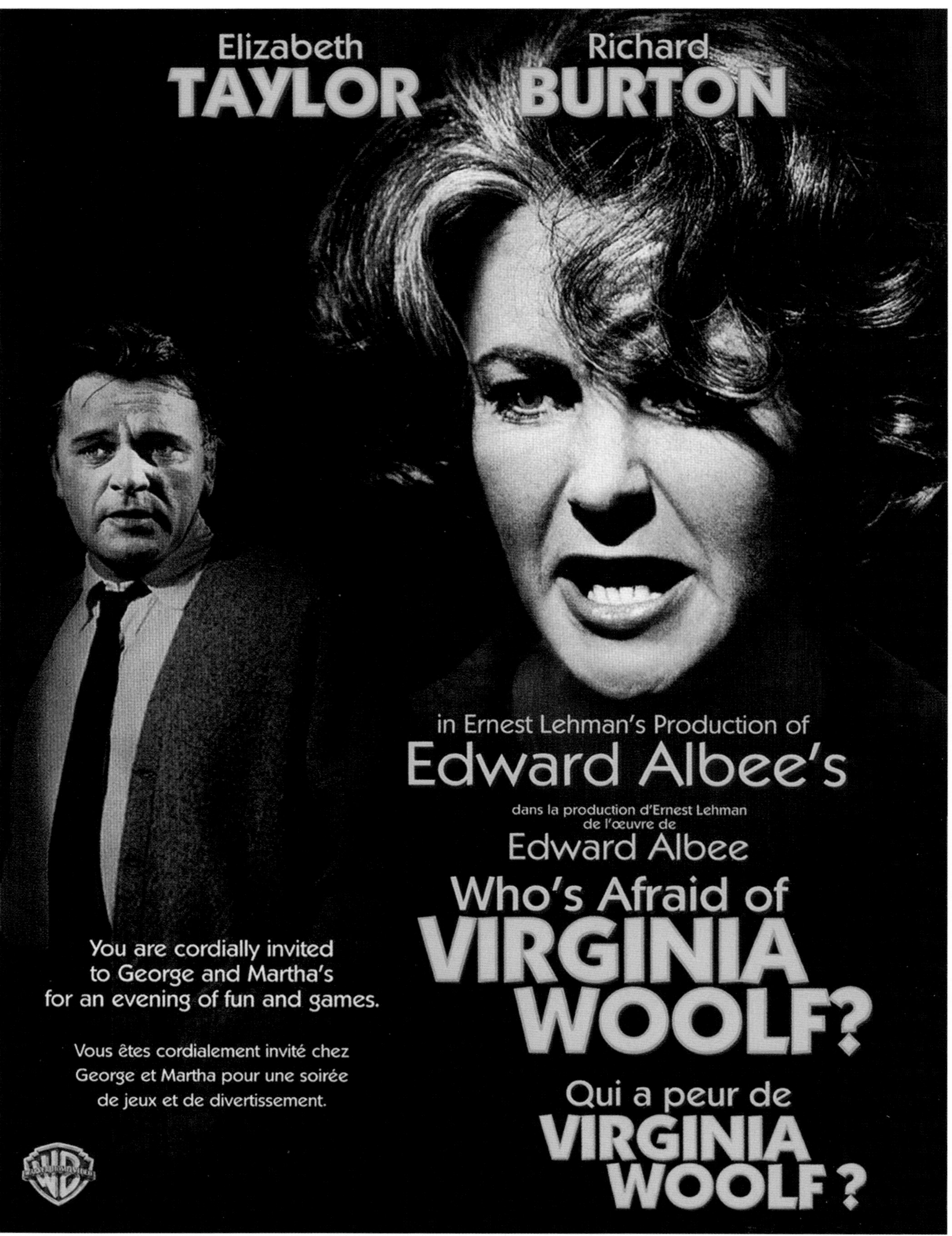

Kate Cameron of The New York Daily News wrote: "Elizabeth Taylor is nothing less than brilliant as the shrewish, slovenly, blasphemous, frustrated, slightly wacky, alcoholic wife of a meek, unambitious assistant professor of history at a university, over which her father reigns as president."

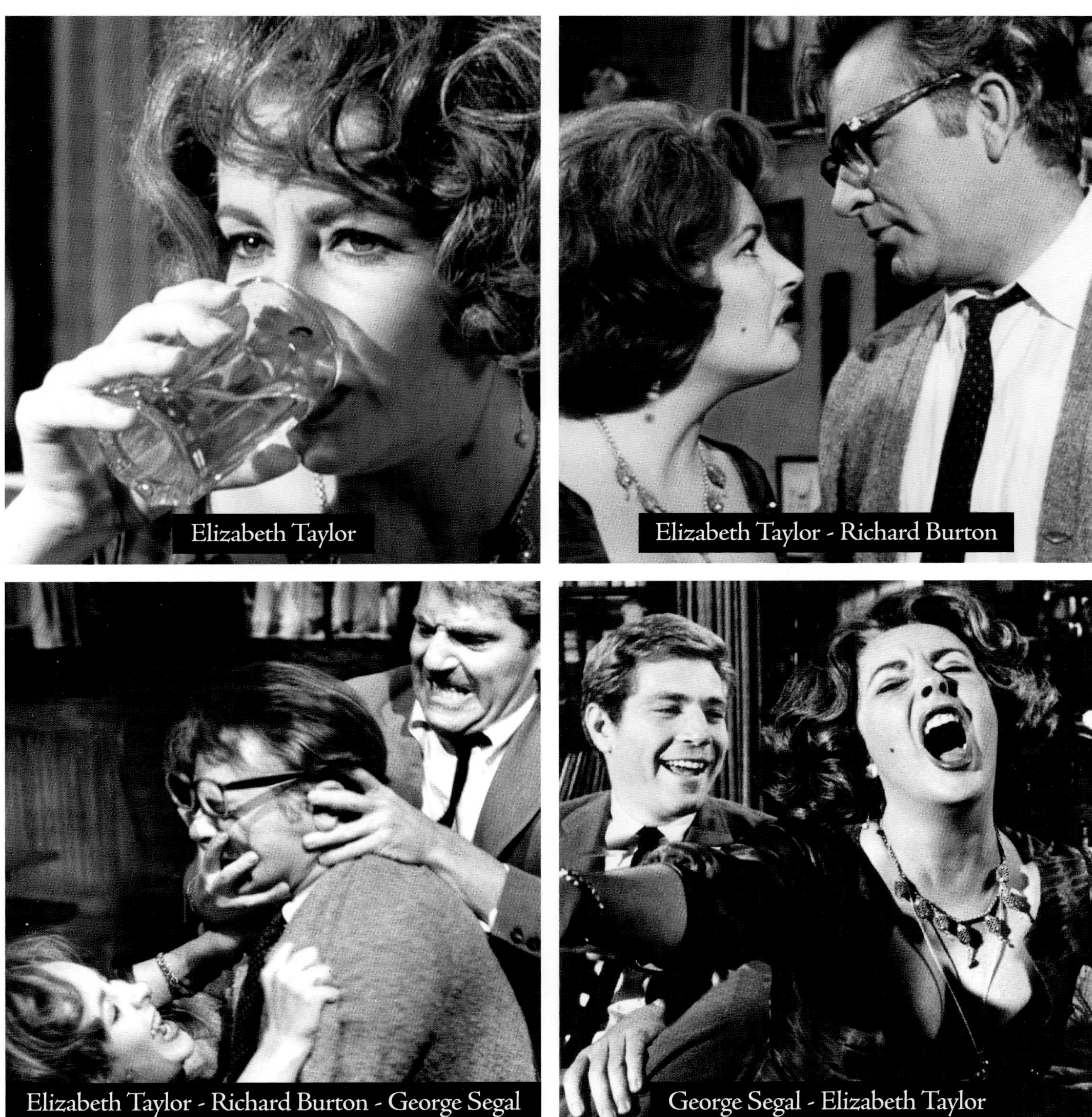

Elizabeth Taylor

Elizabeth Taylor - Richard Burton

Elizabeth Taylor - Richard Burton - George Segal

George Segal - Elizabeth Taylor

Burton and Taylor fell in love on the set of the 1963 film "Cleopatra," and though both were married at the time, they divorced their spouses and married each other. Subsequently, they divorced again and, to nobody's surprise, they remarried again and divorced again.

Producers Max Bialystock and Leo Bloom make money by producing a sure-fire flop.

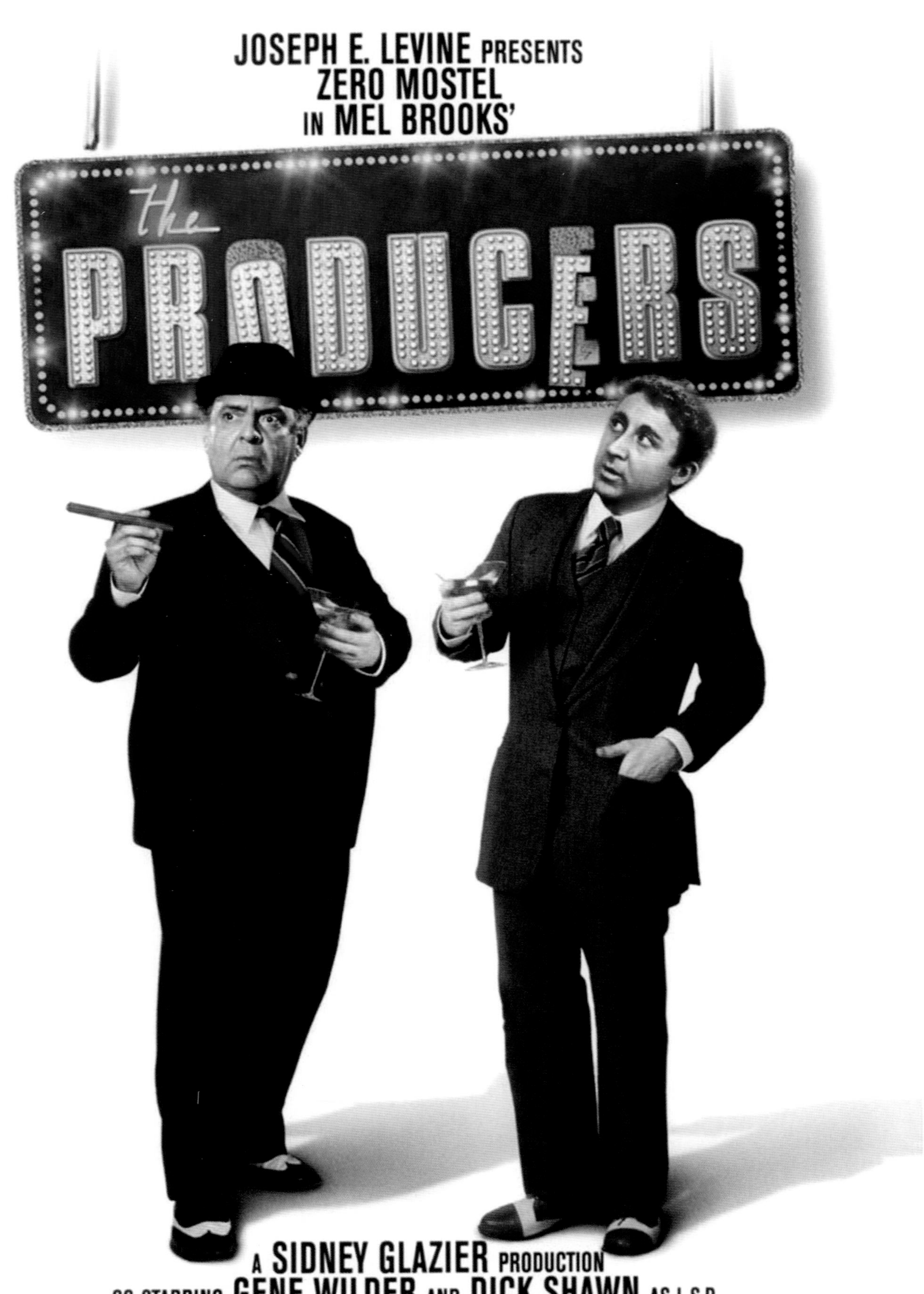

Time Out wrote: "Brooks' first feature, an absolutely hilarious and tasteless New York Jewish comedy about Broadway."

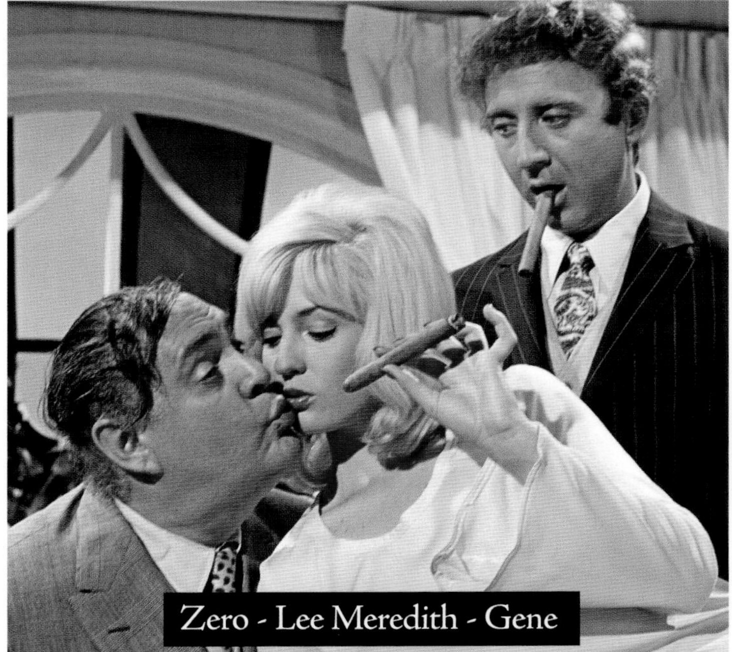

Zero - Lee Meredith - Gene

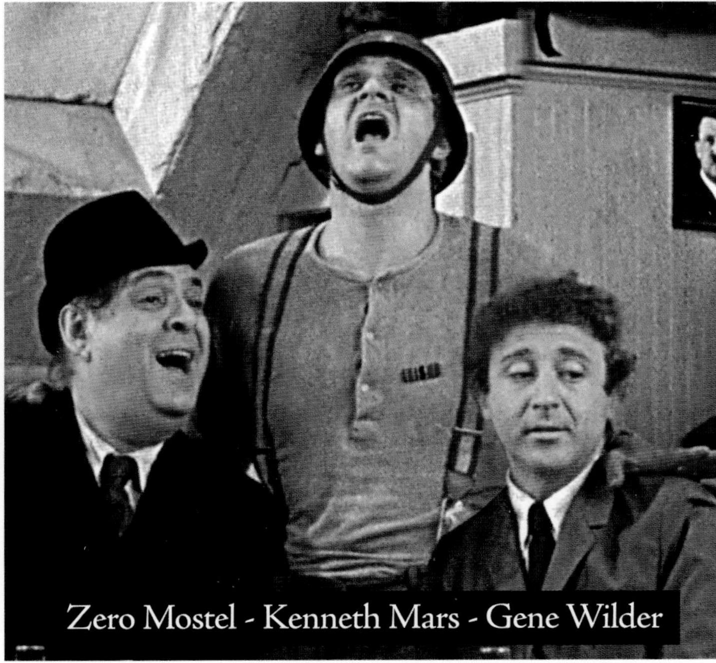

Zero Mostel - Kenneth Mars - Gene Wilder

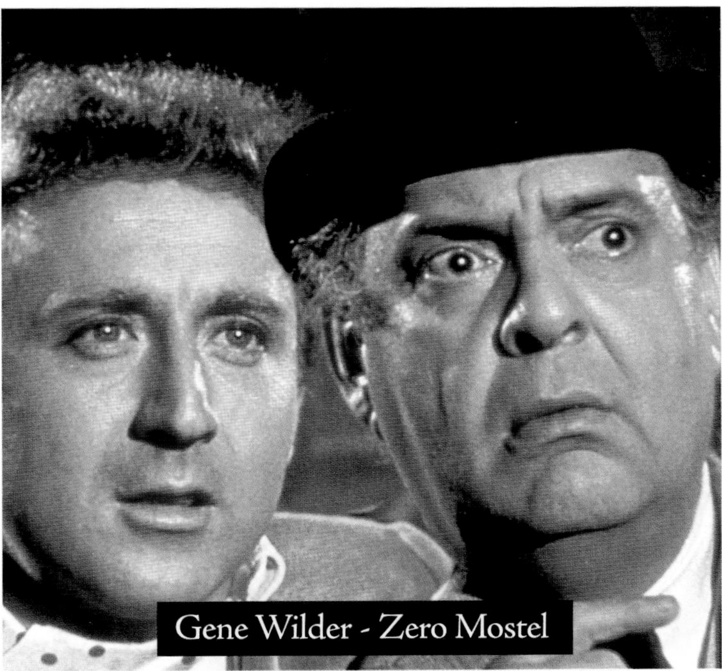

Gene Wilder - Zero Mostel

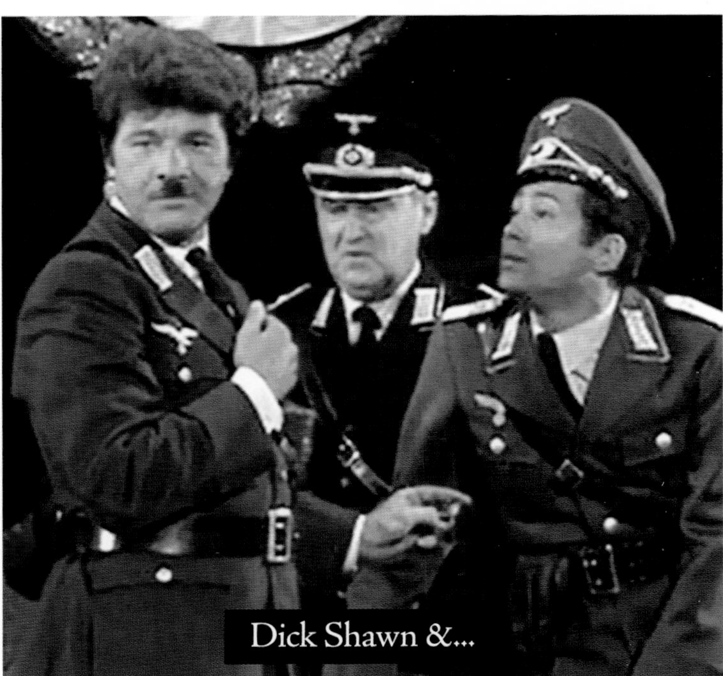

Dick Shawn &...

"The Producers" was the first of Mel Brooks' 11 blockbusters that the world took to its bosom.

When I was 19, I saw Zero Mostel performing at the corner of 42nd St. & Broadway mocking Adolf Hitler by ranting in German double-talk. Two years later, as a member of an Army show, I wowed an audience by doing my impression of Zero's impression of Hitler.

Zero Mostel was a fine painter and many of his works of art were purchased by The Metropolitan Museum. Zero's public career was shortened after being blacklisted by the infamous House Un-American Activities Committee.

An African American police detective is asked to investigate a murder in a racially hostile town.

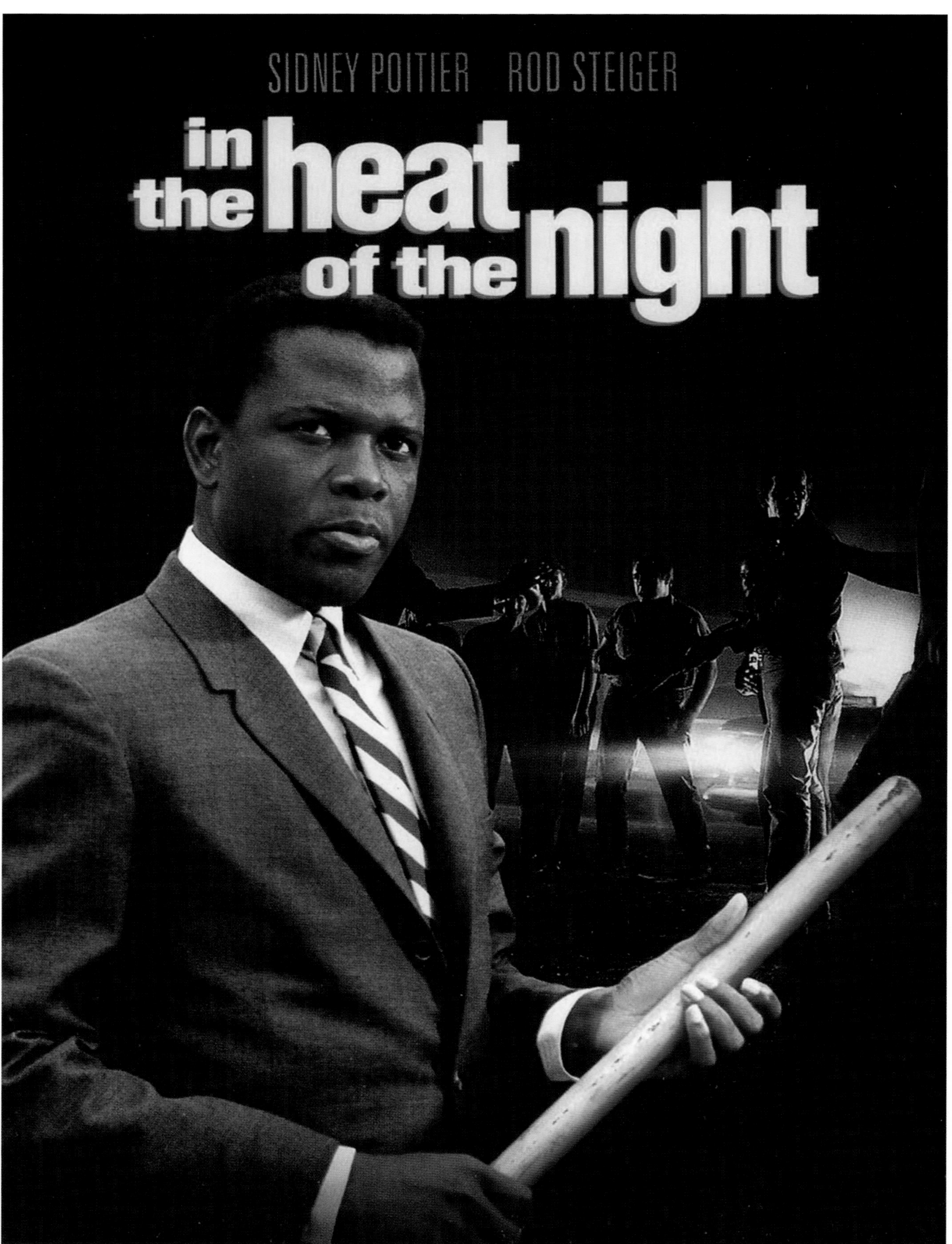

Wanda Hale of New York Daily News wrote: "It's a pleasure watching two splendid actors such as Sidney Poitier and Rod Steiger play a game of cat and mouse in the exceptional murder mystery, 'In the Heat of the Night.'"

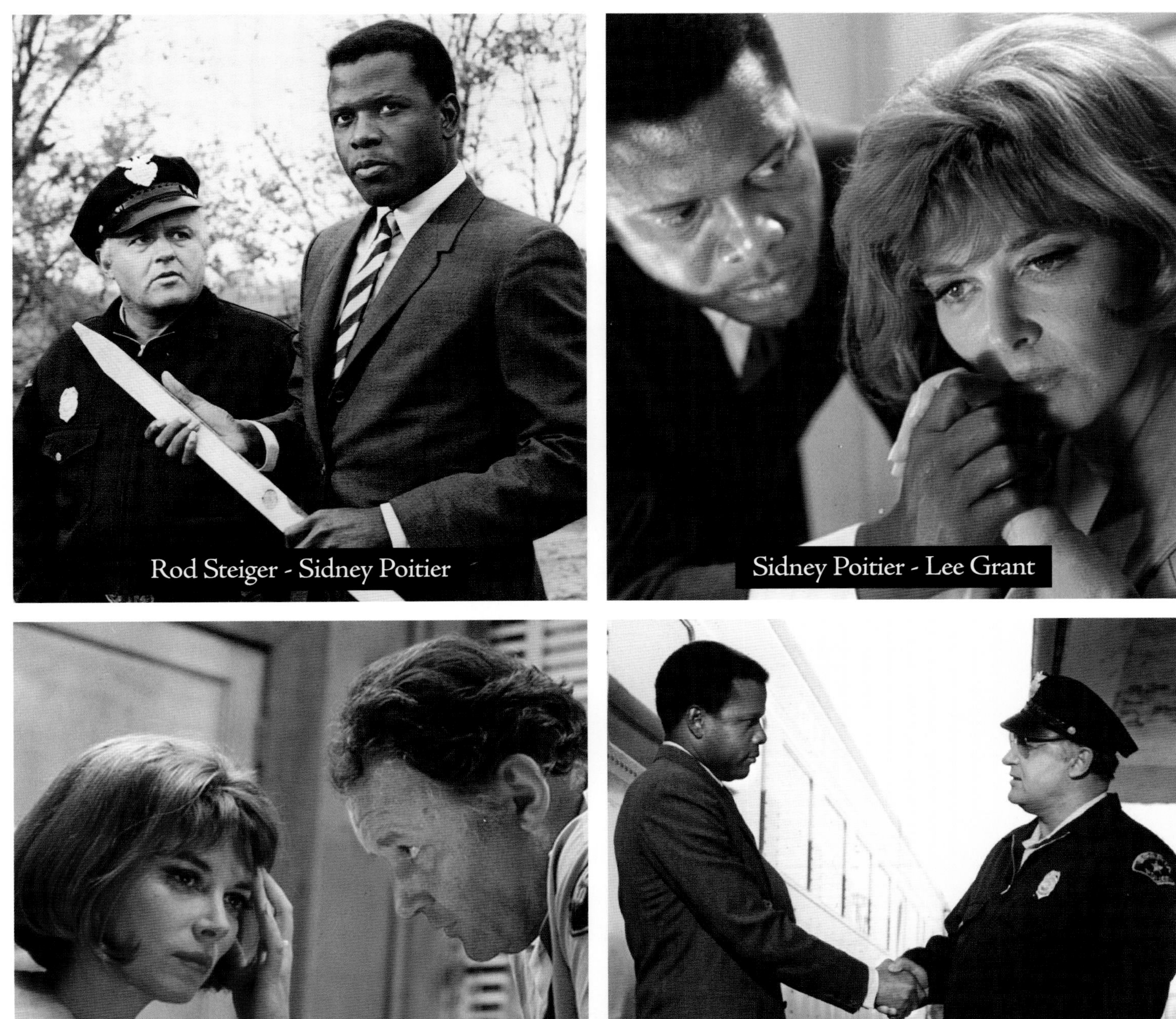

Rod Steiger - Sidney Poitier

Sidney Poitier - Lee Grant

Lee Grant - Rod Steiger

Sidney Poitier - Rod Steiger

This film, besides breaking color barriers by starring Sidney Poitier, also featured Lee Grant who, earlier, had been hounded by The House Un-American Activities Committee for upholding the laws of our Constitution by standing up for the rights of minorities.

Paul, a conservative young lawyer, marries the vivacious Corie. Their highly passionate relationship descends into comical discord in a five-flight New York City walk-up apartment.

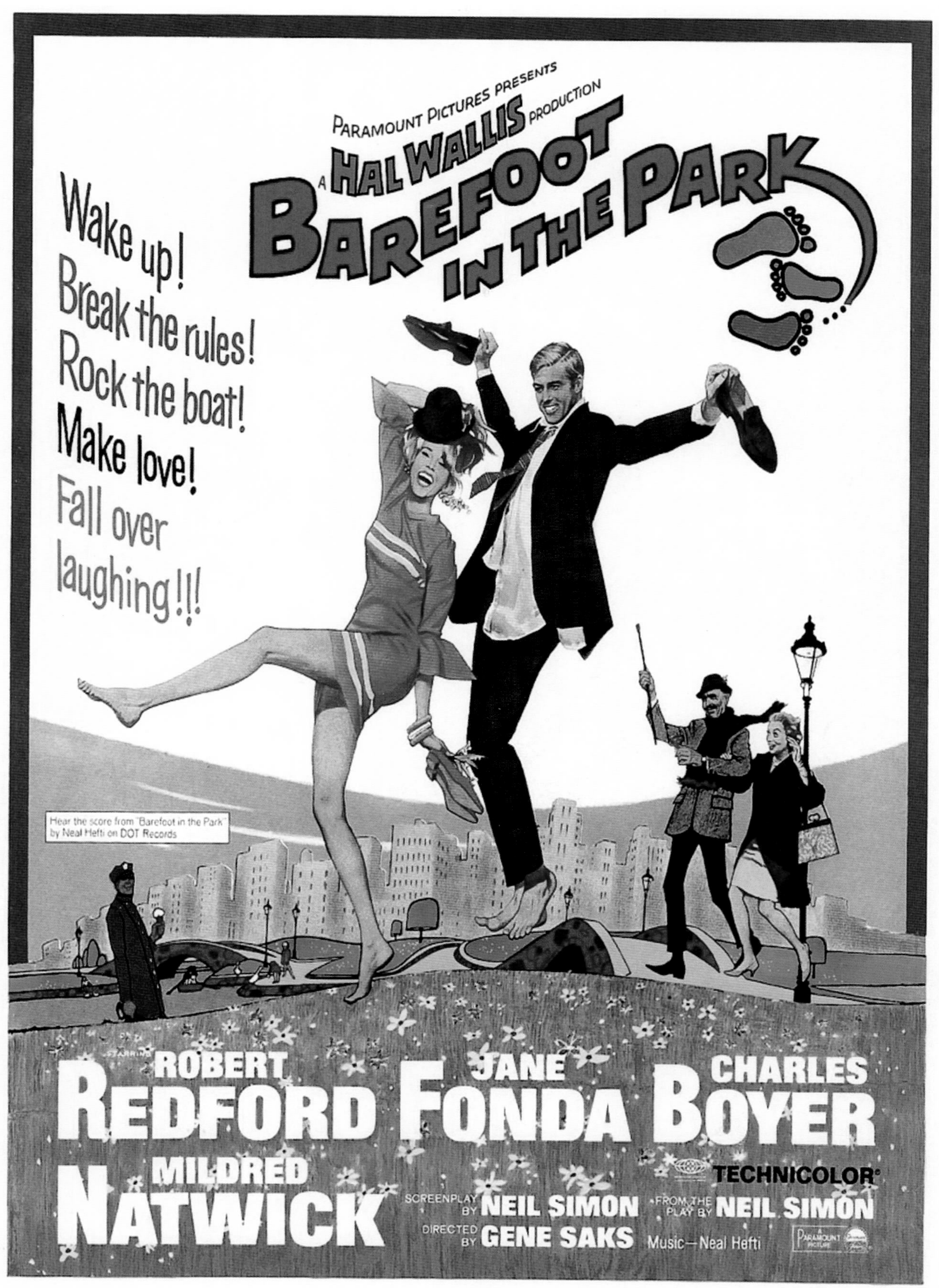

Emanuel Levy wrote: "The adaptation of Neil Simon's Broadway smash hit makes for lighthearted entertainment buoyed by the good chemistry between the newlyweds, Jane Fonda and Robert Redford."

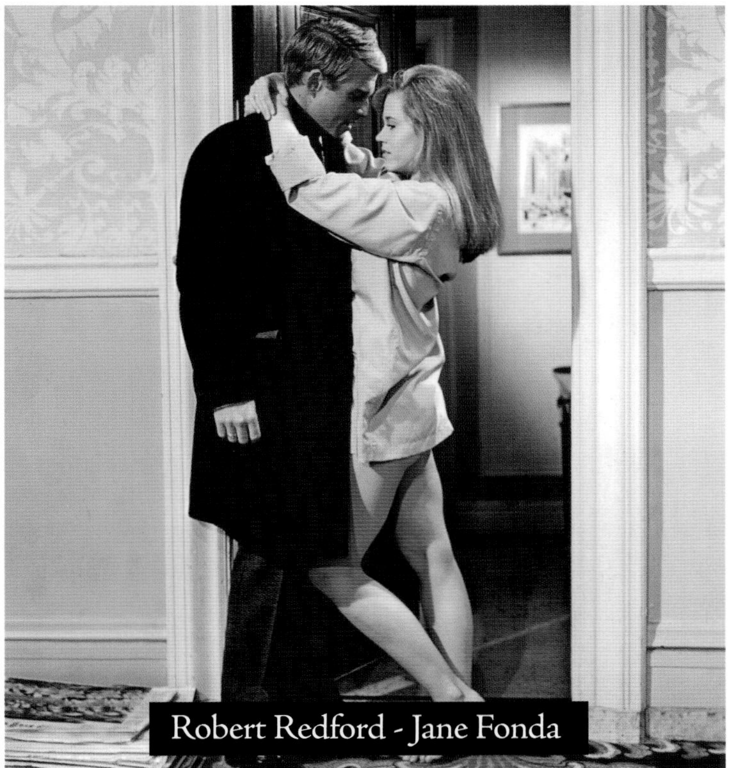
Robert Redford - Jane Fonda

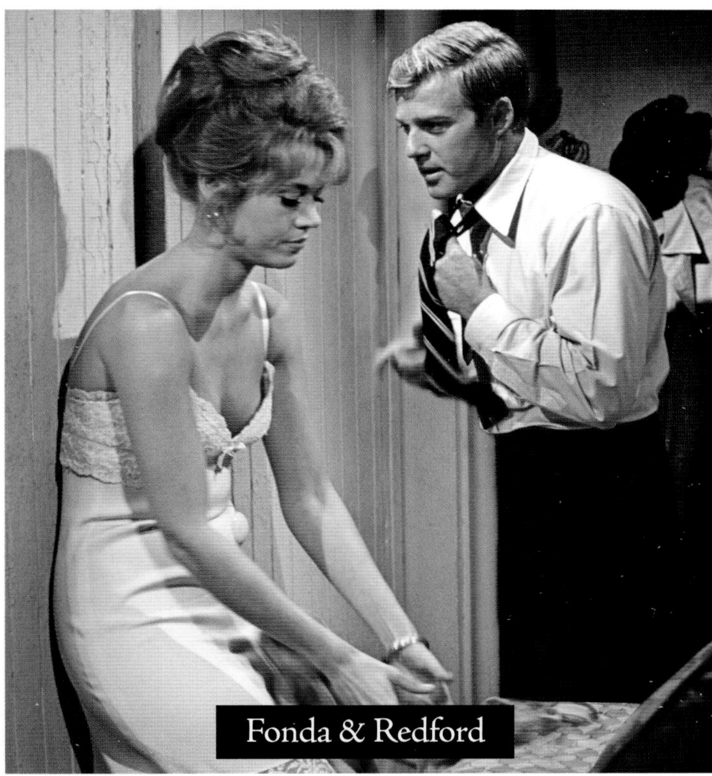
Fonda & Redford

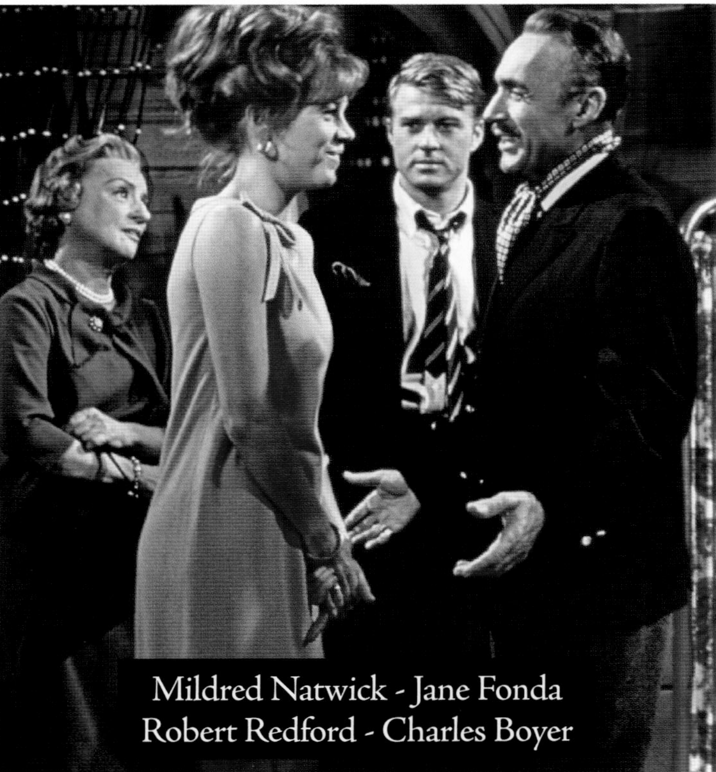
Mildred Natwick - Jane Fonda
Robert Redford - Charles Boyer

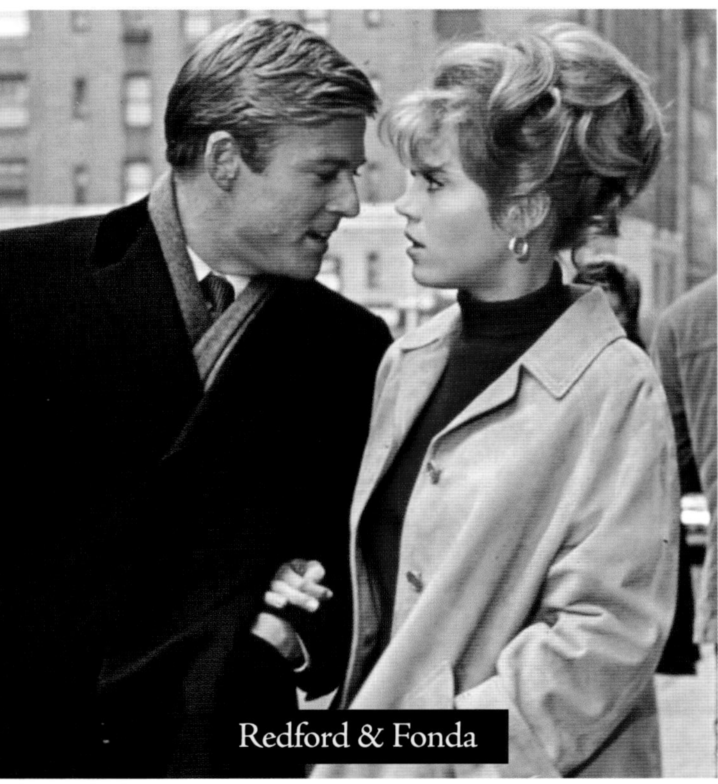
Redford & Fonda

It is guaranteed that any film written by Neil Simon that starred Robert Redford and Jane Fonda would be both entertaining and totally irresistible.

The journey of young aspiring actor as he tries to extricate himself from overly protective parents and two too many girlfriends, while struggling to meet the challenge of his lack of talent.

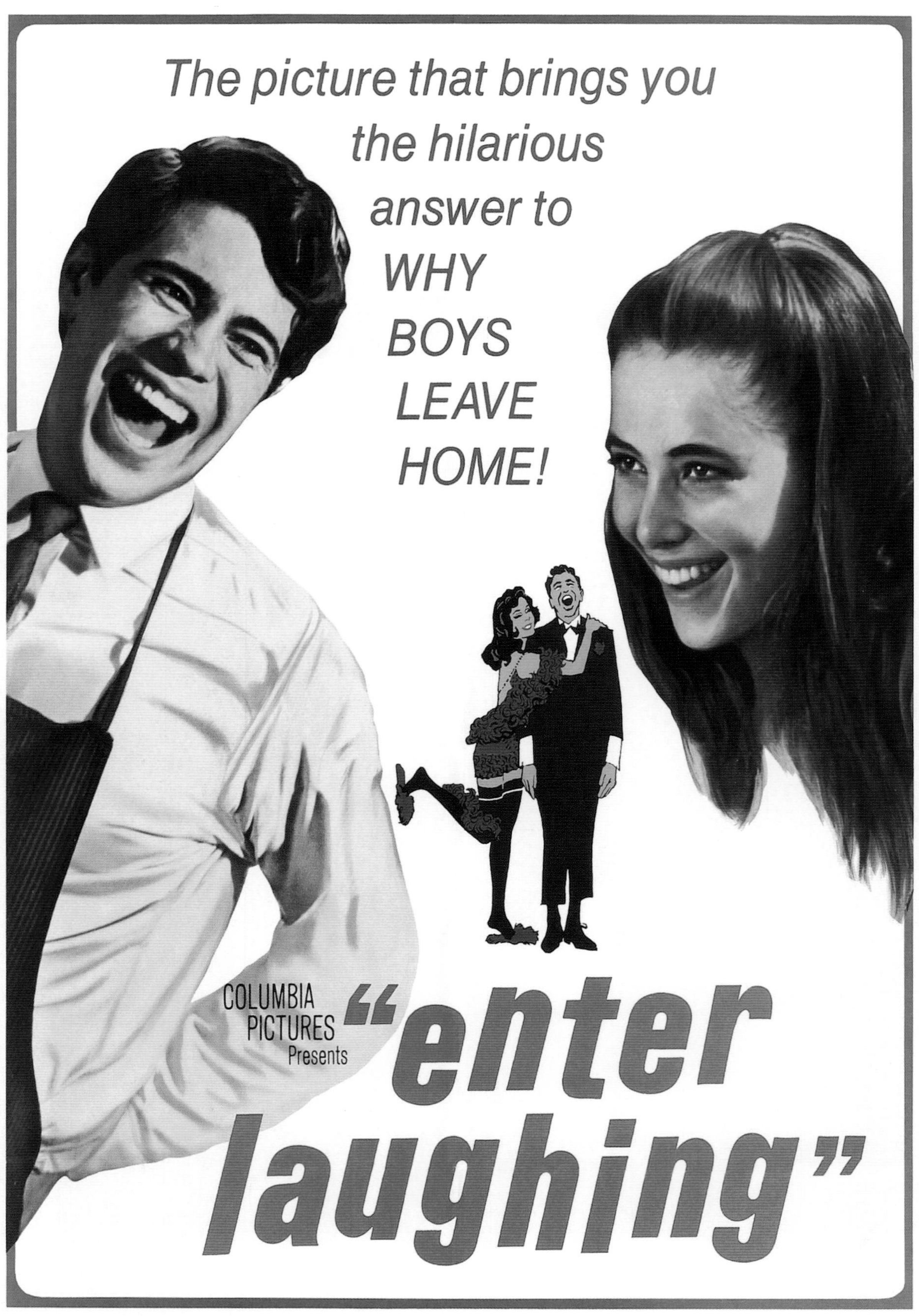

Roger Ebert of The Chicago Sun-Times wrote: "A low-pressure, quietly amusing story based on Carl Reiner's entry into show business."

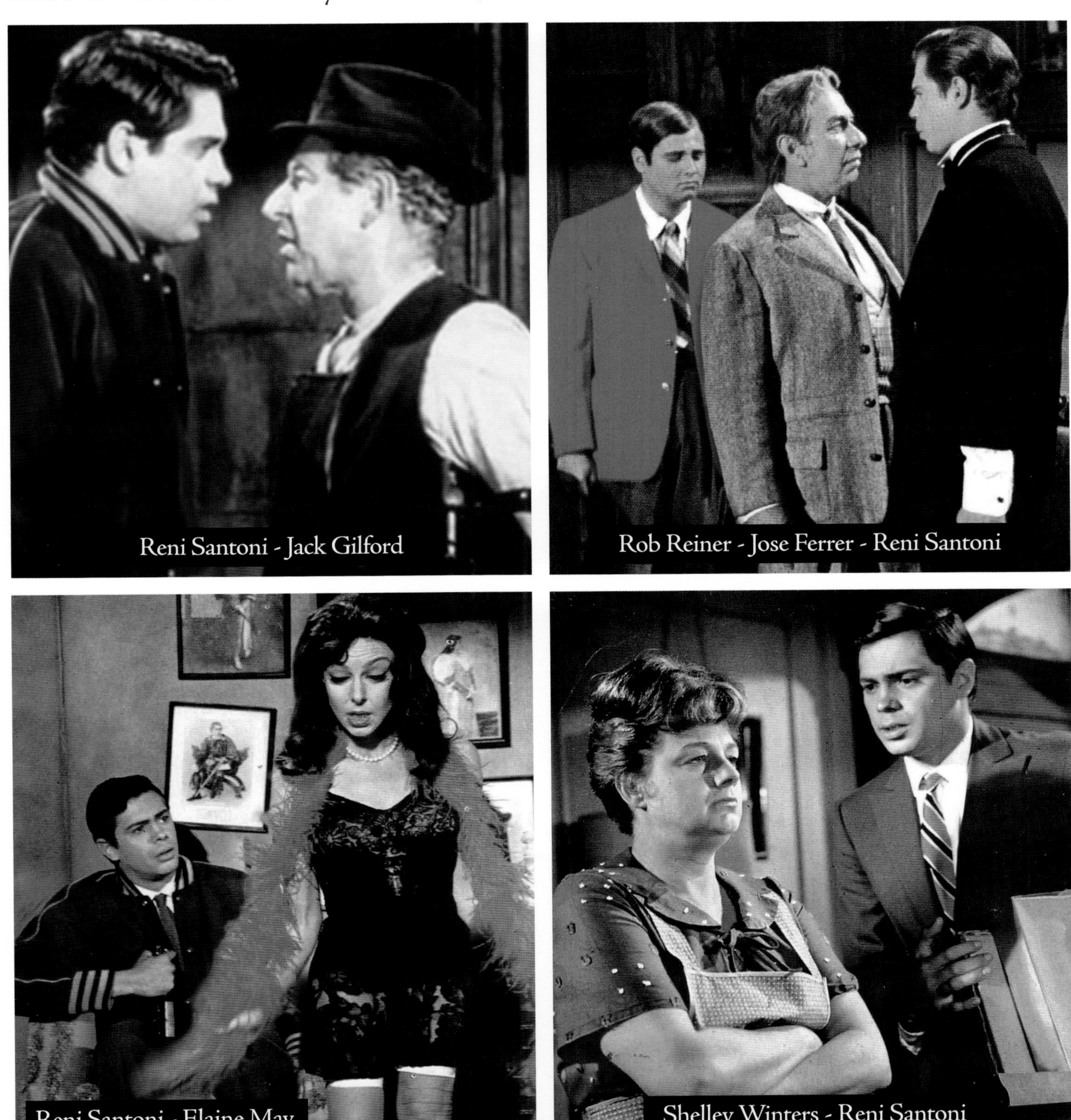

Reni Santoni - Jack Gilford

Rob Reiner - Jose Ferrer - Reni Santoni

Reni Santoni - Elaine May

Shelley Winters - Reni Santoni

This was my first foray into motion pictures and I was excited to be directing an adaptation of my first novel, "Enter Laughing," which had been adapted into a play by Joe Stein.

I was blessed with having a dream cast that made my labor of love come to life.

A couple is challenged when their daughter introduces them to her African American fiancé.

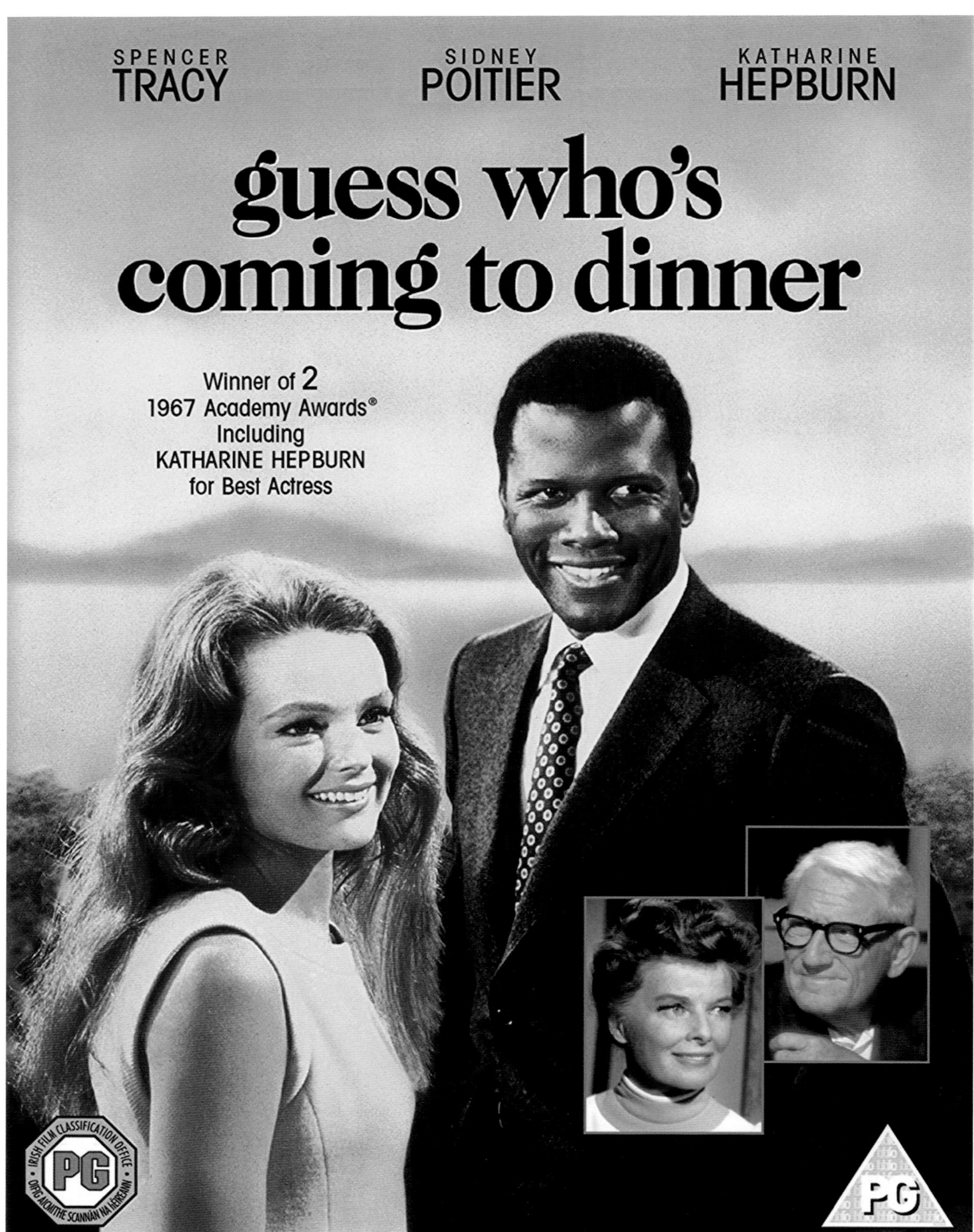

Roger Ebert of Chicago Sun-Times wrote: "On its own terms, this film is a joy to see, an evening of superb entertainment."

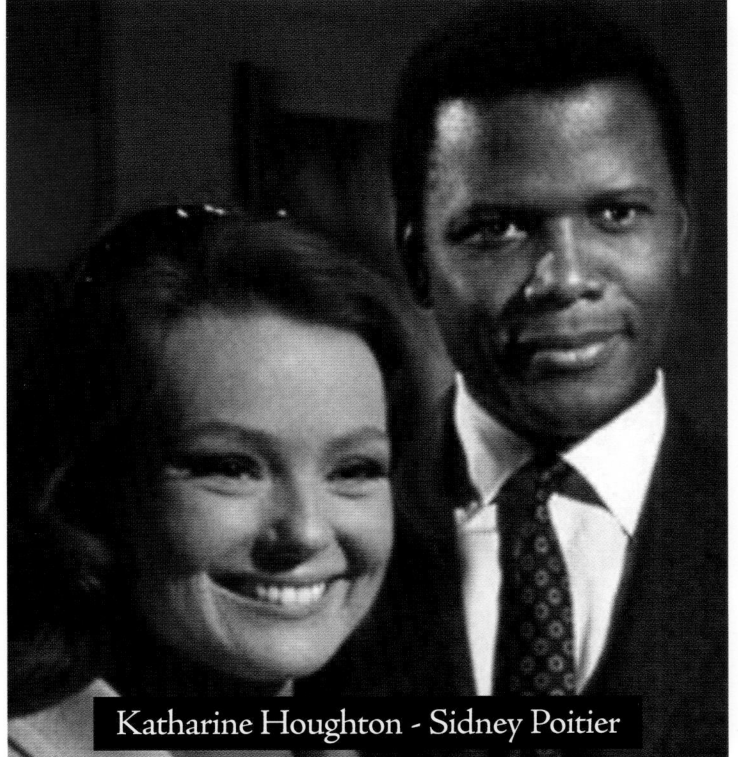

Katharine Houghton - Sidney Poitier

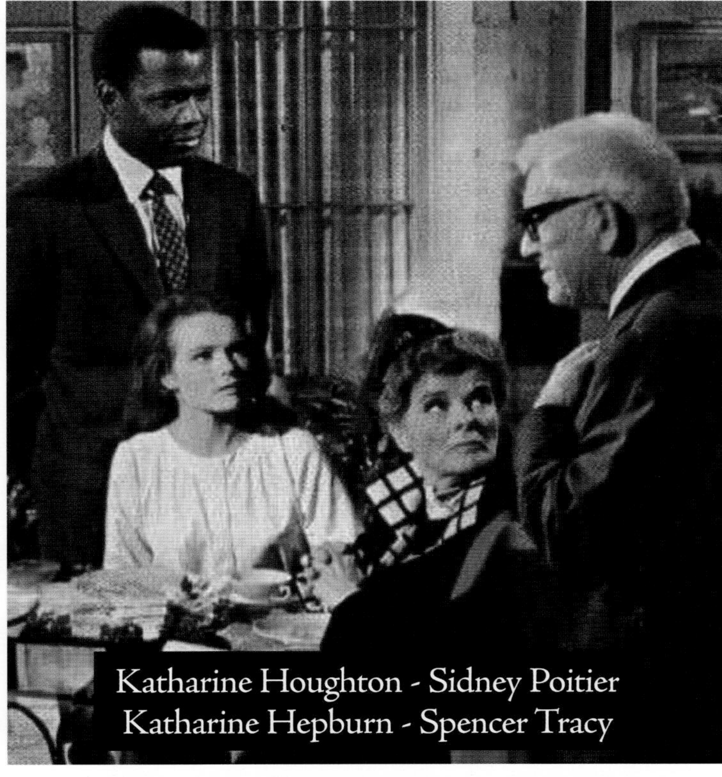

Katharine Houghton - Sidney Poitier
Katharine Hepburn - Spencer Tracy

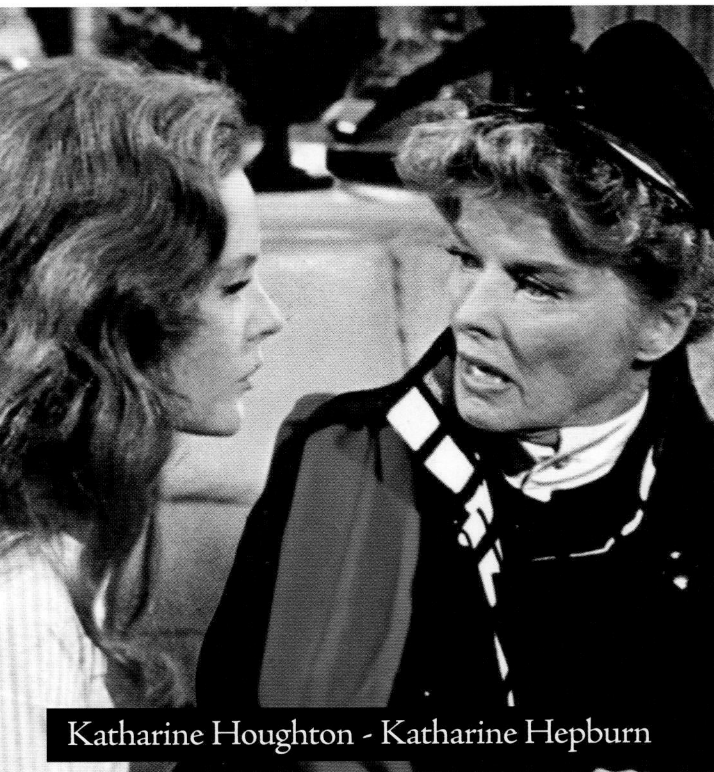

Katharine Houghton - Katharine Hepburn

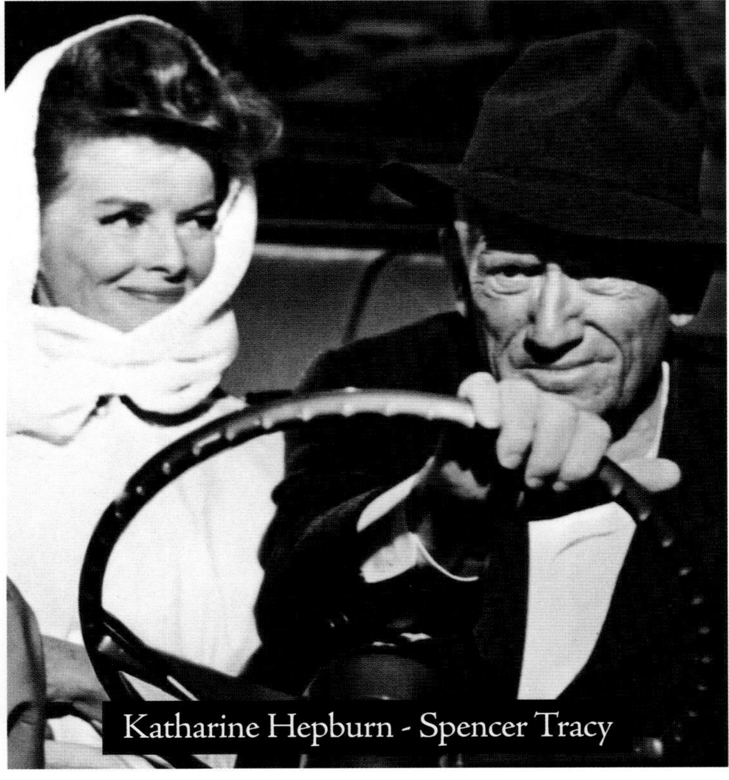

Katharine Hepburn - Spencer Tracy

"Guess Who's Coming To Dinner" followed Sidney Poitier's appearance in "In The Heat Of The Night," "A Raisin in the Sun" and "The Defiant Ones," all socially conscious films.

This was the ninth and final film in which Katharine Hepburn and Spencer Tracy co-starred.

A disillusioned college graduate finds himself torn between his older lover and her daughter.

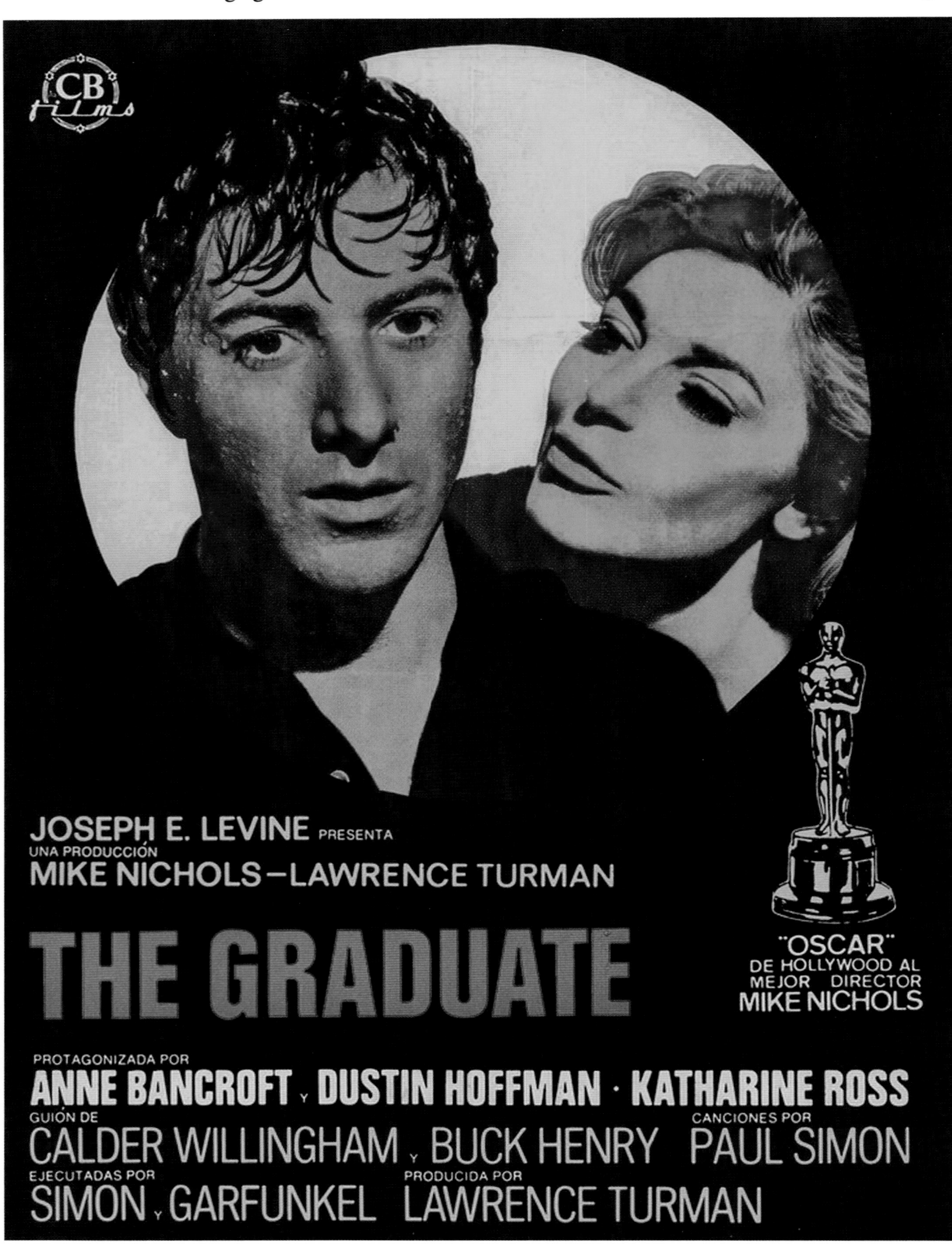

David Edelstein of New York Magazine/Vulture wrote: "Be agog at Anne Bancroft's Mrs. Robinson in some of the most hilariously icky seduction scenes ever filmed."

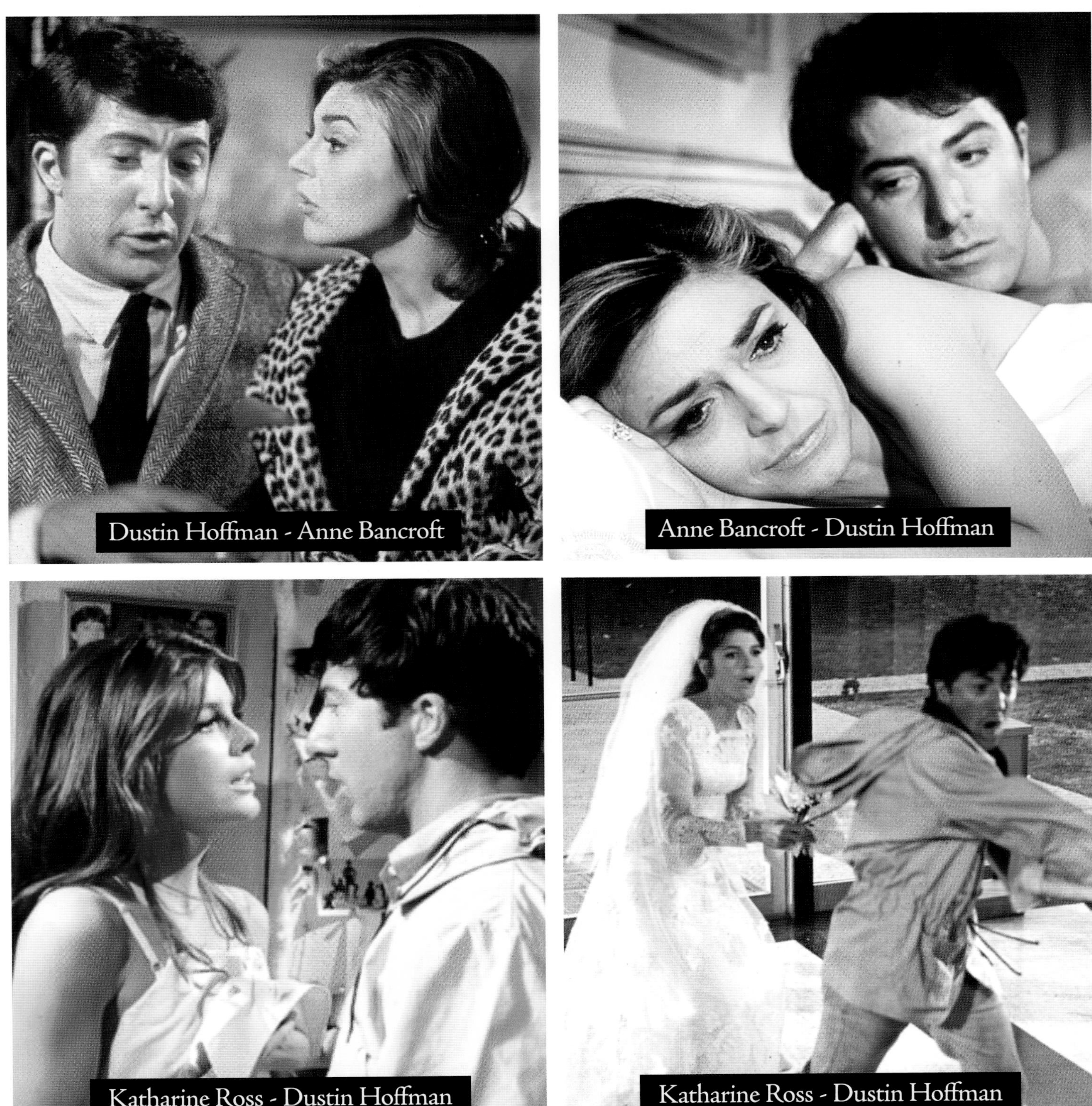

Dustin Hoffman - Anne Bancroft

Anne Bancroft - Dustin Hoffman

Katharine Ross - Dustin Hoffman

Katharine Ross - Dustin Hoffman

"The Graduate" was Dustin Hoffman's break-out film and the one that followed Anne Bancroft's award-winning performance in "The Miracle Worker."

Estelle Lebost and her husband Carl Reiner loved this film and loved spending many happy evenings in the company of Anne Bancroft and her husband Mel Brooks.

When deaf mute Singer moves to a small city to be near his only friend confined in a hospital, he grows attached to his landlady's sensitive 16-year-old daughter.

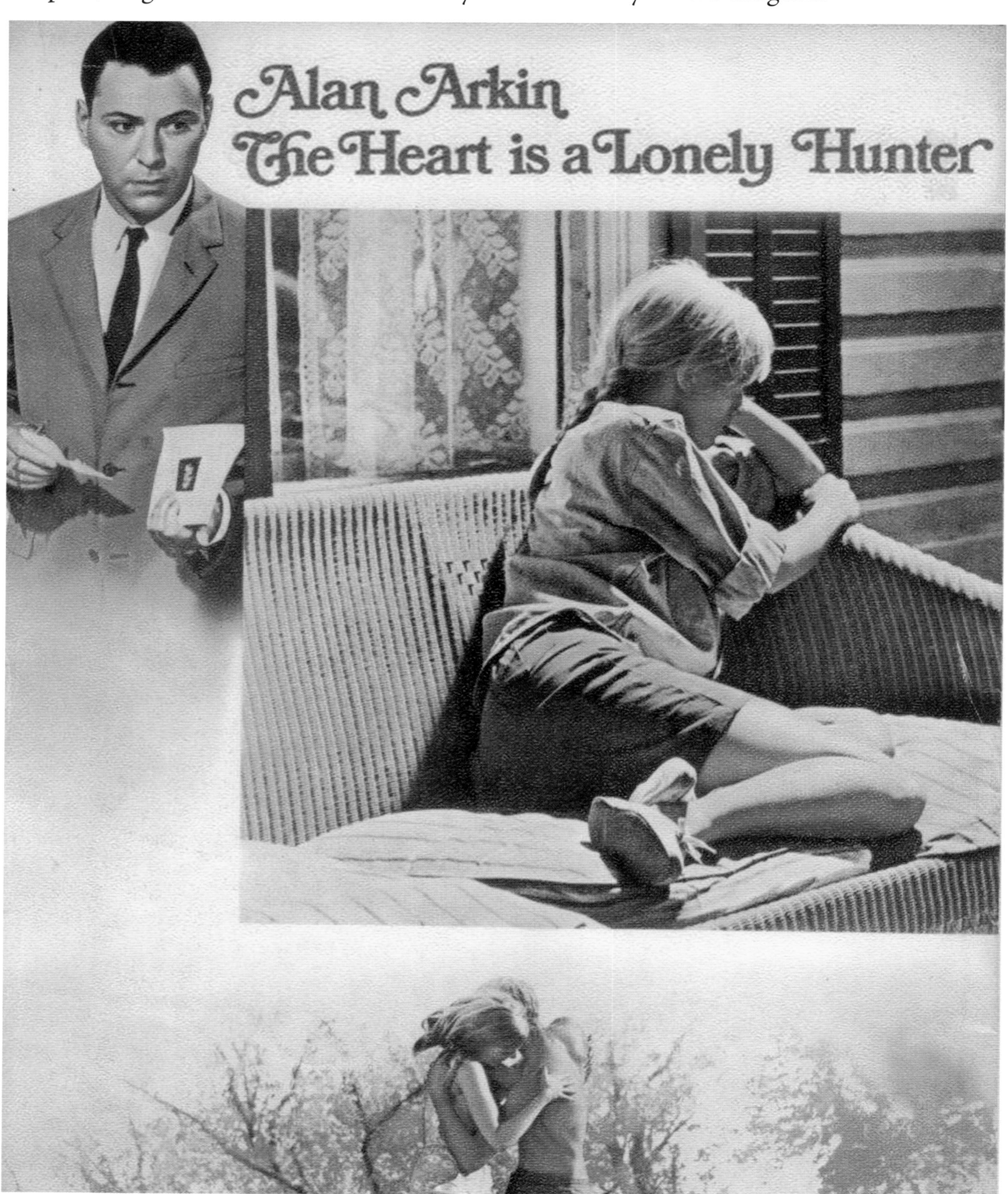

The New York Times wrote: "Alan Arkin's performance is extraordinarily deep and sound. His use of his hands seems quite normal and personal, and when he walks in the night, using his hands to talk to himself, it's a perfect dramatic expression of what thinking is."

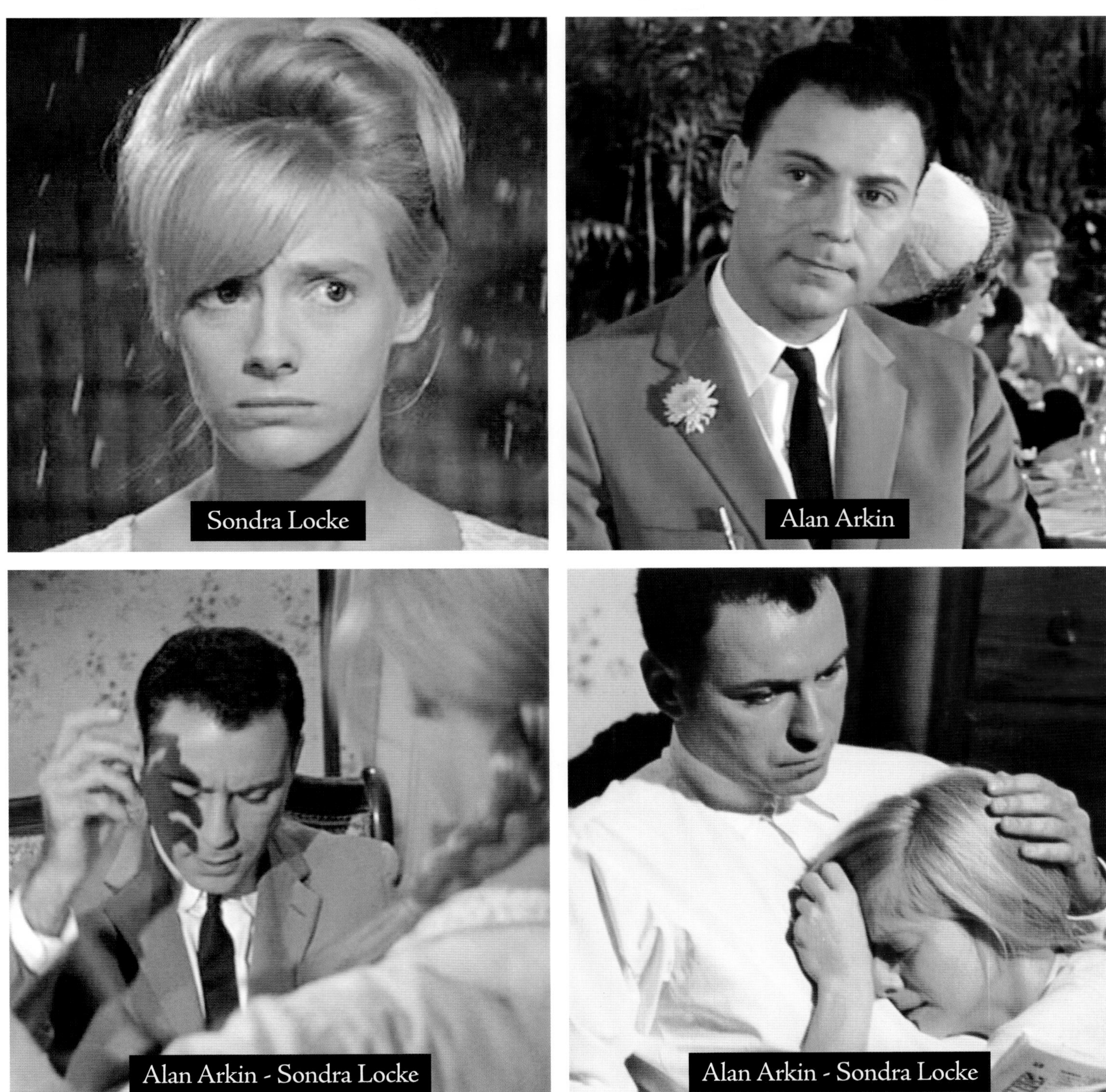

Sondra Locke

Alan Arkin

Alan Arkin - Sondra Locke

Alan Arkin - Sondra Locke

By playing a deaf mute, Alan Arkin showcased his extraordinary abilities to flesh out the characters he played. In "The Russian's Are Coming," he actually learned to speak Russian, in "The Pink Panther," as Inspector Jacques Clouseau, he affected a perfect French accent, and in "Catch 22," he gave a moving performance as Yossarian.

Two friends try sharing an apartment, but they're as different as night and day.

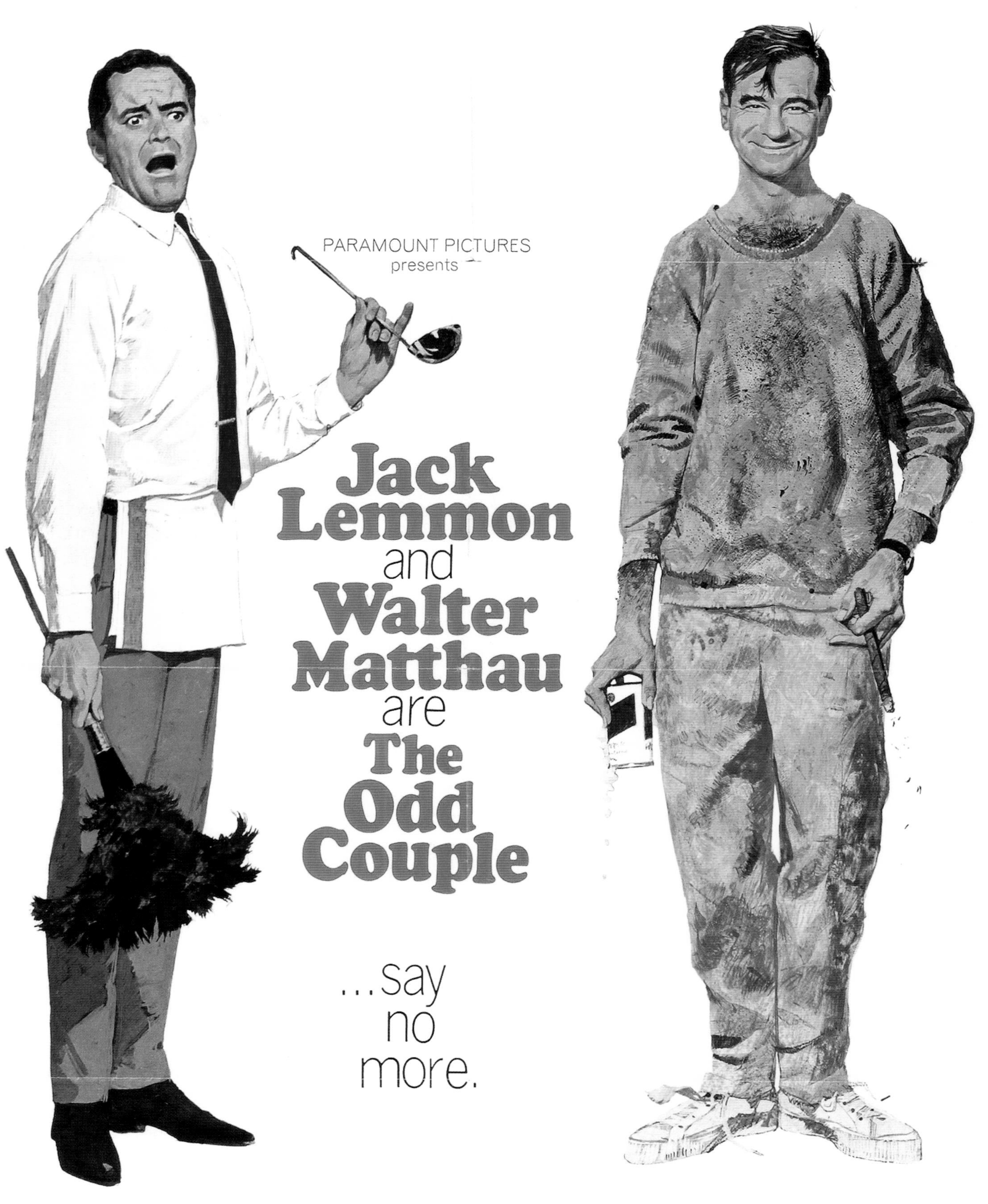

James Plath of Family Home Theater wrote: "Simon's 'The Odd Couple' is proof that smart writing and adult themes can still make for a fun evening at your family home theater."

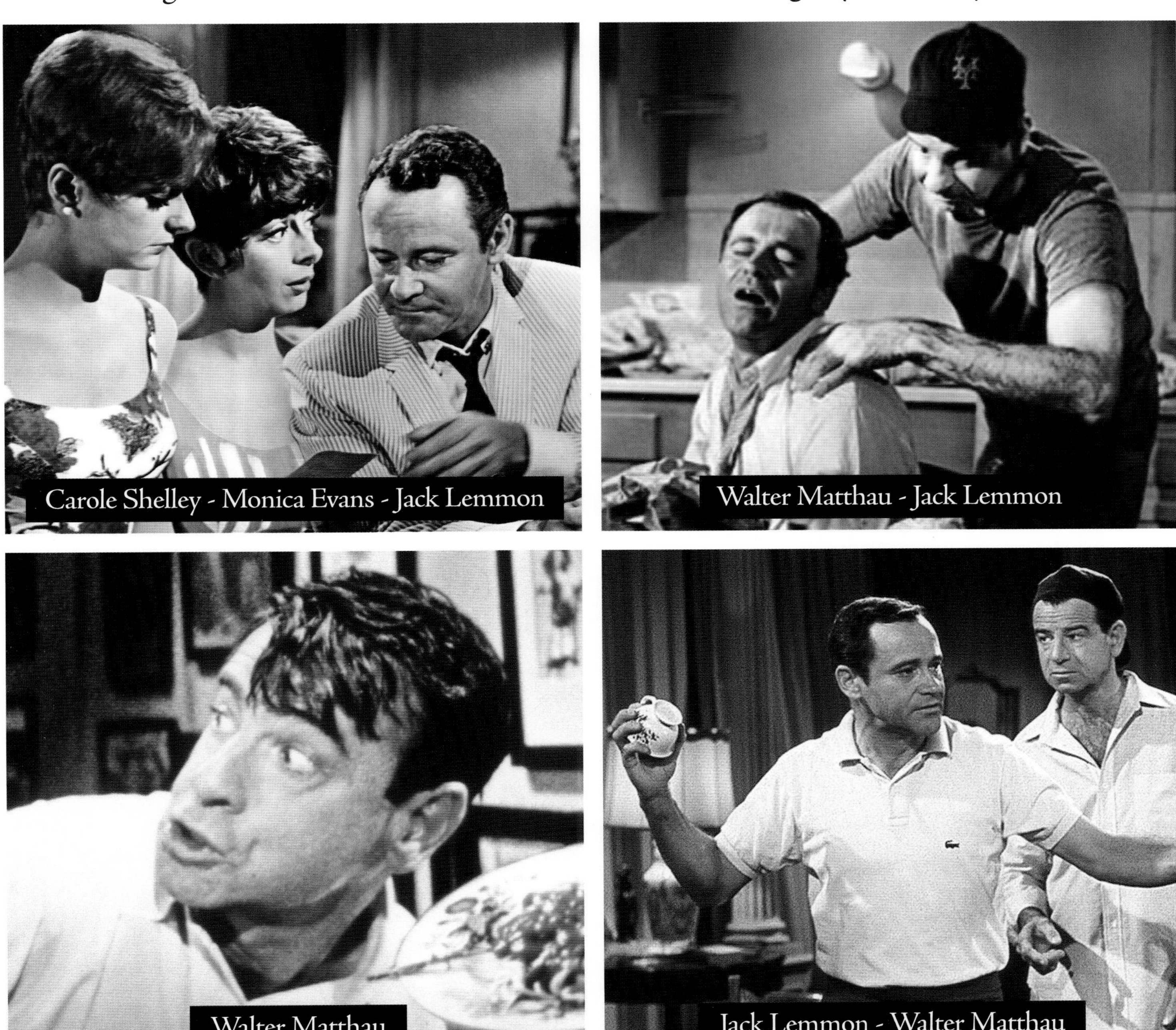

Carole Shelley - Monica Evans - Jack Lemmon

Walter Matthau - Jack Lemmon

Walter Matthau

Jack Lemmon - Walter Matthau

Had I not been working on "The Sid Caesar Show," I would have accepted Neil Simon's invitation to star in "Come Blow Your Horn," his very first Broadway show. Were I available I would have taken Neil's offer and I'd be able to say that: "I appeared in the very first of the thirty-four hit Broadway plays that were authored by the amazing Neil Simon."

In 1965, Neil Simon's play which starred Walter Matthau and Art Carney, "The Odd Couple," opened on Broadway. In 1970, "The Odd Couple" was adapted for television and played for five years with Tony Randall and Jack Klugman in the lead roles. In 2015, CBS resurrected the show, which now stars Matthew Perry and Thomas Lennon.

The life of Fanny Brice, famed comedienne and entertainer. We see her rise to fame as a Ziegfeld girl, subsequent career and her relationship with Nick Arnstein.

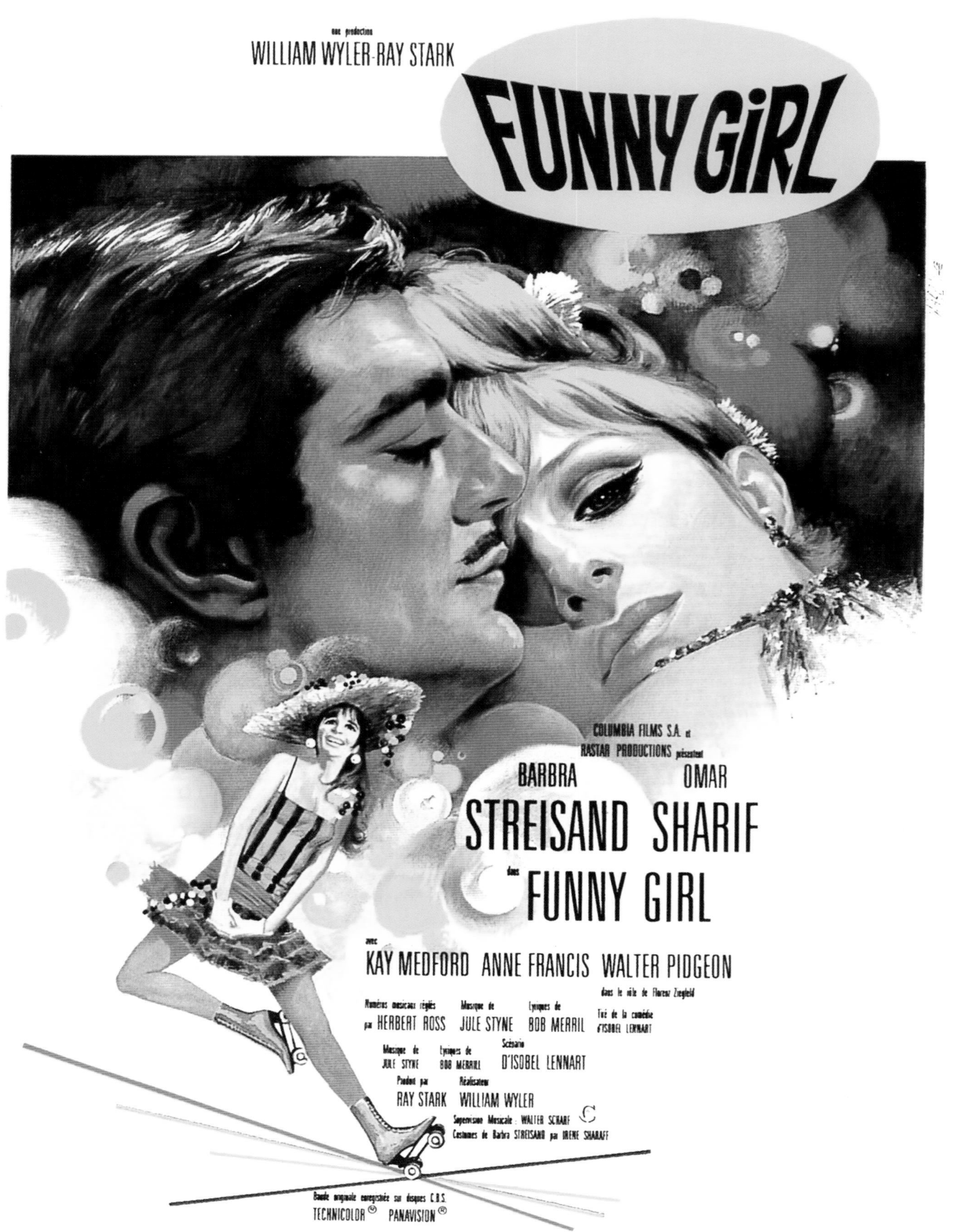

Michael W. Phillips, Jr. of Goatdog's Movies wrote: "Streisand gives a natural, unforced performance, easily one of the three or four best Best Actresses in Oscar history."

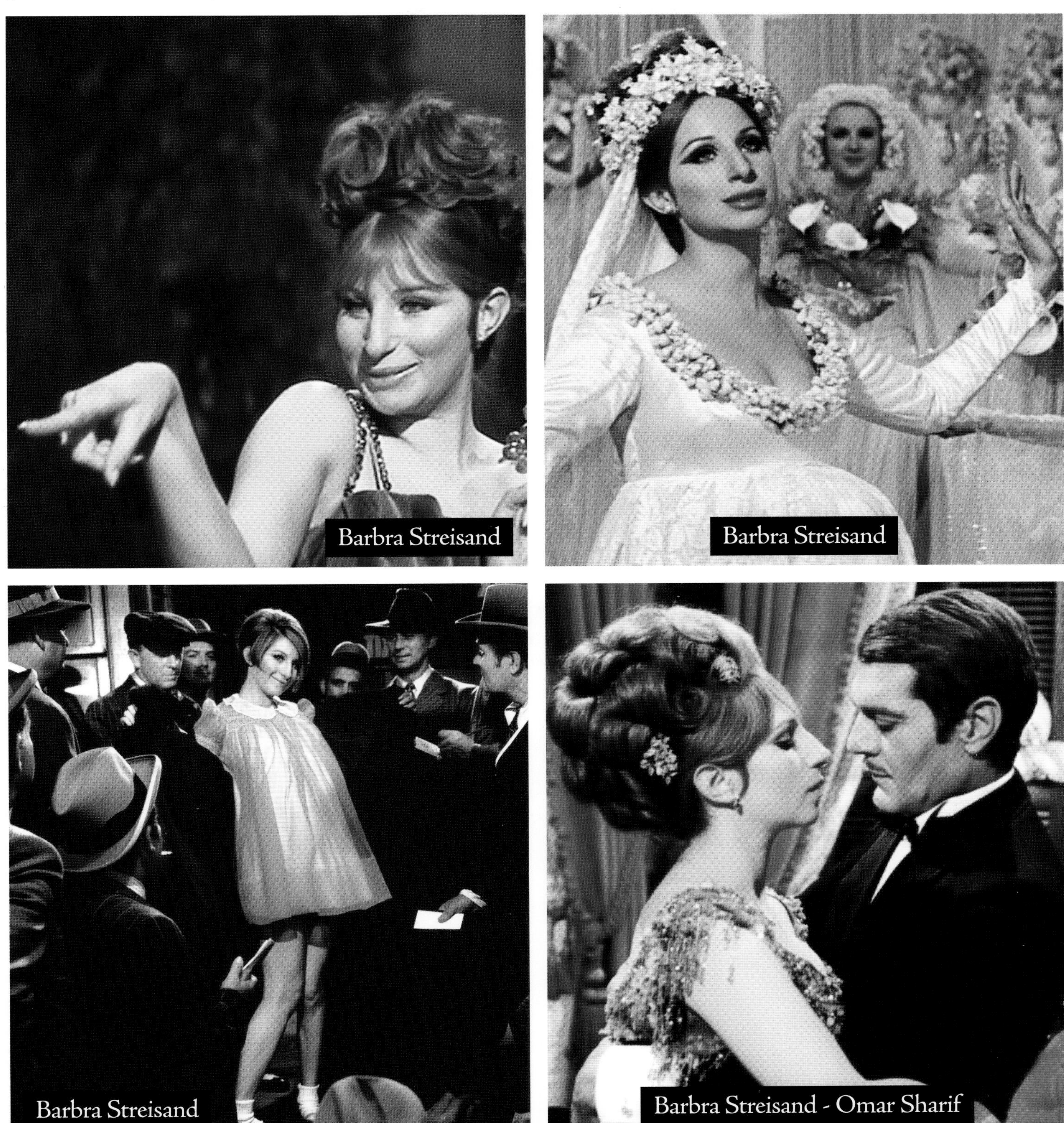

Barbra Streisand

Barbra Streisand

Barbra Streisand

Barbra Streisand - Omar Sharif

Barbra Streisand can sing, dance, act, impersonate, write, direct and produce. She is the only septuple-threat in show business and in her first film, "Funny Girl," for which she won an Oscar, she used five of her seven talents; in "Yentl" and "Prince of Tides" she showed off the last two.

Young Oliver Twist runs away from an orphanage and meets a group of trained pickpockets.

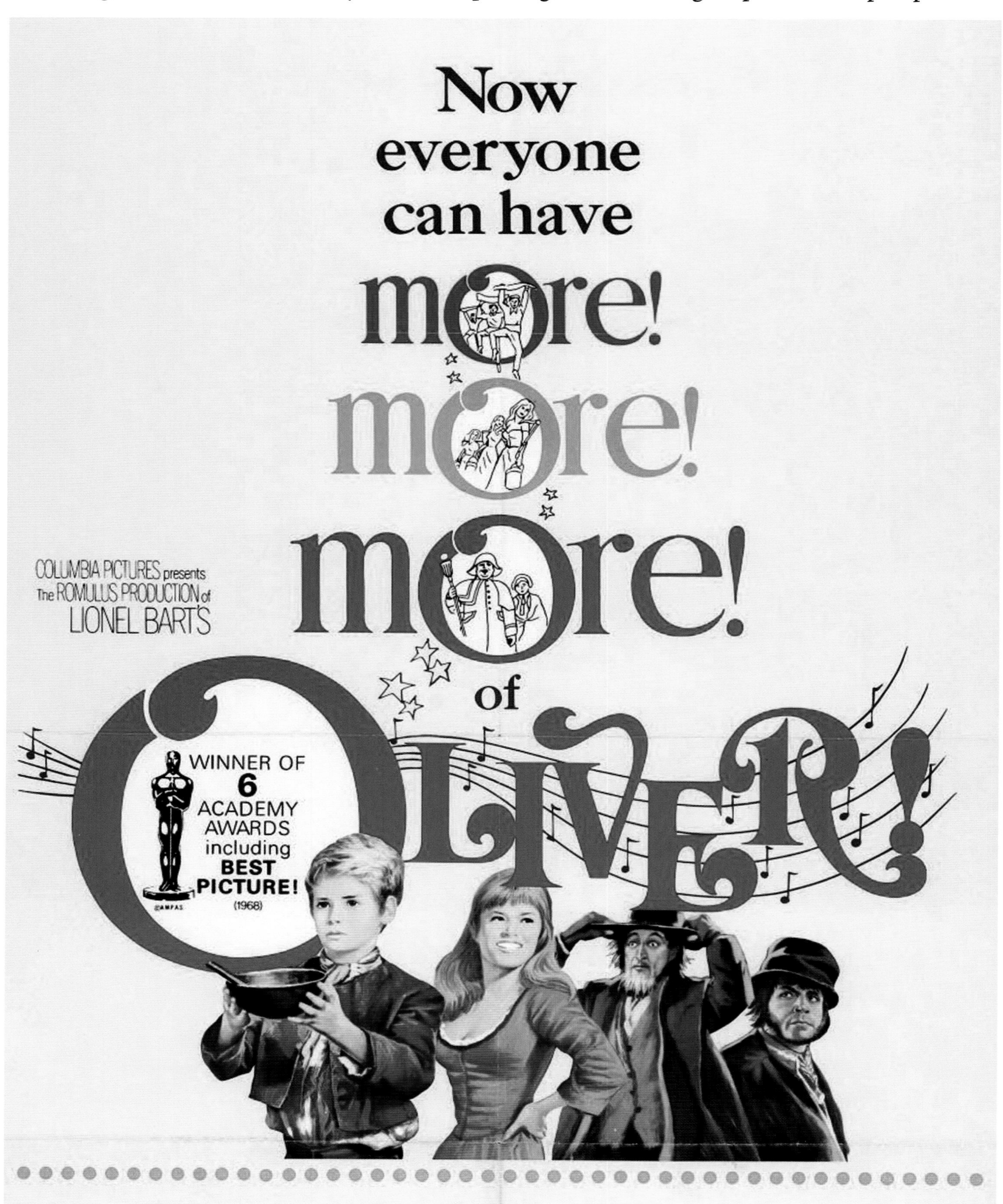

Wanda Hale of New York Daily News wrote: "'Oliver!' is a timeless classic that will be as lovable in 10 or 20 years as it is today."

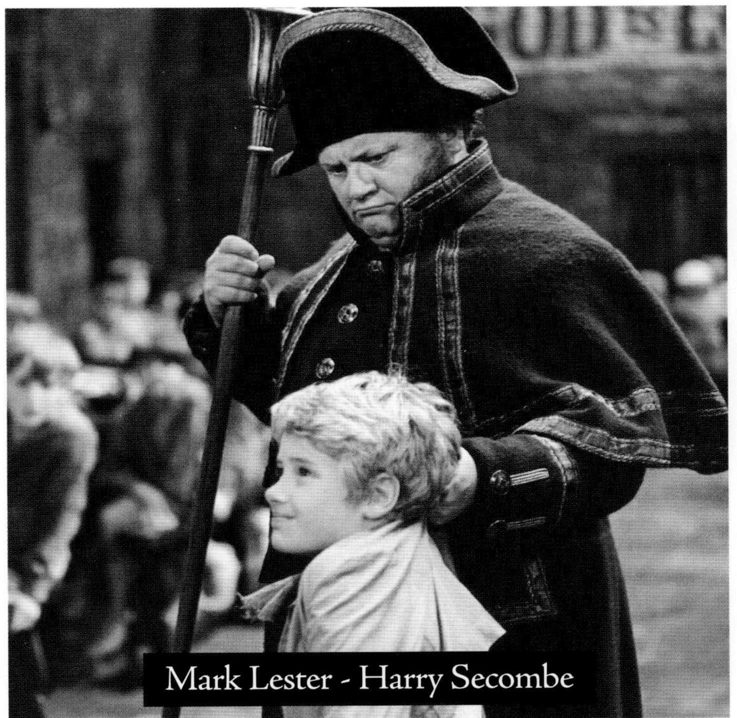
Mark Lester - Harry Secombe

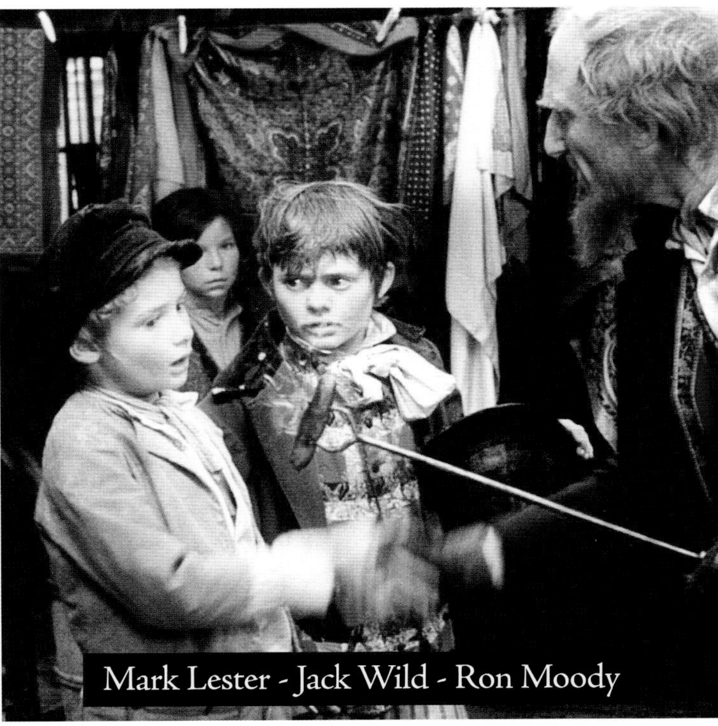
Mark Lester - Jack Wild - Ron Moody

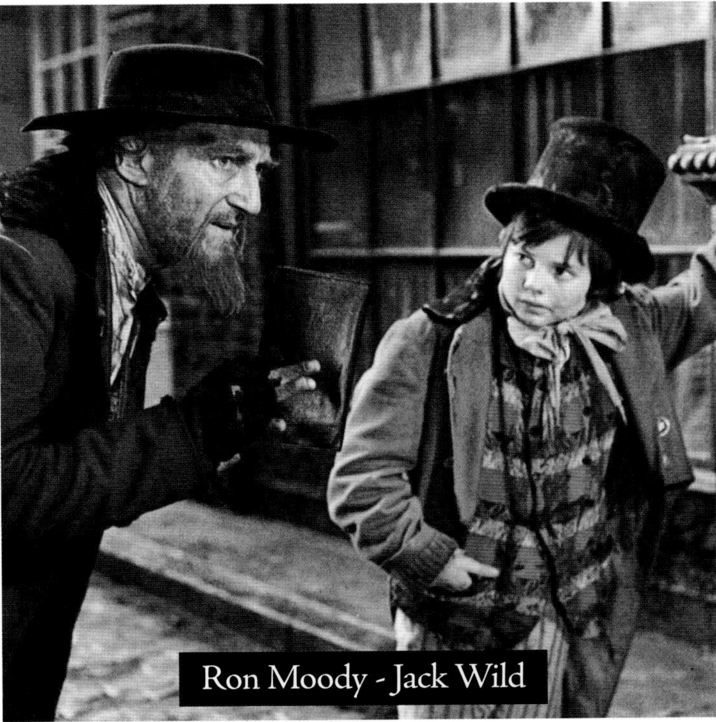
Ron Moody - Jack Wild

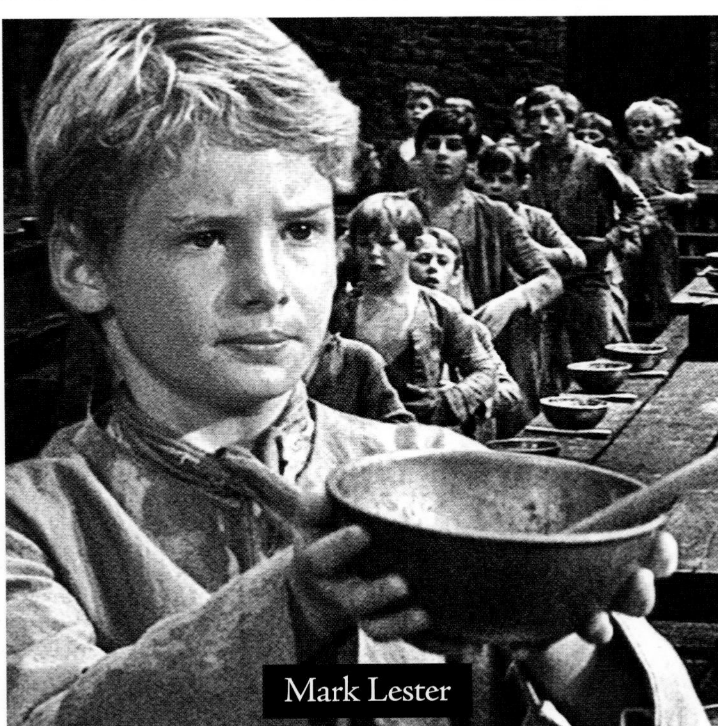
Mark Lester

I wonder how many of you have children who emulated Oliver by holding out their empty bowl and shouting, "More! More!"

At the 41st Academy Awards, "Oliver!" was nominated for eleven Oscars and won six. The film's Art Director, Terry Marsh, won his Oscar for recreating, on the backlot of Shepperton Studios, the streets and houses Charles Dickens' London.

Story of a brilliant silent-film comic whose talent is overshadowed by his ego.

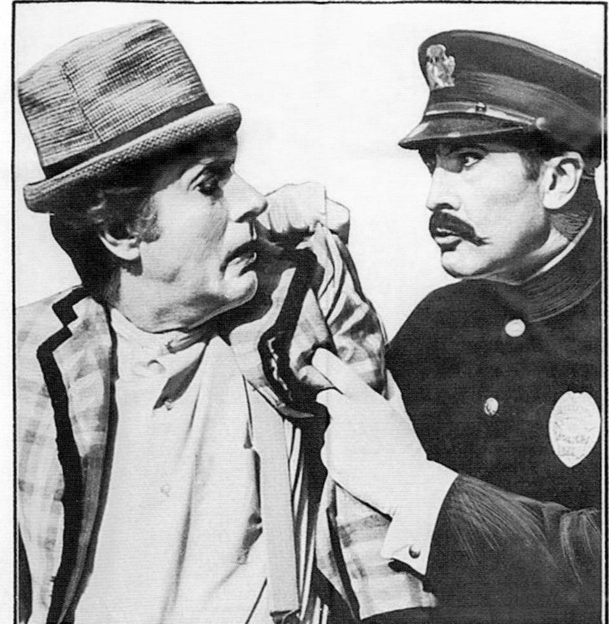

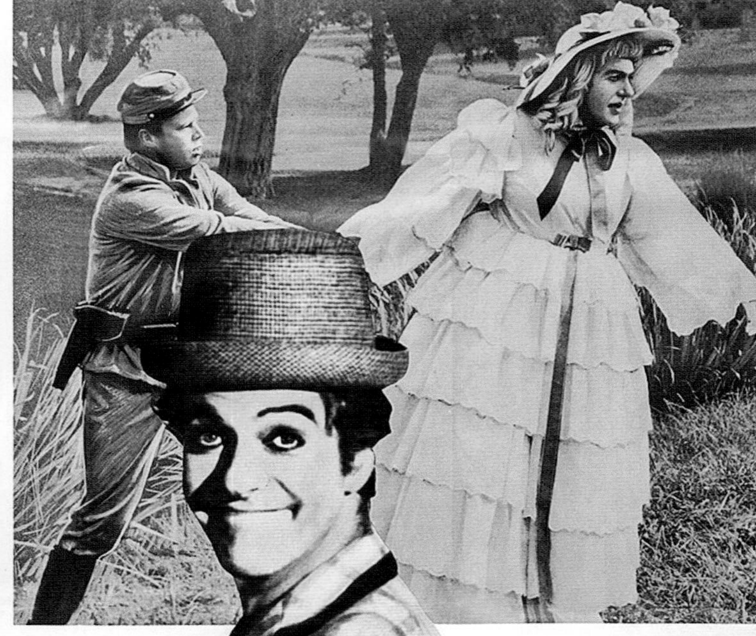

COLUMBIA PICTURES
Presents

"THE COMIC"

starring
DICK
VAN DYKE
MICHELE
LEE
MICKEY
ROONEY

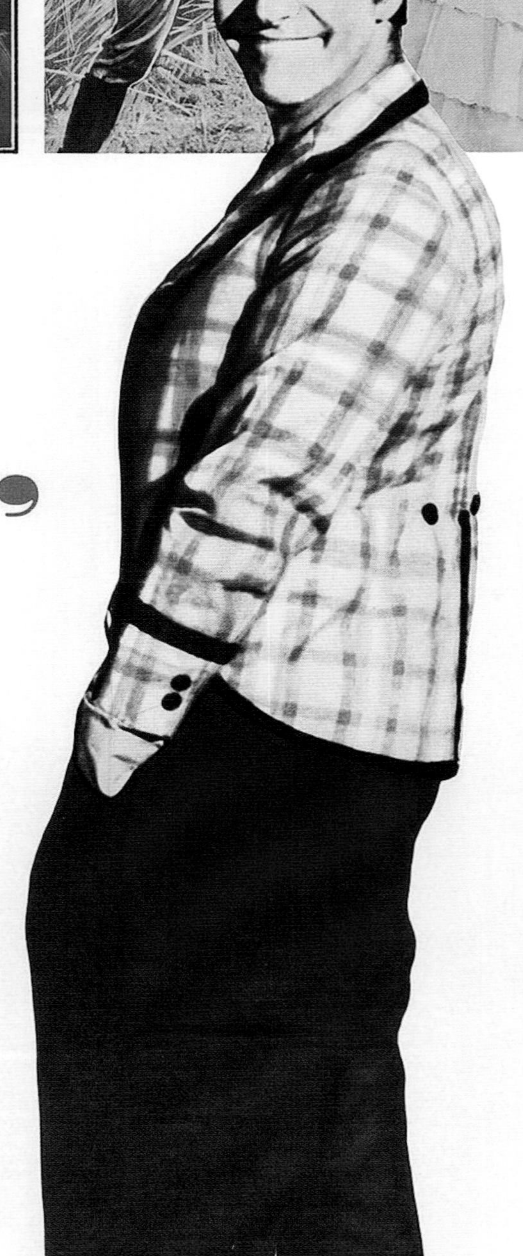

Fernando F. Croce of CinePassion wrote: "Custard mixes with arsenic in Reiner's bright meditation on slapstick."

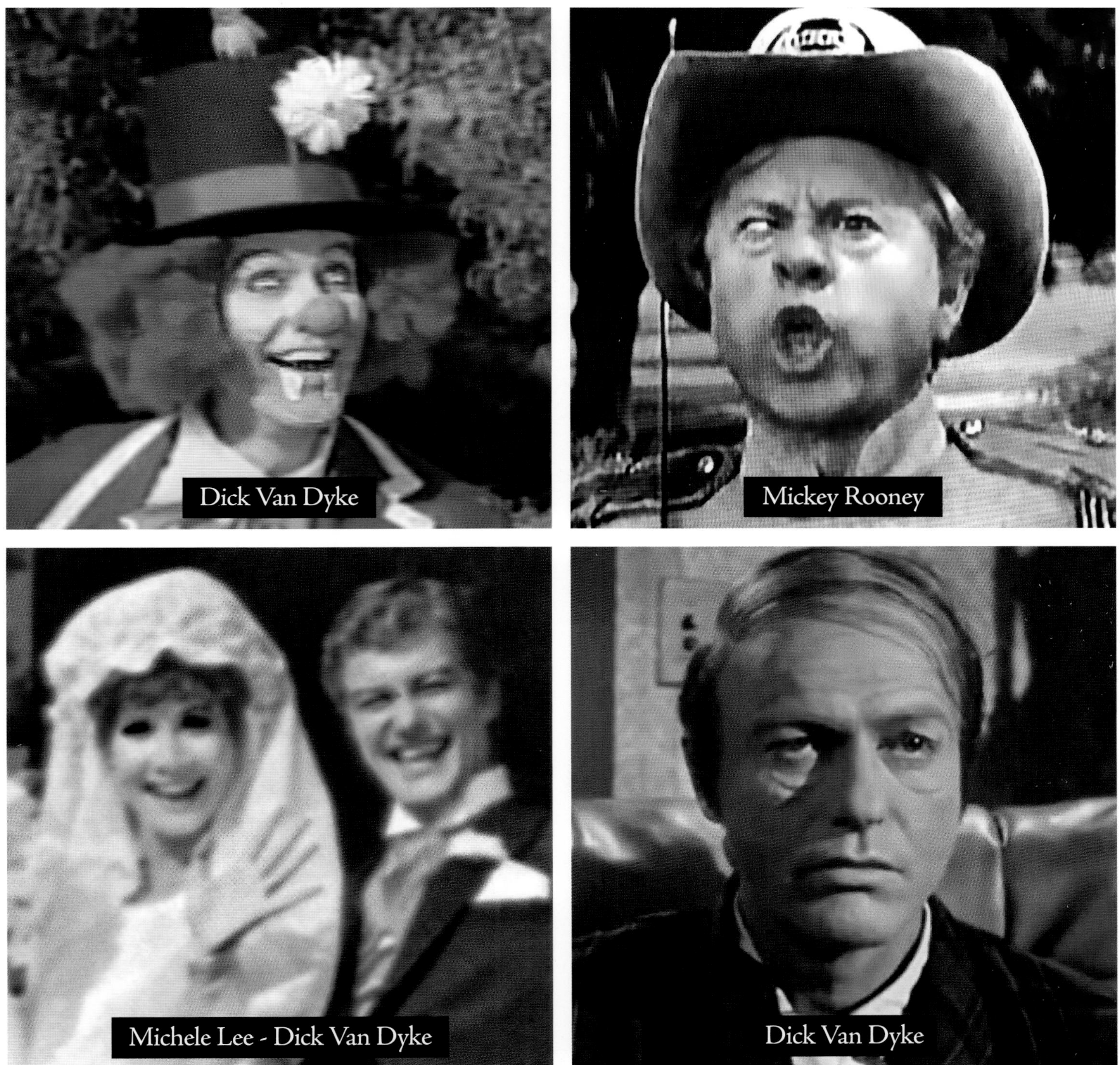

Dick Van Dyke

Mickey Rooney

Michele Lee - Dick Van Dyke

Dick Van Dyke

Mickey Rooney, who played "Cock-eye," was Hollywood's most versatile actor, who could sing, dance and play every musical instrument, but could not cross his eyes. At some expense we had a prosthesis made but it reddened his eye, which required us to have an optometrist on the set.

Dick Van Dyke's performance as Billy Bright, an egocentric silent film star was for me, worthy of an Oscar. In one sad scene, Billy's wife, Michele Lee, informs him that the estranged son he is attempting to kidnap is not theirs, but their neighbor's child.

A Texas dishwasher quits his job and heads to New York City dressed as a cowboy in hopes of becoming a prostitute and meets a street con man who becomes his pimp.

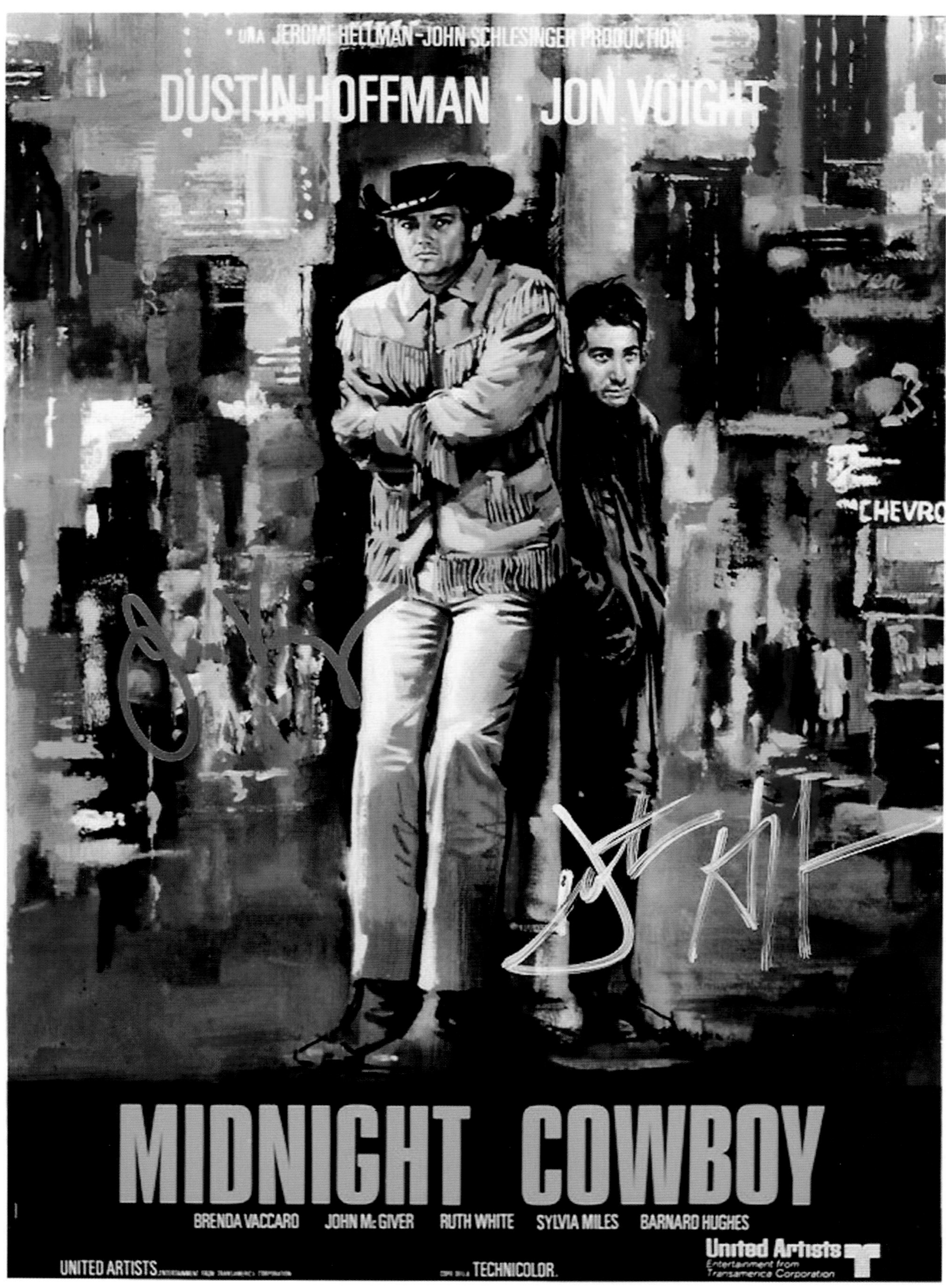

Gene Siskel of Chicago Tribune wrote: "I cannot recall a more marvelous pair of acting performances in any one film."

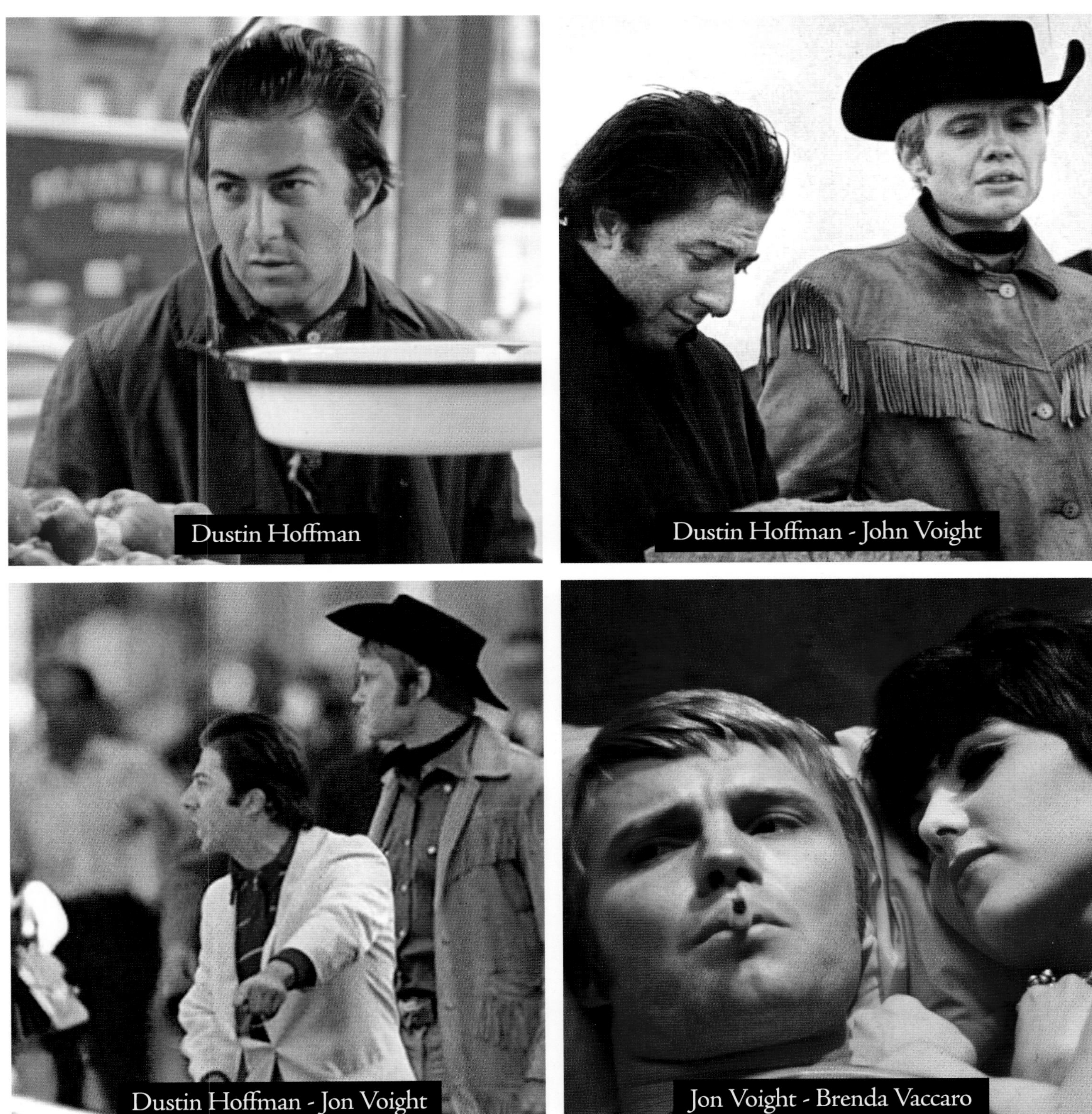

Dustin Hoffman

Dustin Hoffman - John Voight

Dustin Hoffman - Jon Voight

Jon Voight - Brenda Vaccaro

In squiring his new male prostitute about town, the limping Dustin Hoffman shouts at a cab driver who almost runs him over, "Hey, I'm walkin' here! I'm walkin' here!" Those words and his delivery still make me smile. John Voight's first customer is played by Brenda Vaccaro, who pays him twenty dollars for his overnight 'services.'

Documentary filmmakers Bob and Carole attend a group therapy session. The newly "enlightened" couple chastise their closest friends, Ted and Alice, for not coming to grips with their true feelings. Ted and Alice humor their friends, but it is obvious that there is sexual tension at work within the foursome.

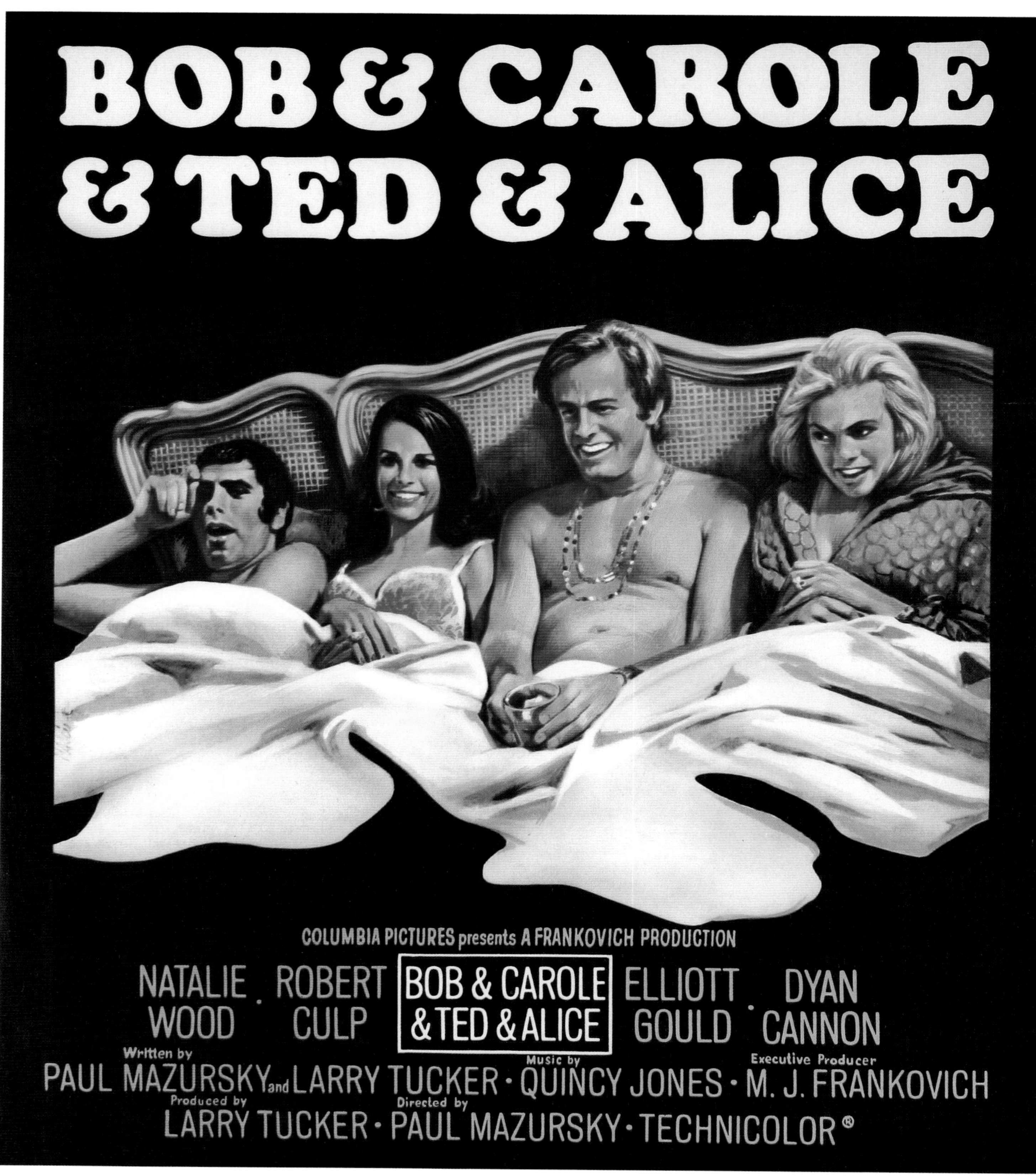

Roger Ebert of The Chicago Sun-Times wrote: "The genius of 'Bob & Carole & Ted & Alice' is that it understands the peculiar nature of the moral crisis for Americans in this age group, and understands that the way to consider it is in a comedy."

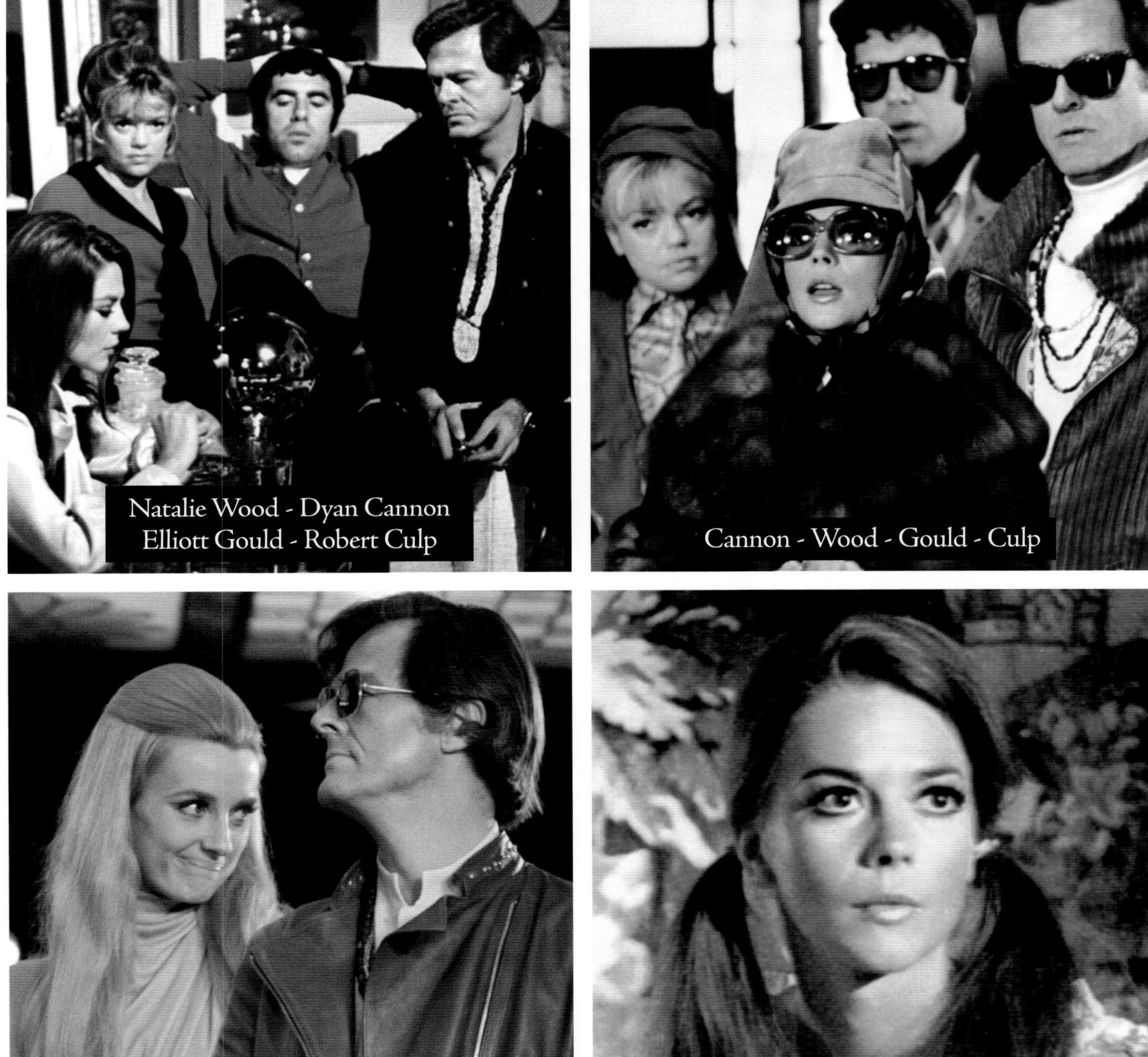

Natalie Wood - Dyan Cannon
Elliott Gould - Robert Culp

Cannon - Wood - Gould - Culp

Celeste Yarnall - Robert Culp

Natalie Wood

This film grossed thirty-one million dollars by showing curious young filmgoers how two couples might behave in a double bed.

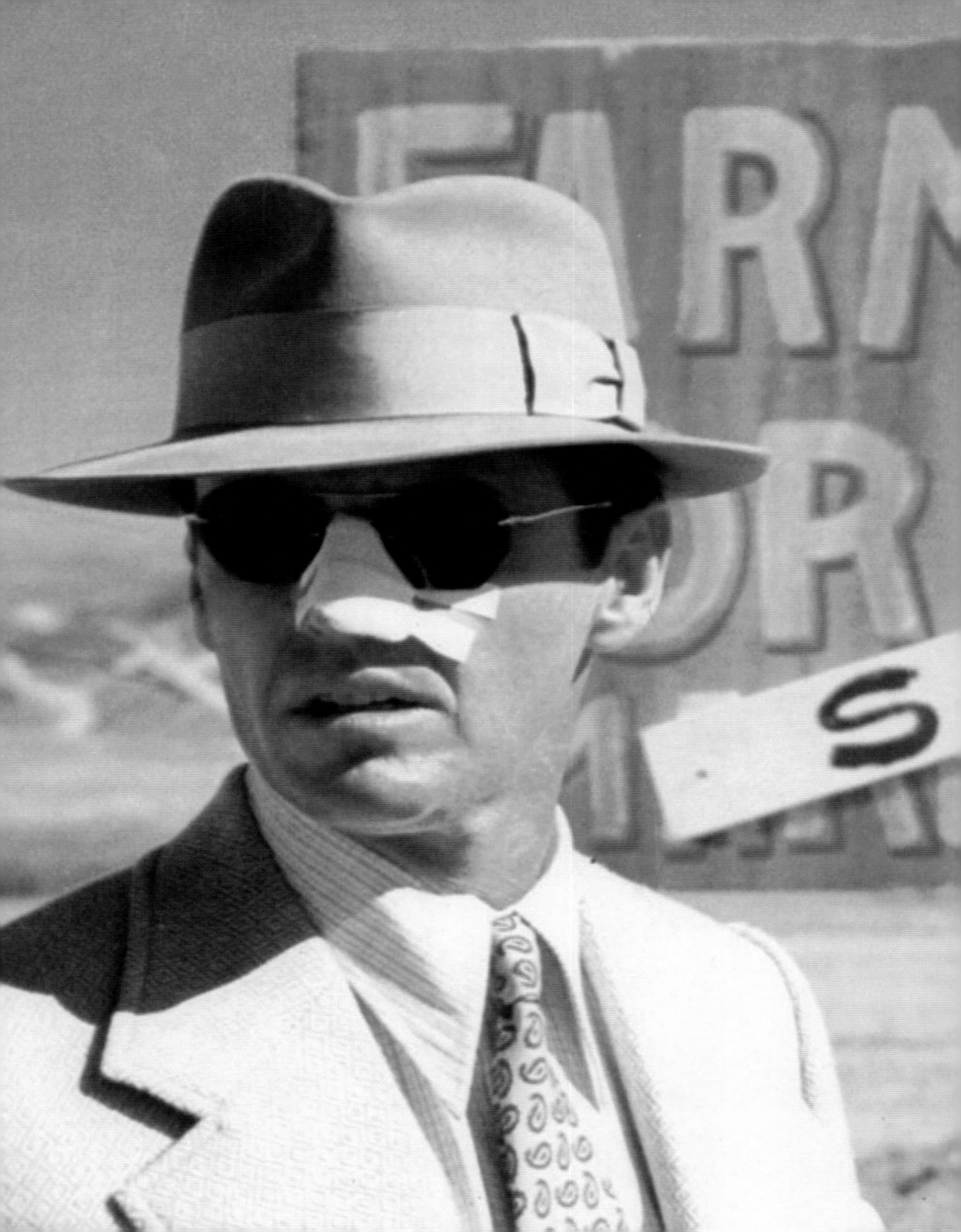

the 70s

When New York attorney George Segal meets Trish Van Devere, he schemes to eliminate his senile mother, because he fears her behavior will lead to his girlfriend's departure.

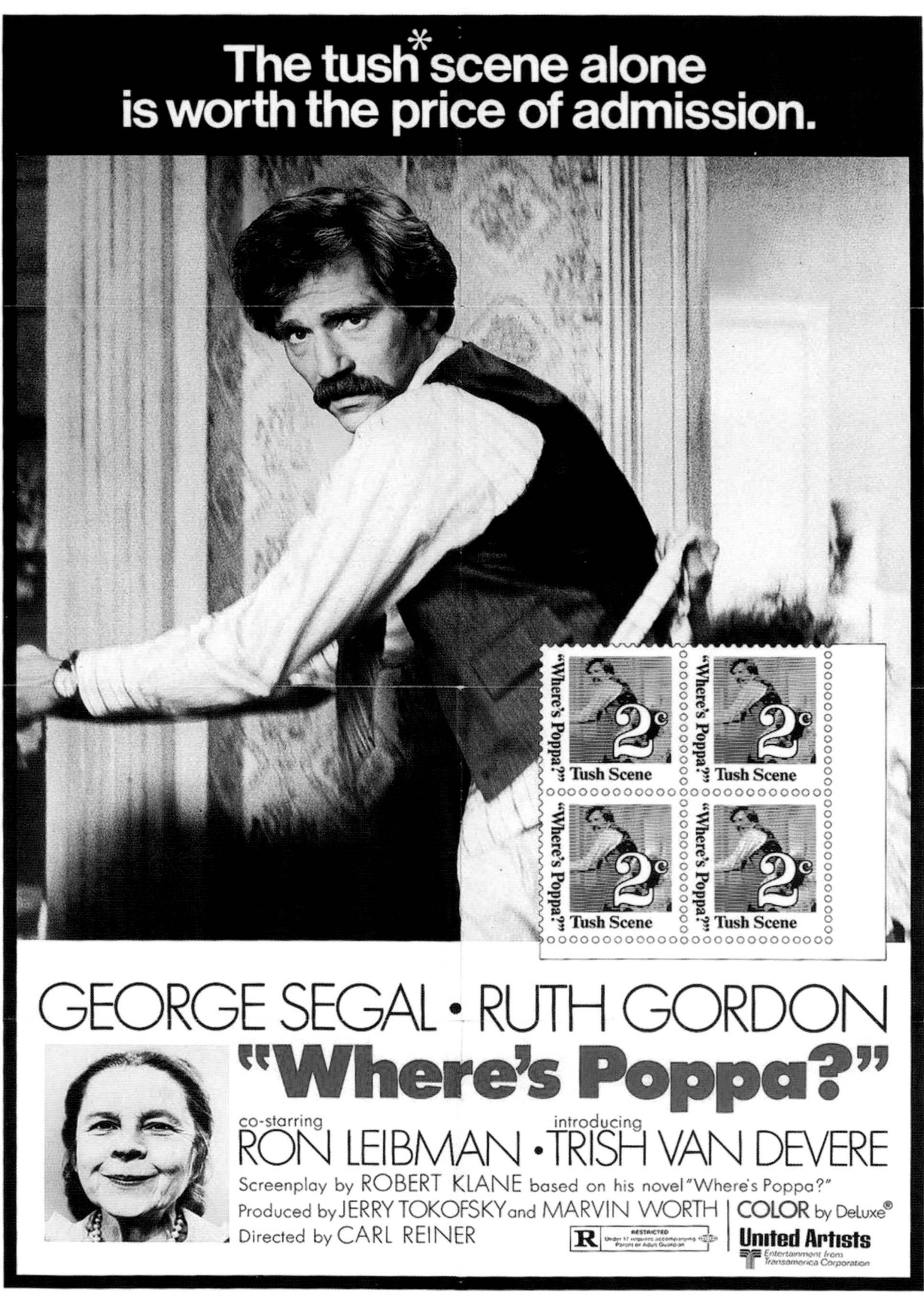

Roger Greenspun of The New York Times wrote: "'Where's Poppa?' doesn't succeed all the time, but it succeeds often enough to satisfy a taste for comedy that has not had much nourishment this season. 'Where's Poppa?' nourishes us with a desperately funny film."

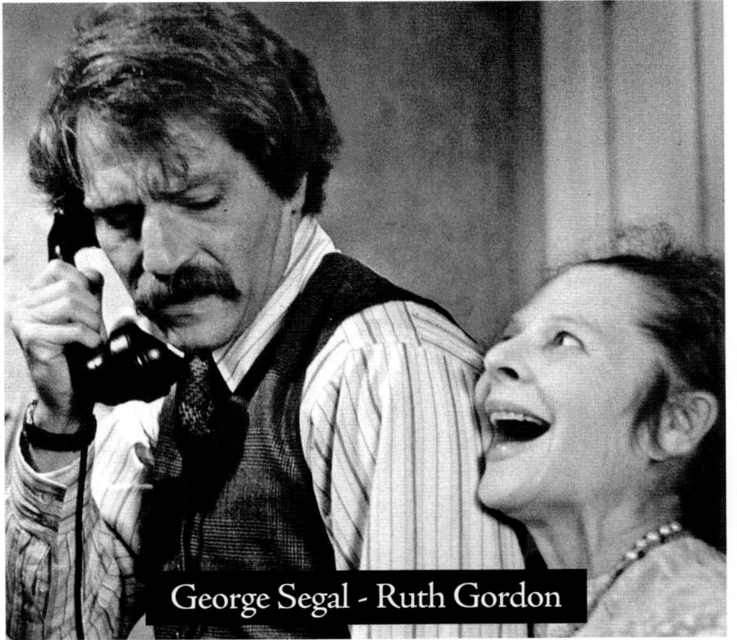
George Segal - Ruth Gordon

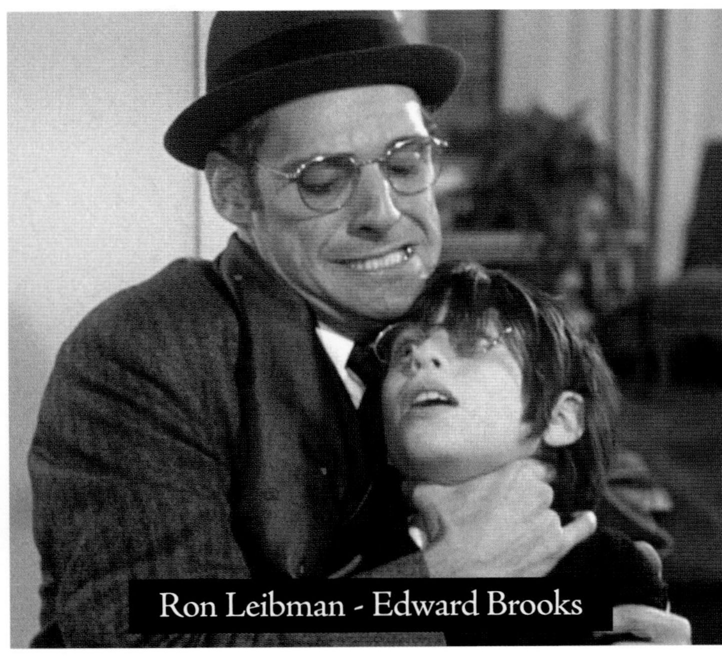
Ron Leibman - Edward Brooks

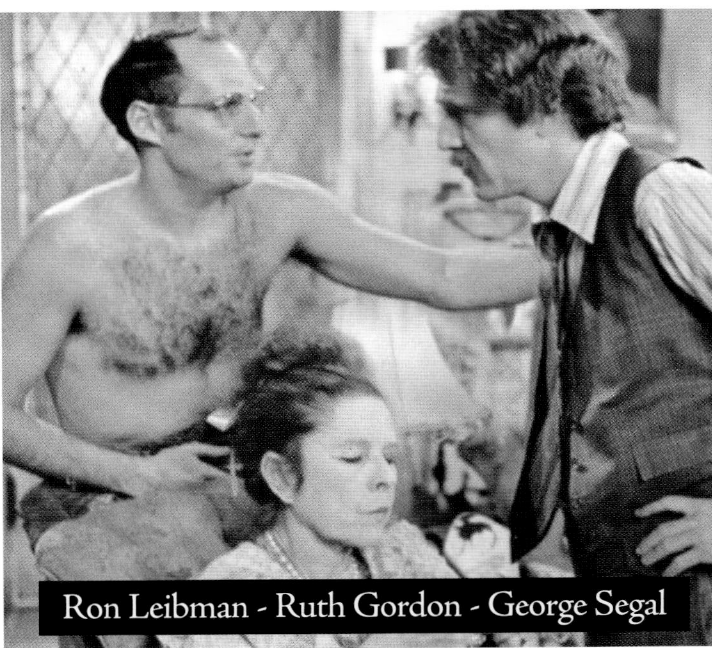
Ron Leibman - Ruth Gordon - George Segal

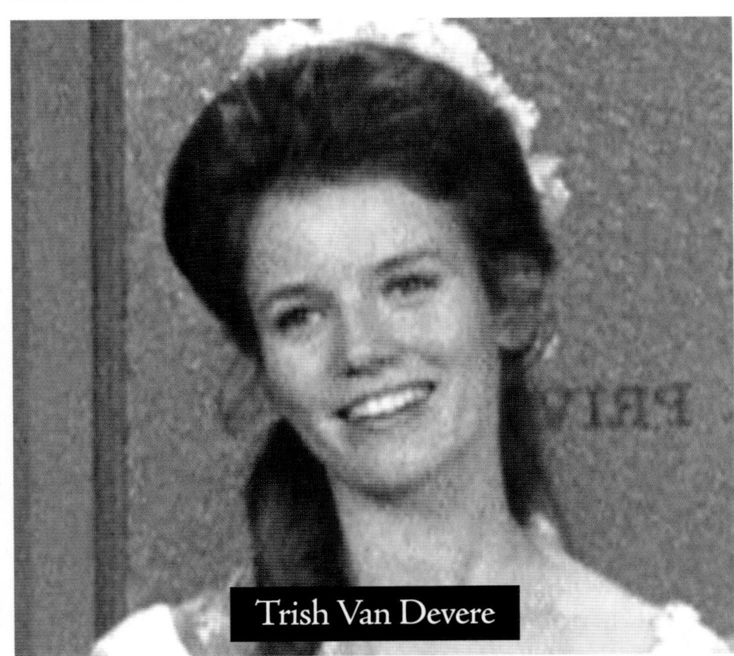
Trish Van Devere

In 1970, I was asked to read the novel, "Where's Poppa?," and if I liked it, would I be interested in directing the movie version? I remember thinking, "*In today's conservative market, there is no way that this movie will ever be accepted and that's a pretty good reason to do it.*"

To my surprise, not only was it accepted, but it keeps having rebirths. Any film where the hero wins the hand of a pretty maiden and has his tush kissed by his mother, can't miss.

The proud father of Edward, the boy being choked, is Mel Brooks.

The daring screenplay was adapted from a novel written by Robert Klane.

The staff of a Korean War field hospital use humor and high jinks to keep their sanity.

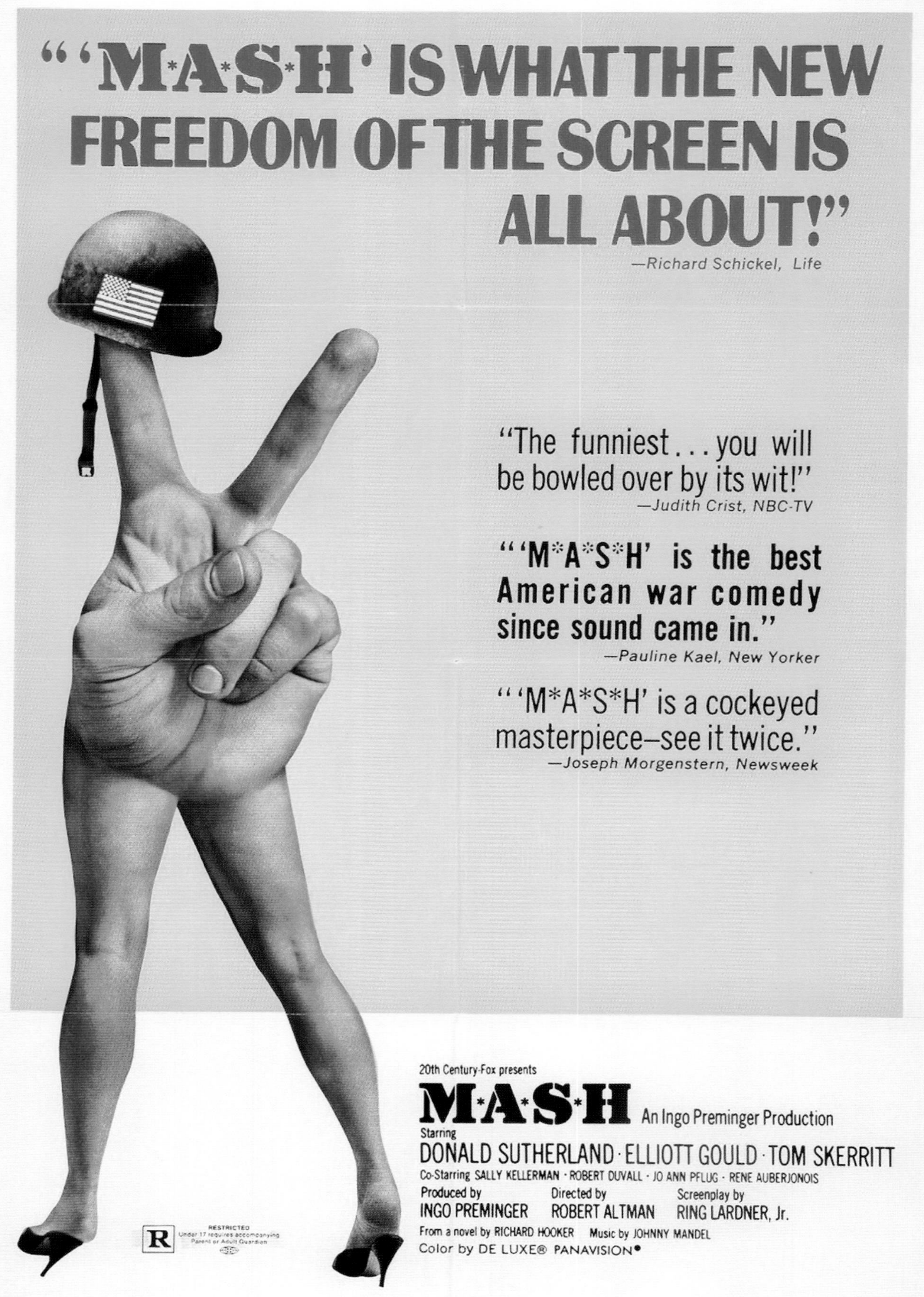

TIME Magazine wrote: "'M.A.S.H.,' one of America's funniest bloody films, is also one of its bloodiest funny films."

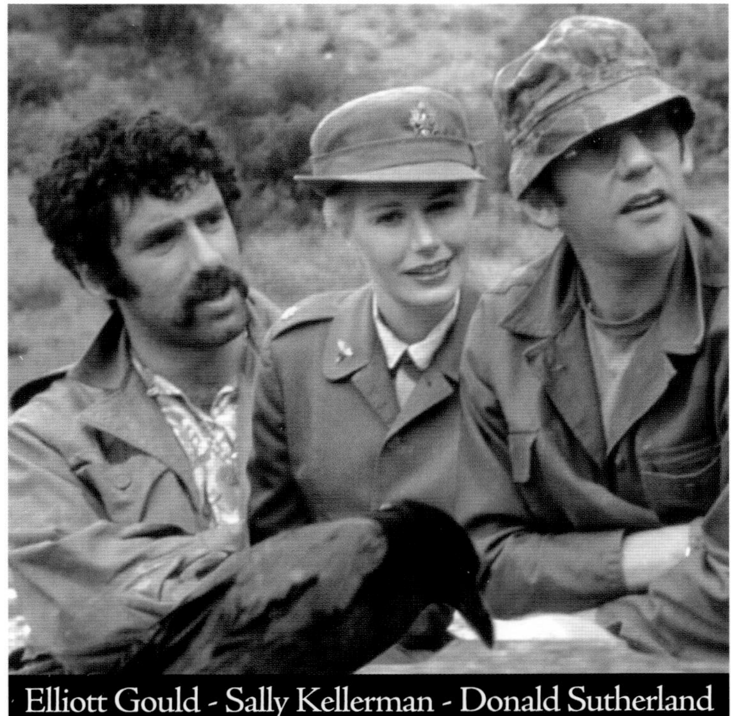
Elliott Gould - Sally Kellerman - Donald Sutherland

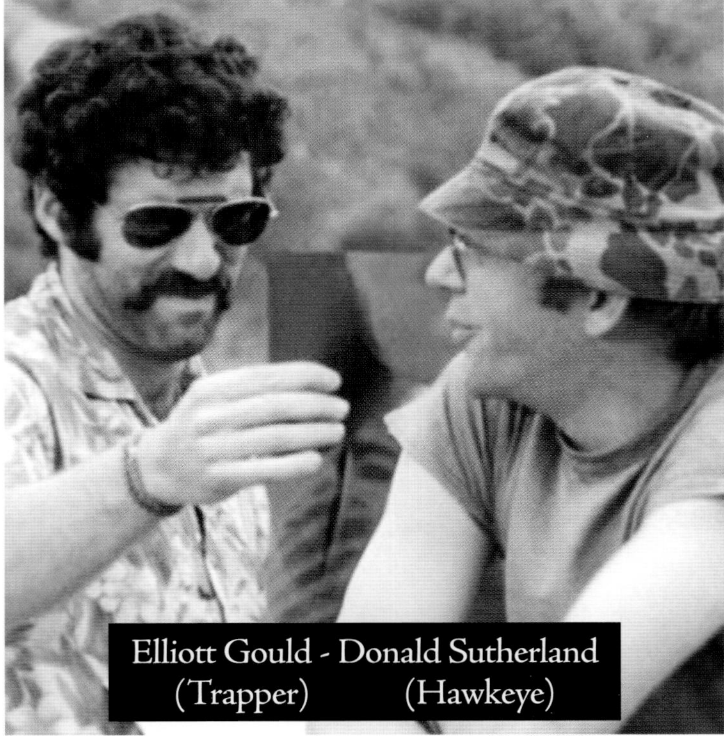
Elliott Gould - Donald Sutherland
(Trapper) (Hawkeye)

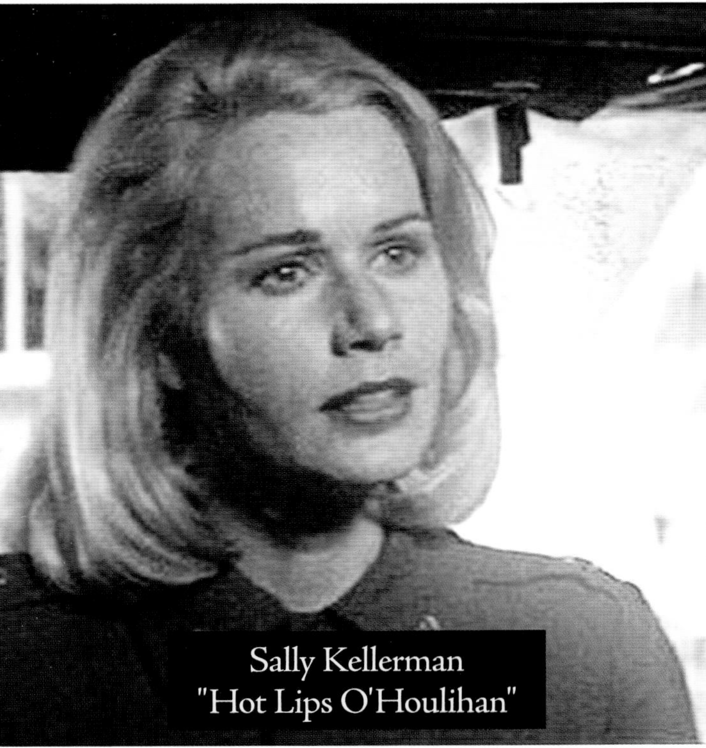
Sally Kellerman
"Hot Lips O'Houlihan"

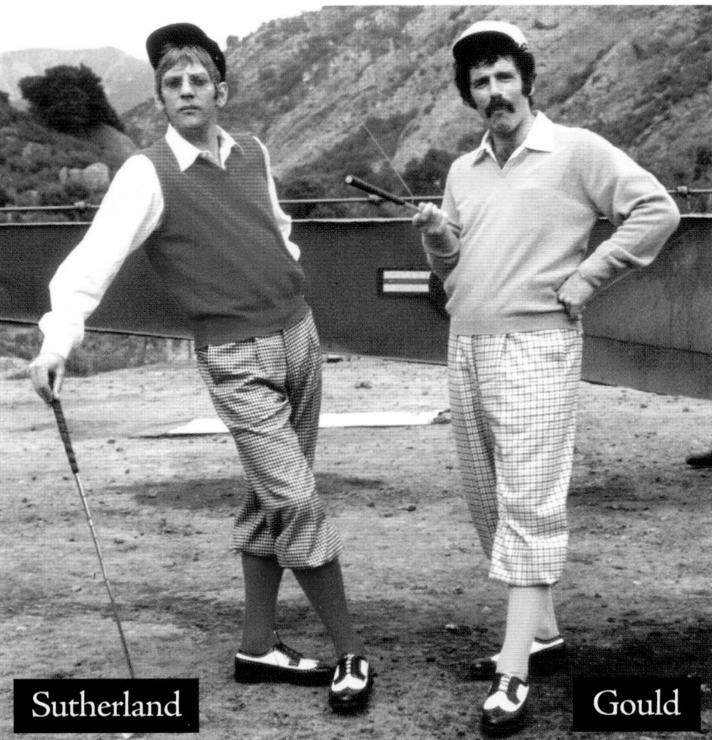
Sutherland Gould

I've always admired the "Hot Legs" in this avant-garde poster, which I'm pretty sure were modeled by the desireable "Hot Lips O'Houlihan."

The film "M*A*S*H*" grossed 81.6 million dollars and the TV show it spawned, which starred Alan Alda, Jamie Farr and Loretta Swit, continues to gross and gross and gross...

An eccentric woman meets an equally odd man at a group therapy session.

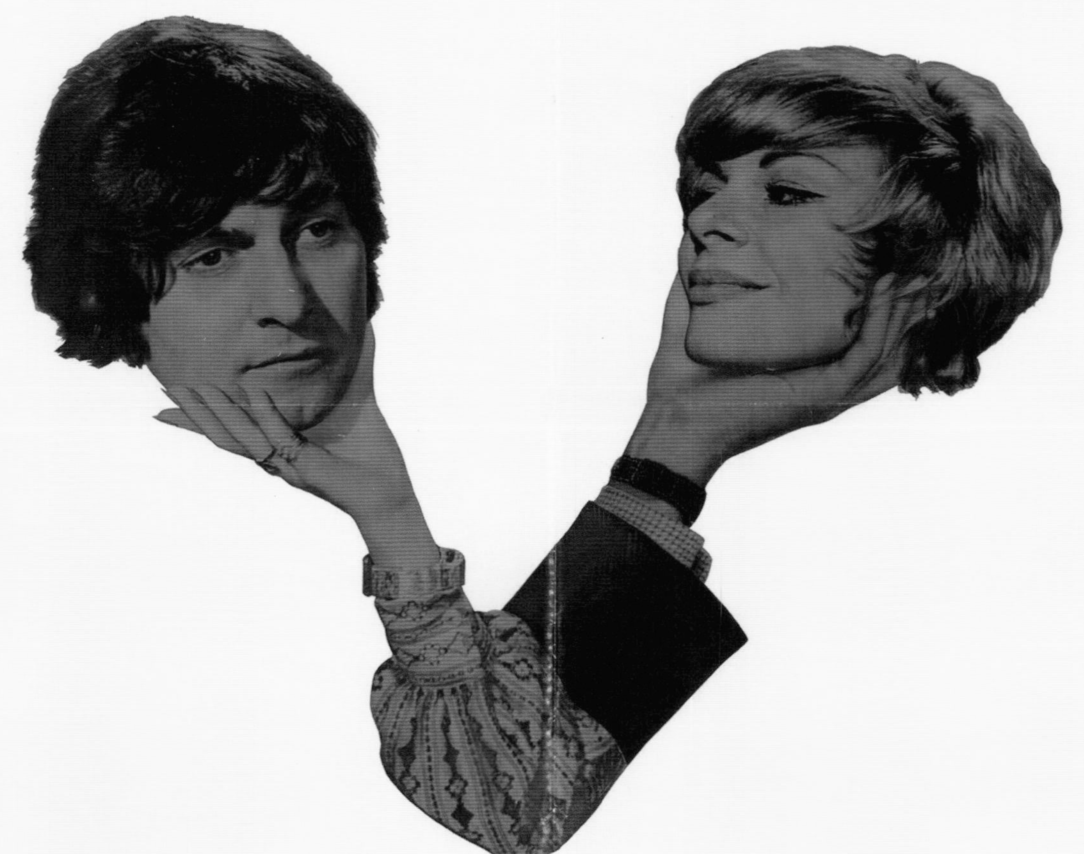

Justin Remer wrote: "A surprisingly warm and funny look at neurotic love in the early '70s."

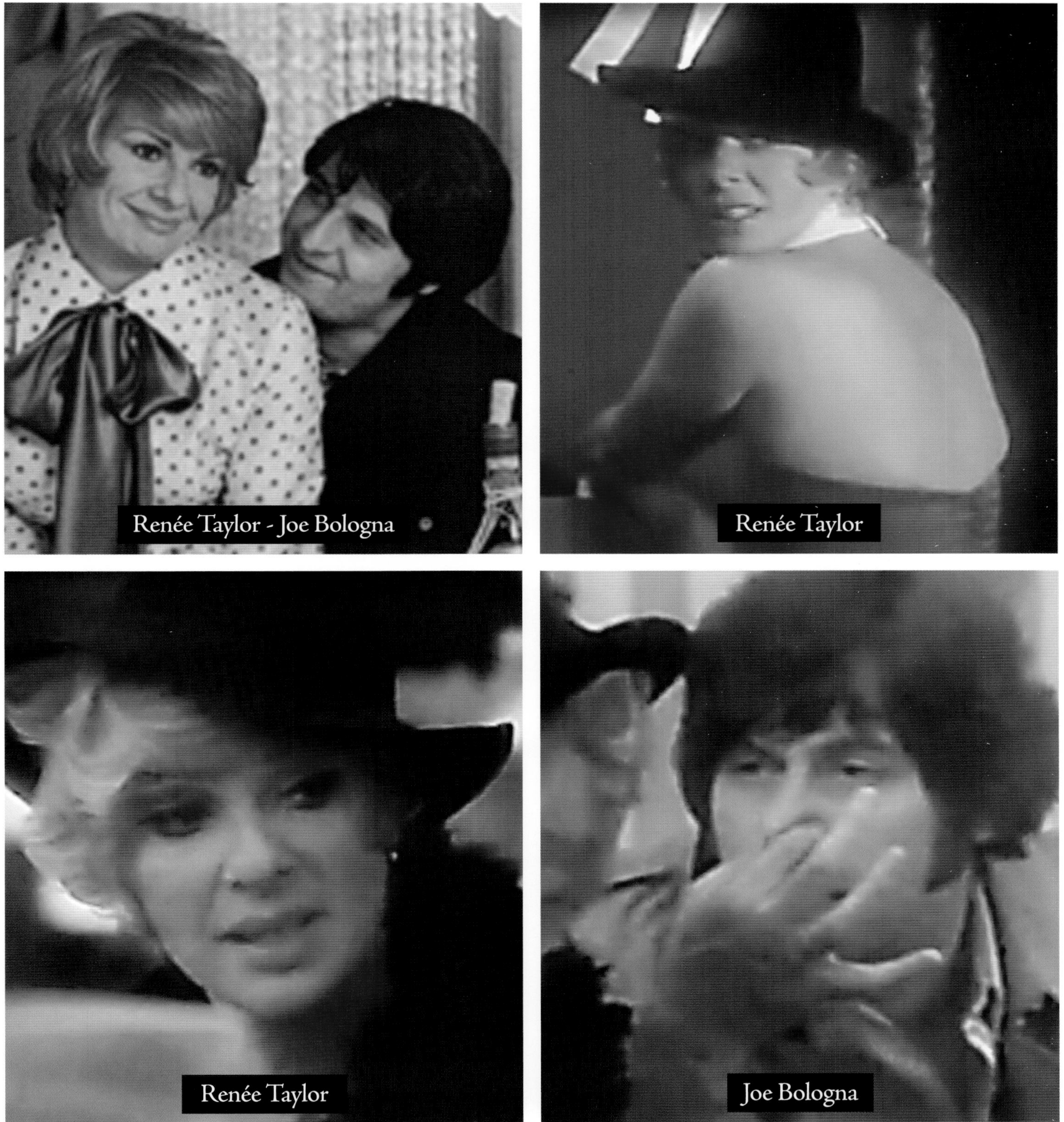

Renée Taylor - Joe Bologna

Renée Taylor

Renée Taylor

Joe Bologna

In the film, Renée Taylor had a discussion with her husband about her nightclub debut performance that provoked me to explode with laughter. Renée asked Joe, "Now, tell me the truth, what did you think about my performance?" He answered, "It stunk! It really stunk!!!"

If you want your face to smile for 90 minutes, watch "Made For Each Other" on YouTube.

A female girlie club entertainer in Weimar Republic era Berlin romances two men while the Nazi Party rises to power around them.

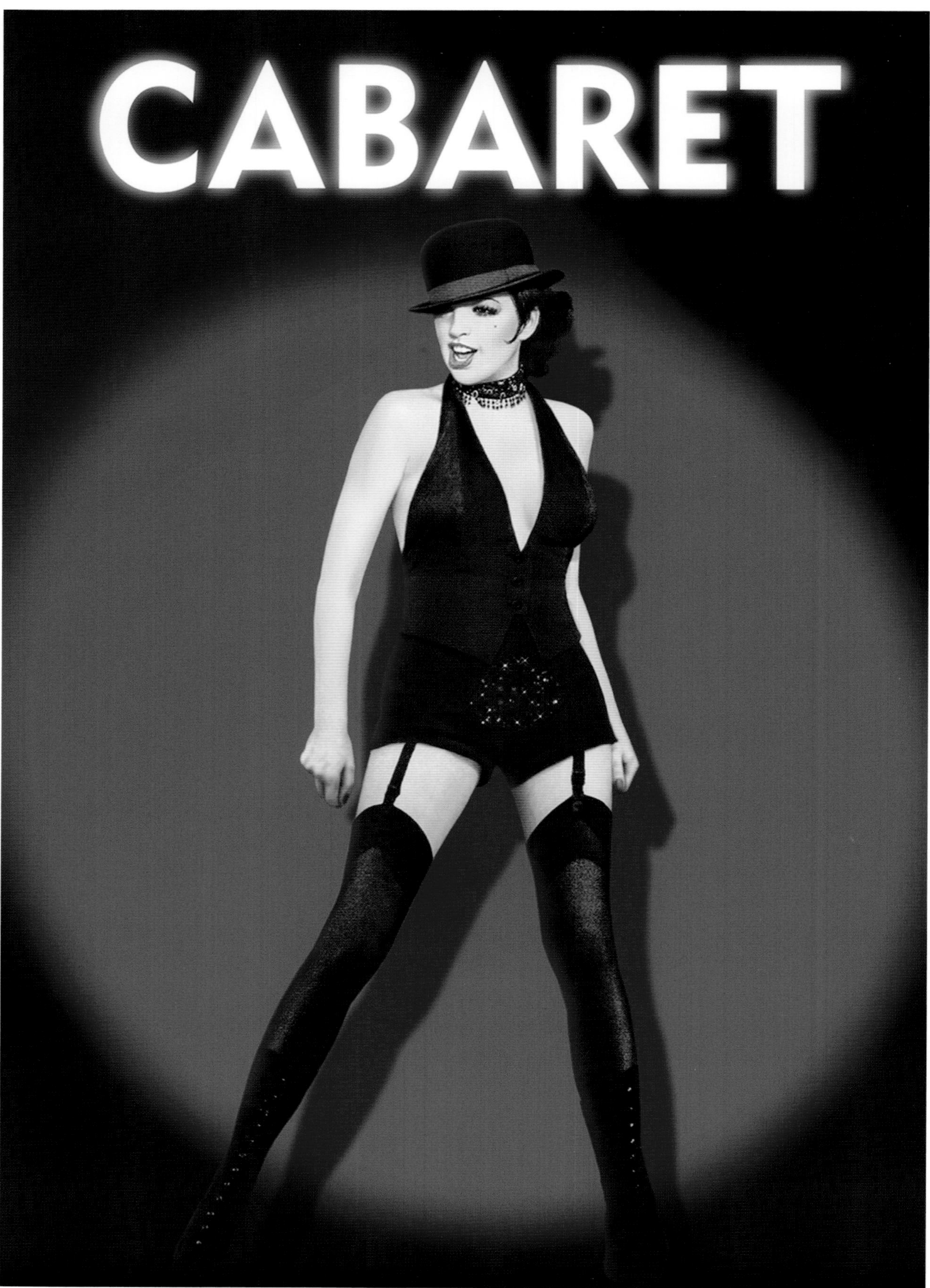

Peter Bradshaw wrote: "'Cabaret' is secure in its status as a stylish, socially conscious classic directed and choreographed with electric style by Bob Fosse. 'Cabaret' is drenched in the sexiest kind of cynicism and decadent despair."

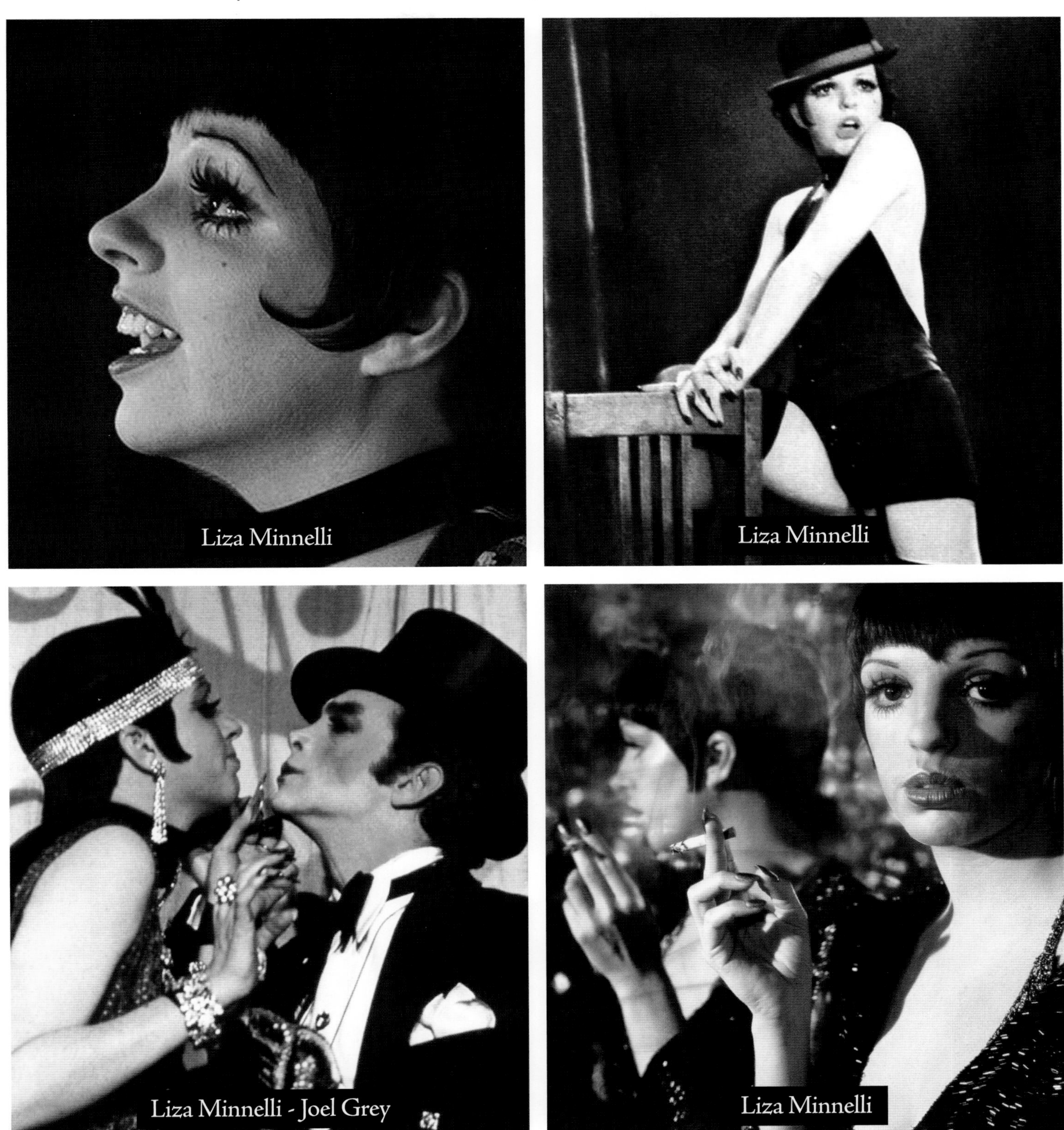

Liza Minnelli

Liza Minnelli

Liza Minnelli - Joel Grey

Liza Minnelli

With Joel Grey as the MC, Bob Fosse as the director and Liza Minnelli as the star, playing Sally Bowles, it would be surprising if "Cabaret" had not won the eight Oscars that it did.

The aging patriarch of a crime dynasty transfers control of his empire to his reluctant son.

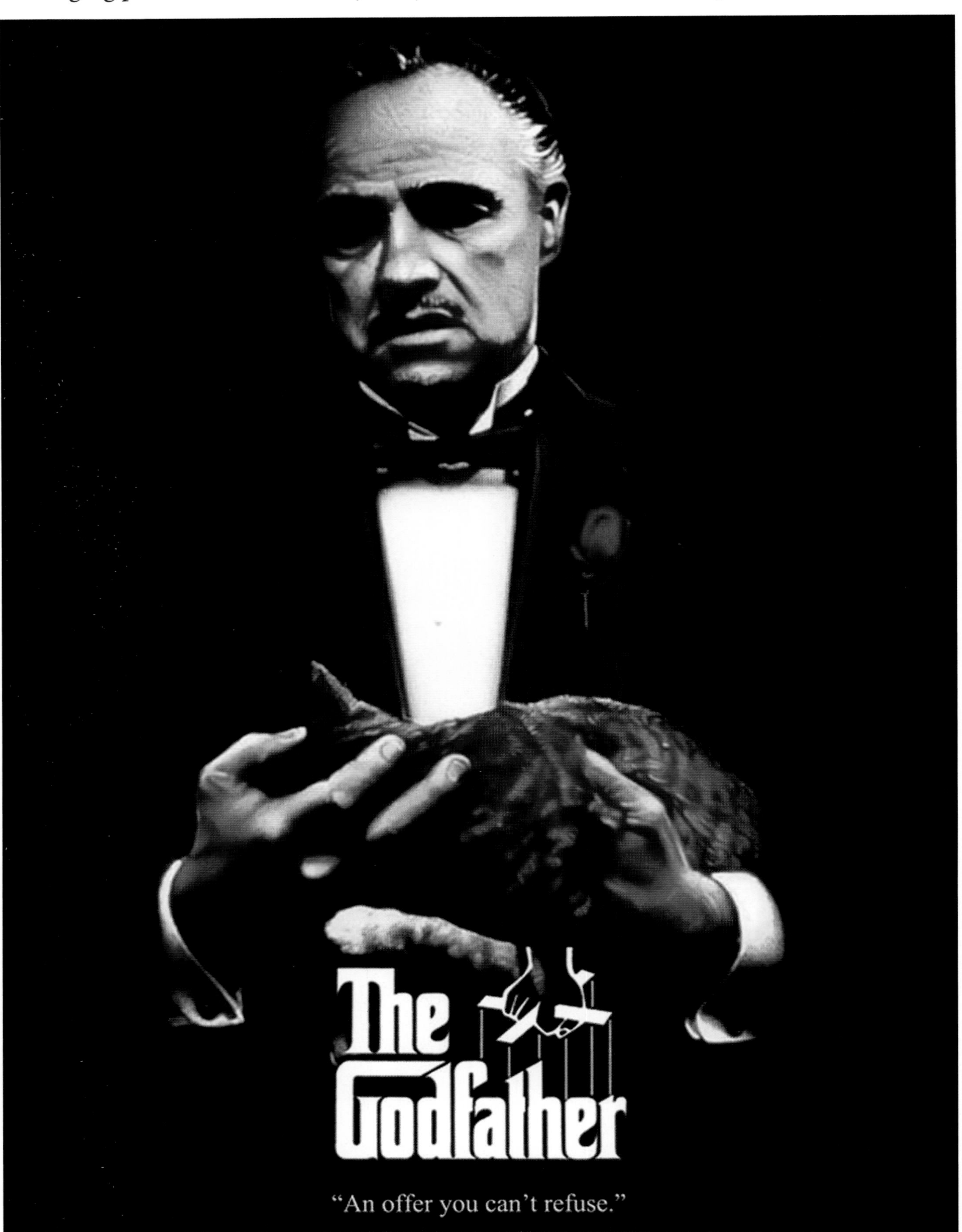

Wanda Hale of New York Daily News wrote:"Brando is the strong magnet that will draw fans to 'The Godfather.' But behind-the-scenes creativity is of equal value to this towering film."

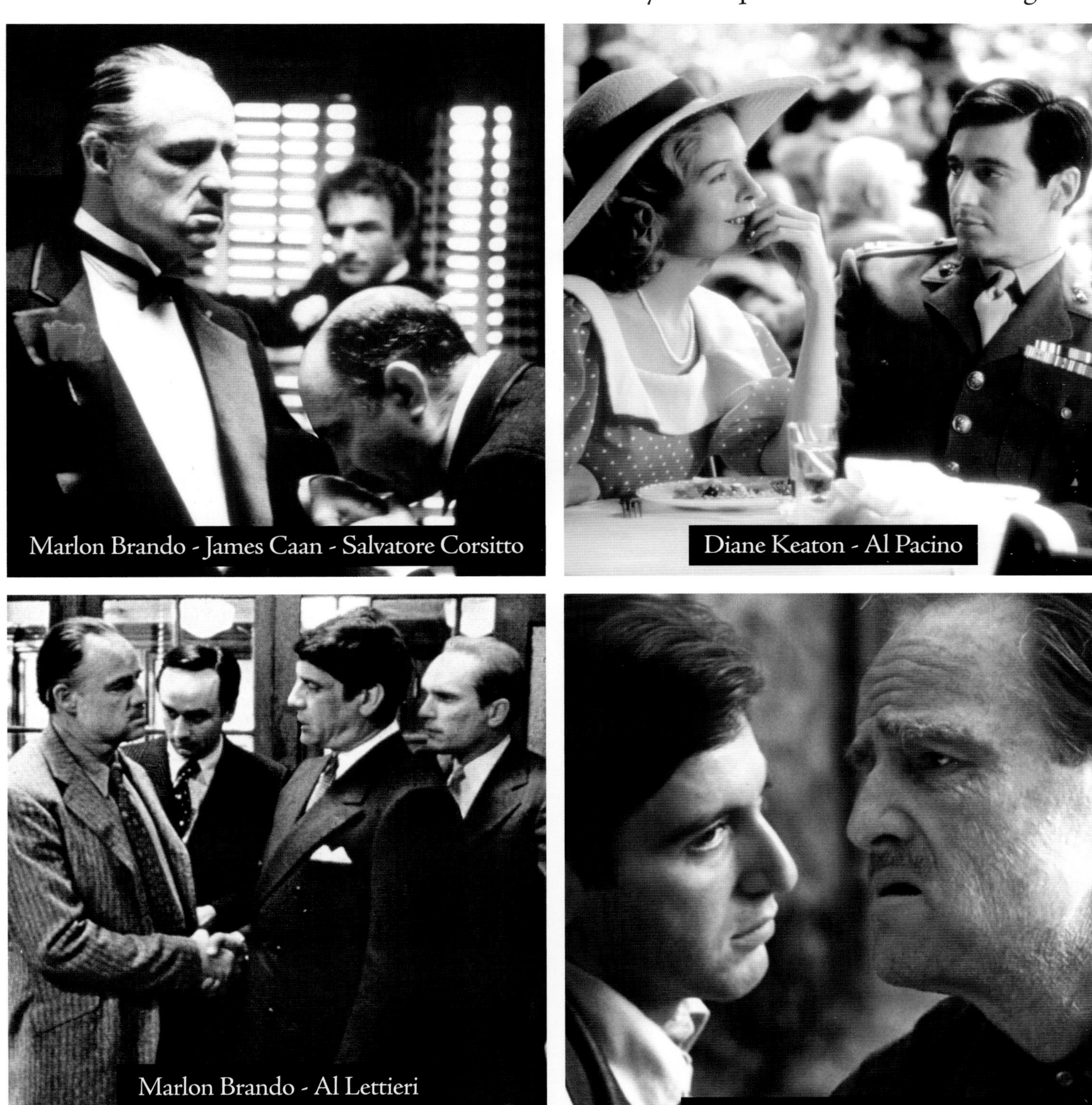

Marlon Brando - James Caan - Salvatore Corsitto

Diane Keaton - Al Pacino

Marlon Brando - Al Lettieri
John Cazale - Robert Duvall

Al Pacino - Marlon Brando

Brando was forever improvising. I read that the cat pictured in the poster which he's holding in his hands, he had, seconds earlier, picked up from the floor. And who knows where he got the idea to enhance his character's fearsome persona by putting prosthetics in his cheeks, prosthetics that might have helped garner him his second Oscar.

During the Great Depression, a con man finds himself saddled with a young girl who may or may not be his daughter, and the two forge an unlikely partnership.

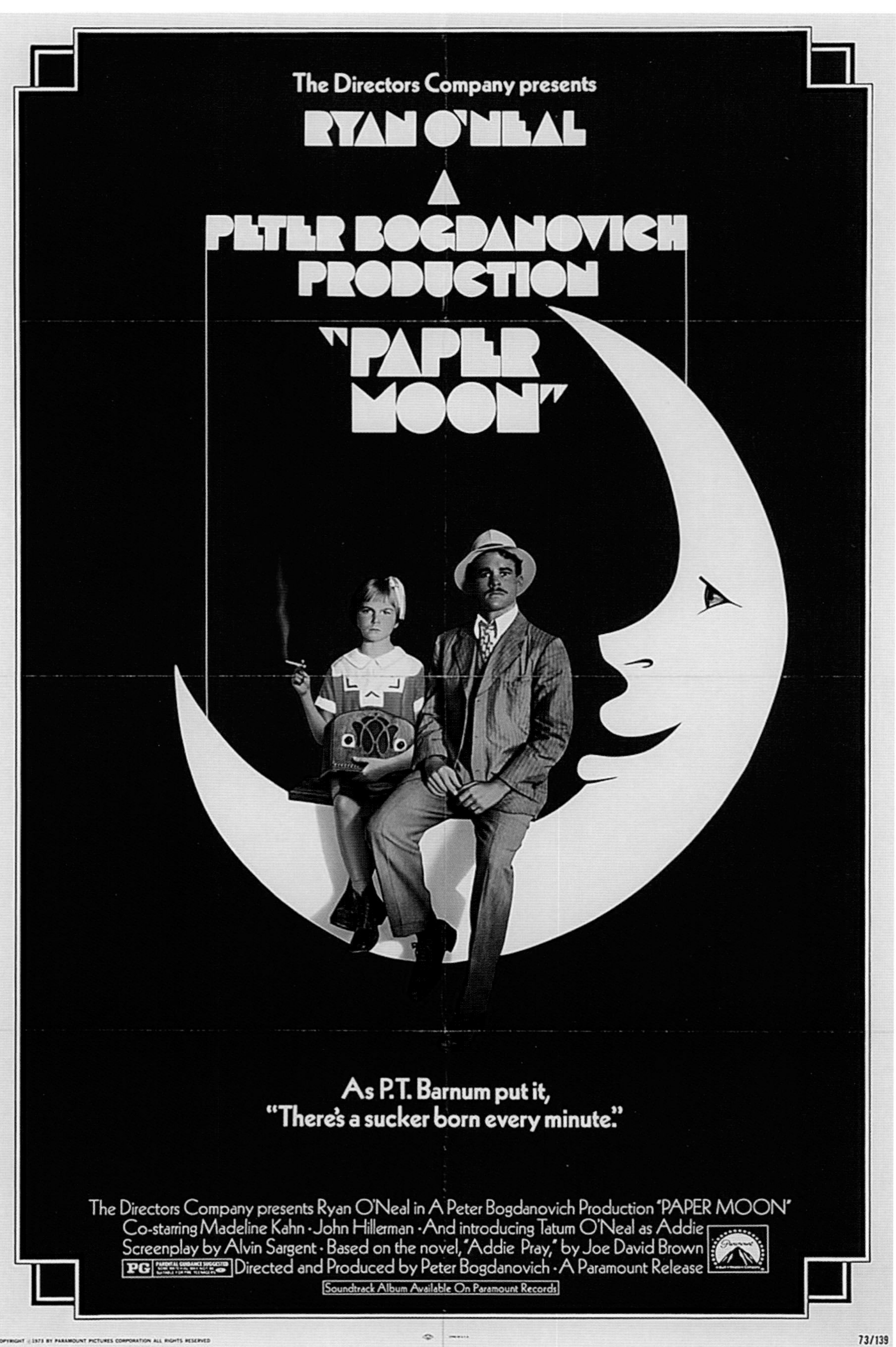

Roger Ebert of Chicago Sun-Times wrote: "I wonder how many moviegoers will be prepared for the astonishing confidence and depth that Tatum brings to what's really the starring role."

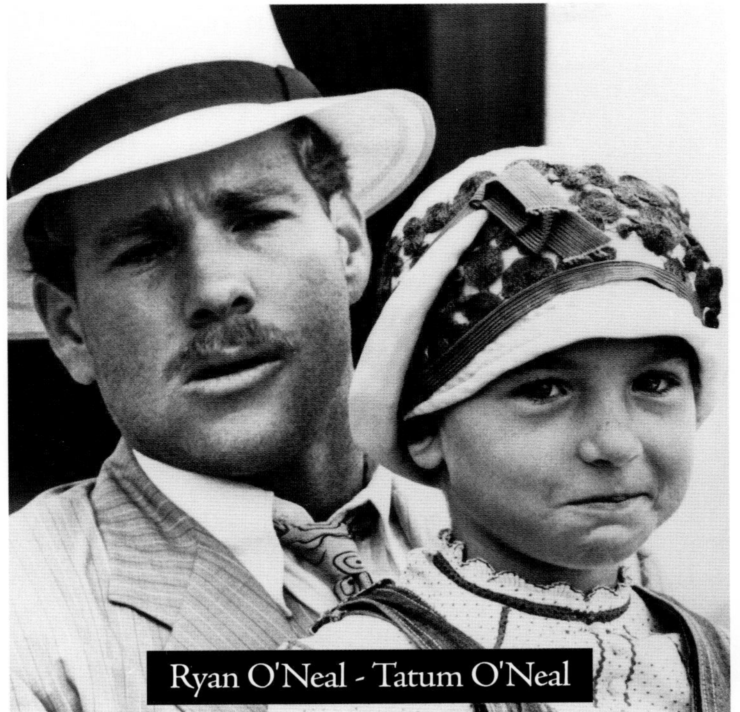
Ryan O'Neal - Tatum O'Neal

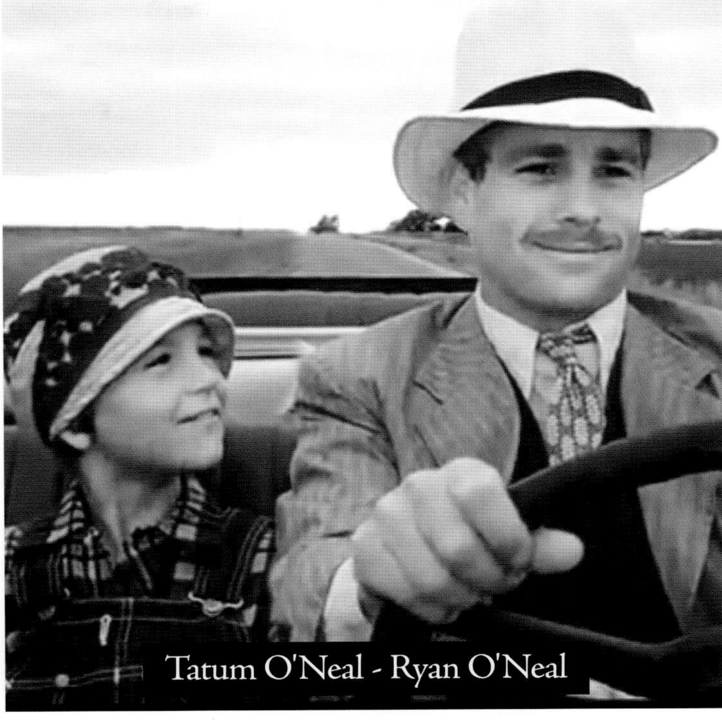
Tatum O'Neal - Ryan O'Neal

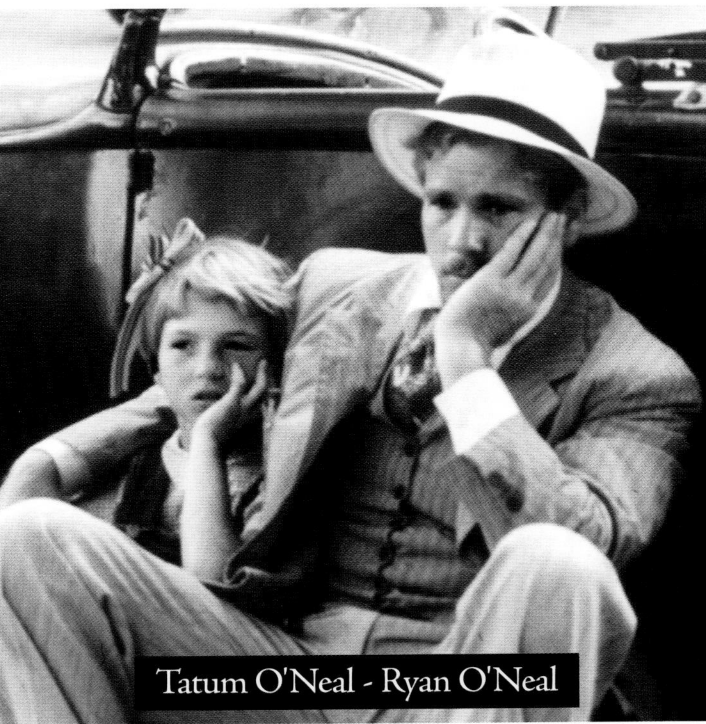
Tatum O'Neal - Ryan O'Neal

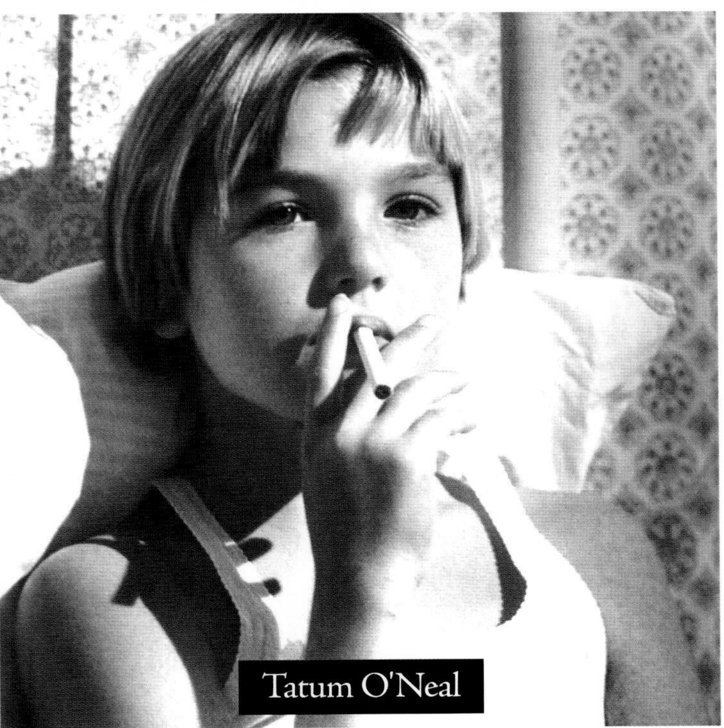
Tatum O'Neal

Being the daughter of Joanna Moore and Ryan O'Neal no doubt helped Tatum O'Neal give the remarkably sophisticated performance she did.

I was about to commend the director, Peter Bogdanovich, for having a cigarette created that contained shredded lettuce instead of tobacco when I learned that smoking lettuce is just as unhealthy as smoking tobacco.

In Chicago in September 1936, a young con man seeking revenge for his murdered partner teams up with a master of the big con to win a fortune from a criminal banker.

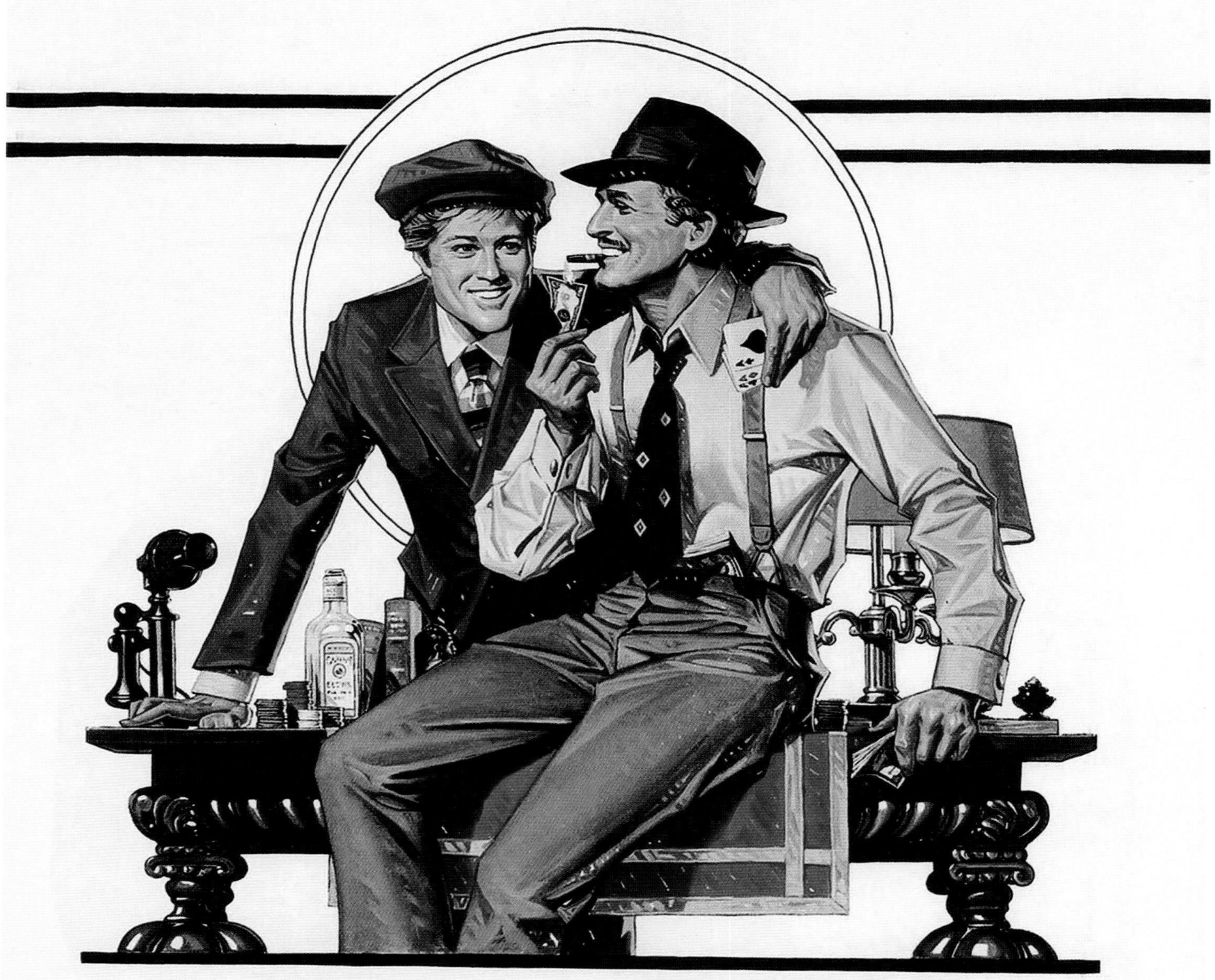

PAUL NEWMAN ROBERT REDFORD
ROBERT SHAW
IN A BILL/PHILLIPS PRODUCTION OF
A GEORGE ROY HILL FILM
THE STING
A RICHARD D. ZANUCK/DAVID BROWN PRESENTATION

Vincent Canby of The New York Times wrote: "'The Sting' looks and sounds like a musical comedy from which the songs have been removed."

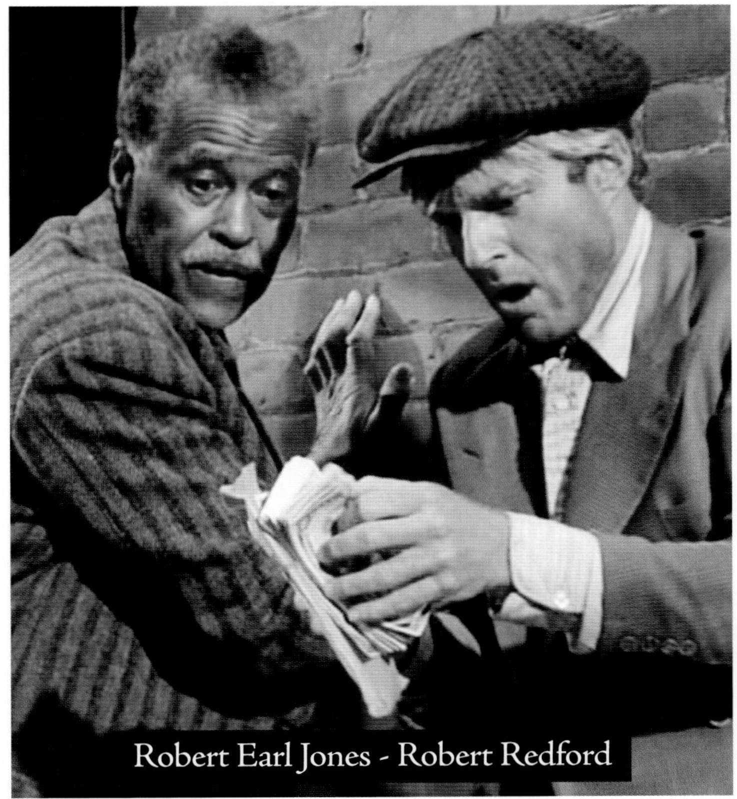
Robert Earl Jones - Robert Redford

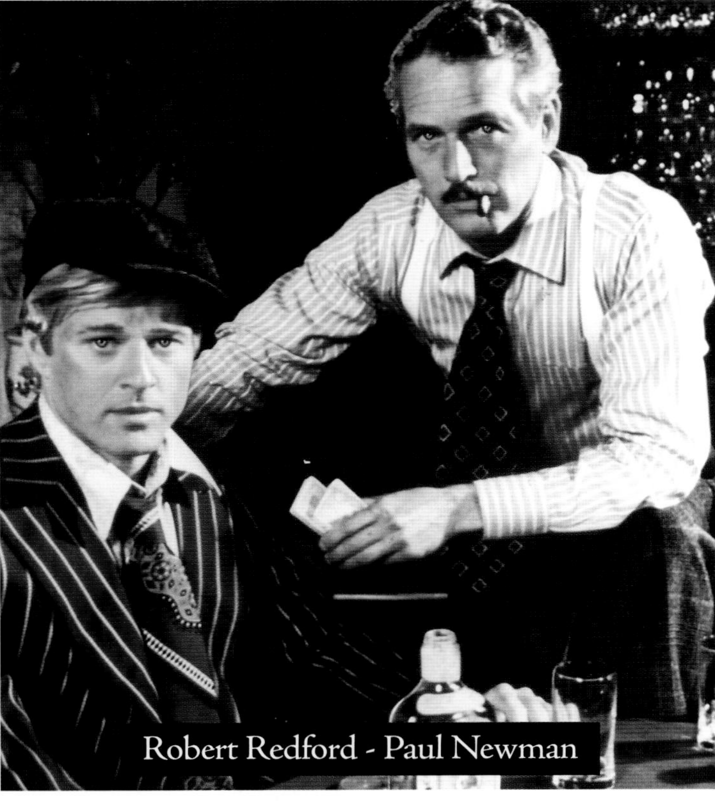
Robert Redford - Paul Newman

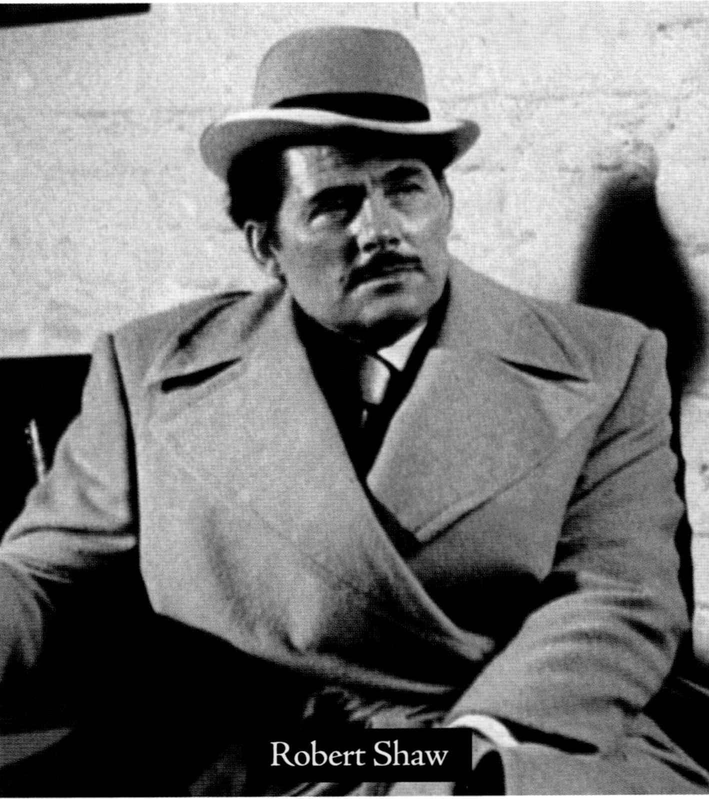
Robert Shaw

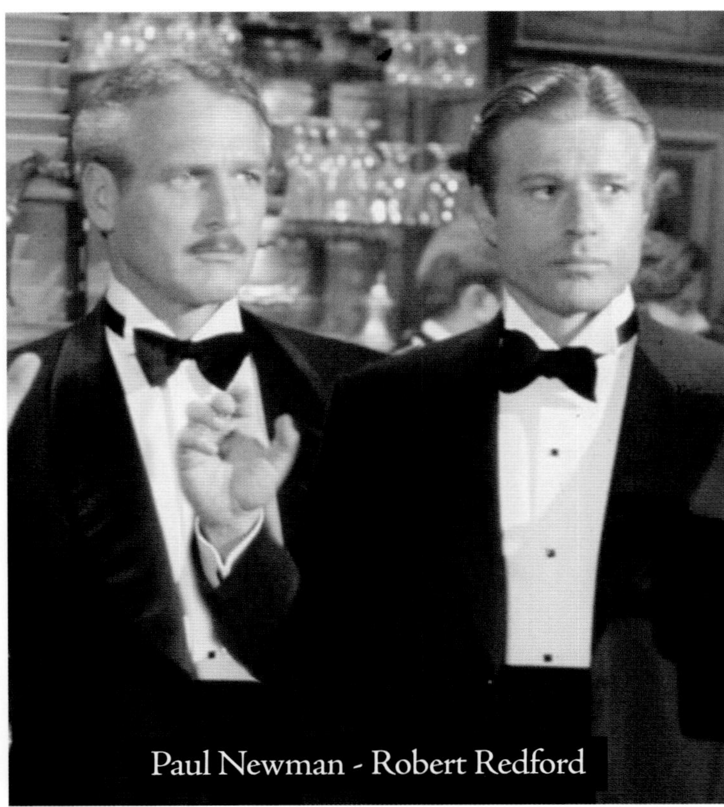
Paul Newman - Robert Redford

You will only enjoy this film if you get a kick out of watching two of the handsomest, most charming, talented actors swindle wicked big-time crooked swindlers who get what they deserve.

In order to ruin a western town, a corrupt politician appoints a black sheriff, who promptly becomes his most formidable adversary.

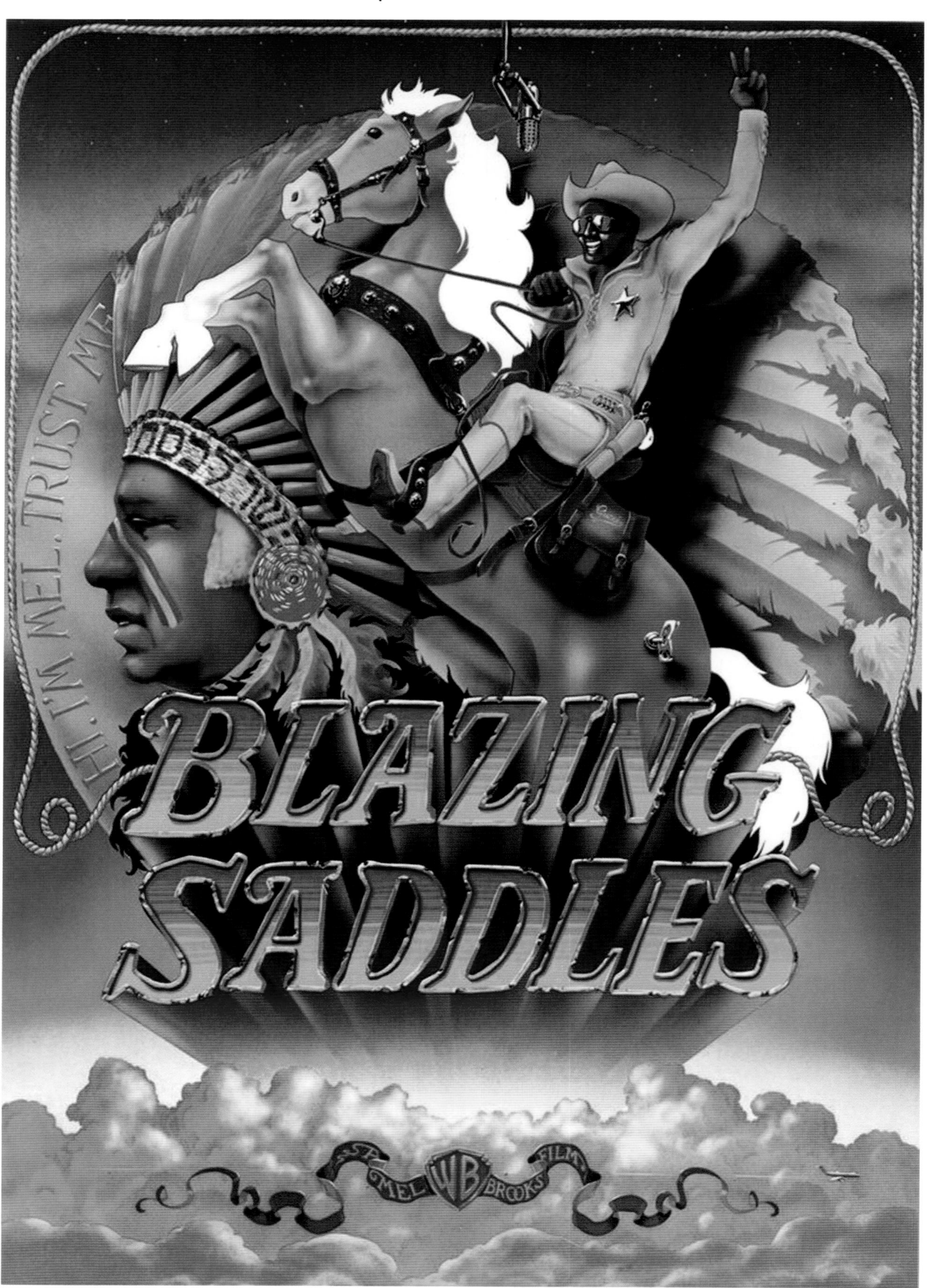

Sean Axmaker of Stream on Demand wrote: "More than simply a loving spoof of Hollywood westerns, 'Blazing Saddles' is one of the funniest movies ever made... and one of the most audacious satires of racism to come out of Hollywood."

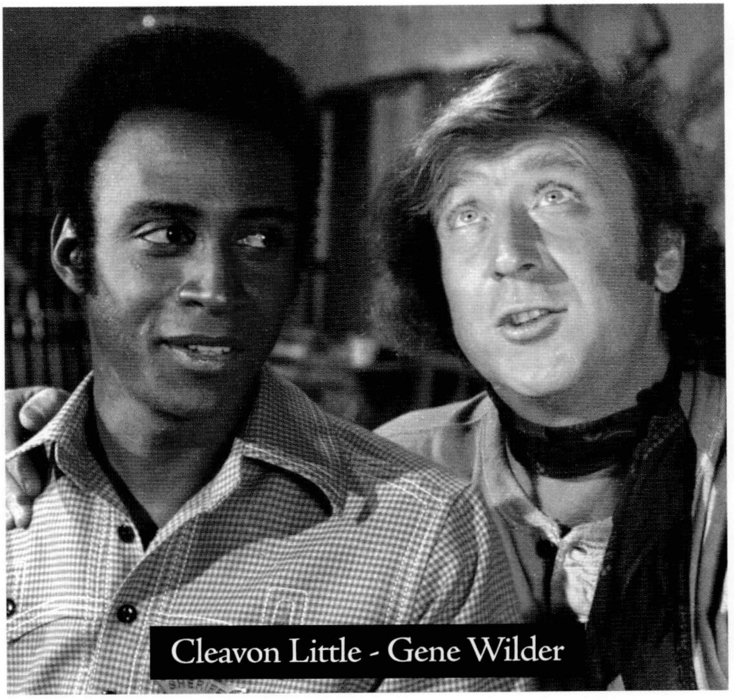
Cleavon Little - Gene Wilder

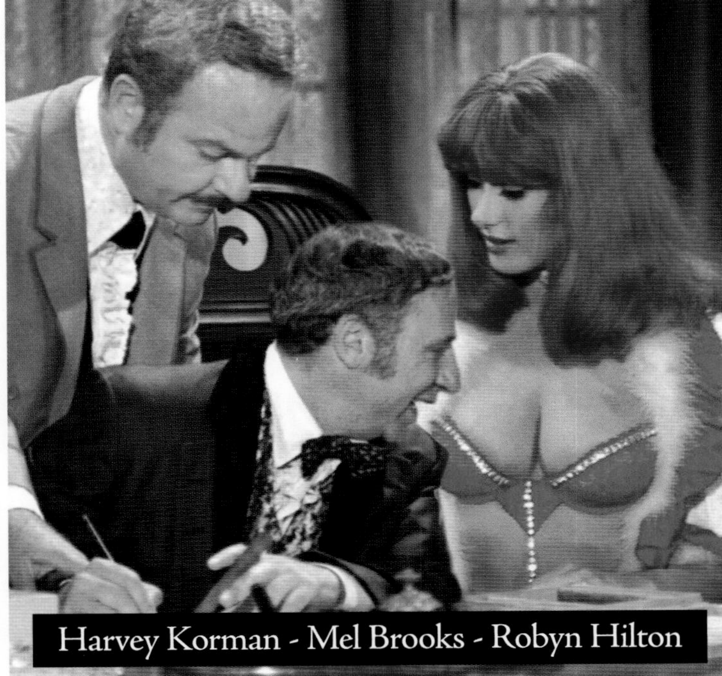
Harvey Korman - Mel Brooks - Robyn Hilton

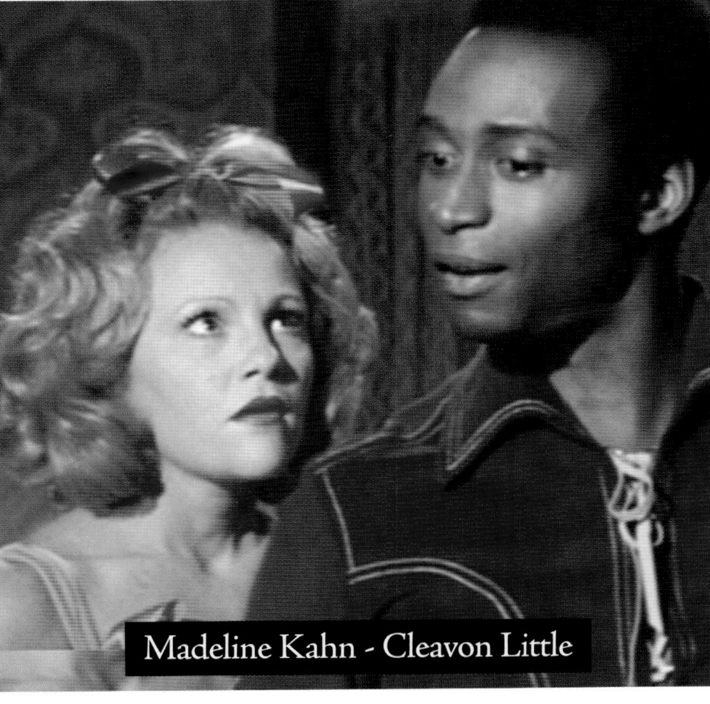
Madeline Kahn - Cleavon Little

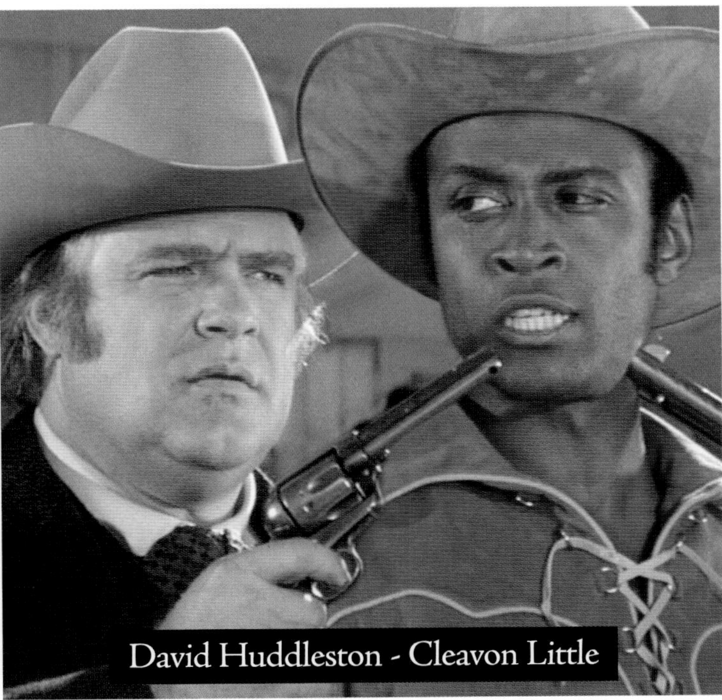
David Huddleston - Cleavon Little

With the perfect cast working with a fine screenplay, which contained a scene where cowboys sit around a fire eating beans and loudly passing wind, Mel again proved my theory:

"Any sexy, dirty, racist or offensive joke is totally acceptable as long as it's funnier than it is dirty, sexy, racist or offensive."

In 2017, I followed suit with a children's book, "You Say God Bless You For Sneezing & Farting."

Struggling to prove that he is not insane, the American grandson of the infamous scientist travels to Transylvania where he discovers the process that reanimates a dead body.

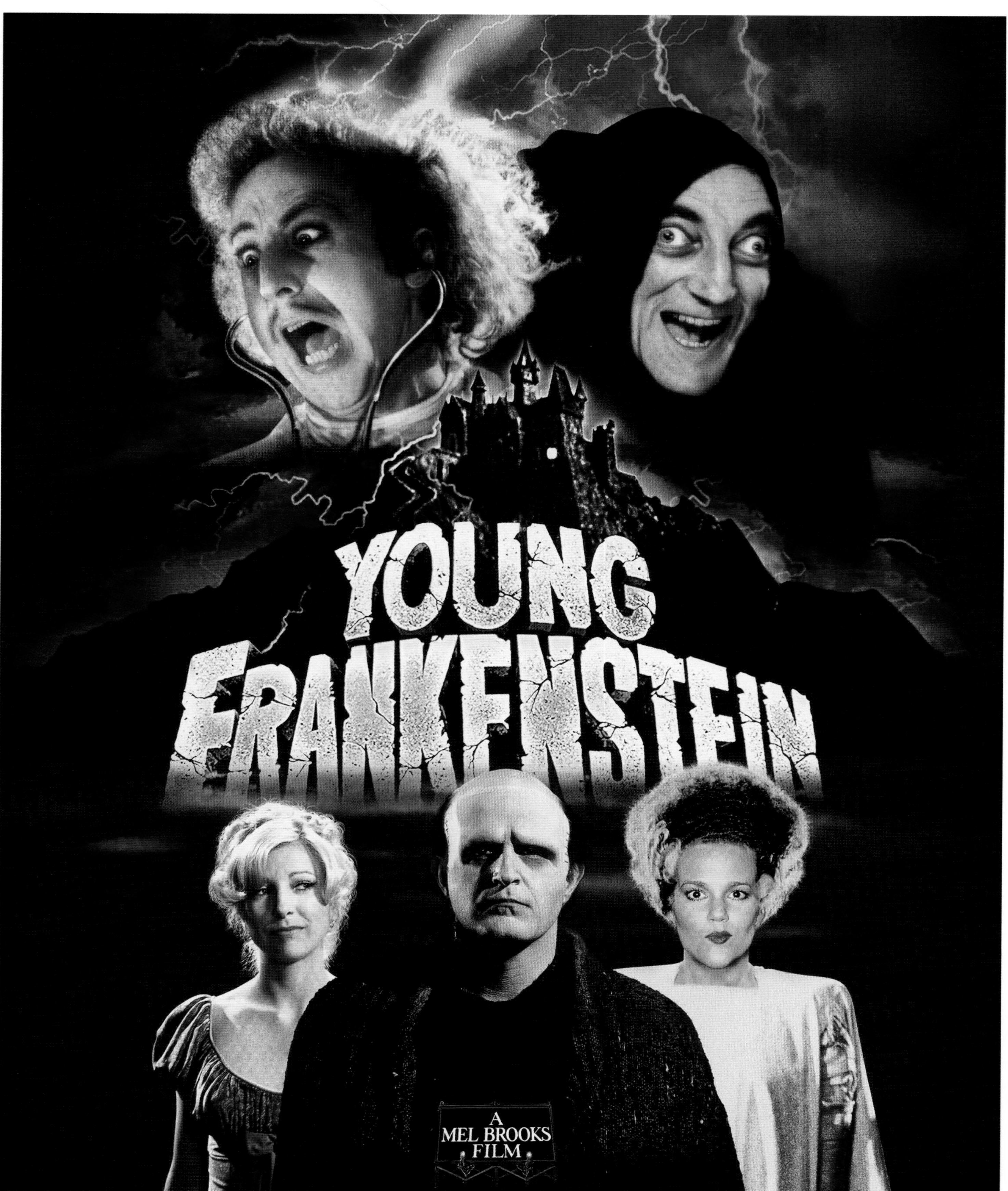

Roger Ebert wrote: "'Young Frankenstein' is Mel Brooks' most disciplined and visually inventive film. It also happens to be very funny."

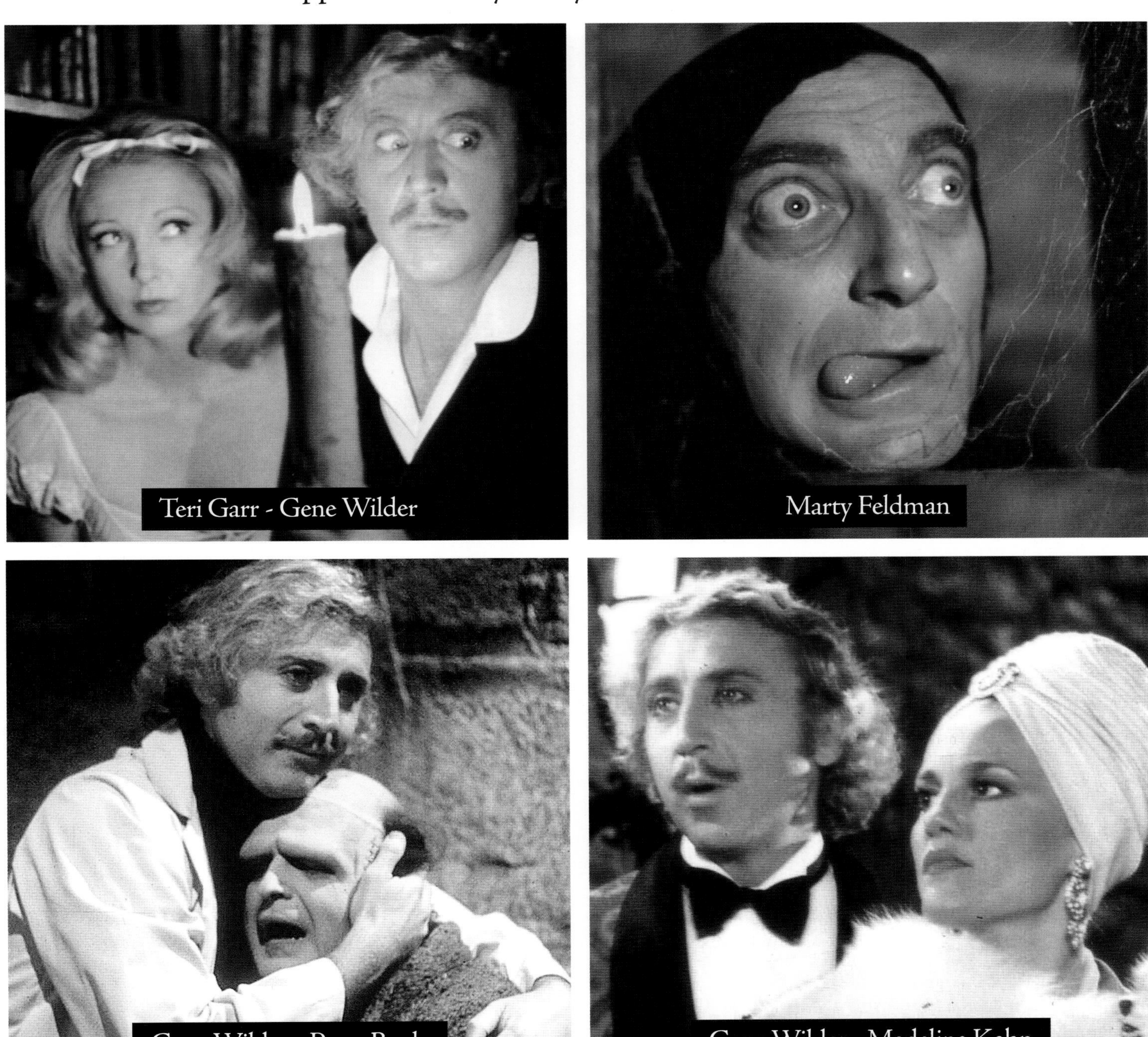

Teri Garr - Gene Wilder

Marty Feldman

Gene Wilder - Peter Boyle

Gene Wilder - Madeline Kahn

The first time I saw Mel's "Young Frankenstein" I heard the audience screaming with laughter long and hard enough to make it a classic. My favorite line in the film, which contains just four words, was delivered by Cloris Leachman when describing her relationship with Dr. Frankenstein: "HE VAS MY BOOOOOOOOOOOOYFRIEEEND!!!!!!!!!!!!"

In this film, Madeline Kahn, who never ceased to create memorable characters, created one who finds The Monster attractive and invites him to bed with her. At the apex of their love making, she bursts into an operatic version of "Ah, Sweet Mystery of Life."

A private detective gets caught up in a web of deceit, corruption and murder.

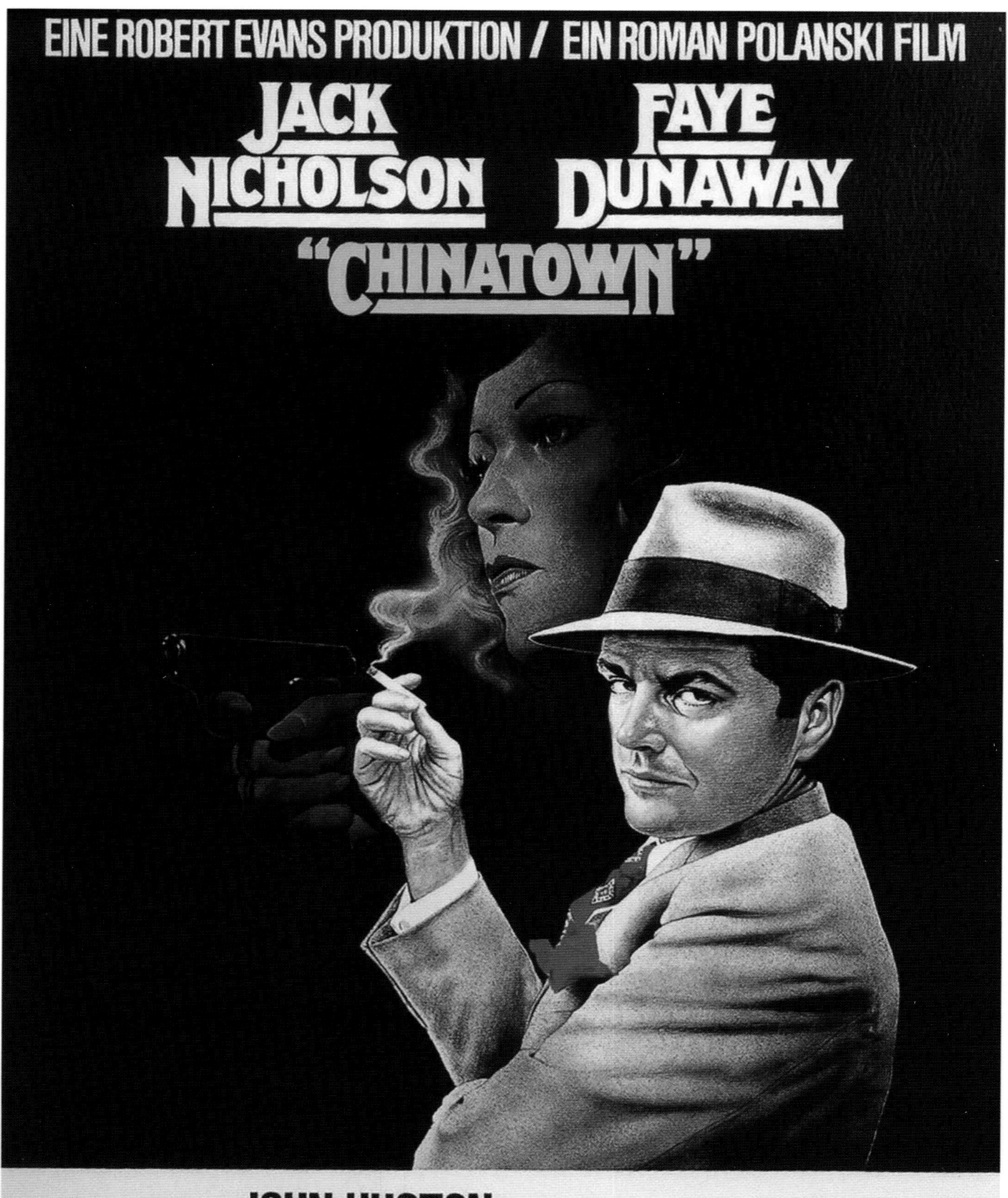

Vincent Canby of The New York Times wrote: "A new private-eye melodrama that celebrates not only a time and a place (Los Angeles) but also a kind of criminality that to us jaded souls today appears to be nothing worse than an eccentric form of legitimate private enterprise."

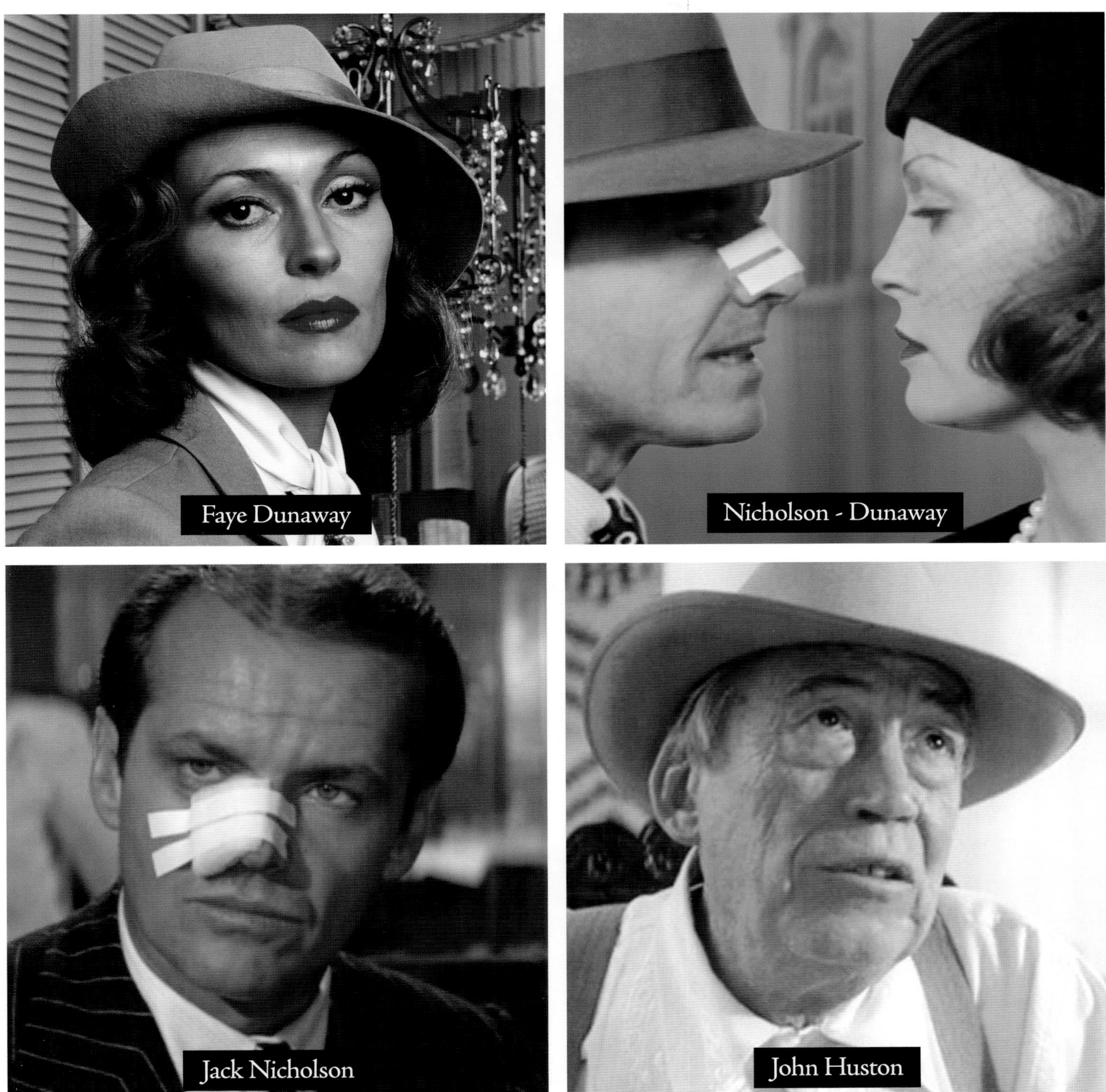

Faye Dunaway

Nicholson - Dunaway

Jack Nicholson

John Huston

One of the most upsetting scenes ever filmed was where Roman Polanski, to convince Jack Nicholson not to stick his nose where it doesn't belong, puts the tip of his knife up Nicholson's left nostril and slices it open. An equally anguishing moment is when we learn that John Huston's character raped his fifteen year old daughter and left her with child.

A true story of a man who robs a bank to pay for his homosexual lover's sex change operation, the robbery becoming a hostage situation and a media circus.

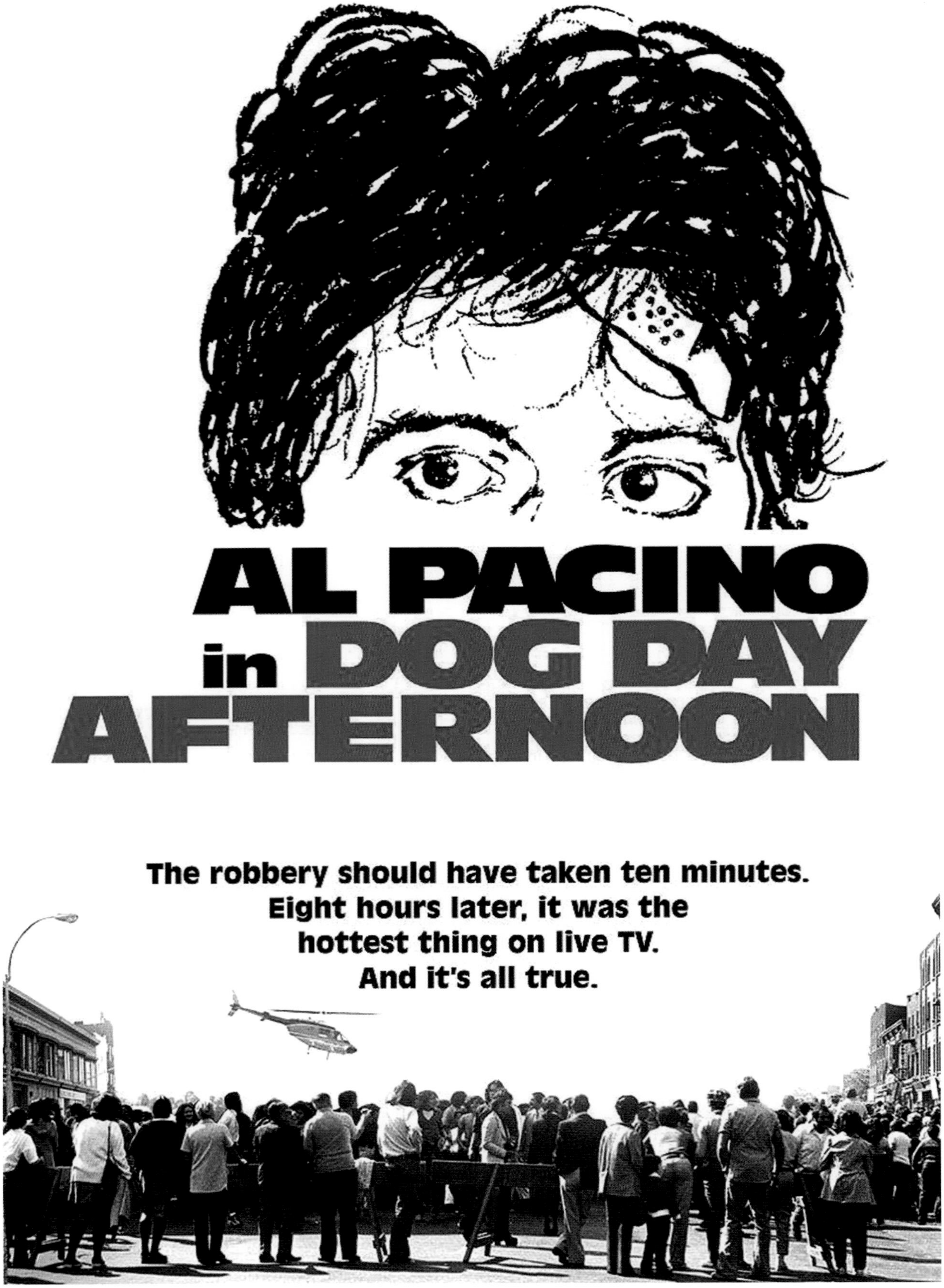

AL PACINO
in DOG DAY
AFTERNOON

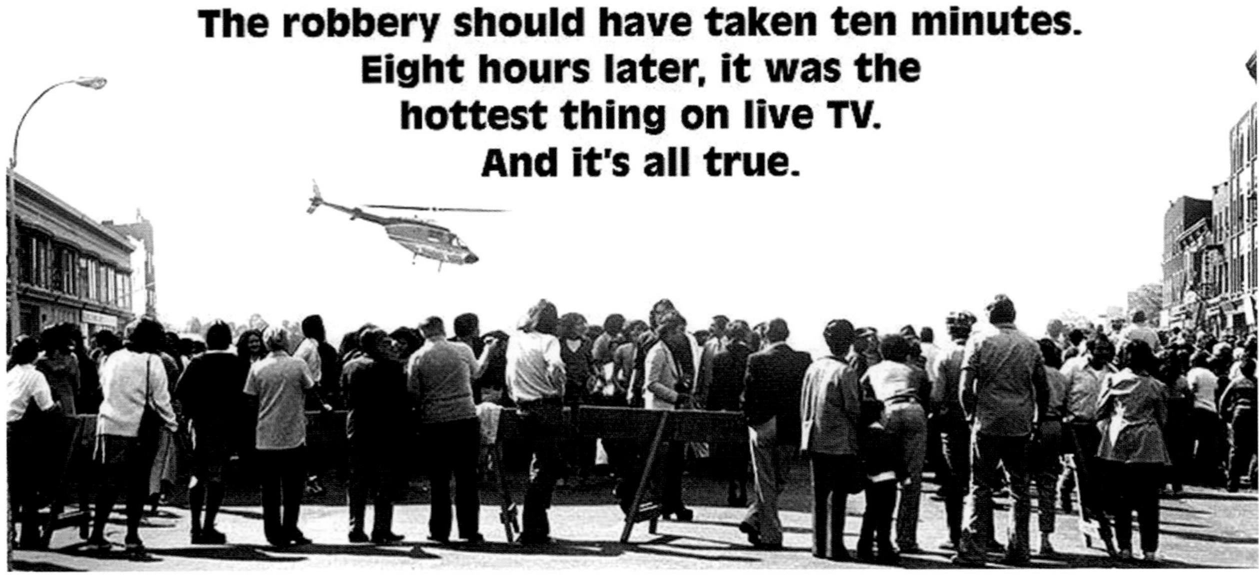

Cole Smithey wrote: "As much as it is about a deeply troubled individual, 'Dog Day Afternoon' is about a shift toward exploitation in the American media via live television."

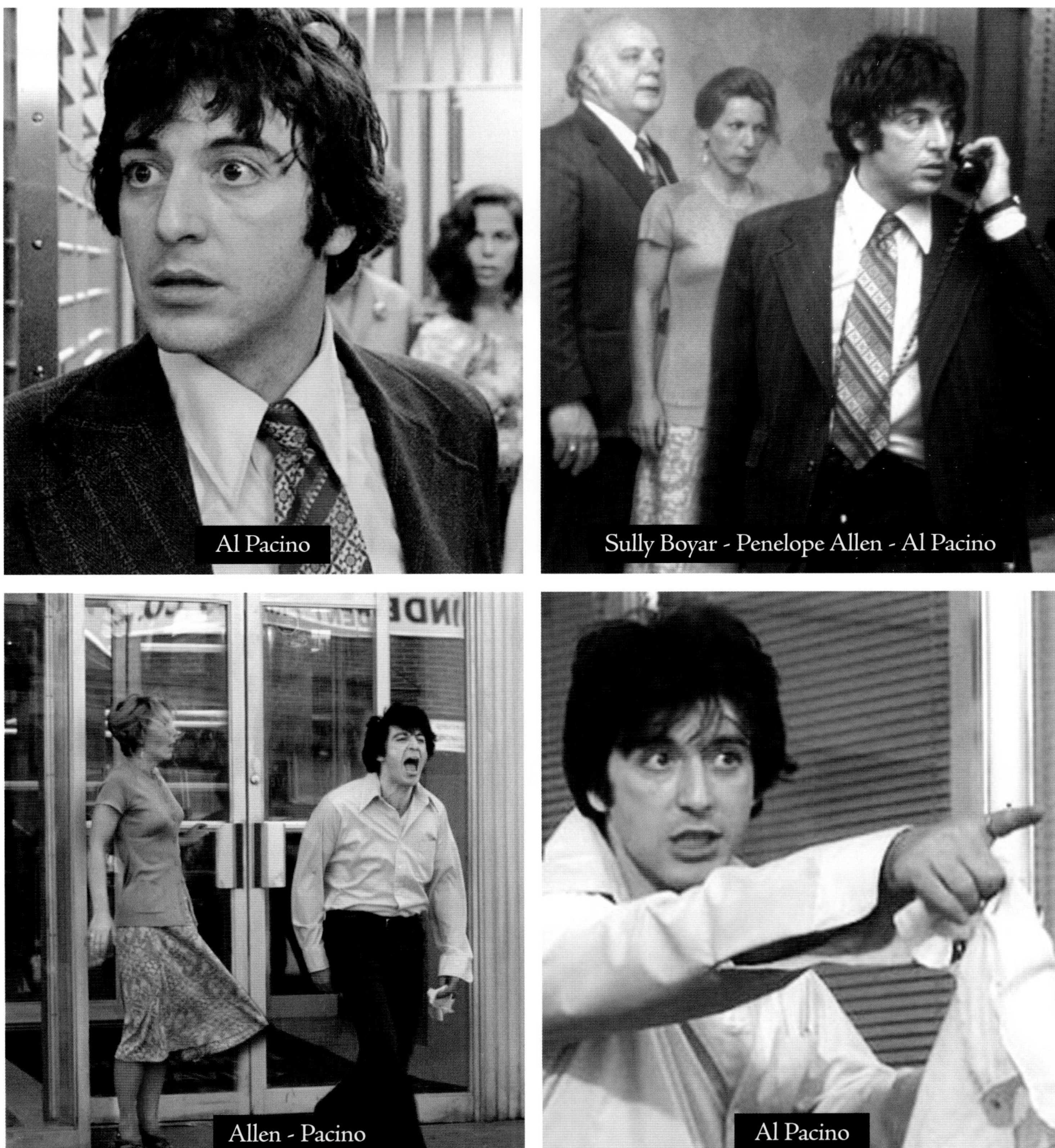

Al Pacino

Sully Boyar - Penelope Allen - Al Pacino

Allen - Pacino

Al Pacino

His performances in "The Godfather," "Serpico" and "Dog Day Afternoon" brought five foot, seven inch Al Pacino the recognition, money and fame he richly deserved.

A criminal pleads insanity after getting into trouble again and once in the mental institution rebels against the oppressive nurse and rallies up the scared patients.

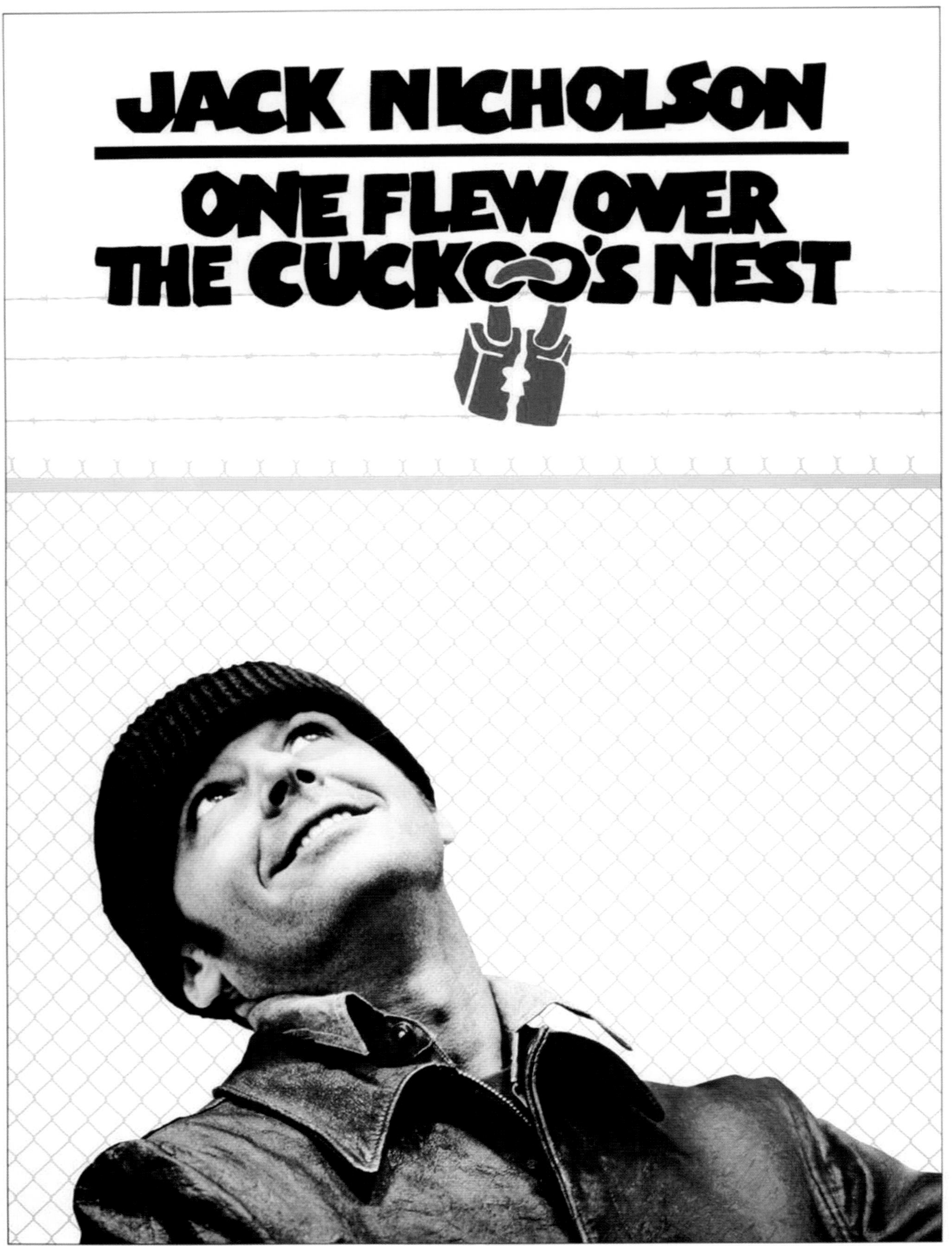

Kathleen Carroll of New York Daily News wrote: "Nicholson explodes on the screen in a performance so flawless in timing and character perception that it should send half the stars in Hollywood back to acting school."

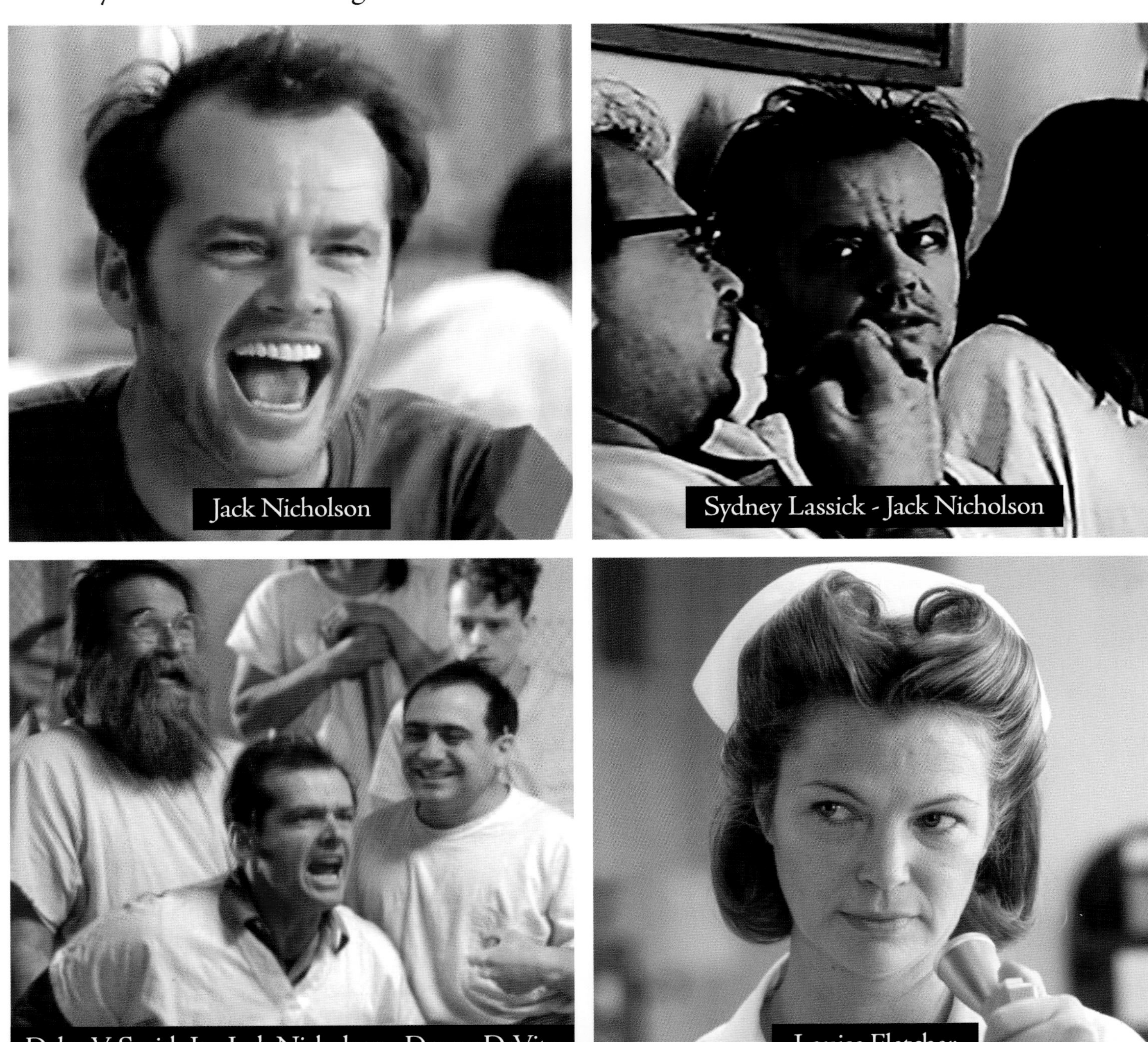

Jack Nicholson

Sydney Lassick - Jack Nicholson

Delos V. Smith Jr. - Jack Nicholson - Danny DeVito

Louise Fletcher

This film was the second film in history to win five Oscars: Best Picture, Best Actor, Best Actress, Best Director and Best Screenplay. Jack Nicholson went on to win two more Oscars, one for "Terms of Endearment" and the other for "As Good As It Gets."

Louise Fletcher, who played Nurse Ratched, was named the fifth-greatest villain in film history and second-greatest villainess, behind Margaret Hamilton as "The Wizard of Oz's" Wicked Witch of the West.

The Washington Post reporters Bob Woodward and Carl Bernstein uncover the details of the Watergate scandal that lead to President Richard Nixon's resignation.

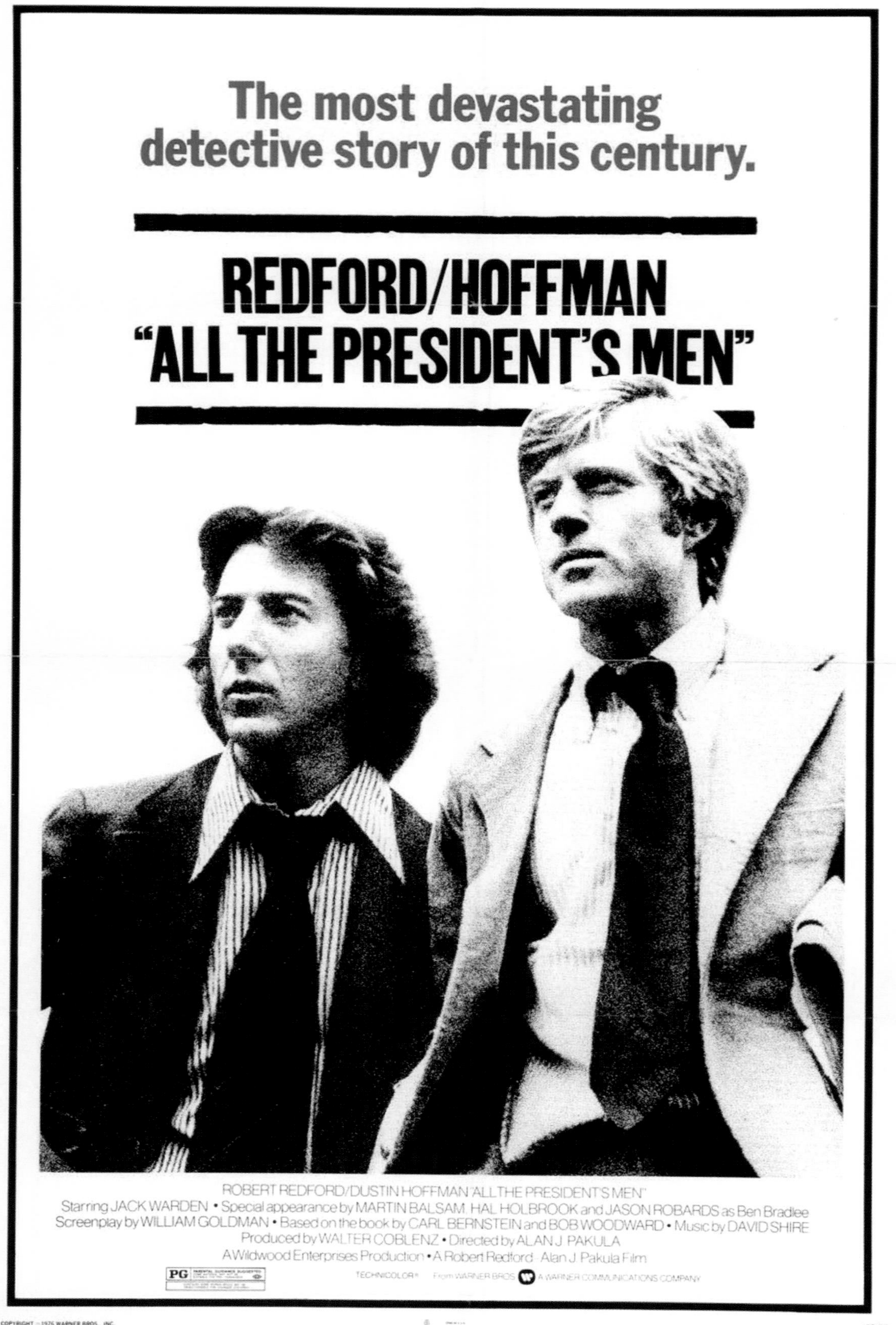

Matt Brunson of Creative Loafing wrote: "This superb film has long been acknowledged as a classic political thriller, but watching it in today's climate reveals its increasingly significant value as a time capsule piece and a victory lap for American journalism."

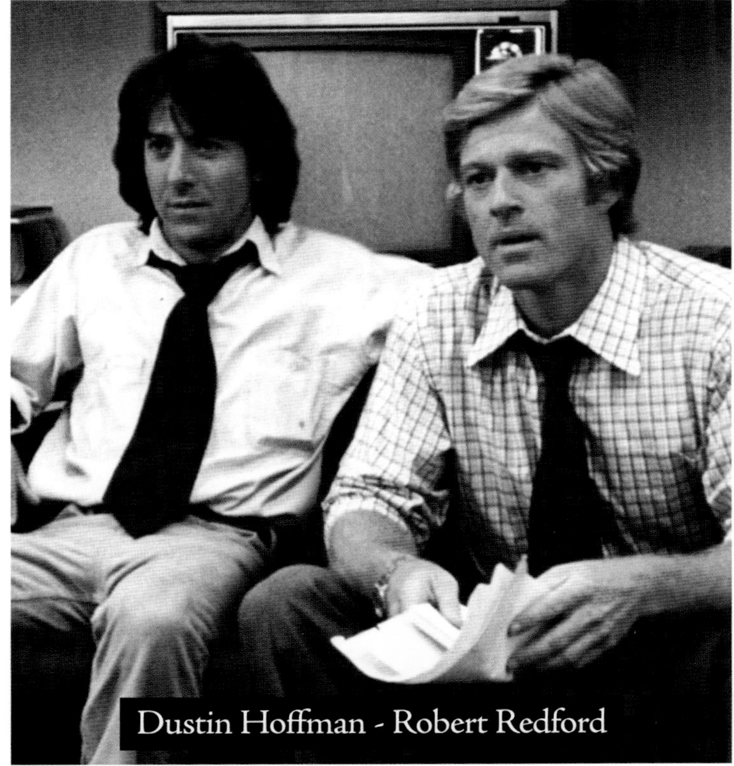

Dustin Hoffman - Robert Redford

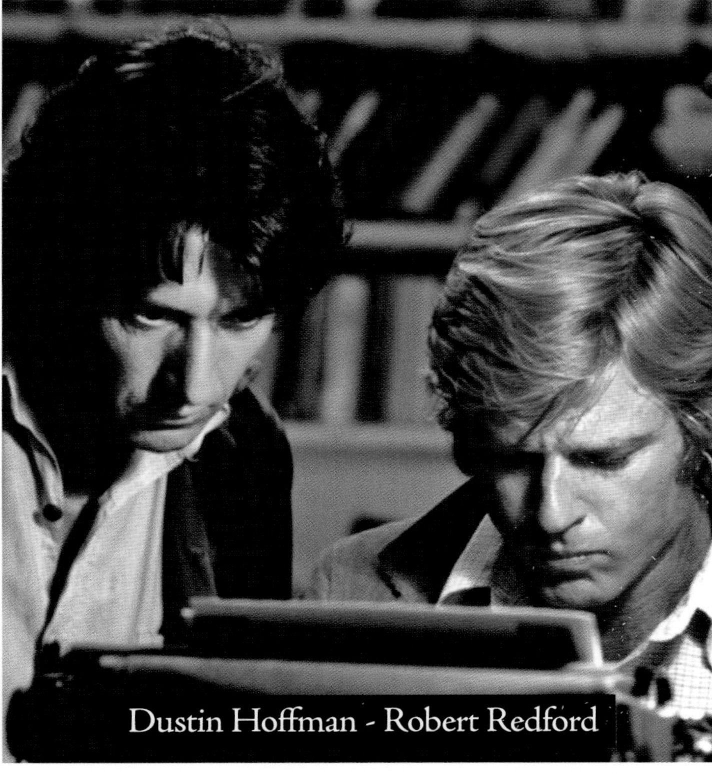

Dustin Hoffman - Robert Redford

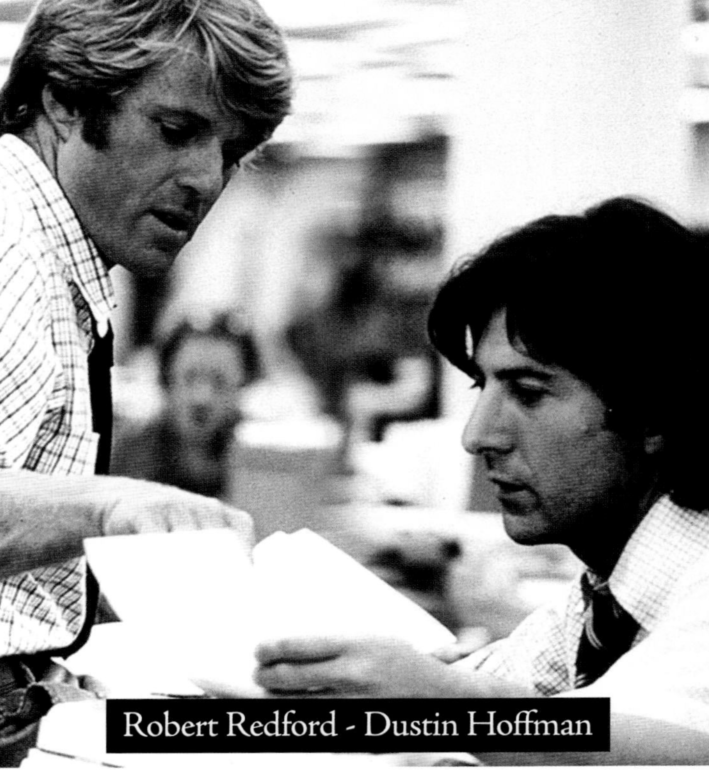

Robert Redford - Dustin Hoffman

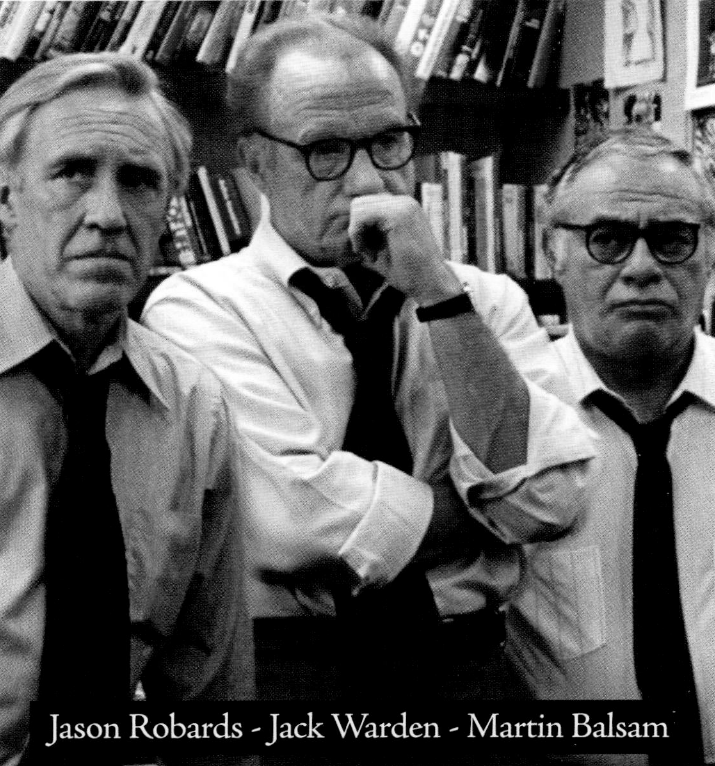

Jason Robards - Jack Warden - Martin Balsam

The investigative reporting that Carl Bernstein and his partner, Bob Woodward, did during the Watergate scandal, Woodward continued doing in the 2016 Russian-Trump election scandal.

A television network cynically exploits a deranged former anchor's ravings and revelations about the news media for its own profit.

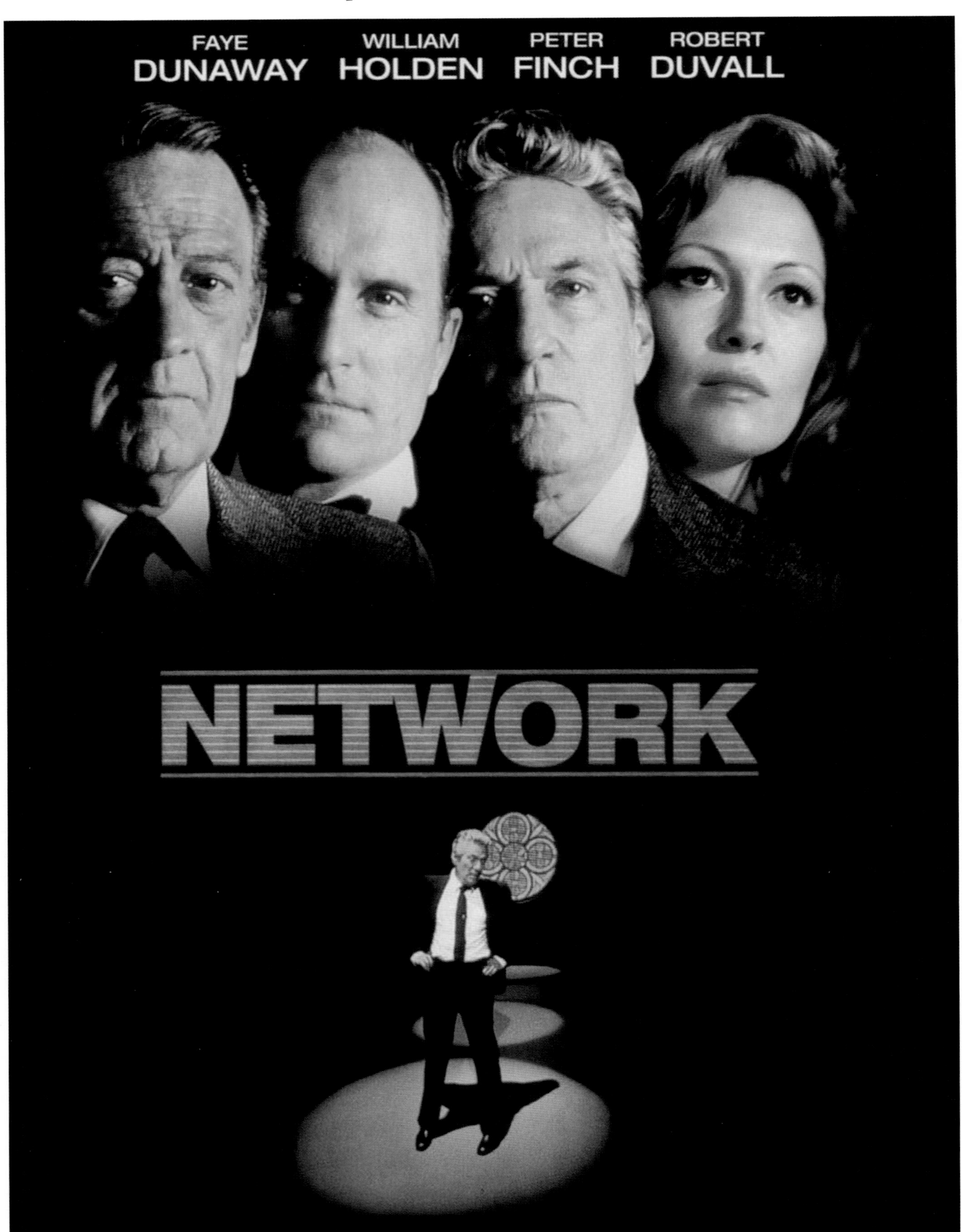

Vincent Canby of The New York Times wrote: "'Network' is a brilliant, cruelly funny, topical American comedy that confirms Paddy Chayefsky's position as a major American satirist."

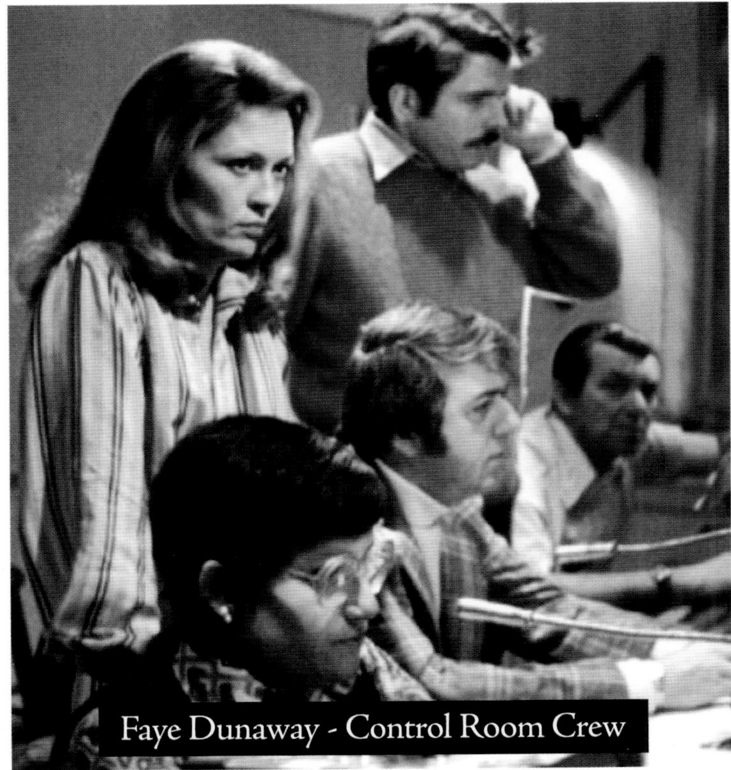
Faye Dunaway - Control Room Crew

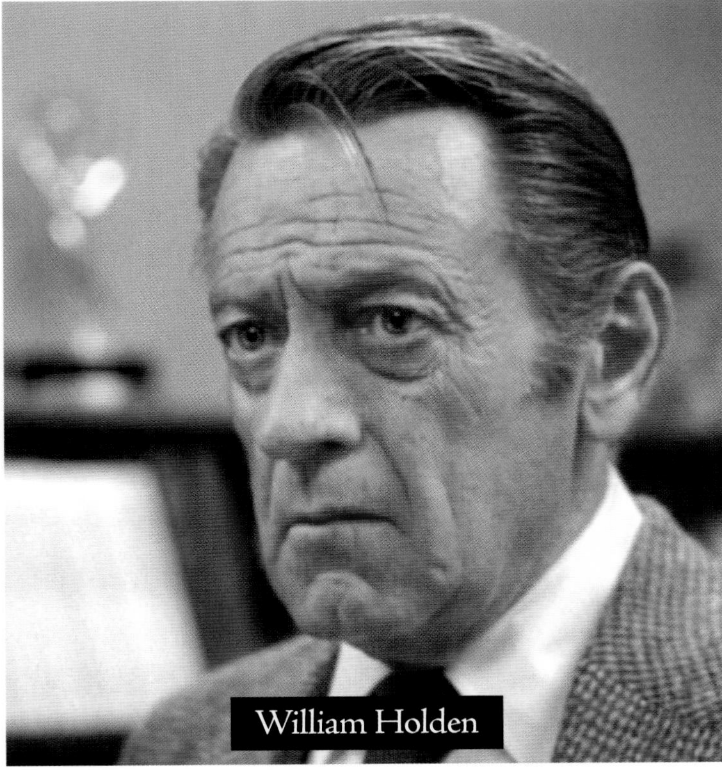
William Holden

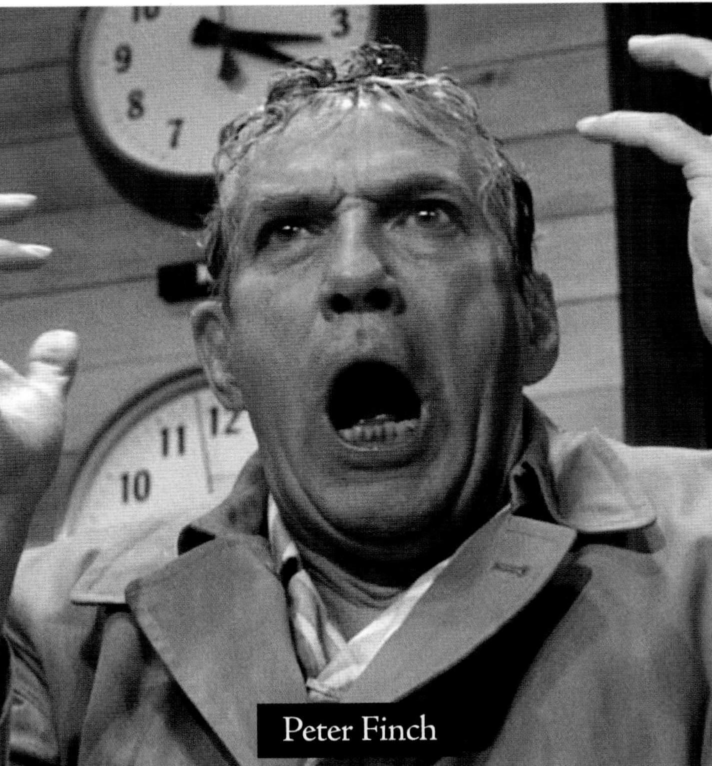
Peter Finch

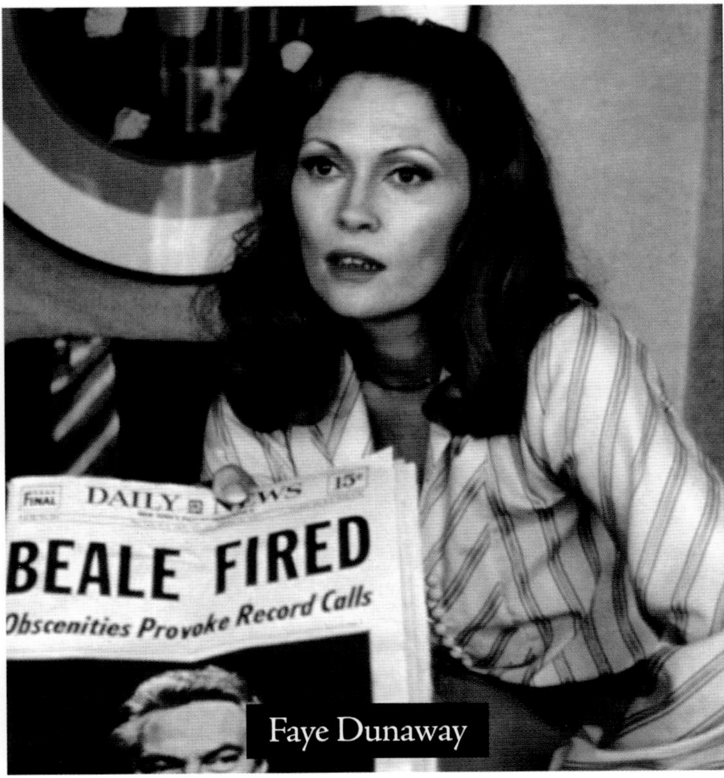

Faye Dunaway

I'll wager that whoever saw Peter Finch as anchorman Howard Beale in "Network," has never forgotten his screaming, "I'M AS MAD AS HELL, AND I'M NOT GOING TO TAKE THIS ANYMORE!" I sure haven't.

Rocky Balboa, a small-time boxer, gets a supremely rare chance to fight heavy-weight champion Apollo Creed in a bout in which he strives to go the distance for his self-respect.

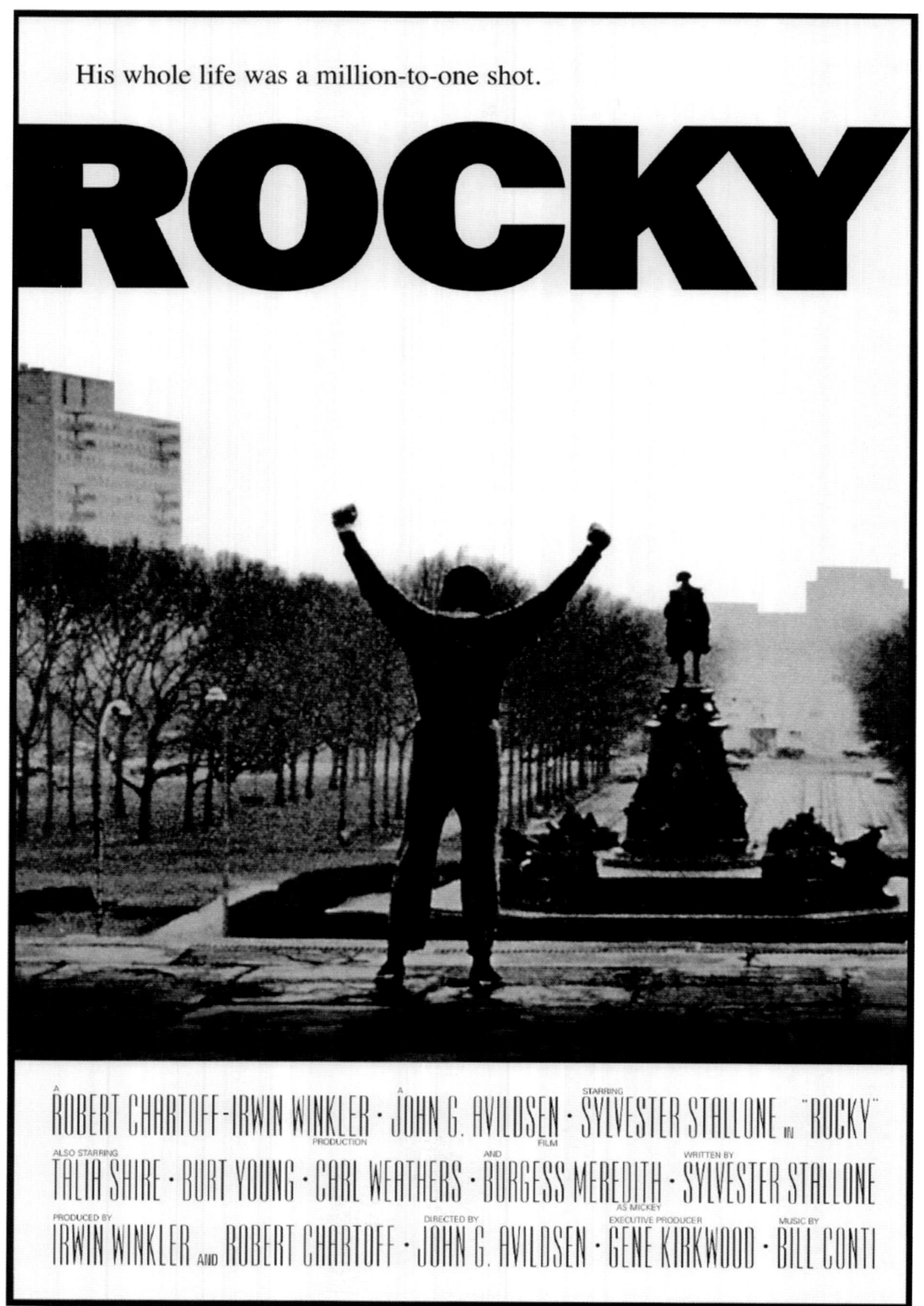

Roger Ebert wrote: "'Rocky' is an immensely involving movie about a punk club fighter who gets a crack at the world championship. 'Rocky' is also a love story about a hero who is played with supreme confidence by Sylvester Stallone who becomes the hottest new star of 1976."

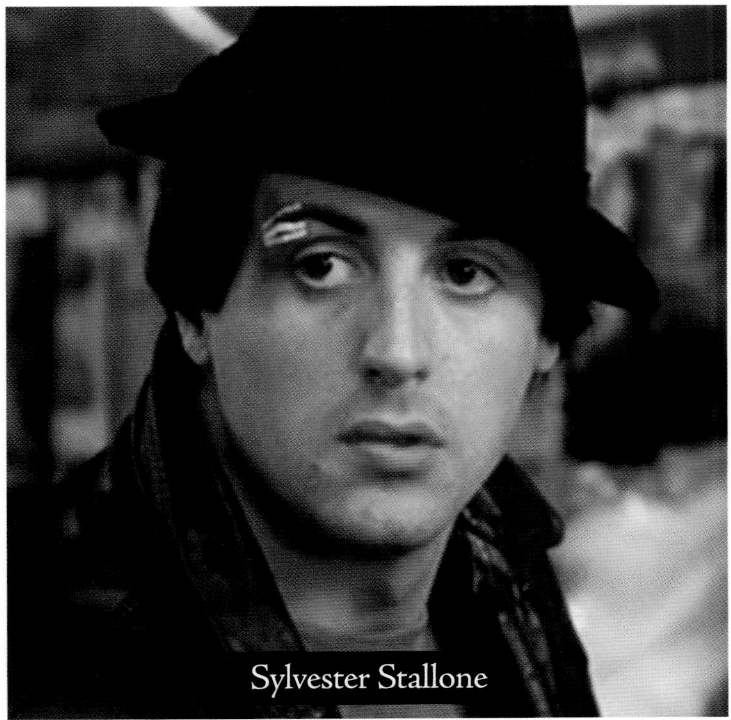
Sylvester Stallone

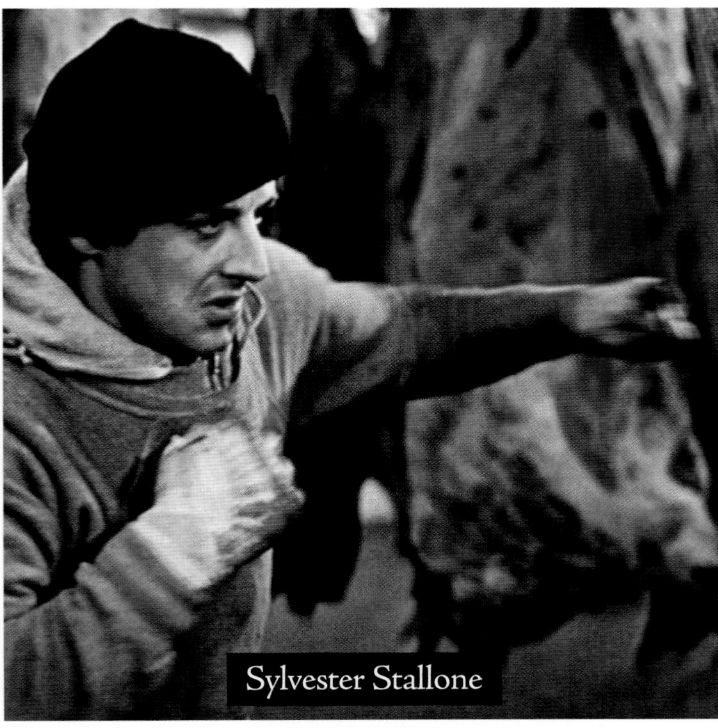
Sylvester Stallone

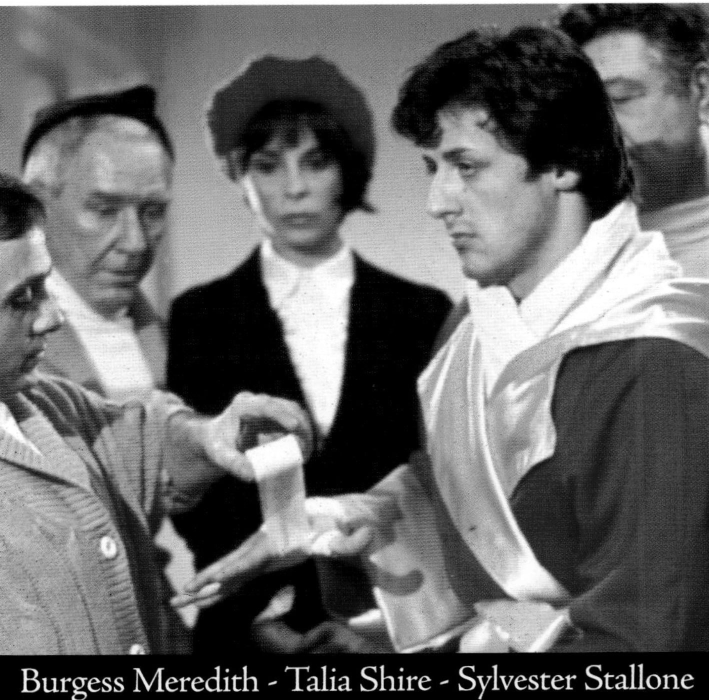
Burgess Meredith - Talia Shire - Sylvester Stallone

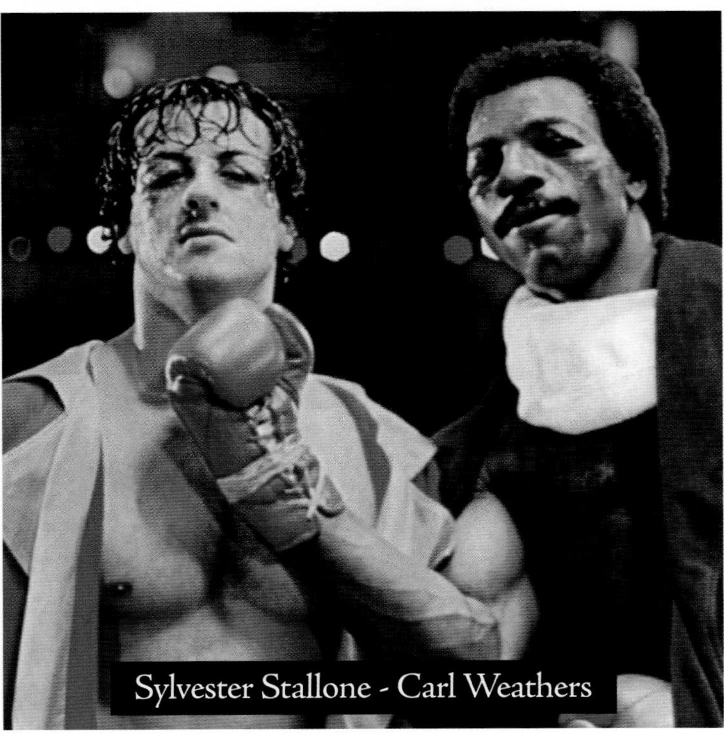
Sylvester Stallone - Carl Weathers

Sylvester Stallone wrote the script for "Rocky" and even though he only had 106 dollars in his pocket, he turned down a 300,000 dollar offer from a major studio. Had he sold it, his movie would have missed winning three Oscars. It takes courage to make the right decision and Stallone, like Rocky, had the courage.

A mentally unstable Vietnam War veteran works as a night-time taxi driver in New York City, where the perceived decadence and sleaze feeds his urge for violent action, while attempting to save a preadolescent prostitute in the process.

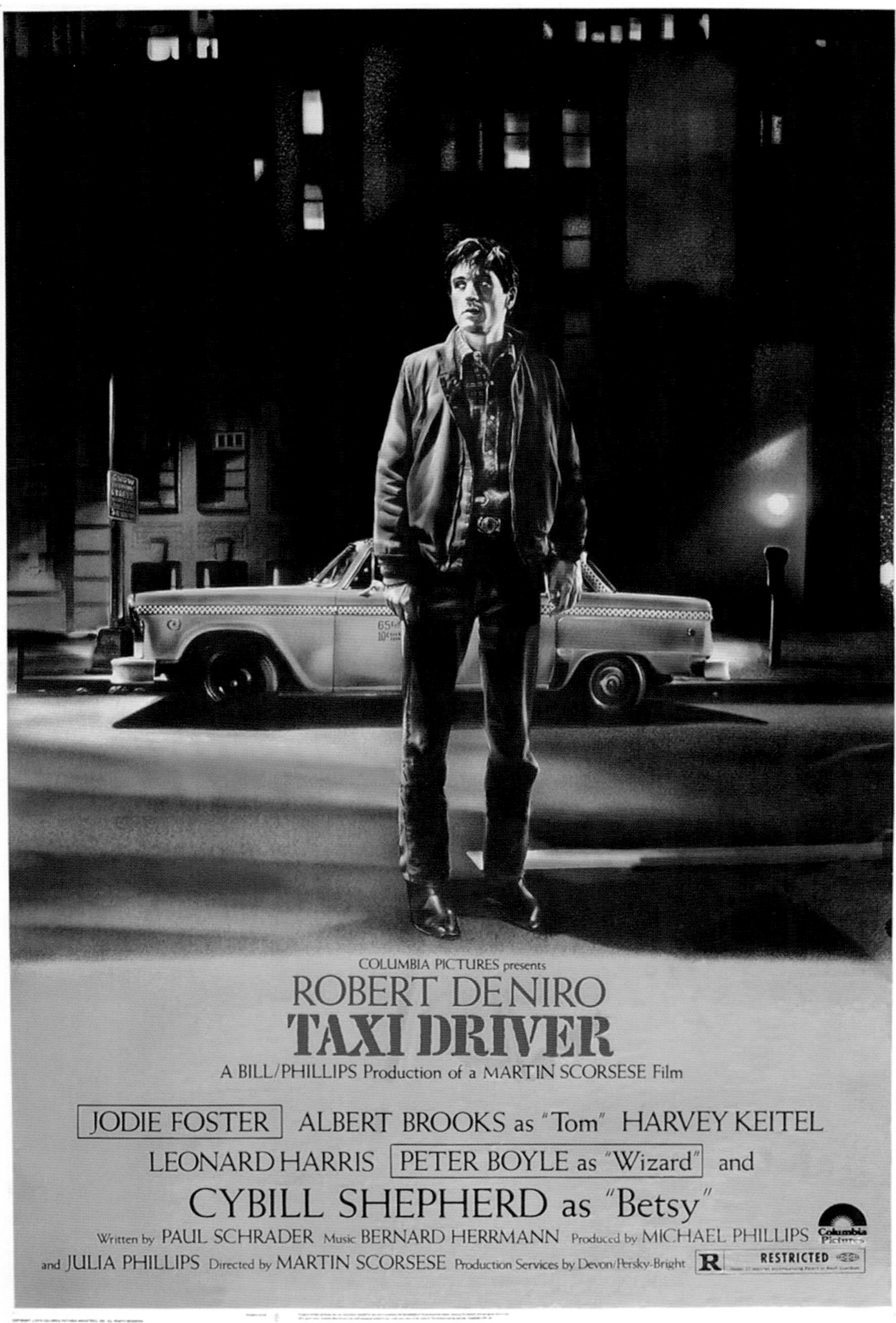

Daily Variety wrote: "De Niro's performance is both riveting and unnerving in this film that will stay with you forever. Assassins, mass murderers and other freakish criminals more often than not turn out to be the quiet kid down the street. 'Taxi Driver' is Martin Scorsese's frighteningly plausible case history of such a person."

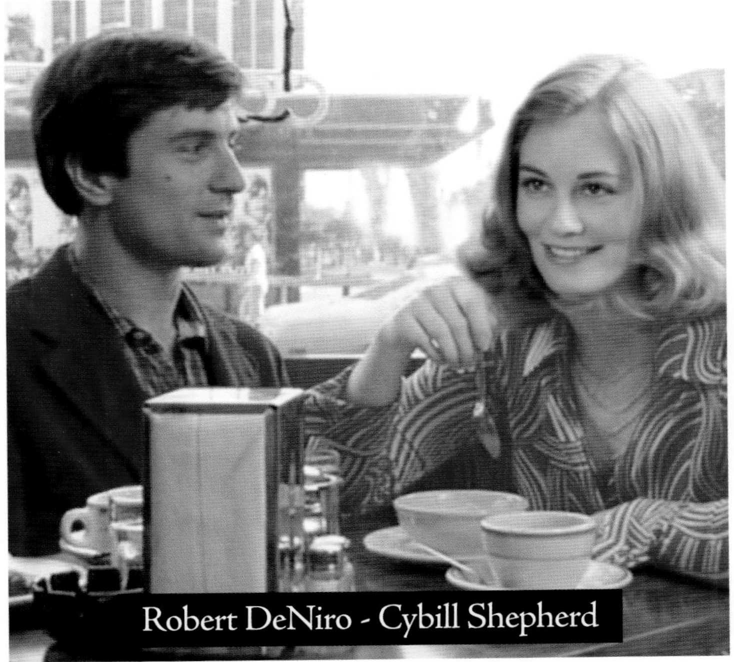
Robert DeNiro - Cybill Shepherd

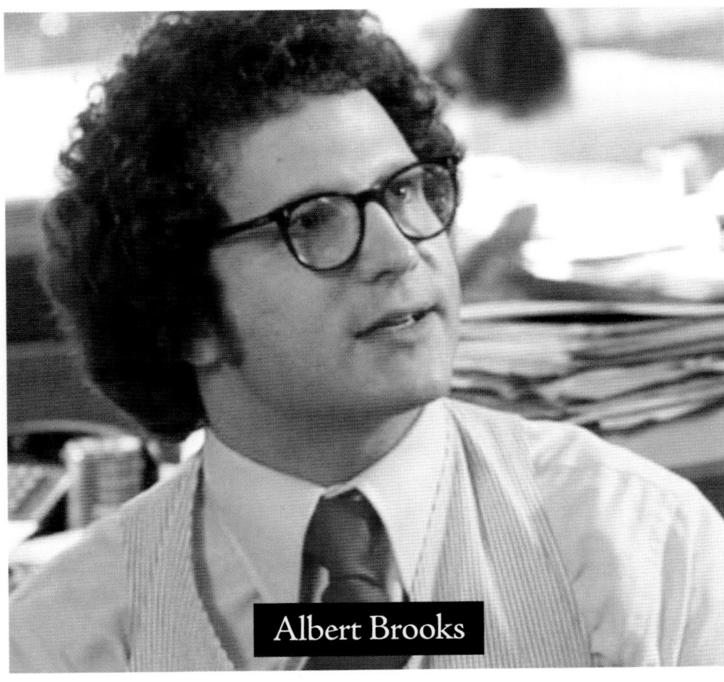
Albert Brooks

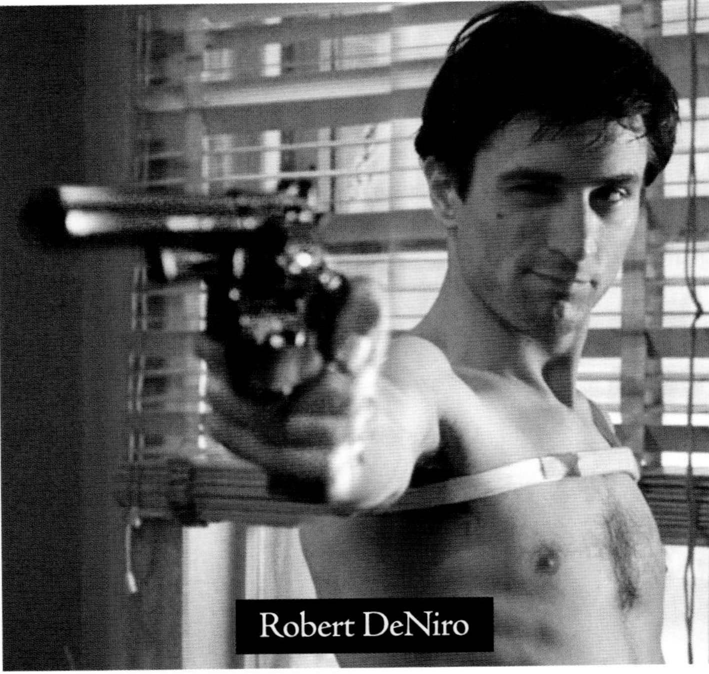
Robert DeNiro

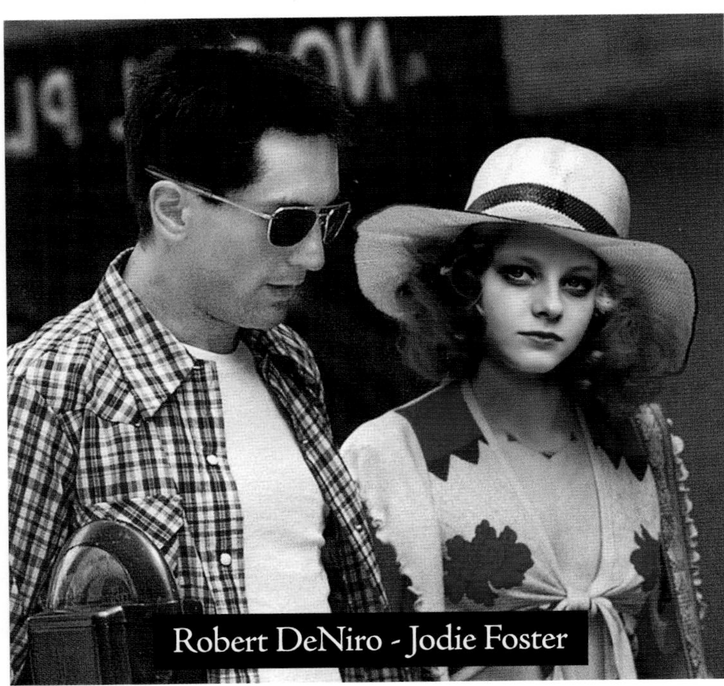
Robert DeNiro - Jodie Foster

Jodie Foster, who was fourteen years old when she played a fourteen year old street walker, went on to become a successful director. Her first effort, "Little Man Tate," was a critical and commercial success, grossing $25,010,896.

Robert DeNiro dated Cybill Shepherd, the girl Albert Brooks desired, and it wasn't until Albert wrote and directed his own films that Albert succeeded in getting the girl.

When God appears to an assistant grocery manager as a good natured old man, the Almighty selects him as his messenger for the modern world.

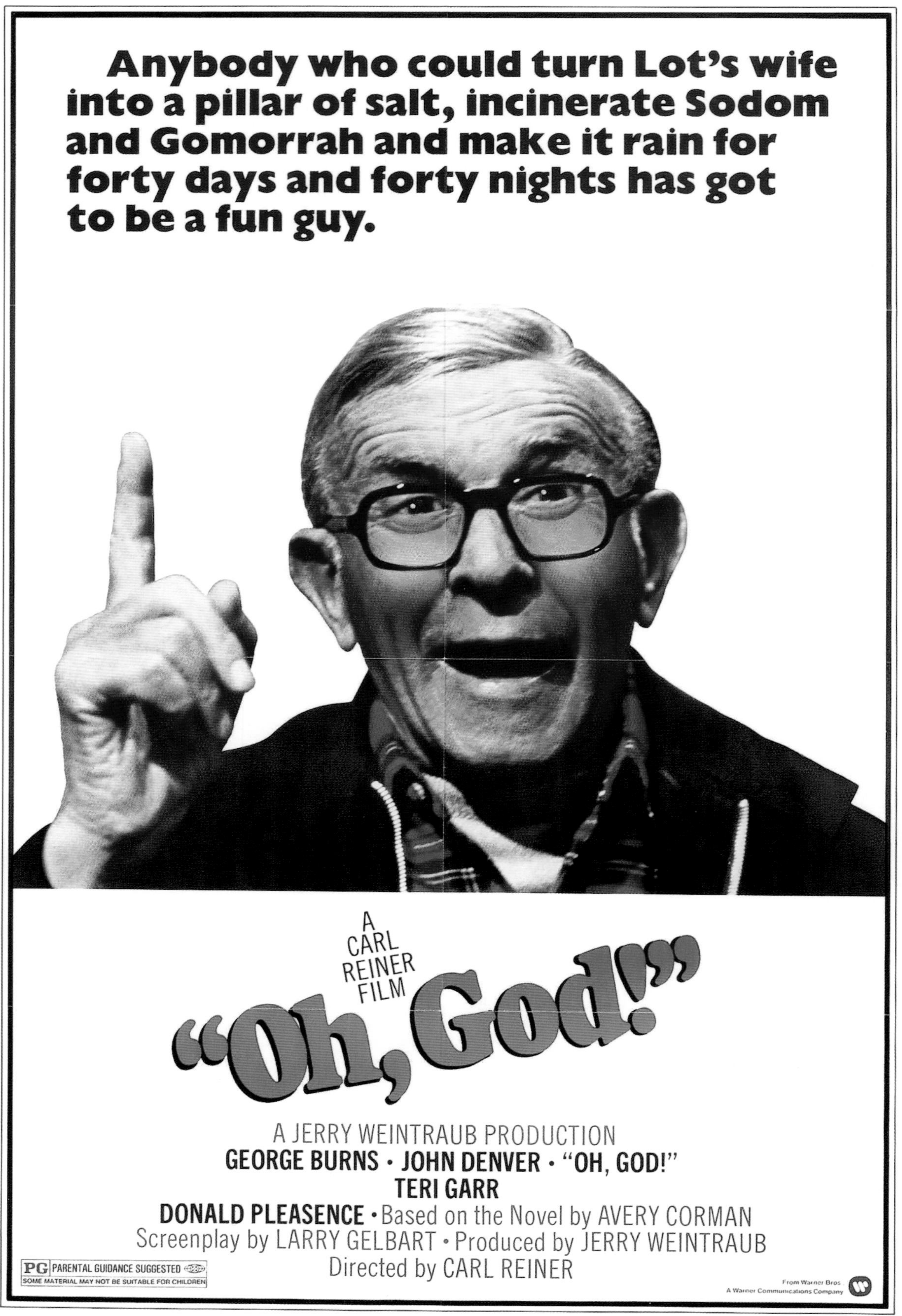

Roger Ebert wrote: "'Oh, God!' is a treasure of a movie: A sly, civilized, quietly funny speculation on what might happen if God endeavored to present himself in the flesh yet once again to forgetful Man."

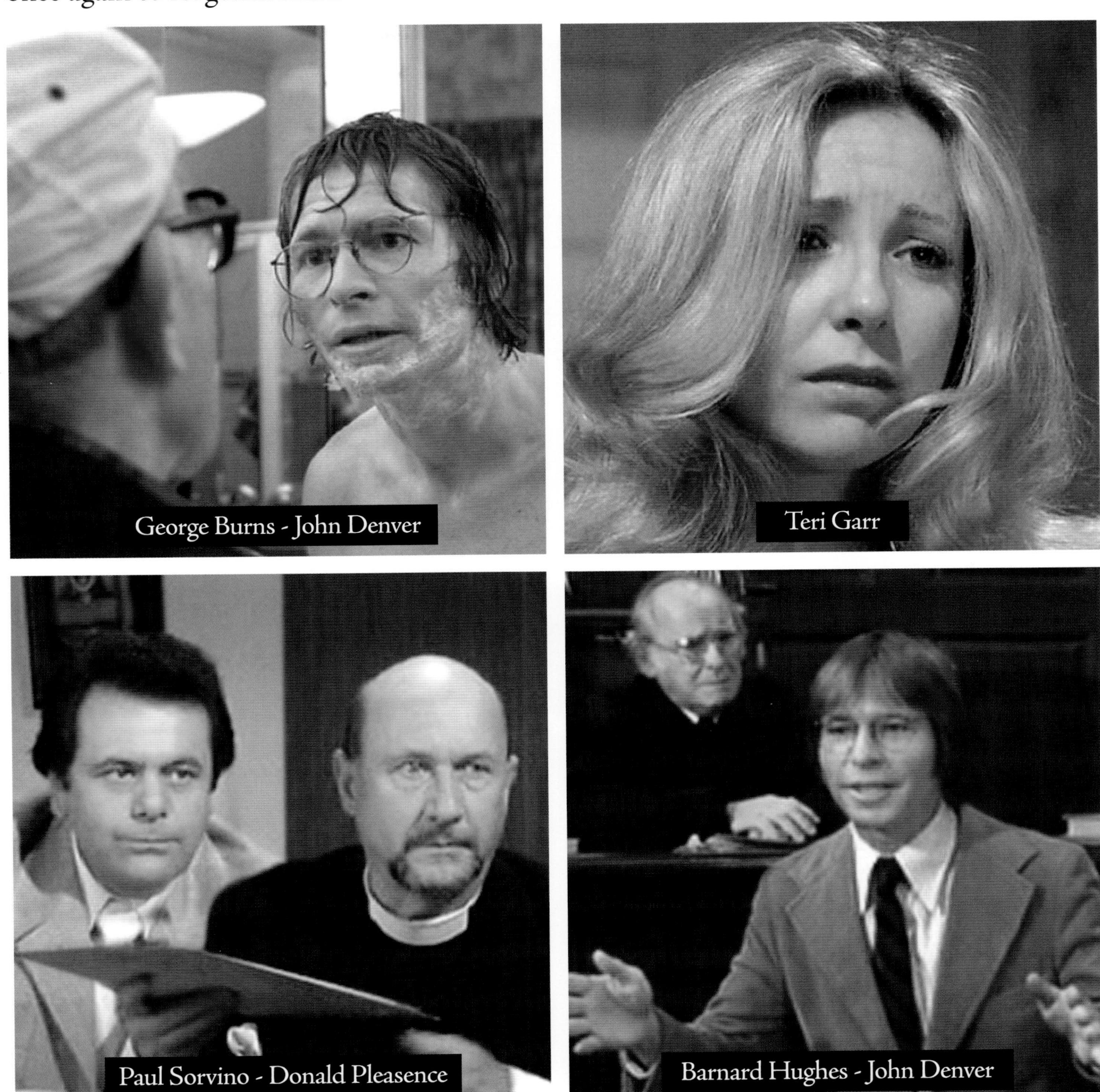

George Burns - John Denver

Teri Garr

Paul Sorvino - Donald Pleasence

Barnard Hughes - John Denver

After performing so well with the lovely and talented Teri Garr, John Denver was offered and refused many film roles, as he much preferred to write songs, sing them and tour with his band. Sadly, he left us prematurely in 1997, when piloting an experimental plane whose engine malfunctioned, crashing into a mountain.

Neurotic New York comedian Alvy Singer falls in love with the ditzy Annie Hall.

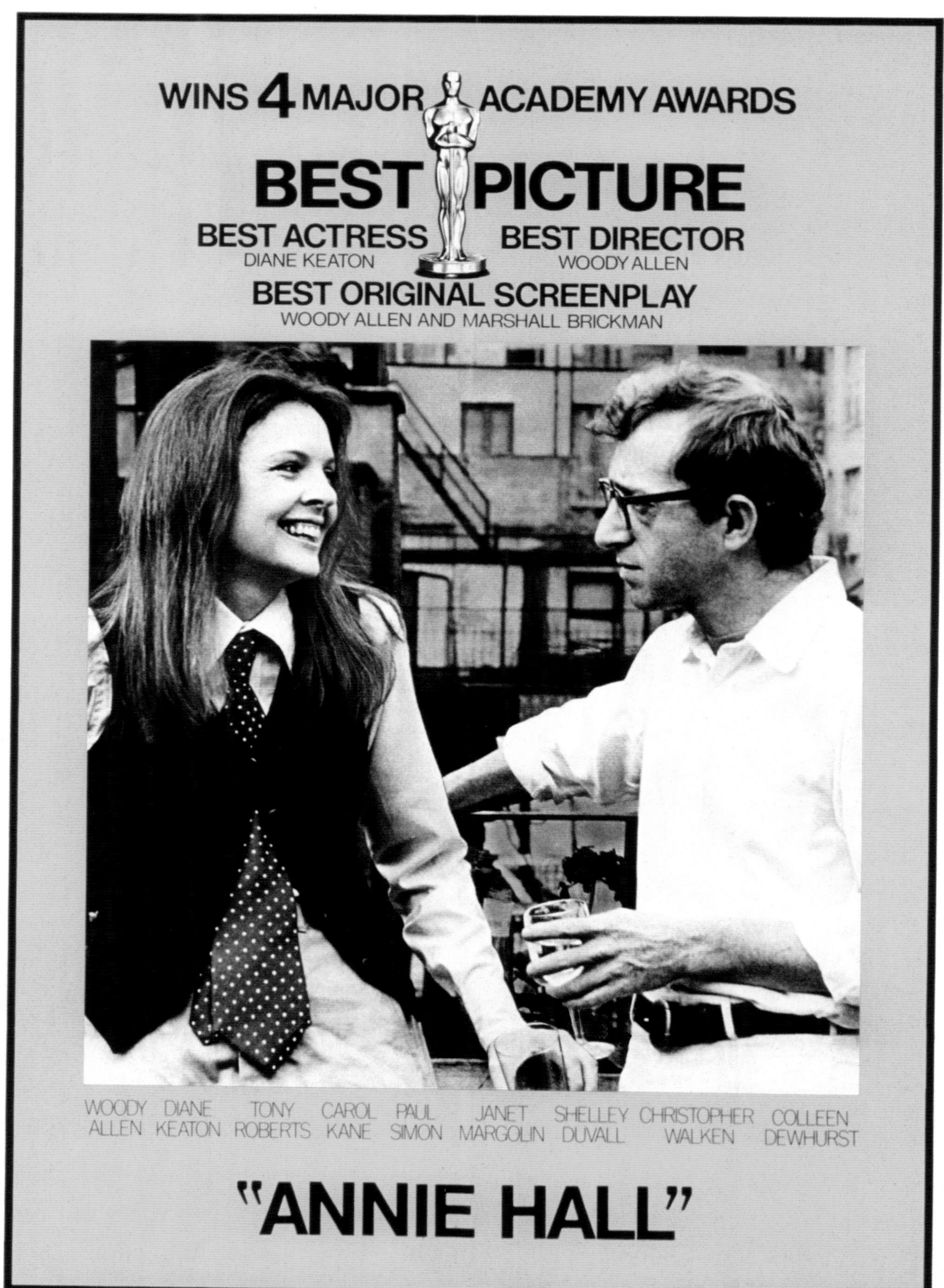

Roger Ebert wrote: "'Annie Hall' contains more intellectual wit and cultural references than any other movie ever to win the Oscar for Best Picture."

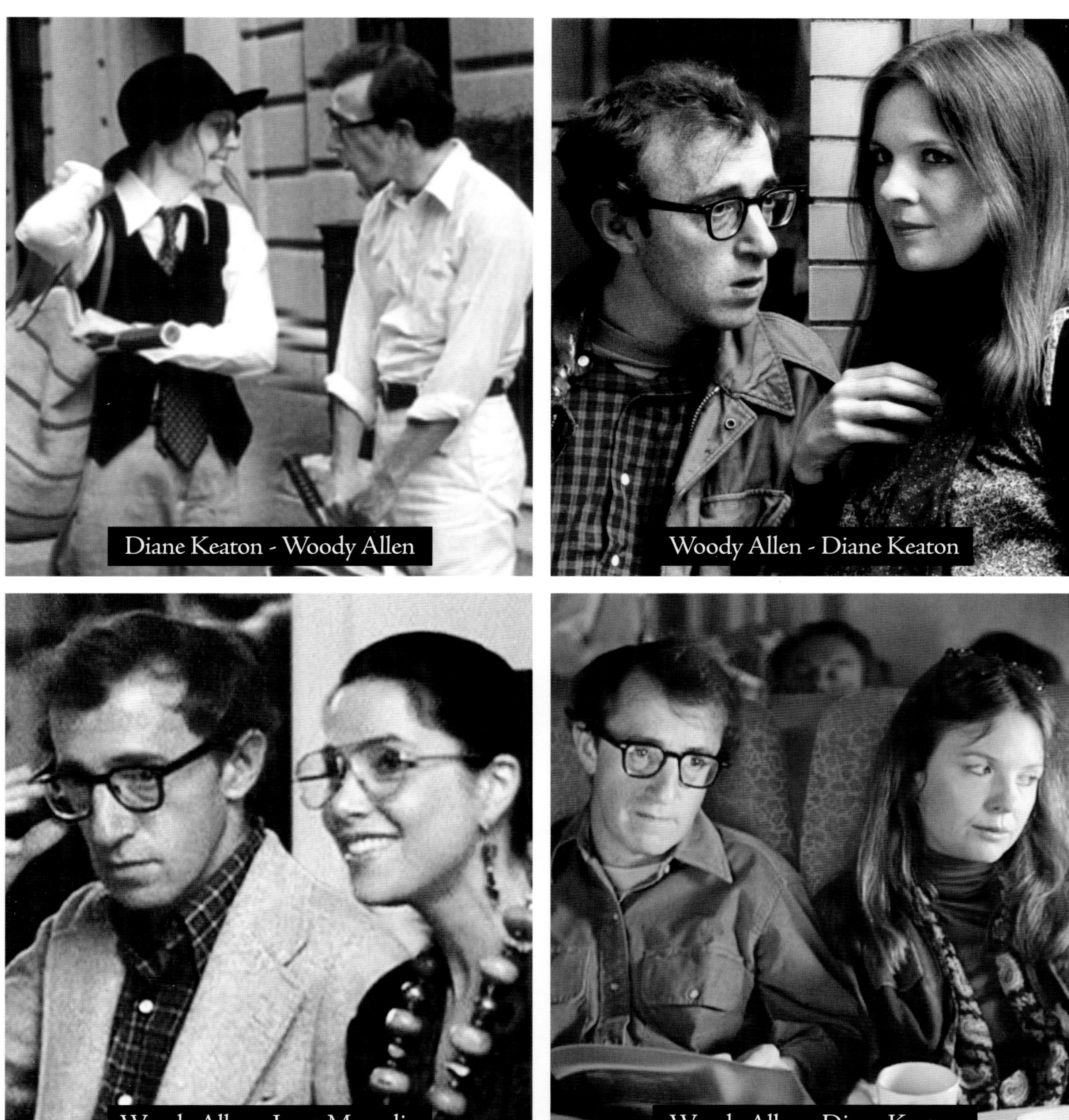

Diane Keaton - Woody Allen

Woody Allen - Diane Keaton

Woody Allen - Janet Margolin

Woody Allen - Diane Keaton

I consider Woody a true genius. He made forty-six brilliant comedies and the only one that, as far as the critics were concerned, did not shine as brightly was "Melinda and Melinda." I enjoyed it and, to remember why I did, I intend to watch it again.

1951: Andy Schmidt is in his last year of college. Taking life easy and always a saucy joke on his lips, he manages to win fellow student Mary's heart. But getting a job after college turns out to be much harder than he expected so he attempts to be a wrestler. To avoid getting beaten up, he stages the fights–and incidentally invents show-wrestling.

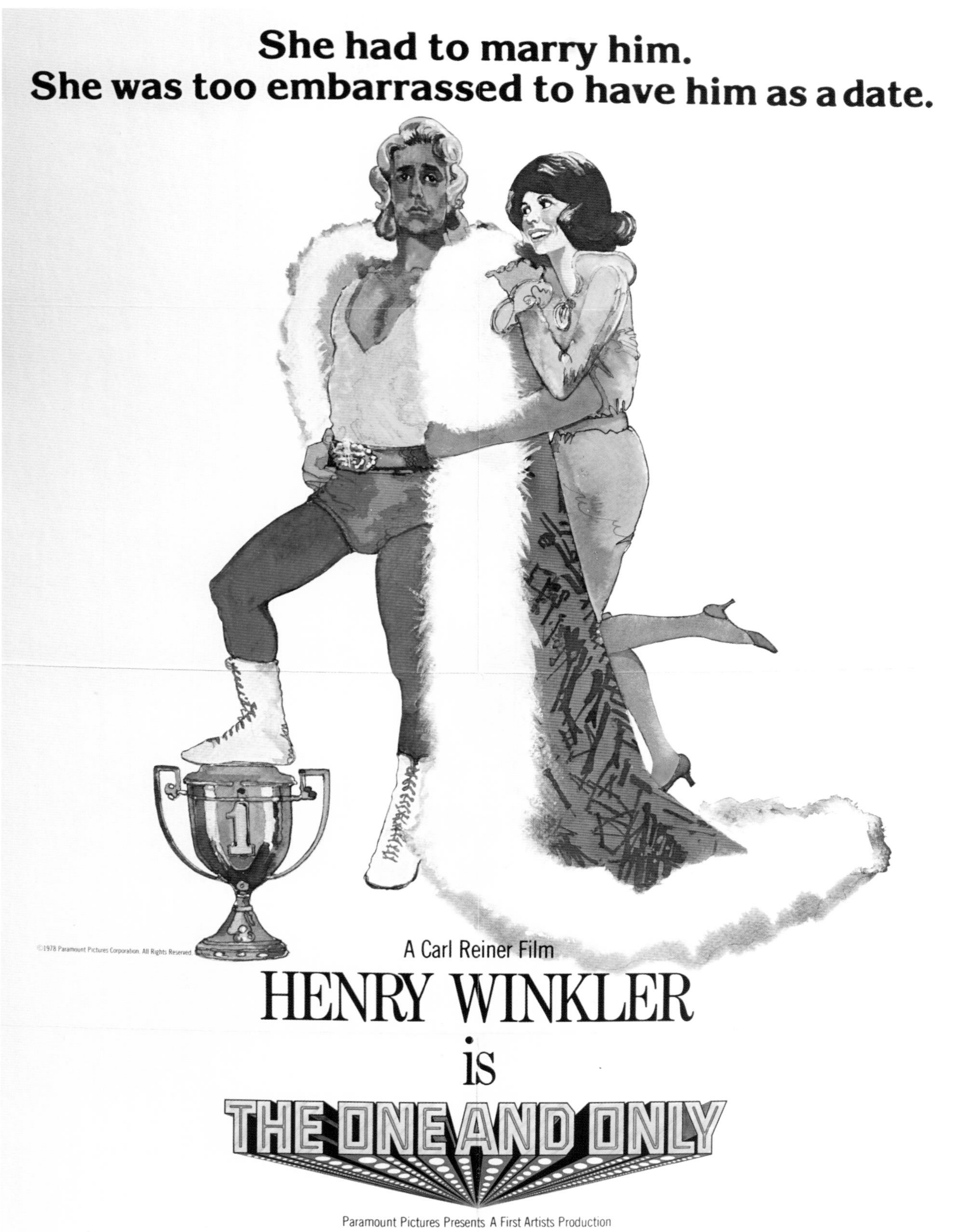

Roger Ebert wrote: "The film has many funny moments that it owes to Kim Darby's innate charm. Henry Winkler selflessly throws himself into his role and becomes a conceited and foppish wrestler. He ultimately ends up competing while wearing a blond wig and mink underwear.

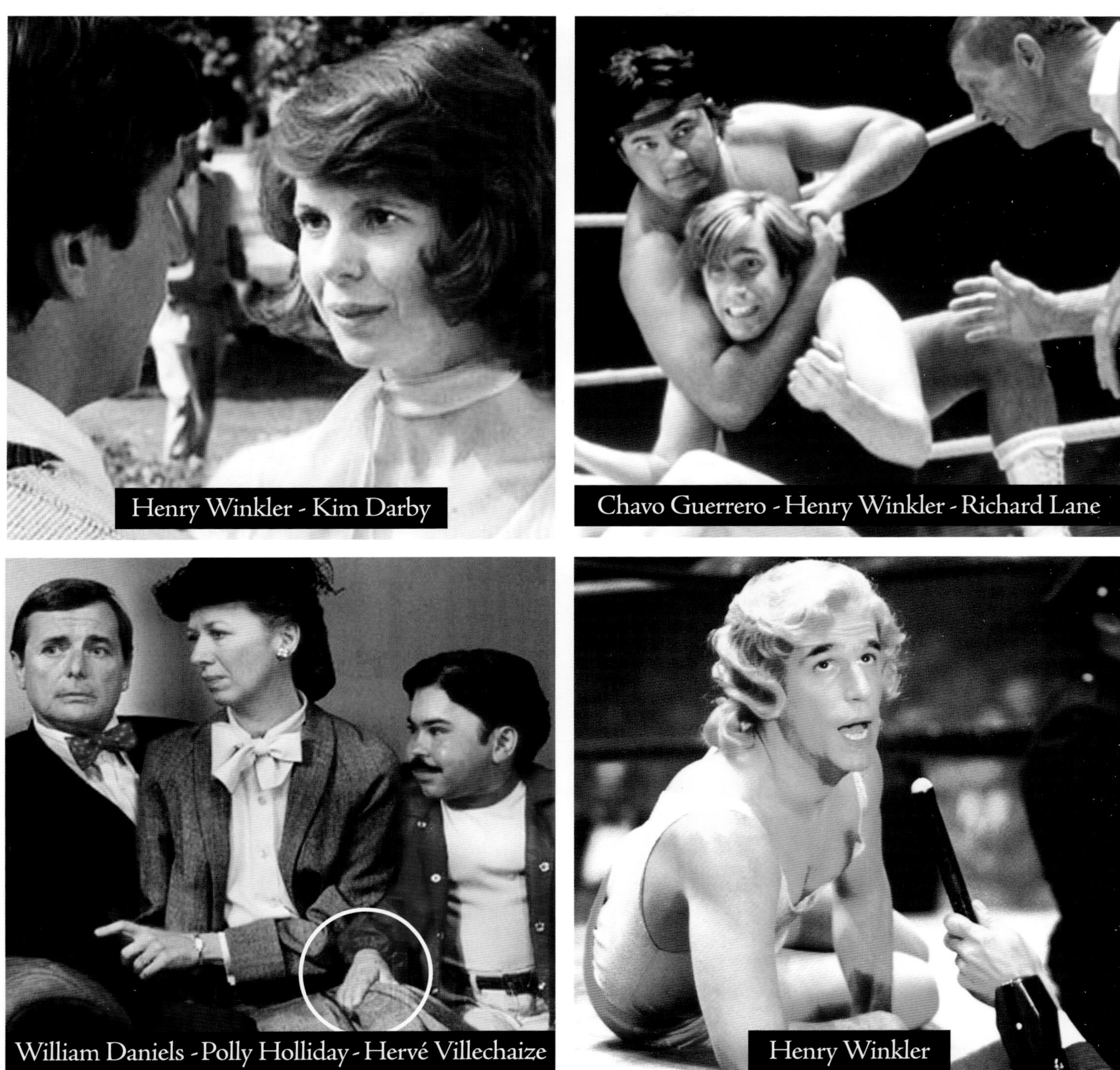

Henry Winkler - Kim Darby

Chavo Guerrero - Henry Winkler - Richard Lane

William Daniels - Polly Holliday - Hervé Villechaize

Henry Winkler

Henry Winkler, who weighed but 149 pounds, convinced audiences that he could win matches with wrestlers three times his size.

I still smile when I recall the debonaire 3 foot, 11 inch Hervé Villechaize strolling down the street with Henry Winkler and asking him in a high-pitched, French-accented voice, "D'you wanna cuppa coffee?"

A pushy, narcissistic filmmaker persuades a Phoenix family to let him and his crew film their everyday lives, in the manner of the ground-breaking PBS series "An American Family." However, instead of remaining unobtrusive and letting the family be themselves, he can't keep himself from trying to control every facet of their lives "for the good of the show".

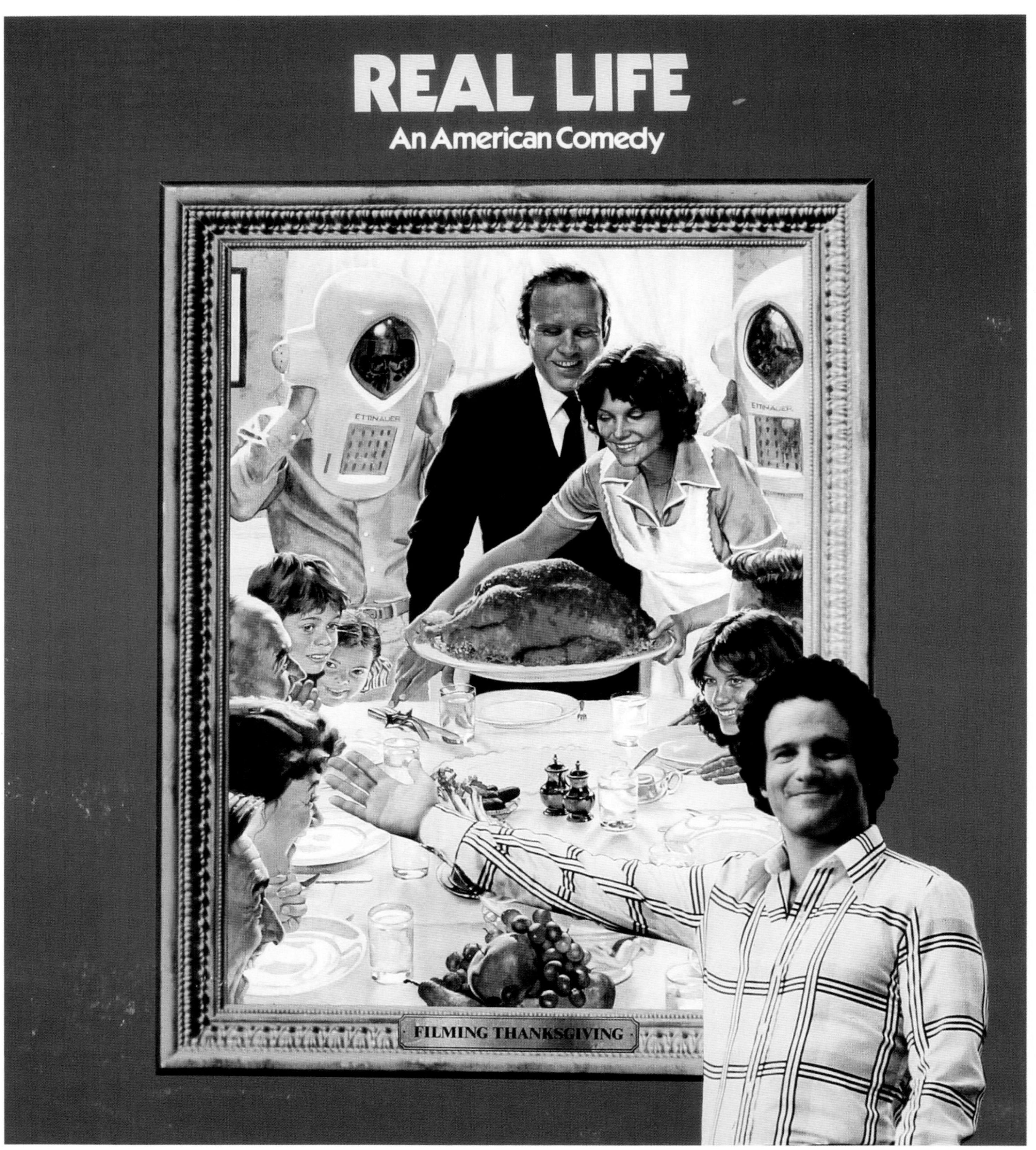

Steve Sandberg from Movie Marathoning wrote: "It would seem impossible for a movie to be both distinctly ahead-of-its-time and undeniably quaint, for a story that feels like part of the genesis of modern reality television. Albert Brooks' directorial debut is a metatextual mockumentary-within-a-mockumentary that satirizes the concept of filmed reality. 'Real Life' is incredibly smart and insightful."

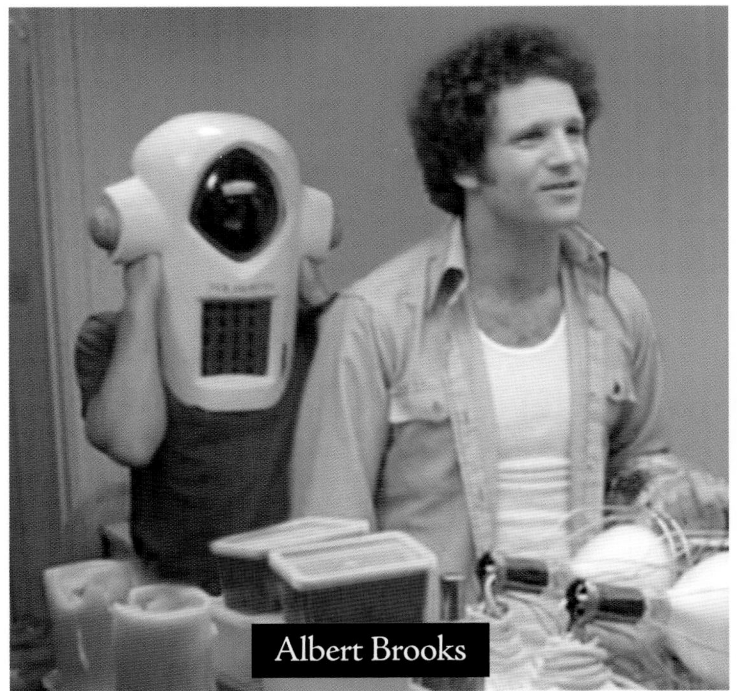
Albert Brooks

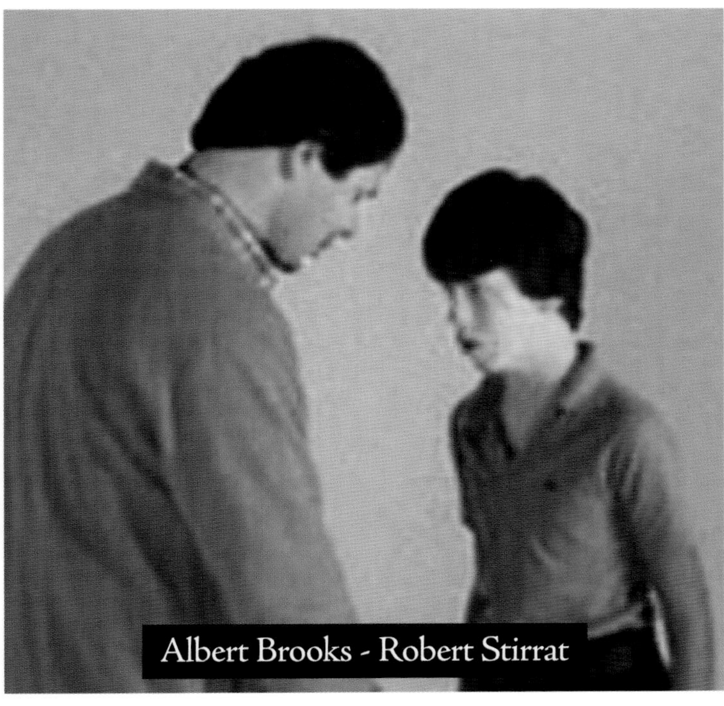
Albert Brooks - Robert Stirrat

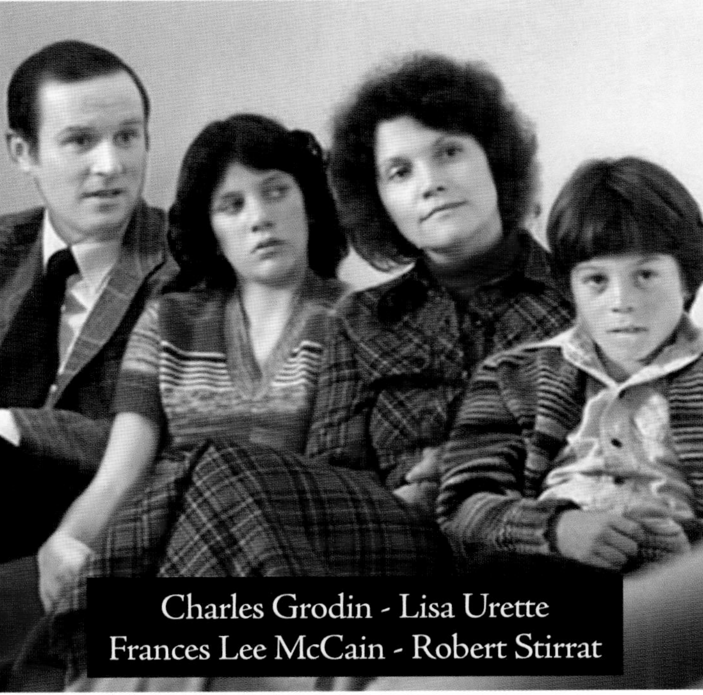
Charles Grodin - Lisa Urette
Frances Lee McCain - Robert Stirrat

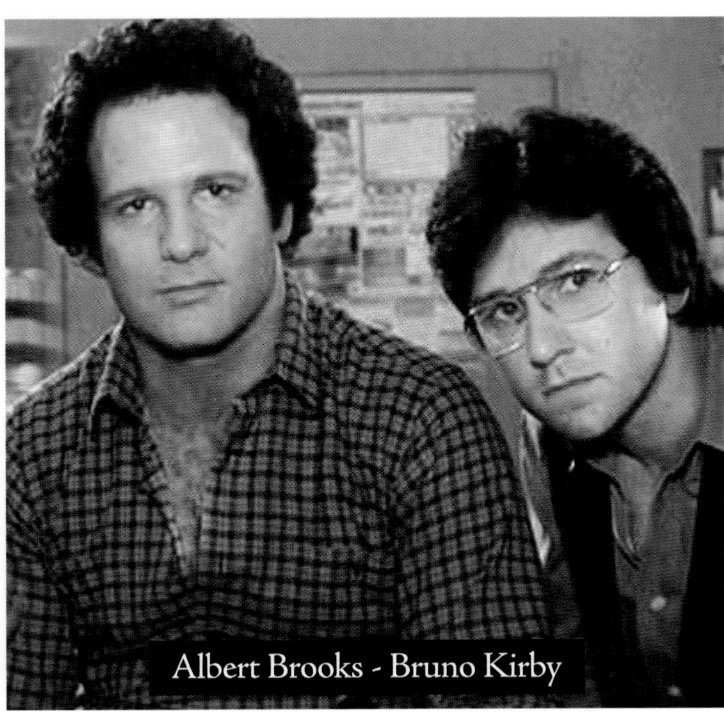
Albert Brooks - Bruno Kirby

Albert Brooks was sixteen when my son, Rob, told me that Albert was the funniest guy ever. Rob was right and one night, in my home, he had me laughing so hard that I left the room. I feared that, if I had stayed, I'd have passed out.

An idiotic man struggles to make it through life on his own in St. Louis.

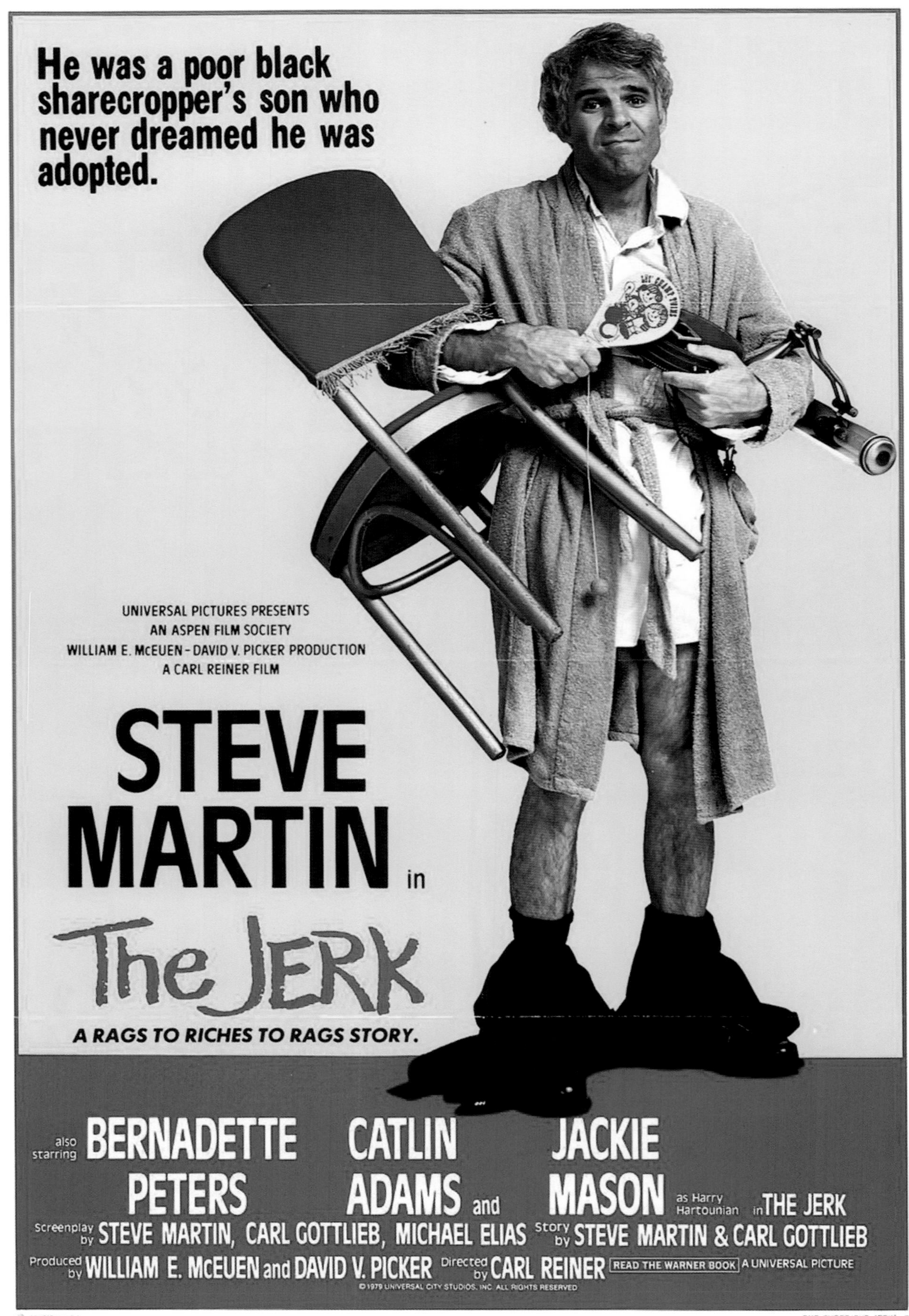

Douglas Reid wrote: "'The Jerk' is simply the funniest most understatedly clever movie ever produced." The audience agreed and bought $73,000,000 worth of tickets.

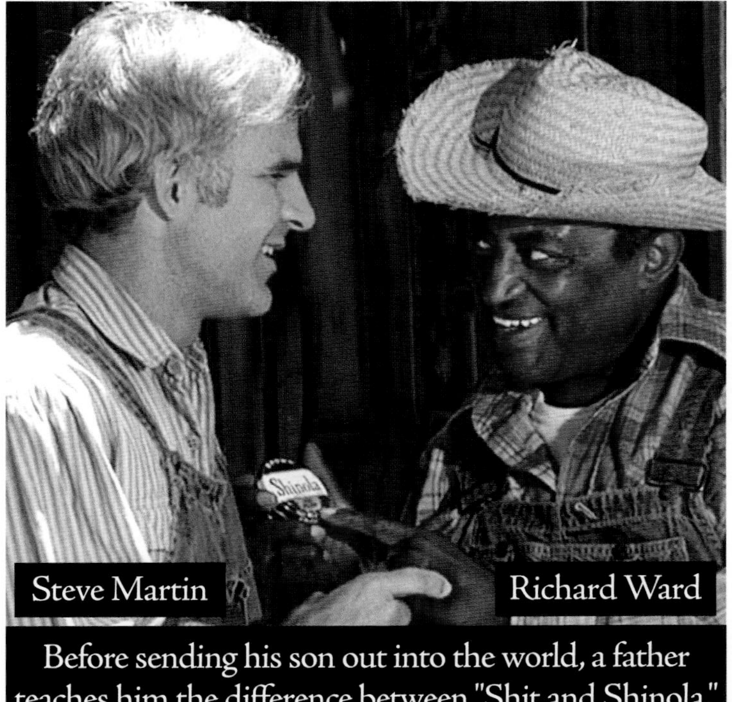

Steve Martin Richard Ward

Before sending his son out into the world, a father teaches him the difference between "Shit and Shinola."

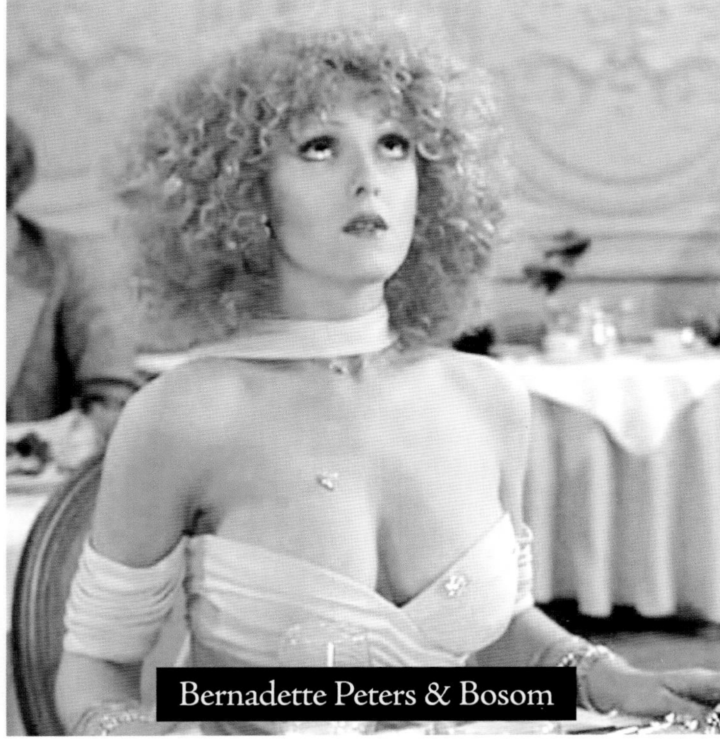

Bernadette Peters & Bosom

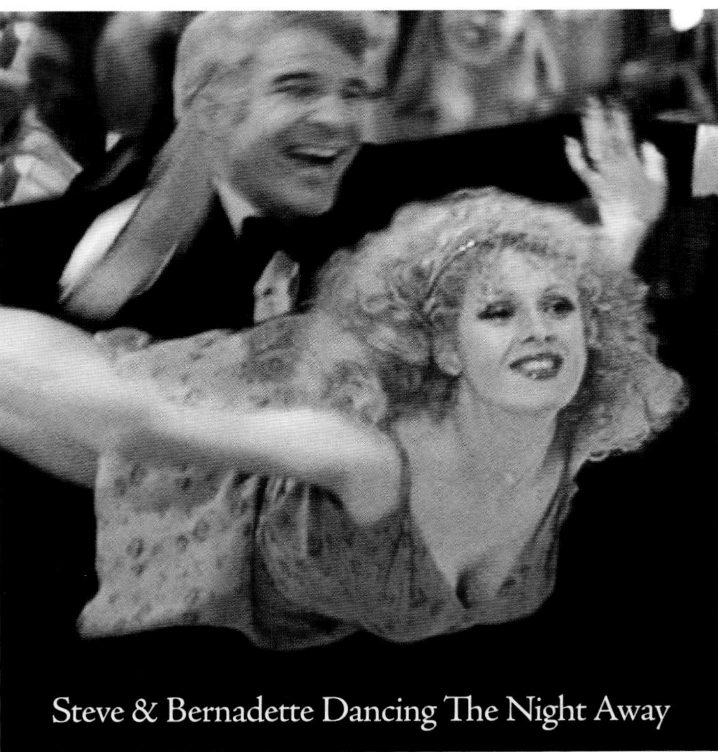

Steve & Bernadette Dancing The Night Away

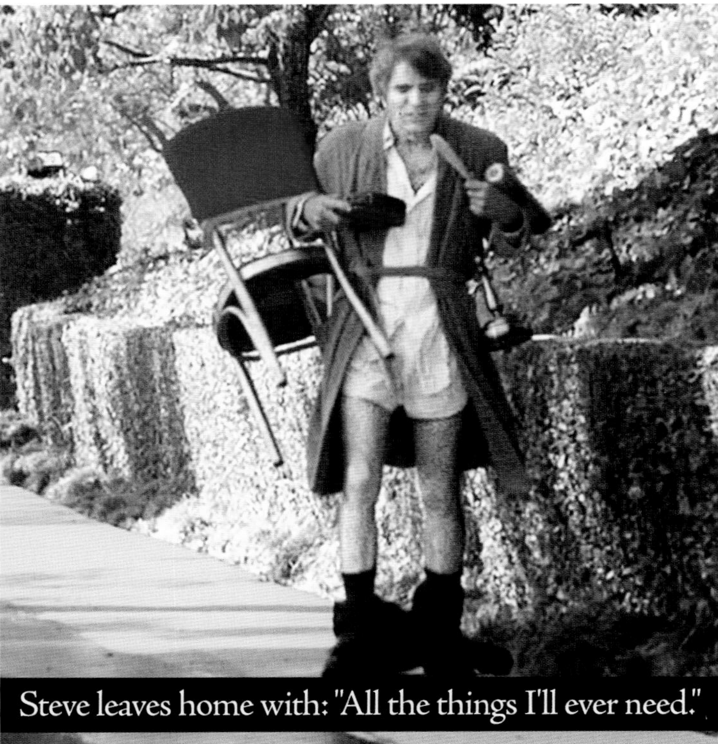

Steve leaves home with: "All the things I'll ever need."

After "The Jerk," Steve and I went on to make three more films, "The Man with Two Brains," "All of Me" and "Dead Men Don't Wear Plaid." Steve Martin is an author, a playwright, a banjoist, a classic and modern art expert, a sleight of hand magician, a loving husband and a doting father of a darling six year old girl.

Ted Kramer's wife leaves her husband, allowing for a lost bond to be rediscovered between Ted and his son, Billy. But a heated custody battle ensues over the divorced couple's son, deepening the wounds left by the separation.

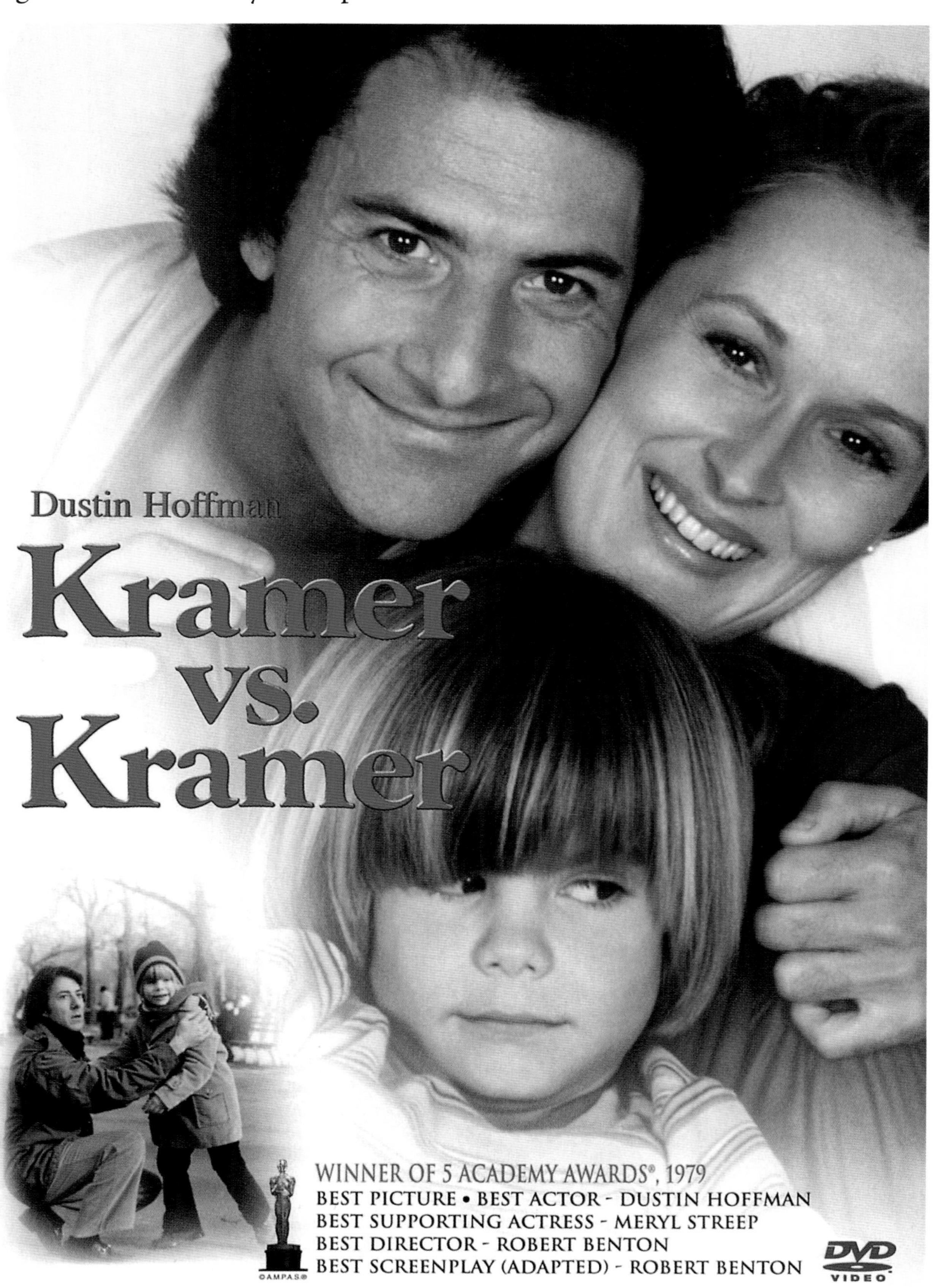

Vincent Canby of The New York Times wrote: "'Kramer vs. Kramer' is densely packed with such beautifully observed detail. It is also superbly acted by its supporting cast, including Jane Alexander, Howard Duff, and George Coe."

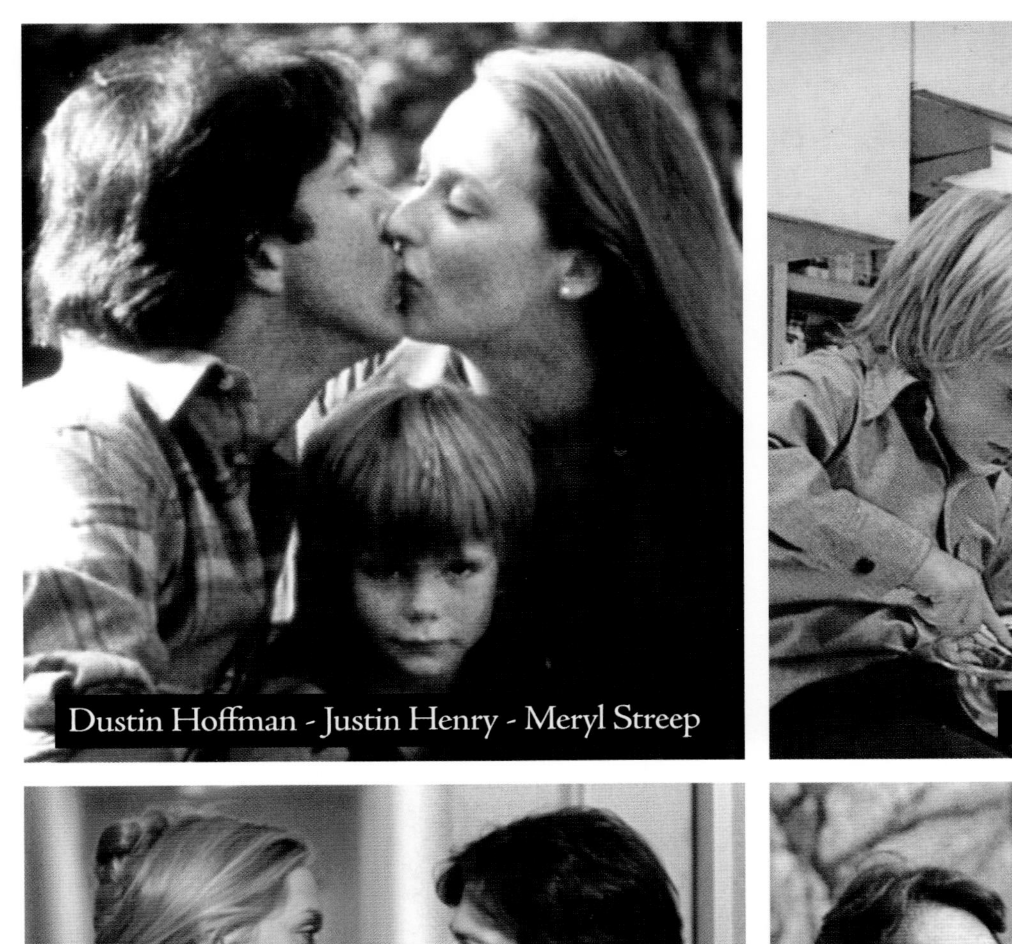

Dustin Hoffman - Justin Henry - Meryl Streep

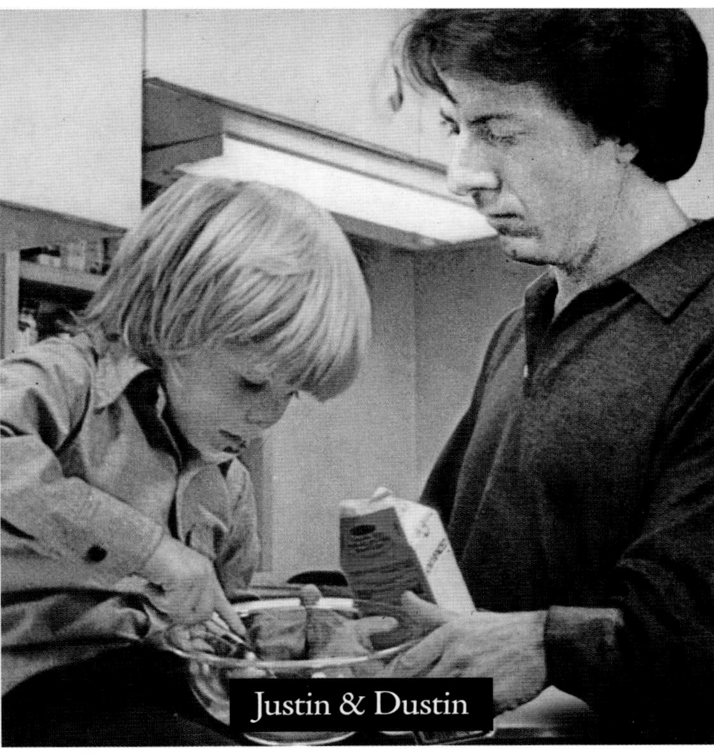

Justin & Dustin

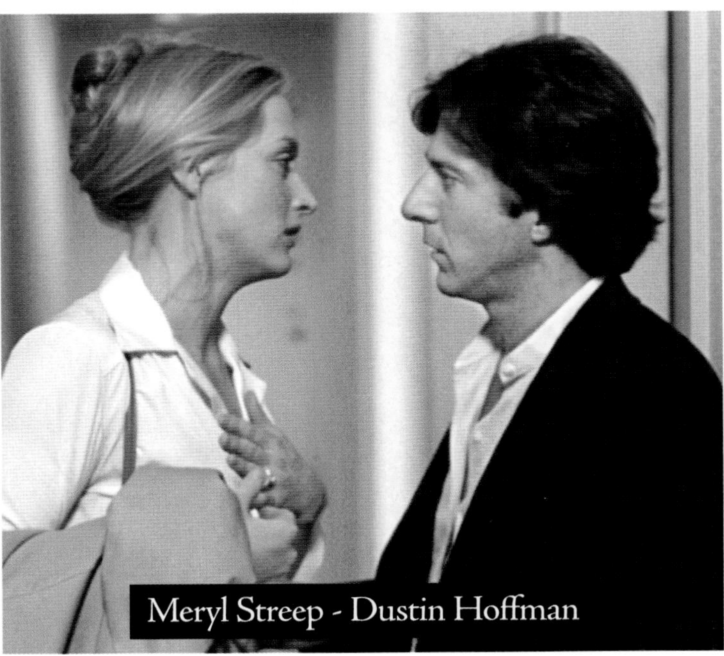

Meryl Streep - Dustin Hoffman

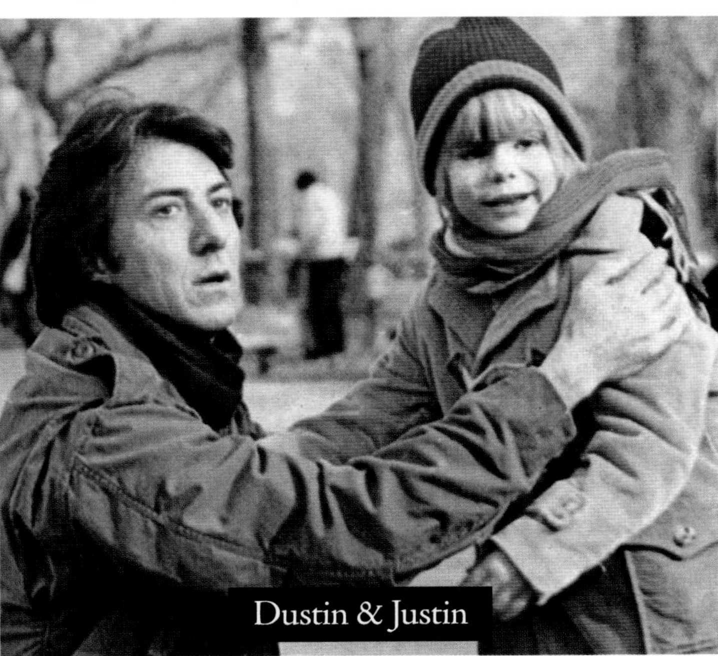

Dustin & Justin

Both Meryl Streep, who that year won an Oscar for Best Supporting Actress, and Dustin Hoffman, for Best Actor in a Leading Role, went on to deliver many renowned works of film art and continue to do so.

I've always said that Meryl Streep is the finest and most versatile actor working today, and that was even before I saw her performance as Florence Foster Jenkins.

A young single mother and textile worker agrees to help unionize her mill despite the problems and dangers involved.

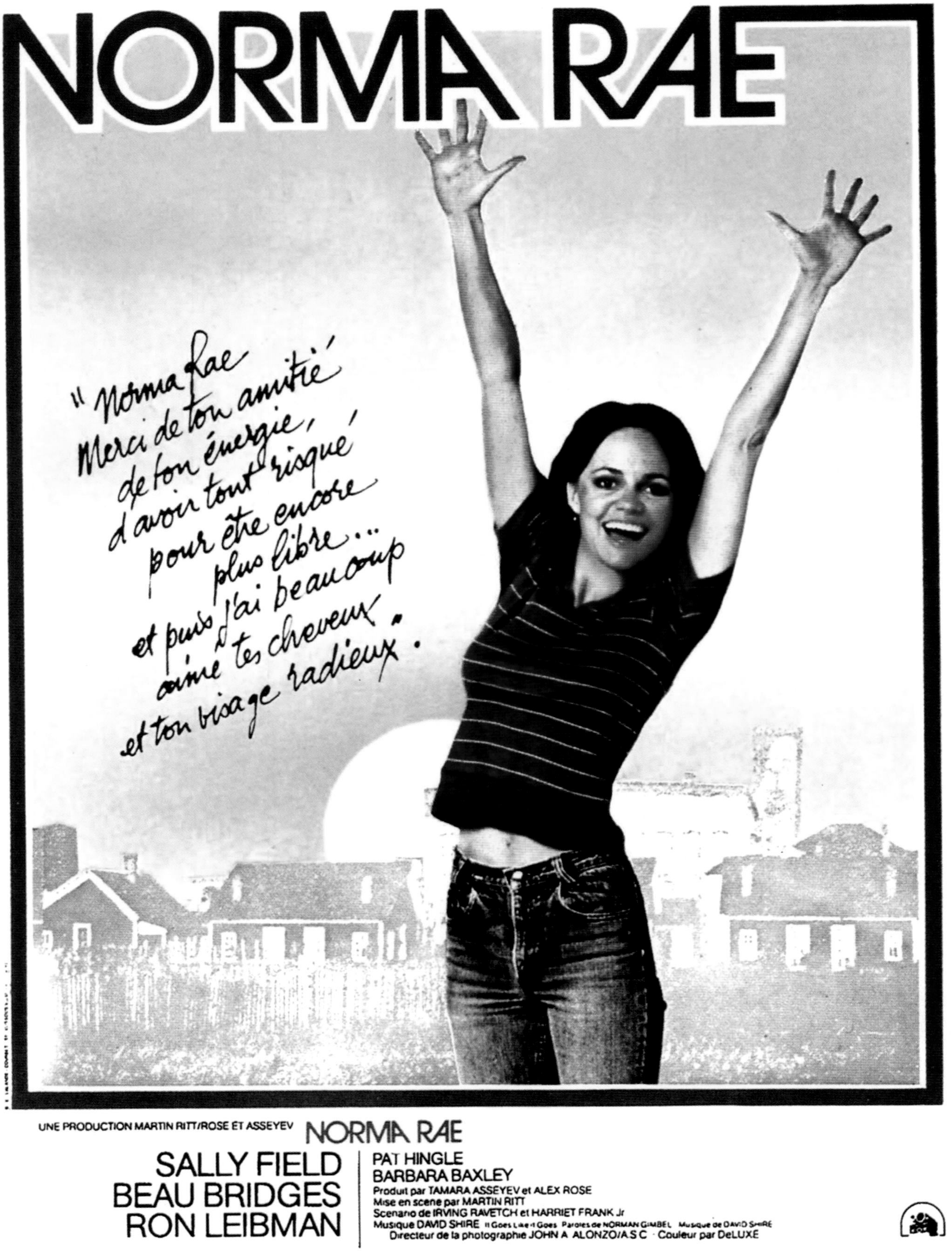

NORMA RAE

" Norma Rae
Merci de ton amitié
de ton énergie,
d'avoir tout risqué
pour être encore
plus libre...
et puis j'ai beaucoup
aimé tes cheveux
et ton visage radieux".

UNE PRODUCTION MARTIN RITT/ROSE ET ASSEYEV NORMA RAE

SALLY FIELD
BEAU BRIDGES
RON LEIBMAN

PAT HINGLE
BARBARA BAXLEY
Produit par TAMARA ASSEYEV et ALEX ROSE
Mise en scene par MARTIN RITT
Scenario de IRVING RAVETCH et HARRIET FRANK Jr
Musique DAVID SHIRE It Goes Like it Goes Paroles de NORMAN GIMBEL Musique de DAVID SHIRE
Directeur de la photographie JOHN A. ALONZO/A.S.C · Couleur par DeLUXE

Vincent Canby of The New York Times wrote: "'Norma Rae' is a seriously concerned contemporary drama, illuminated by some very good performances and one, Miss Field's, that is spectacular, where she demonstrates that she's an actress of dramatic intelligence and force."

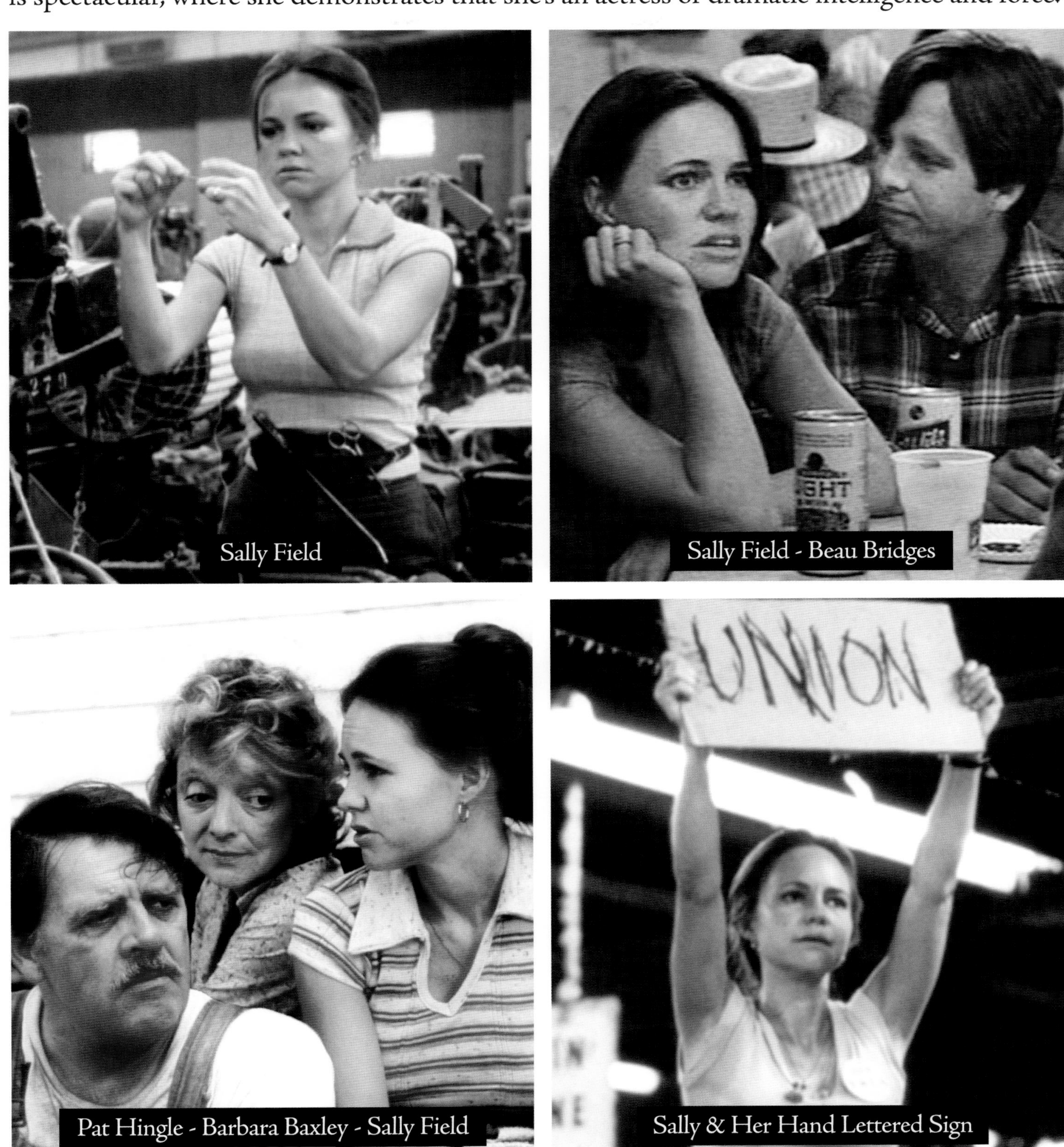

Sally Field

Sally Field - Beau Bridges

Pat Hingle - Barbara Baxley - Sally Field

Sally & Her Hand Lettered Sign

Sally Field as Norma Rae brought hope and rays of sunshine into many lives. You can see why I, who appreciate great actors and great trade union organizers, loved this film.

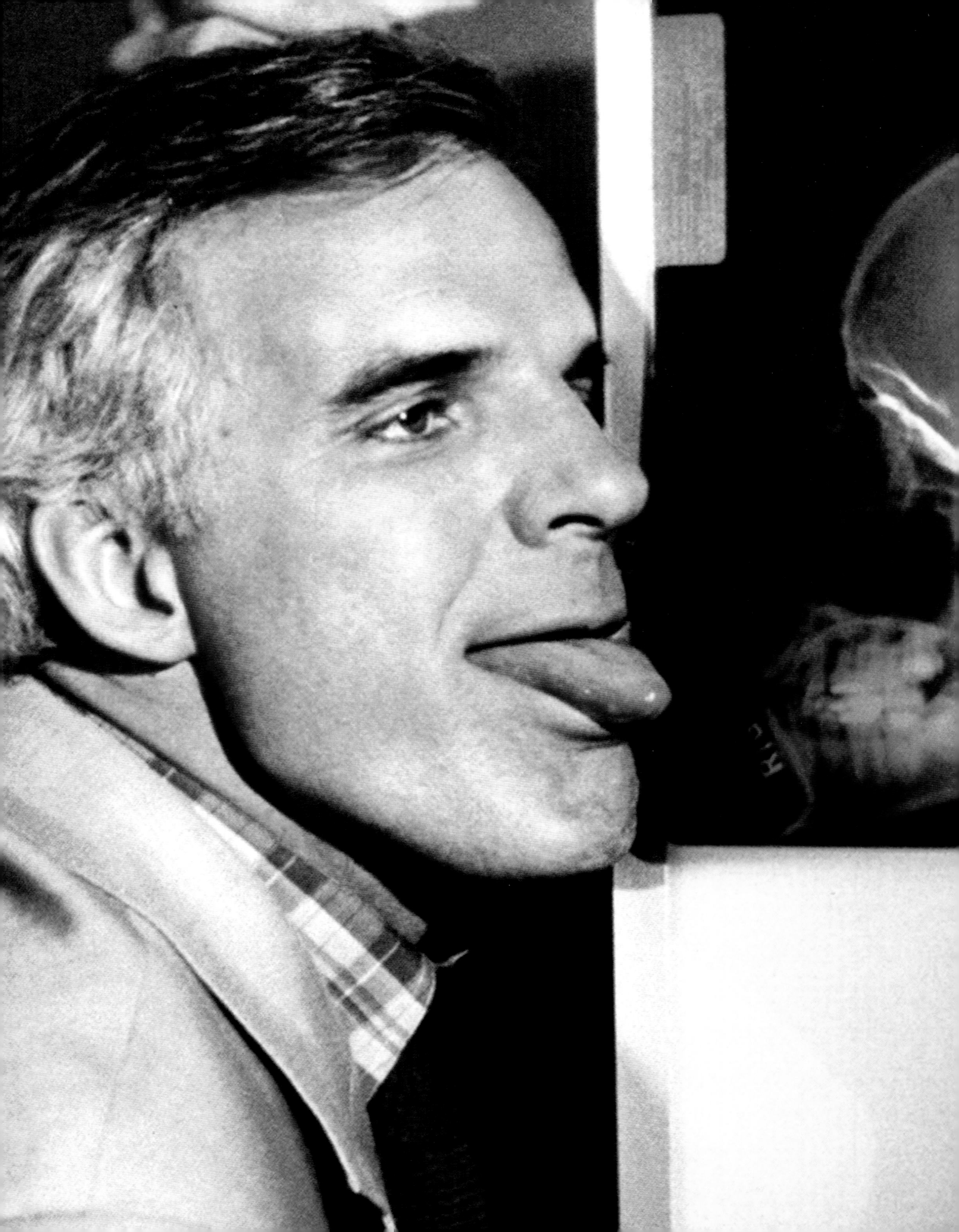

the 80s

Biographical story of Loretta Lynn, a legendary country singer who rose from humble beginnings in Kentucky to super-stardom and forever changed the sound and style of country music.

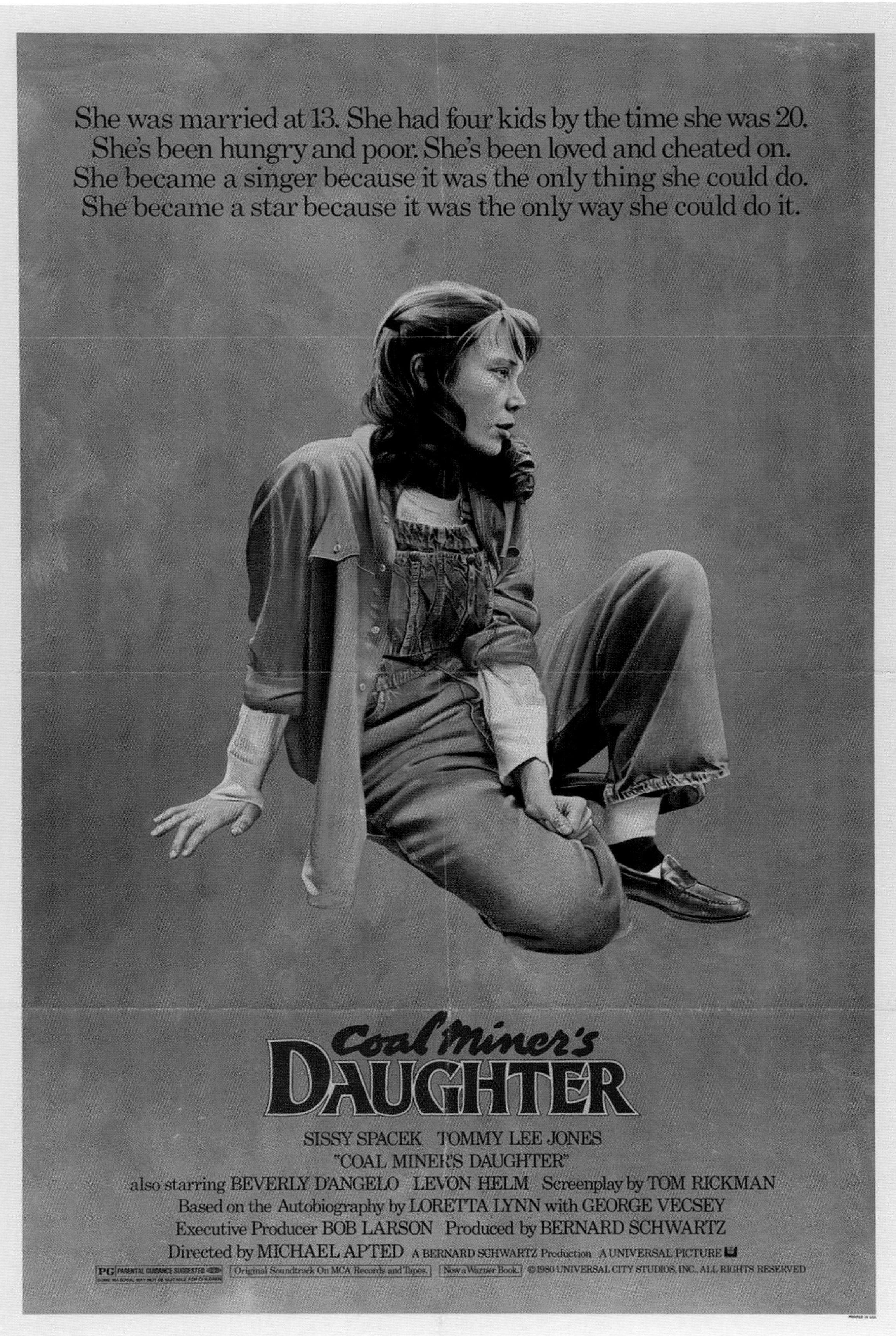

Oliver Gruver of Wichita, wrote: "Arguably the greatest bio-pic ever produced is this one about Loretta Lynn and starring Sissy Spacek. Sissy Spacek is a national treasure and her performance as Loretta Lynn is outstanding and deserves being rewarded with an Oscar."

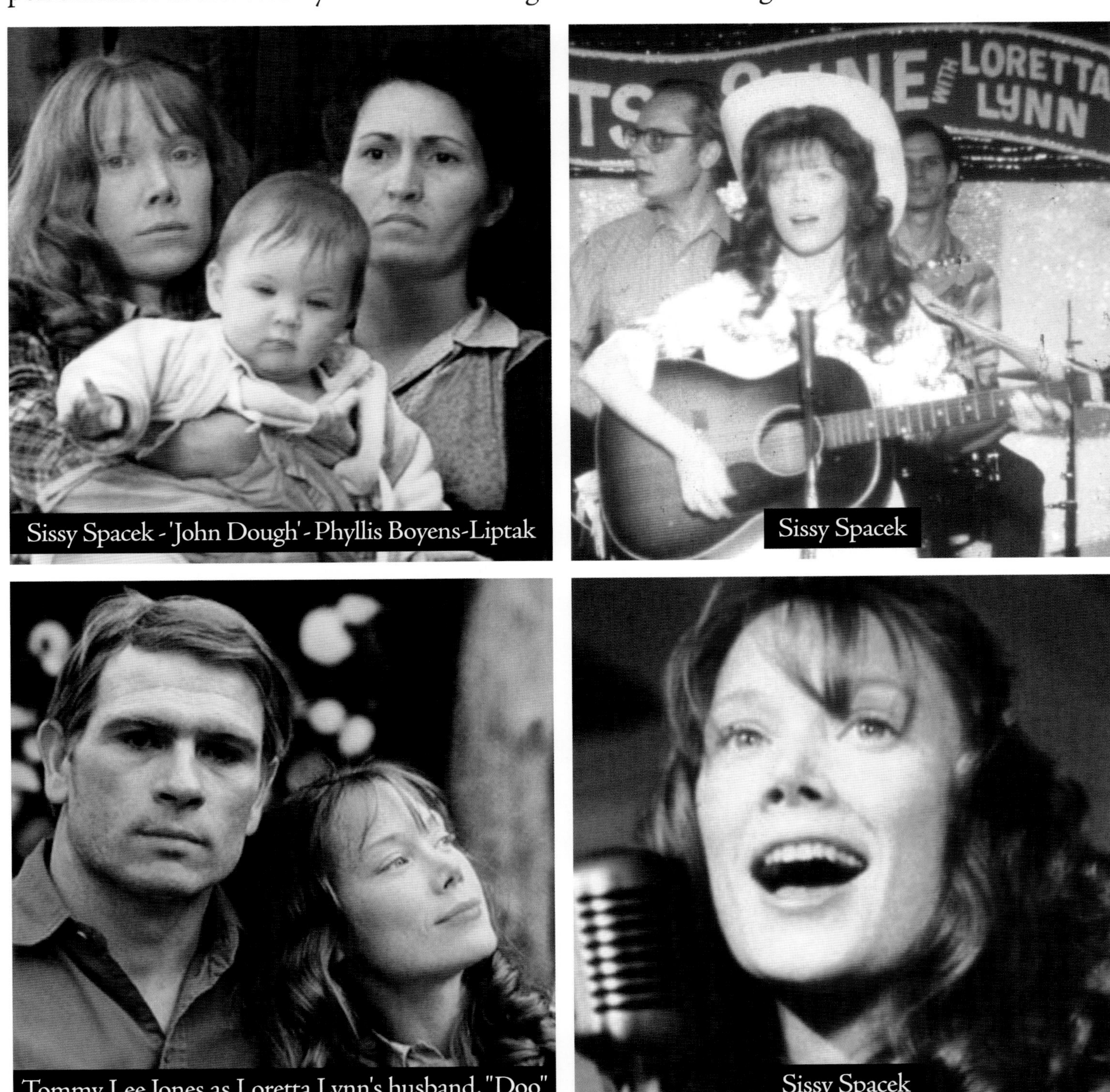

Sissy Spacek - 'John Dough' - Phyllis Boyens-Liptak

Sissy Spacek

Tommy Lee Jones as Loretta Lynn's husband, "Doo"

Sissy Spacek

Soon after Sissy Spacek was awarded The Oscar for her performance as Loretta Lynn, I had the pleasure to work with Sissy when I engaged her to play an unbilled role with Steve Martin in "The Man with Two Brains." Had I given her credit, she probably would have won a second Oscar for her speaking role as a disembodied brain kept alive in a jarful of "Windex."

The accidental death of the older son of an affluent family deeply strains the relationships among the bitter mother, the good-natured father, and the guilt-ridden younger son.

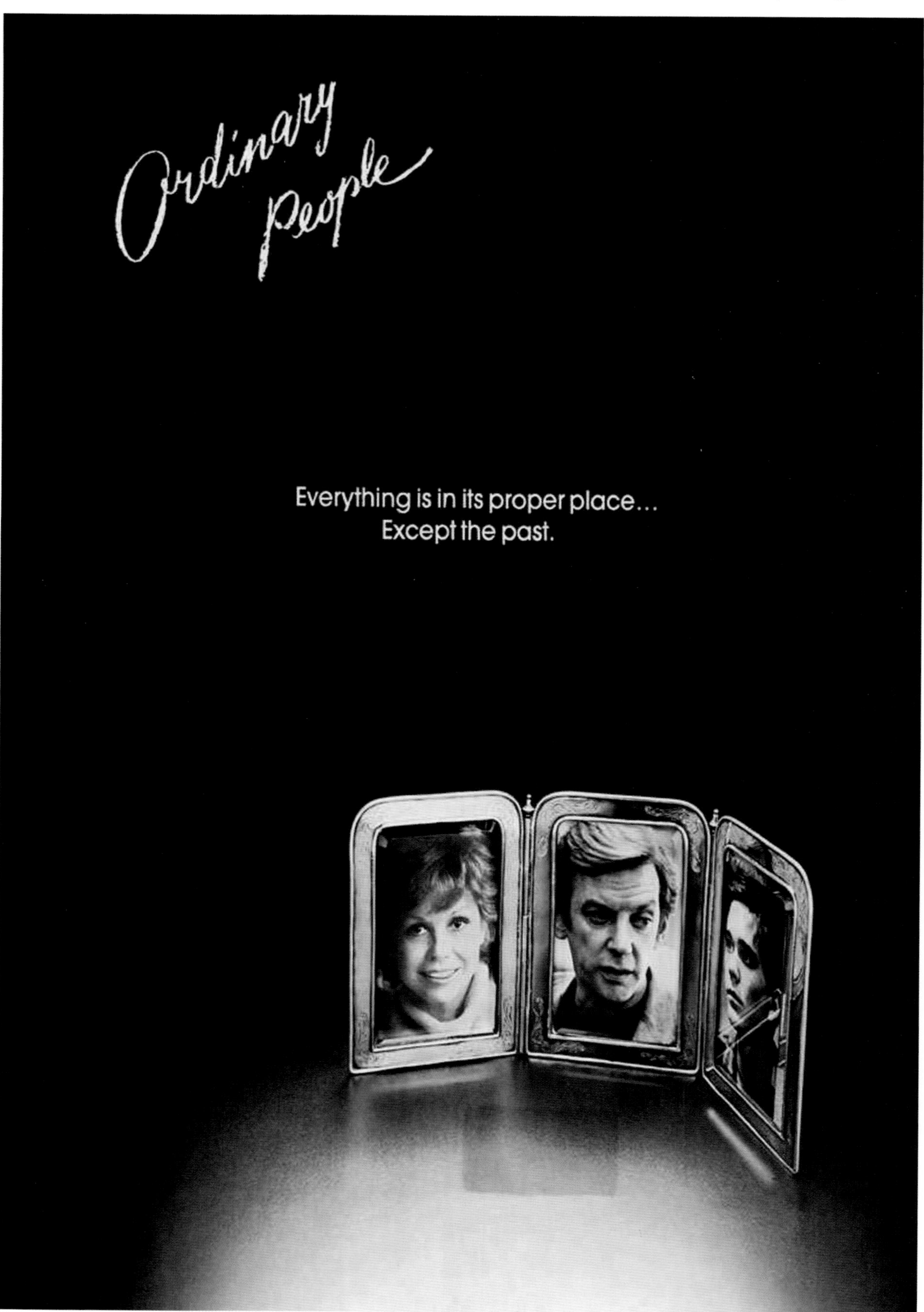

David Sterritt of Christian Science Monitor wrote: "Under Redford's direction, even the smallest scenes practically leap off the screen."

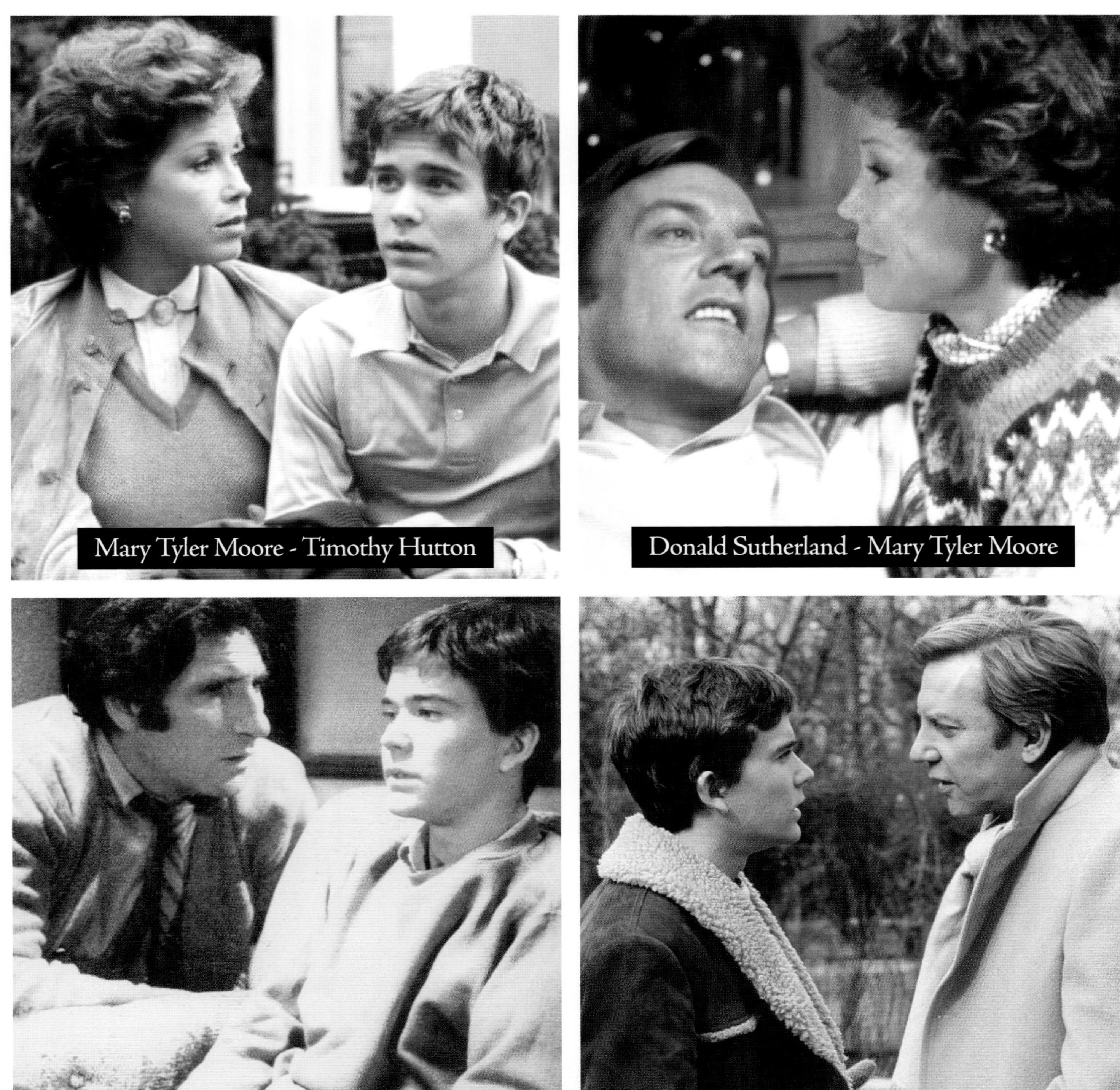

Mary Tyler Moore - Timothy Hutton

Donald Sutherland - Mary Tyler Moore

Judd Hirsch - Timothy Hutton

Donald Sutherland - Timothy Hutton

This award winning film resonated for me because of my involvement with Mary Tyler Moore's career and the personal story of her son's death, which mirrored the film's storyline.

Robert Redford offered Mary a major role in this film after seeing how sad she looked while strolling on a beach in Malibu.

Three female employees of a sexist, egotistical, lying, hypocritical bigot find a way to turn the tables on him.

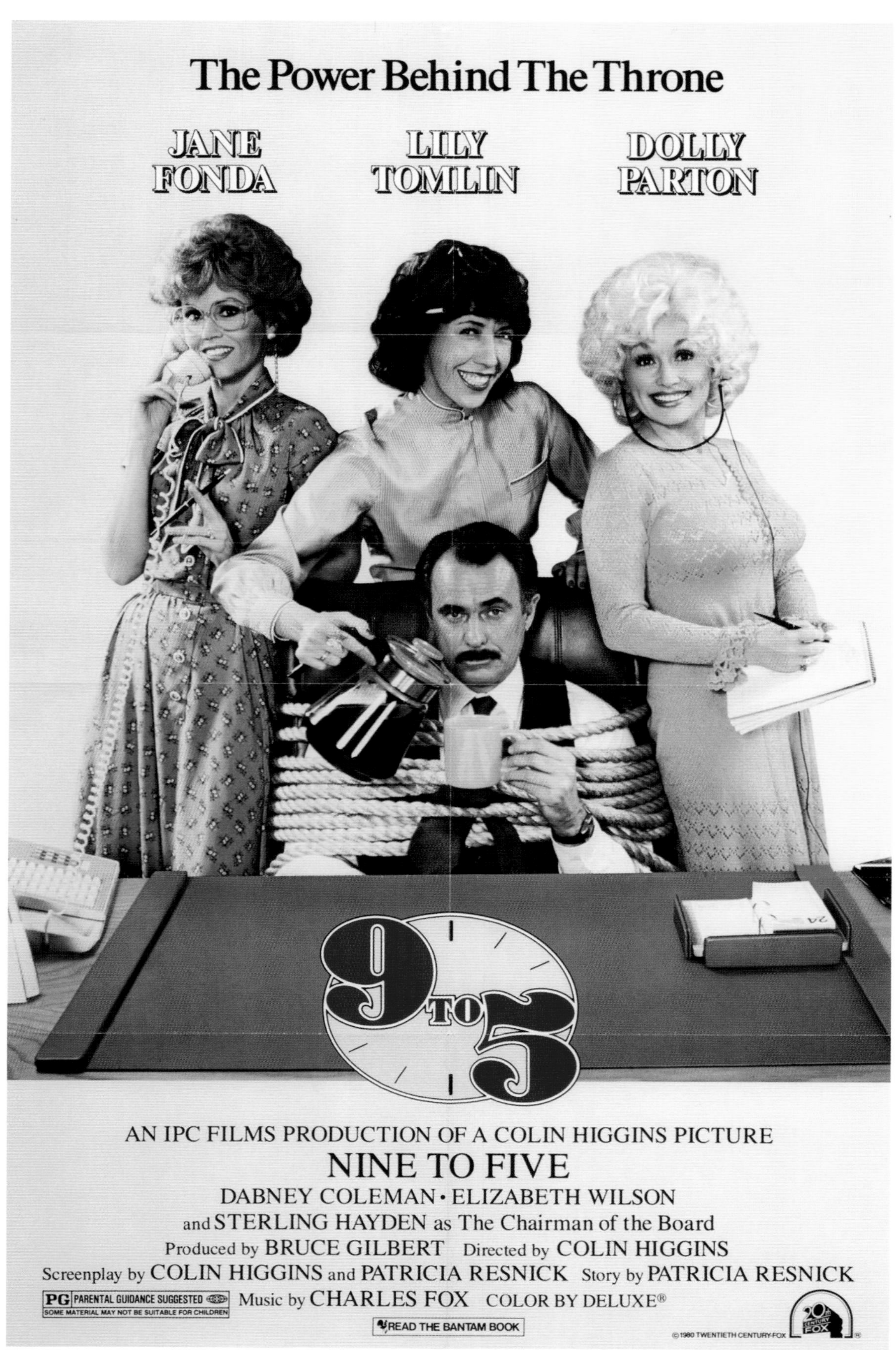

Chuck O'Leary of FulvueDrive-in.com wrote: "A frequently hilarious comic revenge fantasy that struck a chord with people from all walks of life."

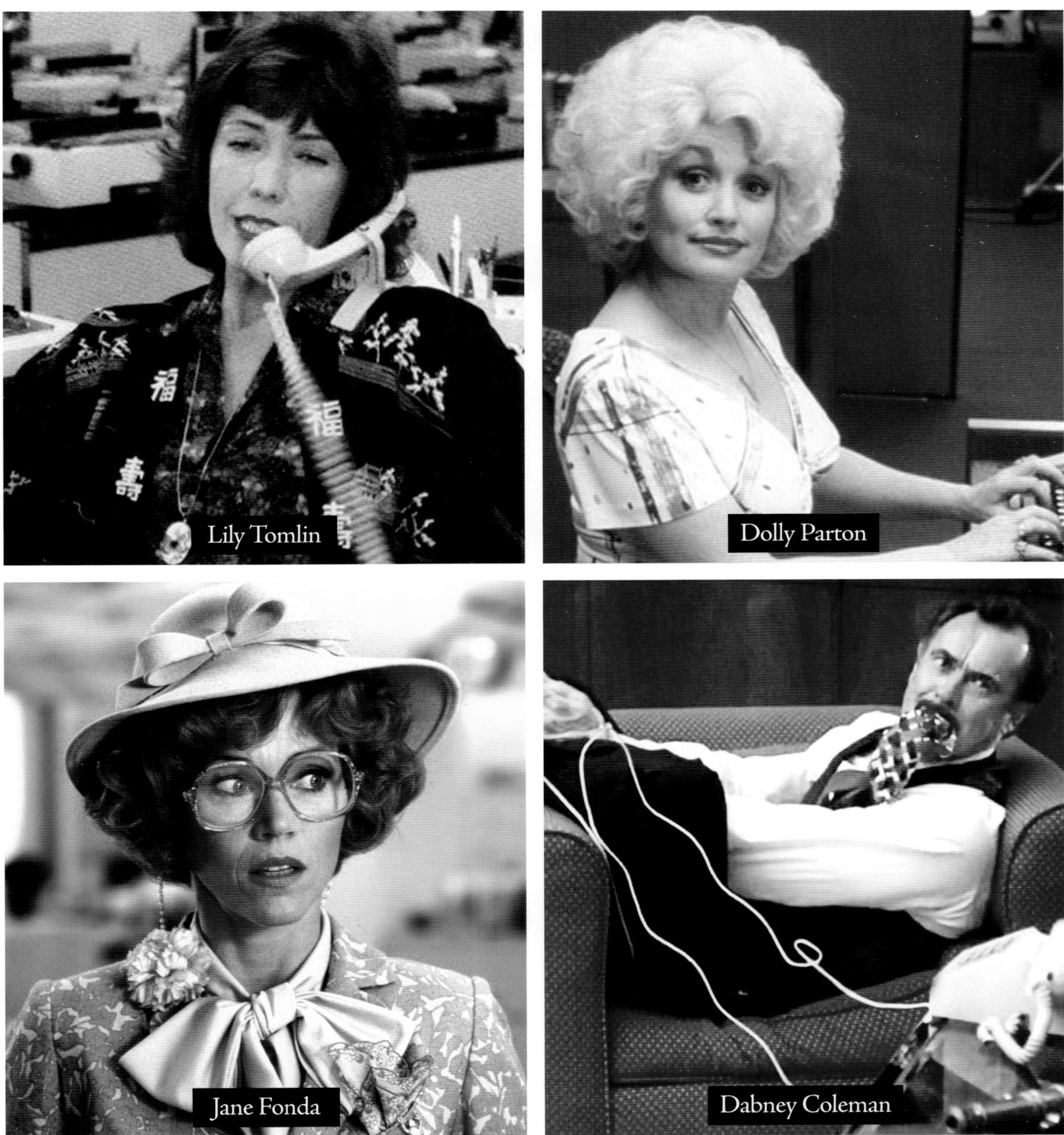

Lily Tomlin

Dolly Parton

Jane Fonda

Dabney Coleman

Like "The Count of Monte Cristo," this is another great comeuppance film. I so enjoyed watching these three talented and beautiful women deftly bring justice to a dastardly deserving villain. If you haven't seen it, see it.

A surgeon rescues a heavily disfigured man who is mistreated while scraping a living as a side-show freak. Behind his monstrous facade, there is revealed a person of intelligence and sensitivity.

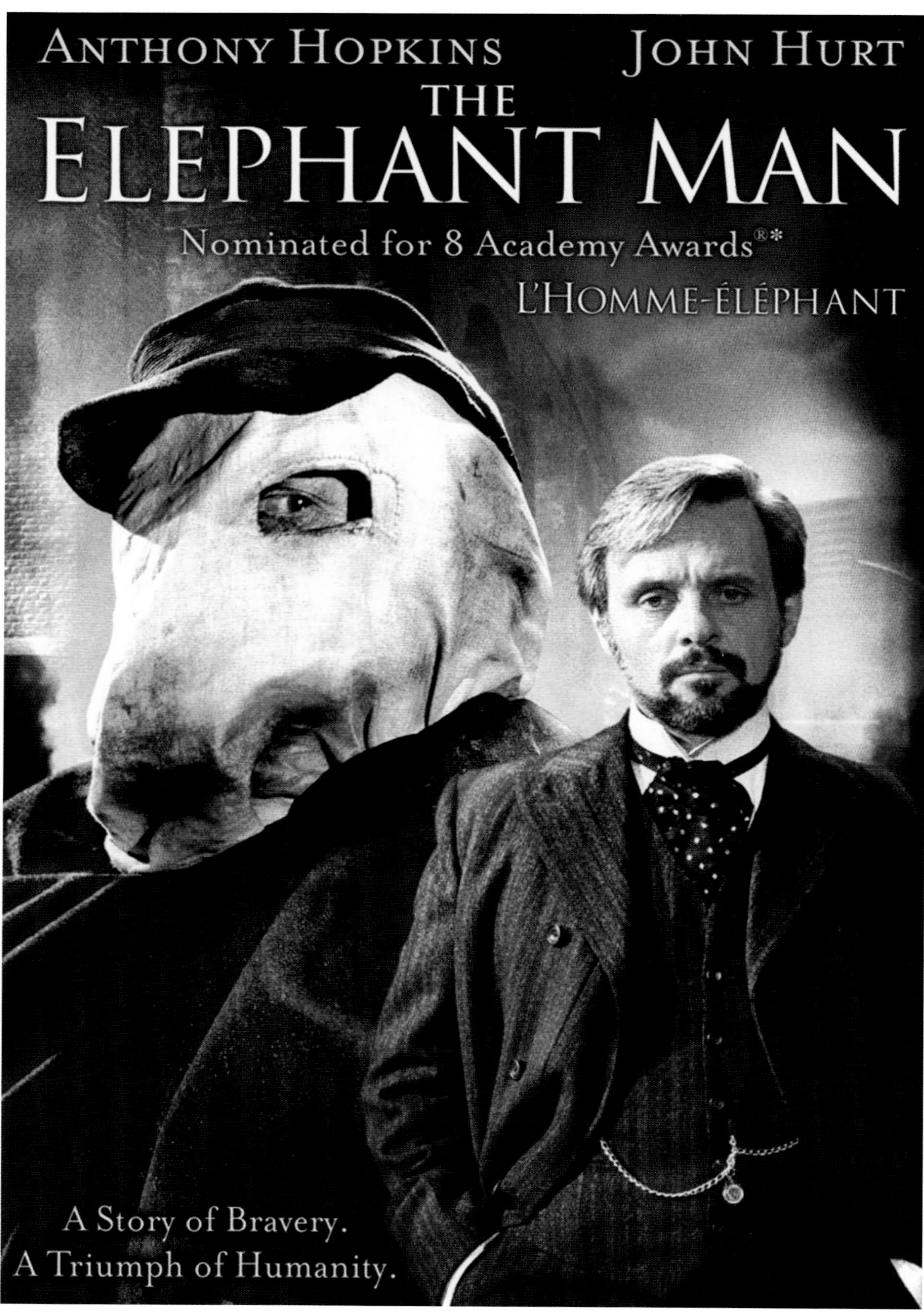

Richard Brody of The New Yorker wrote: "The powerful depiction of Merrick, played by John Hurt, moves a viewer from revulsion and fear to empathy and tenderness. That's the very movement of the story itself."

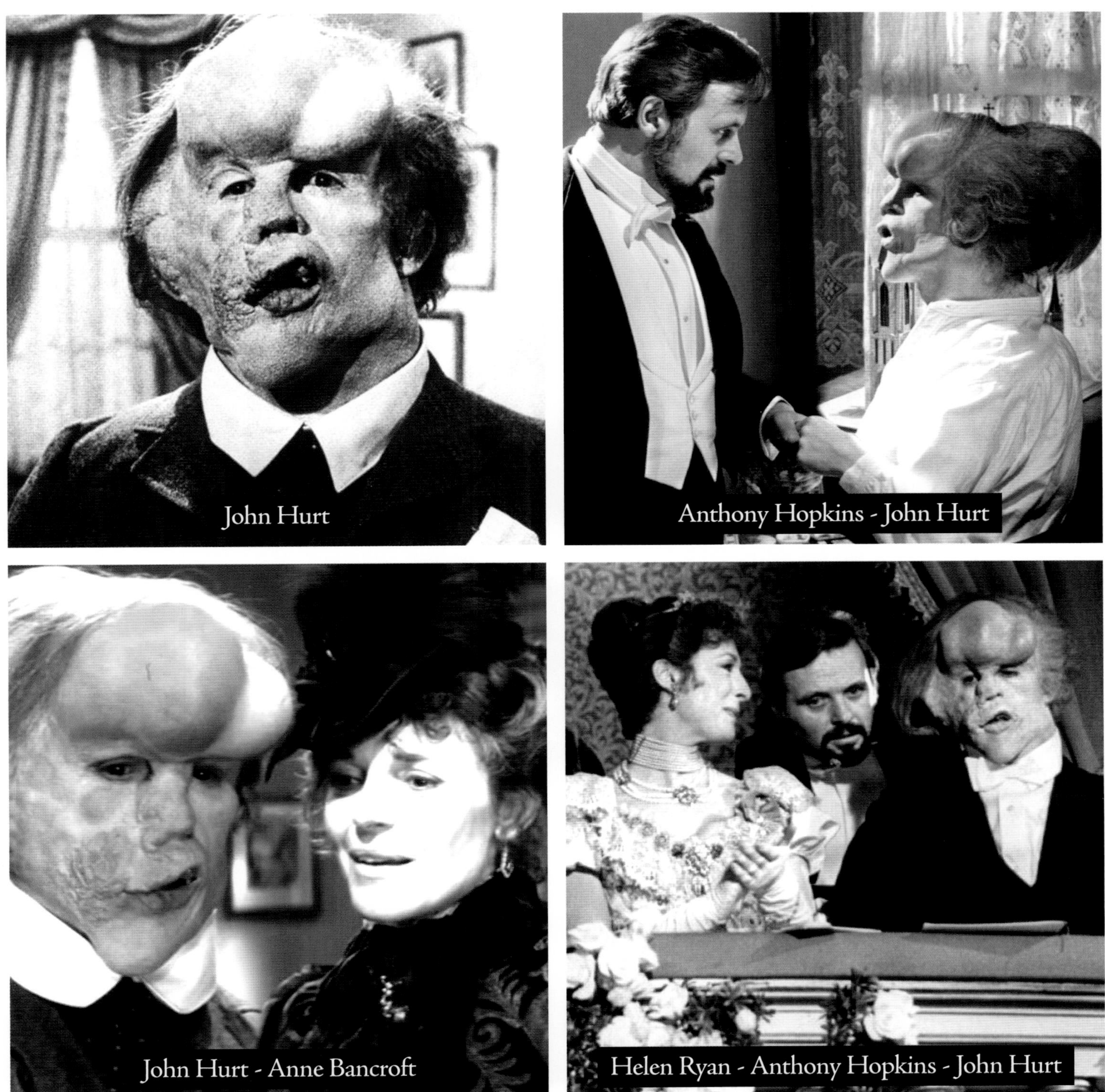

John Hurt

Anthony Hopkins - John Hurt

John Hurt - Anne Bancroft

Helen Ryan - Anthony Hopkins - John Hurt

Mel Brooks, who had given us some of the funniest films of all-time, produced this moving, uplifting film. He was fortunate to secure the services of his wife, Anne Bancroft, to play Mrs. Kendal, the woman who introduces Merrick to the works of Shakespeare.

To see more of Mel Brooks' successful efforts you have but to turn the page.

Mel Brooks brings his one-of-a-kind comic touch to the history of mankind covering events from the Old Testament to the French Revolution in a series of episodic comedy vignettes.

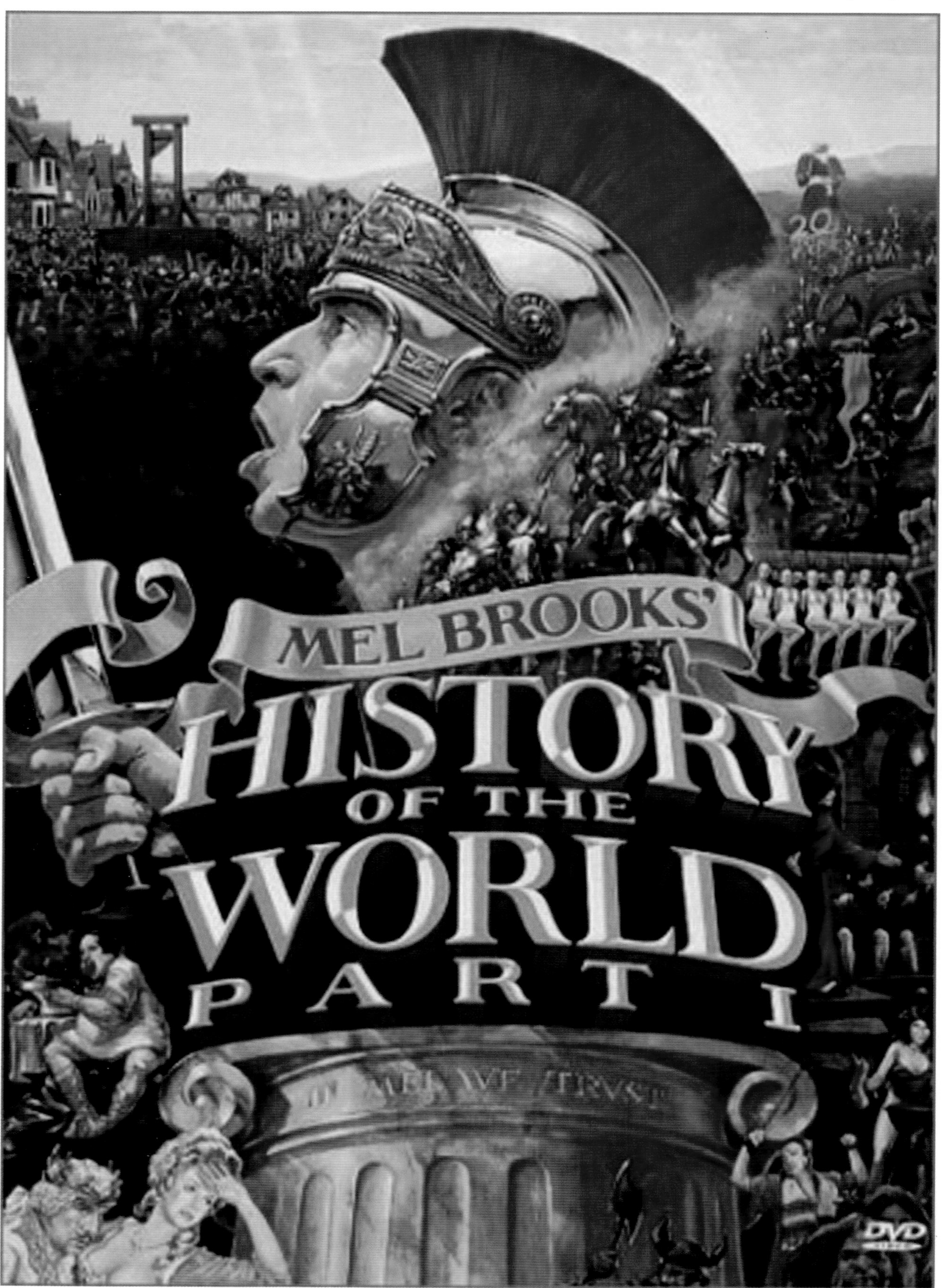

Critic Widgett Walls wrote: "The fact that there has been no 'History of the World Part II' is ample proof that God hates us all."

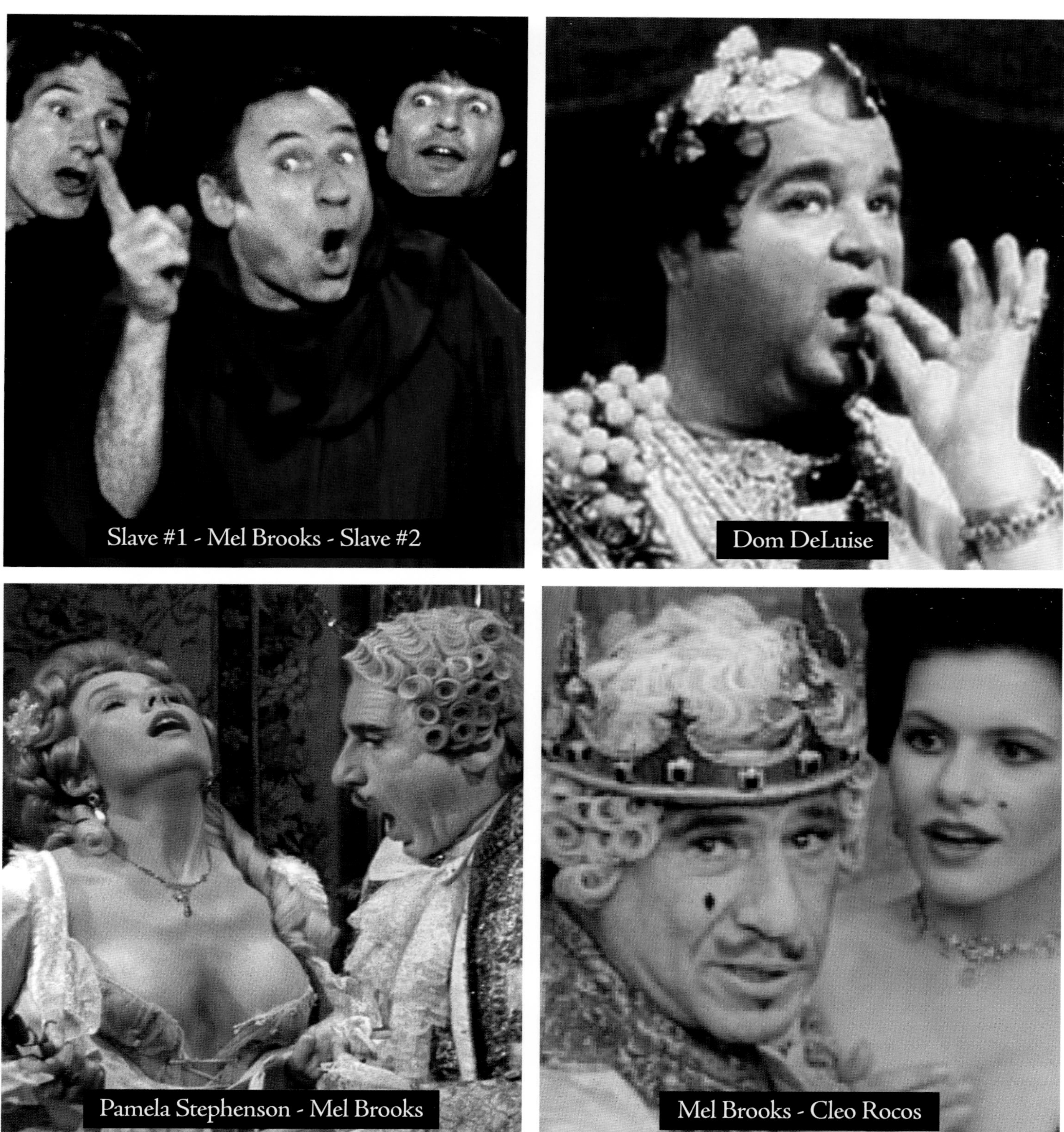

Slave #1 - Mel Brooks - Slave #2

Dom DeLuise

Pamela Stephenson - Mel Brooks

Mel Brooks - Cleo Rocos

Mel Brooks invited Dom DeLuise and one hundred and eight other comic actors to appear in this film and all accepted, including Orson Welles. Mel Brooks cast himself as The King, giving him the opportunity to deliver the film's iconic line, "IT'S GOOD TO BE THE KING!"

A radical American journalist becomes involved with the Communist revolution in Russia and hopes to bring its spirit and idealism to the United States.

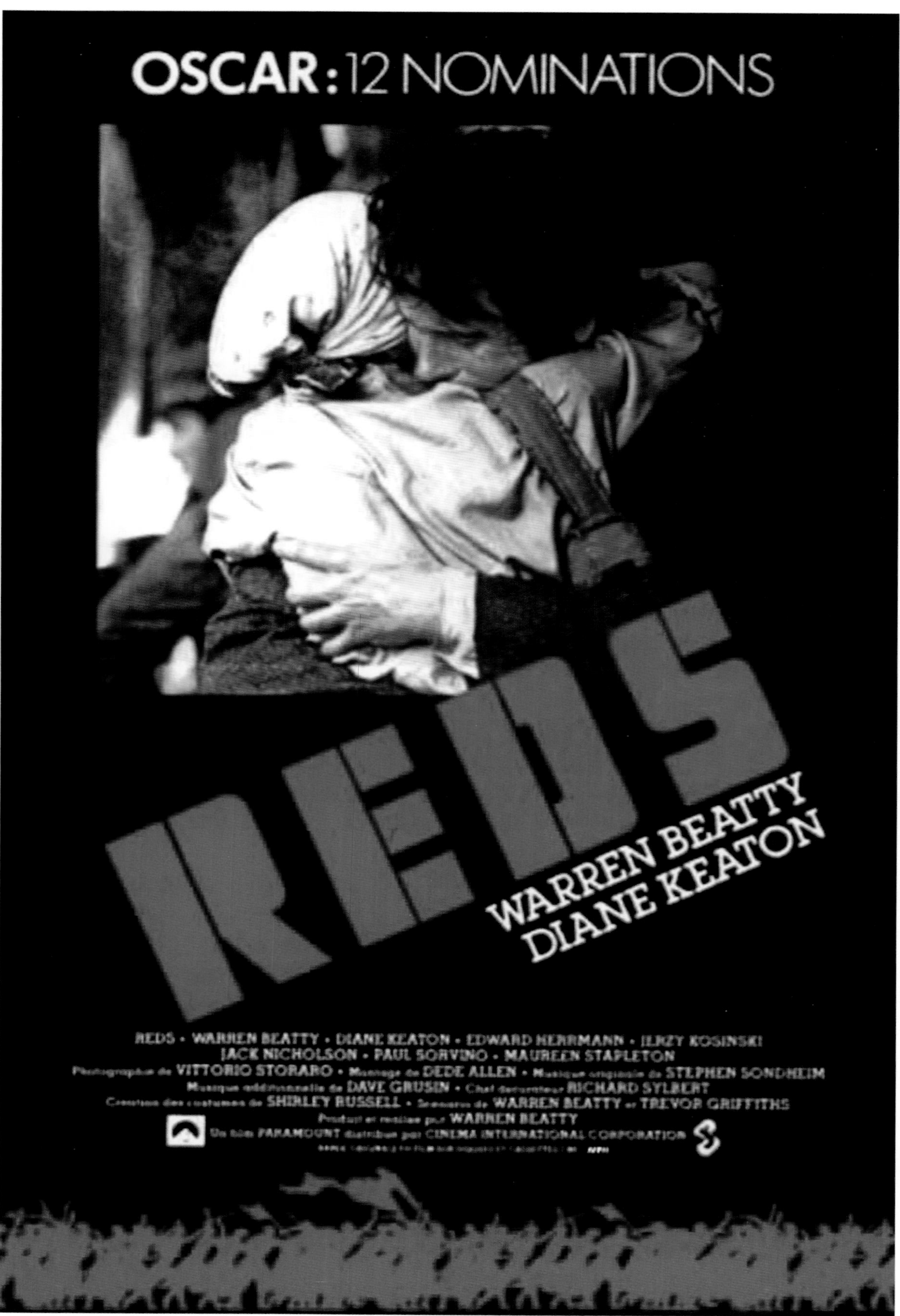

Wesley Lovell of Cinema Sight wrote: "Warren Beatty's political epic features superlative performances and speaks to the inner-rebel in each of us."

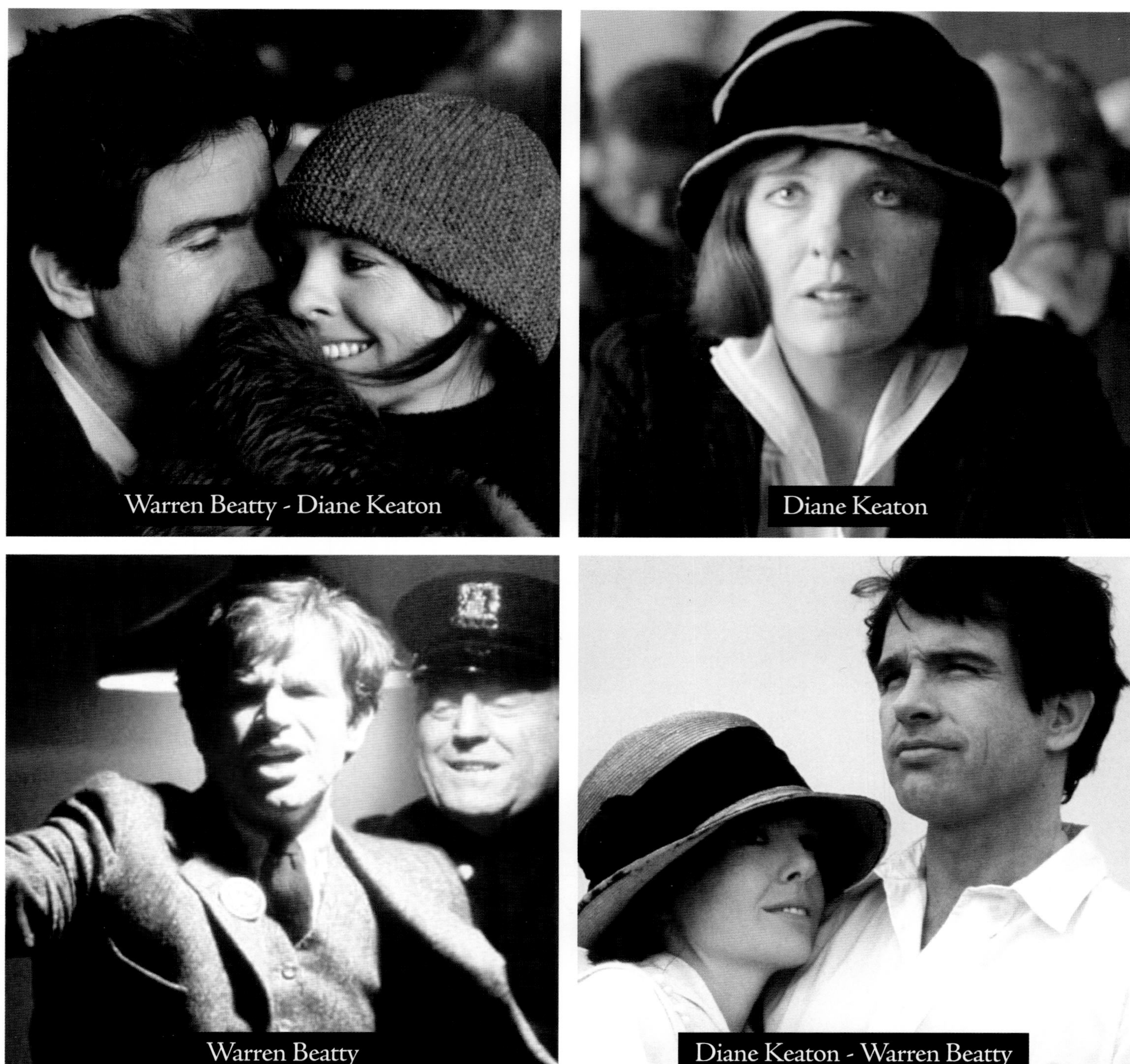

Warren Beatty - Diane Keaton

Diane Keaton

Warren Beatty

Diane Keaton - Warren Beatty

"Reds" is not about Communism, but about a particular era, and a particularly moving kind of American optimism that had its roots in the 19th century.

Warren Beatty wrote, directed and starred as John Reed in "Reds," a film that was a forward thinking, optimistic venture. Had the world taken to heart what John Reed was proposing, we'd be living on a planet where all the nations' leaders were sensible and peace-loving and its inhabitants, happy and carefree.

Norman is a curmudgeon with an estranged relationship with his daughter Chelsea. At Golden Pond, he and his wife nevertheless agree to care for Billy, the son of Chelsea's new boyfriend, and a most unexpected relationship blooms.

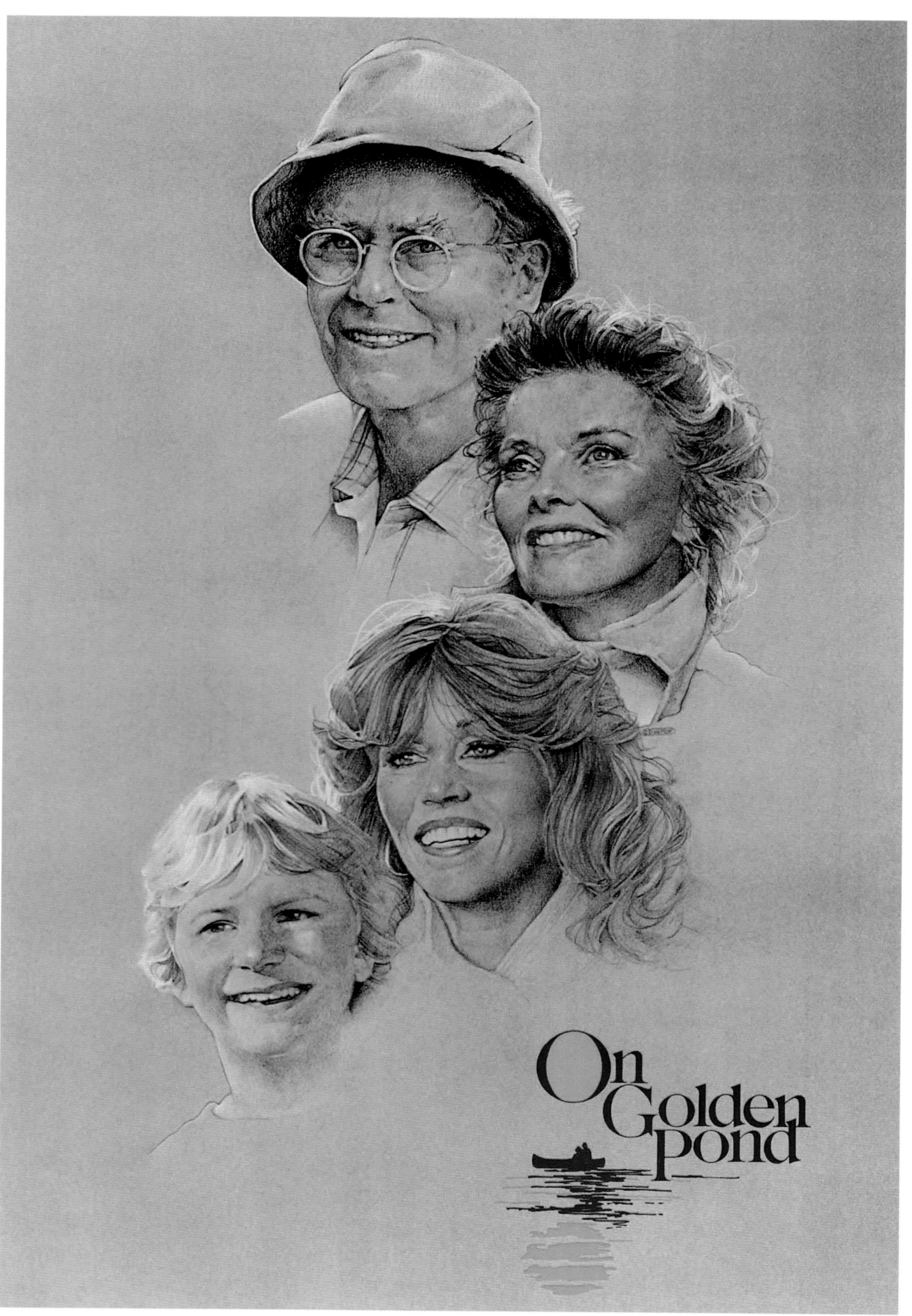

Roger Ebert wrote: "'On Golden Pond' is a treasure for many reasons. We could believe in its major characters and their relationships, and what they felt for one another. There were moments when the movie was witness to human growth and change."

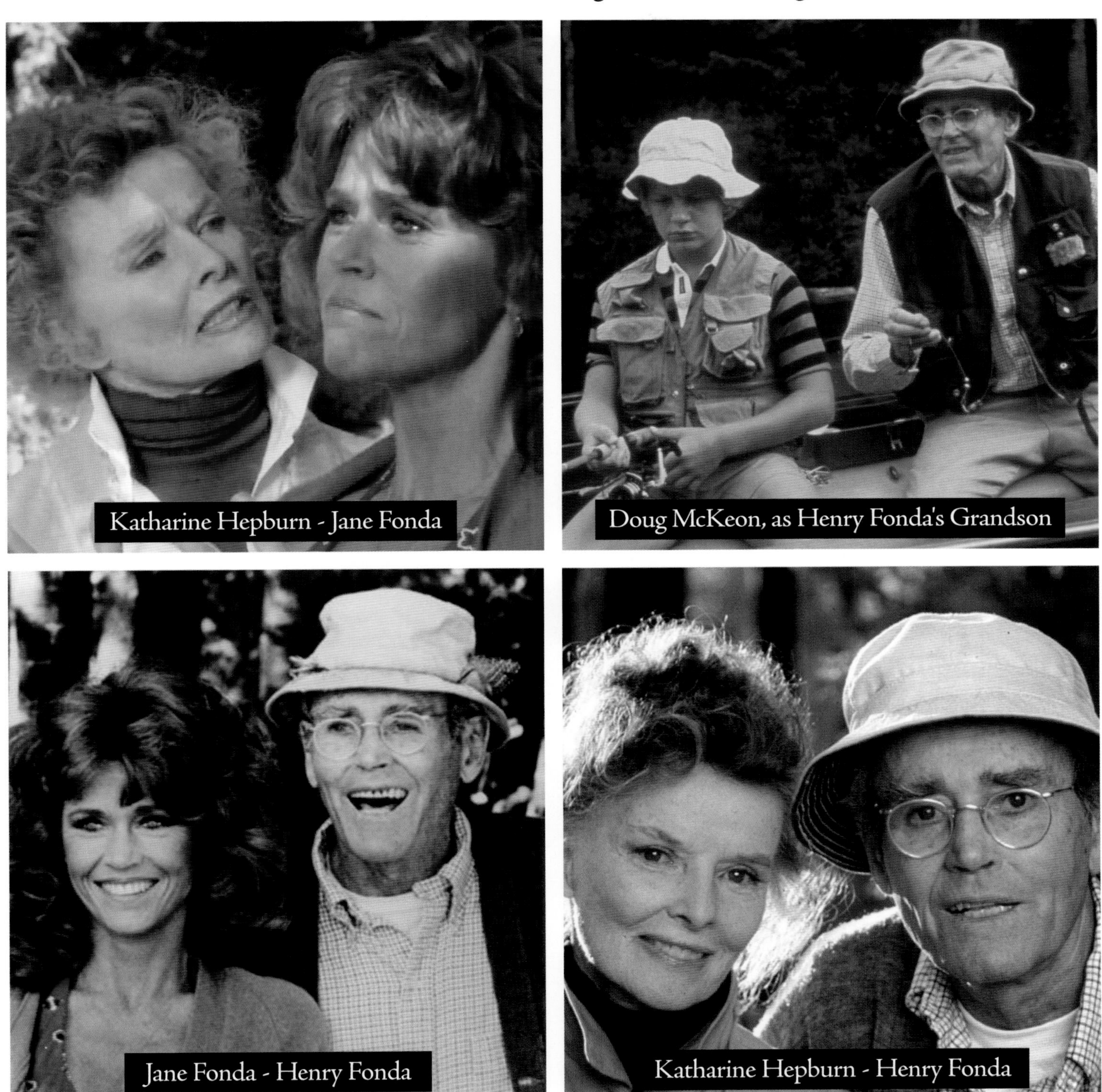

Katharine Hepburn - Jane Fonda

Doug McKeon, as Henry Fonda's Grandson

Jane Fonda - Henry Fonda

Katharine Hepburn - Henry Fonda

This was a family film in which Henry Fonda and Katharine Hepburn perform as husband and wife and Jane Fonda, their daughter. Before they did this film Henry Fonda and Jane had been estranged, and the film, which treated the subject of alienated parents and children, was instrumental in the two establishing a loving relationship.

Film noir parody with a detective uncovering a sinister plot. Characters from real noirs appear as scenes from various films are inter-cut.

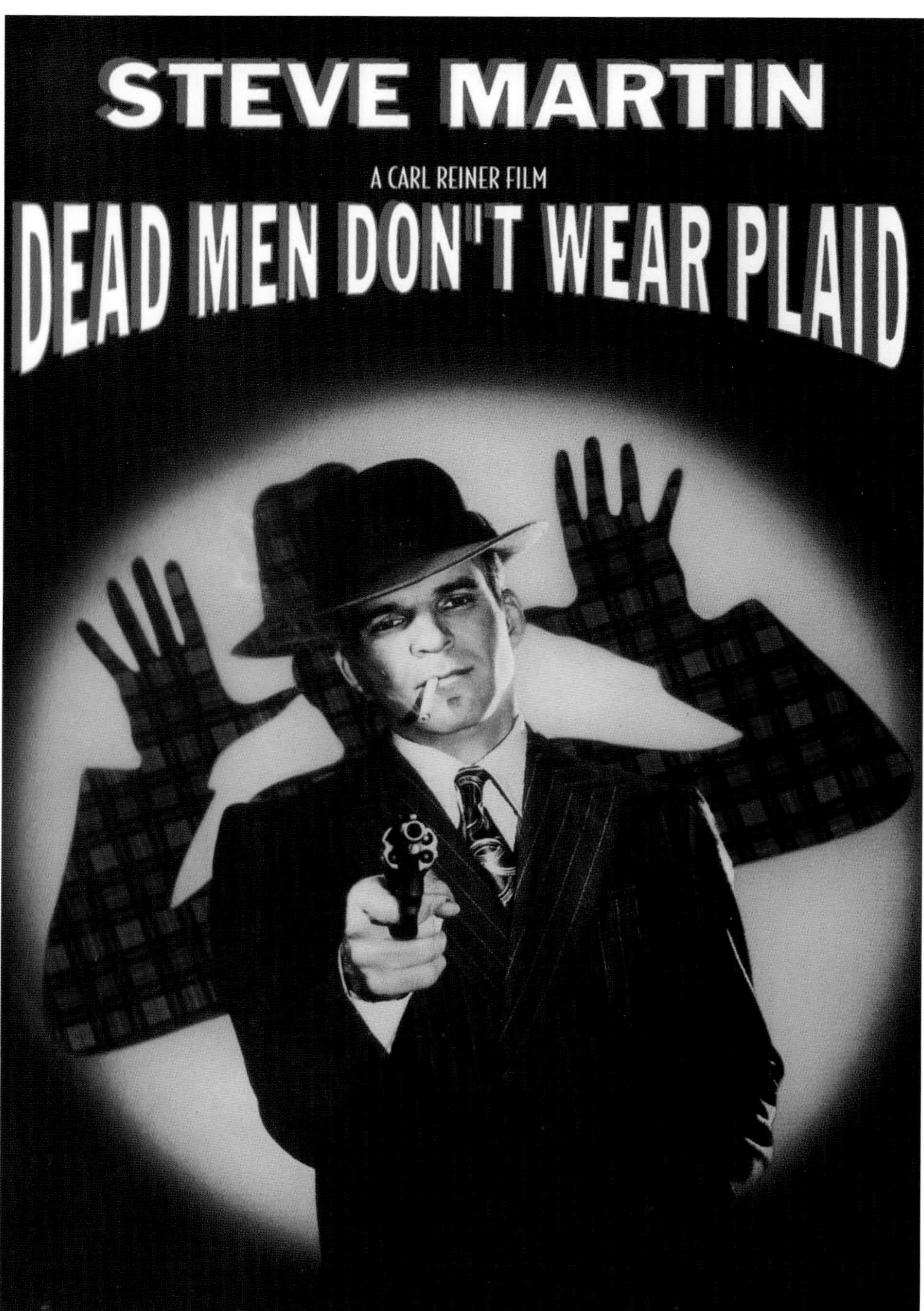

Frederic and Mary Ann Brussat of Spirituality and Practice wrote: "'Dead Men Don't Wear Plaid' is a thoroughly entertaining spoof of Hollywood private eye movies."

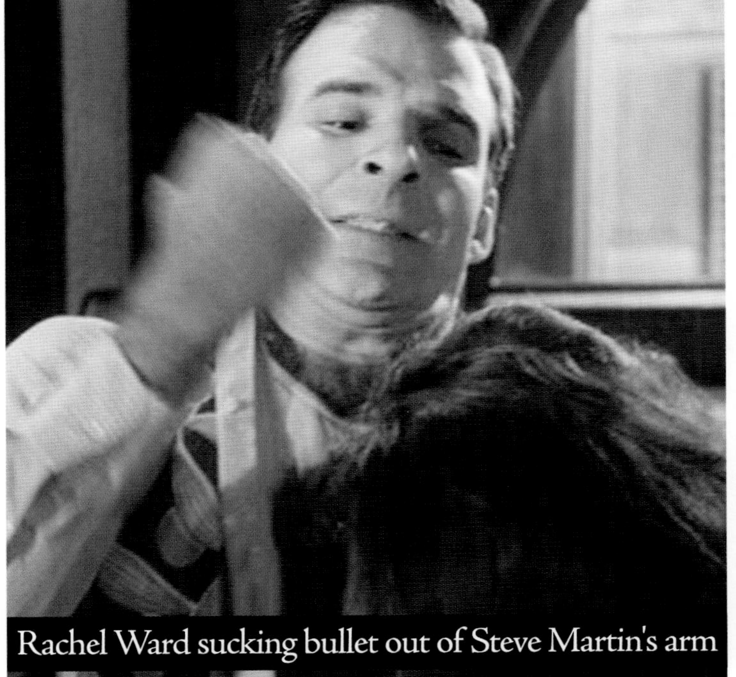

Rachel Ward sucking bullet out of Steve Martin's arm

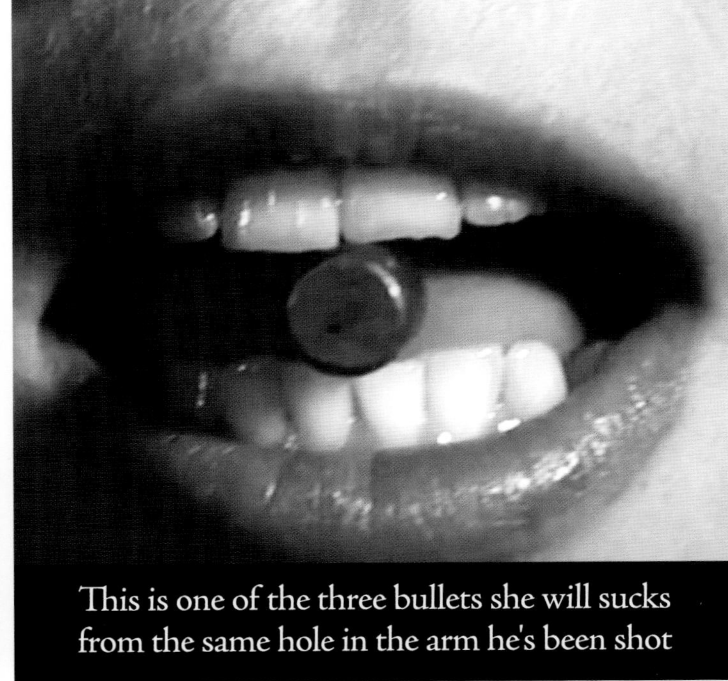

This is one of the three bullets she will sucks from the same hole in the arm he's been shot

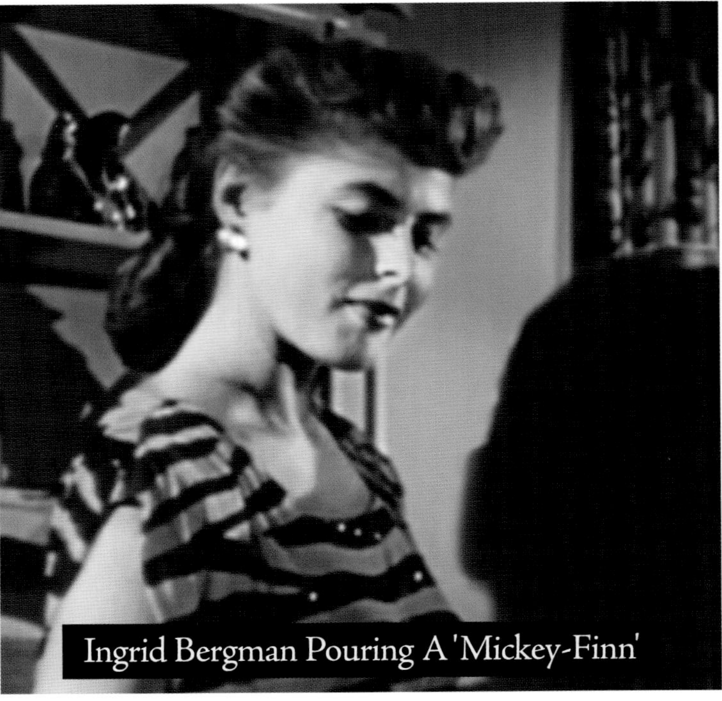

Ingrid Bergman Pouring A 'Mickey-Finn'

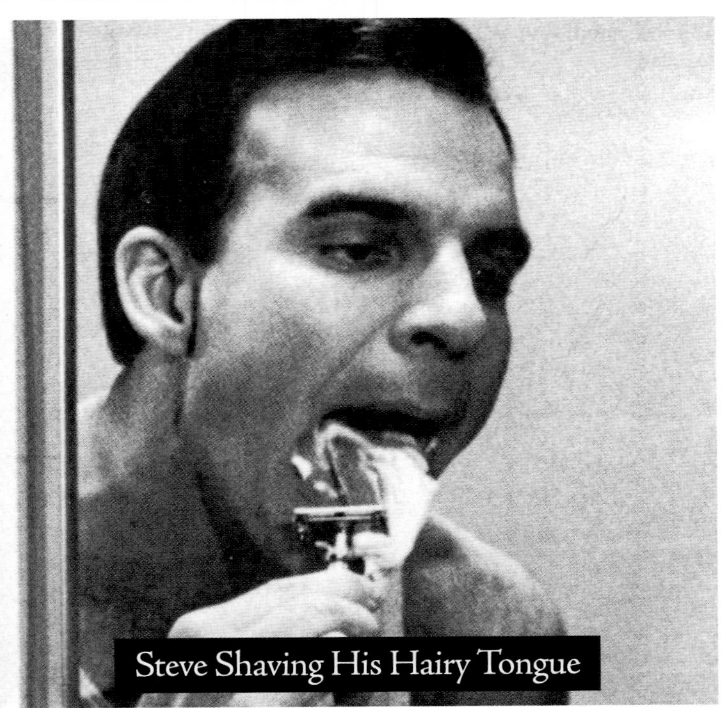

Steve Shaving His Hairy Tongue

By using clips from black and white detective films, we knitted together one in which Steve Martin, as a detective, interacts with great actors from the past. Above, Ingrid Bergman offers Steve a stiff drink to ease the pain in his wounded arm. The drink addles his mind and makes his tongue feel hairy, which he hastens to shave.

Following are photos of a number of the all-star cast with which Steve (Rigby Reardon) interacts during this bogus Film Noir classic.

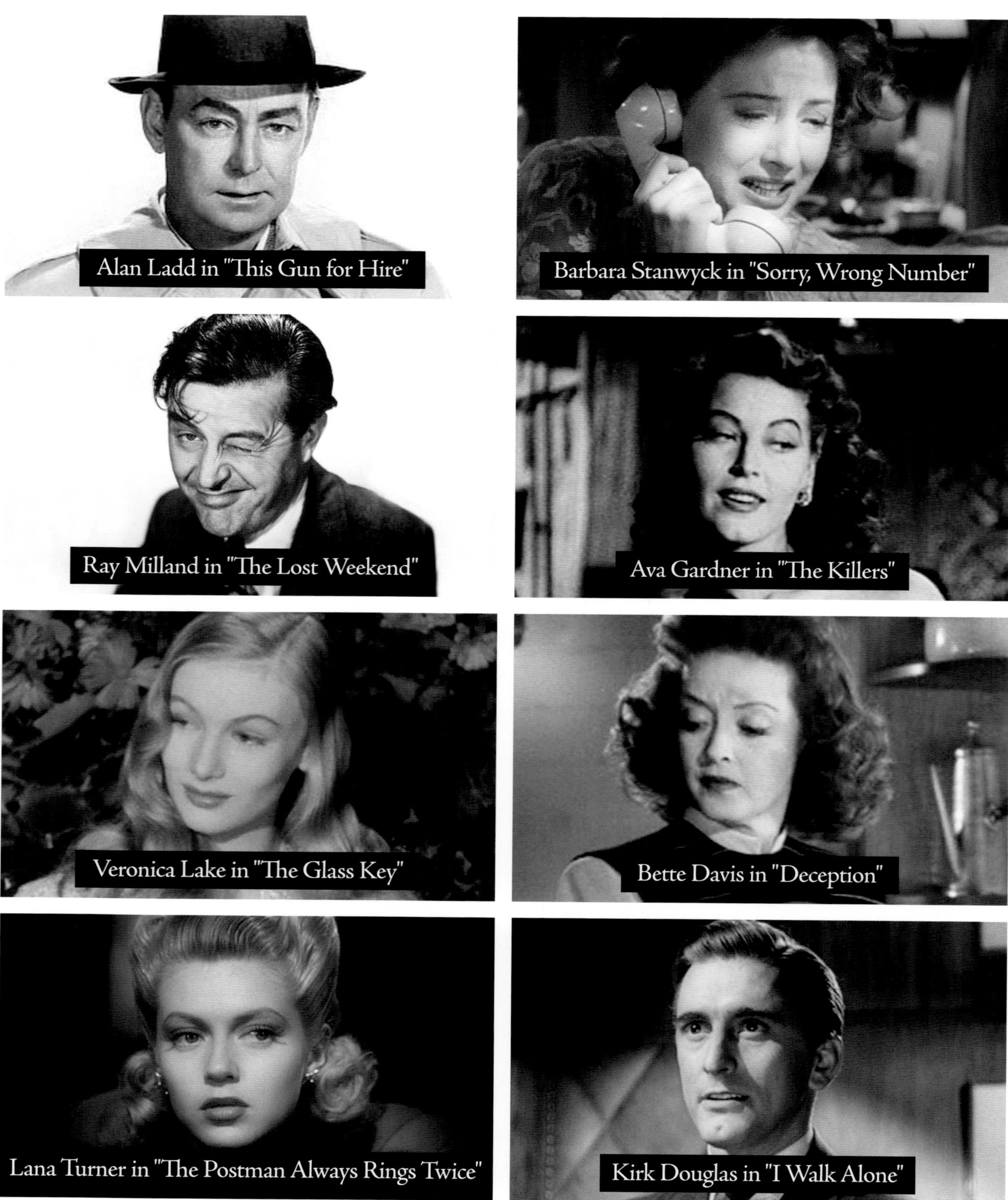

Alan Ladd in "This Gun for Hire"

Barbara Stanwyck in "Sorry, Wrong Number"

Ray Milland in "The Lost Weekend"

Ava Gardner in "The Killers"

Veronica Lake in "The Glass Key"

Bette Davis in "Deception"

Lana Turner in "The Postman Always Rings Twice"

Kirk Douglas in "I Walk Alone"

These are some of the great stars who never knew they would, and would never have agreed to play bit parts in Steve Martin's exciting comedy opus.

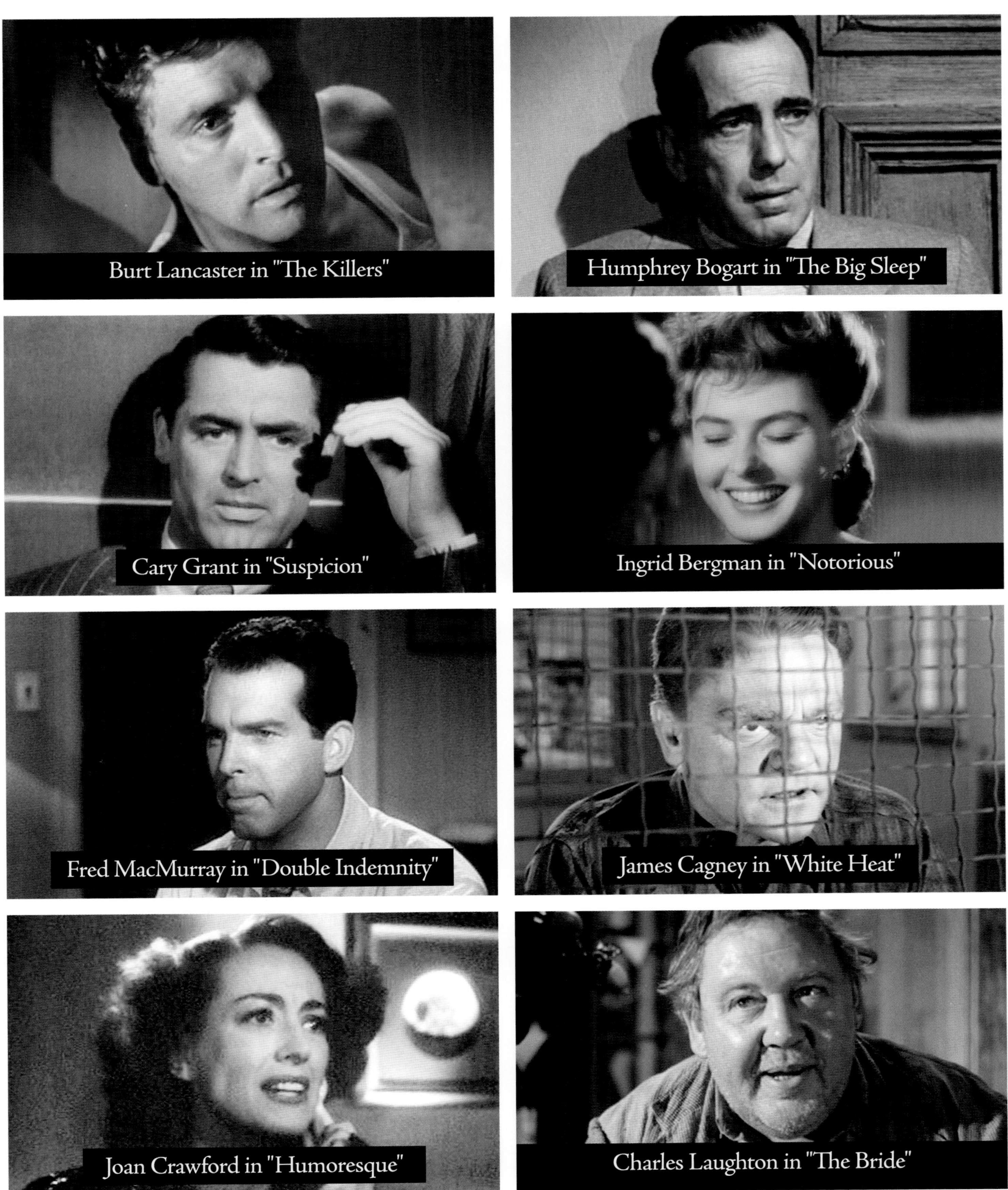

Burt Lancaster in "The Killers"

Humphrey Bogart in "The Big Sleep"

Cary Grant in "Suspicion"

Ingrid Bergman in "Notorious"

Fred MacMurray in "Double Indemnity"

James Cagney in "White Heat"

Joan Crawford in "Humoresque"

Charles Laughton in "The Bride"

Those of you who can complete The New York Times Sunday crossword puzzle may understand the thrill I derived from putting this people puzzle together.

A young aspiring writer befriends a Jewish scientist and his lover Sophie, a Polish, Catholic survivor of the German Nazi concentration camps.

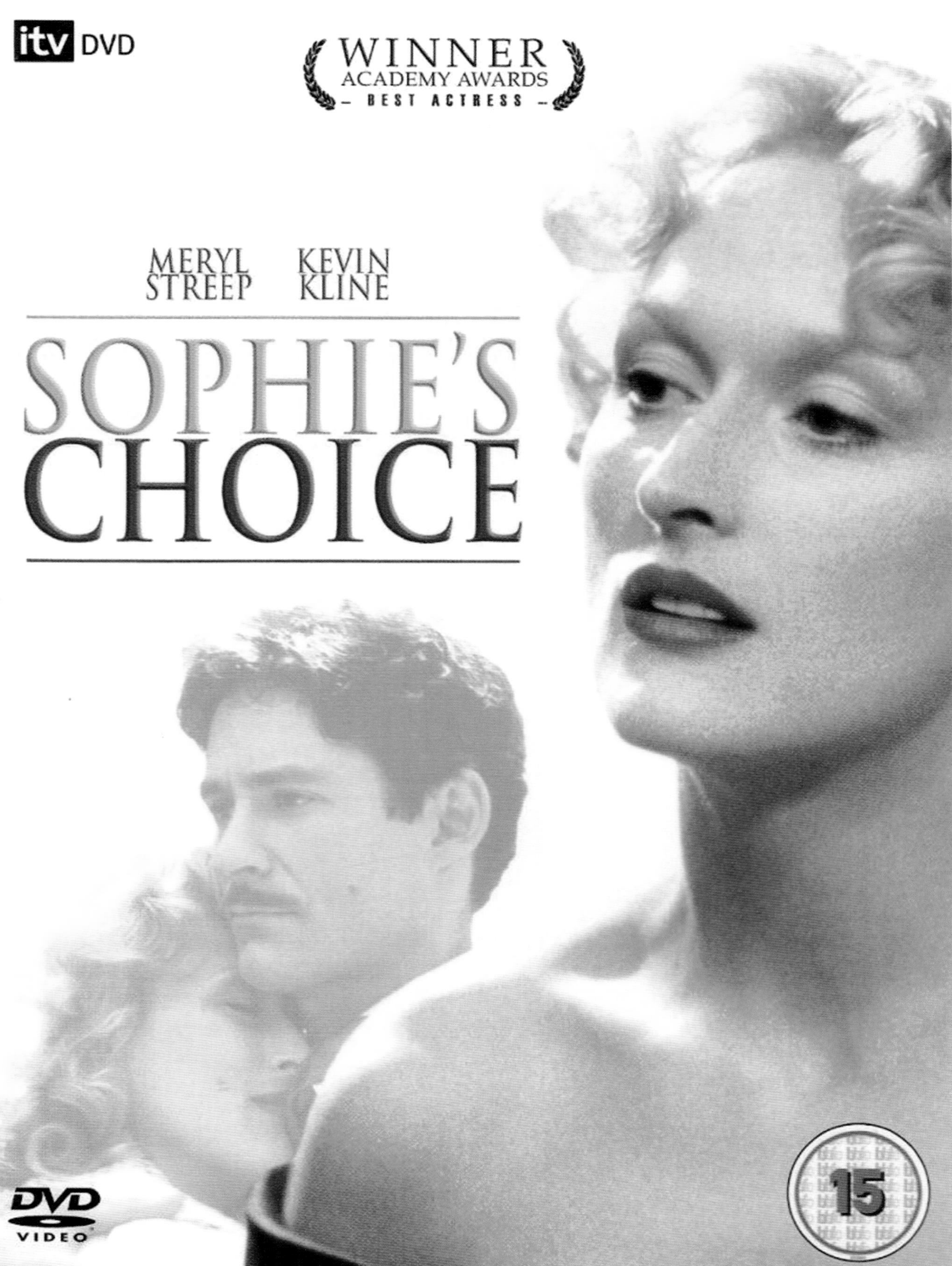

Roger Ebert of Chicago Sun-Times wrote: "So perfectly cast and well-imagined that it just takes over and happens to you. It's quite an experience."

The plot centers on a tragic decision that Sophie was forced to make with her children on her entry into Auschwitz. Her painful decision ends with her son being taken to a labor camp and her daughter, to a gas chamber.

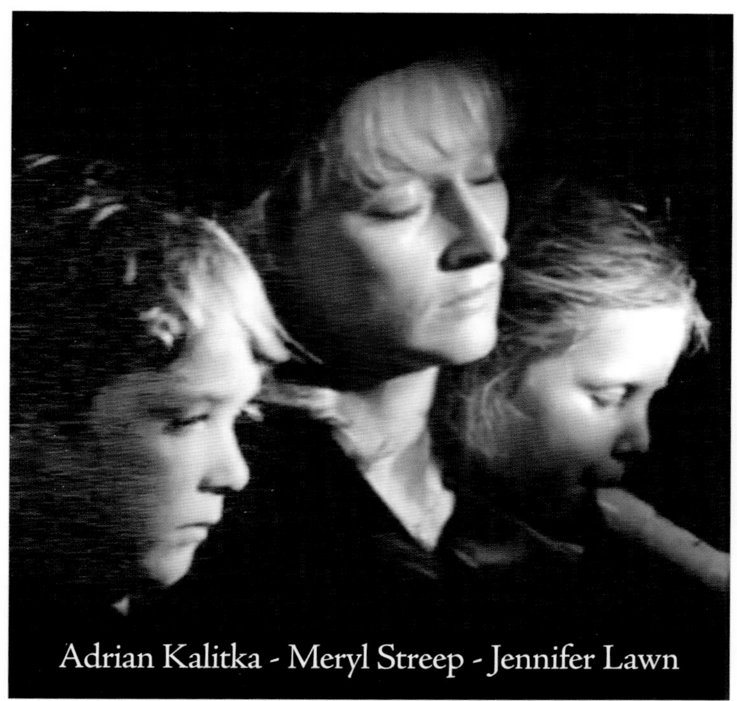
Adrian Kalitka - Meryl Streep - Jennifer Lawn

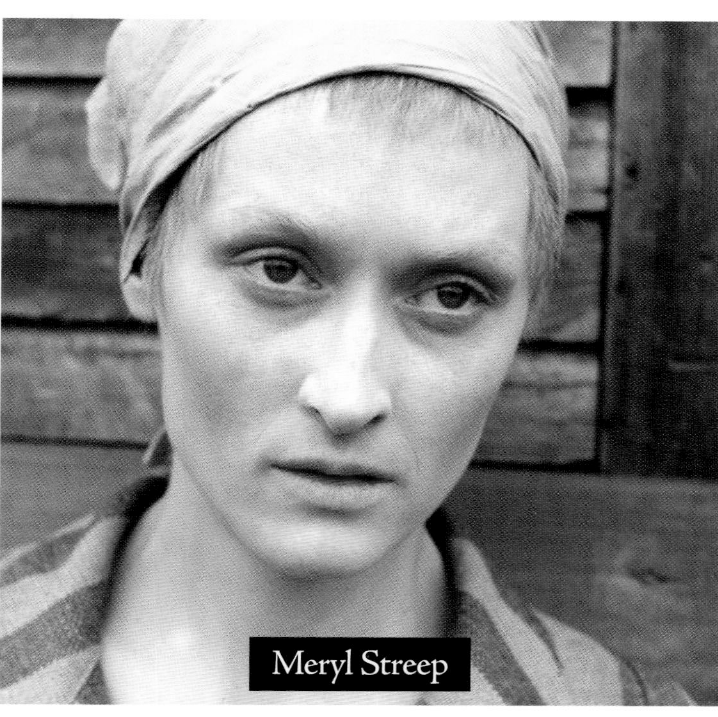
Meryl Streep

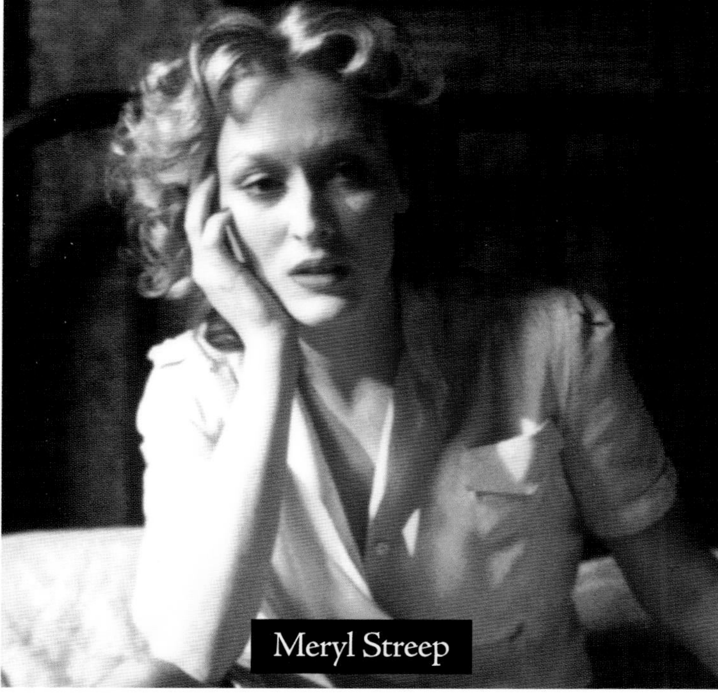
Meryl Streep

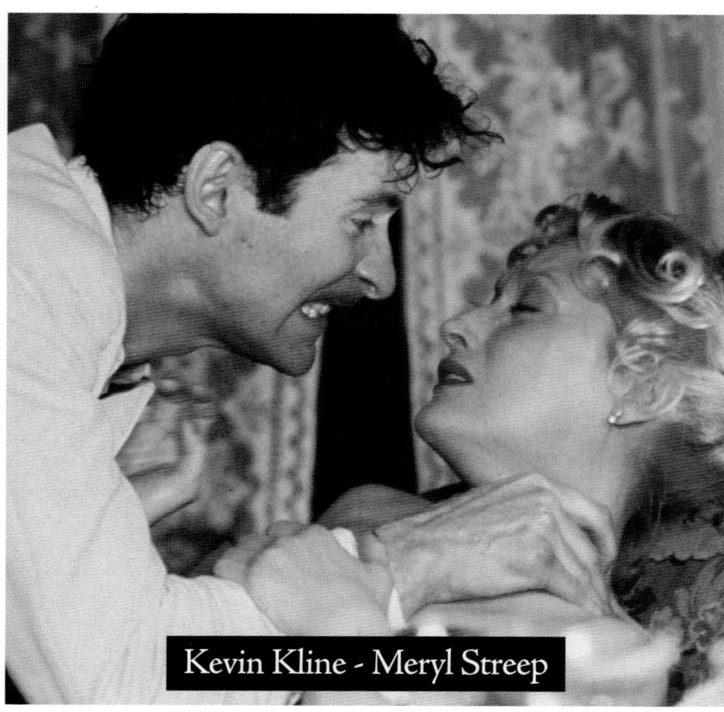
Kevin Kline - Meryl Streep

For her touching portrayal of the tortured mother, Meryl Streep received her second Oscar.

I didn't think it was possible to become a bigger fan of Meryl Streep, but my admiration for her increases with every new film she makes.

Michael Dorsey, an unsuccessful actor, disguises himself as a woman in order to get a role on a trashy hospital soap.

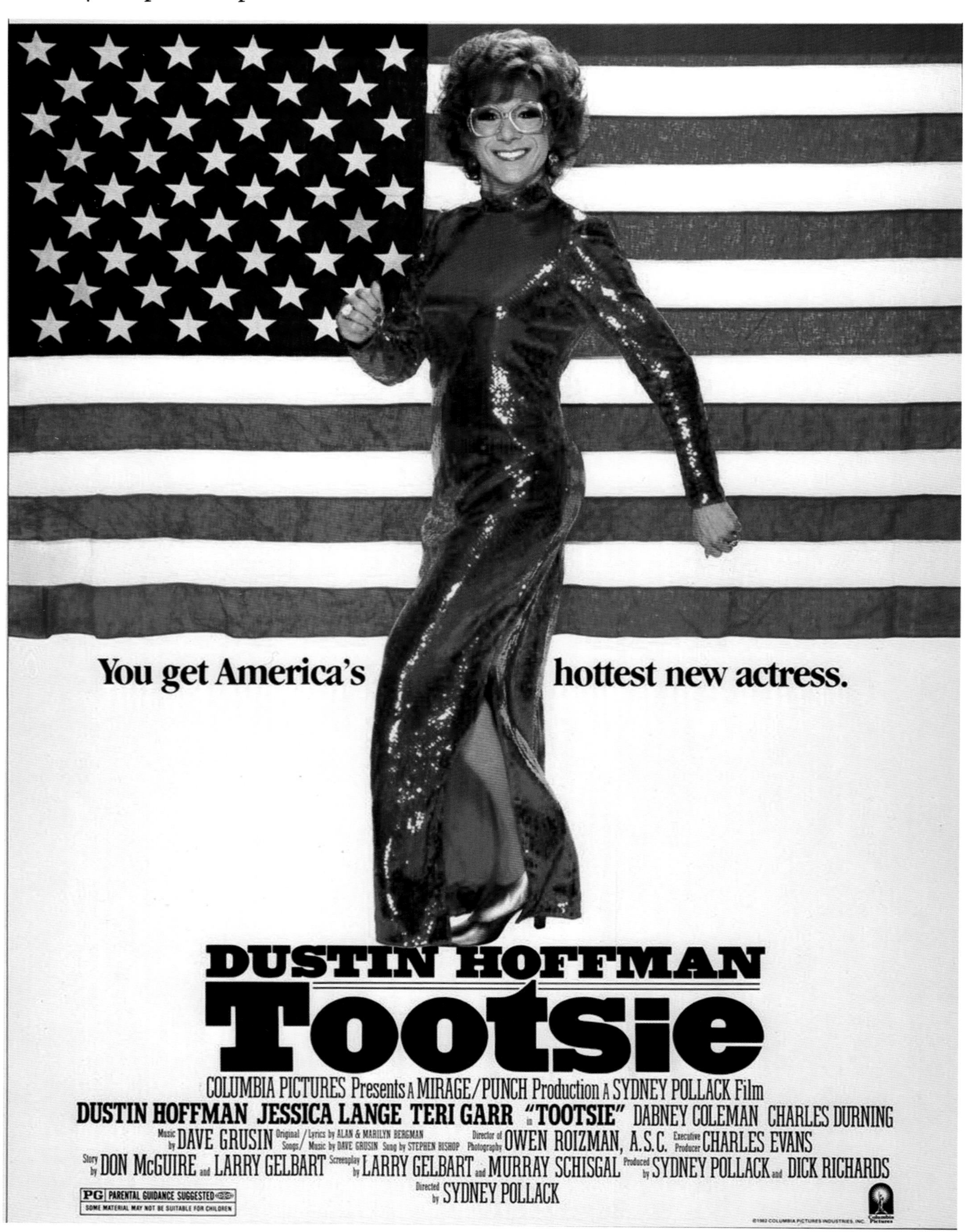

Vincent Canby of The New York Time wrote: "'Tootsie' is the best thing that's yet happened this year. It's a toot, a lark, a month in the country."

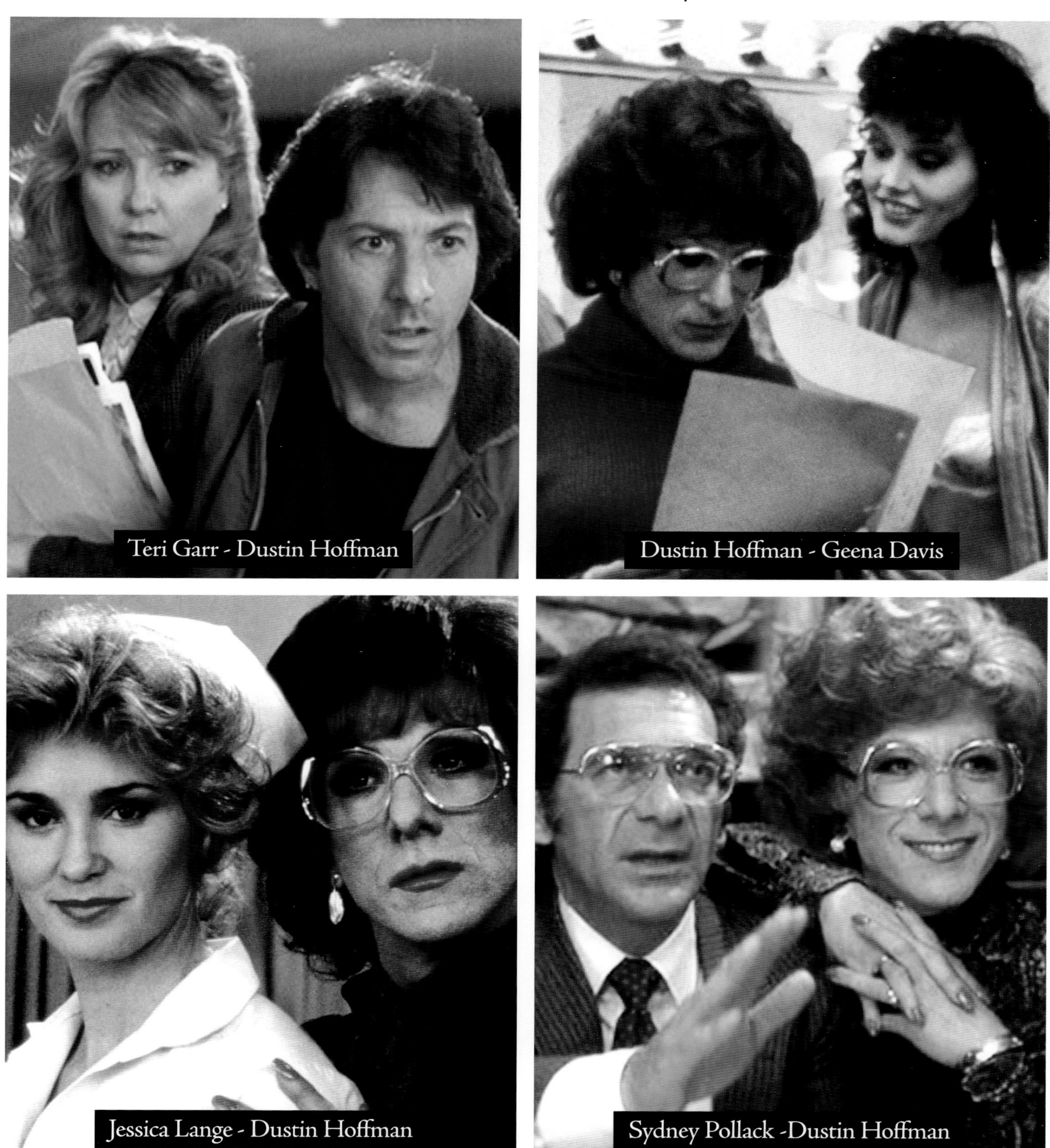

Teri Garr - Dustin Hoffman

Dustin Hoffman - Geena Davis

Jessica Lange - Dustin Hoffman

Sydney Pollack -Dustin Hoffman

It's hard to believe that Dustin Hoffman, a pleasant looking man, can, with very little makeup, morph into a beautiful, almost desirable, young woman.

Forty-one years earlier Jack Benny had made the original version of the film, and Mel Brooks paid homage to him by mounting a new version in which he added songs and dances.

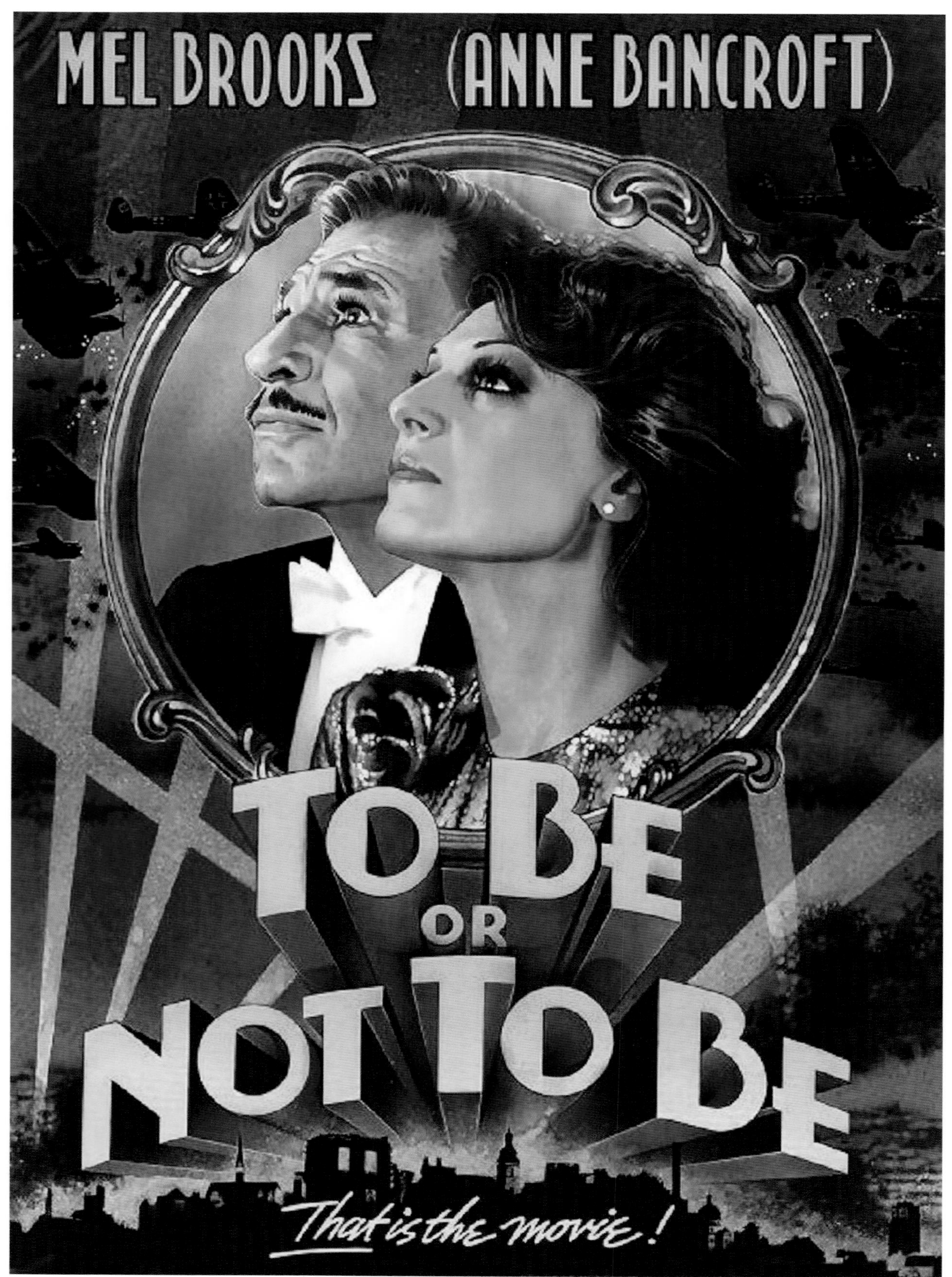

*Anne Bancroft received an Oscar for her role in "The Miracle Worker."

As The New York Times critic put it: "Everybody can relax. Mel Brooks' remake of Ernst Lubitsch's 1942 classic, 'To Be or Not to Be,' is smashingly funny."

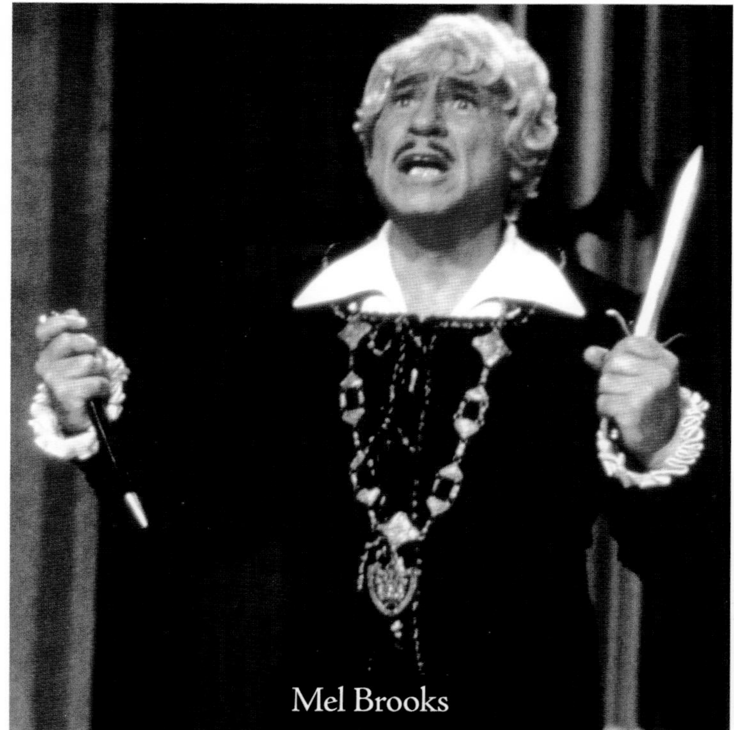
Mel Brooks

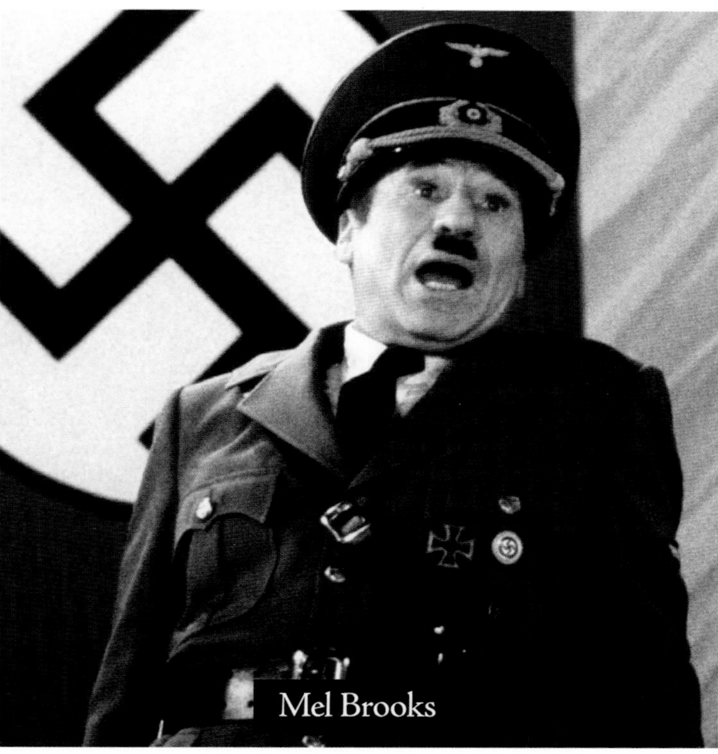
Mel Brooks

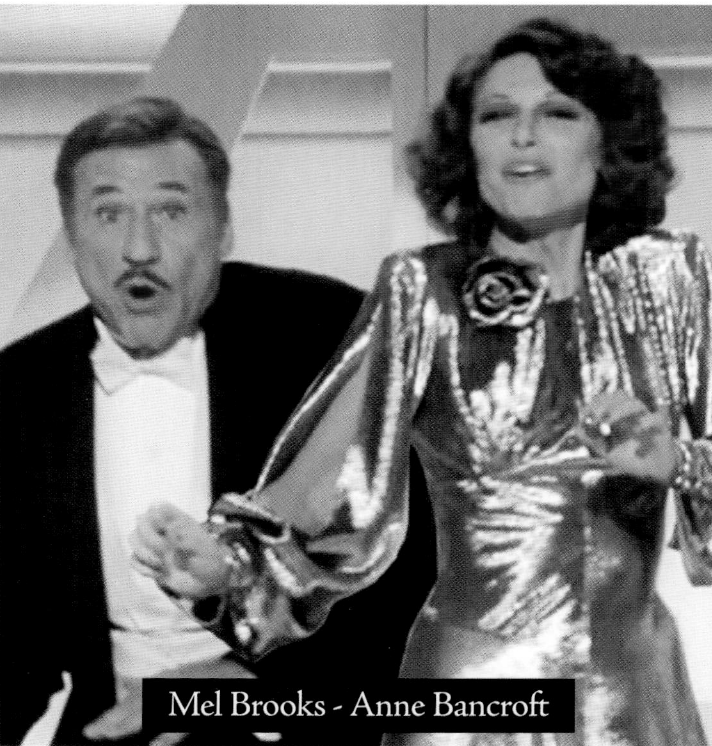
Mel Brooks - Anne Bancroft

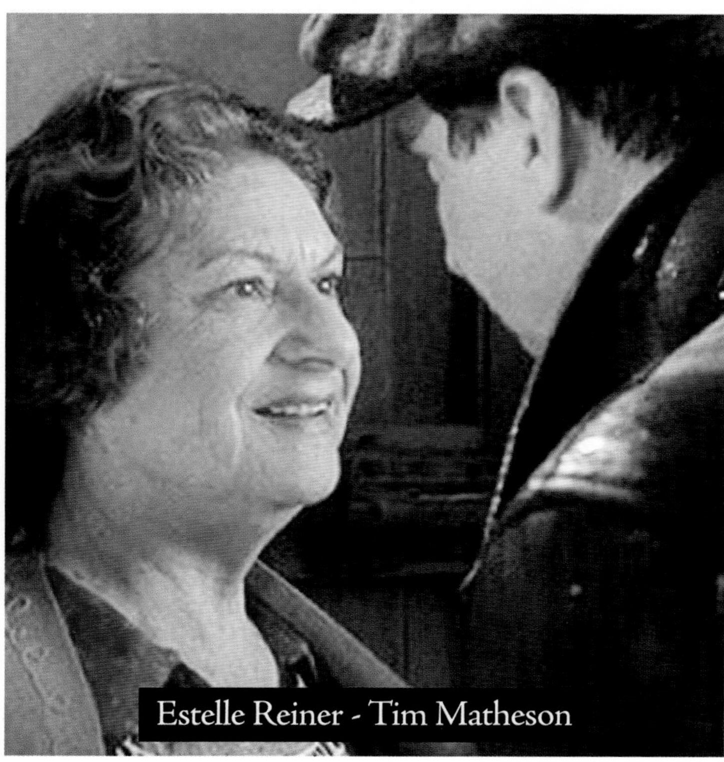
Estelle Reiner - Tim Matheson

Mel Brooks was searching for a co-star who owned a silver dress, was beautiful and could act, sing and dance. Luckily, he found one in his own home, Anne Bancroft.

My all-time favorite actress, who portrayed the wardrobe mistress, was my life partner of 65 years. Estelle (Lebost) Reiner also bore me three extraordinary children, Robbie, Annie and Lucas.

A Jewish girl disguises herself as a boy to enter religious training.

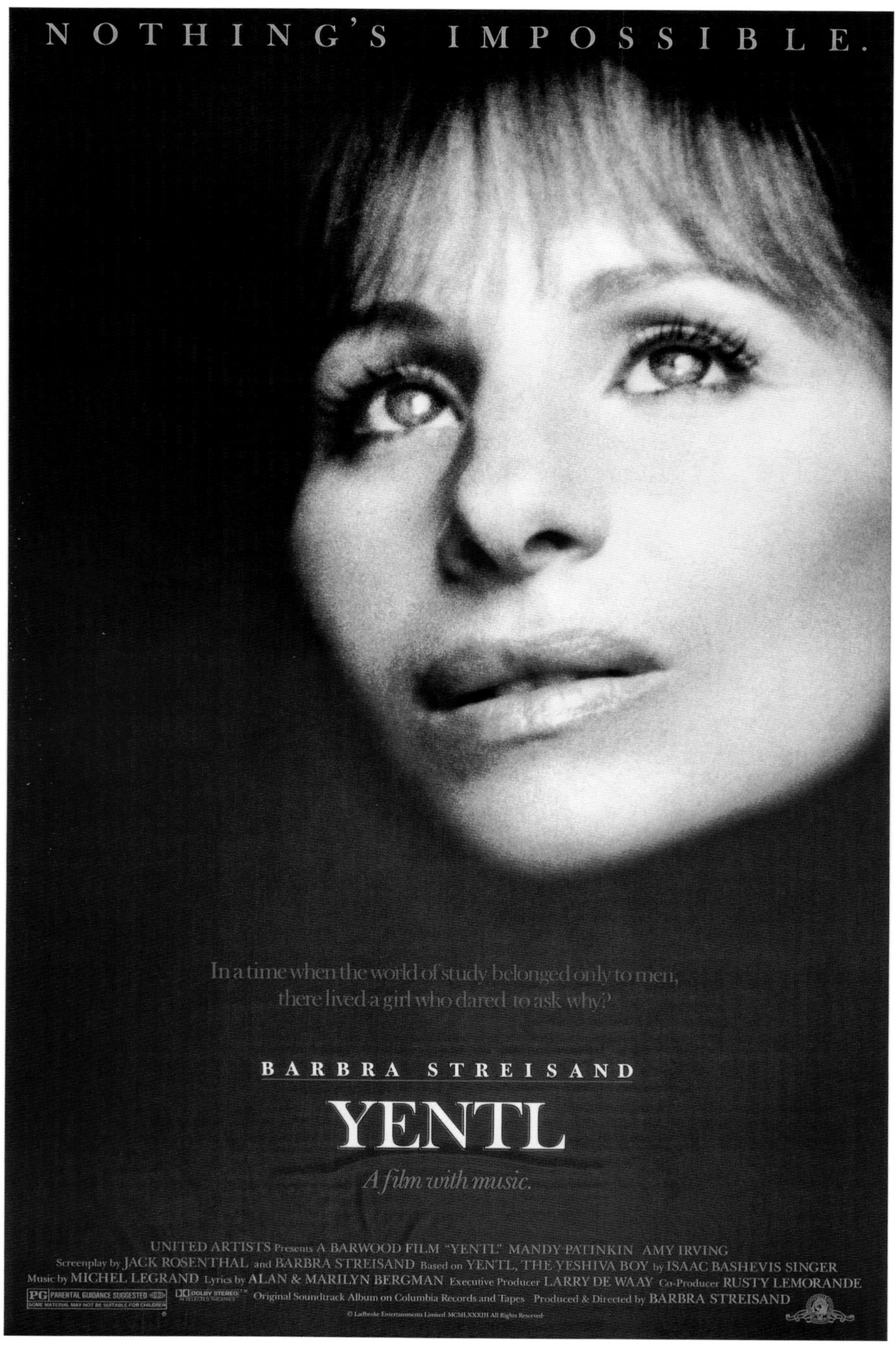

Christian Toto of What Would Toto Watch? wrote: "'Yentl' is all about, who else? Miss Streisand. But her vast talents turn a gender-bending fable into a winner."

James Sanford of Kalamazoo Gazette wrote: "Perhaps Streisand's finest hour, on all fronts."

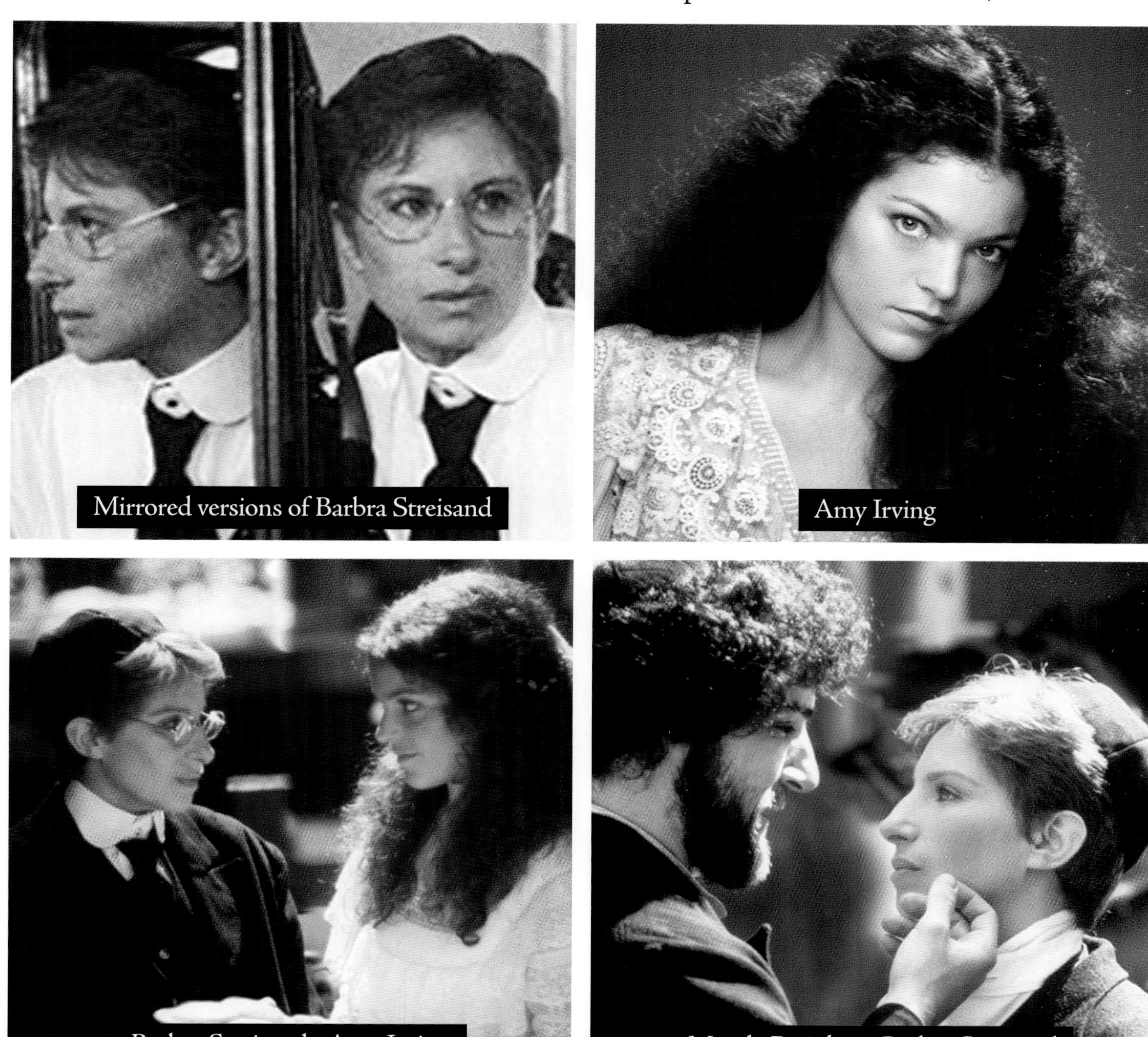

Mirrored versions of Barbra Streisand

Amy Irving

Barbra Streisand - Amy Irving

Mandy Patinkin - Barbra Streisand

It is my humble opinion that Barbra Streisand is one of the most, if not the most, all-around talented and versatile performers on film, stage or recordings.

Barbra Streisand made her West Coast debut in 1960 at "The Coconut Grove." I invited Dick Van Dyke to join me to see this up and coming singer and when she stepped on stage, he mumbled, "Not very attractive." After hearing her sing the opening number, he whispered, "That is one of the most beautiful girls I've ever seen."

A brain surgeon marries a femme fatale, causing his life to turn upside down. Things go more awry when he falls in love with a talking brain.

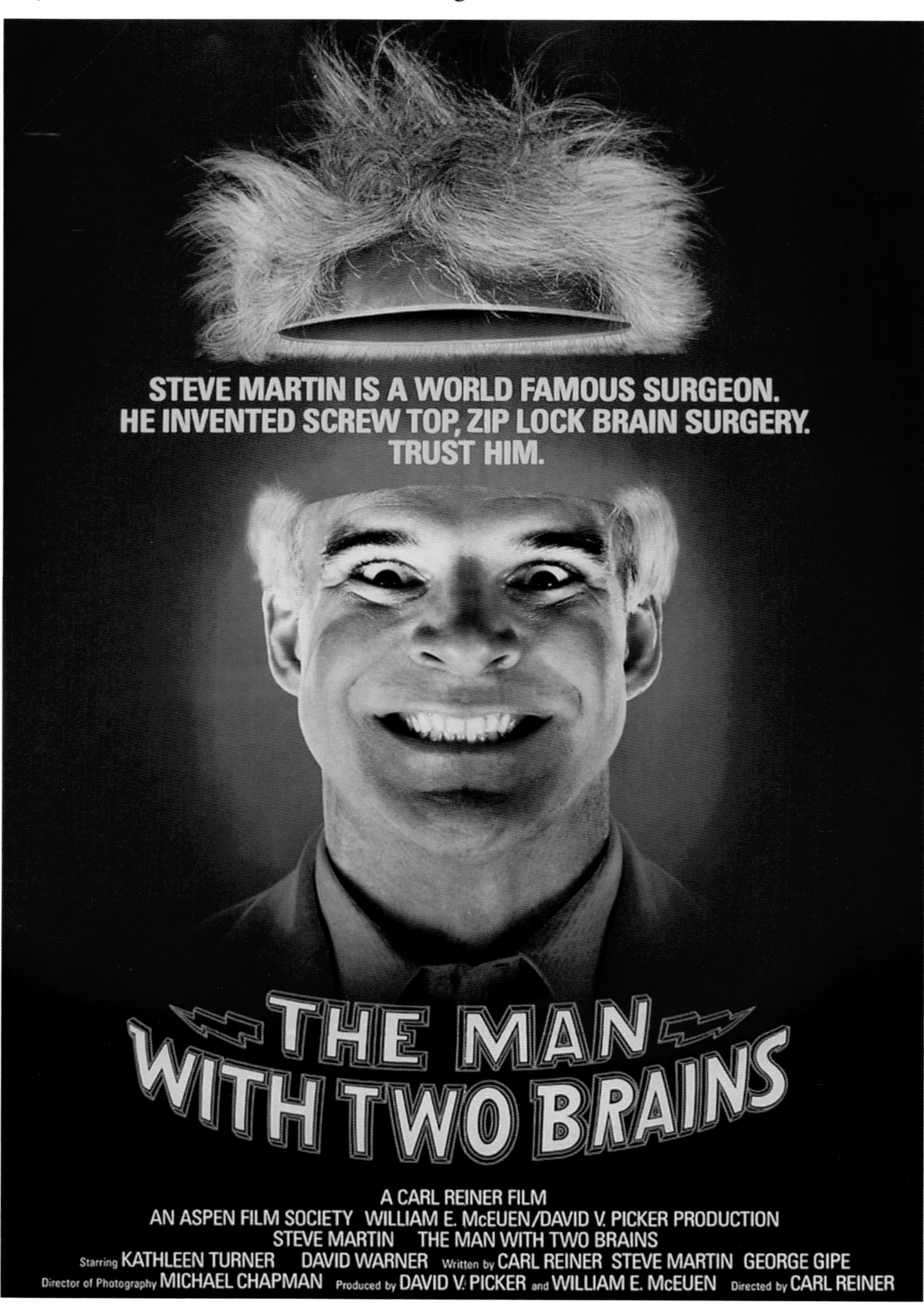

Scott Weinberg of eFilmCritic.com wrote: "Martin's at his wildest and craziest in this seriously silly sci-fi spoof."

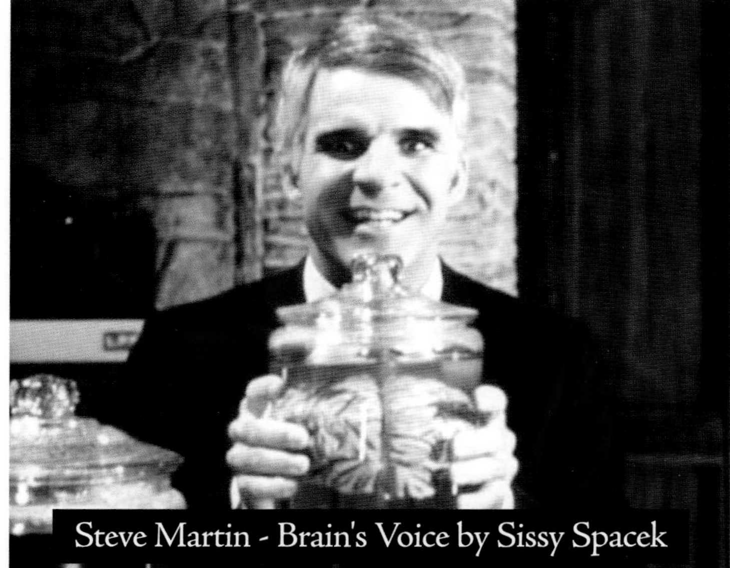
Steve Martin - Brain's Voice by Sissy Spacek

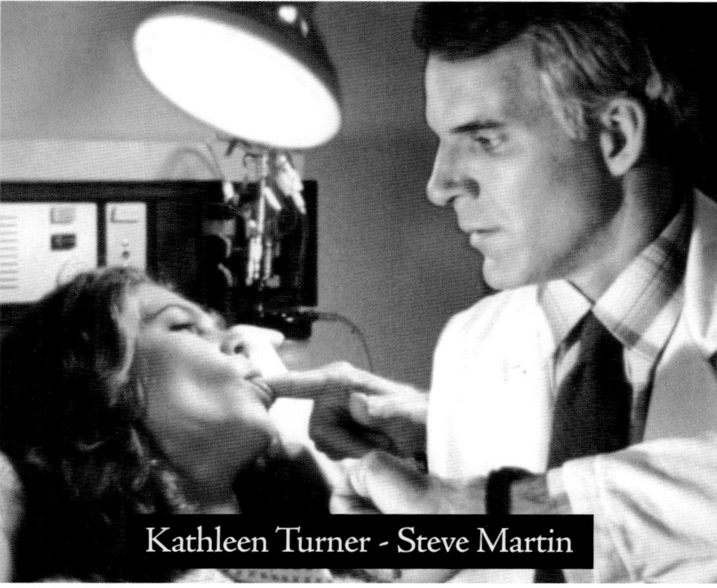
Kathleen Turner - Steve Martin

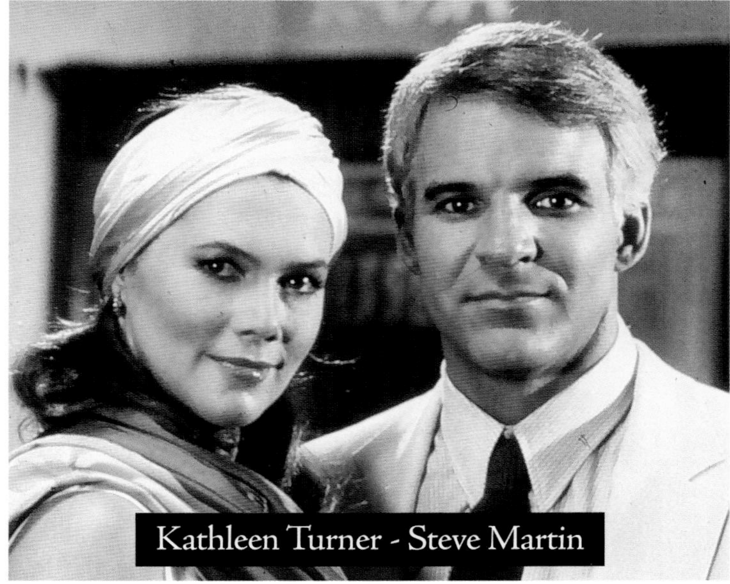
Kathleen Turner - Steve Martin

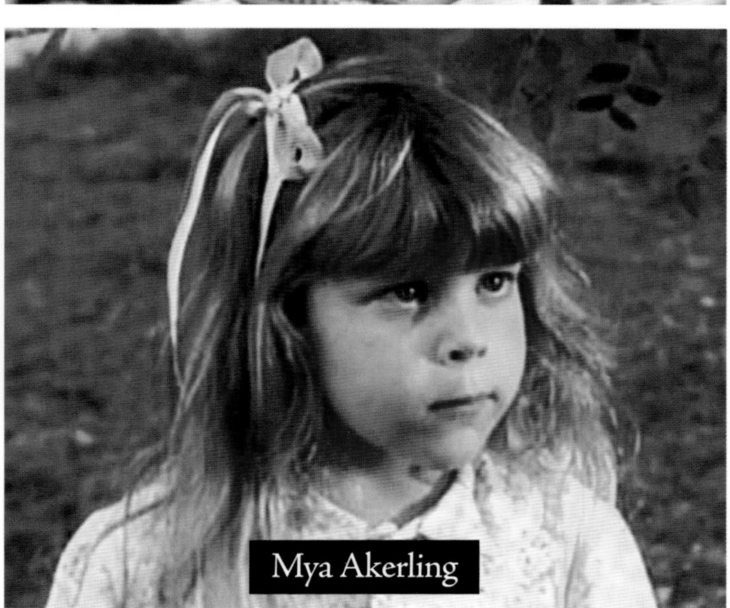
Mya Akerling

Steve Martin plays a brain surgeon who invented a novel way of keeping a disembodied brain alive by floating it in Windex. On his way to find a body for his brain, he accidentally runs over a pedestrian, Kathleen Turner, a beautiful recipient for his beloved brain.

To keep Kathleen alive, Steve tells a four year old bystander to do the following:

"Get to a phone and call the E.R. of North Bank General Hospital, 932-1000 and have them set up O.R. 6 immediately and contact anesthesiologist Isadore Tuerk, 472-2112 beep 12. Send an ambulance with a paramedic crew and light I.V., D-5 and W, KVO... repeat my instructions!"

To everyone's amazement, the darling four year old repeats those complicated instructions word for word. Because perfection cannot be perfected, I had no need to ask for a second take from the four year old genius.

"Spinal Tap," one of England's loudest bands, is chronicled by film director Marty DeBergi on what proves to be a fateful tour.

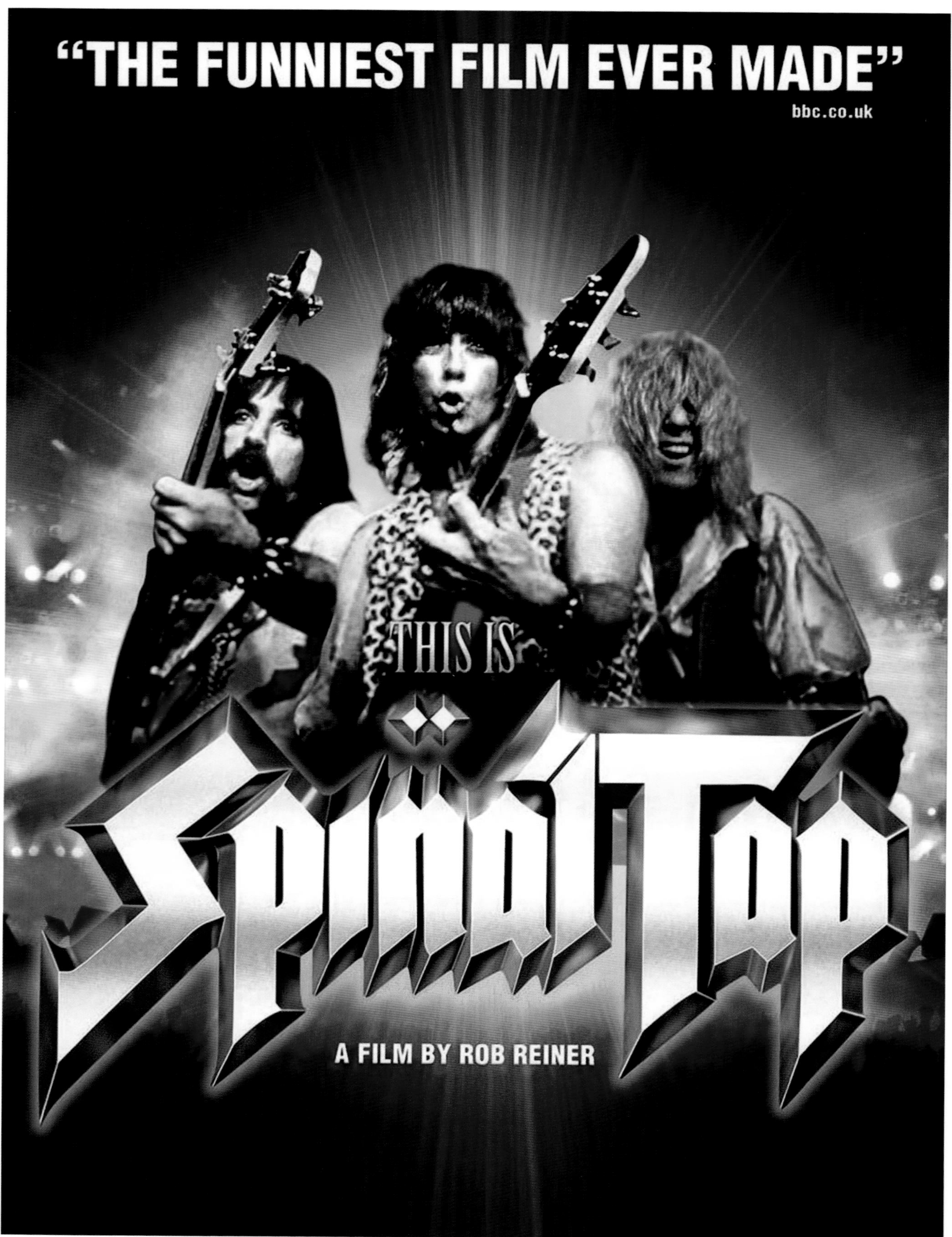

Roger Ebert wrote: "'This Is Spinal Tap,' one of the funniest movies ever made, is about a lot of things, but one of them is the way the real story is not in the questions or in the answers, but at the edge of the frame."

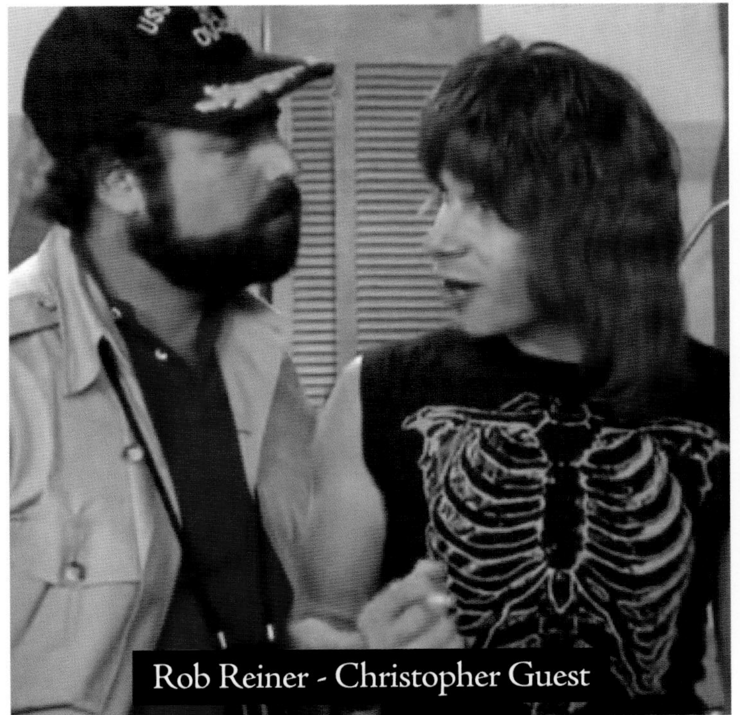
Rob Reiner - Christopher Guest

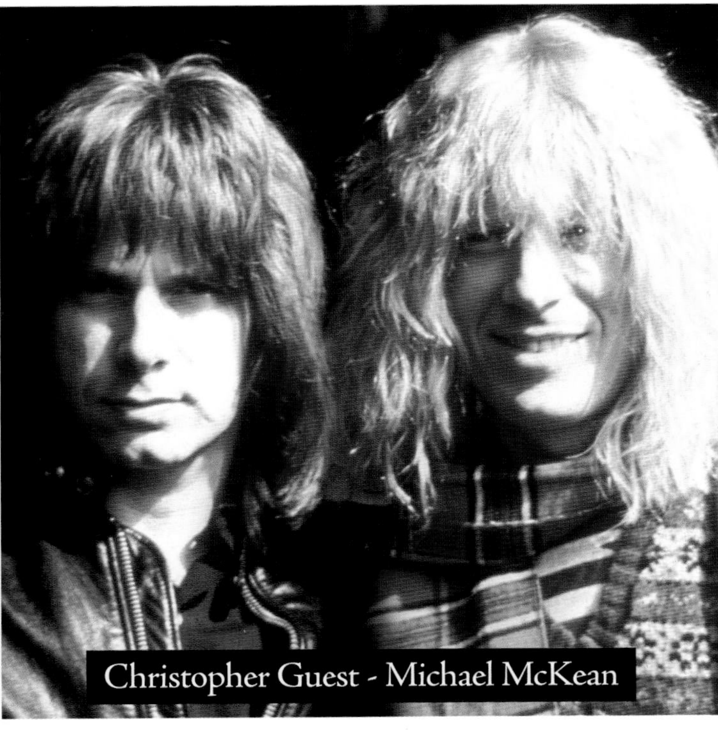
Christopher Guest - Michael McKean

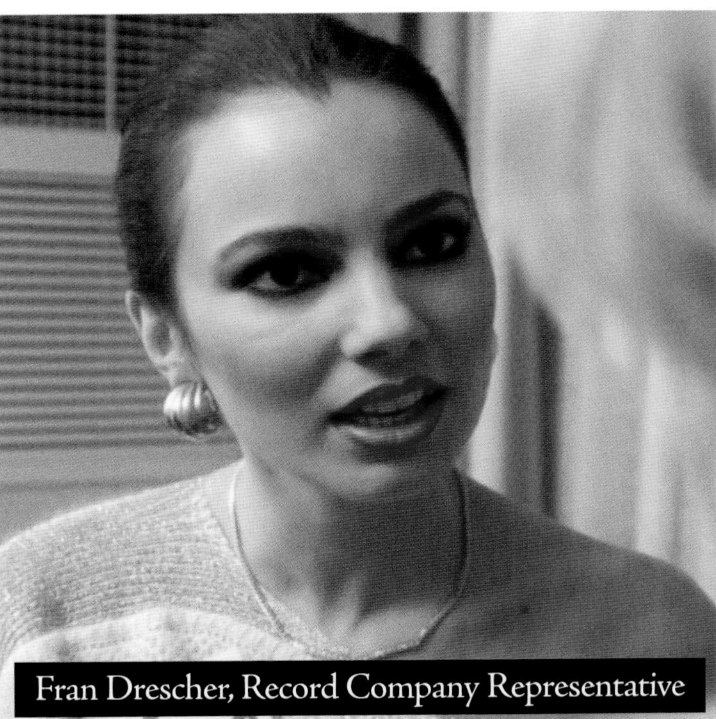
Fran Drescher, Record Company Representative

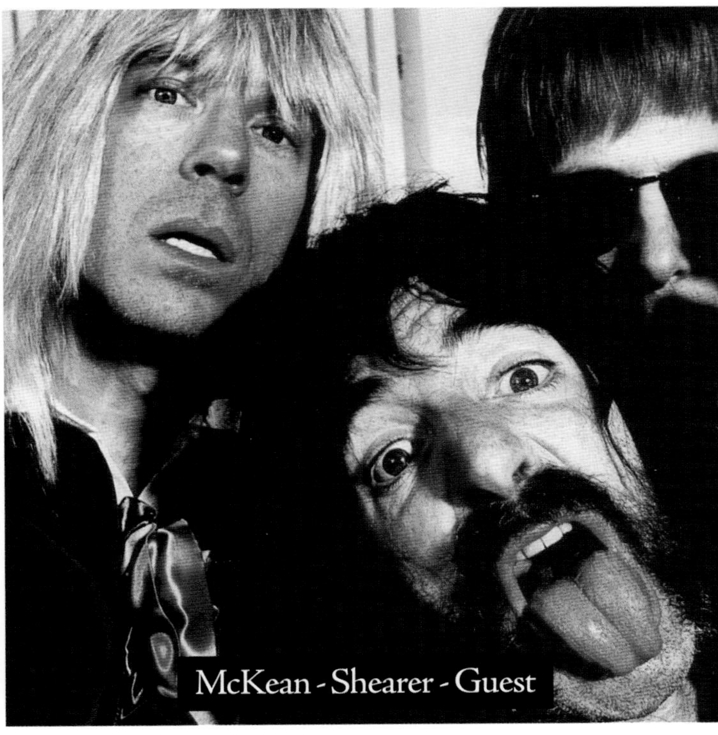
McKean - Shearer - Guest

I fully agree with the above critique written by Roger Ebert and I would say that even if the director, Rob Reiner, wasn't a very very close relative.

"Spinal Tap" had no script but the cast ad-libbed what ultimately became quotable dialogue. (On a scale from one to ten, the film is a definite "eleven, which is one better than ten.")

A husband and wife in their 30s decide to quit their jobs, live as free spirits and cruise America in a Winnebago.

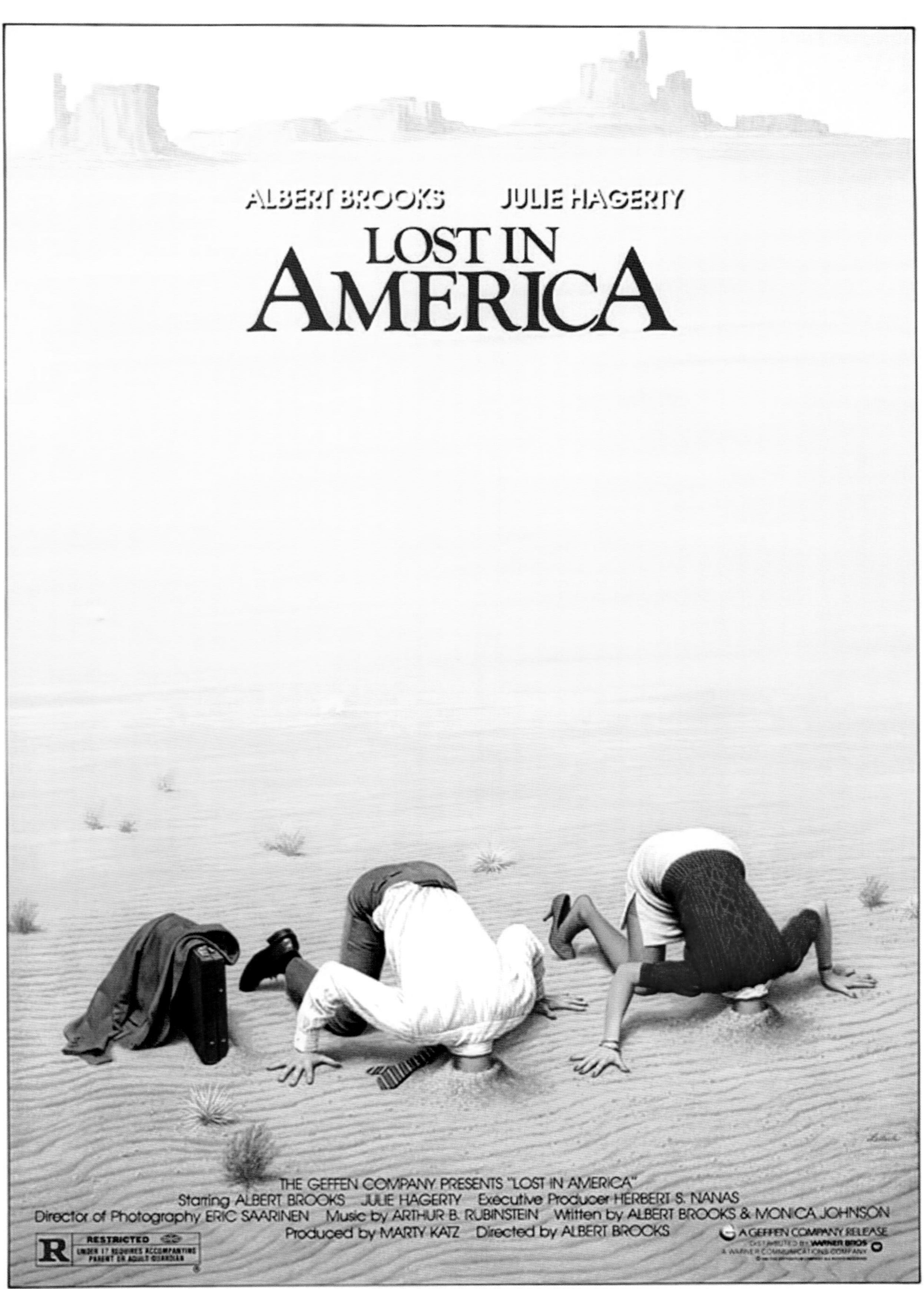

Janet Maslin of The New York Times wrote: "A yuppie mid-life crisis is in the offing, and Albert Brooks has made it the basis for 'Lost in America,' an inspired comedy in his own dryly distinctive style. Mr. Brooks is laugh-out-loud funny, largely because so much of what he has to say is true."

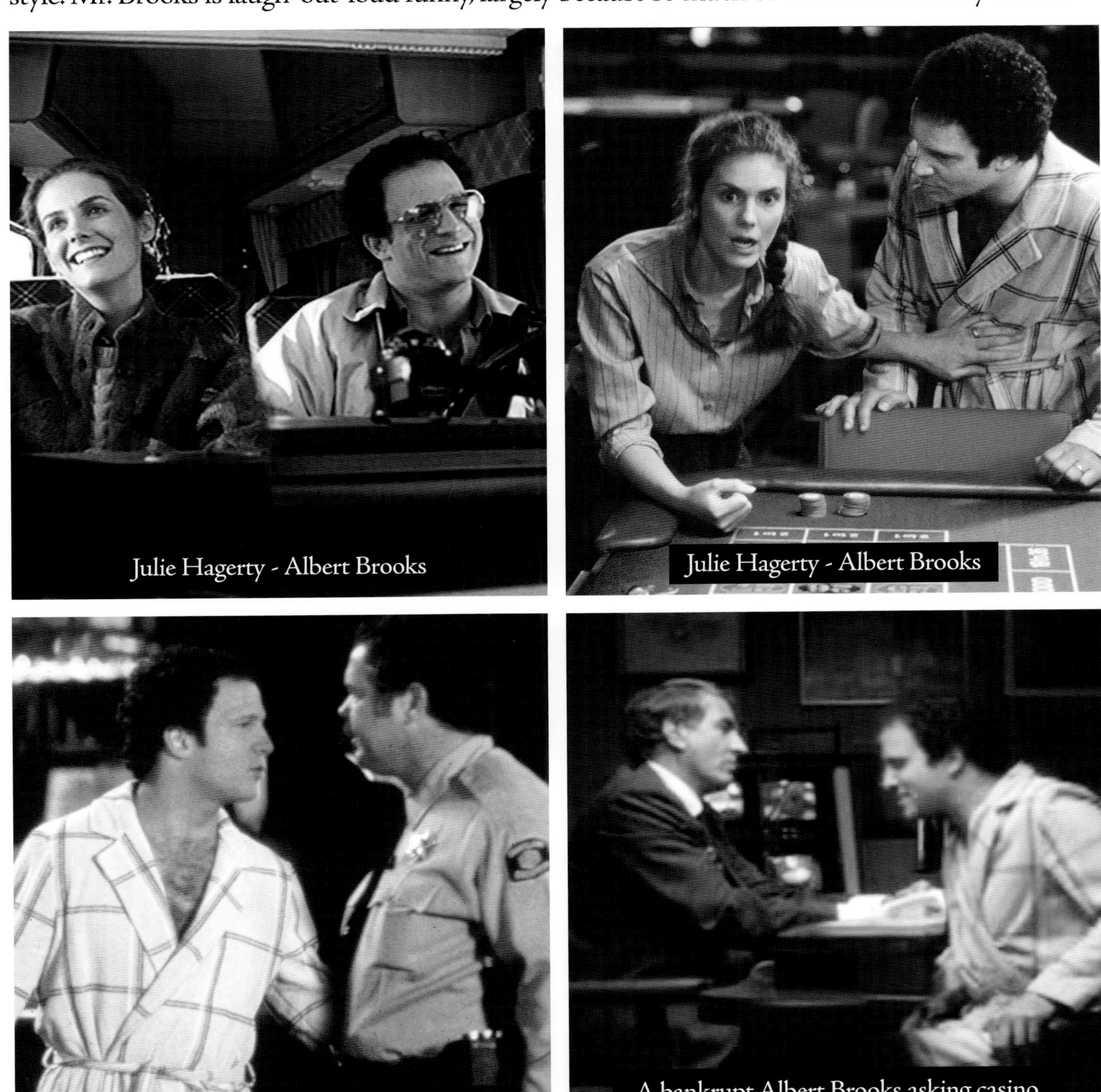

Julie Hagerty - Albert Brooks

Julie Hagerty - Albert Brooks

Albert Brooks - John C. Reade

A bankrupt Albert Brooks asking casino owner, Garry Marshall, to forgive the debt he incurred at the roulette wheel

If you need a pick-me-up, pick up a copy of any film that was directed, written or performed by Albert Brooks, watch it, and if your spirtits aren't lifted, they're apparently not liftable.

An overworked air-traffic controller takes his family on a beach vacation but is soon beset by a series of mishaps.

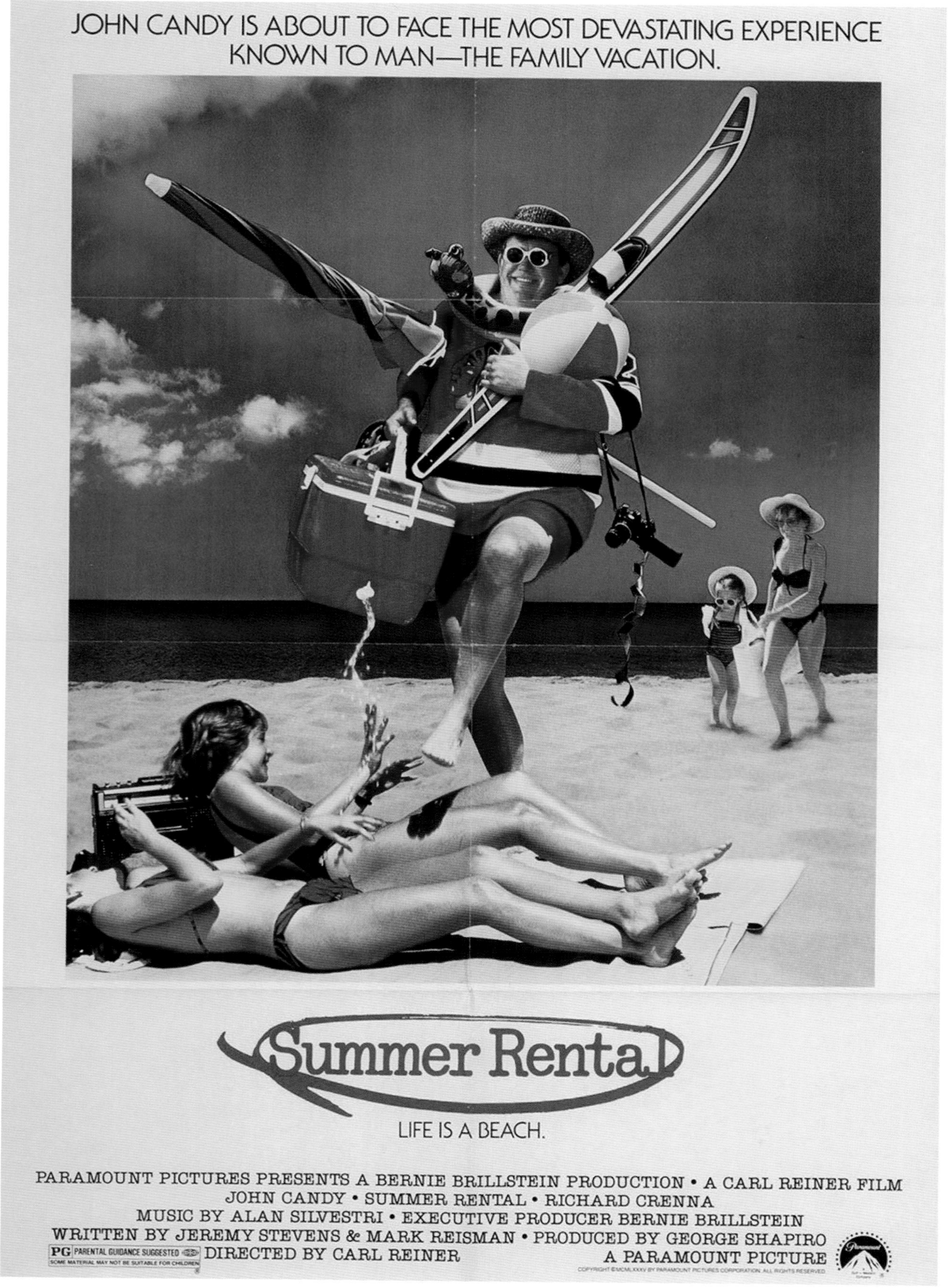

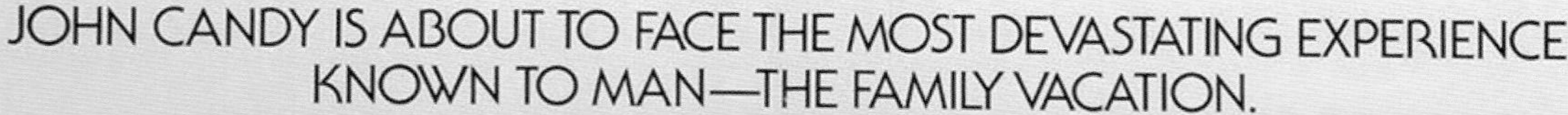

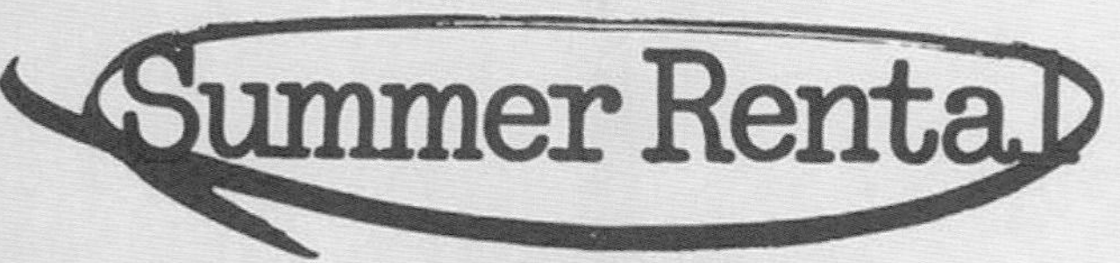

LIFE IS A BEACH.

PARAMOUNT PICTURES PRESENTS A BERNIE BRILLSTEIN PRODUCTION • A CARL REINER FILM
JOHN CANDY • SUMMER RENTAL • RICHARD CRENNA
MUSIC BY ALAN SILVESTRI • EXECUTIVE PRODUCER BERNIE BRILLSTEIN
WRITTEN BY JEREMY STEVENS & MARK REISMAN • PRODUCED BY GEORGE SHAPIRO
PG PARENTAL GUIDANCE SUGGESTED SOME MATERIAL MAY NOT BE SUITABLE FOR CHILDREN DIRECTED BY CARL REINER A PARAMOUNT PICTURE

MaximumCheese of IMDb wrote: "This movie is about having a good time. There's no violence, no crude sexual comedy, just the legendary John Candy, surely one of the best comics of the past 30 years, doing what he does best, making us laugh."

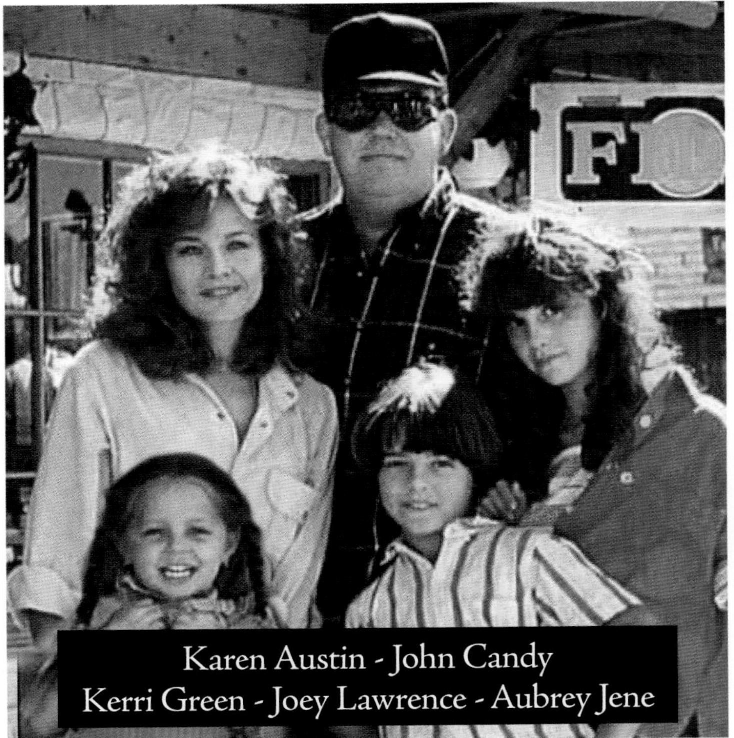

Karen Austin - John Candy
Kerri Green - Joey Lawrence - Aubrey Jene

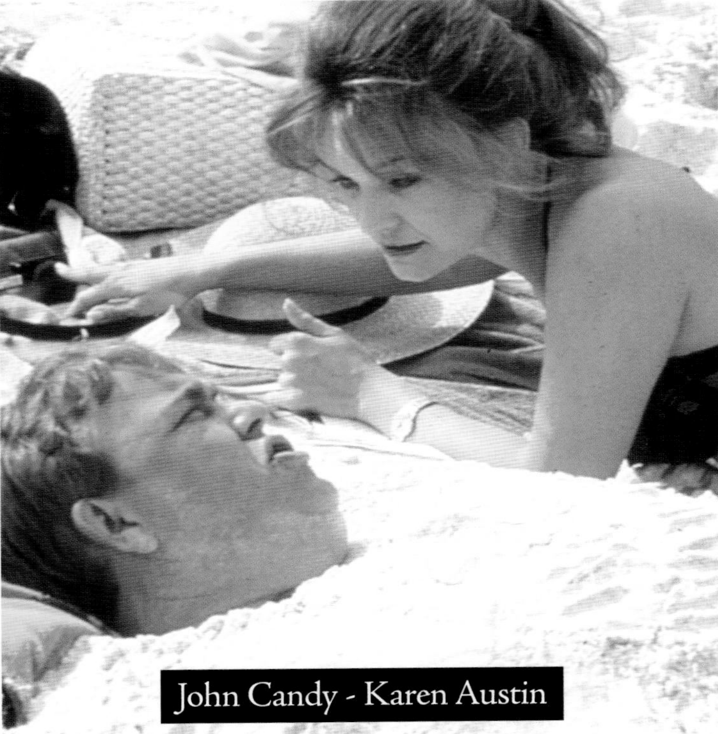

John Candy - Karen Austin

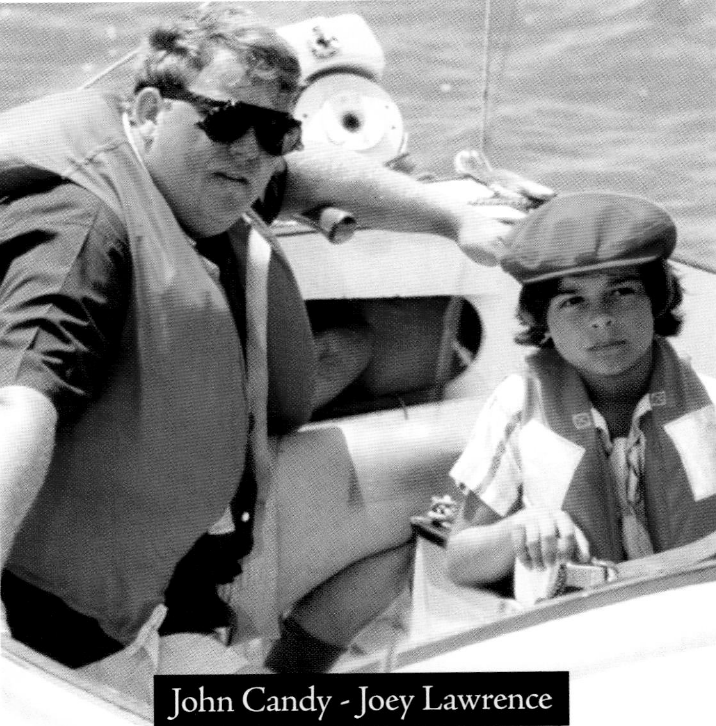

John Candy - Joey Lawrence

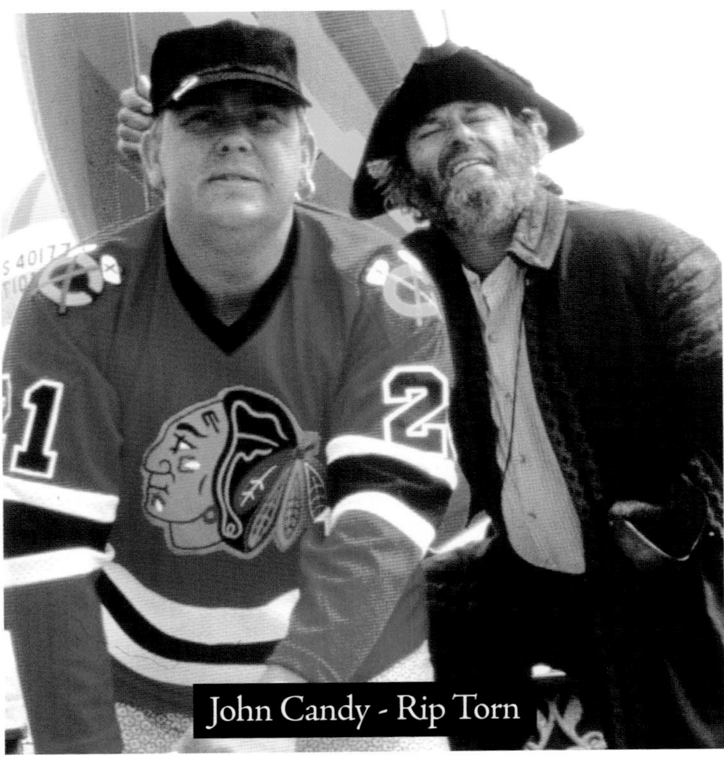

John Candy - Rip Torn

My experience making this film was nothing but pleasure as John Candy and the cast were a joy to be around and, when I wasn't directing, I was spending happy time with my wife, Estelle, enjoying life in St. Petersburg, sunny Florida's sunniest city.

A college student plans a cross-country trip to get laid, but ends up traveling with a young woman. They hate each other, so naturally...

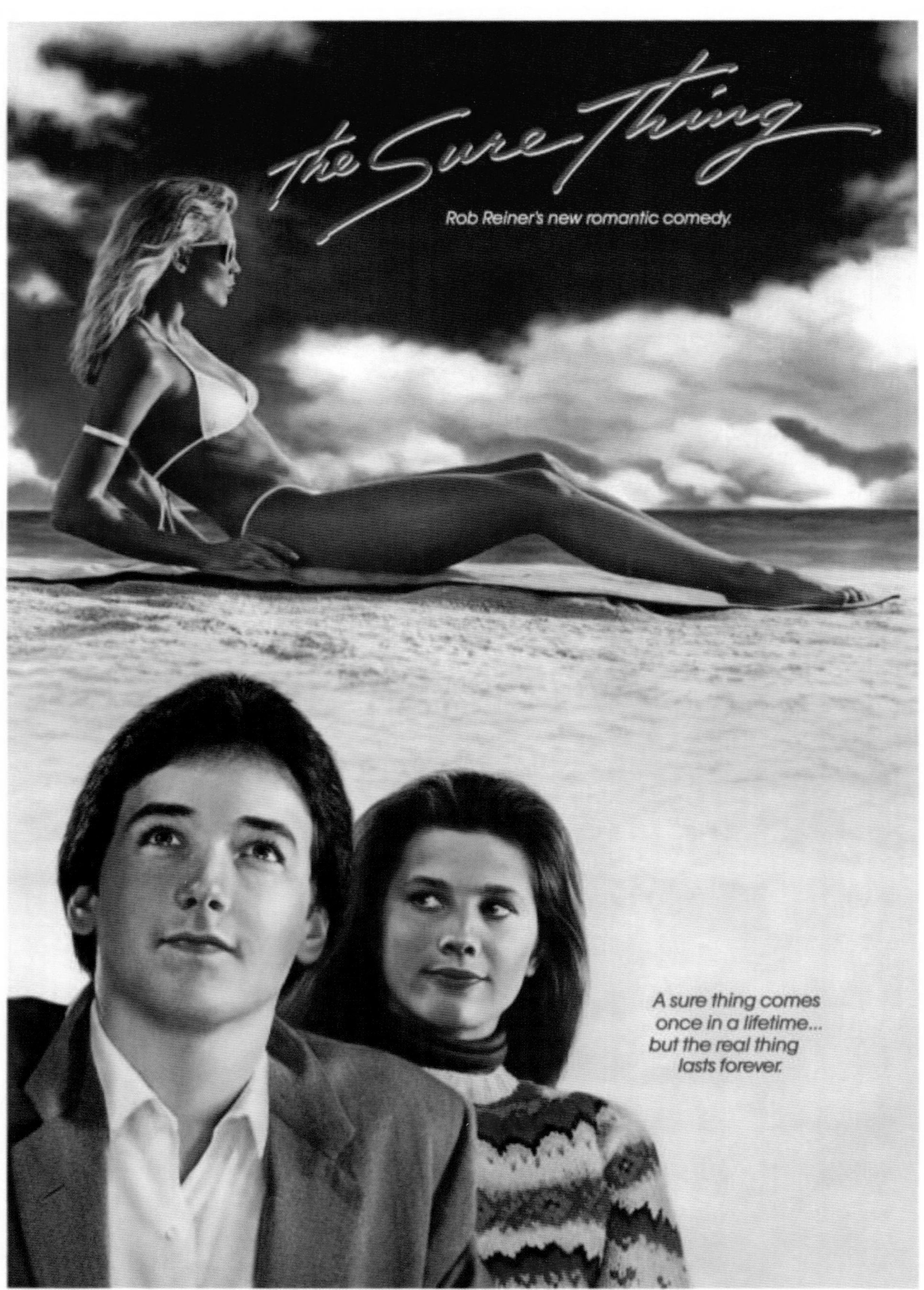

Roger Ebert wrote: "'The Sure Thing' is a small miracle. Although the hero of this movie is promised by his buddy that he'll be fixed up with a 'guaranteed sure thing,' the film is about how this kid falls genuinely in love, not with 'the sure thing,' but with a girl of his choice."

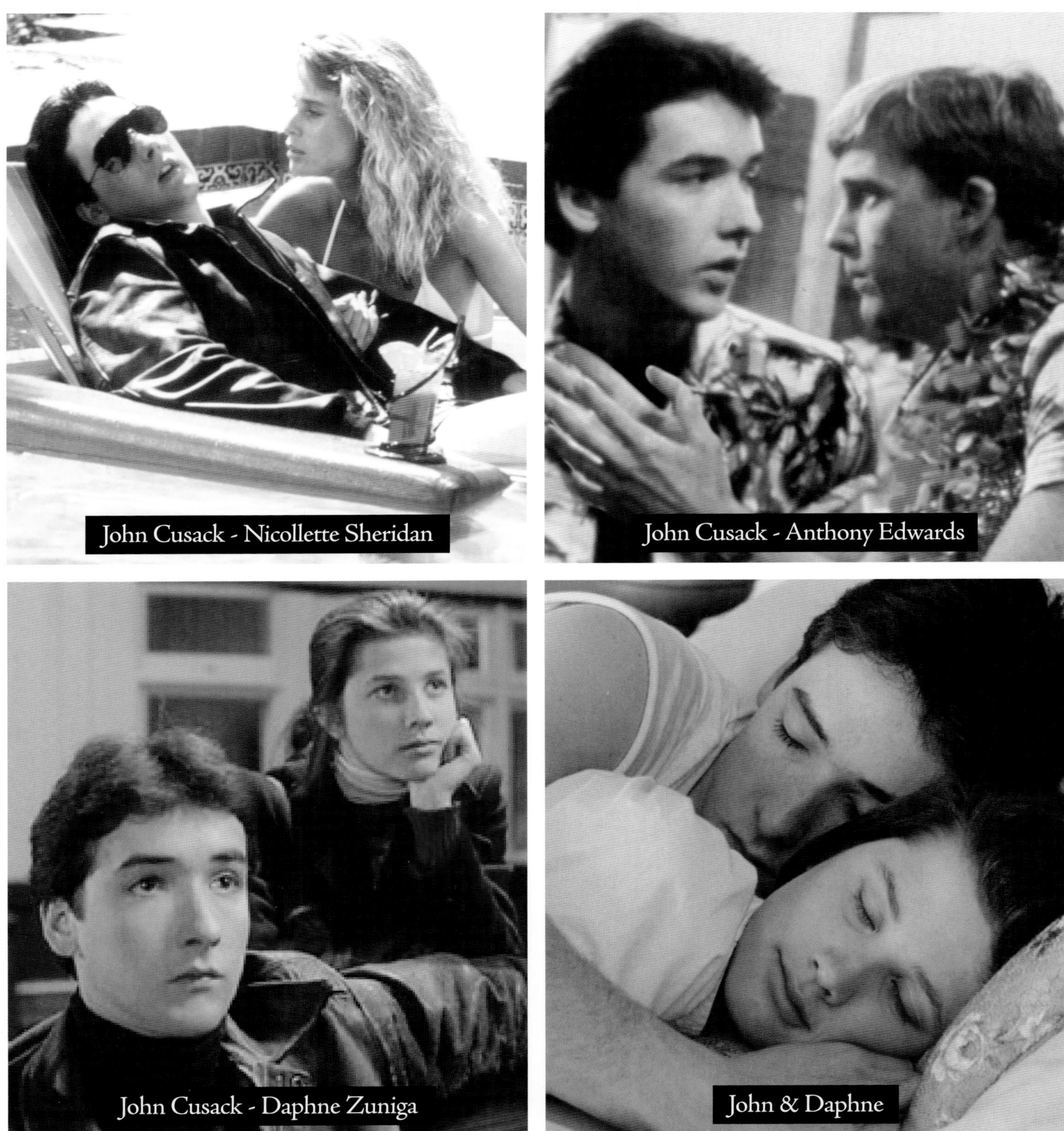

John Cusack - Nicollette Sheridan

John Cusack - Anthony Edwards

John Cusack - Daphne Zuniga

John & Daphne

This was a break out film for both John Cusack and Daphne Zuniga. Mel Brooks chose Daphne Zuniga to play Princess Vespa in his now classic "Spaceballs."

In 20th-century colonial Kenya, a Danish baroness/plantation owner has a passionate love affair with a free-spirited big-game hunter.

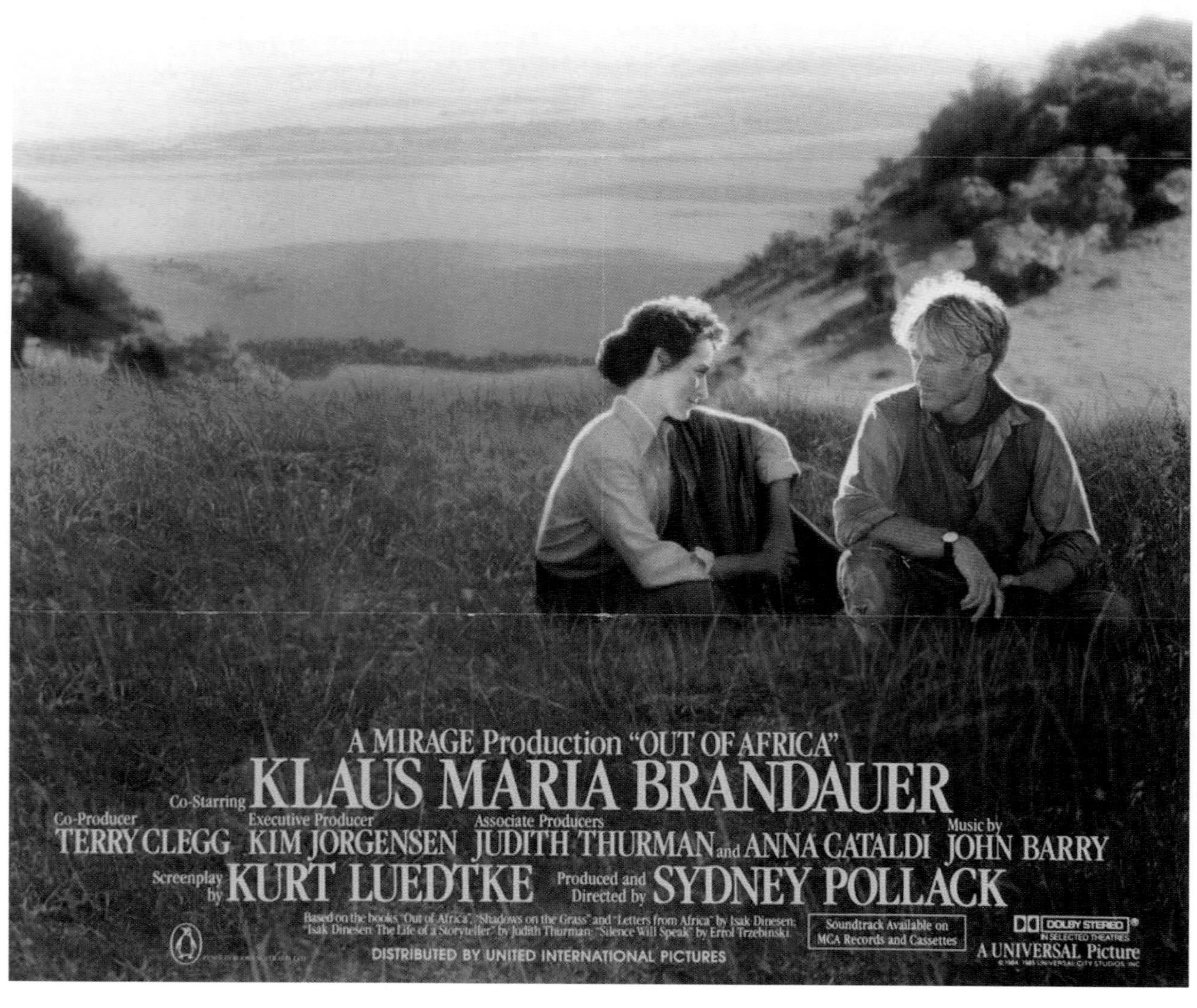

Roger Ebert wrote: "'Out of Africa' is a great movie to look at, breathtakingly filmed on location. It is a movie with the courage to be about complex, sweeping emotions, and to use the star power of Meryl Streep and Robert Redford without apology."

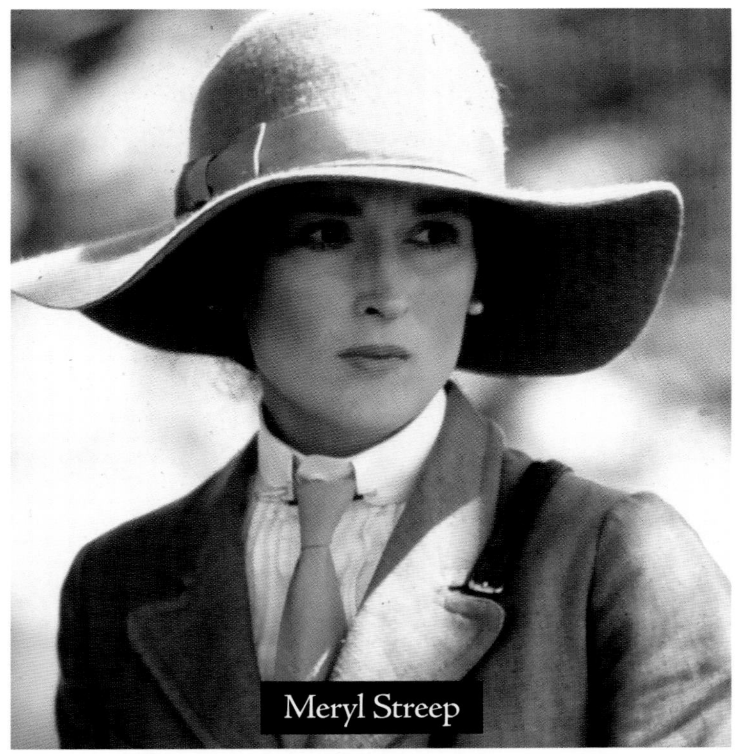
Meryl Streep

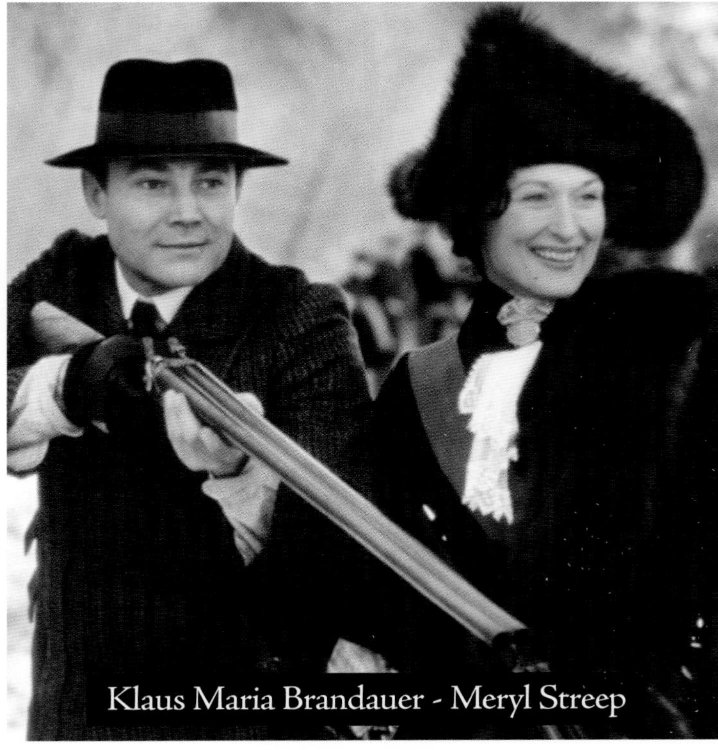
Klaus Maria Brandauer - Meryl Streep

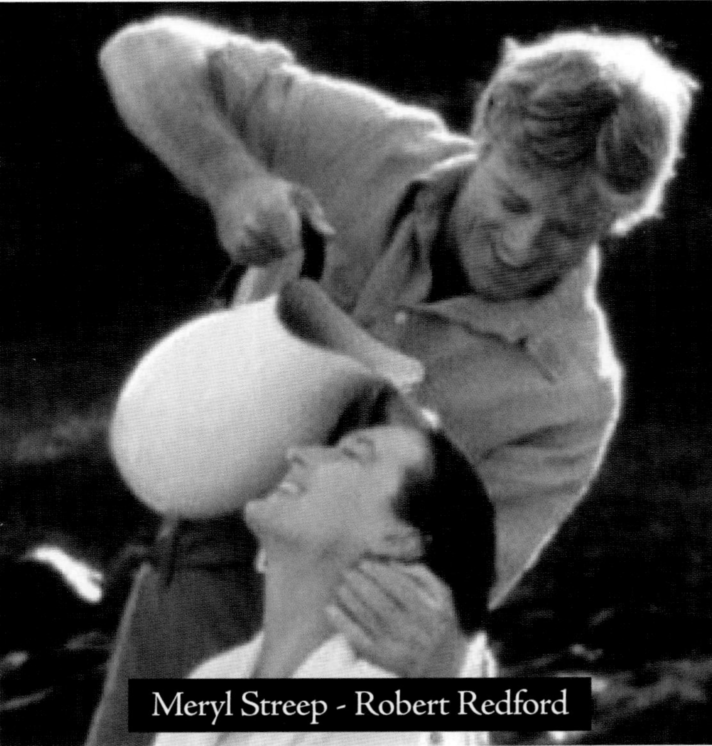
Meryl Streep - Robert Redford

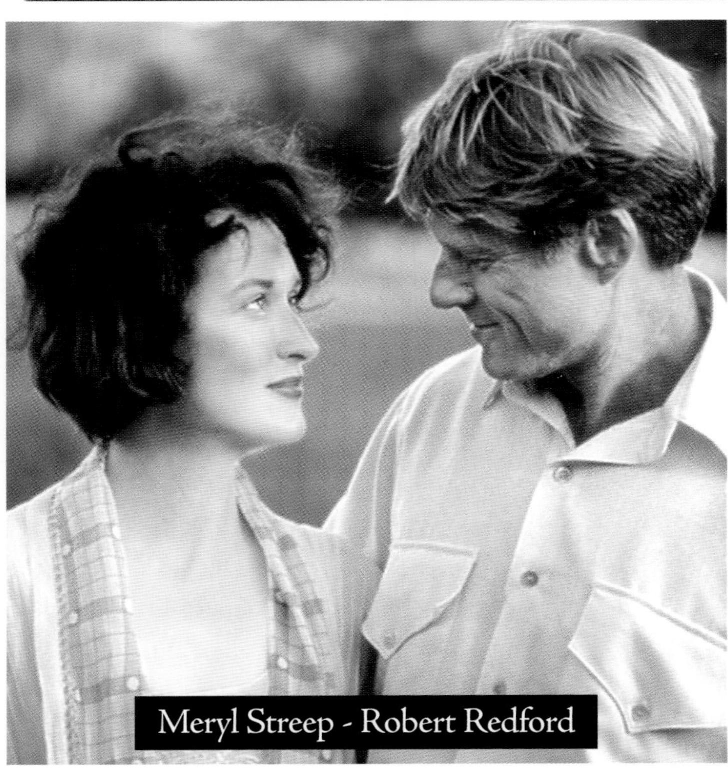
Meryl Streep - Robert Redford

In his review, Roger Ebert spoke for me, as I am a charter member of the Meryl Streep "Can-Do-No-Wrong Fan Club." I am also a life-long fan of Robert Redford, a trustee on the National Resources Defense Council, who is doing positive things to help sustain our environment and planet.

A black Southern woman struggles to find her identity after suffering abuse from her father and others over four decades.

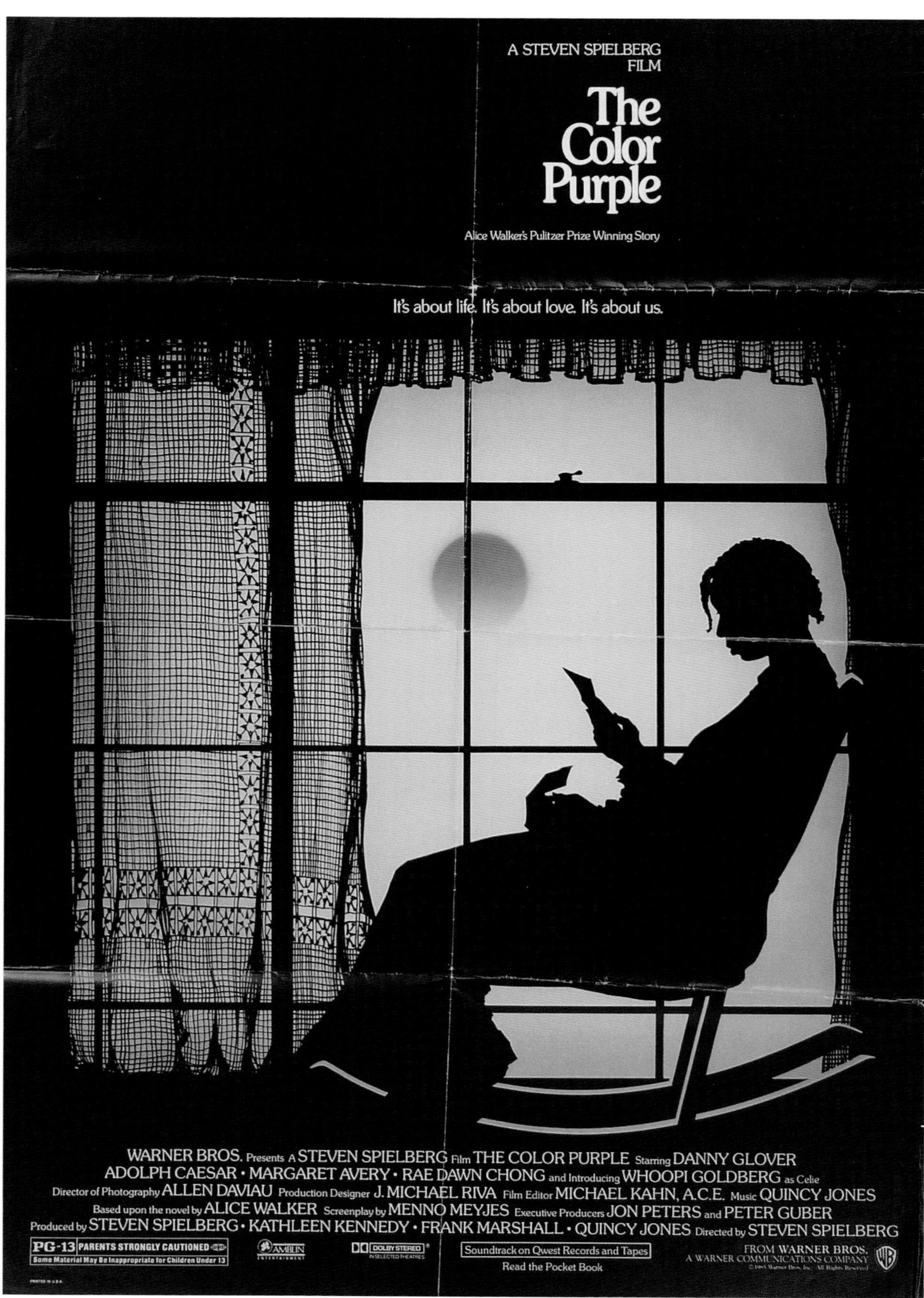

Everybody concurred with Roger Ebert, who wrote: "The affirmation at the end of 'The Color Purple' is so joyous that this is one of the few movies in a long time that inspires tears of happiness, and earns them. It's the year's best film."

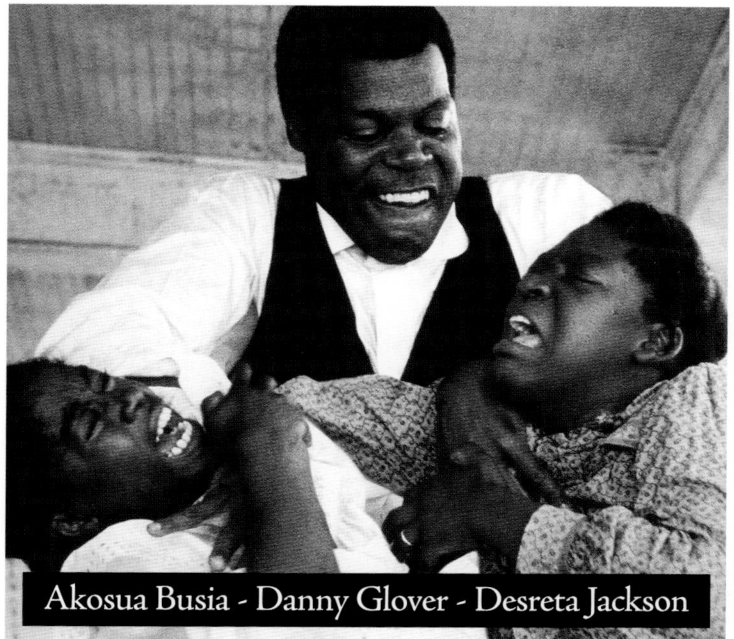
Akosua Busia - Danny Glover - Desreta Jackson

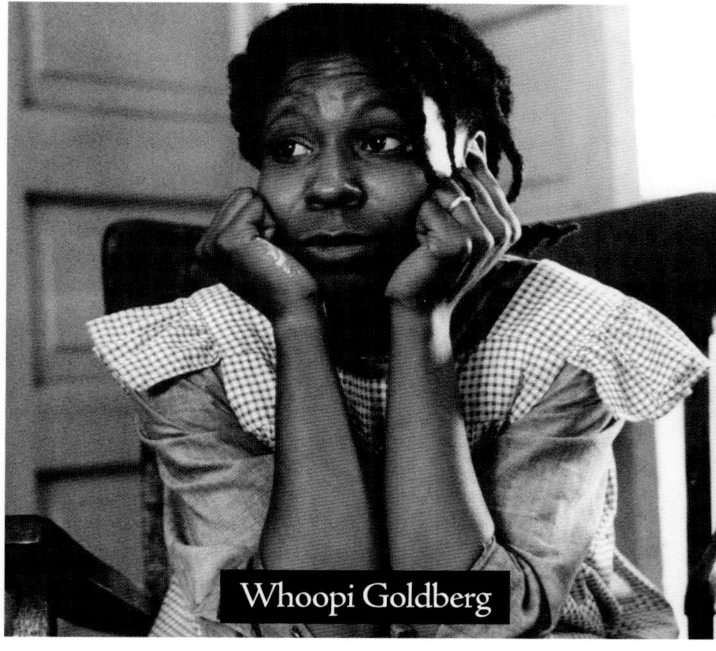
Whoopi Goldberg

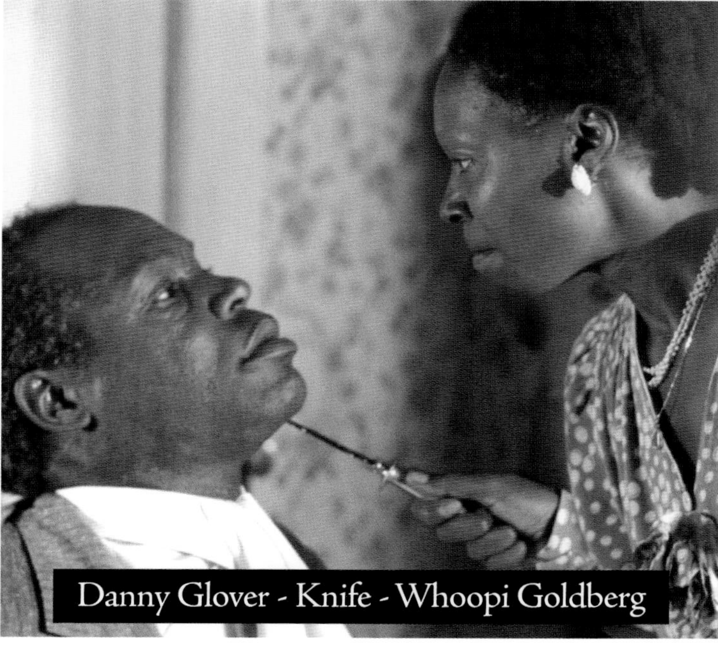
Danny Glover - Knife - Whoopi Goldberg

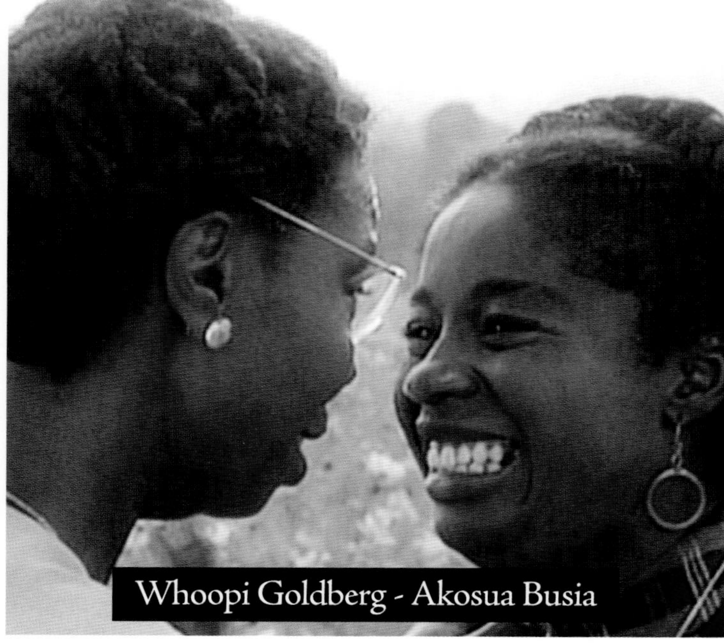
Whoopi Goldberg - Akosua Busia

Whoopi Goldberg gives a magnificent performance playing Celie Johnson, who endures rape, sexism and a tyrannical husband. I was not surprised because, on Broadway, I had seen Whoopi's One Woman Show, where she depicted a Valley Girl-ish teenager, a streetwise hustler thief named Fontaine, a cripple, a little girl and a Jamaican. She did all these without leaving the stage to change makeup or costumes.

Tonight I'm going to treat myself by clicking on YouTube and typing in, "Whoopi Goldberg: Direct from Broadway (1985)." If you like treating yourself, do likewise.

After the death of a friend, a writer recounts a boyhood journey to find a missing boy.

WIL WHEATON RIVER PHOENIX COREY FELDMAN JERRY O'CONNELL KIEFER SUTHERLAND

STAND BY ME

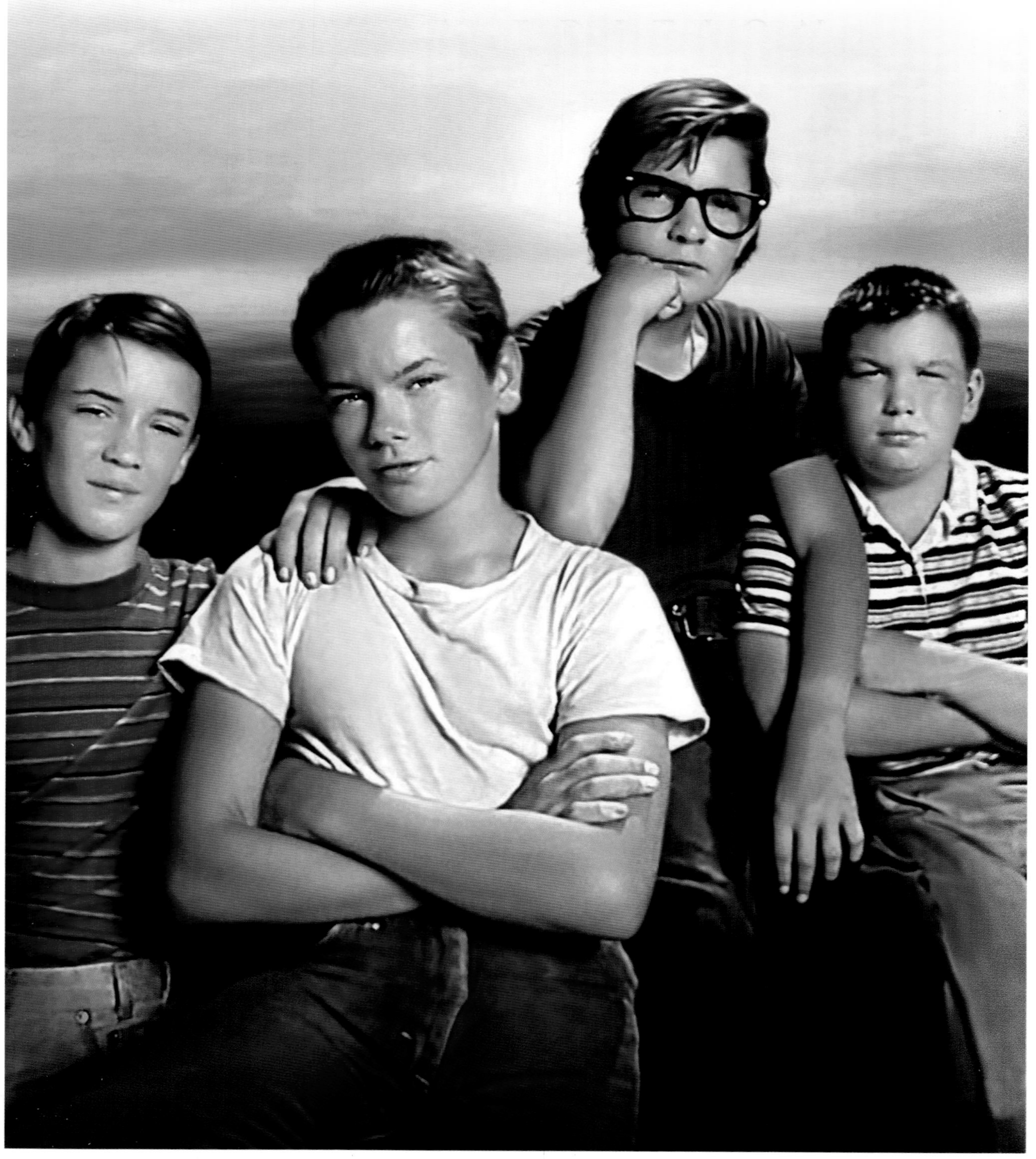

Sheila Benson of The Los Angeles Times wrote: "It stands, sweet and strong, ribald, outrageous and funny, gamy around the edges, but a treasure absolutely not to be missed."

Chris Nashawaty of Entertainment Weekly wrote: "Good luck choking back the tears, folks."

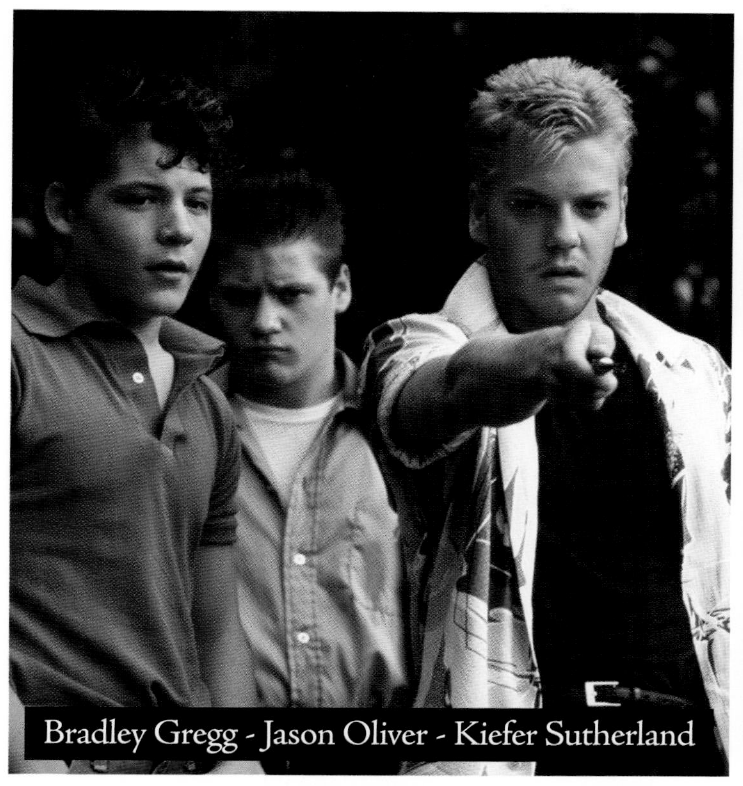

Bradley Gregg - Jason Oliver - Kiefer Sutherland

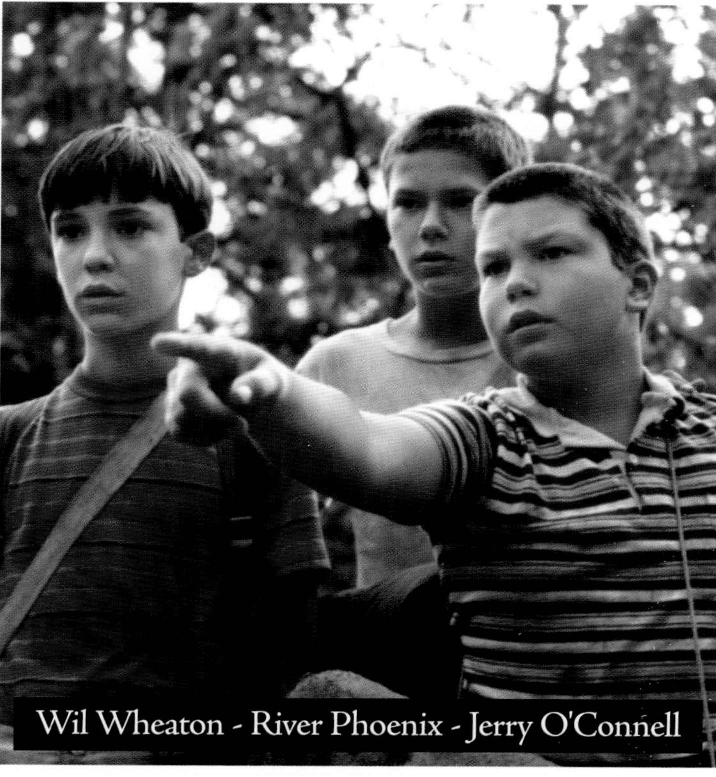

Wil Wheaton - River Phoenix - Jerry O'Connell

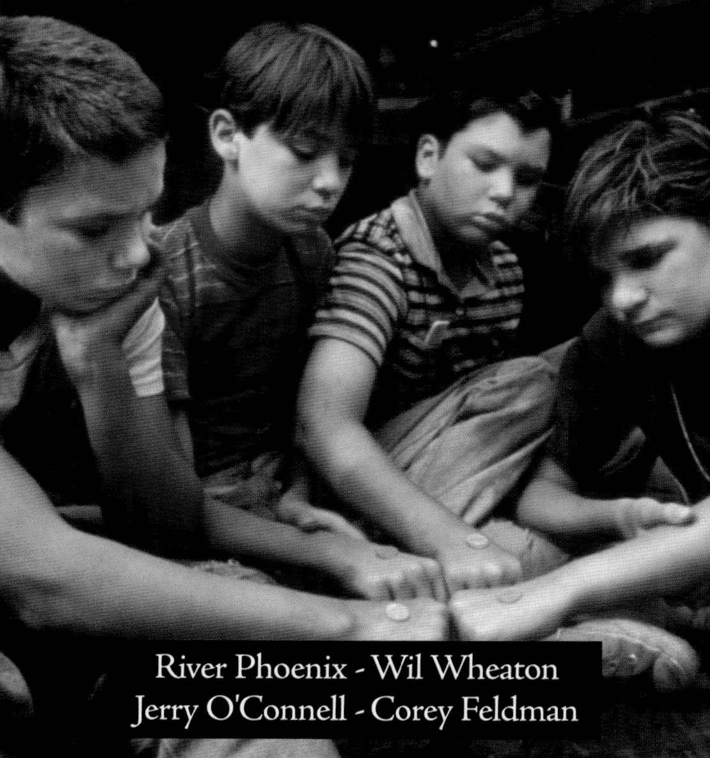

River Phoenix - Wil Wheaton
Jerry O'Connell - Corey Feldman

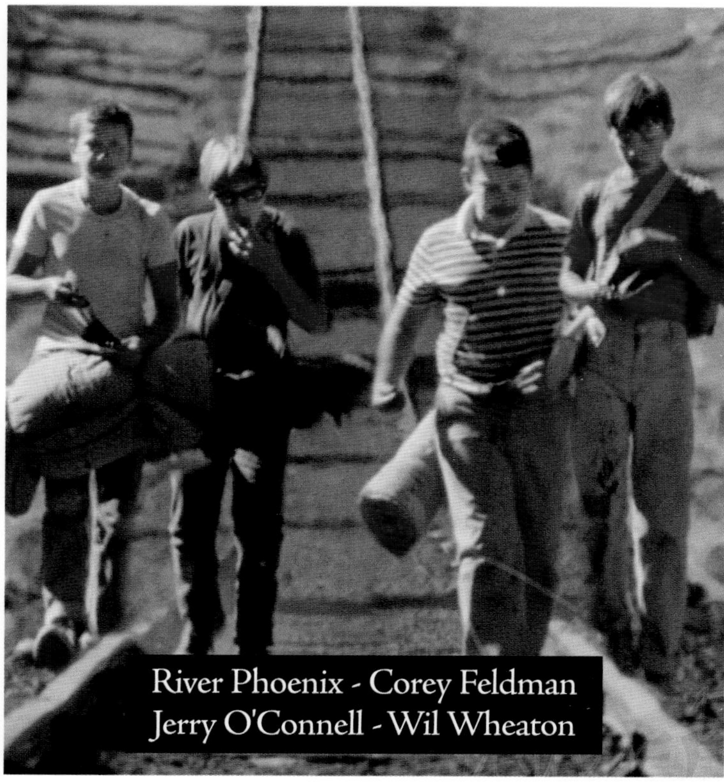

River Phoenix - Corey Feldman
Jerry O'Connell - Wil Wheaton

Only the hardest of hearts and the strongest of eyelids would be able to choke back the tears of this movie directed by the up-and-coming young filmmaker Rob Reiner.

Between two Thanksgivings two years apart, Hannah's husband falls in love with her sister Lee, while her hypochondriac ex-husband rekindles his relationship with her sister Holly.

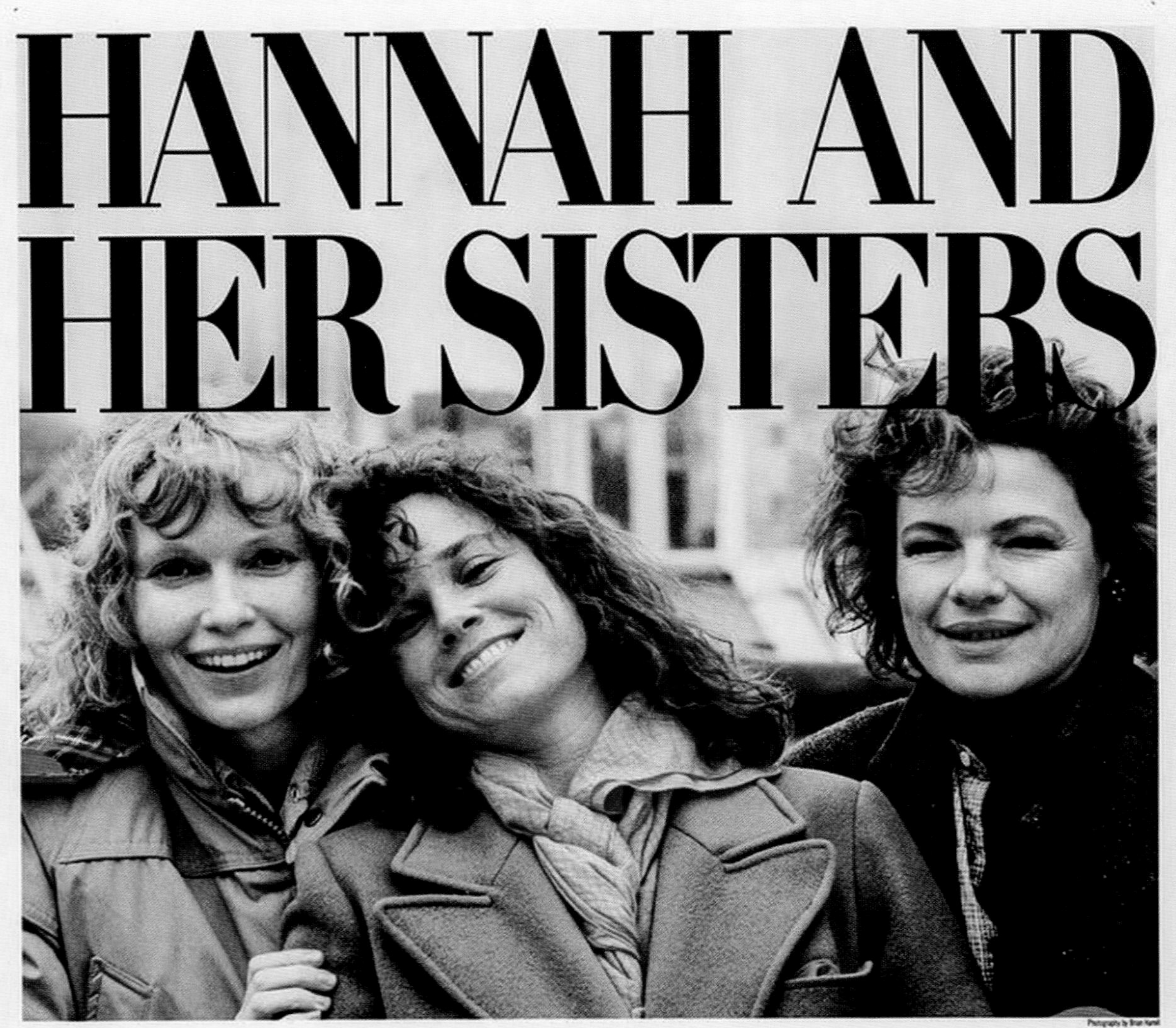

WOODY ALLEN MICHAEL CAINE
MIA FARROW CARRIE FISHER
BARBARA HERSHEY LLOYD NOLAN
MAUREEN O'SULLIVAN DANIEL STERN
MAX VON SYDOW DIANNE WIEST

A JACK ROLLINS and CHARLES H. JOFFE Production
Editor SUSAN E. MORSE A.C.E.
Director of Photography CARLO Di PALMA A.I.C.
Executive Producers JACK ROLLINS and CHARLES H. JOFFE
Produced by ROBERT GREENHUT
Written and Directed by WOODY ALLEN

PG-13 PARENTS STRONGLY CAUTIONED
An ORION PICTURES Release
Color by DeLuxe®

Roger Ebert of The Chicago Sun-Times wrote: "Woody Allen's 'Hannah and Her Sisters,' the best movie he has ever made, is organized like an episodic novel, with acute little self-contained vignettes adding up to the big picture. Perfection is boring, but boring is the very last word to describe 'Hannah and Her Sisters,' which just may be a perfect movie."

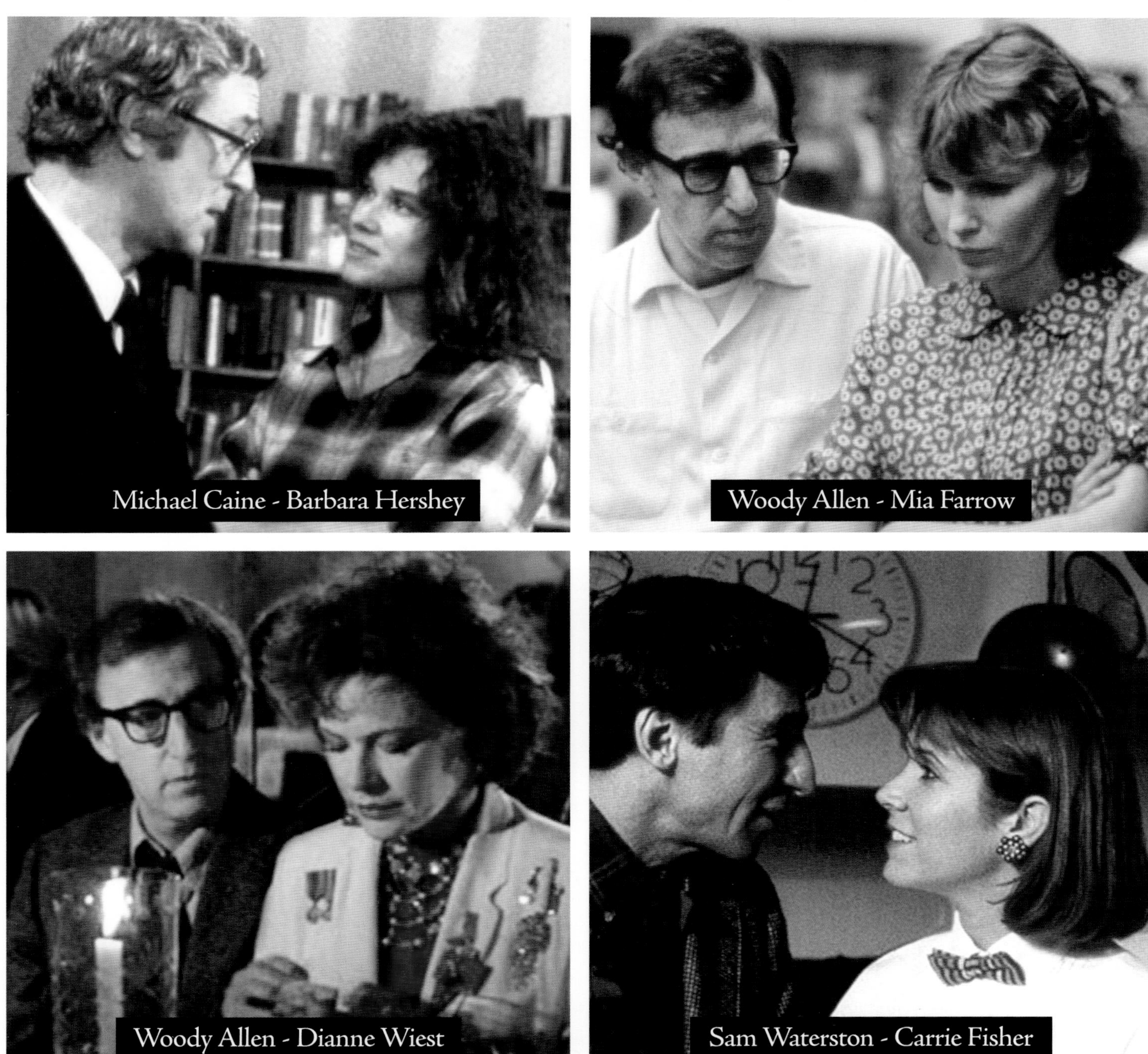

Michael Caine - Barbara Hershey

Woody Allen - Mia Farrow

Woody Allen - Dianne Wiest

Sam Waterston - Carrie Fisher

The fact that he created thirty-seven brilliant plays makes us look upon William Shakespeare as a true genius. I contend that because Woody Allen has written forty-eight highly entertaining films, the word genius also applies to him.

So that Woody knows how I feel about his work, I'm planning to send him an autographed copy of this entertaining book.

Three actors accept an invitation to a Mexican village to perform their onscreen bandit fighter roles, unaware that it is the real thing.

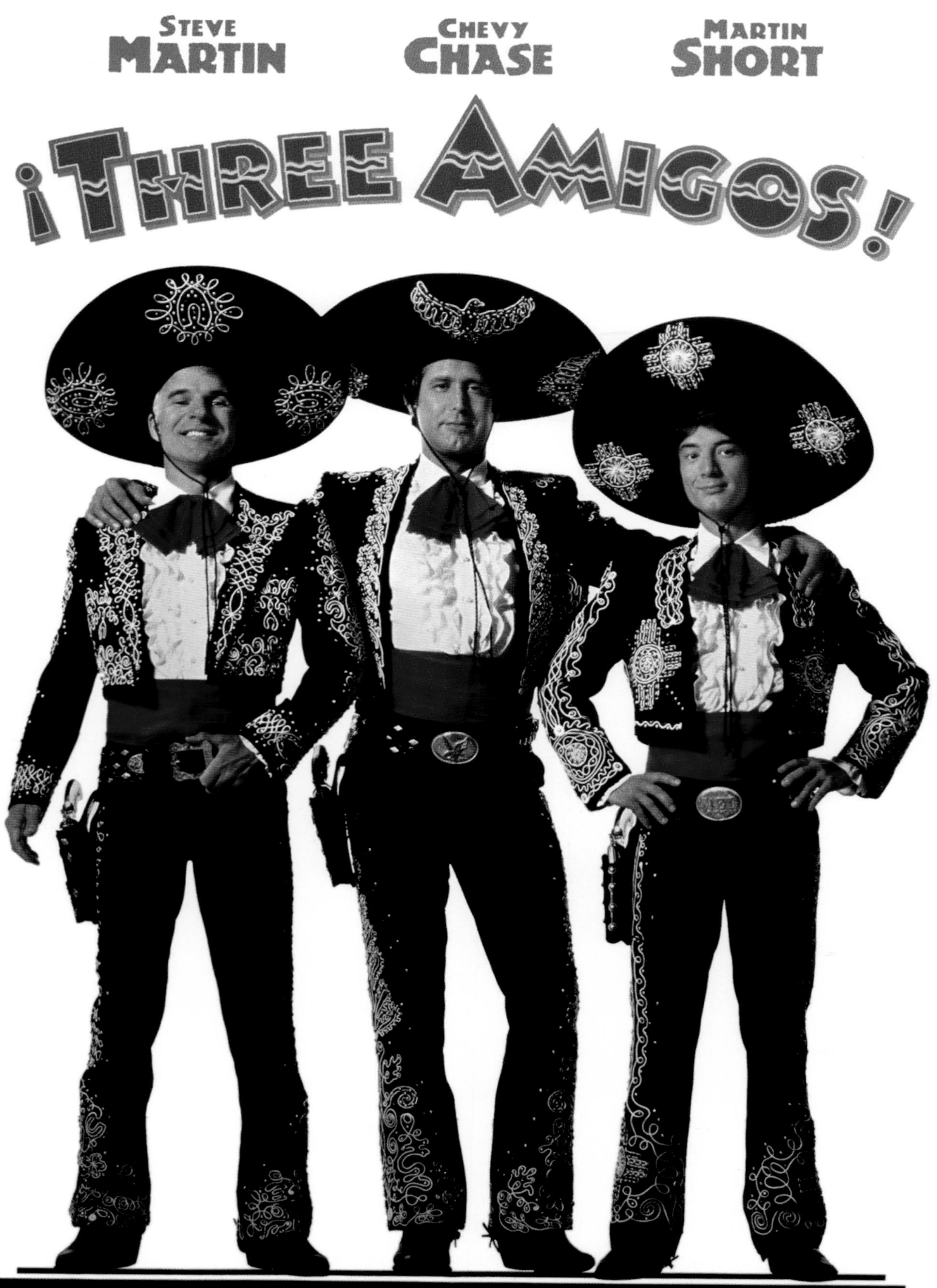

Patrick Goldstein of The Los Angeles Times wrote: "'Three Amigos' is a goofy delight. It's like a cross between a big-budget 'Three Stooges' movie and a Hope-Crosby road picture, with dozens of old cowpoke gags thrown in to spice up the brew."

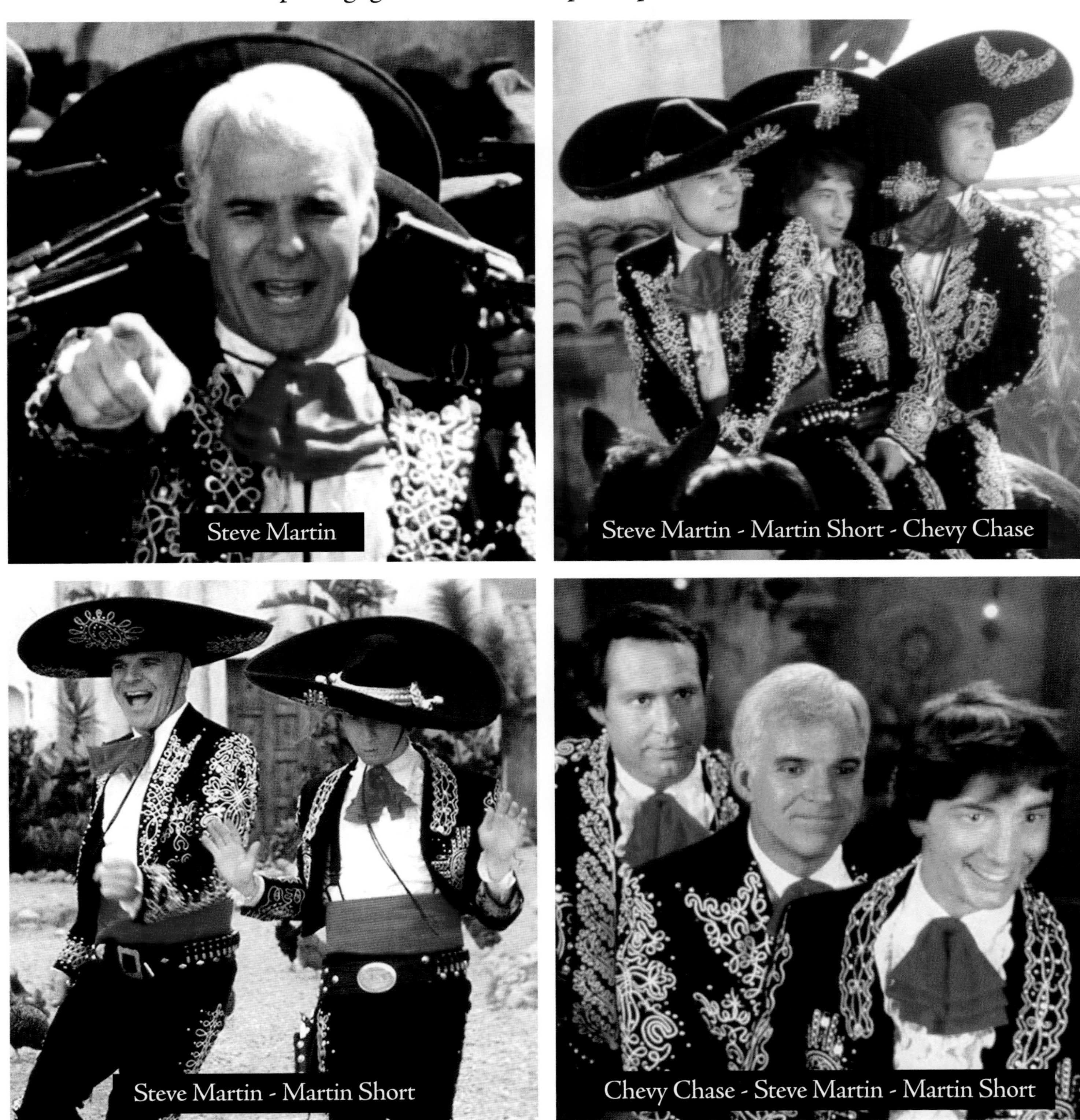

Steve Martin

Steve Martin - Martin Short - Chevy Chase

Steve Martin - Martin Short

Chevy Chase - Steve Martin - Martin Short

What I enjoyed most about this movie was imagining the fun these three talented comedians were having. I'm sure between scenes Marty Short, who is a one man Ringling Brothers Circus, took on the guise of the rotund TV host, Jiminy Glick, and had the cast and crew roaring.

A high-school gym teacher has big plans for the summer, but is forced to cancel them to teach a "bonehead" English class for misfit goof-off students. Fortunately, his unconventional brand of teaching through fun field trips begins to connect with them, and even inspires ardor in some.

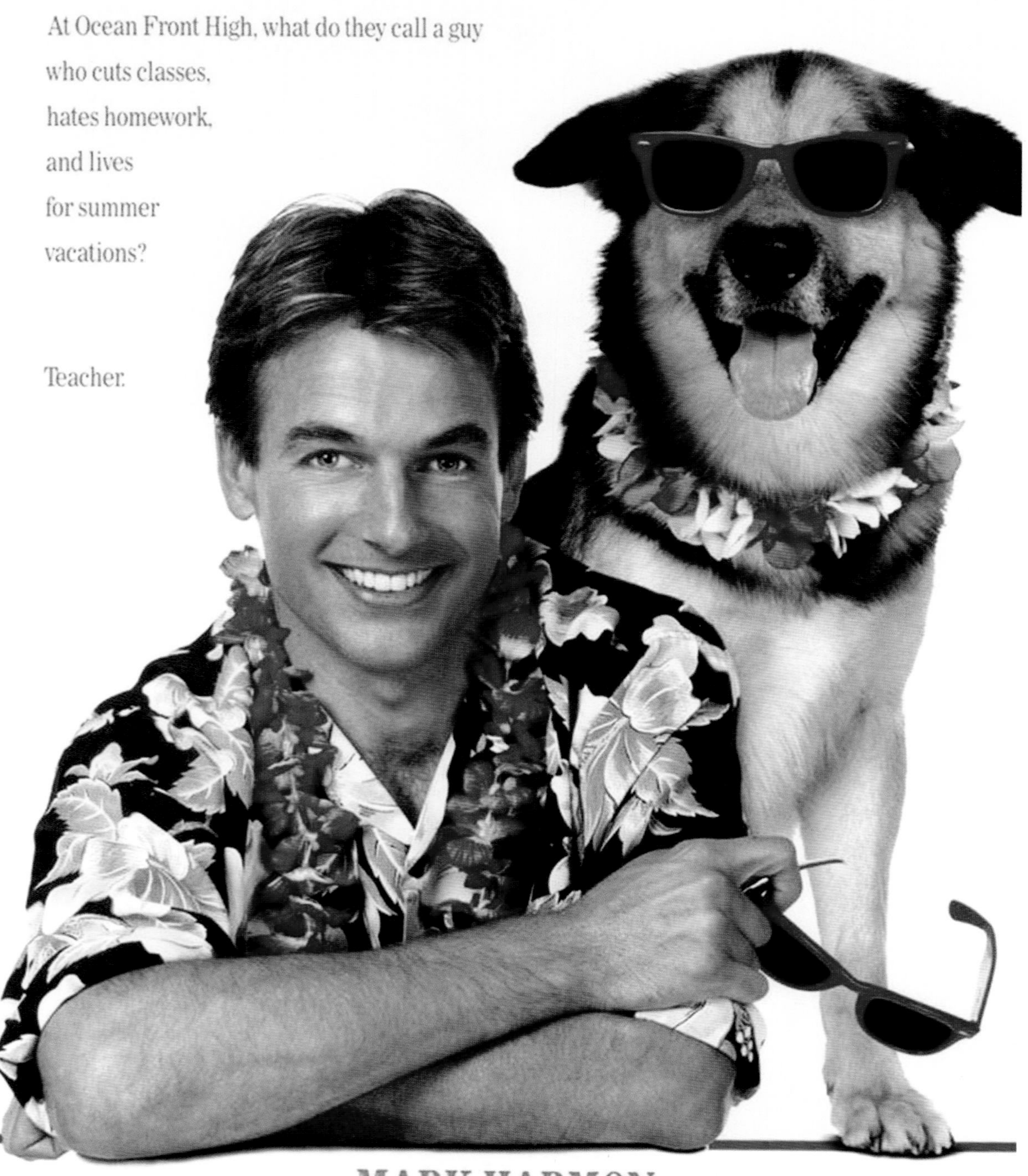

Brian Orndorf, a most perceptive critic, wrote: "'Summer School' might lack a hipster razor edge, but its funny bone personality is larger than life. It's a film I adore for its purity of intentions."

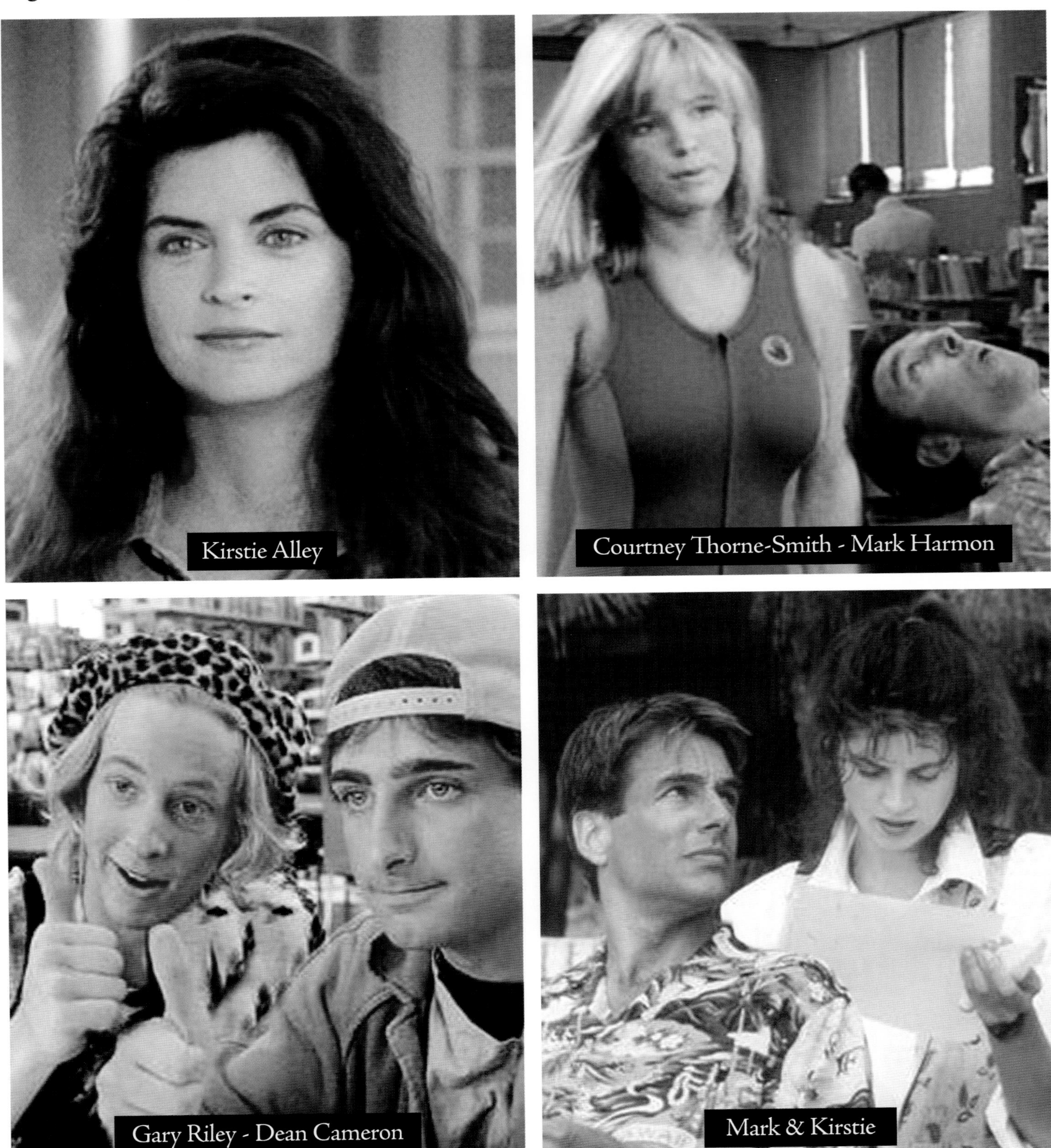

Kirstie Alley

Courtney Thorne-Smith - Mark Harmon

Gary Riley - Dean Cameron

Mark & Kirstie

And it's a film I loved directing because of the fun-loving cast that included the beautiful Kirstie Alley and handsome Mark Harmon, one of the most genuine human beings in our business.

While home sick in bed, a young boy's grandfather, Peter Falk, reads him a story called "The Princess Bride," which concerns a farmhand named Westley, who rescues his true love Princess Buttercup from the odious Prince Humperdinck.

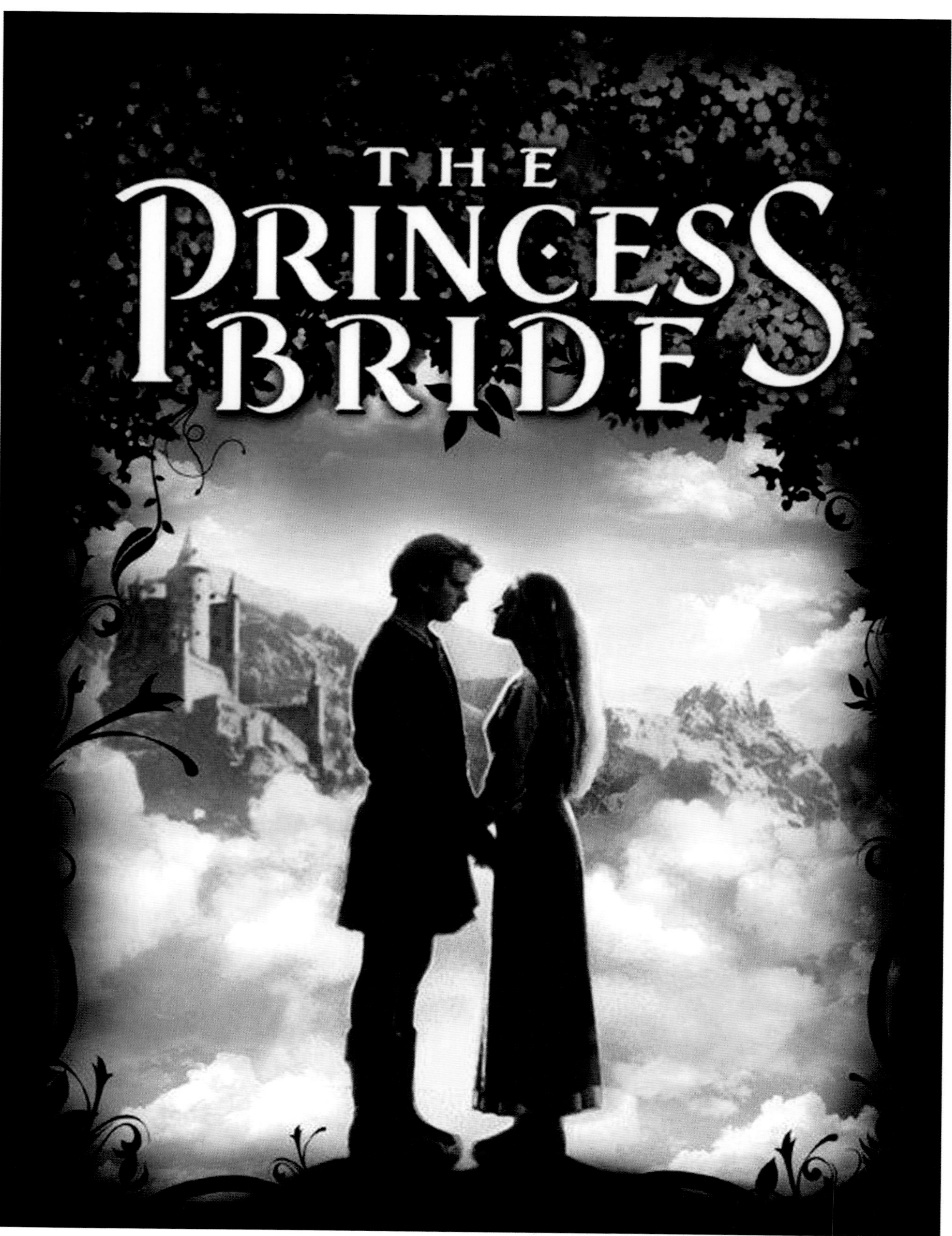

David Nusair of Reel Film Reviews wrote: "It is not difficult to see why 'The Princess Bride' has become a classic in the years since its release," and I, Carl Reiner, give thanks to William Goldman for writing a screenplay that has these wonderful quotable lines.

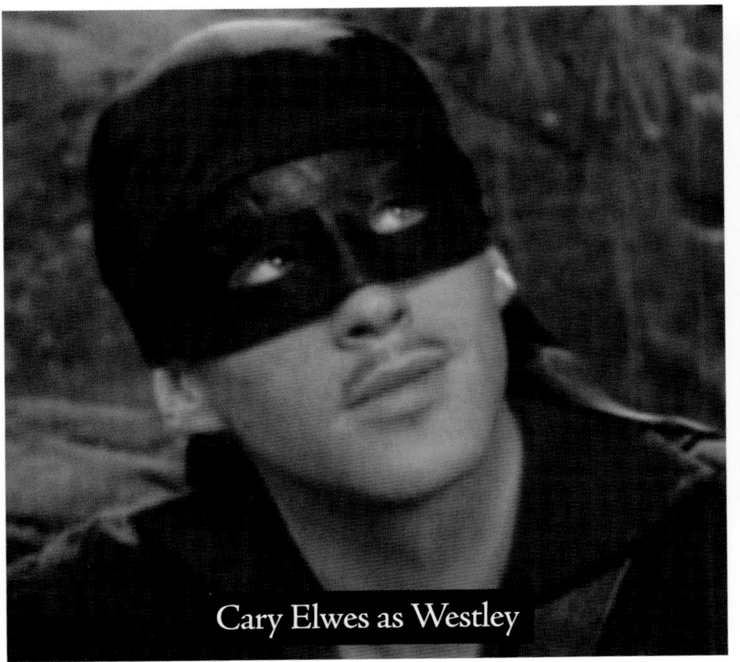

Cary Elwes as Westley

"As you wish."

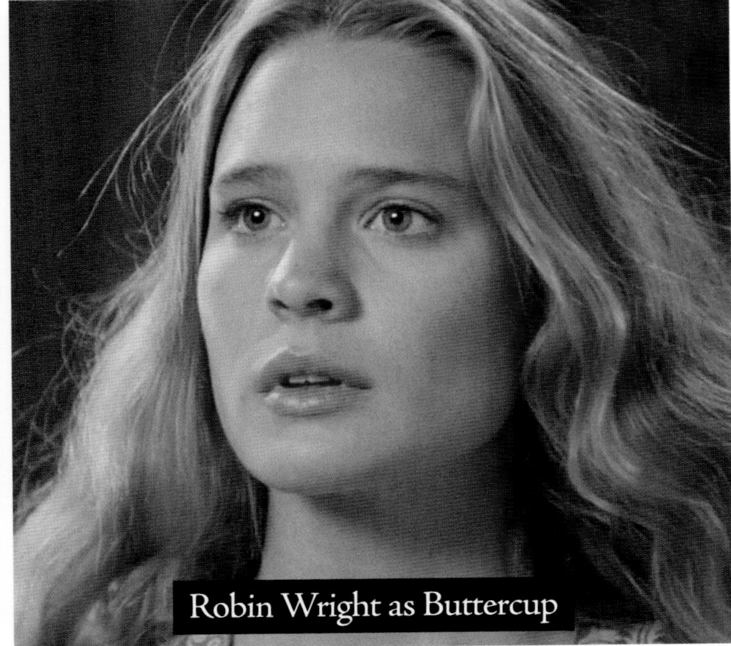

Robin Wright as Buttercup

"You mock my pain?"

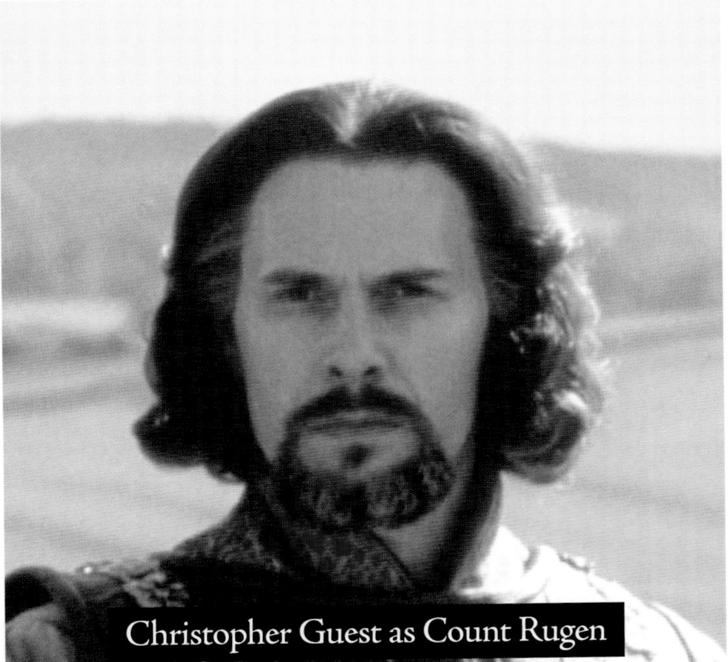

Christopher Guest as Count Rugen

"Your princess is quite a winning creature... her appeal is undeniable."

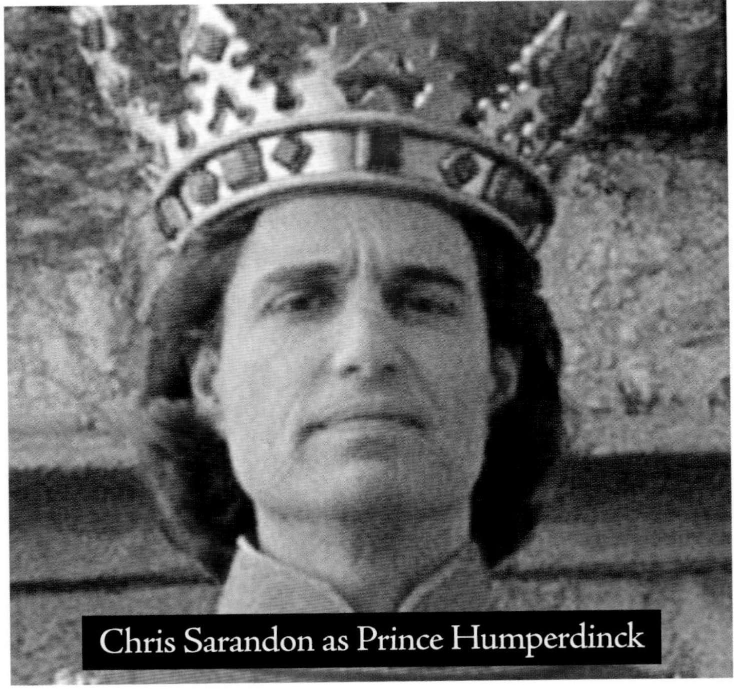

Chris Sarandon as Prince Humperdinck

"That may be the first time in my life a man has dared insult me."

Not because this is one of my all-time favorite movies or because my son directed it, but for my, and I hope, your viewing pleasure, I have added two more pages of photos and quotes.

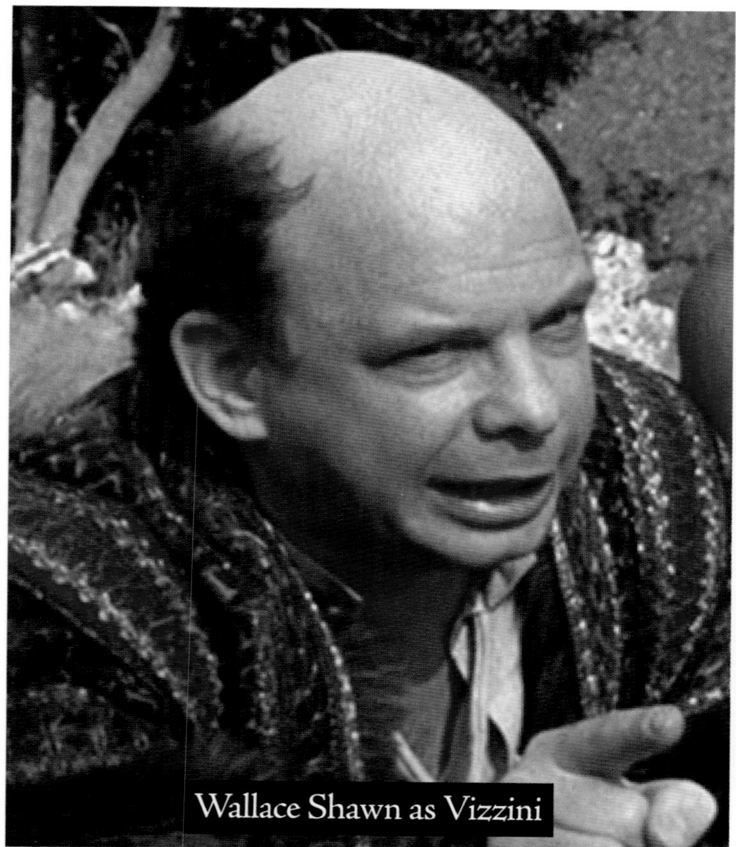
Wallace Shawn as Vizzini

"Inconceivable!"

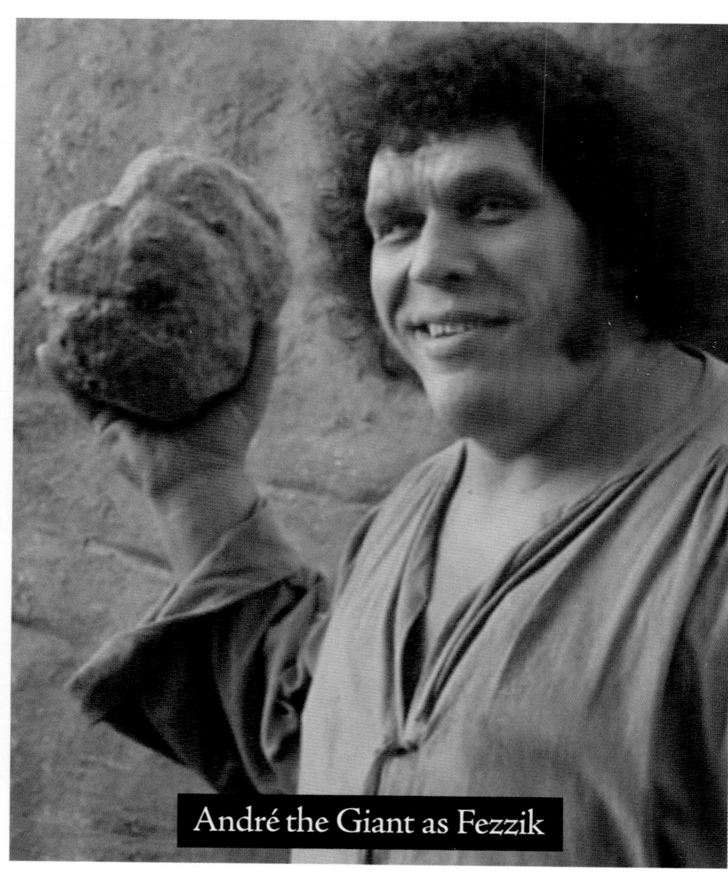
André the Giant as Fezzik

"It's not my fault I'm the biggest & the strongest."

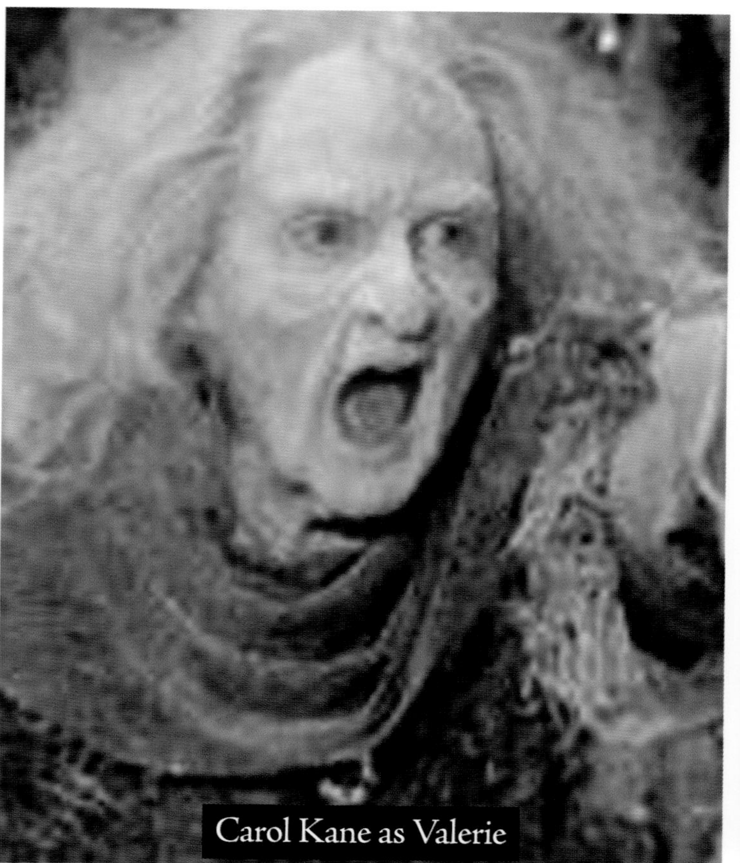
Carol Kane as Valerie

"I'm not a witch, I'm your wife."

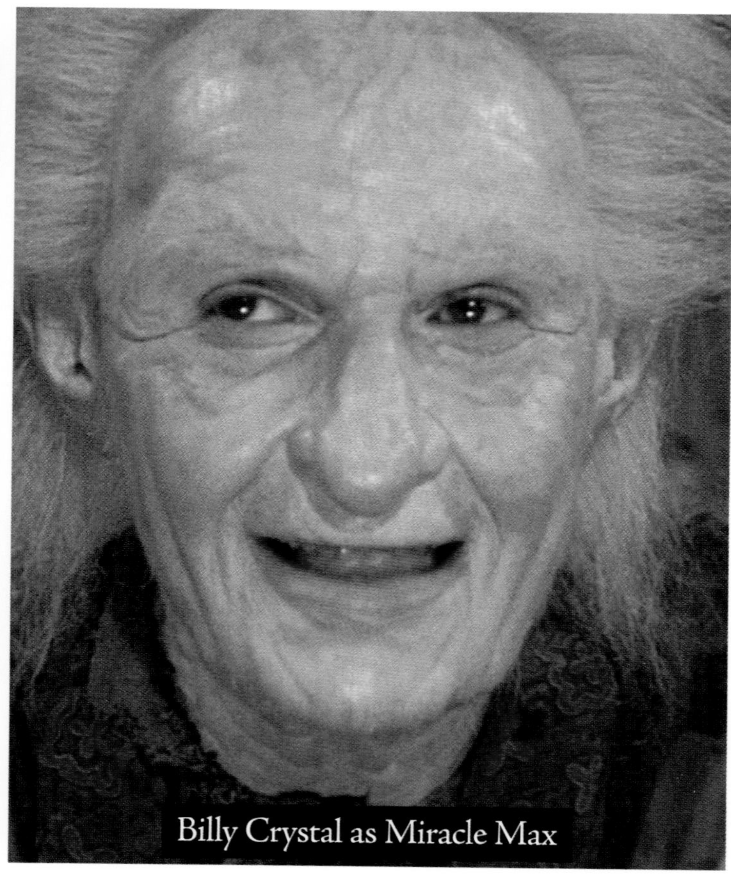
Billy Crystal as Miracle Max

"Good luck storming the castle."

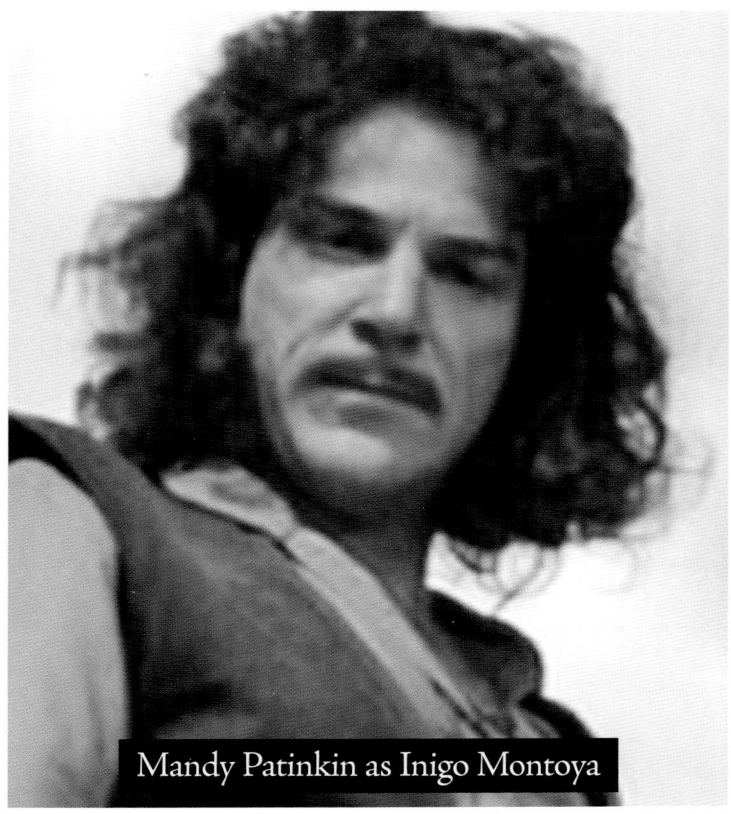
Mandy Patinkin as Inigo Montoya

"Hello. My name is Inigo Montoya. You killed my father. Prepare to die."

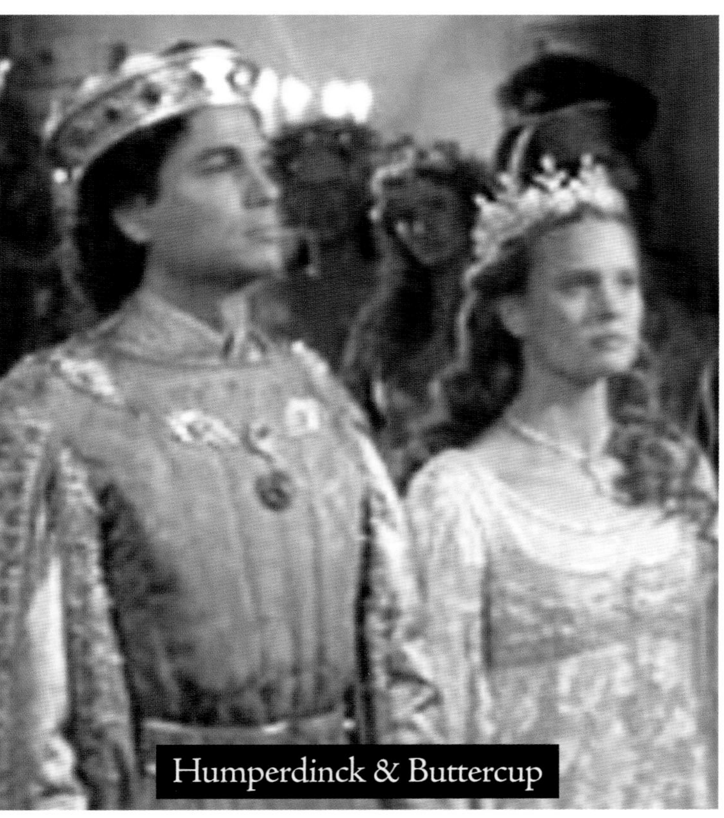
Humperdinck & Buttercup

(Eager to be a groom and equally eager not to be a bride)

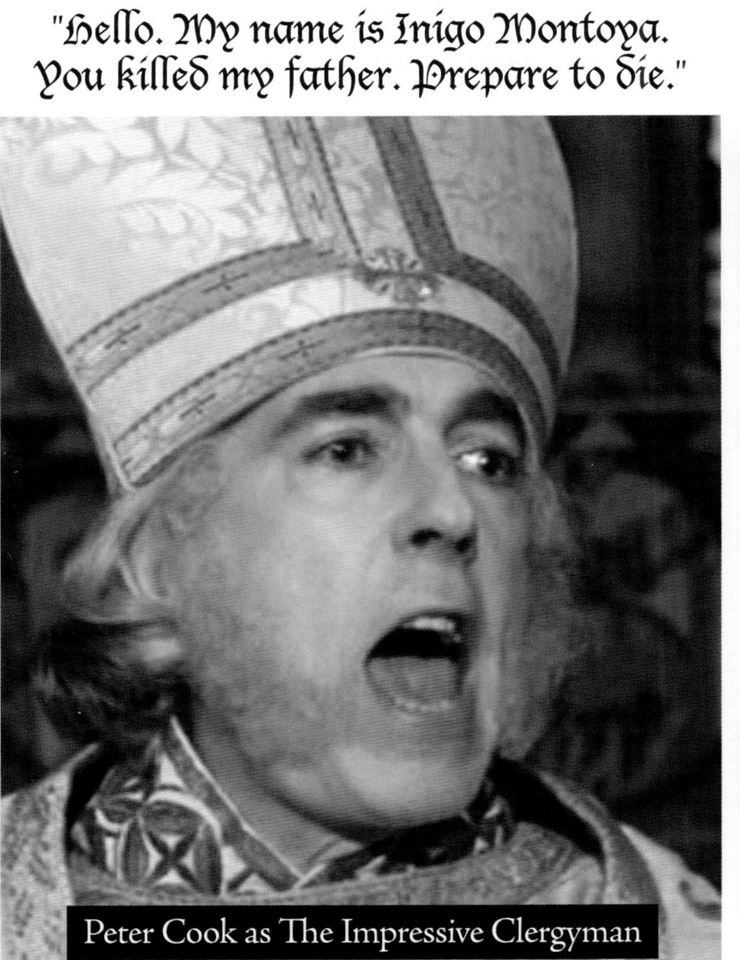
Peter Cook as The Impressive Clergyman

"Mawage, that bwessed awangment."

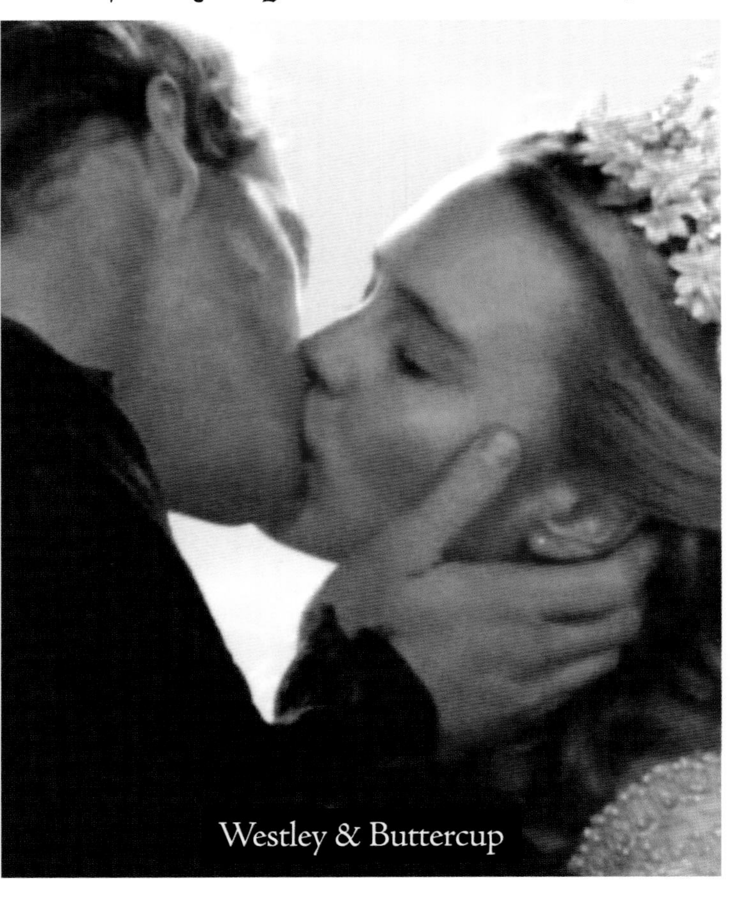
Westley & Buttercup

The kiss heard 'Round the kingdom

The large-nosed C.D. Bales is in love with the beautiful Roxanne; she falls for his personality but another man's looks.

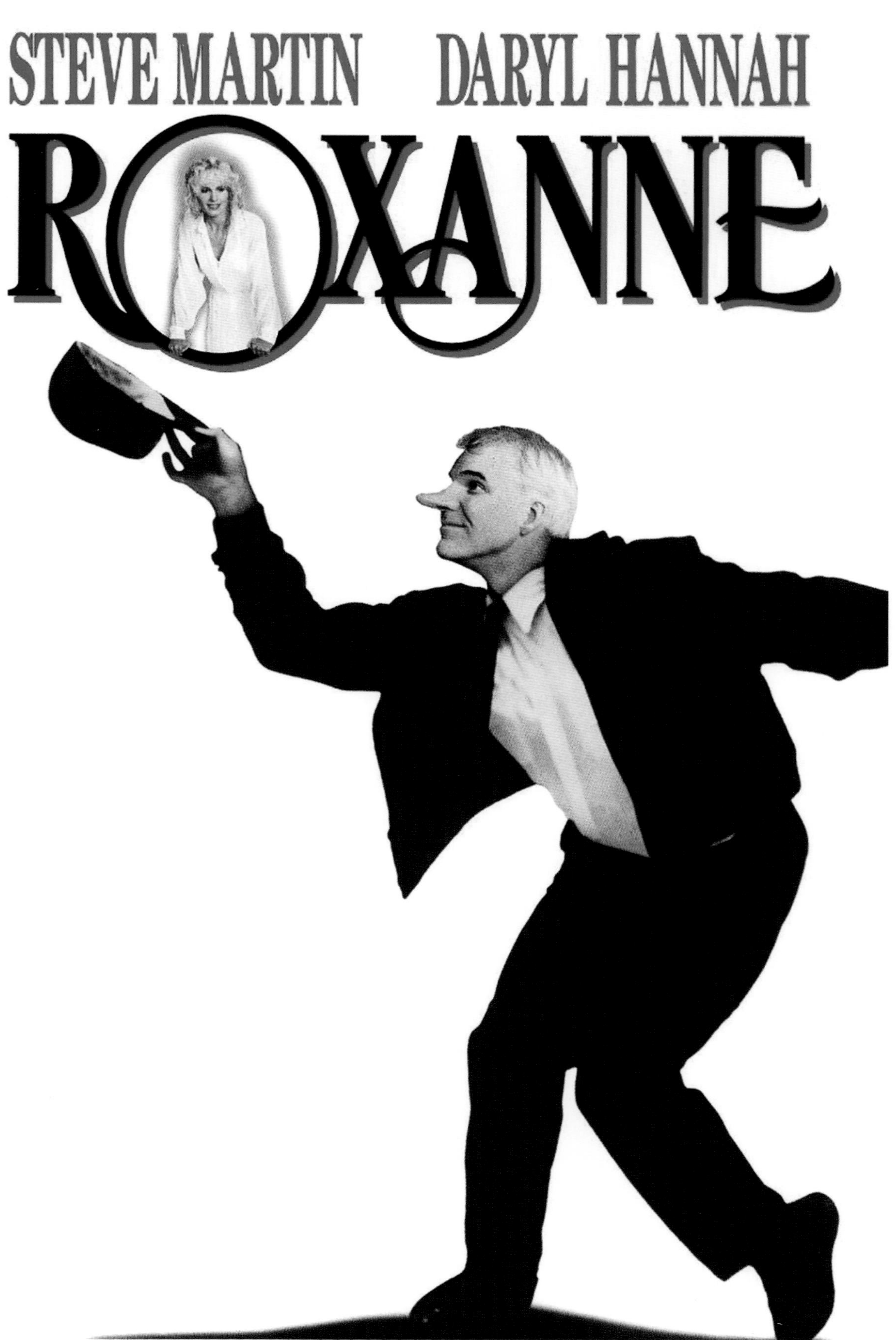

Janet Maslin of The New York Times wrote: "The nose itself is a perfect prop for a man who began his career with a fake arrow through his head, a man who has since evolved from a coolly absurdist stand-up comic to a fully formed, amazingly nimble comic actor."

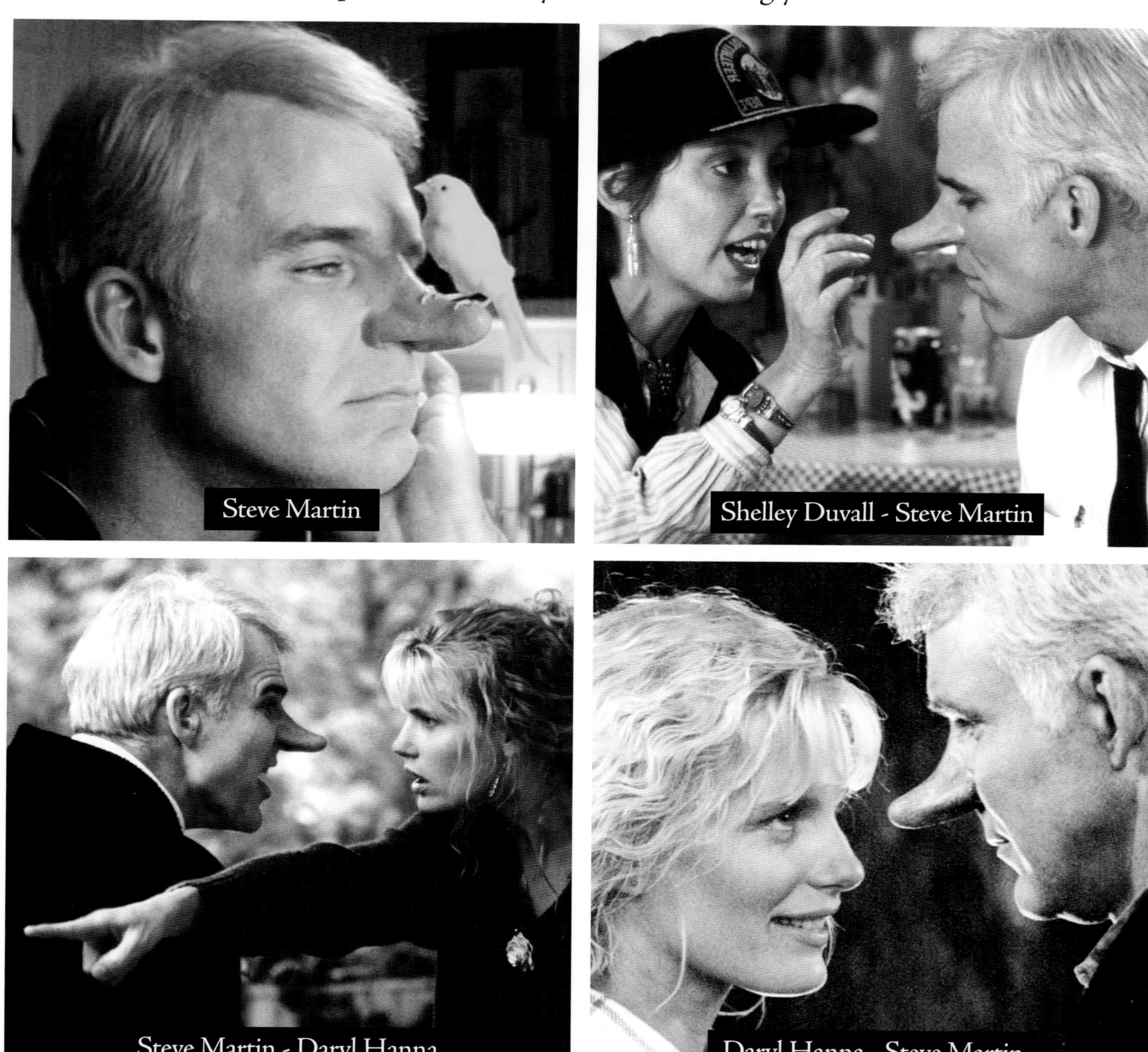

Steve Martin

Shelley Duvall - Steve Martin

Steve Martin - Daryl Hanna

Daryl Hanna - Steve Martin

I wholeheartedly agree with Janet Maslin, but the witty line that Steve delivers as Cyrano, "It is not the size of your nose that counts, it's what's in it," was not written by Cyrano's author, Edmond Alexis Rostand, but ad-libbed by my wife, Estelle Reiner, when in a discussion about the efficacy of rhinoplasty.

A few years later, Steve phoned Estelle and asked her permission to use that line, which, of course, she was thrilled to give.

Loretta Castorini, a bookkeeper from Brooklyn, New York, finds herself in a difficult situation when she falls for the brother of the man she has agreed to marry.

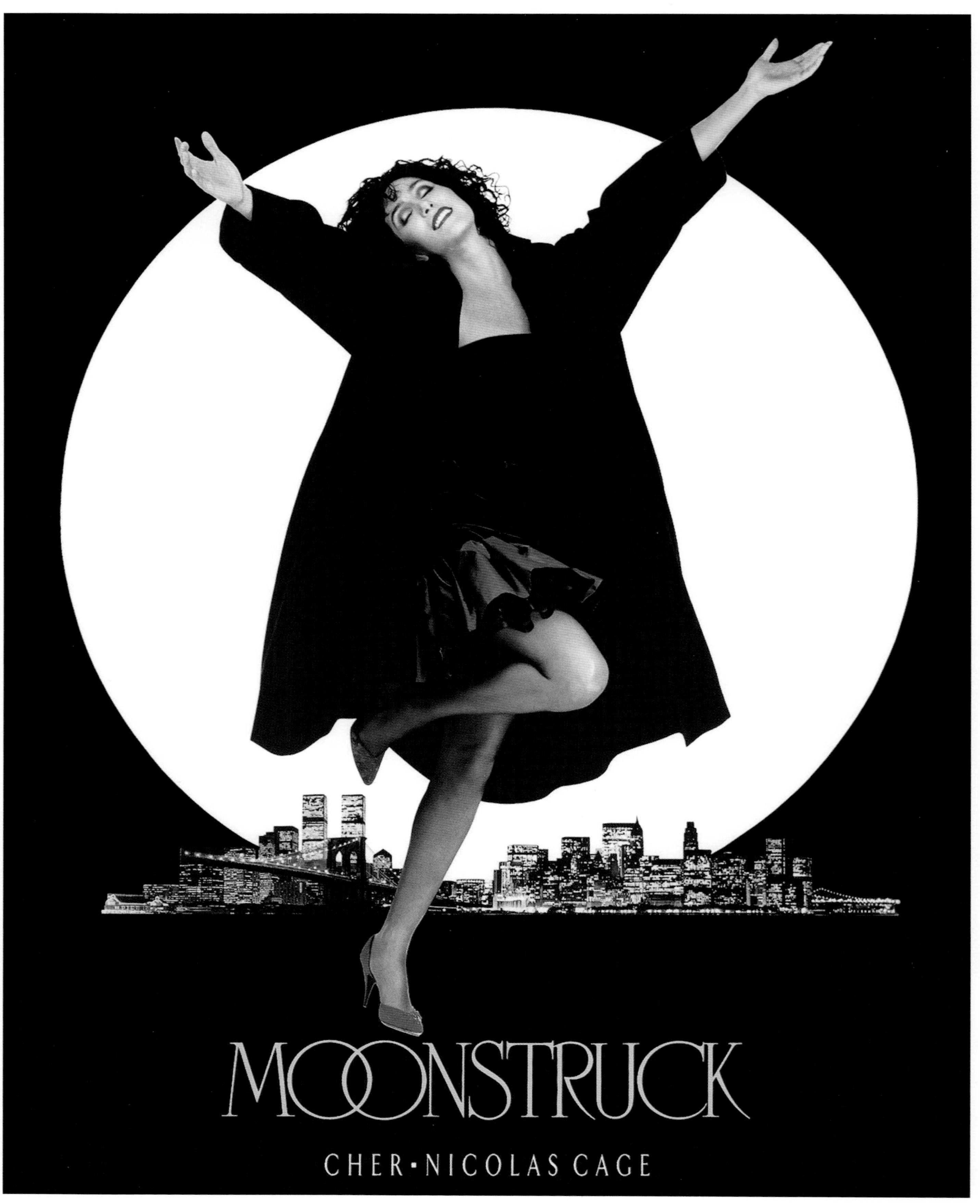

Chris Chase of Daily News wrote: "This film makes you want to sing 'Boheme,' walk in the moonlight and move to Brooklyn."

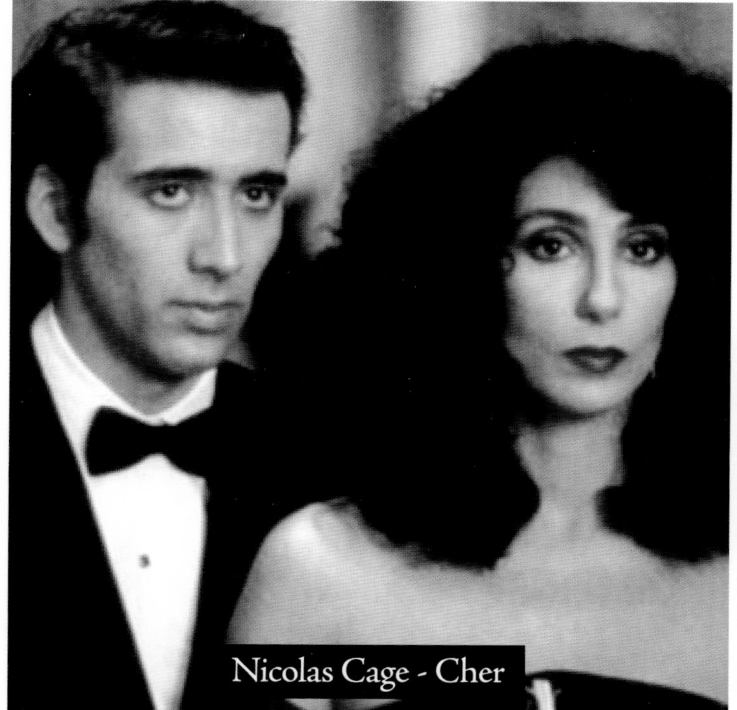
Nicolas Cage - Cher

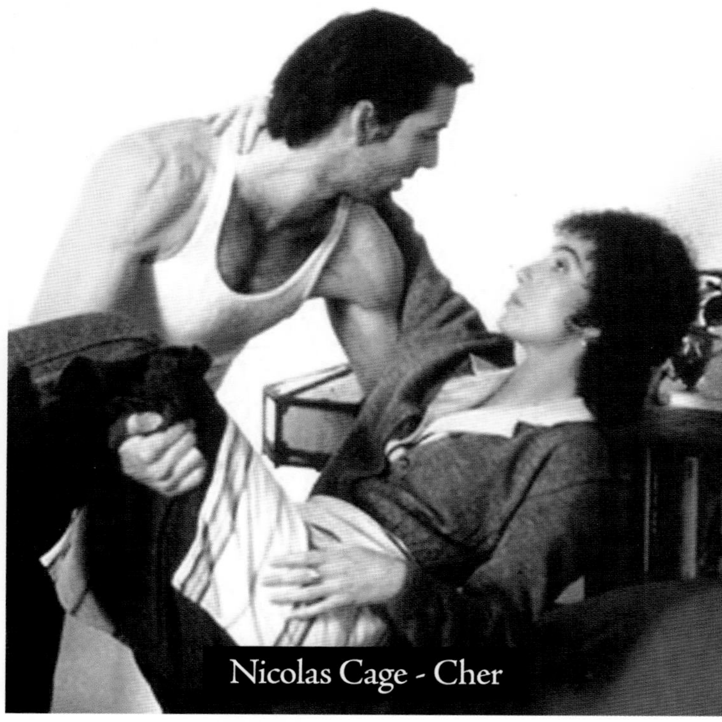
Nicolas Cage - Cher

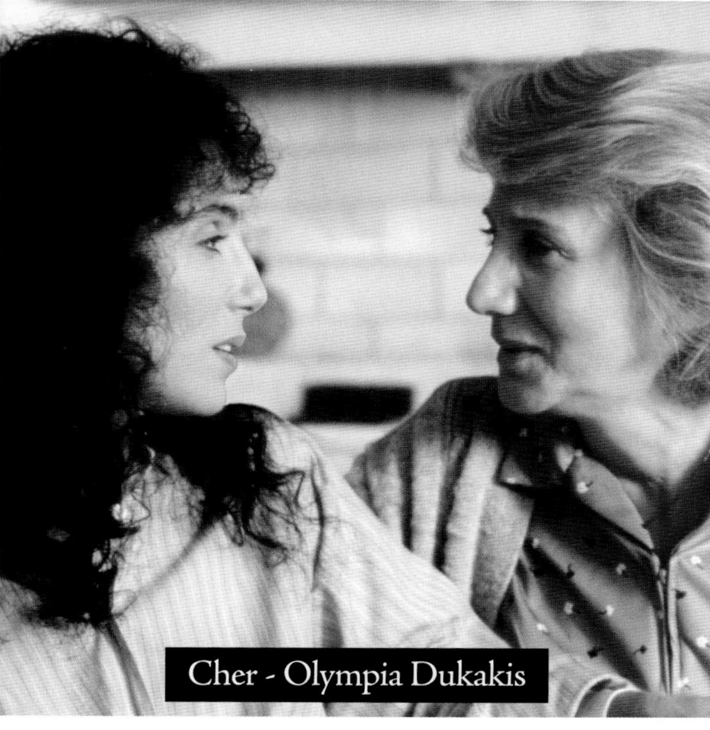
Cher - Olympia Dukakis

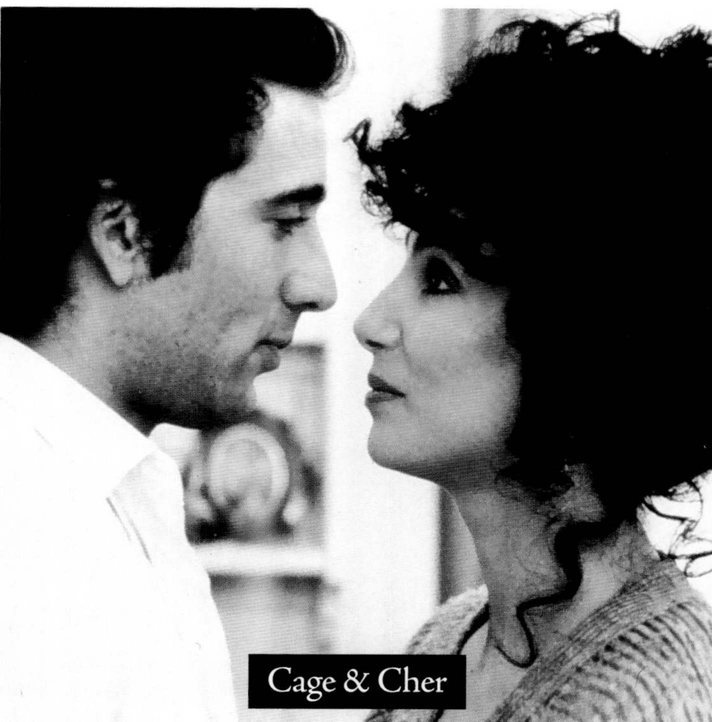
Cage & Cher

After a successful television career partnering with her husband, Sonny Bono, Cher embarked on a successful film career. In her sixth movie, "Moonstruck," for which she won an Oscar, she had this memorable exchange:

Nicolas Cage: "I'm in love with you."

Cher: (slaps him and shouts) "Snap out of it!"

A Manhattan single meets a man through her Jewish grandmother's matchmaker.

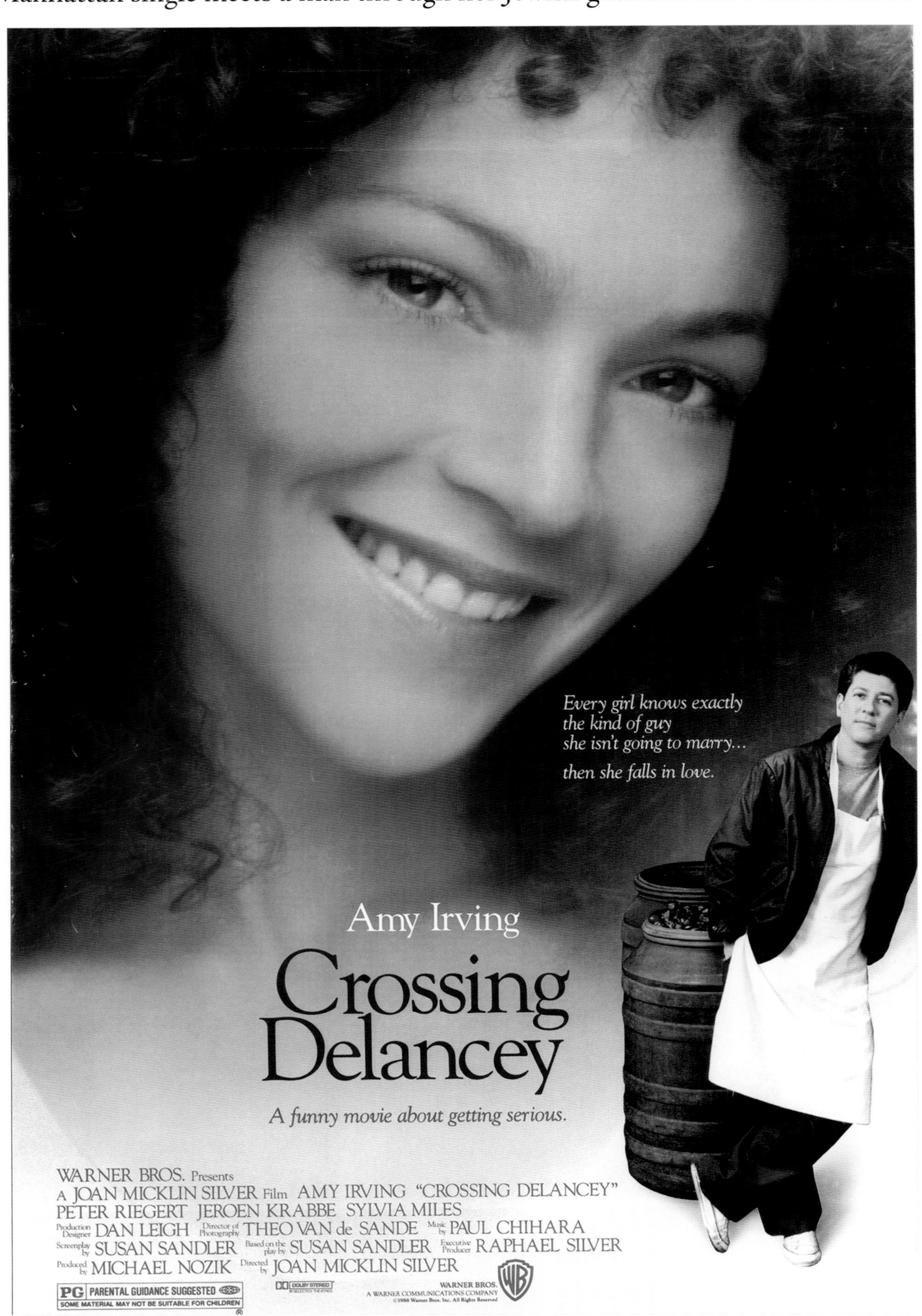

David Nusair of Reel Film Reviews wrote: "An affable, thoroughly charming little romance that benefits substantially from Amy Irving's compelling performance."

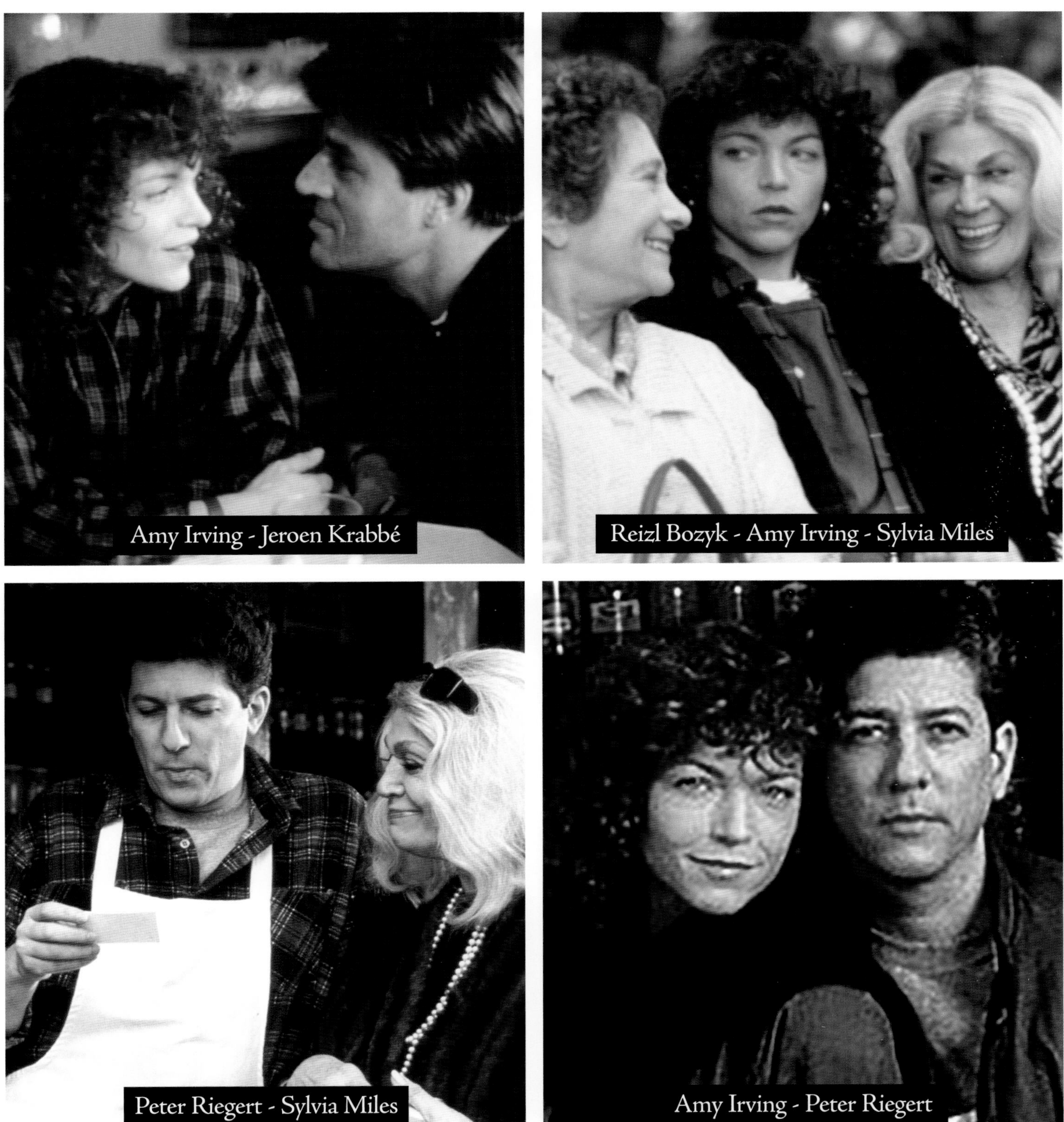

Amy Irving - Jeroen Krabbé

Reizl Bozyk - Amy Irving - Sylvia Miles

Peter Riegert - Sylvia Miles

Amy Irving - Peter Riegert

Had it not been for my daughter, Annie, my son Lucas and my daughter-in-law, Maud, I'd have missed enjoying this lovely romance between a beautiful bookstore clerk (Amy Irving) and a lower east side dill pickle maker (Peter Riegert). Check it out if you don't mind happy endings.

When a secretary's idea is stolen by her boss, she seizes an opportunity to steal it back by pretending she has her boss' job.

WORKING GIRL

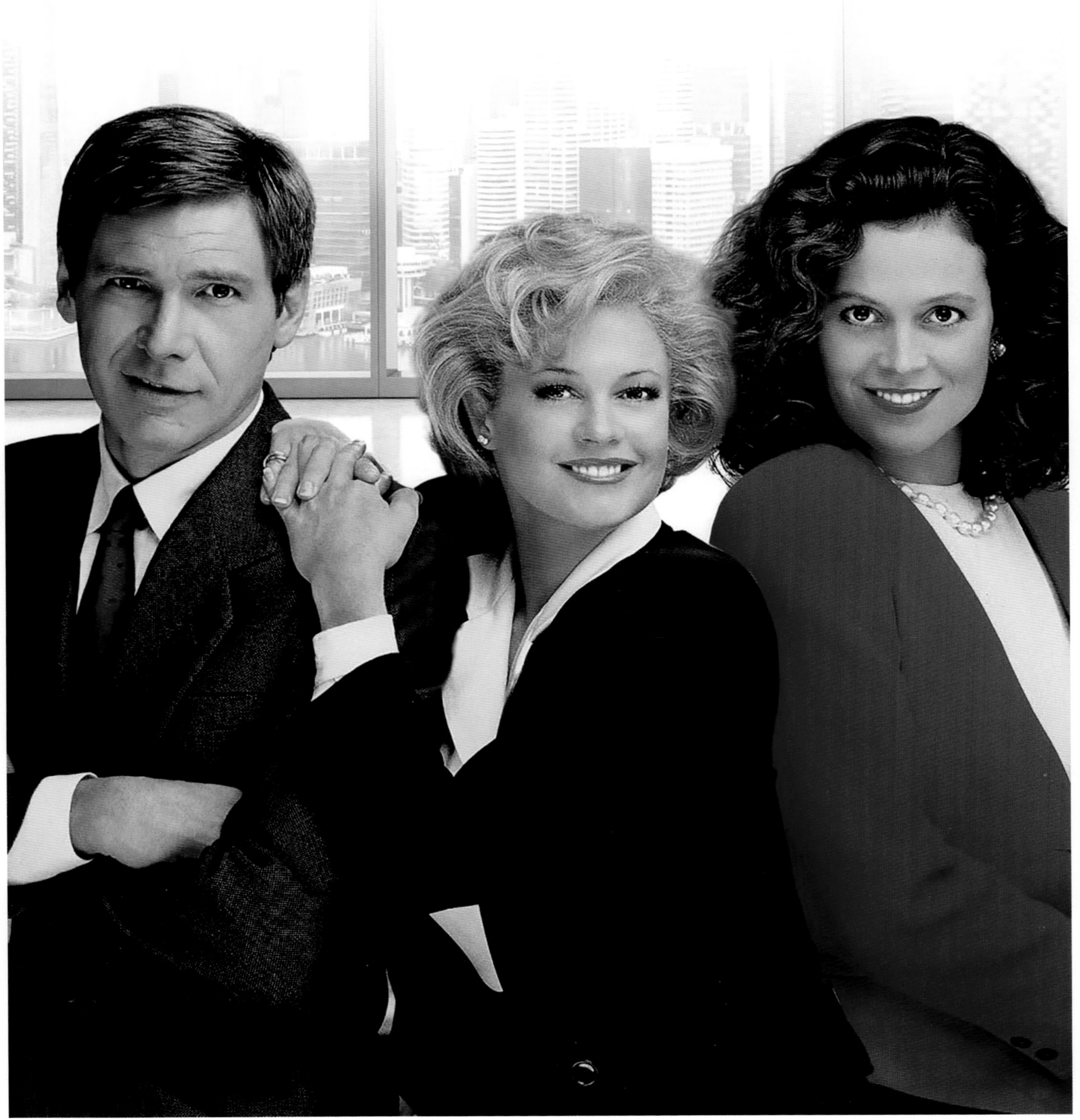

Variety wrote: "'Working Girl' is enjoyable largely due to the fun of watching scrappy, sexy, unpredictable Melanie Griffith rise from Staten Island secretary to Wall Street whiz."

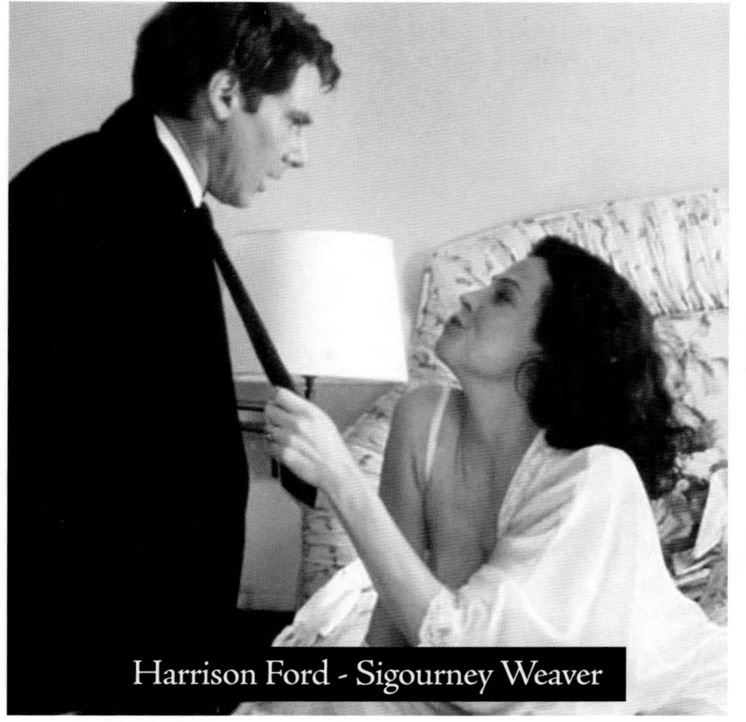
Harrison Ford - Sigourney Weaver

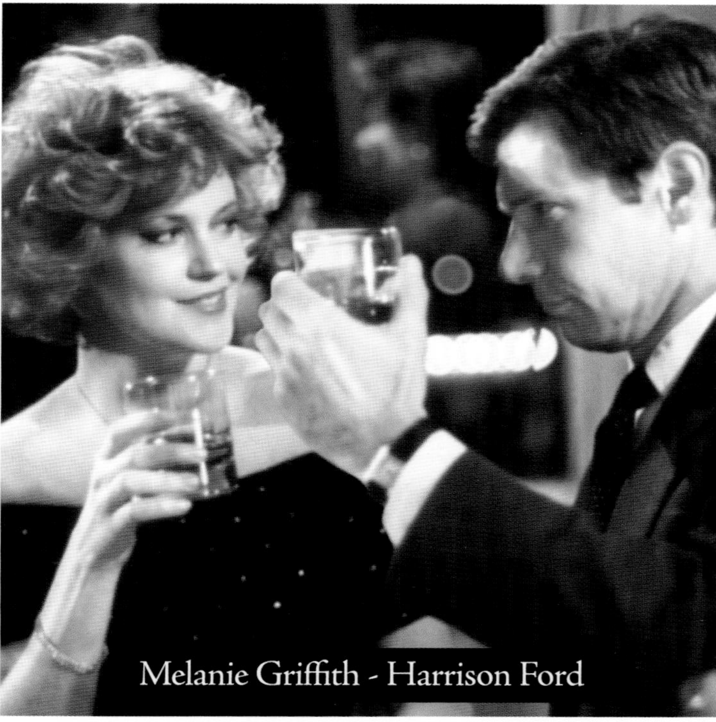
Melanie Griffith - Harrison Ford

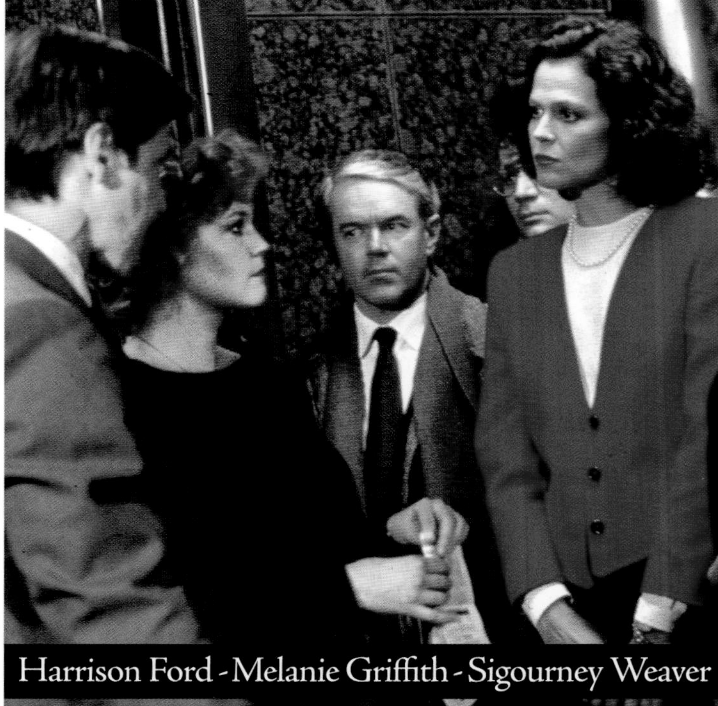
Harrison Ford - Melanie Griffith - Sigourney Weaver

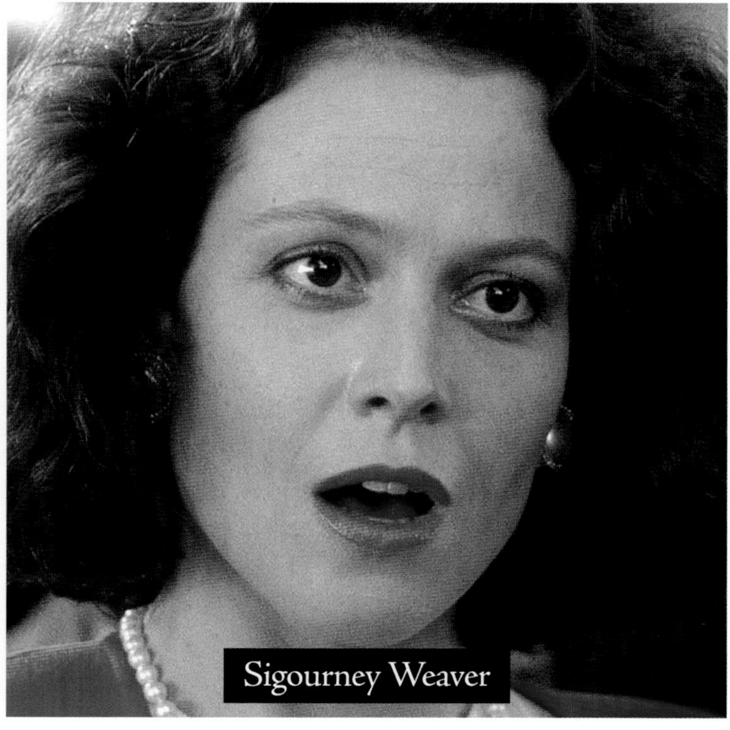
Sigourney Weaver

I so enjoy comeuppance films such as "The Count of Monte Cristo," "The Princess Bride," "The Net," "The Adventures of Robin Hood" and this latest, "Working Girl."

I was so pleased when, at the end of the film, the self-centered executive, Sigourney Weaver, who has been mean to her underlings, asks Harrison Ford, "Jack, help me out here..." and silently he just stares at her and watches her crumble.

Two con men try to settle their rivalry by betting on who can swindle a young American heiress out of $50,000 first.

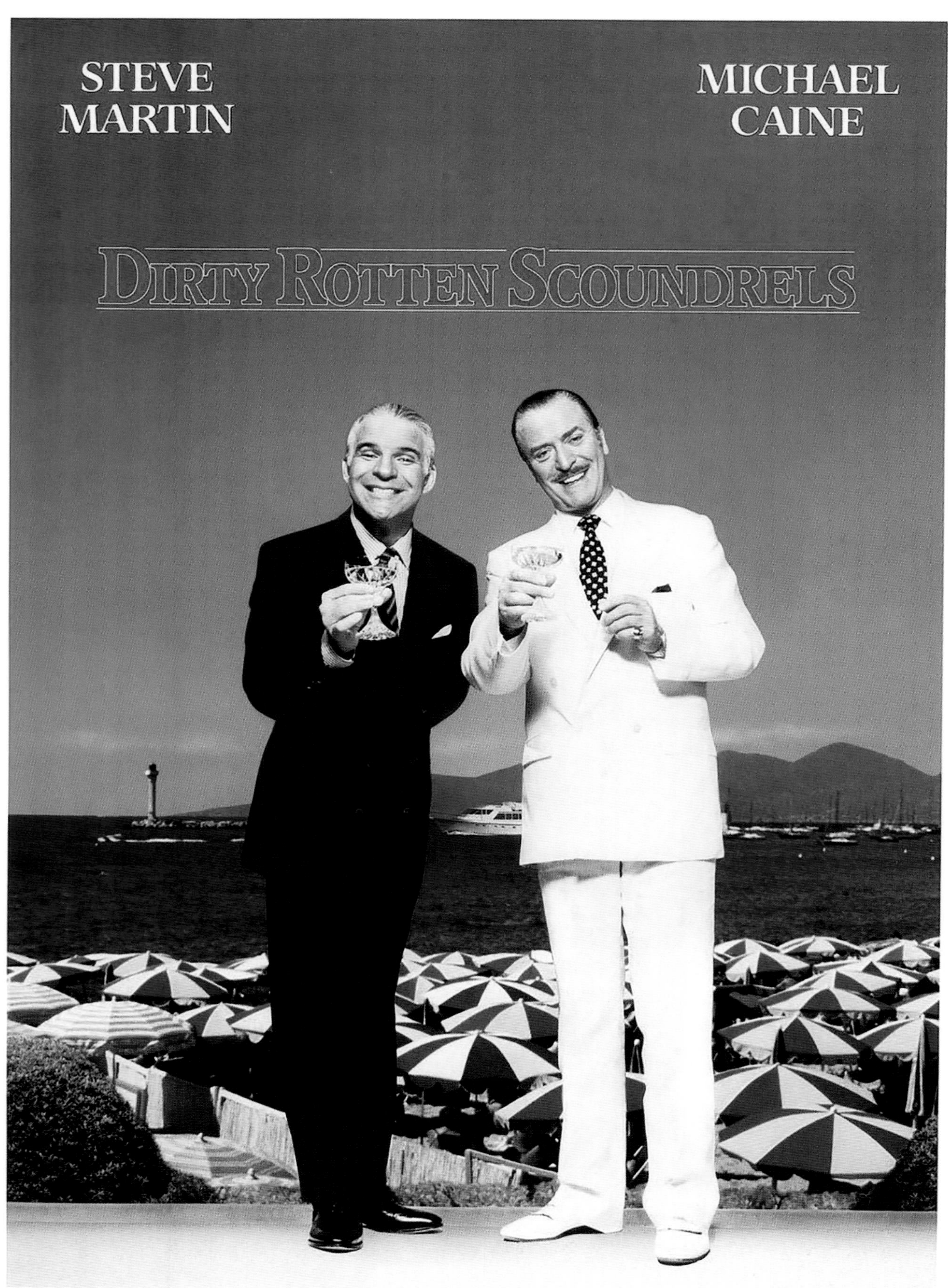

Hal Hinson of Washington Post wrote: "Martin, the most eloquent of physical clowns–the Baryshnikov of comedy–is at his most inspired. He parodies feelings, attitudes, states of mind that one would think were exempt from it, and his caricature of dapper suavity is killingly precise."

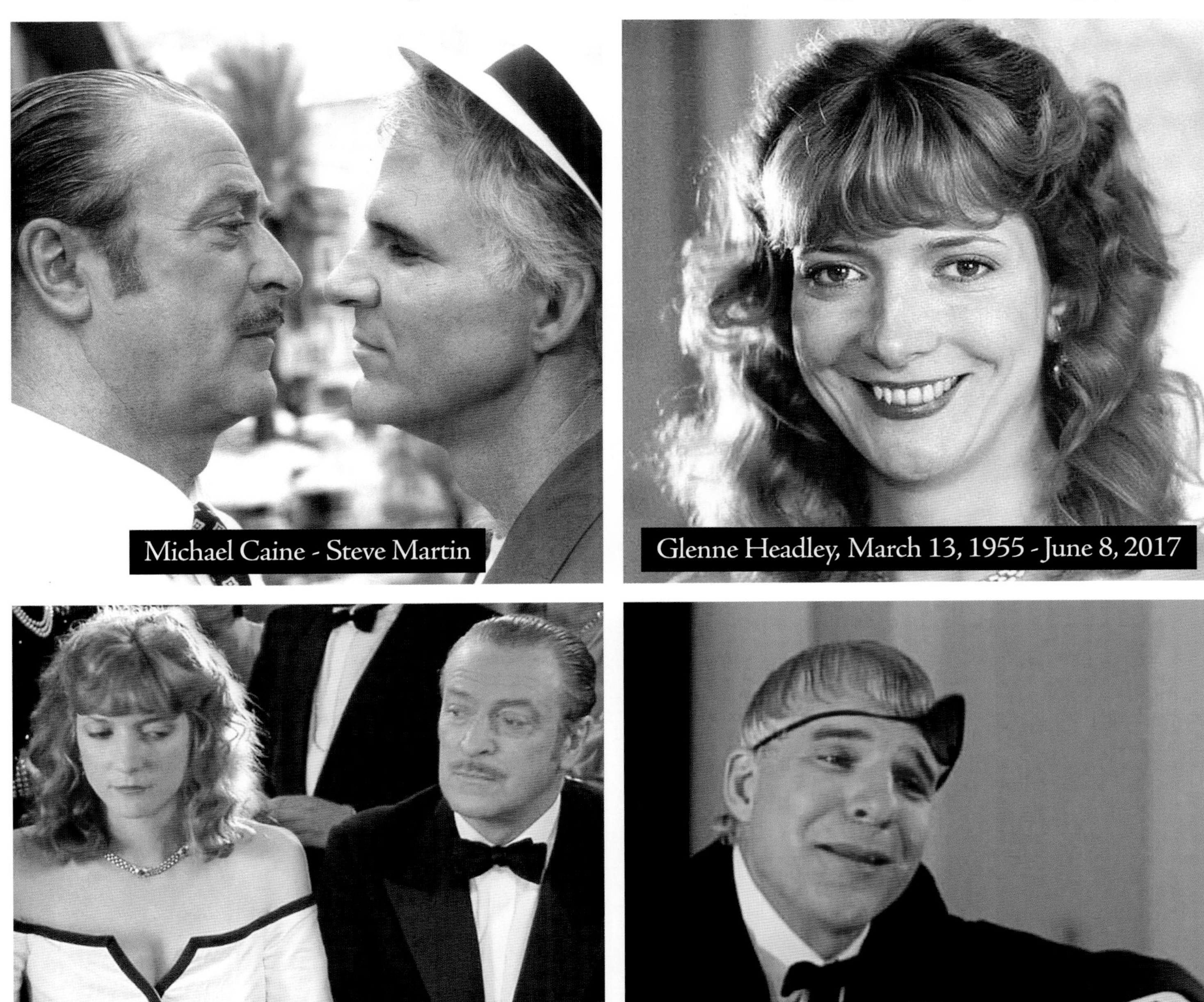

Michael Caine - Steve Martin

Glenne Headley, March 13, 1955 - June 8, 2017

Glenne Headley - Michael Caine

Steve Martin

I've never laughed any harder then I did when Steve Martin, who is sitting at dinner, asks Michael Caine, "Excuse me. May I go to the bathroom?"

Caine answers, "Of course you may."

At the table, Steve, with a minimum amount of straining, bears down, smiles, then says, "Thank you."

In London, four very different people team up to commit armed robbery, then try to doublecross each other for the loot.

JOHN CLEESE WANDA JAMIE LEE CURTIS KEVIN KLINE MICHAEL PALIN

6' 5' 4

6' 5' 4'

A Fish Called Wanda

A New Comedy About Sex, Murder and Seafood.

Jonathan Rosenbaum of Chicago Reader wrote: "Like many of the best English comedies, much of the humor here is based on character, good-natured high spirits, and fairly uninhibited vulgarity."

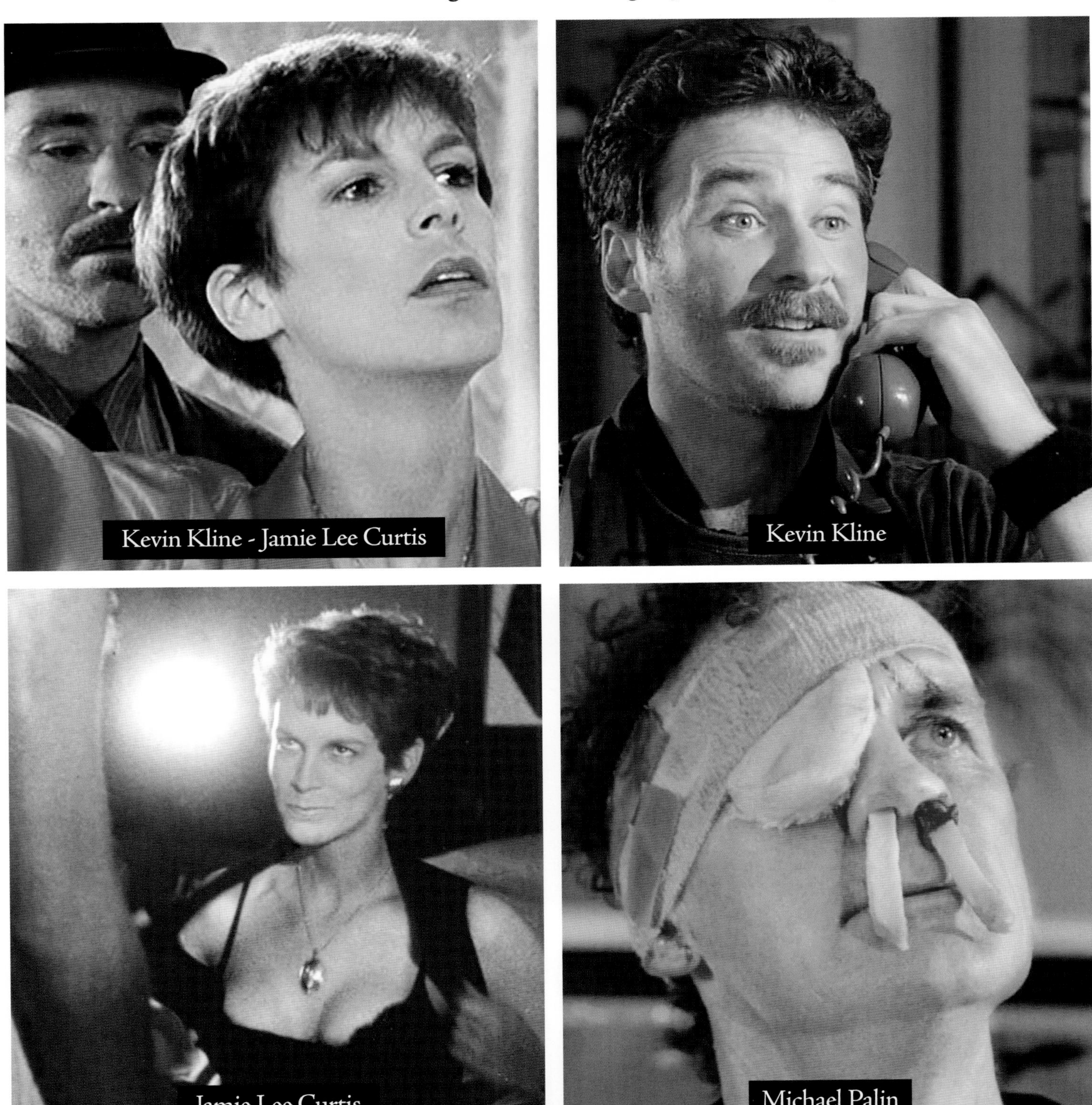

Kevin Kline - Jamie Lee Curtis

Kevin Kline

Jamie Lee Curtis

Michael Palin

For those of us who also derive pleasure from great comedy, John Cleese, Michael Palin and Kevin Kline do not disappoint.

Besides vulgarity, it had sexuality in the form of a beautiful bosom that Jamie Lee Curtis obligingly bared for the pleasure of all.

Selfish yuppie Charlie Babbitt's father left a fortune to his savant brother Raymond and a pittance to Charlie; they travel cross-country.

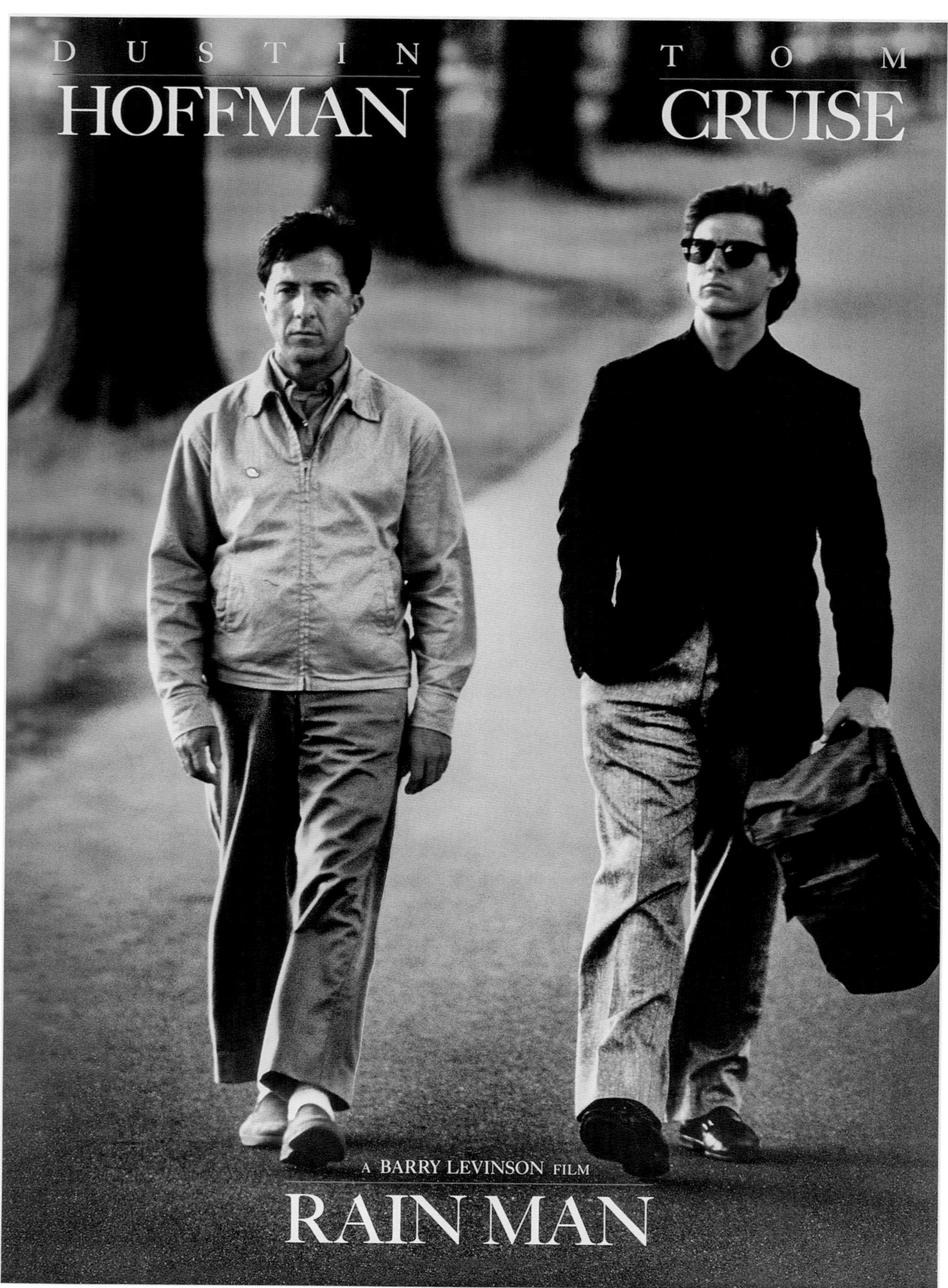

Elliot Panek of Common Sense Media wrote: "This is a quiet, understated gem of a film, one that richly rewards the patient viewer with an unforgettable emotional experience."

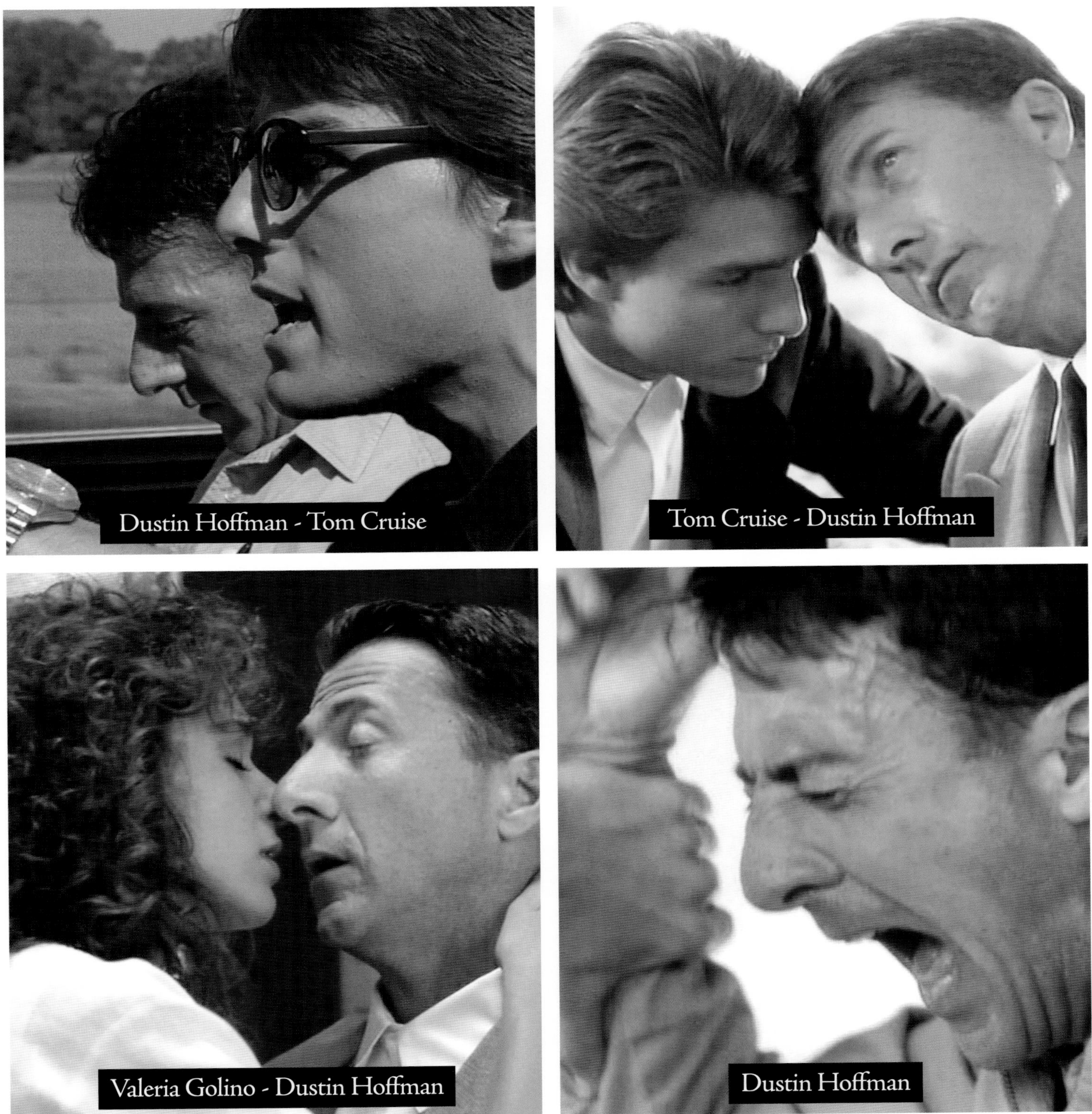

Dustin Hoffman - Tom Cruise

Tom Cruise - Dustin Hoffman

Valeria Golino - Dustin Hoffman

Dustin Hoffman

Dustin Hoffman is the king of delivering quotable lines.
In "The Graduate:" "Mrs. Robinson, are you trying to seduce me?"
In "Midnight Cowboy:" "We're walkin' here... we're walkin' here!"
In "Rain Man:" "I'm an excellent driver... excellent driver."

Bert Rigby is a coal miner who, during a strike, decides to break into show-business.

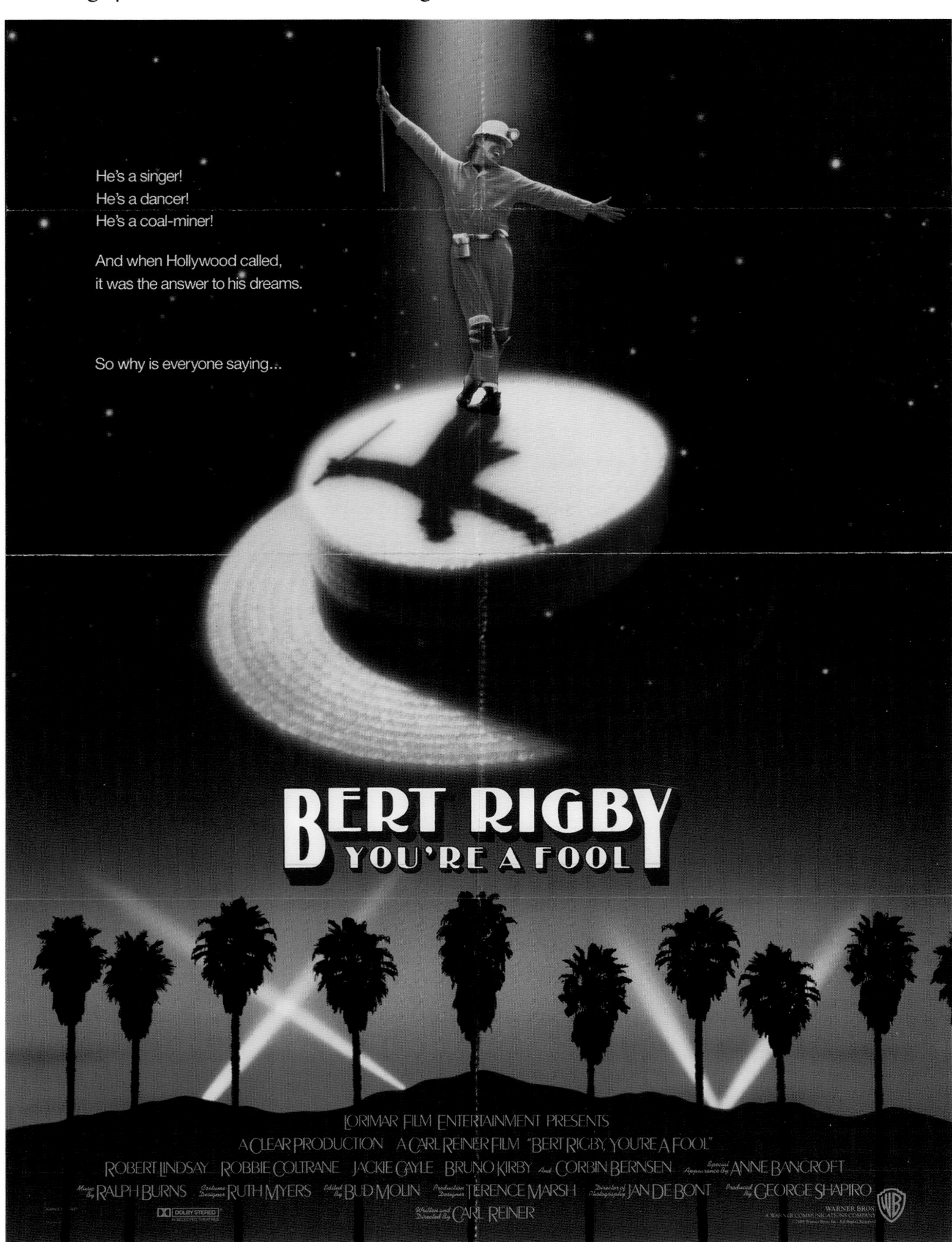

Scott Weinberg of eFilmCritic wrote: "I expected very little and received a nice treat."

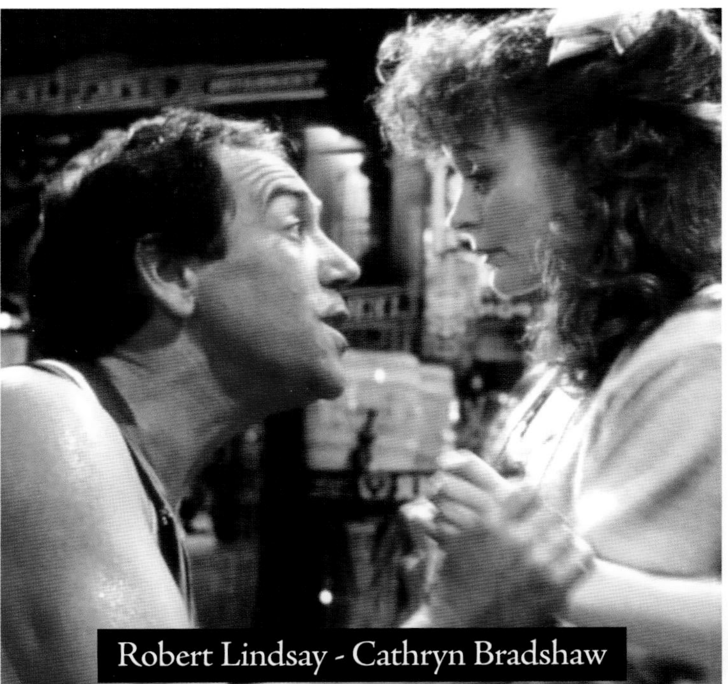
Robert Lindsay - Cathryn Bradshaw

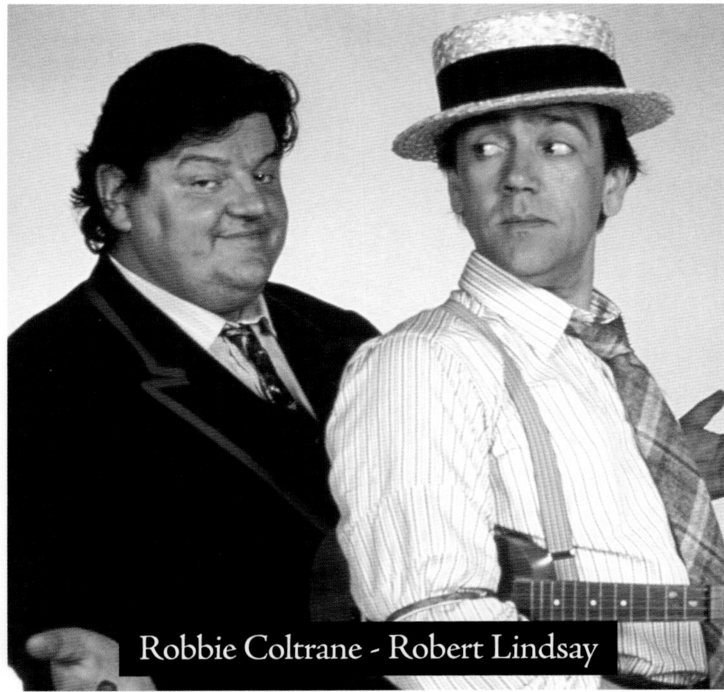
Robbie Coltrane - Robert Lindsay

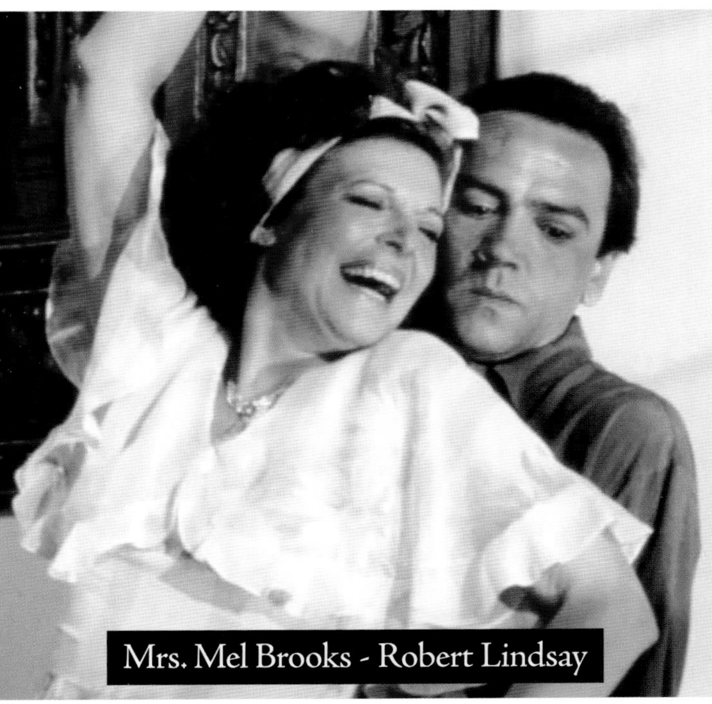
Mrs. Mel Brooks - Robert Lindsay

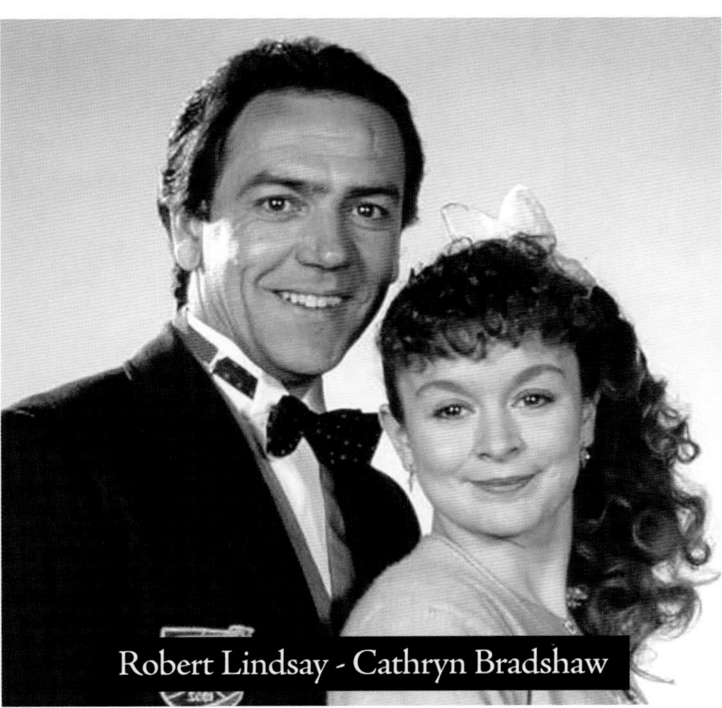
Robert Lindsay - Cathryn Bradshaw

I first saw Robert Lindsay on Broadway in "Me & My Girl" and was so impressed that I asked if he'd be interested in starring in a film musical. He said "Yes," and in six weeks, I fashioned the screenplay and twelve weeks later I delivered a completed film.

"Bert Rigby, You're A Fool," one of my favorite endeavors, grossed an impressive $75,000,000.

For the dancing sequence, I asked Mel Brooks if he would help us secure the services of his lovely wife, Anne Bancroft. He did and, to this day, I am beholden to him.

Cathryn Bradshaw's sweet face honestly reflects the very sweet person she is.

Harry and Sally have known each other for years, and are very good friends, but they fear sex would ruin the friendship.

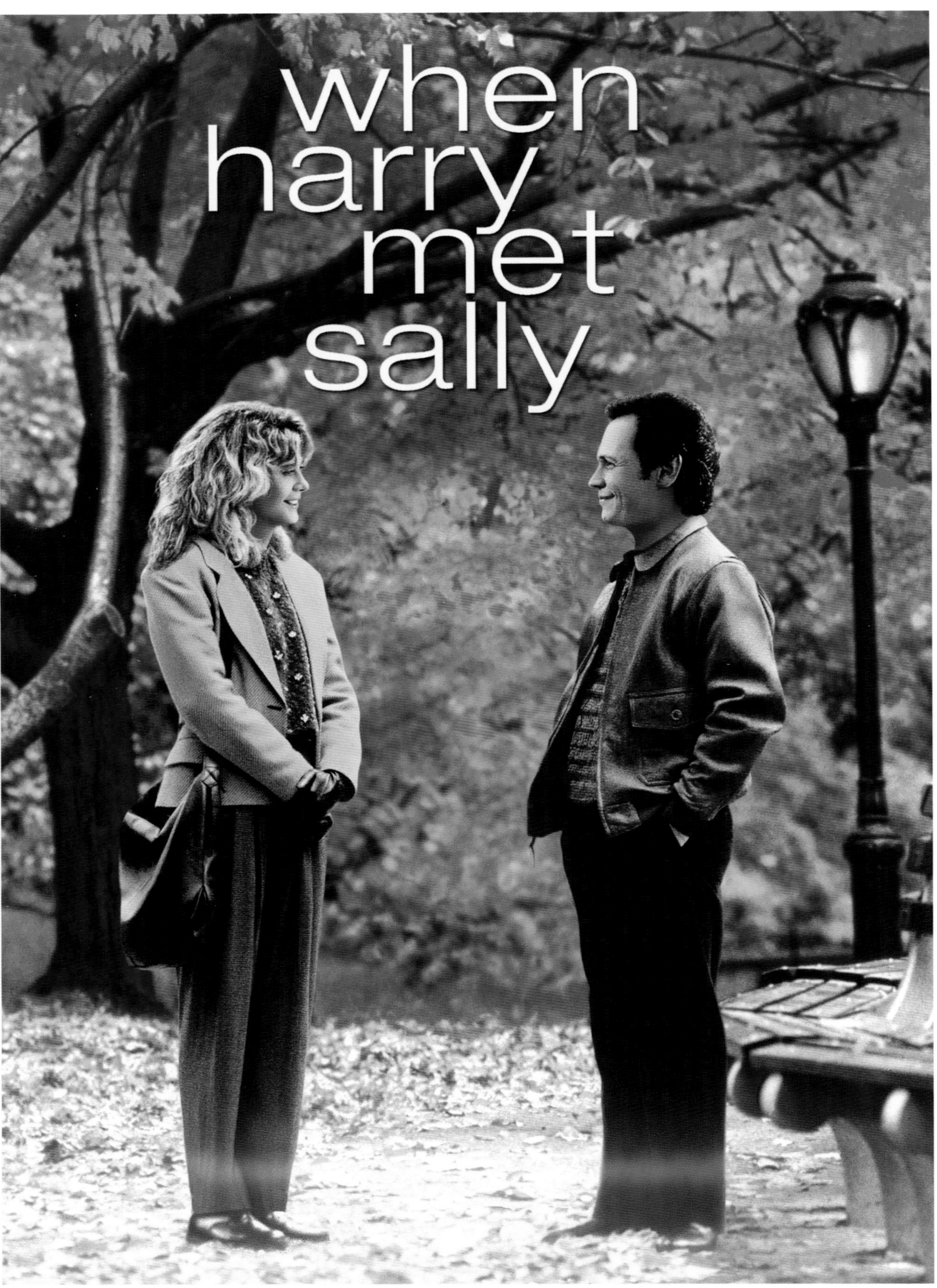

Tim Brayton of Antagony and Ecstasy wrote: "An outright masterpiece of romance, comedy, and cinema itself."

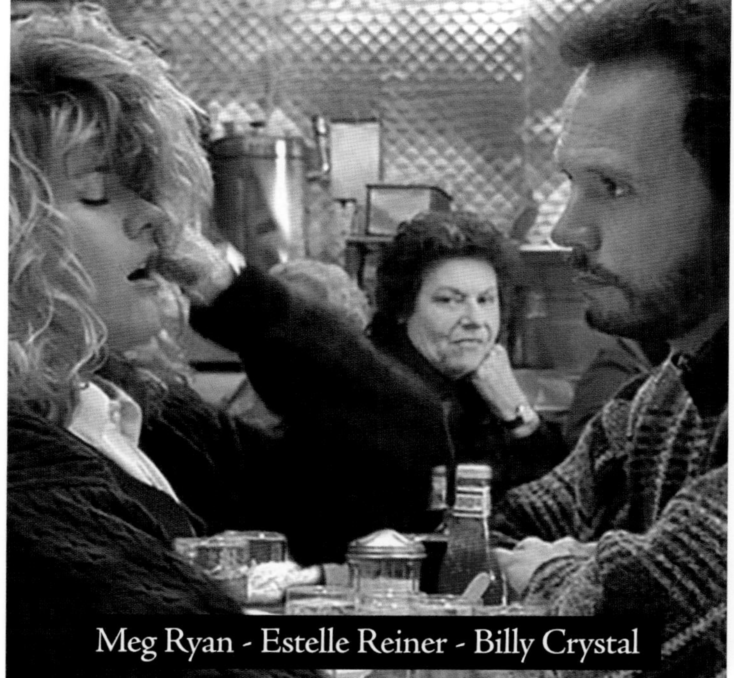

Meg Ryan - Estelle Reiner - Billy Crystal

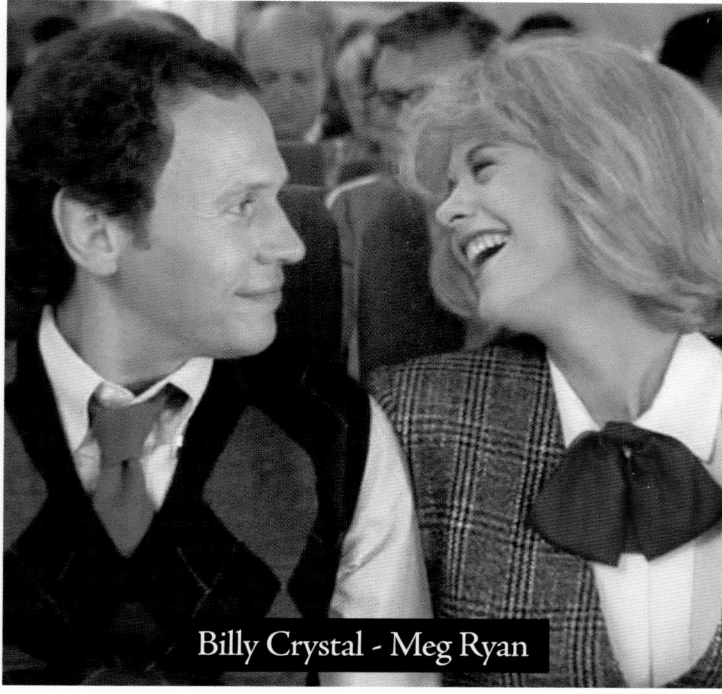

Billy Crystal - Meg Ryan

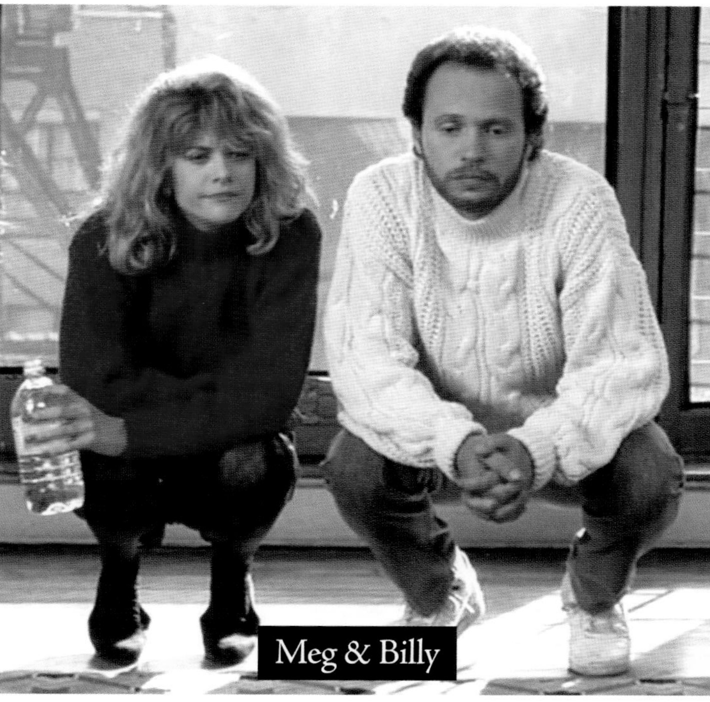

Meg & Billy

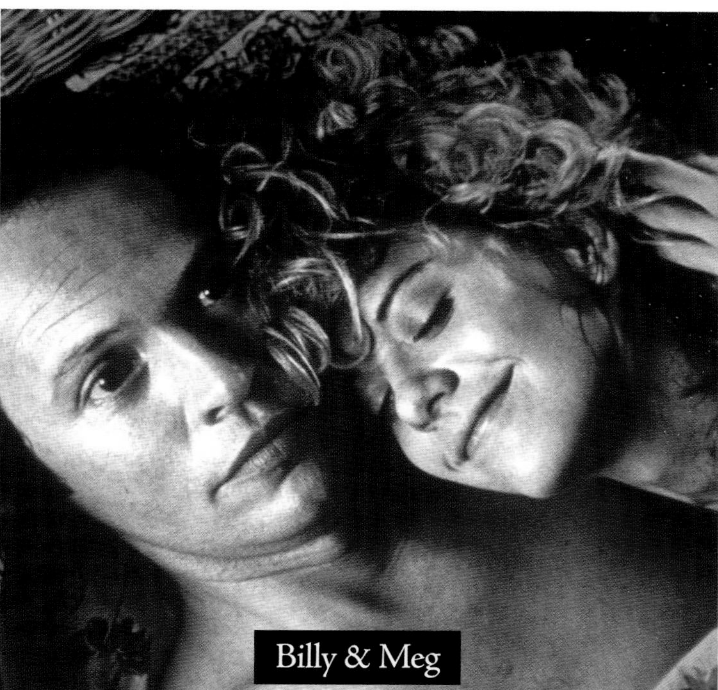

Billy & Meg

This movie launched Billy Crystal's career as a leading man and brought world-wide attention to someone who deserved the attention.

As for Meg Ryan, along with "Sleepless in Seattle" and "You've Got Mail," "When Harry Met Sally" is, arguably, her most popular and endearing effort.

In the first photo, the woman leaning on her fist is my wife, Estelle, who delivered the line, "I'll have what she's having," which is fifth on the American Film Institute's list of most quotable lines.

An old Jewish woman and her African-American chauffeur in the American South have a relationship that grows and improves over the years.

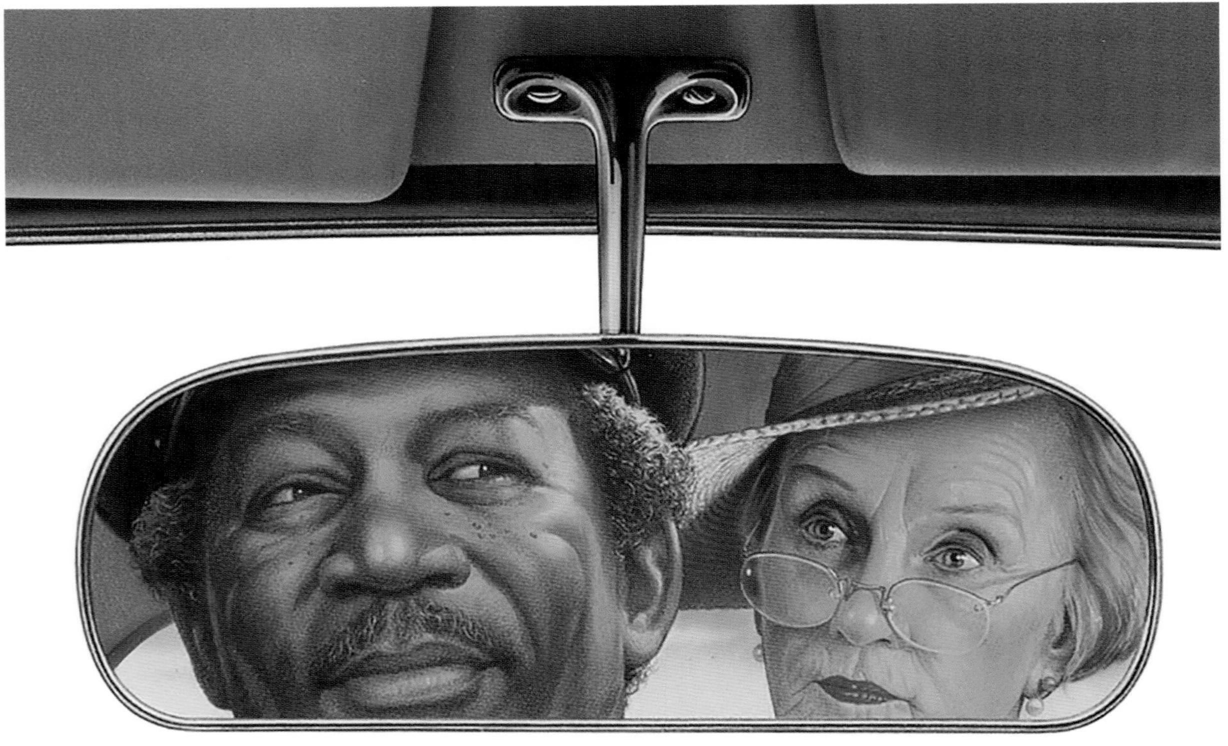

MORGAN
FREEMAN

JESSICA
TANDY

DAN
AYKROYD

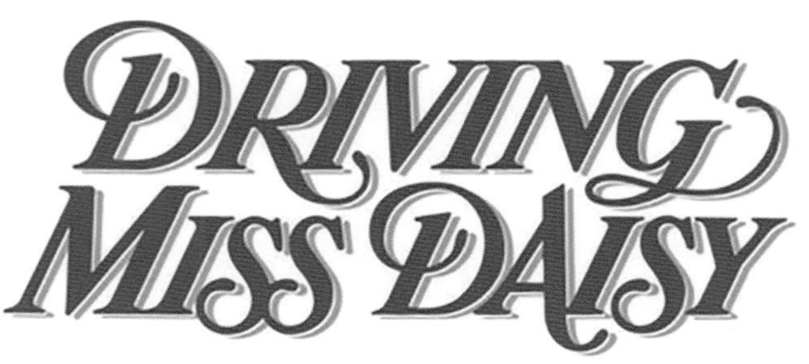

Desmond Ryan of The Philadelphia Inquirer wrote: "'Driving Miss Daisy' spans a quarter-century in the intricate relationship of a Southern dowager and her chauffeur, and it is a movie that invites you to appreciate the passage of time in more than one way."

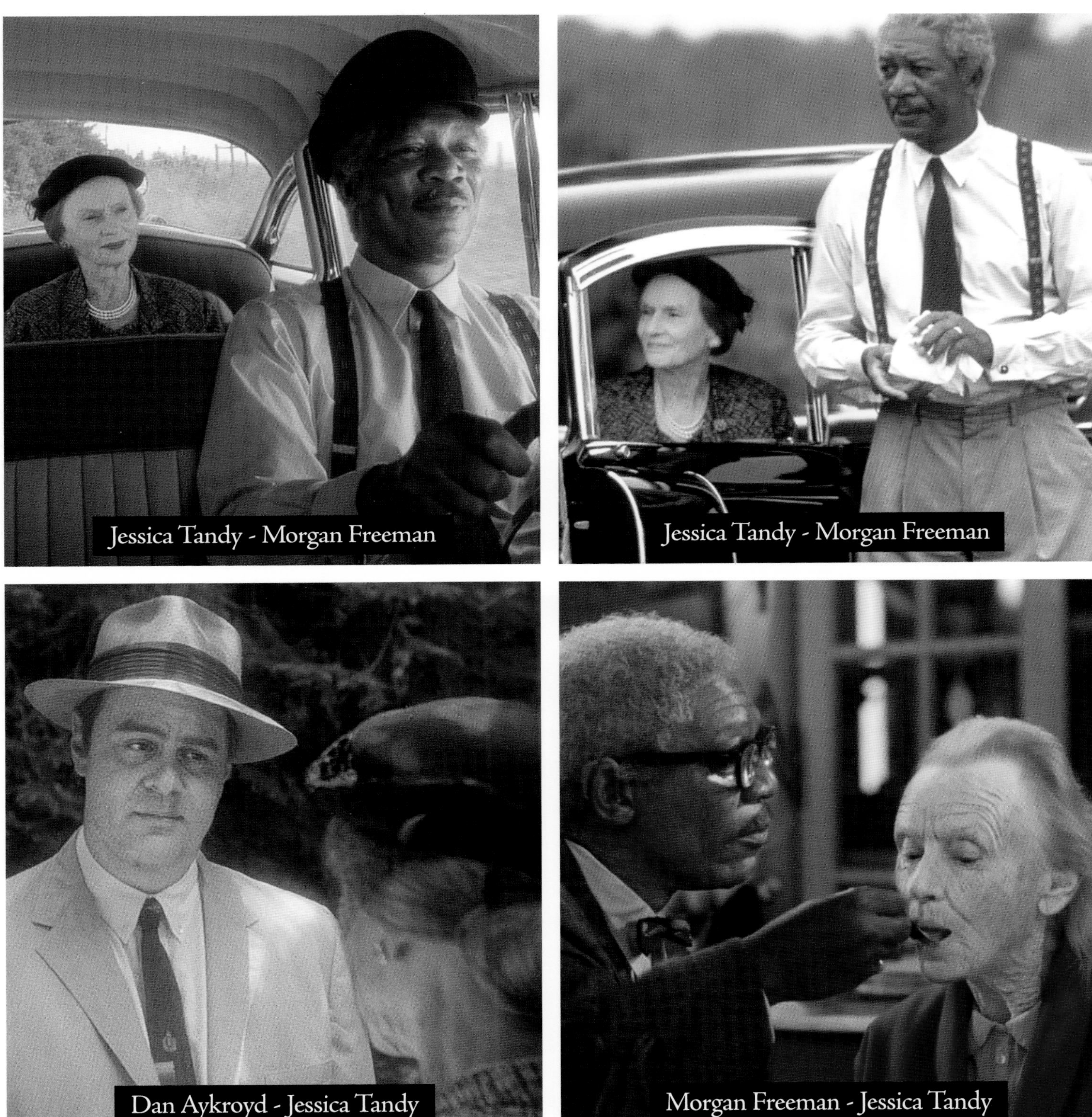

Jessica Tandy - Morgan Freeman

Jessica Tandy - Morgan Freeman

Dan Aykroyd - Jessica Tandy

Morgan Freeman - Jessica Tandy

This film successfully demonstrates how, when a wealthy lady's health declines and she needs her chauffeur's assistance, their racial divide narrows. He is not just a driver, but one who can take care of her and be her friend.

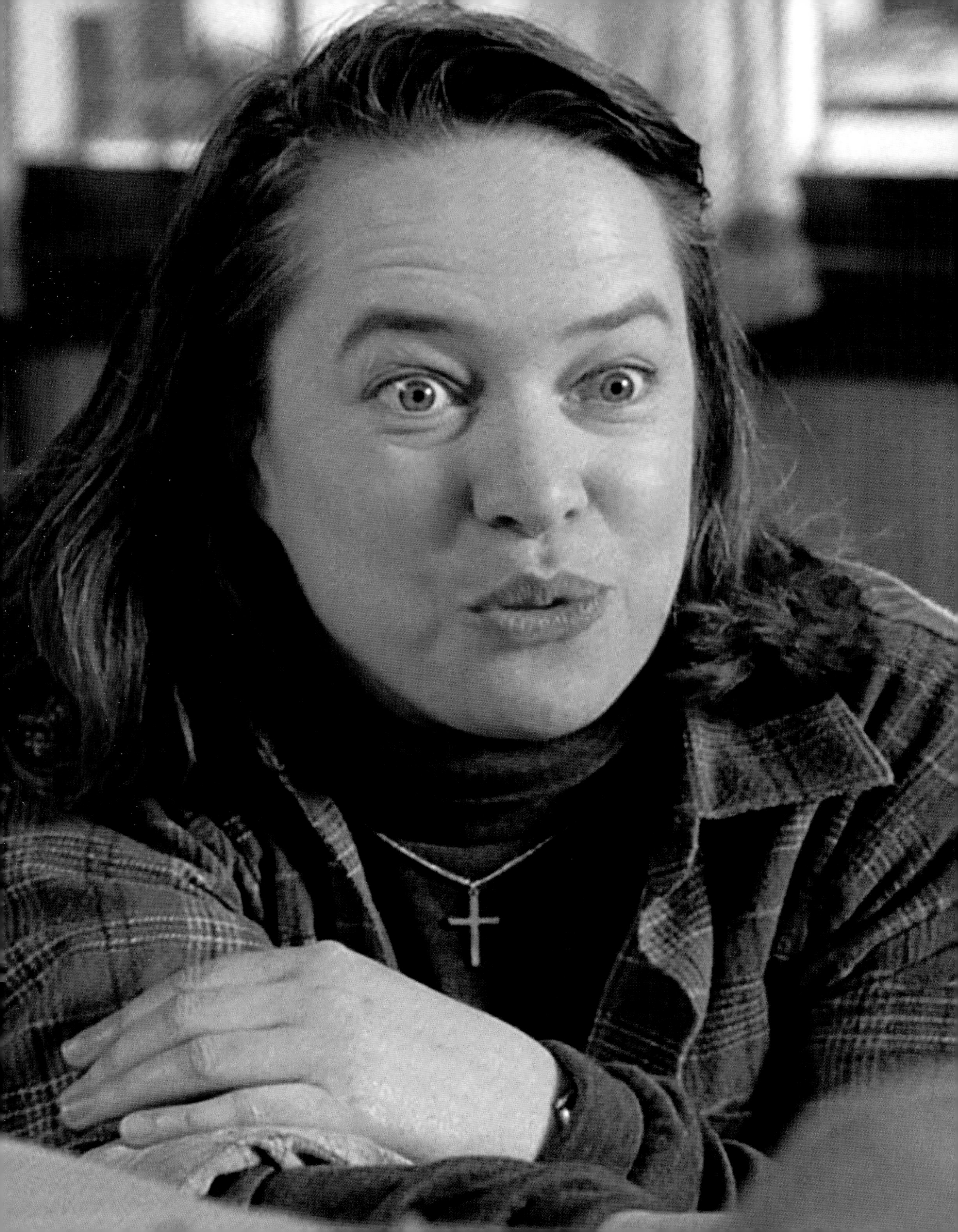

the 90s

After a famous author is rescued from a car crash by a fan of his novels, he comes to realize that the care he is receiving is only the beginning of a nightmare of captivity and abuse.

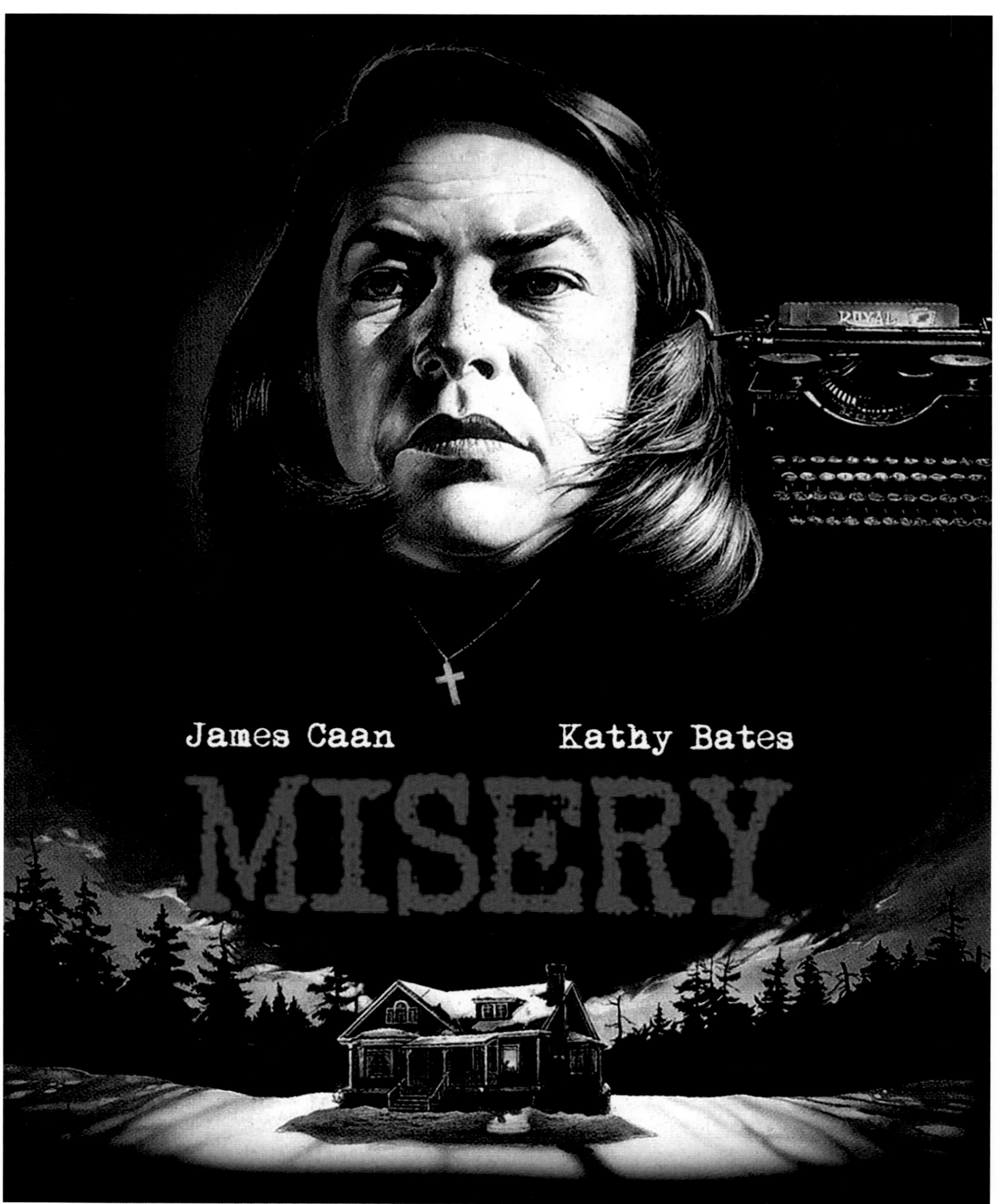

Dave Kehr of Chicago Tribune wrote: "Like any good work of popular culture, Rob Reiner's film of Stephen King's best-selling book 'Misery' functions on more than one level."

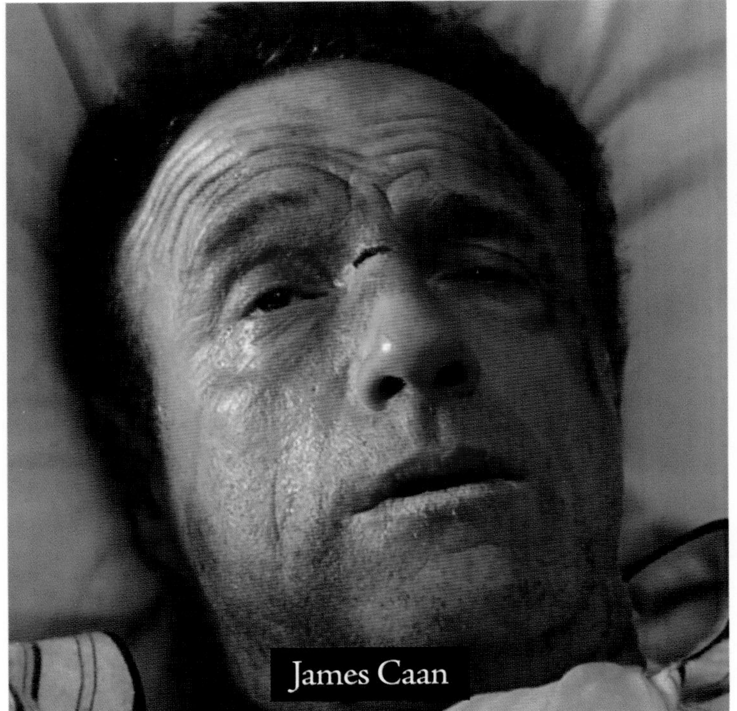

James Caan

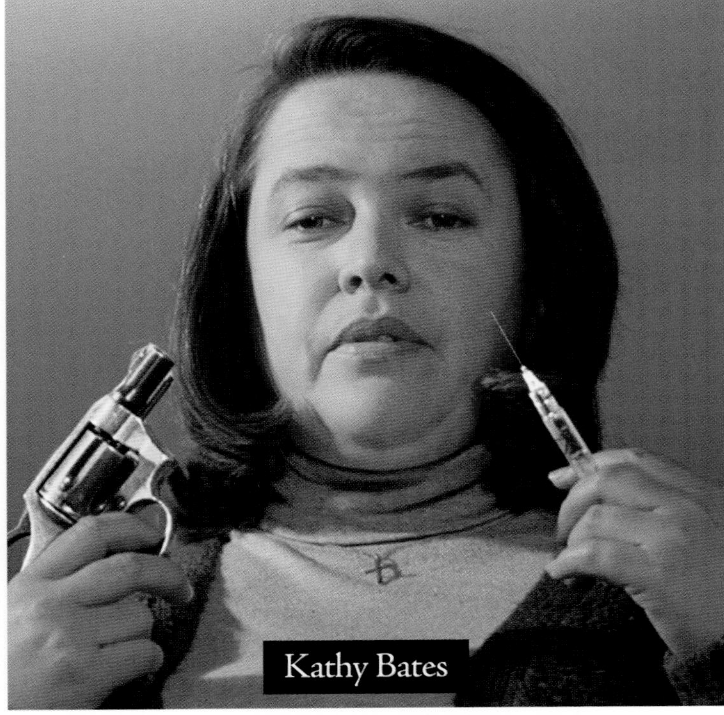

Kathy Bates

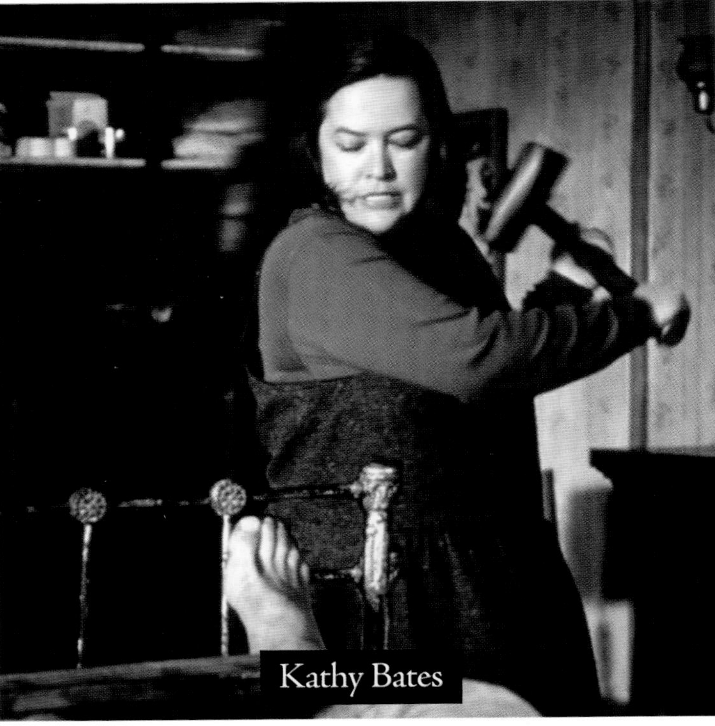

Kathy Bates

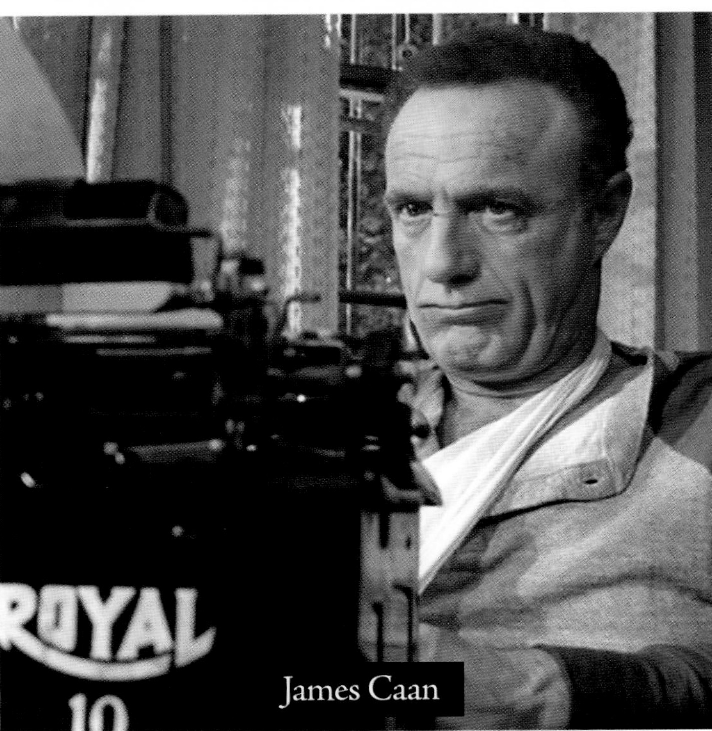

James Caan

Kathy Bates is beloved by all and has never, to my knowledge, smashed a man's foot with a sledge hammer. However, in the film, she does it so violently and expertly you'd swear she'd done it before, but happily, her victim, played by James Caan, lived to write a best-seller about the painful treatment he received from a certifiable nut case.

"Misery" is one of the myriad of films in which that fine director, Rob Reiner, was involved.

A frustrated woman's life gets even more frustrating once she gets into an affair with a man who suffers a fatal heart attack after their fling.

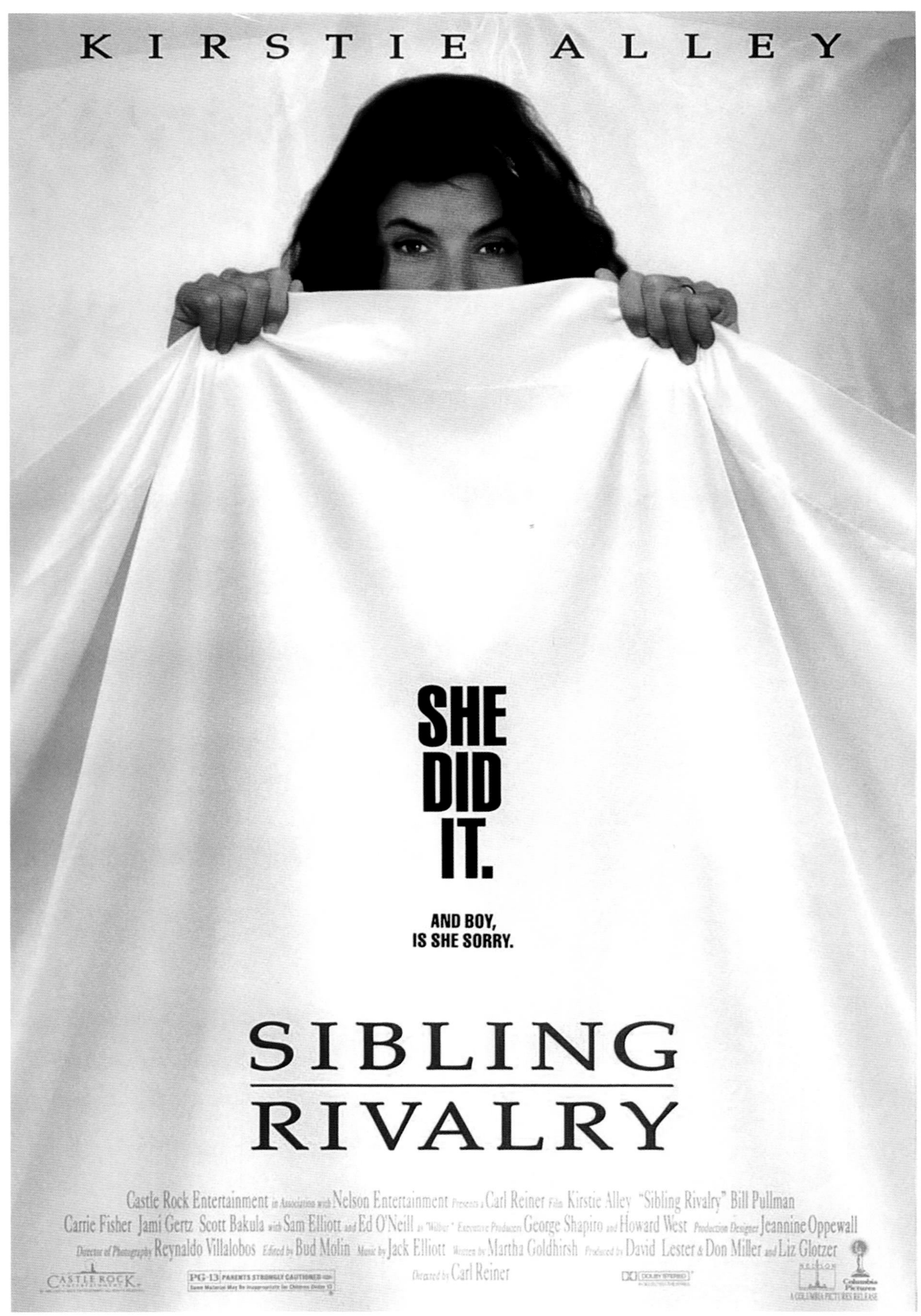

Michael Grost of Classic Film and TV wrote: "Pleasant farce comedy with likable characters."

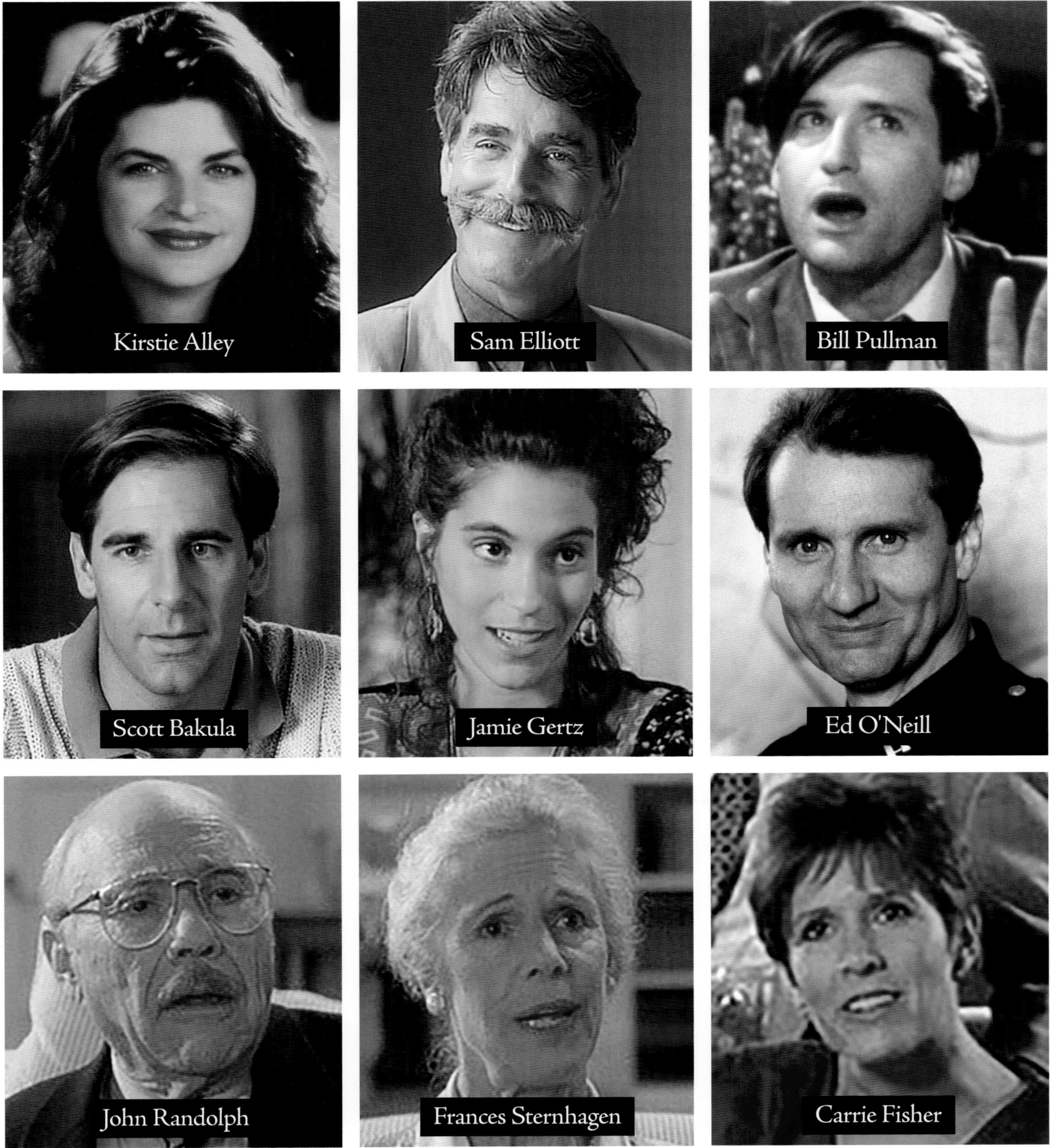

Kirstie Alley
Sam Elliott
Bill Pullman
Scott Bakula
Jamie Gertz
Ed O'Neill
John Randolph
Frances Sternhagen
Carrie Fisher

I not only liked the likable characters the reviewer referred to, I loved them. I loved directing them and I loved their performances and I loved looking at their faces. What I hate is that Carrie Fisher is no longer with us.

A filthy rich businessman bets a corporate rival that he can live on the streets of L.A. without the comforts of home or money, which proves to be tougher than he thought.

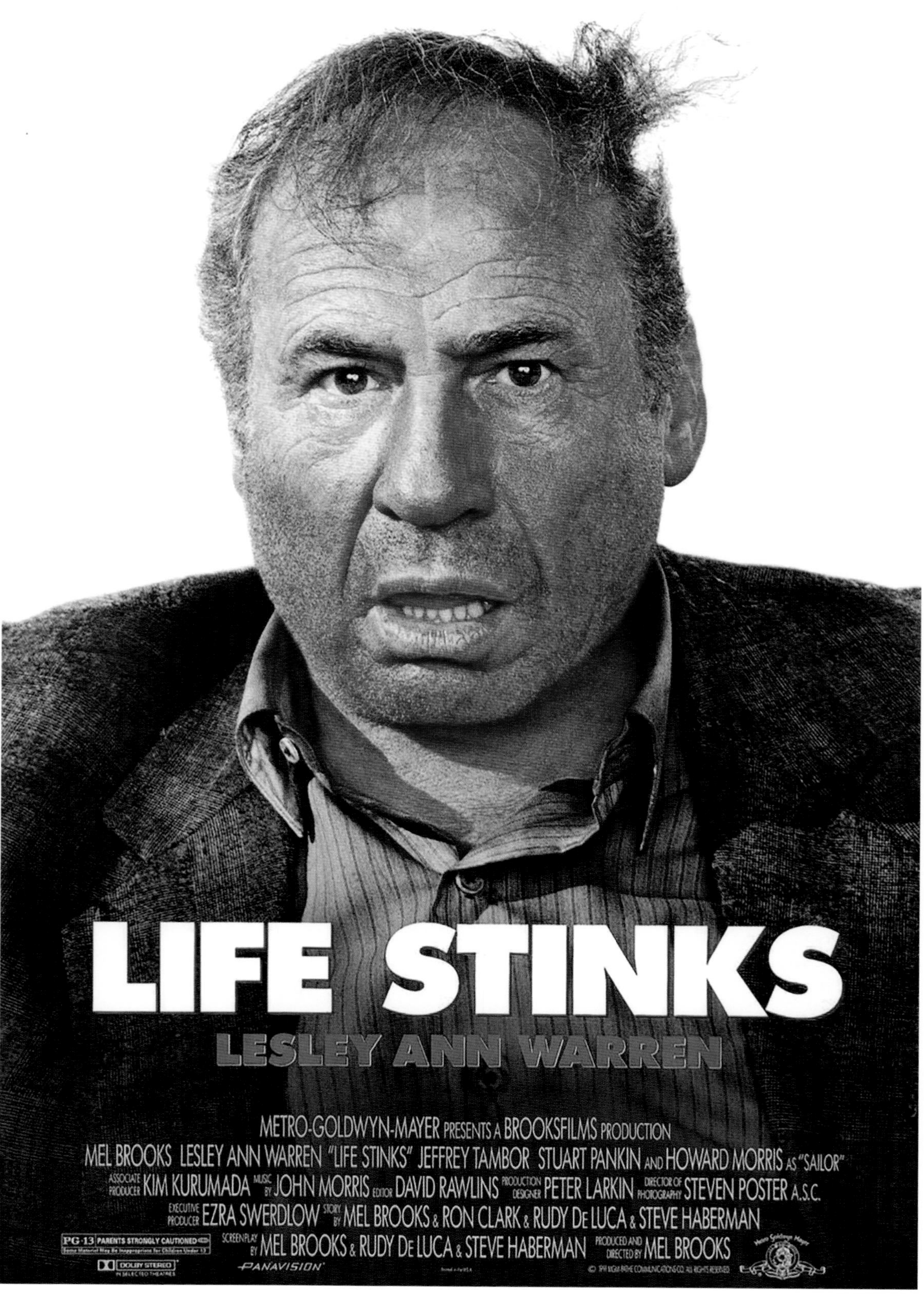

Alex Sandell of Juicy Cerebellum wrote: "Good message, bad comedy."

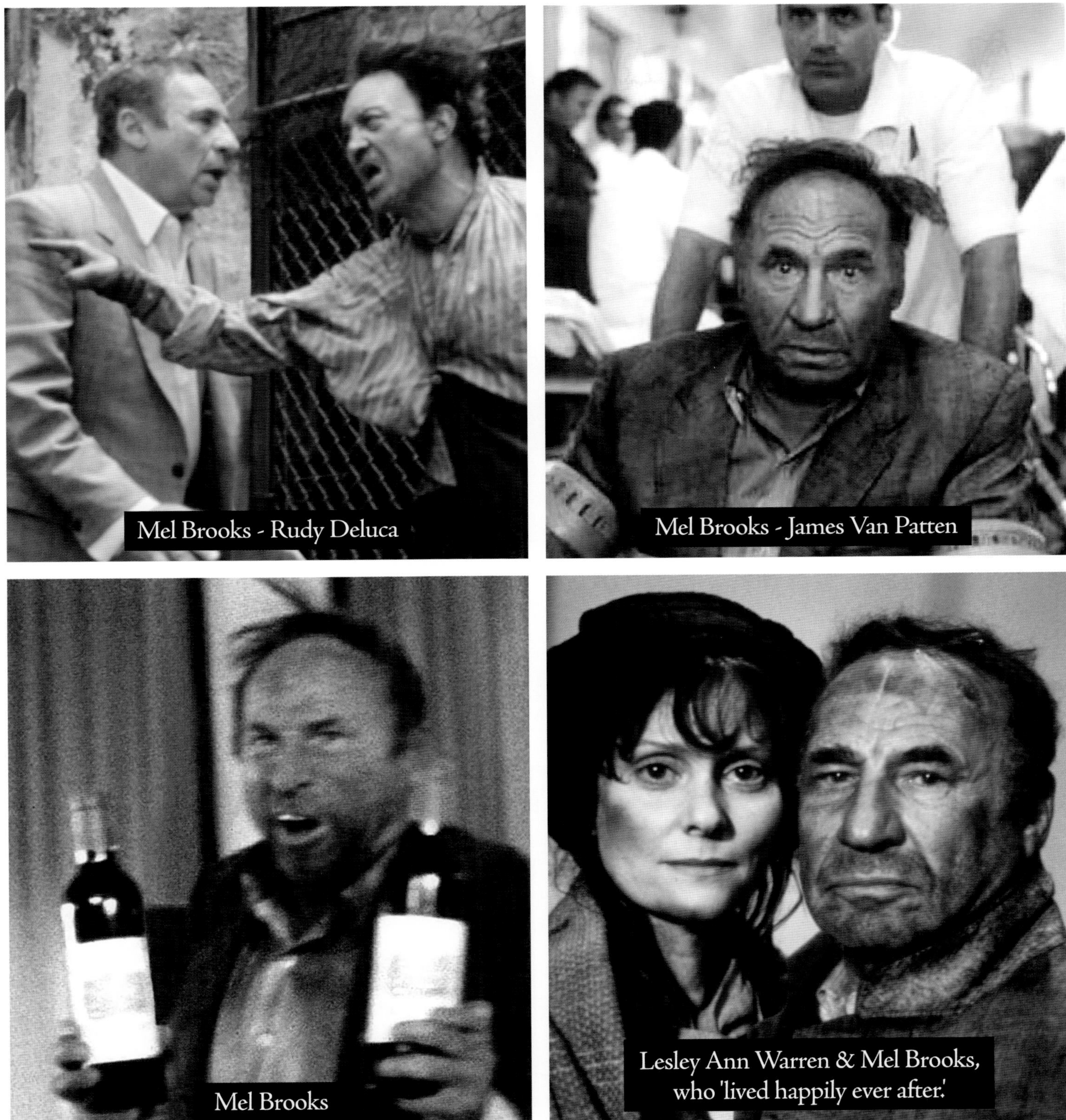

Mel Brooks - Rudy Deluca

Mel Brooks - James Van Patten

Mel Brooks

Lesley Ann Warren & Mel Brooks, who 'lived happily ever after.'

After nine successful films, Mel Brooks proved that the old adage "You can't win'em all" is true. Perhaps Mel did "Life Stinks" to compete with the mild reviews I received for "Sibling Rivalry."

This film is worth watching just to see the scene where Mel Brooks and Rudy Deluca pick and eat bread crumbs they find on each other's face.

Two best friends set out on an adventure but it soon turns around to a terrifying escape from being hunted by the American police as these two girls escape for the crimes they committed!

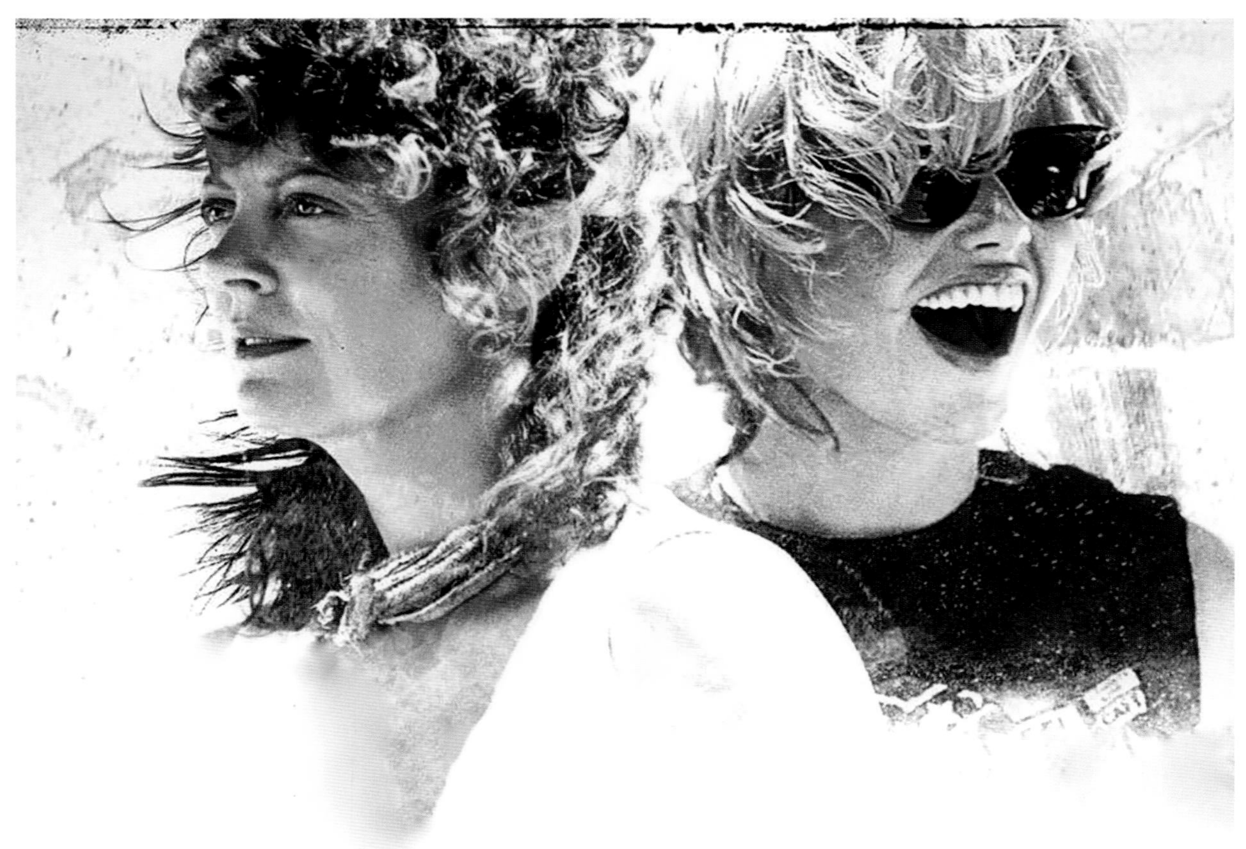

THELMA
& LOUISE

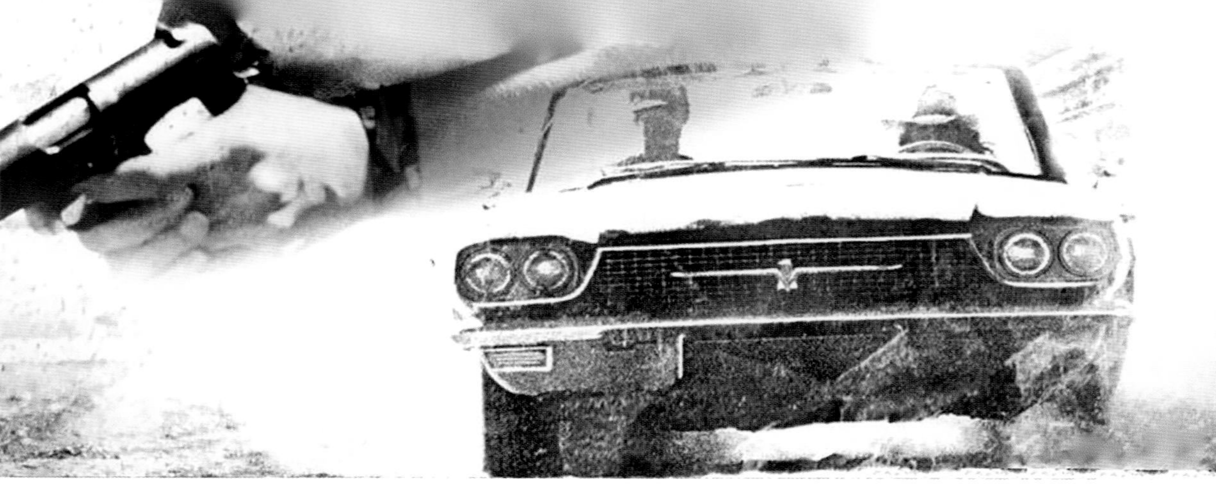

Kathleen Carroll of The New York Daily News wrote: "'Thelma & Louise' is a rare thrill—a gleefully offbeat road movie in which two women, instead of the usual footloose fellas, exult in the heady freedom of America's lonesome highways."

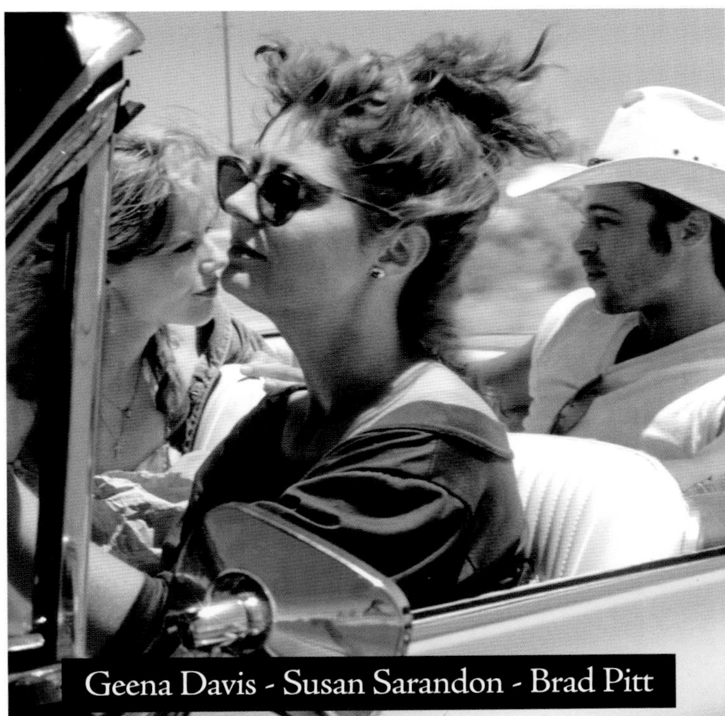
Geena Davis - Susan Sarandon - Brad Pitt

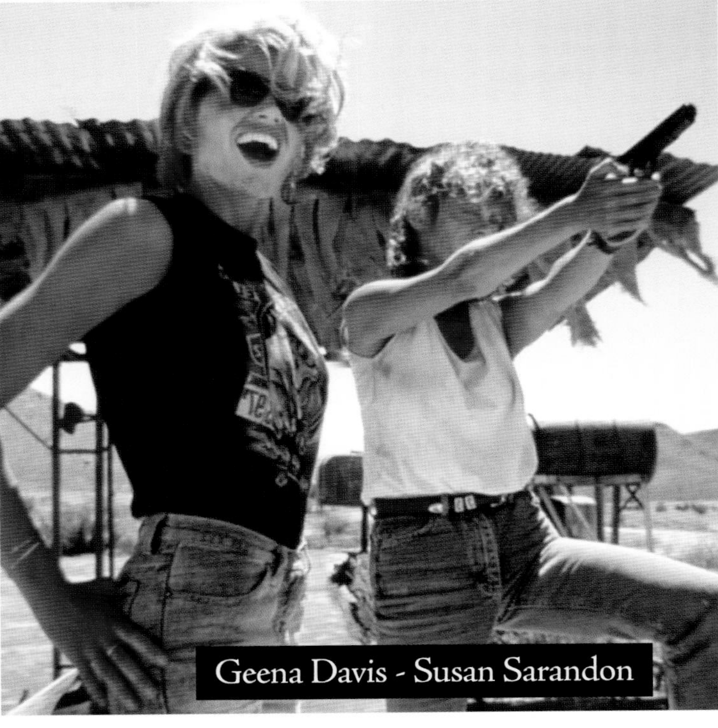
Geena Davis - Susan Sarandon

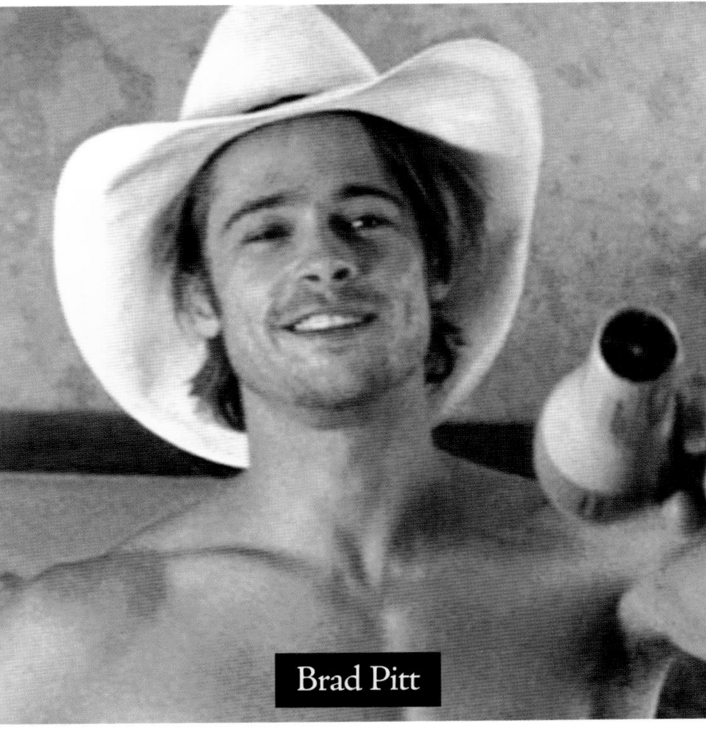
Brad Pitt

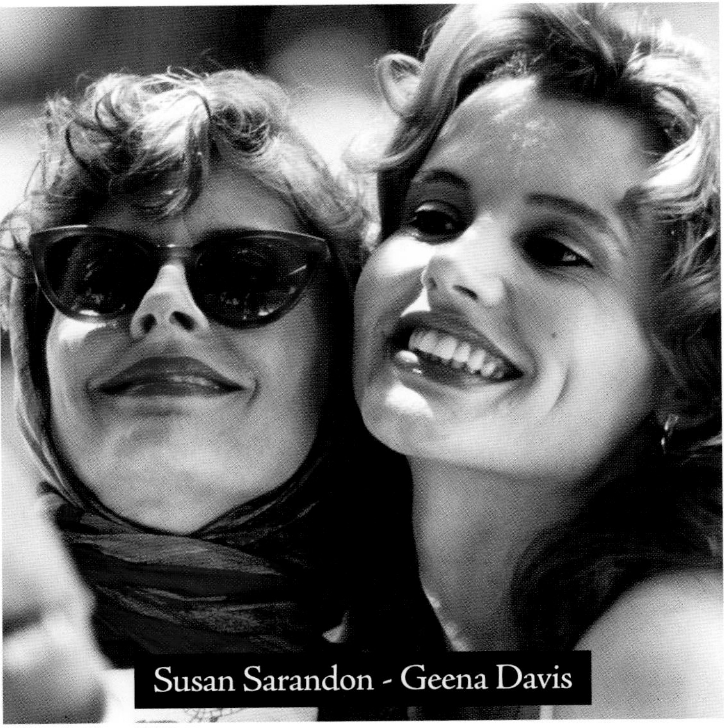
Susan Sarandon - Geena Davis

This was the 30th film of the 112 films in which Susan Sarandon appeared, the 10th film in Geena Davis' career and the breakout performance for the soon-to-be-star, Brad Pitt.

Once again, proving that crime does not pay, Louise drives off a cliff in the Grand Canyon, killing both herself and Thelma.

The troubled and controversial life of the master comedy filmmaker Charles Chaplin.

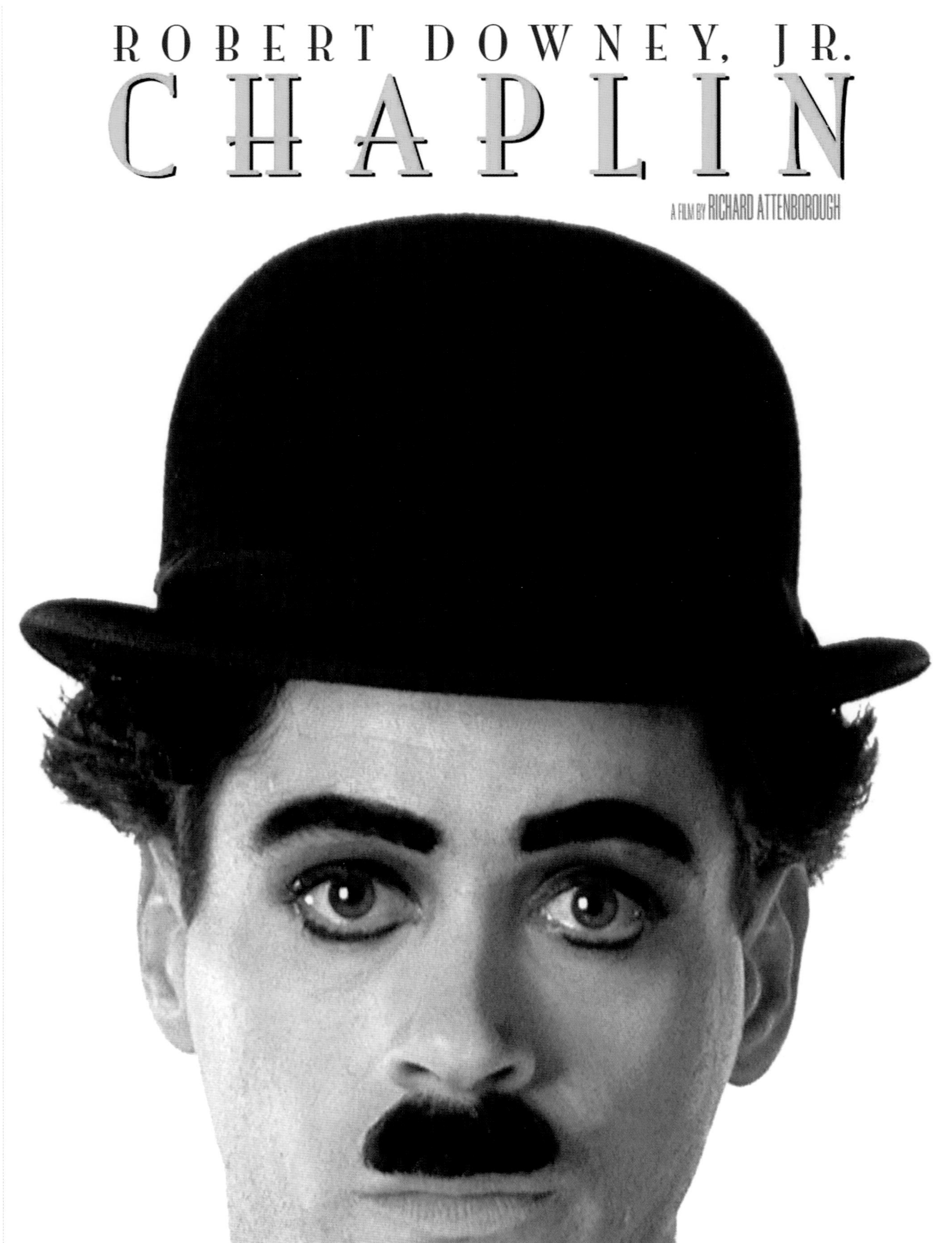

Time Out wrote: "Attenborough's very traditional biopic is a disappointment."

Scott Nash of Three Movie Buffs wrote: "Might be of interest to fans of the great comic, but as entertainment it ultimately fails."

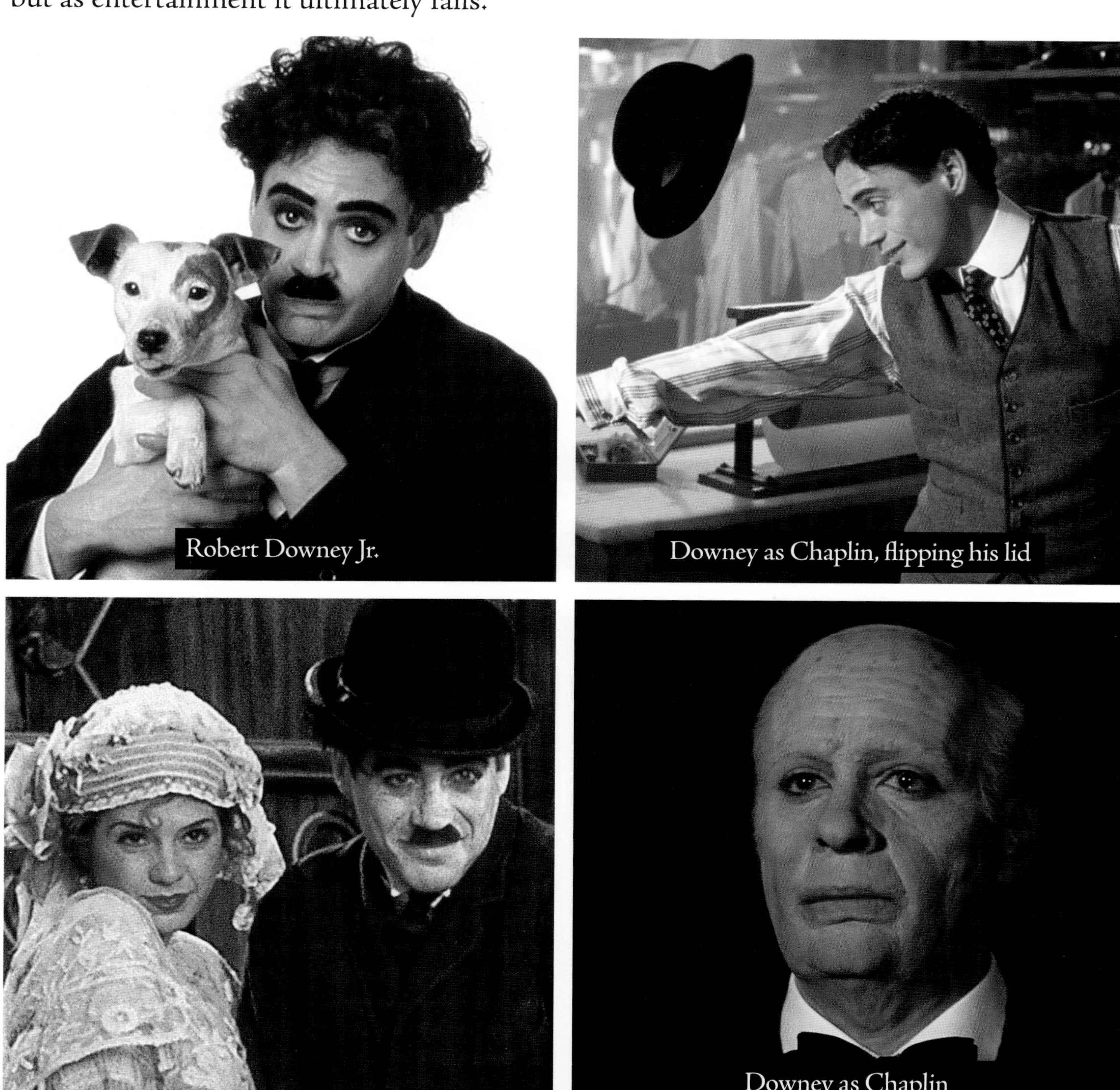

Robert Downey Jr.

Downey as Chaplin, flipping his lid

Marisa Tomei - Robert Downey Jr.

Downey as Chaplin accepting his Honorary Oscar

Here's another set of reviewers with whom I disagree. The film I saw was made by an extraordinarily talented man, Robert Downey Jr. He did a perfect impression of Charlie Chaplin, the gifted actor, writer, director, producer and industry pioneer whose films, incidentally, out-grossed all of his competitors.

Marines, accused of murder, contend they were acting under orders.

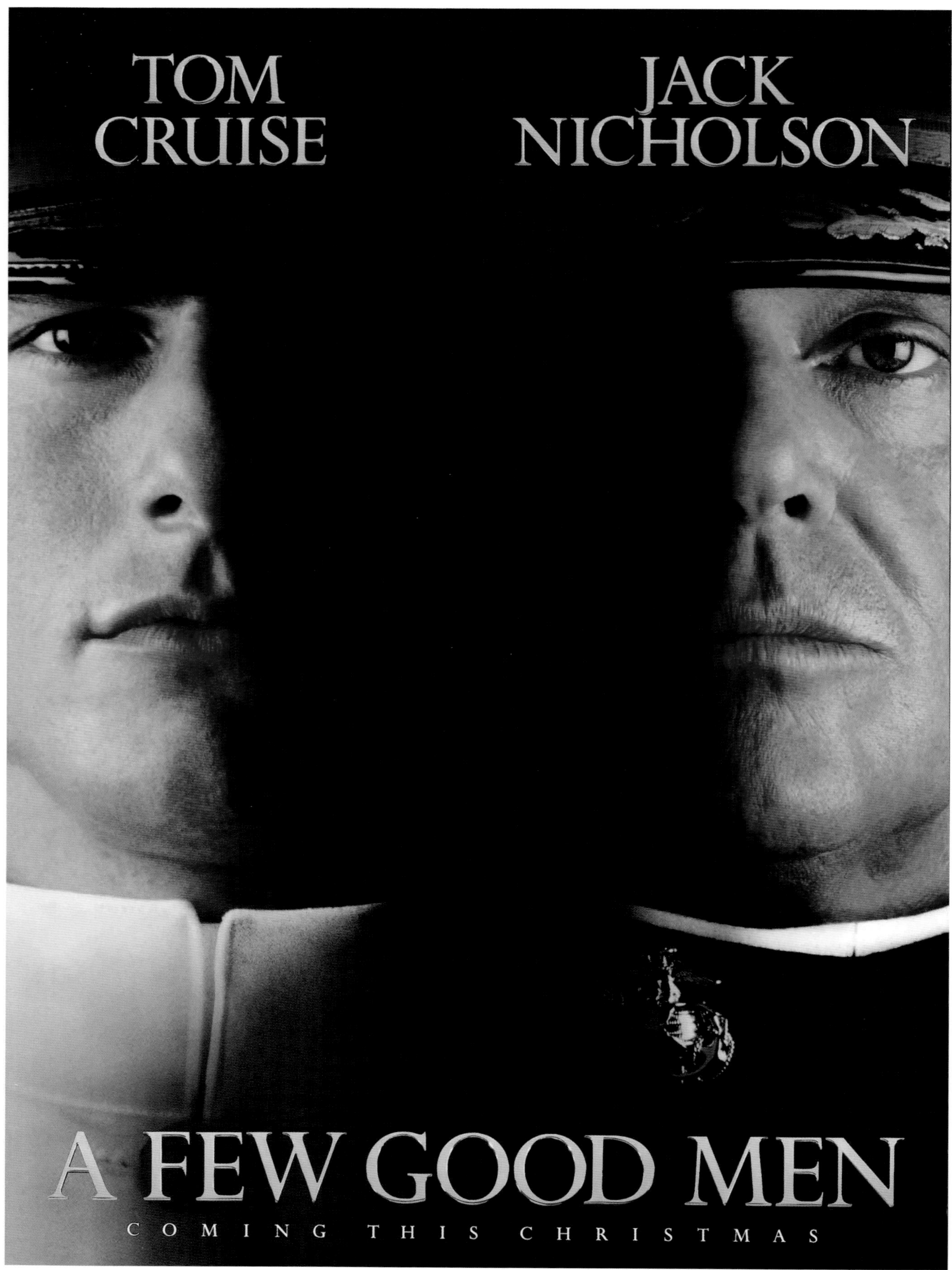

As the film critic, Gene Siskel, noted: "The driving force of the story is watching Cruise's character develop some backbone and staying power."

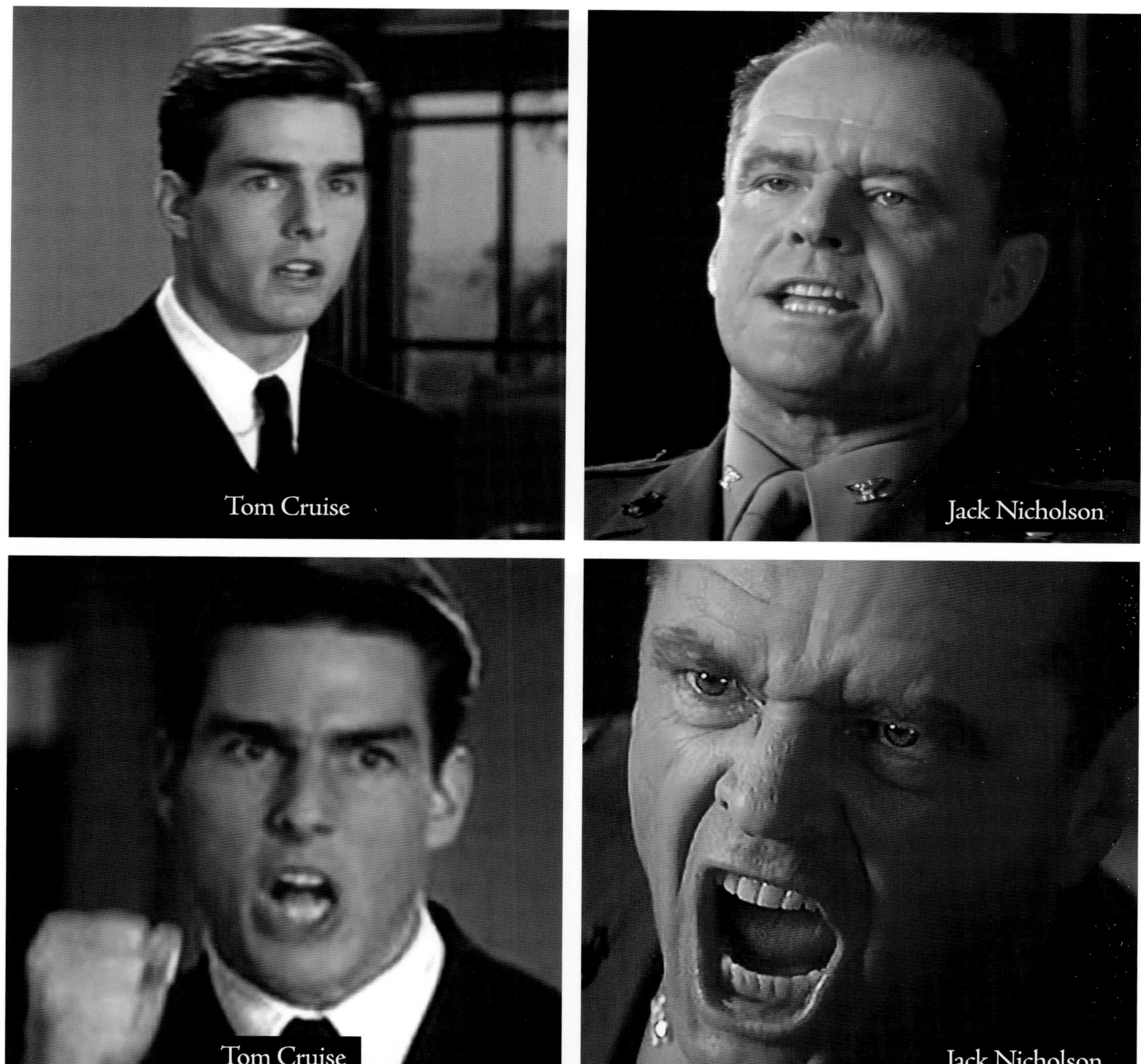

Tom Cruise

Jack Nicholson

Tom Cruise

Jack Nicholson

And as I note, "Rob Reiner just keeps turning out one great film after another!"

Anyone who has seen the film will never forget this shouted exchange between Tom Cruise and Jack Nicholson:

"YOU WANT ANSWERS?"

"I WANT THE TRUTH!"

"YOU CAN'T HANDLE THE TRUTH!"

A spoof of the late 80s and early 90s suspense thrillers and murder mysteries, including "Basic Instinct," "Sleeping With The Enemy," "Cape Fear" and others. A cop/attorney (yes he's both) is seduced by a woman while his wife is having an affair with a mechanic.

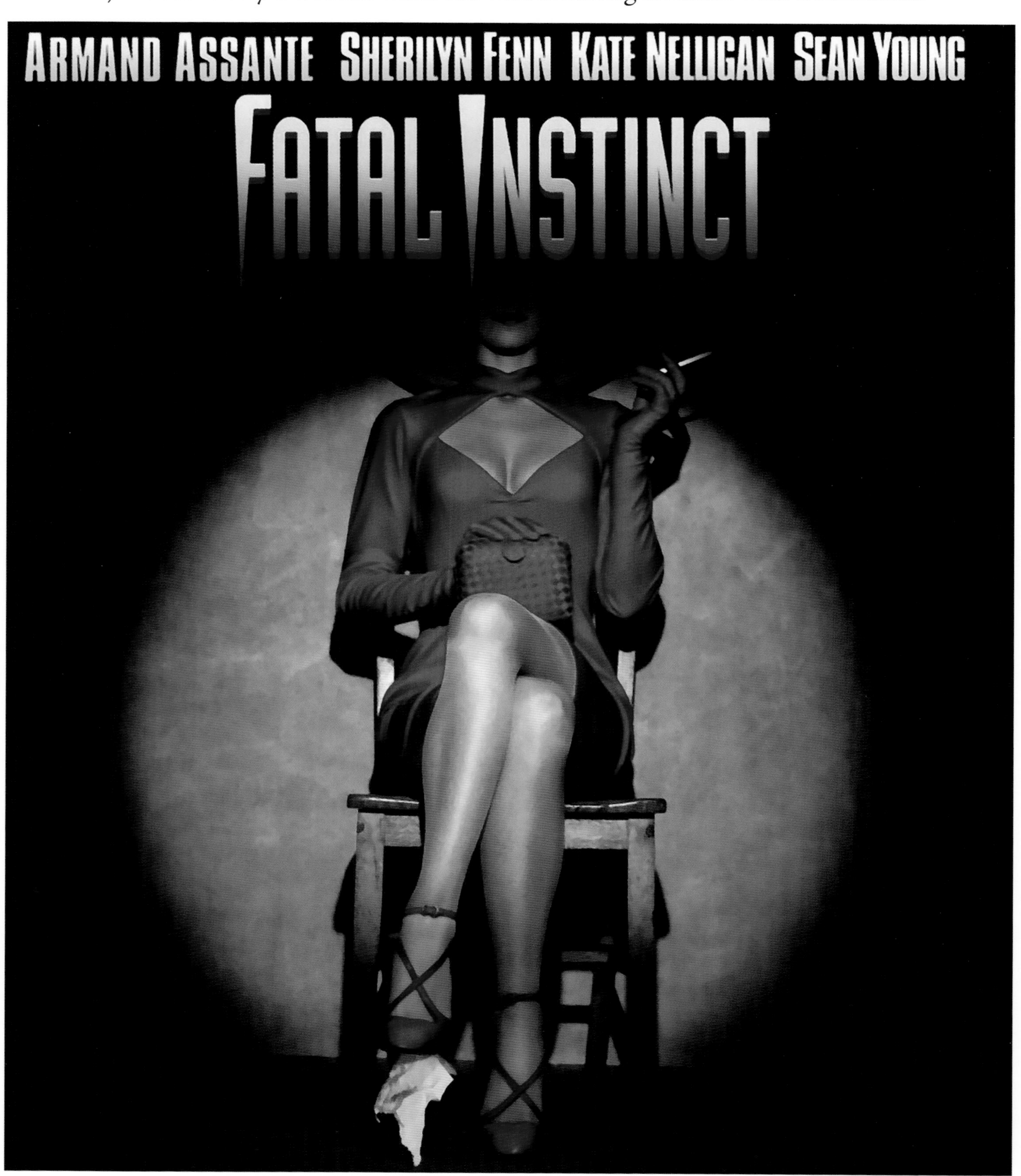

Reviewers wrote: "A continuously ineffective parody." "Small jokes buried under elaborate set-ups." "Sight gags repeated to the point of exhaustion." "Lacking in both inspiration and ingenuity."

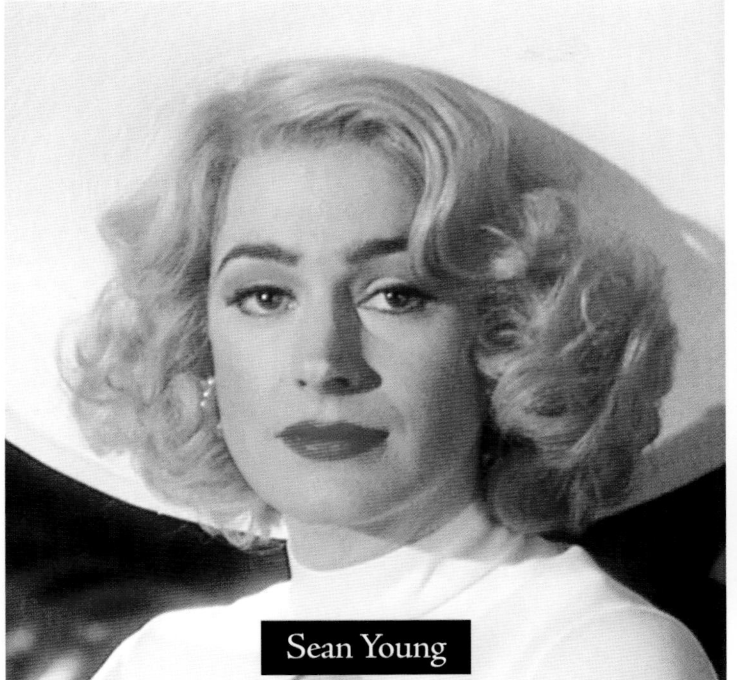
Sean Young

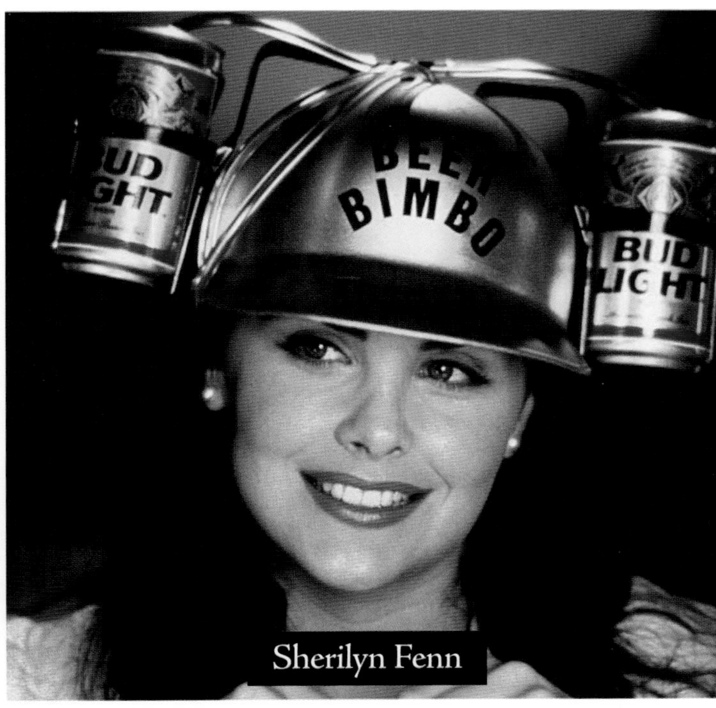

Sherilyn Fenn

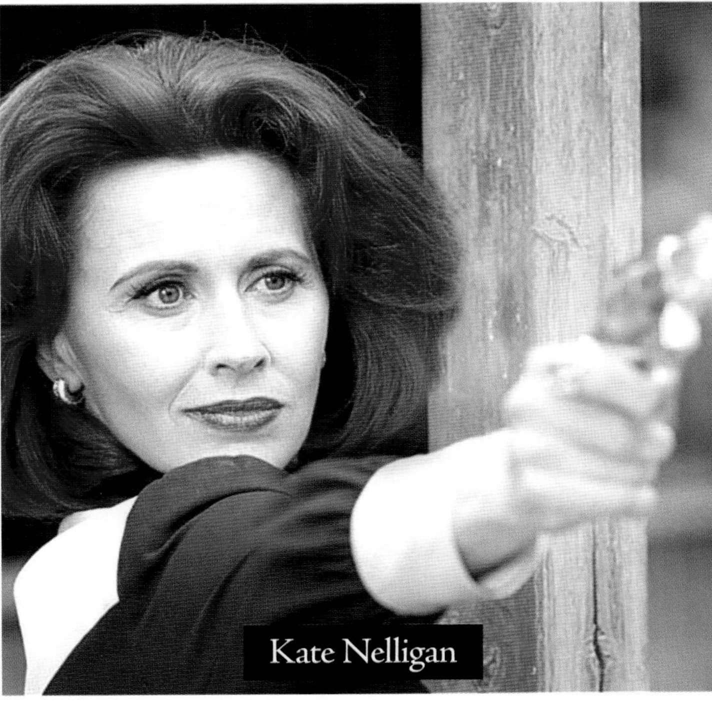
Kate Nelligan

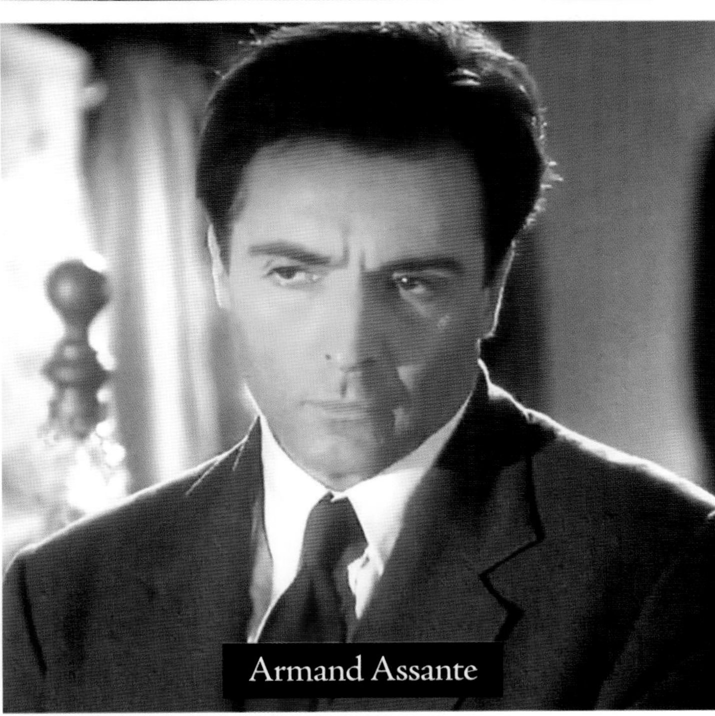
Armand Assante

Unfortunately, the audience was not privy to the review I received from Aaron Davis, this book's graphic designer, who said, "Carl, don't listen to the critics, this is one of my favorite films." Sadly, the audience went along with the critics, but there is no denying the film starred three very attractive women and one good-looking guy.

"Fatal Instinct" might have done better at the box office had I taken Mel Brooks' suggestion and titled the film "Frontal Attraction."

In German-occupied Poland during World War II, Oskar Schindler gradually becomes concerned for his Jewish workforce after witnessing their persecution by the Nazi Germans.

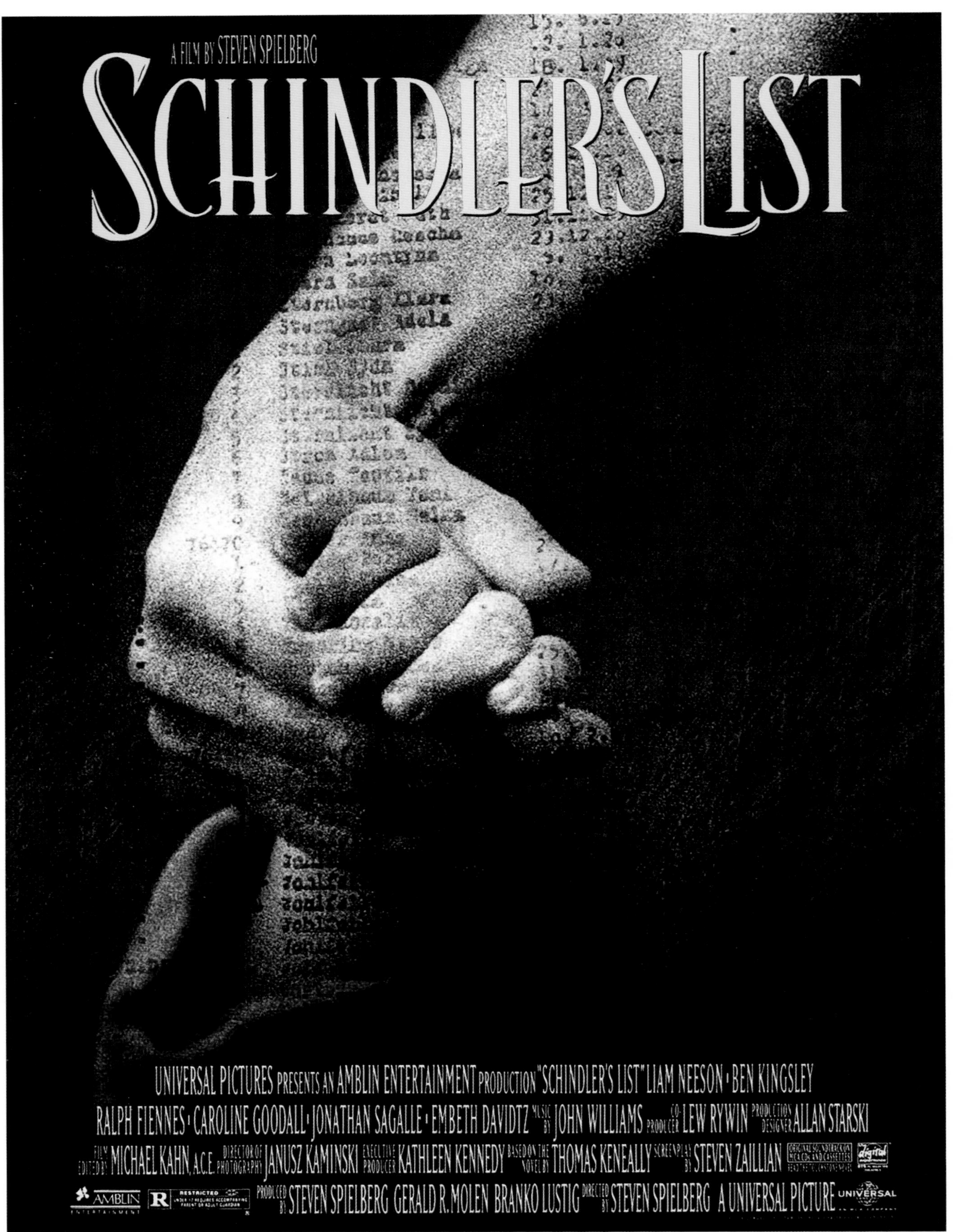

Michael Wilmington of The Chicago Tribune wrote: "With seemingly effortless grace and skill, 'Schindler's List' balances fear and exaltation, humor and horror, love and death."

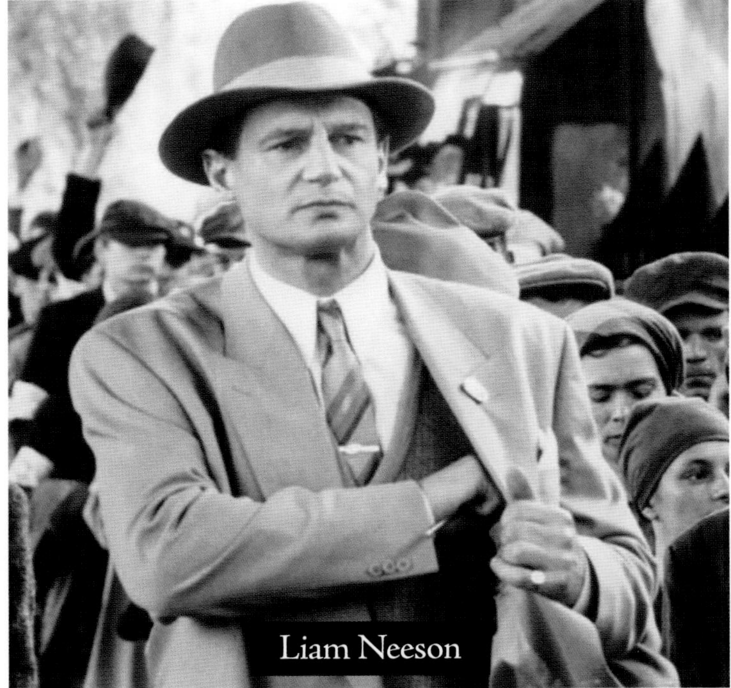

Liam Neeson

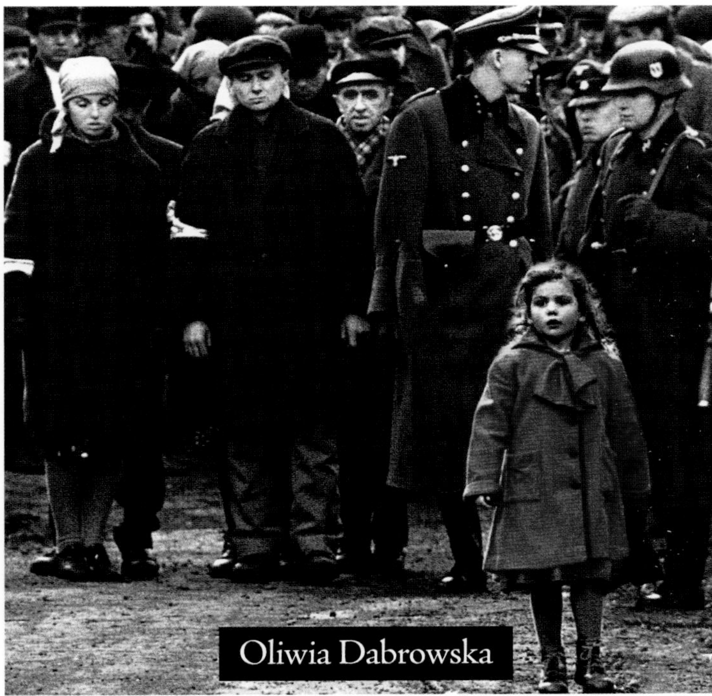

Oliwia Dabrowska

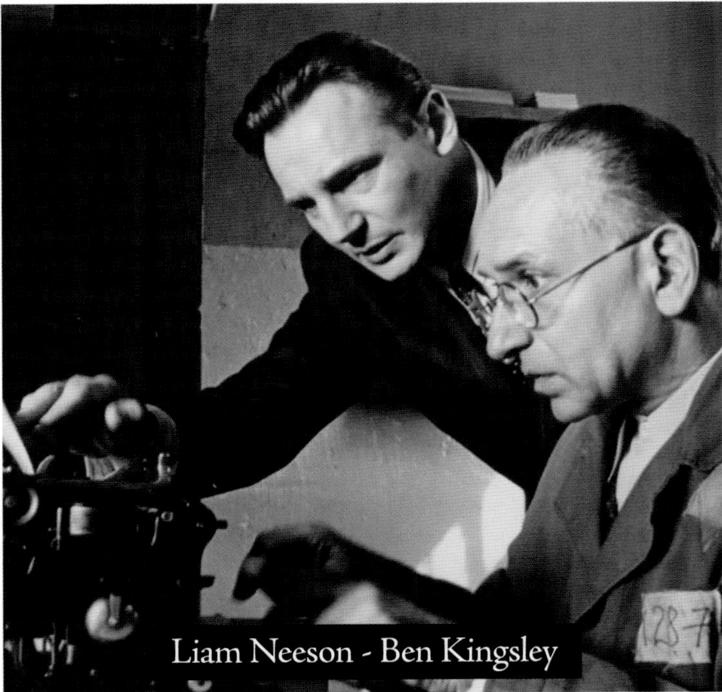

Liam Neeson - Ben Kingsley

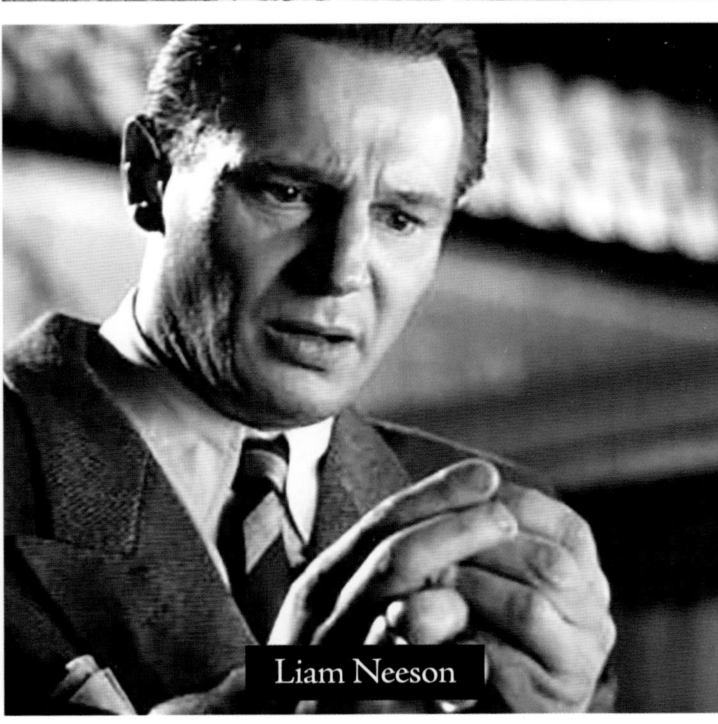

Liam Neeson

Oskar Schindler, a greedy German businessman and a member of the Nazi party, became an unlikely humanitarian when he turned his factory into a refuge that saved 1100 Jews from being gassed at Auschwitz.

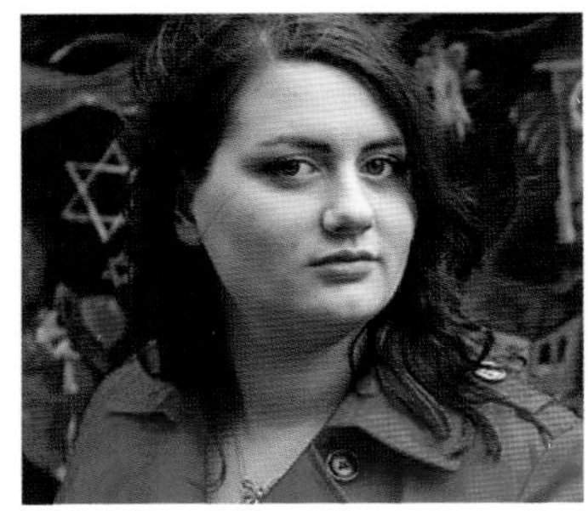

I'm happy to report that Oliwia Dabrowska, the little girl in the red coat, is now this lovely woman in the red coat.

A butler who sacrificed body and soul to service in the years leading up to World War II realizes too late how misguided his loyalty was to his lordly employer.

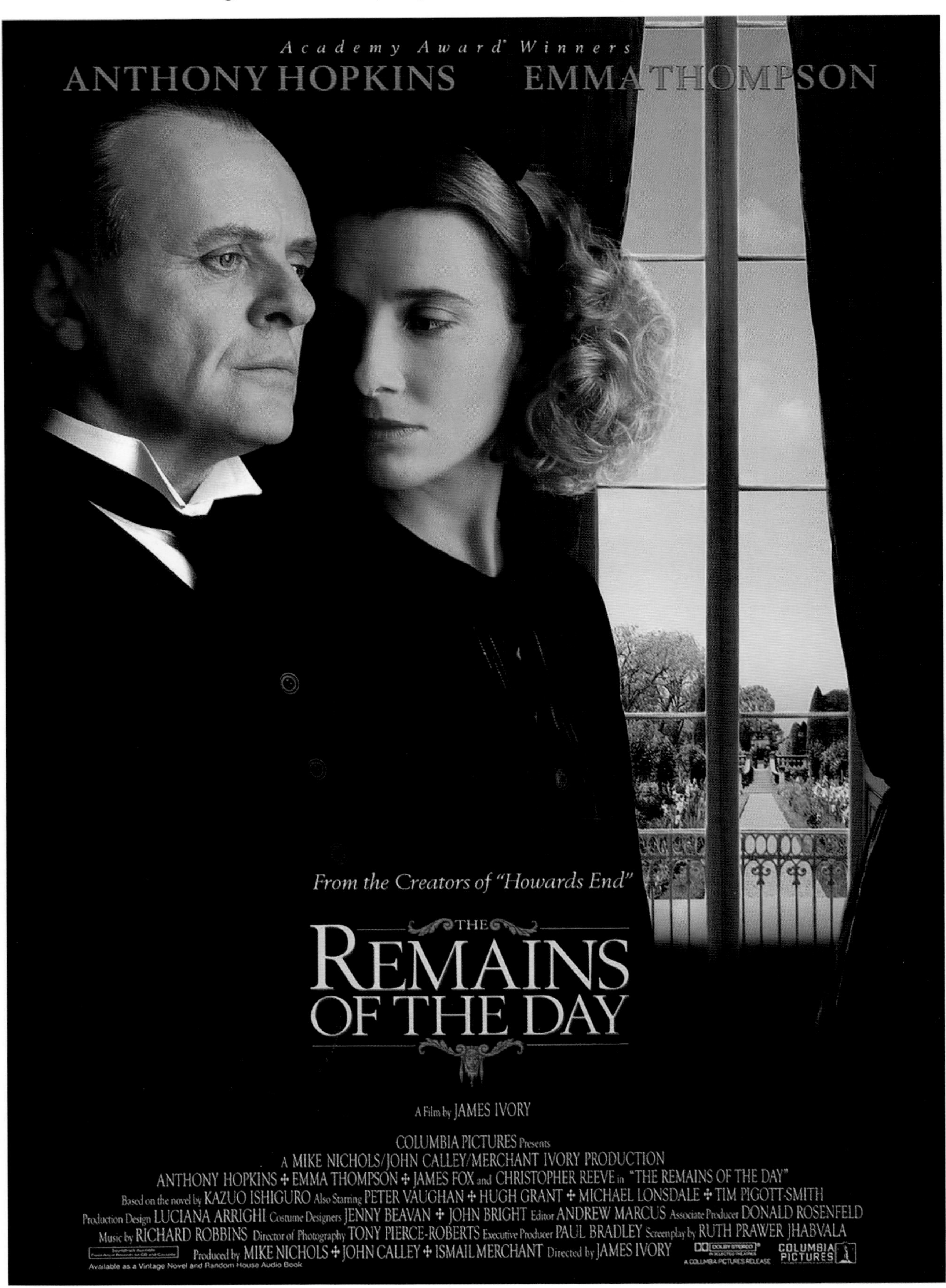

Todd McCarthy of Variety wrote: "All the meticulousness, intelligence, taste and superior acting that one expects from Merchant Ivory productions have been brought to bear."

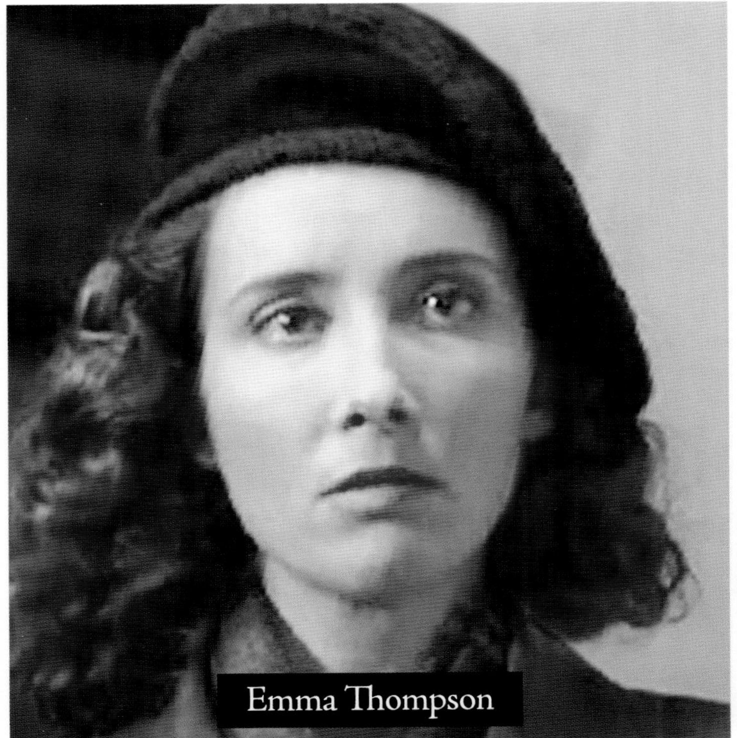
Emma Thompson

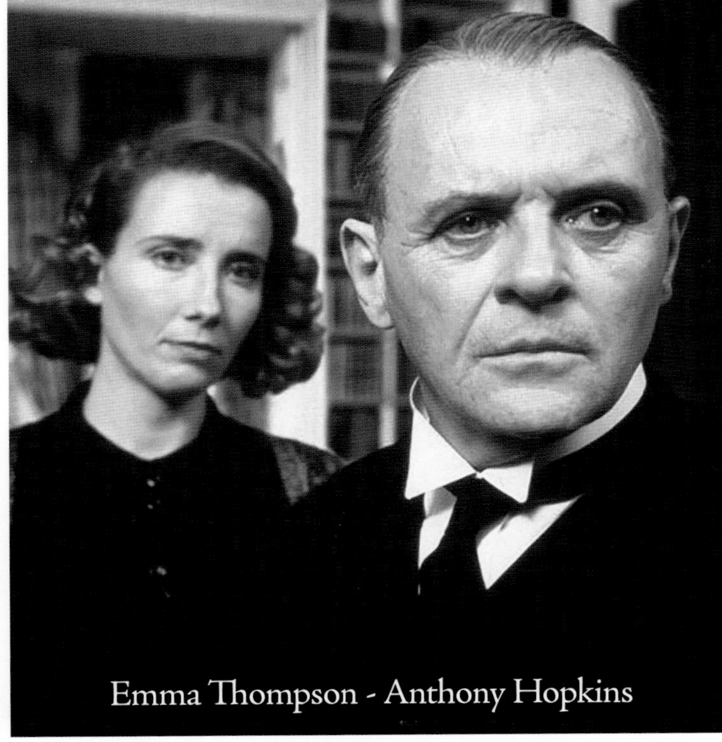
Emma Thompson - Anthony Hopkins

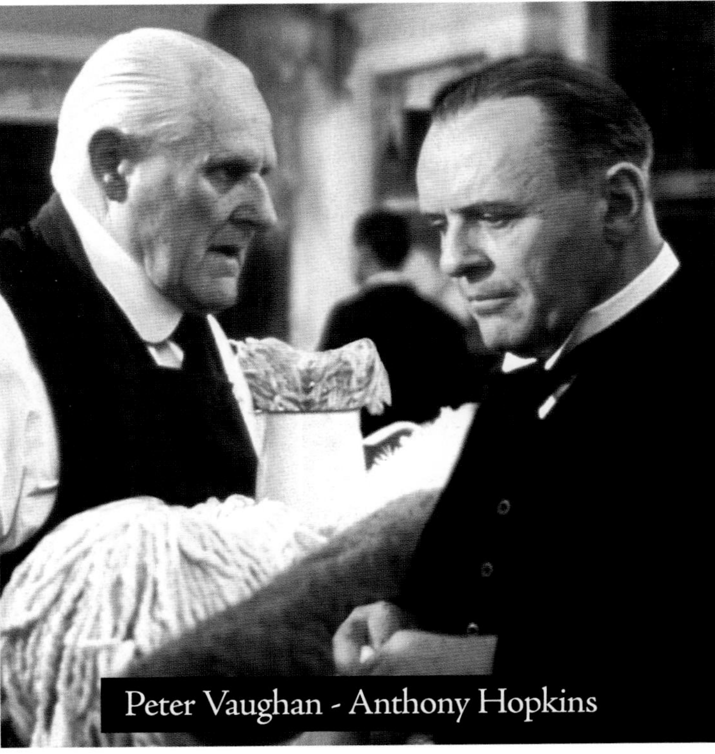
Peter Vaughan - Anthony Hopkins

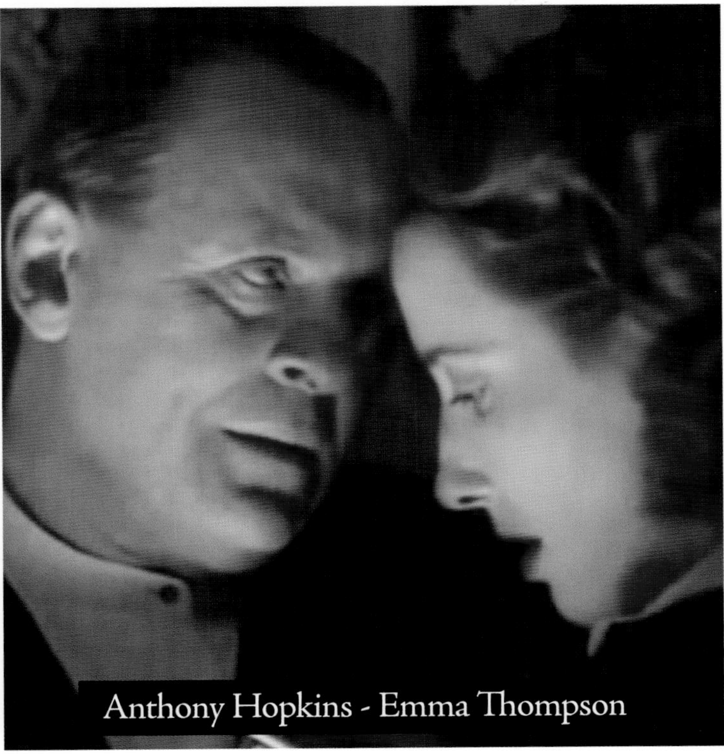
Anthony Hopkins - Emma Thompson

I met Emma Thompson at an L.A. film preview and had the pleasure of telling her that I've admired everything she's ever done, which includes "Remains of the Day," "Howard's End" and "Sense and Sensibility," in which she starred and wrote the screenplay. Every time I see her perform, I marvel at her ability to move me. I also like her looks.

An ambitious but troubled movie director tries his best to fulfill his dream, despite his lack of support.

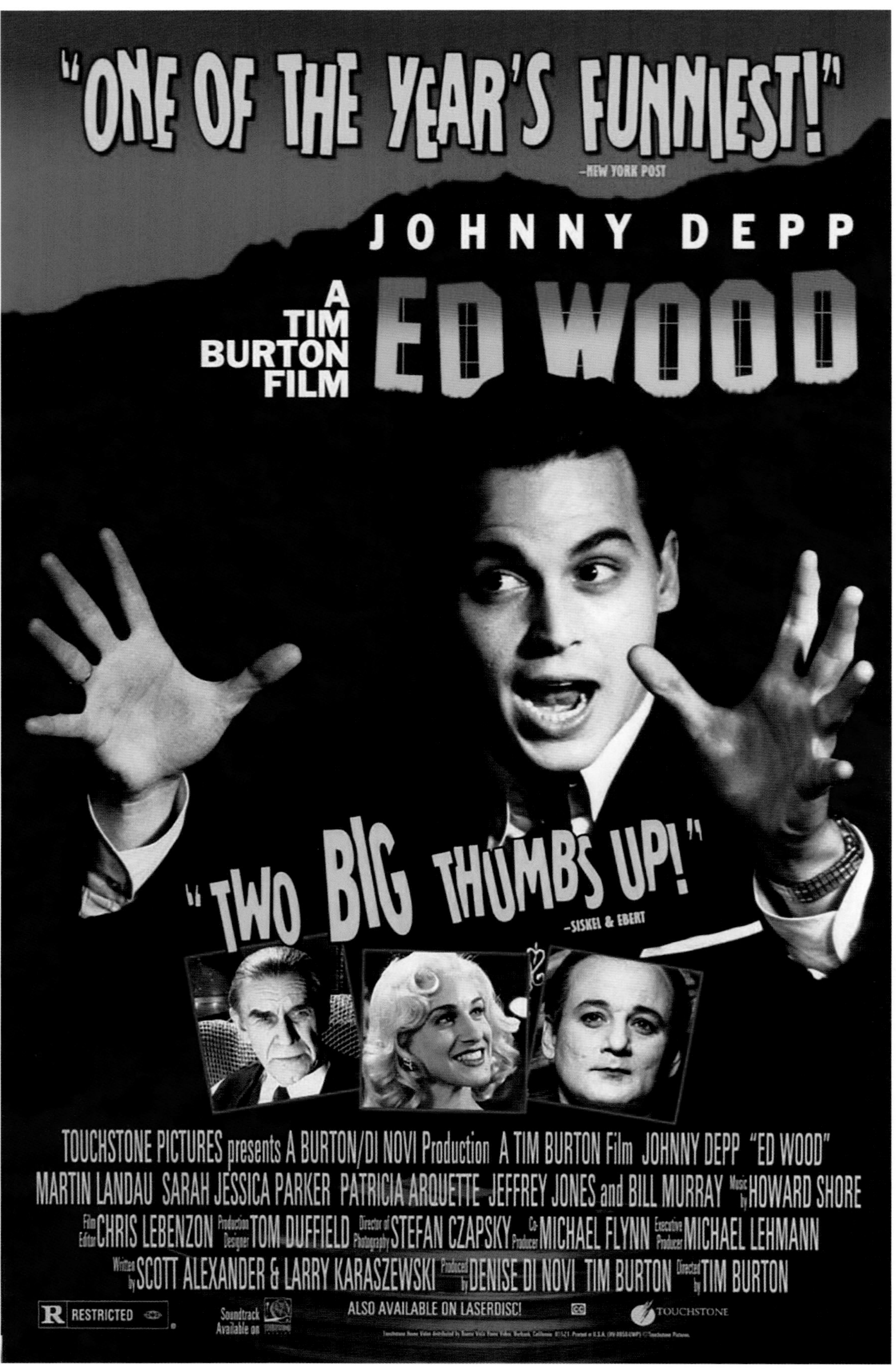

Peter Travers of Rolling Stone wrote: "Outrageously disjointed and just as outrageously entertaining, the picture stands as a successful outsider's tribute to a failed kindred spirit."

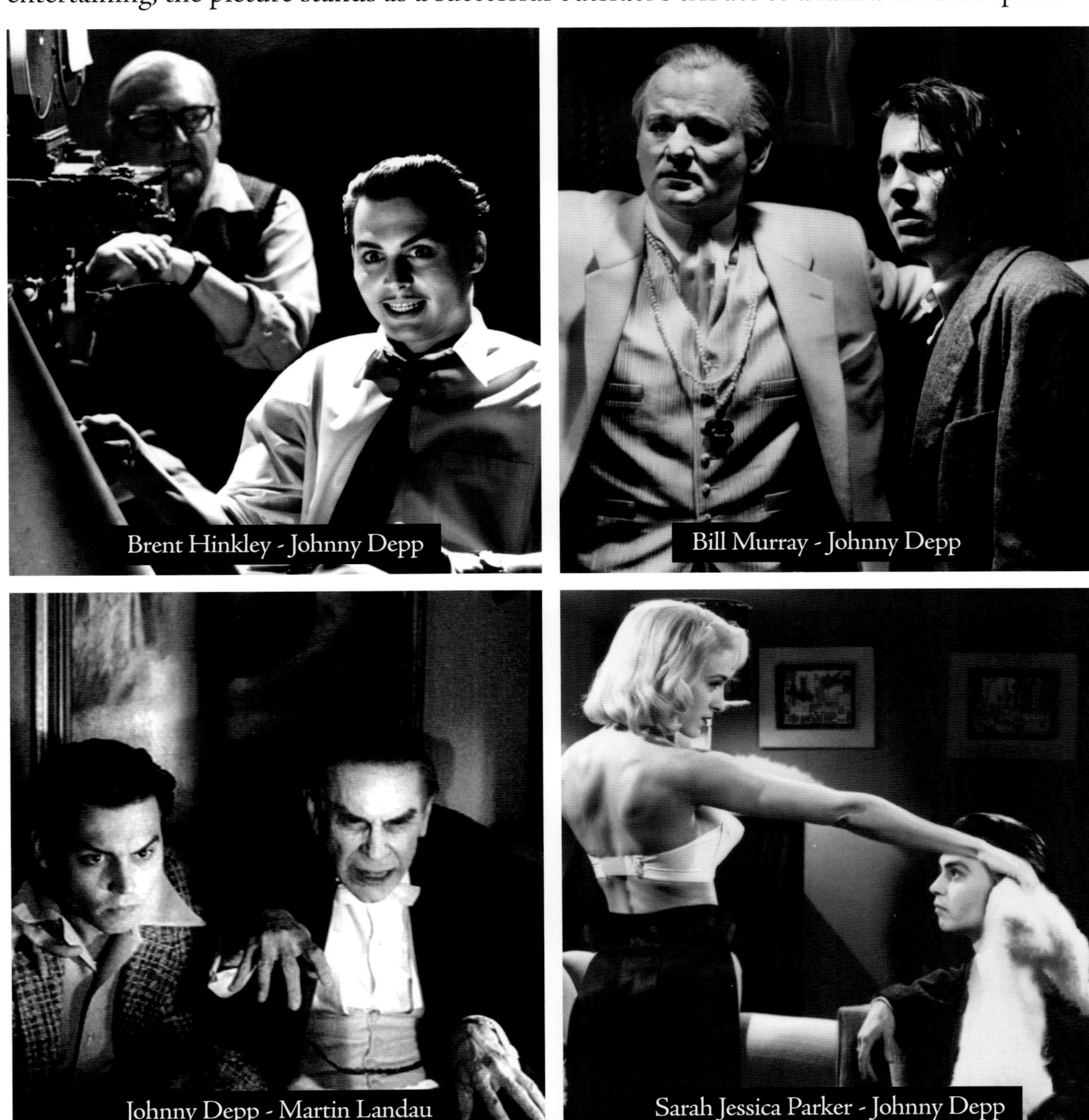

Brent Hinkley - Johnny Depp

Bill Murray - Johnny Depp

Johnny Depp - Martin Landau

Sarah Jessica Parker - Johnny Depp

"Ed Wood" had three minor stars, cost $18 million to make and grossed $5.9 million. So why did I laugh ten times as much as I did when I saw "It's a Mad, Mad, Mad, Mad World," that cost $9.4 million, grossed $60 million and had twelve major stars? Could it be that I laughed ten times as much because "Ed Wood" is ten times as funny as "Mad World?"

While not intelligent, Forrest Gump has accidentally been present at many historic moments, but his true love, Jenny Curran, eludes him.

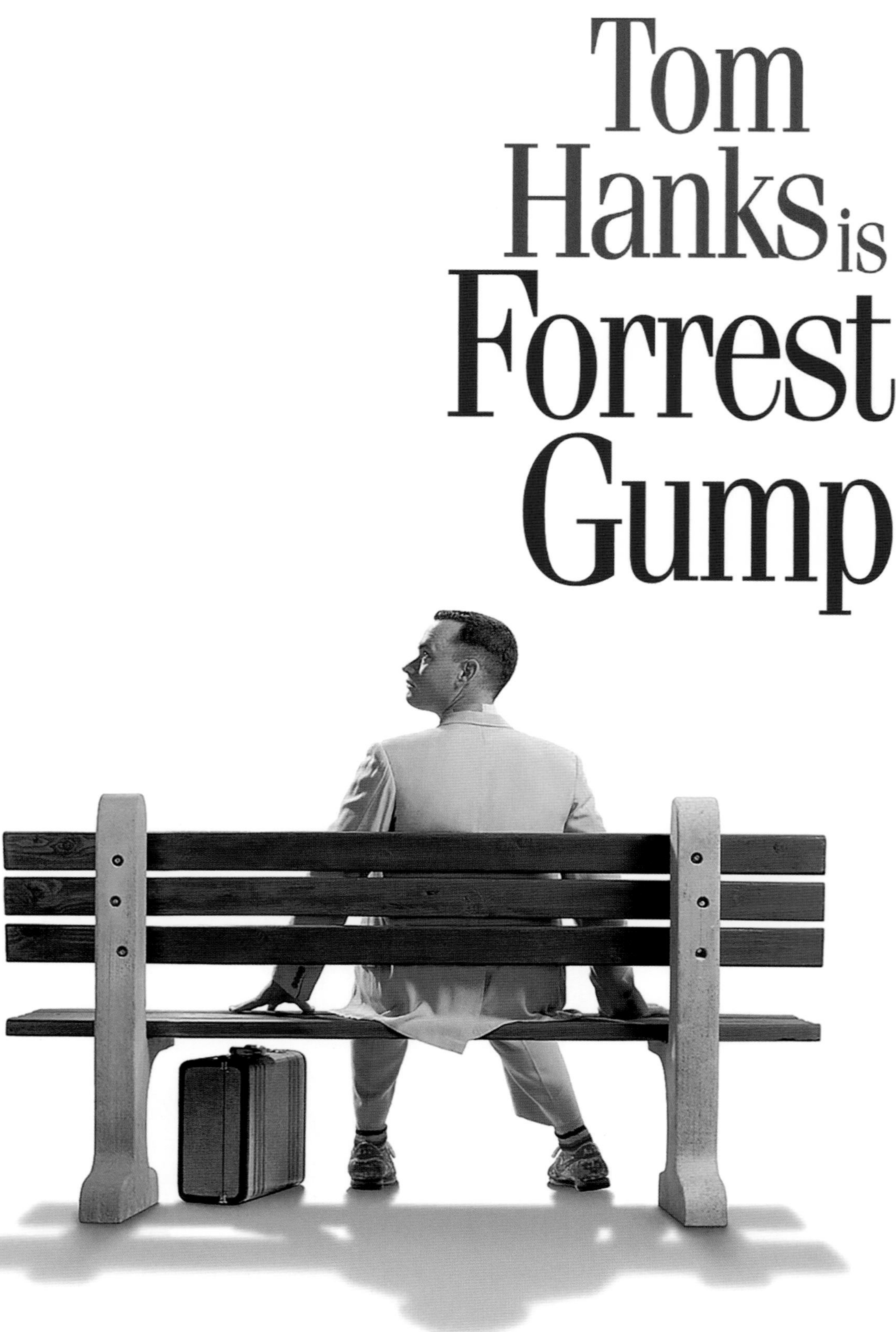

Dennis King of Tulsa World wrote: "It's a lovely and wise story told with honesty and acted out with unassuming grace. To his collection of medals, trophies and kudos, Forrest Gump should add an Oscar or two."

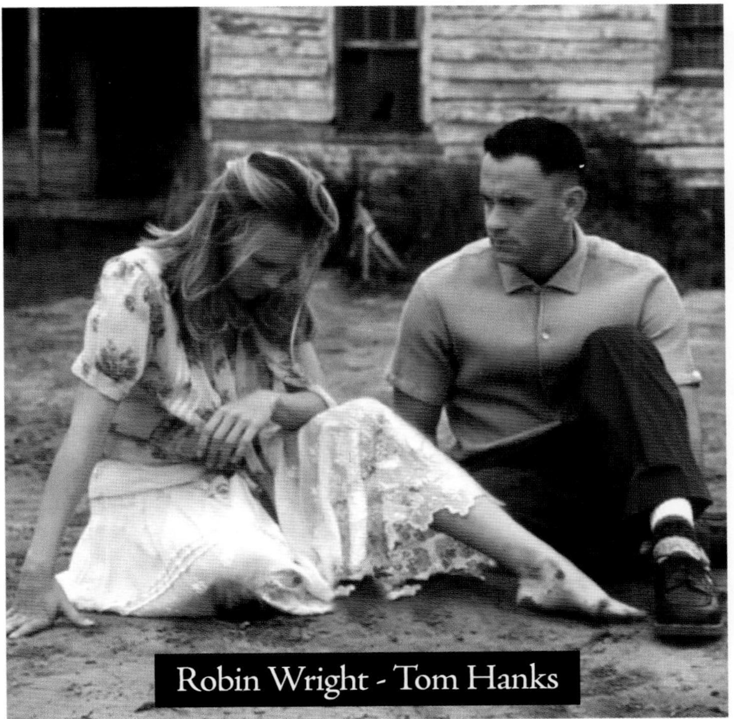
Robin Wright - Tom Hanks

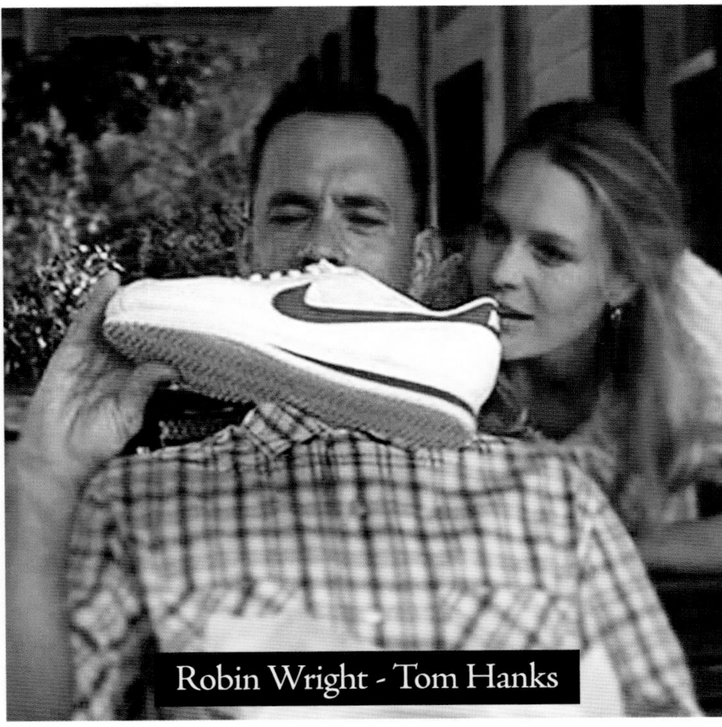
Robin Wright - Tom Hanks

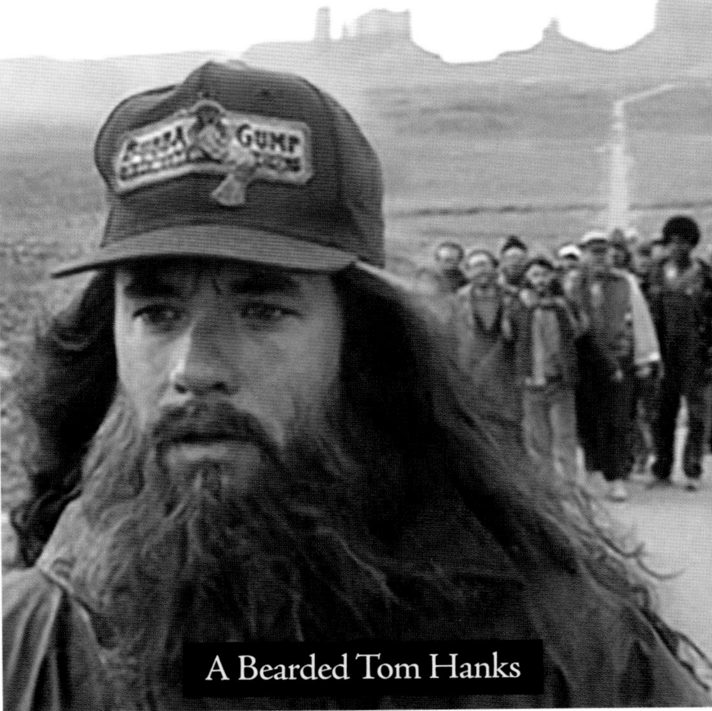

A Bearded Tom Hanks

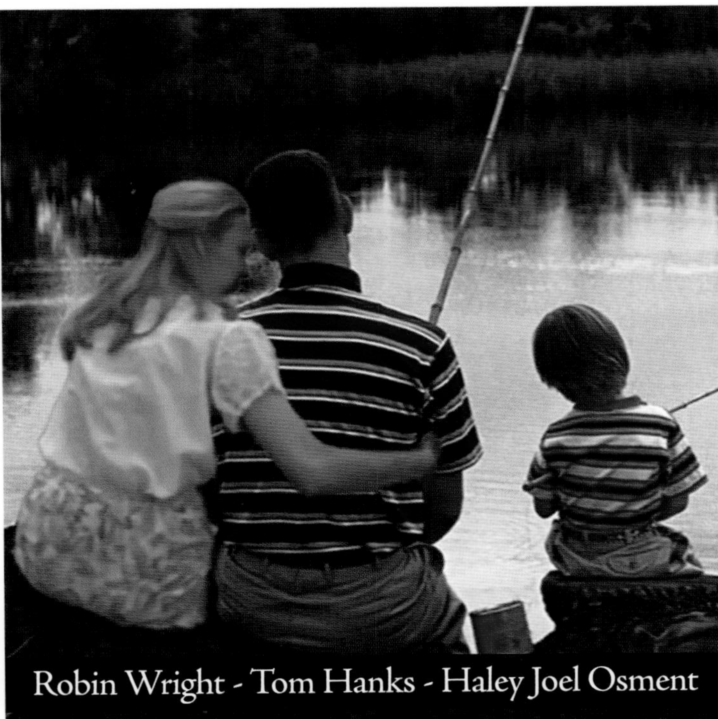
Robin Wright - Tom Hanks - Haley Joel Osment

"Forrest Gump" deserved the six Oscars it won, as did Tom Hanks for his portrayal of Forrest Gump, who I can still hear saying, "Life is like a box of chocolates. You never know what you're going to get." When considering the scope of Tom Hanks' film output, I've no doubt that, if he were British, he'd be dubbed "Sir Thomas Hanks."

Two imprisoned men bond over a number of years, finding solace and eventual redemption through acts of common decency.

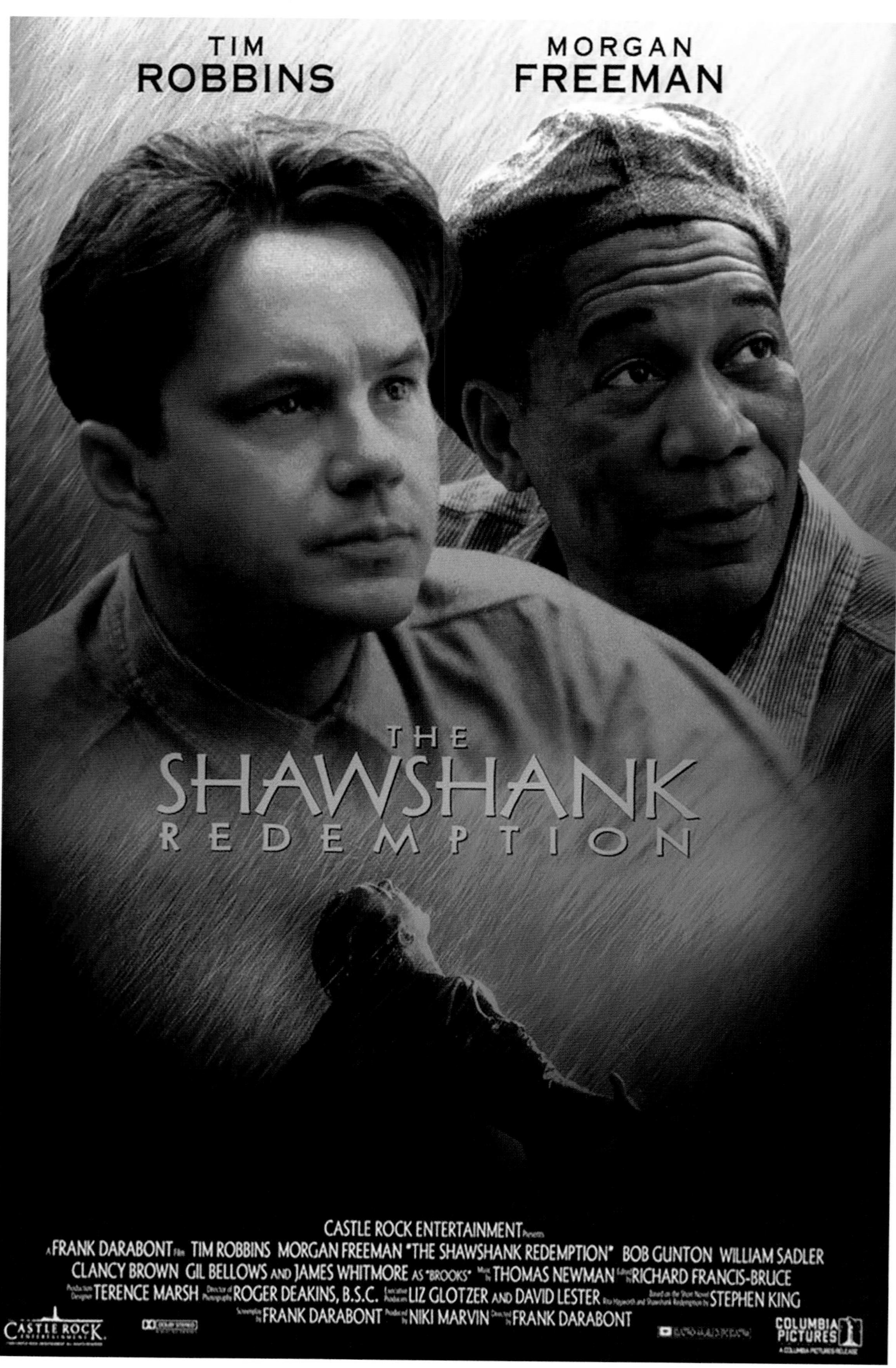

Janet Maslin wrote in the New York Times: "The conspiracy in 'The Shawshank Redemption' takes shape slowly and carefully, displaying an overall subtlety that's surprising in a movie of this genre. In the end, like Andy (Tim Robbins) and Red (Morgan Freeman), it gets to where it wanted to go."

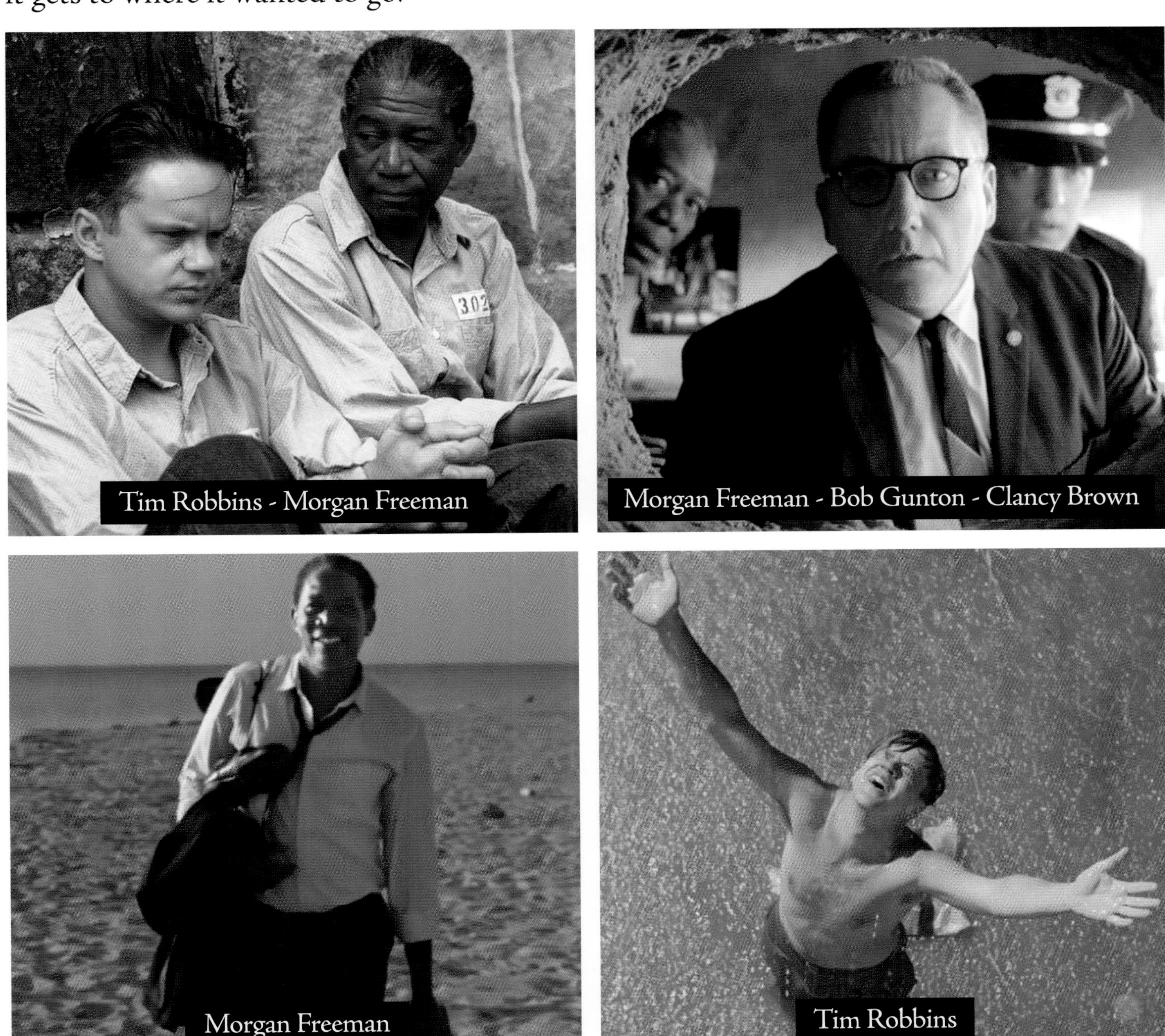

Tim Robbins - Morgan Freeman

Morgan Freeman - Bob Gunton - Clancy Brown

Morgan Freeman

Tim Robbins

I love this film and not because my son, Rob, produced it. I admit, though, that I would have loved it a tad more if the villainous prison warden, who was exposed for his money laundering operation, had not committed suicide. It'd be so much more satisfying if instead, he'd been imprisoned for life in one of the hell-holes he used to punish starving inmates.

About the film's narrator: If there is a God, and he could speak, I'm certain his voice would sound exactly like Morgan Freeman's.

Over the course of five social occasions, a committed bachelor must consider the notion that he may have discovered love.

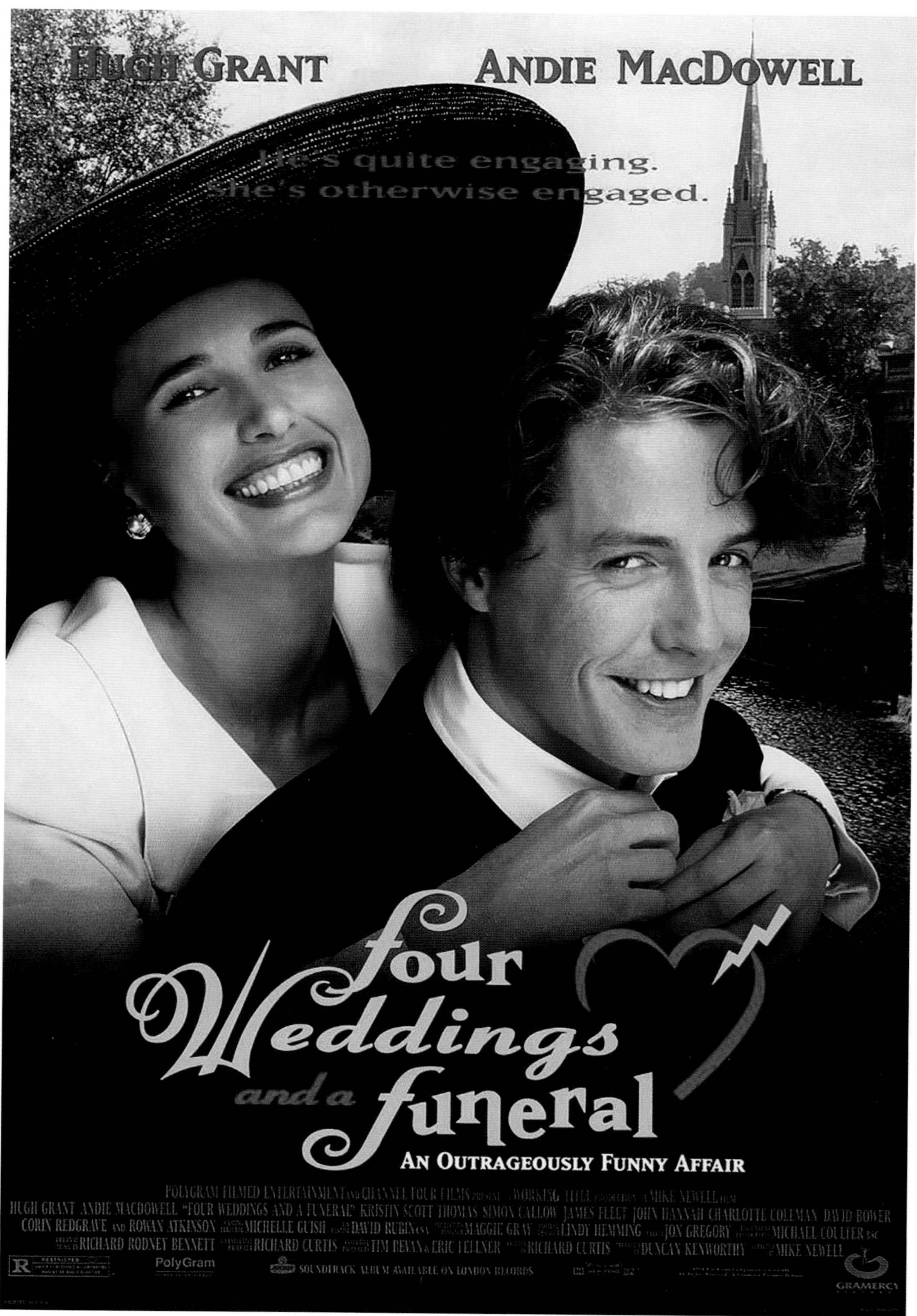

Kenneth Turan of the Los Angeles Times: "Deftly written by Richard Curtis and directed by the versatile Mike Newell, 'Four Weddings' is as good as its word, breezily following a small circle of friends through every one of the events the title promises."

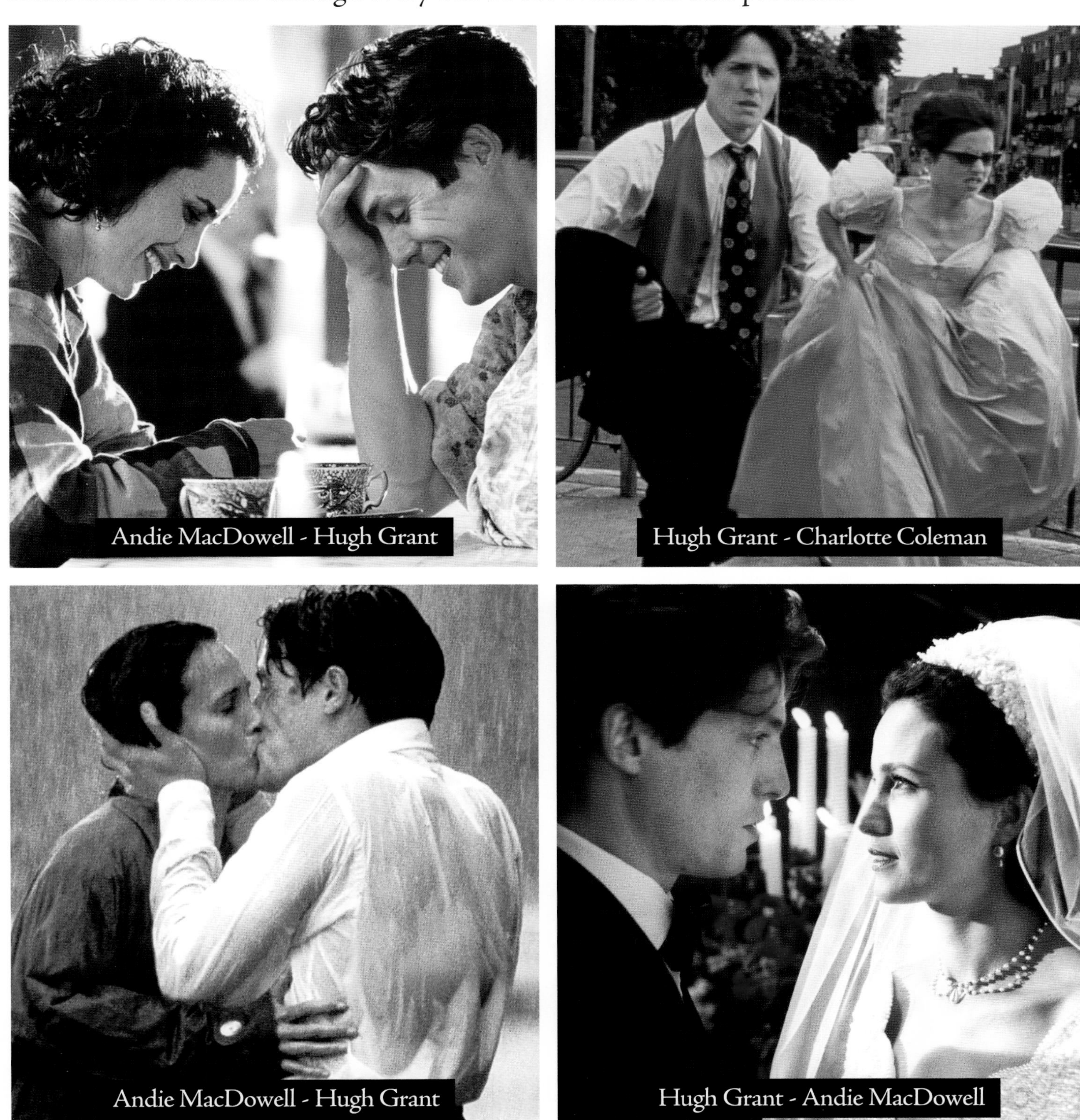

Andie MacDowell - Hugh Grant

Hugh Grant - Charlotte Coleman

Andie MacDowell - Hugh Grant

Hugh Grant - Andie MacDowell

How many of you, besides myself, enjoyed the experience of watching two people, who were obviously meant for each other, not realize they were meant for each other until the very end when they realized they were meant for each other?

Comedy-drama about a widowed U.S. president and a lobbyist who fall in love. It's all above-board, but "politics is perception" and sparks fly anyway.

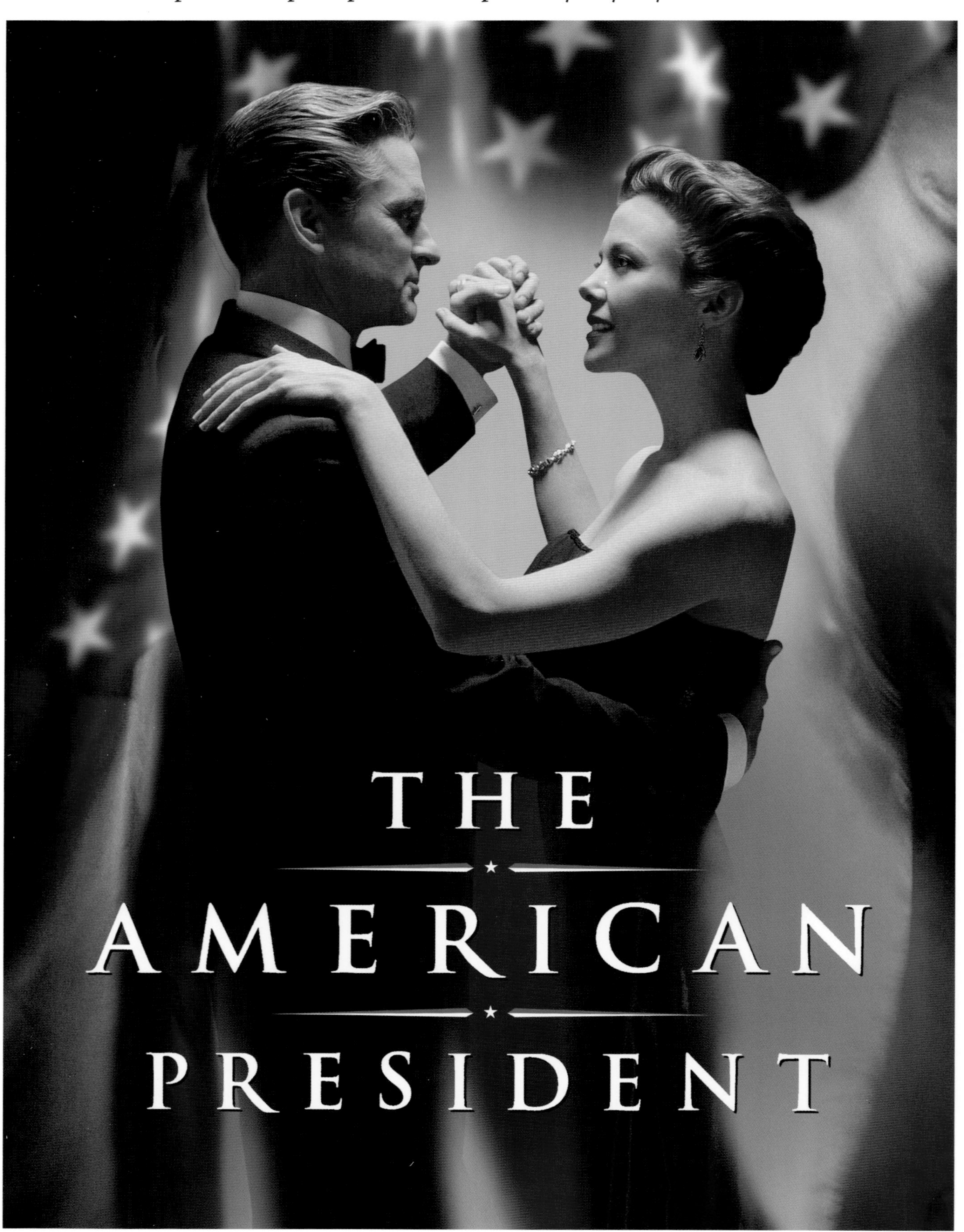

Janet Maslin of The New York Times wrote: "With great looks, a dandy supporting cast, a zinger-filled screenplay by Aaron Sorkin and Mr. Douglas twinkling merrily in the Oval Office, 'The American President' is sunny enough to make the real Presidency pale by comparison."

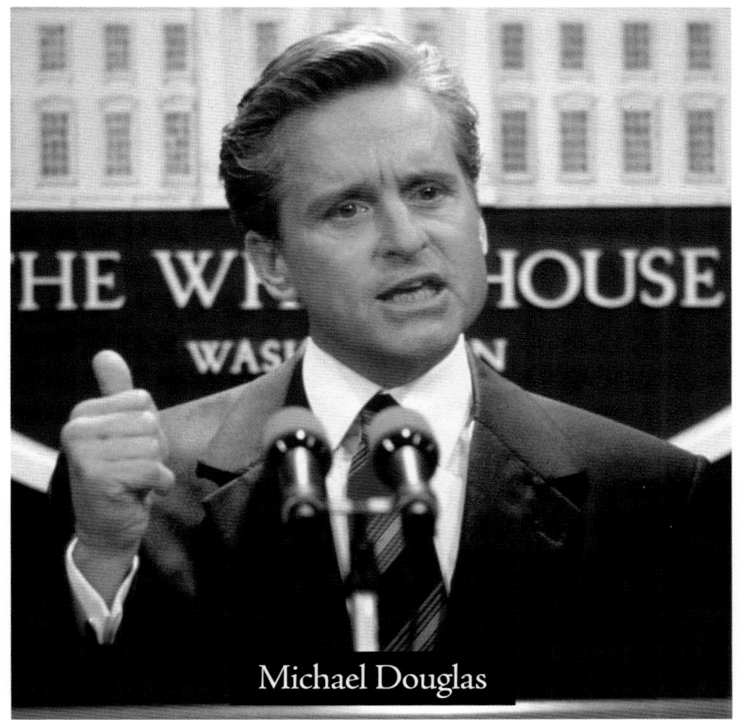

Michael Douglas

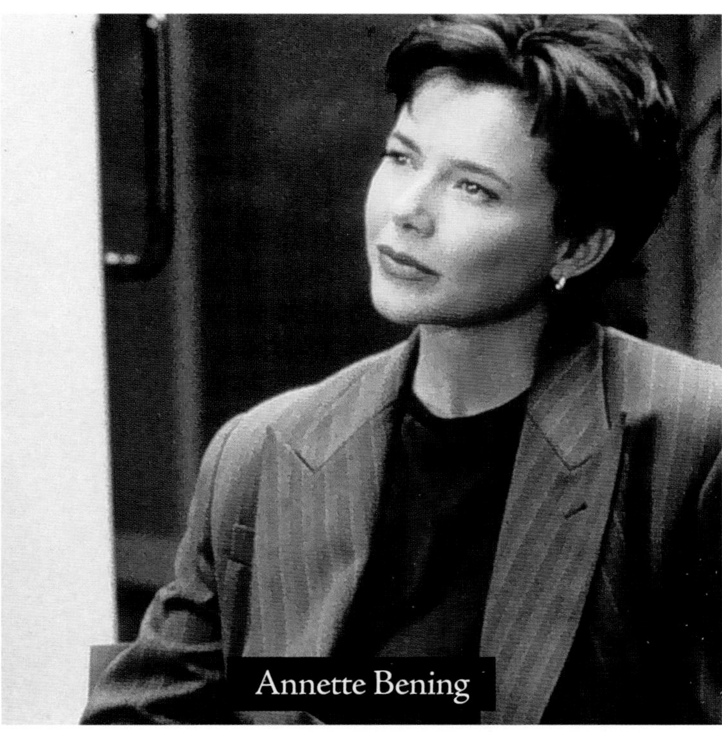

Annette Bening

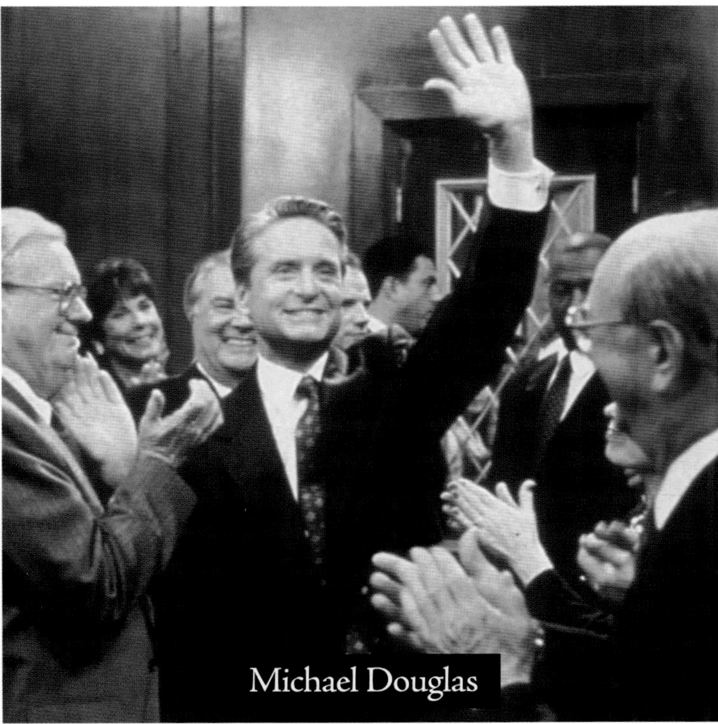

Michael Douglas

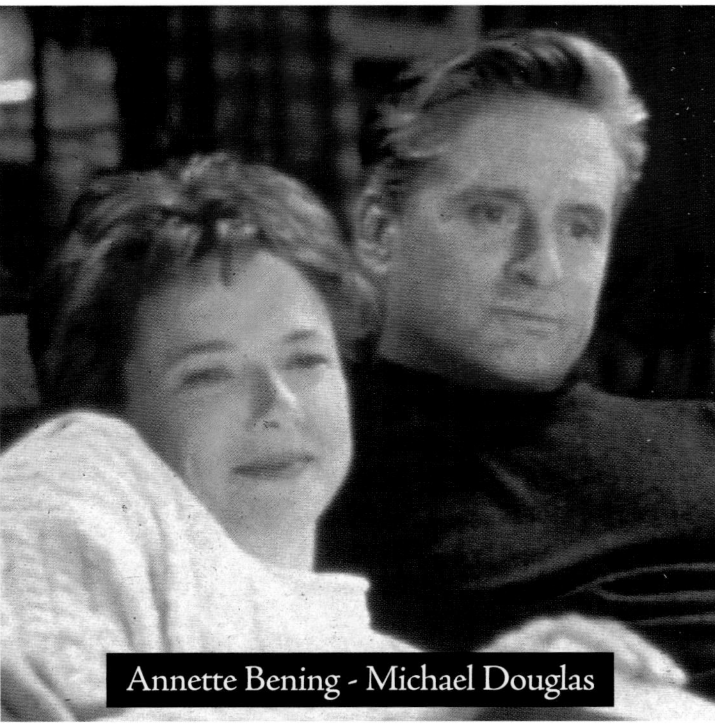

Annette Bening - Michael Douglas

I particularly enjoyed the romance that developed between Annette Bening, the environmentalist, and Michael Douglas, the presidential candidate.

The reason "The American President" is so effective is due to the director, Rob Reiner's, understanding of politics and his ability, if called upon, to be our nation's President.

Rich Mr. Dashwood dies, leaving his second wife and her three daughters poor by the rules of inheritance. The two eldest daughters are the titular opposites.

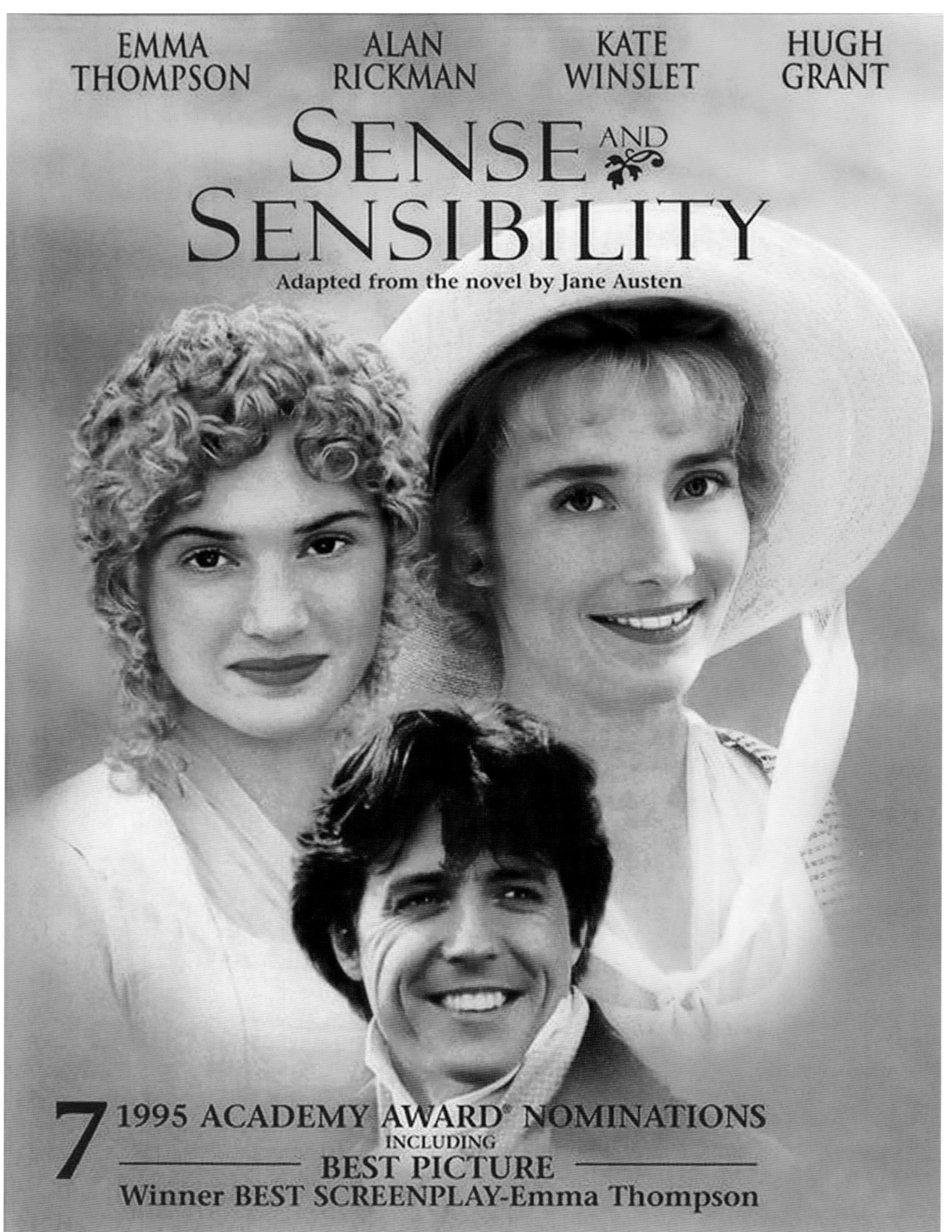

Todd McCarthy from Variety wrote: "Emma Thompson's screenplay of Jane Austen's novel manages the neat trick of preserving the necessary niceties and decorum of civilized behavior of the time while still cutting to the dramatic quick."

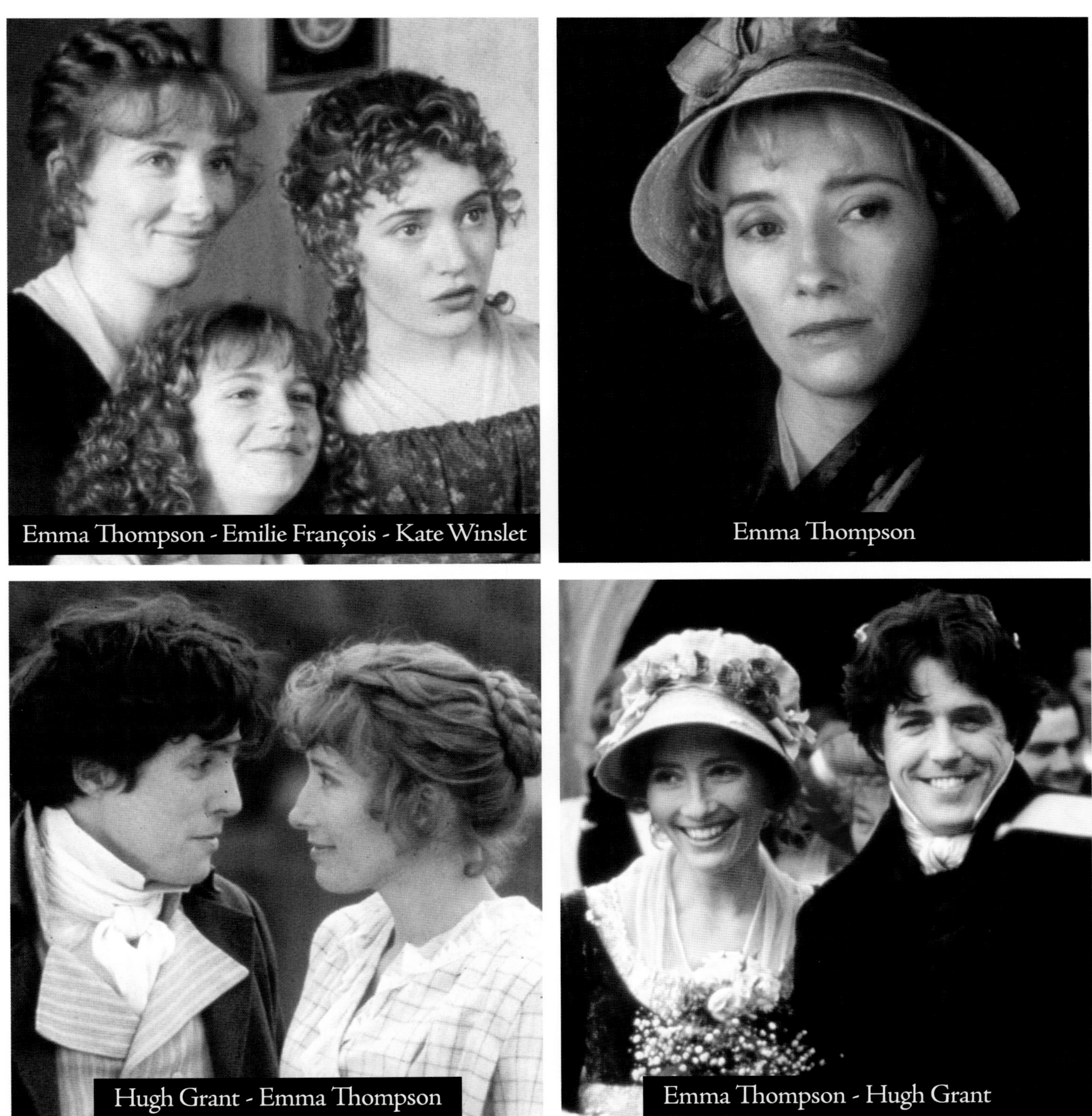

Emma Thompson - Emilie François - Kate Winslet

Emma Thompson

Hugh Grant - Emma Thompson

Emma Thompson - Hugh Grant

I became a fan of Hugh Grant when I saw him in "Love Actually," "Four Weddings and a Funeral" and, this year, as Florence Foster Jenkins' husband.

To remind you how I feel about Emma Thompson, check page 295.

A computer programmer stumbles upon a conspiracy, putting her life and the lives of those around her in great danger.

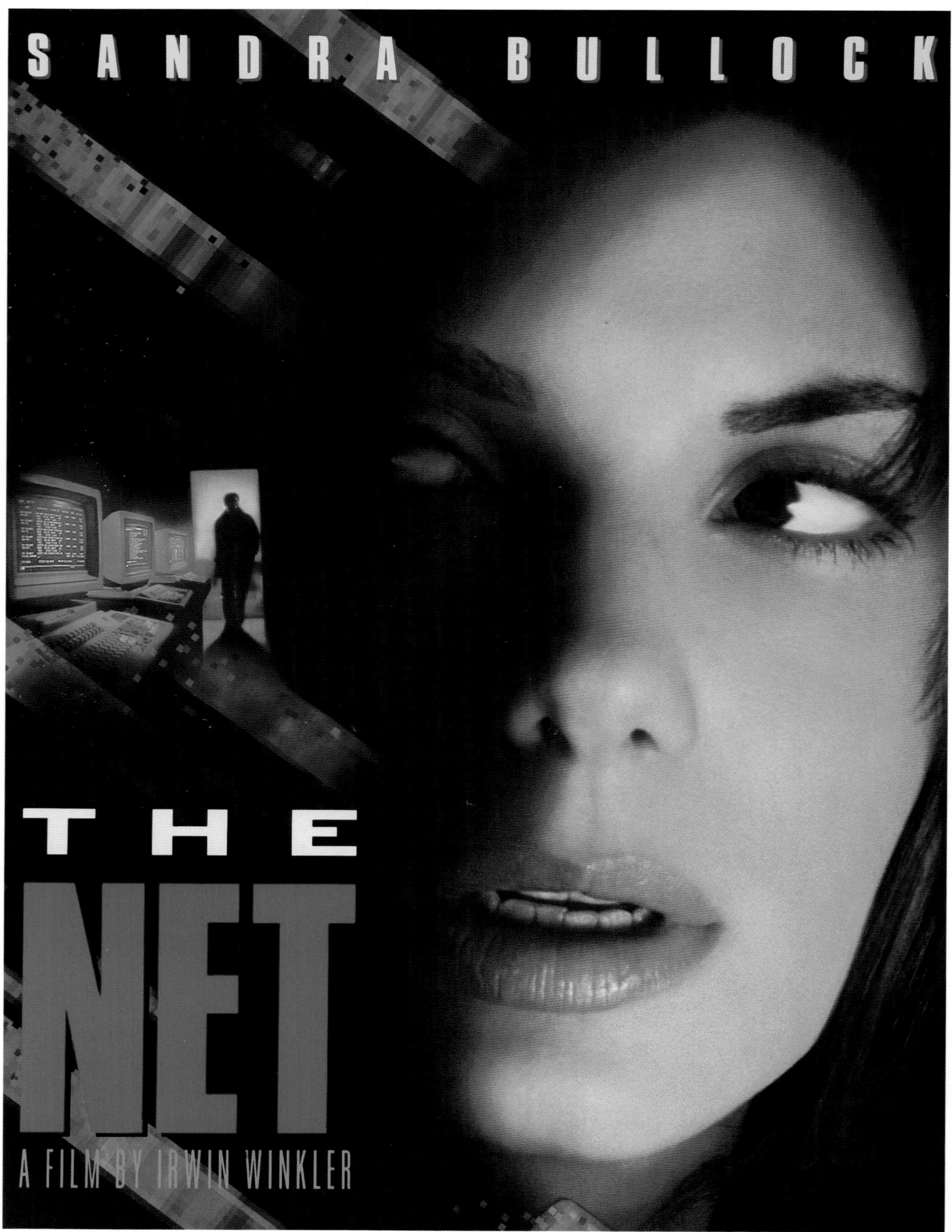

Mick LaSalle of the San Francisco Chronicle: "A strong enough suspense thriller, a high-tech version of one of those spiraling nightmares in which an innocent person is chased by assassins and wanted by the police."

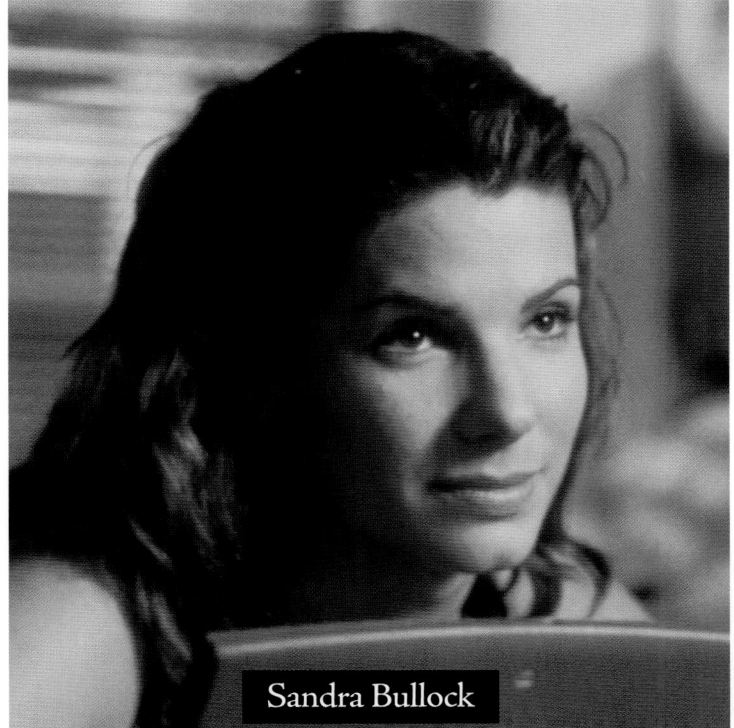

Sandra Bullock

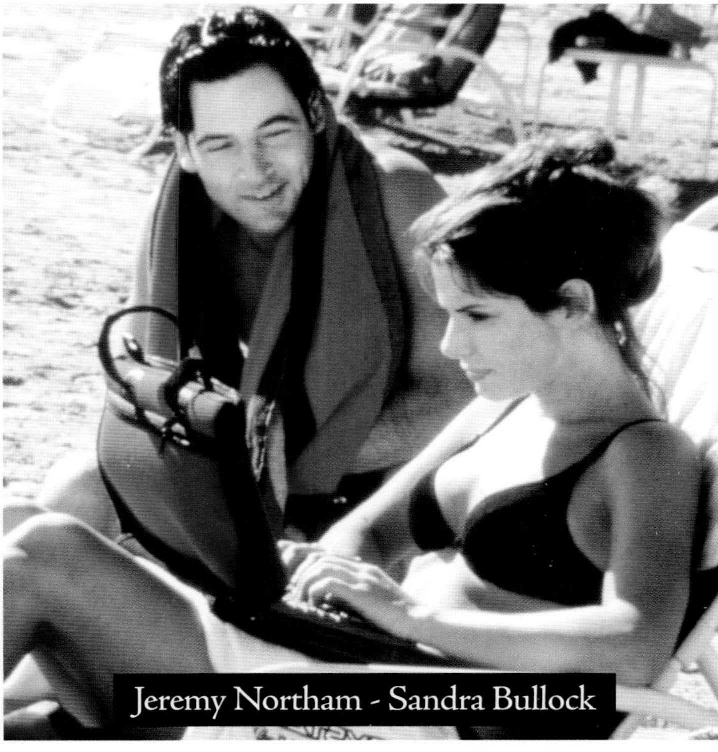

Jeremy Northam - Sandra Bullock

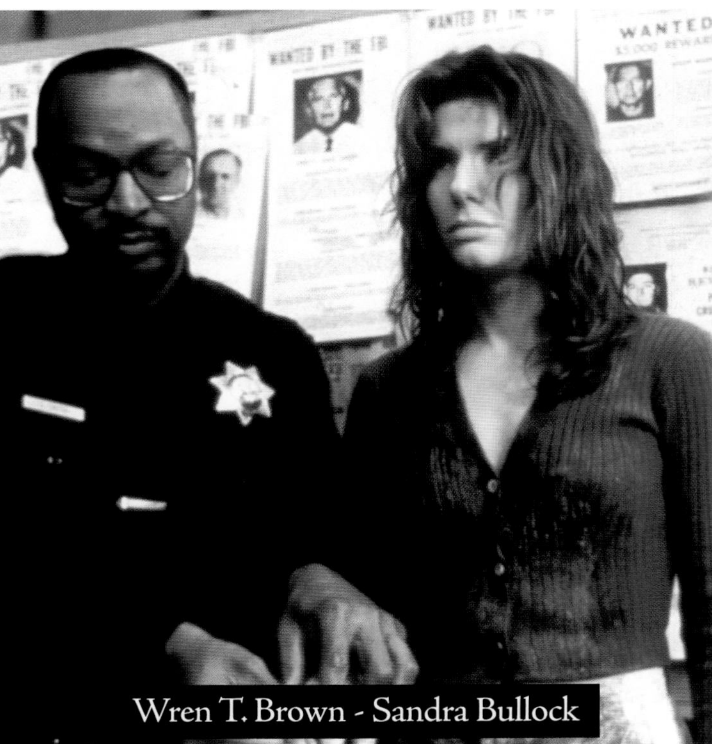

Wren T. Brown - Sandra Bullock

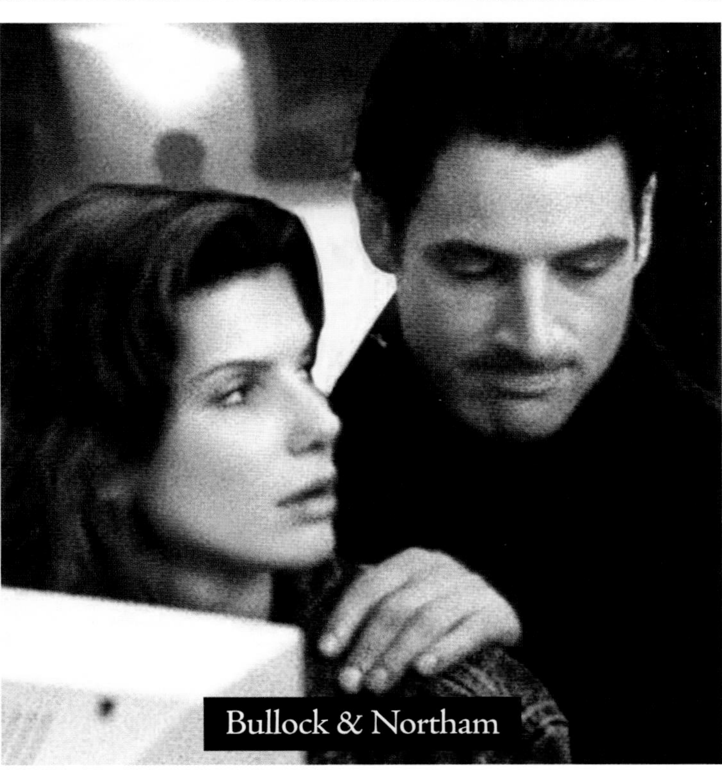

Bullock & Northam

I've often said Sandra Bullock is one of my favorite actresses and I was so happy to tell her how much I admired her when, this year, I did a cameo role with her in "Ocean's 8." I can't wait to see her and the all-female cast of thieves... which is due out in the Summer of 2018.

A Mississippi district attorney and the widow of Medgar Evers struggle to finally bring a white racist to justice for the 1963 murder of the civil rights leader.

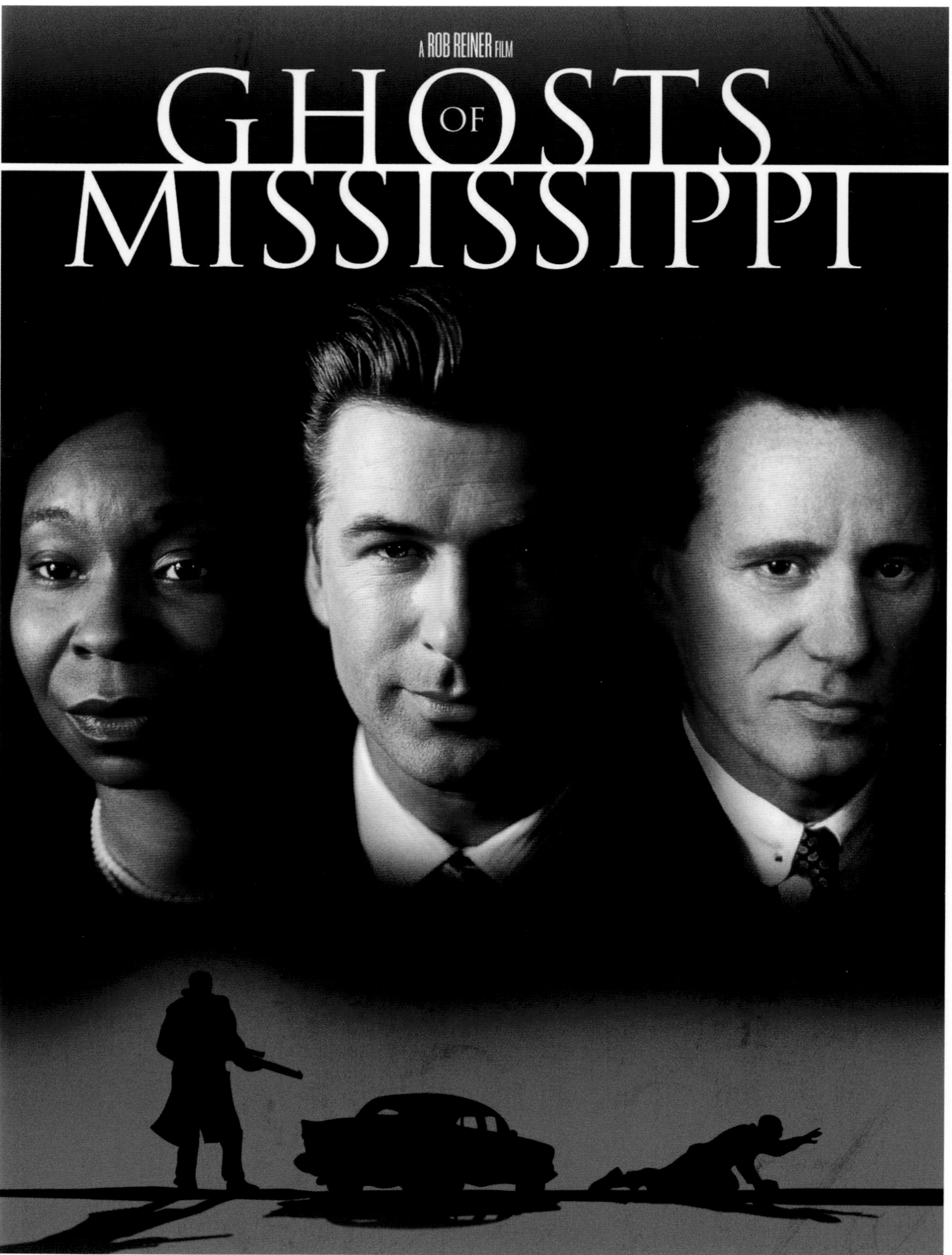

Frank Ochieng from Movie Eye wrote: "Reiner's intermittently preachy but nevertheless powerful and poignant portrait of hostility and racial strife during one of the ugliest chapters in contemporary American history."

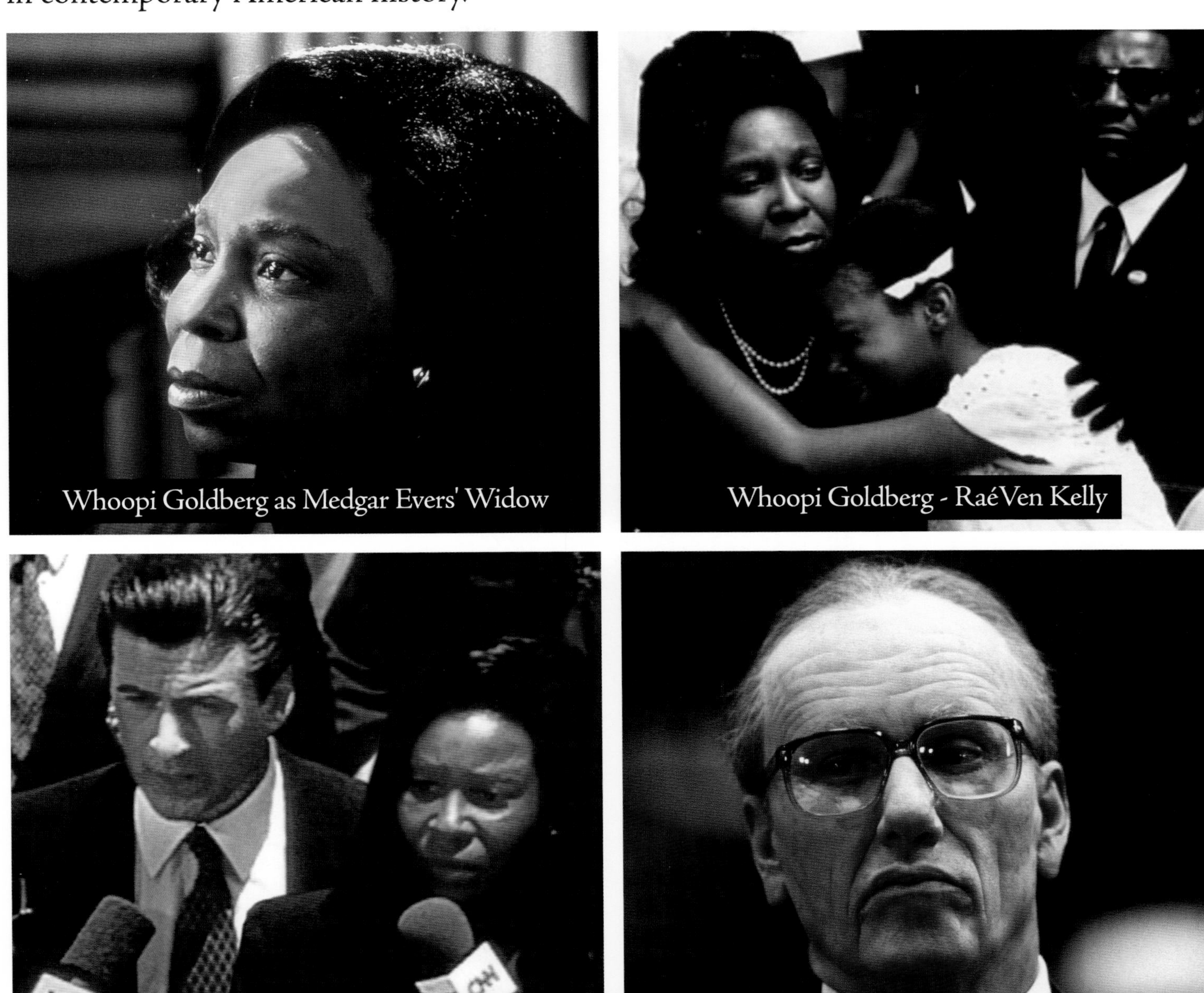

Whoopi Goldberg as Medgar Evers' Widow

Whoopi Goldberg - RaéVen Kelly

Alec Baldwin - Whoopi Goldberg

James Woods

The "Ghosts of Mississippi," another of Rob Reiner's directorial achievements, is high on my list of 'comeuppance' films. It was so satisfying to see the villainous, hate spouting racist, Byron De La Beckwith (James Woods), convicted and sentenced to life imprisonment for the murder of civil rights leader Medgar Evers.

On Oprah's show, her guest, Medgar Evers' widow, Myrlie, offered Rob the wallet her son was carrying when Beckwith shot him in the back. Rob was touched and, after saying he didn't feel right about accepting it, Mrs. Evers reached into the wallet, pulled out her son's poll tax receipt and presented it to Rob.

A neurotic, twice-divorced sci-fi writer moves in with his mother to solve his problems.

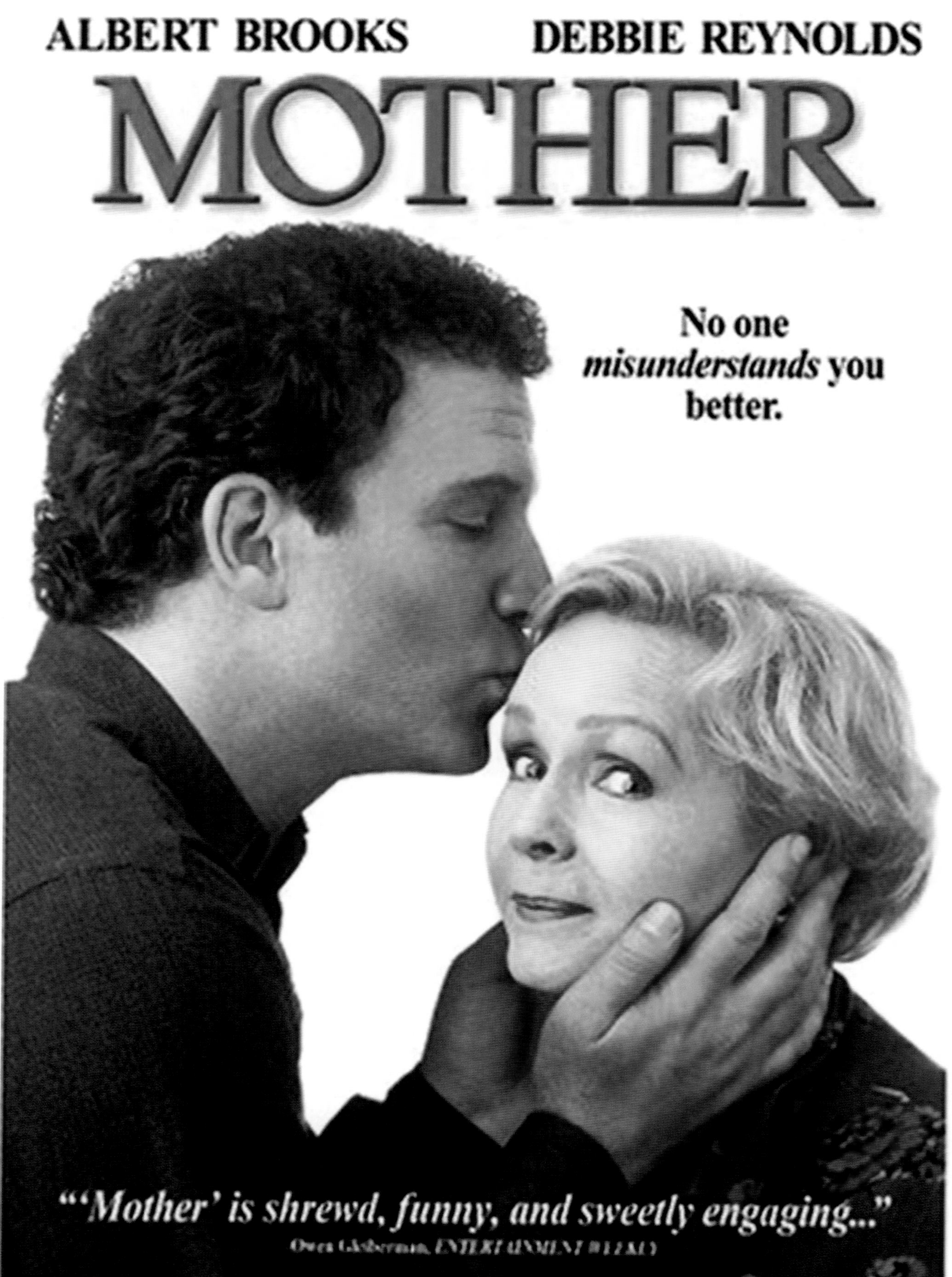

Roger Ebert from the Chicago Sun-Times wrote: "It wasn't the automatic laughter produced by slam-dunk punch lines, but the laughter of recognition, of insight, even sometimes of squirmy discomfort, as the truths hit close to home."

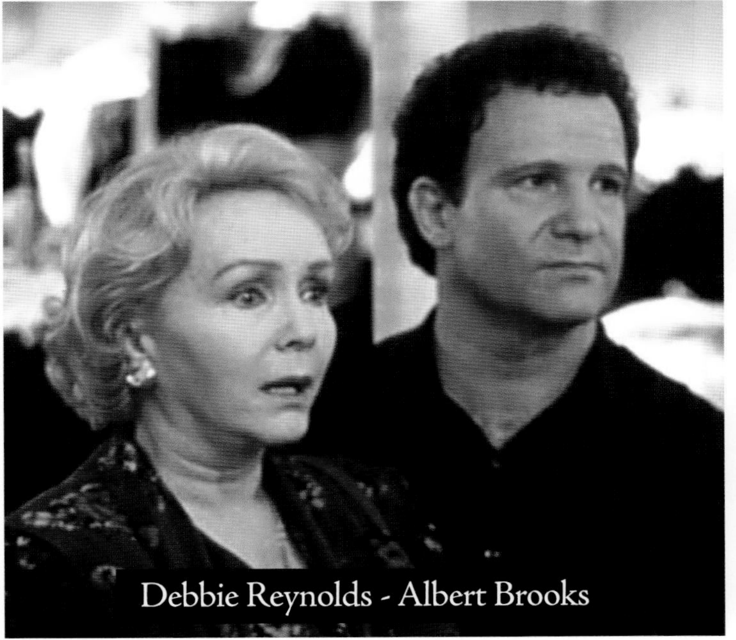
Debbie Reynolds - Albert Brooks

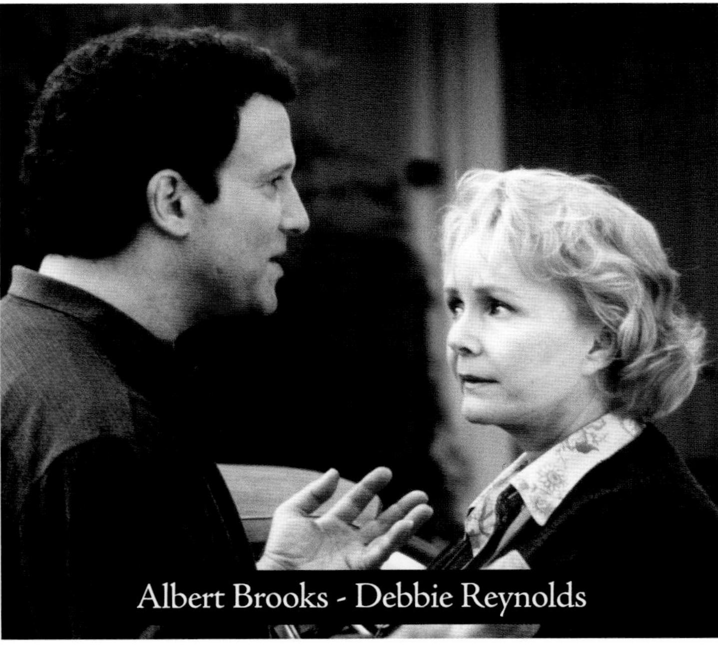
Albert Brooks - Debbie Reynolds

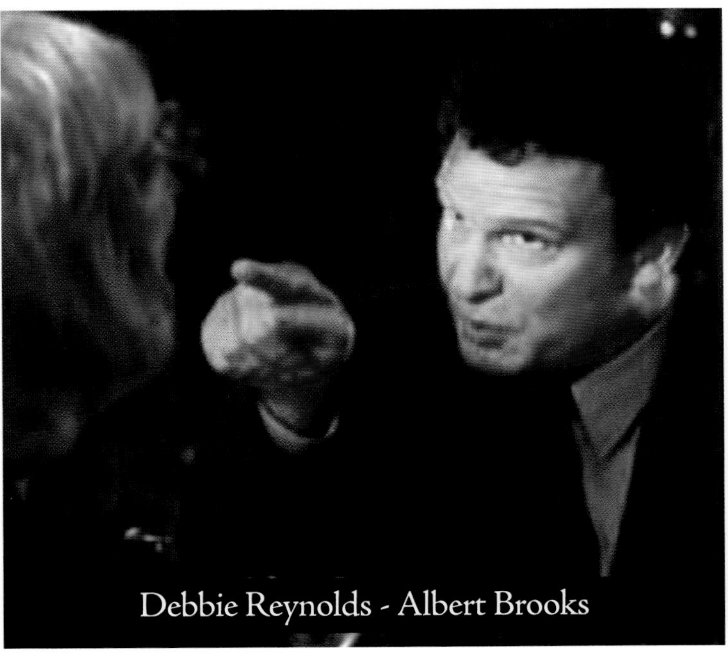
Debbie Reynolds - Albert Brooks

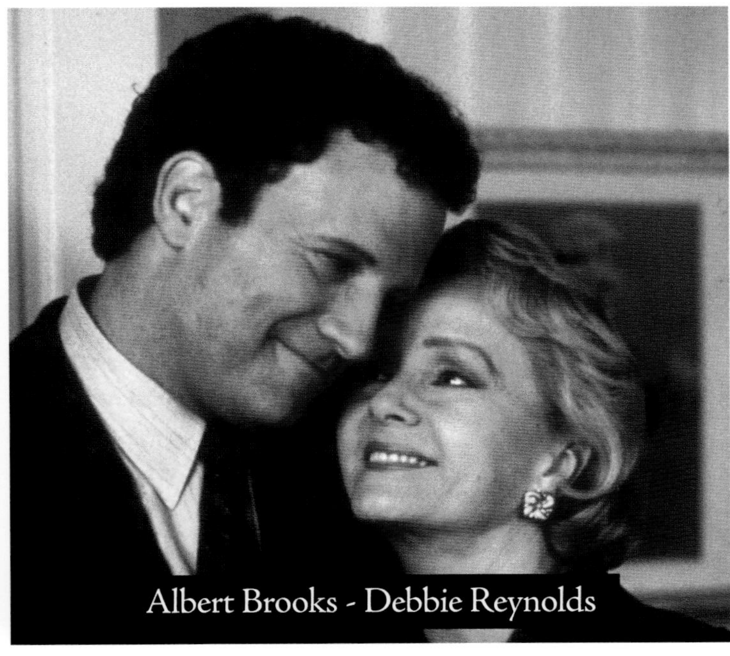
Albert Brooks - Debbie Reynolds

I met Debbie Reynolds when I performed in "Gazebo." Years later, I directed her TV special, "A Date with Debbie." Her impressions of Zsa Zsa Gabor, Sophia Loren and Bridget Bardot showcased her extraordinary talent and versatility.

In 2016, the world was saddened by a tragedy of Shakespearean proportions. Within two days, sixty year old Carrie Fisher and her eighty-four year old mother, Debbie Reynolds, passed away.

Jerry Lundegaard's inept crime falls apart due to his and his henchmen's bungling and the persistent police work of the quite pregnant Marge Gunderson.

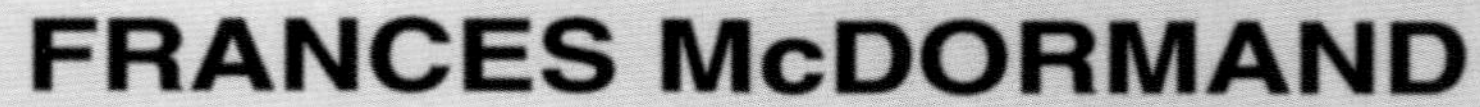

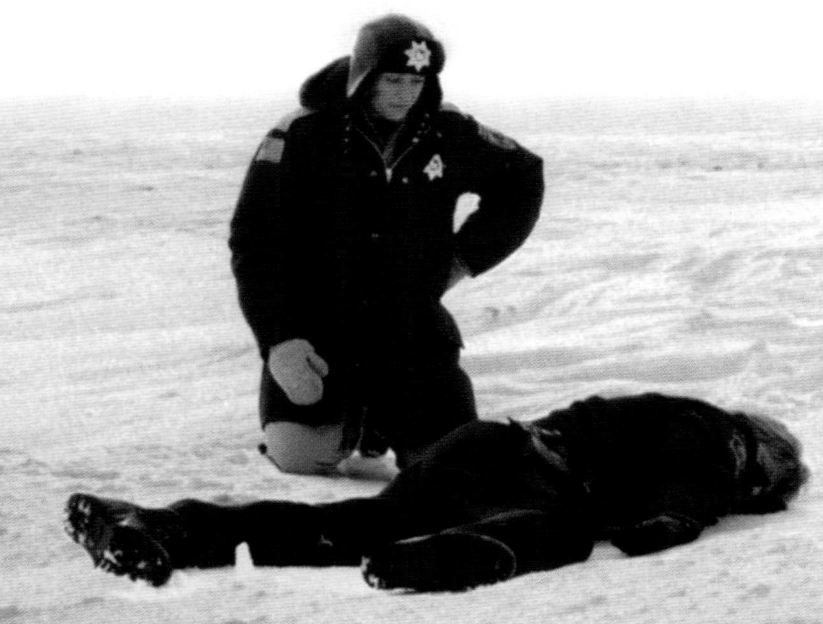

Gene Siskel of The Chicago Tribune wrote: "It's another daring black comedy by Joel and Ethan Coen, one of the most consistently inventive movie making teams of the last decade."

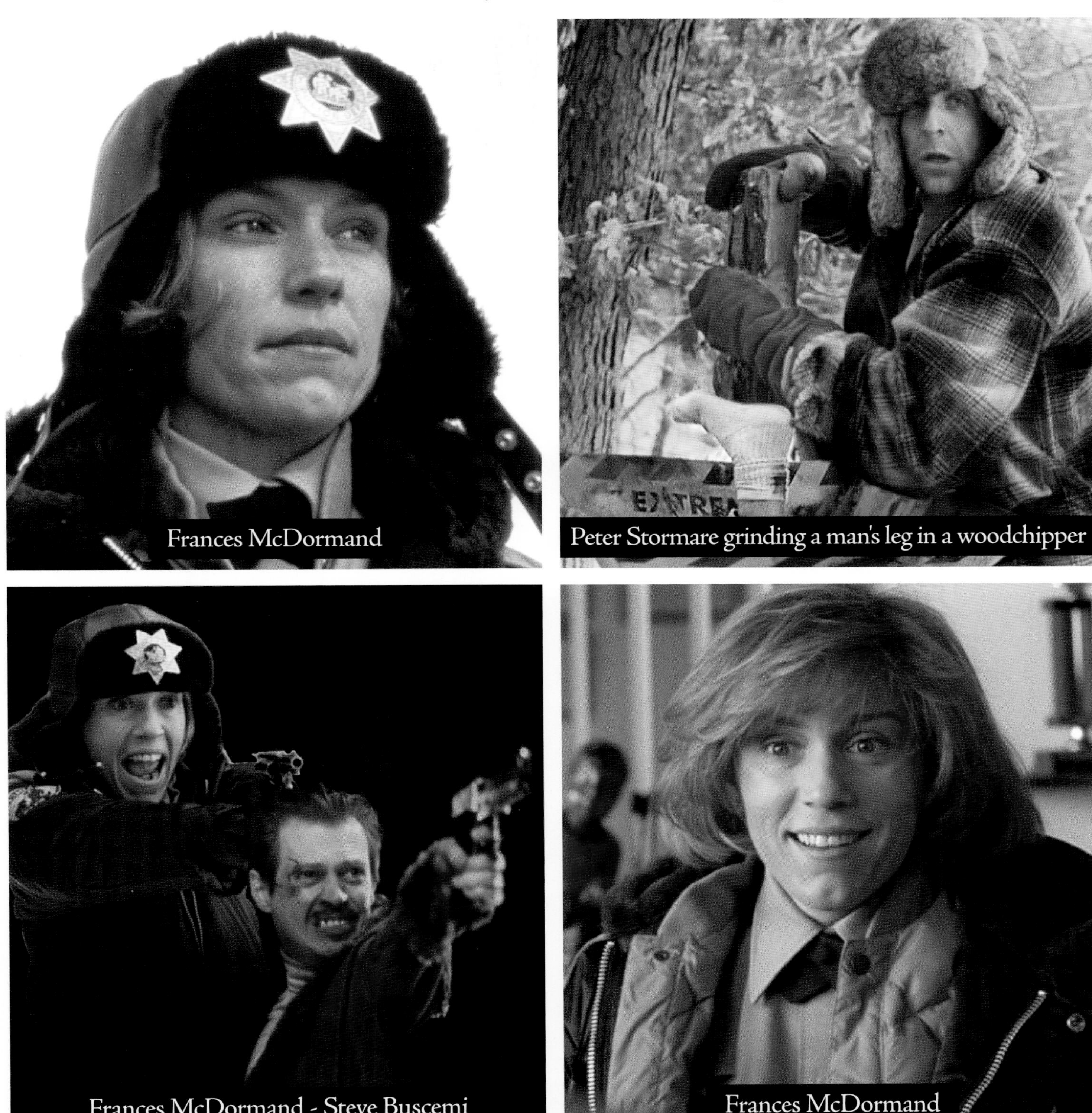
Frances McDormand

Peter Stormare grinding a man's leg in a woodchipper

Frances McDormand - Steve Buscemi

Frances McDormand

From the moment the cleft-chinned, soft voiced Police Officer, Frances McDormand, started to speak with an authentic Minnesota accent, I became a fan and apparently, so did the members of the Academy of Motion Picture Arts and Sciences. In 1996, they presented her with an Oscar for her performance in "Fargo."

A bride's divorced parents find their old feelings for each other during the wedding reception and over the course of the next few days, upsetting the newlyweds' honeymoon.

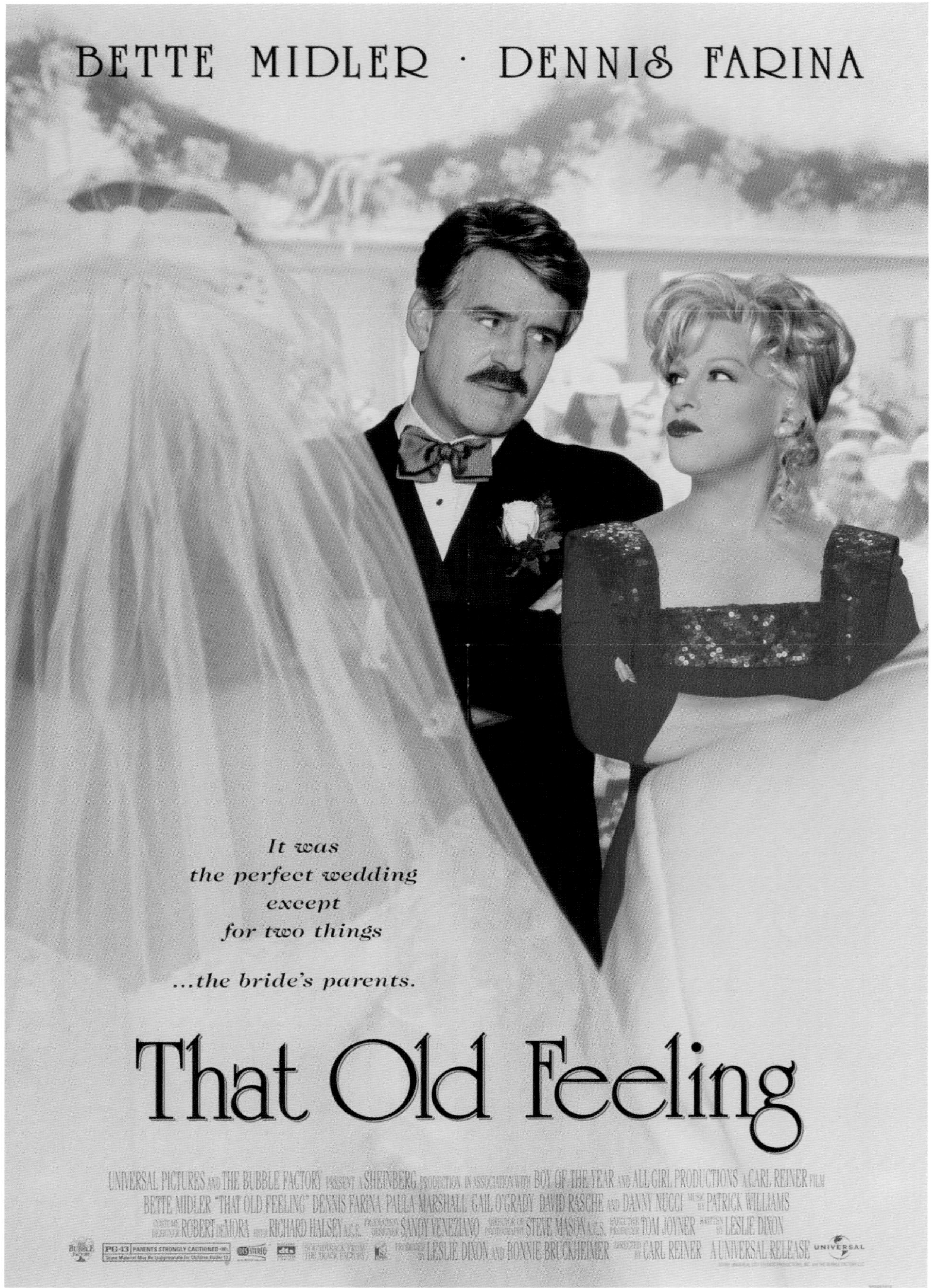

Mike Clark of USA Today wrote: "Reiner benefits from divine intervention from no less than Miss M herself. Bette Midler flings the usual zingers with fang-baring zeal in a part that plays to her brassy strengths."

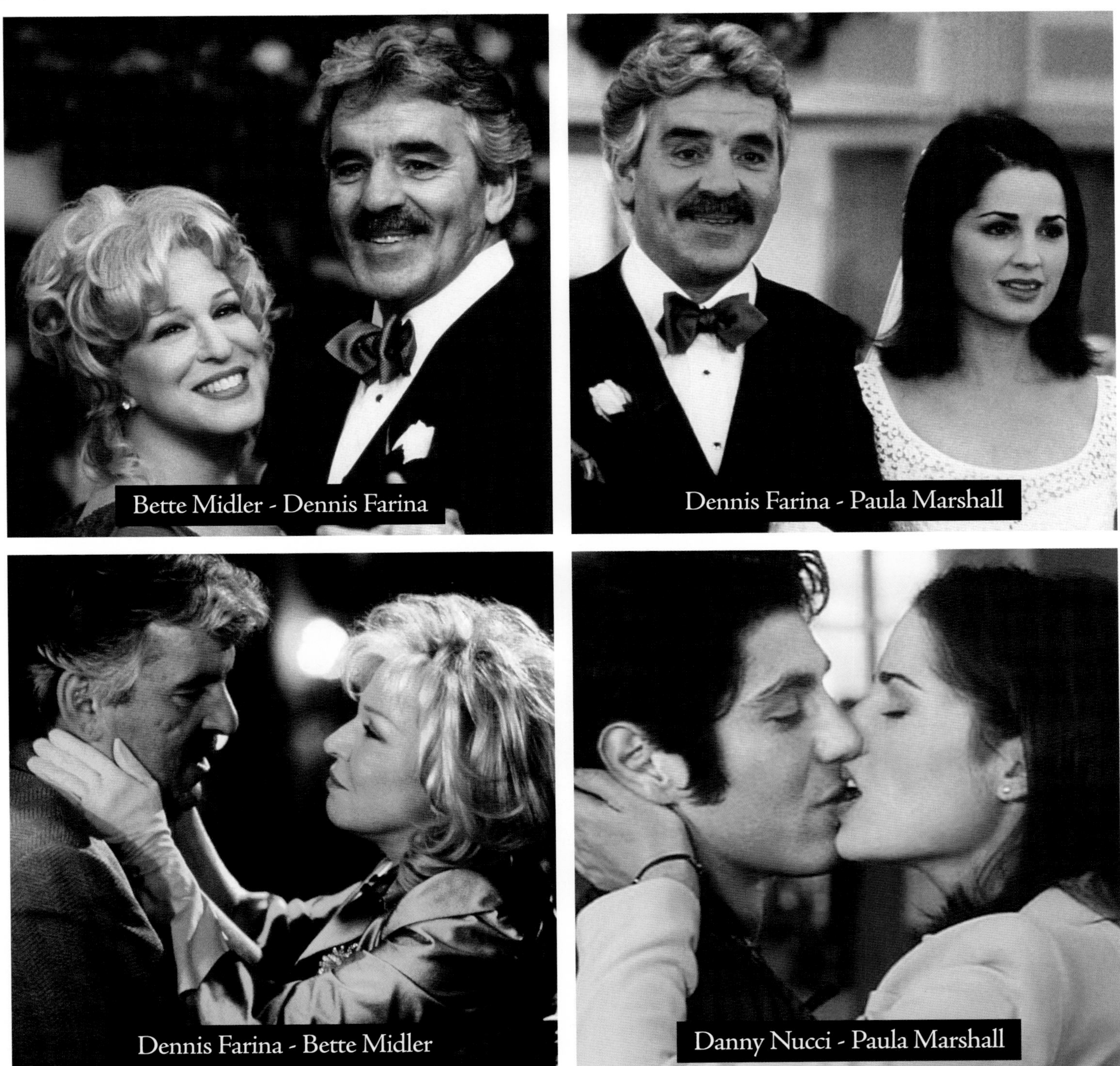

Bette Midler - Dennis Farina

Dennis Farina - Paula Marshall

Dennis Farina - Bette Midler

Danny Nucci - Paula Marshall

If you've never had the opportunity to see the incomparable Bette Midler's one-woman show, you've missed a performer who, every night, has the ability to bring an audience to its feet.

In the film, Paula Marshall, a soon-to-be married socialite, hated Danny Nucci, who played an annoying member of the paparazzi. Ultimately, the unmatched couple fall in love. In real life, Danny Nucci and Paula Marshall did fall in love, marry and have two lovely daughters.

A young Shakespeare, out of ideas and short of cash, meets his ideal woman and is inspired to write one of his most famous plays.

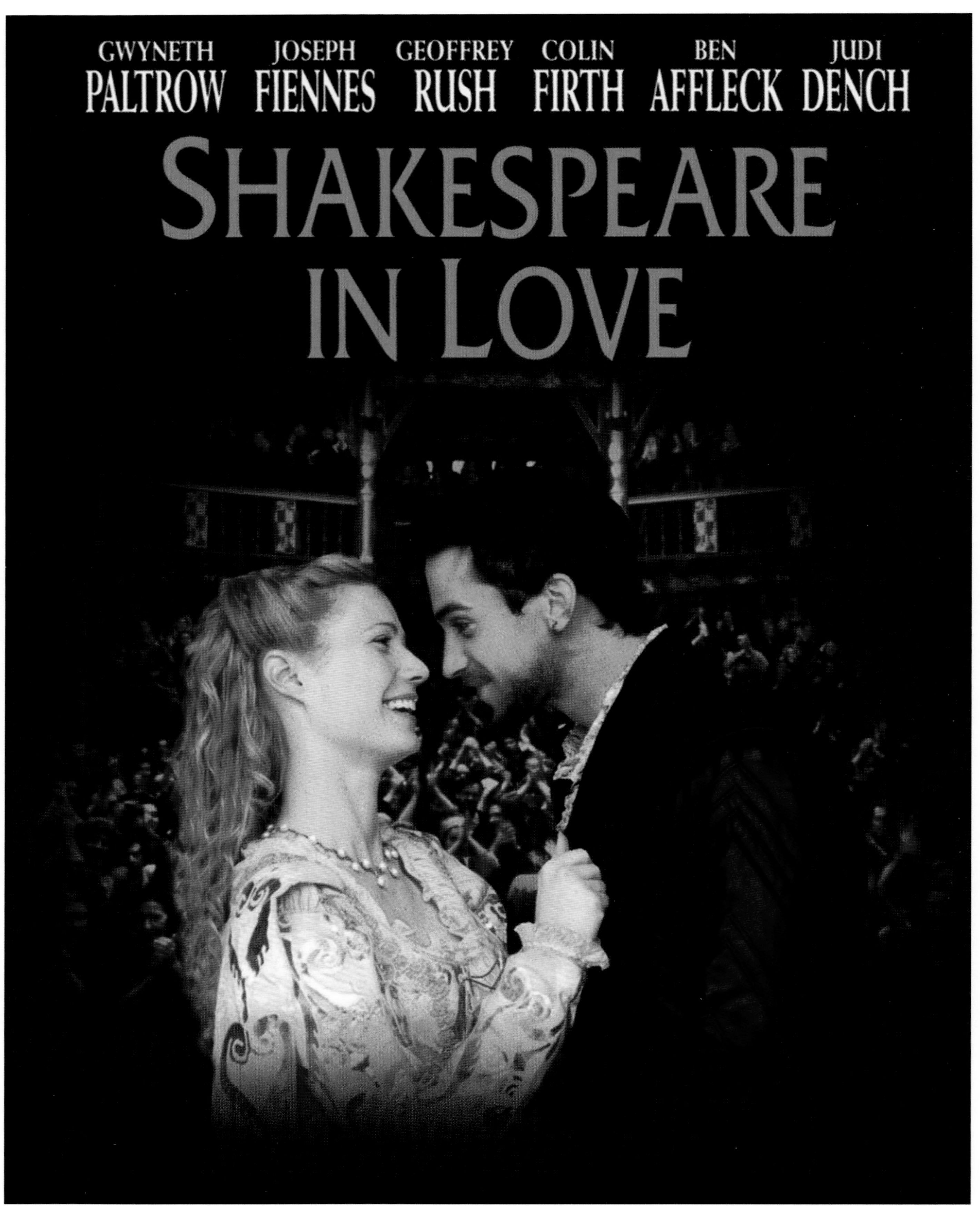

Joe Morgenstern of Wall Street Journal wrote: "Scene after scene engages us as cheerful groundlings, tosses us jokes, toys with our expectations, then sweeps away the boundaries between film and stage, comedy and tragedy so we're open to the power of language and the feelings behind it."

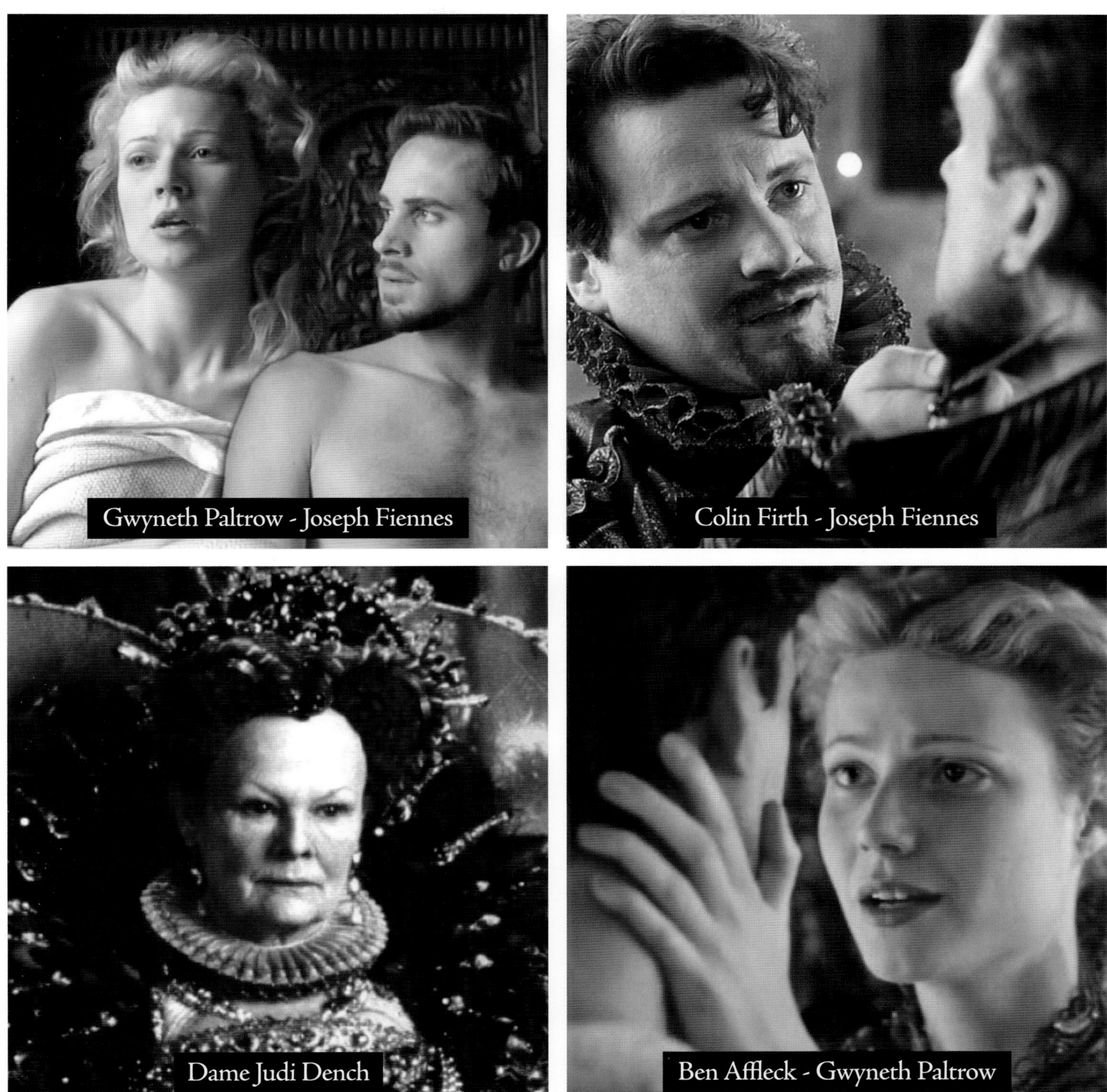

Gwyneth Paltrow - Joseph Fiennes

Colin Firth - Joseph Fiennes

Dame Judi Dench

Ben Affleck - Gwyneth Paltrow

Gwyneth Paltrow's Oscar winning performance in "Shakespeare in Love" was memorable as I found her mother, Blythe Danner's, performance to be when I saw her in "Butterflies Are Free" on Broadway. As always, Dame Judi Dench, as Queen Elizabeth, lights up the screen and makes this enjoyable offering 'enjoyabler.'

After Gilbert and Sullivan's latest play is critically panned, the frustrated team threatens to disband until it is inspired to write the masterpiece "The Mikado".

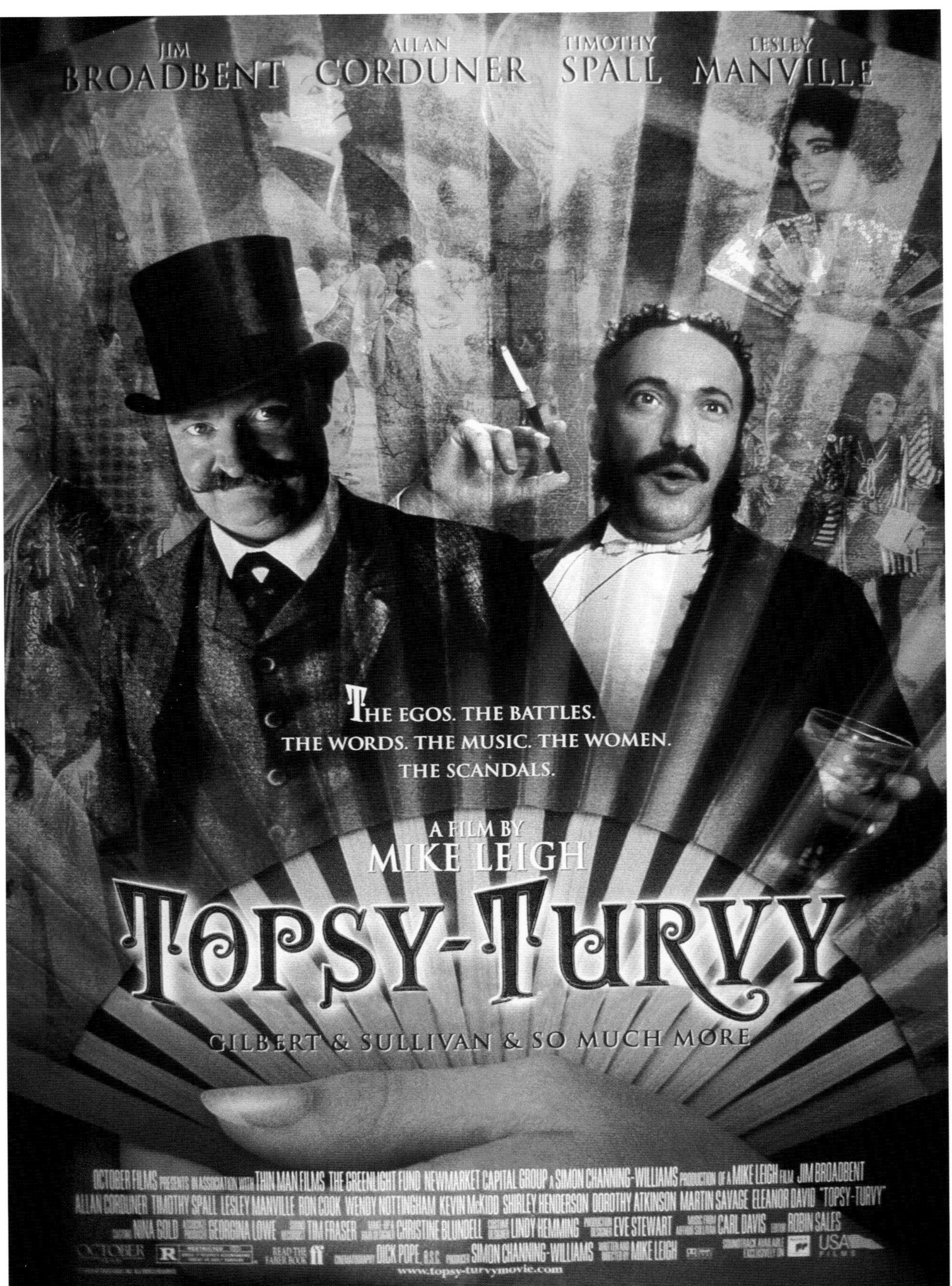

Trevor Johnston of Time Out wrote: "Leigh's cast are beyond compare, and the whole bighearted, splendidly droll celebration of the entertainer's lot surely stands among British cinema's one-of-a-kind treasures."

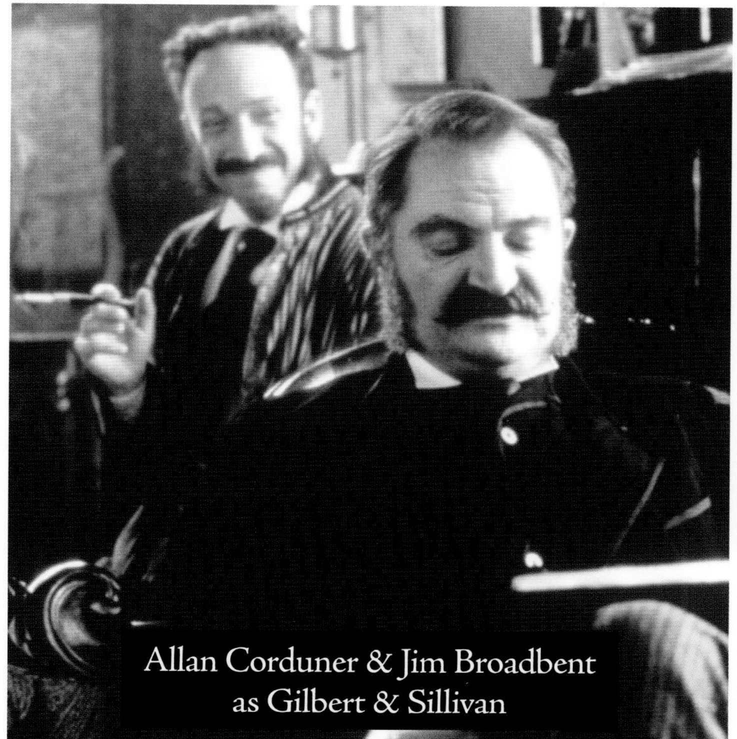
Allan Corduner & Jim Broadbent as Gilbert & Sillivan

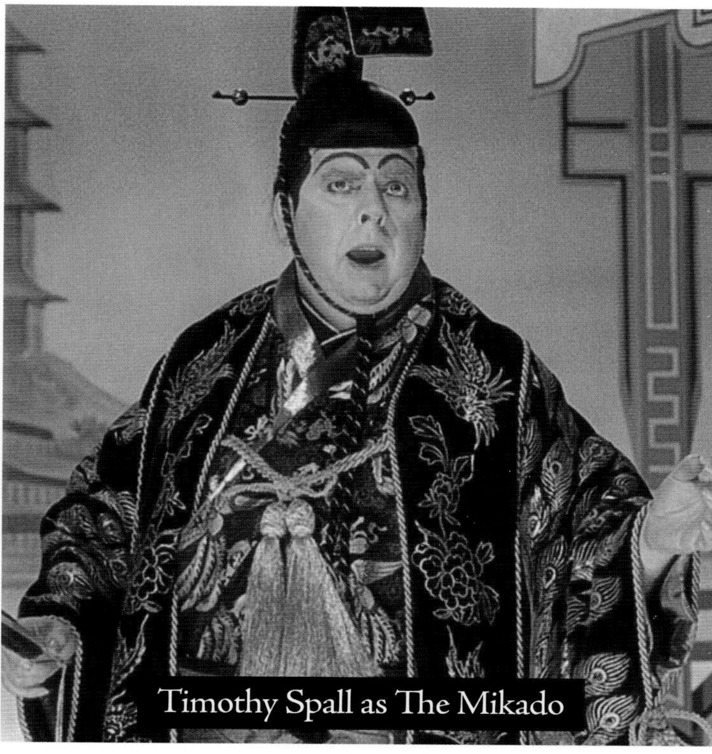
Timothy Spall as The Mikado

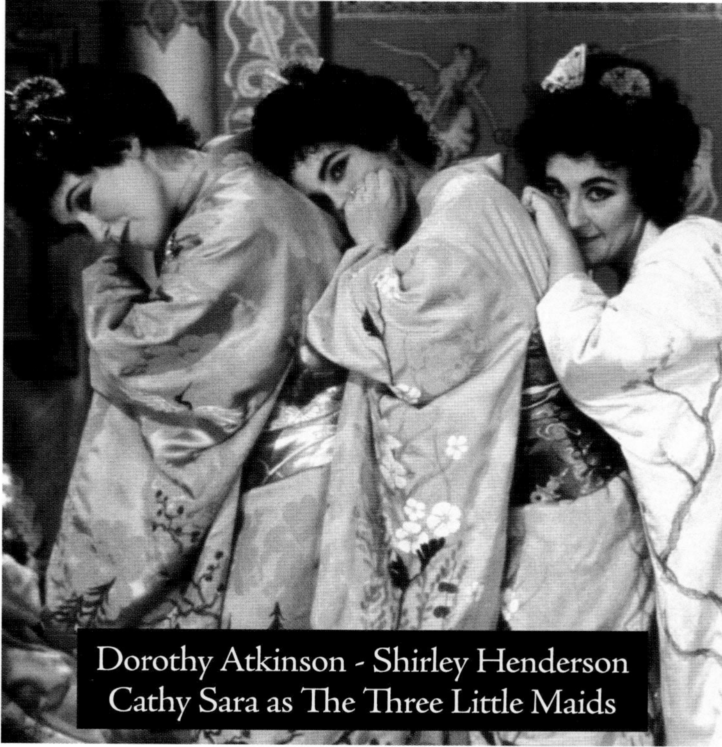
Dorothy Atkinson - Shirley Henderson Cathy Sara as The Three Little Maids

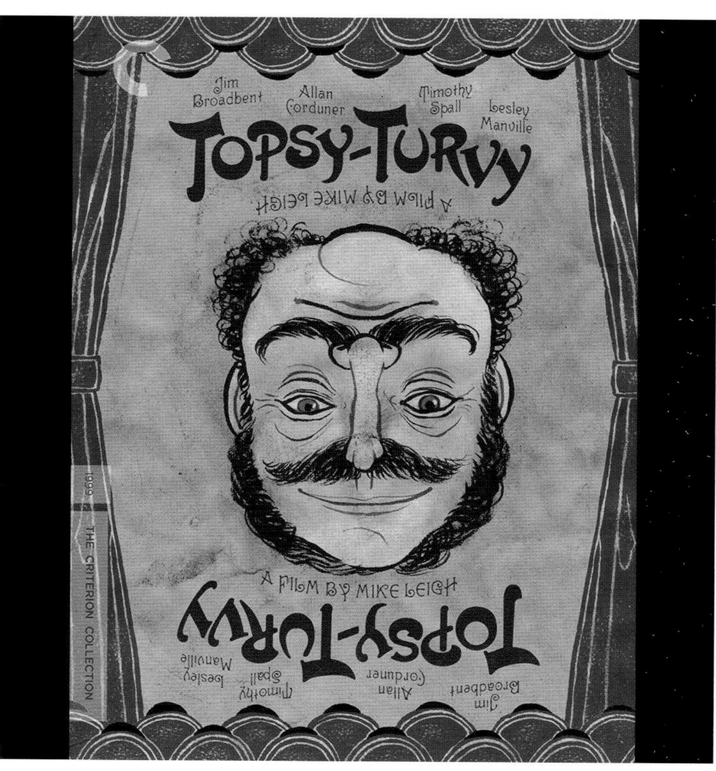

I almost missed seeing this "one of a kind treasure," as I was unaware that "Topsy-Turvy" was about Gilbert and Sullivan. The two gentlemen that wrote these brilliant opperettas, "The Mikado," "H.M.S. Pinafore" and "The Pirates of Penzance," were, in real life, arch enemies.

The life and career of a legendary comedian, Andy Kaufman.

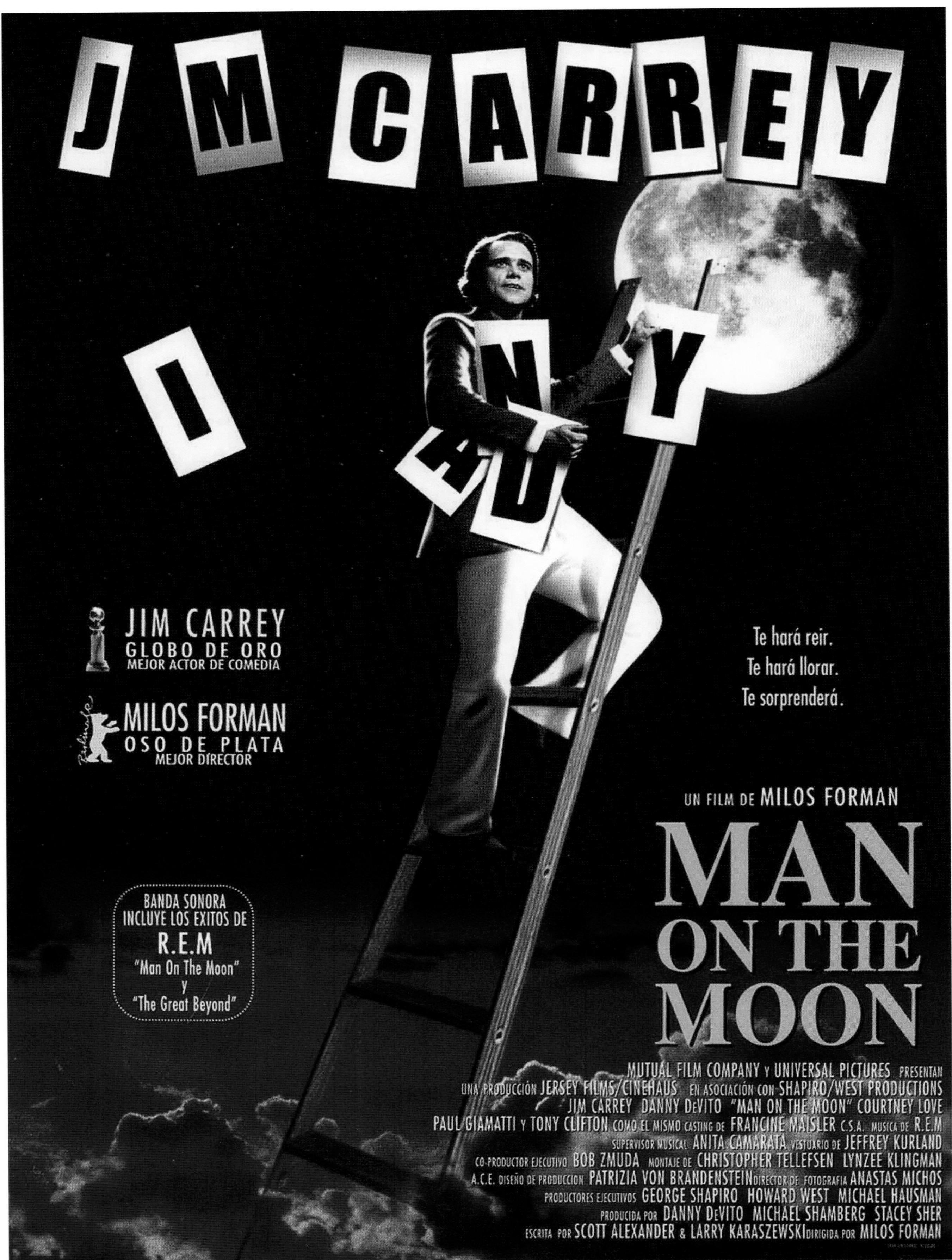

Roger Ebert of At the Movies wrote: "What is most wonderful about 'Man on the Moon,' a very good film, is that it remains true to Kaufman's stubborn vision."

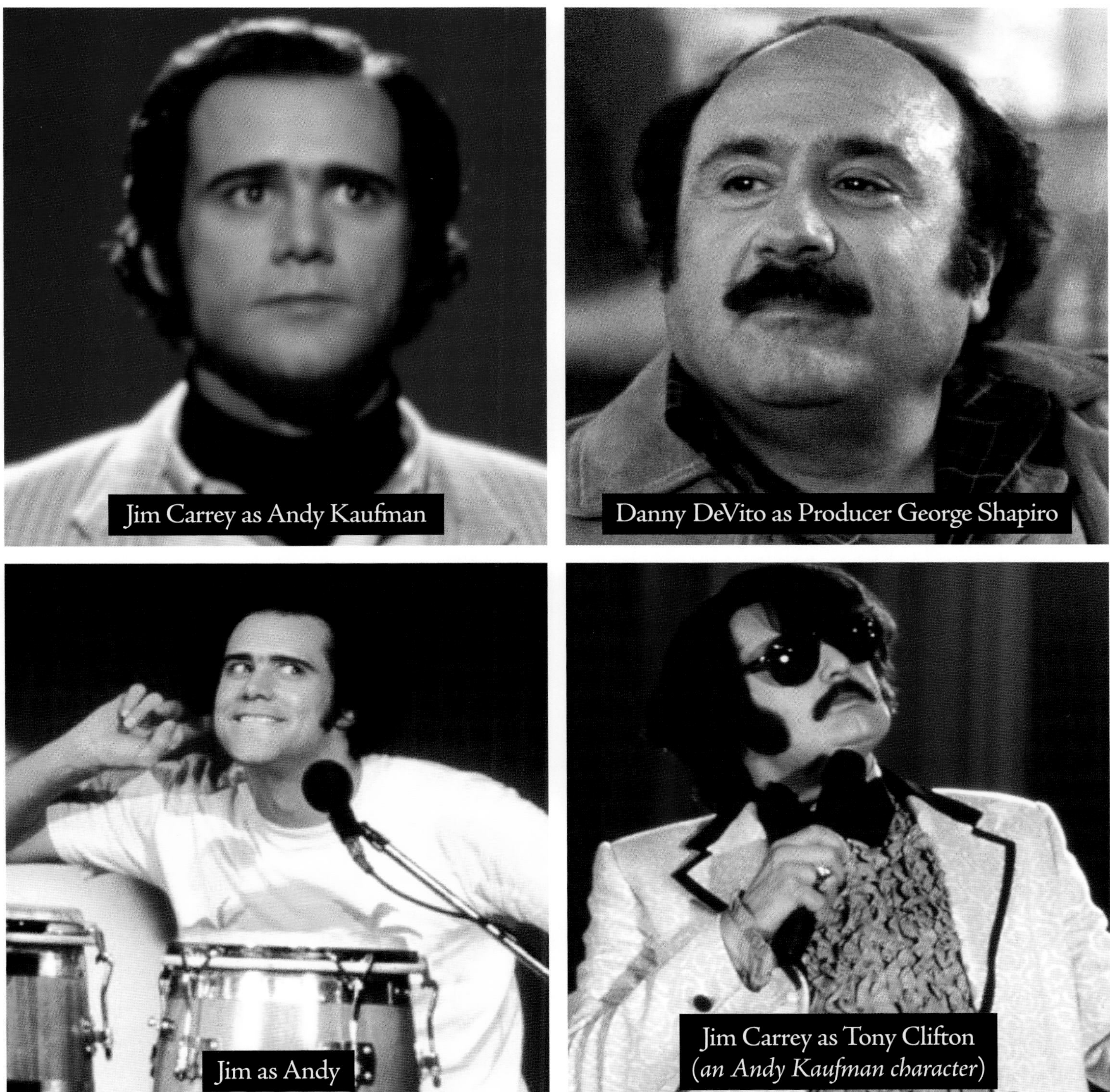

Jim Carrey as Andy Kaufman

Danny DeVito as Producer George Shapiro

Jim as Andy

Jim Carrey as Tony Clifton
(*an Andy Kaufman character*)

This film is close to my heart because I saw Andy Kaufman's very first performance at Rodney Dangerfield's in New York... he had me roaring. I went backstage and introduced myself to Andy, and not long after, I introduced him to my manager/nephew-in-law, George Shapiro, who introduced him to the world. In 1984, at the age of thirty-five, Andy left us and, in 1999, with the film "Man on the Moon," Jim Carrey brought Andy back to life.

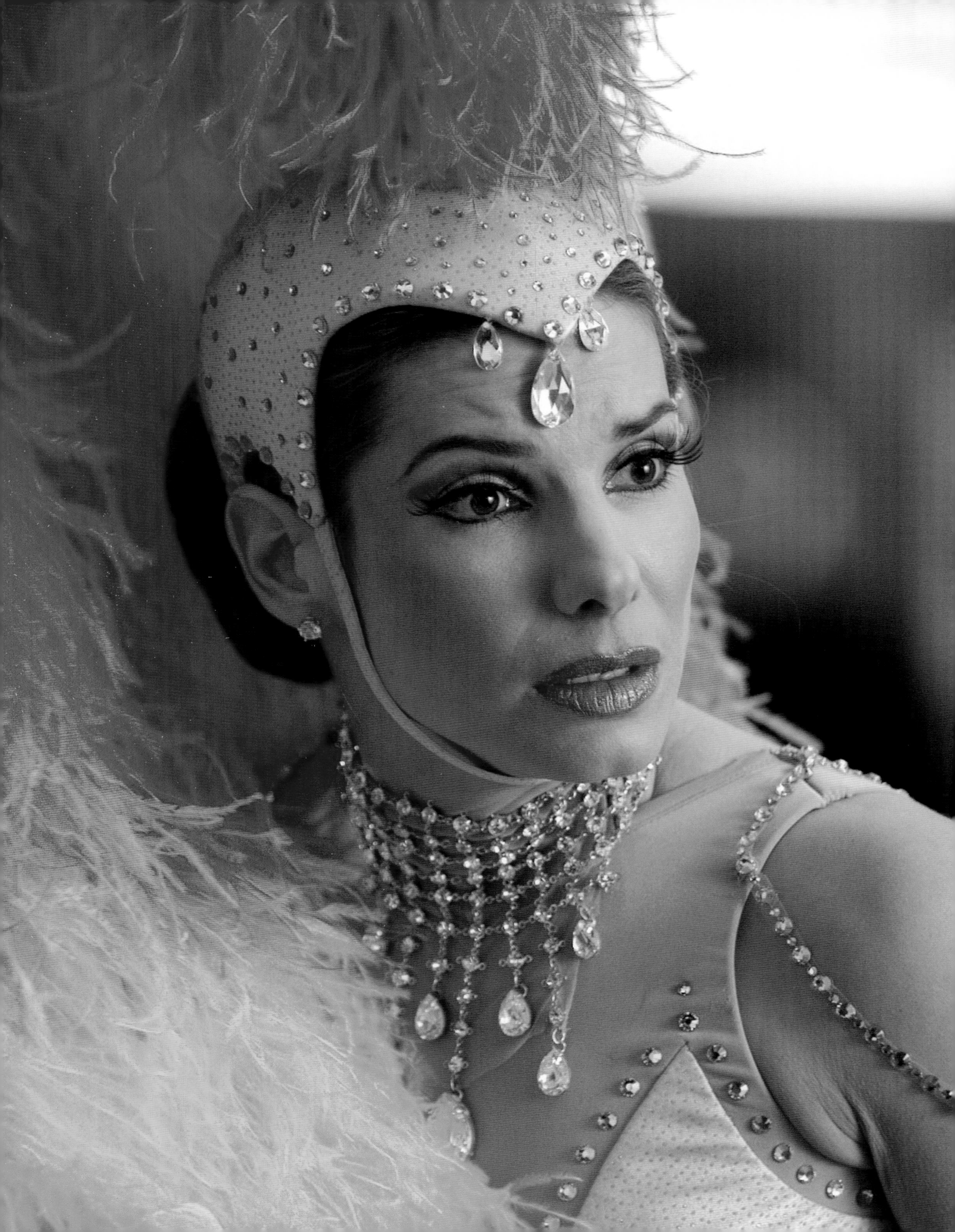

the 2000s

A man who falls in love with the woman who received his wife's heart must decide which woman it is who holds his heart.

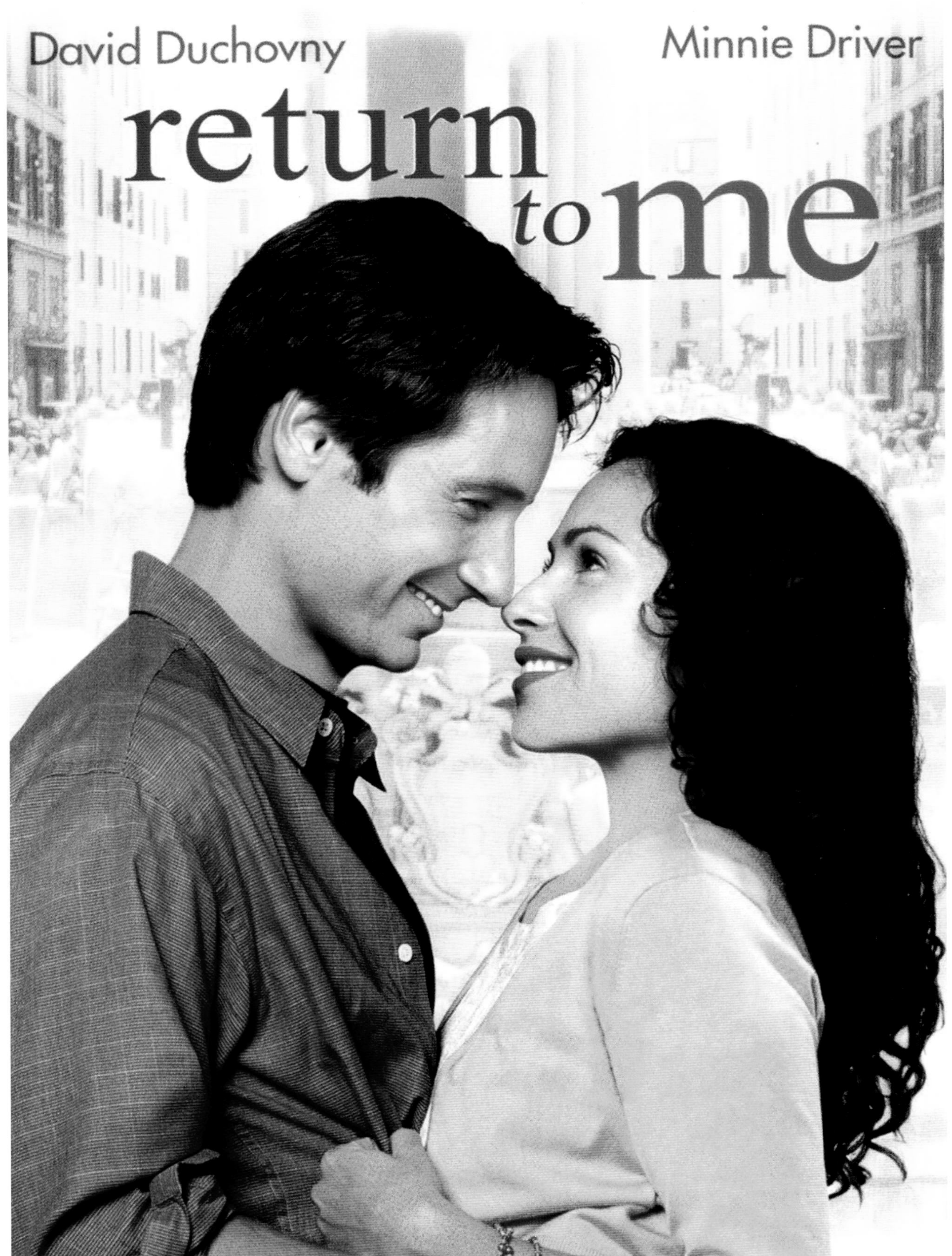

Steven D. Greydanus of Decent Films Guide wrote: "Characters you will care about spending time with, and a charming, hopeful look at love amid the vagaries of life."

Karina Montgomery of Cinerina wrote: "Every time I see this it is better and better. Bonnie Hunt is an amazing writer."

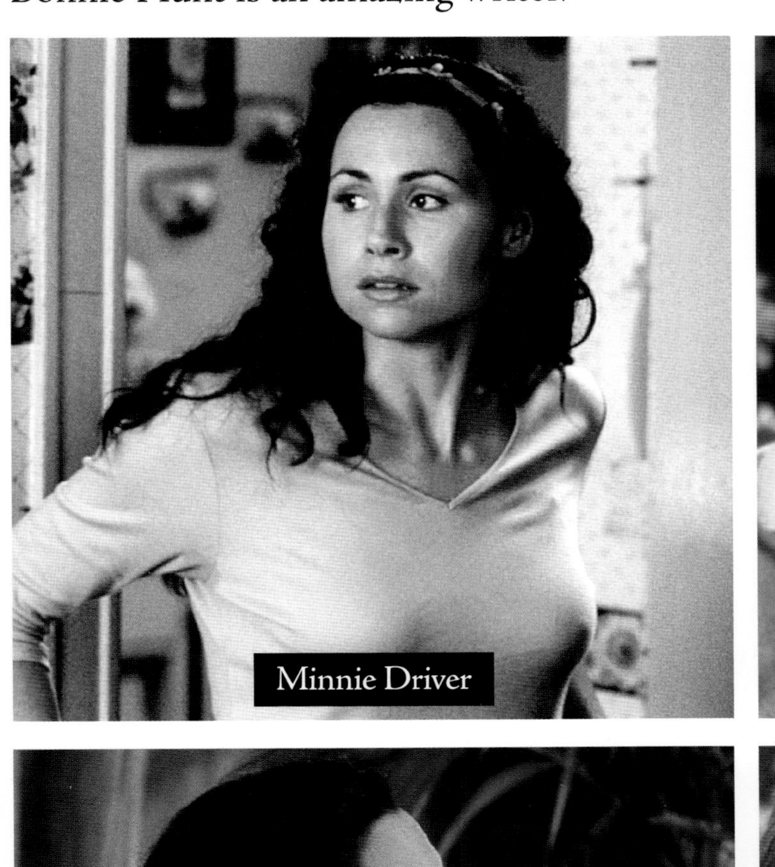
Minnie Driver

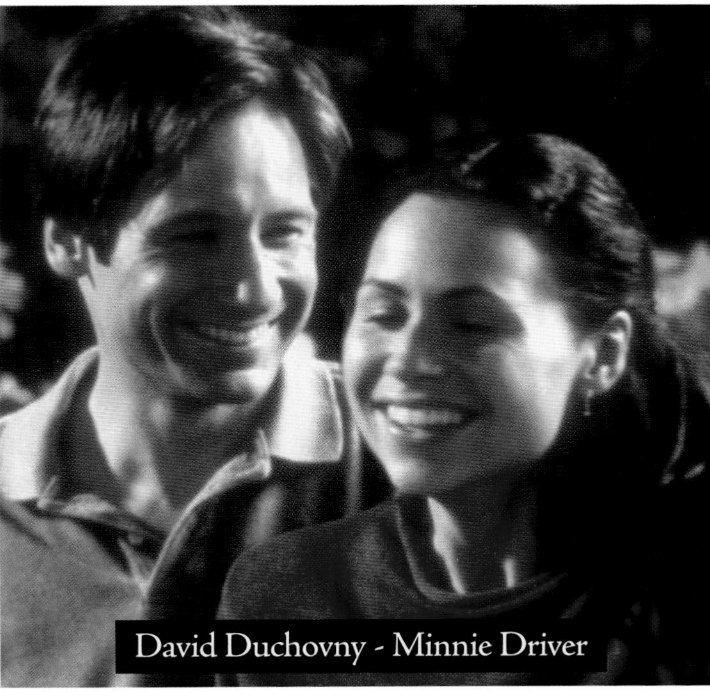
David Duchovny - Minnie Driver

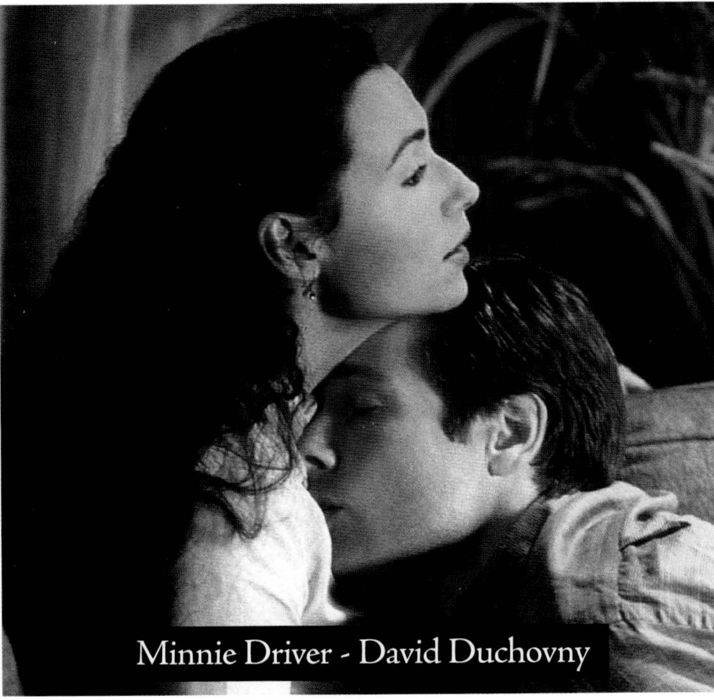
Minnie Driver - David Duchovny

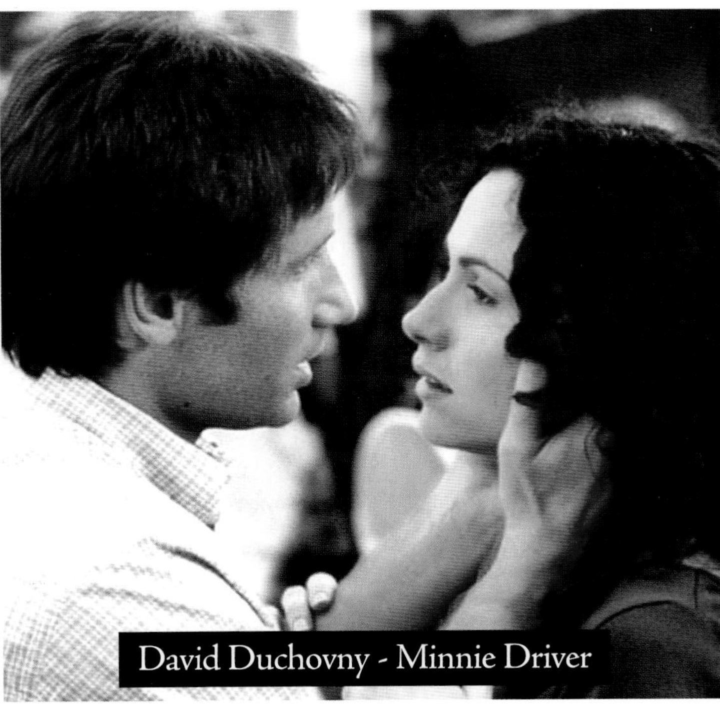
David Duchovny - Minnie Driver

How would you feel if, after your beloved wife passed away, you fell in love with someone who is alive because the donor's heart that beats in her, once belonged to your late wife? Minnie Driver and David Duchovny illustrate beautifully this sad-happy dilemma.

Minnie Driver, who is British by birth, spoke with a credible American accent.

An FBI agent must go undercover in the Miss United States beauty pageant to prevent a group from bombing the event.

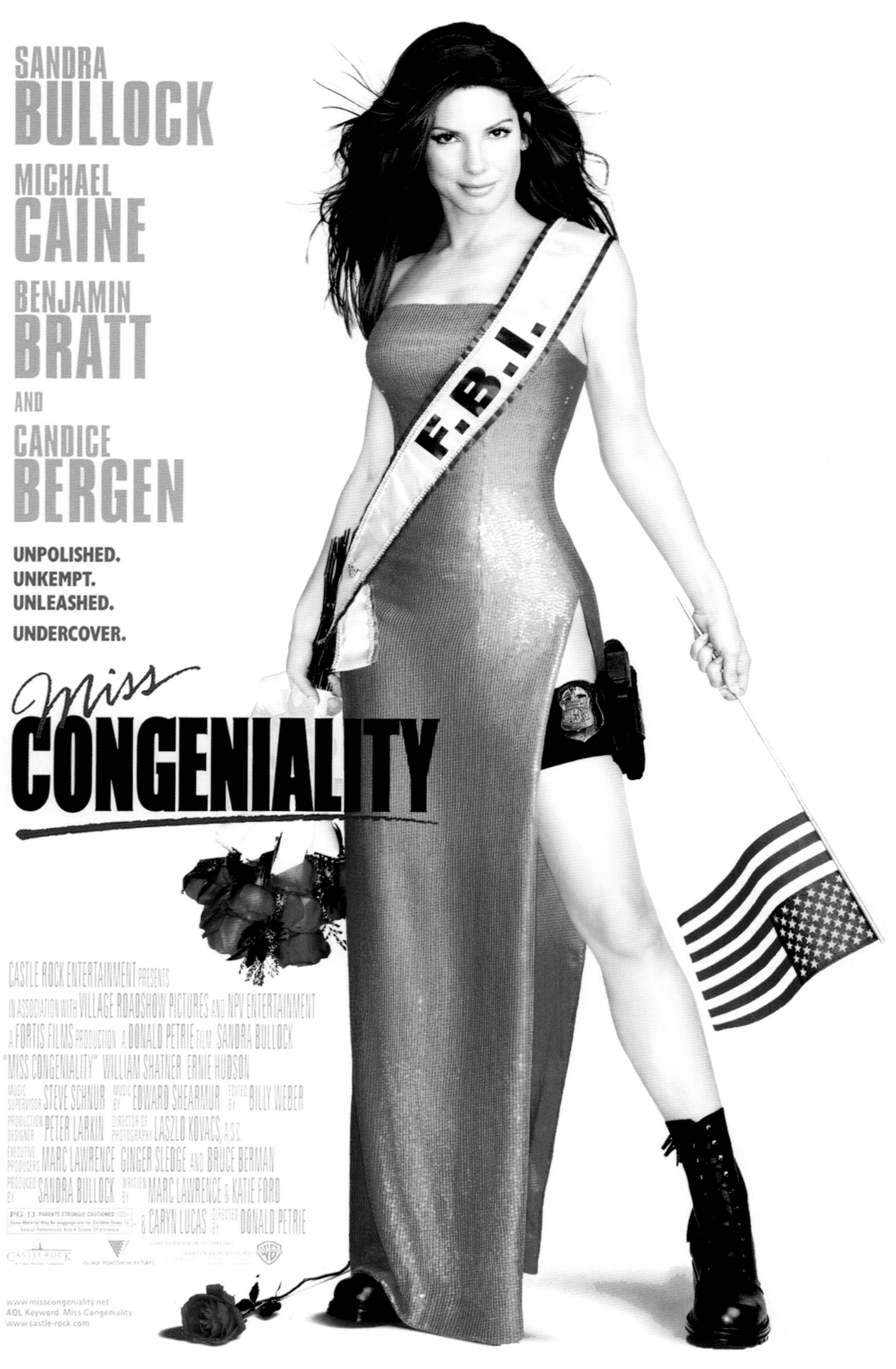

Jay Boyar of Orlando Sentinel wrote: "There's something so friendly and unabashedly silly about this production that it pretty much won me over."

Susan Stark of Detroit News wrote: "For Bullock fans, it's a delight, jolly junk in the season to be jolly."

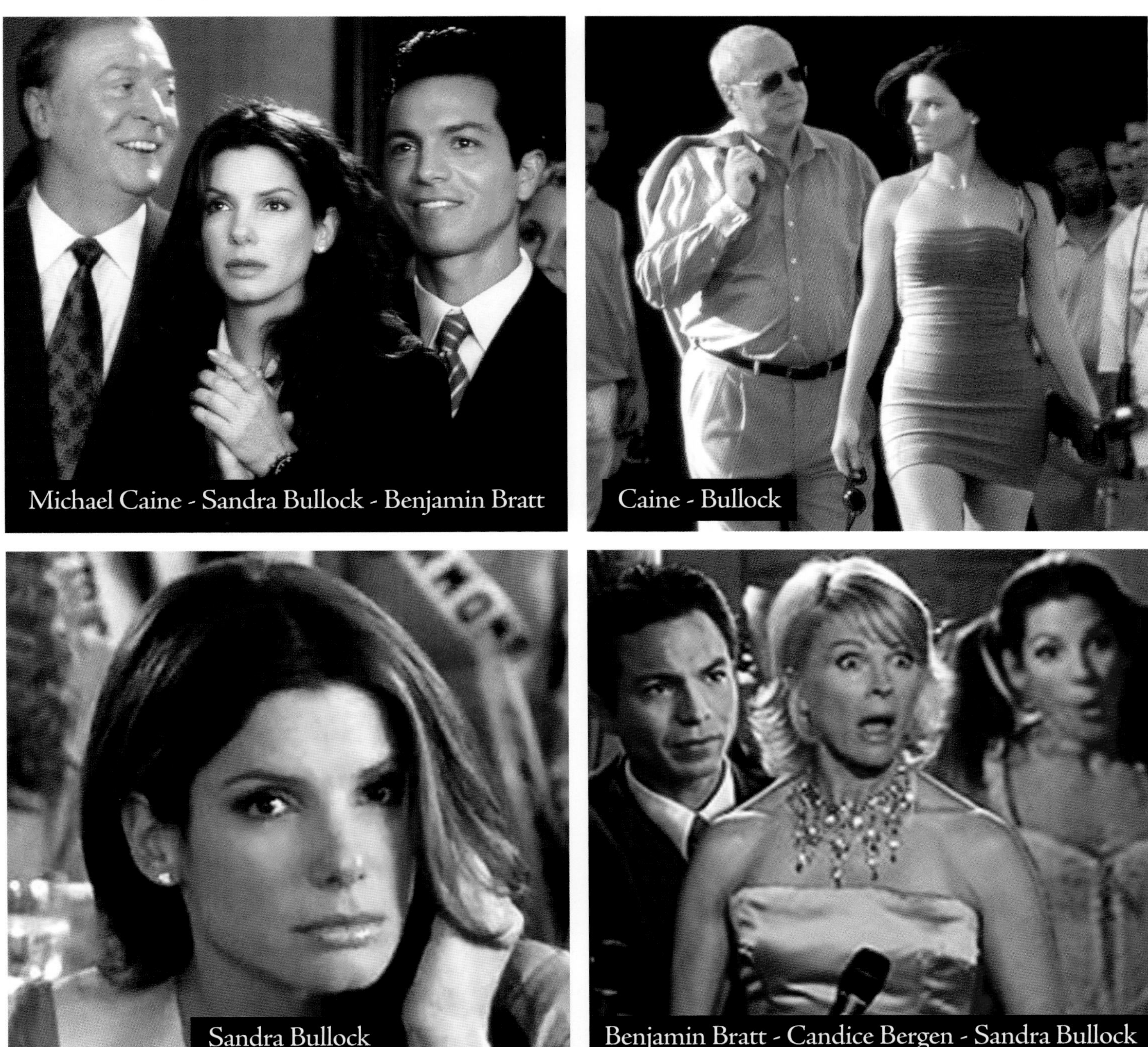

Michael Caine - Sandra Bullock - Benjamin Bratt

Caine - Bullock

Sandra Bullock

Benjamin Bratt - Candice Bergen - Sandra Bullock

Michael Caine, Sandra Bullock's physical training instructor, has just told her and her FBI partner, Benjamin Bratt, of a disgruntled Candice Bergen's plan to wreck the "Miss America Pageant" now and forever by crowning Miss America with an exploding tiara. Agent Sandra helps to abort the tragedy and sees to it that Candice gets her just desserts, arrest and imprisonment.

Thank you Rob Reiner and Castle Rock Productions for this most entertaining film.

An unemployed single mother becomes a legal assistant and almost single-handedly brings down a California power company accused of polluting a city's water supply.

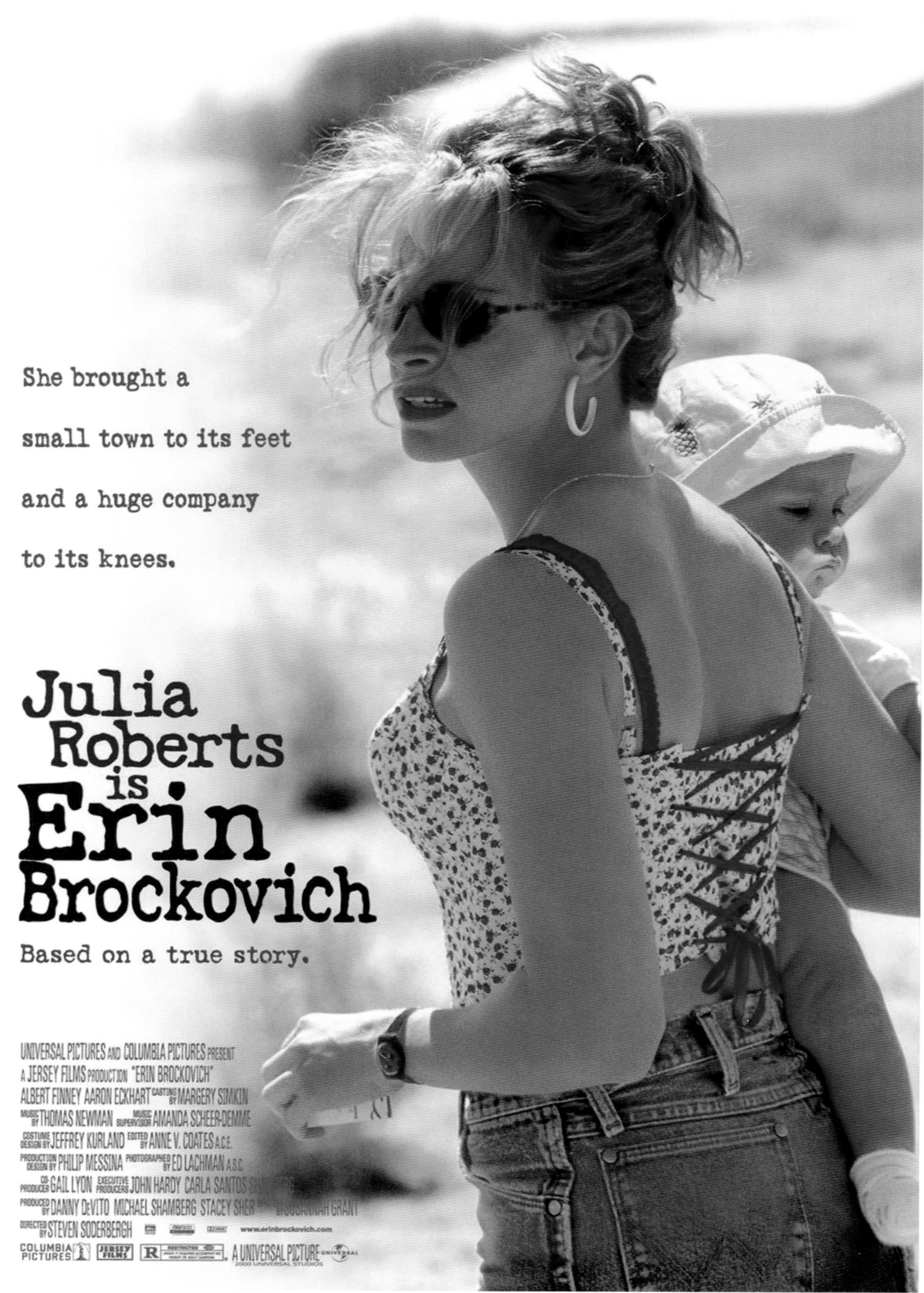

Charles Taylor of Salon.com wrote: "From the opening to the perfect final shot, Roberts is in nearly every scene of 'Erin Brockovich,' and there isn't a second when we're not on her side."

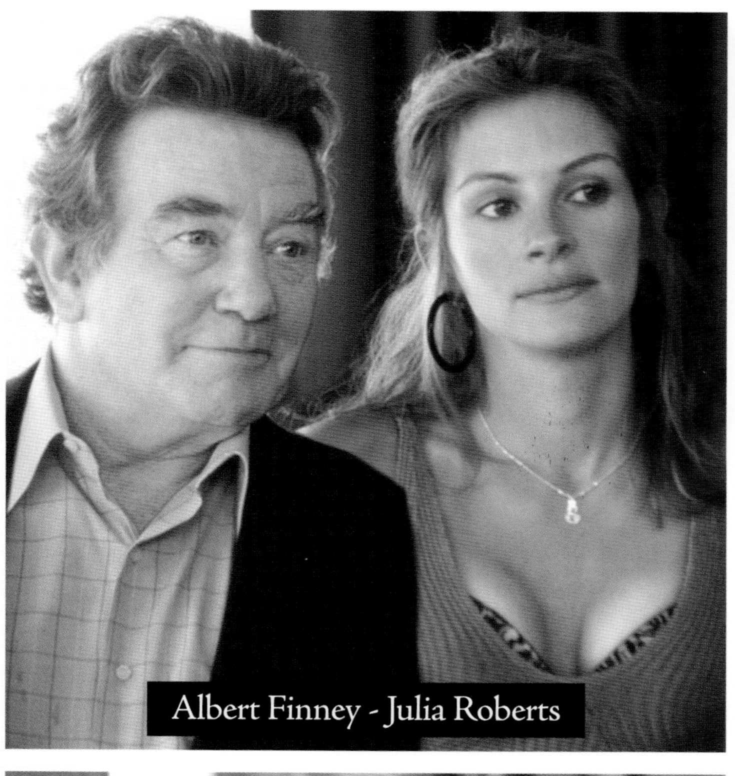
Albert Finney - Julia Roberts

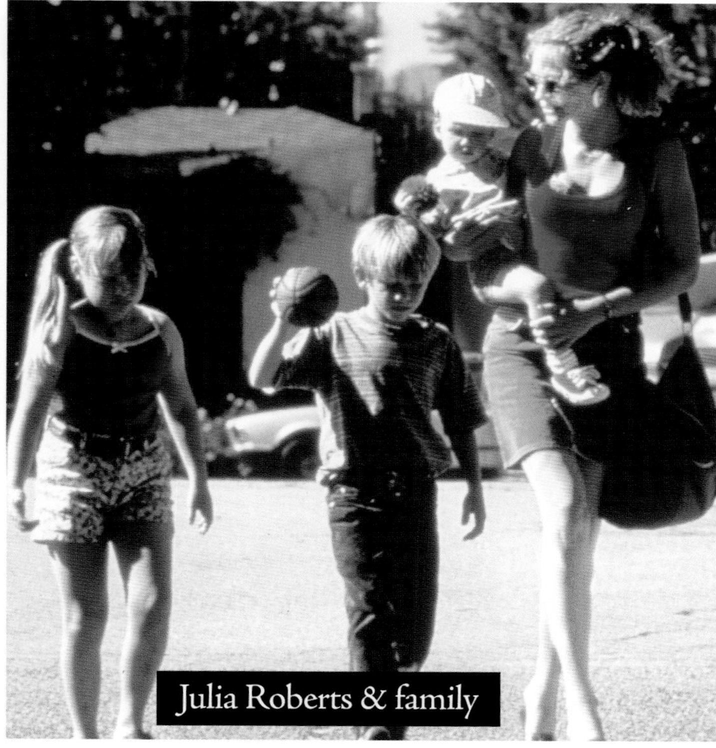
Julia Roberts & family

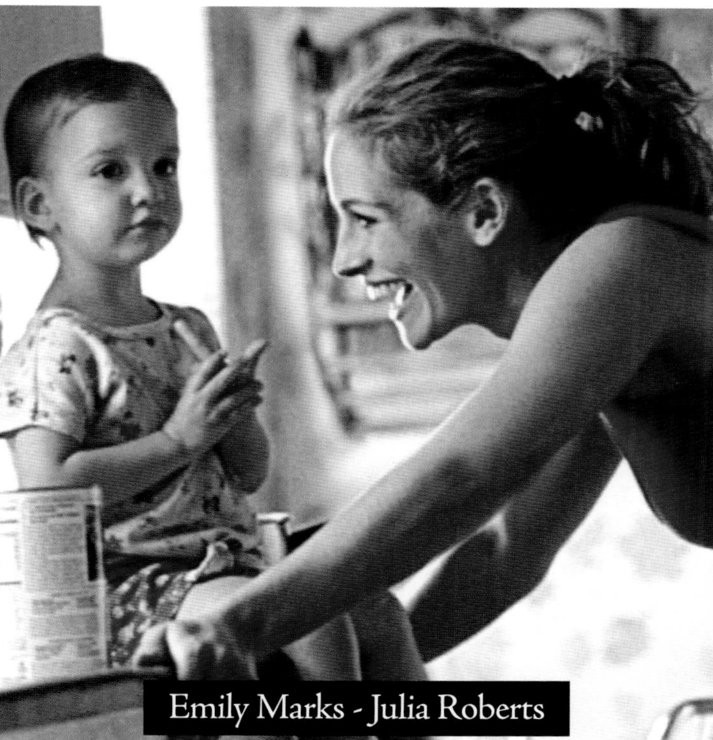
Emily Marks - Julia Roberts

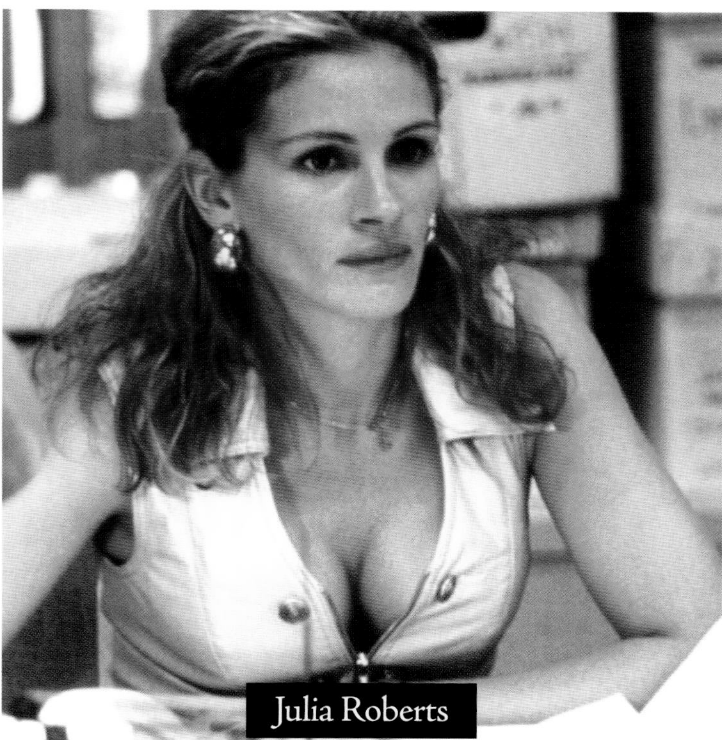
Julia Roberts

Like "The Count of Monte Cristo," "Erin Brockovich" ends with a soul-satisfying comeuppance. I was so happy that I was able to vote for Julia Roberts to receive an Oscar.

In 2017, Julia Roberts was chosen by People Magazine as "The World's Most Beautiful Woman" and I was happy to see that People Magazine agreed with my assessment of her.

Elle Woods, a fashionable sorority queen, is dumped by her boyfriend. She decides to follow him to law school, and while she is there she figures out that there is more to her than just looks.

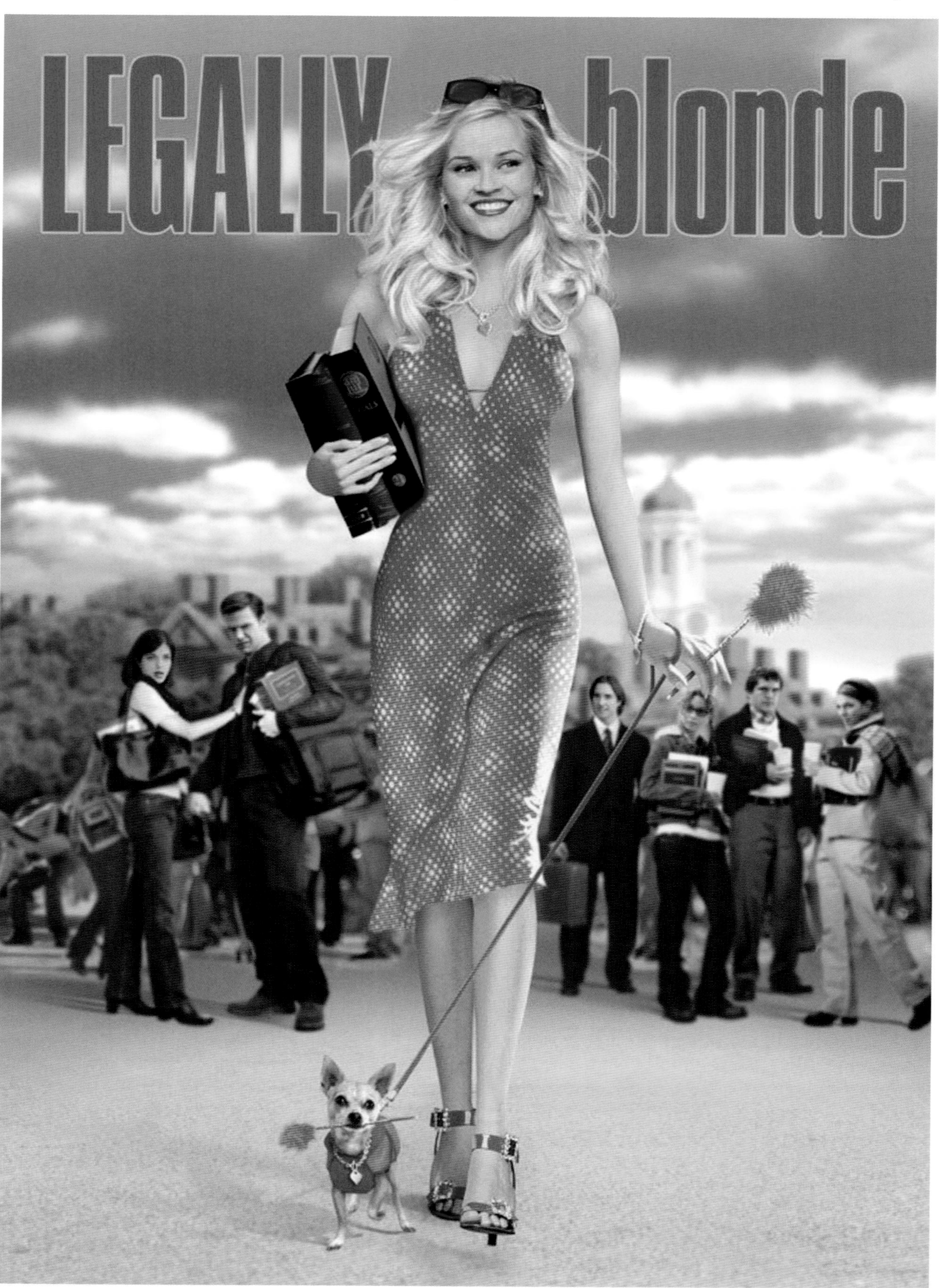

Paul Clinton of CNN wrote: "It's a formula that's well done here with plenty of laughs."

Andrew Sarris of NY Observer wrote: "Ms. Witherspoon won me over right from the start."

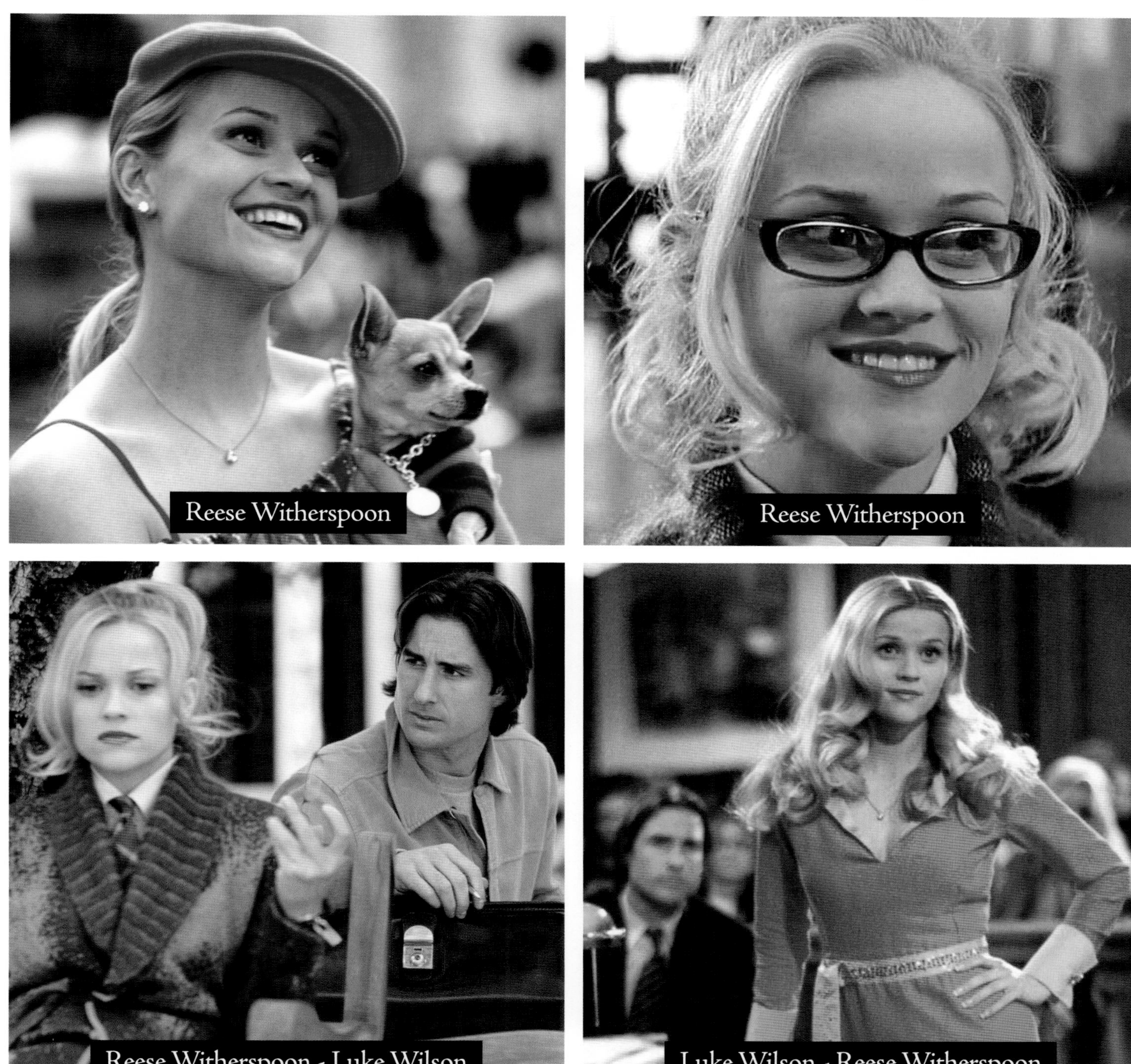

Reese Witherspoon

Reese Witherspoon

Reese Witherspoon - Luke Wilson

Luke Wilson - Reese Witherspoon

Besides the critic, Andrew Sarris, Ms. Witherspoon also won me over as she did the film going audience. This film and "Legally Blond 2: Red, White & Blonde" grossed a combined $232,000,000.

I continue to be amazed at the depth of Reese Witherspoon's talent. Her performance as June Carter, opposite Joaquin Phoenix, in "Walk The Line" has cemented my admiration for her.

I, who am a fan of comeuppance films, so enjoyed the end of this one when Reese Witherspoon gets an opportunity to reject a self-centered boyfriend who once rejected her.

Semi-true story of the Hollywood murder that occurred at a star-studded gathering aboard William Randolph Hearst's yacht in 1924.

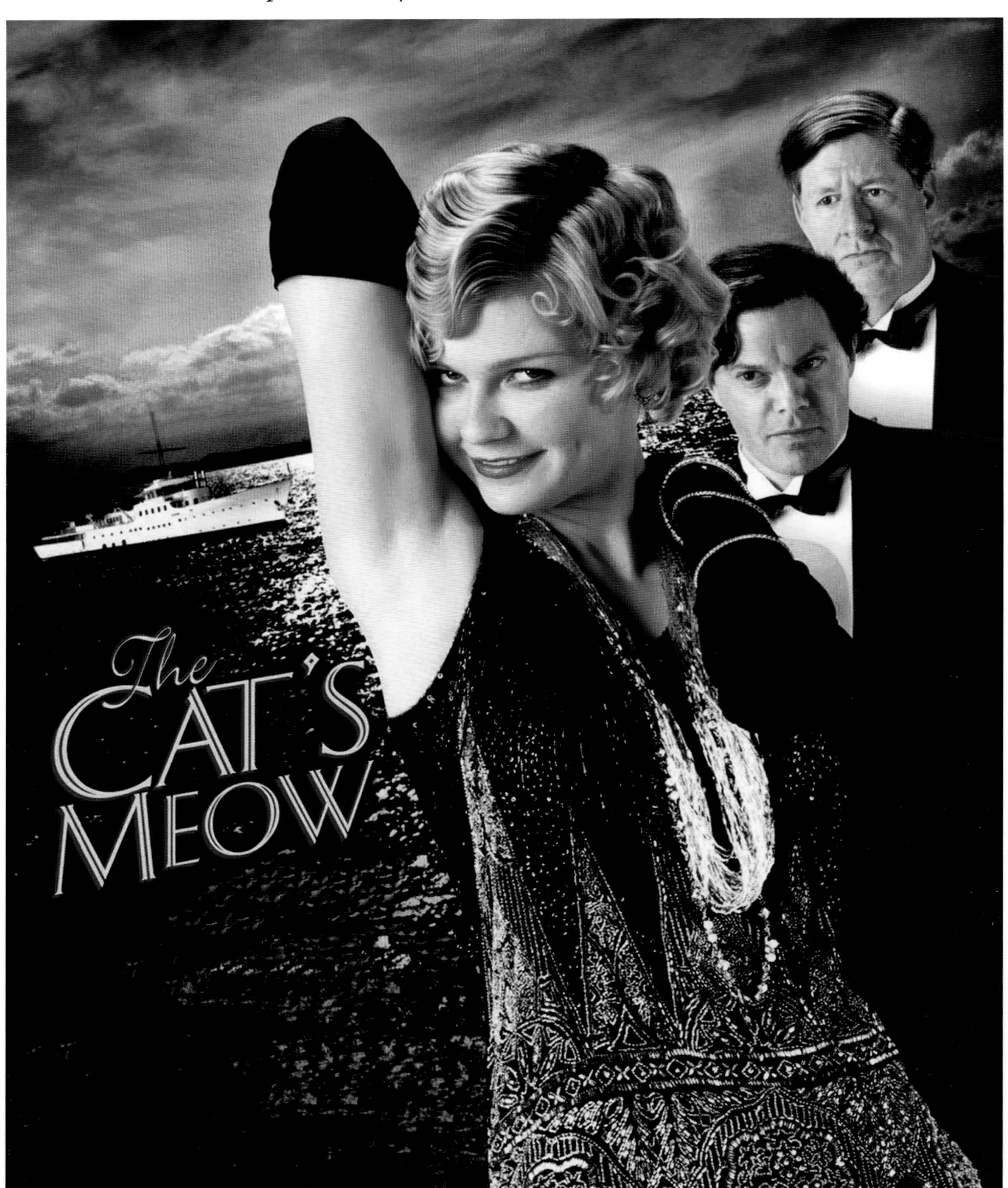

Derek Elley of Variety wrote: "The '20s-set pic is given considerable bounce by a splendid cast, led by Kirsten Dunst in an eye-opening perf as Marion Davies."

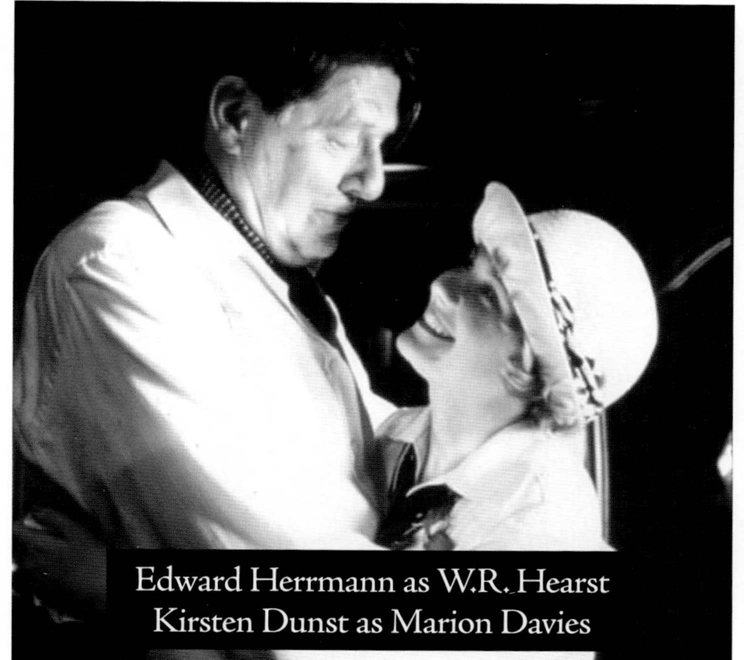
Edward Herrmann as W.R. Hearst
Kirsten Dunst as Marion Davies

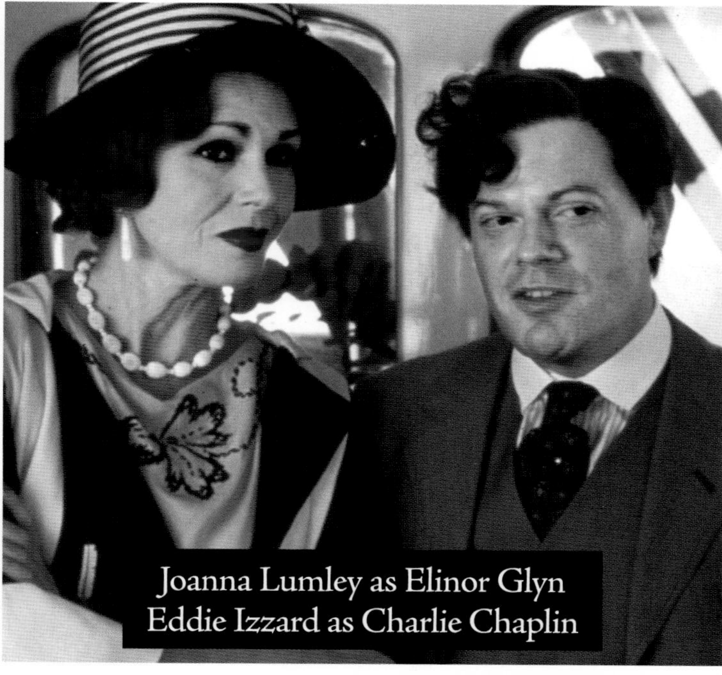
Joanna Lumley as Elinor Glyn
Eddie Izzard as Charlie Chaplin

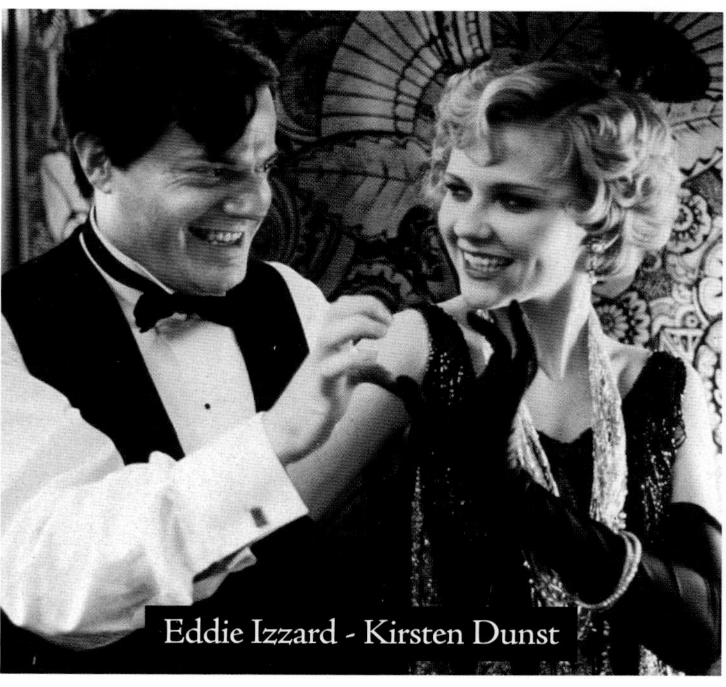
Eddie Izzard - Kirsten Dunst

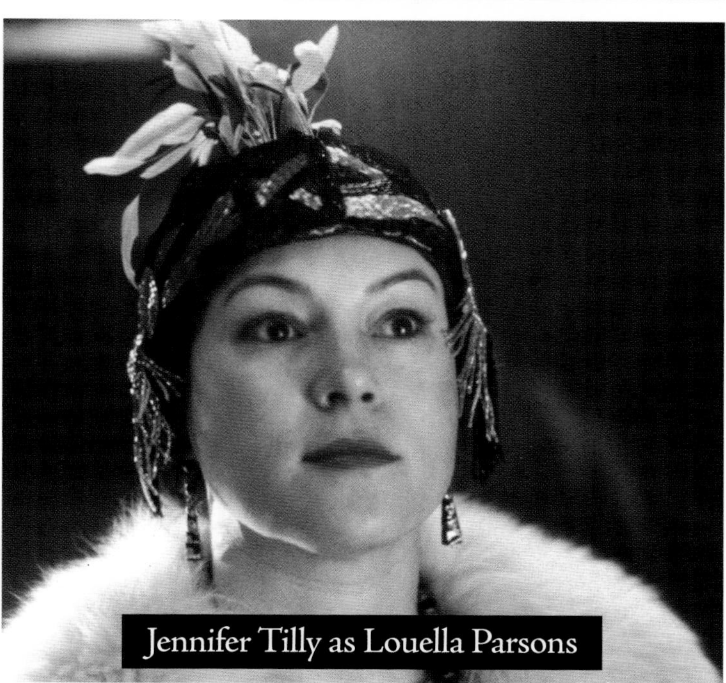
Jennifer Tilly as Louella Parsons

"The Cat's Meow" is a true story based on a lavish party William Randolph Hearst gave aboard his yacht. When Hearst learned that his mistress, the silent film star Marion Davies, was having an affair with Charles Chaplin, he became enraged and killed an innocent man he mistook for Chaplin. With money and jewels, Hearst bribed his guests to keep their mouths shut and one guest, Louella Parsons, he bribed with a weekly gossip column and a radio program. For thirty years in her weak, whiny-voice, Louella Parsons spoke to millions, reporting news items about Hollywood stars that could make or break their careers.

A man is picked up by a fishing boat, bullet-riddled and suffering from amnesia, before racing to elude assassins and regain his memory.

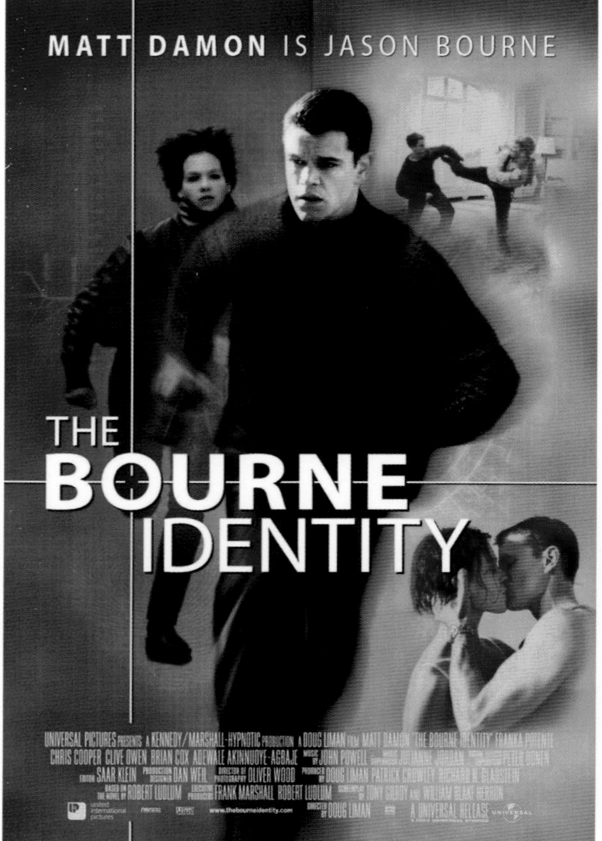

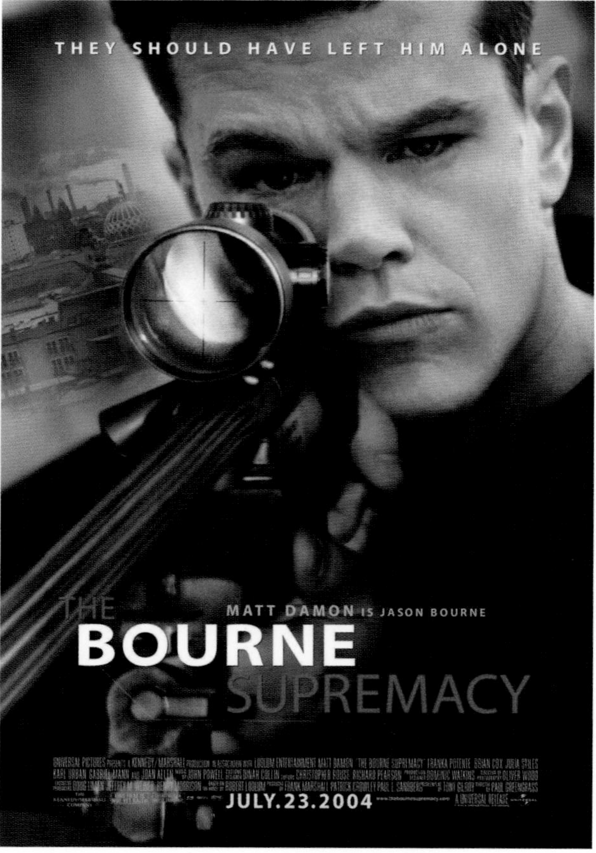

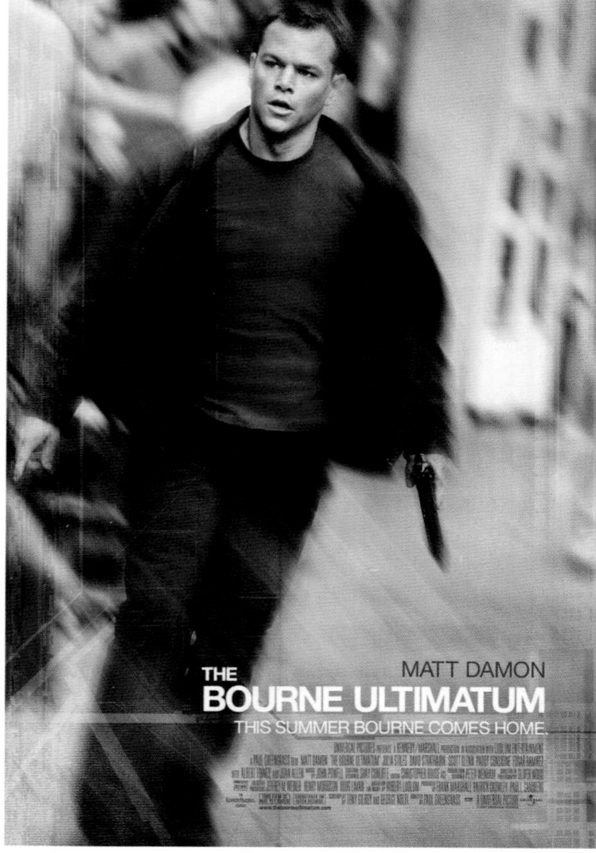

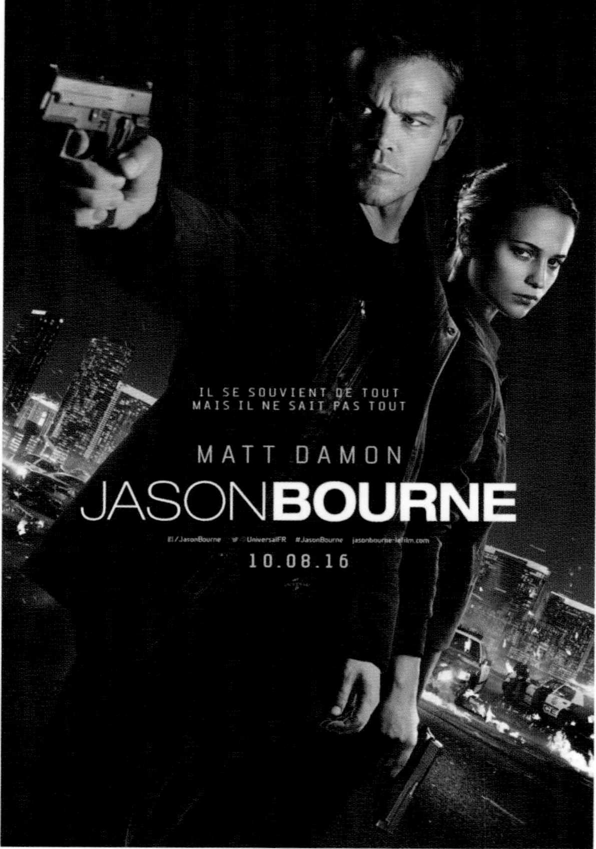

Jess Lomas of Quickflix wrote: "Whether you consider them smart thrillers or paint-by-numbers spy capers, "The Bourne Series" are dynamic interpretations of Robert Ludlum's creative imagination."

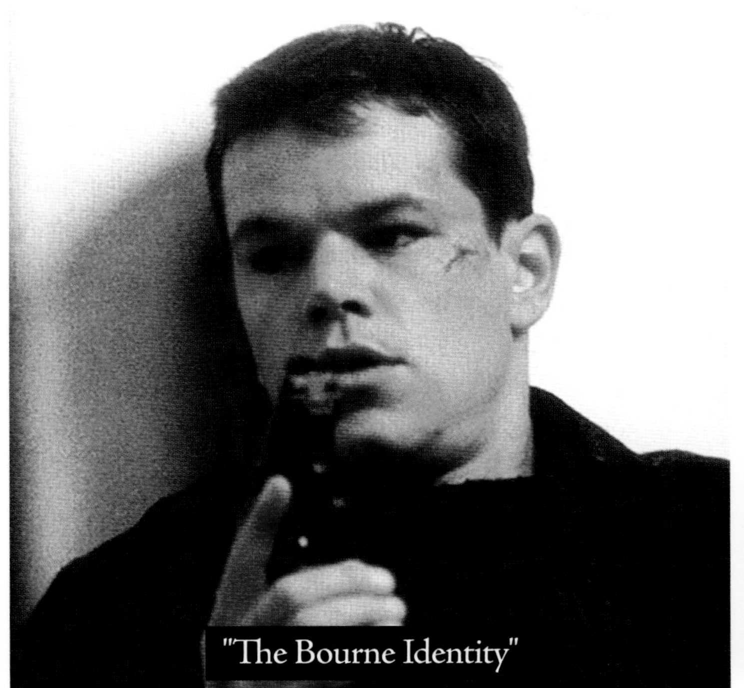
"The Bourne Identity"

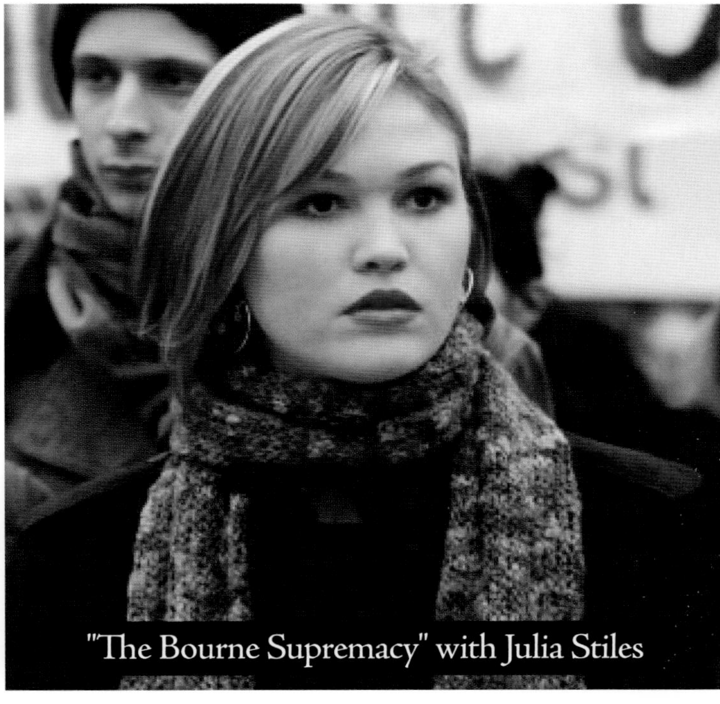
"The Bourne Supremacy" with Julia Stiles

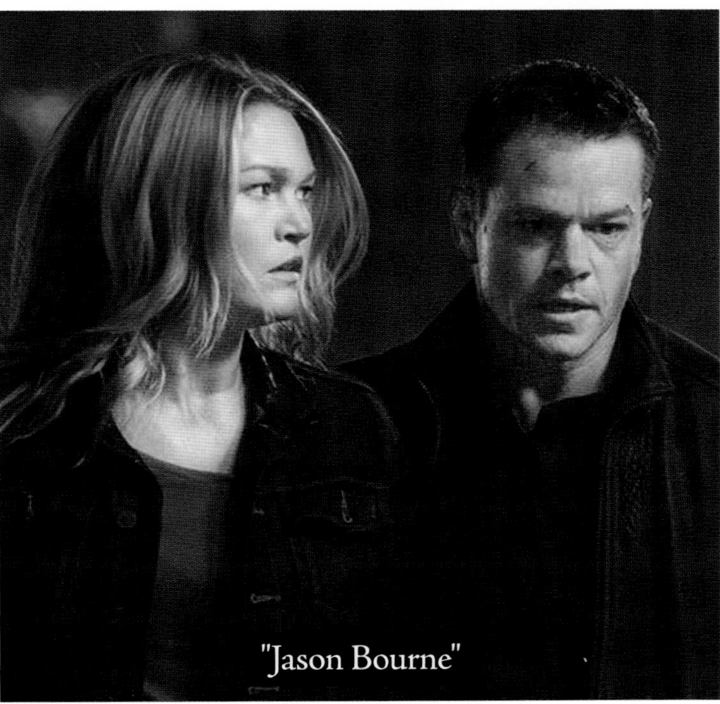
"Jason Bourne"

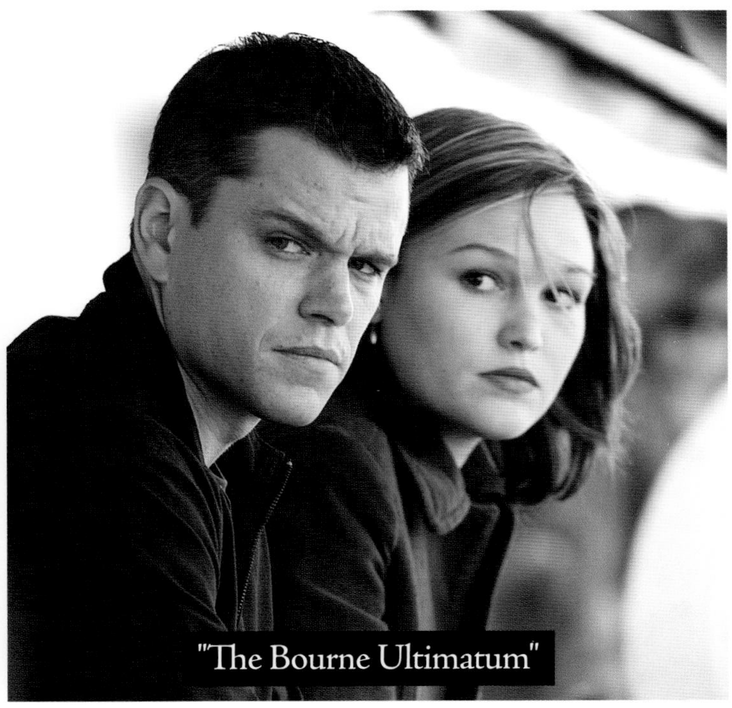
"The Bourne Ultimatum"

My pal Mel Brooks and I are tremendous fans of Jason Bourne and we hope another Bourne movie is gestating and that Matt Damon and Julia Stiles will again be a romantic duo.

Matt Damon is a true renaissance man. He is a great actor, a husband, a father and a philanthropist who co-founded Water.org, a non-profit organization that provides access to safe drinking water and sanitation to the developing countries of Ethiopia, Indonesia and Brazil.

A lawyer decides that she's used too much like a nanny by her boss, so she walks out on him.

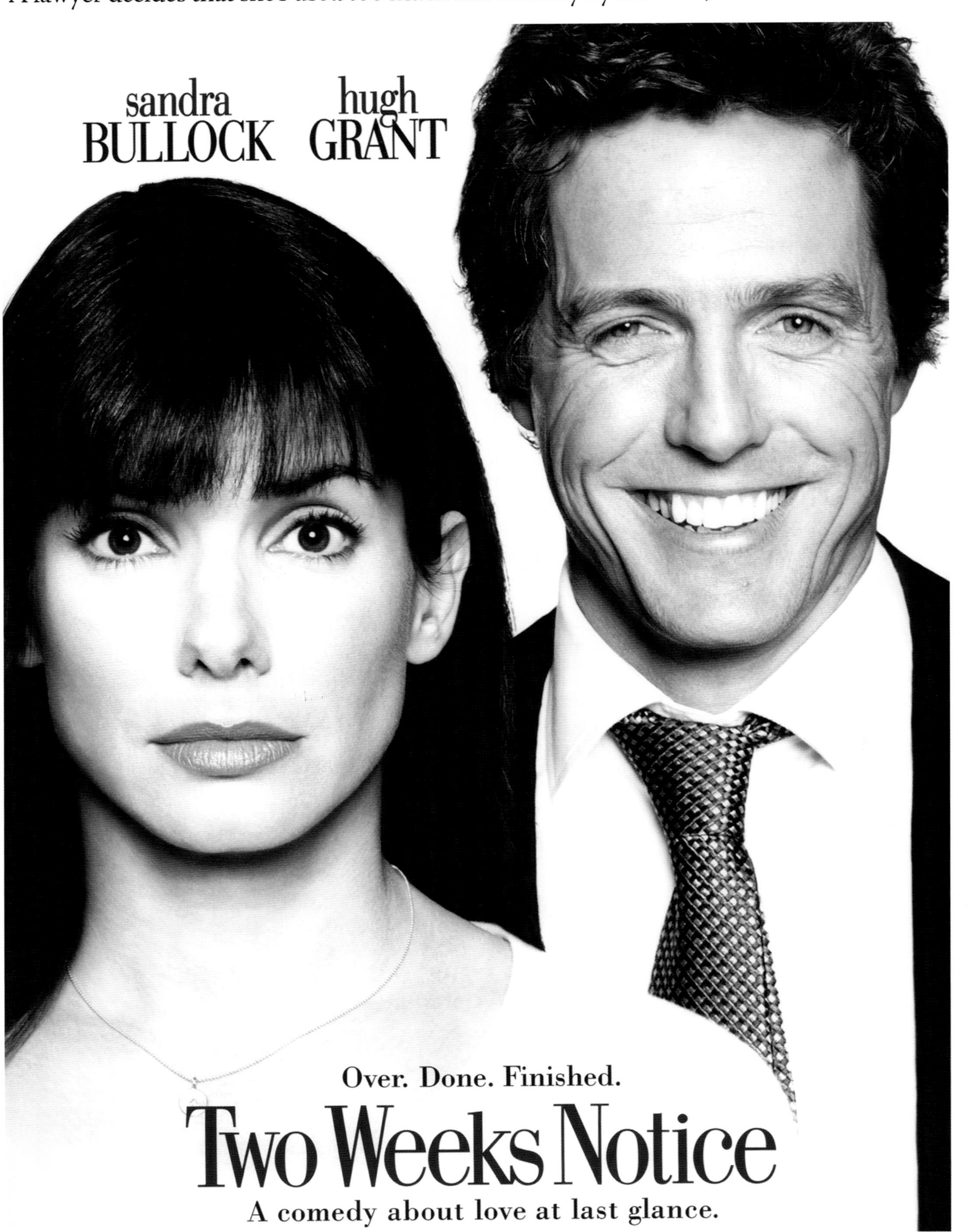

Kevin Carr of Fat Guys at the Movies wrote: "Everything a romantic comedy is supposed to be."

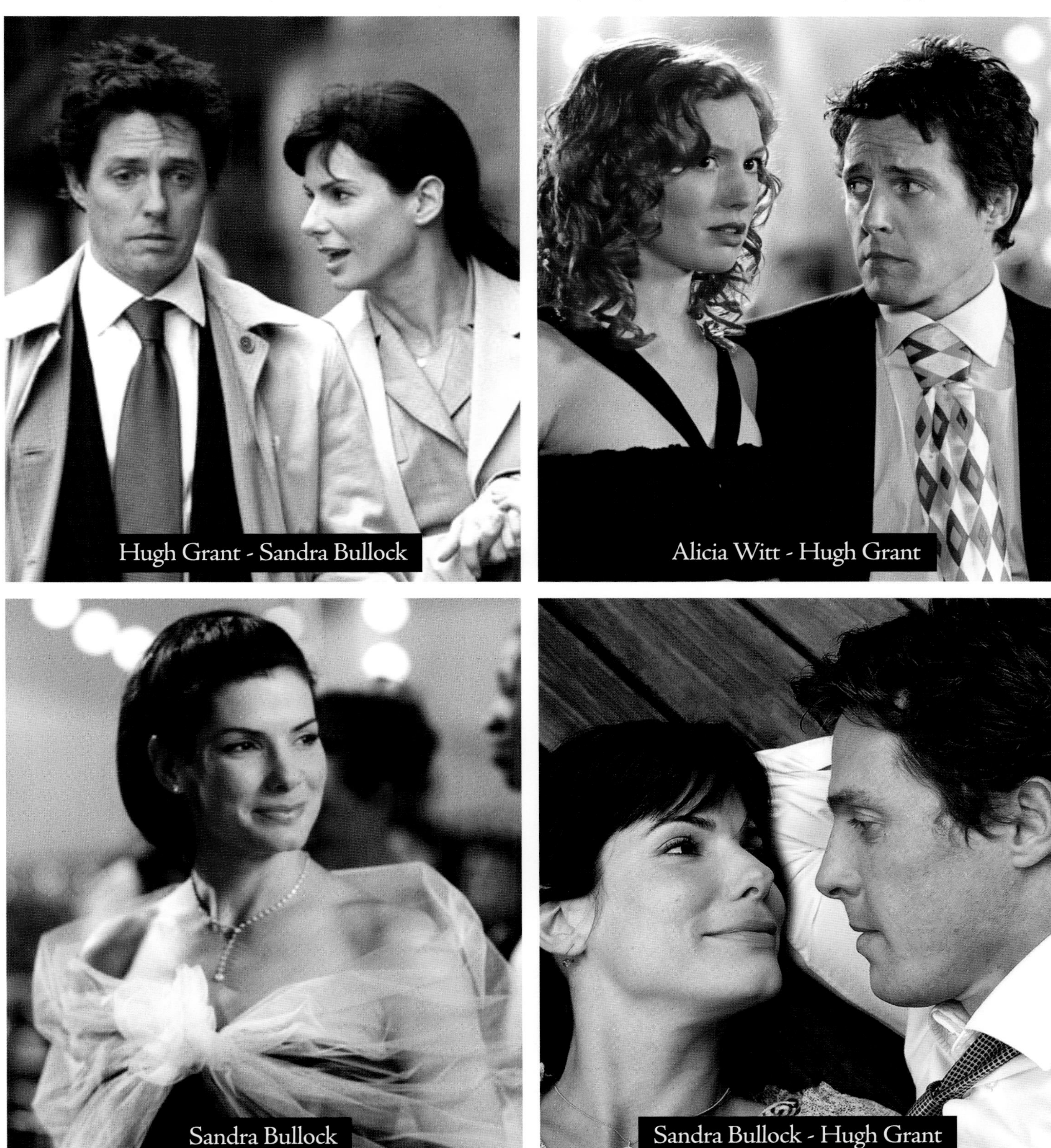

Hugh Grant - Sandra Bullock

Alicia Witt - Hugh Grant

Sandra Bullock

Sandra Bullock - Hugh Grant

What's more fun than seeing two of your favorite actors playing roles that keep them at odds with each other until one hundred and one minutes later, they give you good reason to smile by falling into each other's arms?

A Jewish musician struggles to survive the destruction of the Warsaw ghetto in WWII.

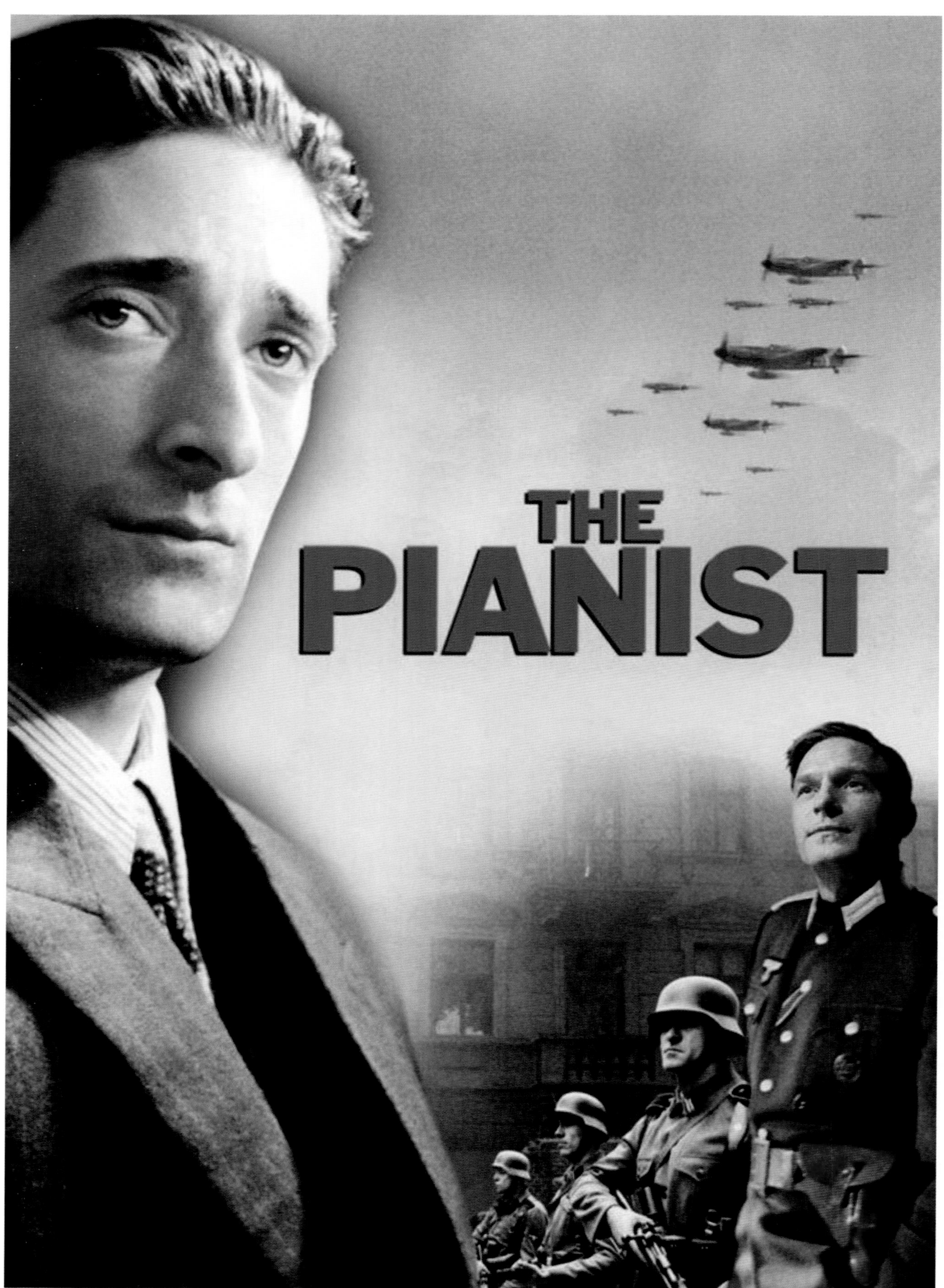

Roger Moore of Orlando Sentinel wrote: "Brody is a sublimely haunting presence at the heart of 'The Pianist.'"

Richard Schickel of TIME Magazine wrote: "We admire this film for its harsh objectivity and refusal to seek our tears, our sympathies."

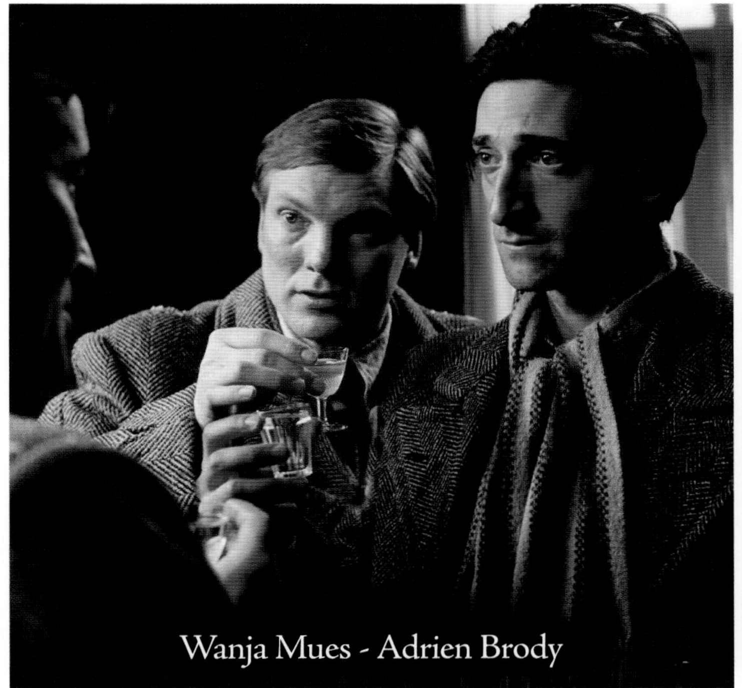
Wanja Mues - Adrien Brody

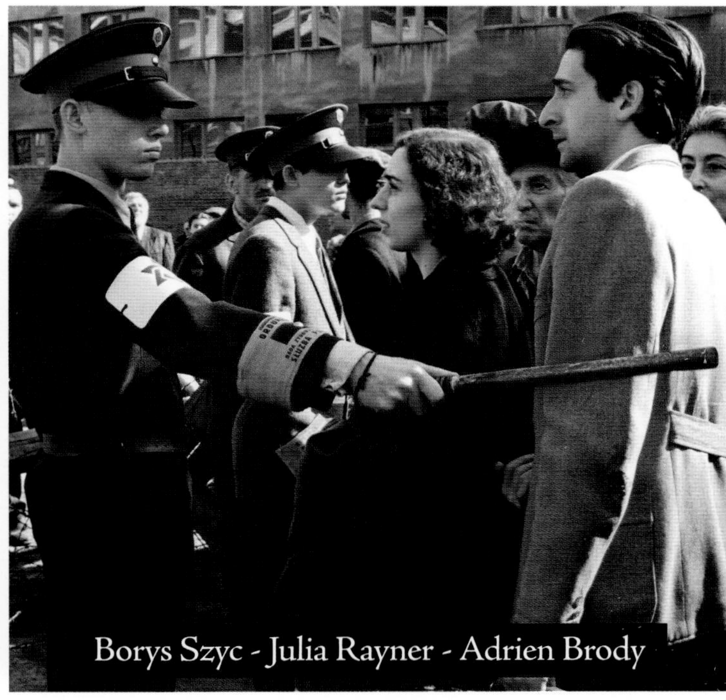
Borys Szyc - Julia Rayner - Adrien Brody

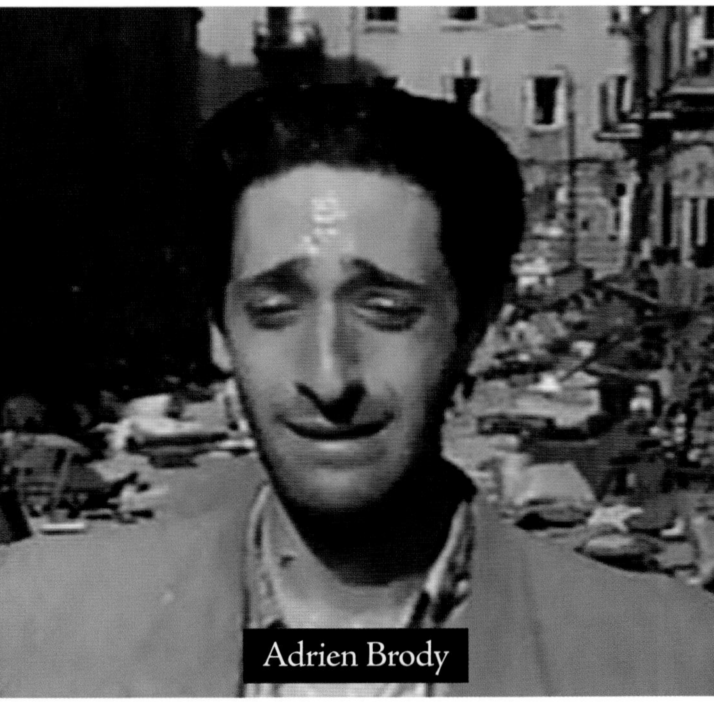
Adrien Brody

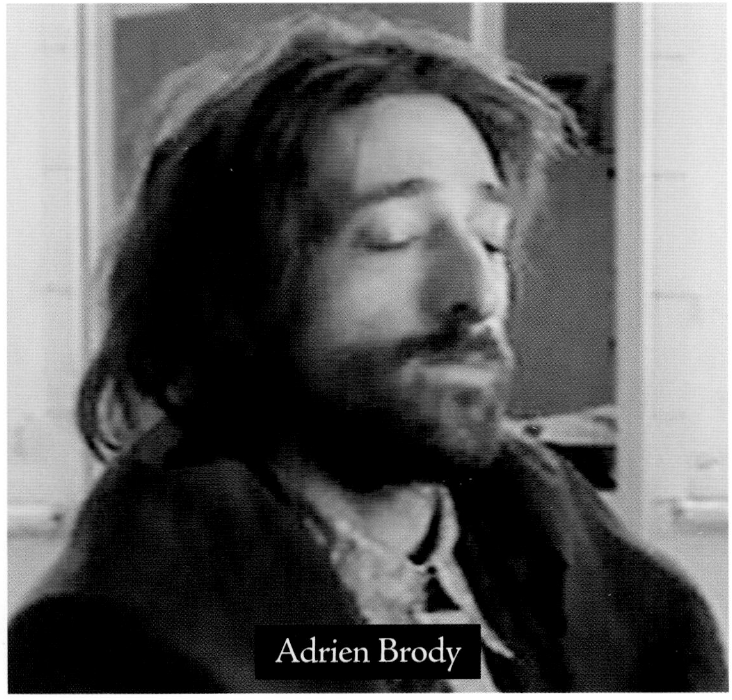
Adrien Brody

This extremely moving film is based on the autobiographical book "The Pianist," a World War II memoir by the Polish-Jewish pianist and composer Władysław Szpilman, who miraculously survived the war and lived to the age of eighty-eight. Had he lived I'm sure that Szpilman would have approved and appreciated both the film and Brody's performance.

Follows the lives of eight very different couples in dealing with their love lives in various loosely interrelated tales, all set during a frantic month before Christmas in London, England.

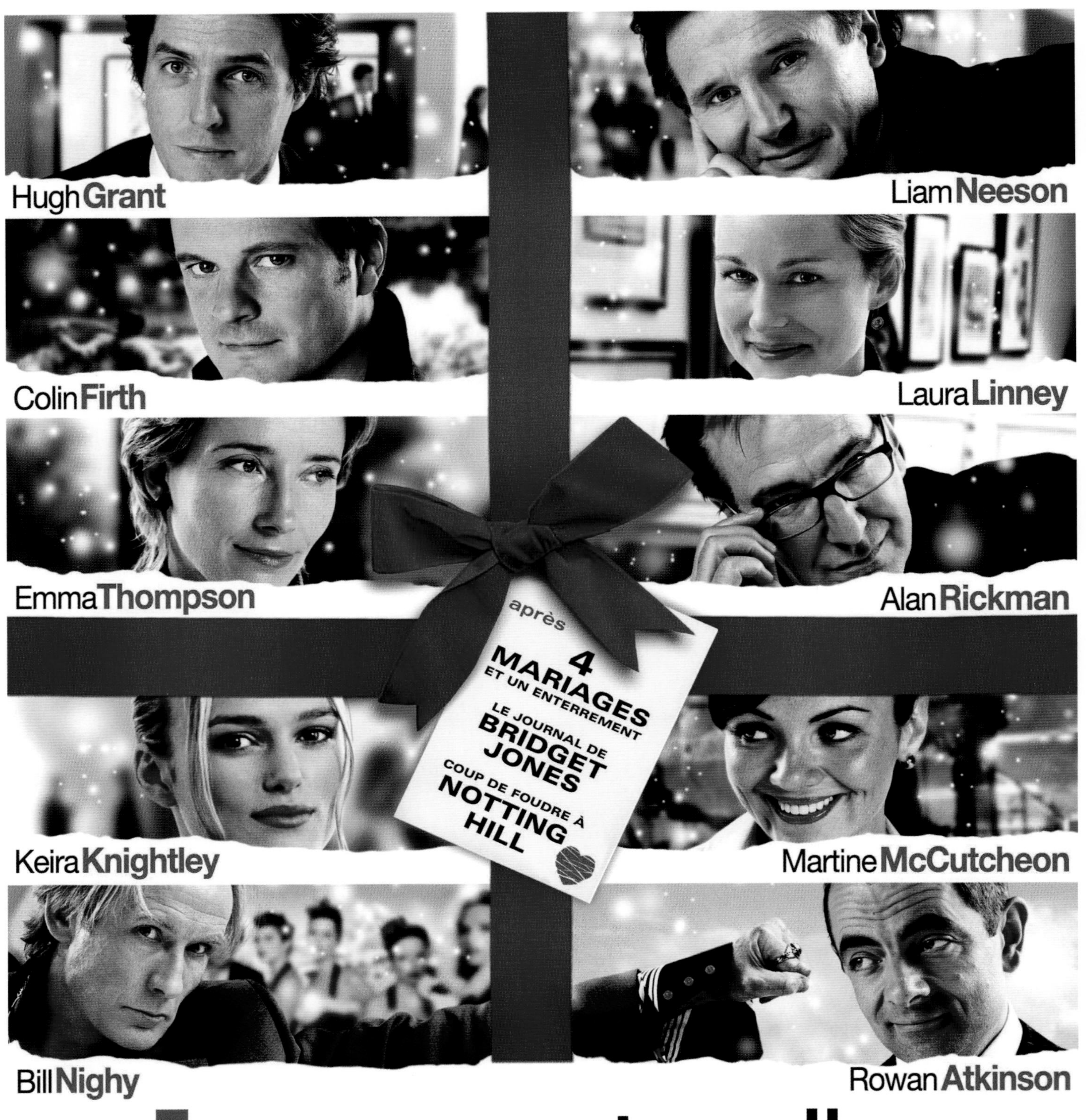

Stanley Kauffmann of The New Republic wrote: "Whatever the actors are given to do they make so delightful–or so delightfully moving–that 'Love Actually' wins out over its wobbles."

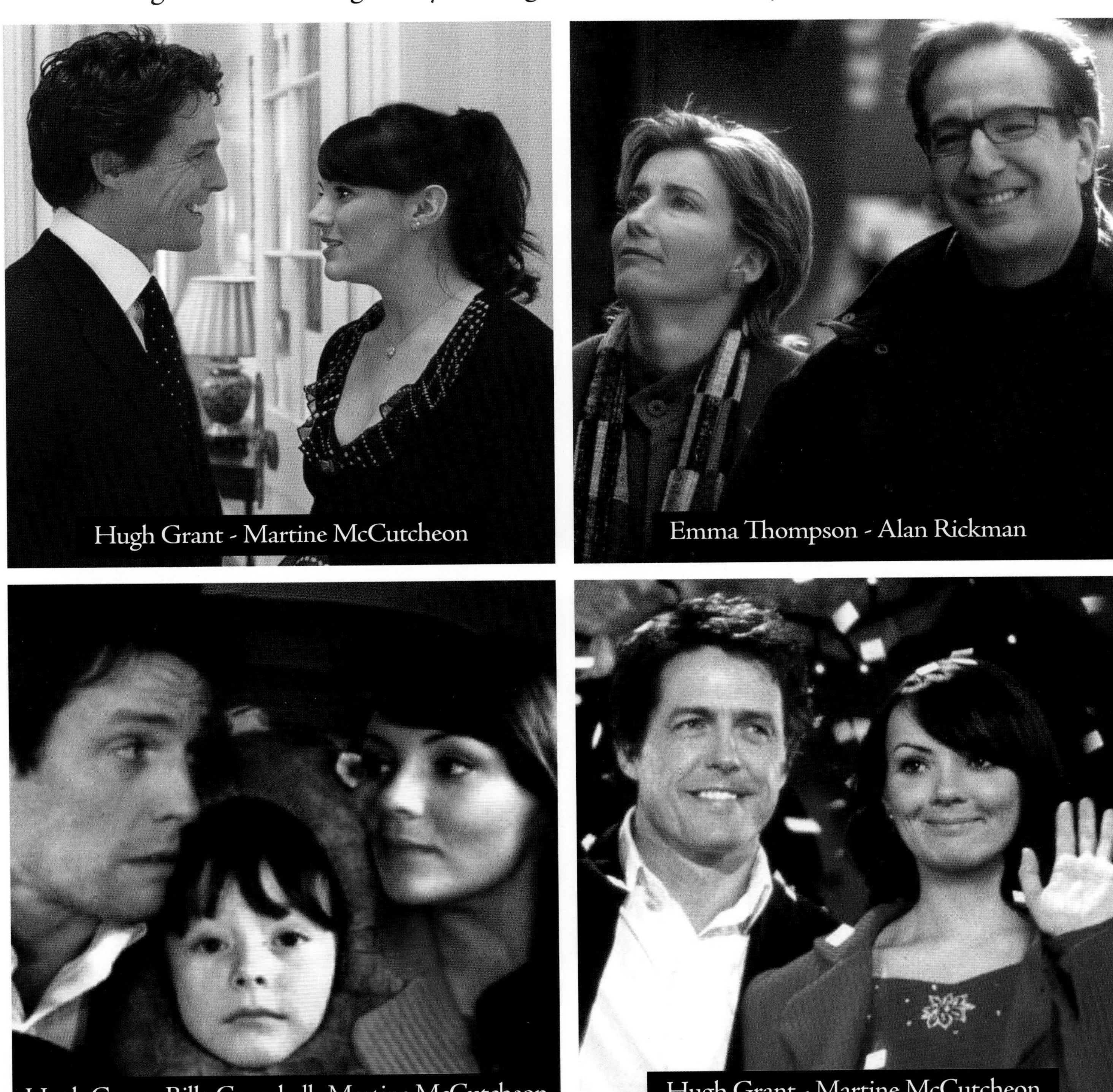

Hugh Grant - Martine McCutcheon

Emma Thompson - Alan Rickman

Hugh Grant - Billy Campbell - Martine McCutcheon

Hugh Grant - Martine McCutcheon

And I, Carl Reiner, of Beverly Hills writes: I didn't see the wobbles that The New Republic critic mentioned. I saw a romantic, feel-good movie that made me feel, not good, but great. I actually loved "Love Actually" and recommend to anyone, who has ever been in love or is on the verge of falling in love or thinking about falling in love again, that you stream this movie and see why I actually love loving this film.

The story of the life and career of the legendary rhythm and blues musician Ray Charles, from his humble beginnings in the South, where he went blind at age seven, to his meteoric rise to stardom during the 1950s and 1960s.

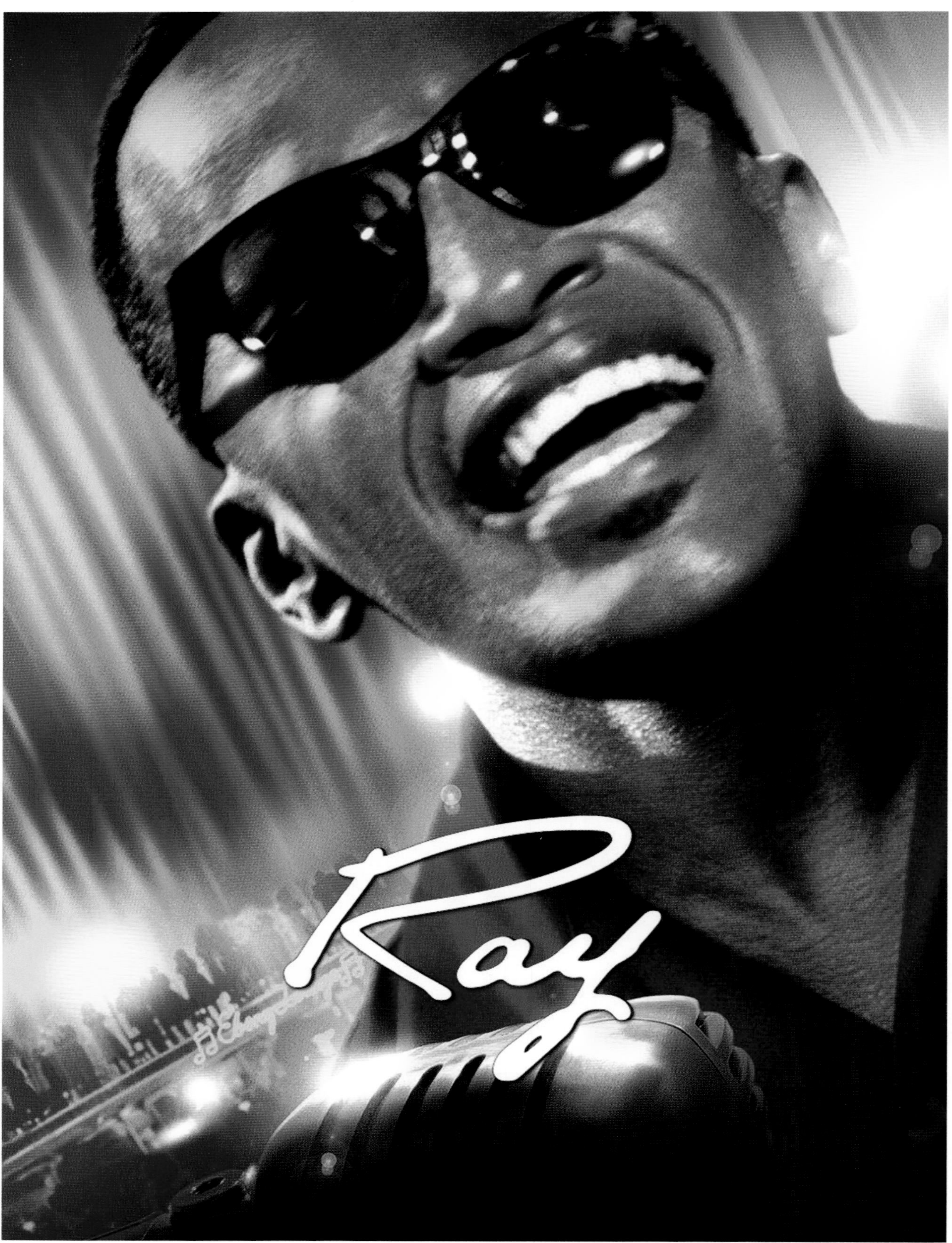

Rex Reed of New York Observer wrote: "Jamie Foxx's all-encompassing performance in the title role more than justifies the early Oscar gossip it has generated."

Teresa Wiltz of Washington Post wrote: "To describe Foxx's performance here is to gush, and so gush we will."

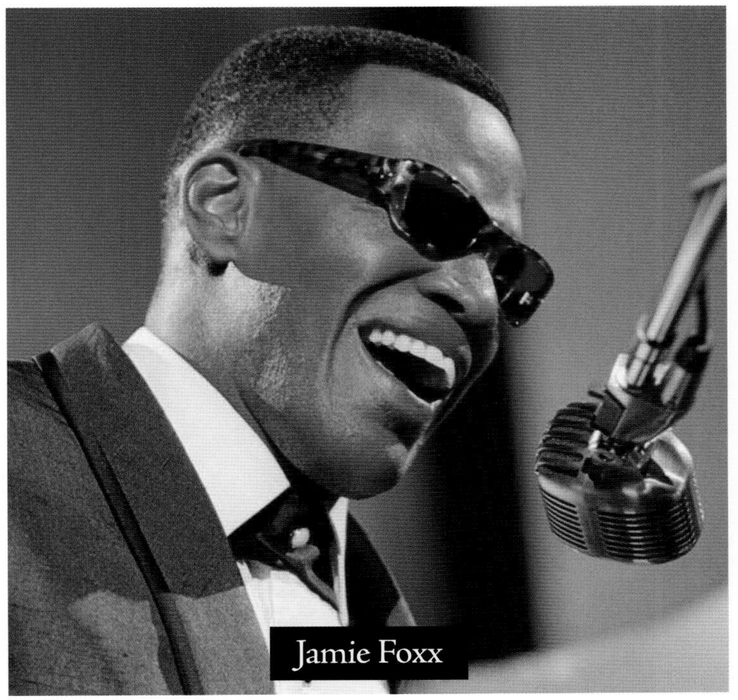
Jamie Foxx

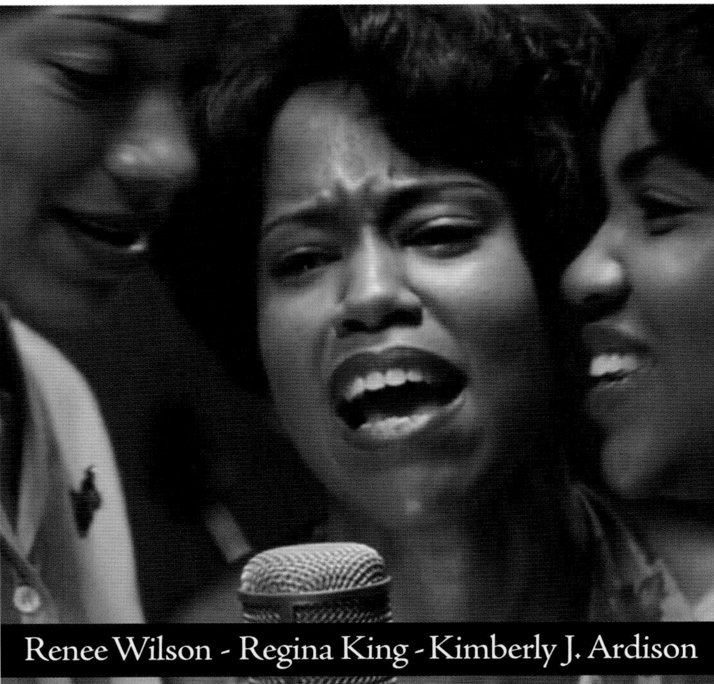
Renee Wilson - Regina King - Kimberly J. Ardison

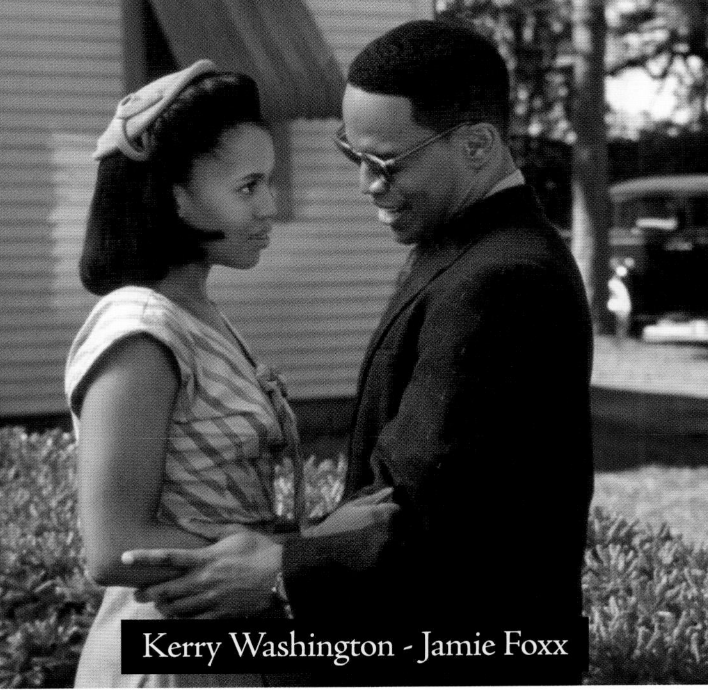
Kerry Washington - Jamie Foxx

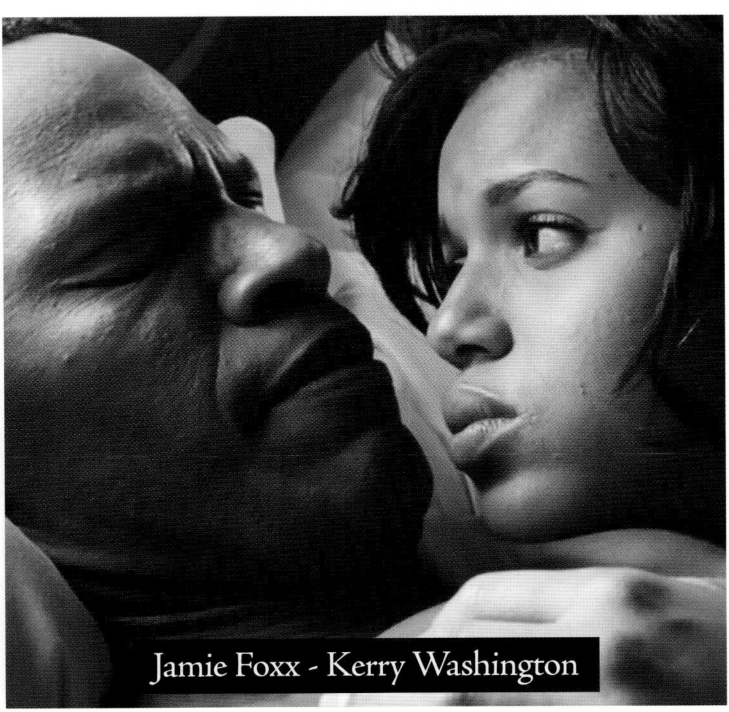
Jamie Foxx - Kerry Washington

And gush I did and so must have the members of The Academy of Motion Picture Arts and Sciences, who, in 2005, presented Jamie Foxx with the Best Actor Oscar. I was amazed to learn that Jamie Foxx did not lip-sync to Ray Charles, but used his own voice to sing Ray Charles' great hits. If I could sing like Jamie Foxx, I'd make a record a day.

Two men reaching middle age with not much to show but disappointment embark on a week-long road trip through California's wine country, just as one is about to take a trip down the aisle.

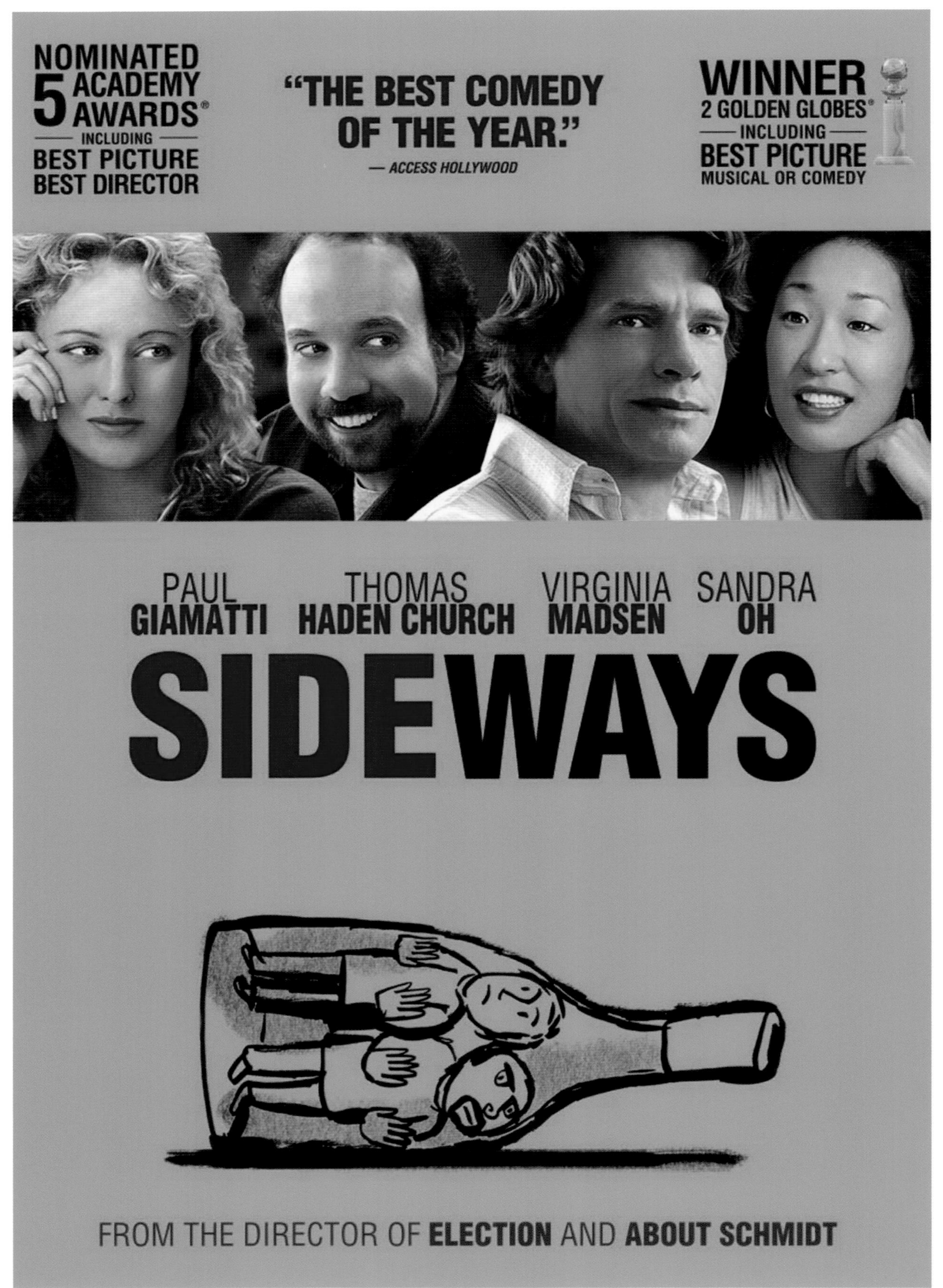

Jay Antani of Cinema Writer wrote: "Giamatti handily raises what could've been a pedestrian road trip romance into the stratosphere of a world-class character study."

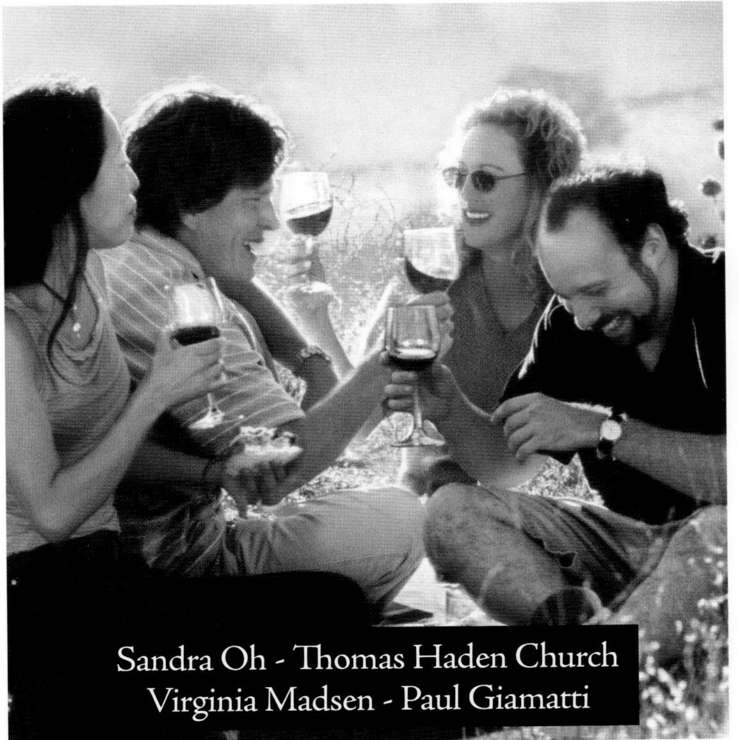

Sandra Oh - Thomas Haden Church
Virginia Madsen - Paul Giamatti

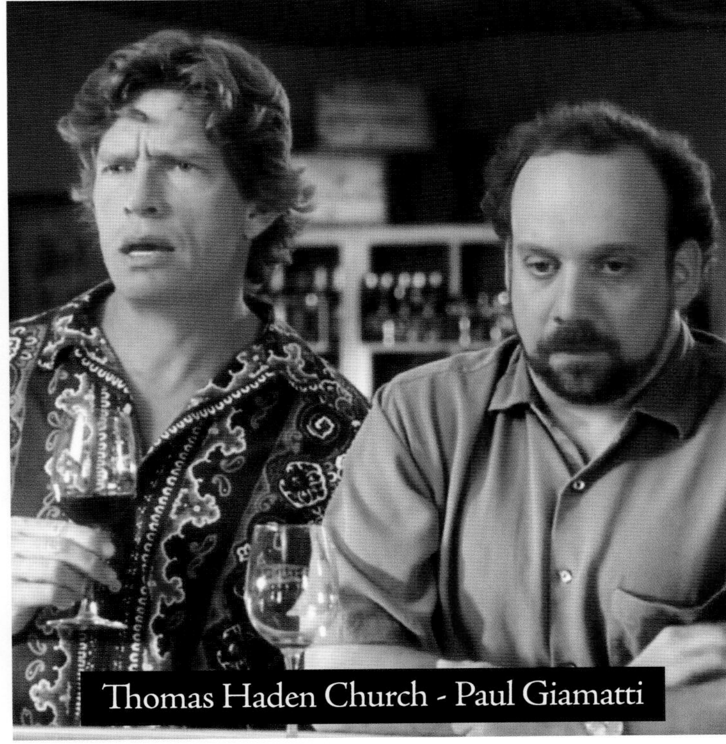

Thomas Haden Church - Paul Giamatti

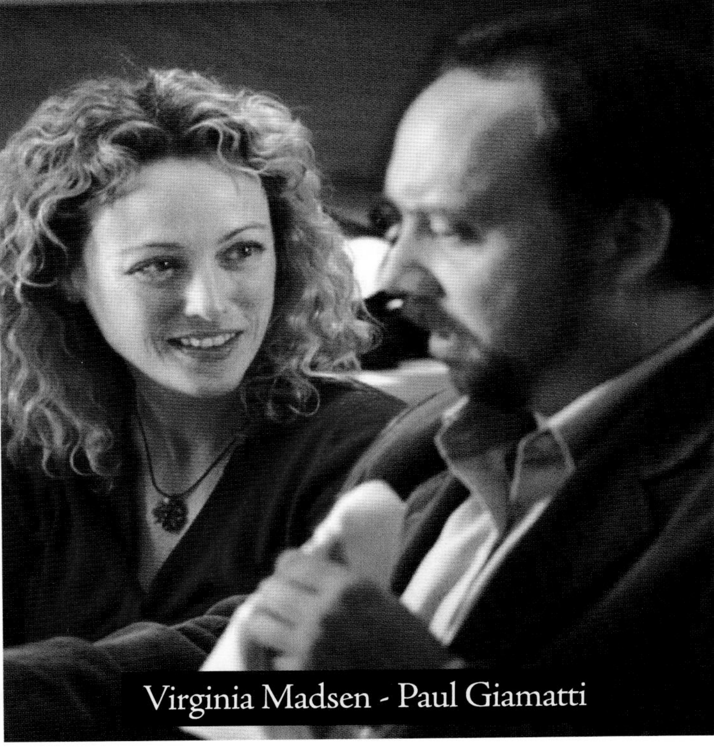

Virginia Madsen - Paul Giamatti

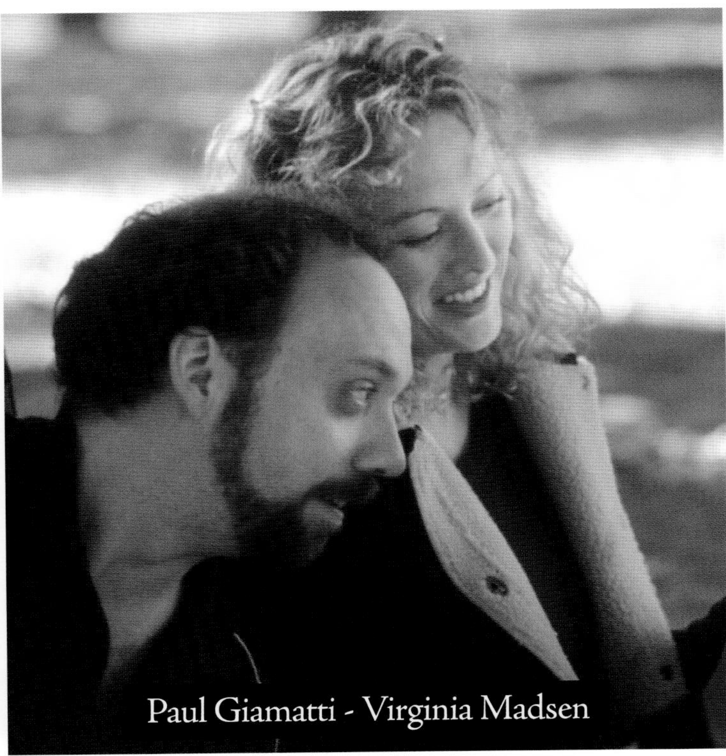

Paul Giamatti - Virginia Madsen

This Oscar winning screenplay treats us to a pleasant weekend roaming around the Santa Barbara wine country. The film's ending is surprising and soul-satisfying as we see the prepossessing Paul Giamatti successfully win the hand of the lovely Virginia Madsen and the hearts of the audience.

A chronicle of country music legend Johnny Cash's life, from his early days on an Arkansas cotton farm to his rise to fame with Sun Records in Memphis, where he recorded alongside Elvis Presley, Jerry Lee Lewis, and Carl Perkins.

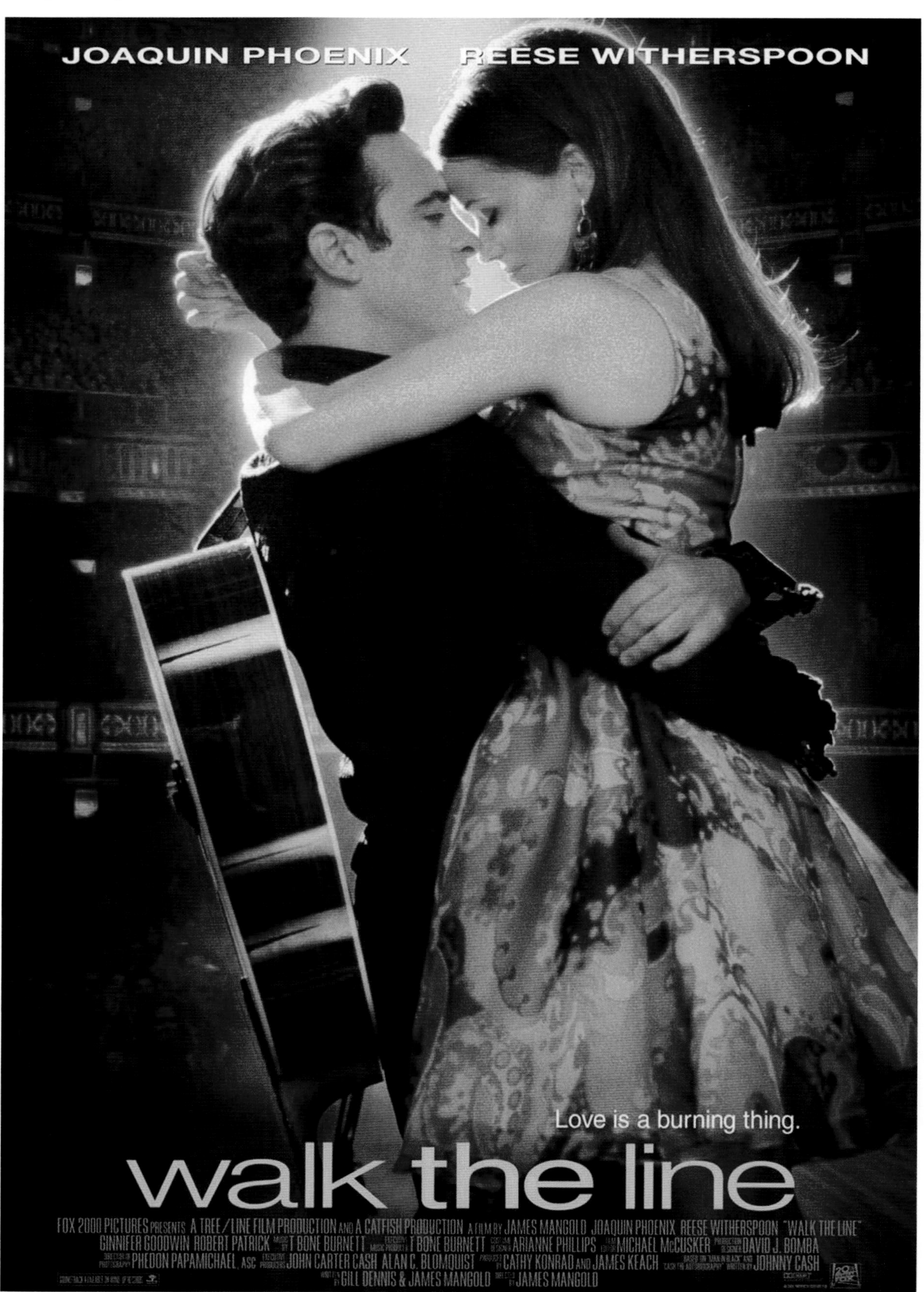

Andrew Sarris of New York Observer wrote: "I advise you catch up with 'Walk the Line,' if only for Ms. Witherspoon's transcendent joyousness as a still-growing legend within a legend."

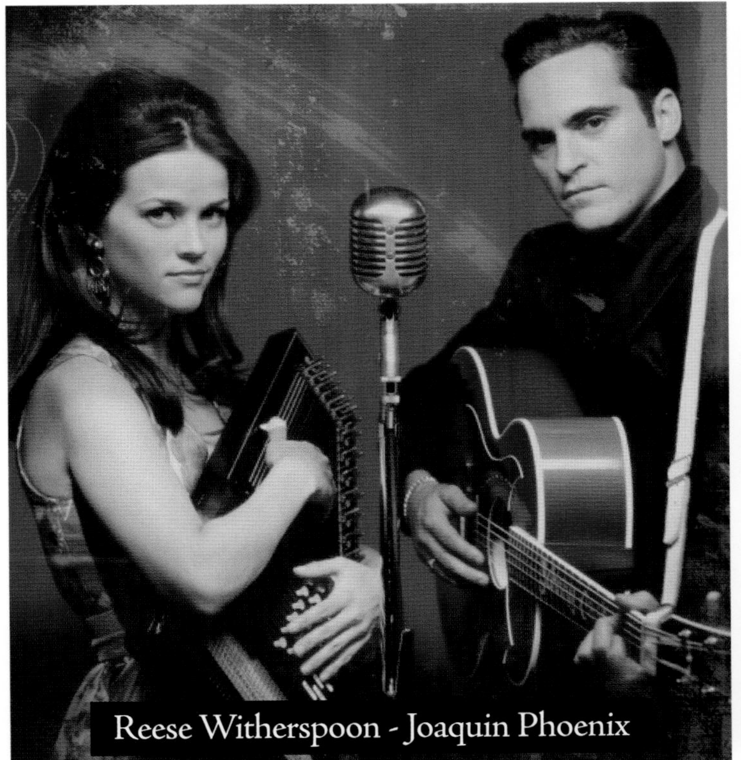
Reese Witherspoon - Joaquin Phoenix

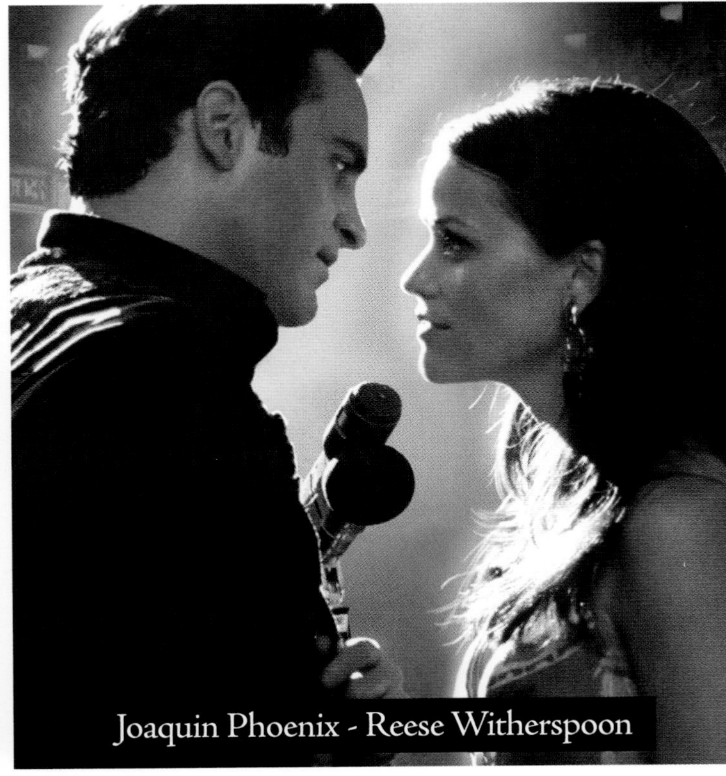
Joaquin Phoenix - Reese Witherspoon

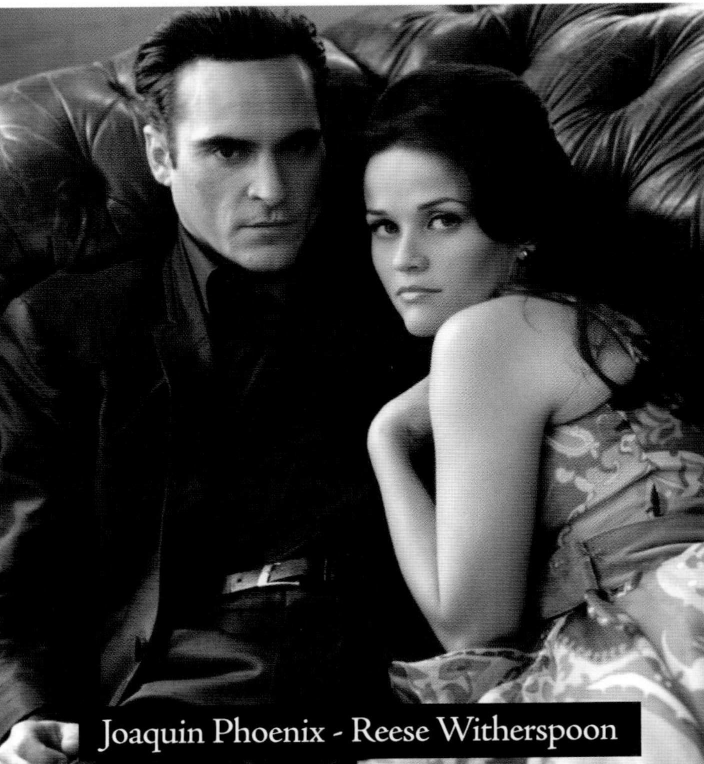
Joaquin Phoenix - Reese Witherspoon

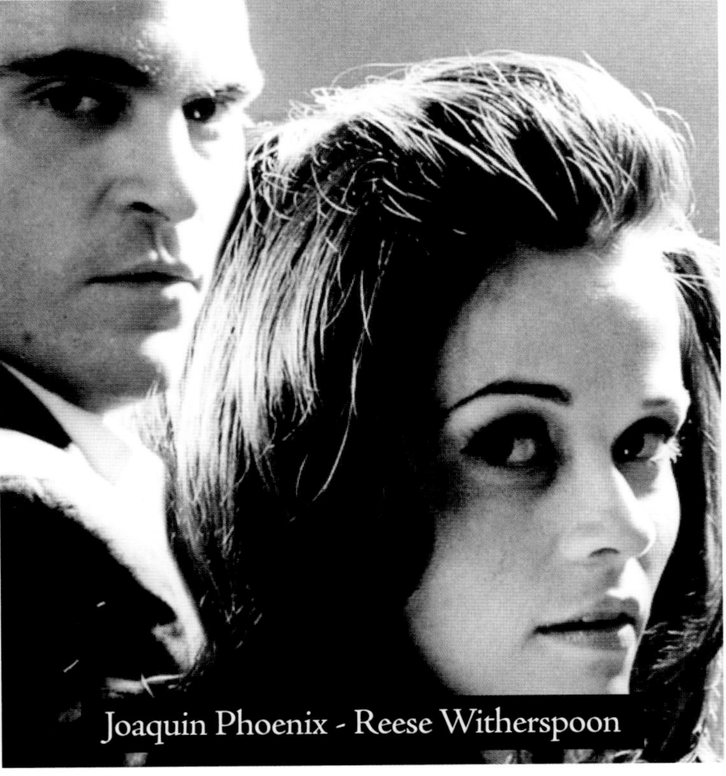
Joaquin Phoenix - Reese Witherspoon

Reese Witherspoon convincingly singing in the style of the country music artist June Carter, once again, demonstrates her versatility. I can't wait to see what Reese chooses to do next. Whatever it is, I know I'm going to enjoy it, talk about it and write about it.

In 1959, Truman Capote learns of the murder of a Kansas family and decides to write a book about the case. While researching for his novel *In Cold Blood,* Capote forms a relationship with one of the killers, Perry Smith, who is on death row.

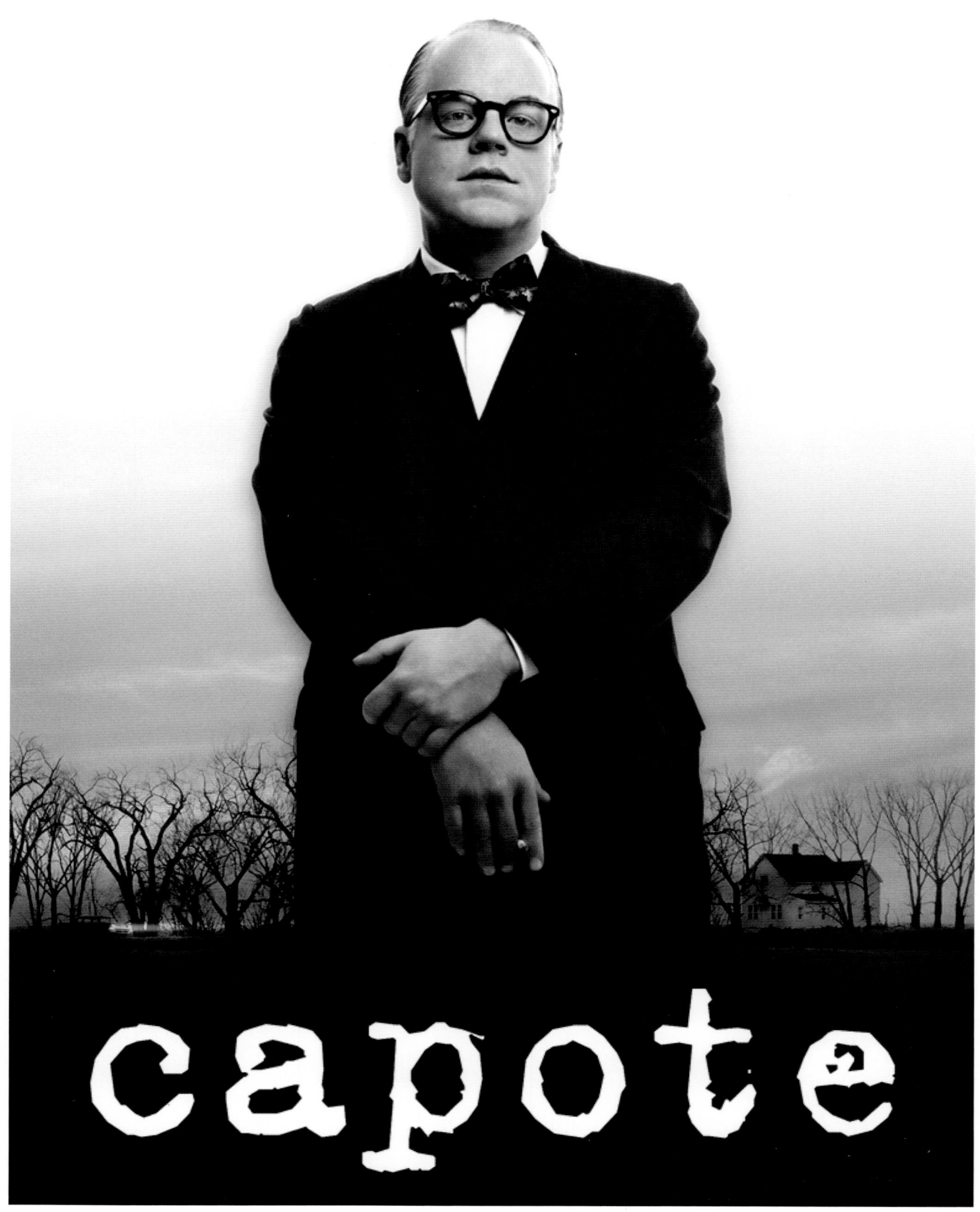

Steve Murray of Atlanta Journal-Constitution wrote: "Hoffman goes beyond impersonation to something close to possession."

Bruce Westbrook of Houston Chronicle wrote: "It's a fully realized look at a time and place, as well as a riveting study of career obsessions warring with a sense of justice."

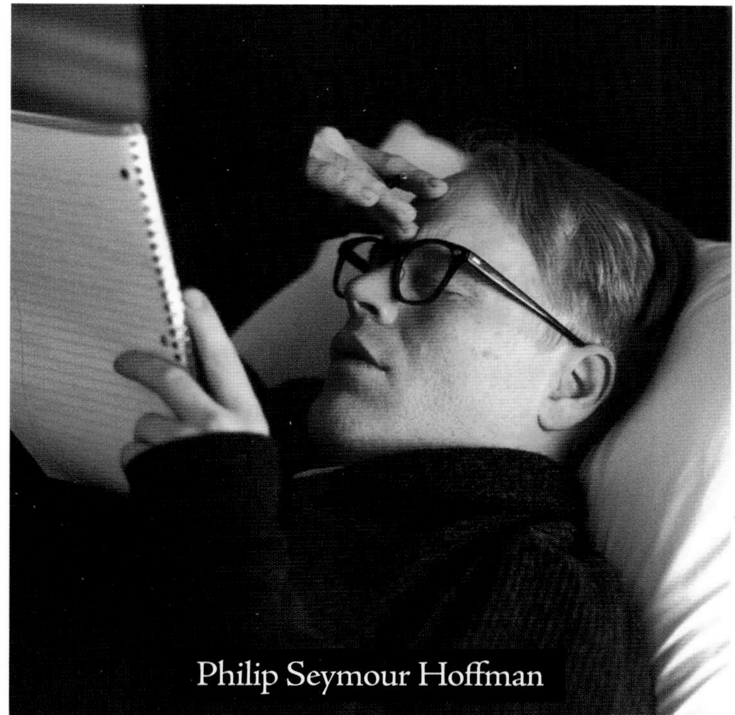
Philip Seymour Hoffman

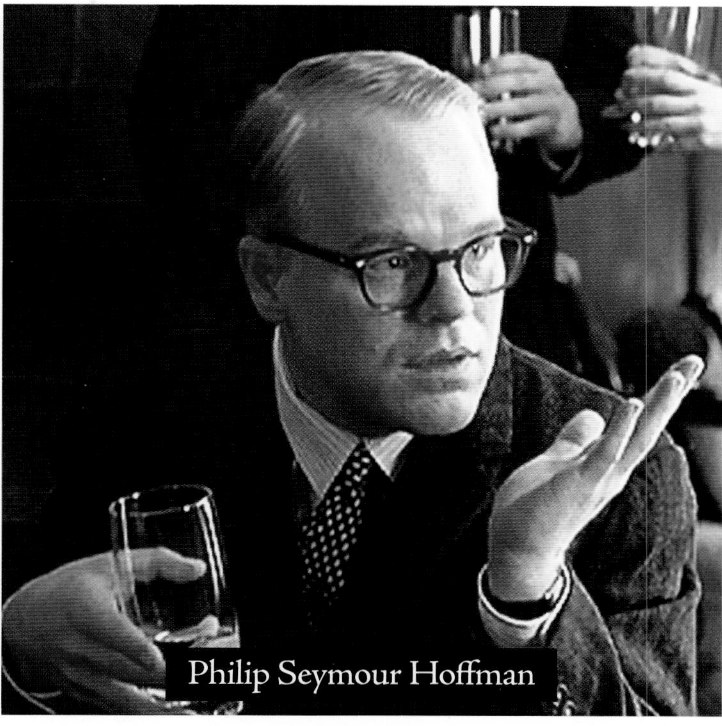
Philip Seymour Hoffman

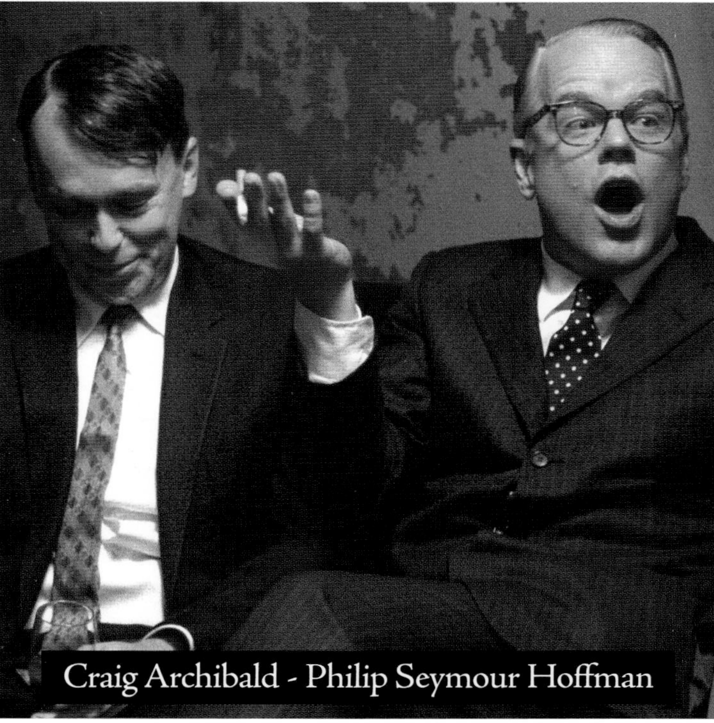
Craig Archibald - Philip Seymour Hoffman

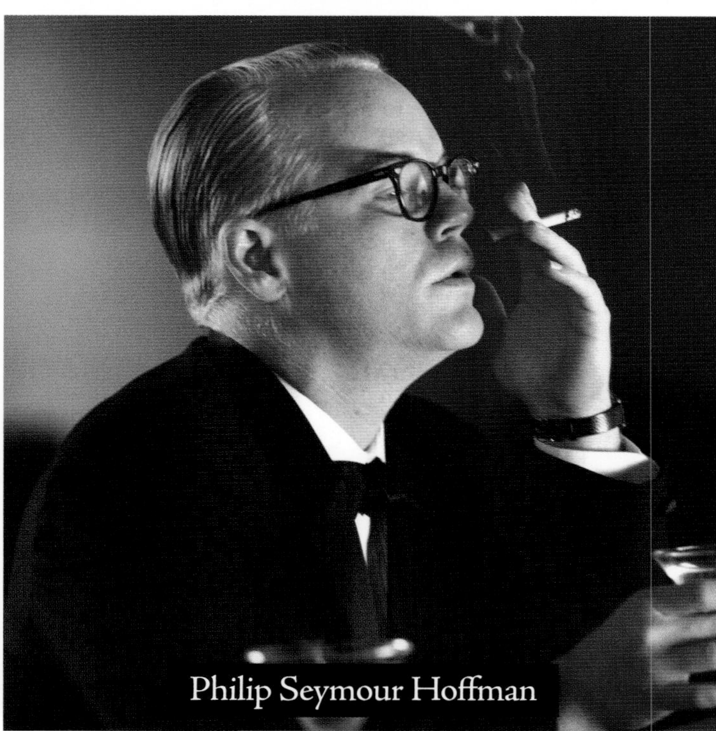
Philip Seymour Hoffman

I truly felt that Philip Seymour Hoffman richly deserved the Oscar he received for his performance. One thing I was amazed to discover is that Hoffman was six feet tall but somehow managed to convince us that he was Truman Capote's height, five foot three.

A smart but sensible new graduate lands a job as an assistant to Miranda Priestly, the demanding editor-in-chief of a high fashion magazine.

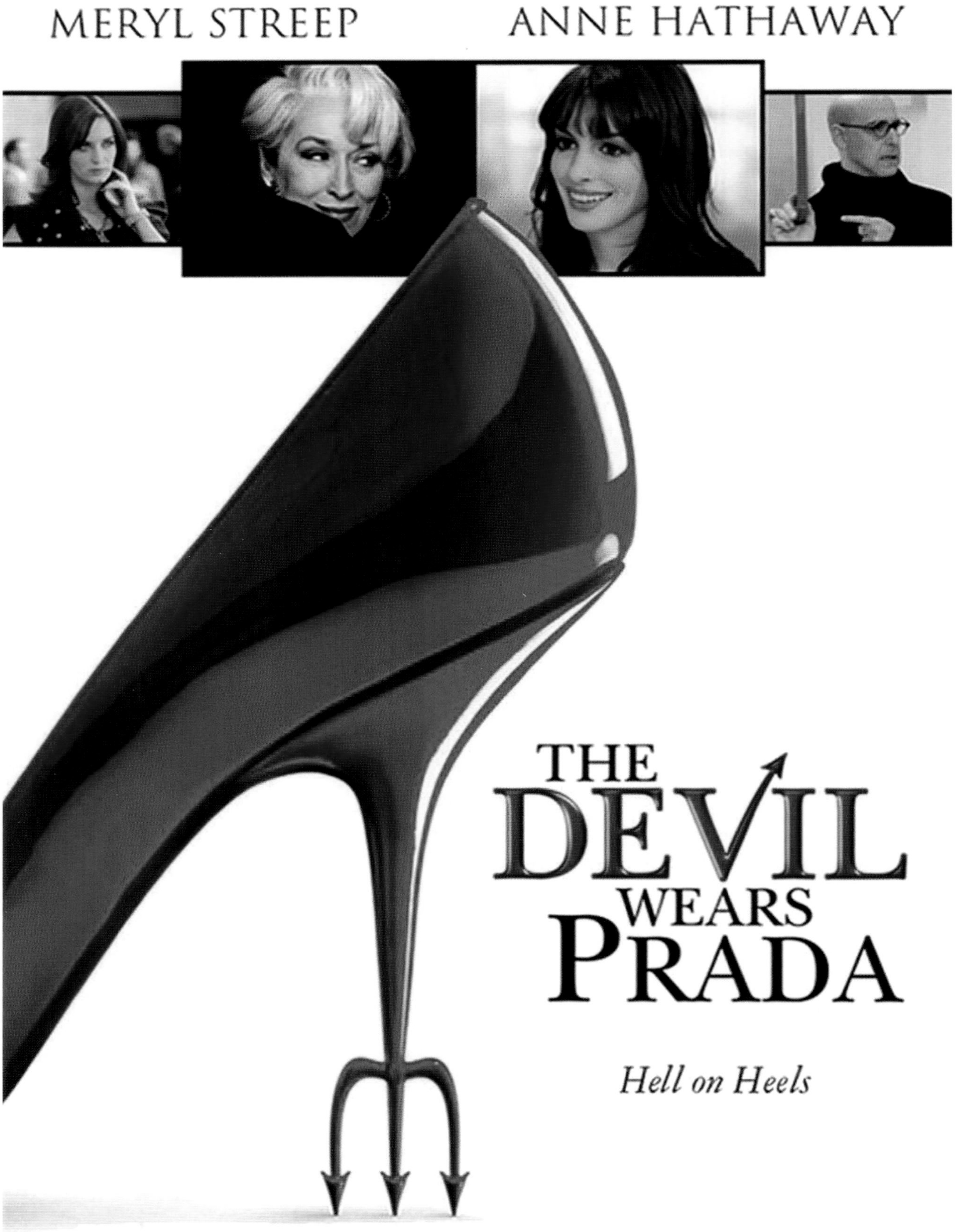

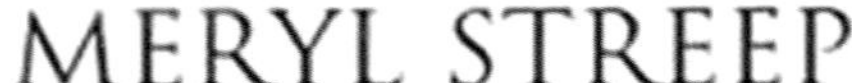

James Berardinelli of ReelViews wrote: "'The Devil Wears Prada' is two films in one: a caustic, energetic satire of the fashion world and a cautionary melodrama."

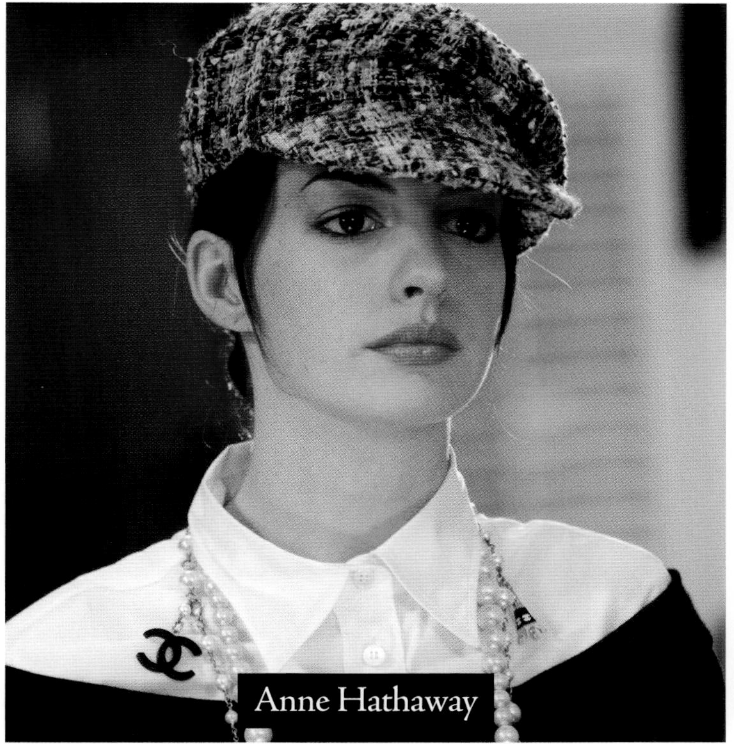

Anne Hathaway

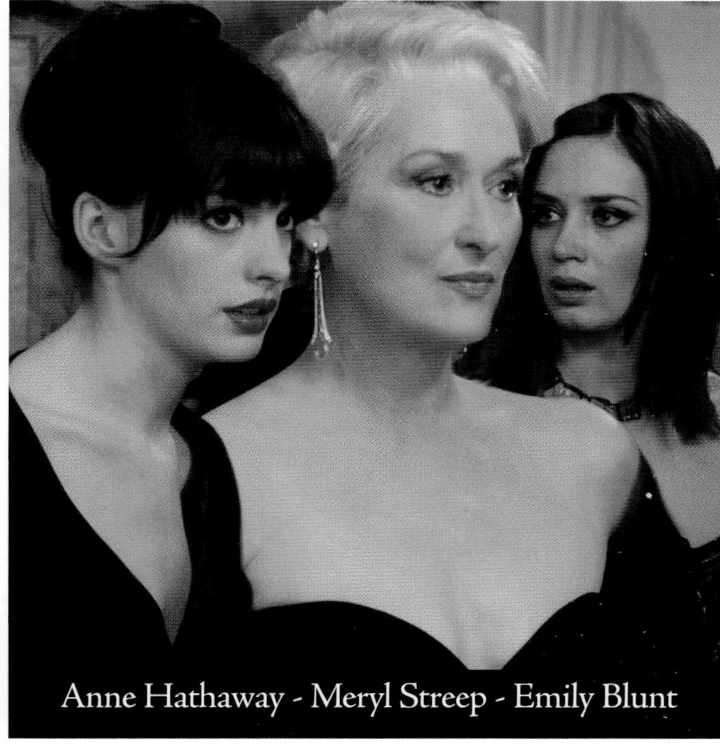

Anne Hathaway - Meryl Streep - Emily Blunt

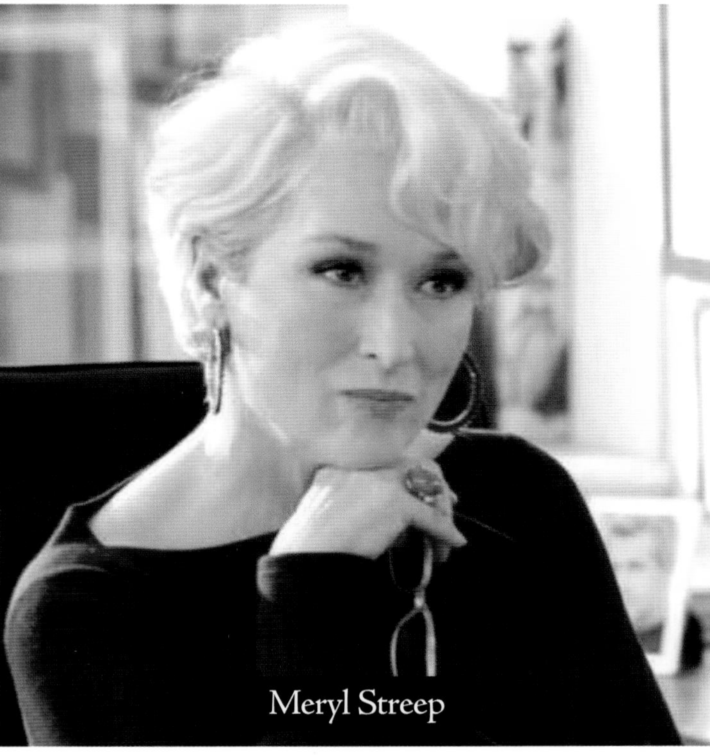

Meryl Streep

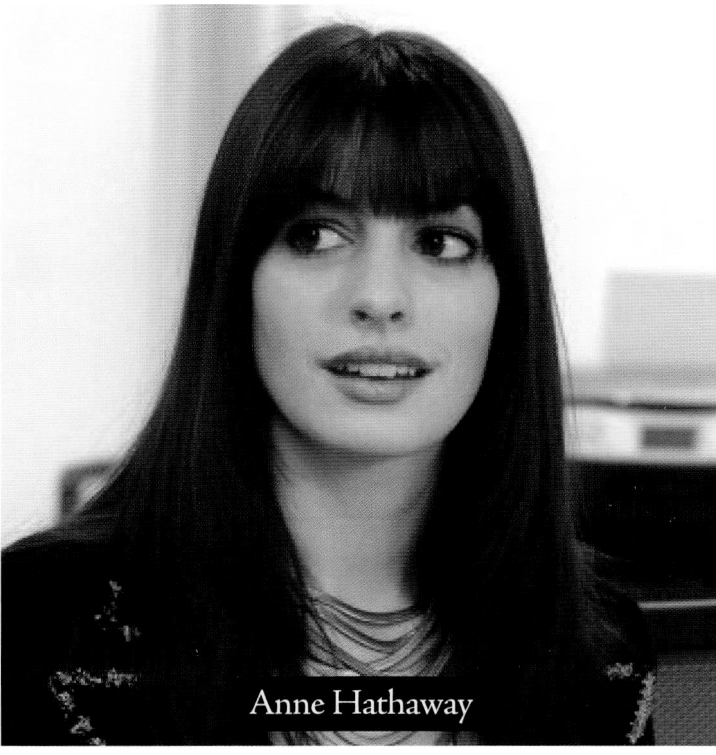

Anne Hathaway

This film was on TV last night and I heard myself saying what I always say when I watch Meryl Streep perform, "She's the best, she's the best!"

Watching the talented actress Anne Hathaway perform made me think, "She can really deliver her lines and she's soooooo attractive!"

Kazakh TV talking head Borat is dispatched to the United States to report on the greatest country in the world. With a documentary crew in tow, Borat becomes more interested in locating and marrying Pamela Anderson.

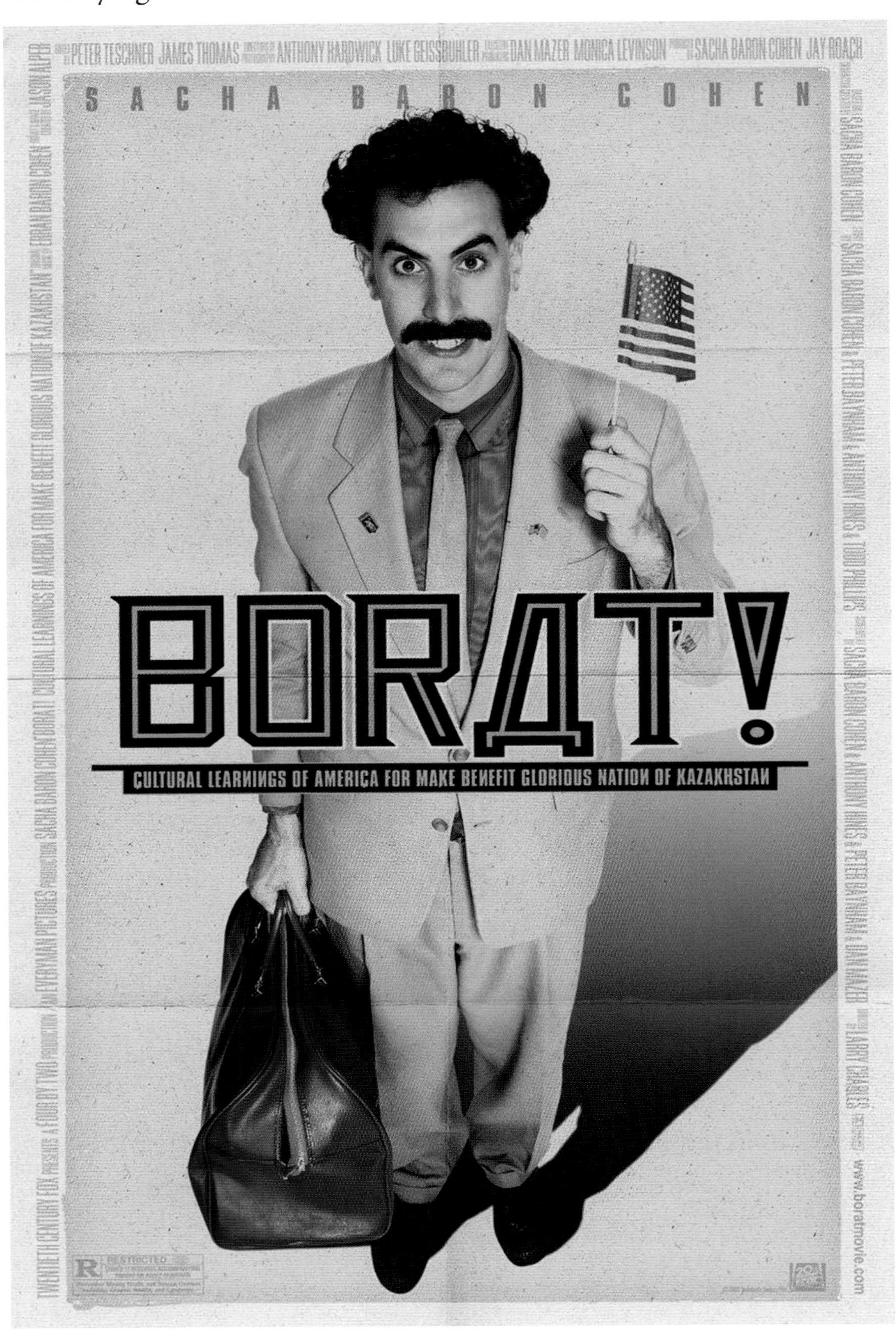

Joe Williams of St. Louis Post-Dispatch wrote: "Borat is a serious work of social criticism. But it's also the funniest movie I've ever seen."

Richard Roeper of Ebert & Roeper wrote: "I did find this to be one of the more inventive, aggressively offensive and insanely tasteless comedies in many a year. And yeah, that's a thumbs-up."

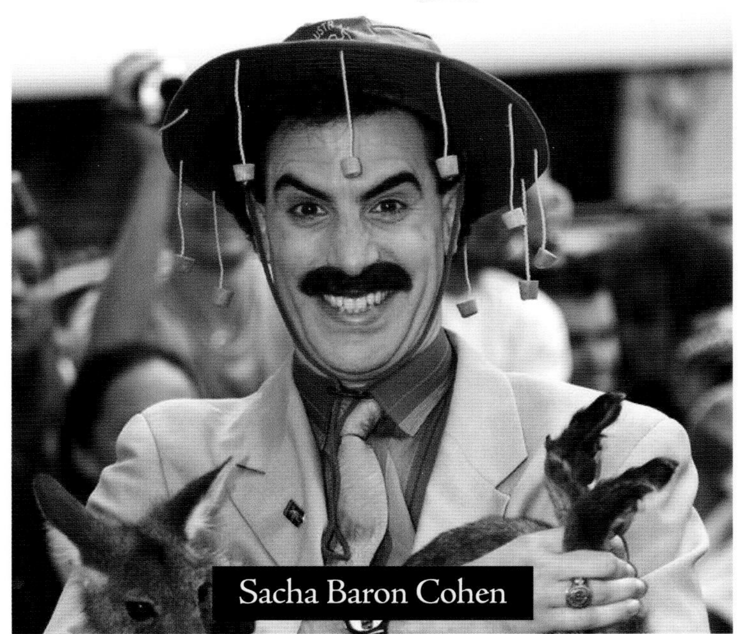
Sacha Baron Cohen

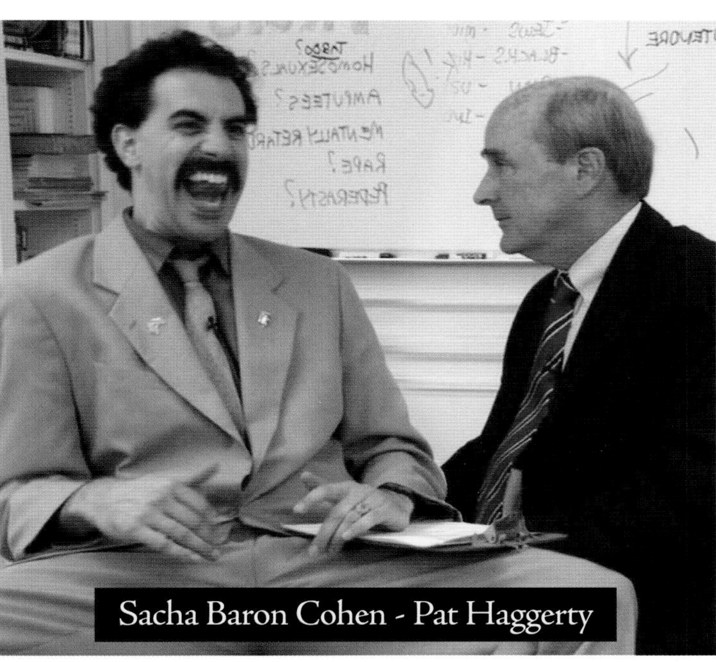
Sacha Baron Cohen - Pat Haggerty

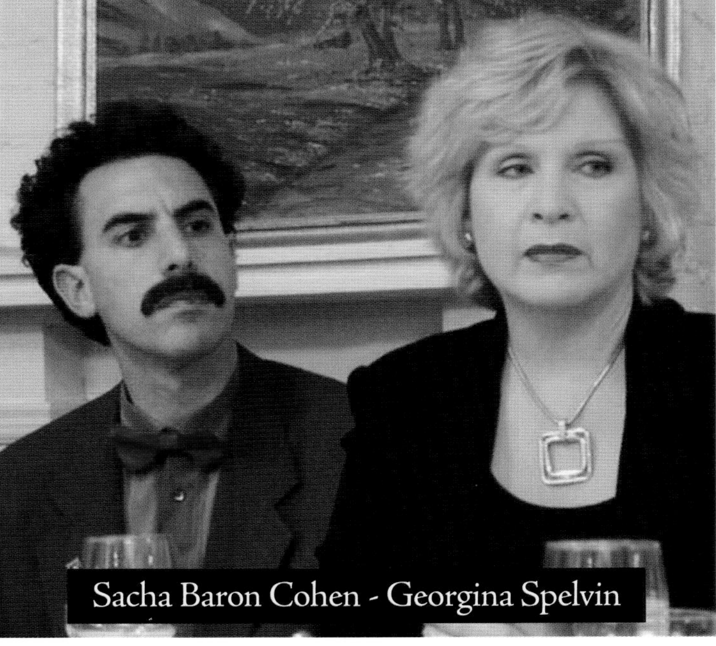
Sacha Baron Cohen - Georgina Spelvin

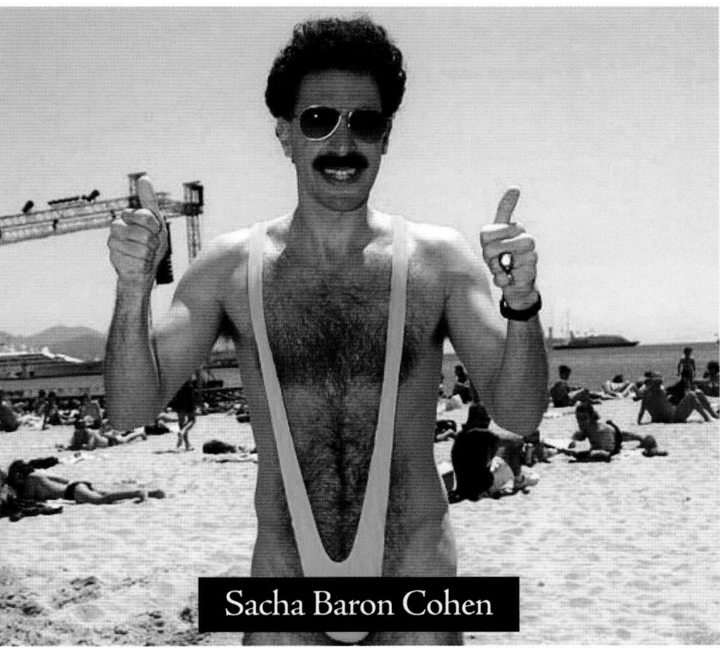
Sacha Baron Cohen

Just when you think that you've seen everything, along comes Sacha Baron Cohen, who created "Borat," a man who found new ways to make you bust your gut laughing. Borat's boorish behavior destroyed more "China shops" than could any rampaging bull.

Mr. Cohen's early incarnation, Ali G, was equally adept at creatively misbehaving and causing elegant women, young and old, to smile broadly as they try to understand his skewed conversation and non-existent table manners.

A family determined to get their young daughter into the finals of a beauty pageant takes a cross-country trip in their VW bus.

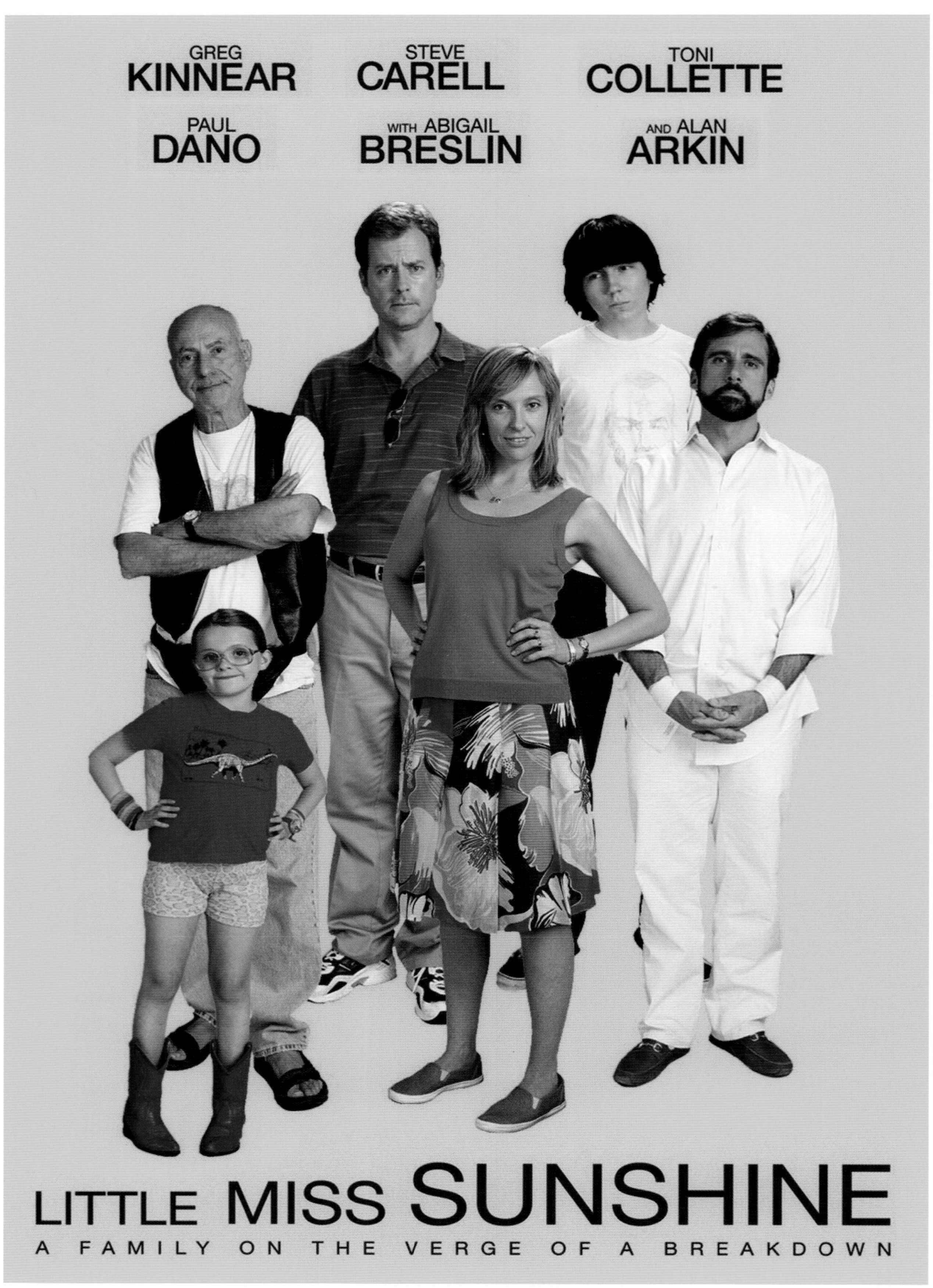

Peter Travers of Rolling Stone wrote: "...a scrappy human comedy that takes an honest path to laughs and is twice as funny and touching for it."

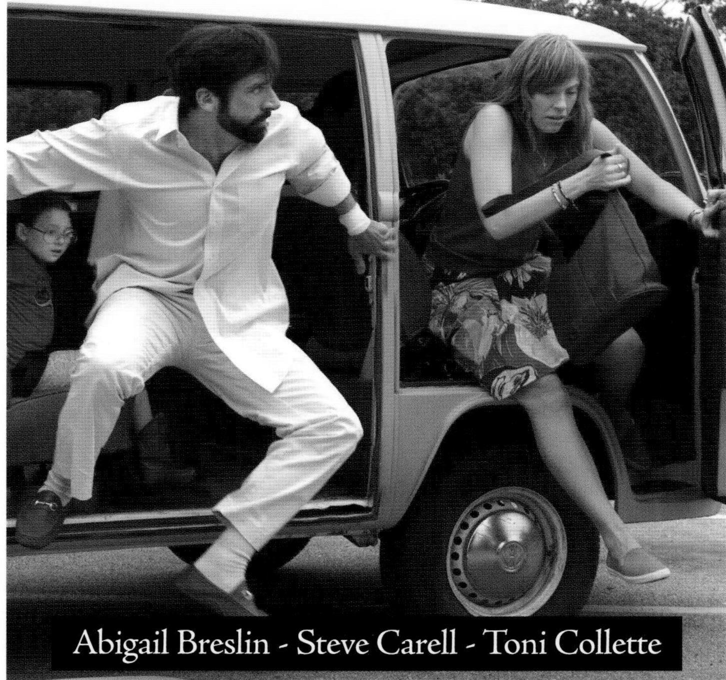
Abigail Breslin - Steve Carell - Toni Collette

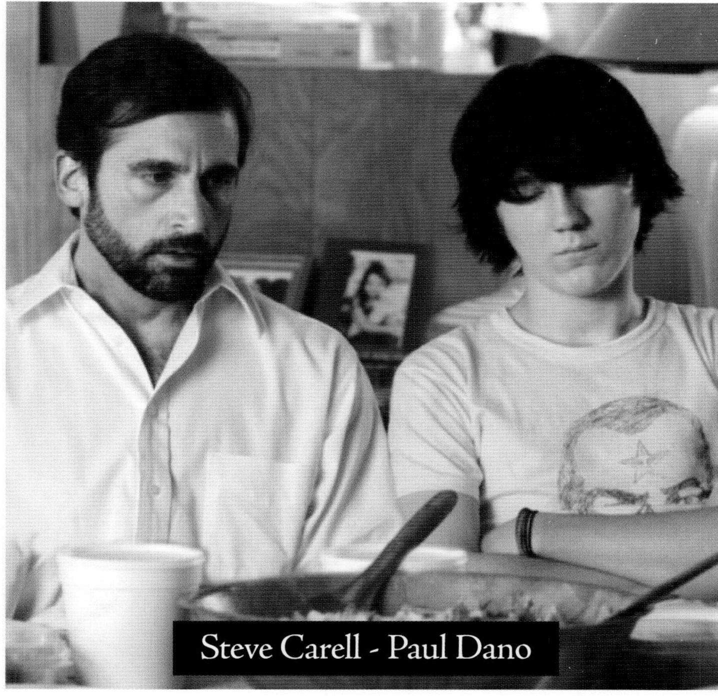
Steve Carell - Paul Dano

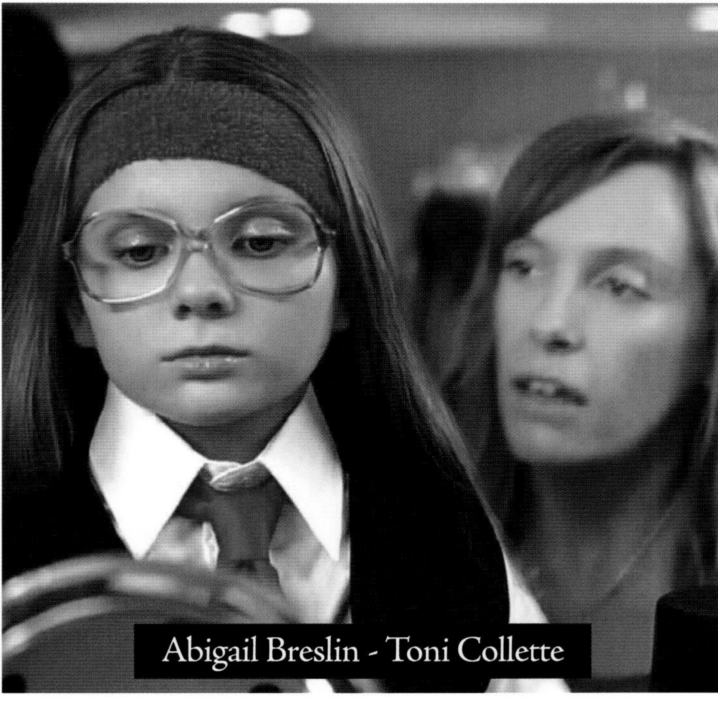
Abigail Breslin - Toni Collette

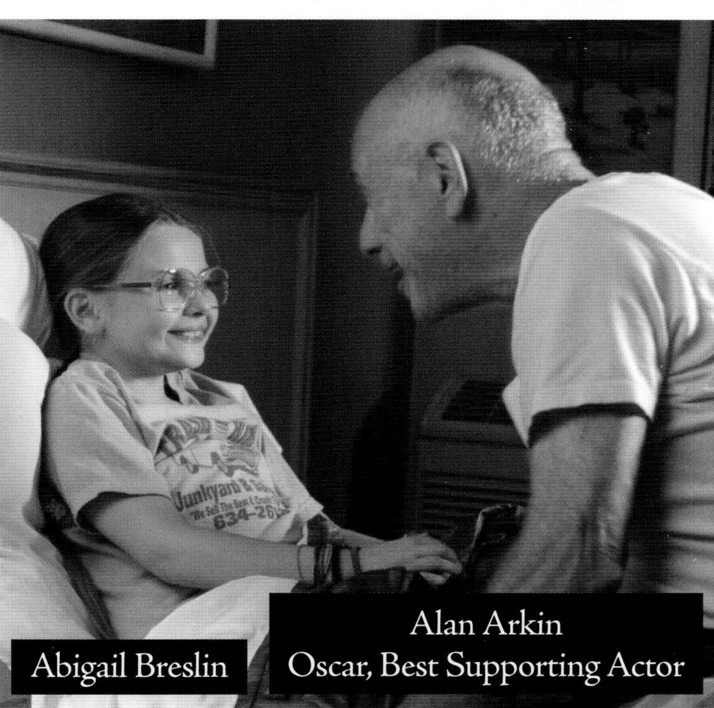
Abigail Breslin

Alan Arkin
Oscar, Best Supporting Actor

I whole-heartedly agree with Peter Travers' review of "Little Miss Sunshine." The cast was superb and I particularly enjoyed Alan Arkin's and Steve Carell's performances.

Steve Carell co-created "Angie Tribeca," one of my favorite TV shows, which stars the irresistible Rashida Jones as Angie.

Alan Arkin, who plays the grandfather in this opus, was a young man when he won a Tony Award for portraying me in the Broadway stage production of my novel, "Enter Laughing."

Two terminally ill men escape from a cancer ward and head off on a road trip with a wish list of to-dos before they die.

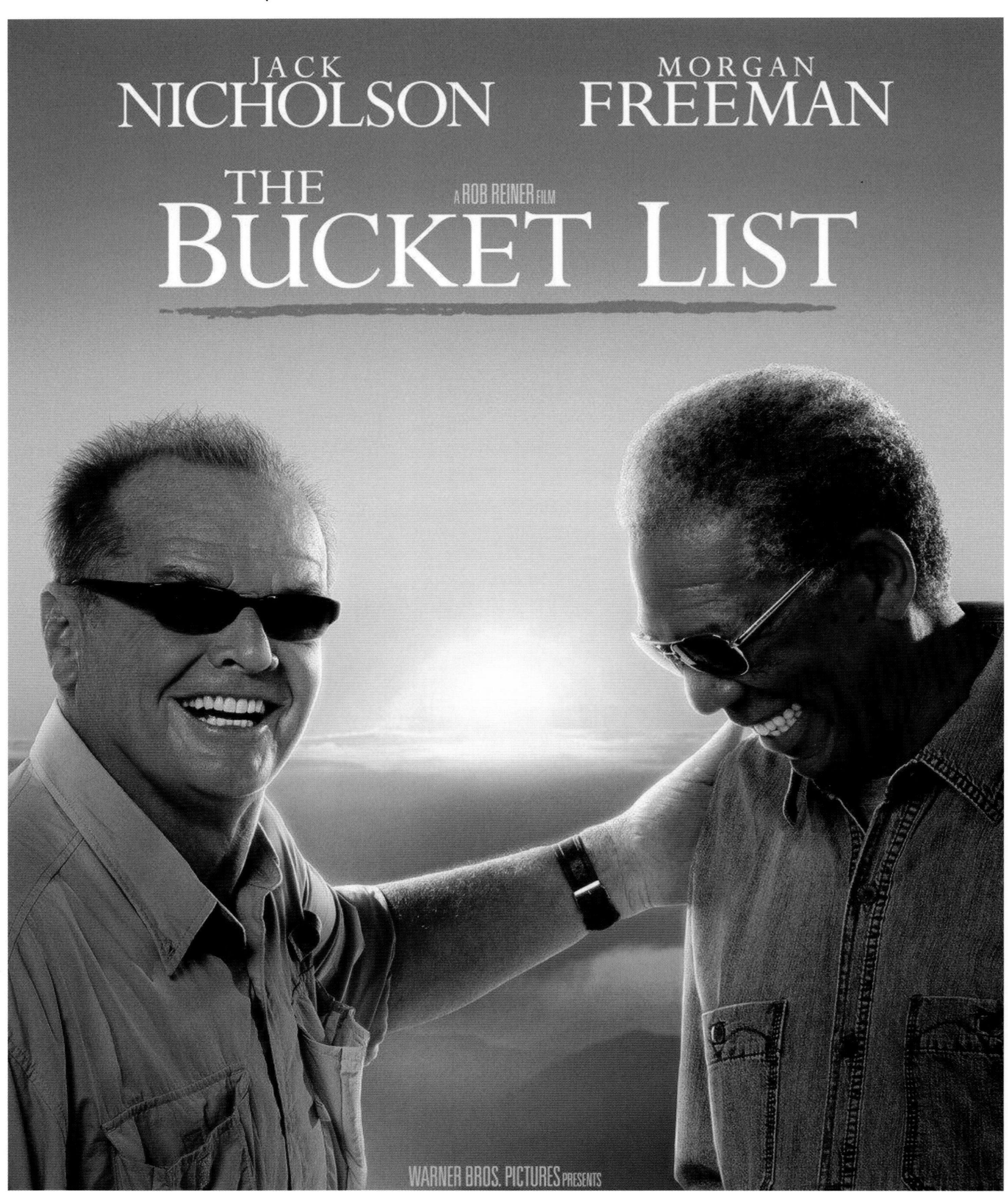

Noel Murray of AV Club wrote: "There are certainly worse ways to spend the holiday season than in the company of two charming old actors, being reminded that human companionship makes life worth living, even as it makes dying a little tougher."

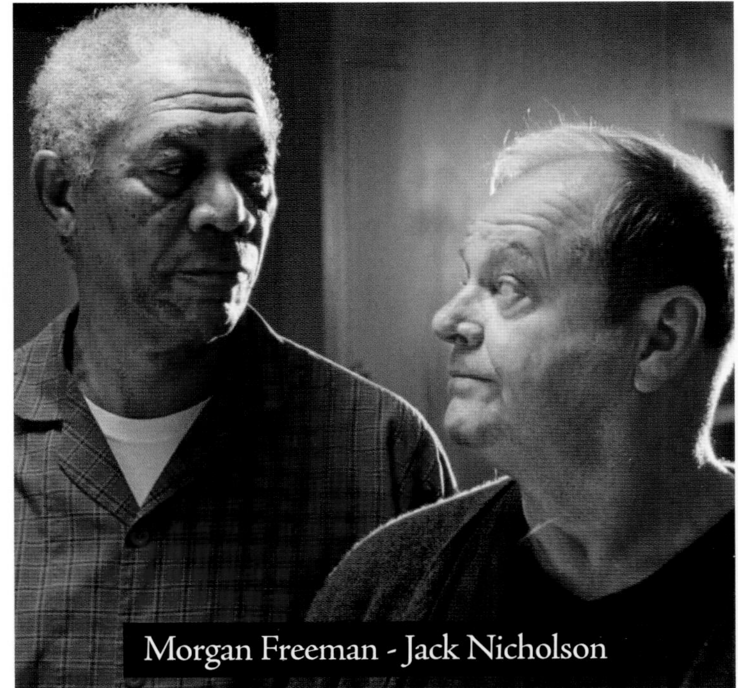

Morgan Freeman - Jack Nicholson

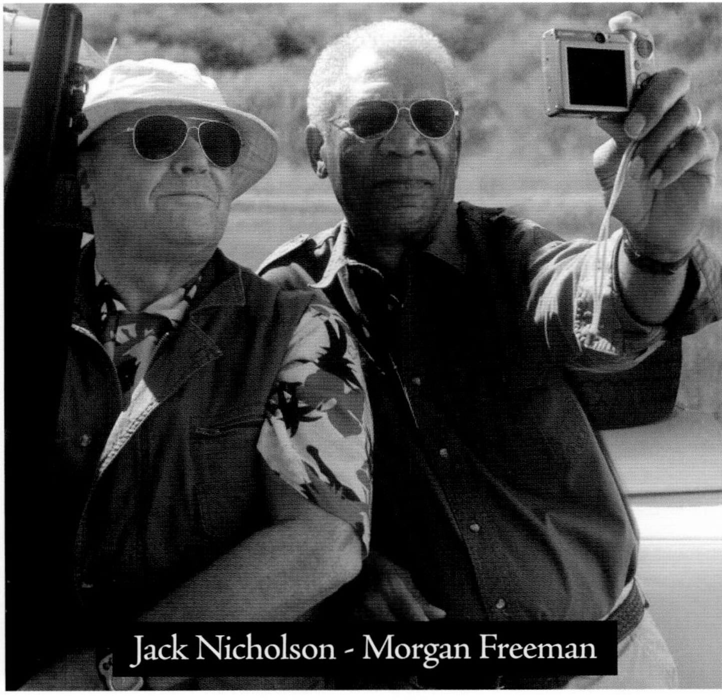

Jack Nicholson - Morgan Freeman

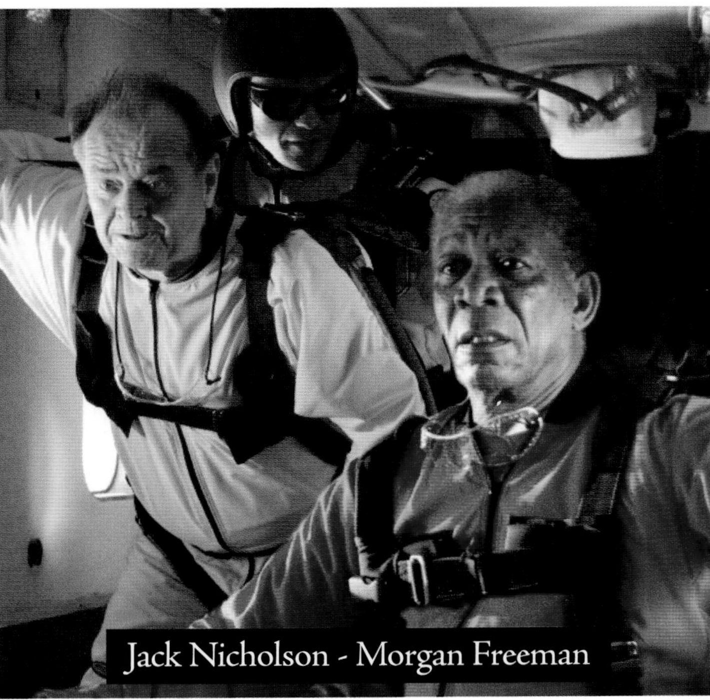

Jack Nicholson - Morgan Freeman

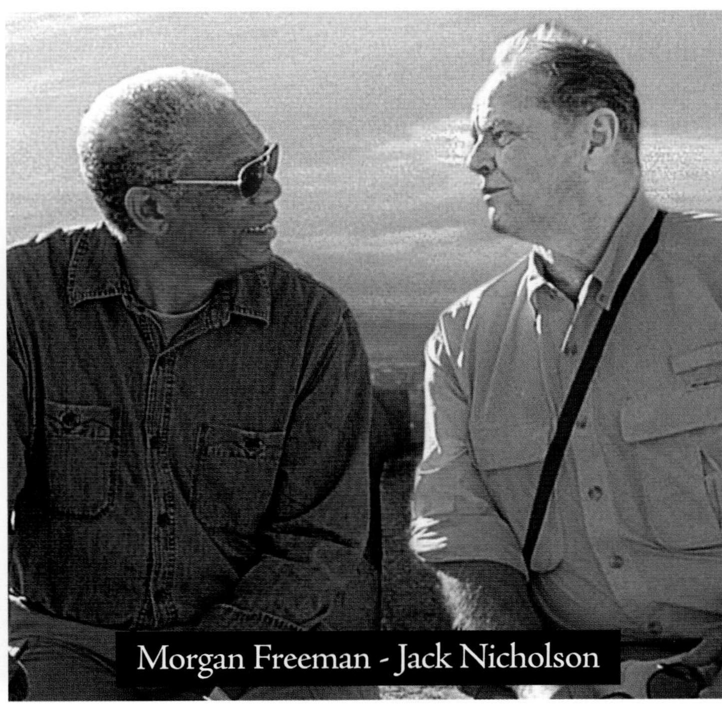

Morgan Freeman - Jack Nicholson

This is the second film that my son, Rob, produced that starred Morgan Freeman and Jack Nicholson. Morgan Freeman in "The Shawshank Redemption" and Jack Nicholson in "A Few Good Men."

As far as my personal 'bucket list,' I'm happy to say that, at ninety-five and eight months, I've lived a full life and if I were to kick the bucket tomorrow, nothing would fall out.

A retired CIA agent travels across Europe and relies on his old skills to save his estranged daughter, who has been kidnapped while on a trip to Paris.

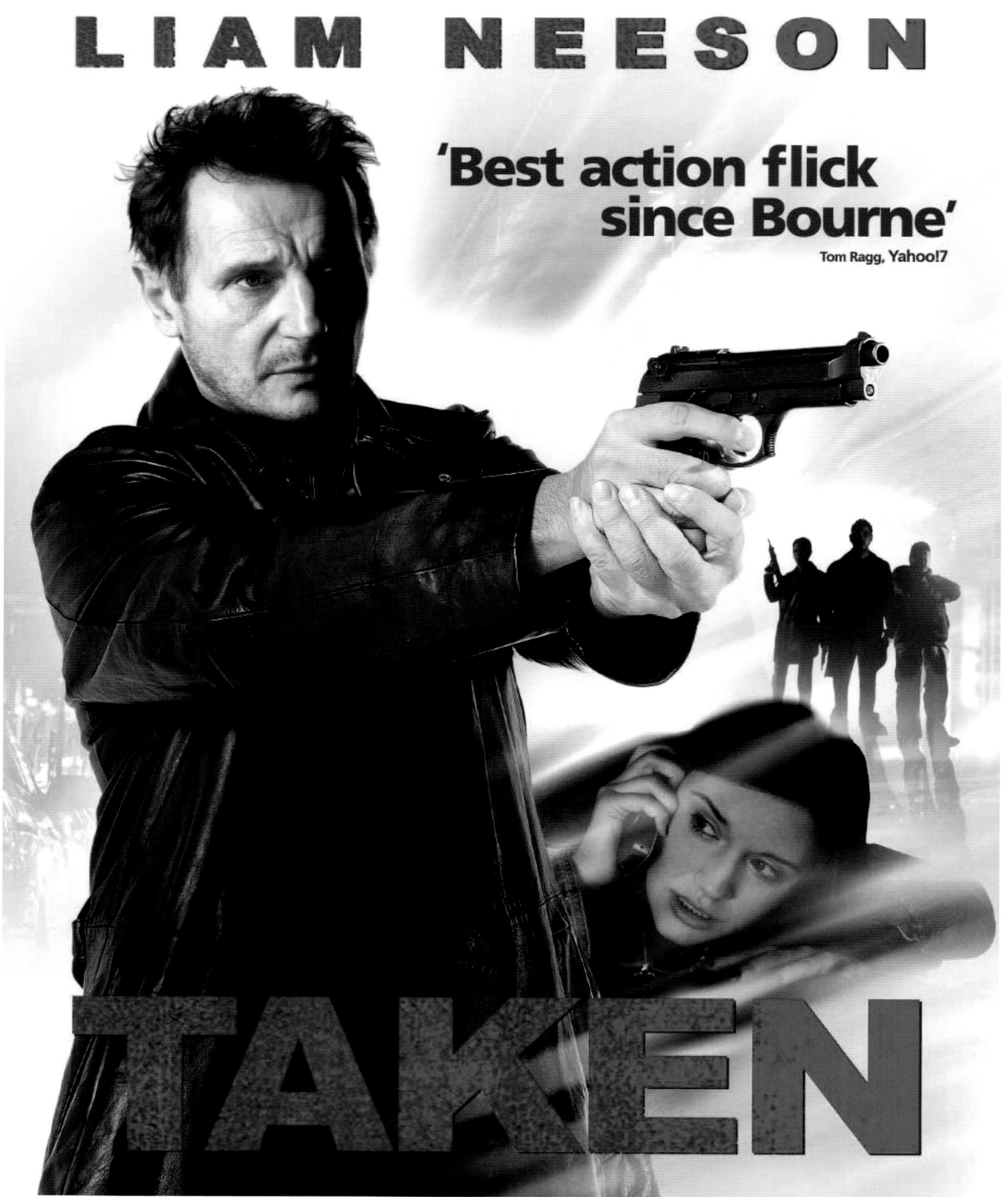

Dave White of Movies.com wrote: "It's so awesome to see Liam Neeson taking out the trash in pursuit of his prized child."

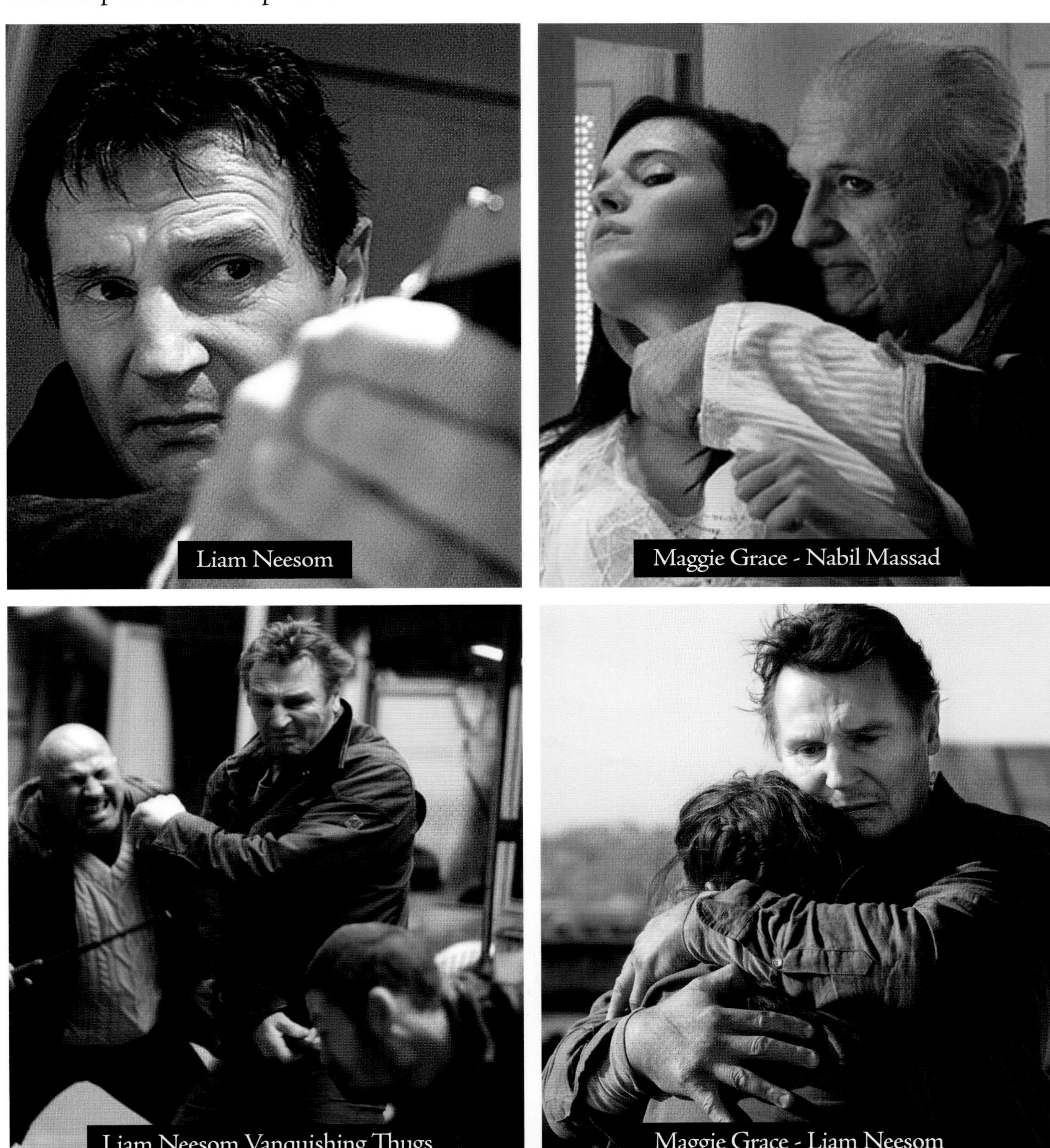

Liam Neesom

Maggie Grace - Nabil Massad

Liam Neesom Vanquishing Thugs

Maggie Grace - Liam Neesom

The first of three heart-pounding and ultimately soul-satisfying 'comeuppance' movies to which my buddy Mel Brooks and I are addicted. Keep 'em comin' and we'll keep 'a watchin'.

A bride-to-be searches for her real father through the hit songs by the '70s group ABBA.

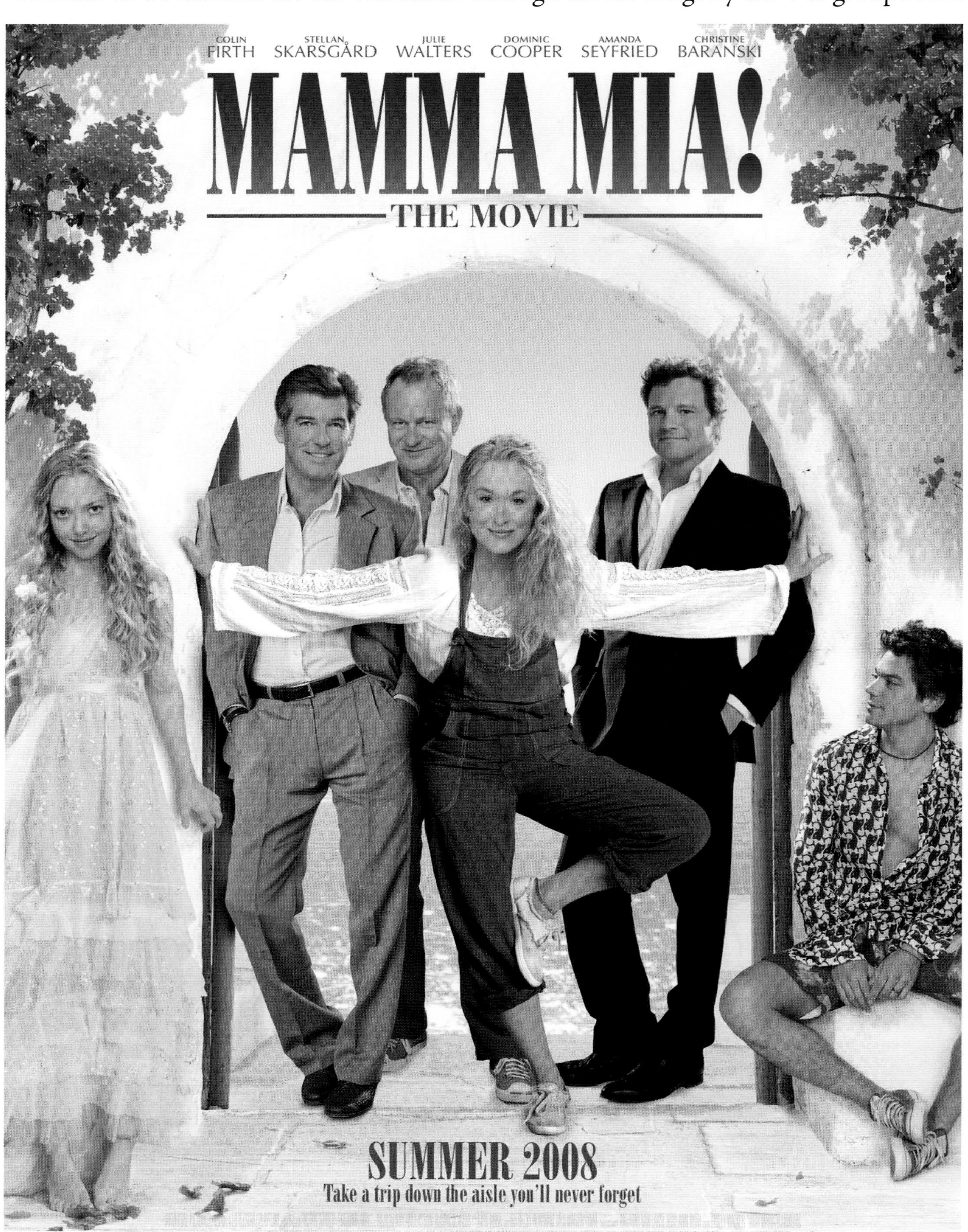

Michael Dequina of The Movie Report wrote: "It would be easy to underrate the deceptively effortless master acting class that Meryl Streep puts on here."

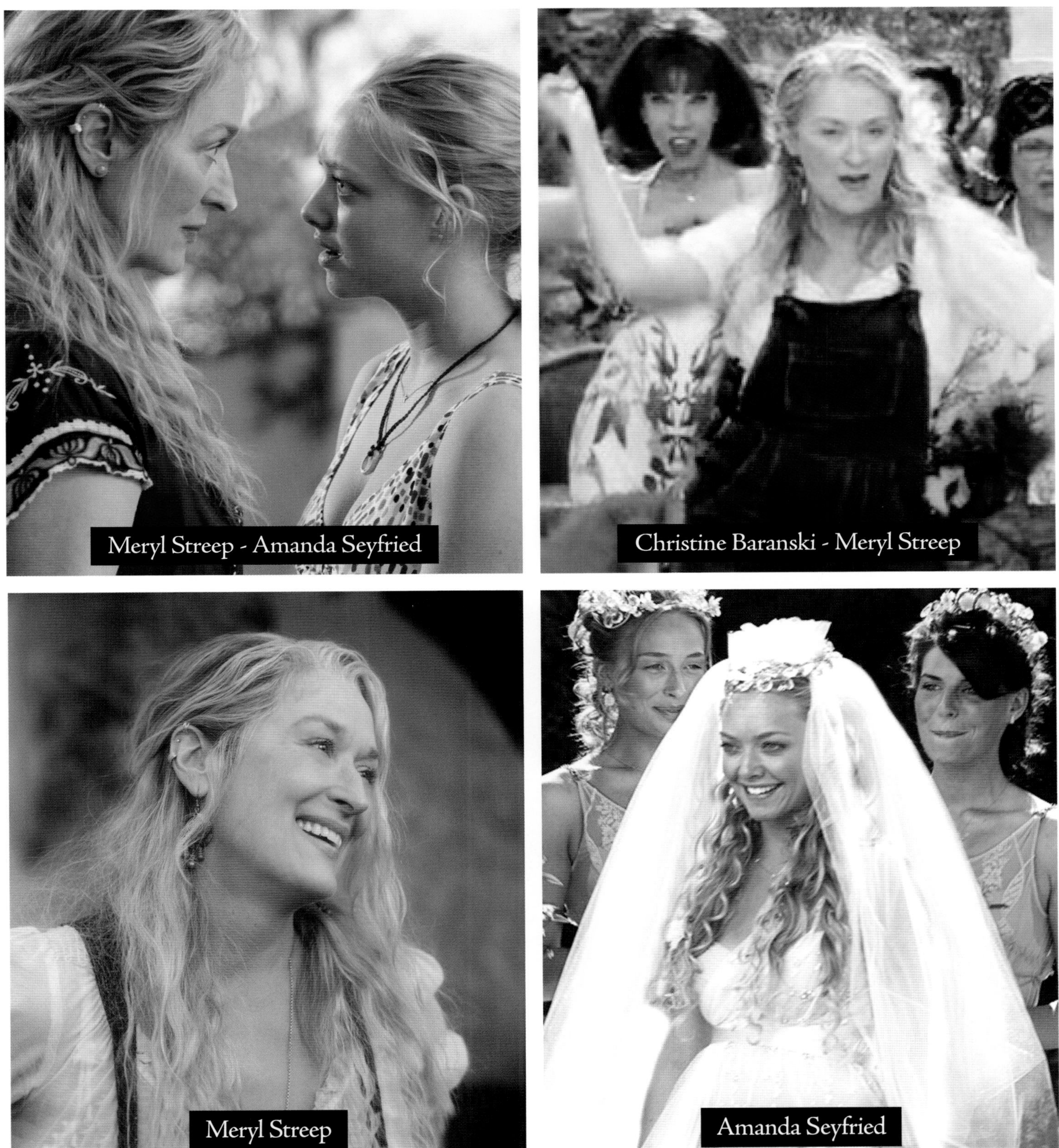

Meryl Streep - Amanda Seyfried

Christine Baranski - Meryl Streep

Meryl Streep

Amanda Seyfried

I've said it many times before and I will keep on saying it, "In my book, (and this is my book) Meryll Streep is, hands down, the finest and one of the most beautiful actresses ever."

A Mumbai teen reflects on his upbringing in the slums when he is accused of cheating on the Indian Version of "Who Wants to be a Millionaire?"

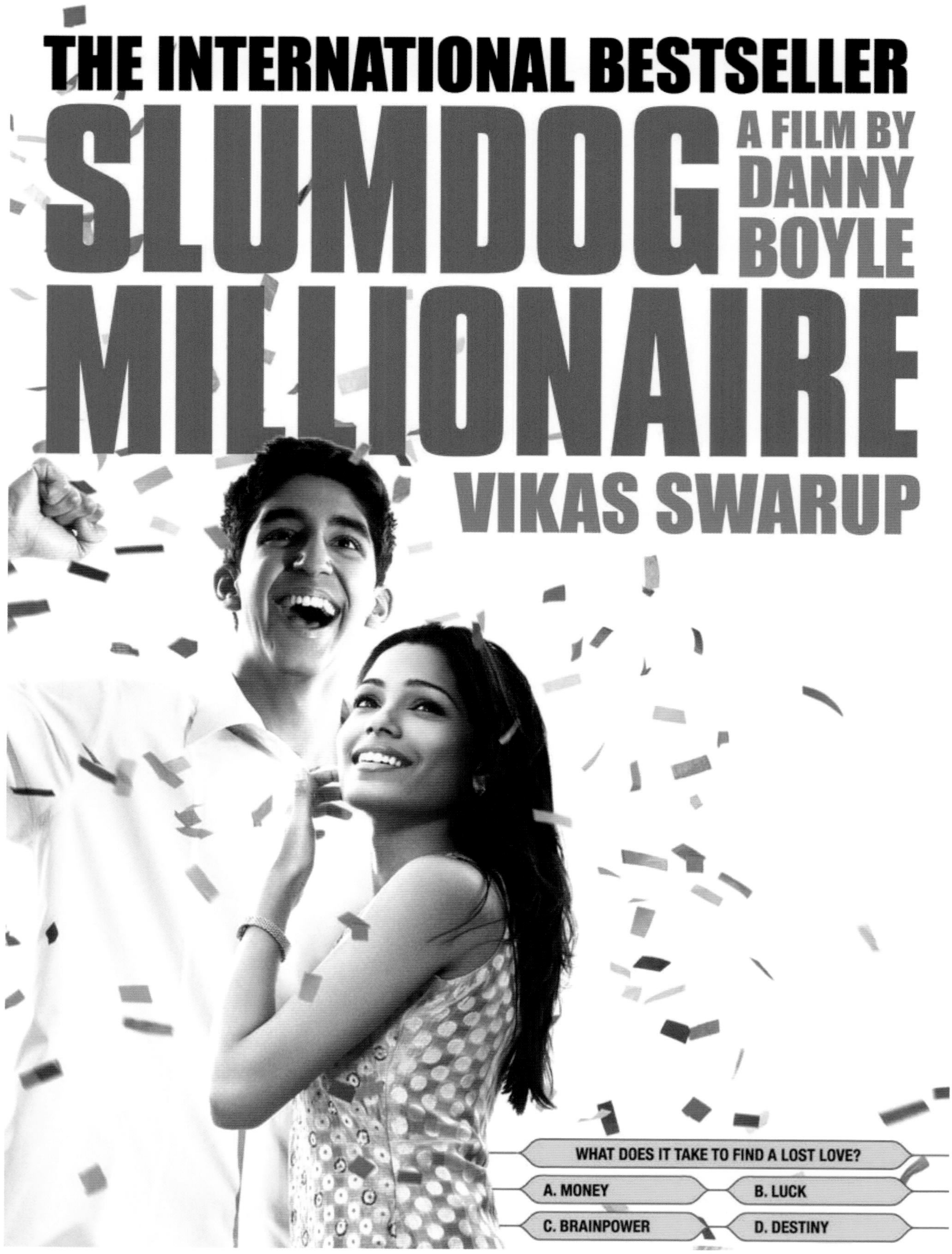

Richard Roeper wrote: "The best movie of 2008."

Jim Vejvoda of IGN Movies wrote: "Heavy with humor, romance and suspense, 'Slumdog Millionaire' is one of the best and most crowd-pleasing films of the year."

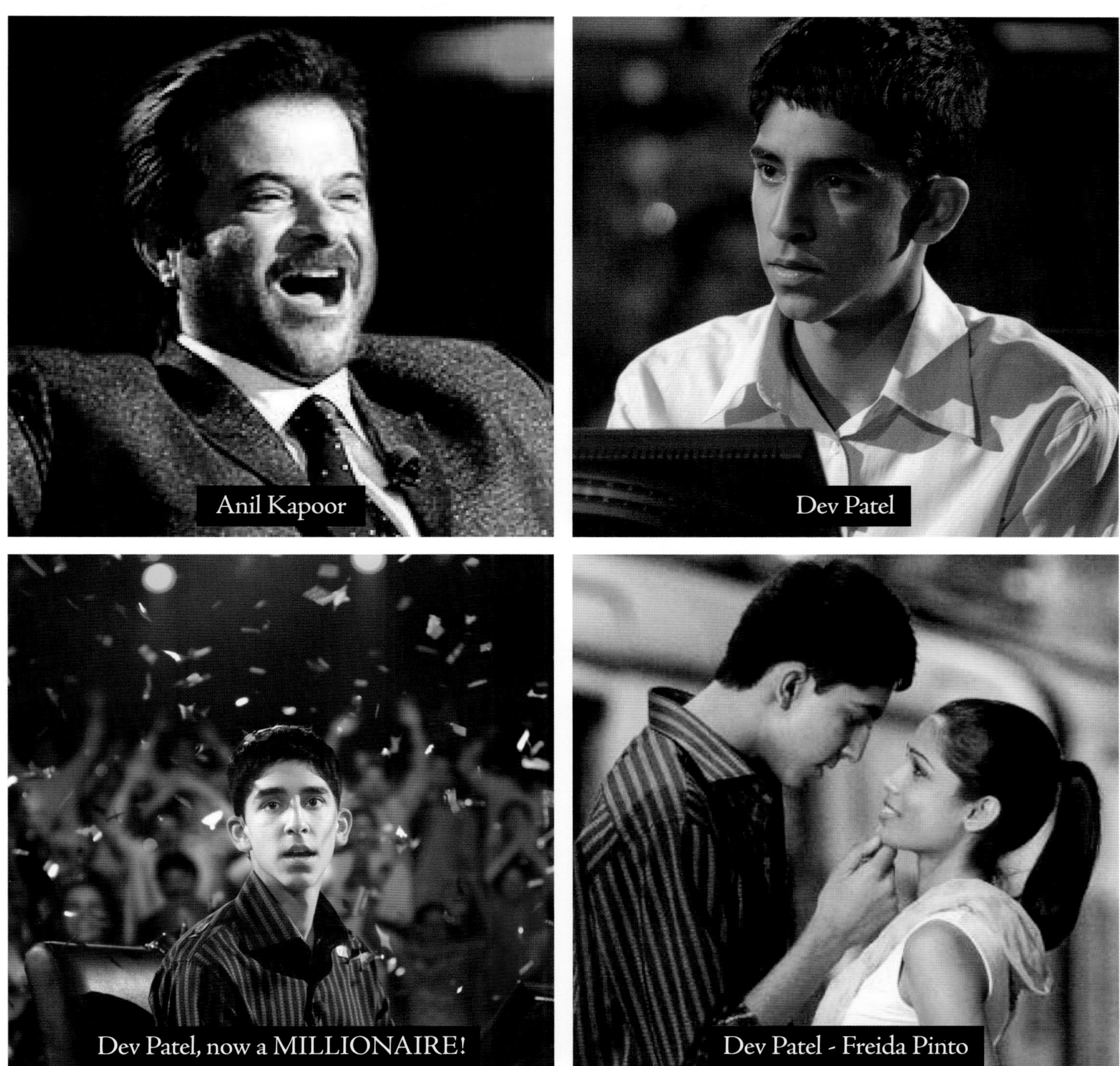

Anil Kapoor

Dev Patel

Dev Patel, now a MILLIONAIRE!

Dev Patel - Freida Pinto

Whoever likes a feel-good movie and wants to see one of the feel-goodest movies of all-time, rent, buy or steal a copy of "Slumdog Millionaire."

I am a devotee of TV's "Who Wants to Be a Millionaire," and every morning, at ten o'clock, I click on ABC and hope to see someone win a million bucks. So far, I've only seen a contestant walk away with $200,000. If before we go to press, someone wins more I will change this number.

A pushy boss forces her young assistant to marry her in order to keep her visa status in the U.S. and avoid deportation to Canada.

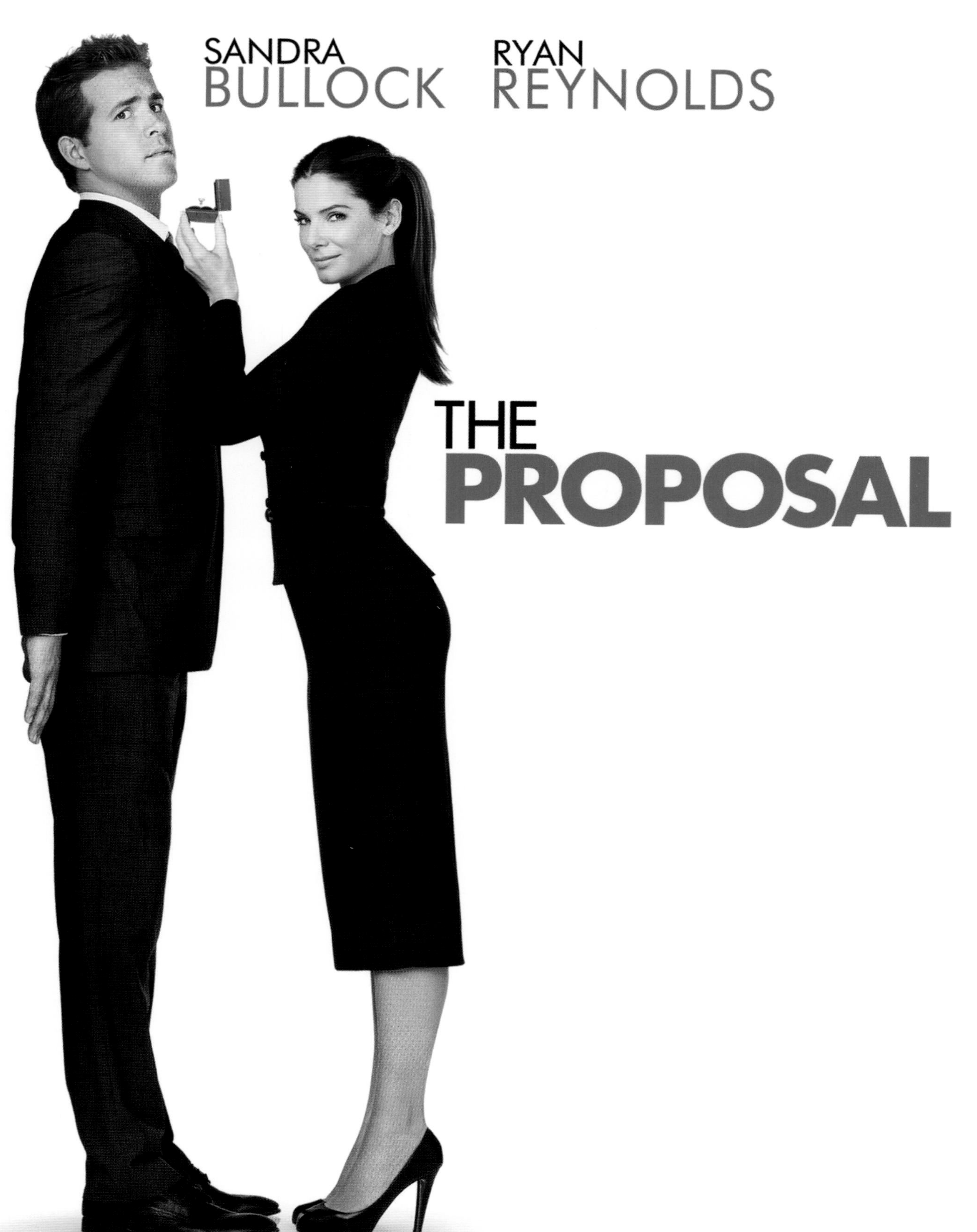

Amy Nicholson of I.E. Weekly wrote: "Thanks to casting and chemistry, this is the first great romantic comedy of the summer."

Perri Nemiroff of CinemaBlend.com: "Simple and clichéd, yet refreshing. As long as you're hell-bent on seeing a romantic comedy, 'The Proposal' will deliver."

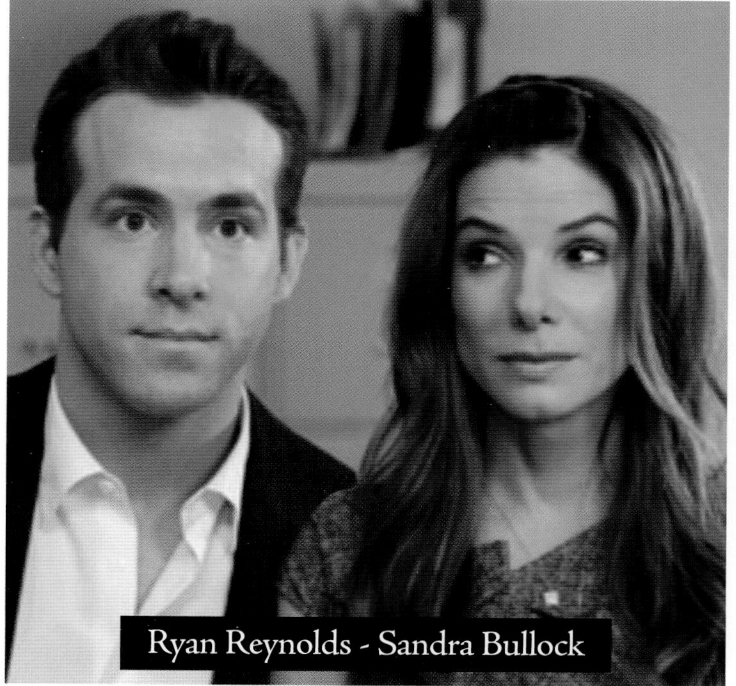
Ryan Reynolds - Sandra Bullock

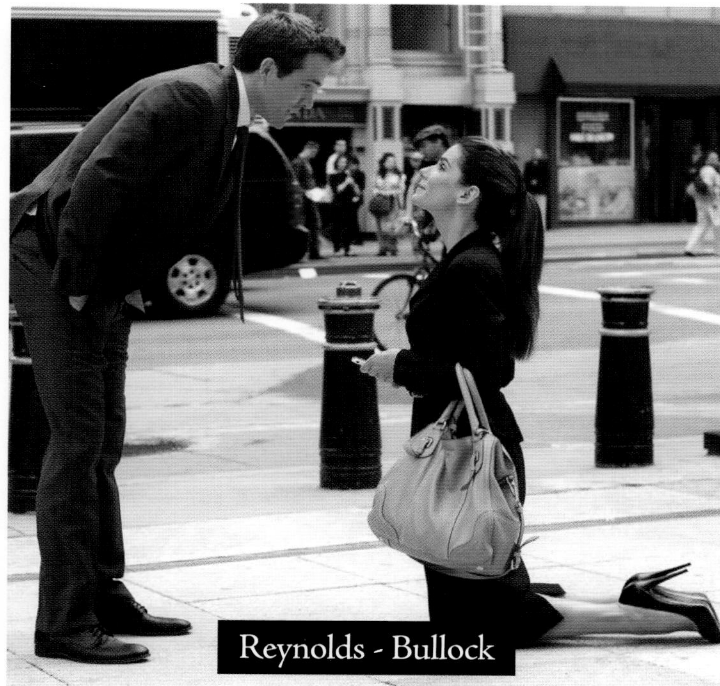
Reynolds - Bullock

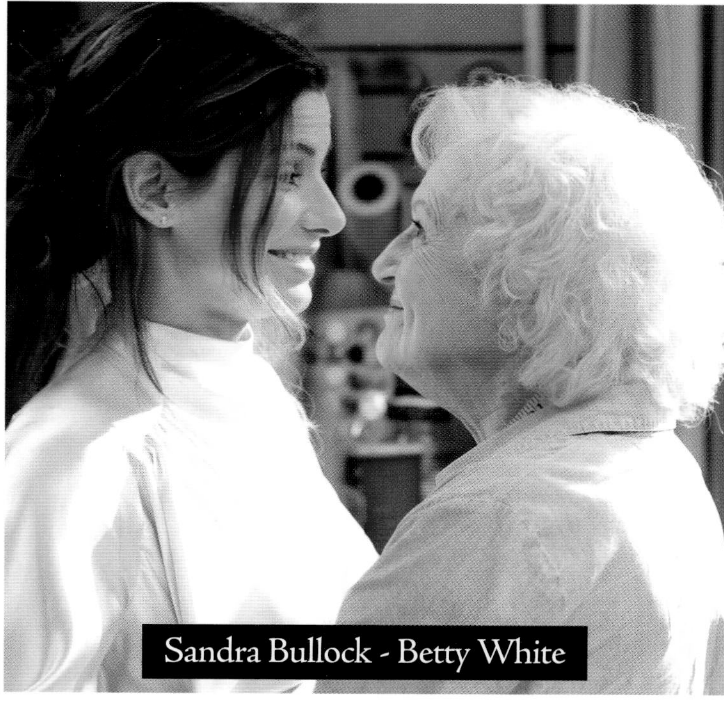
Sandra Bullock - Betty White

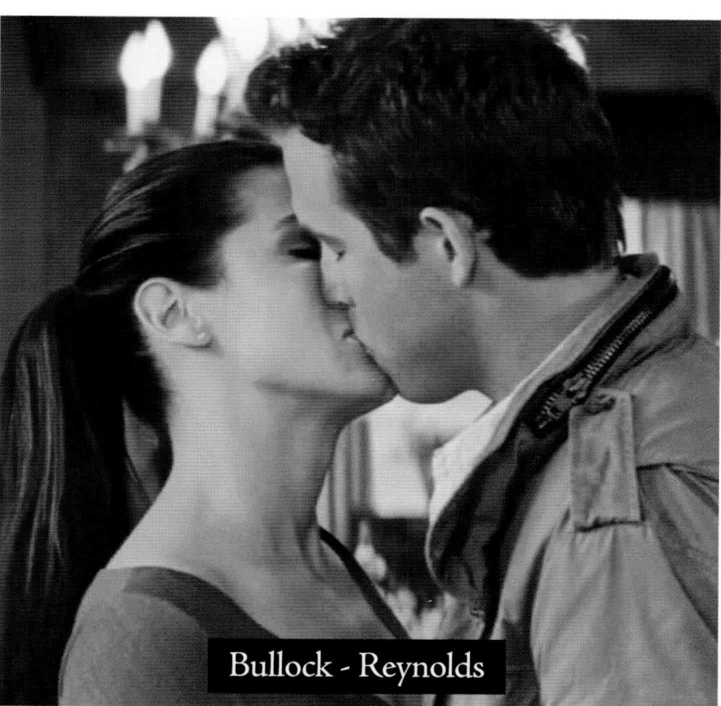
Bullock - Reynolds

One or two critics gave it a thumbs down, but I disagree with those naysayers and agree with the above 'yaysayers.' Joining me in 'yaysaying' was the world-wide public, who bought 317,000,000 dollars worth of tickets, which made it 2009's highest grossing romantic comedy.

Sandra Bullock's multi-layered performance made this film extra-special for me.

In Nazi-occupied France during World War II, a plan to assassinate Nazi leaders by a group of Jewish U.S. soldiers coincides with a theatre owner's vengeful plans for the same.

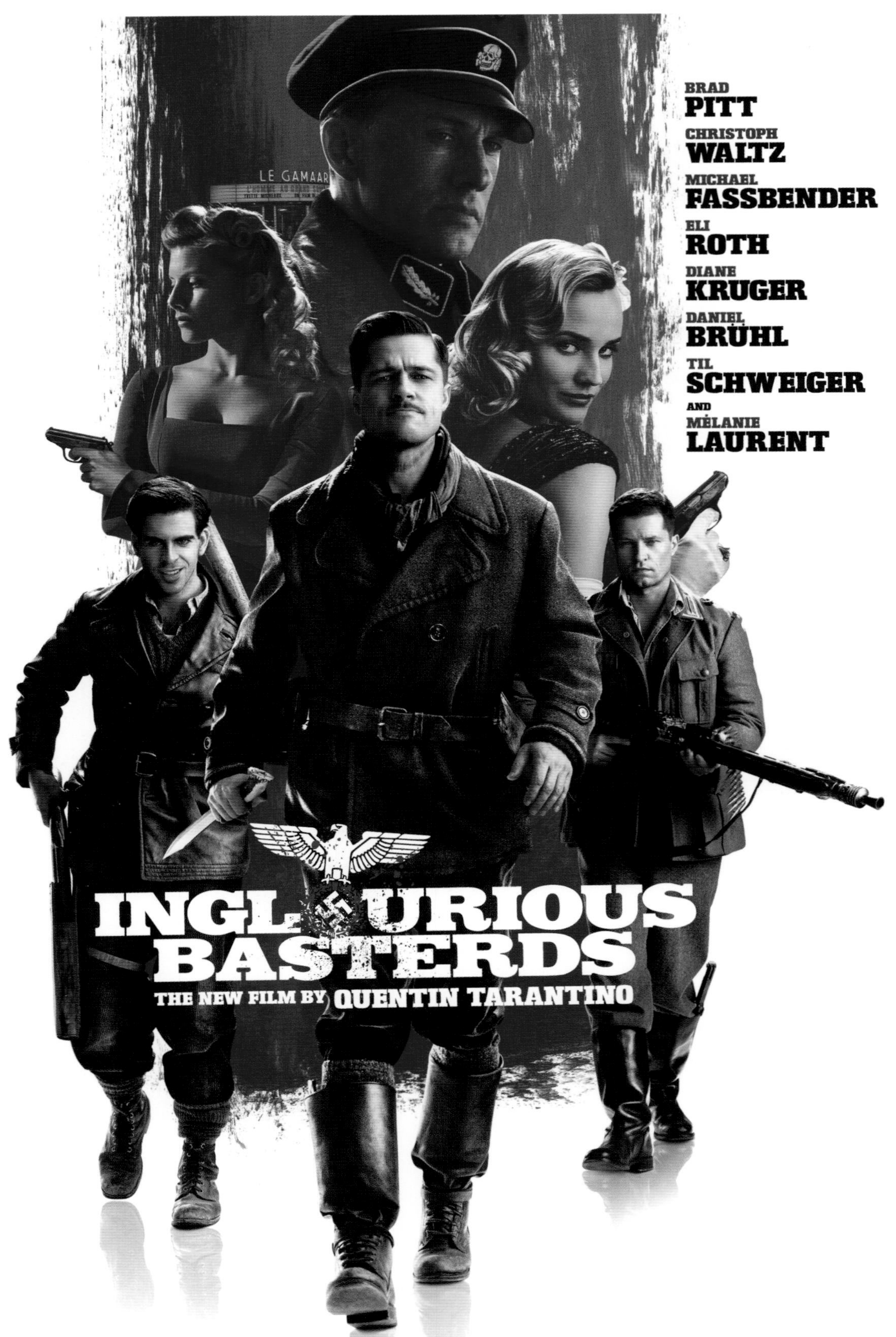

AN INGLORIOUS, UPROARIOUS THRILL-RIDE OF VENGEANCE

Tom Charity of CNN.com wrote: "Christopher Waltz will be unknown to most American audiences, but he's nothing less than sensational as the silky, polyglot SS officer charged by the Fuhrer to root out the remaining Jews in France."

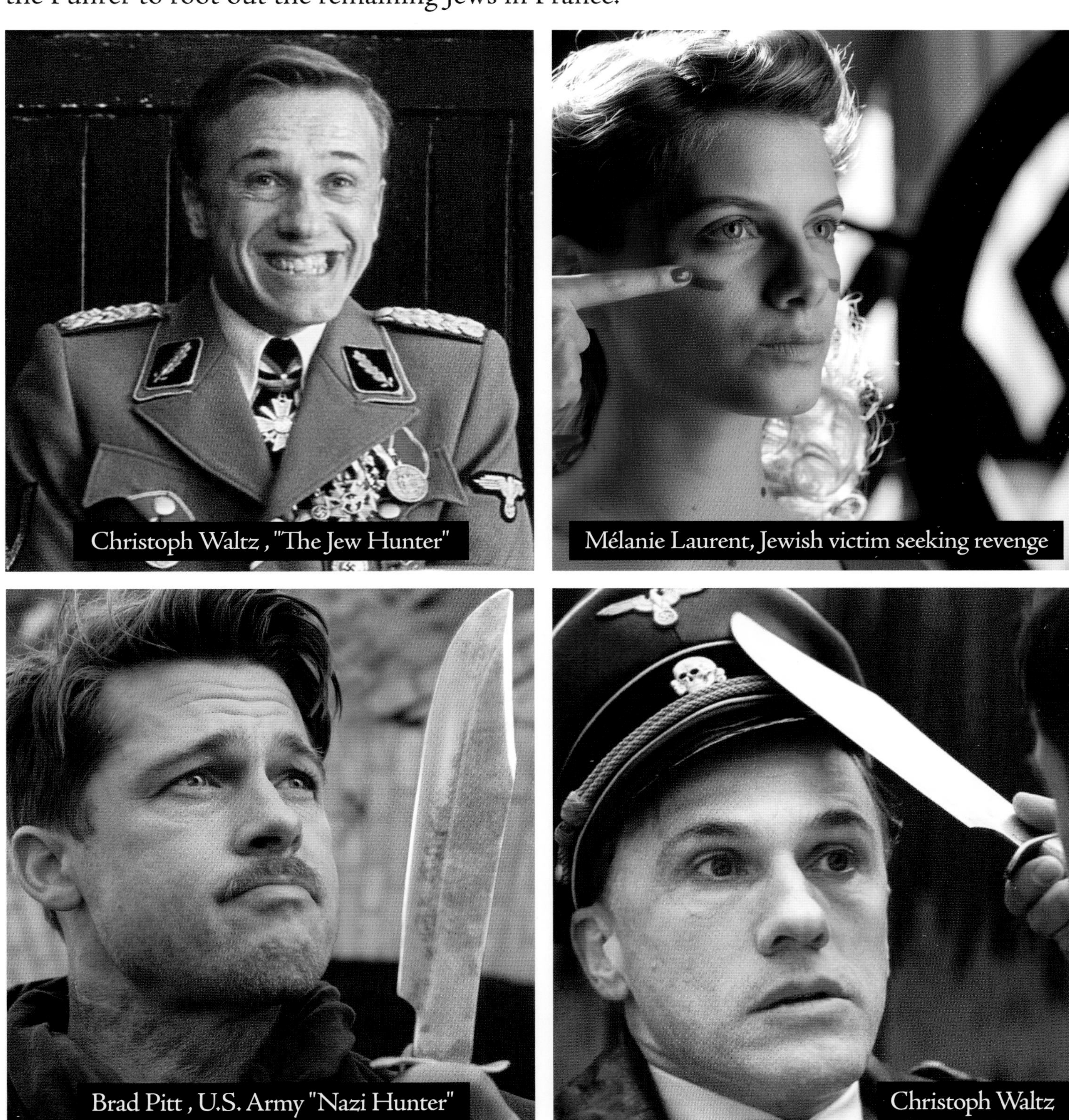

Christoph Waltz, "The Jew Hunter"

Mélanie Laurent, Jewish victim seeking revenge

Brad Pitt, U.S. Army "Nazi Hunter"

Christoph Waltz

Extremely gruesome but also extremely soul-satisfying is the film's ending where Brad Pitt, to insure that the world would never forget a cold-blooded Nazi, who shot and killed Jewish parents and their children, deftly carves a swastika into that Nazi's forehead.

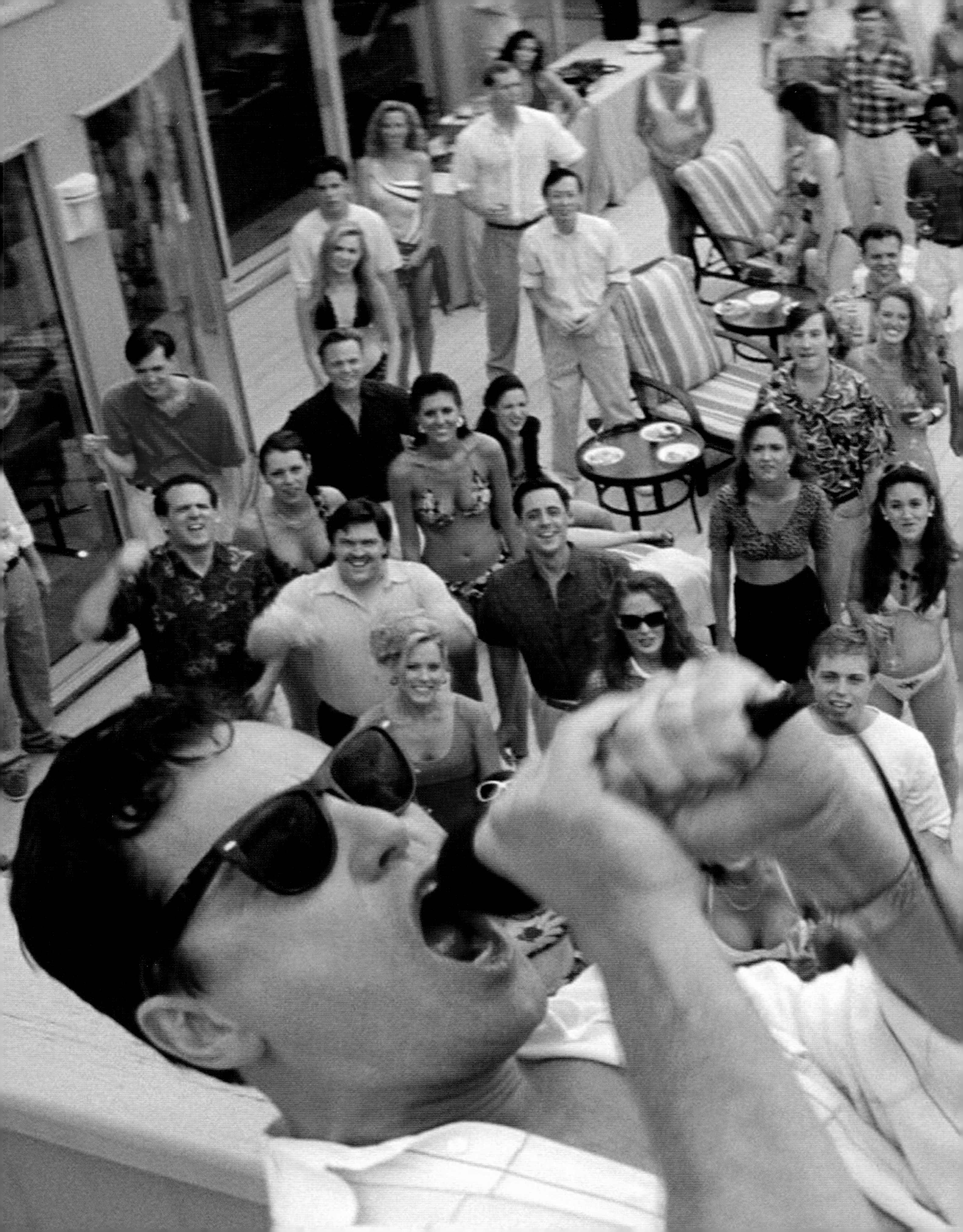

the 2010s

The story of King George VI of the United Kingdom of Great Britain and Northern Ireland, his impromptu ascension to the throne and the speech therapist who helped the unsure monarch become worthy of it.

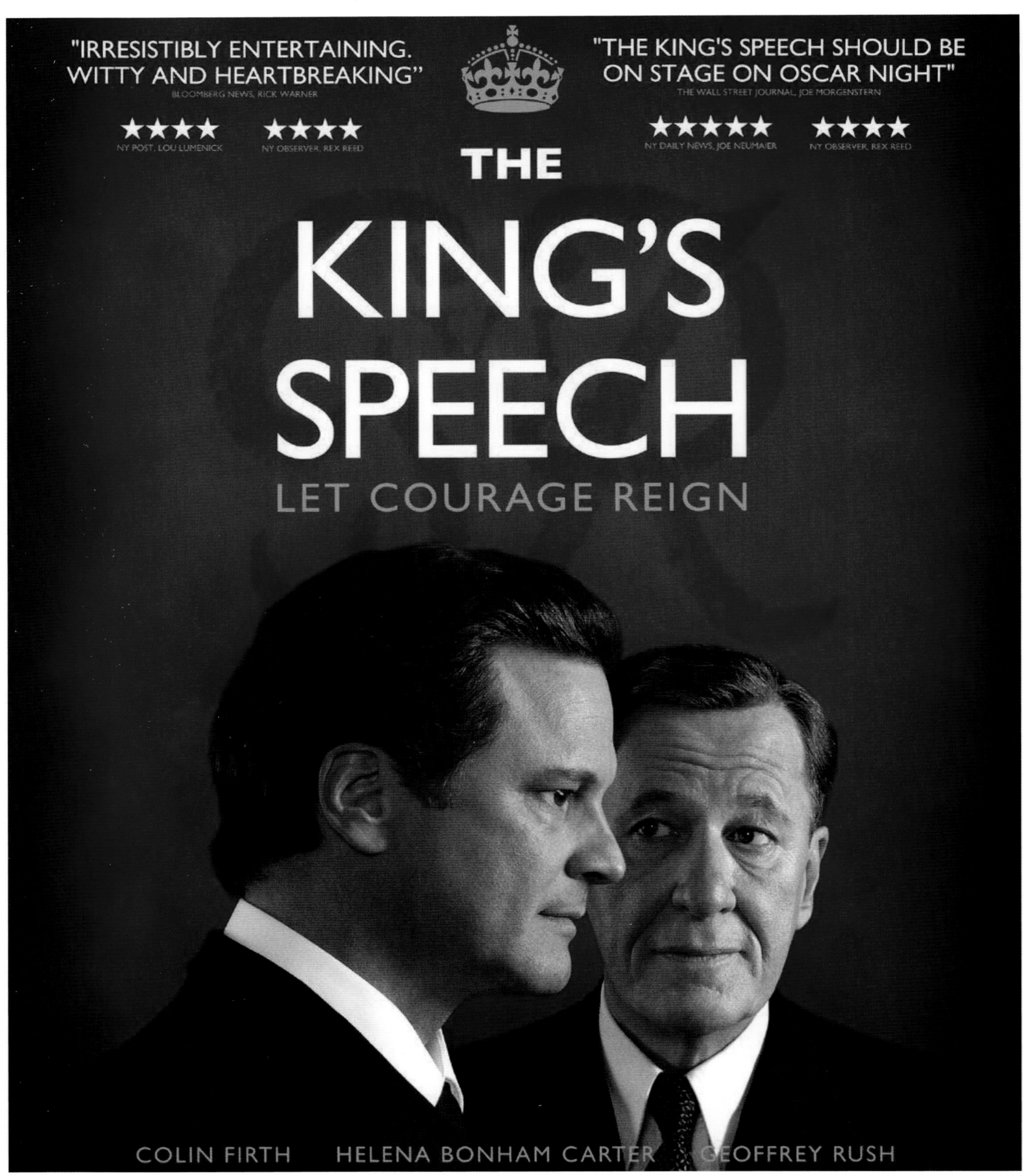

Tom Long of Detroit News wrote: "Classic, rousing entertainment loaded with both humor and poignancy."

Alan Frank of Daily Star wrote: "Watching Firth agonizingly stammer his way through the closing speech at the Empire Exhibition at Wembley Stadium in 1925 is a masterclass in acting."

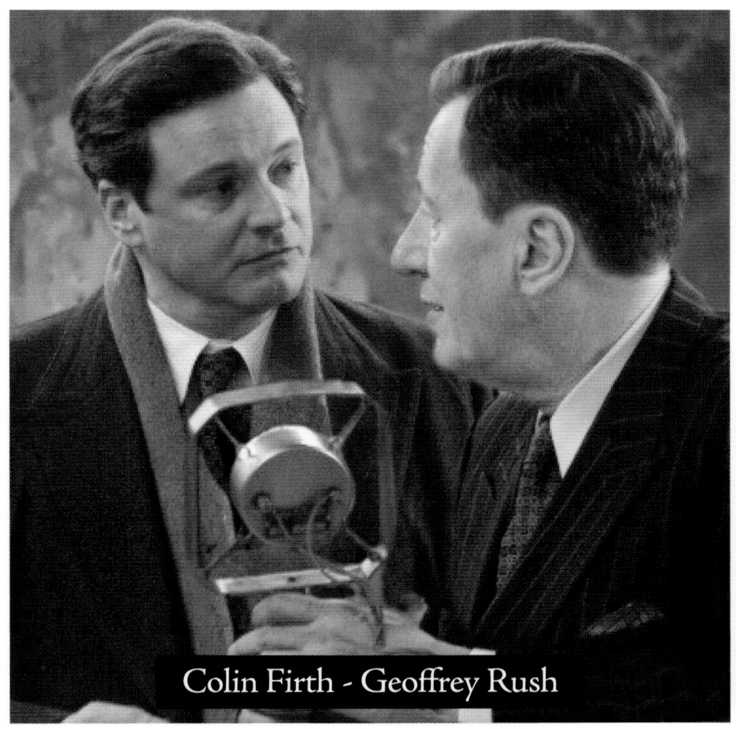
Colin Firth - Geoffrey Rush

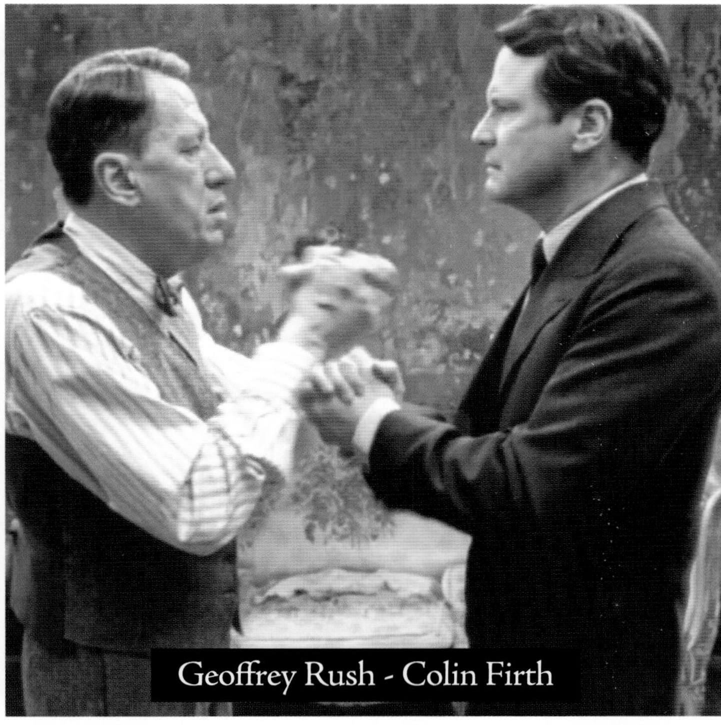
Geoffrey Rush - Colin Firth

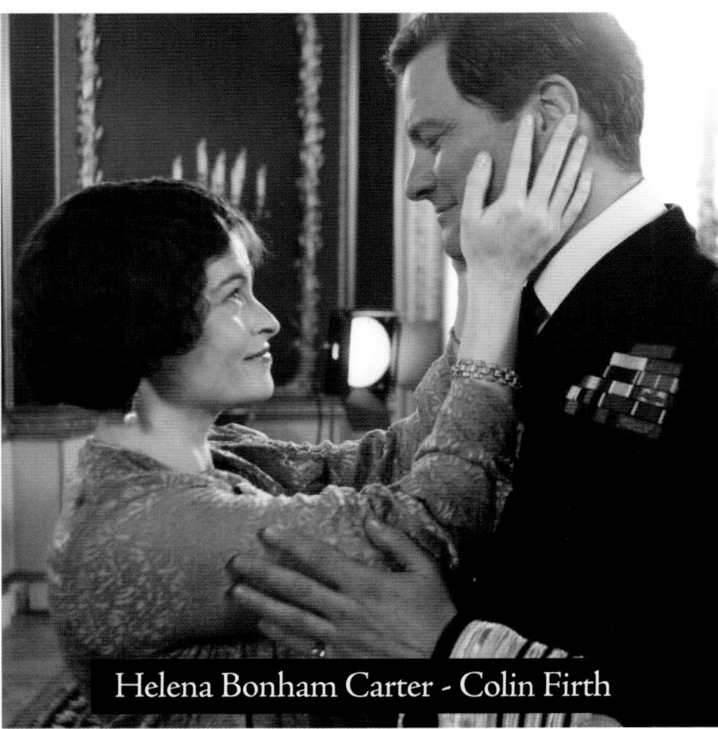
Helena Bonham Carter - Colin Firth

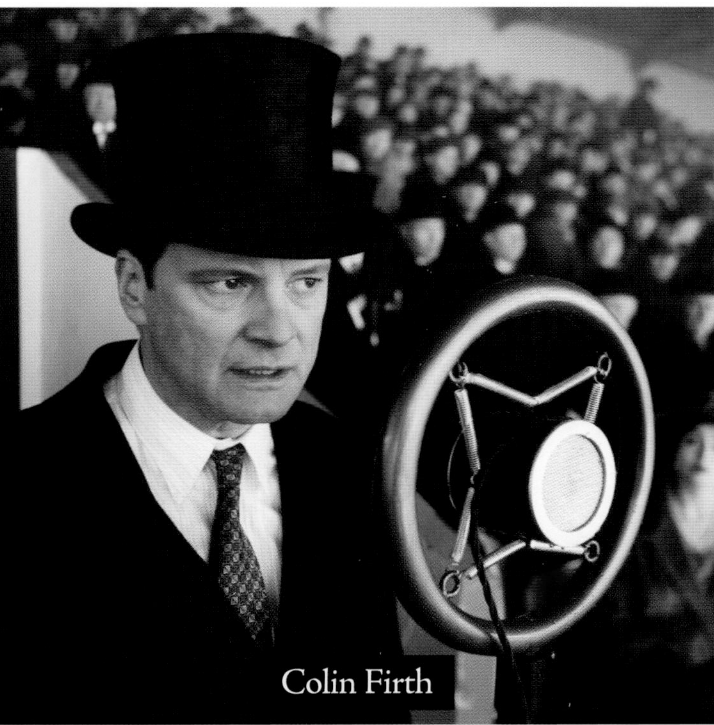
Colin Firth

Watching a speech impaired man struggling to say a few coherent words would not seem very exciting, but I was more than excited when Geoffrey Rush succeeded in helping the King, Colin Firth, make his first war-time radio broadcast.

While on a trip to Paris with his fiancée's family, a nostalgic screenwriter finds himself mysteriously going back to the 1920s every day at midnight.

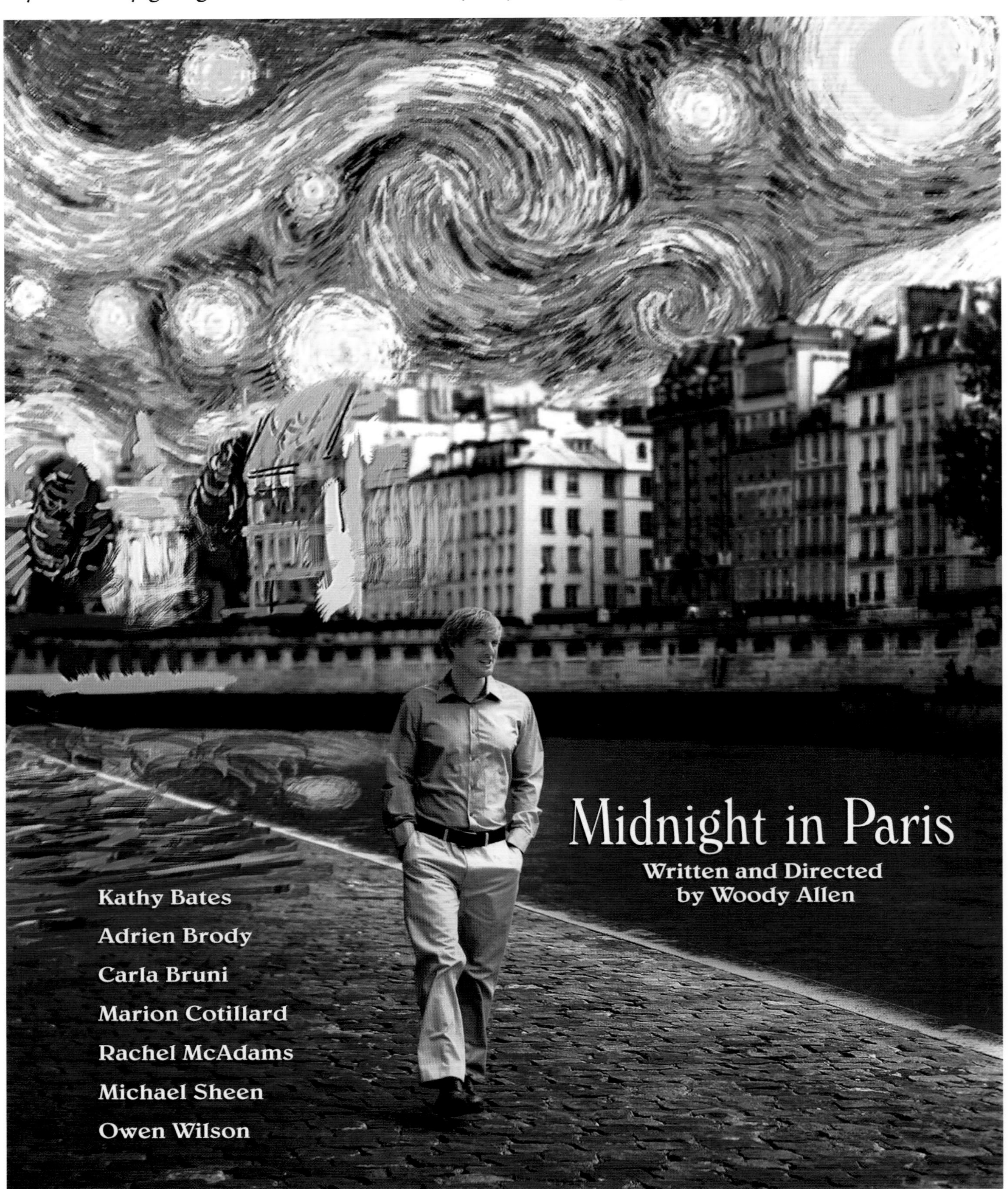

Sean Axmaker of Seanax.com wrote: "...Allen brings his fantasy to life with such affection and joy that he transports us into his dream come true as a shared fantasy."

Lisa Kennedy of Denver Post wrote: "'Midnight in Paris' is charming and clever, at times wickedly astute and hopeful."

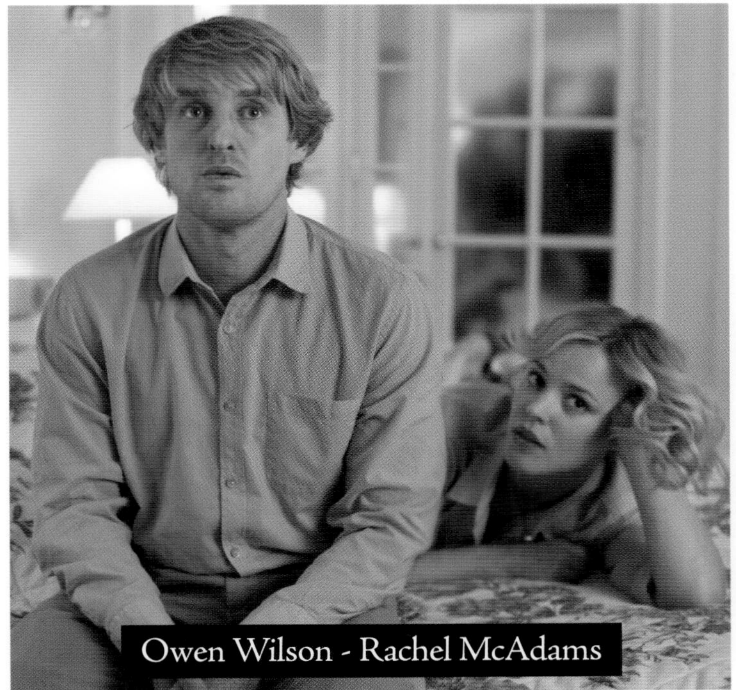
Owen Wilson - Rachel McAdams

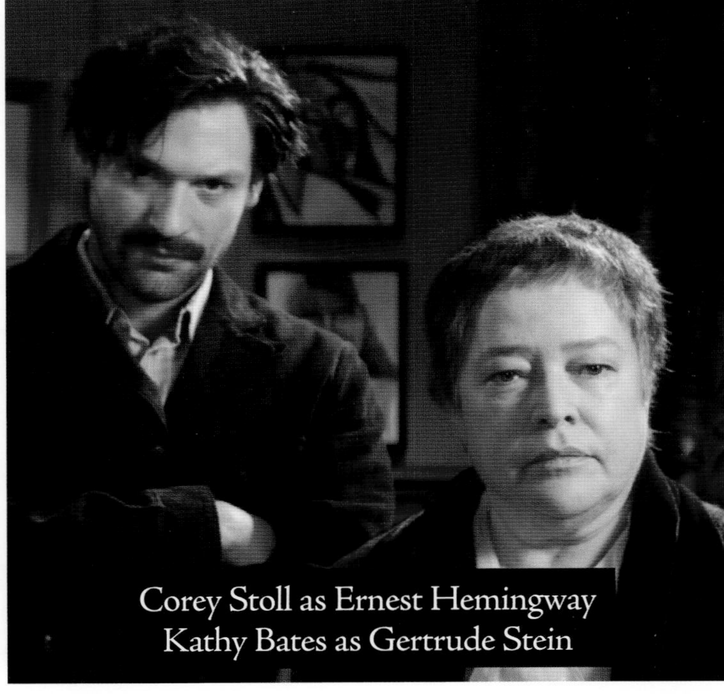
Corey Stoll as Ernest Hemingway
Kathy Bates as Gertrude Stein

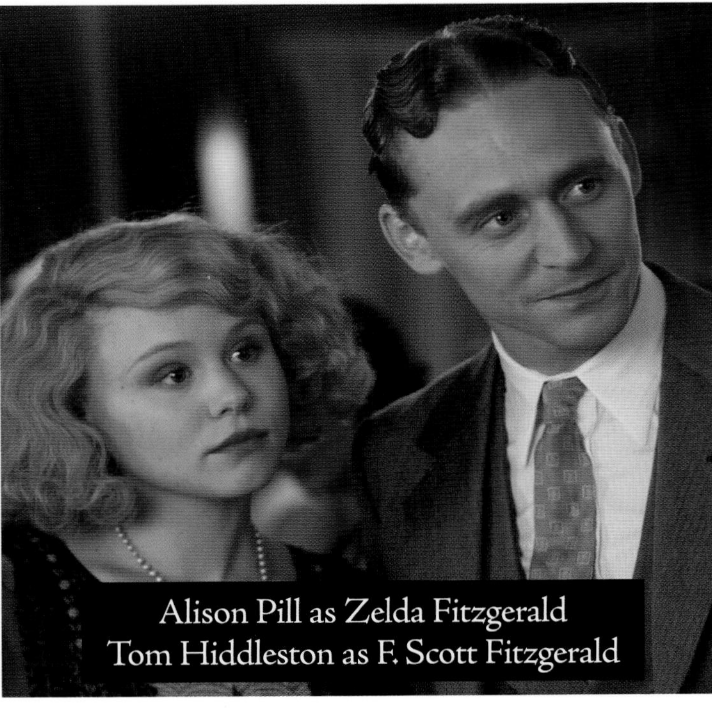
Alison Pill as Zelda Fitzgerald
Tom Hiddleston as F. Scott Fitzgerald

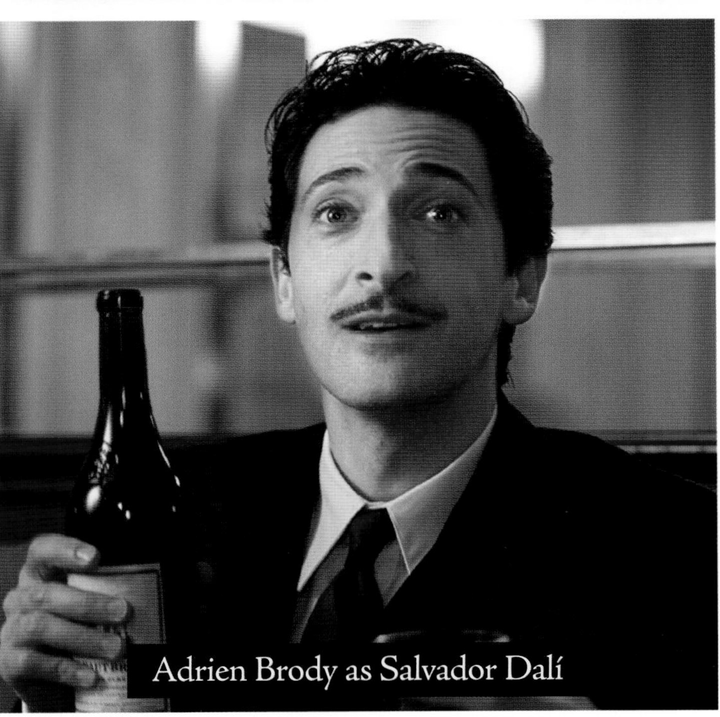
Adrien Brody as Salvador Dalí

My wife and I, who loved Paris, owe a debt of gratitude to Woody Allen for recreating the Paris of yesteryear. He gave us the chance to see how its famous inhabitants conversed, partied, cavorted and how the delightful Can-Can dancers sexily flipped their fluffy skirts and kicked their shapely legs.

A silent movie star meets a young dancer, but the arrival of talking pictures sends their careers in opposite directions.

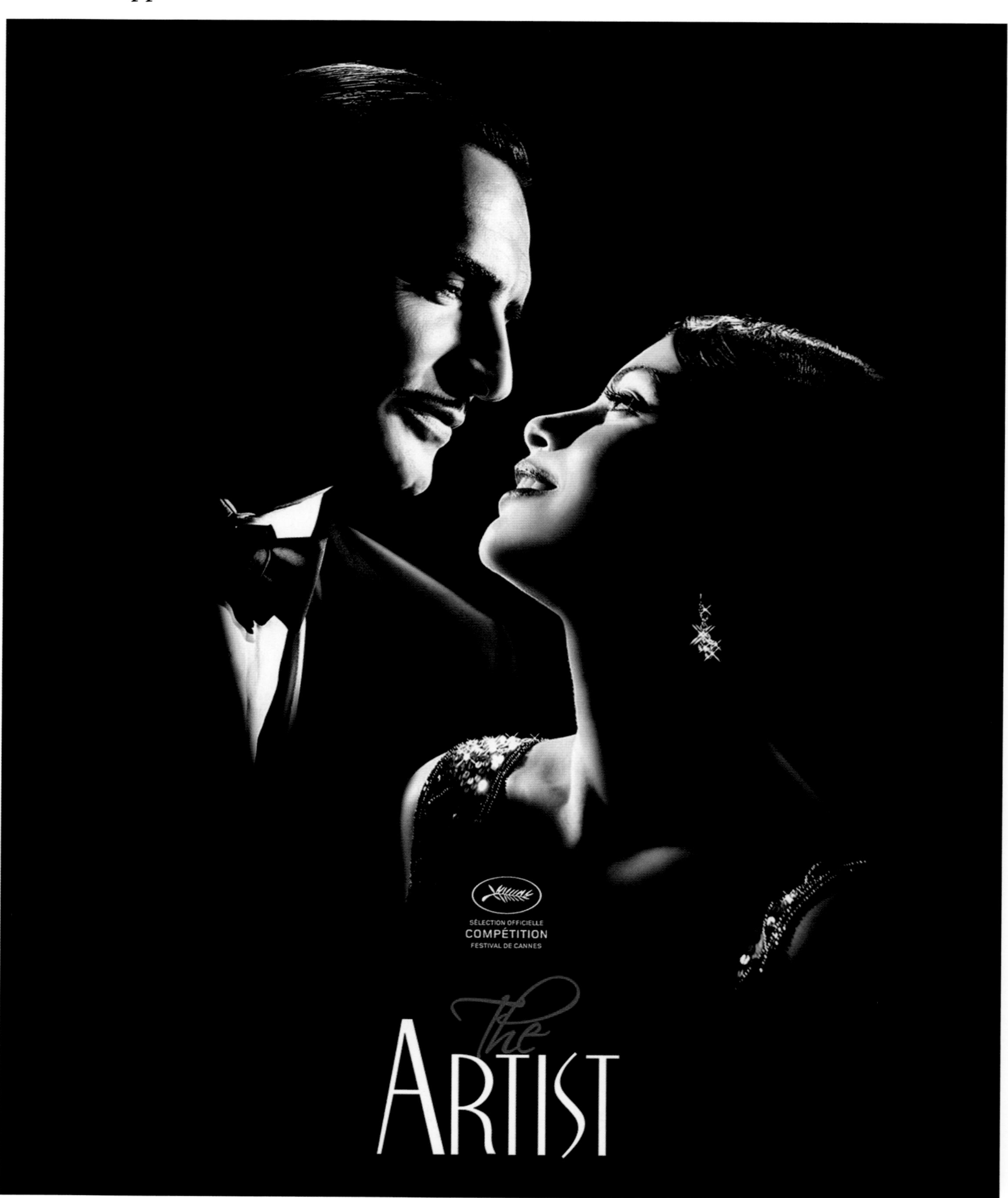

David Elliott of San Diego Reader wrote: "Through it all, Dujardin has great dignity, is hugely likable, and pulls off touches of comic poignancy not far from Chaplin's."

In France it was nominated for ten César Awards, winning six, including Best Actress for Bejo.

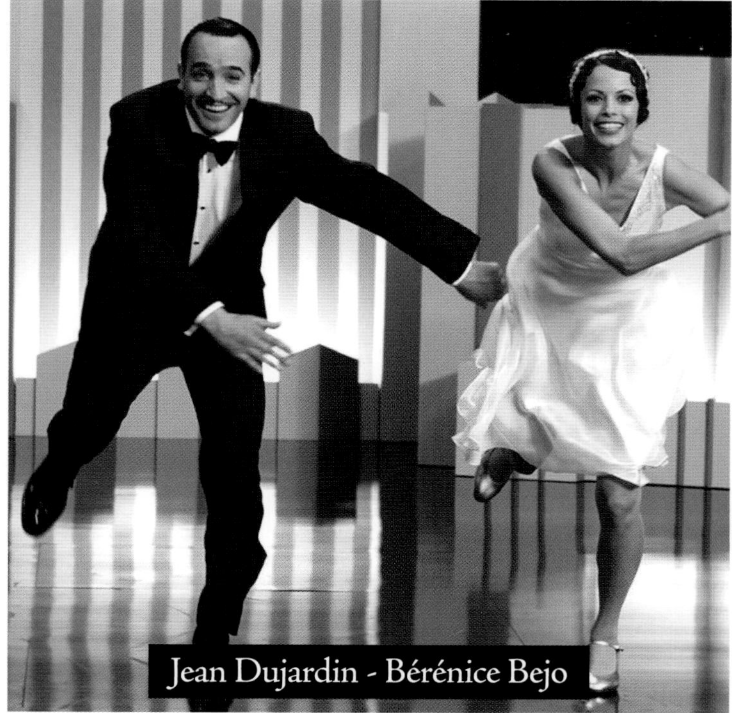
Jean Dujardin - Bérénice Bejo

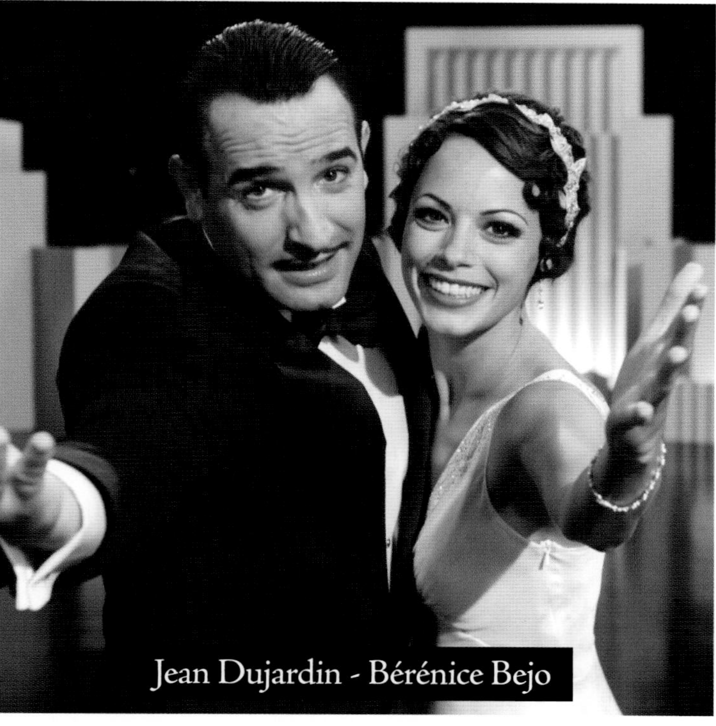
Jean Dujardin - Bérénice Bejo

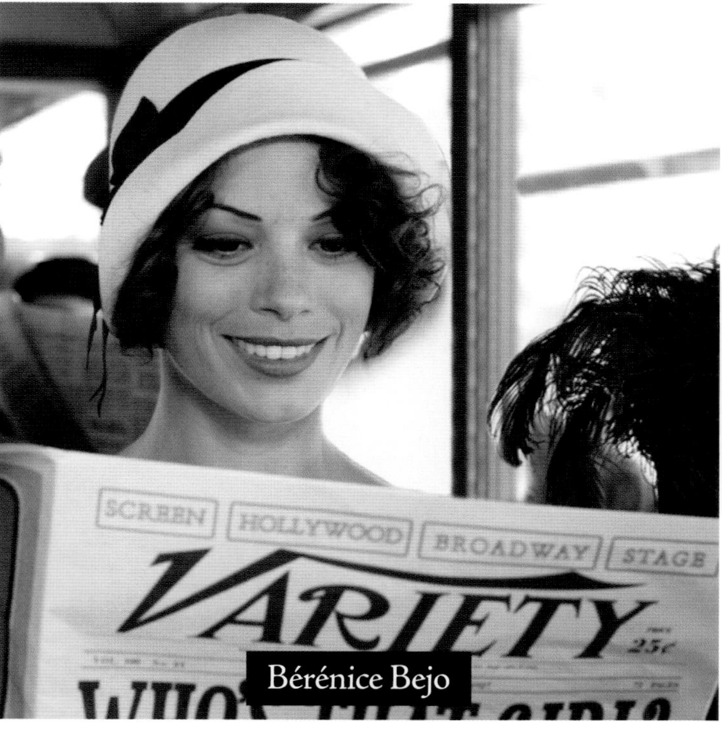

Bérénice Bejo

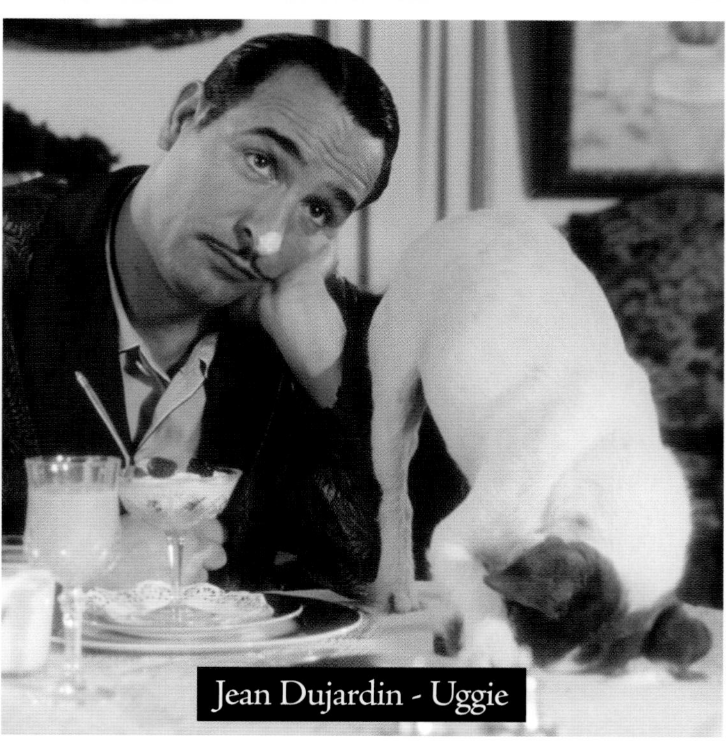
Jean Dujardin - Uggie

Ostensibly, this is a silent film performed by two attractive artists, Jean Dujardin and Bérénice Bejo. Not until the very end do we hear any sounds and with these sounds, happily, an era began for Peppy Miller, the character played by the mellow voiced Bejo, and unhappily an era ended for George Valentin, played by the raspy voiced Dujardin.

An aspiring author during the civil rights movement of the 1960s decides to write a book detailing the African American maids' point of view on the white families for which they work, and the hardships they go through on a daily basis.

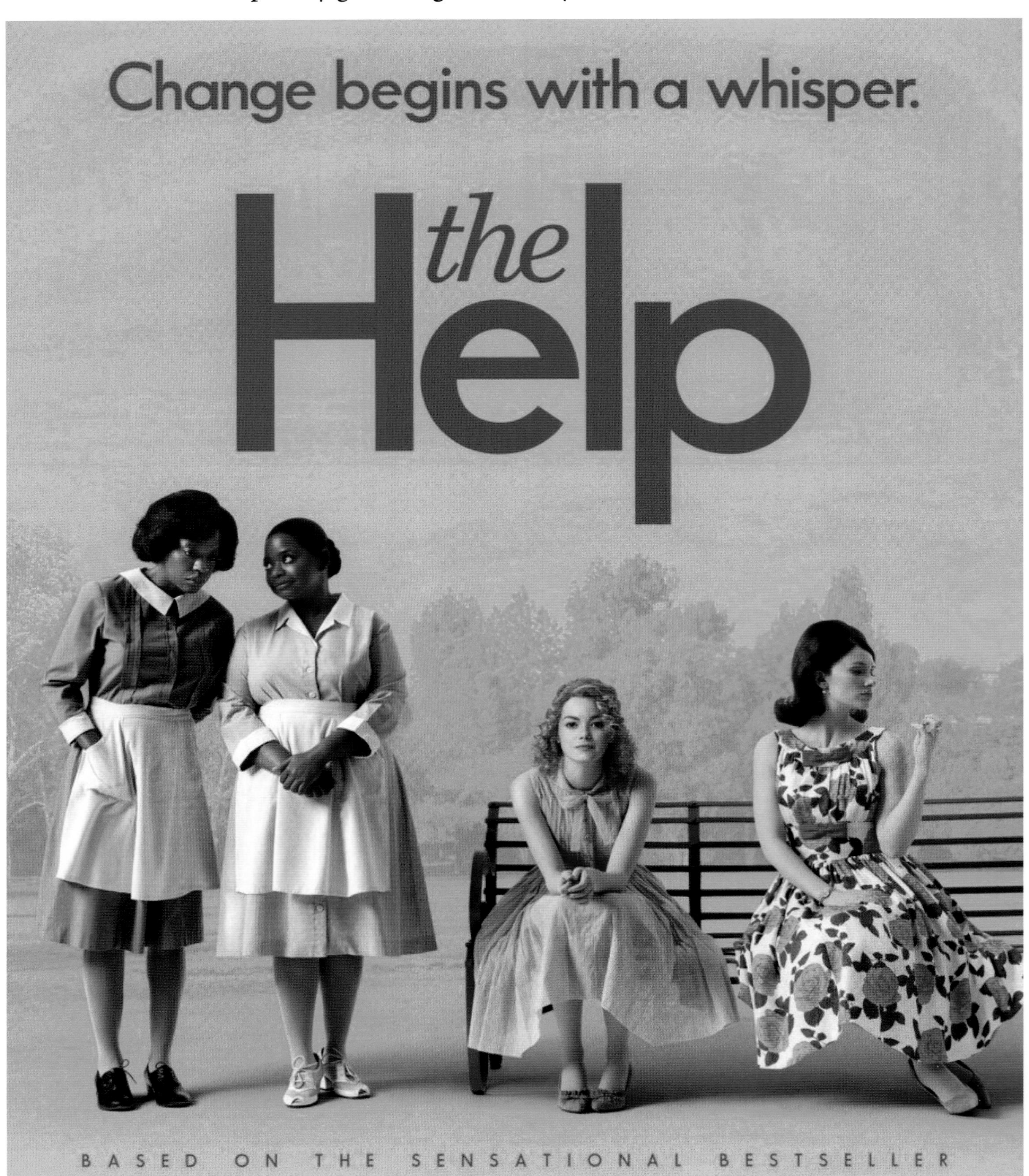

Leonard Maltin of indieWire wrote: "If you lived through that time, it is incredible to contemplate how much has changed (and how much hasn't) over the years, not only in race relations but in attitudes toward women. That's part of the fascination of watching 'The Help.'"

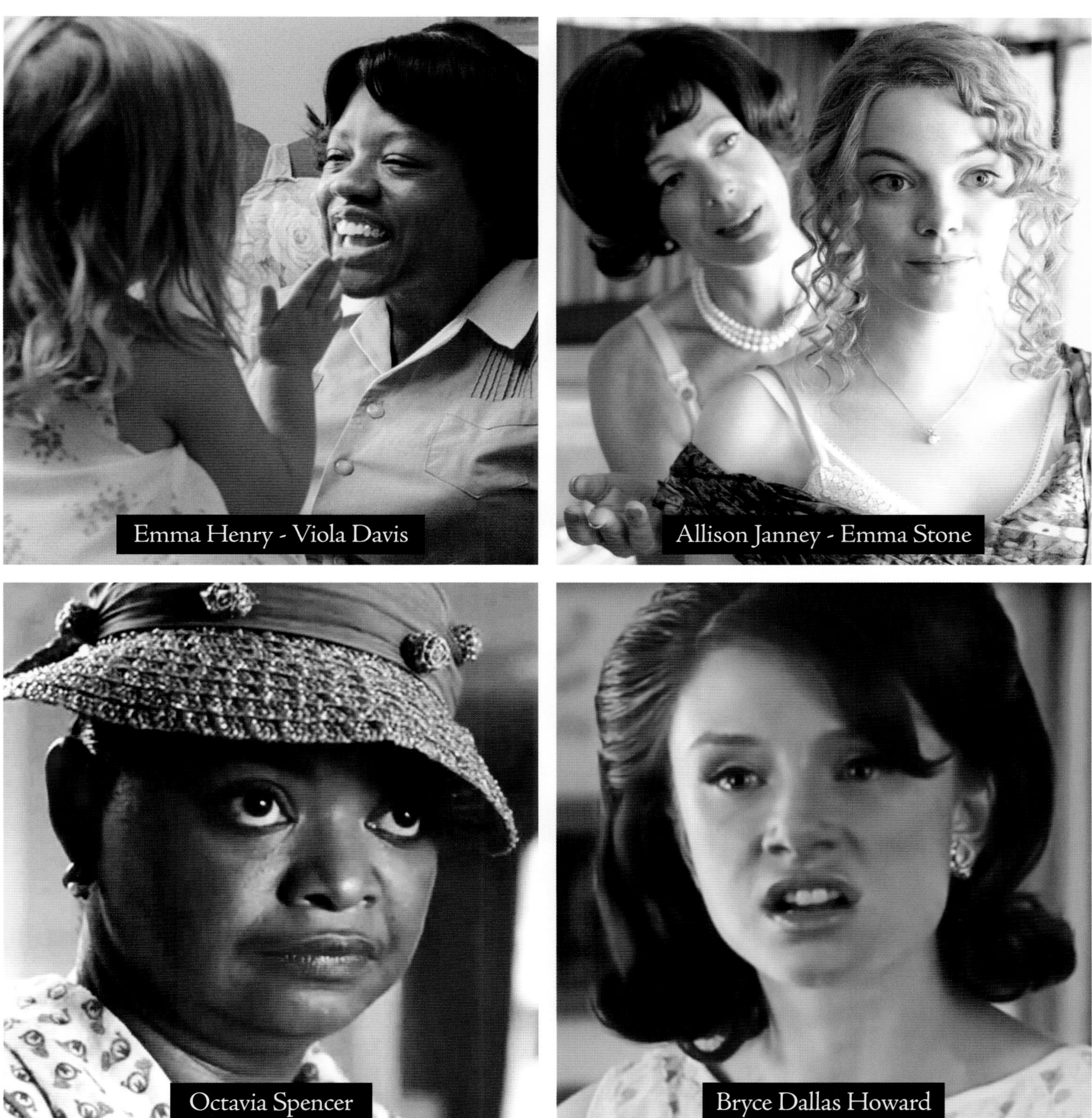

Emma Henry - Viola Davis

Allison Janney - Emma Stone

Octavia Spencer

Bryce Dallas Howard

At the film's end there is a satisfying 'comeuppance' moment when the mean, overbearing 'Lady of the Manor' learns from her overburdened housekeeper, Minny Jackson, that the piece of chocolate pie she enjoys eating so much, contains some of Minny's fresh bowel movement.

Two South Africans set out to discover what happened to their unlikely musical hero, the mysterious 1970s rock n roller, Rodriguez.

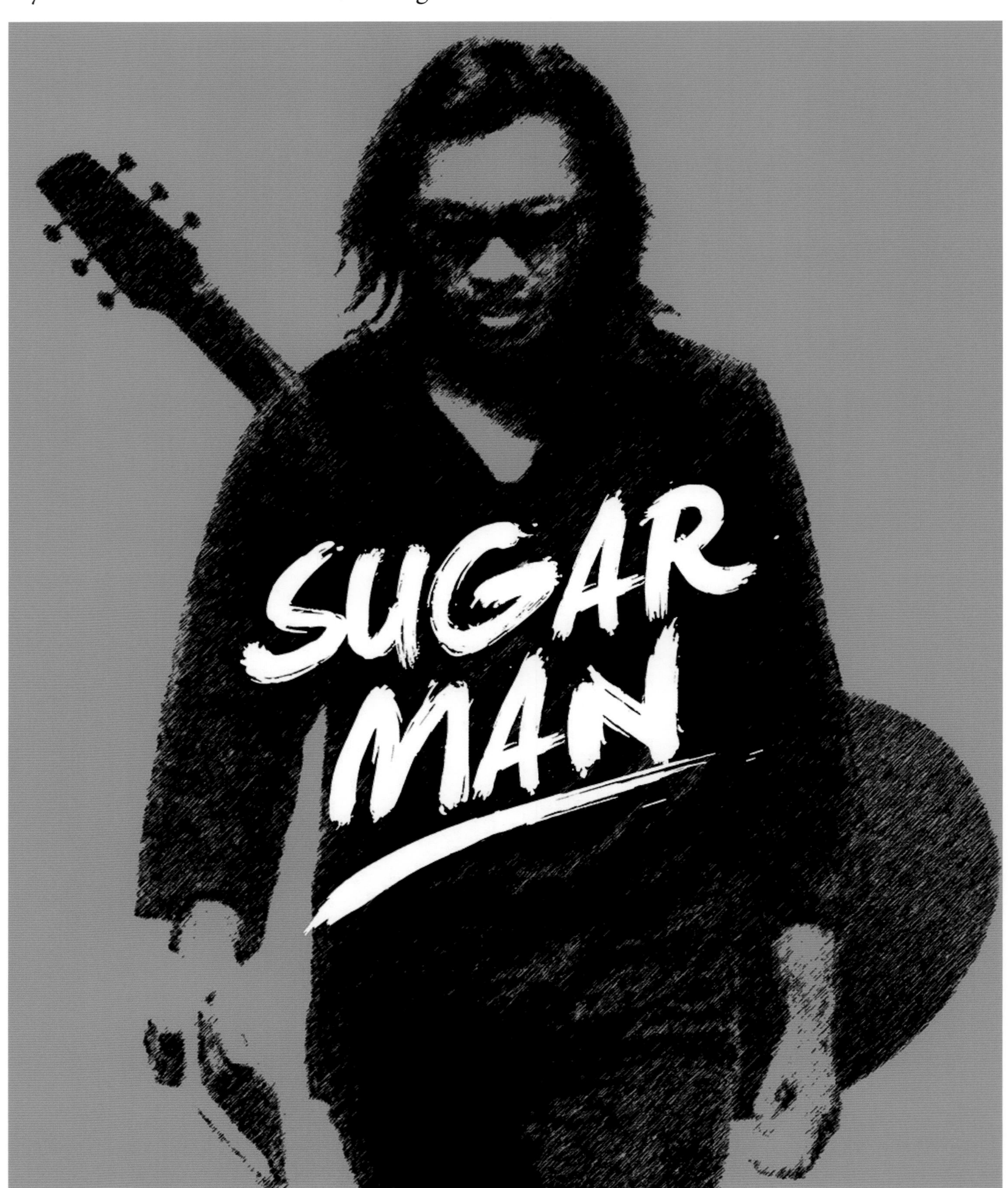

Michael Phillips of Chicago Tribune wrote: "At 85 minutes, it's a tight, sharp achievement, yet one of the things I love about it is simple: It moves to a relaxed rhythm, in sync with its slightly otherworldly subject."

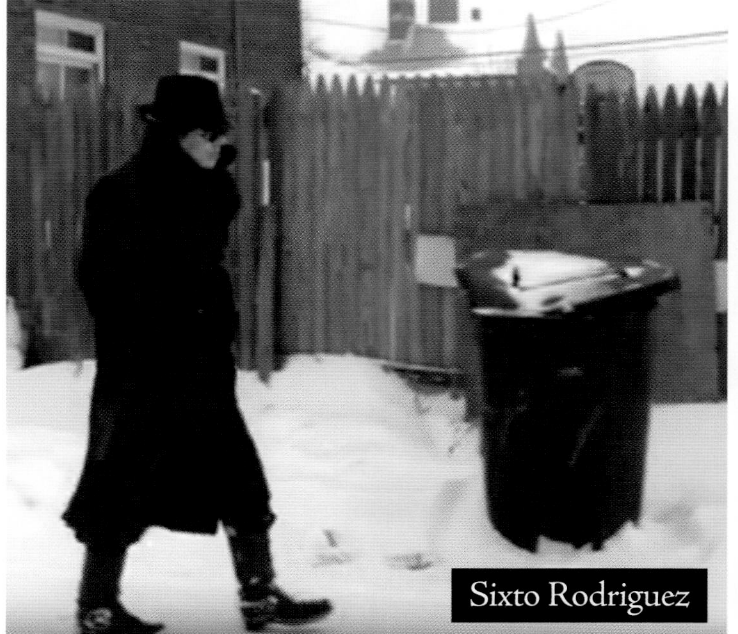
Sixto Rodriguez

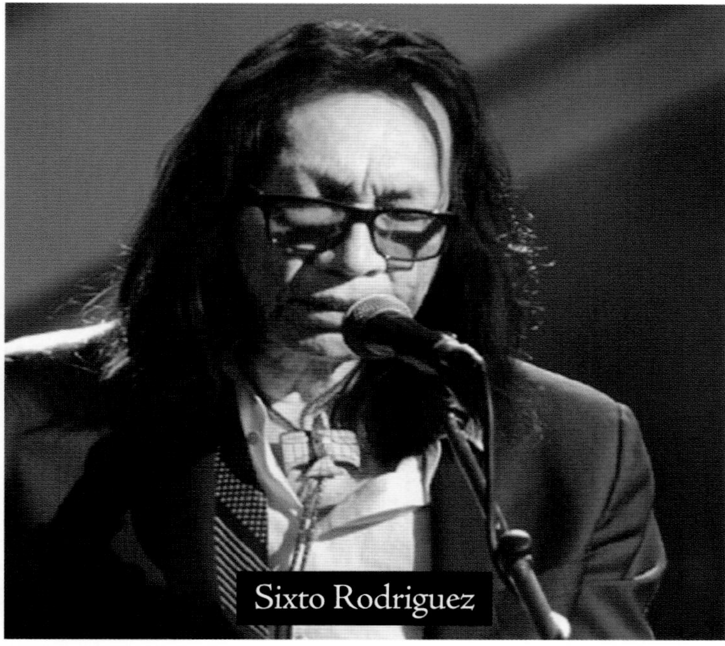
Sixto Rodriguez

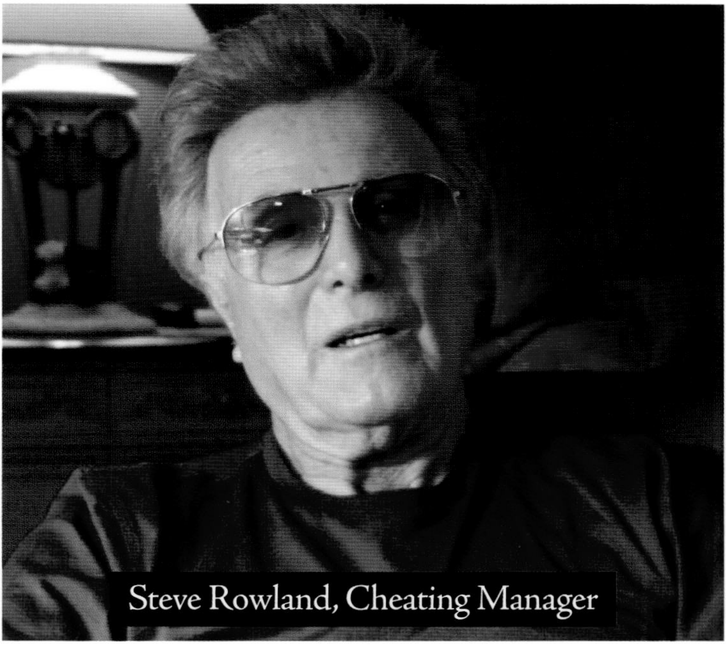
Steve Rowland, Cheating Manager

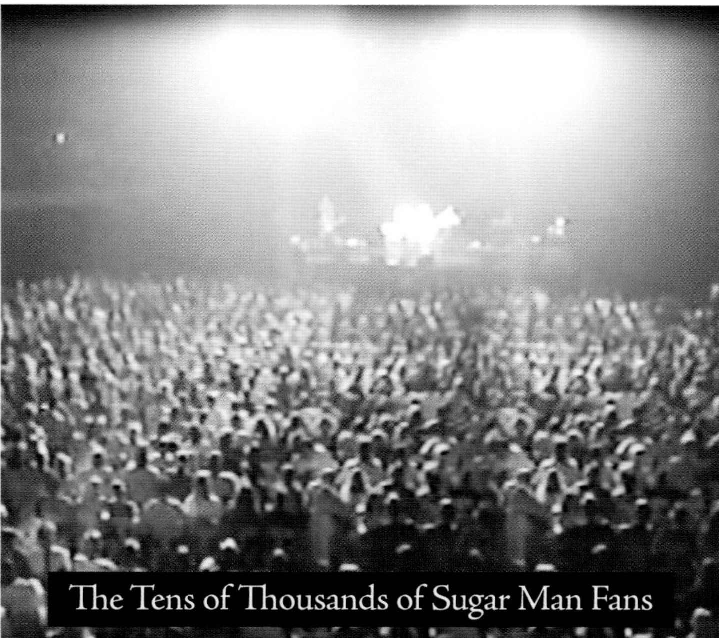
The Tens of Thousands of Sugar Man Fans

This is a true story about Sixto Rodriguez, a musician whose cheating manager booked him into small clubs for minimum wage. At the end we learn that unbeknownst to Rodriguez, his manager had been selling thousands of records to his fans in South Africa. Thankfully, when Rodriguez visits South Africa and plays to a massive, cheering audience, he becomes aware of the scam his manager had perpetrated.

When Malik Bendjelloul, the enterprising director, ran out of money and couldn't afford to buy film, he used his iPhone to finish shooting "Sugar Man."

Monty Wildhorn, an alcoholic novelist of Westerns, has lost his drive. His nephew pushes him to summer in quiet Belle Isle. He begrudgingly befriends a newly single mom and her three girls, who help him find the inspiration to write again.

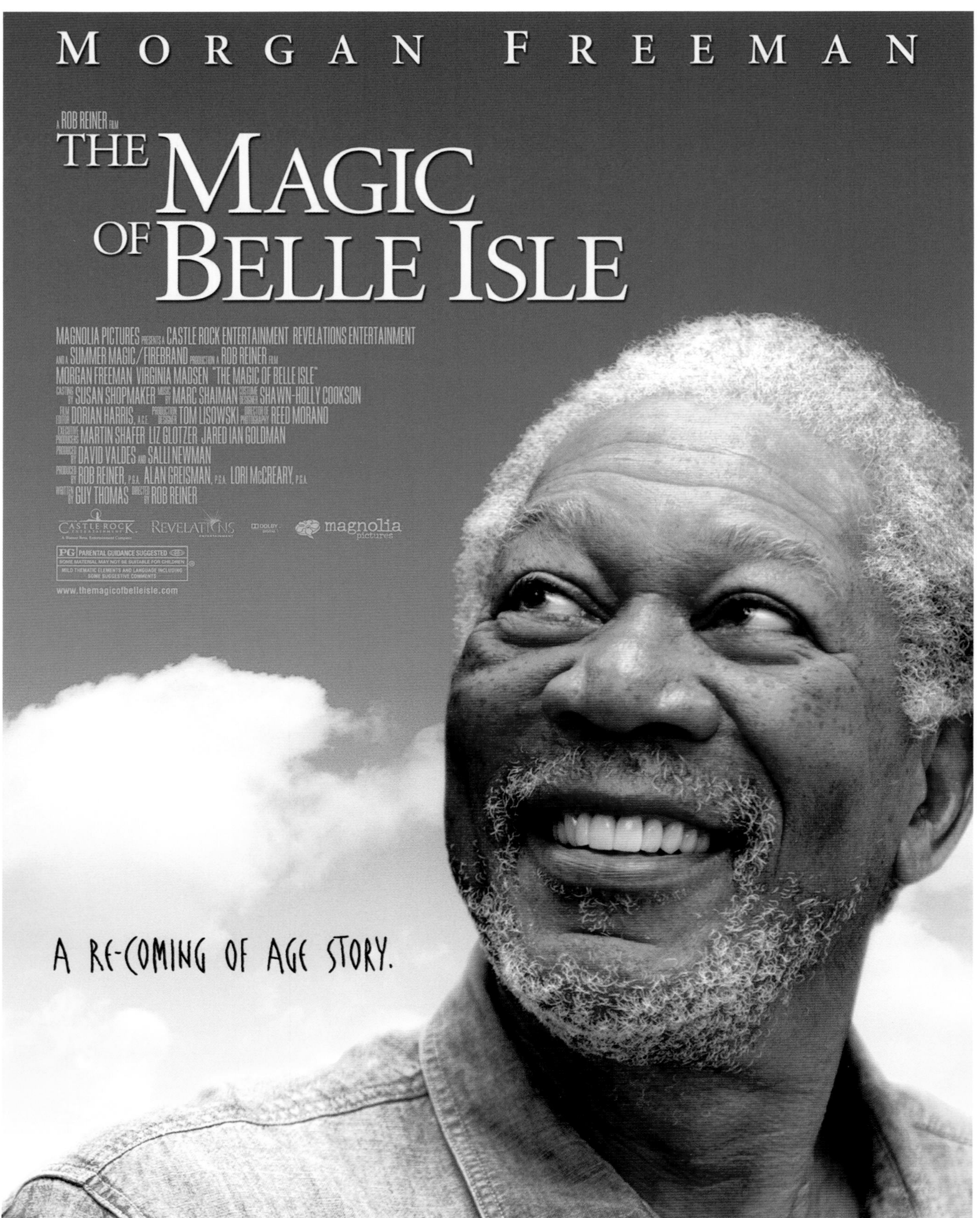

Rex Reed of New York Observer wrote: "You can quarrel with the smiley-face outcome of every ordeal, but the tenderness and optimism are so powerful and ingratiating that only a viewer with the darkest sensibility will go away untouched."

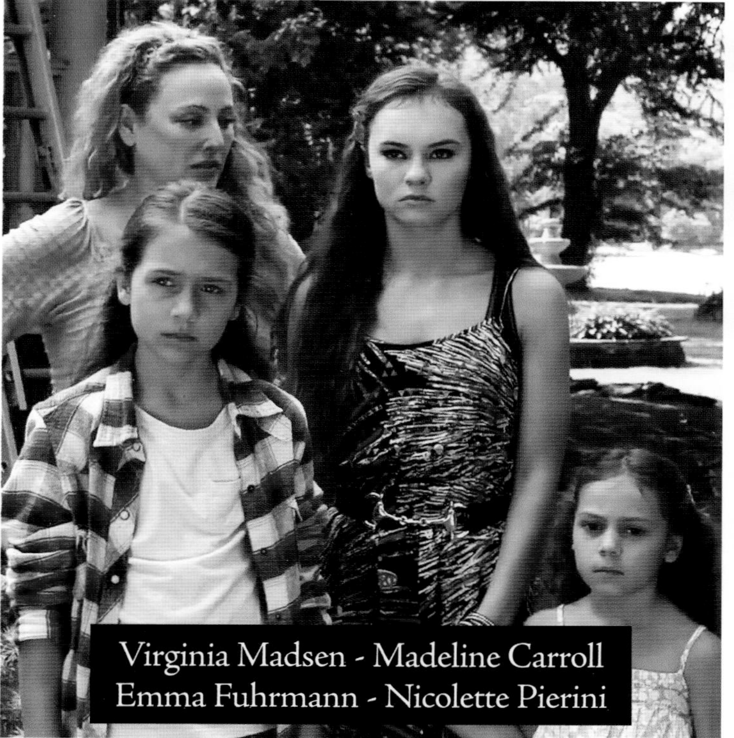
Virginia Madsen - Madeline Carroll
Emma Fuhrmann - Nicolette Pierini

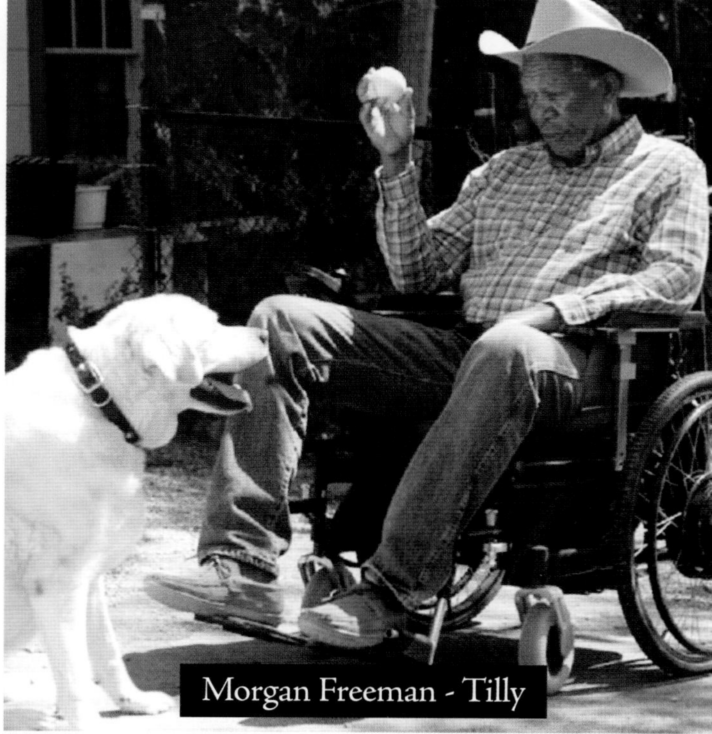
Morgan Freeman - Tilly

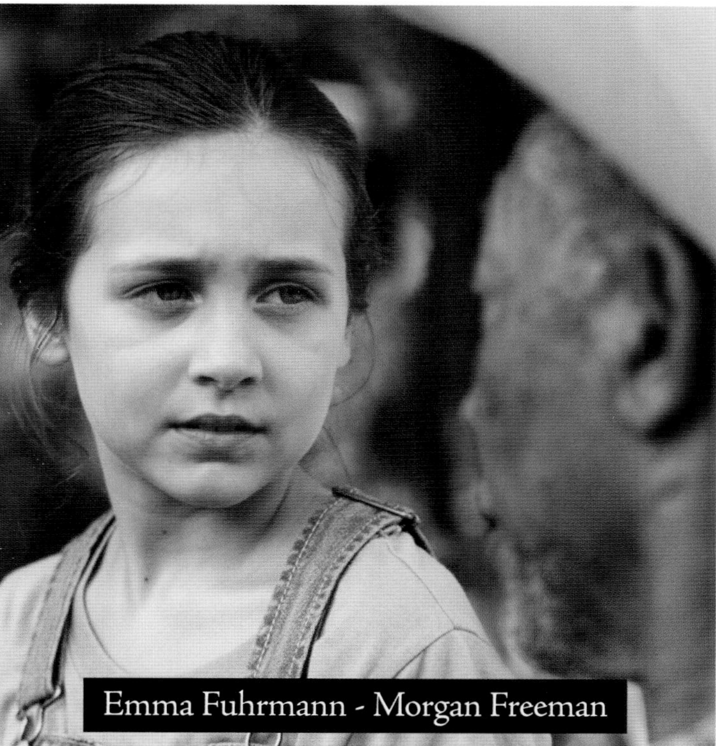
Emma Fuhrmann - Morgan Freeman

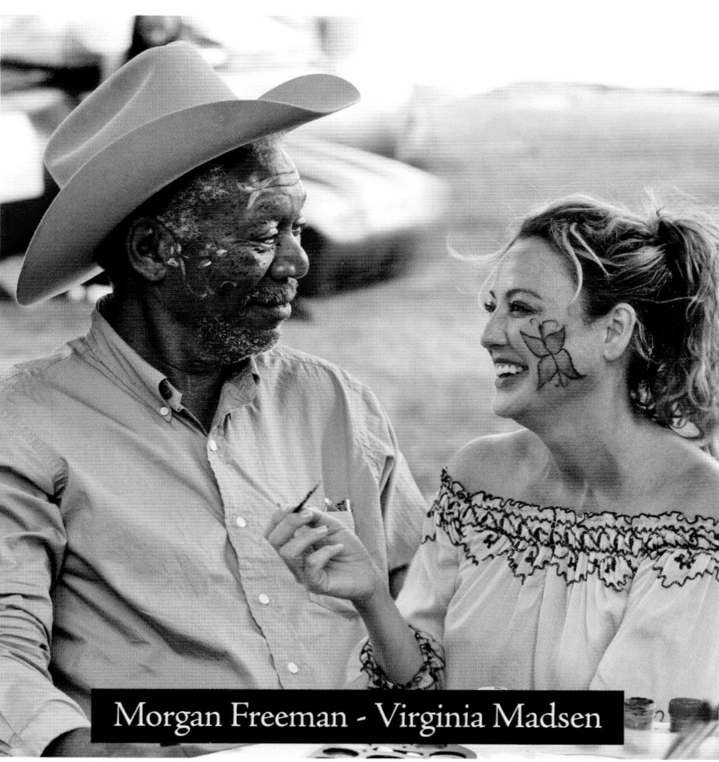
Morgan Freeman - Virginia Madsen

This movie reflects the ability of children and adults of all ethnicities and ages to get along and help each other in times of stress. Once again, it is that fine director, Rob Reiner, who brought this moving film to the theaters, where it played to delighted audiences.

A spelling bee loser sets out to exact revenge by finding a loophole and tries to win as an adult.

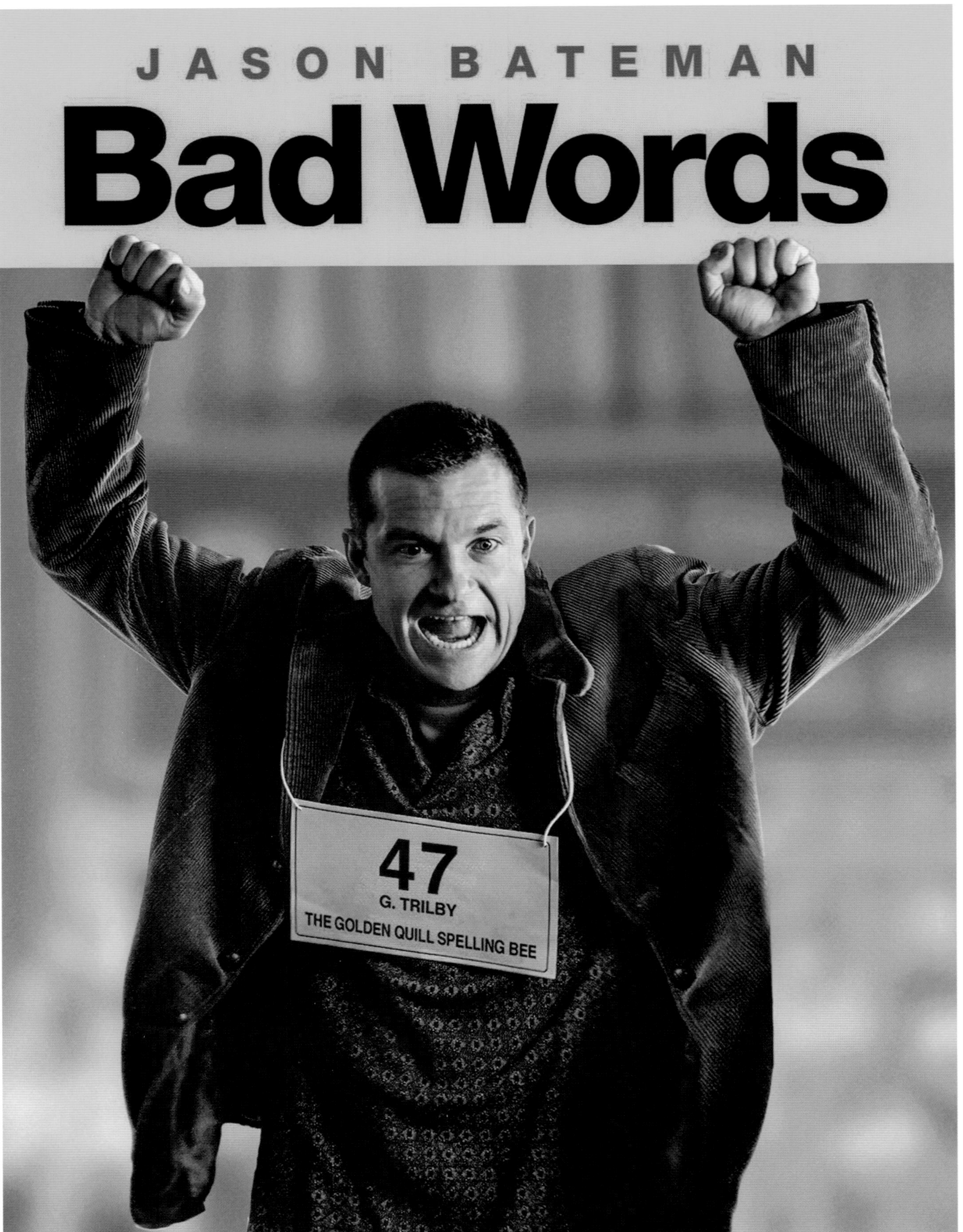

Josh Larsen of LarsenOnFilm wrote: "...a withering send-up of our kid-obsessed culture, in which childhood has been reimagined as a procession of parent-directed accomplishments."

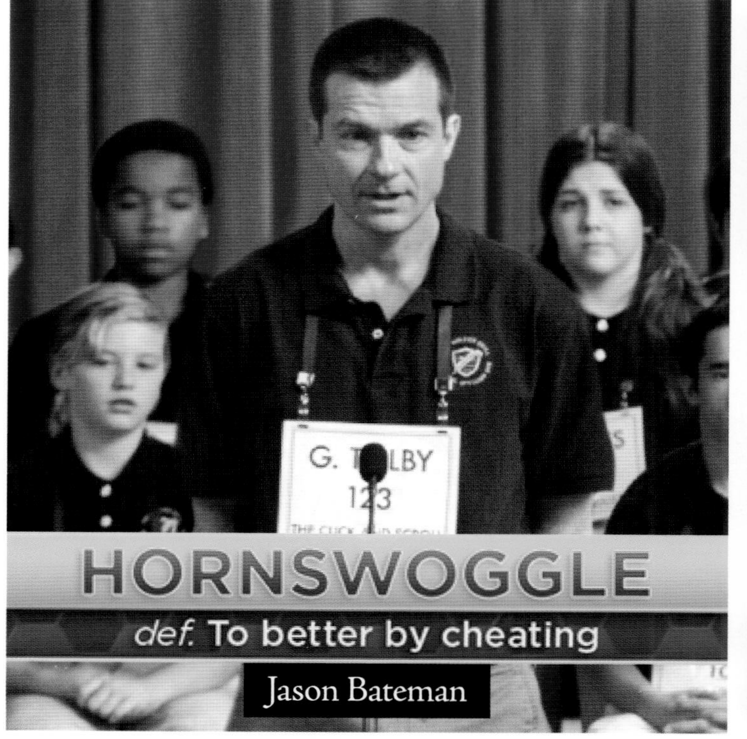

Jason Bateman

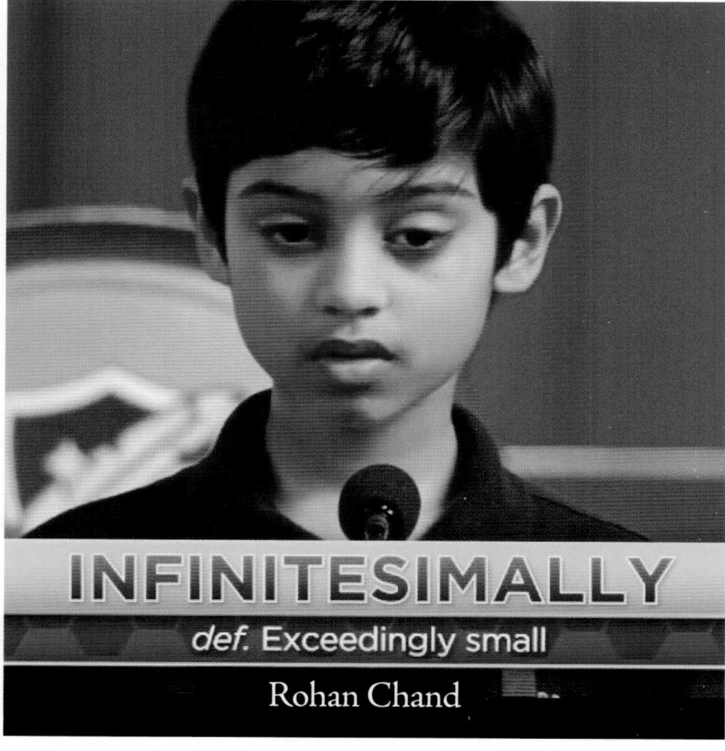

Rohan Chand

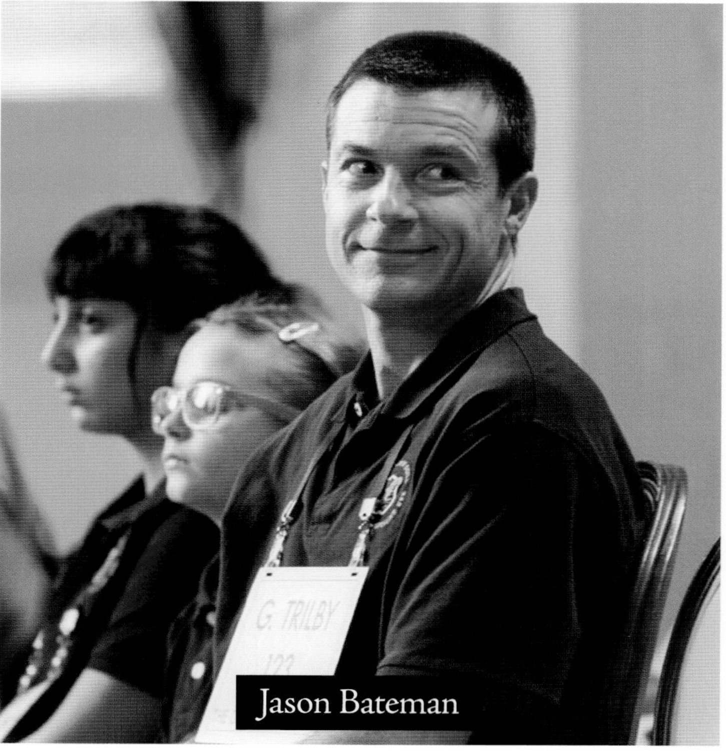
Jason Bateman

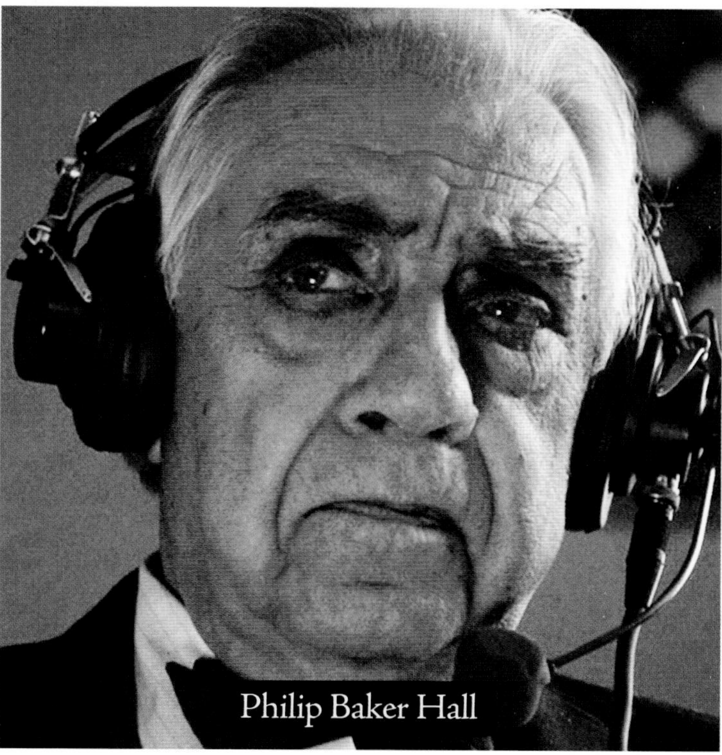
Philip Baker Hall

I particularly love this movie because, and you're not going to believe this, it reminds me of one of my all-time favorites, "The Count of Monte Cristo."

I won't tell you why it reminds me of "The Count of Monte Cristo," because for those who haven't seen it, it'll ruin a very satisfying reveal at the very end.

The true story of Captain Phillips and the 2009 hijacking by Somali pirates of the U.S.-flagged MV Maersk Alabama, the first American cargo ship to be hijacked in two hundred years.

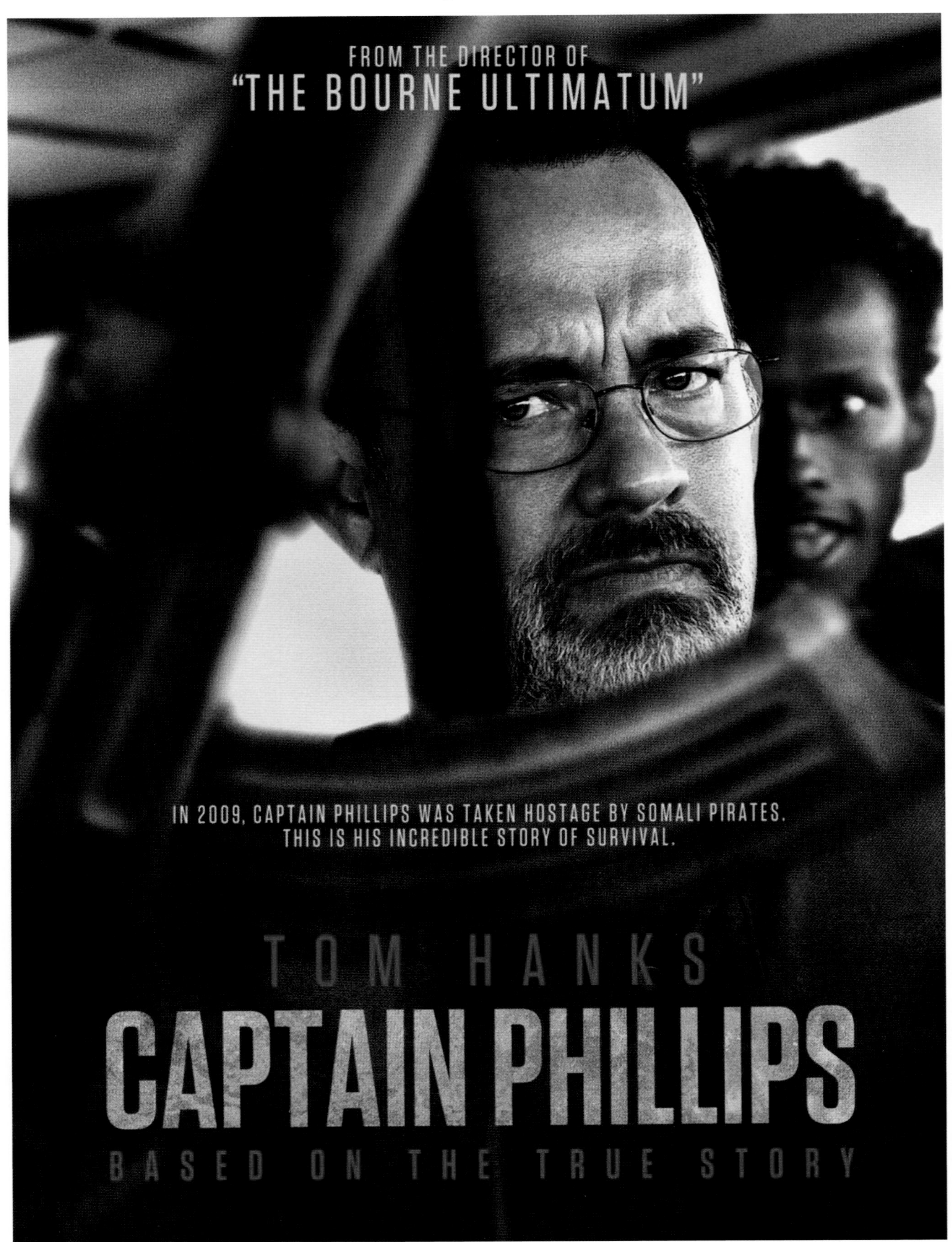

Christy Lemire wrote: "The entire performance is one of the greatest in Hanks' prolific, varied career - a role that gives him a massive arc and the opportunity to show great range."

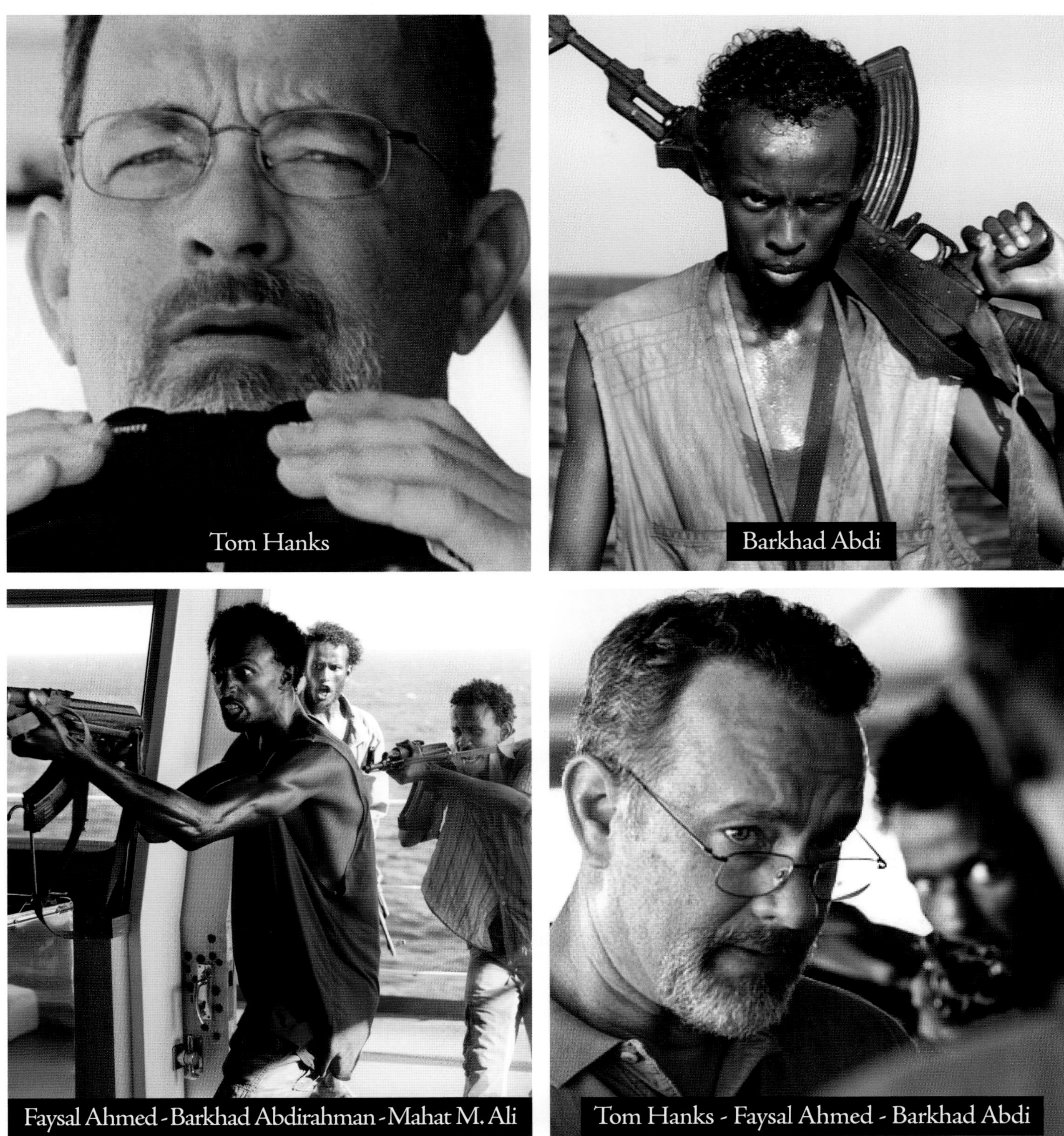

Tom Hanks

Barkhad Abdi

Faysal Ahmed - Barkhad Abdirahman - Mahat M. Ali

Tom Hanks - Faysal Ahmed - Barkhad Abdi

I was about to sing my praises for Tom Hanks' talent, but I remembered that I had sung his praises earlier in the book and there's another Tom Hanks movie coming up later, so I'll save any further praise singing until then.

Based on the true story of Jordan Belfort, from his rise to a wealthy stockbroker living the high life to his fall involving crime, corruption and the federal government.

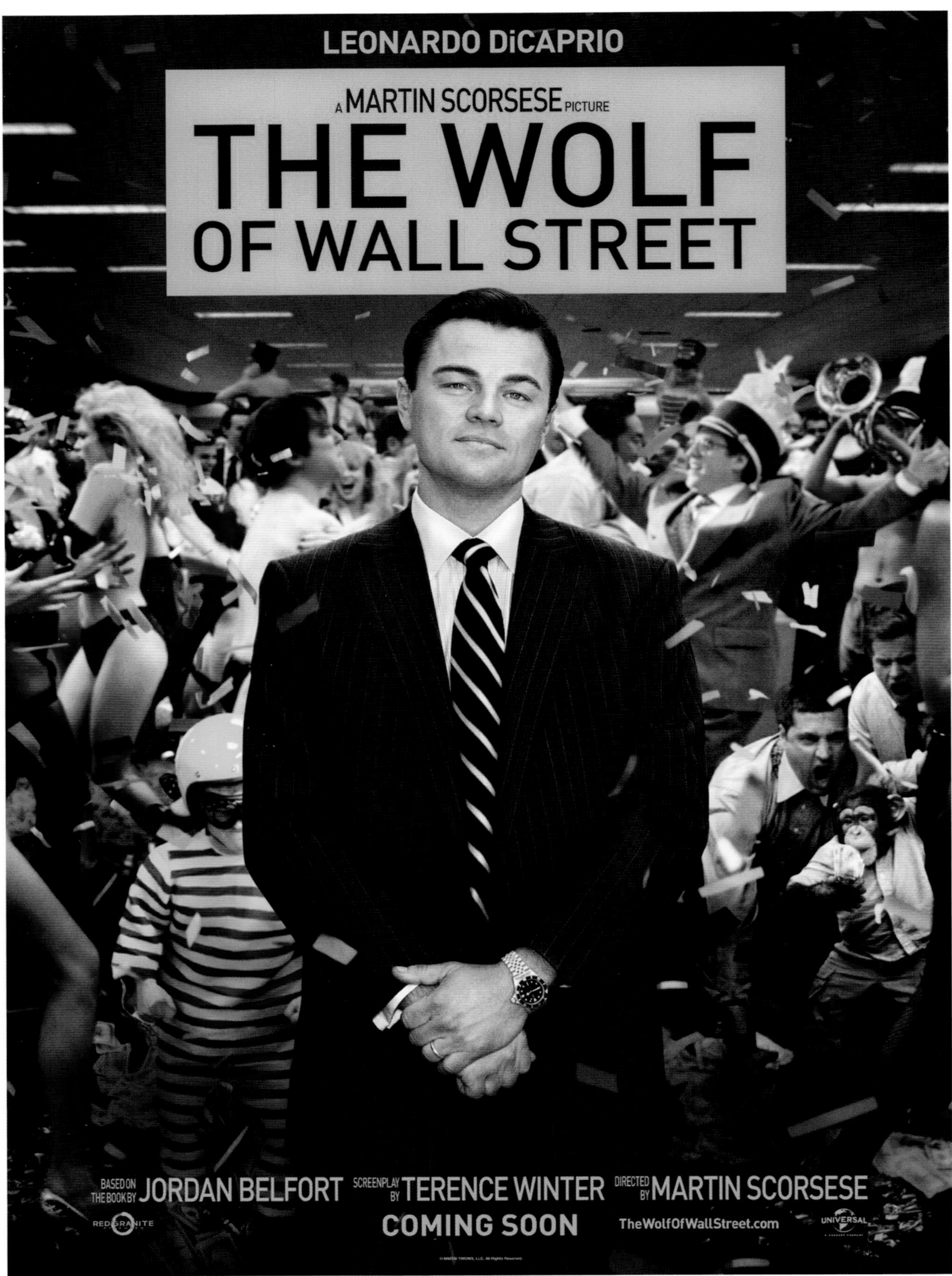

David Thomson of The New Republic wrote: "DiCaprio has hinted before that comedy might be his natural calling–think 'Catch Me If You Can'–but his energy here is not just fun, it's discovery."

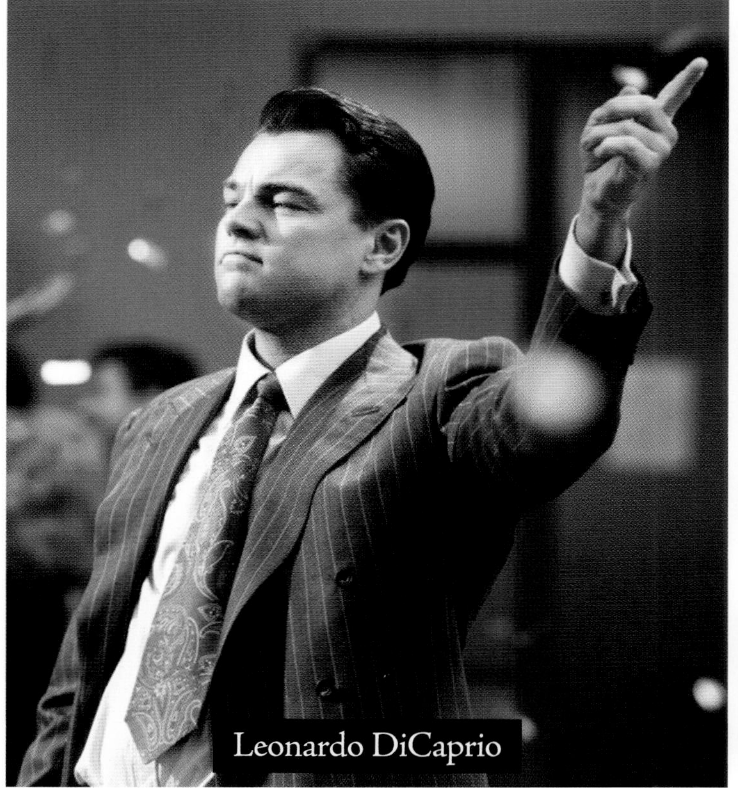
Leonardo DiCaprio

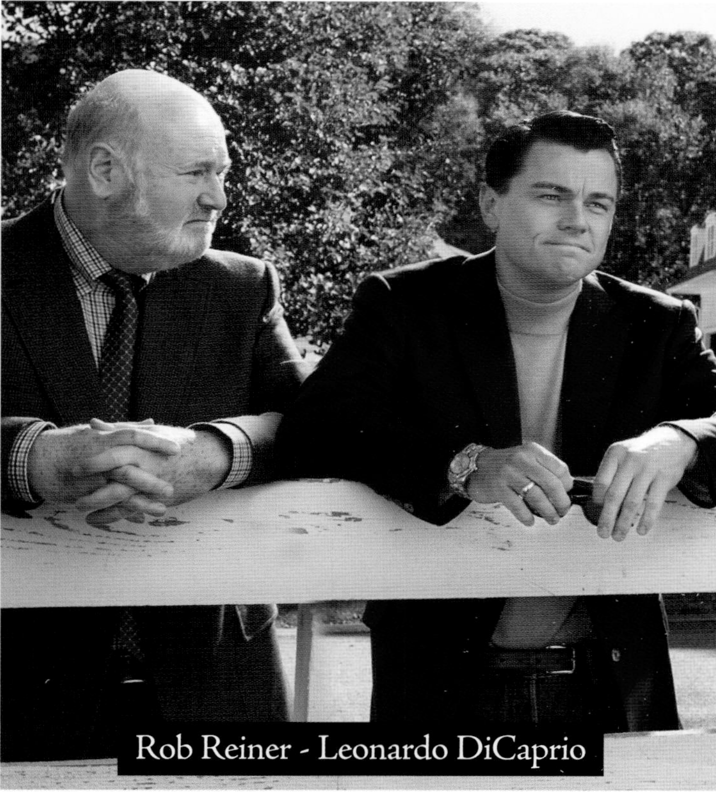
Rob Reiner - Leonardo DiCaprio

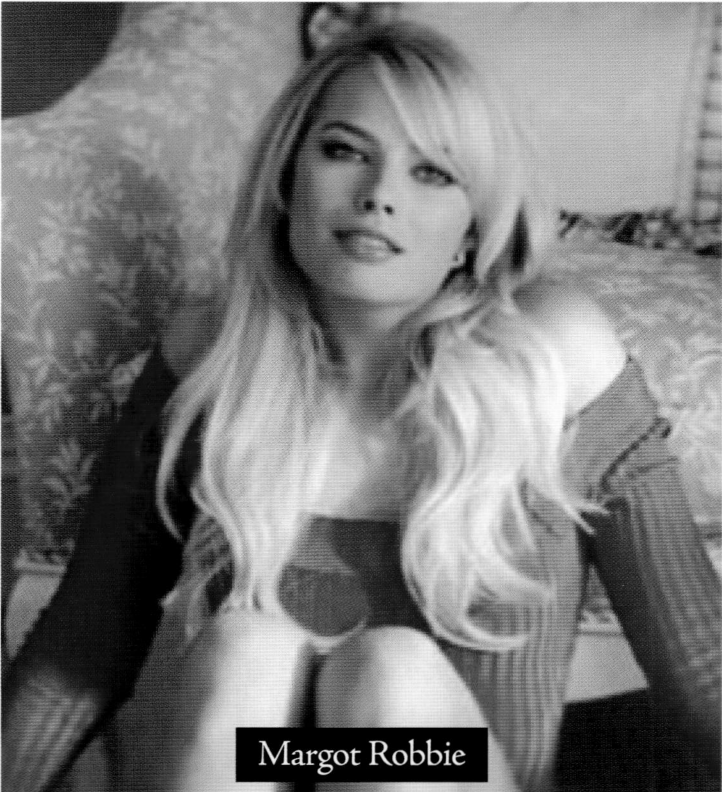
Margot Robbie

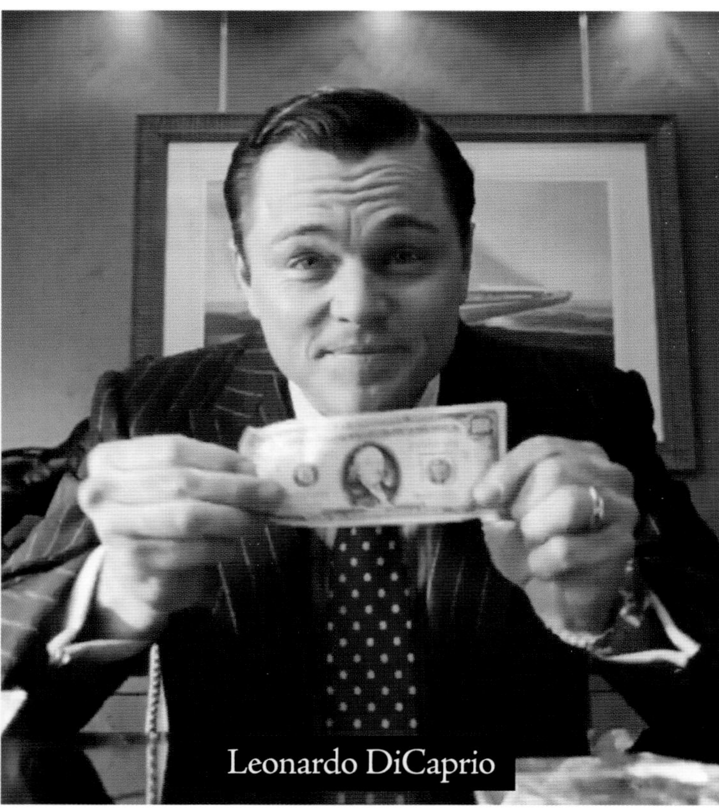
Leonardo DiCaprio

Another discovery for some people might be that Rob Reiner, besides being a producer, director, writer and a "Meat Head," is also a serious and convincing dramatic actor.

A woman, accidentally caught in a dark deal, turns the tables on her captors and transforms into a merciless warrior evolved beyond human logic.

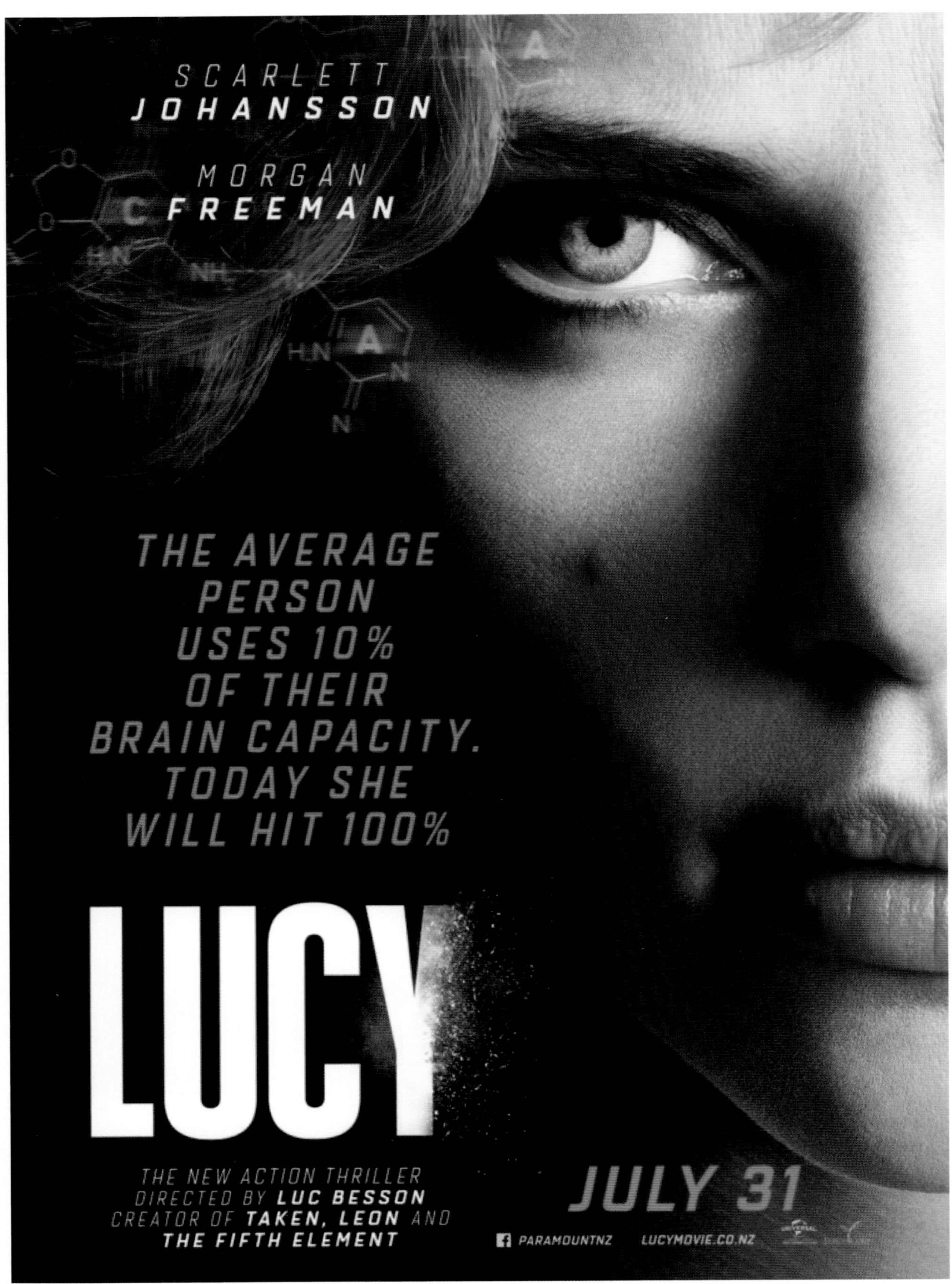

David Sims of The Atlantic wrote: "Let Scarlett Johansson's 'Lucy' grab you by the noodle and zap you into its whacked-out vision of human existence. You'll feel much better for it."

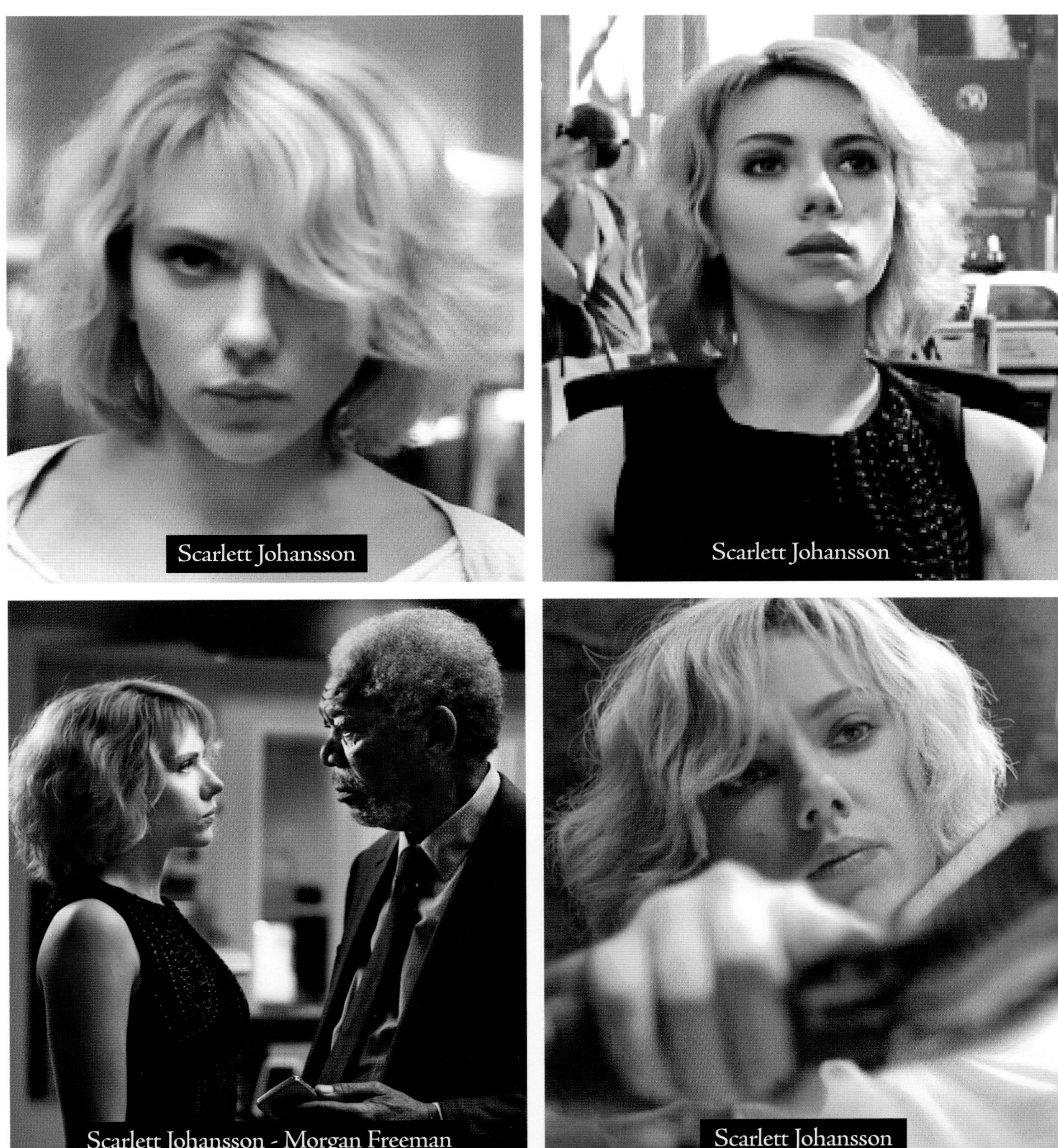

Scarlett Johansson

Scarlett Johansson

Scarlett Johansson - Morgan Freeman

Scarlett Johansson

Any movie in which the lovely and gifted Scarlett Johansson gets the chance to destroy and debilitate dozens of dastardly, deserving dickheads, is my cup of tea.

A recently unemployed single father struggles to get back his foreclosed home by working for the real estate broker who is the source of his frustration.

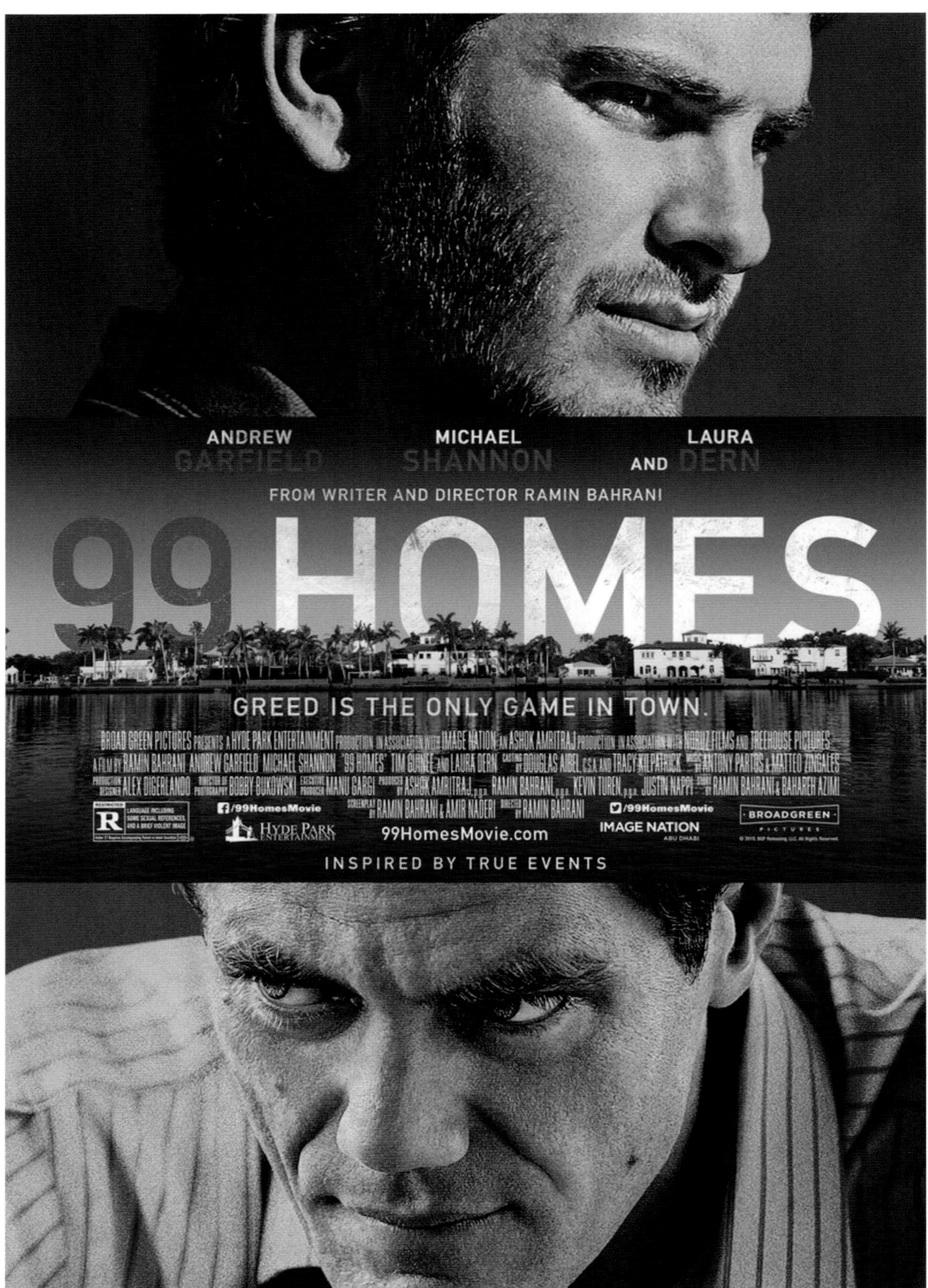

Rafer Guzman of Newsday wrote: "A gripping dramatic thriller about the winners and losers in America's game of mortgage roulette."

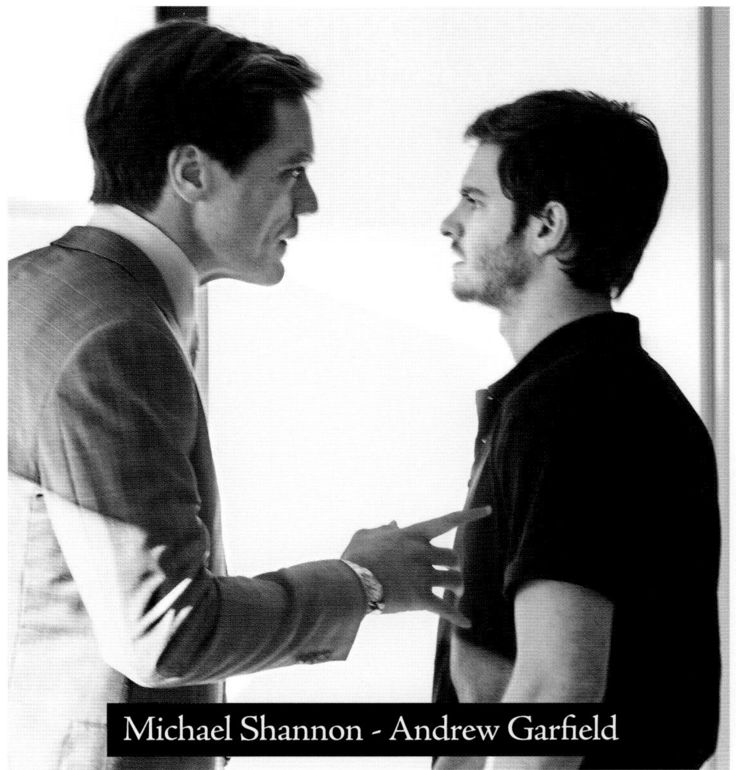
Michael Shannon - Andrew Garfield

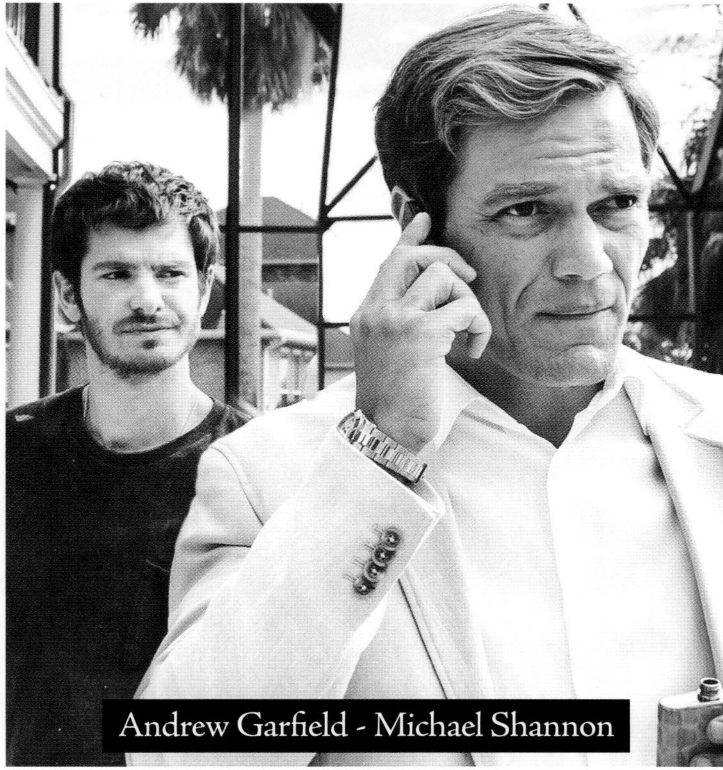
Andrew Garfield - Michael Shannon

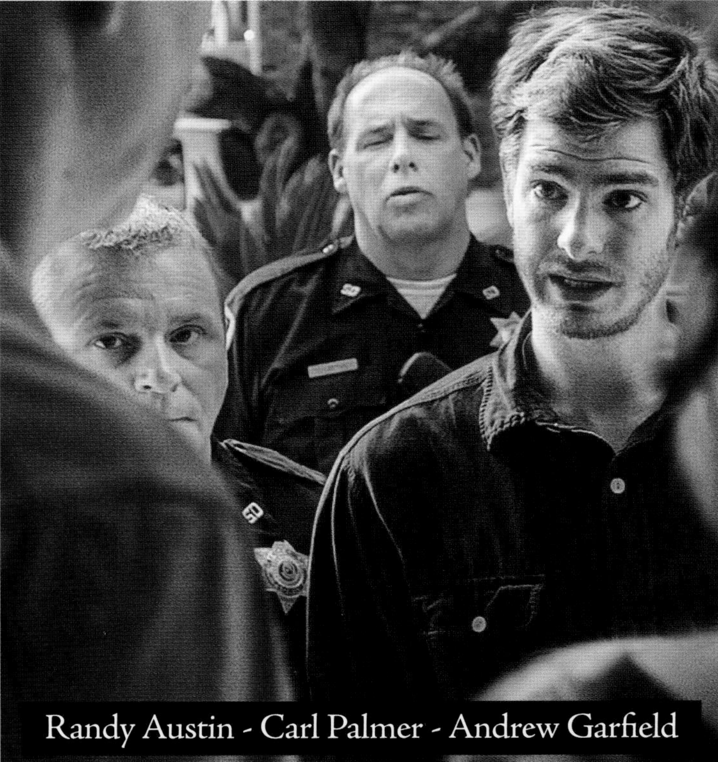
Randy Austin - Carl Palmer - Andrew Garfield

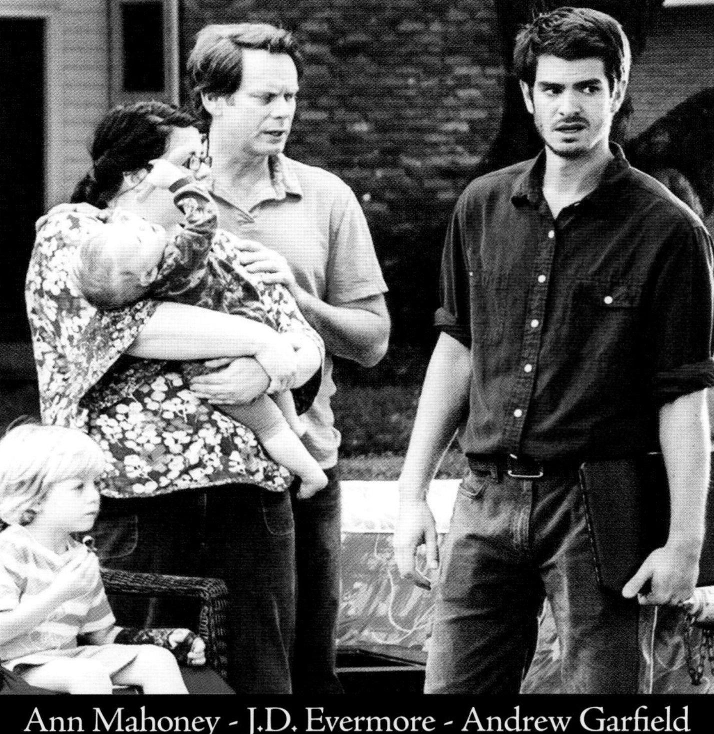
Ann Mahoney - J.D. Evermore - Andrew Garfield

I so admire this film. It clearly exposes the ugly truth about how good and honest people are forced out of their homes by bank foreclosures processed by greedy, unethical realtors, thus burgeoning their personal wealth.

A chronicle of Martin Luther King's campaign to secure equal voting rights via an epic march from Selma to Montgomery, Alabama in 1965.

"A TRIUMPH... OYELOWO'S PERFORMANCE AS MARTIN LUTHER KING IS STUNNING"
BAZ BAMIGBOYE, DAILY MAIL

DAVID OYELOWO

SELMA

TOM WILKINSON CARMEN EJOGO WITH TIM ROTH AND OPRAH WINFREY

ONE DREAM CAN CHANGE THE WORLD

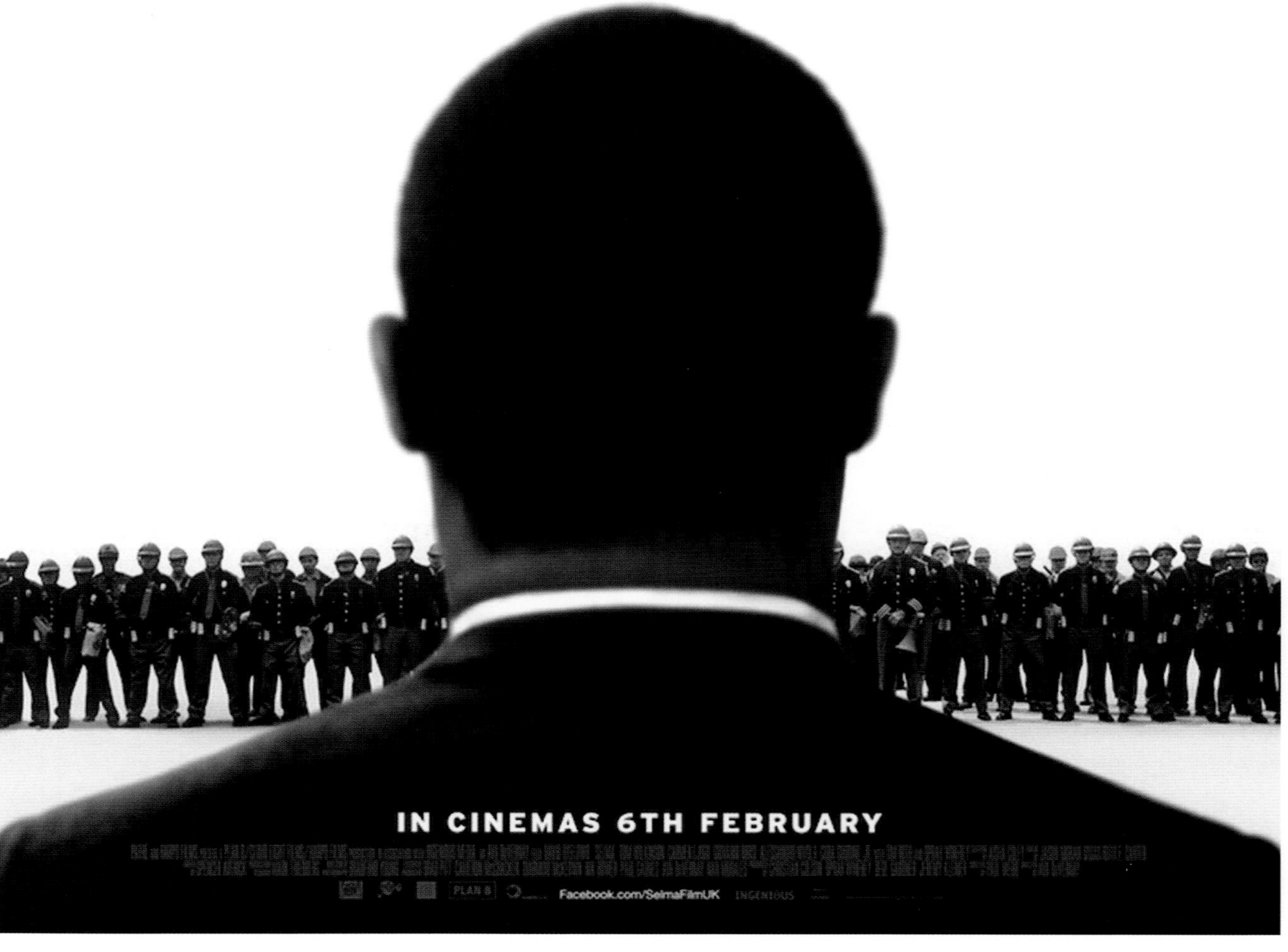

Ty Burr of Boston Globe wrote: "More often than not ... 'Selma' focuses on the one thing we don't expect in a movie about Martin Luther King Jr.–his doubts–and Oyelowo comes through with a deeply felt and quite brilliant performance."

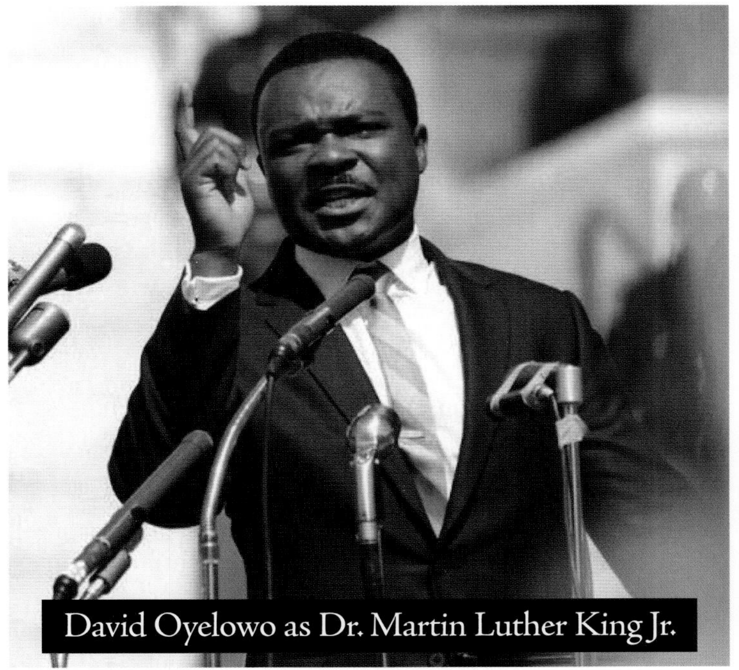
David Oyelowo as Dr. Martin Luther King Jr.

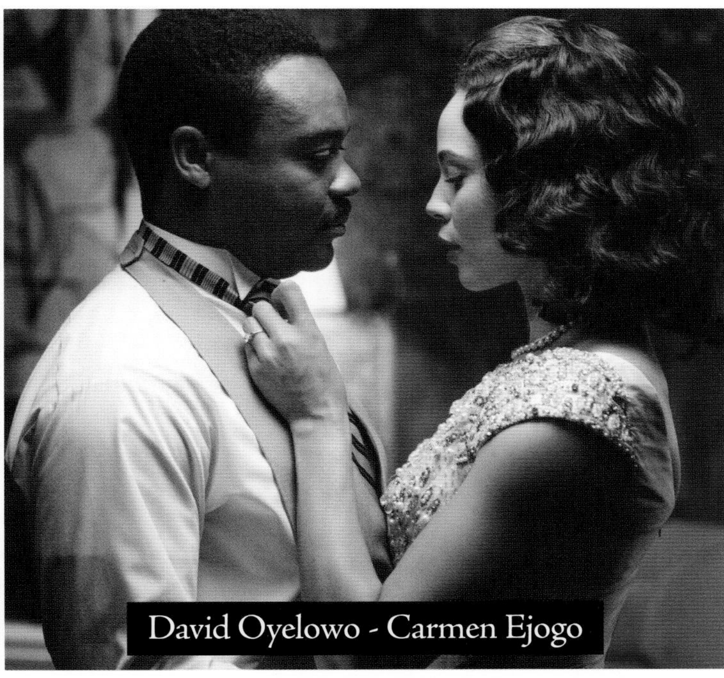
David Oyelowo - Carmen Ejogo

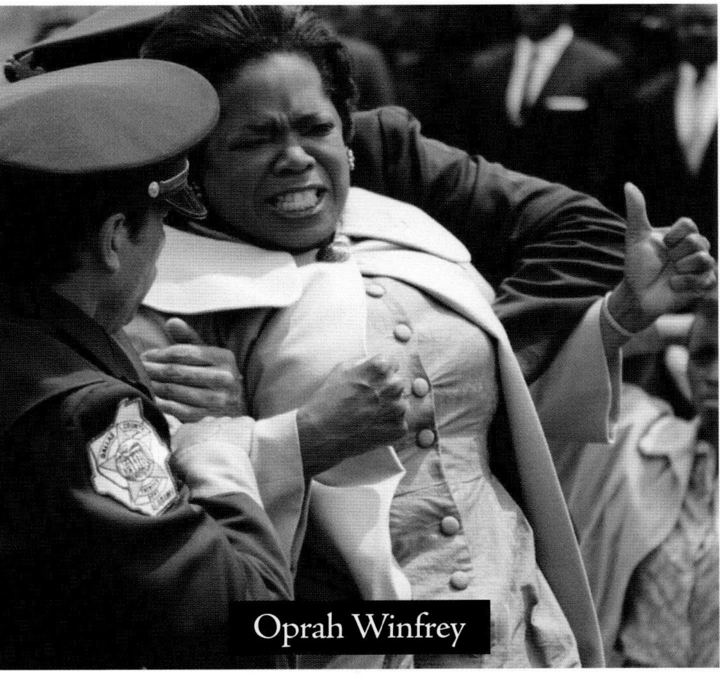
Oprah Winfrey

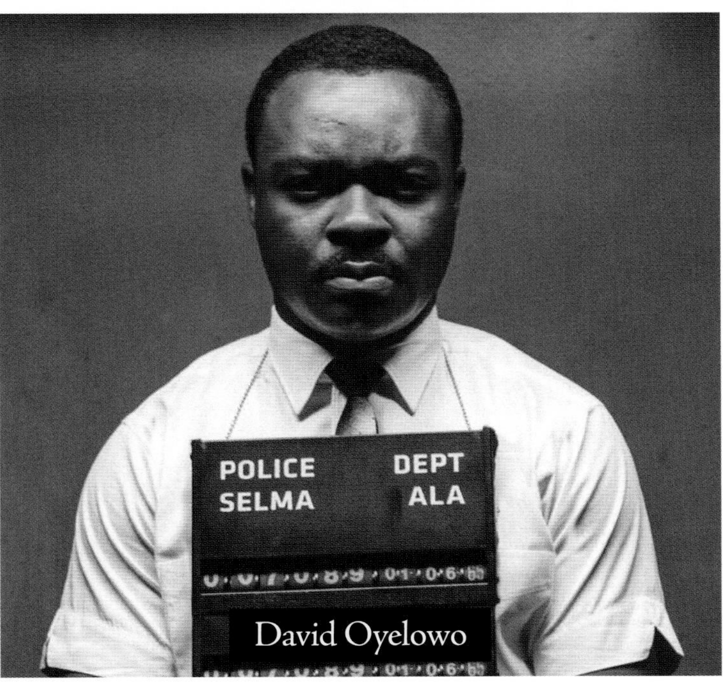

David Oyelowo

We've come a long way since Martin Luther King was in the forefront of the civil rights movement, but sadly there is still a long way to go and our current President is making the long way to go even longer.

Mr. Trump, in case you didn't know, in 1968, three years after Dr. King, an African-American, was arrested, he was shot and killed by James Earl Ray, a white racist. The balcony of The Lorraine Motel, on which Dr. King was murdered, is now the site of the National Civil Rights Museum.

A look at the relationship between the famous physicist Stephen Hawking and his wife.

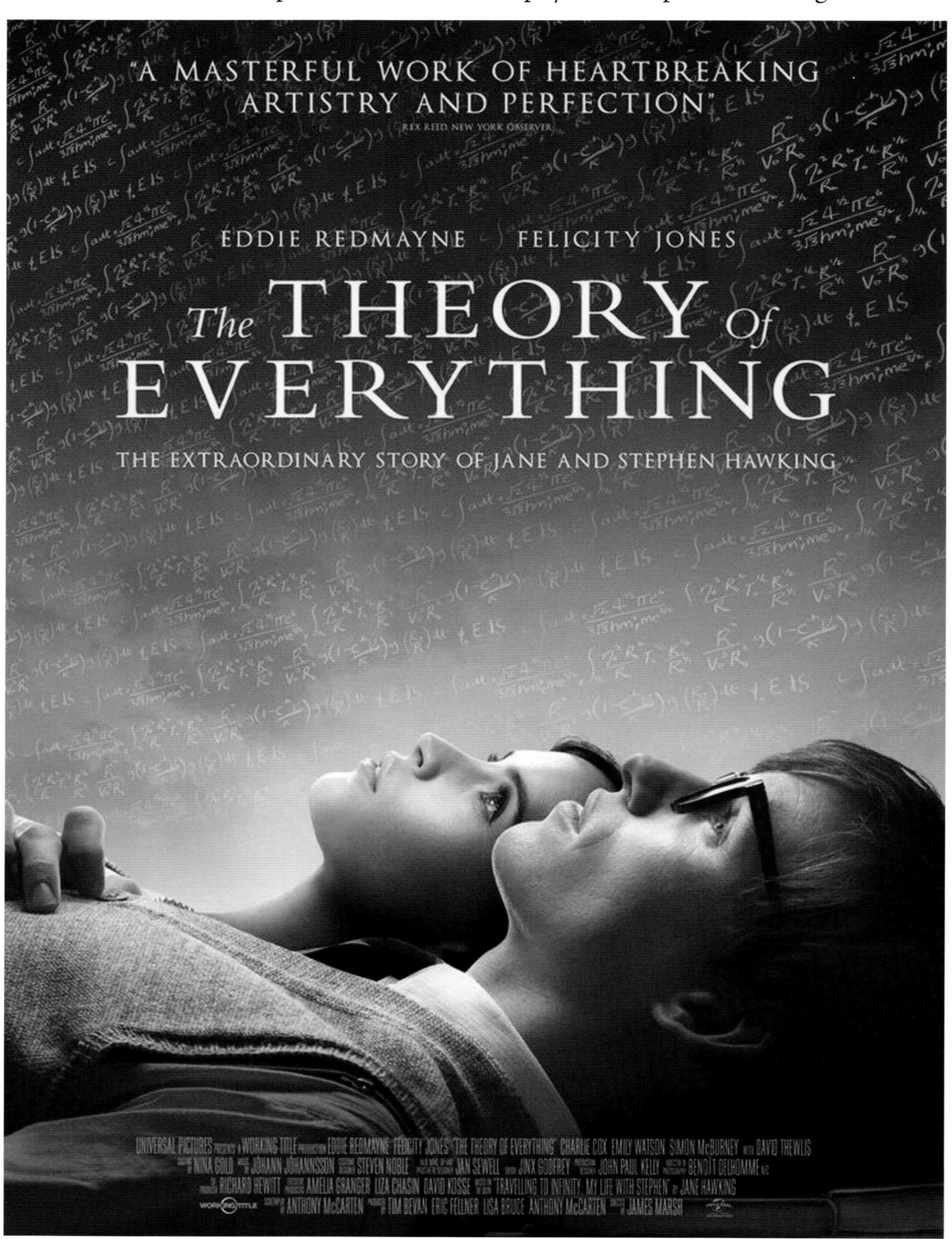

Jim Slotek of Toronto Sun wrote: "There's a mischievous quality to Redmayne that seems a good match with the wit Hawking has always managed to convey with a raised eyebrow and a mechanically-voiced quip."

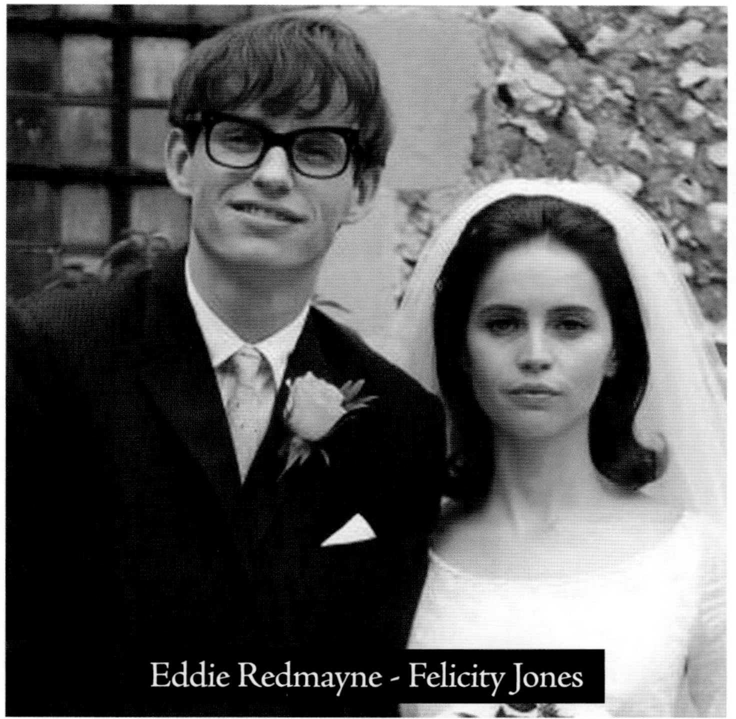
Eddie Redmayne - Felicity Jones

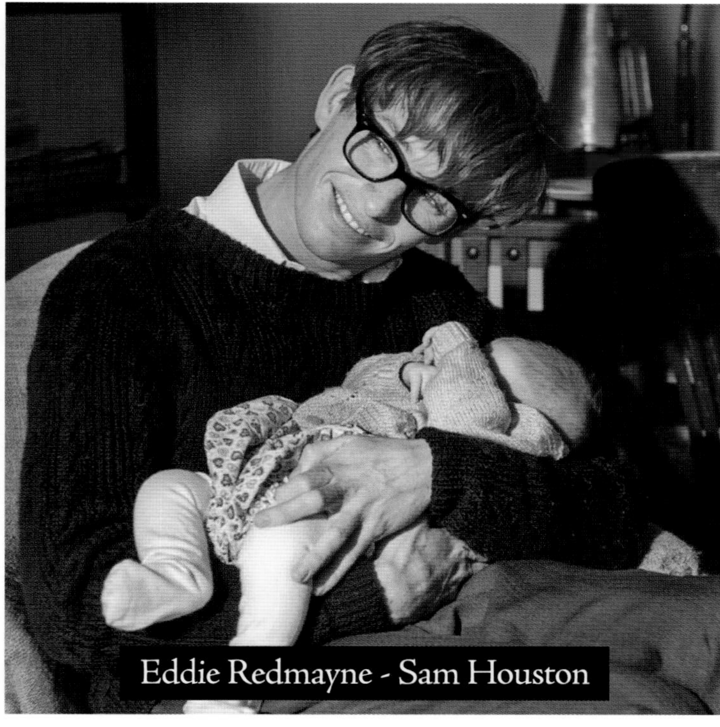
Eddie Redmayne - Sam Houston

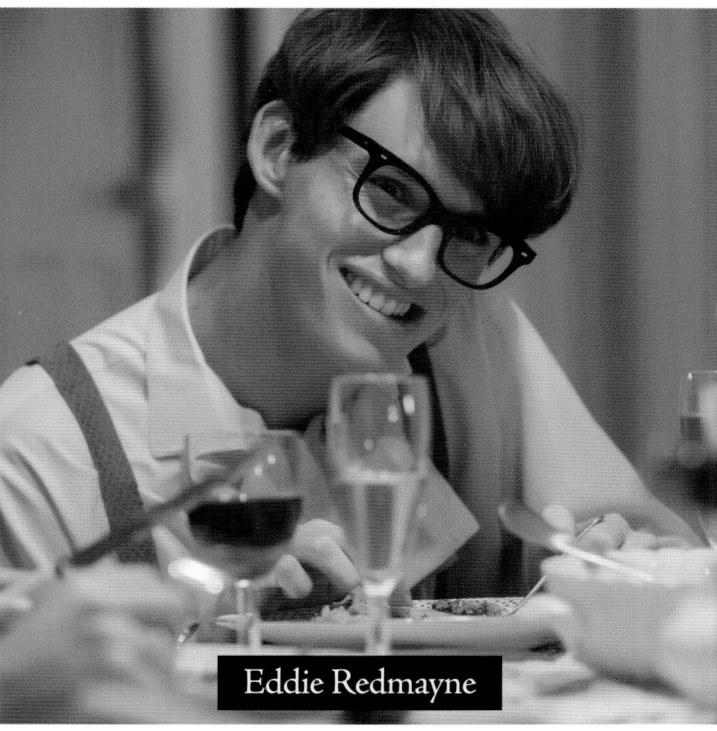
Eddie Redmayne

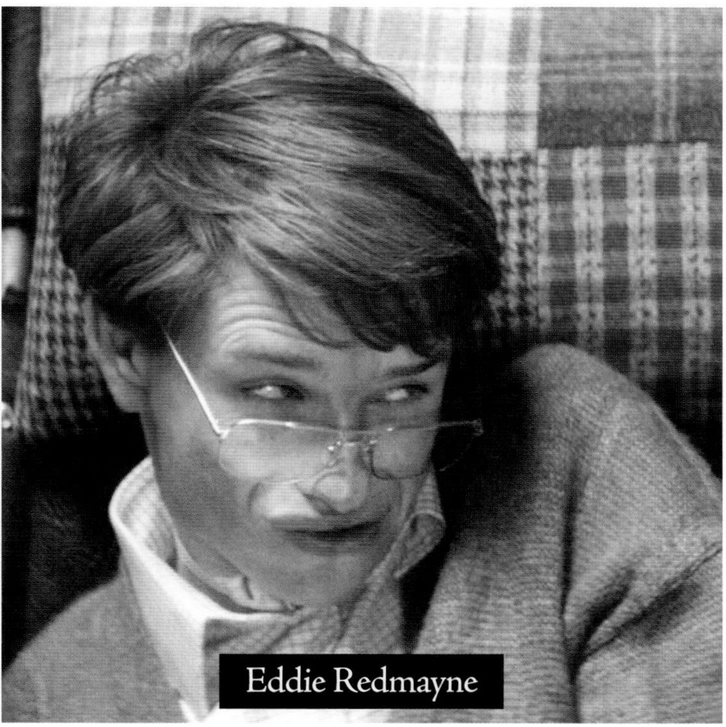
Eddie Redmayne

The brilliant theoretical physicist, Stephen Hawking, has warned that success in creating artificial intelligence would be the biggest event in human history and unless we learn how to avoid the risks it might also be the last event.

For his performance as Stephen Hawking, Eddie Redmayne was awarded the Oscar.

During the Cold War, an American lawyer is recruited to defend an arrested Soviet spy in court, and then help the CIA facilitate an exchange of the spy for the Soviet captured American U2 spy plane pilot, Francis Gary Powers.

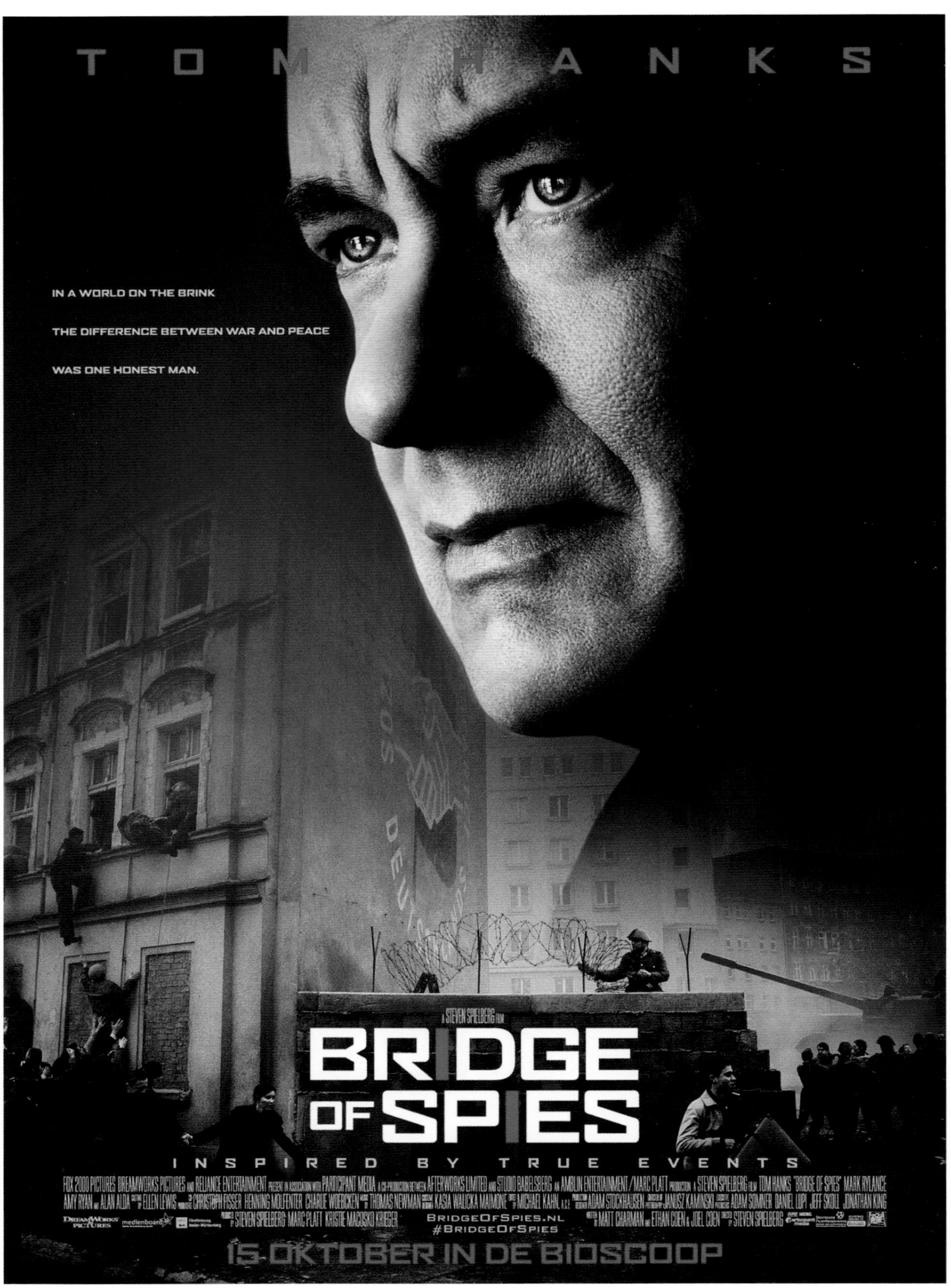

Anthony Lane of The New Yorker wrote: "When a film is as enjoyable as this one, its timing so sweet, and its atmosphere conjured with such skill, do you really wish to register a complaint? Would it help?"

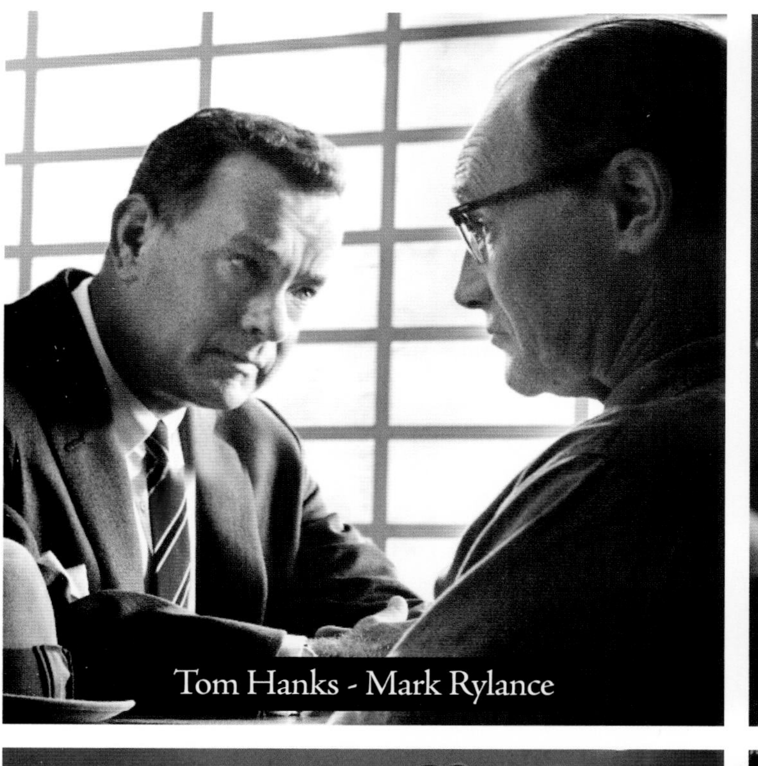
Tom Hanks - Mark Rylance

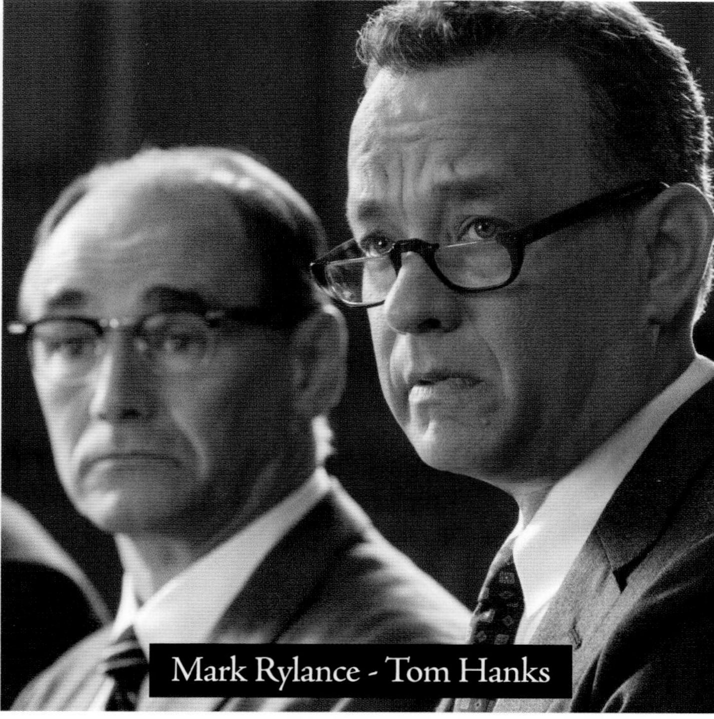
Mark Rylance - Tom Hanks

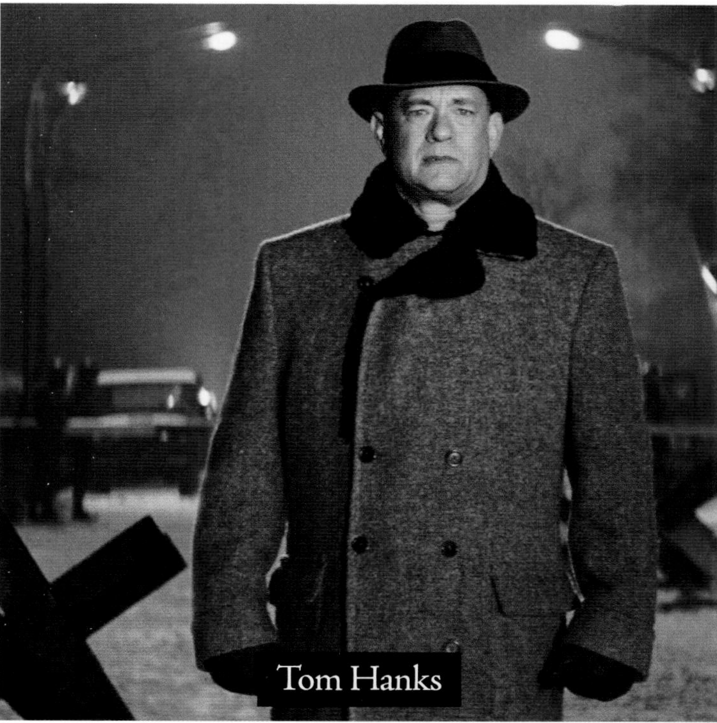
Tom Hanks

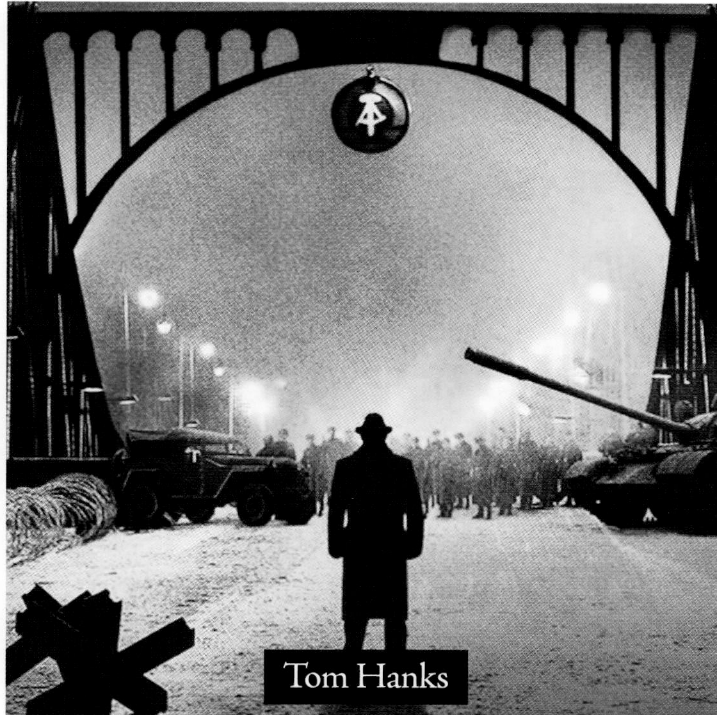
Tom Hanks

After seeing this movie, I thought, *Now, that was a perfect movie! Besides being perfectly written, perfectly directed, it was perfectly cast with Tom Hanks*, who, so far, has won Oscars for his performances in "Forrest Gump" and "Philadelphia." I feel a third might be forthcoming... or at least a nomination.

The true story of how the Boston Globe uncovered the massive scandal of child molestation and cover-up within the local Catholic Archdiocese, shaking the entire Catholic Church to its core.

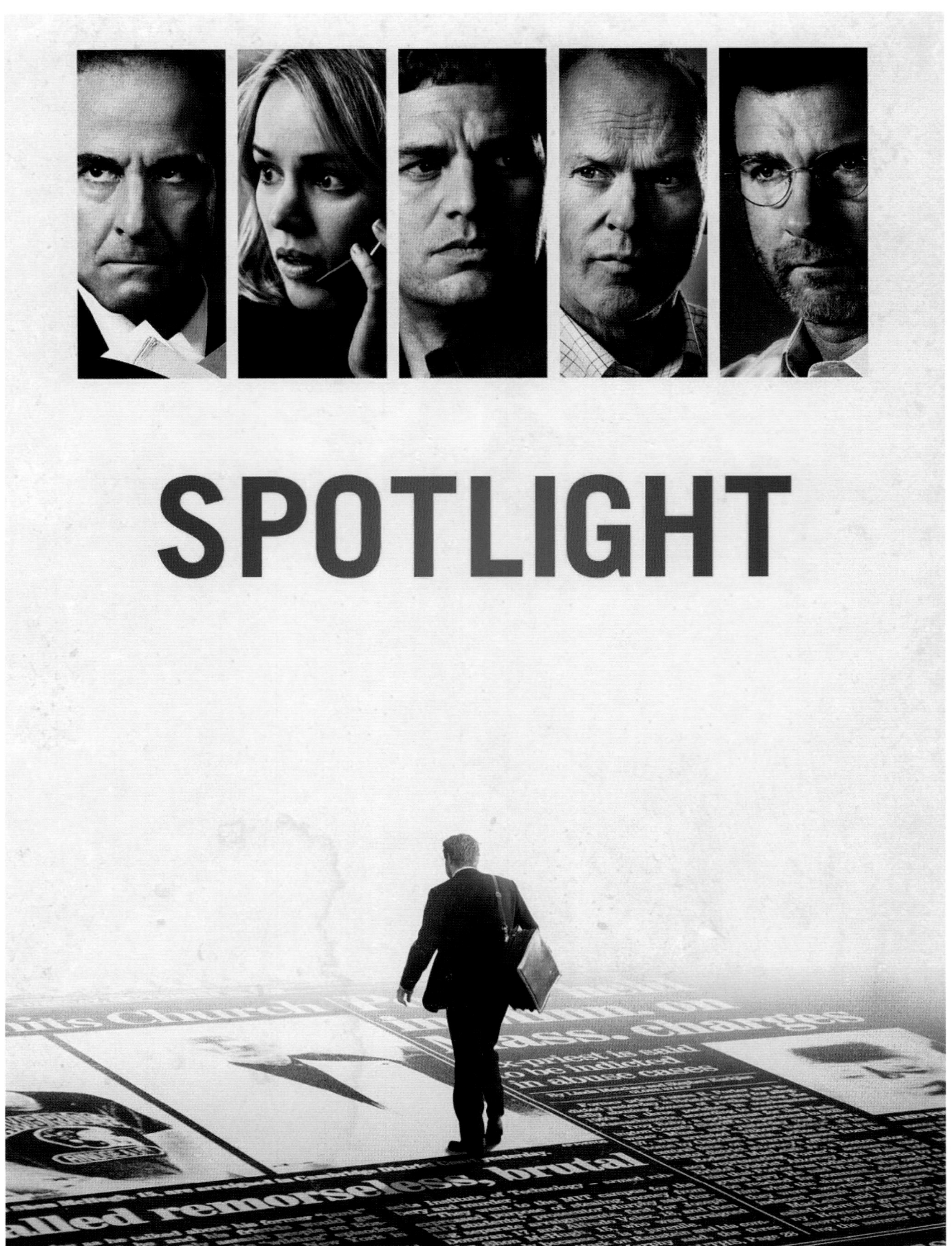

Christy Lemire of ChristyLemire.com wrote: "Like the story being reported within the film, 'Spotlight' is simultaneously emotional and clear-eyed. It's an explosive yet necessary piece of journalism in and of itself. And it's easily one of the year's best."

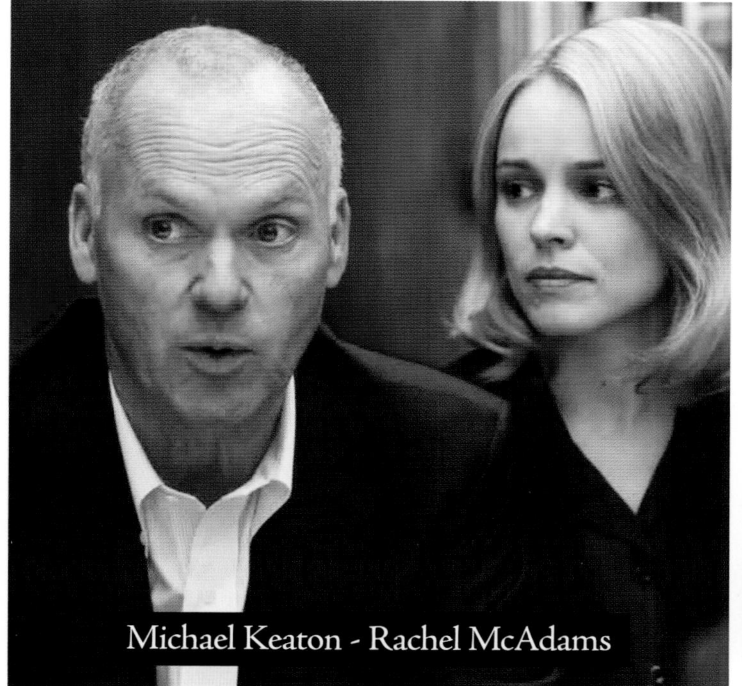

Michael Keaton - Rachel McAdams

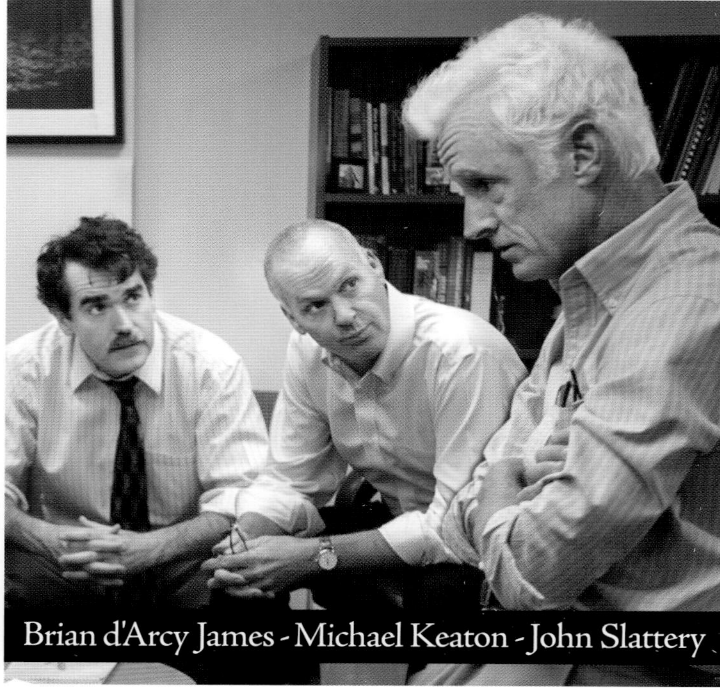

Brian d'Arcy James - Michael Keaton - John Slattery

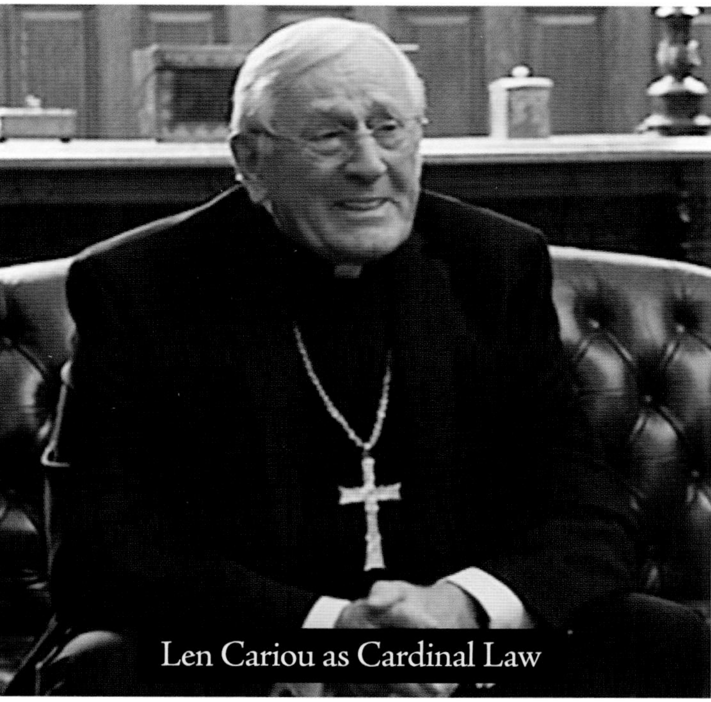

Len Cariou as Cardinal Law

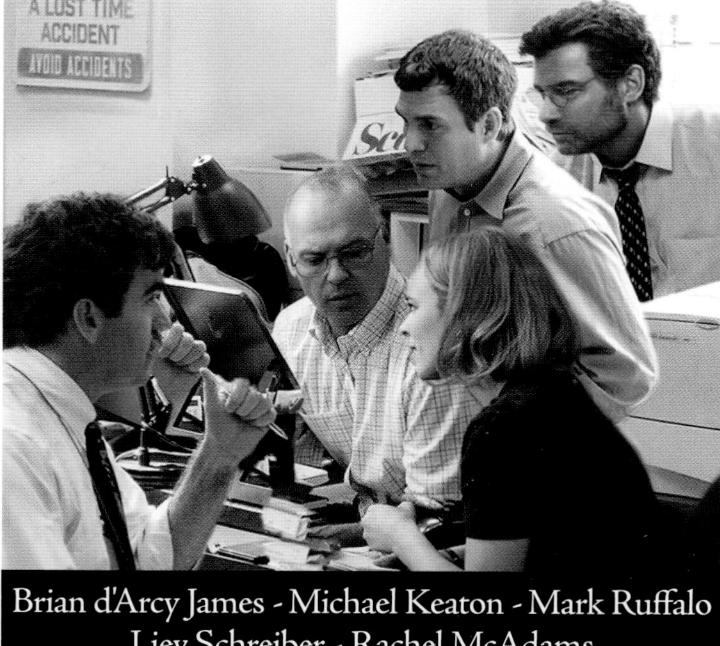

Brian d'Arcy James - Michael Keaton - Mark Ruffalo
Liev Schreiber - Rachel McAdams

The Boston Globe's reporting had a positive effect as it exposed the pedophilia that was being practiced world-wide by a burgeoning number of ordained priests. It was estimated that 4,392 Catholic priests have been accused of sexual abuse by 10,667 victims. Subsequent action by the church leaders triggered a series of reforms that changed the priests' behavior and ultimately renewed the trust of their congregations.

Charlie, a troublesome 18-year-old, breaks out of a youth drug treatment clinic and returns home to Los Angeles where he faces an intervention and is sent to an adult rehab. There, he meets a beautiful, troubled girl, Eva, and is forced to battle with drugs, elusive love and divided parents.

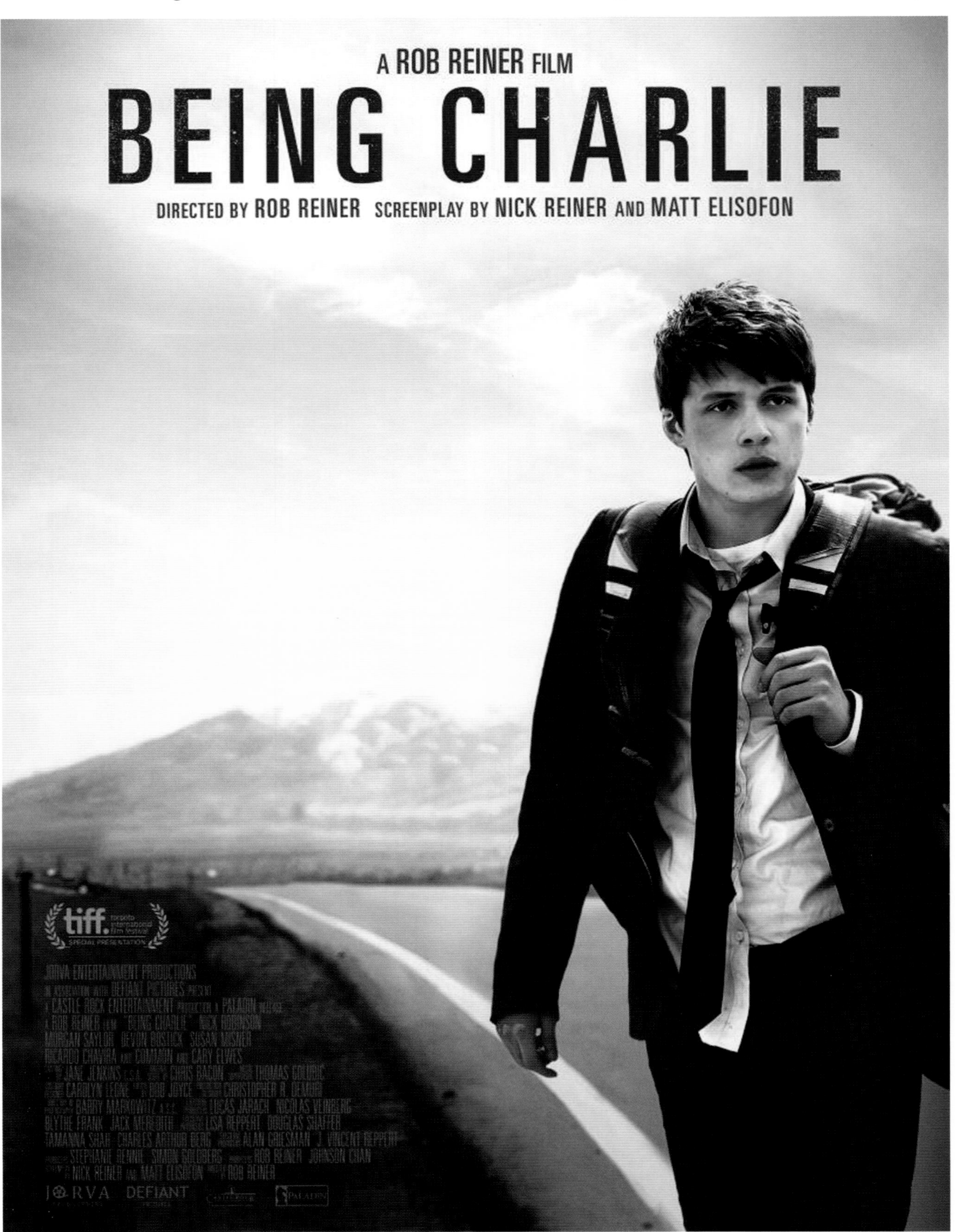

Rex Reed of The New York Observer wrote: "The film is so personal that you watch transfixed, caught up in a life that is constantly enthralling, with a universal appeal that extends beyond the exclusive Hills of Beverly."

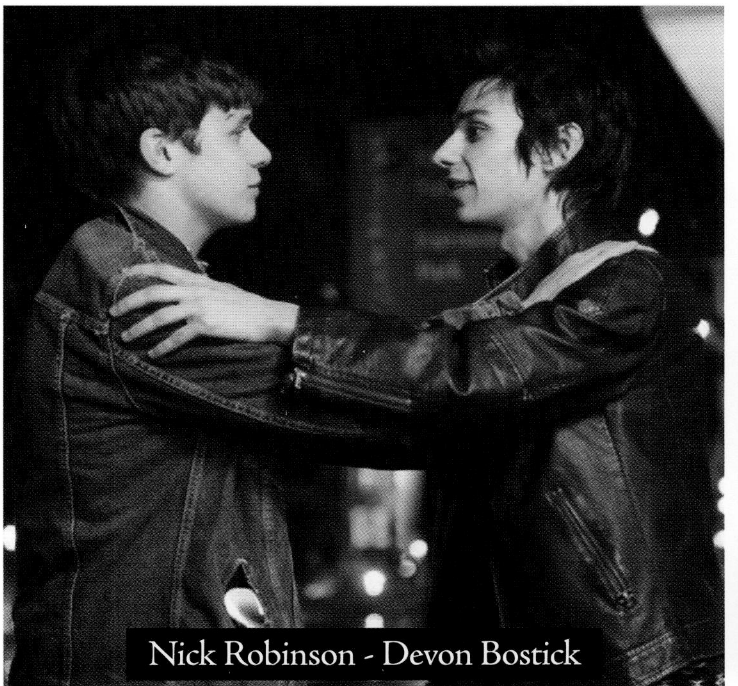
Nick Robinson - Devon Bostick

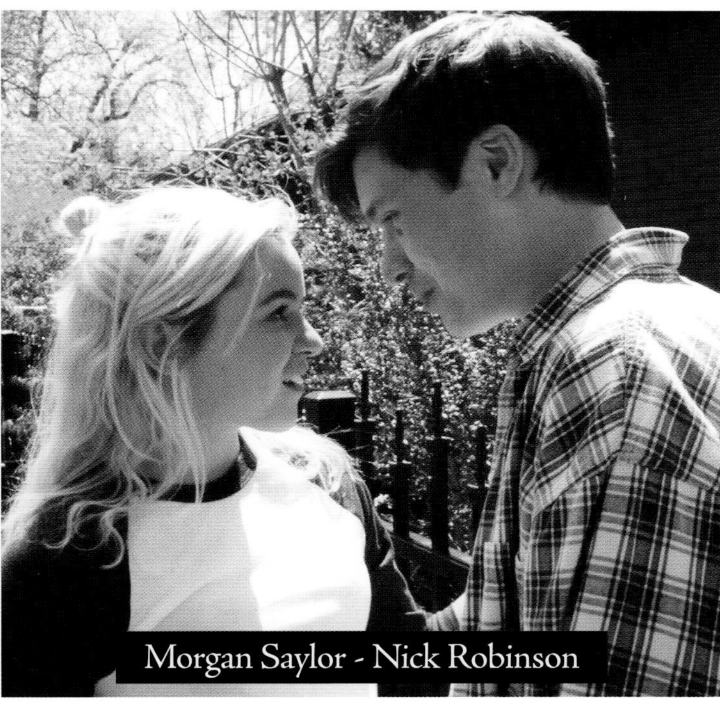
Morgan Saylor - Nick Robinson

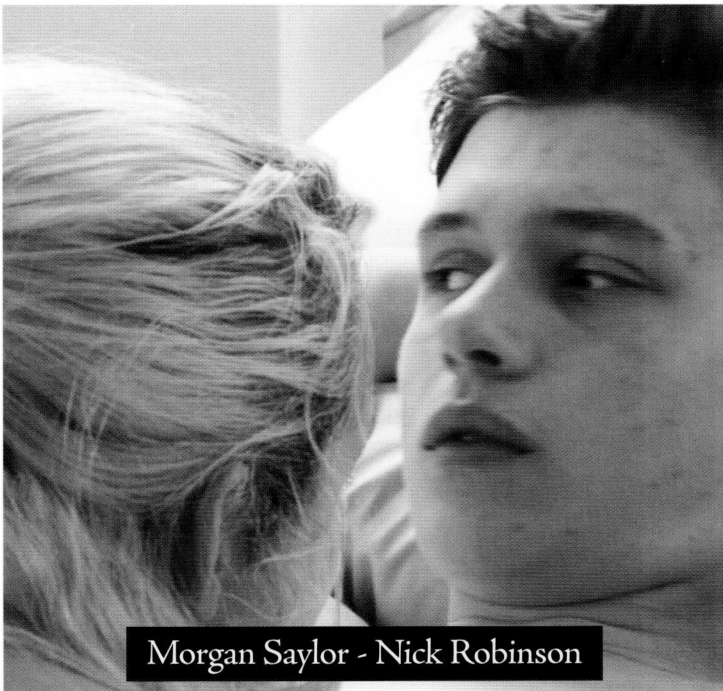
Morgan Saylor - Nick Robinson

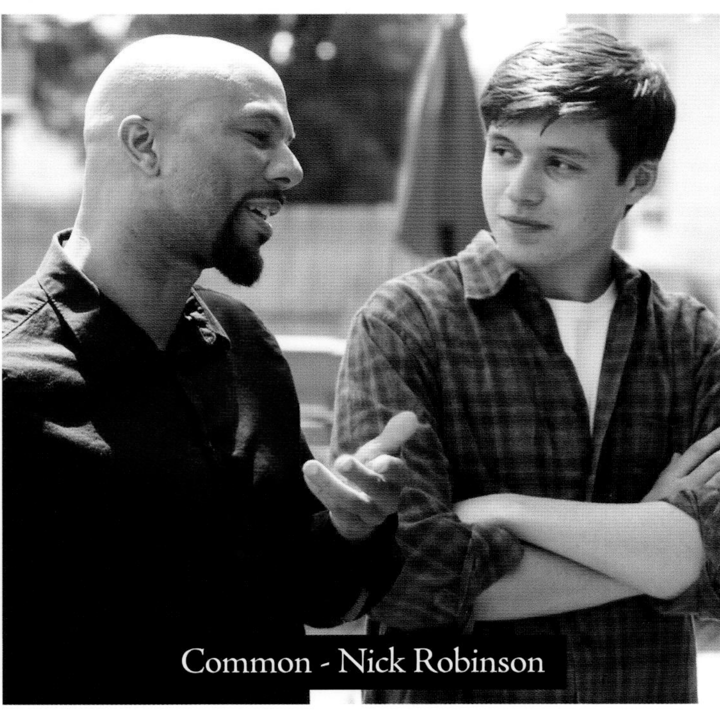
Common - Nick Robinson

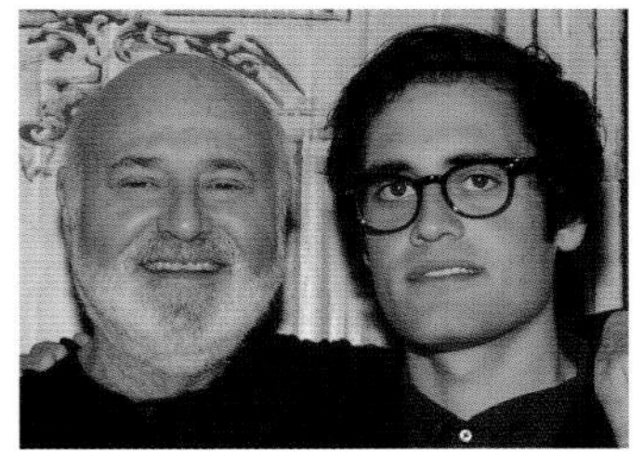

Being the grandfather of the author of a film that depicted his youthful addiction to drugs made it painful to watch but ultimately, after seeing him struggle successfully to conquer his problem, it was elating.

Nick Reiner continues to write films and TV and his father continues to make highly entertaining and informative movies.

A working-class African-American father tries to raise his family in the 1950s, while coming to terms with the events of his life.

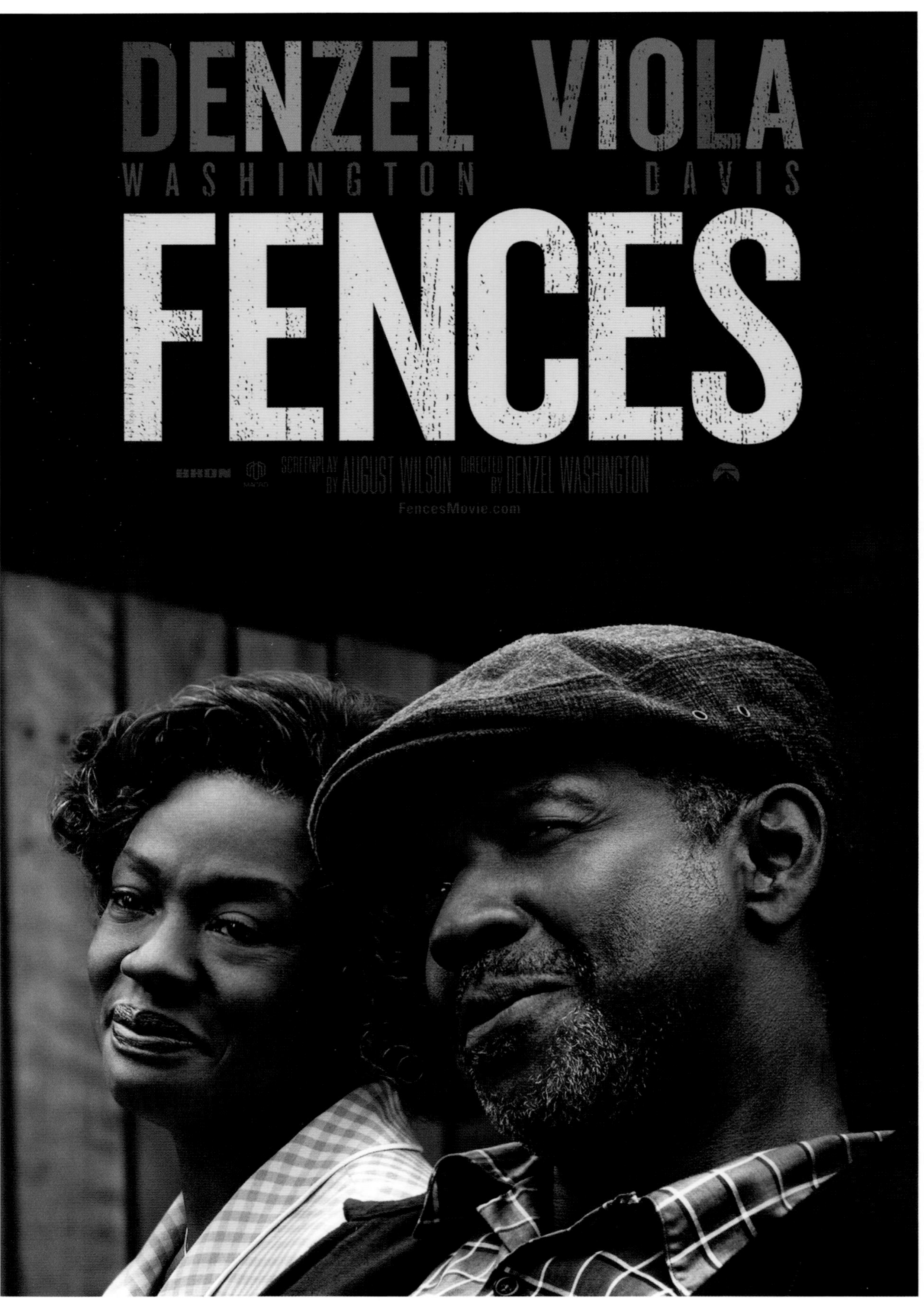

Katie Walsh of Tribune News wrote: "The two lead performances are stunningly complex and deeply human achievements from two of the finest actors working today."

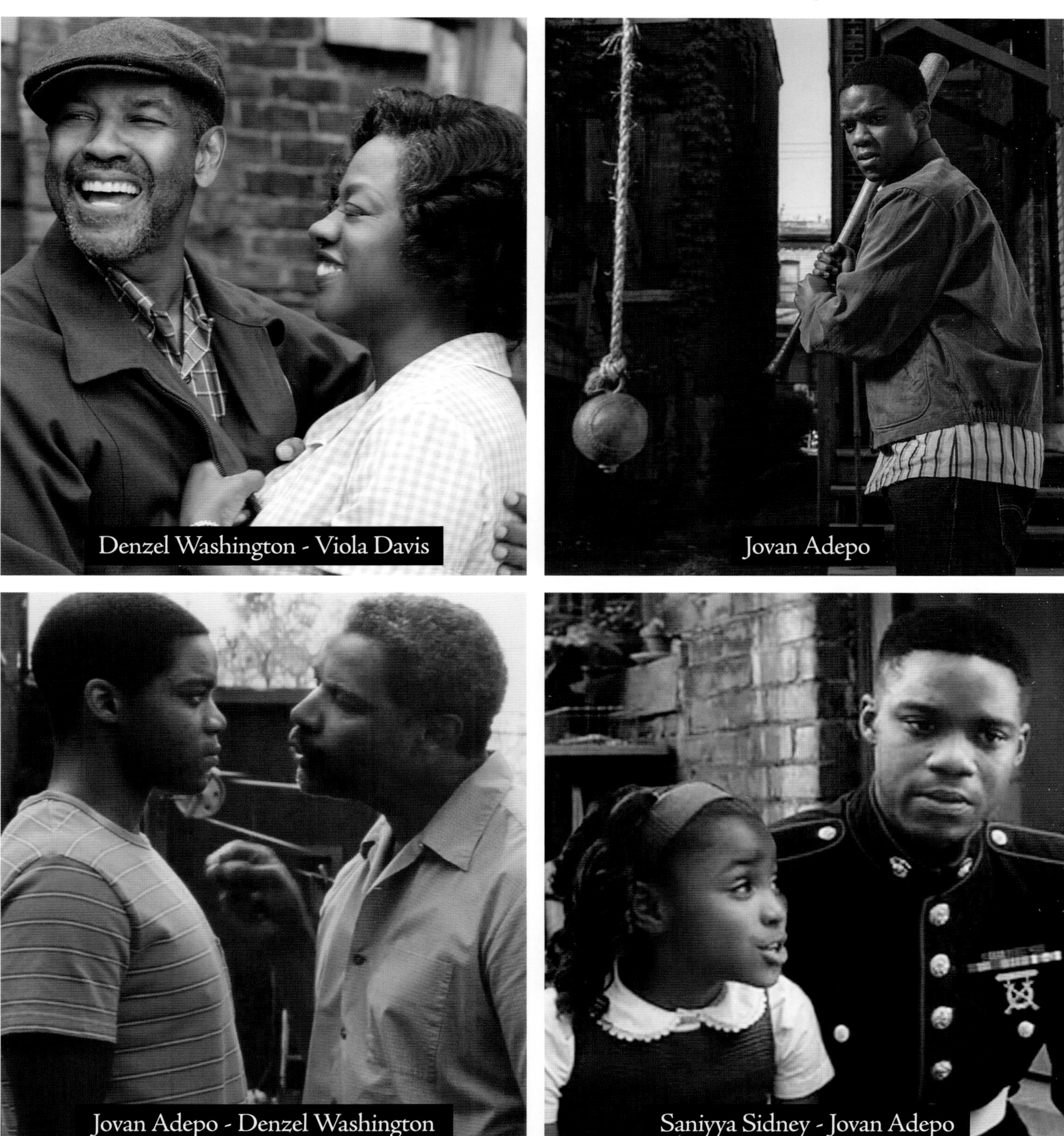

Denzel Washington - Viola Davis

Jovan Adepo

Jovan Adepo - Denzel Washington

Saniyya Sidney - Jovan Adepo

The two fine actors that the reviewer mentioned, Denzel Washington and Viola Davis, are two actors whose work I've always admired. In this film they were shining a light on the racial inequality that still exists even though President Trump denies that it does.

The story of Florence Foster Jenkins, a New York heiress who dreamed of becoming an opera singer, despite having a terrible singing voice.

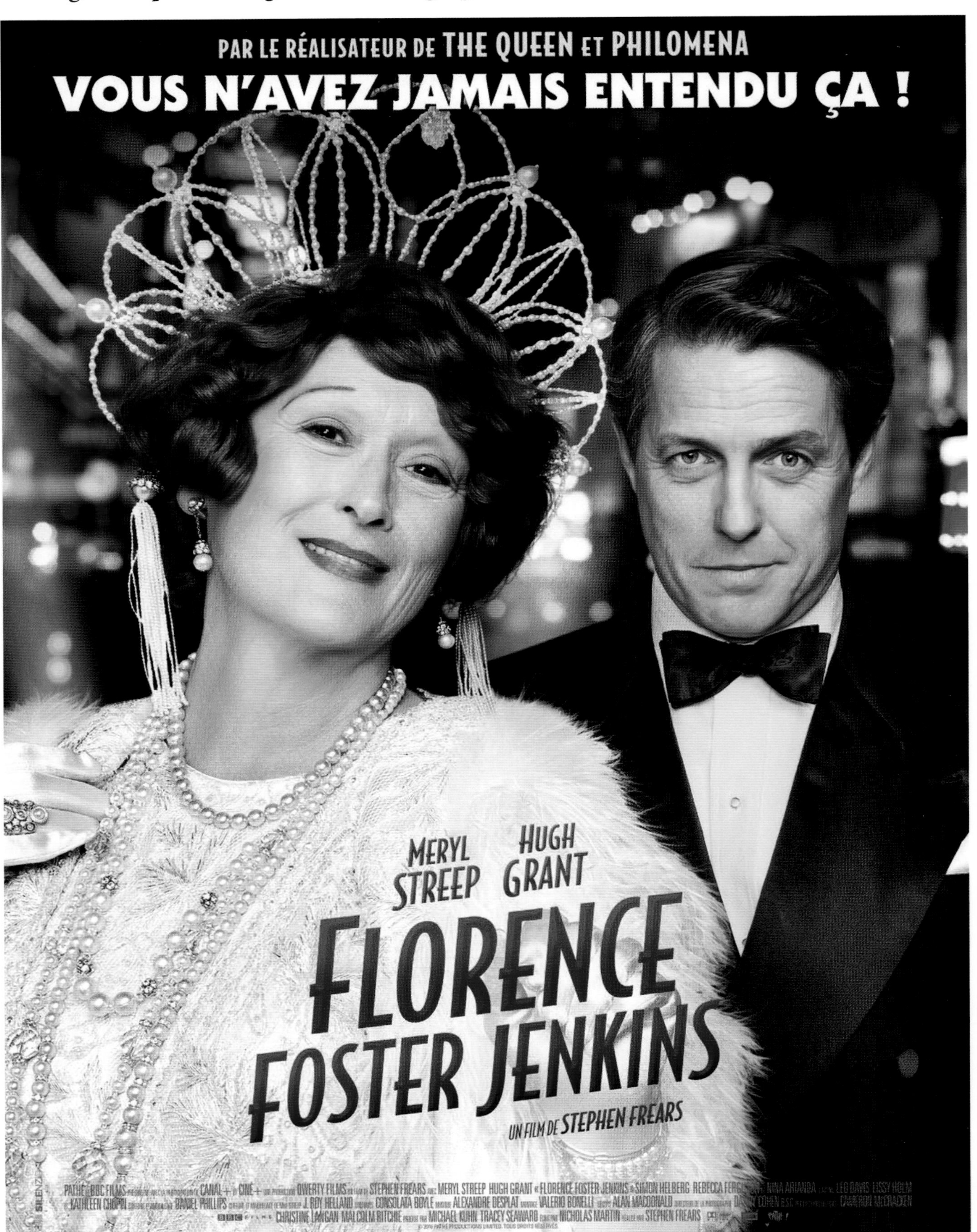

Oliver Jones of New York Observer wrote: "A comic lark that packs a satisfying emotional wallop and continues the balls-to-the-wall career victory lap Meryl Streep has been on since turning 60 years old seven years ago."

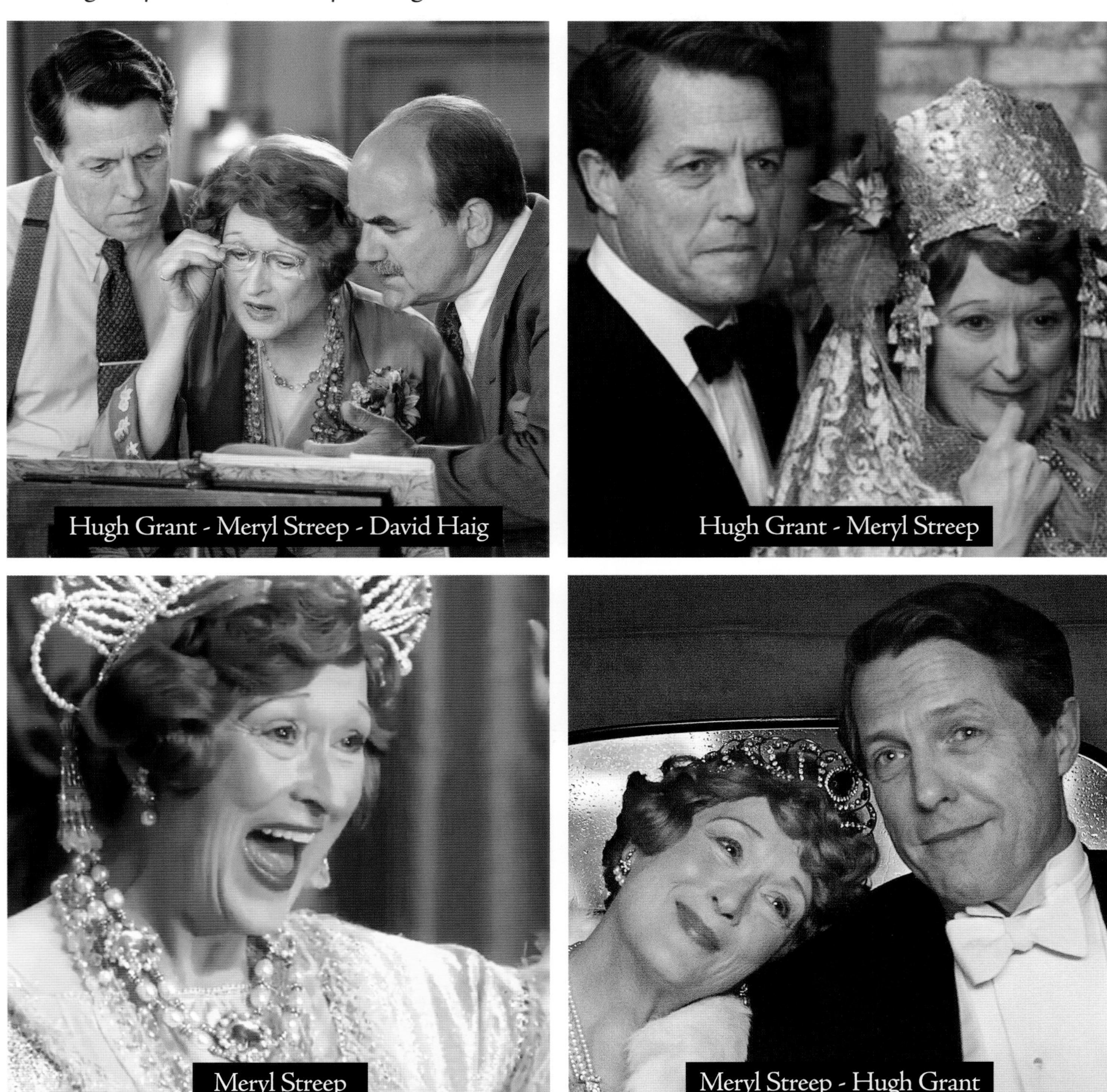

Hugh Grant - Meryl Streep - David Haig

Hugh Grant - Meryl Streep

Meryl Streep

Meryl Streep - Hugh Grant

Meryl Streep won three Oscars and was nominated seventeen times. I expect that before she retires, those numbers will increase.

As Florence Foster Jenkins, Meryl Streep demonstrated her ability to sing further off key than any soprano in history! This is one of the many reasons I'm so in love with Meryl.

The story of a team of female African-American mathematicians who served a vital role in NASA during the early years of the U.S. space program.

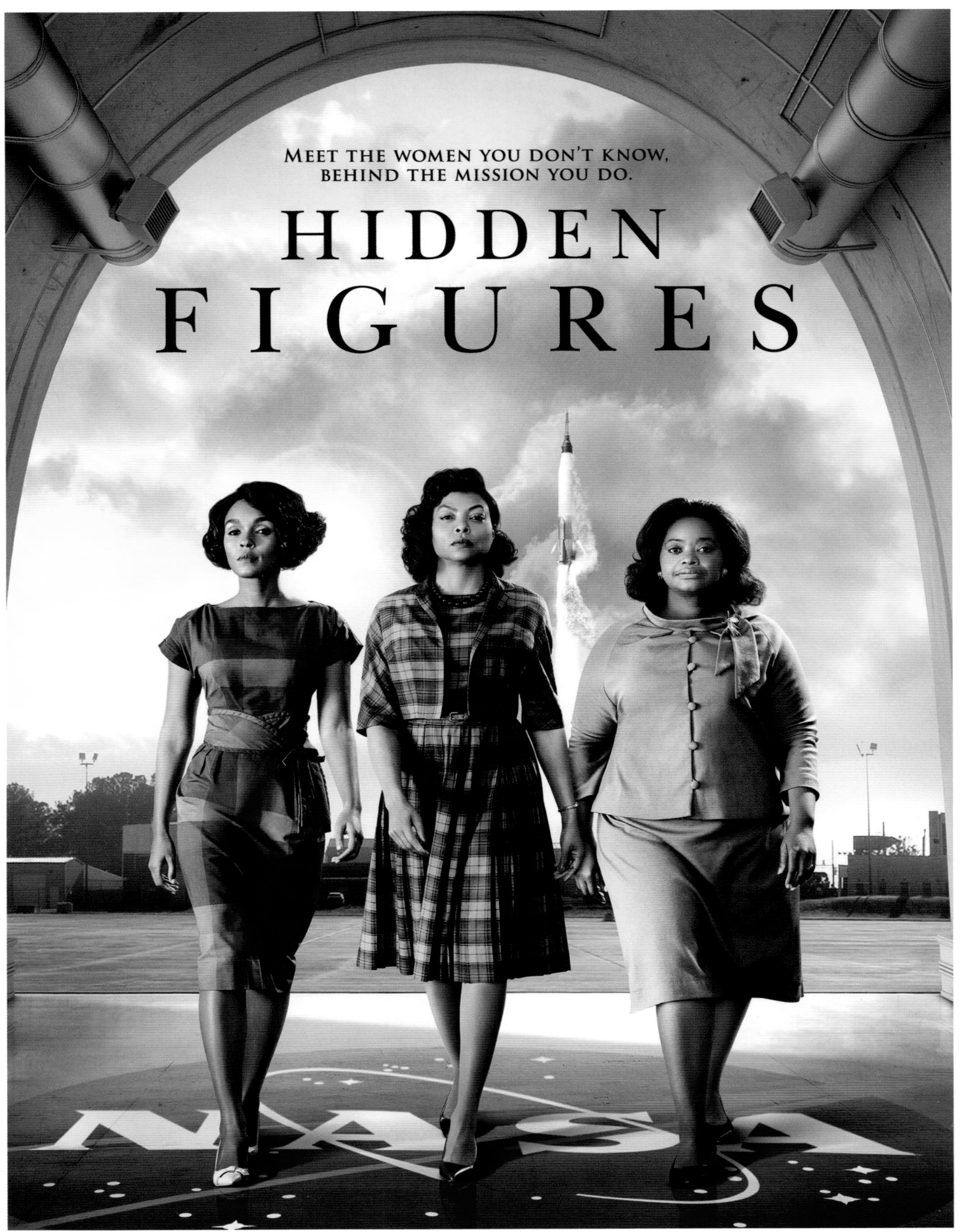

Joe Morgenstern of Wall Street Journal wrote: "The film hews closely to the facts in important respects, and evokes the outrages of the Jim Crow era, as well as the feverish competition of the space race, through the fascinating work of its extraordinary heroines."

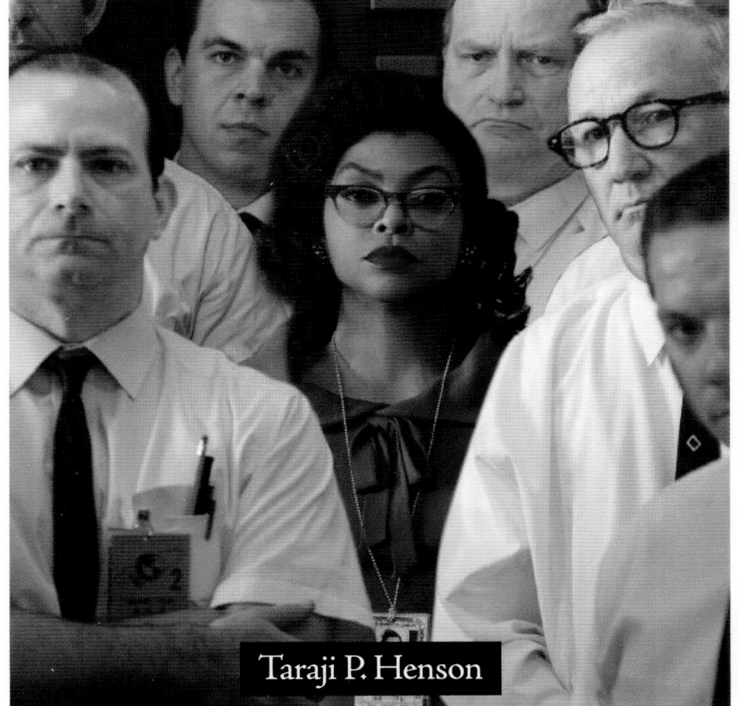
Taraji P. Henson

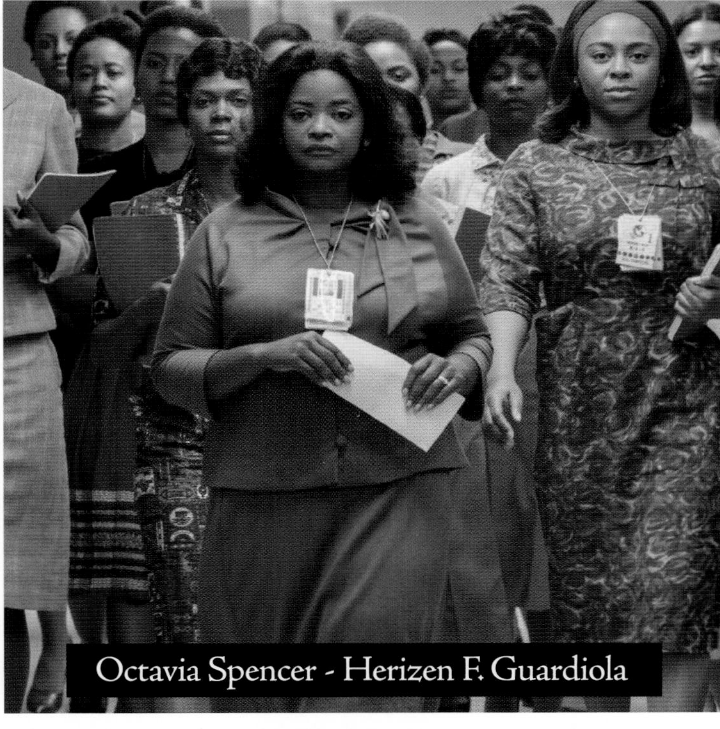
Octavia Spencer - Herizen F. Guardiola

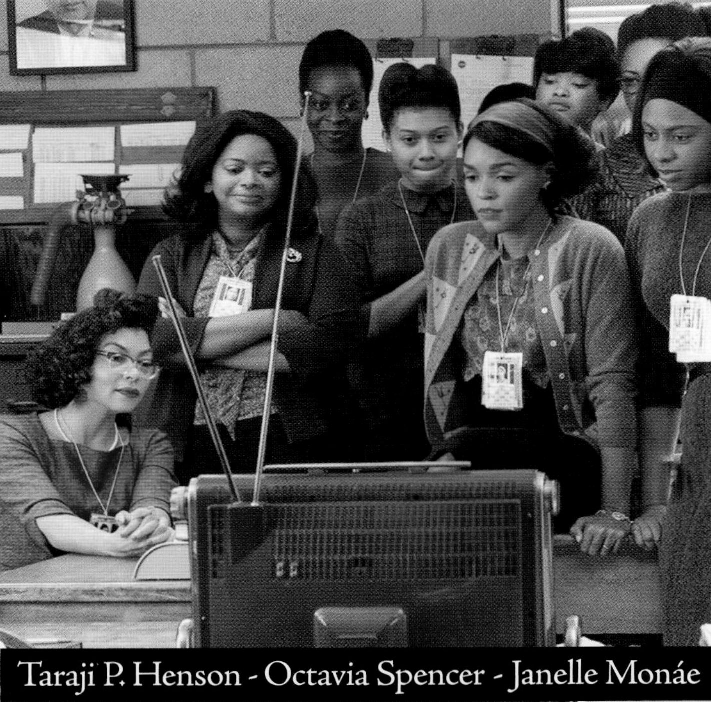
Taraji P. Henson - Octavia Spencer - Janelle Monáe

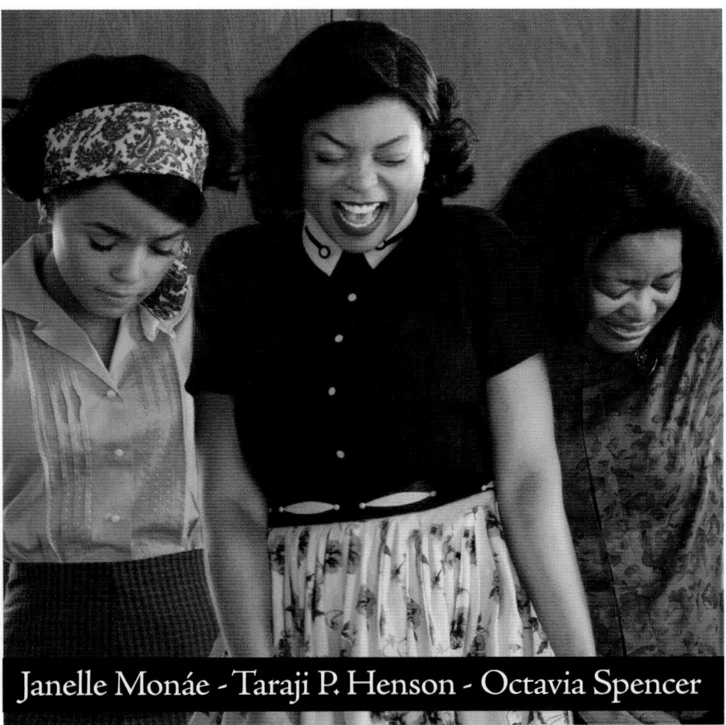
Janelle Monáe - Taraji P. Henson - Octavia Spencer

The efforts of Mary Jackson, Katherine Johnson and Dorothy Vaughan, three African-American women mathematicians, made for a successful space experiment that helped launch the Mercury flight, making John Glenn the first American to orbit the Earth.

I am looking forward to whatever film Taraji P. Henson decides to do next.

A jazz pianist falls for an aspiring actress in Los Angeles.

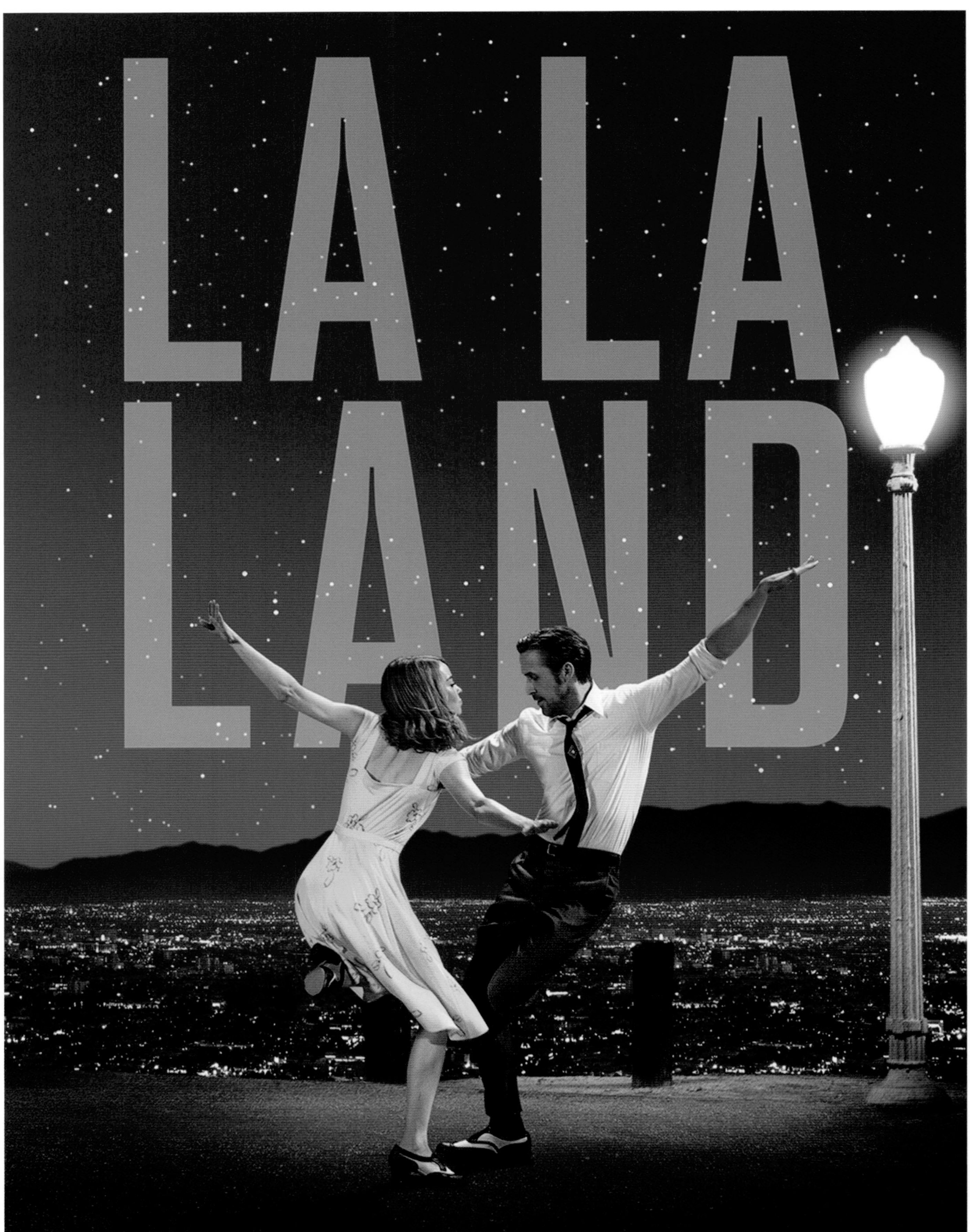

Gary Kramer of Salon.com wrote: "'La La Land' is a worthy showcase for the magnificent Stone's talents, and she is heartbreaking throughout."

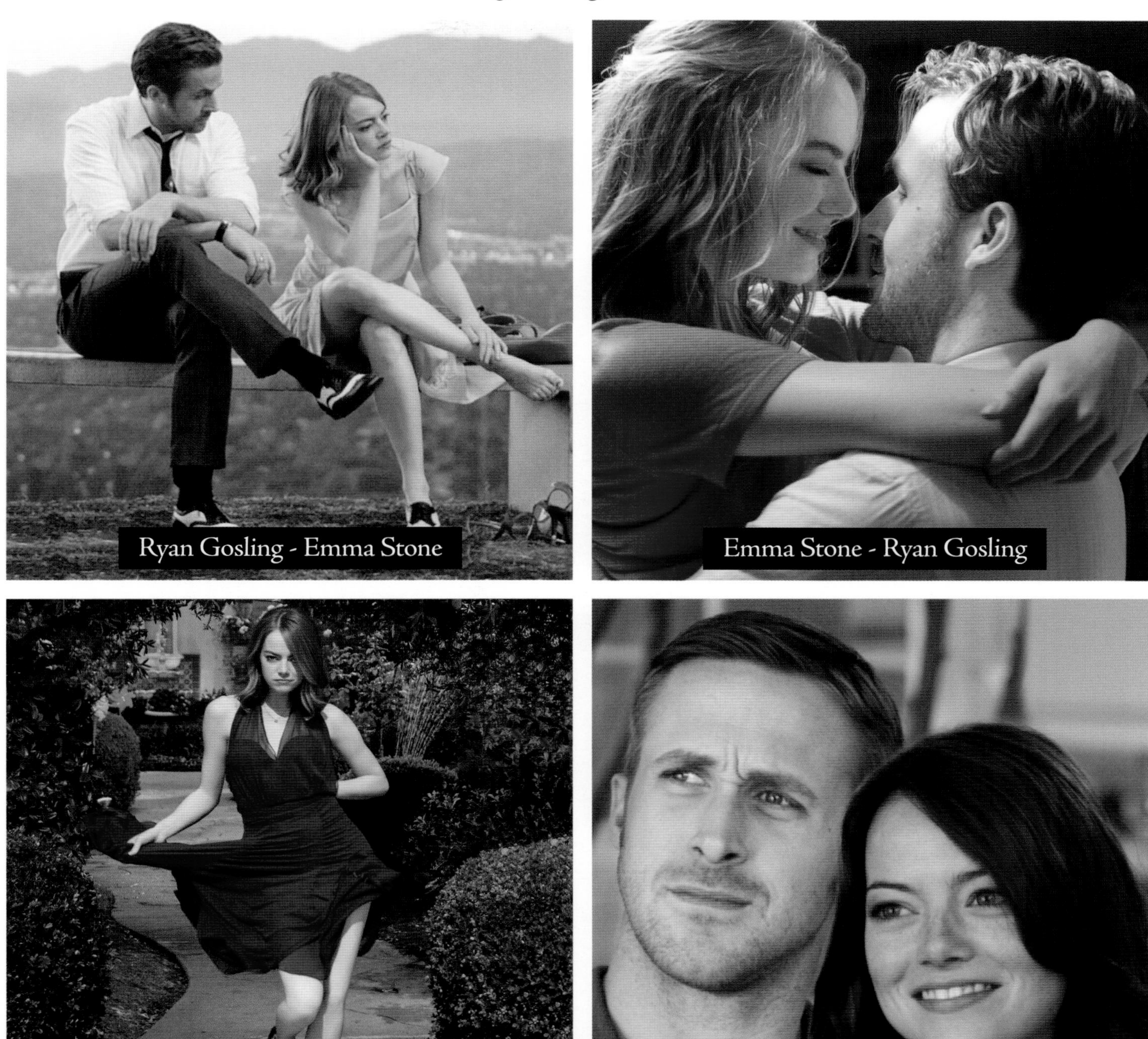

Ryan Gosling - Emma Stone

Emma Stone - Ryan Gosling

Emma Stone

Ryan Gosling - Emma Stone

Emma Stone and Ryan Gosling's opening number was utterly delightful and it was hard to believe that neither had ever before danced. After cramming in six months of tap and ballroom lessons, they became a road show version of Debbie Reynolds and Gene Kelly.

I read this morning that adorable Emma Stone, who deserves to be, is the highest paid actress in the world.

A five-year-old Indian boy gets lost thousands of kilometers from home and is adopted by a couple in Australia. Twenty-five years later, he sets out to find his lost family.

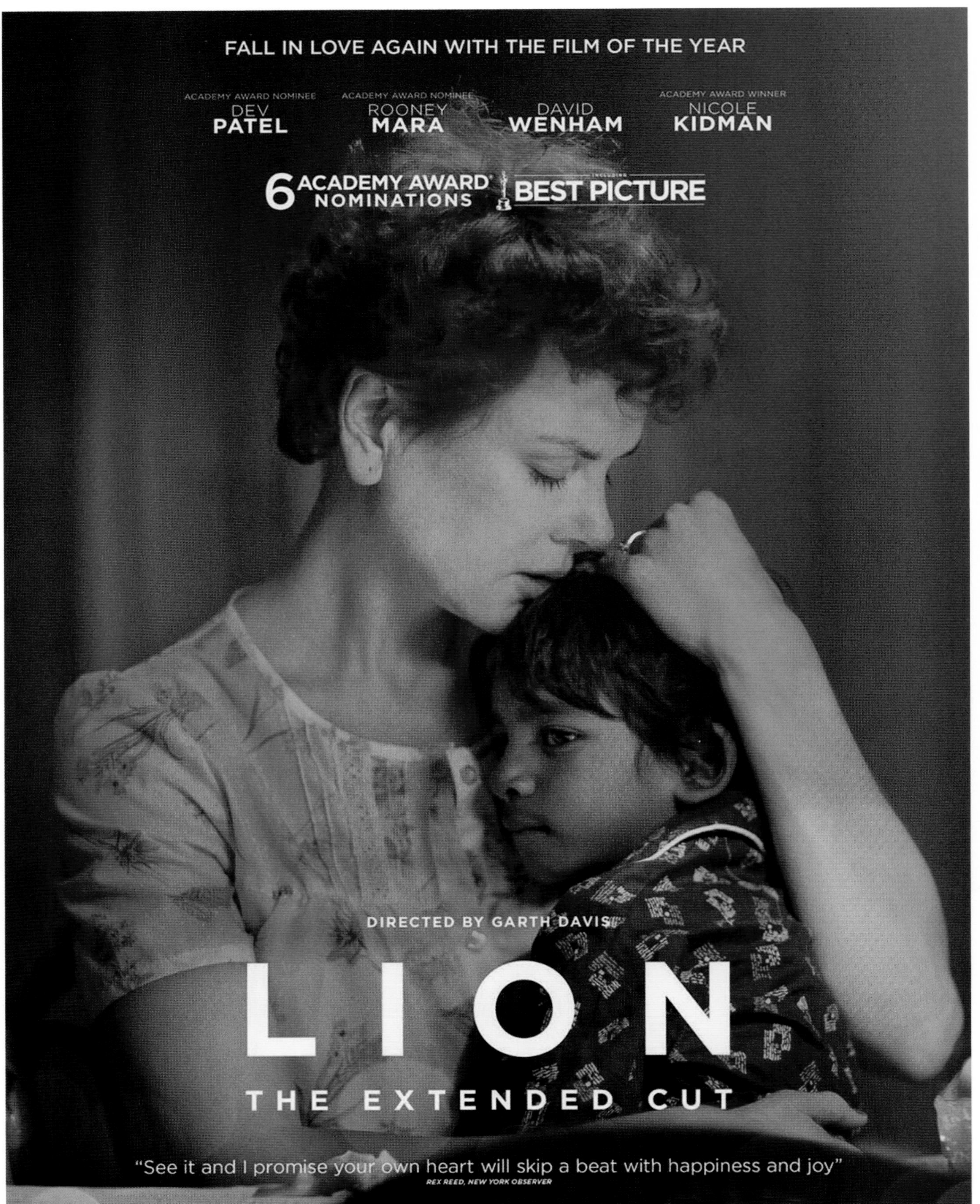

Adam Graham of Detroit News wrote: "Its themes are universal. Everyone has a home, and everyone feels connected to it, no matter how far they travel."

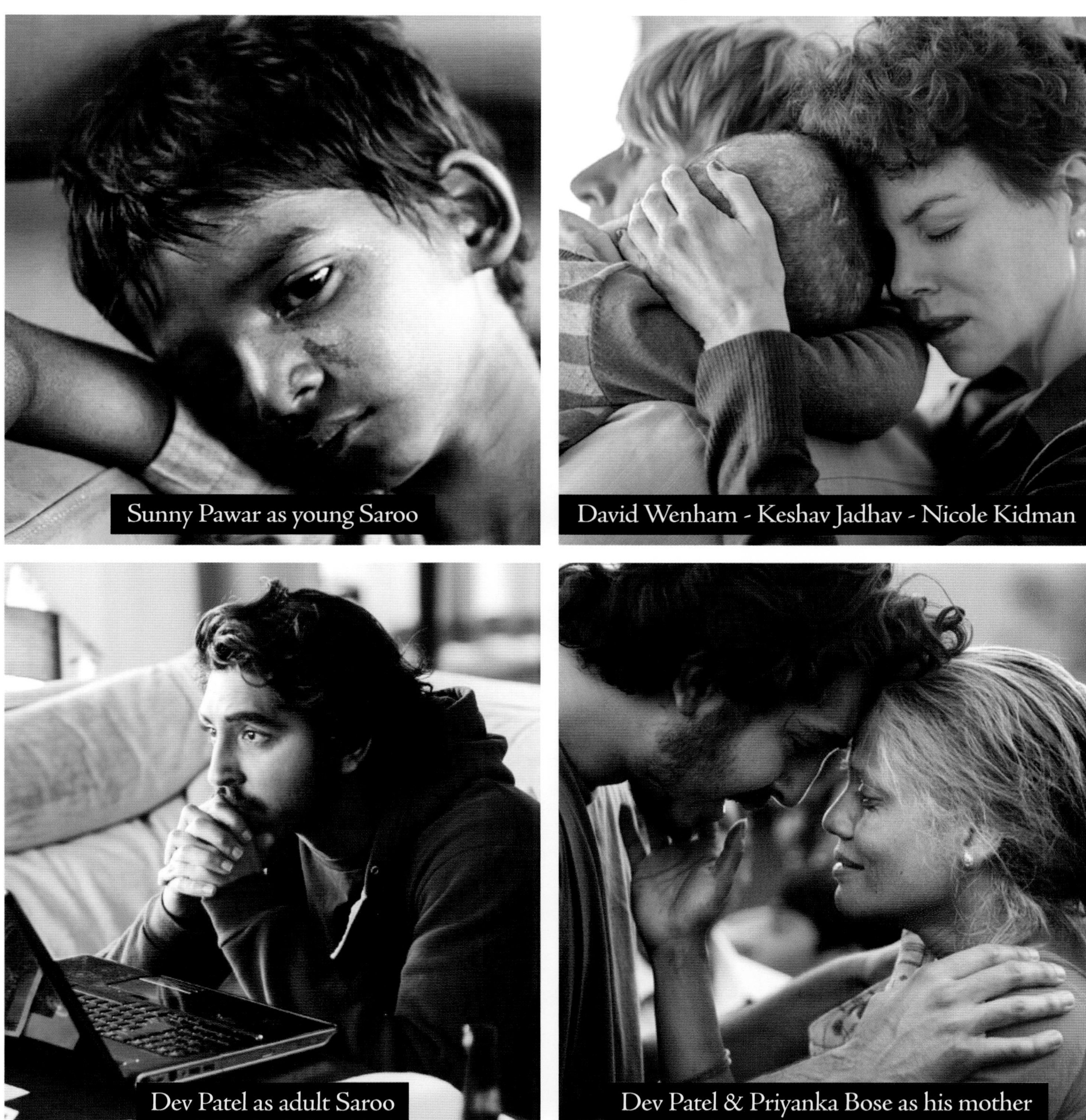

Sunny Pawar as young Saroo

David Wenham - Keshav Jadhav - Nicole Kidman

Dev Patel as adult Saroo

Dev Patel & Priyanka Bose as his mother

Six year old Sunny Pawar gives an astonishing performance as Young Saroo. His character, who is accidentally abandoned at four years of age, grows into a young adult. Saroo searches for and reconnects with his mother who has been dreaming of and waiting for his return.

At the film's end, there wasn't a dry eye on my face or any face in the audience.

Pakistan-born comedian Kumail Nanjiani and grad student Emily Gardner fall in love but struggle as their cultures clash. When Emily contracts a mysterious illness, Kumail finds himself forced to face her feisty parents, his family's expectations, and his true feelings.

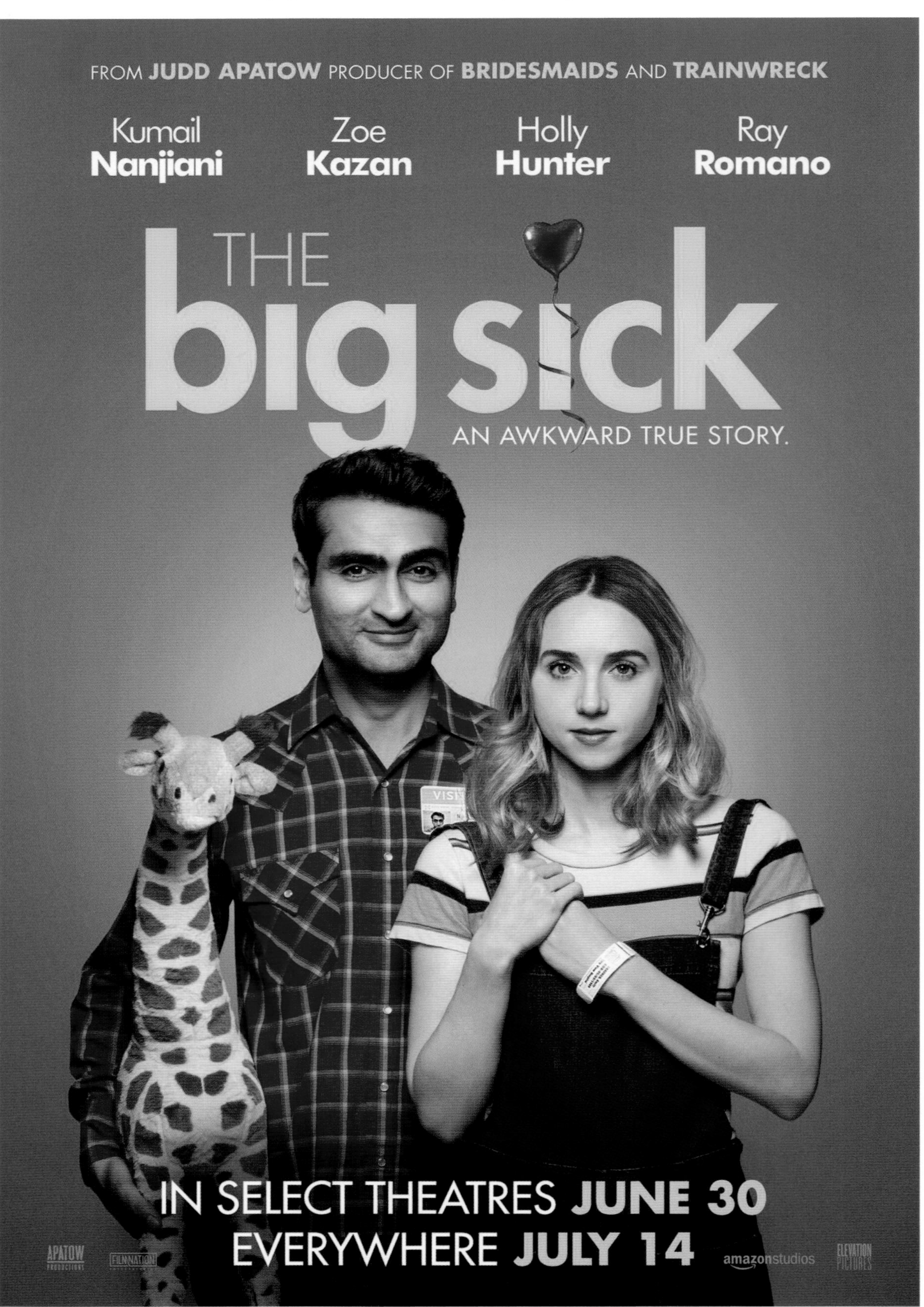

Adam Graham of The Detroit News wrote: "'The Big Sick' has a big heart and shows there are still corners left to explore in romantic comedies; it just takes someone willing to find them."

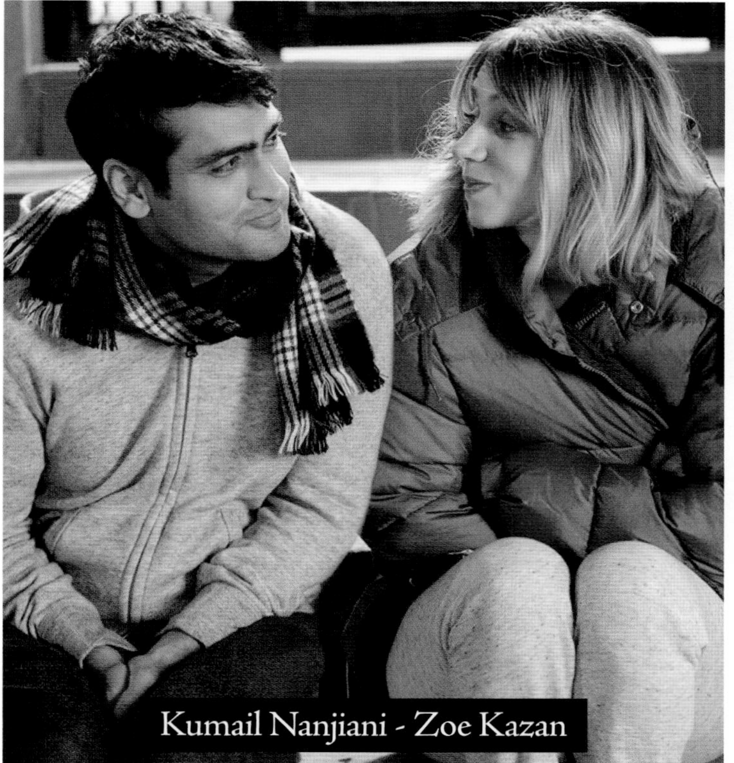
Kumail Nanjiani - Zoe Kazan

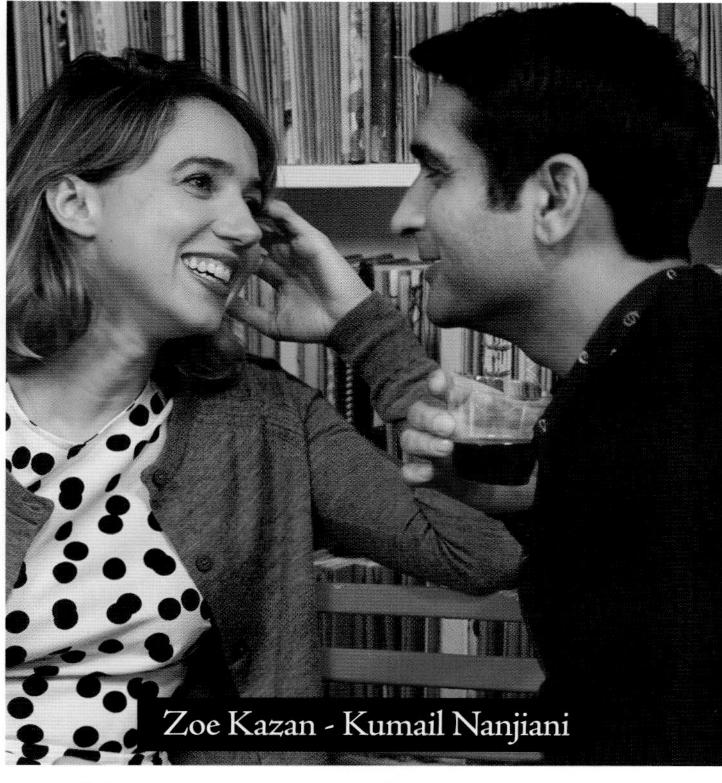
Zoe Kazan - Kumail Nanjiani

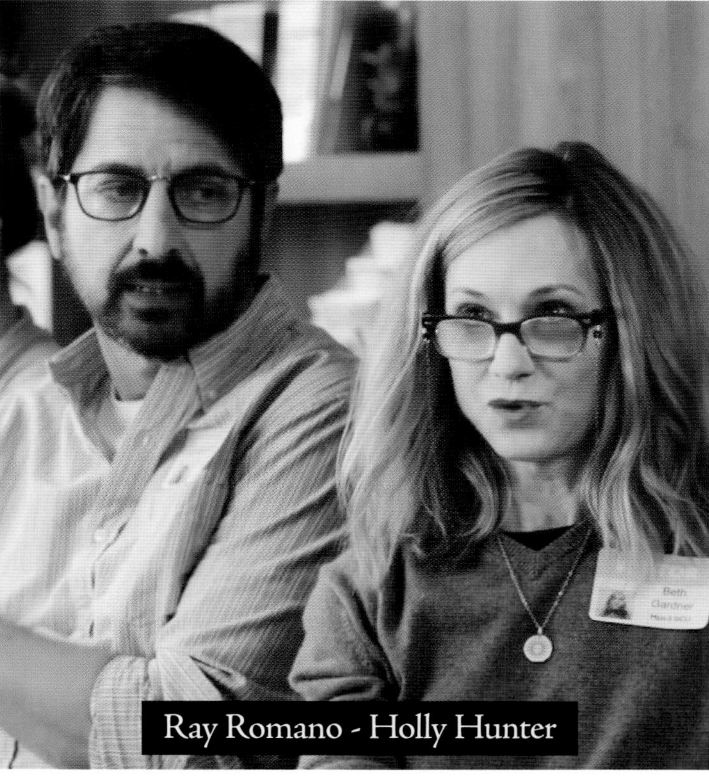
Ray Romano - Holly Hunter

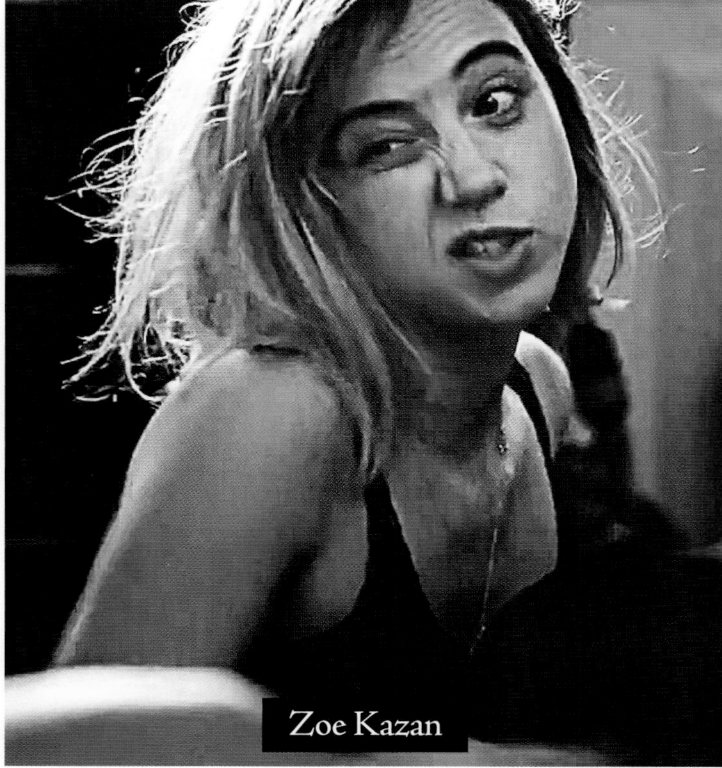
Zoe Kazan

I'm fortunate that Meg Kuehn, the CEO of Kirkus Reviews, when visiting me, sang the praises of "The Big Sick." If she hadn't, I would not have seen this wonderful Michael Showalter directed, Judd Apatow produced film. Thanks, Meg! Thanks, Michael! Thanks, Judd!

The story of U.S. President Lyndon Baines Johnson about his days when he assumed the presidency after the assasination of John F. Kennedy.

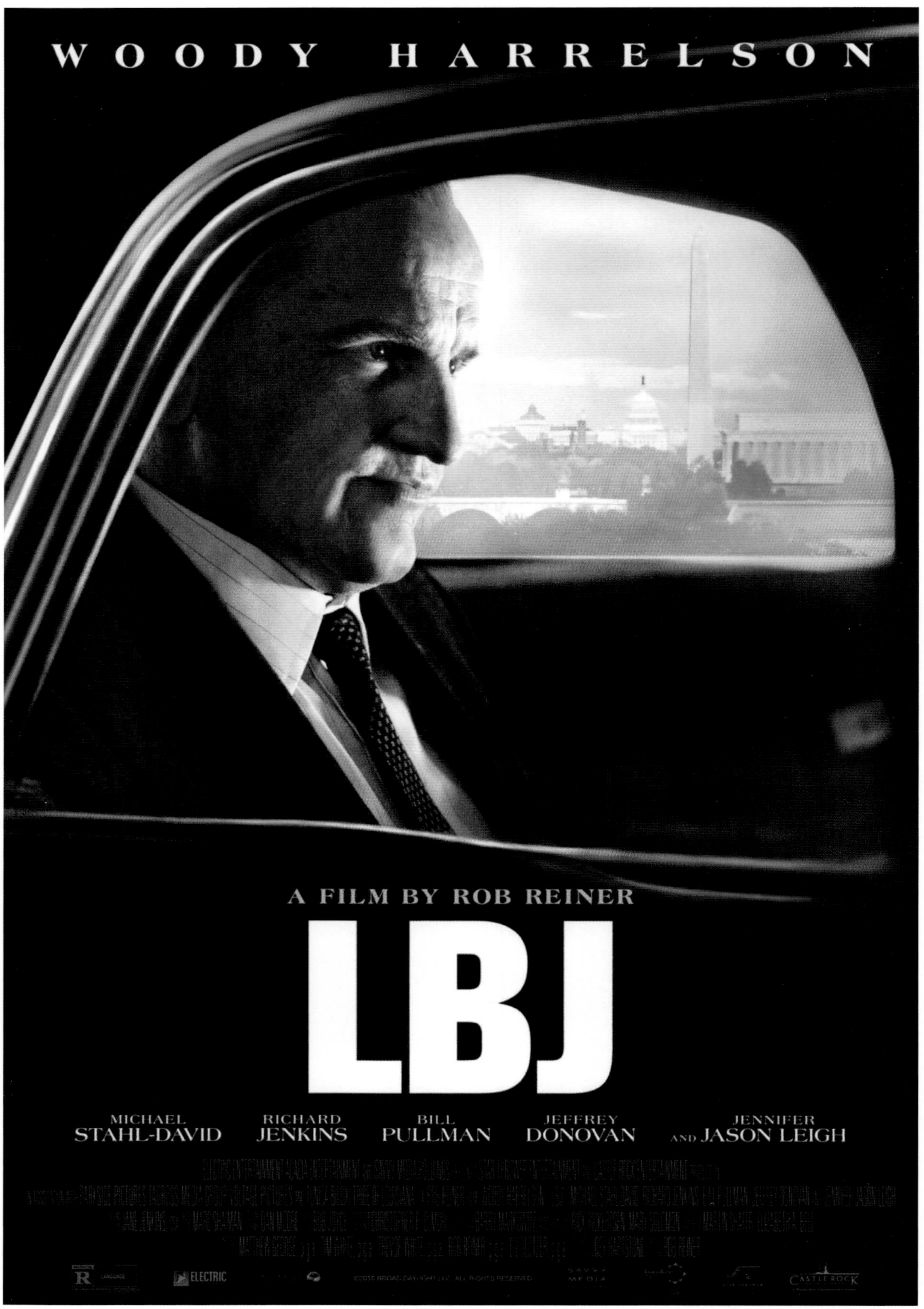

Rex Reed of The New York Observer wrote: "Woody Harrelson in the title role has enough spice to keep the viewer alert and attentive."

Godfrey Cheshire of RogerEbert.com wrote: "Captures a tumultuous political era and one of its most profanely colorful leaders with a good deal of insight and emotional torque."

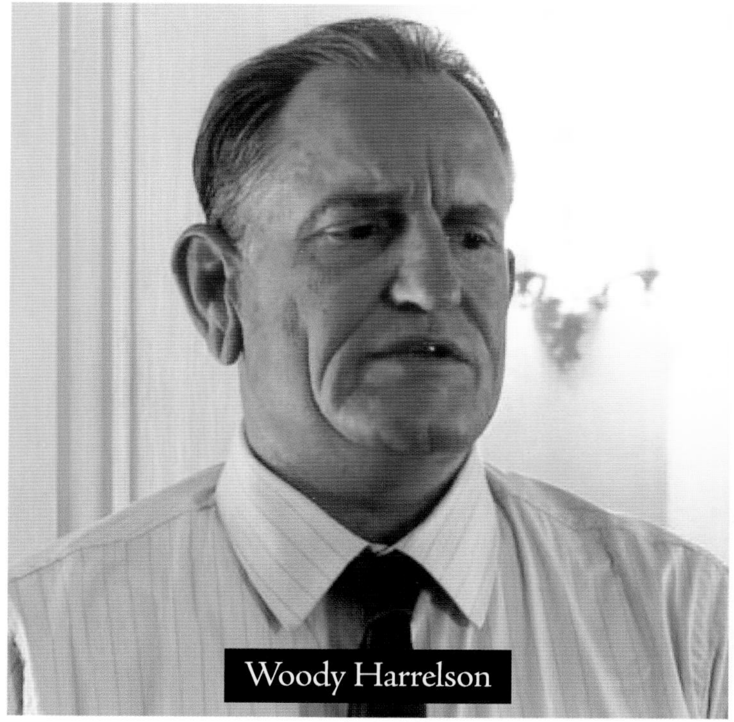
Woody Harrelson

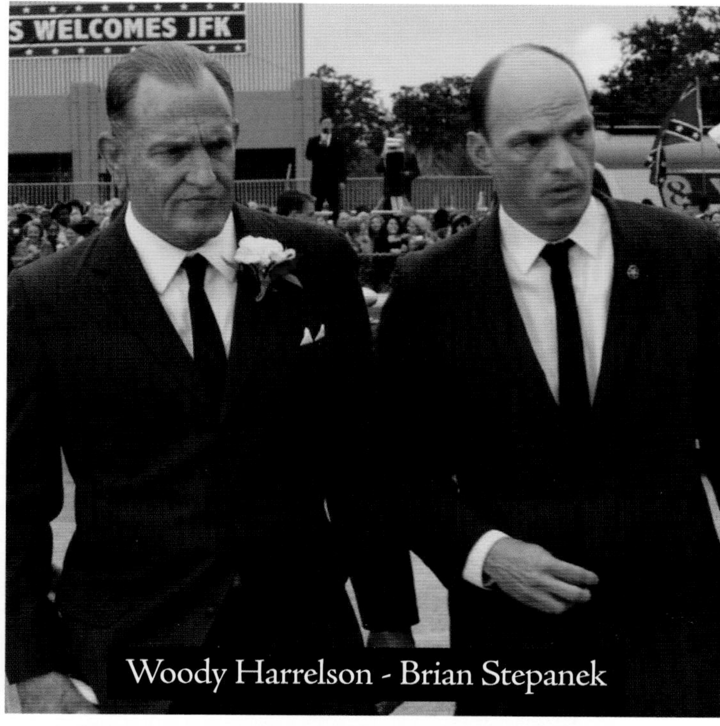

Woody Harrelson - Brian Stepanek

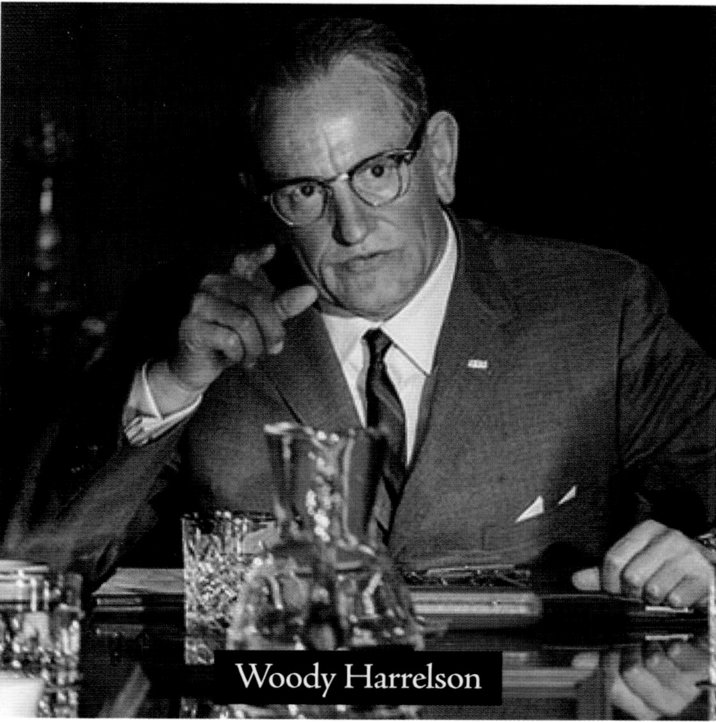
Woody Harrelson

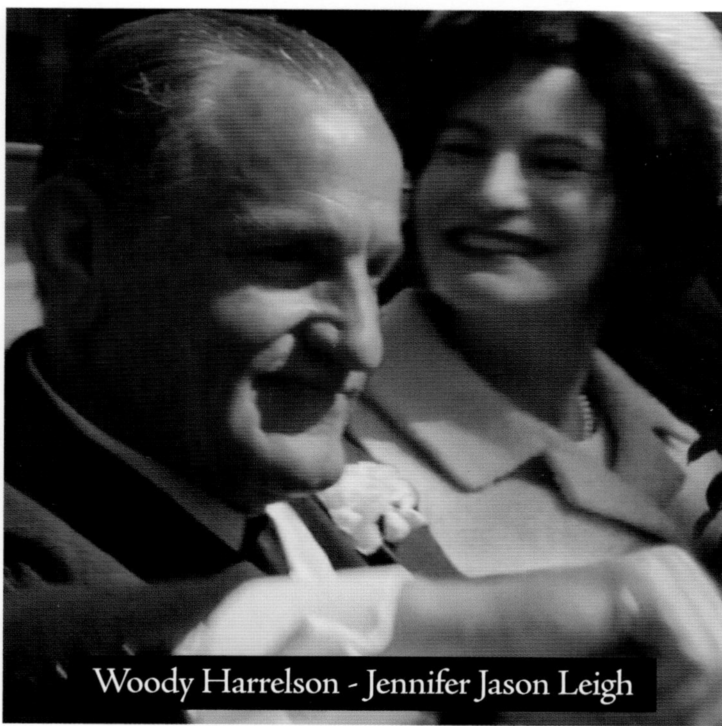
Woody Harrelson - Jennifer Jason Leigh

A few mornings ago, on "The View," I watched the hosts sing the praises of my son's efforts. I'm not surprised that Rob directed another exciting film, his 20th, but who's counting? His proud father, that's who. "Go, Rob, go!"

A group of journalists covering George Bush's planned invasion of Iraq in 2003 are skeptical of the presidents claim that Saddam Hussein has "weapons of mass destruction."

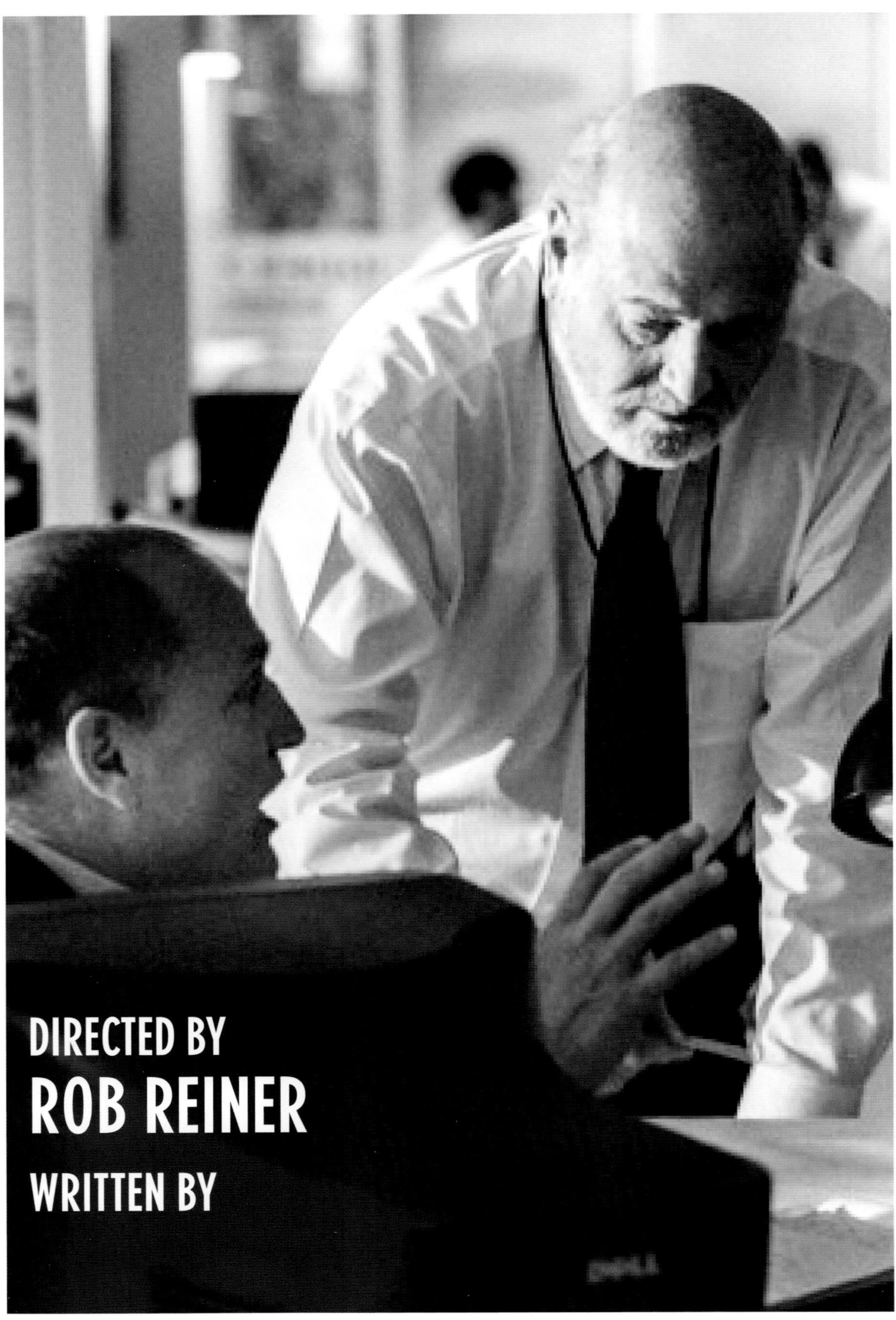

John Walcott, Editor of Knight Ridder, said: "The extraordinary thing about the film is how accurate it is. There are light moments, mostly at the expense of reporter, Warren Strobel, but that's accurate, too. What you see is what really happened, and it is a tribute to a great filmmaker."

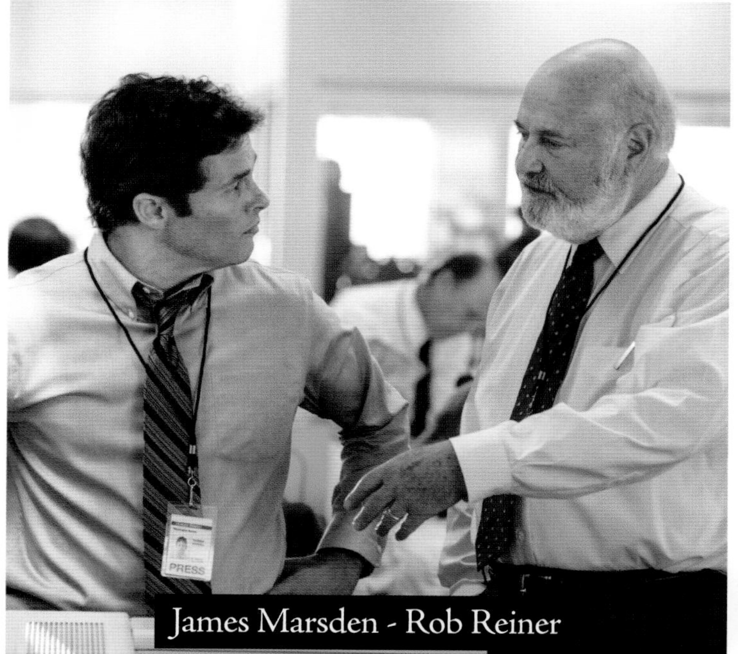
James Marsden - Rob Reiner

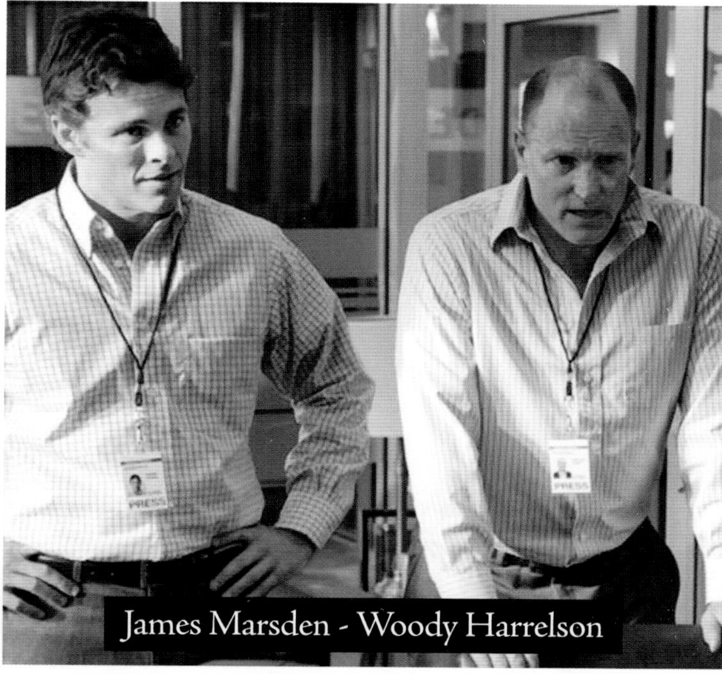
James Marsden - Woody Harrelson

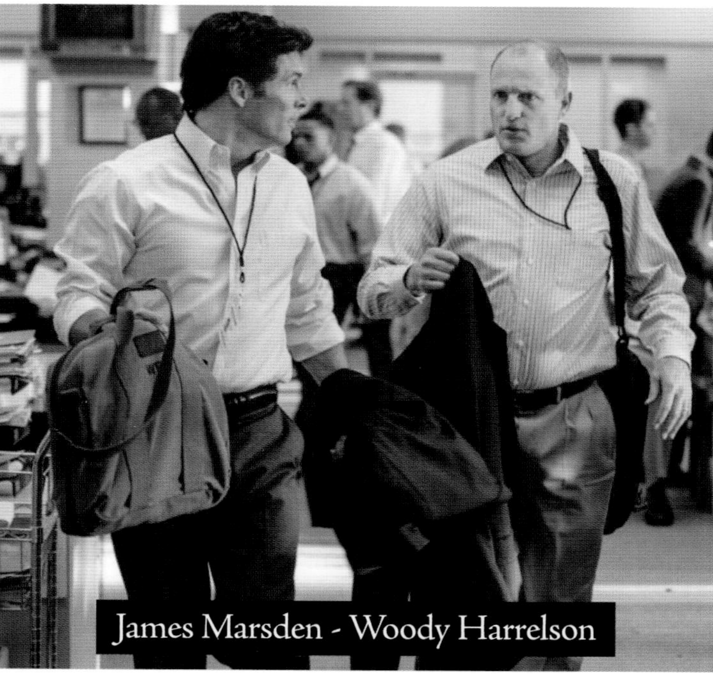
James Marsden - Woody Harrelson

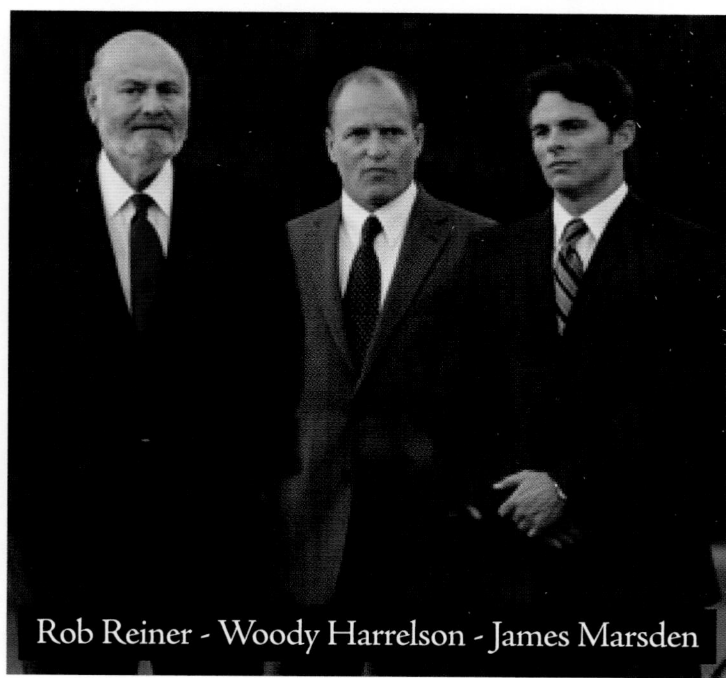
Rob Reiner - Woody Harrelson - James Marsden

Just as I readied this book to go to press, I learned that, after a screening of Rob's new film at The Zürich Film Festival, he and "Shock & Awe" received two sustained standing ovations.

This confirmed the feelings I had after attending a screening of "Shock & Awe." I was shocked and awed by the appearance and truly fine acting performance by Rob, who, at the last minute, stepped in to play the role of John Walcott, the editor of Knight Ridder news organization.

I daresay, this is definitely the most pleasurable way I could end this book.

Six young women emulate the eleven young men of "Ocean's Eleven" by stealing paintings from New York's Metropolitan Museum of Art.

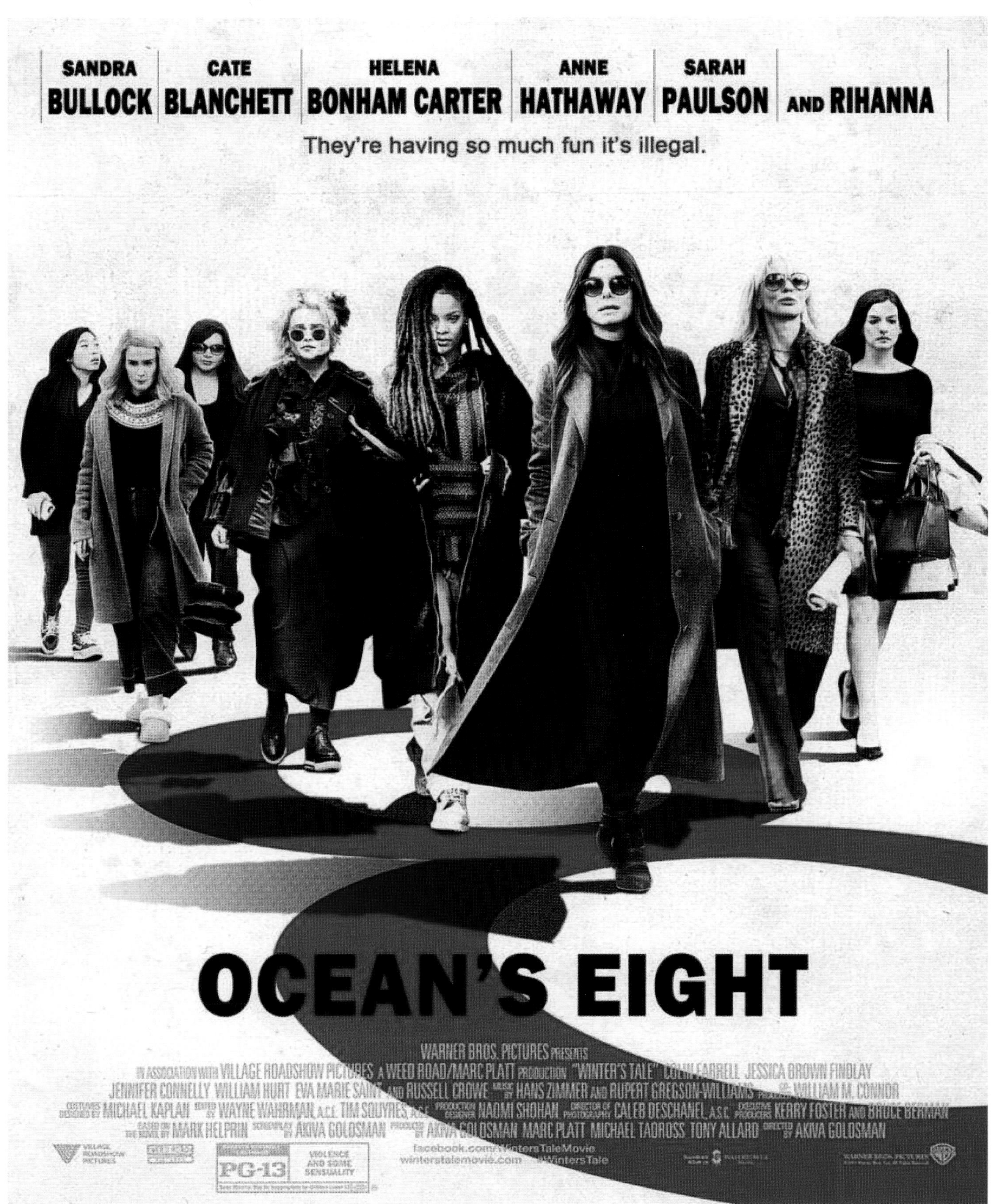

As of this book's printing, the film had not been finished or edited, but I'm sure the film's reviews will mirror the ones that "Ocean's Eleven," "Ocean's Twelve" and "Ocean's Thirteen" received from all knowledgeable critics.

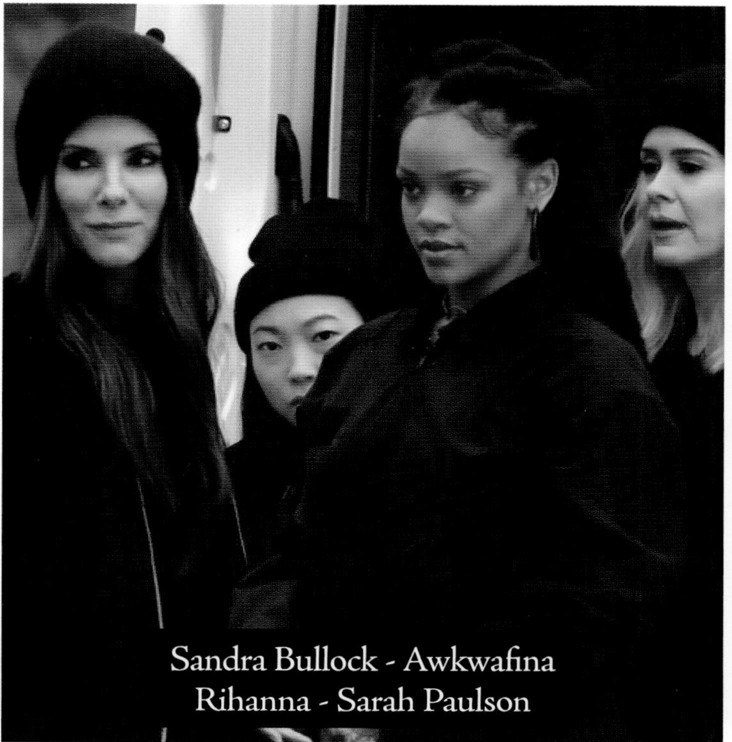
Sandra Bullock - Awkwafina
Rihanna - Sarah Paulson

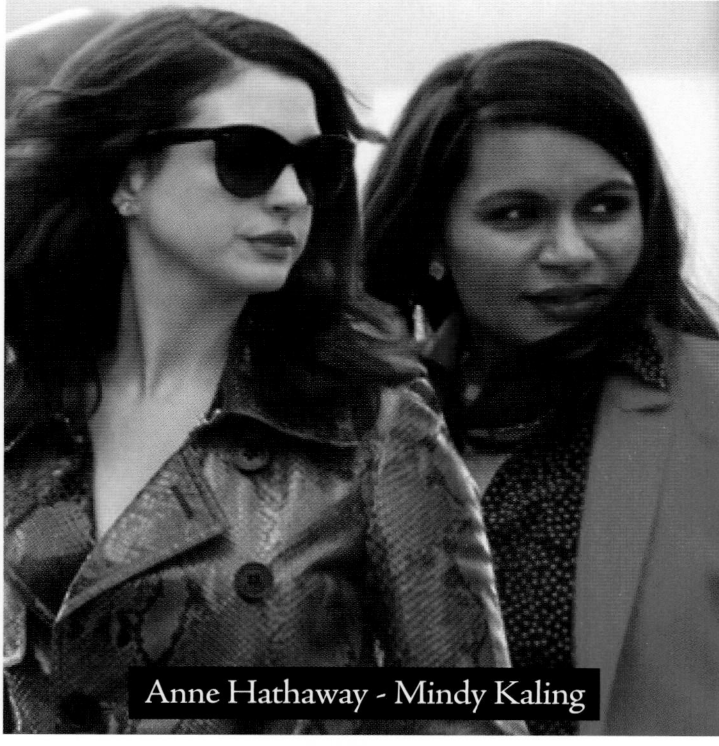
Anne Hathaway - Mindy Kaling

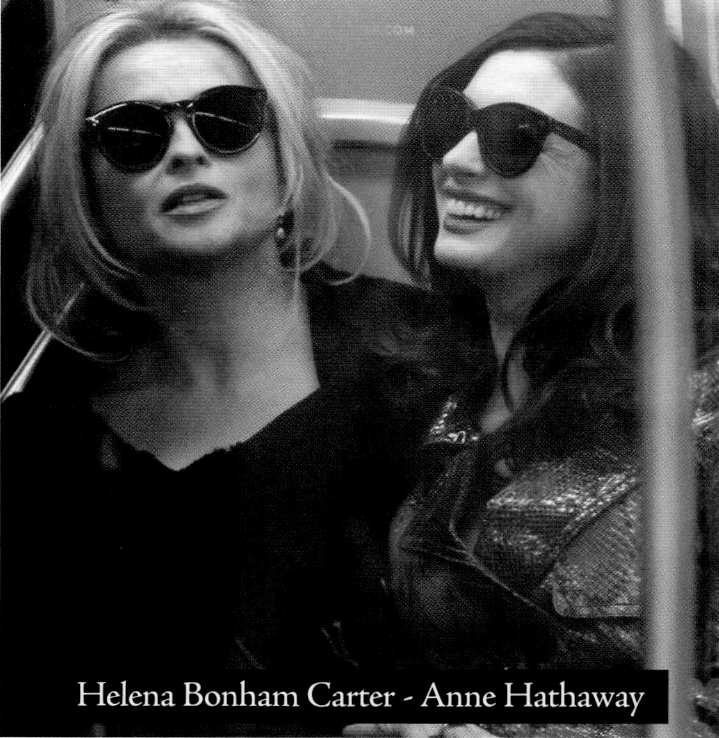
Helena Bonham Carter - Anne Hathaway

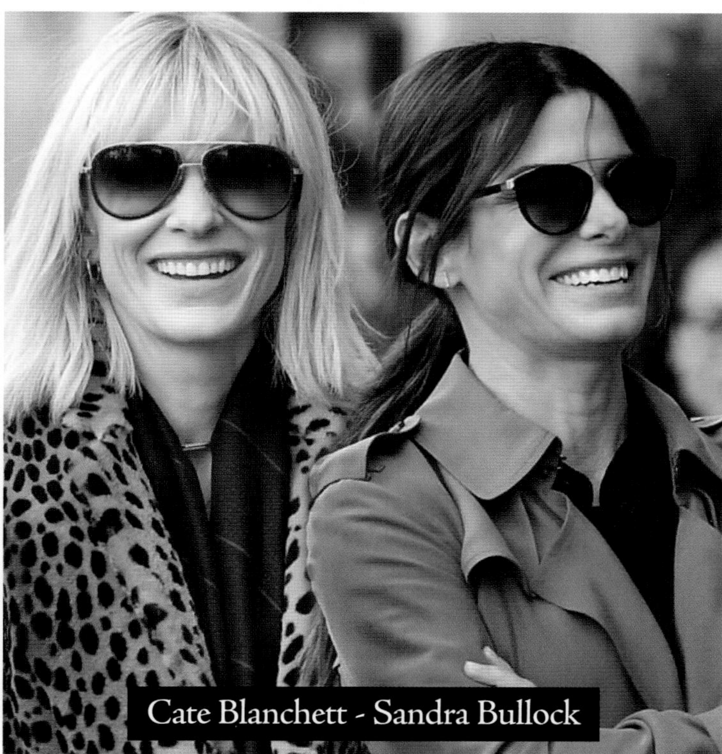
Cate Blanchett - Sandra Bullock

Being cast for a cameo role as Saul Bloom in this film gave me the opportunity to reiterate to Sandra Bullock how highly I esteem her. I told her that anytime my spirits need lifting, I watch her perform as Angela Bennett in "The Net."

If perchance, your favorite movie is not represented, it is only because I never got a chance to see it. I am hoping that I continue to have the ability to enjoy movies and to include how I felt about them in a book I'm contemplating:

"Carl Reiner, Now That You're Ninety-Seven & Not in Heaven, You Can Still Enjoy Watching Films."

I am beholden to Aaron Davis, a brilliant graphic designer, without whose knowledge and artistry this wonderful work would have been just a good idea.

And...

If it were not for publisher, Larry O'Flahavan, whose eye for talent is unerring, as exemplified in his engaging Aaron Davis, you'd never have the opportunity to read this unusual book and the glowing tributes to Larry O'. and Aaron D.

And...

Once again my thanks to Judy Nagy for copy editing the manuscript and putting all my commas, colons, question marks, periods and ellipses where they belong.

And...

Thank you Jessica LeRoy for helping to get our books to our gentle readers.

And...

Thank you Bess Scher for thirty years of steadfast 'aide' and comfort.